D1241769

PENGUIN REFERENCE

THE PENGUIN GUIDE TO COMPACT DISCS AND DVDS YEARBOOK 2002/3

EDWARD GREENFIELD, until his retirement in 1993, was for forty years on the staff of the *Guardian*, succeeding Neville Cardus as Music Critic in 1975. He still contributes regularly to the record column that he founded in 1954. At the end of 1960 he joined the reviewing panel of *Gramophone*, specializing in operatic and orchestral issues. He is a regular broadcaster on music and records for the BBC, not just on Radios 3 and 4 but also on the BBC World Service, latterly with his weekly programme, 'The Greenfield Collection'. In 1958 he published a monograph on the operas of Puccini. More recently he has written studies on the recorded work of Joan Sutherland and André Previn. He has been a regular juror on International Record awards and has appeared with such artists as Dame Elisabeth Schwarzkopf, Dame Joan Sutherland and Sir Georg Solti in public interviews. In October 1993 he was given a *Gramophone* Award for Special Achievement and in June 1994 received the OBE for services to music and journalism.

ROBERT LAYTON studied at Oxford with Edmund Rubbra for composition and with Egon Wellesz for the history of music. He spent two years in Sweden at the universities of Uppsala and Stockholm. He joined the BBC Music Division in 1959 and was responsible for Music Talks including such programmes as *Interpretations on Record*. He contributed 'A Quarterly Retrospect' to *Gramophone* magazine for thirty-four years and writes for the *BBC Music Magazine, International Record Review* and other journals. His books include studies of the Swedish composer Berwald and Sibelius as well as a monograph on the Dvořák symphonies and concertos for the BBC Music Guides, of which he was General Editor for many years. His prize-winning translation of Erik Tawaststjerna's definitive five-volume study of Sibelius was completed in 1998. In 1987 he was awarded the Sibelius Medal and the following year was made a Knight of the Order of the White Rose of Finland for his services to Finnish music. His other books include *Grieg: An Illustrated Life* and he has edited the *Guide to the Symphony* and the *Guide to the Concerto* (OUP). In 2001, at a ceremony to mark the Swedish presidency of the European Union, he was made a knight of the Royal Order of the Polar Star.

IVAN MARCH is a former professional musician. He studied at Trinity College of Music, London, and at the Royal Manchester College. After service in the Central Band of the RAF, he played the horn professionally for the BBC and travelled with the Carl Rosa and D'Oyly Carte opera companies. He is a well-known lecturer, journalist and personality in the world of recorded music and acts as consultant to Squires Gate Music Ltd, an international mail-order source for classical CDs (www.lprl.demon.co.uk). As a journalist he has contributed to a number of record-reviewing magazines, but now reviews solely for *Gramophone*.

THE PENGUIN GUIDE TO COMPACT DISCS AND DVDS YEARBOOK 2002/3
Completely revised and updated

IVAN MARCH,
EDWARD GREENFIELD and
ROBERT LAYTON

Edited by Ivan March
Assistant Editor: Paul Czajkowski

PENGUIN BOOKS

PENGUIN BOOKS

Published by the Penguin Group
Penguin Books Ltd, 80 Strand, London WC2R 0RL, England
Penguin Putnam Inc., 375 Hudson Street, New York, New York 10014, USA
Penguin Books Australia Ltd, Ringwood, Victoria, Australia
Penguin Books Canada Ltd, 10 Alcorn Avenue, Toronto, Ontario, Canada M4V 3B2
Penguin Books India (P) Ltd, 11, Community Centre, Panchsheel Park, New Delhi – 110 017, India
Penguin Books (NZ) Ltd, Private Bag 102902, NSMC, Auckland, New Zealand
Penguin Books (South Africa) (Pty) Ltd, 5 Watkins Street, Denver Ext 4, Johannesburg 2094, South Africa

Penguin Books Ltd, Registered Offices: 80 Strand, London WC2R 0RL, England

This edition first published 2002
1

Copyright © Ivan March Publications, 2002

Set in PostScript Adobe Minion and FF ScalaSans
This book was produced using Librios® authoring & content management technology
Made and printed in Great Britain by Clays Ltd, St Ives plc

CONTENTS

EDITOR'S NOTE
'CD, DVD AND THE FUTURE'

Over the four decades during which our Guides have been published, we have seen three major changes in the world of recording. The first was the coming of stereo, which added so much to the realism and beauty of recorded music and which prompted our first *Stereo Record Guide* in 1960. The second was the coming of cassettes which (with the help of the Dolby noise reduction system) seemed to offer the possibility of giving quality reproduction in a handy format free from those irritating extraneous noises – clicks and pops – which had ruffled the quiet background of vinyl LPs.

But before their full potential was realized, cassettes were upstaged by the coming of a third revolution, the Compact Disc, which apparently offered an ideal solution to all problems, including easy access to any part of the recording. Yet in the early days, the appeal of CDs was often marred by inadequate analogue-to-digital transfers of older recordings, and a matching over-bright, over-present audio image from the sometimes poorly balanced early digital masters. In the course of time, these problems have been all but solved. While there is sadly no current technology at present able to modify a too-bright digital master of the early 1980s, the recording producers learned from experience, and most of the more current CDs can give us an amazing degree of realism, with sound as richly atmospheric as the finest analogue LPs, plus better definition.

More recently, this improvement in naturalism on CD has been extended right back to early mono recordings, transferred from shellac by a remarkable new generation of engineers, led by Mike Dutton and Ward Marston, who use their ears, rather than just monitoring their electronic equipment, to balance the sound in order to match the often excellent quality older collectors recognize from those old 78-rpm discs.

So newer generations of music-lovers are discovering that realistic recording was possible long before the arrival of LPs and stereo, and that when enjoying a great performance from the more distant past, if the transfer of the recording itself is well balanced and full-bodied, it is quite possible to forget the early provenance of the source.

With the arrival of DVD comes the most profound advance of all. Now at last we can watch and *be involved in* the performance itself, almost like being in the theatre, concert hall or opera house – as well as listening to the music in enhanced sound; and if we prefer not to have the visual image, it can be instantly dispensed with.

While this advantage is obvious in the world of ballet and opera (where optional surtitles are also available), to many collectors it may seem less so with orchestral, chamber and instrumental music, or song recitals. But DVD can and does add immediacy to the musical experience. It catches the magnetism between the conductor and the orchestra, between soloist and accompanist, the inter-communication within a small group of musicians, and above all it can convey to a remarkable degree the projection of tension from performers to their audience. Of course, the listener's experience is not quite the same as a live concert. Nothing can equal that. But on the very finest DVDs it is remarkably close to it. This places a huge artistic responsibility on the video director and his cameramen. Ideally one should not be aware of the cameras at all. But when they are in the right place, the result can take domestic listening into a whole new dimension.

So, while we shall all, of course, continue to expand our musical experience with audio recordings on CD (which in real terms cost less than ever), undoubtedly the future lies with DVD – as our present survey is beginning to make clear.

IVAN MARCH

FOREWORD

An astonishing number of new names have joined the composers' roster in our current *Yearbook*, many of whom are not familiar at all. Just as importantly, the reputations of composers who are already known to us are being enhanced by additions to their recorded repertoire. Two outstanding examples will suffice, both from Virgin in their inexpensive 'two-for-the-price-of-one' Veritas reissue series. One, described as 'A Musical Banquet', offers a collection of Renaissance repertoire from Jordi Savall's Hespérion XX. Included is music by Johann Hermann Schein and Samuel Scheidt, plus *Canzonas* from the better-known Giovanni Gabrieli and his all but forgotten contemporary, Giuseppe Guami. The companion set offers Heinrich Biber's astonishing fifteen *Mystery* (or *Rosary*) *Violin Sonatas*, which follow the complete Christian story from the 'Annunciation' to 'Assumption and Coronation of the Virgin' in instrumental terms. The superb playing from the soloist John Holloway has admirable continuo support from Davitt Moroney and Tragicomedia, and Biber's reputation is confirmed as one of the great composers of the latter half of the seventeenth century. DG's Archiv label has also enterprisingly come up with a compilation called '*Bachiana*', a most illuminating disc of pieces by Bach's relatives near and far, which shows the amazing fecundity of the Bachian genes over several generations.

It is not only older music that is being discovered, but also more recently composed repertoire, such as Olympia's steadily growing survey of the unexplored symphonies of Miaskovsky in authentic performances from the Russian Federation Academic Symphony Orchestra under Svetlanov, and (on the ever exploratory Naxos label) the three splendid symphonies of the contemporary New Zealand composer, Douglas Lilburn, which have a distinct Sibelian inheritance and are inspired by the spacious scenery of his own homeland. Another contemporary composer nearer home whose music has been influenced by Sibelius is Arthur Butterworth, who captures the 'faint indefinable air of lonely melancholy brooding' of the North Yorkshire Moors. So far, he is primarily represented on CD by his shorter atmospheric tone poems, but there is no doubt that his symphonies and concertos must follow for his music, like Lilburn's, is invitingly tonal and melodic, and likely to survive.

It is often the smaller labels that discover or rediscover the most interesting new repertoire. Regis, for instance, has been reissuing some of the key recordings from the Unicorn catalogue at budget price, including distinguished complete surveys of Messiaen's piano and organ music, admirably played by Davis Hill and Jennifer Bate respectively. Both sets have the composer's imprimateur. Another highlight from the Regis catalogue is a comprehensive four-disc collection of 'English Anthems from 1540–1990', derived from the Alpha label, splendidly sung by the Magdalen College Choir of Oxford, conducted by Dr John Harper.

The originality and constant inspiration of the Anglican church music of Herbert Howells is confirmed yet again by a memorable Decca anthology from Stephen Cleobury and his King's College, Cambridge Choir, while the specialist Priory Label give us Howell's consistently beautiful *Canticles for Morning and Evening Service*, admirably sung by the Collegiate Songers, under Andrew Millinger. Chandos too, have put us in their debt by completing their coverage of the choral *Sacred Concertos* of Dimitri Bortnyansky (greatly admired by Tchaikovsky) with the recently discovered works for double choir, richly and idiomatically sung by the Russian State Symphonic Capella under Polyansky. And still within the world of Russian vocal music, comes another surprise discovery, a Chant du Monde CD of four superbly dramatic secular cantatas by Rimsky-Korsakov, which casts a new slant on his genius. They too, are very well sung by a Russian Chorus, the Moscow Academy Choir (with excellent soloists) conducted by Viktor Popov.

There have been plenty of Beecham reissues from many sources, including a whole series of his later mono recordings for CBS, now passed on to Sony. But one of the most enterprising and rewarding comes from Somm who have secured the rights to the pre-recorded soundtrack of the justly famous Powell/Pressburger film of Offenbach's *Tales of Hoffmann*, sung in English, by a cast which Beecham picked himself. To Beecham's dismay as a loyal EMI artist, this was originally issued by Decca on mono LP, but now it reappears in greatly enhanced sound, and the calibre of the singing (especially by Bruce Dargavel, who plays all three villainous roles) is fully revealed. Apart from the pleasure to be had from the performance itself, the set becomes a collector's item by including a recording of excerpts of Beecham at the piano – singing through the score for the film's producers, with fascinating if sometimes bizarre enthusiasm. Another treasurable Somm reissue offers

Ansermet's vintage mono recording of the Rossini/ Respighi *La Boutique fantasque* ballet, recorded in Kingsway Hall. This was one of his rare appearances with the LSO, and the orchestra respond brilliantly. At long last the new transfer does Decca's superb ffrr mono recording full justice, notably its magical opening. The coupling is Ansermet's early 78-rpm set of *Petrushka*, with the Suisse Romande Orchestra in better form than they were on later stereo sessions.

The collapse of Nimbus as a recording company has been one of the saddest events of the year, but happily the Brilliant super-super-budget label has acquired the rights to the complete recording of the Haydn Symphonies by the Austro-Hungarian Orchestra under Adam Fischer. Recorded at Esterházy over a period of fourteen years, this is a set to cherish, and it is incredibly inexpensive.

A group of Classics for Pleasure reissues restores Vernon Handley's unsurpassed recordings of the two Elgar symphonies to the catalogue, plus his almost equally fine set of the Symphonies of Vaughan Williams (amongst which the *Fifth* stands out), supplemented by a truly remarkable *Job*, while RCA have reissued the main symphonic cycles recorded by the late and much admired Gunter Wand (Brahms, Bruckner, Schubert). From the same source comes Sir Colin Davis's most recent LSO Sibelius cycle (including *Kullervo*), which now leads the field.

All the major labels have generously celebrated the Walton centenary, covering all his key works, with many different interpretations. Perhaps the most tempting reissue is the RCA Double, which includes vintage accounts of the *Cello*, *Violin* and *Viola Concertos* (played by Piatigorsky, Heifetz and Bashmet, respectively), plus Handley's modern digital recording of the *Sinfonia Concertante* with Kathleen Stott. Previn's still unsurpassed early LSO version of the *First Symphony* completes the package, and it is Previn's superb LSO recording of *Belshazzar's Feast* that has been spectacularly remastered as one of EMI's most desirable Audio DVDs, coupled with the *Second Symphony*, *Portsmouth Point* and *Scapino*.

CONCERTS

In our expanded Concerts section, the ever-fascinating Teldec video illustrating the 'Art of Conducting' is now followed by the first issues in EMI's 'Great Conductors' series, which is made the more valuable by drawing on many broadcast performances, hitherto unavailable on CD. Of course, most of the conductors featured are also well represented in the general collections that follow. Among these, it is sad that almost all the listed vintage Mercury CDs and notably the Detroit/Paray and various Eastman-Rochester recordings, have been withdrawn in England. But the great American orchestras and their conductors are well represented on other labels, and the '*RCA Red Seal Century*' collection includes what is described as 'the first known commercial recording sessions with a full symphony orchestra'. This was the Boston Symphony, conducted by Karl Muck in 1917, playing Tchaikovsky's *Marche miniature* from his *Orchestral Suite No. 1*, which sounds remarkably well, but at the time offered comparatively few problems to the recording horn, as it is piquantly scored for the higher woodwind instruments. Stokowski is also represented here (as he is elsewhere), by a 1927 early electric recording of the closing scene from *Götterdämerung*. The excitement and electricity of the occasion are well captured, but unfortunately the famous Philadelphia strings are not – they sound very undernourished – it would surely have been possible to achieve a better transfer than this!

Ballet music has always been a gramophone staple, and its finest and most comprehensive representation on CD comes in two separate surveys by Richard Bonynge, which stand out both for the sparkle of the orchestral playing and the excellence of the vintage Decca recordings. But alongside a superbly played DG collection from the Berlin Philharmonic under Karajan, there is another CD from the Royal Ballet Sinfonia under Barry Wordsworth which balletomanes should not miss. Described as a '*Tribute to Madame*' it celebrates the enterprise of Dame Ninette de Valois, the 'Mother' of British ballet, by including outstanding scores of works with which she was associated by Arthur Bliss, Constant Lambert, Gavin Gordon and Geoffrey Toye.

The Royal Ballet Orchestra and Sinfonia, under various conductors have additionally made a whole series of delightful CDs of British light orchestral music which has been neatly defined as 'music where the tune is more important than what happens to it'. Its supreme master is Eric Coates and he is additionally well represented in the Composer listing.

INSTRUMENTAL RECORDINGS

One of the most haunting of all brief instrumental records opens that same 'RCA Red Seal Century' collection: Mischa Elman playing Fritz Kreisler's *Sicilienne and Rigaudon* (after Francoeur). It was recorded in 1911 and the sound is frail, but the transfer gives the playing a magical sense of presence carried to us from long ago. There are, of course many fine new instrumental and chamber music CDs, and it is good to find the Takác's Quartet and the Lindsays are both setting out on fresh explorations of the Beethoven *String Quartets*, while a pair of treasurable BBC CDs gathers together many chamber works featuring the celebrated horn player Dennis Brain, including the Beethoven *Piano and Wind Quintet* and *Horn Sonata*, the Brahms *Horn Trio*, the Mozart *Horn Quintet*, and Ibert's *Trois pièces brèves*.

Among piano recordings, Pletnev, who seldom disappoints, has brought his special insights to the Keyboard Sonatas of C. P. E. Bach, while Murray Perahia adds to his laurels and rosette collection with a stylishly magnetic new set of Johann Sebastian's *Clavier Concertos*.

Indeed, piano recordings of Bach's keyboard music, once unfashionable in an age of period instruments, are now proliferating, and no recent issue is more stimulating than Angela Hewitt's Hyperion CD of the seven Bach *Toccatas*, (written in the 'stylus fantasticus' which the young composer had inherited from Buxtehude), while Hewitt's equally perceptive survey of the complete piano music of Ravel now leads the field. Hardly less rewarding is Sara Marianovich's first absolutely complete coverage of Rodrigo's piano music on Sony. I.M. had the privilege of meeting the great Spanish composer not long before he died, and discovered how much he valued his music for the keyboard, and also how disappointed he was that it had been so neglected.

Among a wealth of miscellaneous keyboard recitals by many fine artists, Sviatoslav Richter is generously represented and so, of course is Horowitz, where Sony have brought out a new ten-CD set which they describe as the 'Original Jacket Collection'. Each is housed in its 'original LP sleeve' reduced to CD-size, although the stature of the performances has not shrunk at all. Among the established modern virtuosi, Stephen Hough demonstrates that he too can provide sparkling piano encores to match all those legendary pianists from the past. Benno Moiseiwitsch, admired by Rachmaninov, was undoubtedly among their number and he at last now appears within our pages, but RCA's huge 'Rubinstein Edition' proved overambitious and unmarketable, and many of the individual recital issues have been deleted.

EMI's enterprising Debut label continues to discover talented newcomers, amongst whom two names stand out – the astonishing Korean, Dong-Hyek Lim, and the Macedonian-born Simon Trpčeski, who provides an exciting all-Russian programme. So also does the remarkable Ingrid Jacoby, found on Dutton's mid-price stereo label, giving stunning accounts of Mussorsgky's *Pictures at an Exhibition* and Prokofiev's daunting *Seventh Sonata*.

OPERA

Turning to opera there is plenty to relish, not least a continuing Naxos series of historical recordings of complete sets, which have come out of copyright, and are now usually transferred to CD by Ward Marston. The highlight so far is Decca's first mono LP recording of *Die Fledermaus*, with Gueden, Lipp, Patzak, Dermota and Poell – all in superb voice. The performance is scintillatingly conducted by Clemens Krauss, and many would claim that it has never since been matched.

On EMI we find the celebrated team of Alagna, Gheorgiu and Pappano continuing their serendipitous partnership in outstanding new versions of Massenet's *Manon*, Puccini's *Tosca,* and Verdi's *Il trovatore* (the finest for many years). They also participate in one of the most recommendable DVDs – from Lyon Opéra – of Donizetti's *L'elisir d'amore*, updated visually to the 1920s, but stylishly produced, and great fun to see and hear. Also from EMI comes a definitive new set of Mozart's *Idomeneo*, conducted by Mackerras, with Ian Bostridge in the title role, while Decca offer Massenet's *Thaïs* with Renée Fleming proving an ideal interpreter of the part of the tragic heroine. Solti admirers will be glad also to welcome Decca's 'Solti Wagner Edition', containing his complete performances of all the major Wagner operas outside the *Ring*, now offered individually at mid price for the first time, or together in a box with a further saving.

EMI have also brought out a whole series of operetta recordings, not only from names like Kálmán and Lehár, but also Adam, Benatsky, Lecocq, Messager, Planquette *et al*. The only snag with these inexpensive reissues is the complete absence of texts and translations, or indeed of any kind of proper background documentation. From TER, there are some sparkling new Gilbert and Sullivan recordings by the re-formed D'Oyly Carte Opera company, which has recently made such a success with revivals of *HMS Pinafore,* and *The Mikado* at the Company's traditional home base, London's Savoy theatre, which was built by Richard D'Oyly Carte himself. Chandos have reissued Menuhin's highly enjoyable 1967 version of Mozart's *Abduction from the Seraglio* sung in English, which compares favourably with any of the German-language versions.

Our coverage of vocal recitals (historic and more modern) is now so vast that it is possible to mention only a few, although perhaps the 'RCA Centenary Collection' (the second box devoted to 'the Vocalists') should again be mentioned, alongside Testament's EMI 'Art of Singing' and Romophone's extensive historic coverage. There are countless examples elsewhere of fabulous (and occasionally less fabulous) singing, while the quality of the newest transfers of 'golden age' discs continues to astonish. Two inexpensive Dutton examples stand out, a recital by the Swiss-born Charles Panzéra, who in the 1930s was the foremost interpreter of French song, and a thrilling operatic collection from Helge Roswaenge. He was nicknamed 'the Dane with the High D' and when you hear his performance of the key tenor aria from Adam's *Le Postillion de Longjumeau*, you will know why.

Decca's new vocal series 'The Singers' has proved more disappointing, not least because, unlike their 'Opera Gala label', the texts and translations are only available via a CD-ROM, a policy which has also been applied to the company's recent bargain reissues of complete operas.

DVD

But it is in the new world of DVD that opera recordings have something quite new and special to offer, and already there is a hand-picked group of examples more rewarding than most CD competitors, including Gershwin's *Porgy and Bess*, Handel's *Tamerlano*, Mozart's *Nozze di Figaro* (from Glyndebourne), Mussorgsky's *Boris Godunov* (Gergiev), Offenbach's *La Belle Hélène*, Poulenc's *Dialogue des Carmélites*, Rossini's *La Cenerentola*, Richard Strauss's *Arabella* and *Der Rosenkavalier*, Verdi's *Don Carlos*, *La forza del destino* and *La Traviata*.

The most fascinating and controversial of all is the Decca DVD of the famous Solti audio recording of Tchaikosky's *Eugene Onegin*, which Petr Weigl's newly filmed production of the opera's action has been overlayed. All the vocal parts are mimed by Russian actors who convincingly look their parts, especially the youthful Tatiana, as do all the authentically costumed cast who are filmed against real-life Russian backgrounds. This is obviously a pointer to the future, but while I.M. and E.G. welcome this new kind of operatic experience, R.L. has considerable reservations, mainly about the mismatching of the acoustic of Kingsway Hall – where the recording was made – with the filmed operatic venues which include domestic, ballroom, and open-air scenes.

With a competing pair of DVDs of Schubert's song cycle, *Die Winterreise*, the collector is offered an alternative choice between David Alden's bleakly staged and histrionically desolate presentation of Ian Bostridge and Julius Drake on Warner NVC Arts, or a plainer recital-room performance from Jorma Hyninen and Ralf Gothoni on Arthaus, partly illustrated with visual interludes composed from wintry pictures of the Finnish landscape.

When one turns to the world of ballet there is nothing but gain from DVD: the dazzlingly authentic Kirov Russian *Giselle*; the enchanting Covent Garden Royal Ballet performances of Delibes's *Coppélia*, Herold's *La Fille mal gardée*, and Tchaikovsky's *Nutcracker*; and the Paris Opéra Ballet's powerfully involving realization of Rudolf Nureyev's newly choreographed *Romeo and Juliet*, wonderfully danced by Manuel Legris and Monique Loudière. All these provide a repeatable visual experience, and first-class orchestral playing and recording: they cannot be recommended too highly.

Alongside the video DVDs there are also a few audio DVDs, and SACDS. The SACDs require special and currently expensive playback facilities, and will not reproduce on standard DVD players. They must wait for future appraisal. But the small batch of Audio DVDs issued by EMI, with optional surround sound, are very impressive indeed. They are transferred from quadraphonic masters recorded in the late 1970s, and even on normal stereo equipment the added range and depth of sound is remarkable. We have already mentioned Previn's *Belshazzar's Feast*, but his LSO recording of Holst's *Planets* is even more spectacular, and there are similarly thrilling EMI Audio DVDs of Martinon's complete *Daphnis et Chloé*, recorded in Paris, and Kempe's Dresden performances of Richard Strauss's *Alpine Symphony* and *Also sprach Zarathustra*. There is no attempt to provide pictorial illustrations (as tried unsuccessful by Naxos). Instead, with EMI, the TV screen shows a simple menu listing out the music's subsections, with each illuminated in turn as the performance proceeds.

But our final comment about DVD must return to the instrumental music of Bach, and the Freiburg Baroque Orchestra's video presentation of the six *Brandenburg Concertos*, played in the restored Spegiesaal of Castle Cöthen, where Bach probably lived when they were composed. The performance is superb, the backcloth ideal, and the Freibergers play their period baroque instruments with vigour, finesse and sponteity. This production is as visually illuminating as it is musically satisfying, and considerably more stimulating than an audio recording. This is the way we hope DVD orchestral and instrumental recordings will go in the future.

INTRODUCTION

As in previous editions, the object of *The Penguin Guide Yearbook to Compact Discs and CDs* is to give the serious collector a continuing survey of the finest recordings of permanent music on CD, irrespective of price, but also evaluating the quality of the video and audio DVDs, which are now offering a new kind of musical experience. As most recordings are issued almost simultaneously on both sides of the Atlantic and use identical international catalogue numbers, this *Guide* should be found to be equally useful in the UK and the USA, as it will in Australia, Canada and New Zealand. The internationalization of repertoire and numbers now applies to almost all CDs issued by the major international companies and also by the smaller ones. Many European labels are imported in their original formats, both into Britain and the USA. Those CDs that are only available in England can be easily obtained by overseas collectors via the Web address given on p. xviii.

We feel that it is a strength of our basic style to let our own conveyed pleasure and admiration (or otherwise) for the merits of an individual recording come over directly to the reader, even if this produces a certain ambivalence in the matter of such a final choice. Where there is disagreement between us (and this rarely happens), readers will find an indication of our different reactions in the text.

We have considered (and rejected) the use of initials against individual reviews, since this is essentially a team project. The occasions for disagreement generally concern matters of aesthetics – in the manner of recording balance for instance, where a contrived effect may trouble some ears more than others, or in the matter of style, where the difference between robustness and refinement of approach appeals differently to listening sensibilities rather than involving a question of artistic integrity. But over the years our views seem to have grown closer together rather than having diverged; perhaps we are getting mellower, but we are seldom ready to offer strong disagreement following the enthusiastic reception by one of the team of a controversial recording, providing the results are creatively stimulating.

As playing standards have advanced, our perceptions of the advantages and disadvantages of performances of early music on original (as against modern) instruments seem almost irrelevant. It is the quality of the performance itself that counts. Indeed, so expert is the performer's control of period instruments today (while modern-instrument performances are often influenced by period-instrument style), that sometimes one is hardly aware of the difference, especially in orchestral music.

EVALUATION

Most major recordings issued today are of a high technical standard and offer performances of a quality at least as high as is experienced in the concert hall. In adopting a star system for the evaluation of records, we have decided to make use of from one to three stars. Brackets around one or more of the stars indicate some reservations about a recording's rating, and readers are advised to refer to the text. Brackets around all the stars usually indicate a basic qualification: for instance, a mono recording of a performance of artistic interest, where some allowances may have to be made for the sound quality even though the recording may have been digitally remastered.

Our evaluation system may be summarized as follows:

*** An outstanding performance and recording in every way;

** A good performance and recording of today's normal high standard;

* A fair or somewhat routine performance, reasonably well performed or recorded.

Our evaluation is normally applied to the record as a whole, unless there are two main works or groups of works, and by different composers. In this case, each is dealt with separately in its appropriate place.

ROSETTES (✹)

To certain special records we have awarded a Rosette: ✹.

Unlike our general evaluations, in which we have tried to be consistent, a Rosette is a quite arbitrary compliment by a member of the reviewing team to a recorded performance which, he finds, shows special illumination, magic, a spiritual quality, or even outstanding production values, that place it in a very special class. Occasionally a Rosette has been awarded for an issue that seems to us to offer extraordinary value for money, but that presupposes that the performance or performances are outstanding too. The choice is essentially a personal one (although often it represents a shared view) and in some cases it is applied to an issue where certain reservations must also be mentioned in the text of the review. The Rosette symbol is placed before the usual evaluation and the record number. It is quite small – we do not mean to imply an 'Academy Award' but a personal token of appreciation for something uniquely valuable. We hope that, once the reader has discovered and perhaps acquired a 'rosetted' CD, its special qualities will soon become apparent. There are, of course, more of them now, for our survey has become a distillation of the excellence of CDs issued and reissued over a considerable time span.

DIGITAL RECORDINGS

Nearly all new compact discs are recorded digitally, but an increasingly large number of digitally remastered, reissued analogue recordings are now appearing, and we think it important to include a clear indication of the difference.

All listed CDs are digital *unless* the inclusion of (**ADD**) in the titling indicates Analogue-to-Digital remastering, while of course the term mono is self-explanatory.

The indication **ADD/DDD** or **DDD/ADD** applies to a compilation where recordings come from mixed sources.

LISTINGS AND PRICE RANGES

Our listing of each recording assumes that it is in the premium-price category, unless it indicates otherwise, as follows:
 (M) Medium-priced label;
 (B) Bargain-priced label;
 (BB) Super-bargain label.
See below for differences in price structures in the UK and the USA.

LAYOUT OF TEXT

We have aimed to make our style as simple as possible. So, immediately after the evaluation and before the catalogue number, the record make is given, sometimes in abbreviated form. In the case of a set of two or more CDs, the number of units involved is given in brackets after the catalogue number.

AMERICAN CATALOGUE NUMBERS

The numbers which follow in square brackets are US catalogue numbers if they are different from UK catalogue numbers (and this applies in particular to EMI's 'Great Recordings of the Century' which have a different number on each side of the Atlantic). RCA has now moved over to completely identical numbers. Where a record is available in the USA but *not* the UK, *it will appear in square brackets only*, and that applies especially to some Mercury CDs. But EMI's American label, 'Red Line Classics' is now available in the UK to special order.

There are certain other small differences to be remembered by American readers. For instance, EMI use extra digits for their British compact discs; thus the British number CDM7 63351-2 becomes CDM 63351 in the USA (the -2 is the European indication that this is a compact disc). Prefixes can alter too. The British EMI forte and double forte CZS5 68583-2 becomes CDFB 68583 in the USA; and Virgin Classics VBD5 61469-2 becomes CDVB 61469. We have taken care to check catalogue information as far as is possible, but as all the editorial work has been done in England there is always the possibility of error; American readers are therefore invited, when ordering records locally, to take the precaution of giving their dealer the fullest information about the music and recordings they want.

The indications (M), (B) and (BB) immediately before the starring of a disc refer primarily to the British CD, as pricing systems are not always identical on both sides of the Atlantic. When CDs are imported by specialist distributors into the USA, this again usually involves a price difference. When mid-priced CDs on the smaller labels are imported into the USA, they often move up to the premium-price range. American readers are advised to check the current *Schwann* catalogue and to consult their local record store.

ABBREVIATIONS

To save space we have adopted a number of standard abbreviations in listing record companies, orchestras and performing groups (a list is provided below on p. xix, and the titles of works are often shortened, especially where they are listed several times. Artists' forenames are usually omitted if they are not absolutely necessary for identification purposes. Also we have not usually listed the contents of operatic highlights and collections.

We have followed common practice in the use of the original language for titles where it seems sensible. In most cases, English is used for orchestral and instrumental music, and the original language for vocal music and opera. There are exceptions, however; for instance, the Johann Strauss discography uses the German language in the interests of consistency.

ORDER OF MUSIC

The order of music under each composer's name broadly follows the following system: orchestral music, including concertos and symphonies; chamber music; solo instrumental music (in some cases with keyboard and organ music separated); vocal and choral music; opera; vocal collections; miscellaneous collections. Within each group our listing follows an alphabetical sequence, and couplings within a single composer's output are *usually* discussed together instead of separately with cross-references.

Occasionally (and inevitably because of this alphabetical approach), different recordings of a given work can become separated when a record is listed and discussed under the first work of its alphabetical sequence. The editor feels that alphabetical consistency is essential if the reader is to learn to find his or her way about.

CATALOGUE NUMBERS

Enormous care has gone into the checking of CD catalogue numbers and contents to ensure that all details are correct, but the editor and publishers cannot be held responsible for any mistakes that may have crept in despite all our zealous checking. When ordering CDs, readers are urged to provide their record-dealer with full details of the music and performers, as well as the catalogue number.

DELETIONS

Compact discs regularly succumb to the deletions axe, and many are likely to disappear during the lifetime of this book. Sometimes copies may still be found in specialist shops, and there remains the compensatory fact that most really important and desirable recordings are eventually reissued, often costing less!

Universal Classics have an import service for certain CDs which are not carried in their UK inventory, and these CDs are indicated with the abbreviation IMS in brackets. A small extra charge is made for these discs, which may have to be obtained from Germany or Holland.

COVERAGE

As the output of major and minor labels continues to expand, it is obviously impossible for us to mention every CD that is available within the covers of a single book; this is recognized as a practical limitation if we are to update our survey regularly. Indeed, we have now to be very selective in choosing the discs to be included, and some good recordings inevitably fall by the wayside. There is generally a reason for omissions, and usually it is connected with the lack of ready availability. However, we do welcome suggestions from readers about such omissions if they seem to be of special interest, although we cannot guarantee to include them in a future survey!

ACKNOWLEDGEMENTS

Our thanks are due to our new Penguin editor, Rachael Arthur and also to Roger Wells, especially for his help during the final assembly of all the listings and reviews for this book. Paul Czajkowski, as Assistant Editor, helped with retrieval of earlier reviews (connected with reissues) and contributed a number of specialist reviews, especially in the areas of film music, light music and operetta. He was also responsible for much of the titling – never an easy task – to which Barbara Menard also made an important last-minute contribution.

Alan Livesey and Kathleen March cast an eagle eye over the initial proofing, in particular looking for mistakes in the documentation and musical context. Our team of Penguin copy-editors and proof-readers have also proved themselves indispensable. Grateful thanks also go to all those readers who write to us to point out factual errors and to remind us of important recordings that have escaped our notice.

THE AMERICAN SCENE

CDs are much less expensive in the USA than they are in Great Britain and because of this – so we are told – many bargain recordings available in England are not brought into the USA by their manufacturers. This applies especially to the Universal group, so that Decca, DG and Philips (as well as Eloquence and Panorama, drawn from all three) bargain labels have to be imported by the major US record stores and mail-order outlets. What this means is that while almost any recording mentioned in these pages will be available in the USA, sometimes it will cost more than the buyer might reasonably expect.

Duos and Doubles, where available, remain at two discs for the cost of one premium priced CD in both countries, and here US collectors have a price advantage. However, according to *Schwann*, many excellent lower-priced discs are not issued in the USA. Where a recording is of extra special interest, American collectors can obtain it readily by mail order from England, through the web-site address given. However it will inevitably cost more than it would domestically.

From your many letters, and from visiting record stores in the USA, we know that our *Penguin Guide* is read, enjoyed and used as a tool by collectors on both sides of the Atlantic. We also know that some transatlantic readers feel that our reviews are too frequently orientated towards European and British recordings and performances. In concentrating on records which have common parlance in both Europe and the USA, we obviously give preference to the output of international companies and, in assessing both performers and performances, we are concerned with only one factor: musical excellence. In a 400-year-old musical culture centred in Europe, it is not surprising that a great number of the finest interpreters should have been Europeans, and many of them have enjoyed recording in London, where there are four first-class symphony orchestras and many smaller groups at their disposal, supported by recording producers and engineers of the highest calibre. The early-music period-instrument revolution is also presently centred in London, which seems to add another bias, which is not of our making.

However, the continuing re-emergence of earlier recordings by major American recording orchestras and artists is slowly redressing the balance. Our performance coverage in the present volume – helped by the huge proportion of reissued older records – certainly reflects the American achievement, past and present - particularly the 1930s to 1960s. In that period, Koussevitzky was in Boston; Frederick Stock and, after him, Fritz Reiner, was in Chicago; Mitropoulos, Bruno Walter and Bernstein directed the New York Philharmonic in its heyday; Stokowski and Ormandy were in Philadelphia, and George Szell was creating astonishing standards of orchestral virtuosity in Cleveland. At the same time, Heifetz and Horowitz, Piatigorsky, Rubinstein and Isaac Stern were carrying all before them in the instrumental field. With the current phenomenal improvements in transferring technology, we hope that increasing numbers of the recordings made by these great names from the past will enjoy the attention of the wider public.

PRICE DIFFERENCES IN THE UK AND USA

Retail prices are not fixed in either country, and various stores may offer even better deals at times, so our price structure must be taken as a guideline only. This particularly applies to the line between bargain and super-bargain CDs. Premium-priced CDs cost on average approximately the same number of dollars in the USA as they do pounds in the UK. Harmonia Mundi's Musique d'Abord label (prefix HMA) is described as budget – which it is in the UK – but the American list-price is higher.

Duos and Doubles, Chandos 2 for 1 sets, Delos Doubles, Double Deccas, double fortes, Dyads, Finlandia Ultima & 'Meet the Composer', BMG/RCA Doubles, 2CD &Twofers', Warner Classics Ultimas where available (although they cost less west of the Atlantic) are two-for-the-cost-of-one premium-priced disc the world over. CDCFPD, and the Virgin Classics 2 x 1 Doubles are two-for-the-price-of-one mid-priced CD.

OTHER COMPARABLE PRICES IN THE UK AND USA

Here are comparative details of the other price-ranges (note that sets are multiples of the prices quoted):

(M) Mid-priced series

Includes: Avid; ASV Chandos (including Collect; Enchant); Barbirolli Society; BBC Legends; Classic fM (UK only); EMI Operas (UK only); CRD; Decca/London including Classic Sound, Legends, 'Singers' and Opera Gala; DG (including Originals); Dutton CDLX, CDLXT, CDCLP, 2CDAX, 2CDEA (UK only); EMI (Classics, British Music series, and Great Recordings of the Century); Erato/Warner (UK), Erato/WEA (USA); DHM; Harmonia Mundi Musique d'Abord (USA); Somm; Suite; Mercury; Oiseau-Lyre; Philips; RCA Gold Seal and Living Stereo; Sony; Teldec/Warner (UK), Teldec/WEA (USA); Vanguard; Virgin; Warner Fonit; Westminster.

UK: £10.99; often £9–£10;
USA: $10 and under.

(B) Bargain-priced series

Includes: Calliope Approche (UK only); CfP; Debut; Decca Eclipse (UK only); DG Classikon (UK only); EMI Operetta Series; Harmonia Mundi Musique d'Abord (UK only); HMP; Hyperion Helios, Naim; Philips Virtuoso (UK only); RCA High Performance; Regis; Sony Essential Classics.

UK: £5.50–£7;
USA: Under $7.

(BB) Super-bargain series

Includes: Arte Nova; Arts; ASV Quicksilva (UK only); Belart; Brilliant sets (even lower than super-bargain price); DHM Baroque Esprit; Dutton CDAX, CDBP, CDEA, CDK; Eloquence; Encore; Harmonia Mundi Classical Express; Naxos; RCA Dimension; Navigator (UK only); Warner Apex.

UK: £5–£5.50;
USA: $5–$6.

THE AUSTRALIAN SCENE

We have been fortunate in obtaining for review some recordings from the Australian branch of Universal Classics (responsible for the three key labels, Decca, DG and Philips), who have been making a series of local issues of Decca DG and Philips repertoire of considerable interest, mostly not otherwise available. These are bargain issues in Australia, but because of import costs, are more expensive in the UK and USA. Australian Universal pioneered the reissue of Richard Bonynge's ballet recordings on CD and a seven-disc set of 'The Art of Julian Katchen'. Currently launched is a new 'Australian Heritage' series, which includes a three-disc compilation of the recordings (concertante and solo) of another outstanding pianist from the same era – Noel Mewton-Wood, who has been neglected by the major record companies in the UK.

All these Universal Australian CDs can be purchased via the Australian website:

www.buywell.com

Residents in the UK should be able to obtain them from:

Seaford Music, 24 Pevensey Road, Eastbourne, East Sussex, BN21 3BN. Tel.: 01323 732553

AN INTERNATIONAL MAIL-ORDER SOURCE FOR RECORDINGS IN THE UK

Readers are urged to support a local dealer if he is prepared and able to give a proper service, and to remember that obtaining many CDs involves expertise and perseverance. However, in recent years many specialist sources have disappeared and for that reason, if any difficulty is experienced in obtaining the CDs you want, we suggest the following mail-order alternative, which offers competitive discounts in the UK but also operates world-wide. Through this service, advice on choice of recordings from the Editor of The Penguin Guide to Compact Discs is always readily available to mail-order customers:

> **Squires Gate Music Centre Ltd (PG Dept)**
> **Rear 13, St Andrew's Road South**
> **St Annes on Sea, Lancashire**
> **FY8 1SX**
> **U.K.**
>
> **Tel.: (+44) (0) 1253 782588**
> **Fax: (+44) (0) 1253 782985**
>
> **Web Site Address: www.lprl.demon.co.uk**
> **E-Mail Address: sales@lprl.demon.co.uk**

This organization can supply any recording available in Britain and patiently extends compact disc orders until they finally come to hand. A full guarantee of safe delivery is made on any order undertaken. Please write or fax for further details, or make a trial credit-card order by fax, e-mail or telephone.

❂ THE ROSETTE SERVICE

Squires Gate also offers a try-before-you-buy weekly loan service (within the UK only) so that customers can try out rosetted recordings at home, plus a hand-picked group of recommended key-repertoire CDs, for a small charge, without any obligation to purchase. If a CD is subsequently purchased, it will be discounted and the trial charge waived. Full details sent on request. Currently DVDs are being added to this service.

Squires Gate Music Centre also offers a simple bi-monthly mailing, listing a hand picked selection of current new and reissued CDs, chosen by the Editor of the *Penguin Guide*, Ivan March. Customers of Squires Gate Music Centre Ltd, both domestic and overseas, receive the bulletin as available, and it is sent automatically with their purchases.

ABBREVIATIONS

AAM — Academy of Ancient Music
Ac. — Academy, Academic
ADD — Analogue to digital transfer
Amb. — S.Ambrosian Singers
Ara. — Arabesque
arr. — arranged, arrangement
ASMF — Academy of St Martin-in-the-Fields
(B) — bargain-price CD
(BB) — super-bargain-price CD
Bar. — Baroque
Bav. — Bavarian
BBC — British Broadcasting Corporation
BPO — Berlin Philharmonic Orchestra
BRT — Belgian Radio & Television (Brussels)
Cal. — Calliope
Cap. — Cappriccio
CBSO — City of Birmingham Symphony Orchestra
CfP — Classics for Pleasure
Ch. — Choir; Chorale; Chorus
Chan. — Chandos
CO — Chamber Orchestra
COE — Chamber Orchestra of Europe
Col. Mus. Ant. — Musica Antiqua, Cologne
Coll. — Collegium
Coll. Aur. — Collegium Aureum
Coll. Voc. — Collegium Vocale
Concg. O — Royal Concertgebouw Orchestra of Amsterdam
cond. — conductor, conducted
Cons. — Consort
DDD — digital recording
DG — Deutsche Grammophon
DHM — Deutsche Harmonia Mundi
E. — England, English
E. Bar. Sol. — English Baroque Soloists
ECCO — European Community Chamber Orchestra
ECO — English Chamber Orchestra
ENO — English National Opera Company
Ens. — Ensemble
ESO — English Symphony Orchestra
Fr. — French
GO — Gewandhaus Orchestra
Häns. — Hänssler
HM — Harmonia Mundi
Hung. — Hungaroton
Hyp. — Hyperion
IMS — Import Music Service (Polygram – UK only)

L. — London
LA — Los Angeles
LCO — London Chamber Orchestra
LCP — London Classical Players
LMP — London Mozart Players
LOP — Lamoureux Orchestra of Paris
LPO — London Philharmonic Orchestra
LSO — London Symphony Orchestra
(M) — mid-price CD
Mer. — Meridian
Met. — Metropolitan
min. — minor
MoC — Ministry of Culture
movt — movement
N. — North, Northern
nar. — narrated
Nat. — National
Nim. — Nimbus
NY — New York
O — Orchestra, Orchestre
OAE — Orchestra of the Age of Enlightenment
O-L — Oiseau-Lyre
Op. — Opera (in performance listings); opus (in music titles)
orch. — orchestrated
ORR — Orchestre Révolutionnaire et Romantique
ORTF — L'Orchestre de la radio et télévision française
Ph. — Philips
Phd. — Philadelphia
Philh. — Philharmonia
PO — Philharmonic Orchestra
Qt — Quartet
R. — Radio
Ref. — Référence
RLPO — Royal Liverpool Philharmonic Orchestra
ROHCG — Royal Opera House, Covent Garden
RPO — Royal Philharmonic Orchestra
RSNO — Royal Scottish National Orchestra
RSO — Radio Symphony Orchestra
RTE — Radio Television Eireann
S. — South
SCO — Scottish Chamber Orchestra
Sinf. — Sinfonietta
SIS — Special Import Service (EMI – UK only)
SNO — Scottish National Orchestra

SO	Symphony Orchestra	V/D	Video Director
Soc.	Society	Van.	Vanguard
Sol. Ven.I	Solisti Veneti	VCM	Vienna Concentus Musicus
SRO	Suisse Romande Orchestra	VPO	Vienna Philharmonic Orchestra
Sup.	Supraphon	VSO	Vienna Symphony Orchestra
trans.	transcription, transcribed	W.	West
V.	Vienna	WNO	Welsh National Opera Company

COMPOSERS A–Z

ADAM, Adolphe (1803–56)

La Filleule des fées (ballet): complete.

*** Marco Polo 8.223734-35 (2). Queensland SO, Mogrelia.

Another attractive ballet from Adam, his third, which was first performed in 1849. It shows the composer at his most winningly tuneful, with plenty of rustic-sounding dance numbers interspersed with tenderly beautiful lyrical music, and again one is struck by the seemingly endless melodic invention and the mastery of orchestration. Adam's ability to paint a choreographic picture is also striking: 'Jobin's Dance' in the Prologue, in which he keeps being interrupted by a knock on the door, is a charming example. Adam's wit is irrepressible, while his subtle shifts in metre and harmonic colouring always hold the listener's interest. This makes pleasing home listening, and the recording and performance are both very good.

Giselle (ballet; complete. Choreography: Jean Coralli & Jules Perrot, revised Marius Petipa).

*** Warner DVD 0630 19397-2. Mezentseva, Zaklinsky, Selyutsky, Terekhova, Kirov Ballet, Leningrad Op. & Ballet Theatre O, Fedotov. (Producer: Oleg Vinogradov. V/D: Preben Montell.)

This magnificent live performance of *Giselle*, recorded in 1983 preserves a Russian choreographic pattern and dramatic understanding going back to the ballet's first performance there in 1842. The casting has no weakness. Galina Mezentseva is the epitome of balletic grace in the title role – and her touching performance at the tragic end of Act I is to be surpassed in the second Act, where the opening scene brings more ravishing dancing from Myrtha, Queen of the Wilis (Tatyana Terekhova) and the dazzling corps de ballet. There is intrusive applause here, but it is understandable. Konstantin Zaklinsky as Albrecht and Genndi Selyutsky as Hilarion are hardly less impressive and the solo dances and pas de deux in Act II are memorable. The orchestra plays with warmth, finesse and robust vitality under Viktor Fedotov and is richly and vibrantly recorded, with the slight edge on the violins adding to the brilliant effect of the playing. The camera is almost always where you want it to be with the perspectives imaginatively varied to follow the action. Costumes and scenery are traditional – the setting for Act III is rightly applauded, and it is only the occasionally over-enthusiastic audience response that robs the DVD of a ●.

Le Postillon de Lonjumeau (opera): complete.

(BB) **(*) EMI CZS5 74106-2 (2). Aler, Anderson, Lafont, Le Roux, Ottewaere, Laforge Ch. Ens., Monte Carlo PO, Fulton.

Adolphe Adam's opera *Le Postillon de Lonjumeau* is best known for the hero's spectacular Act I aria with its stratospheric top notes; however, it contains many other charming moments and is given an excellent complete recording in this EMI set. John Aler, heady in tone throughout his range and with no strain on those top notes, is outstanding as the postillion himself, who soon after singing that aria leaves his new bride to become an opera singer. As Madeleine, the abandoned wife, June Anderson is admirably agile, and she brings a vein of toughness to a heroine who, after inheriting a fortune, seeks revenge on her opera singer husband. Her voice, however, is a trifle raw. The story is preposterous, but there is spike behind the fun, which adds point to the music. Thomas Fulton, conducting the Monte Carlo Orchestra, is obviously at home, giving a lively spring to the many ensembles. The sound has atmosphere and clarity, and the CDs offer an inexpensive way to sample this delightful work. The only snag is the lack of texts and translations.

ADAMS, John (born 1947)

El Niño (complete recording).

*** Arthaus DVD 100 220 (CD version on Nonesuch 79634-2 (2)). Hunt Lieberson, Upshaw, White, Theatre of Voices, L. Voices, Berlin Deutsches SO, Nagano. (Director: Peter Sellars. V/D: Peter Sellars.)

El Niño, which might be translated as 'The Babe', began life as an oratorio commissioned by the San Francisco Symphony, but at the same time the Paris Châtelet Theatre asked for an opera, so the final work became what is essentially a staged oratorio. In this respect it broadly follows on after Bach's *Christmas Oratorio* and Handel's *Messiah* in telling the story of the Annunciation and birth of Christ, the journey to Bethlehem, the visit of the Three Kings, Herod's slaughter of the children and the prudent departure of Joseph, Mary and Jesus. The libretto includes Bible texts in the American translation by Richard Lattimore and New Testament Apocrypha, as well as poems by Latin American writers from Mexico and Chile which are sung in Spanish.

The opera staging places the principal singers, chorus and semi-chorus (comprising three countertenors) on a plinth below a huge screen on which is projected a two-hour film (made by Peter Sellars and Yreina Cervántez). The narrative is enacted partly in a desert-like location, where we first encounter the passion of Adam and Eve, and later, as the story of Mary, Joseph and Jesus unfolds, in a contemporary American setting. The visit of the Three Wise Men takes place on wasteland near an airport with jets constantly flying overhead. The massacre ordered by Herod is followed by an angry choral reminder of the slaughter of the Aztecs by Cortès and his troops in Mexico in 1521 .

The work opens with typical Adams throbbing chords, and there is a good deal of this minimalist repetition in the score. The role of Mary is shared by mezzo-soprano and soprano, and the long Annunciation aria set to lyric poetry by Rosario Castellanos (gloriously sung by Lorraine Hunt Lieberson) is an outstanding highlight of the score, as is the same lyricist's soprano/mezzo duet, *Se habla de Gabriel*. Dawn Upshaw, who has more of a narrative role, also sings with great beauty and eloquence.

Much of Willard White's contribution (he takes the part of Joseph) is boldly dramatic recitative, but his performance is still unforgettably powerful. The writing for the three male altos (who together take the part of Gabriel) is imaginatively chorded, and overall the music is consistently invented, if melodically uneven, and the peaceful closing number for mezzo, baritone, male altos and children's chorus is very touching, even if it does not reach the level of inspiration of the opera's early scenes.

It has to be said that much of the visual imagery (apart from the main events of the story) is confusing, even superfluous and does not bear much repetition, but the three principals all sing with moving eloquence and are always worth watching. So there is a good case for the audio version, which includes full texts, as against the video's surtitles. Whether on CD or DVD, the recording is impressively spacious and clear.

ALBÉNIZ, Isaac (1860–1909)

Iberia: Books 1 & 2 (complete); *España, Op. 163*.

*** Teldec 8573 81503-2. Barenboim.

After a long absence Barenboim forsakes the rostrum to return to the piano and provide brilliant and evocative accounts of these famous Spanish pieces. He knows just how to produce a luminous range of Mediterranean colour from the keyboard, and his dynamic shading is full of subtlety. The dance rhythms sparkle, and he can captivate the ear with his languorous rubato. The recording is close but faithful, and this is in every way distinguished playing.

ALBINONI, Tomaso (1671–1751)

Concerti a cinque, Op. 7/3, 6, 9 & 12; Op. 9/2, 5, 8 & 11.

(BB) *** Regis RRC 1095. Francis, L. Harpsichord Ens.

Those looking for a selection of *Oboe Concertos* from both Op. 7 and Op. 9 will find that Sarah Francis is an immensely stylish and gifted soloist. She is accompanied with warmth and grace, and the recording is first-class, transparent yet full and naturally balanced. As a budget-priced Regis reissue this is very attractive indeed.

12 Concerti a cinque, Op. 9.

(B) *** Erato Ultima (ADD) 3984 25593-2 (2). Pierlot, Chambon, Toso, Ferrari, I Sol. Ven., Scimone.

It is good to have Scimone's excellent complete set from the late 1960s available again, confirming once more that Albinoni's concertos are as good as the finest Vivaldi. Pierre Pierlot, with his elegant phrasing and lovely tone, Jacques Chambon (in the *Double Concerto in F*, Op. 9/3) and Piero Toso (in the three concertos for violin) all make impressive contributions. I Solisti Veneti are also on form and the recording is full and naturally balanced. Excellent value at Ultima price.

ALKAN, Charles-Valentin (1813–88)

Esquisses, Op. 63.

(BB) Naxos 8.555496. Martin.

Alkan's *Esquisses* belong to 1861, though the individual pieces were probably composed over the previous decade or more. In all there are 49 little miniatures, some of them lasting under a minute. They are not among Alkan's most brilliant virtuoso pieces, but their range of mood and expression is impressively wide. Some, like *Le Staccatissimo* and *Petit prelude à 3*, suggest the world of Couperin and Rameau, while others, such as *Le Premier billet doux*, are miniature mood pictures. There are occasional foreshadows of things to come (try the Debussian *Les Soupirs* or *Les Diablotins*), but all these pieces, apart from being expertly crafted, are full of imaginative and original touches. Laurent Martin is an excellent player who understands this music inside out. He made a strong impression when this and other recordings appeared in the early 1990s and is generally well served by the recorded sound.

12 Etudes in the Minor Keys, Op. 35; Le Festin d'Esope, Op. 39/12; Scherzo diabolico, Op. 39/3.

(BB) *** Naxos 8.555495. Ringeissen.

The *Douze études dans tous les tons mineurs* are notorious for the fiendish demands they place on the pianist – they are among the most difficult pieces in existence – and are remarkable also for their harmonic originality and sheer imagination. Bernard Ringeissen gives a very brilliant account of them, although Jack Gibbons (on ASV CDDCS 227) and Marc-André Hamelin (on Hyperion CDA 67218) also rise to their challenge (see our main volume). Their couplings are different and their alternative versions more expensive. The 1990 Naxos recording is very faithful, and at this bargain-basement price the attractions of the set are further enhanced by *Le Festin d'Esope*, a rare item on disc and also very impressive here.

ALLEGRI, Gregorio (1582–1652)

Miserere.

(B) **(*) CfP 575 5602. St John's College, Cambridge Ch., Guest – LASSUS: *Missa super'Bell'Amfrit'alterna'* **(*); PALESTRINA: *Missa Veni sponsa Christi*. ***

The 1990 digital recording of this celestial piece from St John's is finely sung, and the three-dimensional balance is very realistic, but the unnamed treble soloist sings less ethereally than his famous predecessors, Alison Stamp and Roy Goodman, with a bold upward leap in the famous repeated phrase.

ALWYN, William (1905–85)

Film Scores, Vol. 2: *The Card:* **suite.** *The Crimson Pirate; Desert Victory: Prologue & excerpts. Green Girdle; In Search of the Castaways: Rhumba; Waltz. State Secret: Main titles & excerpts.* **(i)** *Svengali: Libera me. Take my Life. The Winslow Boy: Suite.*

*** Chan 9959. BBC PO, Gamba; (i) with Bullock, Canzonetta.

Alwyn worked in the British film industry when directors wanted quality writing for their background music. Alwyn's gifts made him an ideal source, and with the scores no longer in existence, Philip Lane's reconstructions from the original soundtracks are most welcome. In *Take my Life* Alwyn composed a pastiche aria for the operatic heroine and wrote a second for *Svengali*, both impressively sung by Susan Bullock. But the highlight here is the delightful suite compiled from the film of Arnold Bennett's *The Card*, with Alec Guinness as the whimsical hero. Both *In Search of the Castaways* and (especially) *Desert Victory* inspired Alwyn to some of his most atmospheric writing, all splendidly played here by the BBC Philharmonic under Rumon Gamba, and given top quality Chandos sound.

ANDERSON, Leroy (1908–75)

Belle of the Ball; Blue Tango; Bugler's Holiday; Fiddle Faddle; Forgotten Dreams; The Girl in Satin; Jazz Legato; Jazz Pizzicato; March of the Two Left Feet; The Penny Whistle Song; The Phantom Regiment; Plink, Plank, Plunk!; Promenade; Sandpaper Ballet; Saraband; Serenata; Sleigh Ride; The Syncopated Clock; Trumpeter's Lullaby; The Typewriter; The Waltzing Cat.

(BB) ** Naxos 8.559125. Orchestra, Hayman.

After playing the classic Mercury account with the Eastman-Rochester Pops Orchestra (432 013-2), this 1989 Naxos recording sounds rather anaemic. This is partly due to the recording, which, though more refined, sounds distant next to the exceptionally vivid Mercury sound. Richard Hayman's performances are good, but the Mercury ones have greater character and come over with tingling immediacy. It is definitely worth paying more for the Mercury CD, although the repertoire is slightly different.

ARNE, Thomas Augustine (1710–78)

(i; ii) *Harpsichord Concerto No. 5 in G min.;* **(iii)** *Organ Concertos Nos. 4 in B flat; 5 in G min.; 6 in B flat;* **(iv)** *Overtures: Nos. 1 in E min.; 2 in A; 3 in G; 4*

in F; 5 in D; 6 in B flat; 7 in D; 8 in G min.; **(i; iv)** *Cantatas: Bacchus and Ariadne; Fair Caelia Love Pretended.* **Arias from: (v)** *Artaxerxes: The Soldier Tir'd;* **(iv; vi)** *Comus: Brightest Lady: Thrice upon thy Finger's Tip; By the Rushy-fringed Bank;* **(vii)** *The Judgment of Paris: O Ravishing Delight;* **(iv; vi)** *Rosamond: Rise, Glory, Rise. The Tempest: Where the Bee Sucks.*

(M) **(*) Decca (ADD/DDD) 470 372-2 (2). (i) ASMF, Marriner; (ii) Malcolm; (iii) Guillou, Berlin Brandenburg O, Klopfenstein (iv) AAM, Hogwood; (iv) Tear; (v) Sutherland, O ROHCG, Molinari-Pradelli; (vi) Kirkby; (vii) Vyvyan, Lush.

Thomas Arne had the knack of writing instantly memorable tunes, though curiously, his most famous piece, *Rule Brittania!*, is not included on this CD. The *G minor Harpsichord Concerto* with its splendidly Handelian opening is a delight. This gives way to a bubbling allegro, with witty interjections from the harpsichord (here supremely played by George Malcolm) followed later by a deliciously insouciant finale, with the minor key adding a certain piquancy. Also included is the alternative version of that same concerto for organ, along with two other organ concertos of comparable invention. Piquant also describes the arias here, mainly from Arne's theatrical works, notably Sutherland's famously radiant account of *The Soldier Tir'd*, and Emma Kirkby's excellent numbers, including the rousing *Rise, Glory Rise.* If the Academy of Ancient Music 1973 version of the *Overtures* is comparatively crude by the standards of present-day period performance (the horns are particularly rough), they still make enjoyable listening as the quality of invention is always stimulating. The two cantatas (recorded in 1969) have many pleasures. Both touching and tuneful, sometimes virtuosic, they pose no problems for Robert Tear. All in all, a delightful addition to Decca's British Collection series, with excellent recordings throughout.

ARNOLD, Malcolm (born 1921)

(i; ii) *Anniversary Overture, Op. 99; Beckus the Dandipratt Overture, Op. 5;* **(iii; ii)** *Carnival of the Animals;* **(iv; iii; ii)** *Concerto for 2 Pianos, 3 hands (Concerto for Phyllis and Cyril);* **(v)** *Guitar Concerto, Op. 67;* **(vi)** *4 Cornish Dances, Op. 91; 8 English Dances, Opp. 27 & 33* **(arr. Farr);** *Fantasy for Brass Band, Op. 114;* **(iii; ii)** *A Grand, Grand Overture, Op. 57;* **(vii)** *Larch Trees, Op. 3;* **(vi)** *Little Suites for Brass Band Nos. 1, Op. 80; 2, Op. 93; The Padstow Lifeboat, Op. 94; 4 Scottish Dances, Op. 59* **(arr. Farr);** **(vii)** *Serenade for Small Orchestra, Op. 26.*

(B) *** RCA (DDD/ADD) 74321 88392-2 (2). (i) BBC Concert O; (ii) Handley; (iii) RPO; (iv) Nettle & Markham; (v) Bream, Melos Ens., composer; (vi) Grimethorpe Colliery Band, Howarth (or composer); (vii) London Musici, Stephenson.

This splendid bargain Double gives a useful and generous survey of shorter Arnold works, not forgetting the brass band music which the superb Grimethorpe players under Elgar Howarth recorded with the composer present. Not surprisingly he gave high praise to Howarth's carefully prepared and winningly spontaneous performances, unerringly paced. Farr's arrangements, too, are extremely effective. The composer himself directs the March, *The Padstow Lifeboat*, with its warning off-key foghorn, based on the pitch of the foghorn at Trevose in Cornwall. The recording is very much in the demonstration bracket.

The short *Anniversary Overture* was written to accompany a Hong Kong fireworks display: it is boisterous and tuneful. Also included is a fizzing performance of Arnold's first orchestral work, *Beckus the Dandipratt*, and the *Double Piano*, originally the 'Concerto for Phyllis and Cyril'. This was written in 1969 for Phyllis Sellick and Cyril Smith when Cyril lost the use of his left hand and he and his wife continued as a highly successful duo. The piano duo here, Nettle and Markham, are obviously captivated by the piece, which they play with much flair and understanding.

Julian Bream's is a classic account of the *Guitar Concerto*, with the composer directing the accompaniment, and the late 1950s recording has worn its years lightly. The other recordings are all modern. The *Grand, Grand Overture* (with its outrageous special effects) was written for the Hoffnung Festival and comes up remarkably effectively here, with Handley as ever a sympathetic advocate.

Larch Trees dates from as early as 1943, written when Arnold was only 21, and is a nostalgic tone poem that instantly reveals his natural feeling for evocative instrumentation. It is very sympathetically played, and Mark Stephenson and London Musici are just as convincingly idiomatic in the charming *Serenade*. Altogether excellent value.

Clarinet Concertos Nos. 1, Op. 20; 2, Op. 115; Scherzetto.

(B) *** Hyp. Helios CDH 55060. King, ECO, Wordsworth – BRITTEN: *Clarinet Concerto Movement*; MACONCHY: *Concertinos*. ***

Designed in part as a tribute to the great clarinettist, Frederick Thurston, Thea King's collection of short concertante works for clarinet makes an exceptionally attractive disc, beautifully recorded and superbly performed. The *Scherzetto* is a delightfully jaunty piece adapted by Christopher Palmer from Arnold's music for the film *You Know What Sailors Are*. Not only Thea King but the ECO (the orchestra in which she has been a distinguished principal for many years) under Barry Wordsworth bring out the warmth as well as the rhythmic drive.

(i) Guitar Concerto, Op. 67; (ii) 8 English Dances, Op. 27 and Op. 33; (iii; iv) Quintet for Brass, Op. 73; (iii; v) Symphony for Brass Instruments, Op. 123.

(M) *** Decca mono/stereo 468 803-2. (i) Fernández, ECO, Wordsworth; (ii) LPO, Boult; (iii) Philip Jones Brass Ens.; (iv) Howarth; (v) Snell.

Boult's 1954 mono set of the *English Dances* is still the best – full of a character and brio that have seldom been matched, and the early mono sound, though lacking in amplitude, is vivid (the bass drum is very realistic). The 1970s recording for the Philip Jones Brass Ensemble is brilliant and clear, as are the superb performances. The *Symphony* is a longish piece, lasting some 26 minutes, and, as one might expect from a former trumpeter, is expertly scored and for unusual forces (horn, tuba, four trumpets and four trombones). Ultimately, the ideas remain a shade facile, but there are powerful sonorities here. The shorter *Quintet* has bubbling outer movements with some interesting quirky harmonies, which frame a somewhat more severe central *Chaconne*. The brilliant digital version of the *Guitar Concerto* is superbly recorded and brings glowing sound from Fernández and the ECO in a fizzing performance, spikily incisive in bringing out the jazz overtones. Fernández makes the haunting melody of the first movement's second subject warm and not sentimental, and the full depth of the blues-inspired slow movement is movingly conveyed.

Guitar Concerto; Serenade for Guitar and Strings.

*** Chan. 9963. Ogden, Northern Sinf., Hickox – BERKELEY: *Guitar Concerto*; WALTON: *5 Bagatelles*. ***

The Arnold *Guitar Concerto* is among the most striking of all his many concertos, with its haunting popular tune for a second subject, its dark, extended slow movement written in homage to the jazz guitarist, Django Reinhardt, and its wittily neo-classical finale. The charming, lyrical *Serenade for Guitar and Strings* which comes as supplement was written by Arnold a couple of years earlier as a trial run for the *Concerto*. Craig Ogden is a consummate soloist in both and he is beautifully recorded. An excellent alternative to Julian Bream's recordings, especially if the Berkeley and Walton couplings are preferred.

(i) 4 Cornish Dances; (ii) 8 English Dances; (iii) Serenade for Small Orchestra; (iv) Sinfoniettas Nos. 1–2; (iii) Sinfonietta No. 3.

(M) **(*) EMI (ADD) CDZ5 74780-2. (i) CBSO, Composer; (ii) Bournemouth SO, Groves; (iii) Bournemouth Sinfonietta, Thomas; (iv) Philh O, Dilkes.

Groves's *English Dances* are affectionately played, if without the excitement of the best available, but the composer's own performance of the less exuberant *Cornish Dances* is excellent. The three *Sinfoniettas* and the *Serenade* all have some attractive ideas – the witty woodwind writing in the finale of the *Second Sinfonietta* is one of several passages that raise a smile, and the slow movements at times have a nostalgic wistfulness. The performances and the

1970s recordings are good, and this collection is certainly worth considering.

ATTERBERG, Kurt (1887–1974)

Ballade and Passacaglia, Op. 38; (i) *Piano Concerto in B flat minor, Op. 37; Rhapsody for piano and orchestra, Op. 1.*

*** CPO 999 732-2. (i) Derwinger, NDR PO, Hanover, Rasilainen.

Atterberg himself made records of his attractive *Ballade and Passacaglia* for Swedish HMV in the dying days of 78 rpm records and the Finnish conductor Ari Rasilainen gives a very good account of it. The *Piano Concerto* is pure kitsch, the Rich Man's 'Warsaw Concerto'. The solo piano writing is unremitting and relentless with hardly a minute's rest and the work is overscored. Dan Franklin Smith recorded it for the ever enterprising Sterling label, but this is the more subtle of the two performances. Even so, not even the artistry of Love Derwinger and the ardour of Rasilainen and the Nord-Deutscher Rundfunk Orchestra, Hanover can save the day. Atterberg struggled for eight long years before finishing the *Piano Concerto*, but it remains one of his feeblest efforts. The *Rhapsody, Op. 1* comes from 1908, the year after he began his studies of electrical engineering, and before he decided to opt for a musical career. It is an accomplished piece, Lisztian in character but very well crafted. The three stars are for the performers and the very acceptable recorded sound – not the music.

AVALON, Robert (born 1955)

(i) *Piano Concerto, Op. 10;* (ii) *Flute and Harp Concerto, Op. 31.*

**(*) Centaur CRC 2482. (i) composer; (ii) Meisenbach, Golden; Houston Foundation for Modern Music O, composer.

The *Piano Concerto* of the Texan composer, Robert Avalon, is a large-scale, accessible work, with an essentially lyrical core. The first movement is effectively written and scored, but at 20' 26" is a shade too long, although its invention does not really falter. The Scherzo is busy and light-hearted, the delicately atmospheric *Andante* is the work's highlight and is quite haunting; the finale sums up what has gone before and ends positively. The *Concerto for Flute and Harp*, written to be played either with string quartet, or string orchestra as here, is texturally attractive, but less tangible in melodic content. However, both works are very well played, with the composer a confident soloist in the piano concerto. The recording is first class, but it is a pity that the notes offer a 'press-type' interview with the composer, instead of offering his analysis of the music.

(i) *Flute Sonata, Op. 26;* (ii) *Violin Sonata;* (iii) *Sextet to Julia de Burgos, Op. 21.*

*** Centaur CRC 2430. (i) Meisenbach; (ii) Lewis; (iii) Lattimore, ens.; composer.

This is an outstanding CD in every respect, and a more rewarding way to explore the music of Robert Avalon than the concerto pairing above. Both the *Violin* and *Flute Sonatas* are inspired works, profoundly lyrical, showing Avalon writing in a highly communicative and appealingly melodic style, yet with his own individual voice. The Adagio of the *Violin Sonata* has real depth of feeling, and the brief moto perpetuo finale ends the piece with infectious brilliance. The *Flute Sonata* is also haunting from the first bar and has a memorably imaginative closing climax to cap the first movement, before the gentle melancholy of the flowing *Adagio*. With the composer at the piano, both performances are outstanding, conveying a natural spontaneity, as at a live performance. The *Sextet*, for soprano, string trio, flute and piano was inspired by Casals, whom the composer greatly admires. A passionate setting of three extraordinarily intense poems by the Puerto Rican poet, Julia de Burgos, it is remarkably colloquial in its Mediterranean style and atmosphere, with the instrumental writing just as ear-catching as the solo line, passionately declaimed here by Jonita Lattimore. The recordings are of great vividness and this collection is highly recommended.

AVISON, Charles (1709–70)

Concerti grossi, Op. 9/1, 4, 6–9.

**(*) Divine Art 2-4108. Georgian Consort.

Charles Avison's set of *Twelve Concertos*, Op. 9 were pulished in London in 1766. Written in four parts, the composer invites the use of keyboard (notably organ) as a replacement for the violin as the concertino soloist. The music is elegant and easy-going, which is reflected in the pleasingly polished and stylish performances by the Georgian Consort, who play the slightly melancholy slow movements with grace and charm. Their double-dotting however could ideally be a shade crisper, and allegros given more bite (although the finale of No. 8 dances agreeably). The recording is natural and the ambience just right and with the reservations expressed this makes enjoyably relaxed listening.

BACH, Carl Philipp Emanuel (1714–88)

Cello Concerto (No. 3) in A, Wq.172.

(M) * DG 445 608-2. Haimovitz, ECO, Davis – BOCCHERINI: *Concerto in B flat* *; HAYDN: *Concerto in C* *.

This CD was made when Matt Haimovitz was still a gifted student in his teens, and if this account of the *A major Concerto* lacks something in refinement, there is no lack of emotional involvement – indeed, the slow movement is a bit too introspective and there is some overheated vibrato that will not be to all tastes. The cello is a bit too up-front, but the recording has no lack of body or warmth. However, this repertoire now is strongly competitive and this CD is outclassed. First choice for the three key Cello Concertos lies with Hidemi Suzuki on BIS CD 807.

Keyboard Sonatas: in F sharp min., Wq.52/4; in E min., Wq.59/1; in D, Wq.61/2; in G, Wq.62/19; in G min., Wq.65/17; in C min., Wq.65/31; Andante contenerezza; Rondos: in A, Wq.58/1; in C min., Wq.59/4; in D min., Wq.61/4.

🏆 *** DG 459 614-2. Pletnev.

Altogether remarkable playing, even by Pletnev's exalted standards. He finds both the wit and depth of this music, and the resource of keyboard colour and refinement of articulation are pretty awesome. And what interesting music it is! He receives very natural recorded sound from the DG team.

BACH, Johann Christian (1735–82)

Amadis des Gaules: Overture & ballet music. Overtures: Endimione; Lucio Silla; Temistocle.

*** CPO 999 753-2. Hanover Band, Halstead.

It's easy to see why London-based J. C. Bach was so successful in his day. These four overtures, written for key opera houses in London and Paris and for the Mannheim Court, are full of bubbling vitality and striking melodic invention and are sprinkled with attractive orchestral colourings throughout. The pastoral flutes contrast well with the drama of the 'hunting' horns, scurrying strings and timpani in the finale of the *Endimione Overture*, and such examples are typical. All the overtures are in the Italian overture form (slow-fast-slow), with central movements of the utmost elegance and grace. The *Amadis des Gaules Overture*, with its crescendi and excited writing, looks to the classical/early romantic period, and one senses a composer embracing all the virtues of a true musical cosmopolitan. The 25-minute ballet music *Amadis* is a delight and includes some vocal items with chorus (curiously not mentioned on the CD leaflet). The final *Tambourin*, with its driving rhythms and bold timpani, is especially enjoyable. Performances and recording are both first class, with Halstead providing the right amount of authentic vigour, while allowing the music's charm to come through.

Harpsichord Sonatas: in E & C min., Op. 5/5–6; in C min.; E flat & A, Op. 17/2–3 & 5.

(M) *** CRD 3453. Black (harpsichord).

Virginia Black plays a modern copy of a Goujon harpsichord, circa 1740, and she is beautifully recorded, the sound clear and robust, with the instrument given a vivid presence (yet not aggressively close) against a warm background ambience. Her account of the two-movement *E flat major Sonata*,

Op. 17/3, with which she opens her recital, immediately catches the listener's ear, and the *Prestissimo* finale of Op. 17/2, which comes second, is most infectious, the articulation admirably crisp. The *Adagio* of Op. 5/5 is elegant and nicely paced, and again the rhythmically winning finale demands and receives easy virtuosity. A most attractive disc.

THE BACH FAMILY, including Johann Sebastian

Heinrich Bach (1615–1692)

Johann Christoph (1642–1703)

Johann Ludwig (1677–1731)

Johann Sebastian (1685–1750)

Cyriacus Wilche (?–1667)

Signr. Pagh (before 1672)

'Bachiana': HEINRICH BACH: *Sonatas Nos. 1; 2; 'à cinque' in C & F for 2 Violins, 2 Violas & Continuo.* JOHANN CHRISTOPH BACH: *Aria: Eberliniana pro dormente Camillo for harpsichord.* JOHANN LUDWIG BACH: *Concerto in D for 2 violins, 2 Oboes & Strings; Orchestral Suite (Overture) in G for 2 Oboes (ad lib.) & Strings.* JOHANN SEBASTIAN BACH: *Concerto in D for 3 Trumpets, Timpani, 2 Oboes, Bassoon & Strings, after BWV 249.* CYRIACUS WILCHE: *Battaglia for 2 Violins, 2 Violas & Continuo.* SIGNR. PAGH: *Sonata & Capriccio in G min. for Violin, 2 Violas & Continuo.*

*** DG 471 150-2. Cologne Musica Antiqua, Goebel.

Johann Sebastian Bach was deeply loyal to his extraordinary family, who over the generations produced an unrivalled tribe of composers. Reinhard Goebel follows up the delvings he did in the 1980s with a wonderfully illuminating disc of pieces by Bach's relatives near and far. JSB himself is represented by a delightful concerto reconstructed from the *Easter Oratorio*, and the most substantial offerings otherwise are the *Overture (Suite)* and *Concerto* by his near-contemporary – a distant cousin – Johann Ludwig Bach, whose music JSB regularly used as Cantor in Leipzig.

Heinrich Bach and Johann Michael Bach (thought to be the pseudonymous Signr Pagh) are from earlier generations, the grandfather and father respectively of JSB's first wife and cousin, Maria Barbara, producing music very typical of their period. The piece by Johann Christoph Bach, brother of Johann Michael, is an inventive set of variations for harpsichord, stylistically looking forward, and brilliantly played here by Leon Berben, while Cyriacus Wilche's *Battaglia*, written in 1659 for two violins, two violas and continuo, is the work of the grandfather of Anna Magdalena, Bach's second wife. Reinhard Goebel and his responsive players present the whole collection with a sure feeling for changing idioms and are brilliantly recorded.

BACH, Johann Sebastian (1685–1750)

Brandenburg Concertos Nos. 1–6, BWV 1046–51.

✹ *** TDK **DVD** DV-BABBC. Freiburg Bar. O, Von der Göltz

It is remarkable that so early in the DVD era we should have such an outstanding set of period-instrument performances of the *Brandenburgs*, appropriately recorded at Castle Cöthen. For while Bach dedicated and sent them to the Margrave of Brandenburg in 1721, they were composed earlier while Bach was Kappellmeister at the Cöthen Court.

The castle's Spiegesaal has been magnificently restored and makes a visually entrancing backcloth for the recordings. The spacious room seems also to have an ideal acoustic for a chamber group, for whether in the larger ensemble used for the *First Concerto* or in the smaller scale of No. 6 the effect is very natural and pleasing. The gambas in the latter work have splendid character.

The Freiburgers play their period instruments with great finesse and warmth. Inner detail is clear, there is no edginess on the strings or linear distortions in the expressively played slow movements. The choice of tempi seems near ideal and Gottfried von der Göltz, who directs proceedings almost impassively but with obvious commitment, plays with an easy virtuosity which is engrossing to watch.

The cameras often cover the players as a group, but also move around among them, and it is fascinating to observe in close-up the pair of horns in No. 1 producing amazing florid passages from simple coils of brass, creating the notes by their controlled embouchures with no valves to press. Similarly the brilliant soloist in No. 3, Friedrich Immer, uses a primitive early trumpet, with his fingers covering and uncovering holes, rather like a transverse flute. The one effect of balance that is less than ideal (though it often happens in the concert hall) is the harpsichord, which can hardly be heard at all in tuttis, although his solo in the *Fifth Concerto*, played with flexible virtuosity, comes over splendidly.

Overall these splendidly alive performances are enormously stimulating and enjoyable. Apart from their very direct musical communication, one learns so much about Bach's contrapuntal writing when the camera directs the eye, without spotlighting, to the performing instruments.

Brandenburg Concertos Nos. 1–6, BWV 1046–51; Suites Nos. 1–4, BWV 1066–9; (i) Violin Concertos Nos. 1 in A min.; 2 in E; (i; ii) Double Violin Concerto in D min., BWV 1042.

(B) ** Ph. Trio (ADD) 470 934-2 (3). ASMF, Marriner; with (i) Szeryng; (ii) Hasson.

The first of the Philips new series of 'Trios' (three CDs in a box, offered for the cost of two mid-priced CDs) is something of a mixed blessing. Like the Duo below, it includes Marriner's outstanding 1980 set of the *Brandenburgs* in which he introduces such distinguished soloists as Szeryng, Rampal and Michaela Petri, and features George Malcolm as an ideal continuo player. But his second Philips recording of the *Orchestral Suites* is no match for his first 1970 ASMF set on Decca, which is still available and sounding pretty good on a single disc (430 378-2). The movements where he has changed his mind – for example, the famous *Air* from the *Suite No. 3*, which is here ponderously slow and mannered – are almost always less convincing, and that reflects an absence of the very qualities of urgency and spontaneity that made the earlier version so enjoyable. Similarly, there are reservations about Szeryng's accounts of the *Violin Concertos*. He had recorded them earlier (also for Philips), with dignity and classical feeling accompanied by the excellent Winterthur Collegium Musicum, with Peter Rybar a responsive partner in the *Double Concerto*. The slow movements of all three concertos were particularly fine. It is a pity that these performances were not included here, for Szeryng's later record with Marriner, in spite of its fuller, more modern recording with an excellent balance, shows rather less spontaneity (and that in the accompaniments as well as the solo playing). In depth of feeling and understanding, the Winterthur accounts are preferable, although the later versions are by no means to be dismissed.

(i) Brandenburg Concertos Nos. 1–6; (ii) Double Violin Concerto, BWV 1043; (ii; iii) Concerto for Violin & Oboe, BWV 1060.

(B) *** Ph. Duo ADD/Dig. 468 549-2 (2). ASMF; (i) Marriner; (ii) Kremer (violin & cond.); (iii) Holliger.

Marriner's 1980 ASMF set of *Brandenburgs* was highly praised by us in our last main Guide as a leading contender among performances on modern instruments. Above all these performances communicate warmth and enjoyment. However, we wrongly attributed the coupled versions of the two double concertos to Henryk Szeryng. In fact the violin soloist is Gidon Kremer, who also directs the accompanying ensemble. In the *Double Violin Concerto* he adopts (by electronic means) both solo roles, so these interpretations cannot be accused of any kind of artistic inconsistency – indeed they have the vigour and forward thrust of a determined advocate, in slow as well as fast movements. The result, although stylish, is rather cool and the same comment might be applied to the *Concerto for Violin and Oboe*, although here Holliger's contribution dominates tellingly, especially in the Adagio. However these comments do not detract from the appeal of the Marriner *Brandenburgs* which, as a Duo, could still be first choice for those not insisting on the use of period instruments and fast tempi.

Brandenburg Concertos Nos. 1–6, BWV 1046–51; (i)
Triple Concerto for Flute, Violin and Harpsichord,
BWV 1044; Orchestral Suites Nos. 1–4, BWV 1066–9.

(B) ** DG (ADD) 463 657-2 (3). Munich Bach O, K.
Richter; (i) with Nicolet, Hetzel, K. Richter.

In the *Brandenburgs* Karl Richter draws superb playing from his Munich orchestra and the recording is
full and clear. His admirers will not be disappointed
with this bargain reissue, but in his German way
Richter puts the music rather into a rhythmic
straight-jacket – witness the first movement of No. 6
which needs more persuasive handling. Fortunately,
in slow movements he allows a greater degree of
expressive relaxation and this also applies in the *Triple*
Concerto where the effect is warmly romantic, partly
because of the rich recorded sound. Aurèle Nicolet's
flute playing is delightfully fresh and in the slow movement Richter provides a neat keyboard embroidery.
But in the outer movements the harpsichord is less
attractively focused and rhythmically very insistent.
Richter's account of the *Orchestral Suites* is more
heavy-handed, less spontaneous; moreover he fails to
observe the 'double-dotting' convention in the overtures. All-in-all this set is primarily of historic interest.

Brandenburg Concertos Nos. 1–6; Orchestral Suites
Nos. 2 in B min., BWV 1067; 3 in D, BWV 1068.

(B) *(*) Teldec Ultima 0630 18944-2 (2). VCM,
Harnoncourt.

It is a sign of the maturing art of authentic performance that Harnoncourt's digital set of *Brandenburgs*,
recorded in the early 1980s, sounds so laboured.
Speeds are slow and rhythms heavy. There is some
expert playing, both solo and ensemble, but the artificially bright and clinically clear recording gives an
aggressive projection to the music-making. Although
the unnamed solo flautist in the *Second Orchestral*
Suite is nimble enough, the orchestral playing in both
suites could have more finesse and is variable in
rhythmic character. Harnoncourt's earlier analogue
versions of all these works are preferable, but even
these have been upstaged by many recent recordings.

Clavier Concertos Nos. 1–7, BWV 1052–8.

❀ Sony SK 89245 (Nos. 1, 2 & 4); SK 89690 (Nos. 3, 5–7).
Perahia, ASMF.

When the first of these two Sony CDs appeared we commented that it seemed certain that Murray Perahia's set
of the Bach solo keyboard concertos was set to sweep
the board. And so it proves. The performances are
totally pianistic, with Perahia's lightness of rhythmic
touch in allegros and deliciously crisp ornamentation
communicating an exhilarating yet intimate sense of
joy. Slow movements are warmly expressive helped by
the elegant fullness of the Academy strings and, as
may be expected, the elysian *Largo* of the *F minor*
Concerto is exquisitely played, and the whole of the
following *F major* is irresistible on every count. The
many individual touches are never self-aware, but

seek to display Bach's music with the freshness of
rediscovery, creating a continuing subtlety of colour
and feeling. Beautifully balanced recording too. In
short the effect here is to put aside any consideration
of period 'authenticity' and instead give this wonderfully life-enhancing music an ageless universality.

Clavier Concertos Nos. 1 in D min., BWV 1052; 3 in
D, BWV 1054; 5 in F min., BWV 1056; 6 in F, BWV
1057.

(BB) *** Warner Apex 0927 40819-2. Katsaris, Franz
Liszt CO, Rolla.

We thought well of these exhilarating performances
when they first appeared at full price in the mid-
1980s. Now that they are on the Apex budget label
their claims on the collector are even stronger. The *F*
major is a transcription of the *Fourth Brandenburg*
Concerto, and the others also derive from earlier
works. Cyprien Katsaris possesses the most remarkable technique and feeling for colour, which are to be
heard to excellent advantage in this vividly recorded
and well-filled disc. He has an astonishingly vital
musical personality and keyboard resource. The playing of the Liszt Chamber Orchestra, surely one of
the very finest chamber ensembles in the world, is
splendidly supportive. Exciting and imaginative performances all round and splendid value for money.

(i) Clavier Concertos Nos. 1 in D min., BWV 1052; 4
in in A, BWV 1055; 5 in F min., BWV 1056. (ii) Triple
Clavier Concertos Nos. 1 in D min.; 2 in D, BWV
1063/4; Quadruple Clavier Concerto in A min., BWV
1065; (iii) Double Violin Concerto in D min., BWV
1043.

(B) *** Erato Ultima (ADD) 3984 26997-2 (2). (i) Pires,
Gulbenkian Foundation CO, Paillard; (ii) Dalberto,
Queffélec, Devoyon, Gautier (pianos), Jean-François
Paillard CO, Paillard.

An excellent compilation on Ultima, well worth its
modest cost for those who enjoy the Bach keyboard
concertos on the piano – as do we. In the solo works
the crisp amd nimble fingerwork of Maria João Pires
is a joy in the allegros, while Corboz provides plenty
of lift, and the orchestral strings are not too ample.
The famous *Largo* of the *F minor Concerto* is beautifully serene and throughout the sound balance is fresh
and believable. The multiple concertos are no less
enjoyable with buoyant outer movements, although it
is again the lyrical freshness of the slow movements
that make the performances distinctive (especially
that of the *Triple Concerto*). The four pianists (Michel
Dalberto, Anne Queffélec, Pascal Devoyon and
Jacques Gautier) change places for each of the concertos, and the very agreeable recording provides better
inner clarity than often happens with harpsichord
versions of these works. Pierre Amoyal and Gérard
Jarry are well matched in the *Double Violin Concerto*,
and the slow movement comes off well. Here there is a
touch of edginess on the timbre of the solo violins,
but not enough to disqualify a recommendation.

Jean-François Paillard provides excellent support, although the recordings date from the 1970s and the style of the strings makes no concessions to period instrument manners. Most enjoyable, just the same.

(i) Guitar Concerto in E (trans. from Violin Concerto No. 2, BWV 1042, arr. Williams); Aria (Andante from Unaccompanied Violin Sonata No. 2, BWV 1003, arr. Williams); Chaconne (from Unaccompanied Violin Partita No. 2, BWV 1004, arr. Williams); Lute Suites (arr. for guitar) Nos. 1–2, BWV 995–6.

(M) *(*) Sony (ADD) SMK 89612. Williams; (i) with ASMF, Sillito.

Bach himself was a prodigious rearranger, so there is no possible objection to the *Second Violin Concerto* being heard on the guitar. Indeed, with careful balancing, and Kenneth Sillito and the ASMF strings providing a lively accompaniment, the first movement works well in John Williams's transcription. The *Adagio* is then given an improvisatory feel, and the work ends buoyantly. However, in the following *Aria* (from BWV 1003) the deliberation of the soloist is very didactic and the famous *Chaconne* simply fails to come off, with an almost complete absence of tension throughout. The *Lute Suites* are very successful, but they are also alternatively available (on Sony SBK 62972) with the *Third Lute Suite* and the *Prelude and Fugue, BWV 999–1000*.

Violin Concertos Nos. 1–2, BWV 1041/2; in G min. (from BWV 1056); (i) Double Violin Concerto, BWV 1041

(BB) *** RCA 74321 68002-2. Zukerman, ECO; (i) with Garcia – VIVALDI: *Concertos, RV 187 & 209.* ***
(BB) *** EMI Encore (ADD) CDE5 74720-2. Perlman, ECO, Barenboim; (i) with Zukerman.

Zukerman virtually upstages his friend and colleague Perlman in a splendid set of the Bach *Violin Concertos*, also with the ECO, but digitally recorded in the early 1990s, producing attractively bright, lithe string textures, cleaner and more transparent than on the HMV disc. Moreover, he offers equally fine accounts of two top-class Vivadi concertos as a bonus. The Bach performances have great vitality and Zukerman's solo line in all three slow movements is very beautiful, particularly felt and moving in the *A minor*, using a wide range of dynamic and equally moving in the lovely cantilena of BWV 1056. In the interplay of the *Largo* of the *Double Concerto* José-Luis Garcia matches his style and timbre with that of his colleague very successfully indeed. The solo balance is forward, but the violin timbre is naturally caught and the orchestra well in the picture.

This Encore disc was issued just as we were going to print with our last main Guide and was wrongly listed, as we were given to understand that it was a straight reissue of CDC7 47856-2. In the event Zukerman only participates in the *Double Concerto*, where the two famous violinists with their friend and colleague,

Barenboim, are inspired to give a very fine account, one in which their artistry is beautifully matched in all its intensity. Perlman is the soloist in the three other works and plays Bach with great naturalness of feeling: his account of the *A minor Concerto* can scarcely be faulted, even if his tempi will not be to all tastes. He is also most impressive in the slow movement of the *E major*. The *G minor* (arranged from the *F minor Harpsichord Concerto* with its sublime Arioso slow movement) is also finely done, and with excellent modern instrument accompaniments from the ECO this is also a Bach reissue to cherish.

(i) Violin Concertos Nos. 1–2; (i; ii) Double Violin Concerto, BWV 1041/3. (Unaccompanied) Violin Sonata No. 1 in G min., BWV 1001.

*** Avie AV 0007. L. St John; (i) New York Bach Ens.; (ii) with S. St John.

(i-iii) Violin Concertos Nos. 1–2; (i; ii; iv) Double Violin Concerto; BWV 1041/3; (i) (Unaccompanied) Violin Sonata No. 2, BWV 1003: Andante (only).

(BB) (***) Naxos mono 8.110965. (i) Menuhin; (ii) Orchestre Symphonique de Paris; (iii) cond. Enescu; (iv) with Enescu (violin), cond. Monteux.

Lara St John is a first rate Bach violinist, her technique wonderfully assured, her playing lithe and full of communicative intensity. Allegros are exhilaratingly fresh, favouring fleet tempi; indeed some will feel that the outer movements of the *Double Concerto* are too brisk. Yet they set off the simplicity of approach to the beautiful slow movement in which Scott St John is an admirable partner. The lovely *Adagio* of the *E major Concerto* is also played with individuality and imagination. With buoyant, polished accompaniments, this collection is very enjoyable indeed, especially as the unaccompanied *G minor Sonata* is equally rewarding, and the recording throughout real and vivid.

Ward Marston has made impressive transfers of these rightly famous recordings, but we marginally prefer the EMI remastering which is in general smoother and cleaner, if perhaps not always so wide-ranging. The EMI CD (❂ CDH5 67201-2), although it costs more, also includes the young Menuhin's remarkable account of the famous Chaconne from the solo *Partita No. 2 in D minor*. Naxos have chosen instead the Andante from the solo *Sonata No. 2 in A minor*, recorded on the same day as the *Double Concerto* and originally issued as a fill-up with Mozart's *Violin Concerto, K.271a.*

(i) Violin Concerto No. 2 in E, BWV 1042; (ii) Magnificat in D, BWV 243.

*** Sony **DVD** SVD 45983. BPO, Karajan; with (i) Mutter; (ii) Blegen, Mollinari, Araiza, Holl, Berlin RIAS Chamber Ch. (Director: Humphrey Burton.)

There are few better examples on DVD than this of a conductor's magnetism being almost tangible. It is apparent during Anne-Sophie Mutter's fine performance of the *Violin Concerto* although she is given the limelight, but in the *Magnificat* one can feel the whole orchestra, chorus and soloists responding to the conductor, while Karajan's actual movements are minimal, his face all but impassive. This is gloriously old-fashioned Bach, with a large orchestra, and when the camera dwells on the blazing trumpets, one feels almost able to reach out and touch them. It is a thrilling performance, richly and vividly recorded, and one feels right in the middle of it.

Orchestral Suites Nos. 1–4, BWV 1066–9.

(B) *** Erato Ultima 0927 41387-2 (2). E. Bar. Soloists, Gardiner; with Monteverdi Ch. (in No. 1).
*(*) Arthaus **DVD** 100266. Amsterdam Bar. O, Koopman. (Video Director Reinier Hilhorst.)

Gardiner's 1983 set of the four *Orchestral Suites* – after a surprisingly long absence – returns to the catalogue on an Ultima Double, making a strong recommendation for those wanting these works played on period instruments. In his characteristic manner, allegros tend to be fast and lightly sprung with slower movements elgantly pointed. Though the baroque violins using a squeeze technique on sustained notes make for some abrasiveness, Gardiner avoids extremes and, thanks to full and immediate recording, textures are fresh and clear with trumpet and timpani biting through, but not excessively. The unnamed flautist in No. 2 has not the strongest instrumental personality, but plays nimbly enough. At the close of the *First C major Suite*, after the reprise of the *Passepied I*, Gardiner (presumably authentically) interpolates the chorale setting *Dir, dir, Jehova, will ich singen*, BWV 299, taken from a manuscript written jointly by Bach and his wife: this comes as something of a surprise for the unprepared listener.

Just as the Freiburg set of the Bach *Brandenburg Concertos* is one of the jewels in the crown of DVD, so Ton Koopman's comparable set of period instrument performances of the *Orchestral Suites* is one of the great disappointments. They date from 1989 and were recorded in two groups in magnificent baroque settings in the Palace Het Loo, built by William of Orange. The choice of venue for Concertos 1 and 2 brings comparatively opaque sound in which detail registers poorly (especially noticeable in the *Second Concerto*, with solo flute). The acoustic for Nos. 3 and 4 is more open and clearer, but neither is ideal, and one has the image of Koopman at the harpsichord, directing energetically (one might almost say frantically) with his arms, and shaking his jowls, with no sense of a spontaneous vital response emerging from the players – rather a sense of routine expertise. No. 4 is the most successful performance, but in No. 3 the famous *Air* does not register as an affectingly beautiful melody as it should. The camerawork is neither particularly distracting nor in any way inspired.

CHAMBER MUSIC

(Unaccompanied) Cello Suites Nos. 1–6, BWV 1007–12.

(B) *** Sony Double SM2K 89754 (2). Ma.

Yo-Yo Ma's playing has a characteristic rhythmic freedom and favours the widest range of dynamic. The improvisatory effect is seemingly spontaneous and these performances are very compelling indeed, for Ma seems right inside every bar of the music. The first-class recording is very real and natural, with the warm acoustic never blurring the focus. This now appears as a bargain double, a very attractive proposition. But first place for the *Cello Suites* rests with Rostropovich (❂ EMI CDS5 55363-2).

Flute Sonatas Nos. 1–6, BWV 1030–5; in G min., BWV 1020; Partita in A min. (for solo flute), BWV 1013; Trio Sonata in G, BWV 1039.

** Hyp. CDA 67264/5. Beznosiuk, Nicholson, Tunnicliffe; with Kenny (archlute in BWV 1031); with Brown (2nd flute in BWV 1039).

After their success with Handel (see below) these performances by the Beznosiuk/Nicholson/Tunnicliffe team are a disappointment. The playing lacks sparkle, but the group are not helped by the too-reverberant acoustic, which puts a resonant halo round the flute timbre in the solo *Partita*, and prevents internal clarity in the *Trio Sonata*. Moreover the harpsichord is too backwardly placed.

Oboe Sonatas: in G min., BWV 1020 & BWV 1030b; in E flat, BWV 1031; in C, BWV 1033. (Organ) Trio Sonata in C, BWV 529; Well-Tempered Clavier Book II; Prelude & Fugue in C min., BWV 871.

*** Signum SIGCD 034. Hennessy, Parle (harpsichord).

Never mind that these works were not conceived by Bach with the oboe in mind, they sound quite delightful on Gail Hennessy's baroque instrument. Her tone is as pleasing as her playing is stylish; whether in the *Siciliana* of BWV 1031 or the searching *Adagio* of BWV 1033, she provides expressive playing of a high order. She has a fine partner in Nicholas Parle – how beautifully they answer each other in the opening Allegro of BWV 1020, partly because of the excellent balance. The *Trio Sonata*, intended for the organ, works remarkably well in the present arrangement, the finale wonderfully perky and light-hearted.

(i) Viola da gamba Sonatas Nos. 1–3, BWV 1027–9; (ii) Flute Sonatas Nos. 4–6, BWV 1033–5.

(M) *** Sony SMK 89747. (i) Ma, Cooper (harpsichord); (ii) Rampal, Pinnock, Pidoux.

The three sonatas for viola da gamba and harpsichord come from Bach's Cöthen period, and the *G minor* (No. 3) is arguably the highest peak in this particular literature. While Jordi Savall stands supreme (Alia Vox AV 9812), these works can also be very effective on the cello and Yo-Yo Ma leads the field in this instrumentation. He plays with great eloqence and natural feeling. His tone is warm and refined and his technical command remains as ever irreproachable. Kenneth Cooper is a splendid partner; collectors who prefer the sound of a cello to a gamba need not hestitate. The recording has wonderful clarity and presence. However, the colour of the harpsichord does not blend with the cello quite as naturally as with a gamba and there is still a case to be made for the piano as a more appropriate accompaniment.

The *Flute Sonatas*, added for this reissue, make a generous bonus. Rampal plays fluently and in good style. He is particularly impressive in his phrasing of slow movements. The snag is the recording balance, with the flute timbre rich and forward, while the harpsichord (an attractive American instrument, after Hemsch) is relegated to the background. When Roland Pidoux's cello is added to the continuo, the combined sound tends to congeal and detail is opaque. Nevertheless most recordings of the gamba sonatas offer no extra music, so this reissue must still be counted excellent value.

(Unaccompanied) *Violin Sonatas Nos. 1–3, BWV 1001, 1003 & 1005; Violin Partitas Nos. 1–3, BWV 1002, 1004 & 1006.*

(*) Analecta FL 2 3147-8 (2). Ehnes.
(B) ** Teldec Ultima 3984 21035-2 (2). Zehetmair.

James Ehnes, the prize-winning young Canadian violinist, gives traditional readings which may not be quite as distinctive as some, but they have a concentration which, combined with flawless technique, make them constantly compelling. Ehnes tends to favour broad speeds in the slower movements, so that the initial impression of the opening Adagio of the *First Sonata* is one of heaviness. In context, on repeated hearings, the Ehnes approach is readily acceptable, with those slow openings consistent with the unforced concentration of the rest. Final movements tend to be taken fast, with exhilarating results, and with slow movements such as the *Sarabande* of the *Partita No. 1* beautifully tender.

Not only that, Ehnes in the biggest challenge of all, the great *Chaconne* which concludes the *D minor Partita*, crowns the whole sequence with his finest performance, readily sustaining the massive scale. So the minor-key variations of the first half lead with seeming inevitability to the moment of resolution when, at a hushed pianissimo, D minor resolves on D major, with Ehnes at his most dedicated. Excellent recording.

Thomas Zehetmair's style is curiously restless; his line tends to have subtle dynamic surges, a feeling almost of rocking between phrases, and the effect is at times emotionally jagged; even the famous *Chaconne* of BWV 1004 could be more positive. Yet the pieces which depend on running passage-work (the *Courant* of the *Partita in B minor*, the *Gigue* of the *D minor* or the brilliant Presto of the *G minor Sonata*) are played with a wonderful, lightly articulated bravura which

has much imaginative light and shade, while the *Fuga* of the *A minor Sonata* has its simple polyphony well under control without being tense. But in a piece like the *Siciliana* which precedes that Presto of BWV 1001 the improvisational restlessness disturbs Bach's underlying serenity, and elsewhere the feeling that the music runs like a mountain stream, over pebbles certainly but essentially flowing onward, is often disturbed in these readings. The recording is close but faithful and gives a very realistic impression against an acoustic which is not too dry.

Violin Sonatas (for violin & harpsichord) Nos. 1–6, BWV 1014–19.

*** Sony S2K 89469 (2). Carmignola, Marcon.**

This new Sony set of the Six *Violin and Harpsichord Sonatas* from Giuliano Carmignola and Andrea Marcon is outstanding, and could well be a first choice for collectors who do not object to the absence of the *Sonatas for Violin and Continuo* provided by Grumiaux (Philips Duo 454 011-2) and others. The balance between the two instruments is just about ideal, within an acoustic which adds a nice bloom without obscuring detail. The opening *Adagio* of BWV 1014 is immediately compelling, bringing a thoughtful harpsichord introduction, the violin then stealing in sweetly on a gentle crescendo, with ravishing timbre and a natural feeling for the music's line. Throughout the set, allegros have a sense of spirited interplay which captivates: sample the jaunty second movement Allegro of the *E major*, BWV 1016; this is followed by an exquisitely played *Adagio*, and a sparkling bravura finale. Carmignola plays an eighteenth-century baroque violin whose maker is not known, but which has a sonority to match perfectly the copy of a Mietke harpsichord used by Andrea Marcon. The measure here may be short, but the quality is outstandingly high.

Violin and Harpsichord Sonatas Nos. 1–4, BWV 1014–17.

(BB) * HM Classical Express HMX 39557084. Blumenstock, Butt (harpsichord).**

In what is presumably to become a complete set, the first instalment from Elizabeth Blumenstock and John Butt is very promising indeed. At the opening *Adagio* of the *B minor Sonata*, BWV 1014, John Butt's introduction is pleasingly free and thoughtful, and the violin entry on a gentle crescendo is just as compelling. Throughout allegros are engagingly spirited, articulation clean without a hint of didacticism and the interplay between these two artists is constantly stimulating. How delightful is the catchy second movement of the *E major Sonata*, BWV 1016! Elizabeth Blumenstock plays a Strad (and her judicious use of vibrato and refined style are wholly apt for this repertoire); John Butt used a modern copy of a 1646 Ruckers, enlarged in 1780 by Taskin and the two players are beautifully balanced and recorded. Most enjoyable – highly recommended.

KEYBOARD MUSIC

English Suites Nos. 1–6, BWV 806–11; French Suites Nos. 1–6, BWV 8127–.

(BB) *** Warner Apex (ADD). 0927 40808-2 (1-2); 09027 40814-2 (3-4); 09027 40813-2 (5-6) (available separately). Curtis (harpsichord).

Anyone wanting both the *English* and *French Suites* together at a modest cost, played on a fine period harpsichord, will find Alan Curtis's Teldec set excellent value. By putting them together (with the first *English Suite* followed by the first *French Suite* and so on) the twelve works have fitted neatly onto three discs – each available separately. Curtis uses a harpsichord made by Christian Zell of Hamburg in 1928. The sound is resonant but pleasingly so, and the full-bodied character of the sound suits Curtis's lively, comparatively robust approach. His playing is both thoughtful as well as spontaneous. Slow movements go particularly well and there is no feeling of didacticism. Excellent value.

Toccatas: in F sharp min.; C min.; D; D min.; E min.; G min.; G; BWV 910-16.

*** Hyp. CDA 67310. Hewitt (piano).

Bach's famous journey to Lübeck to meet Buxtehude took place in 1705, and the seven keyboard *Toccatas* were almost certainly written in the following decade, while Bach was under the influence of that master's 'stylus fantasticus'. They are freely written, often improvisatory in feeling, theatrical in their bursts of virtuosity, but also include more formal imitative and fugal writing. Angela Hewitt is surely their ideal exponent, responding stylishly and spontaneously to their mood changes – and the bravura flourishes, as at the opening of the *C minor* and *F sharp minor* works. In the latter she is characteristically searching in the *Adagio*, which is to provide the subject of the second of the following pair of fugues, both of which are articulated with spirited clarity.

Hewitt always holds Bach's disparate motivations convincingly together, as in the *G minor*, which, as she comments, can be made to sound uniquely varied and buoyant on the piano, especially the bouncing closing fugue. And how engaging is her sparkling articulation of the first section of the *D major Toccata* with which she ends her programme. We have no hesitation in declaring this the most stimulating and rewarding CD of these complex and episodic works on any instrument, consistently showing Bach's youthful explorations at their most stimulating. The recording is excellent.

KEYBOARD RECITAL COLLECTIONS

(i) *Capriccio on the Departure of a Beloved Brother in B flat, BWV 992; Concerto in D, BWV 972;* (ii) *Chromatic Fantasia & Fugue in D min., BWV 903;* *Goldberg Variations, BWV 988; Inventions Nos. 2 in C min., BWV 773; 6 in E, BWV 777; 8 in F, BWV 779;* (i) *Partita No. 2 in C min., BWV 826; Prélude, Fugue & Allegro in E flat, BWV 998;* (ii) *Sinfonia No. 6 in E, BWV 792.*

(B) (*) RCA 74321 84593-2 (2). (i) Landowska (harpsichord); (ii) Arrau (piano).

The artwork and presentation are appalling: difficult to decipher even with the aid of a strong magnifying glass, ugly and confusing in layout even by the abysmal presentation standards of this (otherwise distinguished and desirable) series. Arrau's record of the *Goldberg Variations* dates from 1942 and occupies the first CD. Although the pianism is obviously distinguished, the tone is very monochrome, thin and papery, and there is a background rumble in the opening theme (which admittedly becomes less intrusive later on). The second CD includes some shorter pieces from Arrau, culminating in a masterly and arresting *D minor Chromatic Fantasy and Fugue*. RL still possesses the original 78rpm disc of the *D major Concerto*, BWV 972 (based on Vivaldi, Op. 3, No. 9) and can testify to the vast superiority of the original over this thin and tinny transfer. Whatever the stature of the playing, this transfer unremittingly strains tolerance throughout.

Capriccio on the Departure of a Beloved Brother, BWV 992; 2-Part & 3-Part Inventions, BWV 772–801; Italian Concerto, BWV 971; 7 Toccatas, BWV 910–16.

(B) *** EMI CZS7 62874-2 (2). Pommier (piano).

Jean-Bernard Pommier has an extensive and impressive discography, ranging from Mozart, Beethoven, Chopin, Debussy to Poulenc. The present set originally appeared in EMI's *Rouge et Noir* series and shows him to be no mean Bach interpreter. He is decently recorded and his playing is vital and will give satisfaction.

French Suite No. 2 in C min., BWV 813; Italian Concerto in F, BWV 971; Partita No. 6 in E min., BWV 830; Toccata in E min., BWV 914.

✿ *** Orfeo C547 011A. Kuschnerova (piano).

Very fine Bach playing here from an artist little known in Britain. Elena Kuschnerova was a pupil of Tatiana Kestner, whose pupils have included Gavrilov and Nikolai Petrov. Since 1992 she has lived in Germany and has, it seems, made records of Prokofiev and Scriabin. Make no mistake, this disc, which derives from a recital given at the Kurhaus, Baden-Baden, in March 2000, is altogether outstanding. Indeed, it is one of the finest Bach recitals on the piano we have had in recent years from a newcomer to the British catalogue. She has a commanding musical presence – the listener is held from beginning to end – and the rhythmic vitality and keenly articulated phrasing betoken a fine musical intelligence. The *C minor French Suite* is wonderfully alive, and both the *E minor Partita* and the *Italian Concerto* are full of spirit and freshness. It was Handel who said that he wrote music 'to make people better', and the present recital leaves the listener feeling exhilarated and purified as only the best Bach playing can. Very good sound.

French Suite No. 5, BWV 816; Fuga a Tre, BWV 953; Fughetta, BWV 961; Italian Concerto, BWV 971; 3 Minuets, BWV 841/3; 2 Minuets, BWV Anh. 114/5; Partita No. 1, BWV 825; 6 Preludes, BWV 924–8 & 930; 6 Little Preludes, BWV 939–43; 999.

(B) *** EMI Debut CDZ5 68700-2. Egarr (harpsichord).

Richard Egarr's CD is one of the EMI Debut series and is a welcome reissue. In it the three major solo pieces, the *Partita in B flat*, BWV 825, the *G major French Suite*, BWV 816, and the *Italian Concerto*, BWV 971, are interspersed with *Preludes*, *Minuets* and a number of other smaller pieces. Egarr plays a copy of a 1638 Ruckers, by Joel Katzman, from which he draws splendid sounds. He is far removed from the rigidity of the sewing-machine school; his playing is unfailingly flexible and musical, and he does not hurry but allows the music to breathe naturally. The recording is pleasing and faithful. An excellent bargain recital.

ORGAN MUSIC

Ton Koopman Novalis Series

Disc 1: (i) *Chorale Prelude: Liebster Jesu, wir sind hier, BWV 730/1; Fantasias: in C min., BWV 562; in G, BWV 562; Passacaglia & Fugue in C min., BWV 582; Preludes & Fugues in D, BWV 532; A min., BWV 543; Toccata, Adagio & Fugue in C, BWV 564; Toccata in D min., BWV 538 (Dorian).*

Disc 2: (ii) *Chorale Preludes: Ich ruf zu dir, Herr Jesu Christ, BWV 639; Nun komm' der Heiden Heiland, BWV 659; Schübler Chorale: Wachet auf, ruft uns die Stimme, BWV 645. Fantasia (Prelude) & Fugue in G min., BWV 542; Partita: O Gott, du frommer Gott, BWV 767; Prelude & Fugue in E flat (St Anne), BWV 552; Toccata & Fugue in D min., BWV 565.*

(B) *** Regis RRC 2042 (2). Koopman (i) Dreifaltigkeits organ, Ottobeuren, Christian Müller organ, Leeuwarden, or Garrels organ, Grote Kerk, Maassluis; (ii) Christian Müller organ, Waalse Kerk, Amsterdam.

Before Ton Koopman began his survey for Teldec he had already begun a series for Novalis, using various Dutch organs. This two-CD set brings together two outstanding recitals, drawn from those CDs. The playing is superb throughout, always using organs admirably suited to Bach's music and all splendidly recorded. The first disc has been put together by Regis to include key items from several individual compilations and to demonstrate three different organs. The brilliant *Fantasia in G*, played with an engagingly light touch, shares the attractive palette of the less familiar *D minor Toccata* with the nickname *Dorian*, and Koopman is equally fluent in the *A minor Fugue*, BWV 543, which also has an exhilarating momen-

tum. All three use the Christian Müller organ at Leeuwarden.

The *Prelude and Fugue in D*, BWV 532, and the mighty *Toccata, Adagio and Fugue on C* are played on the famous organ at Grote Kerk, Maassluis. Both works come from the composer's early Weimar period and demand and receive considerable weight and bravura, as does the equally impressive *Passacaglia and Fugue* and *Fantasia*, BWV 562, both in C minor, which were recorded at Ottobeuren. All three organs are superbly caught by the Novalis engineers.

The second disc brings a complete recital (originally issued on 150 005-2). The Waalse Kerk organ is itself a co-star of this programme, producing magnificent, unclouded sonorities in the spacious tapestry of the *St Anne Prelude and Fugue*, and a wide palette of colour that Koopman uses so effectively in the *Partita* and *Chorale Preludes*. The *Partita* has eight diverse variations but is by no means lightweight. The *Fantasia in G minor* is bold and improvisatory, the fugue swiftly moving and buoyantly paced. The *Chorales* make a contrasting centrepiece, with *Nun komm' der Heiden Heiland* poignantly serene and the famous *Schübler Chorale, Wachet auf*, infectiously jaunty. For the most popular of all Bach's organ pieces Ton Koopman then changes to a more flamboyant style, which he establishes immediately by decorating the opening flourishes so that they become almost a series of trills. The *fugue* proceeds with exhilarating momentum and ends in a blaze of bravura, a very free reading and a most exciting one that would deserve a standing ovation at a live recital. The recording is in the demonstration bracket, the microphones in the right place for a proper illusion of reality.

Chorale preludes: O Mensch, bewein' dein' Sünde gross, BWV 622; Schmücke dich, o liebe Seele, BWV 654; Wachet auf, ruft uns die Stimme, BWV 645; Fantasia & Fugue in G min., BWV 542; Passacaglia in C min., BWV 582; Prelude & Fugue in A min., BWV 543; Toccata & Fugue in D min., BWV 565.

(BB) ** EMI Encore (ADD) CDE5 75215-2. Jacob (organ).

Werner Jacob uses a different organ for each piece, so this is as much a demonstration of different organs as a Bach recital. Certainly, the ubiquitous *D minor Toccata and Fugue*, played with some flair, sounds splendid on the Silbermann instrument at Arlesheim. Jacob plays the chorale preludes reverentially but effectively, his registration unostentatious. The passage-work of the *Prelude and Fugue in A minor* (at St Bavo, Haarlem) is rather blurred, but that comes partly from the style of articulation; it is otherwise a fine performance. The powerfully spacious opening of the *Fantasia and Fugue in G minor* serves to demonstrate the massive tone of the organ of the Marienkirche, Stralsund, but the similar grandeur of the *Passacaglia in C minor*, recorded in Brandenburg, is underlined by Jacob's purposefully deliberate basic tempo. This is an inexpensive way to acquire some fine playing in the German tradition and to sample a number of impressive instruments. The 1970s recordings have transferred well to CD.

VOCAL MUSIC

Complete Cantatas: Hänssler Series with Gächinger Kantorei, Bach-Collegium Stuttgart, Helmuth Rilling

Christmas Cantatas Nos. 1; 36; 61; 63; 65; 91; 110; 121; 132; 133; 153; 190.

(B) *** Häns. CD 94.026 (4). Soloists including Nielsen, Donath, Augér, Watts, Hamari, Kraus, Schreier, Equiluz, Baldin, Huttenlocher, Schöne, Stuttgart Gächinger Kantorei (with Bach Collegium Frankfurt Kantorei, Württemberg CO), Rilling.

This four-CD set collects 12 Christmas cantatas from the complete survey of the cantatas by Helmuth Rilling and reissued during the Bach celebrations of 2000. The present compilation includes some very fine performances, though collectors who prefer period performances should look elsewhere. This will make a good alternative to the *Christmas Oratorio* as a seasonal present – except, of course, for those who have invested in the complete set that appeared in the Bach year. There are no notes or texts but they can be downloaded free of charge on the Hänssler website (www.haenssler-classic.de).

Cantatas Nos. 21; 38; 51; 56; 76; 79; 80; 82; 93; 106; 137; 140; 149.

(B) *** Häns. CD 94.028 (4). Augér, Schreckenbach, Kraus, Heldwein, Harder, Huttenlocher, Hamari, Fischer-Dieskau, Watts, Schöne, Nimsgern, Indiana University Ch. Singers, Stuttgart Bach Collegium; Stuttgart Gächinger Nimsgern; Rilling.

This second four-CD set collects 13 cantatas on the theme 'Praise and thanks, death and eternity' from the complete Rilling survey. The present recordings were made at various dates between 1975 and 1983. Arleen Augér sings in all but three of the cantatas, and Fischer-Dieskau is the soloist in *Ich will den Kreutzstab gerne tragen* and *Ich habe genug*. Obviously this compilation, and its companion above, will not be of interest to those who have invested in the complete box, which was quite competitively priced in 2000, but those wanting a handful of cantatas may find the selection appealing. It includes such masterpieces as *Gottes Zeit ist die allerbest Zeit* (106) and *Jauchzet Gott* (51), which is the only one to have been recorded digitally. As with the dozen Christmas cantatas, there are no notes or texts but they can be downloaded free of charge on the Hänssler website, whose details are listed above.

Complete Cantatas: BIS Masaaki Suzuki Series with Japan Bach Collegium

Cantatas Nos. 40; 60; 70; 90.

*** BIS CD 1111; with Nonoshita, Blaze, Türk, Kooij.

Cantatas Nos. 48; 89; 109;148.

*** BIS CD 1081; with Midori Suzuki, Blaze, Türk, Urano.

Cantatas Nos. 66; 67;134.

*** BIS CD 1251; with Blaze, Sakurada, Kooij.

Cantatas Nos. 73; 144; 153; 154; 181.

*** BIS CD 1221. Nonoshita, Blaze, Türk, Kooij, Bach Collegium Japan, Suzuki.

Cantatas Nos. 119; 174.

*** BIS CD 1131; with Hida, Nonoshita, Sollek-Avella, Sakurada, Kupfer, Kooij.

The Japanese Bach Cantata series under Masaaki Suzuki is far removed both in quality (and cost) from the Brilliant set, which offered the lot for roughly 60p per cantata but in rough-and-ready performances. In our main volume we dwelt at some length on the excellence of the present survey, and the most recent issues to have appeared maintain its standards. There is a lot to be said for the practice of releasing these cantatas a disc or two at a time, so that those who are following them do not have too large an outlay to make at one time. The standards of artistic care and the outstanding quality of the recorded sound make this an odyssey worth making. If forced to choose from among the cycles currently before the public (Rilling on Hänssler, the Harnoncourt–Leonhardt set on Teldec and Karl Richter on DG/Archive), the BIS set would be a very credible first choice.

Cantatas: Gardiner DG Archiv Series

Cantatas for the 11th Sunday after Trinity, Nos. 113; 179; 199.

*** BBC Opus Arte **DVD** OA 0816 D. Kožená, Towers, Padmore, Loges; E. Bar. Sol., Gardiner.

These performances were recorded at St David's Cathedral in Wales during the course of the Bach Pilgrimage that John Eliot Gardiner, the Monteverdi Choir and English Baroque Soloists made in 2000, the 250th anniversary of Bach's death. They began in Weimar on Christmas Day 1999 and ended up at St Bartholomew's Church, New York, on New Year's Eve a year later, having visited Leipzig, Eisenach, Cologne, Arnstadt, Kirkwall and many other places on their journey. The original plan was for DG to record the lot, but in the end only 11 discs were issued (see our main Guide, p.86). The present cantatas, all for the eleventh Sunday after Trinity, were issued on DG 463 591-2. Magdalena Kožená is remarkably fine in the solo cantata *Mein Herz schwimmt im Blut* (BWV 199), and indeed the performances throughout have the crisp, alert quality that distinguishes all this conductor does. In addition, there is a substantial and intelligent documentary lasting some 60 minutes, illuminating their odyssey from Weimar to New York City. The sound is vivid and lifelike, there are excellent notes by Nicholas Anderson, and visually the production is impeccable.

Other Cantata Groupings

Cantatas Nos. 12: Weinen, Klagen, Sorgen, Zagen; 140: Wachet auf, ruff uns die Stimme. Chorales: *Ertöt uns durch dein' Güte, from BWV 22; In dulci jubilo, BWV 729; Jesu bleibet meine Freude (Jesu, Joy of Man's Desiring), from BWV 147; Kommst du nun, Jesu, BWV 650; Nun danket alle Gott, BWV 386; O Jesuslein süss, BWV 493; Liebster Jesu, wir sind hier, BWV 373; Magnificat in D, BWV 243; Missa brevis in A, BWV 234.* Motets: *Der Geist hilft unserer Schwachheit auf, BWV 226; Lobet den Herrn, alle Heiden, BWV 230; Sanctus in C, BWV 237; Orchestral Suite No. 3 in D: Air; (Organ) Prelude and Fugue in G, BWV 541.*

*** EMI **Audio DVD** DVC4 92401-9. Gritton, Milne, Chance, Bostridge, Michael George & Soloists, King's College Cambridge Ch., AAM, Cleobury (organ).

With the boy trebles soaring up with the trumpets in the King's Chapel acoustic, and with a superb team of starry soloists, Stephen Cleobury's vivid account of the *Magnificat* lies at the centre of an extremely satisfying 153-minute concert of Bach's choral music. It is a shame that this is only an audio rather than a video DVD, but the sound is magnificent, whether heard in normal stereo (side A) or surround sound (side B). The *Magnificat* is framed by a pair of Bach's finest and most famous cantatas, *Weinen, Klagen, Sorgen, Zagen*, which after the sinfonia has a glorious extended choral introduction, and the much less familiar *Missa brevis in A*, which also closes with an exultant *Cum Sancto Spiritu*. Its highlight is the flute-decorated *Qui tollis peccate mundi*, beautifully sung by Rachel Brown.

For good measure there are two motets, and the programme is interspersed with chorales, including the famous *Jesu Joy of Man's Desiring*, while Cleobury also slips in the jubilant but little-known *Sanctus in C*, plus Bach's most famous orchestral *Air* as an interlude. To close the programme he plays the ebullient organ *Prelude and Fugue in G* which is followed by a thrilling postlude – a full-throated account of the familiar *Nun danket alle Gott*. Altogether a Bachian feast!

Cantatas Nos. 61: Nun komm der heiden Heiland; No. 147: Herz und Mund und Tat und Leben; Magnificat.

(*) **DVD TDK DV-ADCNH. Korondi, Schäfer, Fink, Bostridge, Maltman, Arnold Schoenberg Ch., VCM, Harnoncourt.

'Glorious Bach!', as this record is described, is an apt title both for the music and the performances under Harnoncourt at his most electrifying; but inexcusably sloppy presentation on DVD seriously undermines this issue. This Advent concert of two seasonal cantatas and the *Magnificat*, recorded live at the beautiful baroque Kloster Melk Monastery, comes with only three tracks lasting respectively 16, 32 and 29 minutes. This is the more absurd given that the *Cantata No. 147* contains the best-loved of all Bach cantata movements, *Jesu, Joy of Man's Desiring*. Did no one in the TDK team conceive of any purchaser wanting to go straight to that favourite item? This flawed presentation seems perversely designed to turn newcomers off DVD, and is the more frustrating when the performances are so fine. With perceptive camera-work Harnoncourt's face is highlighted at the start of each item, his eyes bulging wide, mouth open and eyebrows raised, a man obsessed, wildly determined to get his singers and players to bring out the drama of the music. The Arnold Schoenberg Choir, some forty-strong for the cantatas, is augmented to sixty or so for the *Magnificat*, singing with fervour throughout. Anna Korondi's creamy tone is nicely contrasted with the fresh, bright tones of the first soprano, Christine Schäfer. Unlike the others, Korondi appears only in the *Magnificat*. In slow movements Harnoncourt keeps a characteristic touch of abrasiveness in his period style, but these are highly enjoyable performances which come like a breath of fresh air.

(i) *Cantatas Nos. 82: Ich habe genug; 199: Mein Herze schwimmt im Blut.* **(ii)** *Double Concerto for Oboe & Violin, BWV 1060.*

*** Priory/Carus 83 302. (i) Kirkby; (ii) Arfken, Von der Golz; Freiburg Bar. Ens., Golz.

Emma Kirkby's outstandingly fine account of *Ich habe genug* easily ranks alongside the highly praised baritone versions of Hans Hotter and John Shirley-Quirk (see our main volume). This cantata with its lovely transverse flute introduction (beautifully played here by Karl Kaiser), suits Kirkby's sublimely pure soprano voice admirably and this is claimed to be the first recording of the present E minor version. Kirkby earlier recorded the two principal arias, the lovely *Schlummert ein* as well as *Ich habe genug*, and here her radiant performances are matched by the fresh and stylish playing of the Freiburg Baroque Orchestra with Gottfried von der Golz directing from the violin. What is remarkable about the coupling, *Mein Herz schwimmt im Blut*, is not only the lyrical beauty of the arias, but the way this great baroque soprano invests the recitatives with comparable feeling. Here the obbligato is for oboe, and Katherina Arften is most sensitive in this role, while as a refreshing interlude, she joins the leader and conductor Gottfried von der Golz in the engaging *Double Concerto*, BWV 1060. The accompaniments could hardly be bettered, and the recording ambience and balance are just about perfect. A disc that should be in every comprehensive Bach cantata collection.

Cantatas Nos. 113; 179; 199.

*** Opus Arte **DVD** OA 0816D. Kozena, Towers, Padmore, Loges, Monteverdi Ch., English Bar. Sol., Gardiner.

This DVD offers not just three complete Bach cantatas but an hour-long feature film, celebrating the unique pilgrimage undertaken by Sir John Eliot Gardiner and his regular forces during the year 2000, marking not just the 250th anniversary of Bach's death but the new Millennium. The cantatas selected were those for the 11th Sunday after Trinity, given in a concert at St David's Cathedral in North Wales, the 40th of a monumental series that started on Christmas Day 1999 in the Herderkirche at Weimar with the *Christmas Oratorio* and ended at St Bartholomew's Church, New York, on the Sunday after Christmas, 2000. The three cantatas are very well-chosen, the outer ones from 1723 and 1724 respectively are from Bach's Leipzig period, the central one for solo soprano dates from 1714 when Bach was in Weimar. Gardiner characteristically relies on fresh young voices, with the Monteverdi Choir typically bright and incisive, matched by the four soloists. The tenor, Mark Padmore, is excellent, the countertenor, Williams Towers, and the young German baritone, Stephan Loges, are consistently firm and clear. But it is the Czech soprano, Magdalena Kozena, who wins first honours with her superb singing in the solo cantata, *Mein herze schwimmt im Blut*. Aptly, she also appears in the St David's sequence in the feature film, one of the eleven venues visited.

The film is far more than a travelogue, even though each venue is vividly illustrated. Gardiner necessarily takes the starring role, explaining the sequence. He is even shown climbing a dauntingly precarious ladder up to the top of the tower at the wonderful perpendicular-style church at Blythburgh in Suffolk, where the motet *Jesu meine Freude* was given. We also see the party arriving by plane in Orkney for the concert at Kirkwall, before they go on to what Gardiner describes as the spiritual climax of the whole experience, the concert given on 28th July 2000 – the exact anniversary of Bach's death – in the isolated Church of St Columba on Iona, a place of worship for 14 centuries.

Major choral works

Mass in B min., BWV 232.

(B) *** Virgin 2 x 1 VBD5 61998-2 (2). Kirkby, Van Evera, Iconomou, Immler, Killan, Covey-Crump, D. Thomas, Soloists from Tölz Boys' Ch., Taverner Consort & Players, Parrott.

Parrott, hoping to re-create even more closely the conditions Bach would have expected in Leipzig, adds to the soloists a ripieno group of five singers from the Taverner Consort for the choruses. Speeds are generally fast, with rhythms sprung to reflect the inspiration of dance; however, the inner darkness of the *Crucifixus*, for example, is conveyed intensely in its hushed tones, while the *Et resurrexit* promptly erupts with a power to compensate for any lack of traditional weight. Soloists are excellent, with reduction of vibrato still allowing sweetness as well as purity, and the recording, made in St John's, Smith Square, is both realistic and atmospheric. But first choice still rests with Gardiner (DG 415 514-2).

St John Passion, BWV 245.

*** TDK **DVD** DV-BAJPN. Türk, Suzuki, Blaze, Urano, MacLeod, Bach Coll. Japan, Masaaki Suzuki (includes interview with Masaaki Suzuki).

(B) *** Virgin VBD5 62019-2 (2). Covey-Crump, Thomas, Bonner, Van Evera, Trevor, Taverner Consort and Players, Parrott.

Recorded in Suntory Hall, Tokyo on 28th July, 2000 – the day marking the 250th anniversary of Bach's birth – this is an outstanding version on DVD of the *St John Passion*, a tribute to the work of Masaaki Suzuki in Japan. In a brief interview which comes as supplement he comments on the intensive training in period performance he undertook in Holland, and this performance consistently demonstrates the vigour and sensitivity of his approach to Bach. The interpretation remains very similar to Suzuki's earlier CD account on BIS, with fresh, light textures and generally brisk speeds which yet allow for depth of feeling, and the sense of occasion is irresistible.

Only Gerd Türk as the Evangelist is presented as a soloist in front of the choir, giving an achingly beautiful performance, with his profound involvement all the more evident when seen as well as heard. Türk also sings the tenor arias, and the other soloists, all first-rate, also have double roles, singing in the sixteen-strong choir (4.4.4.4) before stepping forward when needed as soloists: Stephan MacLeod singing Christus as well as the bass arias, Chiyuki Urano singing Pilate and other incidental solos, Robin Blaze a superb alto soloist and the ravishing Midori Suzuki in the two soprano arias. The leaflet offers minimal information and no text, though on DVD one can opt for subtitles in either the original German or the English translation, but not both together.

Andrew Parrott's version offers an intimate performance that yet has sharp focus and plenty of power. Though speeds are generally fast and rhythms resilient, he allows himself a broader tempo for the great final chorus and the concluding Chorale, giving them an aptly expressive weight. The Taverner Consort here has only two choristers per part, with soloists included among the singers, while Rogers Covey-Crump as the Evangelist, light and alert, also sings the tenor arias, and David Thomas as Jesus sings the bass arias. The soprano soloists, Tessa Bonner and Emily van Evera, are both bright-toned and boyish, while the alto, Caroline Trevor, has a counter-tenor-like timbre. In compensation for any lack of weight from the scale of forces, the recording balance keeps the voices well forward, both in solo and in choral work. An outstanding recommendation for those who fancy an intimate but powerfully dramatic view. The *St Matthew Passion* has yet to appear on DVD in a satisfactory version. Meanwhile Gardiner's audio set reigns supreme (DG 427 648-2).

Piano Transcriptions

Chaconne from (Unaccompanied) Violin Partita No. 2 in D min., BWV 1004) (trans. BUSONI).

(BB) (**(*)) EMI Encore mono CDE5 75230-2. Michelangeli (piano) – BRAHMS: *Paganini Variations* (**(*)). MOZART: *Piano Concerto No. 15* (*).

Not surprisingly, Michelangeli plays brilliantly, and if Busoni's influence is increasingly (and excitingly) predominant as the piece proceeds, Bach's structure remains a firm basis for the interpretation. The mono recording is fully acceptable. Michelangeli made few recordings, so this is certainly value for money.

Transcriptions: *Chorales: Ich ruf' zu dir, Herr Jesus Christ; Nun komm der Heiden Heiland; Wachet auf, ruft uns die Stimme. Siciliano in D; Sinfonia in D* (all arr. KEMPFF); *Chorales: Alle Menschen müssen sterben; Das alte Jar vergangen ist; Wenn wir in höchsten Nöten sein* (all arr. HEWITT); *Herzlich tut mich verlangen* (arr. WALTON); *In dulci jubilo* (arr. LORD BERNERS) *Jesu, joy of man's desiring* (arr. MYRA HESS); *Meine Seele erhebt den Herrn* (arr. IRELAND); *O Mensch, bewein deine Sünde gross* (arr. HOWELLS); *Sanctify us by Thy goodness* (arr. COHEN); *Die Seele ruht in Jesu Händen* (arr. BAUER); *Sheep may safely graze* (arr. HOWE); *Passacaglia in C min.* (arr. D'ALBERT).

*** Hyp. CDA 67300. Hewitt.

Predictably, Angela Hewitt brings the widest range of pianistic style to these often highly individual arrangements by a galaxy of famous names. She finds a natural simplicity in those by Kempff, with *Nun komm der Heinden Heiland* relatively sombre to contrast with the delightful sunlit *Siciliano*. A comparable delicacy of touch is used to evoke Myra Hess herself for her famous version of *Jesu joy of man's desiring*, while Hewitt's own arrangements are comparably thoughtful. For contrast there is the full-blooded *In dulci jubilo* of Lord Berners, while Eugen d'Albert's version of the great *Passacaglia in C minor* brings a dynamic and colouristic flamboyance within a powerful structure. A most stimulating collection, immensely varied, yet with a thread of underlying profundity throughout. The piano recording could hardly be more natural.

BAERMANN, Heinrich (1784–1847)

Clarinet Quintet No. 3 in E flat, Op. 23 (arr. for clarinet and string orch).

*** EMI CDC5 57359-2. Wolfgang Meyer, ASMF, Sillito – MENDELSSOHN: *2 Concert Pieces for Clarinet & Basset Horn ***; WEBER: *Clarinet Quintet ***.

Heinrich Baermann was the great clarinettist, principal in the royal orchestra in Munich for most of his career, who inspired not just Weber but Mendelssohn, both of them great admirers of his masterly playing, as well as friends. It makes it very apt to have this grouping of works in a delightful disc from the inspired brother and sister team of Sabine and Wolfgang Meyer. The Baermann *Clarinet Quintet*, originally published in 1820 with optional parts for two horns, is here played with the string quartet parts adapted for string orchestra, the sort of arrangement that Baermann himself might have devised. Evidently influenced by the Weber *Quintet*, written just before, the fluency of the clarinet writing goes with an unpretentious structure built on clear if not specially memorable themes. Wolfgang Meyer as soloist with Kenneth Sillito and the Academy is revealed as just as brilliant and persuasive a clarinettist as his sister.

BALAKIREV, Mily (1837–1910)

Symphony No. 1 in C.

(M) (***) BBC Legends mono BBCL 4084-2. BBC SO, Beecham – RIMSKY-KORSAKOV: *Le coq d'or: Suite*; BORODIN: *Prince Igor: Polovtsian Dances.* (***)

Balakirev's *First Symphony*, though still neglected, is among the very greatest of Russian symphonies, built on strong, memorable themes, with a ravishingly beautiful slow movement. Yet when Beecham recorded it for EMI in 1955 his usual spark of inspiration was missing in a cautious studio run-through. Here, for a radio broadcast the following year, he conducts the BBC Symphony Orchestra with all the warmth, thrust and sparkle missing from the earlier performance, making this BBC Legends issue very welcome. The recording may be mono, but it is clear and well-balanced, as it is in the enjoyable fill-ups: the colourful suite from Rimsky-Korsakov's opera, *Le coq d'or*, and the *Polovtsian Dances* from Borodin's *Prince Igor*, complete with chorus.

BALFE, Michael (1808–70)

The Bohemian Girl (complete).

(M) ** Decca 473 077-2 (2). Thomas, Power, Summers, Cullen, De Carlo, RTE Philharmonic Ch., Nat. SO of Ireland, Bonynge.

Sir Thomas Beecham famously revived Balfe's most celebrated opera, *The Bohemian Girl*, at the time of the Festival of Britain in 1951, but it took another four decades for a complete recording to appear. The Irishman Michael Balfe was extraordinarily successful in his own day, writing no fewer than 21 English operas, three in French and four in Italian. His lyrical facility comes out at its most charming in *The Bohemian Girl*, with the heroine's aria, 'I dreamt I dwelt in marble halls', justly still popular as a separate number.

While Richard Bonynge, with his gift for springing rhythms and moulding phrases persuasively, is the ideal conductor for this opera, he is not particularly well served by either the Irish orchestra or the principal singers, most of whom sound fluttery and even uncertain, perhaps badly caught by the microphones. Patrick Power, as the hero, Thaddeus, has a light, lyrical tenor, which sounds well enough until it is stressed, when it acquires a throaty bleating tone on top.

Nova Thomas as the heroine, Arline, is at once throaty-sounding and fluttery, yet bright on top, not helped by her curious vowel sounds. Jonathan Summers is the strongest in the cast, as Count Arnhem, but even he has sounded better-focused on disc; while the bass tones of John de Carlo as Devilshoof, King of the Gypsies, are marred by his unashamedly aspirated style in florid passages. A separate cast of actors is lined up for the spoken dialogue. The recording, too, being slightly recessed, is not up to the usual standards Decca gives to Bonynge, but now at mid-price in Decca's 'British Collection', it remains the only way to sample this engaging work.

BANTOCK, Granville (1868–1946)

Hebridean Sea Poem No. 1: Caristiona; Omar Khayyám: Prelude and (i) Camel Caravan; Orchestral Scene No. 1: Processional; Song of Songs: Prelude; Thalabala the Destroyer (symphonic poem).

*** Hyp. CDA 67250. RPO (i) with Ch., Handley.

This is one of the most attractive and certainly the most enterprising of Hyperion's series of Bantock collections. The style of the music may be eclectic but its ripeness of inspiration is in no doubt, and Handley and the RPO give performances of great commitment and power, while the splendidly wide-ranging recording is vividly realistic. Not least so in the richly Tchaikovskian *Thalabala the Destroyer*. Bantock had been conducting a number of all-Tchaikovsky concerts, including *Francesca da Rimini*, before writing his tone poem and the influences are obvious. But it remains a splendidly successful piece in its own right, full of melodic and orchestral appeal.

Elsewhere, and especially in the *Prelude to The Song of Songs* and *Omar Khayyám*, Wagnerian and Straussian influences are equally strong, along with Eastern exoticism, which also comes to the fore in the early *Processional*. But this is not cheap music and the programme overall is a most rewarding collection that could not be better presented.

BARATI, George (1913–96)

(i) *Symphony No. 1 (Alpine)*; (ii) *Chant of Darkness*; (i) *Chant of Light*.

(BB) **(*) Naxos 8.559063. (i) Budapest SO, Kováks; (ii) Czech Rad. SO, Válek.

Although Richard Strauss wrote a rather more famous *Alpine Symphony*, the title is the only thing his and Barati's work have in common. The latter was written in 1963, and although serialism is inherent in its structure, it is far from being an inaccessible work. For most listeners, it will be the colourful orchestration, with a huge battery of percussion instruments, and bold orchestral effects (some of which are very

loud indeed) that make the most impression. The central *Andantino tranquillo* starts and ends quietly if broodingly. The finale is energetic if angular, with plenty of punctuated brass interspersed with more lyrical passages. The work certainly makes an impact, though its coherence is not immediately apparent. The two orchestral pieces are late works the *Chant of Darkness* was written as an expression of mourning for the composer's daughter who had died of cancer in 1992. It is an obviously sincere elegy, with an understandably melancholic atmosphere, and while it is interspersed with some more dramatic passages, its 16 minutes are unremittingly bleak. The *Chant of Light* occupies a similar sound-world, but is not quite so desolate. First-rate performances and recordings from both sets of orchestras and conductors, but this is not a collection to recommend unreservedly.

BARBER, Samuel (1910–81)

Adagio for Strings; (i) *Piano Concerto*; (ii) *Violin Concerto*; (iii) *Four Part Songs*.

(M) **(*) ASV PLT 8501. (i) Joselson, LSO, Schenck; (ii) Shapira, Russian PO, Sanderling; (iii) Joyful Company of Singers, Broadbent.

The new recording here is the *Violin Concerto* with Itsai Shapira and Russian forces. Shapira is Juilliard trained and a warm, lyrical player, though he is not as dazzling in the finale as many of his rivals. Stern, or among younger players, Joshua Bell, are to be preferred. We liked Tedd Joselson's record of the *Piano Concerto* with the LSO and Andrew Schenck when it first appeared in the mid-1980s, and though it is not finer than the John Browning, it is still very competitive. The choral pieces make a welcome bonus. All the same, for a mid-price introduction to this composer, the mid-price Sony disc of the three concertos (the violin with Stern and Bernstein, the piano with Browning and Szell, and the cello with Yo-Yo Ma and Ormandy) remains the one to have.

(i) *Cello Concerto, Op. 22*; (ii) *Piano Concerto, Op. 38*; (iii) *Violin Concerto, Op. 14*.

(M) **(*) Sony (DDD; ADD) SMK 89751. (i) Ma, Baltimore SO, Zinman; (ii) Browning, Cleveland O, Szell; (iii) Stern, NYPO, Bernstein.

It is good to see that Stern's inspired account of the *Violin Concerto* has been sensibly recoupled. It has warmth, freshness and humanity and the slow movement is glorious. The (originally CBS) forward balance for the orchestra is less than ideal, but the recording is otherwise very good.

With his masterly sense of line, Yo-Yo Ma also gives a richly lyrical reading of the *Cello Concerto*. Here the subtleties of the reading are enhanced by having the soloist naturally placed in relation to the well-balanced orchestra.

The *Piano Concerto* never quite adds up to the sum of its parts, although its slow movement is atmospherically haunting. The brilliant performance by its dedicatee is not helped by the shallowness of the spotlit piano sound, hard in the outer movements with fierce tuttis. However no one could say that the playing is uncommitted, and this CD is well worth having for the other two concertos.

(i) Cello Concerto, Op. 22; Symphony No. 2, Op. 19; Medea – Suite, Op. 23.

✪ (**) Pearl mono GEM 0151. (i) Nelsova; New SO, Composer.

Samuel Barber recorded these three pieces for Decca in 1950 and they appeared on three separate 10 inch yellow label LPs. Though they weren't of the 'highest fi' they were superior to the thin and scrawny Ace of Clubs transfers in the 1960s. This is their first appearance on CD in very good transfers that have plenty of presence and detail, though the pitch problems that beset the opening bars of the finale of the Second Symphony have proved intractable. The ideas of the Cello Concerto have a vernal freshness and youthful innocence which still casts a spell and Zara Nelsova's commanding and pioneering account long remained the only one available. It is sad that the grievous neglect of the eloquent and powerful Second Symphony prompted Barber to succumb to self doubts and withdraw all but the middle movement. The work is wonderfully lyrical and the rather Stravinskyan Medea suite is highly effective and imaginative. Later versions of all three pieces have more polished orchestral playing and the composer could obviously have done with a little more rehearsal with his ad hoc orchestra. All the same there is a special quality and authority about these performances that makes them very treasurable.

(i) Violin Concerto, Op. 14; Music for a Scene from Shelley, Op. 7; Souvenirs (ballet suite), Op. 28; Serenade for Strings, Op. 1.

(BB) *** Naxos 8.559044. (i) Buswell; RSNO, Alsop.

In her superb Naxos series of Samuel Barber's music Marin Alsop with the Royal Scottish National Orchestra backs up the masterly Violin Concerto with the witty and delightfully parodic ballet, Souvenirs, and two early works, the evocative Scene from Shelley and a long-neglected three-movement Serenade, which is based on a string quartet written when Barber was 18, and anticipates the Adagio for Strings. James Buswell is a refined, sensitive soloist, warm without being soupy, if not quite as individual as Isaac Stern in his vintage version with Bernstein (now ideally coupled with John Browning's powerful, pioneering version of the Piano Concerto and Yo-Yo Ma's searching account of the Cello Concerto – a generous triptych).

BARTÓK, Béla (1881–1945)

Concerto for Orchestra; Dance Suite; Divertimento; Hungarian Sketches; The Miraculous Mandarin:

Suite; Music for Strings, Percussion & Celesta; Romanian Folk Dances.

(B) *** Double Decca 470 516-2 (2). Chicago SO, Solti.

A self-recommending collection of Solti's digital Bartók recordings. His Chicago performances may not quite have the searing intensity of his classic LSO accounts of the major works here, but the extra warmth of the later readings bring out more the lyrical qualities to the music. The Divertimento is superbly done too, incisive and full-bloodied, and the Hungarian and Romanian dances have all the atmosphere one could wish for. In short, this is excellent value in the Double-Decca series and brings typically fine Decca sound.

(i) Concerto for Orchestra; (ii) Dance Suite; (iii) Divertimento for Strings; (ii) Music for Strings, Percussion & Celesta; (iv) Rhapsody No. 1; (ii) The Wooden Prince (ballet suite).

(B) ** Finlandia Ultima 8573 81965-2 (2). (i) R. Stockholm PO, Davis; (ii) Toronto SO, Saraste; (iii) Helsinki Strings, Csaba & Géza Szilvay; (iv) Noras, Finnish RSO, Saraste.

These are all very good performances, which are recommendable at budget price without any of them being an outright first choice. Andrew Davis conducts what is a really impressive account of the Concerto for Orchestra recorded in 1996, although there is a certain want of bloom on the sound. (It originally appeared coupled with the Lutoslawski Concerto for Orchestra and was restored in that coupling in 2001 on Warner Apex 0927 40619-2.) The likes of Reiner, Karajan and Daniele Gatti (in 1997) to name only a few, still give greater satisfaction. Much the same must be said of the remaining few. Saraste gives us half an hour of The Wooden Prince, a well-chosen suite, decently played and recorded, and an acceptable rather than exceptional Music for Strings, Percussion and Celesta.

Concerto for Orchestra; Music for Strings, Percussion & Celesta.

(M) ** Orfeo (ADD) C551 011B. Bav. RSO, Kubelik.

Kubelik served as chief conductor of the Bavarian Radio Symphony Orchestra for 18 years, and this account of the Concerto for Orchestra was recorded in March 1978 during his tenure; the Music for Strings, Percussion and Celesta comes from a guest appearance three years later. There is much to impress, though neither displaces existing recommendations.

Collection: (i; ii) Concerto for Orchestra: Elegia (only); (ii; iii; iv) Piano Concerto No. 2: Adagio; (i; ii) Music for Strings, Percussion and Celesta: Allegro molto; (v) Suite No. 1, Op. 3: Allegro vivace; (iii; vi) Sonata for Two Pianos and Percussion: Assai lento – Allegro molto; (vii) Contrasts for Violin, Clarinet and Piano; (viii) Mikrokosmos: Book VI; (ix) Bluebeard's Castle (extracts).

(B) * Decca (ADD/DDD) 470 129-2. (i) Chicago SO; (ii) Solti; (iii) Vladimir Ashkenazy; (iv) LPO; (v) DSO, Dorati; (vi) Vovka Ashkenazy, Corkhill, Smith; (vii) Engegard,

Schmid, Schiff; (viii) Kocsis; (ix) Berry, Ludwig, LSO, Kertész.

As can be seen from the roster of artists above, these are all first-class performances in superb sound. Bartók, however, is not a composer suited to such a collection of bits and pieces, and this is not likely to entice newcomers to his music. A better option would be the Double Decca compilation of complete works, in similarly excellent performances, which gives a much better perspective of this composer's output (448 276-2).

Piano Concertos Nos. 1–3.

(B) ** Sony SK 89732. Bronfman, LAPO, Salonen.

These 1996 performances have not taken long to resurface at a more competitive price bracket. Yefim Bronfman is a master pianist and takes all the technical challenges easily in his stride. But the readings as a whole do not take fire in the way that the very finest do. The orchestral playing is cultured rather than characterful and readers wanting all three concertos on one disc will do better with Schiff (Teldec 0630 13158-2) or Kocsis (Philips 446 366-2) or, at mid-price, Anda (DG 447 399-2).

(i) Piano Concerto No. 3; For Children, Book I, Nos. 22, 30, 31, 40

(*) Pearl mono GEM 0148. Kentner, BBC SO, Boult – LISZT: Recital. (**)

Louis Kentner and the BBC Symphony Orchestra under Sir Adrian Boult gave the first public European performance of the Piano Concerto No. 3 and took it into the BBC Studios the following day (28 February 1946). This is a newly discovered set of 78rpm acetates. Although première performances have that sense of first discovery that is highly communicative, the present broadcast is a disappointment. Kentner's artistry is not well served here, for the piano is horribly forward and masks much of the orchestral detail. It is altogether too poorly balanced to convey more than a scant idea of the playing. The four pieces from For Children are from commercial discs and sound much better.

(i) Piano Concerto No. 3; (ii) Sonata for Two Pianos and Percussion.

(BB) **(*) EMI Encore (ADD) CDE5 74991-2. (i) Ogdon, Philh. O, Sargent; (ii) Lucas, Holland, Fry – SHOSTAKOVICH: Piano Concerto No. 2. ***

Ogdon gives a fine performance of the Third Concerto although Sargent's accompaniment lacks the last degree of brilliance – the result brings out neither the joy nor the poetry of the work at the fullest intensity. The Sonata for Two Pianos however, receives a stimulating performance from the husband and wife team: it is not always as sparkling as it might be (the finale runs down a little) but rarely have two-pianists achieved such fine technical and emotional rapport in this music.

(i) Violin Concerto No. 2; Solo Violin Sonata.

(B) *** Virgin 2 CD VBD5 62053-2 (2). Tetzlaff; (i) LPO, Gielen – JANACEK: Concerto; Sonata; WEILL: Concerto. ***

(M) (***) EMI mono CDM5 74799-2. Menuhin; (i) Philh. O, Furtwängler.

Christian Tetzlaff gives a serious and likeable account of the Violin Concerto with the LPO. He does not press it into service as a mere vehicle for his own display but, on the contrary, is completely at its service. He gets very good support from Gielen and copes well with the formidable difficulties of the Solo Sonata. Very good recording and valuable couplings make this well worth considering.

EMI's 'Great Recordings of the Century' series restores the second of Menuhin's four versions of the Bartók concerto made in the Abbey Road Studios in 1953 with Furtwängler at the helm. It comes not with the pioneering 1947 version of the Solo Violin Sonata, which the great violinist had commissioned, but a later, 1957 account. Whichever modern version you might have, this is mandatory listening for anyone who cares about this great music, and it sounds splendid in this new transfer.

Divertimento for Strings.

*** ECM 465 778-2. Camerata Bern, Zehetmair – SCHOENBERG: Verklaerte Nacht; VERESS: 4 Transylvanian Dances. ***

While this expertly played account of the Divertimento by the admirable Camerata Bern led by Thomas Zehetmair does not displace the Norwegian Chamber Orchestra under Iona Brown to which we assigned a ● (Chan. 9816; see p.114 of our main guide), it gives it a good run for its money. Those who are attracted by the coupling, an eloquent reading of Verklärte Nacht and the fine Transylvanian Dances of Sándor Veress, should consider this as an alternative. The recording is very present and lifelike.

Rhapsody No. 1 for Cello and Orchestra.

(BB) *** Warner Apex 0927 40600-2. Noras, Finnish RSO, Saraste – ELGAR: Cello Concerto; DVORAK: Cello Concerto. **(*)

Bartók only scored the first of his two Rhapsodies (originally written for violin and piano) for cello and orchestra, and very effective it is on the responsive bow of Arto Noras. The piece is in two sections, Lassu and Friska, and the contrasts between the lyrical and fiery elements are managed here with aplomb. Good though not oustanding recording, with the cello dominating the sound picture.

CHAMBER AND INSTRUMENTAL MUSIC

(i) Contrasts for Clarinet, Violin & Piano; (ii) String Quartet No. 6 in D; (iii) Allegro Barbaro; Dance Suite; Romanian Folk Dances.

(M) **(*) ASV PLT 8502. (i) Stanzeleit, Collins, Fenyö; (ii) Lindsay Qt; (iii) Frankl.

The Lindsays' performances of the Bartók *String Quartets* were rightly praised on their original release in the early 1980s, and this account from that cycle of the *Sixth* is powerful and expressive, and excellently recorded. Peter Frankl's performances of the piano music has splendid fire and spirit, though the piano tone is not flatteringly caught by the engineers. The *Contrasts* are vibrant, and the sound is exceptionally brilliant, but collectors may find this a bit too closely recorded for comfort.

String Quartets Nos. 1–6.

(*) Simax PSC 1197 (2). Vertavo Qt.

(***) Pearl mono GEMS 50147 (2). Juilliard Qt.

The Vertavo Quartet is a Norwegian group that has been in existence for nearly two decades and has been playing the Bartók quartets for 15 years. They bring a refreshing ardour and commitment and great vitality to the cycle. All the same, their ensemble is not always flawless, and at a time when there are such imposing accounts as the Végh (Audivis V 4809) or the Takács, our current first choice (Decca 455 297-2), for all their spirited dedication, they must take second place.

Pearl offers new transfers of the famous integral set that American Columbia made in 1950 and Philips issued some years later on its ABL label and that was for long the yardstick by which others were judged. Although all the quartets had been recorded before, this was the first set to be made by the same artists. The Juilliards went on to re-record them in stereo, but there is certainly something special about this pioneering set – a sense of discovery and of awe. It is a core recommendation in the Bartók discography and has been very well transferred.

PIANO MUSIC

Piano Music Vol. 1: *Andante for Piano; 3 Hungarian Folksongs from Csík; 15 Hungarian Peasant Songs, Sz.71; 3 Rondos on Folk Tunes, Sz.84; 7 Sketches, Op. 9b; Sonata, Sz.80; Suite, Op. 14.*

(BB) **(*)** Naxos 8.554717. Jandó.

Piano Music Vol. 2: *Dance Suite; Improvisations, Op. 20; Petite Suite; Romanian Christmas Carols; Romanian Folk Dances Nos. 1–6; Slovakian Dance; Sonatina.*

(BB) **(*)** Naxos 8.554718. Jandó.

The benchmark set of the Bartók piano music is the Philips survey by Zoltán Kocsis, which runs to seven volumes, all of which are listed in our main volume. Jenö Jandó is very well served by the Naxos engineers and gives far more than just serviceable accounts of this repertoire but does not really challenge his countryman. His playing is thoroughly idiomatic without being really special. The Jandó set is a third of the price, but in terms of musical distinction and the excellence of the recorded sound, the Kocsis survey is worth more than three times the price.

Dance Suite; Marche funèbre from Kossuth; 4 Pieces; Rhapsody No. 1 (**extended version and shortened version**).

*** Ph. 464 639-2. Kocsis.

The latest issue in Kocsis's distinguished ongoing coverage of Bartók's piano music includes the composer's transcription of the orchestral *Dance Suite*; the result is technically challenging, but Kocsis plays it with panache. The so-called 'long version' of the *Rhapsody No. 1* originated for piano solo in 1904. From it a year later he derived the concertante version, Op. 1, adding a new introduction. Subsequently, at the request of his publisher, the composer devised a much shorter abridged version of the original solo work. Both solo versions are included here.

BAX, Arnold (1883–1953)

(i) *Coronation March;* **(ii)** *November Woods;* **(iii)** *Oliver Twist: Fagin's Romp; Finale.* **(iv)** *Tintagel;* **(v)** *Fanfare for the Wedding of Princess Elizabeth.*

(M) ** Decca mono/stereo 473 080-2. (i) LSO, Sargent; (ii) ASMF, Marriner; (iii) Nat. PO, Herrmann; (iv) LPO, Boult; (v) Philip Jones Brass Ens.

Some good things here, though this collection as a whole feels rather bitty. Boult's classic mono *Tintagel* is lively and highly atmospheric, and though the 1955 sound is slightly limited, it still makes quite an impact. Marriner, hardly a conductor associated with Bax, gives us an effective account of the fine tone-poem *November Woods*, with the haunting, windswept atmosphere well caught in the vivid and warm (Philips) sound, though it does not eclipse Boult's classic Lyrita account (alas no longer current). Sargent's vigorous 1954 recording of the *Coronation March* (mono) is well known, and the seven minutes of music for *Oliver Twist* and the *Fanfare* are pleasing enough. However, this CD, lasting under 49 minutes, is not generous by today's standards, even at mid-price.

Violin Sonatas: in G min. in One Movement; No. 1 in E; Ballad; Legend.

*** ASV CDDCA 1127. Gibbs, Mei-Loc Wu.

The *G minor Sonata* in one movement is an early piece, dating from 1901 and composed when Bax was still a student at the Royal Academy and subsequently withdrawn. The *First Sonata* was written in 1910 in the wake of a passionate affair with a Ukrainian girl, but Bax re-wrote the second and third movements during the war, and himself gave its première in 1920 with Paul Kochanski (for whom Szymanowski composed his two concertos). The *Ballad* and *Legend* are wartime pieces and not otherwise available. Those who have these artists' earlier record of the *Second* and *Third Sonatas* (CDDCA 1098; see our main guide) will need no further prompting to acquire this. Robert Gibbs and Mary Mei-Loc Wu are sympathetic and persuasive Baxians. Excellent sound.

BEACH, Amy (1867–1944)

Piano Trio in A min., Op. 150; String Quartet in One Movement, Op. 89; Violin Sonata in A min., Op. 34.

*** Arabesque Z 6747. Polk; Lark Qt.

This splendid triptych confirms the calibre of Amy Beach's chamber music, which was written over a period of four decades. The early *Violin Sonata* (1896), which introduces this highly recommendable collection, opens most beguilingly on the bow of Diane Pascal, its warm lyricism pervading the first movement and the equally melodically fluent *Largo*. A scintillating Scherzo acts as a bridge between them, with its centrepiece looking back lyrically to the opening movement. The finale, if not to be taken too seriously, is more passionate, and in the development neatly produces a three-part fugue.

The elliptical *String Quartet* dates from 1921 and is wholly different in mood, with a haunting Gallic atmosphere, the more surprising as the material includes Alaskan folk themes. The *Piano Trio* (1938) draws on older material 'docketed away' in the composer's head (including an early song), its *espressivo* lighter, more romantic in feeling, with the finale dancing along to a catchy, syncopated 'Eskimo' theme. The performances here are first class (Joanne Polk, the pianist, especially worthy of mention) and so is the recording. Most enjoyable and highly recommended.

Piano Trio in A min.; Romance for Violin & Piano. (i) Songs: 3 Browning Songs; Canzonetta; Chanson d'amore; Ecstasy; Elle et moi; Ich sagte nicht; Je demande à l'oiseau; A Mirage; Nahe des Gelibten; Rendezvous; 3 Shakespeare settings; Stella viatoris; Wir drei.

**(*) BIS CD 1245. Romantic Chamber Group of L.; (i) with Kirkby.

The Romantic Chamber Group of London play warmly and certainly romantically, but they are recorded in a resonant acoustic, and both the *Piano Trio* and (especially) the *Romance* create something of the atmosphere of the Palm Court. We are admirers of both the composer and Emma Kirkby, but here she swoons up unabashedly to the climax of the opening song, *Ecstasy*, and *Stella viatoris* is unleashed with comparable ardour. *A Mirage* is more restrained, and the Shakepeare and Browning settings have charm, even if it cloys just a little. The French and German settings are attractive in their innocent way, and Emma Kirkby is her sweet-voiced self, and certainly at her best in the sparkle of the closing *Elle et moi*. But she fails to convince us that Amy Beach's songs can find a place in the recital room rather than the salon.

Evening Hymn, Op. 125/2; Help us O God, Op. 50; Jubilate; Lord of all Being, Op. 146; Nunc Dimittis; Peace I leave with You; Te Deum.

*** ASV CDDCA 1125. Harvard University Ch., Somerville; Johnson (organ) – THOMPSON: *Choral Music.* ***

Amy Beach's flowing lyrical gift is consistently appealing in these comparatively straightforward but highly eloquent settings. They range from the early serene *Peace I leave with you* and the simple *Nunc Dimittis* – both *a capella* and from 1891 – and the passionate *Jubilate* with its exuberant organ accompaniment (1905), to the richly harmonized *Evening Hymn of 1934* and *Lord of all Being* for four-part choir and organ, which has more obvious dissonance, but remains in the musical mainstream. Excellent, committed performances from the Harvard Choir, with the collection made the more attractive by the alternation of items by Randall Thompson.

BEETHOVEN, Ludwig van (1770–1827)

Piano Concertos Nos. (i) 1 in C, Op. 15; (ii) 2 in B flat, Op. 19.

⚫ (***) Testament mono SBT 1219. Solomon, Philh. O., (i) Herbert Menges, (ii) Cluytens.

Piano Concertos Nos. (i) 3 in C min., Op. 37; (ii) 4 in G, Op. 58.

⚫ (***) Testament mono SBT 1220. Solomon, Philh. O., (i) Menges, (ii) Cluytens.

Piano Concerto No. 5 (Emperor).

⚫ (***) Testament mono SBT 1221. Solomon, Philh. O, Menges – MOZART: *Sonatas Nos. 11 and 17.*

Olympian performances from Solomon are restored on the Testament label in altogether exemplary sound. The Beethoven concertos with the Philharmonia Orchestra under Herbert Menges and André Cluytens (in Nos. 2 and 4) have been out many times since they were made in the 1950s but have never sounded richer and fresher than they do here. Solomon never interposed his own personality between the composer and listener and his performances celebrate a dedication to musical truth and a timeless purity that place him among the keyboard giants. This is great Beethoven playing.

(i) Piano Concertos Nos. 1–5; (ii) Choral Fantasia, Op. 80.

(B) *(*) Ph. Trio (DDD/ADD) 470 938-2 (3). Brendel; (i) Chicago SO, Levine; (ii) LPO Ch., LPO, Haitink.

Brendel's 1983 Chicago set of the concertos was intended to prove how much more effective live recording is than studio performances, but the results – recorded at Orchestra Hall Chicago – belie that, especially compared with his splendid later set with Rattle, which were recorded in the studio, *after* live performances. Anything Brendel does has mastery, but compared with the earlier studio recordings with Haitink and the Concertgebouw, this sounds self-conscious and less, rather than more, spontaneous.

The recorded sound gives a good sense of presence but is badly balanced and the loud applause is intrusive.

Piano Concertos Nos. 1 in C, Op. 15; (i) 2 in B flat, Op. 19; Für Elise.

(BB) (***) Naxos mono 8.110638. Schnabel, LSO (i) LPO, Sargent.

Schnabel's performances appeared on LP briefly in the days of the World Record Club and more recently on the Arabesque label. They reigned supreme in the 1930s, when they first appeared, and still make for powerfully compelling listening 70 years on. Mark Obert-Thorn's transfers do justice to the vitality and beauty of sound that Schnabel commanded.

Piano Concertos Nos. 1 & 4.

*** Ph. 462 782-2. Brendel, VPO, Rattle.

Brendel's third and finest recording of the Beethoven concertos, already praised by us as a set (Ph. 462 781-2), now appears on three separate CDs. Although they are studio recordings each was recorded after a live performance, and this consistently tells in the spontaneity of the music-making. These are unashamedly modern-instrument performances, with full-bodied orchestral sound and a wide range of pianistic colour and dynamic.

In No. 1 Rattle immediately sets the scene with a strong, forward-looking introduction, and Brendel's crisp articulation in the outer movements (and neat touches of wit in the finale) balances with the poised, intensely shaped account of the beautiful central Largo. The rare coupling with No. 4 works well, with its highly poetic, yet expansive opening and in the *Andante* the orchestra weightily contrasts with Brendel's gentle response, which triumphs so touchingly to make way for the joyfully vigorous finale.

(i) Piano concerto No. 1 in C, Op. 15; Symphony No. 7 in A, Op. 92; Overture, Coriolan, Op. 62.

*** Arthaus **DVD** 100 148. (i) Perahia; LSO, Solti. (V/D: Humphrey Burton.)

This is a straight recording directed by Humphrey Burton of a concert at London's Barbican Centre in 1987. The camerawork is discreet and unfussy and the sound impeccably balanced throughout. Nothing distracts the viewer or listener from Beethoven. In spite of some over-emphatic gestures, Solti's accounts of both the *Coriolan Overture* and the *Seventh Symphony* are very fine, and at no point are the LSO sound rough or rhythms overdriven. These are cultured and dedicated performances in every way and in the concerto Murray Perahia is unfailingly thoughtful, intelligent and imaginative. A memorable concert, and the first-rate recording will give much pleasure.

Piano Concerto No. 2.

(B) (***) RCA Double mono 74321 845952 (2). Kapell, NBC SO, Golschmann – CHOPIN: *Sonata 2*; DEBUSSY: *Children's Corner*; KHACHATURIAN: *Piano Concerto* (***); PROKOFIEV: *Piano Concerto No. 3* (***); RACHMANINOV: *Rhapsody on a Theme of Paganini*

(with SHOSTAKOVICH: *3 Preludes*; SCHUBERT: *Impromptu; Ländler; Moment musical; Waltzes*). ***

This RCA Double is a welcome tribute to the incomparable William Kapell, but readers should note that Naxos is embarking on a complete Kapell series, which may offer more logical couplings. The transfers are decent, but the hideous artwork makes it difficult to decipher the notes.

Piano Concertos Nos. 2–3.

*** Ph. 462 783-2. Brendel, VPO, Rattle.

As in the *First Concerto*, Rattle opens the *Second* with a strongly rhythmic, yet resiliently classical tutti, and Brendel's response shows how close is this musical partnership, both in the reflectively serene *Adagio*, and in the engaging finale. No. 3, with one of Beethoven's most imaginatively developed opening movements, again shows these two artists working in absolute rapport, with the elysian Largo wonderfully sustained in its rapt beauty and the finale lilting joyously. The often subtle use of light and shade continuously illuminates this music-making and the recording balance is most satisfying.

(i) Piano Concerto No. 2 in B flat; (iii) Symphony No. 9 in D min.

*** TDK **DVD** DV-EC10A. (i) Pletnev (ii) Mattila, Urmana, Moser, Schulte; Swedish Radio Ch., Eric Ericson Chamber Ch., BPO, Abbado. (Producer Paul Smaczny. Video Director Bob Coles.)

This concert, recorded in the Philharmonie on 1 May 2000, was the tenth conducted by Abbado to mark the centenary of the foundation of the Berlin Philharmonic on 1 May 1882. Pletnev's account of the *B flat Concerto* is immaculate, both artistically and technically, and a model of its kind: expressive eloquence tempered by sureness of musical judgement and taste. In short, it is wonderfully fresh and exhilarating. The *Ninth Symphony*, which Karajan had given on this date in 1963, has a fine line-up of soloists, together with the legendary Eric Ericson Choir and the Swedish Radio Choir, and is a hardly less fine performance, direct and powerful. It comes with a 20-minute documentary with commentaries and subtitles in English, French, German, Italian, Spanish and Japanese.

Piano Concertos Nos. 3 in C min., Op. 37; 4 in G, Op. 58; Rondo in C, Op. 51/1.

(BB) (***) Naxos mono 8.110639. Schnabel, LPO, Sargent.

(M) *(*) Sony (ADD) SMK 89581. Gould, NYPO, Bernstein.

Schnabel re-recorded these concertos after the war with Issay Dobrowen, but this pre-war set, made when he was recording the sonatas for HMV's Beethoven Sonata Society volumes, long dominated the musical scene. Schnabel was about fifty when he embarked on this mammoth enterprise, and the 1933 versions of the *Third* and *Fourth Piano Concertos* with Malcolm Sargent conducting the LPO have long been absent from the catalogues. Their return in these fine transfers is welcome: Schnabel's insights are always special, and although they do not occupy quite the same awesome pinnacle as the sonatas in Schnabel's Beethoven discography, they are still memorable.

Glenn Gould made an impressive account of the *First Piano Concerto* with Vladimir Golschmann in the 1950s, and we recall a wonderful performance of the *B flat Concerto* from the same period with Kurt Sanderling. (He also gave a memorable Festival Hall performance in the late 1950s.) He is said to have modelled early performances of the *Fourth* on the war-time Schnabel recording with Frederick Stock, although the present account is very different. Here, alas, Gould is too idiosyncratic and eccentric to command universal appeal, and these performances are for his followers rather than Beethoven's.

(i) Piano Concertos Nos. 3 in C min., Op. 37; 5 in E flat (Emperor); Piano Sonata No. 5 in C min., Op. 10/1; Andante favori in F; Für Elise, WoO 59; (ii) Choral Fantasia, Op 80.

(B) **(*) Double Decca (DDD/ADD) 468 906-2 (2). Ashkenazy with (i) VPO, Mehta; (ii) Cleveland Ch. & O. cond. Ashkenazy

Ashkenazy's digital Beethoven Piano Concerto cycle of the early 1980s was the first to be issued on CD. (Nos. 1, 2, and 4 are already available on a companion Double Decca set, 468 558-2; see our main volume.) They were generally more relaxed and spontaneous sounding than the somewhat aggressive Solti Chicago set of the 1970s, though only in the finale of the *Emperor* does the more recent approach bring a slackening of tension that reduces the impact of the reading. The spaciousness of the first movement combined with clarity of texture is most persuasive, and so too is the unusually gentle account of the slow movement. The relaxed approach works well in the *Third Concerto* because, even though it is slower than the earlier recording, it sounds more spontaneous and has fewer distracting agogic hesitations than before. The slow movement is more lyrical, and the finale has much more charm – an excellent performance. Both receive vividly warm recordings, and Mehta accompanies well, though with no particularly memorable insight. Ashkenazy's 1976 account of the *Op. 10/1 Sonata* is both thoughtful and alert, with the freshness of approach silencing any criticism, and the recording is excellent. The vibrantly characterful account of the *Choral Fantasia* was recorded at the time of his later, third set of the Beethoven concertos (1987) where Ashkenazy directed from the keyboard. It makes a compelling bonus.

Piano Concerto No. 3; (i) Triple Concerto for Violin, Cello & Piano, Op. 56.

**(*) Simax PSC 1183. Berezovsky; (i) with Svensson, Rondin; Swedish CO, Dausgaard.

This fifth volume in Simax's Beethoven series with Thomas Dausgaard and the Swedish Chamber Orchestra follows the regular pattern of presenting the composer in a more closely focused setting than usual. More than most Beethoven recordings using a chamber orchestra, this one clearly conveys an intimate scale, with the music in close-up, bringing the sort of impact that early audiences might have expected. Pianissimos are all the more striking in contrast with the sharp, clear fortissimos. So the opening tutti of the *Third Piano Concerto* initially takes one aback by the forward balance of the woodwind, with the strings less prominent than usual, and with a dry but helpful acoustic suggesting a relatively small venue such as Beethoven might have expected. Equally, at the start of the *Triple Concerto* the hush of the opening is extreme, quickly expanding in a sunburst crescendo, linking this in originality to the similarly hushed opening of the *Fourth Concerto*.

All this pays tribute to the conductor, Thomas Dausgaard, and the soloists match him well, with Boris Berezovsky in the *Third Concerto* also drawing on a very wide dynamic range. Despite the relatively small scale, he opts for Beethoven's last and longest cadenza in the first movement, weightily done but with the most delicate half-tones in the development of second subject material. Outer movements are on the fast side, with influences from period performance practice, yet the slow movements in both concertos are taken at very measured speeds, with Berezovsky allowing himself ample expressive freedom. The finale of the *Piano Concerto* sparkles, thanks to the pianist's exceptionally clean articulation, with passage-work perfectly even. In the *Triple Concerto* the violinist, Urban Svensson, with rather edgy tone as recorded, may not be a perfect match, and Berezovsky rather than the cellist, Mats Rondin, is very much the leader of the team, but the clarity of texture on every level makes for an exceptionally fresh reading.

Piano Concertos Nos. 4 in G, Op. 58; 5 in E flat (Emperor).

(BB) **(*) Regis (ADD) RRC 1047. Brendel, VSO, Hans Wallberh or V. Pro Musica SO, Mehta.

(BB) ** EMI Encore CDE5 74721-2. Zacharias, Dresden State O, Vonk.

It is good that Regis have reissued at budget price Brendel's 1959 Vox performances, originally available on Turnabout in England. Many count these readings the finest of all his Beethoven concerto interpretations and certainly they have a fresh spontaneity which is very appealing. Both are deeply satisfying. In No. 4 the orchestral accompaniment is unimaginative: the first movement tutti for example is rhythmically stodgy. But Brendel's control of phrase and colour is such that his reading rides over this impediment and the contrasts of the slow movement are strongly and poetically made. It is noteworthy that he uses the second of the cadenzas written for the work, one not generally heard.

The *Emperor* is a bold and vigorous reading and here Brendel is well supported by the young Zubin Mehta and the Vienna Pro Musica Symphony Orchestra. The performance is without idiosyncrasy, yet strong in style and personality, the slow movement raptly serene to contrast with the vitality of the outer movments. In both concertos the piano is well captured and in spite of the shrill, thin strings (cleanly remastered) the warm resonance brings a fully acceptable overall effect.

Christian Zacharias is much admired in Germany, and these well-recorded performances of the *G major* and *Emperor*, made in the late 1980s, have a lot going for them, including supportive playing from the Staatskapelle Dresden and Hans Vonk. The articulation is clean and vital, and there are some sensitive tonal shadings and much pianistic finesse, but in the slow movement of the *Emperor* he lacks real breadth and weight. We are so well served in this repertoire that only the most masterly will do.

Piano Concerto No. 5 in E flat (Emperor), Op. 73.

(M) (***) BBCL mono 4074-2. Moiseiwitsch, BBC SO, Sargent – RACHMANINOV: *Piano Concerto No. 2.* (**)

(i) Piano Concerto No. 5 (Emperor); Piano Sonatas Nos. 8 in C min. (Pathétique); 23 in F min. (Appassionata).

(B) (**(*)) EMI mono. CDZ5 74800-2. Edwin Fischer; (i) Philh. O, Furtwängler.

(i) Piano Concerto No. 5 (Emperor); Piano Sonata No. 23 (Apppassionata).

*** Ph. 462 783-2. Brendel; (i) VPO, Rattle.

Brendel and Rattle combine to present the *Emperor Concerto* as the culmination of their outstanding cycle, weighty and commanding yet resilient, with a gloriously rich, flowing *Adagio* and a finale which is jauntily rhythmic and full of elation. As throughout this impressive series the acoustic of the Musikverein is attractively spacious, yet detail is always clear. The account of the *Appasionata* is comparably distinguished, the obvious product of maturity, with the central variations especially thoughtful, and the finale making a most satisfying conclusion. Again most realistic sound.

Some older readers may remember Moiseiwitsch's magisterial and noble *Emperor*, for it was a performance that lingered in the memory and was long spoken of with awe. It comes from one of the BBC Wednesday Concerts at the Royal Festival Hall and was recorded only a month before his death. It is not always finger-sure in the finale – he was, after all, 73 – but it has a wisdom and sense of architecture and line that carry all before it. Sargent and the BBC Symphony give excellent support, although the recording does not have the clarity and transparency of a good studio recording of the period. However, connoisseurs of the piano – and of great music-making – should not neglect this opportunity of collecting it.

Edwin Fischer's 1951 recording of the *Emperor* with Furtwängler and the Philharmonia is one of great classics of the gramophone, an *Emperor* both imperious and imperial. The two *Sonatas* were recorded the following year (also at Abbey Road) and are equally valuable. However the current transfer of the *Concerto* yields a rather opaque, not very refined orchestral texture, though full-bodied enough, and the piano timbre too is somewhat bass-heavy.

(i) Piano Concerto No. 5 in in E flat (Emperor), Op. 73; (ii) Cello Sonata in G min., Op. 5/2.

(BB) (***) Naxos mono 8.110640. Schnabel; (i) LSO, Sargent; (ii) Piatigorsky.

Schnabel's *Emperor* was recorded in 1932 (he subsequently re-made it after the war with the Philharmonia Orchestra and Alceo Galliera) when he was at the height of his powers and had London at his feet. It long occupied a dominant position in the catalogue – and rightly. Schnabel had met Piatigorsky in the 1920s when he was leading the cello section of the Berlin Philharmonic under Furtwängler, and together with Carl Flesch they formed a piano trio in the 1920s. Alas, they made no records, and this 1934 set of the *G minor Cello Sonata* is the sole representation of Schnabel's collaboration with the great cellist. It is very distinguished indeed, although Piatigorsky's post-war set of all five sonatas with Solomon has the greater poise.

Violin Concerto in D, Op. 61.

(M) (***) EMI mono CDM5 67583-2 [567584]. Milstein, Pittsburgh SO, Steinberg – BRAHMS: *Violin Concerto.* (***) ✪

(***) Testament mono SBT 1228. Kogan, Paris Conservatoire O., Vandernoot – MOZART: *Violin Concerto No. 5.* (***)

(BB) (***) Naxos mono 8.110909. Kreisler, Berlin State Op. O, Blech – MENDELSSOHN: *Violin Concerto* ***. (with BACH: *Unaccompanied Violin Sonata No. 1, BWV 1001: Adagio* (***).

**(*) Sony SK 89505. Bell, Camerata Salzburg, Norrington – MENDELSSOHN: *Violin Concerto.* **(*)

(BB) (***) Naxos mono 8.110946. Szigeti, British SO, Walter – MOZART: *Violin Concerto No. 4.*(***)

(BB) *(*) CfP 574 8782. Huggett, OAE, Mackerras – MENDELSSOHN: *Violin Concerto.* *(*)

(i) Violin Concerto; (ii) Romances Nos. 1 in G, Op. 40; 2 in F, Op. 50.

(BB) *** EMI Encore (ADD) CDE5 74973-2. Y. Menuhin; (i) VPO, Silvestri; (ii) Philh. O, Pritchard.

A spacious and magisterial account of the Beethoven concerto from Milstein. One of the finest ever recorded, it can rank alongside the greatest of the past and surpass most of the present. The Brahms coupling belongs among the greatest concerto records ever made.

It is good to have Menuhin's first (1960) stereo recording with Silvestri back in the catalogue; it is far preferable to his later versions with Klemperer and Masur. This is a noble performance, very comparable with his mono record with Furtwängler, but of course the sound is greatly improved. Silvestri is surprisingly classical in his outlook and the VPO provide an accompaniment of great character. Menuhin's warmth and humanity show in his instinctive shaping of phrases, and his slightly slower tempi add breadth and boldness to a design than can easily be spoiled by ill-judged emphasis. His playing in the slow movement is particularly lovely, and the intonation here is rock-steady. The *Romances* are simple, straightforward accounts, not quite as memorable as the concerto. The remastering is vividly successful, with the orchestra clear and quite full-bodied.

Leonid Kogan's mono account of the Beethoven *Concerto* comes from 1957 and, like the Mozart concerto that completes the present CD, was never issued at the time. Kogan re-recorded the work with Constantin Silvestri two years later in stereo so that, although the Paris version was passed for release, it was withheld for obvious reasons. Testament have put us in their debt by issuing it now, for it is a reading of the greatest distinction. It has purity and nobility, as does its successor, but there is a slightly freer quality (Tully Potter's sleeve note calls it 'carefree') and a spirituality that makes it well worth considering.

Fritz Kreisler was undoubtedly among the greatest of all violinists; his playing was for the lyrical tradition of the instrument the equivalent of Heifetz's astonishing technical control and dazzling bravura. Yet as Heifetz was also a fine lyricist, so Kreisler's technique was unassailable; but his lyrical gifts predominated, his tone was glorious, his phrasing, with its gentle touches of the characteristic portamenti of his time, unforgettable. He is at his very peak in this wonderful, poetically rich account of the Beethoven *Concerto*, particularly the ravishing account of the *Larghetto*, which causes one to catch the breath at the rapt, elysian quality of its expressive climax, while the finale releases the tension and is engagingly light-hearted. In Mark Obert-Thorn's splendid transfer the 1926 recording, one of the very first made electrically (in the warm acoustic of the Berlin Singakademie), is astonishingly lifelike, and brings Kreisler's violin vividly into one's presence. One immediately forgets its early provenance, so richly communicative and moving is this playing, with the Mendelssohn coupling hardly less magical. Whichever recordings of the Beethoven you already have this one is a must, with the Bach *Adagio* making a treasurable encore.

Szigeti's searching and magical account of the concerto enjoys legendary status. Its last incarnation was on HMV's plum-label Treasury series during the 1970s, and it is (we believe) new to CD. Made in 1932, when he was at the height of his career, it has the refinement and purity for which he was famous. It belongs among the foremost versions of the concerto on record and is not to be missed in this fine new Naxos transfer.

Joshua Bell's reading has plainly been affected by having a chamber group as partners: the Camerata Salzburg under their period-influenced conductor, Sir Roger Norrington. The opening tutti of the Beethoven is clean and crisp rather than powerful,

and the opening of the slow movement brings minimal use of vibrato by the strings, echoing period practice, giving an ethereal quality. As for the soloist, his tone seems sparer than in his Decca recordings, clean and bright rather than warmly romantic, aided by the recording quality, which is relatively dry, so giving less bloom to the violin tone.

It is a powerful performance, but on a smaller scale than usual, but clarity goes with concentration, and a speed rather faster than usual in this long first movement brings an extra tautness and plenty of light and shade, bringing mystery in the central development section. After his own impressive cadenza, just as long and demanding as the regular Kreisler one, Bell then refuses to linger over the coda in a romantic way, consistent with the whole approach. The slow movement is relatively light and delicate, with clean, pure tone from Bell, and the relative intimacy of the reading comes out more clearly than ever in the finale, with crisp timpani. There too Bell plays his own cadenza with plentiful double-stopping immaculately performed. A strong, distinctive reading, well-coupled with a similar if more mercurial reading of the Mendelssohn, but hardly a primary recommendation.

The opening timpani strokes are not very arresting in Monica Huggett's 'authentic' version, although later Mackerras achieves incisive enough tuttis. Yet overall this is not a performance that convinces by either its emotional power or its serenity in the slow movement, which is comparatively uninvolving.

First choice among modern recordings rests with Kremer (Teldec 9031 74881-2) or Perlman (EMI CDM5 66900-2) although Schneiderhan is very special (● DG 447 403-2).

(i) *Triple Concerto for Piano, Violin and Cello, Op. 56;* (ii) *Piano Concerto No. 3, Op. 37.*

(BB) *** EMI Encore ADD/Dig. CDE5 74722-2.
Zacharias; (i) Hoelscher, Schiff, Leipzig GO, Masur; (ii) Dresden State O, Vonk.

The soloists in Masur's version of the *Triple Concerto*, led by the cellist Heinrich Schiff, make a characterful but finely integrated trio – a balance of responsibility suggested by Beethoven's own priorities in this work. Their rhythmic flair prompts Masur in turn to give one of his most sparkling Beethoven performances on record, and even the opening tutti is better sprung than those of most principal rivals. The long span of the first movement is firmly held together, the brief slow movement has inner intensity without being overweighted, while the finale is ideally clear and light. The sound is both full and detailed. This remains among the very finest of digital versions and Zacharias's analogue account of the *C minor Concerto* makes an appealingly fresh coupling. With lively support from Hans Vonk, his playing sparkles in the outer movements, and the central Largo is both warmly lyrical and gravely poetic in feeling. Again, excellent sound. A real bargain.

Romances for Violin and Orchestra, Nos. 1 in G, Op. 40; 2 in F, Op. 50.

(M) *** CRD (ADD) CRD 3369. R. Thomas, Bournemouth SO – MENDELSSOHN: *Violin Concerto;* SCHUBERT: *Konzertstück.* ***

The purity of Ronald Thomas's intonation (particularly important in the double-stopping at the start of Op. 40) makes for sensitive, clean-cut readings which, along with the Schubert *Konzertstück*, provide enjoyable if unexpected couplings for the Mendelssohn *Concerto*. The recording is first rate.

SYMPHONIES

Symphonies Nos. 1–9.

(M) *(*) Teldec 3984 27838-2 (6); 8573 83085-2 (1 & 2); 8573 83060-2 (3); 8573 82891-2 (4 & 5); 8573 83061-2 (6); 8573 83062-2 (7 & 8); 8573 83063-2 (9). Berlin State O, Barenboim (with Isokoski, Lang, Gambill, Pape & Berlin State Op. Ch. in No. 9).

Barenboim, even more than most of today's conductors, has a lifelong devotion to the work of Furtwängler, a point that is regularly reflected in his current readings of the Beethoven symphonies. Speeds tend to be broad in the Furtwängler manner, often very broad, as in the first movements of the *Eroica* and *Ninth*, and he encourages a fair degree of flexibility within movements. This is the orchestra with which he has worked regularly over his years with the Deutsche Oper in Berlin, and they are certainly responsive to his demands. But what undermines most of these performances is a curious lack of tension. In taking a broad, flexible view the essential factor, as the finest Furtwängler performances demonstrate, is that the expressive freedom must seem to develop spontaneously. In that Barenboim, while still achieving creditable results, tends to fall short. The result is a series of run-throughs rather than genuine performances, not helped by a rounded recording that could with advantage have been brighter. So this set, whether taken as a whole or sampled individually, can be recommended only to Barenboim devotees.

Symphonies Nos. 1–9; Overture: Egmont; Missa solemnis, Op. 123.

(***) RCA mono 74321 66656-2 (6 + 1). NBC SO, Toscanini; with (i & ii) Robert Shaw Chorale; (i) Farrell, Peerce, Scott; (i; ii); Merriman; (ii) Marshall, Conley, Hines.

There could be no greater contrast than that between those pre-war giants, Weingartner and Furtwängler on the one hand and Toscanini and the NBC Symphony Orchestra on the other. This new refurbishment of the Toscanini Beethoven Symphonies and the *Missa Solemnis* comes on six CDs together with an additional disc comparing the present transfers with earlier issues, or alternatively in three double-disc boxes, available separately. If

you were to use an astronomical analogy, you might speak of Toscanini's Beethoven as having the concentration of a white dwarf by the side of Furtwängler's red giant. In any event those who want these classic and electrifying performances are going to find the sound dramatically improved, warmer and less strident. It was the pianist-critic Peter Stadlen whose spoke of Weingartner's 'lean-beef' Beethoven interpretations, and we hope that his incomparable cycle with the Vienna Philharmonic and the LPO will be restored to currency within the lifetime of this volume.

Symphonies Nos. 1 in C, Op. 21; 8 in F, Op. 93.

(*) Sony **DVD SVD 46363. BPO, Karajan. (V/D: Ernst Wild.)

Symphonies Nos. 2 in D, Op. 36; 3 in E flat, Op. 55, (Eroica).

(*) Sony **DVD SVD 46365. BPO, Karajan. (V/D: Ernst Wild.)

Symphonies No. 4 in B flat, Op. 60; 5 in C min., Op. 67.

(*) Sony **DVD SVD 46366. BPO, Karajan. (V/D: Ernst Wild.)

Symphonies Nos. 6 in F, Op. 68, (Pastoral); 7 in A, Op. 92.

(*) Sony **DVD SVD 46367. BPO, Karajan. (V/D: Ernst Wild.)

Karajan's Beethoven has been part of our staple diet since his 1947 account of the *Ninth Symphony*. His first complete cycle was made with the Philharmonia Orchestra in mono, and reigned supreme in the early LP era. Then came the classic 1963 cycle with the Berlin Philharmonic in stereo, which in some respects he never surpassed. His second Berlin set was issued in 1977, and offered some impressive readings (4, 5, 7 and 9) while later on came a third set in digital sound.

DG issued a number of recordings from the 1970s on video, and subsequently on laserdisc, and the present performances, which date from the early 1980s. The laserdiscs were generously filled: Nos 1, 2, 6 and 8 were all accommodated on one disc, though the *Pastoral*, a 1967 recording, suffers from rather pallid, hazy colours. The sound of the new Sony recordings is first class in every way, though the camerawork tends to be restricted to the same limited number of shots. (Hugo Niebeling's direction in the 1967 *Pastoral* was more imaginative.)

All the same, it is good to see as well as hear Karajan and the Berlin Philharmonic. It goes without saying that the orchestral playing is of the highest standard but at the same time it must be admitted that they do not have the same immediacy and spontaneity of the 1950s and 1960s performances. No. 1 is beautifully played yet curiously lifeless. No. 8 certainly does not match the post-War Vienna Philharmonic or the 1963 set in electricity.

The 1967 *Pastoral* had enormous grip (as did the 1963 LP) and held the listener in the palm of its hand, while this newcomer is much less fresh. So this Beethoven set is recommended but without the enthusiasm that Karajan so often inspired.

Symphonies Nos. 1–2.

*** DG 471 487-2. BPO, Abbado.

Unlike the later symphonies in Abbado's Berlin cycle, these first two were recorded in the smaller hall of the Philharmonie in Berlin. Yet the sound is in no way limited and if anything a degree warmer than the rest with clearer detail. Light and resilient with clean attack and speeds generally on the fast side, they make an impressive coupling, with the defiant radicalism of the young Beethoven fully conveyed. In this latest DG series Abbado uses new scholarly editions of all nine symphonies prepared by Jonathan Del Mar, and while Zinman's Zurich Tonhalle performances (Arte Nova 74321 63645-2) are even more strongly influenced by the revelations of period-instrument Beethoven, Abbado's readings will admirably suit those collectors seeking a balance with a more traditional heritage and the playing of the Berlin Philharmonic is superb.

Symphonies Nos. (i) 1–2; (ii) 3 (Eroica); (i) Overtures: Coriolan; Fidelio; The Ruins of Athens (with March alla Turca).

(B) **(*) Teldec Ultima (ADD) 3984 21335-2 (2). (i) Bamberg SO; (ii) Hamburg State PO; Keilberth.

These recordings date from the late 1950s and were first noticed in our Penguin Guide to Bargain Records (1966). Keilberth proved a first class Beethoven conductor but the Telefunken LP transfers were unacceptably fierce. The sound is now immensely improved, still bright and vivid, but with plenty of weight in the bass. The first two symphonies are a great success with both first movement exposition repeats included. No. 1 is wonderfully crisp and sprightly; No. 2 has comparable vitality, well observed detail, and the slow movement is warm and serene. The Eroica is fresh and dramatic, well paced and gripping, although here the exposition repeat is not observed. The overtures are also full of life and drama, although here the recording of the Bamberg violins is at times rather less refined. The brief encore, the Marcia alla Turca, is played with great gusto.

Symphony No. 2 in D, Op. 36.

(M) (***) BBC mono BBCL 4099-2. RPO, Beecham – BRAHMS: Symphony No. 2. (***)

The Second Symphony was the work of Beethoven that Beecham most enjoyed, and he gives an electrifying performance, recorded in the BBC Studio at Maida Vale in December 1956, sadly not in stereo but with clear, well-balanced mono sound. The reading is typical of Beecham, if anything even more magnetic than his EMI studio recording, fiery in the outer movements and warmly persuasive in the Larghetto slow movement, affectionately moulded at a steady speed. An excellent coupling for Beecham's incandescent Edinburgh Festival account of the Brahms symphony.

Symphonies Nos 2; 6 (Pastoral).

(BB) (***) Dutton mono CDBP 9716. Berlin Op. O, or LPO, Kleiber.

It is too easily forgotten that Erich Kleiber (father of Carlos) was, in the 1920s, a supreme conductor alongside Walter, Toscanini and Klemperer – one whose career temporarily suffered when, during the Hitler period, he went to live in South America. His fine recording of the Pastoral Symphony, fresh and alert, was made for Decca in 1948, following up his mould-breaking account of the Fifth for that company, one of the earliest LPs. He recorded No. 2 in Berlin much earlier in 1929; equally strong and magnetic, with full-bodied sound, remarkable for its period. Typically excellent Dutton transfers.

Symphony No. 3 (Eroica); Overture: Coriolan.

(M) (***) Sony mono SMK 89887. RPO, Beecham.

Symphony No. 3 (Eroica); Overtures: Egmont; King Stephen; The Ruins of Athens.

(M) *(*) DG 455 603-2. VPO, Abbado.

Symphony No. 3 in E flat (Eroica), Op. 55 Overtures Leonora Nos. 1–2.

(M) (***) EMI mono CDM5 67740-2 [567741]. Philh. O, Klemperer.

Symphony No. 3 (Eroica); Overture: Leonora No. 3.

(**(*)) Testament (mono) SBT 2242 (2). Royal Danish O, Klemperer – BRAHMS: Symphony No. 4; MOZART: Symphony No. 29. (**(*))

In the concert hall Beecham conducted the Eroica more than most Beethoven symphonies (over 40 times), but he recorded it only once in 1951–2 during the period when he was contracted to American Columbia (CBS). Though it is in mono only, the rare combination of qualities – power as well as elegance, warmth without romantic distortion – makes for a magnetic reading. Beecham is credited with disparaging remarks about Beethoven, but he was plainly in awe of his mastery in the Eroica. The first movement is marked by extremes of dynamic, while the Funeral March has a natural gravity at a steady, measured pace, with the Scherzo rhythmically bouncy rather than hectic, and the finale thrustful as well as elegant. One specially notes the distinctive sound of Dennis Brain's horn at key moments. The Coriolan Overture is comparably powerful and dedicated. Bright, clearly detailed sound.

Recorded in April 1957 on Klemperer's last visit to conduct the Royal Danish Orchestra in Copenhagen, this version of the Eroica is even more magnetic than either of his studio recordings with the Philharmonia, fine as they are, the one in mono from 1955 now re-transferred in EMI's 'Great Recordings of the Century' series (CDM5 67740-2) listed above, and the second in stereo from 1961 (CDM5 66793). Though the playing in a live account is not quite so polished, the tension is consistently keener, the dramatic points more positive, and the overall sense of a great occasion vividly conveyed. The mono sound is not so well-balanced as in the studio recordings, but the ear very soon adjusts. The Beethoven *Overture*, like the Brahms and Mozart symphonies which also come on the first of the two discs in this the set, derives from a concert Klemperer conducted in January 1954, and though the slow introduction brings some rough ensemble, and the recording is rougher too, not at all kind to the trumpet in the famous off-stage call, the weight and intensity of the performance come over strongly, with the main allegro fiercely dramatic.

The 1954 recording of the *Leonora Overtures Nos. 1 and 2*, and the 1955 mono version of the *Eroica* were among the first recordings Klemperer made with the Philharmonia Orchestra, and their success immediately revealed his full strength. This *Eroica* is one of his supreme achievements, with speeds generally more urgent than in his 1961 stereo version (on CDM5 66793-2, with the *Grosse Fuge* sounding appropriately monolithic). The more spacious later version is keenly concentrated, and the remastered stereo weightily re-enforces the work's magnificence. However many will prefer the even greater incisiveness of the earlier mono version recorded in Denmark.

Abbado's earlier recording with the VPO presents an account of the *Eroica*, recorded live, that, for all the beauty of playing lacks dramatic tension. Its general absence of idiosyncrasy and the safe speeds might for some make it an agreeable version to live with, and the recording is pleasantly spacious, more than usually capturing the fine acoustics of the Musikvereinsaal in Vienna. The overtures make quite a good bonus, but it is the main work that counts, of which there are too many preferable recommendations, including Abbado's newest version, to make this release competitive.

Symphonies Nos. 3 (Eroica); 4.

*** DG 471 488-2. BPO, Abbado.

Abbado's reading of the *Eroica* is at once robust, dramatic and refined, with the lessons of period performance clearly taken on board. Though the tempo for the *Funeral March* slow movement is flowing rather than measured, with light pianissimos, the dedication is intense, with high dynamic contrasts building up in this live reading into a deeply affecting coda. The finale is brisk and urgent, yet string textures are transparent, as they are throughout. In No. 4 too speeds are on the fast side, yet the mystery of the slow introduction is magical, while the Adagio slow movement at a flowing speed is sweet and relaxed in its lyricism, with the power of the outer movements fully conveyed. A splendid more traditional alternative to Zinman's Tonhalle coupling of the same two symphonies (Arte Nova 74321 59214-2).

Symphonies Nos. 5; 6 (Pastoral).

*** DG 471 489-2. BPO, Abbado.

Recorded live like the rest of his cycle, Abbado's account of No. 5 is urgently dramatic in the first movement, smoothly refined in the slow movement

and by turns strong and mysterious in the Scherzo, with high dynamic contrasts and an extra repeat of the Scherzo section, as prescribed in the Jonathan Del Mar edition, making an ABABA structure as in the *Fourth* and *Seventh Symphonies*. The finale then expands at full power, with the timpani well caught. The *Pastoral* brings the biggest contrast with Abbado's earlier Vienna recording, when all five movements are faster and lighter than before, bringing out the freshness of inspiration far more effectively. Altogether a superb coupling, hard to beat.

Symphonies Nos. (i) 5; (ii) 6 (Pastoral); (iii) 7; Overtures: Egmont; Leonora No. 3.

(B) ** Teldec Ultima 0630 18946-2 (2). (i) Hamburg State PO; (ii) Bamberg SO; (iii) BPO; Keilberth.

The second Keilberth Ultima is less successful than the first, although the early stereo remains impressively vivid. In the *Fifth Symphony* Keilberth's leisurely speed for the first movement at first seems lacking in tension, but in fact it is beautifully controlled, and the comparably slow speed for the Andante also makes for some stylish playing. But the Scherzo is ridiculously snail-like, and the Finale, as though to compensate, is taken so quickly that it does not match the rest of the performance. The *Pastoral*, however, is uncontroversial – a direct, straightforward account, with nicely turned playing, the brook flowing serenely, and a characterful scherzo and storm sequence. However the climaxes at the end of both outer movements do not expand as dramatically as they might, and in the finale this means less contrast than usual for the peaceful coda, even though it is played gently and beautifully.

For the *Seventh Symphony* Keilberth has the advantage of excellent playing from the Berlin Philharmonic. However the performance does not quite hang together as does Colin Davis's outstanding RPO version from the same period (EMI CZS5 69364-2), and Keilberth seems a degree unwilling to produce a yielding, lilting beat, even when the dance is at its most 'apotheotic'. Both overtures are a success, with the Berlin players rising to a brilliant burst of virtuosity in the coda of *Leonora No. 3*.

Symphonies Nos. 6 (Pastoral) in F, Op. 68; 8 in F, Op. 93.

(M) (***) Sony mono SMK 89888. RPO, Beecham.

As in his other Beethoven interpretations, Beecham treats the *Pastoral Symphony* as far more than an evocative programme-piece. Unlike so many conductors in the romantic tradition, he tends to prefer steady speeds, not even hesitating in the traditional place before the second subject of the first movement. The result is wonderfully fresh as well as elegant, while he takes the *Andante* second movement at a slow tempo, finely pointed, allowing himself expressive freedom in the birdsong at the end. The rustic jollity of the Scherzo leads to a fiercely dramatic account of the Storm and an exuberant reading of the finale at a fast-flowing tempo. These were Beecham's only recordings of the *Pastoral* and of the *Eighth*, even though they were favourites with him among the Beethoven symphonies. No. 8 is comparably brisk and buoyant in the outer movements, relaxed in the middle movements, with the second movement *Allegretto* winningly sprung. Transfers of the mono 1951–2 recordings bring commendably clean textures with good inner detail.

Symphony No. 7 in A, Op. 92.

(M) *** BBC Legends BBCL 4076-2. Hallé O, Barbirolli – MOZART: *Symphony No. 35* ***; WAGNER: *Siegfried Idyll* (***).

(M) ** Decca 470 256-2. VPO, Karajan – HAYDN: *Symphony No. 104 (London).* ***

Beethoven's *Seventh Symphony* was probably Barbirolli's favourite among the nine, and thus it is strange that he never made a commercial recording of it. This live account, recorded by BBC engineers at the Royal Festival Hall in April 1968, is therefore very cherishable indeed, with bright, full stereo sound in which the horns bray out superbly. The ensemble may not always be ideally polished, but few will worry about that when the energy and thrust of the performance are so compelling. After a weighty account of the slow introduction Barbirolli then adopts a tempo for the main Allegro which allows plenty of spring in the dotted 6/8 rhythms. The finale too is taken at a tempo which permits fair articulation of the string semiquavers, and characteristically Barbirolli keeps the tempo steadier than most, even through the plain dotted episodes which so often invite a speeding up. Conversely, Barbirolli's speeds for the middle two movements are on the fast side, with an aptly flowing *Allegretto* and a really fast presto for the Scherzo where, following the custom of the time, he omits most of the repeats. With typically warm-hearted accounts of the Mozart and Wagner items for coupling, this makes a splendid addition to the Barbirolli discography.

Karajan's Decca recording of the *Seventh* dates from 1959 and, being produced by John Culshaw, was very well recorded in the Sofiensaal, although in the tuttis the horns don't penetrate the texture as vibrantly as they might. The interpretion does not match his later DG versions, yet the Vienna Philharmonic are in very good form, especially in the simple eloquence of the *Allegretto*, the scherzo springs to life vividly and the finale, if not earth-shaking, has plenty of impetus. The main attraction of this Legends reissue is the superb coupled account of Haydn's *London* Symphony.

Symphony No. 7; (i) Egmont (overture and incidental music; complete).

*** Simax PSC 1182. Swedish CO, Dausgaard; (i) with Bonde-Hansen,

Recordings of Beethoven symphonies using limited forces have become relatively common, but far more than most Dausgaard's version of the *Seventh Symphony* and *Egmont* incidental music captures an intimate scale while losing nothing in power and bite. Speeds are on the fast side, and textures clear, with the small string section sharply focused and horns braying dramatically. The *Egmont* music begins with an astonishingly brisk account of the *Overture*, minutes shorter than usual, but it works dramatically, with a big pause on 'Egmont's death' and an exhilarating account of the 'Battle Symphony' coda – repeated later at the end of the suite. Henriette Bonde-Hansen is the fresh-toned soprano in the two songs, given a less forward balance than usual for a soloist.

Symphonies Nos. 7–8.

*** DG 471 490-2. BPO, Abbado

Abbado's coupling of Nos. 7 and 8, taken from his complete Berlin cycle, recorded live, brings performances at generally brisk speeds that combine robust power and refinement. The result is more impressive even than his highly praised earlier coupling with the VPO (DG 423 364-2). Dynamic contrasts are heightened, and the description 'Little One' of No. 8 is again in no way apt, when the outer movements are so dramatic and the middle two winningly direct, avoiding mere charm while maintaining refinement. Only in the hectic tempo for the finale is there a reservation, when the recording, well-balanced in the Philharmonie, obscures the rapid semiquaver articulation. But this remains an outstanding disc.

Symphony No. 9 in D min. (Choral), Op. 125.

*** DG 471 491-2. Mattila, Urmana, Moser, Quasthoff, Swedish R. Ch., Ericson Ch., BPO, Abbado.

(BB) *(*) RCA 74321 68005-2. Wiens, Hartwig, Lewis, Hermann, Hamburg State Op. Ch., NDR SO, Wand.

Already in his live recording of the *Ninth* for Sony (SK 62634), made in 1996, Abbado indicated that his approach to Beethoven was changing, influenced by a study of period practice. Here in his 2000 version, recorded as part of his complete cycle for DG, he takes the process a degree further, even faster and more incisive in the first movement, sharper and cleaner in the Scherzo, and even more flowing in the slow movement as well as deeply dedicated. Though in the finale the new account does not quite find the degree of relaxed joy of the 1996 version, the extra incisiveness and fine solo and choral singing, with big dynamic contrasts, makes for a very exciting conclusion to a performance which overall is among the very finest available, and can be recommended alongside the bargain versions by Zinman (Arte Nova 74321 65411-2) and Mackerras (CD-CFP 6071).

Originally issued by EMI, Günter Wand's 1986 version is a rugged interpretation, thrusting and not always very refined. The very opening brings no mystery whatever, with the orchestra recorded close and made thicker through bass-heaviness. However, the scherzo is wild in its jollity and the drum-and-fife episode of the finale is free and easy, adding to an almost operatic feeling. The ruggedness extends to the slow movement, with the violins of the North German Radio Orchestra not always ideally sweet. At times ensemble is rough, and soloists and chorus are not ideally well drilled. Even at budget price this is far from a top choice, but Wand's admirers should not be too disappointed.

CHAMBER MUSIC

Cello Sonatas Nos. 1–2, Op. 5/1–2; (i) 3, Op. 69; 4–5, Op. 102/1–2.

(BB) (***) Naxos mono 8.1101949/50. Casals, Horszowski; (i) Schulhof (with *Minuet in G*) – BRAHMS: *Cello Sonata No. 2.* (***)

Cello Sonatas Nos. 1–2, Op. 5/1–2; Horn Sonata, Op. 15 (arr. cello); 7 Variations on 'Bei Mannern'.

(BB) *** Naxos 8.555785. Kliegel, Tichman.

Cello Sonatas Nos. 1–5; 7 Variations on 'Bei Mannern'; 12 Variations on 'Ein Mädchen' (both from Mozart's Die Zauberflöte).

(M) **(*) Sony SM2K 89870 (2). Ma, Ax.

Casals recorded the *A major Sonata, Op. 69*, with Otto Schulhof in 1930, the *Minuet in G* occupying the last side. He subsequently recorded the *C major, Op. 102, No. 1* with Mieczyslaw Horszowski and completed the set in Paris not long before the outbreak of war. Their magisterial set of the Brahms comes from 1936 and was long the yardstick by which newcomers were judged – including Casals' subsequent post-war versions.

With the Sony set from Yo-Yo Ma and Emanuel Ax there are balance problems in the first two (Op. 5) sonatas, with the piano often masking the refined lines drawn by Ma. In the remaining sonatas, Opp. 69 and 102, the balance is much better judged and throughout the sound quality is well focused and truthful. Emanuel Ax often produces a big, wide-ranging tone which must have posed problems when related to the more introvert style of the cellist. Ma plays with great sensitivity and imagination, even if there are times when one might think his *pianissimo* a bit overdone. The two sets of Mozartean variations have been added for the reissue, but not the companion Handel set.

The cellist Maria Kliegel made a number of impressive concerto recordings for Naxos not long after the label was established. Her return in this first of two Beethoven discs is specially welcome, when (as before) her playing instantly conveys a natural gravity and magnetism. So the long, slow introductions to each of Beethoven's *Op. 5 Sonatas* establish the Beethovenian flavour of the works, early but already strong and characterful. With subtle tonal shading the dedication of the slow sections is sharply contrasted with the exuberance of the Allegros, with the American pianist, Nina Tichman, an excellent partner, clear and incisive, springing rhythms infectiously. The variations on the theme from *Die Zauberflöte* are regularly included in sets of the Beethoven cello sonatas, but it is rare to have the *Horn Sonata* given in its cello adaptation. Though not all the horn writing fits the cello well – as at the very start – Kliegel and Tichman give a fresh, compelling performance, like the rest

very well-recorded. No doubt the other *Cello Sonatas* will follow.

(i) Cello Sonatas Nos. 3 in A, Op. 69; 5 in D, Op. 102/2; (ii) Piano Trios Nos. 4 in D (Ghost), Op. 70/1; 5 in E flat, Op. 70/2; in E flat, WoO 18; 10 Variations on 'Ich bin der Schneider Kakadu', Op. 121a.

(B) *** EMI (ADD) CZS5 74382-2 (2). Du Pré; with (i) Kovacevich; (ii) Barenboim, Zukerman.

It is remarkable that EMI have not thought to couple these two discs together before. Recorded betwen 1965 and 1970 they have the qualities of spontaneity and inspiration that have made all Du Pré's subsequent recordings so memorable. Comparing the *Cello Sonatas* with rival versions one cannot help but notice the extra expressive urgency which marks these interpretations, making them intensely vivid. The very opening of the *D major Sonata* underlines an unbuttonned quality in Beethoven's writing and when, after the hushed intensity of the slow introduction of Op. 69, the music launches into the allegro, both artists soar away fearlessly.

More remarkable still is the range of expressiveness in the slow movement of Op. 102/2. Du Pré's tone moves from full-blooded fortissimo to the mere whisper of a half-tone, and with Beethoven providing the indication Adagio con molto sentimento it is completely fitting that Du Pré and Bishop (Kovacevich) allow the fullest range of rubato, finally making almost any recorded rival sound comparatively superficial. There may be one or two detailed technical faults, but rarely have artists so young reached such depths of emotion in Beethoven on record.

Similarly in the *Trios*, the *Ghost* brings from all three artists playing of such hushed intensity that the result feels like a live performance. Some may find the playing a little self-indulgent, but the feeling for light and shade is remarkable, and anyone who responds to the emotional content of these great works will find their presentation here an enthralling experience. The Abbey Road sound balance is exemplary and the CD transfers most natural and vivid.

Piano Trios Nos. 3, Op. 1/3; 10 (14 Variations in E flat), Op. 44; 11 (Variations on 'Ich bin der Schneider Kakadu'), Op. 121a.

*** MDG 303 1052-2. Trio Parnassus.

Piano Trios Nos. 5 (Ghost); 6, Op. 70/1–2.

*** MDG 303 1053-2. Trio Parnassus.

We commented favourably in our main edition on the Trio Parnassus's disc of the *E flat* and *G major Trios* of Op. 1 for Musikproduktion Dabringhaus und Grimm. The remaining trios, plus the *Kakadu* and *Op. 44* variations, are hardly less satisfying. Indeed, now that the splendid Vienna Piano Trio on Nimbus is no longer in circulation they can be thought of as the best of the recent versions of these pieces. The playing is unfailingly musical, and the recordings are fresh and vivid.

Piano Trio No. 7 (Archduke); 10 (Variations on an Original Theme); 11 (Variations on 'Ich bin der Schneider Kakadu').

(BB) **(*) Virgin x 2 VBD5 62007-2 (2). Castle Trio – SCHUBERT: *Piano Trio No. 2; Sonatensatz.* ***

Those looking for a period-instrument performance of the *Archduke Trio* could well be satisfied with the American Castle Trio. They are generous with repeats, particularly in the Scherzo, playing throughout with vitality, bold accents and plenty of spirit. Indeed at times, in its energy, the music-making has a slightly unsettled quality, and the *Andante cantabile* could ideally be more mellow and relaxed. However, Lambert Ortis's fortepiano (a copy of an 1824 Graf) is not in the least shallow or clattery. Its bright timbre and the sparkling articulation especially suit the two sets of *Variations*, which are presented with great character and charm. The Schubert coupling is even finer.

Septet in E flat, Op. 20.

(B) **(*) DG (ADD) 469 766-2. BPO Octet (members) – MENDELSSOHN: *Octet.* **(*)

An amiable, refined performance (originally on Philips) from the excellent Berlin Philharmonic group, with plenty of life in the outer movements but rather a solemn view taken of the slow movement. The recording is first class – many will like its warmth and amplitude – and the new coupling is more generous than the previous issue of this performance.

String Quartets Nos.1 in F, Op. 18/1; 13 in C sharp min., Op. 131

(M) (***) Teldec mono 8573 83024-2. Calvet Qt.

String Quartets Nos. 5 in A, Op. 18/5; 8 in E min., Op. 59/2.

(M) (***) Teldec mono 3984 28413-2. Calvet Qt.

The Calvet Quartet was founded in 1919 but changed personnel in the late 1920s. They are nowadays scarcely represented at all on record but were held in high esteem in their day. They first recorded the Debussy *Quartet* and later, the slow movement of Florent Schmitt's *Piano Quintet* with the composer himself (most recently reissued on EMI now deleted 'Composers in Person' series), together with quartets by Schubert and Ravel. At the outbreak of war they disbanded, two of their number, Léon Pascal and Daniel Guilet (as Guilevitch became) forming their own ensembles. The latter gave us the pioneering set of the Arriaga quartets on Nixa and went on to lead the Beaux Arts Trio until 1969. Thanks to the advocacy of Nadia Boulanger the Calvet gave two complete Beethoven cycles in the late 1920s and went on to record a handful of them: the *F major, Op. 18, No. 1* and the *C sharp minor, Op. 131* and the *A major Op. 18, No. 5* in 1936 and the *E minor Rasumovsky* in 1938. Readers will soon forget the dryness of the acoustic: such is the compelling quality of the playing that sonic limitations are soon forgotten. The Calvet have great finesse, a wide dynamic range and variety of tone colour. A Gallic sensibility and lightness of touch

in matters of phrasing and accent are in strong evidence as is their lyricism and sweetness of tone. Tempi are wonderfully natural and unforced throughout, and the readings are thoughtful and thought-provoking, involved and involving. The *A major, Op. 18, No. 5*, is among the finest we have heard. The war inhibited the dissemination of these performances in Britain and America and for most modern listeners, these handsomely presented and expertly annotated readings will be a first encounter and something of a discovery. Outstanding music making.

String Quartets Nos. 2 in G; 5 in A, Op. 18/2 & 5.

*** MDG 307 0855-2. Leipzig Qt.

We were much impressed with the natural and unaffected musicianship of the Leipzig Quartet in the first two of their Op. 18 set (Nos. 1 & 4; MDG 307 0853-2), listed in our main volume. This successor is every bit as fine and gives much pleasure. These readings are full of character, and their apt tempi and total dedication to the score are difficult to fault. They can be recommended alongside the very best and are accorded first-class sound as natural and well balanced as the playing.

String Quartets Nos. 7–9 (Rasumovsky), Op. 59/1–3; 10 in E flat (Harp), Op. 74.

*** Decca 470 847-2 (2). Takács Qt.

The Takács offer a highly auspicious and successful start to what will be a complete cycle. They omit the *F minor, Op. 95* and so are able to accommodate the *Rasumovskys* and *Harp* on two CDs instead of the usual three. These are sober and perceptive readings, which make one think anew about this great music. The slow movement of the *E minor, Op. 59, No. 2*, taken more slowly than usual, is searching, and generally they find the right tempi to enable the music to speak effortlessly. Technically impeccable playing, well thought through and scrupulously attentive to detail (with all repeats made), this is a set to rank alongside the very best and the recording is of Decca's finest quality.

String Quartets Nos. 9 in C (Razumovsky), Op. 59/3; 10 in E flat (The Harp), Op. 74.

*** Harmonia Mundi HMC 905252 Turner Qt.
** Praga PR 256014. Vlach Qt.

The Turner Quartet all come from Philippe Herreweghe's Orchestre des Champs Elysées and have made quite a name for themselves in recent years. These are fine, dedicated performances with well-judged tempi and articulate and vital rhythms. They do not rush things in the finale of Op. 59, No. 3 and find the right tempo for the *Presto* movement of Op. 74, which is so often rushed off its feet. The vibrato-less opening of Op. 74 for all its splendidly transparent textures may prompt some listeners to long for the warmer, more full blooded sonority of modern instruments. But both readings are well thought-out, and distinguished by accomplished and refined musicianship.

These Praga performances derive from a complete cycle the Vlach Quartet recorded live in the 1960s for Prague Radio. They have something of the concentration that distinguishes the live performance and naturally are less polished than they would have been had they been made in the recording studio. The sound is a little wanting in bloom, and there is a certain wiriness above the stave. Both are thoroughly musical performances without being among the primary recommendations.

String Quartets Nos. 12–16; Grosse Fuge, Op. 133.

(B) **(*) Sony SB3K 89897. Juilliard Qt.

Sony does not give the date of these Juilliard recordings anywhere in the booklet nor on the discs themselves, merely noting both copyright and performance as 2002. It does state that the set consists of previously released material, and presumably this is from the 1980s, since Earl Carlyss is listed as the second violin (nowadays it is Joel Smirnoff). In any event, the performances are far from negligible and the set is economical: Op. 127 and Op. 131 occupy the first disc, Op. 132 and Op. 135 the last, and Op. 130 and the *Grosse Fuge* the remaining CD. Vital, intelligent readings, competitively priced and decently enough recorded.

String Quartets Nos. 12, Op. 127; 15, Op. 132.

*** MDG 307 0854-2. Leipzig Qt.

We can only echo our welcome to the Leipzig accounts of Op. 18, Nos. 1 and 4 in our main Guide. They are a first-class ensemble, totally free from expressive exaggeration and surface gloss. Their readings are impeccable artistically and technically immaculate, and MDG gives them first-class sound. Musical through and through and strongly recommended.

String Quartet No. 13, Op. 130; Grosse Fuge, Op. 133.

*** ASV CDDCA 1117. Lindsay Qt.

It is almost two decades since the Lindsays gave us their impressive Beethoven cycle on ASV. Here they repeat the *Cavatina*, each time subtly modified, so that the listener can proceed either with that and the *Grosse fuge*, (Tracks 1–6) or Beethoven's second thoughts (Tracks 1–4, 7 & 8) with the appropriate musical preparation, another performance of the *Cavatina*. The *Grosse Fuge* is given a shattering performance, crisper and more urgent than before, easily lyrical before the regular finale, an ultimate demonstration of the players' reponsiveness.

What is striking in these performances compared with the earlier ones is the extra intensity, the hushed tension conveyed as in a live performance, making this a far more searching experience. Both Op. 130 and the *Grosse fuge* have a freshness and keenness of response that bring home to you anew the greatness of this music. The Lindsays play not just as if they have lived a whole lifetime in the presence of this work but as if they are discovering it for the first time. The opening movement is perfectly paced – the *Adagio*

opening having all the space that it needs – and the allegro unfolding at the *tempo giusto*. Indeed this is a performance that soon has you forgetting the players and concentrating on the score. Late Beethoven is beautified at its peril which is why the directness of utterance the Lindsays have cultivated is so convincing. They may not have the brilliance and virtuosity of the Alban Berg (EMI) or the Emerson, but they speak with a naturalness and understanding that makes for a far more satisfying musical experience. Along with the Quartetto Italiano, the Talich and, of course, the Végh, the Lindsays occupy the commanding heights and are splendidly recorded.

Violin Sonatas Nos. 1–10 (complete); 'A Life with Beethoven' (documentary by Reiner Moritz).

**(*) DG DVD 073 014-2 (2). Mutter, Orkis.

Violin Sonatas Nos. 5 in F, Op. 24 (Spring); 9 in A, Op. 49 (Kreutzer). 'A Life with Beethoven' (documentary by Reiner Moritz).

** DG **DVD** 073 004-9 (2). Mutter, Orkis.

This hour-long documentary follows Anne-Sophie Mutter and Lambert Orkis during their year preparing and touring the Beethoven sonata cycle. The performances were recorded at the Théâtre des Champs Elysées in 1999. To follow them over an extended period yields useful insights, though the playing, particularly that of the distinguished violinist, will strike some as being at times just a bit self-regarding: there are some intrusive expressive exaggerations at times during these always highly accomplished and intelligent performances. However, the complete set yields considerable rewards and is probably a better investment than the single disc. Good straightforward camerawork and excellent sound. Subtitles for the English-language documentary are also available in German and French.

Violin Sonatas Nos. (i) 1 in D, Op. 12/1; (ii) 7 in C min., Op. 30/2; (iii) 8 in G, Op. 30/3.

*** Concert Recordings WFYI Indianapolis IVCI 1998. (i) Baak, Epperson; (ii) Roussev, Eguchi; (iii) Prunaru, De Silva. Website: www.violin.org

These excellent performances were recorded live by three prize-winners at the 1998 International Violin Competition of Indianapolis, for one of the rules of the semi-final is that each of the soloists shall choose and play a Beethoven violin sonata. All three performances here are polished and full of vitality, fully conveying the urgency of live music-making and in each case demonstrating a true partnership between the two artists. The performance of the *C minor Sonata* is especially fine, but the *G major* is hardly less vivid and gripping. The earlier *D major Sonata* is a little plainer, but has strong classical feeling. A most enjoyable disc, realistically recorded. For a complete set of the *Violin Sonatas* first chioce lies with Kremer and Argerich (DG 447 058-2).

Violin Sonatas Nos. 3 in E flat, Op. 12/3; No. 5 in F (Spring), Op. 24; No. 9 in A (Kreutzer), Op. 47.

(BB) (***) Naxos mono 8.110954. Busch, Serkin.

Op. 12, No. 3 and the *Spring Sonata* come from the early 1930s, and the *Kreutzer* was recorded in New York in 1941. In their day they were – understandably perhaps – rather overshadowed by the celebrated Kreisler records with Franz Rupp as pianist for the HMV Beethoven Sonata Society. However, these transfers leave no doubt as to the fine musicianship and aristocratic finesse of this playing. Adolf Busch was a Beethovenian of rare quality, and Serkin was at his most responsive and sensitive at this period.

PIANO MUSIC

Piano Sonata No. 3 in C major, Op. 2/3.

** Appian Recordings APR 5632. Arrau – BRAHMS: *Piano Sonata No. 3.* (*)

After he recorded his Beethoven cycle for Philips in 1964–5, Arrau dropped the *C major Sonata, Op. 2, No. 3,* from his active repertory, taking it up again only at the time of his Prague recital in 1976. In his hands it has a weight and depth almost worthy of middle-period or even later Beethoven. The slow movement has more depth than his earlier studio account, and the performance holds the listener throughout. Although Solomon played the mercurial finale with greater lightness, this is a performance that is worth hearing. The sound is very acceptable, though it is a bit forward and shallow, but perfectly natural, even if the Czech Radio engineers do not do full justice to the unusually rounded, perfectly focused and rich sonority.

Piano Sonatas Nos. 8 (Pathétique); 14 (Moonlight); 15 (Pastoral); 17 (Tempest); 21 (Waldstein); 23 (Appassionata); 26 (Les Adieux).

(BB) **(*) Decca Eloquence (ADD) 467 487-2 (2). Backhaus.

In the early days of LP Backhaus was Decca's star Beethoven pianist, and he recorded all the piano concertos and sonatas for this label in the Indian summer of a long and distinguished career. Not all ears take readily to his self-consciously authoritative and often brusque manner, yet he found spontaneity in the recording studio, and also an unmistakable Beethovenian spirit. The finest performances here are of the *Waldstein* and *Appassionata* (fully three-star). His interpretations had changed little if at all over the years, but had never before been caught on disc so realistically, and this coupling was one of the key Beethoven LPs in the early stereo era. The other works also spring to life here, but his somewhat unyielding manner is less suited to the opening of the *Pastoral Sonata*, although he is at his best in the finale. The surprise is the *Moonlight Sonata*, much more resilient than we had remembered. The recordings (dating from between 1959 and 1964) provide an appropriately bold, full-blooded piano image.

Piano Sonatas Nos. 8 (Pathétique); 14 (Moonlight); 23 (Appassionata).

(BB) ** CfP (ADD) 575 5612. Chorzempa.

Daniel Chorzempa is best known as an occupant of the organ loft, but here he shows himself equally impressive as a piano virtuoso. His 1971 CfP coupling of Beethoven's three most popular sonatas remains competitive, if lacking a little in sparkle, the interpretations of a very serious young man who knows what he is doing. The simplicity and clarity of his style is well caught in a recording that is notable for its warm sonority.

Piano Sonatas Nos. 13–14 (Moonlight), Op. 27/1–2; 30 in E, Op. 109.

* DG 453 457-2. Pires.

Maria João Pires has been much (and rightly) admired in the Mozart concertos and sonatas and in the Schubert *Moments musicaux* and *A minor Sonata,* D.784 she recorded for DG. Her Beethoven recital, on the other hand, is a disappointment: she is for the most part curiously unengaged, and whether in the familiar *Moonlight* or in Op. 109 remains uninvolved and uninvolving. The engineers place her rather close to the microphone.

Piano Sonatas Nos. 23 in F (Appassionata), Op. 57; 32 in C min.

(M) (*) Orfeo mono C530 001B. Wilhelm Backhaus (with BACH: *Prelude and Fugue*, MOZART: *Sonata in G, KV 283).*

This is a very unappealing disc and shows Backhaus in a most unfavourable light.

Piano Sonatas Nos. 30–32.

(B) **(*) Hyp. Helios CDH 55083. Kinderman.

William Kinderman is the author of a study of *Beethoven's Diabelli Variations* (Oxford, 1987) and an accomplished pianist. He made a fine recording of the *Diabelli Variations,* and the present 1998 recording of Beethoven's last three sonatas is far from negligible. There are deeper and more searching performances to be had, but Kinderman brings scholarly insights to bear in these masterpieces. Unfortunately, the sound is by no means as distinguished as on his *Diabelli* disc.

VOCAL MUSIC

Missa solemnis in D, Op. 123.

(BB) *** Arte Nova 74321 87174-2. Orgonasova, Larsson, Trost, Selig, Swiss C Ch., Zurich Tonhalle O, Zinman
(B) **(*) Teldec Ultima 0630 18945-2 (2). Mei, Lipovšek, Rolfe-Johnson, Holl, Arnold Schoenberg Ch., COE, Harnoncourt.
(M) **(*) BBC BBCL 4093-2 (2). Zylis-Gara, Hoffgen, Tear, Arie, New Philh. Ch. & O, Giulini – SCHUBERT: *Symphony No. 4.* ***

Following up his superb cycle of the Beethoven symphonies, using modern instruments while taking note of period practice, David Zinman with the Tonhalle Orchestra offers an equally exhilarating account of the *Missa Solemnis* on the Arte Nova label at super-bargain price. Again, fast speeds are the rule in a performance which at every point highlights the drama of the liturgy, making the words fresh and clear, helped by bright, immediate singing from the Swiss Chamber Choir, by the sound of it not a small body. Zinman brings out the joy of *Et resurrexit* as well as of the final *Dona nobis pacem*, made the more intense after Beethoven's dramatic military intrusion has been swept away. Dedication is still part of the equation in this exceptional performance, well-recorded.

Like Levine's performance of a year earlier, Harnoncourt's was recorded live at the Salzburg Festival, but it represents the new, post-Karajan era at that grandest of music festivals. Like Harnoncourt's Beethoven symphony cycle, this performance conveys the dramatic tensions of a live occasion, with finely matched forces performing with freshness and clarity. The rather distanced sound makes the results marginally less involving than either the Levine version (DG 435 770-2) or the sparer but inspired Gardiner account (DG 429 779-2), which remain at the top of the list, yet at Ultima price Harnoncourt remains fully competitive.

The BBC radio recording of Giulini in the *Missa Solemnis*, made in St Paul's Cathedral in 1968 as part of the City of London Festival, brings a characteristically expansive performance which, in the absence of Giulini's studio recording for EMI from the catalogue, is well worth investigating. Though the sound is far more variable than in the studio performance, with some odd balances, the formidable echo is largely tamed, and the concentration is keener. For coupling on the second CD comes a biting account of Schubert's *Tragic Symphony*, a reading that certainly justifies that nickname.

Fidelio (complete).

(**) Arthaus **DVD** 100074. Benacková, Protschká, MacLaughlin, Archer, Lloyd, Pederson, ROHCG Ch. & O, Dohnányi. (Director: Adolf Dresden, V/D: Derek Bailey.)

Very well-cast with Christoph von Dohnányi a dedicated interpreter, the Arthaus DVD of *Fidelio* presents Adolf Dresden's production at Covent Garden in 1991, updated to late Victorian times. The first scene opens in a squalid flat, more appropriate for Berg's *Wozzeck*, with Rocco and Jaquino looking like uniformed officials from some continental railway-company. Leonore, the powerful Gabriela Benacková, makes little pretense of looking like a man with her long hair in a snood hanging down her back. The squalor persists, with Act II set in the deepest dungeon, reached down a long vertical ladder. None of this helps the drama much, except that Pizarro, presented as an army officer in cocked hat and epaulettes, emerges as a terrifying villain, obsessed with power, determined to have his revenge for earlier slights. The singer is Monte Pederson – tall, handsome and menacing, singing with fine focus and power, an unforgettable portrayal. Benacková sings magnificently too, beautifully matched by Marie McLaughlin as Marzelline. There is no weakness in the rest of the cast either, with

Josef Protshcká as Florestan singing powerfully and without strain, so that the duet with Leonore, *O namenlose Freude*, is clearer, more precise and less squally than usual. Sadly, the sound of the voices is spoilt by a glassy edginess, and the dry Covent Garden acoustic has been treated to some extra reverberation.

BELLINI, Vincenzo (1801–35)

Norma (opera; complete).

*** Arthaus **DVD** 100 180. Sutherland, Elkins, Stevens, Grant, Opera Australia Ch., Sydney Elizabethan O, Bonynge. (V/D: Sandro Sequi.)

(M) *** Decca (ADD) 470 413-2 (3). Sutherland, Horne, Alexander, Cross, Minton, Ward, LSO Ch. & O, Bonynge.

Recorded live at the Sydney Opera House in 1978 (not 1991 as the box seems to imply), this Australian Opera production by Sandro Sequi is chiefly valuable for presenting Dame Joan Sutherland in one of her most important roles when she was still at the peak of her powers. Her two audio recordings date from early and late in her career, where this provides an important bridge, with *Casta diva* finding Dame Joan in glorious voice, at once powerful, creamily beautiful and wonderfully secure.

With sets by Fiorella Mariani it is a traditional production, springing no surprises, encouraging the diva to relax in the role, never more so than in her big duet with Adalgisa, *Mira o Norma*, ending in a dazzling account of the cabaletta, where Margeta Elkins equally sparkles, and Richard Bonynge draws light, crisply sprung playing from the orchestra.

Less satisfying is the singing of Ronald Stevens as Pollione, powerful and heroic, but rather too coarse for Bellinian cantilena. Clifford Grant by contrast could hardly be more cleanly focused as Oroveso. The sound is a little dry, not as full-bodied as in the finest fully digital recordings, but the sharpness of attack heightens the dramatic thrust of Bonynge's conducting.

Sutherland's mid-sixties set has now been re-issued at mid-price as part of Decca's 'Compact Opera Collection'. However, there is no printed libretto, only a CD Rom facility which carries full text and translation via a computer. The full-priced set remains available (425 488-2).

BENATZKY, Ralph (1884–1957)

L'Auberge du cheval blanc (operetta): complete.

(B) ** EMI (ADD) CZS5 74070-2 (2). Bourvil, Forli, Dens, Ervil, Germain, René Duclos Ch., Paris Conservatoire O, Nuvolone.

The Czech composer Ralph Benatzky had quite a distinguished career in the field of light music and operetta during the first half of the twentieth century and is chiefly remembered for his Johann Strauss pastiche *Casanova* (1928) and, especially, for *The White Horse Inn* (1930). The present operetta enjoyed some success in the 1930s, both in Paris and on Broadway.

Its mixture of the styles of operetta and early musical is attractive: there are waltzes alongside the dance rhythms of the day. The end of Act I, with its faint jazz beat over which a wordless chorus and soprano float, is most winning. There are several such touches throughout this score, which begins with a yodelling song, a theme running through the score. Other highlights include a fully fledged *Tyrolienne* in Act II, along with a drunken version, complete with hiccoughs, in the same act. There is also a lively tango duet and some melting waltzes, some with off-stage choruses, which are quite haunting. Alas, there are absolutely no texts – or even notes in English – so only those fluent in French will have any idea what's going on. The performance is quite a good one, with voices suited to this style of music and with lively characterizations. The 1962 recording is quite vivid, although some voices are very closely miked. Fans of operetta and music theatre should find this worth exploring as a rarity, despite the pitiful packaging.

BENDA, František (1709–86)

Violin Concertos: in D; D min.

(BB) *** Naxos 8.553902. Suk or Pfister, Suk CO, Christian Benda – JAN JIRI BENDA: *Concerto in G.* ***

Of these two concertos, the *D minor* is certainly the finer, for it has a memorably gentle slow movement and a buoyantly lively finale, which Christian Benda and his Chamber Orchestra relish for its sparkling vitality. Both soloists play most elegantly and if these works are not highly individual they are both enjoyable when so sympatheically presented. The recording too cannot be faulted.

BENDA, Jan Jiři (1713–52)

Violin Concerto in G.

(BB) *** Naxos 8.553902. Suk, Suk CO, Christian Benda – FRANTISEK BENDA: *Concertos in D; D min.* ***

Jan Jiři Benda was a member of a celebrated Bohemian family of musicians, and his *G major Concerto* sparkles with vitality in the outer movements (with a faint flavour of Bach) and has a rather fine solo cantilena as its centrepiece. Josef Suk is highly sympathetic and dazzles the ear in the sharply pointed rhythms of the finale. Excellent, polished accompaniments and full natural recording. This disc is well worth its modest cost.

BENJAMIN, Arthur (1893–1960)

Romantic Fantasy for Violin, Viola & Orchestra.

(BB) *** Arte Nova 74321 89826-2. Schmid, Raiskin, Berlin SO, Shambadal – BRITTEN; BRUCH *Double Concertos.* ***

Arthur Benjamin's *Romantic Fantasy* for violin, viola and orchestra is best-known in the searingly brilliant recording made by Jascha Heifetz and William Primrose, but a modern version as fine as this, at once warmly expressive and polished, is very welcome, particularly with an ideal coupling in the Britten and Bruch *Double Concertos* for the same combination. First-rate orchestral playing and well-balanced recording.

BENNETT, Richard Rodney (born 1936)

(i) Piano Concerto No. 1; (ii) (Saxophone) Concerto for Stan Getz; (iii) Dream Sequence. Film music from: (iv) Four Weddings and a Funeral; Murder on the Orient Express: Waltz.

(M) *** Decca (ADD/DDD) 470 371-2. (i) Kovacevich, BBC SO, Gibson; (ii) Harle, BBC Concert O, Wordsworth; (iii) Lloyd Webber, Composer; (iv) Hollywood Bowl O, Mauceri.

Richard Rodney Bennett wrote his *Piano Concerto*, a work involving complex, endlessly fluttering figuration, especially with Stephen Bishop (Kovacevich) in mind. It is one of his most thoughtful works, music that replays the detailed study possible on CD, particularly in a performance as dedicated as this, and the 1971 (Philips) sound emerges especially vivid in this transfer. The *Concerto for Stan Getz* (1990) is an unashamedly cross-over piece, an enjoyable mixture of jazz and film music styles, melodic and colourful, offering the soloist plenty of opportunity to explore the instrument's colour. The famous *Waltz* from *Murder on the Orient Express* receives a most winning performance here (complete with a whoosh of steam to get it going!) The haunting piece from *Four Weddings and a Funeral* and the gentle *Dream Sequence* provide contrast. This is an excellent CD, and the sound is bright and vivid.

BERG, Alban (1885–1935)

Violin Concerto.

(BB) *** Warner Apex 0927 40812-2. Zehetmair, Philh. O, Holliger – HARTMANN: *Concerto funèbre*; JANACEK: *Concerto.* ***

On this inexpensive Apex disc Zehetmair plays with great sensitivity and a natural eloquence, and many will prefer this to Mutter on DG. That has tremendous brilliance and panache but Zehetmair's less sensational reading brings one closer to the heart of this poignant music. Moreover, apart from the price advantage, he offers more interesting couplings in the form of the Hartman *Concerto funèbre* and the fragmentary Janáček *Concerto* of 1927–8. The recording, made at The Maltings in Snape, is of exemplary clarity and has great presence, making this triptych a very real bargain.

(i) *Violin Concerto*; (ii) *Lyric Suite*: excerpts; (i) 3 *Orchestral Pieces, Op. 6*; (iii) *Piano Sonata, Op. 1*; (iv) *Lulu: Suite*; (ii; v) 5 *Orchestral Songs on Picture-Postcard Texts*; (iv) *Wozzeck*: 3 excerpts.

(BB) **(*) Ph. Duo (ADD/DDD) 470 531-2 (2). (i) Kremer, Bav. RSO, Davis; (ii) Berlin SO, Ashkenazy; (iii) Brendel; (iv) Pilarczyk, LSO, Dorati; (v) Balleys.

It is a sign of the times when a bargain Duo entitled '*The Essential Alban Berg*' appears, and it certainly provides an ideal way to explore this composer inexpensively, even if not all the performance are quite the very best. Kremer's 1984 recording of the *Violin Concerto* is a little problematic, for all its emotional intensity and accomplishment. There is an element of narcissism here. Kremer often stresses the music's self-pity: the solo posturing at bars 43–57 of the second movement is unappealing and so too is the withdrawn, nasal tone of the chorale.

Besides providing an admirable accompaniment for the *Concerto*, the Bavarian Radio Orchestra gives a fine account of themselves in the *Op. 6 Pieces*, and Sir Colin Davis makes much of their refined textures and powerful atmosphere – this really is a compelling performance. The Philips sound has remarkable clarity and definition, completely truthful, while in the *Concerto* the balance between the violin and orchestra is perfectly judged.

Ashkenazy's account of the three pieces Berg chose from his *Lyric Suite* to arrange for string orchestra is exceptionally well played and recorded, while Brendel's 1982 recording of the highly chromatic *Piano Sonata* is a strong reading with good sound for a live recording (and, mercifully, a very silent audience). Dorati's exceptionally vivid and analytical 1961 recordings of the *Lulu* and *Wozzeck* excerpts (originally Mercury) are well worth having, even if Helga Pilarczyk's sometimes abrasive, under-the-note singing in the vocal passages tends to mar one's enjoyment slightly. The *Five Orchestral Songs on Picture Postcard Music* with texts by Peter Altenberg were written in 1912 and are full of imagination and haunting colouristic affects, a huge orchestra achieving much delicate and subtle detail – twelve-tone music at its most approachable.

Wozzeck (complete).

(BB) *** Naxos 8.660076-2. Falkman, Dalayman, Qvale, Wahlund, Stregard, Stockholm Royal Op. Ch. & O, Segerstam.

Recorded live at the Royal Opera in Stockholm with three performances edited together, the Naxos issue offers one of the most powerful, intense accounts of this atonal opera ever put on disc. Segerstam proves a strong, thrusting interpreter, tautly holding the drama together, with the impact heightened by the vividness of the recording; powerful, immediate and atmospheric, even if the strings are set behind the woodwind, one of the almost inevitable discrepancies in any live recording. There are stage noises too, but the magnetism of the performance and the consist-

ency of the singing with no weak member of the cast quickly make you forget any slight flaws. Though the Sprechstimme ('sing-speech'), is sometimes free – again not surprisingly – the great merit of all the singers is their musicality, with the Captain and the Doctor less caricatured than usual, and with a firm, central account of the title-role from Carl Johan Falkman. Katarina Dalayman is also superb as Marie, singing with character as well as beauty. A detailed synopsis is provided in the booklet and a complete libretto in German but no translation. An excellent issue which at Naxos price should tempt collectors to experiment with a challenging work that in a performance like this is deeply moving. Dohnányi with Waechter and Silja (on Decca 417 348-2) remains the top premium-priced choice, but this Naxos version is very competitive.

BERKELEY, Lennox (1903–89)

Guitar Concerto.

*** Chan. 9963. Ogden, Northern Sinf., Hickox – ARNOLD: *Guitar Concerto*; WALTON: 5 *Bagatelles*. ***

The Berkeley *Concerto*, one of his last works, begins atmospherically with a duet for two unaccompanied horns, relaxed in its mood, gaining in this performance under Richard Hickox from relatively urgent speeds. It leads via a mysterious slow movement to a finale which starts with a sly quotation from Rodrigo's *Concierto de Aranjuez*. Craig Ogden gives a commanding performance.

Symphony No. 1; Serenade for Strings.

*** Chan. 9981. BBC Nat. O of Wales, Hickox – M. BERKELEY: *Horn Concerto; Coronach*. ***

This first instalment of the Chandos Berkeley series, celebrating father Lennox and son Michael, brings two of Berkeley senior's strongest, most approachable works, both dating from early in his career, when the influence of his teacher, Nadia Boulanger, and of French neo-classicism was at its strongest.

The *First Symphony* is one of Lennox Berkeley's most luminous and captivating scores, Gallic in feeling and with a strong sense of momentum and purpose. Completed in 1940, it hardly reflects the mood of the time. Now that the composer's own recording on a Lyrita LP is no longer available, this superbly shaped account is the only recording – and very good it is too, both well shaped and finely paced. The four movements, lasting half an hour, are set in a conventional symphonic pattern, in which airy neo-classical procedures are mixed with organic growth in an echo of Sibelius. It is a fresh and beautifully written work, prompting a strong, committed performance from the BBC National Orchestra of Wales under Richard Hickox, which has been superbly recorded. This symphony deserves to become popular, for its ideas resonate in the mind long afterwards.

The *Serenade for Strings* always sounds fresh no matter how often you hear it. In four compact movements, it is a delightful piece, carefree until the final

Lento, where, reflectively, Berkeley touches deeper emotions. In Hickox's hands it comes off splendidly. The BBC National Orchestra of Wales again play with zest and sensitivity, and the recording is extremely vivid and present. Recommended with enthusiasm.

BERKELEY, Michael (born 1948)

(i) *Horn Concerto* (for horn and string orchestra); *Coronach* (for strings).

*** Chan. 9981. BBC Nat. O of Wales, Hickox; with (i) Pyatt – L. BERKELEY: *Symphony No.1; Serenade*. ***

Michael is the eldest of Lennox Berkeley's three sons, and apart from his creative activity is a well-known voice on BBC Radio 3, where he worked for many years as an announcer, and on BBC TV. He studied composition with his father and with Richard Rodney Bennett. (He is also active as an administrator: he is artistic director of the Cheltenham Festival.)

Unlike the works of his father on this CD, the two by Michael are among the darkest and most intense that he has written, giving a sharpness otherwise missing on the disc. *Coronach* is a lament for string orchestra, which explores the 'complex emotions of grief; the rage and anger as well as the sadness'. It builds up powerfully in the manner of a funeral dirge, with a quotation from the Scottish ballad, 'The Bonny Earl of Moray'. The *Horn Concerto* in two movements is more powerful still. Written in 1984, it represents a new departure for the composer in its often gritty, uncompromising tone. Yet it makes an immediate emotional impact, with the naggingly energetic first movement giving way to a deeply thoughtful and spacious slow movement. David Pyatt is the superb soloist, magnetically bringing out the logic of each development, with Hickox and the orchestra equally powerful in support. Full, brilliant sound.

BERLIOZ, Hector (1803–69)

Overtures: *Béatrice et Bénédict; Le Carnaval romain, Op. 9; Le Corsaire, Op. 21; Rob Roy; Le Roi Lear, Op. 4.*

**(*) Chan. 8316. SNO, Gibson.

Rob Roy is the rarity of the late Sir Alexander Gibson's Berlioz collection. It adds an aptly Scottish tinge to the CD, even when the traditional melodies – *Scots Wha Hae* at the opening – are given distinctly Berliozian twists. It is if anything even wilder than the other overtures, and with its anticipations of *Harold in Italy* finds Gibson and his SNO at their most dashingly committed. *King Lear*, another rarity, also comes out most dramatically, and though *Béatrice et Bénédict* is not quite so polished, the playing is generally excellent. With first-rate recording, this is attractive enough, but the original dates from 1982, and this should have been reissued at mid-price.

Symphonie fantastique, Op. 14; Overtures: Béatrice et Bénédict; Le Carnaval romain; Le Corsaire.

(B) CfP (ADD) 575 5622. Hallé O, Loughran.

(i) *Symphonie fantastique, Op. 14*; (ii) *Roméo et Juliette, Op. 17*.

(M) ** Westminster (ADD) 471 242-2 (2). (i) Vienna St. Op. O, Leibowitz; (ii) Resnik, Turp, Ward, LSO Ch. & O, Monteux.

(i) *Symphonie fantastique, Op. 14*; (ii) *Roméo et Juliette, Op. 17* (excerpts).

(**) Testament mono SBT 1234 (i) French Nat. RO; (ii) Paris Opéra O, André Cluytens.

Symphonie fantastique, Op. 14; Roméo et Juliette: Scène d'amour.

**(*) Telarc CD 80578. Cincinnati SO, Järvi.

Paavo Järvi's impressive version of the *Symphonie fantastique*, generously coupled with the love scene from *Roméo et Juliette*, celebrated his arrival as the new music director of the Cincinnati Symphony Orchestra. With vivid Telarc recording, engineered by Jack Renner, the brilliance of Berlioz's orchestration is brought out in finely detailed sound with textures clarified. The interpretation is fresh and clean-cut, with relatively spacious speeds, yet next to the finest versions there is a lack of spontaneity and dramatic thrust, making it very much a studio account. First choice still remains with Colin Davis on Philips (464 692-2).

Leibowitz's *Symphonie fantastique* has no great claim to greatness in either performance or execution, and the 1958 recording, while basically full, suffers from a rather dry and claustrophobic acoustic. Monteux's 1962 *Roméo et Juliette* has a robust, idiomatic strength, which helps one to forgive some of the rough patches in the ensemble and recording, the former indicating a lack of rehearsal. We have come to expect high standards of refinement and discipline in this work (set by Munch and Colin Davis *et al*), although, of course, any Monteux performance is worth hearing. The CD is well packaged and includes texts and translations.

This Cluytens performance of the *Symphonie fantastique* is not the same as that included in the 'Great Conductors' compilation (see Concerts below) and derives from a mono recording made in the Salle de la Mutualité in 1955. It originally appeared on Columbia 33 CX1439 and was coolly received in *The Gramophone* magazine, when it was up against some pretty formidable competition. It is well shaped but not, perhaps, as spontaneous as the concert performance this partnership gave on their Japanese tour, which the EMI disc includes. Nor is *Roméo seul* and the *Scène d'amour* as well played as rival versions, though it has the merit of being straightforward, unaffected and felt.

James Loughran's Hallé account of the *Symphonie*, which dates from the mid-1970s is disappointing, heavy in places and rarely really exciting, although there are touches that reveal this conductor's character and freshness of approach. Of the three Overtures offered as makeweight, *Le Corsaire* is vivid enough, with a strong contribution from the trombones, but not really exilarating, and the finest performance here is *Béatrice et Bénédict*, where the lyrical writing shows Loughan and his players at their best. Throughout the recording is excellent, vivid, yet warm and refined. First choice for the *Symphonie fantastique* still rests with Sir Colin Davis's 1974 Concertgebouw recording (Philips 464 692-2).

(i) *Requiem Mass (Grande messe des morts)*; (ii) *Grande symphonie funèbre et triomphale*; (iii) Choral music: *Tantum ergo; Le Temple universel; Veni creator.*

(B) ** Decca (ADD/DDD) 467 479-2 (2). (i) Riegel, Cleveland Ch. & O, Maazel; (ii) Montreal Ch. & SO, Dutoit; (iii) Soloists, Heinrich Schütz Ch. & Chorale, Norrington.

Especially in comparison with Dutoit's exhilarating 1985 digital account of the *Symphonie funèbre*, Maazel's version of the *Requiem*, with the choir set at a distance, is relatively uninvolving. The recording offers clean, truthful 1978 Decca sound. The *Tuba mirum*, with its spectacular brass, is certainly physically impressive, and here the chorus is boldly focused, but overall Maazel's reading is comparatively unimaginative and no match for Previn's version in the same price range (EMI CZS5 69512-2).

The rare choral items add much to the value of this set, showing Berlioz in an unfamiliar and rewarding light, particularly when two of the three choral works have a piquant harmonium accompaniment. The *Tantum ergo* and *Veni creator* are late works, and both contrast the choir with solo voices, the latter almost like the slow movement of a vocal concerto grosso, while *Le Temple universal* is for double choir. It was inspired by the visit of a huge French Choir to London's Crystal Palace in 1860. At the close 4,000 French singers sang *God Save the Queen*, and the audience rose to its feet and responded with *La Marseillaise*. Berlioz intended that the two choirs should sing the same words in English and French, but Norrington manages with rather smaller forces and has both groups singing in French. The effect is undoubtedly stirring, for there is much of the spirit of the French national anthem, and the (originally Argo) recording from the late 1960s is first rate. This reissue has, alas, no texts or notes at all, but it is at bargain price.

(i) *Requiem Mass, Op. 5 (Grande messe des morts)*; (ii) *Roméo et Juliette* (orchestral music); (ii; iii) *La Mort de Cléopâtre*.*

(M) ** Sony (ADD) SM2K 89565 (2). (i) Burrows, French R. Ch., French Nat. RO & PO; (ii) NYPO; (iii) Tourel; all cond. Bernstein.

Berlioz's *Requiem Mass* is an elusive work to bring off on record, and Bernstein's 1975 version came close to conveying its full power. His style is moulded and consciously persuasive, with an ample acoustic making the chorus sound even bigger than expected, and the result is an aural picture that is both dramatic and atmospheric. In the *Rex tremendae* Bernstein's expansiveness is well within the scale of the music, and in the *Lacrimosa* his fast and urgent direction is irresistible in its wave-like rhythm. The remastered sound is good. The performance of the most popular orchestral movements from *Roméo et Juliette* is fully acceptable, although the 1959 sound is not quite so impressive. The same can be said for Jennie Tourel's 1961 *La Mort de Cléopâtre*, made late in her career when she was not in the freshest of voice. Her account seems rather literal, though the unatmospheric, dry sound doesn't help. Texts and translations are included.

(i) *Roméo et Juliette, Op. 17*; (ii) Overtures: *Béatrice et Bénédict; Le Corsaire; Les Francs-juges; Le Roi Lear; Waverley*.*

✪ (B) *** Ph. Duo (DDD/ADD) 470 543-2 (2). (i) Borodina, Moser, Miles, Bav. R. Ch., VPO; (ii) LSO; all cond. Davis.

Sir Colin Davis's first recording of *Roméo et Juliette* is now over 30 years old – although this is hard to believe. It long reigned supreme in the catalogue, but on this bargain Duo Philips have chosen to reissue the later 1993 recording, which is likely to do the same for another thirty! In this Vienna performance, Sir Colin's interpretive approach remains basically unchanged – yet, like vintage wine that has matured, it offers greater depth, colour and body. He has the advantage of fine soloists, and Olga Borodina has the full measure of the Berlioz style. Thomas Moser is no less ardent and idiomatic, and Alastair Miles is a more than acceptable Friar Laurence. Apart from its all-round artistic excellence, this scores over all-comers in sheer quality of sound, which reproduces the whole range of Berlioz's luminous orchestration in all its subtle colourings in remarkable detail and naturalness. The perspective is natural and the orchestral texture astonishing in its transparency. It is no surprise to discover that the sound-picture is the work of Volker Strauss. The five superbly played and recorded overtures (dating from 1965, except *Béatrice*, which dates from 1977) make this an exceptional bargain on the Philips Duo series, though sadly, no texts are included.

BERNSTEIN, Leonard (1918–90)

West Side Story: The Making of the Recording.

*** DG DVD 073 017-9. Te Kanawa, Carreras, Troyanos, Ollmann, Bernstein. (V/D: Chris Swann.)

With narration from Bernstein himself, this classic feature film about the making of the controversial opera-style recording of *West Side Story* gives a vivid portrait of the composer at work. His unique combination of toughness, warmth, shining charisma and overwhelming genius is vividly conveyed. There is no false modesty in his approach to a work which he had written over 30 years before but never previously conducted. For the first time he had studied it in depth, and was surprised and gratified that it is 'so funky'. He goes on to explain that although it had been tiring listening to play-backs, the experience of recording it 'made me feel very young. It sounds as though I wrote it yesterday'. It is good to see Bernstein's obvious joy as he starts to conduct Kiri Te Kanawa in *I Feel Pretty*, but his bursts of irritation when someone fails to carry out his instructions are just as telling. The contrasting characters of the four principals come over well, notably the feisty Tatiana Troyanos, and on DVD it is most helpful to have no fewer than twenty-eight chapter points, letting you find any passage quickly. But above all this film is important in giving so illuminating an insight into the character of a great musician and his work.

This is of course a supplement to the recording and does not include a complete video performance, only excerpts. The complete audio recording is available on DG 447 958-2, or together with *Candide* on 429 734-2.

BERWALD, Franz (1796–1868)

Symphonies Nos. 3 (Singulière); 4 in E flat; Elfenspiel.

*** Chan. 9921. Danish Nat. RSO, Dausgaard.

Only a month separates the two symphonies: the *Singulière* was written in March 1845, and the *Fourth in E flat* in April. Neither was performed in Berwald's lifetime, and the *Singulière* had to wait until 1905, 60 years after its composition, before it was heard. In their day the best all-round version of the two symphonies was by Sixten Ehrling and the LSO on Decca, and the fine DG set by Neeme Järvi and the Gothenburg Orchestra remains the most economical buy. But the sheer excellence of the Danish Orchestra's playing of these sparkling and original pieces is not in question nor is the quality of the sound. A minor point: the Chandos cover refers to the *E flat Symphony* as *Sinfonie naïve*, a title that Berwald specifically rejected by the time he gave the autograph score to Auber in Paris some years later. A strong recommendation, nevertheless. However, first choice for a complete set of the four symphonies rests with Sixten Ehrling on BIS 795/6.

BIBER, Heinrich (1644–1704)

Mystery (Rosenkranz) Violin Sonatas (complete).

☼ (BB) *** Virgin VBD5 62062-2 (2). Holloway, Moroney, Tragicomedia.

(B) **(*) Signum SIGCD 021 (2). Reiter, Concordia.

Biber's emergence as one of the great composers of the 17th century is more than ever borne out by his set of *Mystery* (or *Rosary*) *Sonatas* for violin and continuo, which is surely his instrumental masterpiece, and which tells the Christian story in instrumental terms. There are 15 Sonatas divided into three groups: *The Five Joyful Mysteries* (The Annunciation; Visit-

ation; Nativity; Presentation of the Infant Jesus; and the Twelve-year old Jesus in the Temple); *The Five Sorrowful Mysteries* (Christ on the Mount of Olives; the Scourging at the Pillar; Crowning with Thorns; Carrying of the Cross; and the Crucifixion) and *The Five Glorious Mysteries* (The Resurrection; Asension; Descent of the Holy Ghost; Asumption of the Virgin; and Coronation of the Virgin). The work ends with an expressively powerful extended slow *Passacaglia*, which becomes steadily more complex.

Each of the Sonatas has an introductory Prelude followed by variations and dance movements. The programmatic element, where is appears, is usually limited to the opening section, as in the very first Sonata, where the soloist represents the Annunciation with a flourishing bravura passage, or in the touching *Lamento* which opens No. VI, or the powerful hammering of the nails in Sonata 10 (The Crucifixion). That effect is accentuated by the use of scordata, where the solo violin's strings are retuned, affecting the instrument's sonority. The solo writing is immensely demanding and of these two fine recordings it is John Holloway whose strong instrumental personality is the most telling, David Moroney (chamber organ or harpsichord) and Tragicomedia provide an imaginative continuo, using viola da gamba, lute, harp and a regal for the Crowning with Thorns. The Concordia version on Signum is rather more intimate and less flamboyant, although Walter Reiter is obviously deeply involved in the music and this too is a fine performance. But the Virgin set is a clear first choice, with a recording that gives the most vivid presence to the soloist.

BIRTWISTLE, Harrison (born 1934)

An Interrupted Endless Melody; Duets for Storab; Entra'ctes and Fragments; 9 Settings of Niedecker; The Woman and the Hare.

*** Black Box BBM 1046. McFadden, Watson, Nash Ens., Brabbins

Entitled '*The Woman and the Hare*' after the most ambitious work on this disc, a setting of a text specially written by David Harsent, this collection of Birtwistle chamber works spans his whole career, from *The Entractes* and *Sappho Fragments* of 1962–4, his uncompromising style already established along with his love of a ritualistic structure, to the Harsent setting of 1999. Harsent was the librettist for Birtwistle's opera, *Gawain*, but when his verses proved too long for the composer's purpose, he set the salient lines for soprano and interwove them with recitations of the rest, to striking effect. In response to the verses, the music evokes the wildness of nature and of man himself in a sequence of fragments that characteristically still holds firmly together, thanks also to the performers here, including the soprano Claron McFadden and the reciter, Julia Watson. The Niedecker settings were developed from what began as a tribute to Elliott

Carter on his ninetieth birthday, again built on brief evocative images, while the *Duets for Storab* (1983) take their inspiration from a legendary Neolithic king and comprise duets for two unaccompanied flutes with echoes of Stravinsky. *An Interrupted Endless Melody* was written in 1991–4 in memory of the oboist, Janet Craxton, with a single melody varied by strongly contrasted accompaniments on the piano. A fascinating collection, vividly recorded.

Pulse Shadows.

*** Teldec 39842 68672-2. McFadden, Arditti Qt, Nash Ens., De Leeuw.

This sequence of laments, inspired by the cryptic verses of the poet, Paul Celan, is one of the most moving of Birtwistle's later works. In it he interleaves two works that had a separate genesis – his nine settings of Celan and the nine pieces for string quartet – making a two-tier sequence of over an hour, which among much else enshrines the composer's response to the Holocaust. The figure of Celan has a special fascination for Birtwistle, a Romanian-Jewish poet who gravitated to Paris, but who continued to write in German, reflecting the influence of the Expressionist poets like Georg Trakl, prime inspirer of Schoenberg and his school.

In this version the English translations of Paul Hamburger are used for all the poems except one, *Todtnauberg*, which is recited in English while the song is sung in German. Whatever the influences, Birtwistle's writing is totally distinctive, not just in his response to the strangely allusive poems of Celan, but in his equally cryptic writing for string quartet in the intervening pieces. The eighteen sections, most of them brief, far from seeming fragmentary, hang together in a kaleidoscope of sharp inspiration, superbly realized here by all the performers, not least the soprano, Claron McFadden, totally unfazed by the cragginess of the writing and helped by the vividly immediate sound.

BISHOP, Henry Rowley (1786–1855)

Shakespearean song settings: *Come Live with Me; Come, Thou Monarch of the Vine; Flower of the Purple Dye; Hark, Hark, Each Spartan Hound; Lo! Hear the Gentle Lark; It was a Lover and his Lass; Lo! Oh! Never Say that I was False of Heart; Now the Hungry Lions Roar; Orpheus with his Lute; Should He Upbraid; Sing Willow; Spirits Advance; Take, Oh! Take those Lips away; That Time of Year; Under the Greenwood Tree; Welcome to This Place; When that I was a tiny little Boy; Who is Sylvia, What Is She? (2 versions).

(M) *** Decca 470 381-2. Musicians of the Globe, Pickett.

This is a peach of a disc, originally issued on Philips (as recently as 1999) and unaccountably ignored. It includes music composed, adapted and arranged for Shakespeare productions at Covent Garden in 1816–21.

There is an abundance of delightful songs here, matching the charm of the most famous number, *Lo! Hear the Gentle Lark*. The rustic feeling runs through all these pieces, typified in such numbers as *It was a Lover and his Lass*, with its hint of Scottish colour, or the hunting horns of the *Hark, Hark, Each Spartan Hound*, and the gently lilting *Welcome to This Place*. Some are more robust and substantial, such as the six-minute *Spirits Advance*, with the ghost of Weber not too far away; *When that I was a tiny little Boy* has the simple charm of a folk-song; *Now the Hungry Lions Roar* starts in appropriately leonine style, yet ends with great delicacy and is another highlight. These essentially simple songs/arias are performed in imaginative orchestrations, with over a dozen singers (in solo, duets and ensembles) adding to the colour and variety of the programme. The sound is full and perfectly balanced, and this CD is strongly recommended.

BIZET, Georges (1838–75)

L'Arlésienne: Suites Nos. 1 & 2; Patrie Overture, Op. 19; Symphony in C.

(**(*)) Testament mono SBT 1235 French Nat. RO, Cluytens.

In French music there is a lot to be said for the special Gallic sonority the National Radio Orchestra produces. André Cluytens' 1953 account of the *Symphony in C* with this orchestra was the first on LP. It is worth recalling that Bizet's youthful Symphony had only entered the repertoire in 1935 when the English Bizet scholar, D.C. Parker discovered the autograph in the Paris Conservatoire library.) It is an eminently stylish account and has a refreshingly unaffected quality about it. The finale is completely unforced with great lightness of touch and clarity of articulation. The same goes for the *L'Arlésienne – Suites*, also from 1953. Very good mono sound and a worthwhile addition to the Bizet discography.

La Jolie Fille de Perth: Suite.

(*) Testament SBT 1238 French Nat. RO, Cluytens – RAVEL: *Daphnis et Chloé suites etc*; ROUSSEL: *Le festin de l'araignée*. *

Unfussy, straightforward and fresh even if the last ounce of polish is missing. But this CD is a must for the coupling, Cluytens's inspired and atmospheric account of Roussel's *Le festin de l'araignée*.

Symphony in C; Jeux d'enfants (suite), Op. 22; *Suite bohémiennes.*

(BB) *** DG Eloquence (ADD) 469 689-2. French Nat. R. O, Martinon – DEBUSSY: *Danse sacrée et danse profane* ***; SAINT-SAENS: *Morceau de concert* ***.

Martinon's performance of the *Symphony* is engagingly fresh, among the very best versions to have appeared after Beecham, and both *Jeux d'enfants* and *Suite bohémiennes* are captivating in his hands. These classic accounts from the early 1970s had hardly been issued when they were peremptorily deleted. Excellent recording, too. This is one of the best bargains on DG's Eloquence label.

Carmen (opera; complete).

*** Columbia Tristar **DVD** CDR 10530. Migenes-Johnson, Domingo, Raimondi, Esham, French National RSO and Chorus, Maazel. (V/D: Franco Rossi.)

Filmed on location in the most atmospheric of sites, few operatic films add so vividly to the music as this version of *Carmen*, directed by Franco Rossi. It starts with a striking visual coup: the credits are shown with merely the murmur of a bullring crowd in the background, while a matador is seen playing with a bull. He finally brings his sword down for the kill, and Bizet's opening *Prélude* thunders out.

The film is set to a recording specially made in the studio, and issued on CD by Erato. An excellent performance, under Lorin Maazel, on DVD it projects as sharply dramatic, with Placido Domingo at his finest and Julia Migenes-Johnson the most vibrantly characterful of Carmens. Ruggero Raimondi makes a noble Ecamillo, and though Faith Esham's voice is not ideally sweet as Micaela, it is a tender, sensitive performance. The sound is first rate, and having the singers miming to the music is not too distracting. The DVD is markedly sharper in focus than the equivalent VHS. No booklet is provided, just a leaflet, with only sketchy details given, even of the cast. First CD choice rests with Karajan's DG set with Baltsa, Carreras and Van Dam (410 088-2).

Carmen: highlights.

(BB) ** EMI Encore CDE5 74955-2. (From complete recording with Bumbry, Vickers, Freni, Paskalis, Paris Opéra Ch. & O, Frübeck de Burgos.)

Frübeck de Burgos's account of 1970 was the first to use the original 1875 version of Bizet's score, without the cuts that were made after experience in the theatre, and with spoken dialogue instead of the recitatives which Guiraud composed after Bizet's early death. The EMI Encore disc offers a comprehensive selection (76 minutes) from a set with a less-than-compelling Carmen in Grace Bumbry, who sings with firm tone but too rarely with musical or dramatic individuality. Vickers makes a strong Don José and Paskalis a rich-toned Escamillo, so with the opera well paced this makes a more than acceptable and well-recorded sampler, even if the synopsis is very sparse.

BLAKE, Howard (born 1938)

Clarinet Concerto.

(B) *** Hyp. Helios CDH 55068. King, ECO, Composer – LUTOSLAWSKI: *Dance Preludes*; SEIBER: *Concertino*. ***

Howard Blake provides a comparatively slight but endearing *Clarinet Concerto* which is played here with great sympathy by Thea King, who commissioned the work. At budget price this is even more attractive.

BLISS, Arthur (1891–1975)

(i) *Antiphonal Fanfare for 3 Brass Choirs*; (ii; iii) *Cello Concerto*; (i) *Fanfare for the Lord Mayor of London*; *Flourish for 2 Brass Orchestras (Greetings to a City)*; (iii) *Introduction and Allegro*; (iv; v) *Introduction and Allegro for Violin and Orchestra*; (iii) *Meditations on a Theme of John Blow*; (iv; v) *Theme and Cadenza for Solo Violin and Orchestra*; (vi) *Things to Come: Suite*; (iv) *Welcome to the Queen*.

(M) **(*) Decca (ADD/DDD) 470 186-2 (2). (i) Philip Jones Brass Ens., Howarth; (ii) Cohen; (iii) RPO, Wordsworth; (iv) LSO, Composer; (v) Campoli; (vi) NPO, Herrmann.

A generally worthwhile Bliss anthology. CD 1 comprises a 1993 Argo recording of the *Cello Concerto* – composed for Rostropovitch – the advantage of which is that it gets better as it goes along. The *Larghetto* is much more attractive than the comparatively weak first movement, and the finale gathers the best of the composer's ideas, including the main theme of the opening movement. The flamboyantly scored *Introduction and Allegro*, which has a striking lyrical idea, and the amiable if rambling *Meditations on a Theme of John Blow* complete this well-played and spectacularly recorded CD. CD 2 includes the composer's own vigorous performances of the works for violin and orchestra with Campoli, which were (unbelievably) recorded in 1955, although the vivid sound only hints at their age with its comparative lack of overall opulence. The composer's own account of the rumbustious *Welcome to the Queen* is enjoyable, but it is a pity his recording of the *Things to Come* suite wasn't chosen instead of Bernard Herrmann's version. That is acceptable but lame in comparison, with the famous *March* – perhaps Bliss's best piece – lacking the swagger of the composer's own account. The three vibrant *Fanfares* make unusual and interesting bonuses, and this CD is an excellent summation of the Bliss style.

Piano Quartet in A min; Bliss; The Rout Trot; Triptych (for piano). (i) Angels of the Mind (for voice and piano); 4 Songs (for voice, violin and piano).

*** ASV CDDCA 1126. De Pledge, Chamber Domaine, with (i) Meyerhoff.

This accomplished ensemble bring us some Bliss rarities, including the first recording of the early *Piano Quartet in A minor* (1915) and the *Triptych* for piano (1971). The former, written when he was in his early twenties, is well crafted, though Bliss has not yet found his own voice: the debt to Vaughan Williams and English folksong is still to be discharged. The jazzy *Bliss* and *The Rout Trot* are well done, as is the *Triptych*, which is muscular and well held together. There are moments when one's thoughts turn to John Ireland, though the writing is still very characteristic. *Angels of the Mind* is another late piece of some quality, which Helen Meyerhoff sings with great musical intelligence though less vocal beauty. The recording is dryish and more air is needed round the aural image.

Song cycles: 2 *American Poems* (Millay); 7 *American Poems; Ballads of the Four Seasons* (Li-Po); *A knot of riddles; 2 Nursery rhymes* (Cornford); 3 *Romantic songs* (Walter de la Mare); 4 *Songs. The Tempest* (incidental music). Other songs: *Angels of the mind; At the window; A Child's prayer; Auvergnat; Elegiac sonnet; Fair is my love; The fallow deer at the lonely house; The hammers; In praise of his Daphnis; Rich or poor; Simples; 'Tis time I think by Wenlock town; Three jolly gentlemen; The tramps; When I was one-and-twenty.*

*** Hyp. CDA 67188/9. McGreevy, Spence, Herford, Sturrock, Nash Ens., Brabbins.

The very variety of this splendid collection of Bliss's songs will come as a surprise to many, for the composer refused to be limited by the usual constraints of the English tradition, let alone to be influenced by the folk tradition. The collection spans the full extent of his composing career, from a boyhood song like the Housman setting, *'Tis time, I think, by Wenlock town*, through to two of his last works, *A Knot of Riddles* for baritone and 11 instruments and *Angels of the Mind* another song-cycle for soprano and piano setting poems by Kathleen Raine, a work he wrote not on commission but simply for his own enjoyment. Geraldine McGreevy is the outstanding soloist in that and the other soprano items, and the others also respond sensitively to Bliss's distinctive word-setting, often helped by sharply rhythmic accompaniments. It is striking how often Bliss liked to have more than a piano in accompaniment, not just in *A Knot of Riddles* but in such an isolated song as his *Elegiac Sonnet* for tenor, string quartet and piano to words by Cecil Day Lewis, written for the memorial concert commemorating the pianist, Noel Mewton-Wood. Kathleen Sturrock is the excellent pianist in most of the songs, with members of the Nash Ensemble ever-stylish in the rest. First-rate recording. A most valuable, comprehensive essay, 'An introduction to Arthur Bliss as Songwriter' by Giles Easterbrook, is included in the booklet.

BLOCH, Ernest (1880–1959)

Enfantines, Five Sketches in Sepia; In the Night; Nirvana; Piano Sonata; Visions and Prophecies.

*** Chan. 9887. Fingerhut.

Bloch composed relatively little for the piano: the majority of the smaller pieces on the disc, *Enfantines, Five Sketches in Sepia, In the Night* and *Nirvana,* come from the period 1921–3. The *Piano Sonata* was written in the mid-1930s at the time he was working on *Voice in the Wilderness* for cello and orchestra, which is very much in the spirit of his *Hebrew Rhapsody, Schelomo.* At the time he made a cello and piano transcription of the new six-movement work. A little later he produced a completely overhauled reworking of the piece

for solo piano, calling it *Visions and Prophecies*. This omits the cadenza and the final movement of *Voice in the Wilderness* and re-works the remainder. The dramatic movements (1, 3 and 5) depict the Old Testament prophets while the remainder evoke the visions. Bloch's muse is essentially rhapsodic and improvisatory and his piano writing cries out for the colours of the orchestra. Much of the writing is amorphous and wanting in direction, but it is difficult to imagine it better played than it is here by Margaret Fingerhut or more naturally recorded.

BOCCHERINI, Luigi (1743–1805)

Cello Concerto in B flat (arr. Grützmacher).

(M) * DG 445 608-2. Haimovitz, ECO, Davis – C. P. E. BACH: *Concerto in A;* HAYDN: *Concerto in C.* *

Matt Haimovitz produces a big (almost schmaltzy) tone and his rather impulsive manner, pressing forward and then holding back, disturbs the natural flow of the piece. There are much more recommendable versions of this concerto.

String Quartets, Op. 32/1–2; String Quartet in A, Op. 39.

(BB) *** Naxos 8.555042. Borciani Qt.

String Quartets, Op. 32/3–6.

(BB) *** Naxos 8.555043. Borciani Qt.

We already have an excellent set of the six *Op. 32 Quartets* written in 1780, played on period instruments by the Esterházy Quartet on Teldec (8573 85565/66-2). Now the Quartetto Borciani offer an equally accomplished alternative on modern instruments, which have plenty of character and vitality and are always sensitive to Boccherini's gentle touches of expressive melancholy, as in the *Larghetto* of the C major, Op. 32/4. They also catch admirably the mood of the opening movement of the first of the set in E flat, marked *Allegretto lentarello e affettuoso.* But they have an advantage over the Teldec set in including Boccherini's later *A major Quartet,* Op. 39 (1787), which has a particularly touching *Grave* third movement, most affectingly played here. The Naxos recording is vivid and truthful and there are excellent notes, whereas the Teldec set is very sparsely documented.

String Quintets: in E, Op. 13/5, G.275; in G minor, Op. 37/13, G.348; in F minor, Op. 37/19, G.351.

*** Hyp. CDA 67287 Vanburgh Qt, with Lester.

With over a hundred cello quintets among his works, the *E major,* G.275, makes an obvious first choice, when the third movement Minuet is the music universally associated with the very name of Boccherini. It is particularly refreshing in the Vanburgh performance to hear it in context with the work's other three movements; their approach pays obvious tribute to period practice in the choice of tempo, far faster than one usually associates with 'Boccherini's Minuet', light and crisp. The other movements are comparably striking, starting with a leisurely first movement marked amoroso, and ending with a relaxed Rondo finale, marked sotto voice, with much pointed dialogue between the instruments.

The format of a string quintet with two cellos instead of two violas was very much Boccherini's special genre. Himself a cellist, it allowed him to free at least one of the cellos from following the bass line, so as to soar lyrically. Both the other quintets here were composed in 1789, eighteen years after the *E major*, and regularly rely on the characteristic Boccherini device of quickly switching between major and minor keys – the striking minor-key openings of both works promptly lead to the relative major keys, with interplay of tonality back and forth. In the *G minor* Boccherini again uses the rare marking 'amoroso' in the Larghetto slow movement, before leading in the finale to a movement which has something of the flavour of Haydn in *Sturm und Drang* mood, not a rondo but a compact sonata-form structure. Vividly recorded with such fine performances, both polished and refreshing, with Richard Lester a perfect partner for the prize-winning Vanburgh Quartet, this is an outstanding disc in every way.

BORODIN, Alexander (1833–87)

In the Steppes of Central Asia; Prince Igor: Polovtsian Dances.

(BB) **(*) EMI Encore (ADD) CDE5 74763-2. Philh O, Cluytens – RIMSKY-KORSAKOV: *Capriccio espagnol* etc. MUSSORGSKY: *Night on the Bare Mountain.***(*)

From Cluytens come a beautifully controlled performance of *In the Steppes of Central Asia* and a lively *Polovtsian Dances*, both enjoyable. The 1958 recording sounds astonishingly well, with only a touch of thinness betraying its age. Part of an attractive bargain CD of Russian show-pieces.

(i; ii) *Symphonies Nos. 2 in B min.; (iii) 3 in A min.; (i; iv; v) Prince Igor: Overture; Polovtsian Dances.*

(BB) *** Decca (ADD) 467 482-2. (i) LSO; (ii) Martinon; (iii) SRO, Ansermet; (iv) Solti; (v) LSO Ch.

Martinon's electrifying account of the *B minor Symphony* remains unsurpassed. Notable for its fast tempo for the famous opening theme, the strong rhythmic thrust suits the music admirably; the scherzo is vibrant, the slow movement, with a beautifully played horn solo, is most satisfying, and the finale is a blaze of colour. The early 1960s sound is astonishingly vivid. Solti's *Prince Igor Overture* is both unexpectedly romantic and very exciting: there is no finer version in the catalogue. The same can be said of the *Polovtsian Dances*, with splendid choral singing, even if the chorus takes a little longer to warm up than in the famous Beecham version. Both items date from 1966 and have vintage Decca sound.

If the playing of the Suisse Romande Orchestra is not a match for the LSO, Ansermet brings out all the colour in his alive and spontaneous account of the *Third Symphony*, with some delightful moments from the SRO woodwind. Any slight reservations are swept aside, however, when the rest of the programme is so stimulating, and this makes a splendid bargain on the Eloquence label.

String Quartets Nos. 1 in A; 2 in D.

*** Chan. (ADD) 9965. Borodin Qt.

Borodin had a more highly developed interest in chamber music than any of his Russian colleagues of 'The Five', fostered, no doubt, by his studies abroad in Heidelberg and in Italy. The *First Quartet* had occupied him over a long period, the best part of the 1870s, while the *Second* was composed in the course of a few summer weeks in 1881 when he was in the country at Zhitovo. It is one of the most lyrical quartets in the repertoire, and its familiarity prompts some music-lovers to underrate its consummate mastery of form. Its very luxuriance has aroused some critical hackles, but as Gerald Abraham put it, 'romantic languor and the pervading blandness of its textures run the danger of being considered cloying, yet Borodin avoids this by virtue of the music's latent muscularity'. The Borodins made this classic recording in 1979, and it remains the yardstick by which all others are judged.

String Quartet No. 2 in D.

(M) (**(*)) BBC mono BBCL 4063-2. Borodin Qt. – RAVEL: *Quartet* (**(*)); SHOSTAKOVICH: *Quartet No.8.*(**(*))

The Borodins made their professional debut in 1946, though it was not until 1955 that they assumed their present name. Such was their refinement of sonority, wonderful blend and superb unanimity of ensemble that they soon acquired a legendary reputation. This performance and its companions come from 1962, when the Edinburgh Festival concentrated on Russian music and artists and when the Borodin Quartet made their first appearance in Britain. After Edinburgh they recorded the Shostakovich and Borodin quartets at the Decca studios (425 541–2). This performance is not quite its equal, although it has great immediacy and flair; in any event, it is still worth having and sounds very good for its age.

Prince Igor: Polovtsian Dances.

(M) (***) BBC Legends mono BBCL 4084-2 RPO & Ch, Beecham – BALAKIREV: *Symphony No. 1*; RIMSKY-KORSAKOV: *Le coq d'or: Suite.* ***

Though this live broadcast performance is less polished than Beecham's studio version, and comes in mono instead of stereo, it is the full version with chorus, making a powerful fill-up to the superb account of the Balakirev symphony.

BORTNYANSKY, Dmitri (1751–1825)

Sacred Concertos Nos. 30–35.

*** Chan. 9956. Russian State Symphonic Capella, Polyansky.

The fifth issue completes the Chandos set of Bortnyansky's Sacred Concertos for single choir. (The others are on Chan. 9729, 9783, 9840 and 9878 – see our main volume). Certainly the claim in the notes by Philip Taylor that this fifth collection represents Bortnyansky's crowning achievement in the genre is well borne out here, and the present disc might be a good place to start exploring the series for Tchaikovsky himself declared that the *Concerto No. 32* (*Lord let me Know mine End*) with its ethereal opening is the finest of the set. But the other works are also very beautiful. No. 30 creates an opening mood of rich serenity, although the singing is deeply felt; No.31 opens with expansive, very Russian-sounding textures. No. 33 is very moving too and No. 35 is full of calm acceptance and optimism of spirit. Performances and recording are of the very highest standard.

Sacred Concertos for Double Choir Nos. 1–10.

*** Chan. 9922. Russian State Symphonic Cappella, Polyansky.

To supplement their outstanding performances of the 35 *Sacred Concertos for Single Choir*, the Russian State Symphonic Cappella here undertake, with equal success, the hardly less beautiful works for double choir, which have only recently been discovered. They are mostly Psalm settings, and have a radiant simplicity. But throughout, Polyansky and his singers make rich use of the composer's antiphonal interplay, and although these settings are often more peaceful, less expressively extrovert than many of the works for single choir, their effect is hardly less potent.

There is moving depth and intensity of response in the centrepiece of the very first concerto, *I will worship towards Thy Holy Temple*, with the music then taking vigorous flight in the closing section. At the opening of the fifth, the flowing lines of *The heavens declare the Glory of God* are ecstatic in religious feeling, and that same fervour is mirrored in the finale of No. 7, *For thou alone art Holy*, with its exciting closing accelerando.

Nos. 8, *Ye People sing a Song*, and the elysian, soaring No. 9, *Praise ye the Lord*, are each condensed into a single movement, with the part-writing particularly concentrated. But the whole set shows Bortnyansky's consistency of inspiration to which these Russian singers respond with great eloquence. First class recording.

BOULEZ, Pierre (born 1925)

Pli selon pli.

*** DG 471 344-2. Schäfer, Ensemble InterContemporain, Boulez.

First composed in 1957 but repeatedly revised since, *Pli selon pli* is a key work in Boulez's development, a portrait of the poet, Mallarmé, setting his texts to craggy vocal lines that blossom in such a performance as this, with Christine Schäfer singing radiantly. Boulez has recorded this piece, well over an hour long, twice before, but this definitive version is the first to take account of his last revision in 1989. With vivid sound the composer brings out the contrast between the complex textures of the outer movements and the chamber-like precision of the three central settings of Mallarmé or 'Improvisations' as he calls them. The recording was made after a series of live performances, so that the talented players of Ensemble InterContemporain convey rapt concentration in obedience to the composer-conductor's precise demands, magnetic from first to last.

BOWEN, York (1884–1961)

Horn Quintet; Piano Trio; Rhapsody Trio.

(M) *** Dutton CDLX 7115. Endymion Ens.

In the years leading up to the First World War, York Bowen, born in 1884, was generally counted as one of the great hopes of British music, far more widely performed and appreciated than such a contemporary as Arnold Bax. After the war, though he continued to write new works till he died in 1961, he was seriously neglected, evidently content to be one of the most respected of composition teachers. These three superb chamber works, dating respectively from 1927, 1926 and 1945, bear out the quality of his writing, a composer never afraid to write a good tune, offering well-made works that never seem routine, particularly in outstanding performances like these. The *Horn Quintet* is a glorious piece, with Stephen Stirling magnificent in the central horn part, and if the main motif of the first movement reminds one of Vaughan Williams's *Fifth Symphony*, York Bowen was writing almost 20 years earlier. One looks forward to hearing much more.

String Quartets Nos. 2 in D min., Op. 41; 3 in G, Op. 46b; (i) Phantasy-Quintet for Bass Clarinet & String Quartet, Op. 93.

*** British Music Society BMS 426CD. Archaeus Qt.; (i) with Timothy Lines.

Here is yet another record of York Bowen's chamber music to confirm that he is more of a major figure in British music than has hitherto been thought. The two *String Quartets* are remarkably similar in atmosphere and layout and were probably written about the same time, around the end of the First World War. The *Second Quartet in D minor*, with its hauntingly melodic first movement, was published in 1922 as the recipient of a Carnegie Trust Award and soon forgotten. The *Poco lento* is unforgettably nostalgic and the busily folksy finale of contrasting brilliance, offset by more appealing lyricism.

The *Third Quartet* opens with another lovely melodic contour reminding one a little of Dvořák, with the slow movement following in the same mood of intimate melancholy. The finale matches the pattern of the last movement of No. 2, opening with pizzicati, and leading to a dashing main theme and a warmly lyrical counterpart.

The bass clarinet does not dominate the *Phantasy-Quintet*, but adds a beguiling touch of darkness to its texture, interwoven with solo interludes. The work is continuous, opening and closing in gentle reverie, but with quixotic tempo changes in its middle sections. Highly sympathetic performances and excellent recording ensure this CD receives a strong recommendation.

BOYCE, William (1710–79)

Overtures Nos. 1–12; Concerti grossi: in B flat; B min.; & E min.

(B) *** Chan. Double 6665 (2). Cantilena, Shepherd.

Though these works do not have quite the consistent originality which makes the Boyce *Symphonies* so refreshing, the energy of the writing – splendidly conveyed in these performances – is recognizably the same, with fugal passages that turn in unexpected directions. Cantilena's performances readily convey the freshness of Boyce's inspiration, and this is one of the most recommendable of all their recordings, the more attractive for being re-issued as a bargain Double. They are oddly balanced but the sound is both atmospheric and vivid and provides a refreshing musical experience.

Symphonies Nos. 1–8, Op. 2.

(M) *** Decca 473 08102. AAM, Hogwood.

Christopher Hogwood and the Academy of Ancient Music turn in performances that are every bit as lively and well played as Trevor Pinnock's rival set with the English Concert, and perhaps more sensitively shaped. By comparison, Pinnock sounds just a bit bright and business-like, making the Hogwood top choice among the period instrument versions, especially at its new mid-price in Decca's 'British Collection'. Excellent recording.

BRAHMS, Johannes (1833–97)

Academic Festival Overture, Op. 80; Tragic Overture; Variations on a Theme by Haydn, Op. 56a; (i) Rhapsody for Alto, Chorus and Orchestra, Op. 53.

(M) * Decca (ADD) 470 254-2. VPO, Knappertsbusch with (i) West – WAGNER: *Siegfried Idyll.* *

This programme would have been an attractive addition to the catalogue had the performance been of high calibre, but one cannot believe that Decca thought Knappertsbusch's slow and stodgy Brahms collection was suitable for inclusion in its Legends series for, with its pretty sloppy playing and ponderous tempi, it is not really recommendable at all. The *Rhapsody* is a mite better in some respects, especially as the rarely recorded Lucretia West, with her opulently burnished contralto, will interest collectors of

recordings of seldom heard singers. The 1957 sound, rather thick and tubby, is not especially ingratiating.

Piano Concertos Nos. 1 in D min., Op. 15; 2 in B flat, Op. 83.

(B) ** Teldec Ultima 0630 18948-2 (2). Leonskaya; Philh. O, Inbal or Leipzig GO, Masur.

(i) *Piano Concertos Nos. 1; 2; Academic Festival Overture; Tragic Overture.*

(B) **(*) Sony (ADD) SB2K 89905 (2). (i) Serkin; Cleveland O, Szell.

(i-iii) *Piano Concertos Nos. 1 in D min., Op. 15; (i; iii; iv) 2 in B flat, Op. 83; (i; v) Variations & Fugue on a Theme by Handel, Op. 24 (orch. Rubbra); Variations on a Theme by Handel, Op. 56a.*

(B) **(*) Double Decca 470 519-2 (2). (i) Ashkenazy; (ii) Concg. O; (iii) Haitink; (iv) VPO; (v) Cleveland O.

Serkin's 1968 account of the *First, D minor Concerto*, his third on LP, brought tremendous command and grandeur. This is undoubtedly a memorable performance and the support from Szell and the Cleveland Orchestra has great power. In the *Second, B flat major Concerto* Serkin achieves an ideal balance between straightforwardness and expressiveness, while the slow movement has a genuine 'inner' intensity, with some wonderfully expressive playing by the Cleveland principal cellist. Serkin choses a comparatively slow speed for the finale, but the flow and energy of the music are not impaired and the Hungarian motifs of the second subject sparkle with point and wit. The CBS/Sony recordings have been considerably improved in the current remastering, but in No. 1 the piano tone is not as full as one would ideally like and the balance still lacks a natural perspective. However, in No. 2 the piano tone has more body and the orchestral sound is fuller too; in both works the hall ambience contributes to a Brahmsian orchestral sonority. The two overtures are brilliantly played, the *Academic Festival Overture* being particularly ebullient.

Ashkenazy gives a commanding and magisterial account of the solo part of the *First Concerto* that is full of poetic imagination. The performance is very impressive indeed, and there is superlative playing from the Concertgebouw Orchestra. The soloist is placed rather closely, but the sound in general is very vivid. The *Second Concerto*, with the VPO, is not as successful. It is spacious in conception and thoughtful in detail, but curiously lacking in impulse, with cautious speeds, and overtly expressive in the lyrical episodes of the second movement. The slow movement is very beautiful and the finale offers the proper contrast, but in the last resort, in spite of the excellent recording, this is slightly disappointing.

For the fill-ups, Ashkenazy adopts the role of conductor: the *Haydn Variations* receives an excellent performance in very plush Cleveland sound – sound which also brings out all the vibrant colour in Rubbra's extravagant orchestration of the *Variations and Fugue on a Theme by Handel* – a substantial bonus –

which is similarly well played and is highly enjoyable. A mixed bag then, but worth considering by Ashkenazy admirers.

Leonskaya is an impressively direct and powerful Brahmsian, inclined to be stoic, but also thoughtful in her lyrical moments. Eliahu Inbal proves a more successful partner for her than Masur, and the Philharmonia provide a passionate opening for the *D minor Concerto*, although the secondary material is much more considered. Overall this is a spacious rather than a fiery reading and it lacks the electricity of the finest versions. The *B flat Concerto*, very broadly conceived, gives an impression of massiveness and is even less spontaneous in feeling, although the finale brings a lighter touch. These artists are given excellent, modern, digital recording, but their performances are no match for those of Gilels.

Piano Concerto No. 2 in B flat, Op. 83.

(BB) (**) Naxos mono 8.110671. Horowitz, NBC SO, Toscanini – TCHAIKOVSKY: *Piano Concerto No. 1.* (***) ☻

This Horowitz/Toscanini version of the Brahms *B flat Concerto* dates from around the same time as their famous coupled recording of the Tchaikovsky *B flat minor Concerto*. Both were made in Carnegie Hall, but the Brahms, recorded in 1940, has the advantage of fairly full orchestral sound, although the piano timbre is shallow. But this very leonine account will not appeal to all tastes. While the first movement has undoubted lyrical strength, Toscanini generates little Brahmsian expansiveness (and Horowitz matches his lean textures with bare pedalling). For all its energy and bravura we are not drawn into the tension of the performance as we are in the Tchaikovsky, and only in the finale does Horowitz's scintillating fingerwork restore the *grazioso* feeling. Mark Obert-Thorn's admirably vivid transfer cannot be faulted.

(i–iii) Piano Concerto No. 2 in B flat, Op 83; (ii; iv) Symphony No. 1 in C min., Op. 68; (ii; v) Academic Festival Overture, Op. 80; (ii; iv) Hungarian Dances, Nos. 3 in F; 6 in D; 17 in F sharp min.; 18 in D; 19 in B min.; 20 in E min; Variations on a Theme by Haydn, Op. 56a.

(B) *** DG (ADD/DDD) 469 298-2 (2). (i) Gilels; (ii) BPO; (iii) Jochum; (iv) Karajan; (v) Abbado.

If the programme appeals, there's nothing to quibble with here: Gilels's outstanding account of the *Second Piano Concerto* remains one of the most impressive versions on disc, his partnership with Jochum producing music-making of real distinction. Karajan's 1964 recording of the *First Symphony* is generally regarded as the best of his several recordings of this work and remains one of the top choices; his account of the *Haydn Variations*, dating from the same period, is impressive too, and the *Hungarian Dances*, recorded in 1959, have great panache and brilliance. Abbado's digital *Academic Festival Overture* completes this excellent two-CD Panorama set, and the re-mastered sound is excellent.

Violin Concerto in D, Op. 77 – see also under Symphonies 3–4.

☻ (M) (***) EMI mono CDM5 67583-2 [567584]. Milstein, Pittsburgh SO, Steinberg – BEETHOVEN: *Violin Concerto.* (***)

*** Sony SK 89649. Hilary Hahn, ASMF, Marriner – STRAVINSKY: *Violin Concerto.* ***

(BB) (***) Dutton mono CDBP 9710. Neveu, Philh. O, Dobrowen – RAVEL: *Tzigane;* SUK: *4 Pieces.* (***)

The EMI mono Milstein/Steinberg recording originally appeared on Capitol in Britain and was long treasured. Returning to it after many years, its stature impresses more than ever before. It is quite simply glorious: a performance of surpassing beauty, its virtuosity effortless, and with a tremendous breadth, warmth and eloquence. There is, above all, a nobility here that shines through. Milstein re-recorded it in the 1980s in Vienna with Jochum – superbly, too – but this remains in a class of its own.

Hilary Hahn adds one more to the list of powerful readings of this most demanding of violin concertos recorded by women virtuosos, often at the beginning of their careers. Her very first entry establishes her total command, coupled with a purity and precision which make for a magnetic reading from first to last. Her love of this concerto, established in early childhood, gives rise to a sense of spontaneity as she seamlessly draws together the many contrasted thematic motifs, sensitively matched by the full and incisive playing of the Academy under Sir Neville Marriner. In the first movement the balance of the violin is ideal, allowing plenty of bite in the bravura passages of double-stopping, as well as a breath-taking pianissimo in the mysterious, meditative bars just before the final bravura passage of the exposition. The close balance means that Hahn is much less hushed in the slow movement, but then her urgent reading of the finale is given extra impact. It was her personal decision to have the Stravinsky *Concerto* as an unexpected coupling, a work which, as she sees it, for all its fundamental contrast of idiom, can be related to its composer's career very much as Brahms's can to his. In any case it makes a unique and provocative coupling, particularly when Hahn's reading of that later work is even more distinctive than that of the Brahms.

Not surprisingly the Dutton transfer of Ginette Neveu's legendary account of the Brahms concerto is even more realistic and full-blooded than the EMI version (CDH7 61011-2). That is coupled with her magnetic account of the Sibelius concerto, whereas Dutton choses music by Ravel, Suk and others.

(i) Violin Concerto in D, Op. 77; (ii) Double Concerto for Violin, Cello & Orchestra in A min., Op. 102.

*** DG 469 529-2. Shaham, Wang, BPO, Abbado.

It makes an ideal and generous coupling having Brahms's two concertos for stringed instruments on a single disc, and these are outstanding versions of both works. The *Violin Concerto* comes in a live recording which in its urgency and sense of drama is among the most impressive for a long time. Speeds in the outer movement, are faster than is common these days, so that the first movement with high contrasts of mood as well as of dynamic, is compellingly taut. The slow movement is at once warm and steady, while the finale at a daringly impulsive Allegro dances along to bring out the second marking, giocoso. Though the *Double Concerto* was recorded under studio conditions, there too the impression is of spontaneous music-making. With warm interplay between Shaham and the cellist, Jian Wang, the first movement, after a reflective opening cello solo, is tautly dramatic, the slow movement is ripely songful and in the finale, as in the *Violin Concerto*, the folk-dance element is sparklingly brought out. A splendid supplement to Abbado's fine Brahms symphony cycle with the Berlin Philharmonic, and a first choice for those wanting a pairing of these two concertos.

Double Concerto for Violin, Cello & Orchestra in A min., Op. 102.

(BB) (***) Naxos mono 8.110930. Thibaud, Casals, Barcelona O, Cortot – DVORAK: *Cello Concerto.*(***)

Collectors who grew up in the 1930s and 1940s will probably have got to know the *Double Concerto* in the Thibaud–Casals version with the Barcelona Orchestra conducted by Cortot. It is a performance of incandescent intensity and humanity, which reigned supreme until the Heifetz–Feuermann set came along. This new transfer is probably as good as any we are likely to get. The 1929 original was scrawny and strident, and Mark Obert-Thorn has succeeded in taming it more successfully than did Dutton – almost his only failure!

(i) Serenades Nos. 1 in D, Op. 11; 2 in A, Op. 16; (i) Liebeslieder Waltzes, Op. 52 & 65.

(M) **(*) Orfeo (2CD) C008 102A. (i) VSO, Bertini; (i) with Sieghart, V. Singverein der Musikfreude.

Gary Bertini's account of the opening movement of the *D major Serenade*, with its rollicking horns, has a boisterous quality which is engaging, and throughout both works he draws much fine playing from the Vienna Symphony Orchestra; the woodwind provide appealing colour. Bertini maintains a good momentum for the *Adagio* slow movements, which is sensible enough, but he captures the relaxed atmosphere better in Op. 16 than in Op. 11. The resonant recording sounds rich-textured at lower dynamic levels, but in fortissimos the opulence also brings a touch of heaviness. However, there is much agreeable warmth here and the reissue throws in a second CD with an equally agreeable performance of the seductive *Liebeslieder Waltzes*, liltingly sung by the Vienna Singverein, although Ingrid Sieghart is not a soloist to banish memories of more famous names.

SYMPHONIES

Symphonies Nos. 1–4.

(B) **(*) RCA 74321 89103-2 (2); or 74321 89102-2 (Nos. 1 & 3); 74321 89101-2 (Nos. 2 & 4). North German RSO, Wand.

(M) *(*) Chan. 9776 (4). LSO, Järvi.

Symphonies Nos. 1–4; Academic Festival Overture; Tragic Overture; Variations on a Theme of Haydn.

(BB) ** Ph. Trio 470 942-2 (3). Phd. O, Muti.

Symphonies Nos. 1–4; Academic Festival Overture; Tragic Overture; Variations on a Theme by Haydn; (i) Alto Rhapsody.

(BB) *(*) Virgin VB5 62081-2 (4). Houston SO, Eschenbach; (i) with Vejzovic & Houston Symphony Male Ch.

Günter Wand's Brahms set is highly recommendable for providing spontaneously compelling readings of all four works very well played. RCA have carefully remastered the 1982–3 recordings (as far as is possible with digital masters) and the sound balance seems fuller, with the tendency to shrillness on violin tone now less problematic; certainly the effect gives the playing plenty of bite. Wand's is a consistently direct view of Brahms, yet the reading of each symphony has its own individuality. No. 1 has striking impetus throughout, and the *Second* (the finest of the four) is a characteristically glowing but steady reading, with the recording adding fullness and bloom. In the *Third* the foward thrust returns excitingly in the outer movements, yet overall Wand's wise way with Brahms, strong and evenly paced, works beautifully. The reading of No. 4 initially seems understated, but the remastering with its rather more expansive sound adds to the weight and strength of what is a generally satisfying conclusion of a fine cycle. Wand's admirers need not hesitate. The two discs are available separately.

The Philips engineers faced in 1989 with recording in the difficult Philadelphia venue only gradually overcame their problems. It follows that Muti's set, too, is inconsistent, generally offering crisp, beautifully played readings, which are distinguished without being strongly characterized, occasionally dull and lacking in tension. Individually the most desirable of the four is No. 3 and that would make a fine separate issue with its original coupling, the *Alto Rhapsody* beautifully sung by Jessye Norman. This has been omitted here to get the set onto three CDs.

Even though it is in the budget range, with its extravagant layout on four discs (partly caused by the inclusion of the first-movement exposition repeats in the first three symphonies) Eschenbach's set could compete only if the Houston performances were truly outstanding, which they are not. They are beautifully played and very well balanced and recorded. But Eschenbach, highly musical Brahmsian as he is, has not yet entirely mastered the art of bringing a performance fully to life in the recording studio. No. 1 is singularly lacking in a strong profile, for here the conductor's easy, lyrical style works least well: the effect is more like a final rehearsal than a vivid consummation. In spite of a fine introductory horn solo, the finale hangs fire and really comes together only in the coda. The conductor's recessive manner may in theory be more suitable for the pastoral No. 2, but again, there is simply not enough tension to hold each movement together, until the performance suddenly springs to life in the finale. No. 3 is much more impressive: the first movement immediately generates a stronger electrical charge. It sails off heftily, and there is plenty of momentum in the finale too, with impressive brass playing and the closing pages movingly autumnal. The inner movements, however, tend to sag just a little before the end, although the playing is affectionate and warm. Easily the finest Houston performance is the *Fourth Symphony*, where the tension is consistently maintained and Eschenbach's steady lyrical flow, often impassioned, reminds one of Karl Boehm – and there can be no higher compliment. The *Academic Festival Overture* and *Haydn Variations* are comparatively subdued, whilst the *Tragic Overture*, which is coupled to the *Fourth Symphony*, is equally impressive. One of the highlights of the set is the moving account of the *Alto Rhapsody*. Dunja Vejzovic is in glorious voice and the choral entry is a moment of serene magic, with the Houston Chorus beautifully balanced with solo voice. But as a general recommendation, this Virgin set is a non-starter.

During the late 1980s, Neeme Järvi was among the most active of all recording conductors, with records appearing on many different labels, and the quality has been astonishingly consistent, sounding not at all hasty or slapdash. By Järvi's standards, however, his Brahms cycle is a disappointment, often fussy, sometimes wilful, with playing from the LSO which generally lacks that very quality which marks out most Järvi records: the sense of a genuine performance rather than a studio run-through. Added to that, the Chandos engineers' preference for a wide, reverberant acoustic makes Brahms's heavy orchestral textures sound thick and vague, however great the richness and range of the recording. The lack of definition in the bass is particularly damaging in No. 1. The slackness of ensemble in the outer movements adds to the heaviness of approach and the middle movements are similarly inelegant and lacking charm.

The general comments made above apply to No. 2 as well. The first movement, taken relatively fast, is warmly lyrical but lacks both tension and delicacy. The middle movements miss the charm of Brahms's inspiration, and the finale, taken fast, sounds slapdash, with the lack of definition in the bass making the results even more muddled.

Järvi takes a broad view of No. 3, and the weight of the recording at the very start gives appropriate grandeur – before the thickening of texture which mars this series then obtrudes. Though he responds well to the lyricism, the end result is too heavy-handed, often fussy, with the ensemble no better than in the rest of the series. The effortfulness at the start of No. 4 is typical of Järvi's disappointing approach to this Brahms cycle, and the reservations of the previous symphonies apply here. All in all, it emerges as a none-too-careful studio run-through.

Originally, each symphony was coupled with a Schumann overture, which have now been removed, making each CD particularly ungenerous in playing time. Four discs for the price of two full-price discs is hardly compensation, and makes this set a non-starter. Abbado's Berlin Philharmonic set still holds its place as first choice among modern digital cycles (DG 435 683-2).

Symphony No. 1 in C min., Op. 68; Tragic Overture, Op. 81.

(BB) *(*) Warner Apex 0927 44351-2. NYPO, Masur.

Masur is better attuned to the lyrical *Second Symphony* than to No. 1, but despite some first-rate playng from the New York orchestra the result sounds too easy, lacking in tension until the finale.

Symphonies Nos. 1–2; Academic Festival Overture; Tragic Overture.

(B) *(*) Teldec Ultima 8573 84067-2 (2). Cleveland O, Dohnányi.

Dohnányi's reading of the *First Symphony* sets the pattern for his cycle of recordings as a whole: strong and direct, beautifully controlled and finely textured, but rather lacking in the tensions of live communication. The Teldec recording is rich as well as being naturally balanced, finely detailed and full of presence. However, while this is agreeable enough there are many more distinctive versions available. Moreover The *Second Symphony* is one in which Dohnányi's direct, slightly no-nonsense approach to Brahms pays fewest dividends. Superbly played and recorded and with speeds impeccably chosen, the performance yet fails to catch fire or give the feeling of anything more than a brilliant run-through.

Symphonies Nos. 1 and 3.

(BB) **(*) RCA 74321 68009-2. NDR SO, Wand.

Günter Wand's readings are nothing if not individual. In the opening movement of the *First Symphony*, like Toscanini, he brings fierce intensity to the slow introduction by chosing an unusually fast speed, then leading naturally by modular pacing into the main allegro. The extra unity is clear. There is comparable dramatic intensity in the finale, though the choice of tempo for the main marching melody, far slower than the rest, brings uncomfortable changes of gear. Yet with a sense of spontaneity matching that of a live perfomance, the reading remains convincing. The *Third Symphony*, steadily paced, strong and easy, with the exposition repeat observed, again demonstrates Wand's singularity, here bringing out the work's autumnal moods and ending with a sober view of the finale. The sound in both works is inclined to be edgy on top which affects the violins and, in the *Third Symphony*, underlines the reedy twang of the Hamburg woodwind, especially in the slow movement, while the solo horn is none too secure in his solo in the third movement.

Symphony No. 2 in D, Op. 73.

(M) *** Cala CACD 0531. Nat. PO, Stokowski –
MENDELSSOHN: *Symphony No. 4 (Italian).* ***

(M) (***) BBC mono BBCL 4099-2. RPO, Beecham –
BEETHOVEN: *Symphony No. 2.* (***)

Stokowski's recording of the *D major Symphony* was
one of the last he made, in London in 1978. It is a performance of warmth and power, and for all his free
rubato the effect is totally spontaneous with the
symphonic structure unimpaired, first movement
exposition repeat included. The concert hall acoustic
adds richness and breadth to the sound and the reading itself grips the listener throughout, and after the
reprise of the second subject of the finale the brass
ring out to make a thrilling conclusion. The CD
transfer is first class, and with its equally impressive
Mendelssohn coupling, this is one of Stokowski's very
finest later recordings.

This radio recording of Brahms's *Second Symphony*, always a favourite work with Beecham, comes
from an Edinburgh Festival performance given in
August 1956 which has become legendary. Though the
dry Usher Hall acoustic and the bronchial audience
prevent it from matching in sound Beecham's stereo
recording for EMI (currently withdrawn), the incandescence of the performance makes it magnetic, at
once warm and impulsive in the first movement,
richly expressive in the second and elegant in the
third, leading to the fieriest, most biting account of
the finale, with a marked stringendo in the coda and
wild cheering from the audience before the last chord
has ended. The excitement of the event is vividly
caught despite the limited sound.

Symphonies Nos. 3–4.

(BB) ** DG Eloquence (ADD) 469 756-2. VPO, Boehm.

*Symphonies Nos. 3–4; (i) Violin Concerto; Variations
on a Theme of Haydn, Op. 56a.*

(B) ** Teldec Ultima 8573 84068-2 (2). Cleveland O,
Dohnányi; (i) with Zehetmair.

Continuing his cycle, Dohnányi conducts a clear,
direct reading of No. 3, superbly played and recorded.
In sound so beautifully balanced the often thick
orchestration is made transparently clear as well as
naturally weighty, and this is a version which emphasizes classical values, crisply structured rather than
warmly expressive. In the second movement Andante,
taken on the slow side, Dohnányi does not entirely
avoid squareness, and the horn reprise of the main
third-movement theme is forthright rather than
affectionate. The opening of the finale lacks mystery
and the hemiola rhythms of the second subject, for all
the power of the performance, fail to leap aloft.

The reading of the *Fourth* again brings a strong,
finely controlled reading, lacking only occasionally in
a flow of adrenalin. The slow movement is hushed
and thoughtful, the third clear and fresh in its crisp
articulation, while the weight of the finale is well

caught – even if it is not thrust home at the close as
sharply as it might be.

These detailed criticisms are given merely to suggest why – with such superlative playing and an irre-
proachably direct manner, not to mention
outstanding sound – these performances finally lack
something in Brahmsian magic and memorability.

Similarly Zehetmair's is a warm and thoroughly
musical account of the *Violin Concerto*: his timbre is
sweet, and both he and Dohnányi, who accompanies
sympathetically, offer a good response to Brahmsian
lyricism. The Cleveland orchestral playing is beyond
criticism and the Teldec sound balance impressively
natural. But other versions of this concerto have a
much stronger profile and this performance fails to
resonate in the memory.

Boehm's recordings derive from a 1976 boxed set.
The readings are unexpectedly idiosyncratic. Slow
movements, in particular, are unusually slow, and
indeed there is a general lack of the necessary thrust
and impetus in No. 3, until the finale, which then
tapers off to a melancholy coda. No. 4 is overall
rather more impressive (though not in the same
class as Boehm's pre-war 78 set with the Saxon State
Orchestra). Again the finale sparks into life and produces a rousing close. Good analogue recording,
well transferred to CD, but this coupling is very
much an also-ran, even at budget price.

Symphony No. 4 in E min., Op. 98.

(**(*)) Testament mono SBT 2242 (2). Royal Danish O,
Klemperer – BEETHOVEN: *Symphony No. 3; Leonora
No. 3;* MOZART: *Symphony No. 29.* (**(*))

Though the Copenhagen audience in January 1954 is
disagreeably bronchial, and the ensemble is rough by
the standards that Klemperer came to achieve with
the Philharmonia for EMI, the electricity of his reading of Brahms's *Fourth* is most compelling, warmer
and more spontaneously expressive than one might
expect from this rugged conductor. Though in the
Passacaglia of the finale the solo playing is not always
refined, the power of the piece is inescapable, making
one understand the glowing memories of players in
the orchestra as quoted in the Testament note.

CHAMBER MUSIC

Cello Sonatas Nos. 1 in E min., Op. 38; 2 in F, Op. 99.

(**(*)) EMI mono CDC5 57293-2. Du Pré, Barenboim –
BRUCH: *Kol Nidrei.* **(*)

*(i) Cello Sonatas Nos. 1 in E min.; 2 in F, Op. 99; (ii)
in D (arr. of the Violin Sonata in G, Op. 78).*

(B) **(*) RCA 2-CD 74321 84598-2 (2). (i) Ma, Ax; (ii)
Starker, Neriki – RACHMANINOV: *Cello Sonata* **(*);
SCHUMANN: *Adagio and Allegro; Fantasiestücke.* ***

Thanks to Christopher Nupen delving into his great
store of films, we have this long-buried treasure of
unpublished versions by Du Pré and Barenboim of
the two Brahms *Cello Sonatas* as well as Bruch's *Kol*

Nidrei. What is fascinating is to find how different this account of the *Second Sonata* is from the studio recording which Du Pré and Barenboim made in that same period, soon after they had married in 1967 at the height of the Six Day War in Israel. The first movement, at 6'41", is over two minutes shorter than in the studio recording, increasing the passionate urgency of the reading although the repose in the central development section then becomes if anything more intense. Du Pré's characteristic wildness means that intonation occasionally strays, and detail is less cleanly delivered than in the studio performance.

No other movement in either sonata offers quite such a marked contrast, though in each the extra bite of spontaneity adds to the magnetism. Though the mono sound – presumably from the film sound-track – is cramped, with the piano rather shallow and clattery, no devotee of this inspired partnership is likely to be disappointed.

As in the later Sony performances by Ma and Ax (SK 48191) the balance favours the piano, for Ax sometimes produces too thick a sound in climaxes and Ma is, as always, sensitive and smaller in tone. Theirs is an essentially romantic view, and some might find the *E minor Sonata* rather too wayward. They are certainly more measured in their tempi than almost any of their rivals. Ma's *pianissimos* occasionally draw attention to themselves, though the grace and tenderness of his playing is not in question. The claims of these readings reside in their refined lyricism rather than their muscularity, and these artists have splendid rapport. The RCA recording is very truthful. The coupled transcription of the *G major Violin Sonata,* whether or not made by the composer, as is claimed here, is more controversial. Starker plays it boldly, but the cello line generally lies low, and is less well-projected than the piano part. However, the couplings are worthwhile and generous (although the Rachmaninov *Sonata* also has balance problems), and this reissue is certainly worth its asking-price.

Clarinet Quintet in B min., Op. 115.

(BB) *** Warner Apex 0927 44350-2. Leister, Berlin Soloists – MOZART: *Clarinet Quintet.* ***

Karl Leister is no stranger to the Brahms *Clarinet Quintet,* but he has never recorded it more ravishingly than with the Berlin Soloists in 1988. His easy-going lyricism does not mean that there is not a firm overall grip on the proceedings, yet in the elysian slow movement he seems to be tenderly and thoughtfully improvising, and his relaxed warmth is captivating. The mellow grazioso of the Minuet is then followed by a con moto finale which retains the overall mood yet lightens and becomes more passionate as the variations develop. His supporting string group match his playing serenely and they are well balanced and beautifully recorded. A lovely performance, well matched by the Mozart coupling – and this CD is very inexpensive.

String Sextets Nos. 1 in B flat, Op. 18; 2 in G, Op. 36.

(M) *** EMI (ADD) CDM5 74957-2. Y. Menuhin, Masters, Aronowitz, Walfisch, Gendron, Simpson.

Menuhin's group of star players integrate well together and transmit their enjoyment of these warmly lyrical works. The performances are relaxed and agreeably affectionate, with the *G major* work particularly beguiling. Perhaps both opening movements could have more grip, but there is spontaneity here and the mid-1960s recording has retained its original warmth, and now has greater freshness and better definition, without edginess. The humanity of the playing comes over fully.

Violin Sonatas Nos. 1 in G, Op. 78; 2 in A, Op. 100; 3 in D min., Op. 108.

(B) *** Hyp. Helios CDH 55087. Osostowicz, Tomes.

Krysia Osostowicz and Susan Tomes give performances of such natural musicality that criticism is almost disarmed. They phrase with great spontaneity yet with apparently effortless care and artistry, and the interplay between the two partners is instinctive. The Hyperion engineers manage the sound and balance with their customary skill, and theirs is certainly to be preferred to some of the more glamorous rivals now on the market. At its new bargain Helios price this goes straight to the top of the recommended list.

PIANO MUSIC

Piano Sonata No. 3 in F min., Op. 5.

(*) Appian Recordings APR 5632. Arrau – BEETHOVEN: *Piano Sonata No. 3 in C major, Op. 2/3.* **

Piano Sonata No. 3 in F min., Op. 5; 3 Intermezzi, Op. 117; 2 Rhapsodies, Op. 79.

(M) **(*) Sony SMK 89802. Ax.

Emanuel Ax gives an appropriately massive performance of the *F minor Sonata,* but the fortissimo he produces is never ugly and his pianissimo tone is always most refined and of great beauty. The slow movement in particular is played with great tenderness and poetic feeling. There is plenty of space round the aural image and the sound is a joy in itself. Although he is an artist of the highest intelligence, Ax is at times prone to moments of expressive exaggeration and phrases are sometimes self-consciously moulded, almost cossetted, as if he did not quite trust the music to speak for itself. With its attractive encores, this reissue has much going for it, but for all its beauties, and the excellence of the recorded sound, it does not displace Stephen Hough at full price, who also offers the *Ballades* (Hyperion CDA 67237) or Curzon at mid price, coupled with Schubert's last and greatest sonata (Decca 448 978-2).

Arrau had a special feeling for the Brahms *F minor Sonata,* and in this 1978 recital at the Avery Fischer Hall he takes more risks than in his fine commercial recording from 1973. The conception is magnificent, but the sound is not. No details are given of its provenance, but the aural image is too ill-focused, clangorous and brittle to emanate from a radio source and sounds as if it were taken in the wings or in the first few rows. There are far too many microphone bumps. Arrau always has something new to say about great music, but sonic limitations diminish the wider appeal of this reading.

Variations on a Theme by Paganini, Op. 35.

(BB) (**(*)) EMI Encore mono CDE5 75230-2. Michelangeli – BACH/BUSONI: *Partita No. 2: Chaconne* (**(*)); MOZART: *Piano Concerto No. 15* (*).

Michelangeli's prodigious virtuosity here (in 1950) is dazzling, with not a note out of place, and Paganini's own legendary bravura looms over Brahms's variations, although there is no lack of light and shade. The piano recording is shallow on top, but acceptable.

German Requiem, Op. 45.

*** TDK **DVD** DV-MUSIK. Bonney, Terfel, Swedish R. Ch., Eric Ericson Chamber Ch., Berlin PO, Abbado. Video director: Coles.

(M) **(*) DG (ADD) 463 661-2. Janowitz, Waechter, Vienna Singverein, BPO, Karajan.

Abbado's account of the *Requiem* with Barbara Bonney and Bryn Terfel as soloists and the Swedish Radio and Eric Ericson choirs, together with the Berlin Philharmonic itself, was recorded at the Vienna Musikverein in April 1997. It is in every way highly impressive, and there is a moving directness of utterance. We are also spared any attempts at visual gimmickry. This is Brahms pure and simple, with sympathetic and intelligent direction from Bob Coles and the camera completely at the service of the music. Strongly recommended.

Karajan's beautifully refined performance of Brahms's big choral work emerges more vividly in its new Originals transfer, and one enjoys its many beauties, not least Gundula Janowitz's fresh approach to the music. Other versions may convey more immediate power, but although it is not a prime recommendation, this recording will not disappoint Karajan's admirers.

BRITTEN, Benjamin (1913–76)

Clarinet Concerto Movement (orch. Matthews).

(B) *** Hyp. Helios CDH 55060. King, ECO, Wordsworth – ARNOLD: *Clarinet Concertos Nos. 1–2; Scherzetto*; MACONCHY: *Concertinos*.

Benny Goodman, having commissioned Bartók to write *Contrasts*, turned in 1942 to the young Benjamin Britten, then in the United States, to write a concerto for him. Sadly, just before Britten returned to England, Goodman suggested a delay, and the composer never even sorted out the sketches. Colin Matthews, who worked closely with Britten during his last three years, has here fathomed what Britten intended and has orchestrated the result to make a highly attractive short piece, alternately energetic and poetic, with material adroitly interchanged and percussion used most imaginatively. Thea King, as in the rest of the

disc, plays the piece most persuasively, making one regret deeply that it was never completed.

(i) Piano Concerto, Op. 13; (ii) Prelude and fugue for strings, Op. 29.

(B) (**) EMI mono CDZ5 74781-2 (i) Jacques Abram, Philh. O, Menges; (ii) RPO, Del Mar – RUBBRA: *Piano Concerto* (***).

Jacques Abram offers the première recording of the Britten concerto made in 1956. The American pianist was forty-one when he recorded the concerto with Herbert Menges and the Philharmonia Orchestra: it was originally coupled with the Rawsthorne *First Concerto* with Moura Lympany, though later reappeared coupled with the Rubbra. Abram is an effective enough soloist though others find much greater subtlety and poetry in this wonderful score. Norman Del Mar's record of the Britten *Prelude and fugue for strings*, written in 1943 for Boyd Neel and first issued in harness with Lutyens *O saisons, ô châteaux* and the Schoenberg *Suite in G for strings*, is a bright forward recording (as was the original). The sound comes up well and the transfers are faithful to the original.

Double Concerto for Violin, Viola & Orchestra (edited Matthews).

(BB) *** Arte Nova 74321 89826-2. Schmid, Raiskin, Berlin SO, Shambadal – BENJAMIN: *Romantic Fantasy*; BRUCH: *Double Concerto*. ***

The prize-winning young violinist, Benjamin Schmid, and the superb Russian viola-player, David Raiskin, have made a speciality of playing the *Double Concerto* of Britten, giving some 25 performances since 1998 including the premieres in no fewer than ten countries. Written in 1932 when Britten was in his late teens, the work was not heard till 1997, when Colin Matthews prepared a full score from the closely annotated short-score found in the composer's archive at Aldeburgh. It is an elusive work but a fascinating one, warmer and more characteristic than the *Sinfonietta* which Britten nominated as his Opus 1. It inspires the two soloists to a thoughtful reading, not as individual as the premiere recording with Kremer and Bashmet for Erato but more polished, with brilliant accompaniment from the Berlin Symphoniker. The coupling on this super-budget issue could not be more apt or attractive.

(i) Simple Symphony, Op. 4; (ii) Les Illuminations, Op. 18; Nocturne, Op. 60; (iii) Rosa Mystica.

(M) **(*) ASV PLT 8503. (i) Northern Sinf., Hickox; (ii) Rolfe Johnson, LMP, Glover; (iii) Eton Col. Chapel Ch., Allwood.

Any new recording of *Les Illuminations* and the *Nocturne* is inevitably compared with the classic Decca Pears/Britten version, and this ASV recording lacks the intensity and sheer personality, not to mention the clearly detailed projection of that classic account. However, the more atmospheric (though not blurred sound) of the ASV recording brings out other aspects to the score and the performance has its own insights. Readers who do not respond to Peter Pears will find refreshment here, with the opening of the *Nocturne*, for example, very haunting. Anthony Rolfe Johnson's approach is warmly lyrical, and he colours the vocal line with subtle detail, without any distracting idiosyncrasy, while Jane Glover's relaxed direction coaxes some lovely playing from the LMP. The sound is warm and well balanced. Hickox's version of the *Simple Symphony*, though not as electrifying as the composer's own, is beautifully played and among the best of the digital versions, and the short *Rosa Mystica* makes an unusual bonus. Texts are not included.

CHAMBER MUSIC

String Quartet No. 1 in D, Op. 11; 3 Divertimenti, Op. 36.

⚫ *** Challenge Classics CC 72106. Brodsky Qt. – TCHAIKOVSKY: *String Quartet No. 1.* ⚫ *** Available from www.challengeclassics.com.

At the end of February 2002 the Brodsky Quartet gave three outstanding concerts at the Blackheath Concert Halls in which they unexpectedly combined the three numbered quartets of Britten with the three of Tchaikovsky. The result was extraordinarily stimulating, as the present coupling (recorded at The Maltings the previous year) demonstrates. The spontaneity of their playing immediately grips the listener, with the gleamingly luminous opening of the *D major Quartet* bringing a raptly concentrated pianissimo, and this degree of intensity pervades the whole performance.

The crisply impetuous, sardonic Scherzo and the deep feeling of the *Andante calmo* contrast with the bustle of the finale, with its fugato and broad lyrical melody jostling with each other for our attention. The *Three Divertimenti* of 1936 are equally vividly characterized, the flimsy central *Waltz* delectably slight and transparent and full of charm. The recording could hardly be more real and present.

VOCAL MUSIC

Canticles Nos. 1–5; Folksongs, arr. Britten: *The Ash Grove; The Plough Boy; The Foggy Dew; Greensleeves; O Waly Waly; The Sally Gardens; There's none to soothe.*

*** Virgin VC5 45525-2. Bostridge, Daniels, Maltman, Drake, with Brown, Brewer.

Ian Bostridge's heady tenor is ideally suited to the inflections of Britten's music, and here in the *Five Canticles* he gives colourful, vigorously dramatic readings of pieces that can seem wayward, helped by inspired accompaniment from Julius Drake. The longest of the five, No. 2, setting the story of Abraham and Isaac in the words of the Chester Miracle Play, brings the most striking performance, with Bostridge joined by the counter-tenor, David Daniels, each characterfully distinctive, yet well matched. The set-

tings of Edith Sitwell and of T. S. Eliot (with Christopher Maltman as baritone) are also made the more dramatic with high dynamic contrasts, and the *Fifth Canticle*, with harp accompaniment, brings eartweaking textures. The seven folksong arrangements, including the most popular ones, are shared among the three singers. Excellent recording.

(i) *Les Illuminations* (song-cycle), *Op. 18;* (ii) *Nocturne;* (iii) *Serenade for Tenor, Horn & Strings, Op. 31.*

(B) *** CfP 575 5632. Ainsley with (ii) Britten Sinf. wind soloists; (iii) Pyatt; Britten Sinf. Strings; Cleobury.

The ideal triptych of Britten's three great orchestral song cycles finds John Mark Ainsley echoing the example of the inspirer, Peter Pears, in the shading and moulding of each phrase, above all in the *Serenade*, where the brilliant horn-playing of David Pyatt provides an extra reason for recommending the CfP disc. Ainsley's range of expression is wide, and under pressure the voice grows a little rough, as in the final Shakespeare stting of the *Nocturne*. But that is contrasted with an exceptionally beautiful use of the head-voice, with total freedom in the upper register, as in the *Lyke-Wake Dirge* from the *Serenade*. Warm, immediate recording.

OPERA

Death in Venice (opera; complete).

** Arthaus DVD 100 172. Tear, Opie, Chance, Glyndebourne Ch., L. Sinf., Jenkins. (S/D: Stephen Lawless, Martha Clarke. Producer: Dennis Marks.)

This Glyndebourne production of Britten's last opera, based on Thomas Mann's celebrated novella, offers a stark, even brutal view of a piece which originally, thanks both to Britten's score and John Piper's sets, highlighted the beauty of Venice. With Lawless and Clarke, using bare sets by Tobias Hoheise, predominantly black, blotting out the beauty of the city on water, the result seen in close-up is even more claustrophobic in presenting the dilemma of Aschenbach, the celebrated author, who to his horror finds himself passionately attracted to the young boy Tadzio.

Robert Tear's vividly detailed, totally compelling portrayal of Aschenbach is masterly, and his characterization may prompt many to consider the set, even though the voice itself is wanting in bloom, and very different from the moving but more relaxed approach of Peter Pears, for whom the role was written.

Similarly Alan Opie in the multiple baritone roles of characters dogging Aschenbach's path is far more sinister than John Shirley-Quirk, plainly representing evil, and even Tadzio is finally made to leer at Aschenbach, suggesting that he is after all the messenger of evil too, something quite different from Britten's original concept. In the countertenor role of Apollo, Michael Chance is also ideally cast, the opponent of evil and death, finally worsted.

The result is undeniably powerful, and musically the set has a lot going for it – sensitive orchestral playing and Tear and Alan Opie thrillingly involving in a piece that can seem episodic, and with the conductor, Graeme Jenkins, also drawing the threads tautly together.

But the production is another matter: the action is confined within a distinctly cramped, small arena and there is no feeling of space or sense of atmosphere. This shoe-box dimension of the sets really lets the opera down badly. Nor is the recording as ample as one could wish and the piano sound is pretty uningratiating. Thus, vision adds little if anything to the musical experience and, such is its overwhelming claustrophobia, even detracts from it. Subtitles are provided in French, German and Spanish but there is no original English text, which at times would have been helpful.

However, readers will find the pioneering Decca CDs (425 669-2) under Steuart Bedford, with Peter Pears as Aschenbach, James Bowman as the voice of Apollo and John Shirley Quirk in multiple roles, a far more satisfying experience in every way.

The Turn of the Screw (opera; complete).

*** Virgin VCD5 45521-2 (2). Bostridge, Rodgers, Henschel, Tierney, Leang, Wise, Mahler CO, Harding.
(*) Arthaus **DVD 100 198. Field, Davies, Greager, Obata, Stuttgart RSO, Bedford. (Director: Michael Hampe. V/D: Claus Viller.)

Vividly recorded in atmospheric sound at the Snape Maltings, Britten's own concert-hall, with the chamber orchestra regularly adding to the dramatic impact, notably in the writing for timpani, Harding's version on Virgin of this most tautly constructed of Britten's operas brings many qualities to distinguish it from previous recordings. The headily fluent performance of Ian Bostridge in the Peter Pears roles of the Prologue and Peter Quint is specially memorable. Bostridge is lighter with his exceptionally free upper register, creepy though not as darkly sinister as Peter Pears or other predecessors. As the Prologue makes clear, Bostridge and Harding bring a freely volatile, at times improvisatory quality to the music with plenty of light and shade, again helped by the wide-ranging digital recording. Joan Rodgers is very well cast as the Governess, spontaneously expressive, vividly conveying her growing fears without seeming as neurotic as some rivals. It is good too to have not just the role of Miles sung by a boy treble but the role of Flora sung by a girl of the appropriate age rather than an adult. That adds to the horror of innocence corrupted, while Jane Henschel as Mrs Grose and Vivien Tierney as Miss Jessel are first-rate, clear and firm, characterizing well.

The hero of this Arthaus production is Steuart Bedford, who gets vibrant singing and playing from all concerned. Helen Field is a thoroughly convincing governess and the cast is in every respect excellent, even if Machita Obata looks a little too mature for

Flora. A good production, very atmospheric, and with generally unobtrusive video direction.

BRUCH, Max (1838–1920)

Double Concerto in E min., for Clarinet, Viola & Orchestra, Op. 88.

*** Sup. SU 3554-2. Peterkova, Besa, Prague Philh., Bĕvlohlávek – MENDELSSOHN: 2 Concert Pieces; ROSSINI: Introduction, Theme and Variations; Variations in C . ***

Max Bruch's Double Concerto for Clarinet and Viola is as lusciously romantic a work as his ever-popular G minor Violin Concerto, the passionate inspiration of a composer in his mid-seventies. Sadly, it was damned from the start by appearing in 1913 when such uninhibited outpouring was deeply unfashionable. With the viola-player, Alexander Besa, as an inspired partner, the Czech clarinettist, Ludmila Peterkova, includes it in this delightfully off-beat collection of neglected clarinet music, warmly accompanied by Jiri Bĕlohlávek and the Prague Philharmonia. She is an artist who is not only warmly expressive, but sparkles in everything she plays.

Double Concerto for Violin & Viola, Op. 88.

(BB) *** Arte Nova 74321 89826-2. Schmid, Raiskin, Berlin SO, Shambadal – BENJAMIN: Romantic Fantasy; BRITTEN: Double Concerto. ***

At 73 Bruch wrote his ripely romantic Double Concerto, unashamedly ignoring any stylistic developments that had taken place since his youth. Here it is given in its alternative version for violin instead of clarinet. Schmid and Raiskin give a superb performance, flawless in intonation, observing the allegro markings in the second and third movements more faithfully than their direct rivals on RCA, Bashmet and Tretiakov. This comes with the perfect coupling of two other works on the disc for violin, viola and orchestra.

Kol Nidrei, Op. 47.

(**(*)) EMI mono CDC5 57293-2. Du Pré, Israel PO, Barenboim – BRAHMS: Cello Sonatas Nos. 1–2 (**(*)).

Du Pré's account of Bruch's Kol Nidrei, like the Brahms sonatas discovered by Christopher Nupen in his film archive, was recorded in 1968 when the Israel Philharmonic was visiting London. It also sweeps one along in its spontaneous warmth, deeply dedicated in the prayerful first half and passionate at the climax. A most welcome bonus to the store of Jacqueline Du Pré's recordings.

Scottish Fantasy (for violin and orchestra), Op. 46.

(M) *** Decca (ADD) 470 258-2 (2). D. Oistrakh, LSO, Horenstein – MOZART: Sinfonia concertante etc. **(*); HINDEMITH: Violin Concerto ***.

The extrovert 1962 Oistrakh/Horenstein performance of the Scottish Fantasia owes nearly as much to the conductor as the soloist. The expansive dignity of the opening of the brass shows immediately how fine the orchestral contribution is going to be, and Oistrakh's playing throughout is ravishing, enhancing the stature of the work immeasurably. The slow movement is especially memorable, and, with superb 1962 sound, this is one of the top choices for this work, now in Decca's Legends series.

Symphonies Nos. 1 in E flat, Op. 28; 2 in F min., Op. 36; 3 in E, Op. 51.

(B) *** EMI double fforte CZS5 75157-2 (2). Gürzenich O or Cologne PO, Conlon – SCHREKER: *Prelude to a Grand Opera.* ***

In James Conlon's convincing performances, both orchestras (it is not clear which plays which work) emphasize the music's Brahmsian and Schumann-esque derivations. A good case is made for the *Third Symphony* here, with the romantic opening richly done, the slow-movement variations warmly effective, and the Scherzo (which the composer regarded as the finest movement in each of these works) is made to sound original in its scoring. Only the finale lets the piece down. The orchestral playing is committed throughout, even if at times greater drive is needed from the conductor. However, reservations are put to one side when the reissue is not only inexpensive but includes a red-blooded account of Schreker's vividly colourful *Prelude to a Grand Opera.*

BRUCKNER, Anton (1824–96)

Symphonies Nos. 1–9 (complete).

(M) **(*) RCA (ADD) 09026. Cologne RSO, Wand (also available separately: Nos. 1 (09026 63931-2); 2 (09026 63932-2); 3 (09026 63933-2); 4 (09026 63934-2); 5 (09026 63935-2); 6 (09026 63936-2); 7 (09026 639367-2); 8–9 (09026 639368-2 (2)).

Symphony No. 4 (Romantic) (1878 version, Ed. Haas).

(M) *** RCA 74321 93041-2 (2). NDR SO, Wand. – SCHUBERT: *Symphony No. 5 in B flat* *** (includes interview with Wand).

Günter Wand's final survey of the Bruckner symphonies (1974–81) with the Cologne Radio Symphony Orchestra shows him as a dedicated Brucknerian who rarely falters in his majestic progress. His accounts of Nos. 5 and 6 do not match Jochum but elsewhere (in Nos. 2 and 8 particularly) he is sometimes to be preferred.

In No. 1 he uses the 1891 version of the score with its richer tonal palette and makes a very persuasive case for so doing, though some collectors may find the gear change when the second group arrives in the first movement a little disruptive. Nos. 2 and 3 are well structured and, although not as powerful as the very finest versions, the interpretations are well considered and unmannered.

No. 4 is one of the finest of the cycle; Wand holds the score together extremely well and produces distinguished playing from the Cologne Orchestra throughout. But by the side of the *Fourth*, Nos. 5 and 6 are comparatively disappointing. Again there are disruptive changes of gear in the first movement of No. 5; the slow movement on the other hand is very eloquent. More surprisingly, in No. 6 the actual quality of the orchestral playing, particularly in the Scherzo, lets the side down somewhat, but the Cologne players return to full, disciplined form in the *Seventh*, playing with ardour and conviction. Wand incidentally misses out the famous cymbal clash in the slow movement, which is given a reading of great dignity.

The planners were wise to choose the 1979 recording of the *Eighth*, rather than Wand's more recent and less convincing account with the North German Radio Symphony Orchestra. With his Cologne players he gives a reading of natural and unaffected eloquence, well paced and finely structured. The *Ninth* then makes a dignified and spacious close to the series. Tempi are sensible, and again the performance is finely shaped.

As a whole the cycle has much to recommend it. Except in No. 6, Wand is never less than perceptive, and at times he and the fine Colgne Orchestra achieve real inspiration. The studio recordings were made in the Klaus von Bismarck Saal of the West German Radio. They are are all analogue and the current remastering brings much improved sound compared with the older LPs. The acoustic has pleasing warmth and detail is well defined. Though the recordings are not quite in the demonstration category, they are very good indeed, spacious and well balanced.

The symphonies are additionally all available separately at mid price, and alongside the complete set RCA have issued a brand new digital recording of the *Fourth Symphony* (the reading even more spacious than the earlier account), coupled with Schubert's *Fifth Symphony*. Both are 'live' performances, made not long before the conductor died. They are of high calibre, the Schubert particularly warm, gracious and vital, beautifully recorded. Additionally this 2-disc set includes an interview, 'Serving Music with Devotion', illustrated with excerpts from *Symphonies Nos. 4, 5, 6,* and *9*. Being spoken in German, this is perhaps of less interest to English-speaking collectors, although a translation is included in the accompanying booklet.

Symphony No. 00 in F min.; Overture in G min.

(BB) *** Arte Nova 74321 84434-2. Saarbrücken RSO, Skrowaczewski.

Unlike most cycles of the Bruckner's symphonies, Skrowaczewski's with the Saarbrücken Orchestra includes this first attempt at writing a symphony, completed in 1863 when the composer was already in his late thirties. It is a fine performance, very well recorded, making an outstanding bargain. The inspiration is fresh and open with many echoes of Mendelssohn and Schumann, but already there are

Bruckner fingerprints, notably in the hushed and tender slow movement and the Scherzo with its rugged contrasts. The *Overture in D minor* from the same period makes an ideal fill-up with its mysterious slow introduction leading to a light, Mendelssohnian Allgro.

Symphonies Nos. oo in F min. (Study Symphony); o in D min. (Die Nullte).

(B) *** Teldec Ultima 0927 42398-2 (2). Frankfurt RSO, Inbal.

Georg Tintner has included these two early symphonies in his Bruckner cycle and many will turn to those more modern Naxos recordings (see our main volume). But Inbal and his orchestra are in excellent form and they approach both symphonies with total freshness as if they were mature works. The character of the opening movement of *Die Nullte*, a work that at times portends the greatness to come, is immediately caught at the atmospheric opening. This is not an easy movement to hold together, but Inbal succeeds both in retaining tension and in creating a natural forward flow, as he does in the powerful and exciting account of the finale. It is good to have these two early works together and this reissue is one of the most impressive of the Inbal series.

Symphony No. o in D min. (Die Nullte); String Quintet in F: Adagio (arr. for string orchestra).

(BB) *** Arte Nova 74321 75510-2. Saarbrücken RSO, Skrowaczewski.

Written in the winter of 1863–4, this D minor Symphony, universally known as *No. o (Die Nullte)*, brings striking stylistic developments over the *F minor Symphony* completed only months before. The very opening, with its pianissimo ostinato repetitions quickly expanding in crescendo, could only have been written by Bruckner, and much else gives clear foretastes of his mature style, notably the finale with its angular unison passages for heavy brass. The slow movement, characteristically hushed and dedicated, brings clear echoes of middle-period Wagner, notably *Lohengrin*. Skrowaczewski, following the pattern of the rest of his Bruckner cycle, conducts a strong, taut reading, with refined string playing, making an excellent bargain. The string orchestra arrangement of the *Adagio* from the *F major String Quintet* makes an apt coupling.

Symphonies Nos. 1 in C min.; 2 in C min. (original versions).

(B) ** Teldec Ultima 0927 41399-2 (2). Frankfurt RSO, Inbal.

Bruckner's *First* is a rather intractable symphony. The composer's restless alternations of heavy tuttis, energetic passages more lightly scored and lyrical blossoming are less well knit together than in his mature works. Inbal's direct, comparatively brisk approach – with the tempo changes in the first movement convincingly handled – makes quite a good case for the earlier (1866) Linz version, although the lack of opulence in the recording adds to the impression that the end result is lightweight.

In the Frankfurt performance of No. 2, Inbal offers a version which is comparatively close to the 1872 Haas Edition, which, like Tintner's Naxos recording (8.554006), retains the Scherzo and Trio with all repeats and uses the original horn, instead of the clarinet, at the end of the slow movement. The closing string chords are missing here, which brings one up with a start. For the most part the playing is good without being outstanding, and the recording is excellent. However Tintner's account remains first choice for those seeking the composer's first thoughts.

Symphonies Nos. 2 in C min. (1877 version); 4 in E flat (Romantic).

(B) **(*) EMI (ADD) CZS5 74837-2 (2). Dresden State O, Jochum.

Jochum's Bruckner has a special magnetism, though some will have reservations on points of style with his free variation of tempo within a movement, especially his accelerandi in the big crescendi, evident in both these symphonies, recorded in 1975 (No. 2) and 1980 (No. 4); this is a characteristic that occurs throughout his cycle (available in a bargain box). However, Jochum's natural affinity of temperament with the Austrian master gives these massive structures a compelling, unforced concentration that brings out their architectural grandeur. At budget price, this is well worth considering if the coupling is desired. But Chailly on Decca is recommended for No. 2 (436 154-2).

Symphony No. 3 in D min. (1877 version).

(*) Arthaus **DVD 100 320. Bavarian RSO, Solti – STRAVINSKY: *Symphony in 3 Movements*. *(*)

Recorded for television by Bavarian Radio in 1993, this Arthaus DVD offers straightforward video presentations of Solti conducting the Bavarian Radio Orchestra in two sharply contrasted works, with the Bruckner rather curiously coupled with the Stravinsky *Symphony*. Solti is a dramatic Brucknerian rather than a warmly expressive one. The sound as well as the interpretation is bright and incisive, with the orchestral balance on DVD rather light on bass. Dynamic contrasts are extreme, bringing out the monumental quality of the outer movements, with the third-movement Scherzo fiercely rhythmic. It is a characteristic Solti reading, which will please his admirers. However, the Stravinsky coupling is much more controversial.

Symphony Nos. 3 in D min. (1877 version); 8 in C min.

(BB) *** Ph. Duo 470 534-2 (2). VPO, Haitink.

Haitink's was one of the first digital recording of the 1877 version of the *Third Symphony*, which Bruckner embarked on after Hermann Levi had rejected the *Eighth Symphony*, making a number of cuts suggested by the Schalk brothers. This version is favoured by many Bruckner scholars. Questions of editions apart, this is a performance of enormous breadth and majesty, and Philips give it a recording to match. The playing of the VPO is glorious throughout, and even collectors who have alternative versions should consider this magnificent issue. No less enticing is the recording of the *Eight Symphony*, with the same formidable combination of conductor and orchestra, and outstanding engineering (by the doyen of Philips engineers, Volker Strauss), and the results are outstanding. The performance is remarkable for its breadth and nobility, and Haitink has the full measure of its majesty and grandeur. Not only does it possess great dramatic sweep, its slow movement has greater depth than his earlier reading. The VPO play with great fervour and warmth, and the recorded sound is sumptuous. If it doesn't quite match Karajan's magisterial DG accounts, it is still among the most satisfying versions available. In short, these two symphonies make an outstanding bargain on the Philips Duo label.

Symphony Nos. 4 in E flat (Romantic); 5 in B flat.

(BB) ** Ph. Duo 470 547-2 (2). VPO, Haitink.

Haitink's Vienna recording of the *Fourth Symphony* has no want of authority and has predictably fine orchestral playing and a well-defined Philips recording to commend it. But it falls short of the highest levels of inspiration that this conductor can command; there are many moments of eloquence, but there is ultimately more prose than poetry. However, the conductor is on his best Bruckner form in the recording of the *Fifth*, which is superbly recorded and here the orchestral playing is of the very highest quality. The only snag, perhaps, is the slow movement, which is rather on the brisk side: Haitink knocks four minutes off Karajan's timing, yet at the same time succeeds in conveying an unhurried effect. Anyway, this is a performance of nobility and is presented in impressive sound.

Symphonies Nos. 4 in E flat; 7 in E.

(B) ** Teldec Ultima 3984 21338-2 (2). NYPO, Masur.

Kurt Masur's New York account of No. 4, recorded at the Avery Fisher Hall in 1993, has all the breadth and much of the finesse one could ask for. Those with keen memories of the Mehta years can be assured that the orchestra now produces a far more cultured and refined sound. Masur's command of the architecture of the piece is undoubtedly impressive and there is no want of feeling. The weakness lies perhaps in the slow movement, where concentration flags, certainly among the audience. The *Seventh* also comes from a live concert, but it dates from two years earlier, when Masur's relationship with the orchestra was in the bloom of youth and he was working hard to banish the unrefined sonority that was associated with his predecessor. The sound is certainly better blended than before. His opening is very spacious and expansive, with consequent accelerandi later on. The performance is generally more characterful than his Leipzig account and has quite a lot going for it – albeit not quite enough to overcome the unpleasing acoustic of the Avery Fisher Hall, hardly a Bruckner venue. Admirers of this conduc-

tor will find the present two-for-the-price-of-one set good value, and it is certainly preferable to its DG competitor; but Chailly is a much stronger bargain recommendation for the *Seventh*, and at mid price Jochum or Karajan more than hold their own for the *Fourth*.

Symphonies Nos. 5 in B flat; 6 in A (original versions).

(B) *(*) Teldec Ultima R0927 41400-2 (2). Frankfurt RSO, Inbal.

Inbal makes a promising start to the *Fifth Symphony* and gets good playing from the Frankfurt Radio forces. Unfortunately the slow movement is far too brisk to be convincing – lasting 14 minutes as against Jochum's 19 and Karajan's 21. In the *Sixth Symphony* the slow movement is the best part of the performance, with fine string playing, but the reading overall is a little short on personality. After the *Fifth*, the *Sixth* is probably the least well served of Inbal's cycle although the recording is full-bodied and spacious, and has a dramatically wide dynamic range. But for No. 5 one should turn to Sinopoli (● DG 460 527-2) and for No. 6 Chailly (Decca 458 189-2).

Symphony No. 7 in E (original version).

(BB) ** Warner Apex 0927 40817-2. Frankfurt RSO, Inbal.

For excellence of orchestral playing and vividness of recording, Inbal's *Seventh* is well up to the standard of his Bruckner series, using the original scores; but the performance itself, although not lacking an overall structural grip, is without the full flow of adrenalin that can make this symphony so compulsive. The great climax of the slow movement is much less telling without the famous contribution from the cymbals.

Symphony No. 7 in E.

(B) ** DG (ADD) 469 761-2. Chicago SO, Barenboim.

Barenboim's account of the *Seventh Symphony* must be numbered among his more successful ventures in this terrain. He gives a noble account of the first movement and offers some thoughtful and perceptive moments elsewhere. However, the well-lit Chicago sound lacks the cultured sonorities of the Berlin and Amsterdam orchestras, and the performance as a whole has neither the quality of inspiration nor the sheer atmosphere of the very finest versions. This is not a performance that stays in the mind afterwards, as do Karajan's, Haitink's and Jochum's. But first choice rests with Harnoncourt (Teldec 3984 24488-2).

Symphony No. 8 in C min.

*** Decca 466 653-2. Concg. O, Chailly.
*** RCA 74321 82866-2 (2). BPO, Wand.

Chailly reinforces his claims as an outstanding Brucknerian in this incandescent reading of Bruckner's *Eighth* in the Nowak Edition. Despite the refinement of the playing, he conveys an appropriate degree of ruggedness in Bruckner's bold structures, with the wide dynamic range beautifully caught in the splendid Decca recording. The finale, not as bitingly urgent as it can be, in compensation conveys the composer's joyfully unruly inspiration. That Chailly uses the Nowak Edition brings the benefit that though his speeds are as spacious as you could want, the whole symphony is squeezed (as with Boulez – DG 459 678-2) on to a single CD.

Recorded live in the Berlin Philharmonie in January 2001, Wand's reading of the massive *Eighth Symphony* in the Haas Edition brings a deeply dedicated performance, weightier and more expansive than his 1979 version with the Cologne Radio Symphony Orchestra. With full-bodied sound, the power of his interpretation comes over at full force, even if the lack of a true pianissimo means that the slow movement is less poignant than before, warm and open-hearted rather than mysterious, yet superbly controlled over the massive span of the *Adagio*. The tensions of a live event also add to the impact of the performance, with the Scherzo and the finale both conveying a degree of wildness in their thrusting power. A valuable alternative to the earlier version.

Symphonies Nos. 8 in C min. (original 1887 version); 9 in D min. (original version, 1887–96).

(B) **(*) Teldec Ultima 0927 41401-2 (2). Frankfurt RSO, Inbal.

Eliahu Inbal concludes his stimulating series with generally impressive first versions of Nos. 8 and 9. In No. 8 there are considerable divergences from the versions we know, and in both symphonies the playing is often very fine. Inbal is scrupulously attentive to detail; however in No. 9 there is not the sense of scale that is to be found on the best of his rivals.

Symphony No. 9 in D min.

(M) **(*) Decca (ADD) 468 494-2. VPO, Mehta.

There are moments of considerable power in Mehta's reading, which comes from his vintage Decca period in the mid-1960s. The orchestral playing has great splendour, although at the opening of the finale not everyone will respond to the somewhat febrile vibrato on the strings. In overall cogency and sense of mystery this does not match Jochum, but the newly remastered Decca sound is overwhelmingly rich and spectacular. While this last appeared at bargain price on Belart, for collectors where the quality of the recording is paramount, the extra cost will surely not be considered a deterrent. But Bruno Walter's account of No. 9 is very special (● Sony SMK 64483).

BRUMEL, Antoine (c. 1460–c. 1520)

Missa: Et ecce terrae motus; Sequentia: Dies irae, Dies illa.

● (M) *** Sony SMK 89613. Huelgas Ens., Nevel.

Missa: Et ecce terrae motus; Lamentations; Magnificat secondi toni.

*** Gimell CDGIM 026. Tallis Scholars, Philips.

Brumel succeeded Josquin as *maestro di cappella* at Ferrarra. Lassus himself prepared and took part in a performance of the 12-part mass, *Et ecce terrae motus*, in Munich in the 1570s, and this is the only copy of the work that survives. It is not just the contrapuntal ingenuity of Brumel's music that impresses but the sheer beauty of sound with which we are presented. Brumel was not only one of the first to write a polyphonic *Requiem* but the very first to make a polyphonic setting of the sequence *Dies irae, Dies illa*. This is a more severe work than the glorious 12-part Mass which occupies the bulk of this CD, and it is written in a more medieval tonal language. The performances by the Huelgas Ensemble under their founder–director, Paul van Nevel, are fervent and eloquent and vividly bring this music back to life. This recording, made in the ample acoustic of the Irish Chapel in Liège, is resplendent.

The Tallis Scholars are hardly less impressive than the Huelgas Ensemble. In some respects their disc is complementary in that they opt for a different solution to the *Agnus Dei*, which is incomplete in the Munich manuscript. Nevel favours a Danish source that Phillips and his editor reject on the grounds that it uses six voices and voices of different range. The texture in their performance has greater transparency and clarity than the richer, darker sonority of the Nevel. Both can be recommended. However, the re-issued Sony version now has a distinct price advantage and readers who have not already acquired it (or the Hyperion alternative) should lose no time in securing a copy, before Sony delete it again!

BRUSA, Elisabetta (born 1954)

Florestan (orchestral portrait); Nittemero Symphony; Messidor (fantasy); La Triade (symphonic poem).

(BB) **(*) Naxos 8.555266. Nat. SO of Ukraine, Mastrangelo.

Born in Milan, Elisabetta Brusa studied at the Conservatoire, before going on to participate at Dartington and Tanglewood (with a Fulbright bursary), later working with Hans Keller in London. Although she writes 'neo-tonally', her melodic lines are clear, and the ear always senses a key centre. *Messidor* is the most immediately attractive work here, an orchestral fantasy inspired by 'A Midsummer Night's Dream'. It is most fetchingly scored, with a jauntily catchy main theme that reminds one of early Delius, though dissonance clouds the coda. *Florestan* (1997) evokes Schumann's imaginary character. It opens ardently and melodramatically with strings and horns, but it is the atmospherically lyrical music that is the more memorable.

'Rain pours down incessantly' in *La Triade* (1994), an orchestral 'curtain of water', its scenario drawn both by an Aesop fable (with a fox and snake the central characters) and Leonardo da Vinci's description of 'The Deluge'. An impressively drenched orchestral canvas depicts the flooded river and the pair of marooned animals, but the work ends peacefully.

The *Nittemero* ('Night and Day') *Symphony* (1985–88) is scored for 14 players, yet one does not sense any economy of texture and again the ear is immediately struck by the composer's vivid orchestral world. The three-movement work is cyclic, depicting the 24 hours, from midday to midday. The opening Rondo, both rhythmically and lyrically, suggests a busy *Afternoon*, with some striking writing for the solo trumpet, followed by a *Largo* (a passionate, sultry nocturnal, with an exotic background, that recalls Villa-Lobos). Sonata form is reserved for the good-tempered mood of the following morning, where the brass are strongly featured, plus a neo-romantic solo violin cadenza. The work ends very confidently, as does the Adams-like minimalist *Fanfare*, which brings a positive end to the programme.

The performances here are bold and committed and generally well recorded, except that the Ukrainian violins sound thin in their upper range. But this is a promising debut, and worth sampling at Naxos price.

BURGON, Geoffrey (born 1941)

(i) *Requiem;* (ii) *Nunc Dimittis.*

(M) *** Decca 470 380-2. (i) Smith, Murray, Rolfe Johnson, London Symphony Ch., City of L. Sinf., Hickox; (ii) King's College, Cambridge, Ch., Cleobury.

Geoffrey Burgon is best known for the music written for *Brideshead Revisited* and the *Nunc dimittis* used for *Tinker, Tailor, Soldier, Spy,* which is included on this CD. In the *Requiem* his style owes much to Benjamin Britten and, perhaps, early Messiaen. Much of the writing is static in feeling but highly atmospheric. The composer has shown considerable resource in his handling of texture, and, though the melodic invention is unmemorable, the overall impression is quite powerful. The work enjoys committed advocacy from the artists and fine 1981 recording quality. Although the aspiration of the music may not quite be matched by its substance, this score still has the power to hold the listener, and the disc is well worth investigating.

BUSONI, Ferruccio (1866–1924)

Berceuse élégiaque, Op. 42; (i) *Concertino for Clarinet and Small Orchestra; Geharnischte Suite; 2 Studies for Doktor Faust, Op. 51; Tanz–Walzer.*

*** Chan. 9920. (i) Bradbury; BBC PO, Järvi.

The *Geharnischte Suite* is the rarity here. It was written in 1895 during Busoni's time in Helsinki and dedicated to members of his circle there – Sibelius (whose cause he championed in Germany), Armas and Eero Järnefelt, and the writer Adolf Paul. It was revised in 1903, and although not top-drawer Busoni, it is still rewarding and inventive. Neeme Järvi and the BBC Philharmonic produce sumptuous performances of the moving, dream-like *Berceuse élégiaque,* written on the death of the composer's mother, and the inspired *Sarabande and Cortège,* the *Studies for Doktor Faust.* The *Tanz Walzer* also found their way into *Doktor Faust,* where they were used to depict festivities at the Court of Parma. The BBC Philharmonic play with evident commitment, and John Bradbury is the elegant and sensitive soloist in the *Concertino for Clarinet and Small Orchestra.* The sound is first class and in the best traditions of the house.

Berceuse élégiaque, Op. 42; 2 Studies for Doktor Faust, Op. 51; Turandot Suite, Op. 41.

(BB) **(*) Naxos 555373. Hong Kong PO, Wong.

Popularity seems to rest as much on chance as on merit, for it is difficult to understand why the *Turandot Suite* has never become a popular repertory piece. Sir Malcolm Sargent conducted it with the BBC Symphony Orchestra in the late 1950s and early 1960s, but it remains virtually unplayed these days, and only in recent years has it been recorded (by Muti in 1994). Given its bargain price, it should now reach a wider audience. It has all the qualities of melodic appeal (its fifth movement quotes *Greensleeves*), resourceful invention and brilliant orchestral colour that should ensure its popularity. The two *Studies,* the *Sarabande* and *Cortège,* written in preparation for his opera, *Doktor Faust,* remain the composer's masterpiece, highly searching and imaginative music that can claim to be profound, as, indeed, can the *Berceuse élégiaque.* Both performances and recording are very good, and this disc serves as an admirable and inexpensive introduction to a fascinating and underrated master, although on the assumption that Neeme Järvi goes on to record the *Turandot Suite* in his Busoni series, readers may want to hold their hand before acquiring this.

(i) *Piano Concerto. Fantasia contrappuntistica.*

(B) ** Erato Ultima 3984 24248-2 (2). Viktoria Postnikova; (i) French R. Ch. & Nat. O, Rozhdestvensky.

Postnikova's version of Busoni's ambitious concerto is a curiosity. Her characteristic magic and that of Rozhdestvensky keep tensions sustained for much of the time, despite speeds that by most standards are grotesquely slow, but the result is eccentric. The *Fantasia contrappuntistica* makes a valuable fill-up, but other CD versions have managed to fit the concerto on to a single disc. Recording is good, but the choir in the finale sounds dim. Garrick Ohlsson's Cleveland version on Telarc is the one to go for (CD 82012).

BUTTERWORTH, Arthur
(born 1923)

Summer Music, Op. 77.

(M) *** ASV CD WHL 2132. Salvage, Royal Ballet Sinfonia, Sutherland (with Collection of Bassoon Concertos and Concertinos ***.)

Although a concertante piece, led by the soliloquizing bassoon, Arthur Butterworth's unforgettably atmospheric triptych is more like a three-part symphonic poem, organically whole in the way of Sibelius, yet reflecting not the Nordic scenery but the North Yorkshire Moors, which, as the composer tells us, 'despite the exhilaration of sun and wind on the high hills in summertime' (tellingly evoked in the finale), 'there ever seems to be a faint indefinable air of lonely melancholy brooding'. This is imaginatively caught by the soloist here; and Butterworth's subtly vivid use of orchestral colour increases the music's evocation and intensity, reaching a peak in the central *Nocturne*, moving slowly forwards, with its tolling bells and underlying persistent timpani. The performance is altogether first class and so is the recording. It comes within an attractive collection of more lightweight bassoon concertos (see Concerts section below), and the disc is well worth investigating.

BUXTEHUDE, Diderik
(*c.* 1637–1707)

7 Trio Sonatas, Op. 1, BuxWV 252-8.

*** HM HMC 901746. Kraemer, Quintama, Roberts, Börner.
*** Hyp. CDA 67236. Wallfisch, Tunnicliffe, Nicholson.

It seems remarkable that relatively soon after the exploration of Buxtehude's chamber music has begun on CD there should now be three competing recordings of the *Trio Sonatas, Op. 1*, all of high quality. Of the two new sets, the Hyperion recording is rather more intimate than the Harmonia Mundi version. Much depends on the lead violin in these works, and Manfredo Kraemer's virtuosity and strong instrumental personality is reminiscent of Andrew Manze, although of course Elizabeth Wallfisch who leads the Hyperion group certainly does not lack a strong profile and she and her colleagues make an impressive team.

But Kraemer is especially appealing both in the lyrical writing, and in his witty pointing of the rhythmic snaps which are a feature of the splendid *Ciaconna Vivace* which opens the *Fourth Sonata*. In the *Fifth Sonata*, the beautifully recorded harpsichord player, Dirk Börner also shines, while the *Sixth*, with its second movement marked *Con discretione* and extreme volatility of tempo in the third, is a splendid example of Buxtehude's 'stylus fantasticus' which so impressed Bach and which is particularly well handled by Kraemer and his colleagues. In short, both these sets of performances are first class, but to us the Harmonia Mundi disc is marginally the more appealing, and it is very well recorded.

BYRD, William (1543–1623)

The Byrd Complete Edition, Vol. 7: Cantiones sacrae (1589) Nos. 1–8: Deficit in dolore; Domine praestolamur; O Domine adjuva me; Tristitia anxietes; Memento Domine; Vide Domine afflictionem; Deus venerunt gentes; Domine tu jurasti; Propers for Lady Mass from Christmas to the Purification (1605).

*** ASV CDGAU 224. Cardinall's Musick, Carwood.

By the time Byrd came to publish the first Book of his *Cantiones sacrae* in 1589, the position of practising catholics in protestant England had become extremely vulnerable and dangerous. The execution of Mary Queen of Scots in 1586 and the failure of Philip II of Spain's Armada two years later (intended to conquer England and return the Church to the Pope's authority) was the culmination of a period when there had been persecution, savage torture and martyrdom for Jesuit priests in England (of which Edmund Campion was the most renowed).

Byrd was undoubtedly associated with the Jesuits yet, a favourite of the queen, he was allowed to write his music unharmed, and in his *Cantiones sacrae* express the anguish of his fellow catholics. The powerful message of *Deficit in dolore* ('My life has wasted away in grief, and my years in sighing') is very clear, while their fears are expresed in *O Domine adjuva me* ('O Lord help me and I shall be safe'). *Memento Domine* asks for the Lord's direct intervention, and the passionately felt and beautifully set *Vide Domine* is even more explicit.

These beautiful motets are used to frame Byrd's first volume of gradualia, settings of Proper texts for the whole church year, and the fact that the book was allowed to be published is remarkable, even if they could only be used in private devotions. The performances from Andrew Carwood and his fine group are as movingly committed and expressive as ever, and beautifully recorded. The editor, David Skinner, as usual provides the excellent notes.

Cantiones sacrae: Laetentur coeli; Tristitia et anxietas.

*** Proud Sound PROUCD 1149. King's College Ch., London, Trendell – TAVERNER: *Missa Corona Spinea; Audivi vocem de caelo.* ***

The exuberant *Laetentur coeli*, the Advent motet that concludes Byrd's 1589 collection of *Cantiones sacrae*, and the magnificent *Tristitia et anxietas* from the same collection, make a fine supplement to the fresh-voiced performance of Taverner's wide-ranging *Missa Corona Spinea*. Warmly atmospheric recording.

CAMPO, Conrado del (1878–1953)

La divina comedia; Evocacion y nostalgia de los molinos de viento; Ofrenda; 6 Little Compositions.

*** ASV CDDCA 1100. Gran Canaria PO, Leaper.

Conrado del Campo, unlike his close contemporary, Manuel de Falla, has never been appreciated outside Spain, maybe because his music has few nationalistic flavours, echoing instead such composers as Richard Strauss and Liszt. Adrian Leaper with the Gran Canaria Philharmonic, of which he is principal conductor, here offers an attractive collection, well-played, representing the full span of Del Campo's career from *La divina comedia* of 1908, an evocation of Dante's *Inferno* with a warmly lyrical interlude representing Paolo and Francesca, to his last major piece, a 'poetic overture' inspired by the composer's love of windmills, *molinos de viento*. Completed in 1952, the year before he died, it leads to a passionate climax, while *Ofrenda*, dating from 1934, is equally sensuous, with exotic echoes of Respighi, suggesting that Del Campo could have made his fortune as a Hollywood composer.

CANTELOUBE, Marie-Joseph (1879–1957)

Chants d'Auvergne: L'Antouèno; Baïlèro; 3 Bourrées; Lou Boussu; Brezairola; Lou coucut; Chut, chut; La Déläissádo; Lo Fïolairé; Jou l'pount d'o Mirabel; Malurous qu'o uno fenno; Passo pel prat; Pastourelle; Postouro, sé tu m'aymo; Tè, l'co, tè.

☼ (B) *** CfP 575 138-2. Gomez, RLPO, Handley — FAURÉ: *Masques et bergamasques; Pavane.* ***

Jill Gomez's selection of these increasingly popular songs, attractively presented on a bargain-price label, makes for a memorably characterful record which, as well as bringing out the sensuous beauty of Canteloube's arrangements, reminds us, in the echoes of rustic band music, of their genuine folk base. An ideal purchase for the collector who wants just a selection. The inclusion of the charming Fauré works makes this reissue more attractive than ever.

CARTELLIERI, Casimir Anton (1772–1807)

Clarinet Quartets Nos. 1 in D; 2 in E flat; 4 in E flat.

*** MDG 301 1097-2. Klöcker, Consortium Classicum.

Those readers who have already discovered Cartellieri's *Clarinet Concertos* (MDG 301 0527-2) will not need persuading to explore these even more delightful companion chamber works. Their style brings an occasional whiff of Mozart, but is more *galant* than the music of that master, and there are also touches of the kind of wit one finds in Rossini's *String Sonatas*.

Dieter Klöcker plays beguilingly and he is given splendid support from the Consortium Classicum, elegant and fresh, and they are beautifully recorded.

CASELLA, Alfredo (1883–1947)

11 Children's Pieces, Op. 35; 2 Ricercari on the name B.A.C.H, Op. 52; 9 Pieces, Op. 24; 6 Studies, Op. 70.

(BB) *** Naxos 8.554009. Ballerini.

What an interesting composer Casella is and how strange that he is so neglected! Of the three composers of the Ottocento (Malipiero, Pizzetti and Casella), he may well prove the most long-lasting. Born in Turin, he spent his formative years in Paris where he studied with Fauré and rubbed shoulders with such masters as Ravel, Enescu and Stravinsky. The main influences on him in the pre-war years were Mahler, Strauss, Stravinsky and Albéniz, and on his return to Italy he was a great champion of new music. As we go to press we see that his pioneering record of the Bloch *Piano Quintet* with the Pro Arte has been announced for reissue. Like Strauss, his role in the fascist era has attracted the opprobrium of various armchair heroes, usually American academics, who have never faced such realities, but Egon Wellesz, a scholar-composer of proven anti-Nazi credentials, never wavered in his admiration of him. The *Nove Pezzi*, Op. 24, are all exploratory in idiom, reflecting the worlds of Stravinsky, Busoni and Ravel. The third, *In modo elegiaco*, even foreshadows the harmonic world of Frank Martin. The *Children's Pieces* of 1920, dedicated to Castelnuovo-Tedesco, are imaginative and full of resource and charm, the last being reminiscent of the circus music of Stravinsky's second *Little Suite*. The *Ricercari on the name B.A.C.H*, Op. 52 were written for Gieseking in 1932 and are as exploratory in idiom as the charming wartime *Etudes*, Op. 70. Very convincing performances, as intelligent as befits this music, and very well recorded too.

CASTELNUOVO-TEDESCO, Mario (1895–1968)

Guitar Concerto No. 1 in D, Op. 99.

(M) *** Sony (ADD) SMK 89753. Williams, ECO, Groves — RODRIGO: *Concierto de Aranjuez* etc.; VILLA-LOBOS: *Concerto.* ***

John Williams's more recent version of Castelnuovo-Tedesco's engaging concerto with Groves is more vividly recorded than his earlier account with Ormandy and the Philadelphia Orchestra, but that was fresher and had more pace. He is placed far forward here, so that it is not always possible to locate him in relation to his colleagues. But if the sound is unreal as far as perspective goes, it is by no means unpleasing. These artists make the most of the slow movement's poetry and the performance has no lack of charm. The generous couplings and distinguished performances (about which there are few reservations) make this new compilation highly recommendable.

CHABRIER, Emmanuel (1841–94)

Mélodies (complete): *Adieux à Suzon; Ah! petit démon; Ballade des gros dindons; Chanson poir Jeanne; Chants d'oiseaux; Les Cigales; Couplets de Mariette; Credo d'amour; Duo de l'ouvreuse del'Opéra Comique et de l'employé du Bon Marché; L'Enfant; España* (arr. Emile Louis); *L'Isle heureuse; L'Invitation au voyage; Ivresses!; Lied* (De Banville); *Lied* (Mendès); *Le Pas d'armes du roi Jean; Pastorale des cochons roses; Ronde gauloise; Le Sentier sombre; Sérénade; Sérénade de Ruy Blas; Sommation irrespecteuse; Tes yeux bleus; Tout les fleurs; Villanelle des petites canards.*

Folksong arrangements: *Les Plus jolies du pays de France: Bèrgere et chasseur; La Bien-amée; Le Désereur; Entrez, la belle, en vigne; Les Filles de trente ans; Le Flambeau éteint; Le Fleur dorée; Les Garçons de Bordeaux; Joli dragon; Marion s'en va-t-a l'ou; Les Métamorphoses; La Mie du voleur; La Morte de la brune; Nique nac no muse!; Que les amants ont de la peine! Sur le bord de lîle. Ode à la musique.*

*** Hyp. CDA 67133/4. Lott, Burden, Varcoe, Spence, Johnson, McGreevy, Polyphony, Layton.

These two generously filled discs, appropriately subtitled '*Musique adorable!*' offer a wide-ranging selection of Chabrier's songs, as well as the *Ode à la musique* (sung by Geraldine McGreevy with the choral group, Polyphony), and a curious duo for a programme-seller at the Opéra Comique and an assistant at the Bon Marché department store. That jokey piece, with each section ending in a Swiss yodelling song, demonstrates the humorous side of Chabrier, and his lighter manner also comes out in the vocal arrangement of his popular Spanish rhapsody, *España*, made under his supervision by Emile Louis with patter-like words by Eugene Adenis, a fun piece. Yet many of these songs are deeply expressive, even some of those from his earliest period, which date from 1862 when he was only 21. They include a setting of Victor Hugo, *Sommation irrespectuseuse*, which darkly hints at madness, and a setting of Baudelaire's *L'Invitation au voyage*, which has always been eclipsed by the supreme setting of that poem by his friend, Duparc, but which is intensely original, with sustained notes on a bassoon producing distinctive tone-colours (finely played by Ursula Leveaux). The song which opens the second disc, *Tes yeux bleus*, is also most evocative, hinting at Wagner's *Traume*, while that second disc also includes 16 regional folksong settings, bright and characterful. As always in his song recordings for Hyperion, Graham Johnson greatly adds to enjoyment, not only with his ever-sensitive playing but in his comprehensive, scholarly notes. Felicity Lott, Geraldine McGreevy, William Burden and Toby Spence are all in fine voice, singing stylishly.

CHADWICK, George (1854–1931)

Aphrodite; Angel of Death; Overtures: Euterpe; Melpomene; Thalia.

(BB) *** Naxos 8.559117. Nashville SO, Schermerhorn.

Although an American composer, George Chadwick still relates to the world of Brahms and Dvořák, if with an attractive transatlantic flavour in the manner of the *New World Symphony*. But these tone poems and (symphonic) overtures, although substantial and colourful works, are not on that level, and although they have engaging invention, they do not always fully sustain their length. The three overtures are each named after one of the muses. *Thalia* (the music of comedy) highlights Chadwick's particular skill at writing wittily and light heartedly; the more substantial *Melpomene* (the muse of tragedy) was one of the composer's most often performed works during his lifetime, its opening almost *Tristanesque*, while *Euterpe* (the muse of music), is enjoyably colourful.

The *Angel of Death*, one of Chadwick's last orchestral ventures, has a Straussian flavour, and rather melodramatically depicts a dying sculptor's attempt to finish his masterpiece before succumbing to death. It is a flamboyant score, with its ominous low brass chorales, and the drum roll signifying the artist's death is followed by sweeping strings and harp. But the longest work here is the tone poem *Aphrodite*, which lasts just under 30 minutes. With its depictions of 'Moonlight on the Sea', 'Storms', 'Lovers', 'Children playing' and 'The Approach of a Great Army', it suggests the sights the statue of the goddess might witness overlooking the sea. The Nashville orchestra seems thoroughly inside the music and the recording is very good, if not in the demonstration league.

CHAMINADE, Cécile (1857–1944)

Music for violin and piano: *Capriccio, Op. 18; Rondeau, Op. 97; Sérénade espagnole; Valse carnavalesque, Op. 73.* **Music for 2 pianos:** *Danse payenne; Pas des cymbales.* **Songs:** *Alleluia; Auprès de ma mie; L'Amour captif; L'Anneau d'argent; Attente (Au pays de Provence); Bonne humeur; Chanson triste; Ecrin; Espoir; L'Eté je voudrais …; La Lune paresseuse; Maigré nous; Ma première lettre; Menuet; Mignonne; Mots d'Amour; Nice-labette; Ronde d'amour; Si j'étais jardinier; Sombrero; Te souviens-tu?; Viens! mon bien-aimé!; Villanelle; Voisinage.*

*** DG 471 331-2. Von Otter, Fosberg, Sparf, Jablonski.

Those who associate the Victorian favourite composer Cécile Chaminade with slight, genteel piano pieces, will be surprised to find a far greater variety in this winning collection of her songs, as well as pieces for violin and for two pianos. The sparkle and energy of many of them chimes perfectly with the artistry of Anne Sofie von Otter, here at her most vivacious. One may look in vain for any kind of profundity, with the poems chosen by the composer rarely rising above the banale, but the vocal lines are easily elegant and often colourful, and the piano accompaniments unusual and demanding. The picture is completed by equally winning performances of the six instrumental pieces, full of fun and energy.

CHERUBINI, Luigi (1760–1842)

Overtures: Les Abencérages, ou L'Etendard de Grenade; Anacréon, ou L'amour fugitif; Eliza, ou Le voyage aux glaciers du Mont St-Bernard; Faniska; L'hôtellerie portugaise; Les deux journées, ou Le Porteur d'eau; Medée; Concert Overture.

(B) *** EMI double fforte CZS5 75160-2 (2). ASMF, Marriner – WOLF-FERRARI: *Overtures and Intermezzi.* ***

Although Marriner's performance of *Anacréon* does not have the sheer incandescent energy of Toscanini, its close is brilliantly done. All these overtures, which are brimming with attractive invention, are played with characteristic finese and warmth by the Academy of St Martin-in-the-Fields. *L'hôtellerie portugaise* has much dexterity and charm, and the combination of drama, energy and elegance in *Les deux journées* and *Faniska* is most winning. Here, and even more in the witty touches in *Les abencérages*, there are hints of Rossini, but Cherubini's style is that bit weightier and the very fine *Concert Overture*, with its grave opening, is both dramatic and full of grace. Incidentally, it is more substantial than the incorrect playing time given on the leaflet would suggest. An outstanding disc, very naturally recorded at Abbey Road in 1991, again reminding us why Beethoven admired Cherubini.

CHOPIN, Frédéric (1810–49)

Piano Concertos Nos. 1 in E min., Op. 11; 2 in F min., Op. 21.

(M) *** DG (ADD) 463 662-2. Zimerman, LAPO, Giulini.
(BB) *** Regis RRC 1096. Tirimo, Philh. O, Glushchenko.

The CD coupling of Zimerman's performances of the two Chopin *Concertos* with Giulini is hard to beat. Elegant, aristocratic, sparkling, it has youthful spontaneity and at the same time a magisterial authority, combining sensibility with effortless pianism. Both recordings are cleanly detailed, and this makes an obvious candidate for reissue as one of DG's 'Originals'.

Martino Tirimo's performances are worthy to rank alongside those of Perahia and Zimerman. Moreover, they have the advantage of now being in the lowest price range. Tirimo's readings often bring exquisite delicacy and they are totally without barnstorming, yet there is spontaneity in every bar, and both slow movements bring playing where one has an impression of musing reverie. In outer movements passage-work is scintillatingly alive, and finales have a beguiling rhythmic lift. There is strong orchestral support from Glushchenko and the Philharmonia players in the sparkling dance rhythms. Excellent (originally Conifer) recording too.

(i) *Piano Concertos Nos. 1 in E min., Op. 11; 2 in F min., Op. 21; Waltzes Nos. 1–14.*

(B) **(*) Erato Ultima (ADD/DDD) 3984 21089-2 (2). Pires; (i) with Monte Carlo Op. O, Jordan.

With her natural feeling for a limpid musical phrase and her unostentatious poetry, Maria João Pires would seem the ideal soloist for the Chopin concertos. However, she is so anxious not to give the slightest hint of barnstorming that her gently relaxed, coaxing approach to opening movements is inclined to let the ongoing tension slip, particularly in the *E minor Concerto*. The responsibility is clearly hers, for Armin Jordan gives her warm support and secures remarkably refined and polished accompaniments from the Monte Carlo players. Slow movements are another matter. Here she can afford to be poetically serene, yet remain seemingly spontaneous and delight the listener with her simplicity of mood and the ease with which she throws off the filigree decoration. The two closing Rondos, although not glittering, have a delectable lift and, with glowing analogue recording from the late 1970s (the piano timbre particularly pleasing), this Chopin playing is easy to enjoy. Pires's readings are far preferable to Arrau's self-conscious rubato. The second of this pair of CDs offers the *Waltzes* and here, unlike many of her rivals, she does not include the posthumously published pieces, and chooses her own sequence for the basic 14, opening with the *F major* (Op. 34/3), leaving the *Grande valse brillante* (Op. 18) as the penultimate item and ending with another *Valse brillante in A flat* (Op. 34/1). Her rubato is again individual, but she brings a real sense of style to this generally more extrovert pianism, with good judgement and taste, along with an impeccable technique. Only rarely does she fall short of real poetic distinction. The 1984 digital recording, somewhat brighter than the analogue sound afforded the two concertos, is well suited to this repertoire. Admirers of this artist need not hesitate.

(i) *Piano Concerto No. 1 in E min., Op. 11; Etudes: in G flat, Op. 10/5; in E min., Op. 25/5.*

(B) (*(*)) EMI mono CDZ5 74802-2. Lipatti; (i) with Zurich Tonhalle O, Ackermann – GRIEG: *Piano Concerto.* (***)

Lipatti's is a lovely performance, but despite the recent remastering at Abbey Road by Simon Gibson, its sonic limitations (which also apply to the pair of *Etudes*) will prove something of an obstacle to all but his most fervent admirers.

Cello Sonata in G min., Op. 65.

(M) *** Somm SOMMCD 026. Walton, Owen –
RACHMANINOV: *Cello Sonata*. ***
**(*) BIS CD 1076. Thedéen, Pöntinen – SCHUMANN
Adagio & Allegro etc. **(*)

Cello Sonata; Polonaise brillante, Op. 3.

** DG 471 346-2. Maisky, Argerich – DEBUSSY: *Cello
Sonata*; FRANCK: *Cello Sonata*. **

A fine new coupling of the Chopin and Rachmaninov
Sonatas from an excellent new duo, both individually prize-winners, but who play very sypathetically
together, their spontaneous style both passionate
and refined. The slow movement of the Chopin is
presented with winning simplicity. The recording
balance is very good, the sound natural, although at
higher dynamic levels one would have liked rather
more separation.

Torleif Thedéen and Roland Pöntinen give an eloquent and convincing account of the *Cello Sonata*
with a particularly beautiful slow movement, even if
they are not helped by a reverberant acoustic, though
the overall sound is not unpleasing. Most readers will
probably stick with Tortelier (EMI CZS5 74333-2), but
this partnership is well worth considering.

Recorded live in Japan, Maisky's accounts of the
Chopin *Sonata* and *Polonaise* bring some inspired
moments, but as in the other works on the disc the
results are too often self-indulgent. This is perfectly
illustrated in the soaring cantilena of the brief *Largo*,
where the relative simplicity of Tortelier in his EMI
version is so much more moving than the lurching
phrasing of Maisky. A pity, when artists of this calibre
have so much to give. The recording has plenty of
weight, but lacks inner clarity.

PIANO MUSIC

Ballades Nos. 1–4; Nocturnes Nos. 1–20; Scherzi Nos. 1–4; Waltzes Nos. 1–17.

(B) **(*) DG Trio (ADD) 469 350-2 (3). Vásáry.

Vásáry's artistic achievement, as summed up by the
New Grove Dictionary of Music and Musicians, is
quoted on the back of this DG box: '*His virtuosity is
delicate, his phrasing is seductive, and always at the
service of a sensitive poetic imagination*'. Certainly the
Ballades are imaginatively played here and the readings individual in their combination of poetry and
bravura, with the *G minor* outstanding in its romantic
sweep. The *Nocturnes*, too, demonstrate a flexibility in
delicately moulding a Chopin phrase to find the kernel of poetry, even if the relaxation in the melodic line
sometimes seems just a shade calculated. But it is the
Scherzi that show the pianist at his best, played boldly
and brilliantly and with much resilience. The *Waltzes*
offer clean, stylish phrasing and crisp articulation, but
sometimes lack charm, perhaps partly because here
the piano timbre is drier. The recordings were made
in the mid-1960s and are of good if slightly variable

quality. But for the *Ballades* first choice remains with
Perahia (❂ Sony SK 64399), the *Nocturnes* with
Rubinstein (RCA 09026 63049-2) and the *Scherzi* with
Arrau (Philips 442 407-2).

Nocturnes Nos. 1–21.

(B) *** Nonesuch Ultima (ADD) 7559 79564-2 (2).
Moravec.

Ivan Moravec recorded the complete *Nocturnes* in 1965,
but we have not discovered them until now. You have
only to sample the very opening *Nocturne in B flat
minor* to recognize the delicacy of Moravec's touch,
his pliable control of colour and sensitive nuancing.
His playing is intensely felt and poetic, often very
measured and gentle, but magically sustained, as in
the *D flat major*, Op. 27/2. Yet sometimes he ranges
over the widest dynamic, as with the passionate central crescendo of the *C sharp minor*, Op. 27/1, while
the famous *Nocturne in E flat major* could not be
more appealing in its flowing rubato. The analogue
recording is most realistic, the piano timbre warm
and well focused. This is Chopin playing to compare
with the finest on record.

24 Préludes, Op. 28; Préludes Nos. 25–6; Piano Sonata No. 2, Op. 35.

(M) *** DG 463 663-2. Argerich.

The *Préludes* show Martha Argerich at her finest,
spontaneous and inspirational, though her moments
of impulsiveness may not appeal to all tastes. But her
instinct is sure, with many poetic, individual touches.
The *B flat minor Sonata* was recorded two years earlier
in 1975 and its combination of impetuosity and lyricism is distinctly individual. A fine addition to DG's
'Originals'.

Waltzes Nos. 1–19; Impromptus Nos. 1–4 (Fantasie-impromptu).

(BB) * EMI encore (ADD) CDE5 74975-2. Cziffra.

Georges Cziffra's performances date from the 1970s, and
although his technique is not in question, there is a feeling of skating over the edge of the music. The effect is
exacerbated by the thin, almost brittle quality of the
recording, which was poor by 1970s standards, never
mind today. With Rubinstein and Lipatti around, this is
a non-starter and does scant justice to the artist.

RECITAL COLLECTIONS

Andante spianato et Grande polonaise brillante, Op. 22; Ballades Nos. 1–4; Fantaisie-Impromptu, Op. 66; Polonaise-fantaisie, Op. 61.

** BIS CD 1160. Kempf.

Having been greatly impressed by his Rachmaninov
CD, we approached Freddy Kempf's Chopin with
high anticipation. As in his earlier disc, he plays with
great virtuosity, but there are some attention-seeking
touches that make the listener more aware of the
gifted pianist than the great composer. They are

sufficient to diminish the appeal of this eminently well-recorded issue.

Andante spianato et Grande polonaise, Op. 22; Etudes: Op. 10/2 & 5; Op. 25/11; Fantaisie-impromptu, Op. posth.; Nocturnes: Op. 9/1 & 2; Op. 15/2; Sonata No. 3 in B min., Op. 58.

**(*) DG 471 476-2. Yundi Li.

Yundi Li was the first prize-winner of the Warsaw Chopin Competition in 2000 and the first to have won outright since Stanislav Bunin in 1985 – and at barely 18, he is the youngest, too! He comes with glowing tributes from Krystian Zimerman, among others, and gives assured, immaculately clean performances of these pieces. This debut has appeared to much press acclaim, and the recital bears all the hallmarks of modern marketing techniques, with lots of photos of him in white suits, fetching black and white vests and leather jackets, as if he were a male model. His playing is refreshingly free from posturing or ostentation, however. He is obviously a serious artist – perhaps a little too serious, for although the performances are beautifully delivered with impressive technical address, they are a little lacking in the subtlety of tone colour of which the presentation notes speak. The recording has clarity and presence; indeed, perhaps the rather clinical, close balance contributes to the lack of mystery conveyed by some of the recital. There are poetic moments, of course, but we have heard more haunting performances of the *Andante spianato* and the *Nocturnes* than Yundi Li gives us on this occasion.

Ballades Nos. 1, Op. 23; 4, Op. 52; Barcarolle, Op. 60; Etudes, Op. 10/5; Op. 25/7; Nocturnes, Op. 9/2-3; Op. 15/1; Op. 27/1; Polonaise-fantaisie, Op. 61; Waltz in A flat, Op. 16/1.

(BB) *** RCA Stereo/mono 74321 68008-2. Horowitz.

Although the *Andante spianato and Grande Polonaise* is omitted, this super-bargain reissue is a rather more extended recital than its mid-priced predecessor, but again all these performances derive from live recitals. The pair of *Nocturnes* (in E flat major, Op. 9/2 and C sharp minor, Op. 25/7) are in excellent mono from 1957, with the rest coming from between 1979 and 1982. The performances are fabulous; to the end of his career Horowitz's technique was transcendental and his insights remarkable. There is much excitement, but even more that is unforgettably poetic, and not a bar that is predictable. With the sound so realistic, his presence is very tangible. Not to be missed.

CIMAROSA, Domenico
(1749–1801)

Overtures: La baronessa Stramba; Cleopatra; Il convito; Il credulo; Il falegname; L'impresario in angustie; L'infedelt´ fedele; Il matrimonia segreto; Il ritorno di Don Calendrino; Le stravaganze del conte; La vergine del sole; Voldomiro.

*(*) Marco Polo 8.225181. Esterházy Sinf., Amoretti.

A disc of Cimorosa's overtures was sorely needed, but this does not fill the gap. The orchestra plays quite well for Alessandro Amoretti, and one enjoys the often witty melodic invention along the way, but it takes a Beecham or a Toscanni – with a first-class orchestra – to transform such works into something special. As it is, the collection here (which includes the first recording of the Vienna version of the *Il matrimonio segreto* overture) only intermittently displays the sparkle of Cimarosa's invention. The recording is only average, lacking in depth and brilliance in general, with the strings in particular sounding rather thin. At Naxos price, it would be more recommendable.

COATES, Eric (1886–1958)

Orchestral Music, Volume 1: *By the Sleepy Lagoon; Cinderella (A Phantasy); The Jester at the Wedding; London Bridge March; London Suite; Summer Days Suite; Summer Afternoon (Idyll); Symphonic Rhapsodies on: 'I Pitch My Lonely Caravan'; 'I Heard You Singing'; 'Bird Songs at Eventide'. Wood Nymphs (Valsette).*

(BB) (***) Naxos mono 8.110173. O, Composer; with Brownlow.

Orchestral Music, Volume 2: *By the Tamarisk; Calling All Workers; From Meadow to Mayfair Suite; London Again Suite; Springtime Suite; The 3 Bears; With a Song in My Heart Symphonic Rhapsody.*

(BB) (***) Naxos mono 8.110182. O, Composer.

Eric Coates's mastery of the British light classical genre is particularly well demonstrated by the composer's own performances, recorded between 1926 and 1940, which offer a unique authenticity and charm. Both CDs are highly imbued with the flavour of the period: just sample *On the Edge of the Lake* from *Summer Days*, one of Coates's best works, and you are in a sunlit, imaginary world of pre-war Britain, with the composer knowing just how to coax exactly the right sentiment from his players, the effect never cloying or slushy. Similarly, the hushed strings in *Meditation* from the *London Suite* are most touching, while the robust outer movements have plenty of swagger. The Rt. Hon. W. Brownlow, a scion of the Lurgan baronetcy, apparently made a name for himself charging extortionate prices for his recitals, all for charitable causes, and his baritone contributes genuine period charm to *I Pitch My Lonely Caravan*. The first CD also includes *By the Sleepy Lagoon*, familiar as the signature tune of *Desert Island Discs*, while the *Cinderella Phantasy*, the longest work here at some thirteen minutes, is beguilingly romantic.

The second volume opens with his famous wartime march, used in factory broadcasts, *Calling All Workers*. The *Three Bears Phantasy*, with its syncopated rhythms, is even more tangibly descriptive than the *Cinderella* evocation, especially as it is colourfully scored and attractively animated. Coates is in his best English pastoral mood for *Spring Times* and *Meadow to Mayfair*, both suitably rustic, while the more robust writing in the *London Again Suite* is equally enjoyable. Both CDs offer first-rate transfers, and the period flavour of the orchestral playing is very nostalgic.

Cinderella (Phantasy); Dam Busters' March; Joyous Youth (Suite); London Suite; Miniature Suite; The Selfish Giant (Phantasy); The Three Bears (Phantasy).

✪ *** Chan. 9869. BBC PO, Gamba.

This is easily the best Eric Coates collection ever. It is a joy to hear his imaginatively coloured orchestration on a full-sized orchestra with an ample string group and played with such loving warmth and finesse. The Master (as he was affectionately known by his colleagues) or, in Dame Ethel Smyth's equally pertinent description, 'The Man who writes tunes', is splendidly served by these superb performances and Chandos's demonstration-worthy recordings.

The three *Phantasies* were inspired by the stories that Coates's wife read aloud to their son, Austin. The finest is *The Three Bears*, with its opening rhythmic phrase, 'Who's been sleeping in my bed?' and its later, utterly beguiling waltz theme. Coates wrote a very English-style waltz. *Cinderella* boasts another richly romantic example, and two more, both deliciously lightweight, close the *Joyous Youth Suite* and the *Miniature Suite*, which shows the composer at his most elegant and graceful (the opening *Children's Dance* is enchanting).

More robust is the *London Suite*, with its vigorous, pacy evocation of the old Covent Garden Market, using 'Cherry Ripe' as its richly lyrical centrepiece, followed by a romantic portrayal of *Westminster*, complete with chimes. The *Knightsbridge March* finale was famous before the war as the BBC's signature tune for the radio programme with a self-explanatory title: *In Town Tonight*. The programme ends appropriately with *The Dam Busters*, not actually written for the famous film but adapted from a previously composed military march. All orchestral musicians love playing Coates's music: it isn't technically easy, but it is infinitely rewarding, and this is conveyed by the orchestra throughout this wonderfully enjoyable CD.

COLES, Cecil (1888–1918)

Behind the Lines (suite): excerpts: Estaminet de Carrefour. Cortège (orch. Brabbins). Overture: The Comedy of Errors; From the Scottish Highlands (suite); Scherzo in A min.; (i) Fra Giacomo (scena for baritone and orchestra); (ii) 4 Verlaine Songs.

*** Hyp. CDA 67293. BBC Scottish SO, Brabbins; with (i) Whelan; (ii) Fox.

Cecil Coles, a close friend of Gustav Holst, died of wounds received on the Somme in April 1918. His career was brief but brilliant, with a period of study from 1908 on a scholarship in Stuttgart, which led to his being appointed assistant conductor at the Stuttgart Royal Opera House. As a bandmaster in the army during the war, he continued to compose, culminating in the suite *Behind the Lines*, from which the two surviving movements are included on this pioneering disc of his music. The scores were hidden away for over 80 years, until they were unearthed by his daughter, Catherine. What immediately strikes one about all the pieces is their confidence and skill, with clean-cut ideas crisply presented and beautifully orchestrated. The bustling *Comedy of Errors Overture* is typical, a piece that deserves to be in the regular repertory, and the dramatic scena, *Fra Giacomo* for baritone and orchestra to a poem by Robert Williams Buchanan, brings out the influence on Coles of Wagner, a melodramatic monologue, positive and red-blooded. The *Scherzo in A minor* is rather more adventurous stylistically with its angular brass motif at the start, possibly a movement designed to be included in a full symphony, while the *Four Verlaine Songs*, using English translations, sound more German than French in their warmly romantic idiom. The suite, *From the Scottish Highlands*, one of the earliest pieces here, dating from 1906–7, is easily lyrical with a Scottish folk element, ending with a moving *Lament*, but it is the two movements from *Behind the Lines* that capture the imagination most. The first, *Estaminet de Carrefour*, is a jolly genre piece picturing a typical crossroads tavern, while the final *Cortège*, preserved only in short score and sensitively orchestrated by the conductor, is an elegiac piece that in this dedicated performance has a gulp-in-throat quality, bringing home more than anything the tragedy of a career cut short. Splendid performances throughout, not least from the two singers, and warm, well-balanced recording.

CONUS (KONIUS or KONYUS), Julius (1869–1942)

Violin Concerto in E min.

*** DG 471 428-2. Garrett, Russian Nat. O, Pletnev — TCHAIKOVSKY: *Violin Concerto*. ***

Conus was born in Moscow of mixed Italian and French parentage, his name being variously transliterated as Konyus, Konus and Konius. His musical ideas are long marinaded in Tchaikovsky and Rachmaninov, and show not a glimpse of originality. After the First World War, Conus moved to Paris where he taught, returning to his native Moscow in 1940 and dying two years later. The *Violin Concerto* (1898) is the only work of his to maintain a foothold (and a very peripheral one at that) on the repertory. Its tunes are pleasing at the time but ultimately unmemorable, and no one would pretend that it is a masterpiece. Nevertheless, it has been recorded by Heifetz and Perlman no less. David Garrett is the young virtuoso whose account of the Paganini *Caprices* (with accompaniments by Schumann) excited much attention when it appeared some time ago, and this 17-year-old soloist plays it with great conviction and sweetness of tone, and is splendidly partnered by Pletnev and the Russian National Orchestra. Perlman (and Heifetz) remain peerless in this kind of repertoire, but Garrett is impressive too and well worth hearing.

COOKE, Arnold (born 1906)

Clarinet Concerto.

(B) *** Hyp. Helios CDH 55069. King, Northwest CO of Seattle, Francis – JACOB: *Mini-Concerto*; RAWSTHORNE: *Concerto.* ***

Arnold Cooke's music contains an element of Hindemithian formalism, carefully crafted, but the slow movement of this *Concerto* soars well beyond. Thea King makes a passionate advocate, brilliantly accompanied by the Seattle Orchestra in excellent 1982 analogue sound, faithfully transferred. This triptych is the more attractive at bargain price.

COPLAND, Aaron (1900–90)

(i) *Clarinet Concerto*; (ii) *Rodeo: 4 Dance Episodes*; (iii; iv) *Piano Quartet*; (iii–v) *Sextet for Clarinet, Piano and String Quartet.*

(M) *** ASV Platinum PLT 8504. (i) Hosford, COE, Fischer; (ii) Bournemouth SO, Farrer; (iii) Vanbrugh Qt (iv) Roscoe; (v) Collins.

A fine account of Copland's delightful *Clarinet Concerto* from Richard Hosford, who plays beautifully as well as with character, and is admirably supported by Thierry Fischer and the COE. The opening is really quite magical. The *Sextet,* a tersely argued work with sharply etched colours, and the more challenging *Piano Quartet* are still relative rarities, and these 1999 recordings are very welcome indeed. Both receive fine, committed performances by the Vanbrugh Quartet (and the excellent soloists), who bring out plenty of detail and colour in these scores, be it in the vibrant contrasts of the *Sextet* or the haunting beauty of the first movement of the *Piano Quartet.* The recording is ideal, vivid and warm. The well-known *Rodeo* excerpts are brightly done, though the acoustic is a little dry.

CORELLI, Arcangelo (1653–1713)

Concerti grossi, Op. 6/1-12.

(B) ** Chan. 6663 (2). Cantilena, Shepherd.

Corelli's masterly *Op. 6 Concertos* are rich in melodic invention and harmonic resource and were enormously influential in their day. They are now generously represented in the bargain range on CD, and although Adrian Shepherd's Cantilena are excellently recorded, their playing is not as polished as that of Marriner and the ASMF (Double Decca 443 862-2). Their approach is genial, but slow movements are sometimes rather lazy-sounding, while the lively music lacks the pointed rhythms characteristic of the best period instrument performances. Here, choice would seem to lie between the Brandenburg Concert under Roy Goodman (Hyperion Dyad CDD 22011) and Harmonia Mundi's Ensemble 415 under Banchini. Those looking for a bargain will find the modern instrument performances by the Capella Istropolitana under Krechek have much greater vitality than Cantilena (Naxos 8.550402/3).

COUPERIN, François (1668–1733)

Les Goûts-réunis: Nouveaux concerts: Nos. 5–14.

*** Decca O-L 458 271-2 (2). Les Talens Lyriques, Rousset.

Christophe Rousset is an idiomatic and masterly interpreter of this repertoire. *Les Goûts-réunis* or *Nouveaux concerts* come from 1724. Its title, *goûts-réunis,* derives from the contemporary fascination with combining the styles of France and Italy, and *nouveaux* from the fact that only two years earlier Couperin had published his four *Concerts royaux.* Rousset leads elegant and imaginative performances that quite outclass most of the recent competition, and the Oiseau-Lyre team produces sound that is beautifully clean, completely lifelike and perfectly in perspective. This is most civilized music in performances that have the measure of its subtlety.

CUI, César (1835–1918)

Preludes Nos. 1–25.

(BB) **(*) Naxos 8.555567. Biegel.

Of all of members of the 'Kutchka' or 'Mighty Handful' (Balakirev, Borodin, César Cui, Mussorgsky and Rimsky-Korsakov), Cui is by far the least well known. Born in Vilnius, the son of a French officer who had remained in Lithuania after the Napoleonic retreat, he briefly studied with Moniuszko in Warsaw before embarking on a military career (he was an authority on fortifications). His was a talent of minuscule proportions beside those of his four friends, although he was an acerbic, opinionated critic. These *Preludes* have a certain charm, though in *No. 13 in F sharp* the debt to Tchaikovsky is strong – and even stronger in its successor, which is almost a paraphrase of the *Valse à cinq temps* of Tchaikovsky's Op. 72 set. There is also a lot of Schumann and even more Mendelssohn here. Slight and derivative though many of these pieces may be, there is still much worthwhile music among these miniatures, and Jeffrey Biegel gives decent and faithful accounts of them. The recordings come from 1992 and are perfectly acceptable, although the piano has not been perfectly conditioned.

DANZI, Franz (1763–1826)

Horn Concerto in E.

(BB) *** Teldec (ADD) 0630 12324-2. Baumann, Concerto Amsterdam, Schröder – HAYDN; ROSETTI: *Concertos.* ***

Danzi was born in Mannheim and worked in Munich, Stuttgart and Karlsruhe. His *Horn Concerto* is straightforward but attractive. The opening of the first movement is elegant, with flutes decorating the simple orchestration. The Romance is Weberian, smoothly contoured, and pleasing in line, but the pertly amiable closing Rondo is the most winning of the three movements and demands and receives some very nimble tongueing from Baumann who gives a most sympathetic performance overall. The 1969 recording has been pleasingly remastered and sounds smoother and warmer than on its last appearence.

DAQUIN, Louis-Claude (1694–1772)

Nouveau Livre de Noëls Nos. 1–12.

*** Hyp. CDA 66816. Herrick (organ of Church of St Rémy de Dieppe).

Louis-Claude Daquin was a keyboard prodigy, and at the age of six he is reported to have played for the king who correctly predicted his later fame. Daquin became organist at Notre Dame in 1735. He is best known for his *Noëls*, which are often used as piquant organ encore pieces. The composer's title page suggests that they could also be played on harpsichord or violins and woodwind; but they were obviously meant primarily for the organ, and intended for performance at Christmas Mass – acting as seasonal voluntaries, usually heard just before midnight.

Each uses a popular melody to which a cumulative bravura variation style is applied, with the decoration and variants steadily gaining in pace and brilliance. Above all, performances were required to be buoyant and spirited, as indeed they are here, and Christopher Herrick, who registers a colourfully varied palette, obviously enjoys himself throughout. The Dieppe organ seems an ideal choice (sample Nos. 4, 6 or 10) and it is beautifully recorded. Not a disc to play all at once, but very engaging to dip into.

DEBUSSY, Claude (1862–1918)

La Boîte à joujoux; Children's corner (orch. Caplet).

(***) Testament mono SBT 1236 French Nat. RO, Cluytens – RAVEL: *Le Tombeau; Valses Nobles.* (**)

Like *Le Martyre de Saint Sébastien* and the ballet *Khamma, La Boîte à joujoux* was one of those scores that the composer left for others to orchestrate. Caplet's scoring was made in 1923 some five years after Debussy's death. The ballet, effortless and charming in its inventive flow, tells of a triangular love affair among marionettes who live in a large toy box. Cluytens conveys its charm very expertly and gets good playing from his French Radio forces – and a mono recording of outstanding quality for the period

which still impresses today. Both pieces are very enjoyable indeed.

Danse Sacrée et danse profane (for harp and string orchestra).

(BB) *** DG Eloquence (ADD) 469 689-2. Zabaleta, Paul Kuentz CO – BIZET: *Symphony in C; Jeux d'enfants; Suite bohémiennes* ***; SAINT-SAENS: *Morceau de concert* ***.

Nicanor Zabaleta's *Danse sacrée et danse profane* with the Paul Kuentz Chamber Orchestra was recorded in 1967 and comes up well. It is beautifully played. But you should get this disc for the sake of the Bizet couplings, which are a delight.

Danse (Tarantelle styrienne); Sarabande (orch. Ravel).

(BB) *** Virgin 2 CD VBD5 62050-2 (2). Lausanne CO, Zedda – MILHAUD: *La création du monde;* PROKOFIEV: *Symphony No. 1 (Classical)* ***; SHOSTAKOVICH: *Chamber Symphony; Symphony No. 14* **.

Zedda's performances with the Lausanne Chamber Orchestra are neat and polished, full of character and well recorded. The Milhaud and Prokofiev couplings are excellent too, the Shostakovich more controversial.

Images; Jeux; Le Roi Lear (incidental music).

(BB) *** EMI Encore CDE5 75218-2. CBSO, Rattle.

In *Images* Rattle is memorably atmospheric, while in *Jeux* he is just a touch more expansive than most rivals and also more evocative, although he does not depart from the basic metronome markings. Haitink probably remains a first choice in this score, for he has atmosphere and a tauter grip on the music's flow. The *King Lear* excerpts sound splendid. First-rate recording, very vivid but beautifully balanced. At Encore price this is a truly remarkable bargain.

(i) Collection: *Images: Le Matin d'un jour de fête;* (ii) *La Mer: Dialogue du vent et de la mer;* (i) *Nocturnes: Fêtes;* (i; iii) *Pelléas et Mélisande: Mes Longs cheveux;* (i) *La plus que lente;* (ii) *Prélude à l'après-midi d'un faune;* (iv) *Sonata for Flute, Viola and Harp* (finale); (v) *Petite Suite;* (vi) *Préludes (Book 1): La Cathédrale engloutie; La Fille aux cheveux de lin; Minstrels. Suite bergamasque: Claire de Lune.*

(B) ** Decca 470 123-2. (i) Montreal SO, Dutoit; (ii) Cleveland O, Ashkenazy; (iii) Alliot-Lugaz, Henry; (iv) Ellis, Melos Ens.; (v) Labèque Sisters; (vi) Rogé.

It is not clear who would want just one movement each from *La Mer, Nocturnes* or *Images* when you can have all three complete and reasonably priced on, *inter alia,* a Double Decca CD set. But if you are attracted to a sampler of this kind, the present compilation works quite well, thanks partly to the sympathetic performances and partly to sensitive programming. The recordings are all excellent, too.

Jeux; Khamma; La Mer; Prélude à l'après-midi d'un faune.

(M) ** Decca (ADD) 470 255-2. SRO, Ansermet.

It was sensible of Decca to choose to use Ansermet's 1957 version of *La Mer* instead of the later, 1964 one: the earlier version has more tension and atmosphere and is better played. His 1958 *Jeux* has plenty of atmosphere and character, too. The rarely heard *Khamma* (orchestrated by Koechlin) is aurally fascinating: the sinister opening of deep woodwinds and pulsating strings is superbly caught by Ansermet and the Decca engineers. Indeed, the analytical quality of these readings is what makes them fascinating, and, bar certain lapses of intonation and ensemble from time to time, characteristic of the Swiss Orchestra, these performances show Ansermet on top form. The recordings, if a bit thin, have – as always from this source – amazing clarity and vividness.

(i) Jeux; Nocturnes. Prélude à l'après-midi d'un faune; Marche écossaise; (ii) La damoiselle élue.

(**) Testament mono SBT 1212. French RO, Inghelbrecht; with (i) Chorale Marcel Briclot; (ii) Madeleine Gorge; Jacqueline Joly, and Ch.

For younger collectors, the French conductor, Désiré-Emile Inghelbrecht will hardly be a familiar name – understandably enough as his Debussy records have not been in circulation since the 1950s. Nevertheless they have special claims on the serious collector as Inghelbrecht was closely associated with Debussy during the first decades of the century. Although the quality of the orchestral playing leaves much to be desired, there is a sense of music from another age. Among the highlights here is *Jeux*, which has a wonderful breadth and space. The singing in *La damoiselle élue* or in *Sirènes* from the *Nocturnes* is not particularly distinguished but there is an authenticity of feeling that is rather special. Excellent transfers.

Le Martyre de Saint Sébastien (symphonic fragments); *Prélude à l'après-midi d'un faune.*

*** MDG 337 1099-2. Orchester der Beethovenhalle, Bonn, Soustrot – RAVEL: *Ma Mère l'oye; La Valse.* ***

Soustrot gives highly atmospheric, slightly understated but not under-characterized accounts of these scores, with no exaggerated nuances, only unforced music-making. The recorded sound is beautifully balanced too, with the details emerging with both clarity and subtlety. Altogether a most distinguished coupling.

La Mer; Images; (i) 3 Chansons de Charles d'Orléan; Noël des enfants qui n'ont plus de maison.

(**) Testament mono SBT 1213 French RO, Inghelbrecht; (i) with Madeleine Gorge, French R Symph. Ch.

As in the two companion discs, ensemble is pretty rough-and-ready and woodwind intonation insecure and string tone wanting in lustre: the Orchestre National de la Radiodiffusion Française was not on top form. But there is still much to learn from these readings: above all a wonderful sense of space and atmosphere in *Gigues* and the complete absence of any glamorisation. One gets the feeling that this is the unhurried way Debussy should be played and is left understanding why these performances had such a reputation in the 1950s despite the infirmity of the orchestral response.

(i) Première rapsodie (for clarinet and orchestra); *(ii; iii) Danses sacrées et profanes; (iii; iv) Sonata for Flute, Viola and Harp; (v) String Quartet; (vi) 2 Arabesques. (vii) Suite bergamasque: Clair de lune.*

(M) **(*) ASV PLT 8505. (i) Johnson, ECO, Tortelier; (ii) Prometheus Ens.; (iii) Thomas (harp); (iv) Blake, Inoue; (v) Lindsay Qt (vi) Fergus-Thompson; (v) Cherkassky.

Debussy's lovely *First Rhapsody* for clarinet and orchestra (he never wrote a second) brings out the most persuasive qualities in Emma Johnson's artistry. The range of expression, with extreme contrasts of tone and dynamics, make this an exceptionally sensuous performance, yearningly poetic, and well recorded. The Lindsays play with their usual aplomb and panache in the *String Quartet*. There are splendid things here, notably the youthful fire of the opening movement and the finely etched finale. They do not always match the *douceur* and *tendresse* that the Quartetto Italiano, the Hagen and the Melos find, but they are always stimulating. The Prometheus Ensemble provide an attractive performance of the *Danses sacrées et profanes*, and the *Sonata for Flute, Viola and Harp* is sensitively done too by Richard Blake and his partners. Gordon Fergus-Thomson's *Deux Arabesques* are engagingly played, but Cherkassky's account of *Clair de lune* isn't as magical as it might be.

CHAMBER MUSIC

Cello Sonata in D min.

(BB) *** Warner Apex 0927 40599-2. Noras, Rigutto – FRANCK; FAURE: *Cello Sonatas.* ***

** DG 471 346-2. Maisky, Argerich – CHOPIN: *Cello Sonata; Polonaise brillante; FRANCK: Cello Sonata.* **

From Arto Noras and Bruno Rigutto comes as good a performance of the *Cello Sonata* as any in the catalogue (excepting Rostropovich and Britten and, perhaps, the Gendron-Jean Françaix version from the 1960s). Noras was recorded in 1995, and the sound is good. At the price it is a real bargain.

In this live recording from Japan the magnetism of both Maisky and Argerich is clear from first to last – these are musicians whose very presence commands attention. But, alas, the self-indulgence which has often afflicted the performances of such highly individual artists has here become obtrusive; not so much with Argerich – who has the job of matching the vagaries of her wilful partner – but with Maisky, who on this showing seems to find it very hard to maintain a steady speed in almost any music for more than a bar or so. The Debussy, more improvisational in its highly original inspiration, fares better than the Chopin and Franck, though the earlier studio account on EMI made by the same artists is more satisfying, with cleaner textures.

String Quartet in G min., Op. 10.

(B) (**(*)) EMI mono CDZ5 74792-2. Italian Qt. – MILHAUD: *String Quartet No. 12* (***); RAVEL: *String Quartet in F* **(*).

** Simax PSC 1201. Vertavo Qt. – GRIEG: *String Quartet.* **

For long the Quartetto Italiano version from 1965 (Philips) reigned supreme, coupled, of course, with the Ravel, and it is still very highly recommendable (464 699-2). EMI now offers their earliest versions from 1954, and the playing is immensely refined. The booklet annotator maintains that it is, in fact, superior to the later version, but this is not a view that will be widely shared. Of course their ensemble is stunning (in those days they played from memory), but there are some tiny agogic distortions that sound just a little affected. Their later performance is every bit as impeccable technically and completely free from artifice. However, on EMI, in addition to the usual Ravel coupling we have a Milhaud Quartet, also recorded in 1954, with which the Columbia LP originally appeared.

In neither the Debussy nor in the coupled Grieg Quartet would the Vertavo be a first choice, although they make a logical coupling since they share the same key and the Grieg (1878) so clearly influenced the Debussy (1893). The playing is very good but nothing special. Of recent re-issues, the mid-price Melos Quartet is a very strong contender and gained a ◉ in our main Guide (DG 463 082-2), while among newer versions the Belcea Quartet give a fine performance on EMI Debut (CDZ5 74020-2; see our main volume).

Readers may also like to be reminded that the Borodin Quartet's version of the Debussy–Ravel coupling, made when Rostislav Dubinsky was leader, has just become available in Chandos's Historical Series (Chan. 9980). The Borodins recorded this coupling for Virgin in 1989, but this is roughly two decades earlier. (In 1974 Dubinsky was replaced as leader by Mikhail Kopelman, but the documentation does not give the exact date of this performance.)

PIANO MUSIC

2 Arabesques; Children's Corner; Danse Bohémienne; Estampes; L'Isle Joyeuse; Préludes: Les Collines d'Anacapri; La Fille aux cheveux de lin; Minstrels; Feux d'artifice; Le Petit Nègre; Rêverie; Suite bergamasque.

(BB) **(*) Ph. Eloquence (ADD) 468 193-2. Haas.

These recordings come from the early 1960s and serve as a splendid reminder of just how fine an interpreter of French music we lost with the untimely death of Werner Haas in a car accident in 1976. (His first

Debussy LP won a prize from the *Académie du Disque Français*, which Milhaud presented him in 1962.) Like his countryman, Gieseking, with whom he briefly studied, he had a natural feel for both Debussy and Ravel. He is vividly recorded (even if the instrument is too close and a shade bottom heavy) and in this respect others are better served: but these are distinguished performances, and are very competitively priced. As with other issues in Universal's Eloquence label, there are no notes on either the composer or the artist.

Estampes; Images (1894); Images I & II.

(BB) ** Warner Apex 7559 79674-2. Jacobs.

Paul Jacobs has an enviable reputation, and his recording of the *Images* and the *Estampes* have much to recommend them. They were recorded in 1978 in New York, but the sound, though generally acceptable, is a little bottom heavy at times, unpleasingly so (try *Quelques aspects de 'Nous n'irons plus au bois'*, the third of the 1894 *Images*). It is by no means as refined sonically as, say, Zoltán Kocsis's Debussy records (Philips) or Pascal Rogé (Decca), made only a few years later.

Estampes: La Soirée dans Grenade; Jardins sous la pluie; Images: Reflets dans l'eau; Hommage à Rameau; Poissons d'or; Masques; La plus que lente; Préludes: La Fille aux cheveux de lin; La Cathédrale Engloutie; Minstrels; La Terrasse des audiences de clair de lune; Ondine.

(B) *** RCA 2CD (ADD) stereo/mono 74321 846062. Rubinstein – FAURE: *Nocturne No. 3*; FRANCK: *Symphonic Variations for Piano and Orchestra; Prélude choral et fugue*; RAVEL: *Valses nobles et sentimentales; Le tombeau de Couperin*: excerpts; *Miroirs*; SAINT-SAENS: *Piano Concerto No. 2 in G min., Op. 22* (with CHABRIER: *Pièces pittoresques: Scherzo-valse*). ***

The source of these Debussy pieces is not clear, but most were recorded in the 1960s. The excerpts from *Estampes* and *Reflets dans l'eau* are listed as mono (1945) but still sound real and immediate. The performances are poised and refined and have great atmosphere, showing Rubinstein as a natural Debussian. *Jardins sous la pluie* and *Reflets dans l'eau* bring an easy virtuosity, always at the service of the composer. The remastering is most impressive.

Etudes, Books 1–2; Estampes; L'isle Joyeuse.

(BB) *** Regis RRC 1091. Tirimo.

Martino Tirimo offers not only the *Etudes*, played with imagination and much subtlety of colour, but he also includes a set of *Estampes* and *L'Isle Joyeuse*, neither quite as impressive, but still worth having. He is very well recorded and this Regis reissue is very competitive in the cheapest price range. First choice for the *Etudes*, however, remains with Uchida (now at mid-price: ◉ Philips 464 698-2).

Préludes, Books 1–2 (complete).

(BB) *** Regis RRC 1111. Tirimo.

No grumbles about value for money or quality from Martin Tirimo on Regis. His playing is very fine indeed and can withstand comparison with most of his rivals – and apart from the sensitivity of his playing, the recording is most realistic and natural. This could well be a first choice for those wanting a modern digital recording offering the complete set on one disc.

VOCAL MUSIC

Le Martyre de Saint-Sébastien; (i) *3 Ballades de François Villon.*

(**) Testament mono SBT 1214. Collart, Collard, Gayraud, Falcon; (i) Plantey; French RO & Ch., Inghelbrecht.

Ingelbrecht conducted the first performances of *Le Martyre de Saint-Sébastien* in its concert form (André Caplet who was responsible for putting the score into its finished shape conducted the stage première.) His performance is totally dedicated and refreshingly wanting in glamour, and such is the sense of authenticity that it communicates, that its want of finish seems of no account. Readers who really care about Debussy should seek this out.

Mélodies: L'Âme évaporée; Auprès de cette grotte sombre; Beau soir; Chevaux de bois; Les Cloches; Crois mon conseil; L'Echelonnement des haies; Fêtes galantes 1 (En sourdine; Fantoches; Clair de lune); Fêtes galantes 2 (Les Ingénus; Le Faune; Colloque); Green; Je tremble en voyant ton visage; Le Jet d'eau; Mandoline; La Mer; Pour ce que plaisance est morte; Le Son du cor; De soir; Le Temps a laissié son manteau.

(M) *** DG (ADD) 463 664-2. Souzay, Baldwin.

This is one of the great Debussy song recitals of the age. Recorded in 1961, it opened the eyes of many music-lovers of the time to the mastery of these inspired songs. Quite apart from the beauty of his voice itself, it is the sheer intelligence and consummate artistry that Gérard Souzay brings to bear that silences criticism. He is admirably partnered by Dalton Baldwin. Excellent recorded sound.

OPERA

Pelléas et Mélisande (opera; complete).

(M) *** Naïve Radio FranceV4923 (3) Anne Sofie von Otter, Wolfgang Holzmair, Laurent Naouri, Hanna Schaer, Alaina Vernhes, Florence Couderc, R. France Ch. & O National, Haitink.
** Arthaus **DVD** 100 100. Le Roux, Alliot-Lugaz, Van Dam, Soyer, Taillon, Golfier, Schirrer, Lyon Op. Ch. & O, Gardiner. (S/D: Pierre Strosser. V/D: Jean-François Jung.)

Taken from two concert-performances promoted by Radio France at the Theâtre des Champs-Elysées, this live recording offers an inspired reading of Debussy's magical score from Bernard Haitink with a cast that is outstandingly fine. Haitink even in the opening prelude establishes the dedication of his reading, spacious, capturing an intensity that unmistakably evokes a great live event. Though speeds are often on the slow side – with the overall timing of the opera over ten minutes longer than with Abbado in his fine DG set – the thrust of the drama is presented with an extraordinary vividness, largely a question of Haitink's control of tempo, so that climactic moments are thrust home with often chilling impact. Never is there the feeling that this is a static work. The sense of drama is heightened by the recording balance, which more than in most recordings favours the voices, with words crystal clear, and with the orchestra clear rather than sumptuous. The beauty of the score is there, but very much in the service of the drama, not as an end in itself. Though neither of the two principals is a native French-speaker, their performances are totally idiomatic, with Holzmair a fresh, lyrical Pélleas, believably ardent in his obsession with Mélisande, and with von Otter also characterising superbly, tender and subtle, not just an innocent. The Golaud of Laurent Naouri is the more moving, when with his youngish baritone he is such a believable lover, not merely a predator. The others too are first-rate, with firmness and clarity the keynote, with the soprano of Florence Couderc fresh and bright if obviously feminine in this young boy's role. The three discs avoid the need to break in the middle of Act 3, and come in a three-for-the-price-of-two offer, but the CD index points are limited to the beginnings of scenes, not even separating the preludes and interludes, so that the third disc containing just Act 5, has only a single index point.

The Lyon cast is strong: François Le Roux's Pelléas, familiar from Abbado's DG recording, has innocence and vulnerability, and the Mélisande of Colette Alliot-Lugaz is subtly drawn, more so than in her Decca recording with Dutoit. José van Dam, who also recorded the rôle with both Abbado and Karajan, conveys Golaud's torment of spirit to perfection, and it is difficult to fault any of the remaining characters.

Special interest lies in Gardiner's musical direction: he corrects various textual errors and removes the interludes Debussy wrote to cover scene changes in the original production, producing an altogether tauter dramatic experience. Gardiner also lays out the orchestra in the way Debussy had originally directed with a distinct gain in transparency.

The stage director shows no comparable respect for the original: the action is placed indoors in the large room of a château at the turn of the last century at the time when Debussy was composing the opera: so there are no tower, no sea-shore, no forest, no grotto, no sense of the sunless castle and no mystery.

A rather run-down Golaud is seen in a dressing-gown, turning over the past in his mind, and we lose the fountain, the impact of light when the lovers emerge from the vault – and so on. In any profession other than opera production this would be condemned as vandalism, although it is not quite as dire and impertinent as the 1997 Glyndebourne production which pictured Mélisande perched in a chandelier! This performance comes from 1987.

Doubtless the 1992 Welsh National Opera production by Peter Stein, with Boulez conducting and Neil Archer and Alison Hagley in the title rôles, long available on video (DG 072 431-3) and laserdisc (DG 072 431-1), will reach DVD during the lifetime of this volume. It shows a decent respect for Debussy's dramatic conception and is finer and more atmospheric than either of Boulez's CD accounts on Sony.

DELIBES, Léo (1836–91)

Coppélia (ballet; complete. Choreography: Ninette de Valois).

✪ *** BBC **DVD** 1024. Benjamin, Acosta, Heydon, Royal Ballet, ROHCGO, Moldoveaunu. (Production: Ninette de Valois/Anthony Dowell. V/D: Bob Lockyer.)

With this production the Royal Ballet celebrated its return to Covent Garden after the Opera House's two-year closure. Ninette de Valois's choreography and production and Osbert Lancaster's colourful sets of *Coppélia* make a return after twenty years. It was televized in February 2000 and were you to compare a VTR of that broadcast with the present DVD, you would appreciate the greater sense of presence, cleaner focus and altogether firmer image that the new medium offers. In fact the colour is quite spectacular.

Leanne Benjamin's Swanhilda has much charm and the Cuban, Carlos Acosta, brings the appropriate ardour, grace and virtuosity to the role of Franz, while Luke Heydon's Dr Coppélius is exemplary. There is first-class dancing from the Corps and lively, well-paced orchestral playing under Nicolae Moldoveaunu. Moreover, the sound is well defined and musically balanced.

Deborah Bull introduces the ballet and the DVD includes a short feature about the Royal Ballet on the move after the closure of the Royal Opera House, and another on the work of Osbert Lancaster. An altogether delightful set which will give much pleasure.

Coppélia; Sylvia (excerpts).

(BB) ** (*) EMI Encore (ADD) CDE5 75221-2. New Philh. O, Mackerras – MESSAGER: *Les Deux Pigeons* (excerpts); GOUNOD: *Faust: ballet music.* ** (*)

With only three numbers from *Coppélia* and four from *Sylvia* included – admittedly among the most popular movements – this CD captures only a few of the highlights from Delibes's scintillating ballets, but these late 1960s recordings are lively and enjoyable, only a touch dated in sound, and they form part of an enjoyable and inexpensive programme of French ballet music.

Lakmé (complete).

(M) ** EMI CMS5 67742-2 [567745] (2). Mesplé, Burles, Millet, Soyer, Paris Opéra Comique Ch. & O, Lombard.

This EMI version with Alain Lombard conducting Opéra-Comique forces dates from the beginning of the 1970s, just after the much superior Decca Bonynge recording with Sutherland (now on a Double Decca, 460 741-2). Since then the *Flower Duet* has become a top classical pop following a British Arways TV commercial. This is delicately sung by Mady Mesplé and Danielle Millet, but otherwise the singing of Mesplé in the title role is thin and wobbly. Charles Burles sings with some charm as Gérald and Roger Soyer offers strong support as Nilakantha. Lombard conducts with understanding and the recording is agreeable if rather reverberant. However this is hardly a suitable candidate for 'Great Recordings of the Century' (no doubt the choice of French EMI) and the newest Toulouse version with Natalie Dessay, Gregory Kunde, Delphine Haldan and José van Dam, conducted by Plasson, is now a clear first choice (EMI CDC5 56569-2).

DELIUS, Frederick (1862–1934)

(i) Air and Dance; La Calinda (Koanga); Hassan: Intermezzo and Serenade; (ii) In a Summer Garden; Paris; (iii) Sea Drift; (iv) A Song of the High Hills; (ii) A Song of Summer; Summer Night; A Village Romeo and Juliet: The Walk to the Paradise Garden; (v) Cello Sonata.

(M) ** (*) Decca mono/stereo 470 375-2. (i) ASMF, Marriner; (ii) LSO, Collins; (iii) Shirley-Quirk, London Symphony Ch., RPO, Hickox; (iv) Evans, Hoare, Welsh Nat. Op. Ch. & O, Mackerras; (v) Lloyd Webber, Forsberg.

Some notable Delius performances here, the earliest contribution coming from Anthony Collins. Dating from 1953, the mono recorded sound retains its ambient warmth and the glow of sound that made these accounts famous in their day and that is so essential for Delius. *Paris* is full of spontaneous passionate evocation, and Collins's mastery in this repertoire is confirmed in the rest of his items. In his 1980 account of *Sea Drift*, rather than lingering, Hickox is urgent in his expressiveness, but there is plenty of evocative atmosphere, too. John Shirley-Quirk sings with characteristic sensitivity, and the chorus – trained by Hickox – is outstanding; the remastering is excellent. Marriner's 1977 items have always been admired: they are lovely performances, warm, tender and eloquent. They are superbly played and recorded in a flattering acoustic, the sound not in the least bit dated.

(i; ii) Brigg Fair; (iii; i; iv) Piano Concerto; (iv; v) Violin Concerto; (vi) On Hearing the First Cuckoo in Spring; (vii) 2 Pieces for Cello and Piano: Caprice; Elegy.

(M) ** (*) Decca mono/stereo (ADD/DDD) 470 190-2. (i) LSO; (ii) Collins; (iii) Kars; (iv) Gibson; (v) Little; (vi) Welsh Nat. Op. O, Mackerras; (vii) Lloyd Webber, Forsberg.

Anthony Collins's mono 1953 account of *Brigg Fair* is a classic account, its ardour totally English in feeling. The delicate woodwind playing at the opening is most beautiful, while the hazy languor of the string theme, echoed by the horn, is wonderfully gentle in its sentience. The sound is superb for its time, although its coupling with much later stereo and digital recordings might not suit all listeners. That said, there are no poor performances here: Tasmin Little, often shading her tone down to hushed pianissimos in the *Violin Concerto*, is ravishing, with the close of the work bringing a moment of total repose, while Mackerras draws strong, sympathetic playing from the orchestra of the WNO, as he does in *On Hearing the First Cuckoo in Spring*, although here the forwardness and clarity of the recording tends to make the results less evocative than they might be. Jean-Rudolph Kars proves a superb and eloquent advocate of the rare *Piano Concerto* in this persuasive 1969 reading. Gibson provides admirable support, and the recording demonstrates an excellent balance between soloist and orchestra. With the 2 *Pieces for Cello and Orchestra* making a pleasing bonus, this is certainly a worthwhile collection.

(i) *Brigg Fair; Eventyr; In a Summer Garden;* (ii) *A Song before Sunrise;* (i) *A Song of Summer;* (ii) *Summer Night on the River; A Village Romeo and Juliet: The Walk to the Paradise Garden.*

(B) *** CfP (DDD/ADD) 575 3152. (i) LPO; (ii) Hallé O; Handley.

Vernon Handley is an understanding and exciting Delian, and if his tempi are very much his own, he is always warmly sympathetic, fresh and spontaneous. The beautifully played Hallé performances were recorded in 1981 and the digital sound is of EMI's best quality, matching clarity of definition with ambient lustre and rich colouring. This very generous reissue adds three hardly less fine LPO performances recorded in the Henry Wood Hall three years earlier, where the analogue quality is very nearly as good. Handley's approach to *The Walk to the Paradise Garden* is strongly emotional, closer to Barbirolli than to Beecham. Incidently, the variations which make up *Brigg Fair* – one of the disc's highlights – are grouped in six separate bands, a very useful feature, unique on CD.

Violin Concerto.

(BB) (***) Dutton mono CDBP 9735. Sammons, Liverpool PO, Sargent – ELGAR: *Violin Concerto.* (***)
(BB) (**(*)) Naxos mono 8.110951. Sammons, Liverpool PO, Sargent – ELGAR: *Violin Concerto.* (**(*))

Albert Sammons's première account of the Delius *Violin Concerto*, recorded in 1944, is by general consent still unsurpassed even by the likes of Ralph Holmes and Tasmin Little, except in terms of recording quality. The World Record LP transfer by A. C. Griffith (coupled with Moiseiwitsch's 1946 account of the *Piano Concerto*) was very fine, but those who have been surviving on that, may now turn with confidence to these

transfers. Of the two, Dutton is a clear choice, smoother and more detailed as far as the orchestra is concerned, and it does much better justice to Sammons's tone.

Eventyr *(Once upon a Time); Sleigh Ride;* (i) *Song of the High Hills;* (ii) *5 Songs from the Norwegian* (orch. Holten).

*** Danacord DACOCD 592. Aarhus SO, Holten; with (i) Høyer Hansen, Kjøller, Aarhus University Ch., Aarhus Chamber Ch.; (ii) Bonde-Hansen.

Bo Holten and the excellent Aarhus Symphony Orchestra follow up their earlier Danacord disc of Delius's Danish inspirations with this collection of works inspired by Norway, a country to which Delius was specially attracted. His first major visit was in 1887 during a summer vacation while studying at the Leipzig Conservatory, when he spent over six weeks joyfully exploring fjords, moors and mountains. Later that year his Leipzig contemporary, Christian Sinding, introduced him to Grieg, for whom as a Christmas present he wrote *Sleigh Ride*, a piano piece buried for many years that finally surfaced in the composer's orchestration in 1946, long after Grieg's death. It is a jolly little piece, not at all Delian in style, that by rights should have been a popular hit from the start.

The *Five Songs from the Norwegian* were written in gratitude for Grieg's intervention with Delius's father over giving him an allowance so that he could devote himself to composition. Dedicated to Grieg's wife, they are charming pieces, the more seductive in Bo Holten's sensitive orchestrations, with Henriette Bonde-Hansen the delightfully fresh, pure-toned soprano. *Eventyr*, inspired by the folk-tales of Christen Asbjornsen, was written much later, an evocative tone-poem first given in 1919 by Sir Henry Wood, but the most ambitious Delius work inspired by Norway is *The Song of the High Hills*. Though Beecham recorded it in the days of 78 (sadly not currently available on CD), it has been curiously neglected on disc, when over its 25-minute span it offers some of the most hauntingly atmospheric music that Delius ever wrote, notably in the passages for wordless choir. Holten conducts a beautiful, refined performance, which keeps the music moving, never letting it meander, building to powerful climaxes thrillingly recorded with a fine feeling for atmosphere.

Fennimore and Gerda: *Intermezzo; Irmelin: Prelude; Koanga: La Calinda* (arr. Fenby); *On Hearing the First Cuckoo in Spring; Sleigh Ride.*

(B) *** CfP (ADD) 575 3162. LPO, Handley – VAUGHAN WILLIAMS: *Lark Ascending; Wasps Suite* etc. ***

These five favourite Delius items belong to the same 1977 Henry Wood Hall sessions as the LPO items included in the companion Handley collection above. The playing is equally sensitive and the warm, spacious analogue recording is most attractively transferred. The Vaughan Williams items are hardly less attractive.

(i–iii) *Idyll (Once I Passed Through a Populous City)*; **(i–iv)** *Requiem*; **(i; v)** *A Song Before Sunrise*; **(i; iv; v)** *Songs of Farewell.*

(M) **(*) EMI (ADD) CDM5 75293-2. (i) RPO; (ii) Davies; (iii) with Harper, Shirley-Quirk; (iv) Royal Choral Soc.; (v) Sargent.

Delius's *Requiem* was written during the First World War, and his well-known atheism as well as his disillusion with life did not find a responsive echo at the first performance: indeed, the work was written off. Although it is not austere, it is far sparer than most of the composer's other works of the period, and much of it is rewarding. This was its recording première. The *Idyll* is much earlier, or at least its material is, and the music, though uneven in inspiration, is often extremely impressive. These excellent pioneering Meredith Davies performances date from 1968 and still sound excellent, if lacking a little richness by modern standards. The *Songs of Farewell*, dedicated to Eric Fenby, are among the most ambitious works the composer attempted to write after he had become blind and paralysed. Sir Malcolm Sargent conducted the first performance in March 1932, and this, his 1964 account, is committed and warm-hearted in the best tradition of Delius recording. Fenby admitted in the original sleeve note how disconcerted he was initially to find out how thin the basic material was on which the whole structure for double chorus and orchestra was to be founded. True, the musical ideas are not Delius's most memorable, but the writing is still beautiful and will delight all Delians. *A Song Before Sunrise* provides a haunting and atmospheric makeweight. The recordings are excellent for their period.

(i) *A Village Romeo and Juliet* (complete); **(ii)** *Songs of Sunset.*

(M) (***) Somm BEECHAM 12-2. (i) Soames, Hambleton, F. Smith, Sharp, Clinton, Terry, Davies; (ii) Haley, Henderson; BBC Theatre Ch., RPO, L. Select Ch.; LPO, Beecham.

Beecham's radio recording of Delius's opera, *A Village Romeo and Juliet*, issued here on the SOMM label, was made for the BBC Third programme only a week before he went to the EMI studio to record the opera with substantially the same cast. The wonder is how different it is interpretatively. The timing alone provides an indication of the contrast, with the studio recording some eleven minutes shorter than the radio recording in an opera lasting under two hours. Surprisingly, the more expansive radio recording is the one which sounds more passionate at almost every point, with the spontaneity of the live performance far outweighing any advantages of precision and balance in the studio version. With Beecham magic in full flow, the curiously stilted story of the lovers who sacrifice themselves rather than be separated is made tenderly moving, with the energy of the score given its full impact. Though the studio recording is better balanced, it is the radio version which, despite flaws, is

the more atmospheric, with more air round the voices.

Rene Soames, a fine, sensitive tenor, sings with fresh, cleanly-focused tone as the hero in both recordings, yet the radio version again wins out as the more lively. Other singers who appear in both include Gordon Clinton in the sinister role of the Dark Fiddler, and Frederick Sharp as Marti, father of the heroine, Vreli, both strong and clear in a very English way. Fabian Smith, who sings the role of Sali's father, is even firmer than his quarrelling rival, Sharp, and every bit as impressive as the excellent Denis Dowling on the EMI version. More surprising still, Vera Terry as the heroine, Vreli, on the radio recording outshines her EMI rival, Lorely Dyer, who has a distracting flutter in the voice, though at the top Terry's soprano grows shrill. The only pity is that at mid-price Somm have been unable to provide a libretto, and the indexing is limited to just one track per scene.

The revised version of Beecham's 1934 Leeds Festival performance of the *Songs of Sunset* makes a welcome bonus on the second disc. When Somm first issued it on an earlier disc of material from the Beecham archive, the final section was missing, and was replaced on the disc by the equivalent passage from Beecham's later studio recording. Since then the missing section has been discovered, here rounding off an astonishingly vivid and atmospheric live performance of these sensuous settings of poems by Ernest Dowson, with Olga Haley and Roy Henderson the excellent soloists.

DEUTSCH, Adolph (1897–1980)

Film music from: *George Washington Slept Here; High Sierra; Northern Pursuit; The Maltese Falcon; The Mask of Dimitrios.*

**(*) Marco Polo 8.225169. Moscow SO, Stromberg.

Adolph Deutsch's name is not as well known as Steiner, Korngold or Waxman, though he wrote some important scores for Warner films while he was under contract to the studio, from 1937 to 1945. (Incidentally, he later wrote the music to *Some Like it Hot*.) These scores, excellently reconstructed by John Morgan and draped in flamboyant orchestrations, are highly characteristic of Hollywood of the 1940s. Highlights include the opening flourish to *The Maltese Falcon*, with its brooding *film noir* atmosphere, interspersed by melodrama and highly romantic passages. *The Mask of Dimitrios* has some effective atmospheric evocation – the *Blackmail Letter* sequence, for example, where heavy brass, fluttering woodwind, and harp and celesta create plenty of dramatic tension. *The Big Battle* from the war film *Northern Pursuit* is an exciting set piece, a score that uses Beethoven's *Fifth Symphony* as a recurring motif, especially arresting at the end of the film. Although this music is essentially effect over substance, it is certainly presented vividly, with copious and fascinating sleeve notes. But this is for film music buffs rather than for the general collector.

DOHNÁNYI, Ernst von
(1877–1960)

Piano Concerto No. 1 in E min., Op.51; Ruralia Hungarica.

*** Chan. 9649. Shelley, BBCPO, Bamert.

Howard Shelley, the brilliant soloist in Bamert's version of the *Variations on a Nursery Tune* (Chan. 9733), is here the powerful, warmly expressive soloist in a work which first brought Dohnányi success when still a student, the *First Piano Concerto*. With Bamert a dedicated interpreter of this composer, as he is in the rest of his excellent Chandos series, Shelley magnetically sustains the massive length of the outer movements, relishing the Lisztian fluency of the improvisatory writing and bringing a natural gravity to the chorale theme of the Bruckner-like central Andante. As an attractive coupling Bamert conducts the five movements of the orchestral version of *Ruralia Hungarica*, just one of the five folk-based works to which he gave this title. This makes a recommendable alternative to the rival Hyperion version of the *Concerto*, which has the *Second Concerto* for coupling (CDA 66684). Full, vivid recording, not always ideally clear on detail.

DONIZETTI, Gaetano (1797–1848)

L'elisir d'amore (complete).

*** Decca DVD 074-103-9. Gheorghiu, Alagna, Scaltriti, Alaimo, Lyon Op. Ch. & O, Pido

Updated to the 1920s with jolly sets in primary colours, Frank Dunlop's production for Lyon Opera on Decca makes an attractive DVD, very well-produced by Brian Large, involving the same cast as on the excellent Decca CD recording, also made in 1996. As Alagna explains in the 52-minute feature film on the making of the recording, which comes as a valuable supplement, he tries in his characterization of the innocent Nemorino to bring out the youthful rather than the comic element, with results a degree weightier than usual. Angela Gheorghiu as Adina emerges in Act I brandishing a riding-crop, more than a match for Belcore, let alone Nemorino, and singing enchantingly. As Belcore Roberto Scaltriti is young and virile, with Dulcamara equally firm and characterful, arriving in a vintage Rolls-Royce drawing a streamlined caravan. Under Evelino Pido the comedy of the piece fizzes winningly, with something of a circus atmosphere created by the staging.

Lucia di Lammermoor (complete).

(M) **(*) Westminster 471 250-2 (2). Sills, Bergonzi, Cappuccilli, Diaz, Amb. Op. Ch., LSO, Schippers.
(M) ** Decca (ADD) 470 421-2 (2). Caballé, Carreras, Sardinero, Ramey, Murray, Ahnsjö, Amb. Op. Ch., New Philh. O, López-Cobos.

The giving personality of Beverly Sills has never been so warmly conveyed on record as in the formidable performance originally issued on LP by EMI (it was recorded at Abbey Road), now a 1970 Westminster set. Sills's Mad Scene in particular is deeply moving. The initial 'takes' were recorded at the very end of a taxing six hours of sessions in which, like the heroine, Miss Sills was literally at the end of her tether. That tension has been retained in the finished recording and, with glass harmonica adding an authentic – if hideously out-of-tune – dimension to the score, Sills devotees need not hesitate. Her coloratura is as effortless as ever, and though the decorations to the cabaletta of the First Act aria are uncomfortably elaborate, the technical assurance is never in doubt. But, as in the opera house, the voice has an uneven register towards the top of the stave, and when it comes to the sheer beauty of tone she cannot compare with Sutherland. However, her supporting cast is first-rate and so is the vigorous direction of Thomas Schippers. The recording balance is not always consistent, but the sound is full and faithful.

The idea behind the set with Caballé is fascinating, a return to what the conductor, Jésus López-Cobos, believes is Donizetti's original concept, an opera for a dramatic soprano, not a light coloratura. Compared with the text we know, transpositions, paradoxically, are for the most part upwards (made possible when no stratospheric coloratura additions are needed); But Cobos's direction hardly compensates for the lack of brilliance and, José Carreras apart, the singing, even of Caballé, is not very persuasive. This has now been reissued at mid-price as part of Decca's 'Compact Opera Collection'. However, there is no printed libretto, only a CD-ROM facility which offers full text and translation.

DOPPER, Cornelis (1870–1939)

Symphonies Nos. 3 (Remembrant); 6 (Amsterdam).

*** Chan. 9923. Hague Residentie O, Bamert.

We have already had a fine recording of Dopper's *Second Symphony* from Bamert (Chan. 9884), but these are both more attractive, and their pervading geniality is endearing. They are not really programmatic: the title of the jolly *Third* (1905) anticipates the third centenary of the birth of the famous Dutch painter in 1906, which was celebrated with major compositions from a number of Dutch composers. The work is pleasingly if conventionally tuneful, with a strong, rhythmic scherzo; but the finale is perhaps the most striking movement, opening with fanfares, and with a Dvořákian lyrical flavour. The title of the *Amsterdam Symphony* relates to the finale, which celebrates a fair in Amsterdam on the queen's birthday. The Dvořákian flavour persists with the swinging secondary theme and the colourful scoring of the first movement. The contemplative *Adagio* makes a tranquil interlude before another bustlingly vibrant scherzo. The engagingly jaunty finale has no lack of picaresque detail, with its popular tunes, the sounds of the bells of the tramcars, and even snatches of the national anthem. This is not great music, but it is certainly entertaining in performances as lively and well played as these. The recording is well up to the house standards, if perhaps a shade over-reverberant.

DUPHLY, Jacques (1715–89)

Pièces pour clavecin: *Allemande; La de Belombre; La du Baq; Cazamajor; Chaconne; La Forqueray; La Lanza; Médée; Menuets; La Millettina; Rondeau: Le Pothoüin; La de la Tour; La Tribolet; La de Vaucanson; La de Villeneuve.*

** MDG 605.1068-2. Meyerson.

Jacques Duphly published four sets of *Pièces de clavecin* in Paris between 1744 and 1768. This disc draws on all four collections. The music is finely wrought and vital in spirit, very much in the tradition of Couperin, and Mitzi Meyerson has chosen a well-contrasted and well-planned programme. In her earlier 1988 recital for ASV (CDGAU 108; see our main volume) she used a Goble but here turns to the 1998 copy by Keith Hill of a Taskin, which she used in her recent two-CD set of Forqueray suites. Although she plays with great panache and understanding (her playing could not be more idiomatic), the balance is unpleasingly close and the aural image can only be called overbearing. One quickly tires of the sound though Ms Meyerson's mastery of the style is unfailingly impressive. But the ASV disc is the one to go for.

DUREY, Louis (1888–1979)

Mélodies and song cycles: *Le bestiaire; Chansons basques; Epigrammes de Théocrite; Hommage à Erik Satie; Images à Crusoé; Inscriptions sur un oranger; 2 Lieder romantiques; 3 Poèmes de Pétrone.*

*** Hyp. CDA 67257. Le Roux, Johnson.

Louis Durey is the forgotten member of 'Les Six', the group of young French composers nominated in 1920 for their adventurousness. As Graham Johnson points out in his keenly perceptive note for this important issue in Hyperion's French Song Edition, Durey's membership of the group was suspect from the start, and foundered completely when he turned against their inspirational collaborator, the writer and artist, Jean Cocteau. Durey was more tenderly romantic than the others, initially inspired by his love of Debussy, later rejecting the artistic embrace of the eccentric Erik Satie.

All the songs in this illuminating collection date from 1918 and 1919, the brief period leading up to the arrival of 'Les Six', with the composer's own commentary on each group of songs included as well as the texts. An exception is the opening item, *Hommage à Erik Satie*, a song found among Satie's papers on his death, with its stylistic mixture of Poulenc, Stravinsky and Satie himself. The rest reveal a subtly evocative response to French texts and a characterful use of the piano, often angular in the three Basque songs to words by Cocteau and in the twenty-six songs setting *Le bestiaire* of Apollinaire. Unlike his friend, Poulenc, who at the same period set merely a selection of Apollinaire's animal portraits, Durey set all of them, omitting only the four Orpheus poems which punctuate the series. Here Le Roux recites those four extra poems in the appropriate places.

Most of the forty-eight songs in the seven collections are very brief, pointful fragments merely, but the sequence, sensitively devised by Johnson, leads up to Durey's masterpiece, *Images à Crusoe*, which to texts by Saint-John Perse tackles a deeper theme – the alienation of Crusoe from the world when he returned from his desert island. Durey himself was a loner, cutting himself off from the world of Parisian chic, a lifelong communist whose political allegiance sadly seemed eventually to sap the originality so winningly displayed here. Though under pressure Le Roux's baritone has its moments of strain, these are all wonderfully idiomatic performances from singer and pianist alike, ideally recorded and presented.

DUŠEK, Franz Xaver (1731–99)

Sinfonias in E flat (Altner Eb3); F (Altner F4); G (Altner G2).

(BB) *(*) Naxos 8.555878. Helios 18, Oschatz.

Part of Naxos's useful 18th Century Symphony series, these three Dušek symphonies (undated) are pleasing works, with some elegant tunes and nice touches here and there, but the performances, on period instruments, are only just about serviceable, and no more than that, and the dryish sound is not particularly ingratiating.

DUTILLEUX, Henri (born 1916)

(i; ii) Cello Concerto (*Tout un monde lointain*); (ii; iii) Violin Concerto (*L'Arbre des songes*); (i) 3 Strophes sur le nom de Sacher (for unaccompanied cello).

**(*) Virgin VC5 45502-2. (i) Mørk; (ii) Radio France PO, Chung; (iii) Capuçon.

There is only one rival version coupling the two concertos, the Decca account with Lynn Harrell and Pierre Amoyal respectively as the soloists with the Orchestre National (444 398-2), but this new Virgin version this has the benefit of a bonus in the form of the *Trois strophes sur le nom de Sacher* for solo cello commissioned by Rostropovich to celebrate Paul Sacher's seventieth birthday. Truls Mørk is an impressive exponent of *Tout un monde lointain,* though the solo cello is rather too forwardly placed. The recording made in the Salle Olivier Messiaen at Radio France is impressively detailed even if the balance is slightly synthetic (as one finds in radio studios). Renaud Capuçon is recorded in the Salle Pleyel and the splendid recording reveals plenty of orchestral detail, though perhaps Pierre Amoyal has the greater presence. There is not a great deal to choose between the performances: Myung-Whun Chung holds everything together in magisterial fashion. The Virgin disc has the solo piece, played with great authority and fine characterization by Truls Mørk.

Métaboles; The Shadows of Time; Symphony No. 2 (Le Double).

*** EMI CDC5 57143-2. Toulouse Capitole O, Plasson.

(BB) **(*) Arte Nova 74321. Bordeaux Aquitaine Nat. O, Graf.

This new record from the Orchestre du Capitole de Toulouse and Michel Plasson eclipses previous recordings of the *Second Symphony*, not only in terms of vitality and imagination but in the sheer detail and realism of the sound. Not only the symphony (*Le Double*) but also its two companions sound quite marvellous.

The Orchestre National Bordeaux Aquitaine is far from negligible in this repertoire and their playing under the Austrian Hans Graf is spirited and vital, although it does not match the Plasson record in finesse or subtlety. Nor is the recording quite in the same league. Those wanting this repertoire but not willing to spend more than budget price, will naturally want to consider it, but the Toulouse version is more than worth the extra outlay.

DVOŘÁK, Antonín (1841–1904)

Cello Concerto in B min., Op. 104.

(BB) (***) Naxos mono 8.110930. Casals, Czech PO, Szell – BRAHMS: *Double Concerto*. (***)

(B) **(*) Warner Apex 0927 40600-2. Noras, Finnish RSO, Oramo – BARTOK: *Rhapsody No.1* ***; ELGAR: *Cello Concerto* ***.

(M) **(*) Ph. 470 250-2 (2). Schiff, Concg. O, C. Davis – PROKOFIEV: *Sinfonia concertante;* SCHUMANN: *Concerto;* R. STRAUSS: *Don Quixote.* **(*)

(M) *(*) EMI CDM5 67593-2 [567594]. Rostropovich, LPO, Giulini – SAINT-SAËNS: *Cello Concerto No. 1.* **

Cello Concerto; Silent Woods, Op. 88.

**(*) Guild GMCD 7253. Kreger, Philh. O, Yu – HERBERT: *Cello Concerto.* **(*)

(i) Cello Concerto; Slavonic Dances Nos. 5–8, Op. 46/5–8.

(BB) ** Arte Nova 74321 34054-2. (i) Schiefen; Gran Canaria PO, Leaper.

Casals's classic account with the Czech Philharmonic is discussed in our main volume in the EMI transfer made by A. C. Griffith and the late Keith Hardwick, where it is coupled with the Elgar (CDH7 63498-2). The Naxos coupling restores the intensely felt Brahms *Double Concerto* with Thibaud and Casals to circulation. There is not a great deal to choose between Mark Obert-Thorn's transfer of the Dvořák and the EMI version - both have been done with great care –

though if pressed to a choice, we would prefer the slightly more detailed Naxos.

James Kreger, a pupil of Leonard Rose, won the Piatigorsky Award at his time at Juilliard when he was only 18 years old. He first came to wider notice at the Moscow Tchaikovsky Competition in 1974 and has an impressive *curriculum vitae*. His dedication and artistry come across in this fine version of the *Cello Concerto*, whose slow movement is most eloquent. He is rather too forwardly balanced in comparison with the orchestra and draws out the central section of the first movement rather too much, but this is still a rewarding performance, and the addition of the rarely recorded *Silent Woods* is another plus point. In this coupling with the Victor Herbert *Concerto*, was the source of Dvořák's inspiration, he comes into direct competition with Yo-Yo Ma, and some may well prefer Kreger's naturalness of expression. Djong Victorin Yu provides rather routine support, and it is the orchestral response that tips the scales in favour of the Ma performance (discussed in our main Guide).

The excellent Finnish cellist, Arto Noras, gives a sensitive reading of the Dvořák *Concerto* responsively accompanied by Oramo. He is rather too backwardly balanced, but better this than a spotlight, and the orchestra is vividly and warmly caught. There is no lack of vigour, but most impressive are the tender moments, not least the *Epilogue*, raptly done. With fine couplings this is a real bargain.

Philips have reissued Heinrich Schiff's 1980 recording as part of a compilation of four key cello works to celebrate his 50th birthday. It has an exaggerated vein of poetry, akin to the somewhat recessive style of Yo-Yo Ma, but deeply felt with a range of emotion that is satisfying on a smaller scale. It sounds extremely well in its current CD transfer and can be strongly recommended to admirers of this artist.

Guido Schiefen is a very fine player, whose accounts of the Strauss and Pfitzner sonatas we have much admired elsewhere in this volume. He is heard to often impressive effect here, although he tends to waywardness at times. The Gran Canaria Orchestra is an impressive body, although their strings, as balanced on this disc, lack the opulence of the finest rival versions.

Rostropovich's 1977 version of the *Cello Concerto* (with Giulini) is his least successful on record and is a strange choice for EMI's 'Great Recordings of the Century'. He makes heavy weather of most of the concerto, and his unrelieved emotional intensity is matched by Giulini, who focuses attention on detail rather than structural cohesion. Of course there are many beauties here that compel admiration, and the current transfer of the Abbey Road recording is impressive, but this does not begin to match his 1969 recording with Karajan and the Berlin Philharmonic (available at mid price on ❶ DG 447 413-2 or in a celebratory 2-CD compilation with other concertos – DG 471 620-2 – see CONCERTS below).

(i) *Cello Concerto*; (ii) *Serenade for Strings, Op. 22*; *Serenade for Wind, Op. 44*; (iii) *Symphony No. 9 (New World)*.

(B) *(*) Finlandia Ultima 0630 18950-2 (2). (i) Noras, Finnish RSO, Oramo; (ii) St Paul CO, Wolff; (iii) Philh. O, Inbal.

Here a potentially attractive anthology, very well recorded, is let down by a series of performances which fail to be distinctive enough for the listener to want to return to them. Arto Noras is a fine young player, but in the first movement of the *Cello Concerto* the volatile changes of tempo (with an abrupt slowing-down for the second subject) are unconvincing. His performance is discussed in more detail above. The performances of the two *Serenades* from the St Paul Chamber Orchestra are agreeable enough but in the last resort rather bland and undercharacterized, though very well played, with the work for wind instruments much the more pleasing of the two. Inbal's *New World* is not very compelling either. He omits the first-movement exposition repeat and, like his colleague Sakari Oramo in the *Concerto*, his slowing down for the secondary theme sounds mannered. The rest of the performance lacks real magnetism.

(i) *Cello Concerto*; (ii) *Symphony No. 8 in G, Op. 88*.

(M) **(*) Sony SMK 89871. BPO; (i) with Ma, cond. Maazel; (ii) cond. Giulini.

The partnership of the passionately extrovert Lorin Maazel – witness his spaciously powerful orchestral introduction – and the more withdrawn artistry of Yo-Yo Ma is unexpectedly successful in Dvořák's gorgeous concerto, when the recording is so vivid and atmospheric and the orchestral playing superb. Ma's rapt concentration and refined control of colour brings at times an elegiac dimension to the performance, and Maazel accompanies with understanding and great sensitivity, fining down the orchestral textures so that he never masks his often gentle soloist, yet providing an exuberant contrast in orchestral fortissimos. If Ma's playing is characteristically subtle, it is never narcissistic: sometimes there is a mere thread of tone, but it is a magical thread. The orchestra is set back within a warmly resonant concert-hall ambience which lends bloom to the overall sound-picture – the solo cello is most skilfully balanced – and ensures that the pianissimo detail of the Adagio registers naturally.

Giulini's account of the *G major Symphony* is warm-hearted and has those touches of refinement which distinguish this conductor's interpretations. The Berlin Philharmonic too, play most beautifully throughout. But the performance is studio bound and, although not without intensity, refuses completely to take off. Furthermore, Giulini makes comparatively little of the lilting lyrical melody which is the glorious centrepiece of the *Allegretto grazioso*.

(i) *Piano Concerto in G min., Op. 33*; Overtures: *Carnival*; *In Nature's Realm*; *Slavonic Rhapsody No. 2*.

(M) **(*) Westminster 471 266-2. Firkušný; Vienna State Op. O, Somogyi.

If ever there was a 'Great Pianist of the 20th Century' it was Rudolf Firkušný whose omission from the Philips series was scandalous, particularly when lesser pianists such as Previn were included. This is his 1965 recording of the Dvořák concerto which HMV first issued on LP in their Concert Classics series coupled with the *Slavonic Rhapsody No. 2*. Firkušný plays a combination of Wilém Kurz's version (printed below Dvořák's own in the Collected Edition) and his own realization. This aristocrat of the keyboard recorded it subsequently with Kubelik, and most successfully with the Czech Philharmonic and Václav Neuman in 1990 (RCA), which is now deleted. László Somogyi, a pupil of Kodály and Leo Weiner, gets lively performances of the *Carnival Overture* and *In Nature's Realm*, but first choice for the *Piano Concerto* remains with Richter and Kleiber (EMI CDM5 66895-2).

(i) *Violin Concerto in A, Op. 53*; *Romance in F min. Symphonies Nos. 7 in D min., Op. 70*; *8 in G, Op. 88*.

(B) ** Erato/Teldec Ultima 3984 21036-2 (2). Philh. O, Inbal, with (i) Zehetmair.

Inbal's early 1990s Dvořák recordings bring straightforward, well-played if not exactly riveting accounts of the symphonies, lacking something in Czech character and excitement and with a hint of blandness creeping in at times. Zehetmair plays with a clean attack and much brilliance in the *Violin Concerto*, but there is little sense of fantasy. In essence, these performances bring the music into the central Viennese tradition, with the influences of the composer's homeland played down. However, these CDs are inexpensive and the sound is good.

Legends, Op. 59.

(BB) ** Warner Apex 7559 79676-2. Rochester PO, Zinman.

Like the more familiar *Slavonic Dances*, the Op. 59 *Legends* began life in piano duet form and were only later orchestrated with Dvořák's characteristic mastery. The Rochester performances derive from 1984 and, as far as we have been able to ascertain, have not appeared before in Britain. We are fairly close to the orchestra, and the sound needs space to expand a little more. All the same, the performances are persuasive enough, although at under 42 minutes this disc is hardly a bargain. Iván Fischer on Philips 464 647-2 (see our main volume, p.424) is the one to have.

Serenade for Strings in E, Op. 22.

(M) **(*) Decca (ADD) 470 262-2. ASMF, Marriner – GRIEG: *Holberg Suite*. TCHAIKOVSKY: *Serenade*. ***

Marriner's 1970 Decca (originally Argo) account of the *Serenade* is very richly textured, almost velvety, which some may find a bit too indulgent for the innocent simplicity of the music. But after a slightly mannered start, it is hard not to respond to such beguiling and engaging playing. The sound remains rich and full in this 'Legends' transfer, and both couplings are first class.

Serenade for Wind in D min., Op. 44.

(M) *** CRD (ADD) CRD 3410. Nash Ens. – KROMMER: *Octet-Partitas.* ***

The Nash Ensemble can hold their own with the competition in the *D minor Serenade*, and their special claim tends to be the coupling, a Krommer rarity that is well worth hearing. The CRD version of the Dvořák is very well recorded and the playing is very fine indeed, robust yet sensitive to colour, and admirably spirited.

Slavonic Dances Nos. 1–16, Op. 46/1–8 & Op. 72/1–8.

*** Teldec 8573 81038-2. COE, Harnoncourt.

*** Ph. 464 601-2. Budapest Festival O, Fischer.

(M) **(*) Chan. 6641. RSNO, Järvi.

(M) **(*) Decca (ADD) 468 495-2. VPO, Kubelik.

(M) (**) Westminster mono 471 202-2. RPO, Rodzinski.

Harnoncourt's excitingly uninhibited new set of the *Slavonic Dances*, with the Chamber Orchestra of Europe, has received much acclaim and for most collectors its free-running adrenalin will make it an obvious primary recommendation. Recorded live, the sound may not have the richness and colour of Dohnányi's splendid demonstration Decca set made in Cleveland (430 171-2), or indeed Fischer's natural Budapest ambience, but the balance is well judged to achieve maximum projection and brilliance, while at the same time reflecting the acoustic of the Stefaniensaal, Graz, Austria.

As for the playing, it combines great exuberance and virtuosity with vivid colouring. Harnoncourt's direction has tremendous zest and vitality. The *Dumka* character of Op. 46/2 is spectacularly caught, moving from a relaxed lyrical charm and warmly flexible phrasing to spontaneously hot-blooded bursts of energy, with the trombones electrifyingly unleashed. The delicacy of the string and woodwind playing in No. 6 of the first set is particularly beguiling, as is the seductive rubato at the opening of Op. 72/2. Harnoncourt's dramatic contrasts are never more excitingly made than in the sheer verve of the penultimate number (Op. 72/7), balanced by the affectionate ebb and flow of the final *Sousedská*, marked Lento grazioso, quasi tempo di valse. But even here the relaxation of the shapely phrasing is underpinned by an inherent vitality, with the last two chords given a firm finality.

Not surprisingly the playing of the Budapest Festival Orchestra under Iván Fischer is attractively idiomatic and the Philips recording is first-class in every way, richer and more natural than the Teldec sound for Harnoncourt. If by the side of Harnoncourt the performances seem comparatively easy-going, they are certainly not without moments of brilliance, even if they lack the sheer zest which makes the COE playing so compelling. But those who find Harnoncourt too rashly uninhibited will find this a mellower but satisfying alternative set, beautifully played and even more idiomatic in feeling.

Järvi undoubtedly has the measure of this repertoire and he secures brilliant and responsive playing from the RSNO. The recording, made in the SNO Centre, Glasgow, has the orchestra set back in an acoustic of believable depth, but the upper strings are brightly lit and the fortissimos bring some loss of body and a degree of hardness on top, so that after a while the ear tends to tire.

Almost unbelievably, Kubelik's early Vienna Philharmonic recording – the first complete set in stereo – dates from 1955 and was made in the Grosser Saal of the Musikverein, which adds an underlying warmth and atmosphere to a recording which on LP had an unattractivey thin upper range. The remastering has greatly improved the sound: the violins still sound pinched, but the effect is less exaggerated. The performances have plenty of vitality and colour, but the Decca reissue is in most respects eclipsed by Kubelik's later DG version made twenty years later with the Bavarian Radio Orchestra (see below).

Rodzinski's 1955 mono set of the *Slavonic Dances* (recorded by DG) is lively and enjoyable enough, but not so brilliant that it competes with several classic stereo versions. The sound is warm and quite good for the period but not outstanding.

Slavonic Dances Nos. 1–16, Op. 46/1–8; Op. 72/1–8; Overtures: Carnival, Op. 92; Hussite, Op. 87; In Nature's Realm, Op. 91; My Home, Op. 62; Othello, Op. 93. Symphonic Poems: The Golden Spinning Wheel, Op. 109; The Nooonday Witch, Op. 108; The Wood Dove, Op. 110; Symphonic Variations, Op. 78.

(B) *** DG Trio ADD 469 356-2 (3). Bavarian RSO, Kubelik.

This is among the finest of the Universal Trios (three discs for the price of two mid-priced CDs, with excellent documentation) so far issued. Kubelik has a special feeling for Dvořák, and these performances are among his finest on record and they are superbly played, with the *Slavonic Dances* displaying both virtuosity and panache. He is also splendidly dashing in *Carnival*, and the other two overtures, Opp. 91 and 93 – all three linked by a recurring main theme – which Dvořák wrote immediately after his first visit to America in 1892, are comparably successful and full of colouristic subtlety.

The patriotic *Hussite Overture* is superbly passionate, while the opening of *The Golden Spinning Wheel* is gentle and elfin-like. There is some bewitching playing from the woodwind throughout this performance, matched by tender strings and a noble restraint from the trombones. In both *The Water Goblin* and *The Noonday Witch* the dramatic urgency is most compelling, with stabbing rhythms in the former, and the lyrical sections of the score played with much poignancy. *The Wood Dove* is more difficult to bring off but here, as in its companions, there is magic and lustre in the orchestral textures and the atmospheric tension is striking. The *Symphonic Variations* open warmly and graciously, and Kubelik is obviously determined to minimize the Brahmsian associations. The recordings made in the Munich Hercules-Saal between 1973 and 1977 are freshly transferred to CD and generally sound very good indeed.

SYMPHONIES

Symphonies Nos. 1–9.

(M) *** Chan. 9991 (6). SNO, Järvi.

Now reissued at mid-price, this set makes a clear first choice for those wanting first-class digital recordings of these symphonies, the sound full and naturally balanced. There are no fillers, as with Kertész on Decca (and there would have been room for some on the first, second and sixth CDs), but each symphony can now be heard without a break, and Järvi is a consistently persuasive Dvořákian.

Symphony No. 6 in D major.

(M) **(*) Orfeo C 55201B. Bav. RSO, Kubelik. – JANACEK: Sinfonietta.**(*)

Kubelik recorded the glorious D major symphony in the early 1970s with the Berlin Philharmonic and it is still available as part of his complete bargain boxed set – DG 463 158-2 (see our main volume). This broadcast from 1971 is eminently satisfactory, straightforward and idiomatic, though not superior to his Berlin version. But readers who would welcome this particular coupling need not really hesitate. It is musically satisfying and well recorded.

Symphonies Nos. 7 in D min., Op. 70; 9 (New World).

(B) *(**) RCA Double 74321 68013-2 (2). Chicago SO, Levine.

Using modern digital techniques, RCA's Chicago engineers seem unable to recapture the acoustics of Symphony Hall, Chicago with the bloom and naturalness they achieved in the earliest days of analogue stereo. So Levine's virile account of the *Seventh Symphony* is hampered by a sound balance that makes tuttis seem aggressive (particularly the slow movement climax) and the upper strings thin and febrile. The reading itself is direct and well played, but lacks charm: the sparkle of the Scherzo is there, but Levine's inflection of the main idea is less than ideal. The *New World Symphony* is similarly problematic. The reading is lively and exciting, with some excellent playing, but in spite of a fresh transfer the digital recording is rough, again with an edge on the violins and internal congestion in tuttis.

Symphony No. 9 in E min. (From the New World), Op. 95.

*** Sony **DVD** SVD 48421. VPO, Karajan.

(M) (***) Teldec mono 8573 83025-2. Concg. O, Mengelberg. – FRANCK: *Symphony in D minor.* (***)

(BB) ** EMI Encore (ADD) CDE5 74961-2. New Philh. O, Muti – TCHAIKOVSKY: *Romeo and Juliet.* **(*)

Symphony No. 9 (New World). Overtures: Carnaval; In Nature's Realm; Othello.

*** Ondine Double ODE 962-2 (2). Czech PO, Ashkenazy.

Ashkenazy's recording is not only an outstanding new recommendation, but also makes an excellent coupling, offering Dvořák's trilogy of overtures, originally conceived as a group under the title of 'Nature, Life and Love', together with his most popular symphony in a two-for-the-price-of-one package. The performances from this great Czech orchestra are excellent, conveying wonderfully the warmth and thrust of a live experience, with musicians playing their hearts out. In the powerful build-up in the central development section of the first movement, one registers that this is the opposite of a routine performance from musicians over-familiar with a piece. Incidentally, Ashkenazy follows the instruction from Dvořák to ignore the exposition repeats in the first movements of his symphonies. The great cor anglais solo in the Largo slow movement is easily songful, and the flute solo in the central section has a pastoral freshness. The scherzo brings wonderfully crisp articulation and a delectable lilt in the contrasting episodes, while the finale is big and bold with bouncy rhythms. Textures are not ideally transparent, largely a question of the immediate recorded sound, warm rather than clear.

As for the overtures, *In Nature's Realm* vividly evokes a pastoral atmosphere, genial and welcoming, while *Carnival*, opening at a fast and furious pace, is both brilliant and joyful, with *Othello* bitingly dramatic in the main allegro. Though there are many fine versions of the *New World Symphony*, this one is not only among the finest, but offers a unique and apt coupling in its two-disc format.

Karajan recorded this symphony four times with the Berlin Philharmonic (for Polydor in 1940, for Columbia, EMI, in 1958, for DG in 1964 and for EMI/HMV in 1977). This present account comes from February 1985 and appeared originally on both LP and CD on DG 415 509. At the time we thought the playing of the Vienna Philharmonic not quite as refined as the previous Berlin version (which at the time seemed unsurpassed in terms of sheer excitement).

Seeing as well as hearing this performance gives one pause. Does seeing the players and their conductor affect the listener's judgement? Whether or not it equals earlier versions or not, it is certainly a very fine account, its beauty of sonority is quite affecting, and the remaining movements are strikingly fresh.

The sound has an impressively wide dynamic range and the visual direction keeps the eye's attention where it would be in the concert hall. At 43:30 minutes it is perhaps short measure but artistically it is very satisfying and well worth the money.

Mengelberg took up his appointment at the Amsterdam Concertgebouw in 1895 only two years after Dvořák had finished his Symphony, *From the New World*. He gave its Amsterdam première in 1896. Mengelberg conducted it with an enormous lyrical intensity, and gets such eloquent playing in these war-time performances that criticism is almost silenced. Both performances here are strongly narrative, that is they totally compel attention throughout, and the expressive self-indulgence of which his detractors complain, does not unduly disturb. Such is the dramatic fire and ardour of this playing that most listeners will take his mannerisms in their stride. Mind you, he pulls the contrasting idea of the scherzo horribly out of shape, and the end of the first movement is rather steeply faded, perhaps to avoid some blemish, but the sound has striking presence and sonority.

Muti's 1976 *New World* is a sweet and amiable performance, unsensationally attractive but hardly memorable. The recording is quite rich and smooth but makes the great cor anglais melody of the slow movement sound a little bland. The price is low but the competition is ferocious.

CHAMBER AND INSTRUMENTAL MUSIC

String Quartets Nos. 9 in D min., Op. 34; 10 in E flat, Op. 51.

(BB) *** Warner Apex 7559 79671-2. American String Qt.

Although the Dvořák quartets are well served on CD, their representation at bargain price is limited to the fine Naxos series by the Vlach Quartet, which includes these two works differently coupled. The *D minor*, Op. 34, has one of Dvořák's most deeply expressive and affecting slow movements. These 1985 performances are very sensitive and imaginative, and the recorded sound is perfectly serviceable. Strongly recommended alongside the Vlach versions.

String Quartet No. 12 in F (American), Op. 96; (i) String Quintet in E flat, Op. 97.

(BB) *** Warner Apex 0927 44355-2. Keller Qt., with (i) Deeva.

Dvořák wrote the second of his string quintets (the one with the extra viola) in the same period as the popular Op. 96 *Quartet*, similarly using thematic material with American inflections, so that the two works make an apt and attractive coupling. The Keller Quartet give outstanding readings of both works, crisp and fanciful, with light, clear textures and speeds generally on the fast side. The tenderness of the lyricism is beautifully caught in consistently imaginative phrasing, and the Erato recording is beautifully balanced. A real bargain.

String Sextet in A, Op. 48.

(BB) *** Warner Apex 7559 79679-2. Boston Symphony Chamber Players – SMETANA: *Piano Trio*. ***

*(**) EMI CDC5 57243-2. Chang, Hartog, W. Christ, T. Christ, Faust, Maninger – TCHAIKOVSKY: *Souvenir de Florence.* *(**)

This 1983 performance finds Joseph Silverstein leading some eminent colleagues from the Boston Symphony and giving as sensitive an account of Dvořák's endearing *Sextet* as any now before the public. Decent if rather forward recording.

It makes an excellent coupling having on a single disc two of the finest string sextets by Slavonic composers, particularly when it would be hard to devise a starrier line-up of musicians in the ensemble. Sarah Chang's warm individual artistry is superbly matched by players drawn from the Berlin Philharmonic, past and present. The second violin, Bernhard Hartog, is now the leader of the Deutsches Symphony Orchestra in Berlin, while Wolfram Christ during his years as principal viola of the Philharmonic was a superb soloist in Lorin Maazel's recording of Berlioz's *Harold in Italy*. These are players who not only respond to each other's artistry, but do so with the most polished ensemble and a rare clarity of inner texture, not easy with a sextet. The subtlety as well as the energy of Dvořák's *Sextet* is consistently brought out, using the widest dynamic range. This work was written soon after Dvořák had had his big success with the *Slavonic Dances*, and the contrasts of the second movement *Dumka* and the lightness and sparkle of the *Furiant* Scherzo echo that source. Sadly the sound is top-heavy with little bass, the cello registering fully only in the work's gentler moments. On some reproducers the adjective scrawny might describe the string tuttis.

(i) Requiem, Op. 89; Symphonic Variations.

(M) *** Decca (ADD) 468 487-2 (2). (i) Lorengar, Komlóssy, Isofalvy, Krause, Amb. S.; LSO, Kertész – KODALY: *Psalmus hungaricus.* ***

Kertész's outstanding Kingsway Hall recording of the *Requiem* (produced by Christopher Raeburn and engineered by Gordon Parry and James Lock) brings analogue sound in the demonstration class. It is also available on a Double Decca coupled to the much rarer *Mass* (448 089-2 – see our main volume). Here it is equally attractively paired with Kodály's *Psalmus hungaricus*, with Kertész's admirably fresh account of the underrated *Symphonic Variations* – the finest in the catalogue – thrown in for good measure. The new transfers are superb.

Stabat mater, Op. 58; Psalm 149, Op. 79.

(BB) ** (*) Naxos 8.555301/2 (2). Brewer, Simpson, Aler, Gao, Washington Ch. & O, Shafer

Music Director of the Washington Chorus for over thirty years, Robert Shafer conducts his chorus and the Washington Orchestra in a fresh, well-disciplined reading of a work much-loved by the Victorians. The chorus is rather backwardly placed in a recording which otherwise effectively defies the acoustic problems of the Kennedy Center in Washington, but Shafer's clean-cut directness helps to avoid any feeling of sentimentality. He counters the problem of performing a predominantly slow work with steady, flowing speeds. Outstanding among the soloists is Christine Brewer, and John Aler, though not as sweet-toned as usual, sings very sensitively too. The mezzo, Marietta Simpson, is tremulous as recorded, and Ding Gao is clear and reliable in the bass solos. Not a first choice which probably rests with Robert Shaw on Telarc (2CD 80506), although Sinopoli's vibrant operatic approach also pays dividends (DG 471 022-2). However the alternative DG Double from Kubelik includes also the *Ten Legends*, and the analogue recording, made in the Munich Herculesaal, still sounds well (453 025-2).

ELGAR, Edward (1857–1934)

3 Bavarian Dances, Op. 27; Caractacus, Op. 27: Triumphal March; The Light of Life, Op. 29: Meditation; Polonia, Op. 76. Wand of Youth Suites Nos. 1–2, Op. 1a-b.

(B) *** EMI (ADD) CDZ5 75295-2. LPO, Boult.

Sir Adrian's outstanding performances of the *Wand of Youth Suites* catch both the innocence and the intimacy of the music, very much reflecting Elgar's personal world. The fragile charm of the delicate scoring is well realized and there is plenty of schoolboy gusto for the rollicking *Wild Bear* (only playfully wild, of course). The orchestral playing is first-rate and conveys to the listener the conductor's obvious affection for this music. The 1968 recording is of vintage EMI quality and has adapted splendidly to CD remastering, with little loss of ambient warmth. The *Bavarian Dances* are also genuinely inspired, and the climax of *The Marksman* brings a real frisson. *Polonia* was written as a gesture to help Polish refugees at the beginning of the First World War and shows the composer's flair for flag-waving orchestral sounds.

Caractacus, Op. 35: Woodland Interlude. Crown of India Suite, Op. 66; Grania & Diarmid, Op. 42: Funeral March. The Light of Life, Op. 29: Meditation. Nursery Suite; Severn Suite, Op. 87 (orchestral version).

(B) **(*) EMI (ADD) CDZ5 75294-2. RLPO, Groves.

It is good to have these performances by Sir Charles Groves restored to the catalogue. They were recorded in 1969 and 1970, while he was principle conductor of the Royal Liverpool Philharmonic Orchestra. This is all music that he understands warmly, and the results give much pleasure. One does not have to be an imperialist to enjoy any of the occasional pieces, and it is interesting to find the patriotic music coming up fresher than the little interlude from *The Light of Life*, beautiful though that is. Both the *Nursery Suite* (written for Princesses Elizabeth and Margaret Rose) and the orchestral version of the *Severn Suite* (written for a brass band contest) come from Elgar's very last period, when his inspiration came in flashes

rather than as a sustained searchlight. The completely neglected *Funeral March* was written in 1901 for a play by W. B. Yeats and George Moore; it is a splendid piece. The CD transfer retains the bloom of the original recordings.

Cockaigne Overture, Op. 40; Enigma Variations, Op. 36; Introduction & Allegro for Strings; Serenade for Strings, Op. 20.

⚫ (B) *** Teldec Apex 09027 413712-2. BBC SO, A. Davis.

Andrew Davis's collection of favourite Elgar works is electrifying. The very opening of *Cockaigne* has rarely been so light and sprightly, and it leads on to the most powerful characterization of each contrasted section. The two string works are richly and sensitively done. Similarly the big tonal contrasts in *Enigma* are brought out dramatically, notably in Davis's rapt and spacious reading of *Nimrod*, helped by the spectacular Teldec recording. This is surely a worthy successor to Barbirolli in this repertoire and is an outstanding disc in every way. At its new Apex price it is one of the great Elgarian bargains of all time.

Cockaigne Overture; Falstaff; Introduction and Allegro for Strings; Serenade for Strings.

(B) *** CfP (ADD/DDD) 575 3072. LPO, Handley.

Vernon Handley directs a superb performance of *Falstaff*, and the achievement is all the more remarkable because his tempi are unusually spacious (generally following the composer's markings). The playing of the LPO is warmly expressive and strongly rhythmic. *Cockaigne* is also given a performance that is expansive yet never hangs fire. The *Introduction and Allegro* and *Serenade* are digital and date from 1983. They were made in Watford Town Hall, but the balance is closer, the string outline more brightly lit. The *Introduction and Allegro* is passionate, yet with lyrical contrasts tenderly made; the *Serenade* brings a somewhat indulgent treatment of the *Larghetto* and here comparison with Boult is not in Handley's favour. Nevertheless this reissue is a real bargain.

Cockaigne Overture, Op. 40: Froissart Overture, Op. 19; In the South (Alassio), Op. 50; Overture in D min. (arr. from HANDEL: Chandos Anthem No. 2).

(M) **(*) Chan. 8309. SNO, Gibson.

Sir Alexander Gibson's Chandos collection dates from 1983, but it shows him at his best. The Scottish orchestra make a vividly cohesive sound and they are given a brilliant digital recording with a firm bass, though the strings are just a little lacking in richness of timbre. The picture of London is full of bustle and pageantry, with bold brass and flashing percussion, and Gibson's directness serves *Froissart* and the Handel arrangement equally well. *In the South*, too, does not lack impetus, if not matching the famous Silvestri version, and the overall effect is extremely vivid and tangible, even though there are finer individual versions of these works available and the present collection only has a playing time of 54 minutes.

Cello Concerto in E min., Op. 85.

(M) *** Sony SMK 89712. Ma, LSO, Previn – WALTON: *Cello Concerto*. ***

(B) *** Warner Apex 0927 40600-2. Noras, Finnish RSO, Saraste – BARTOK: *Rhapsody No. 1* ***; DVOŘÁK: *Cello Concerto*. **(*)

In its rapt concentration Yo-Yo Ma's recording with Previn is second only to Du Pré. The first movement is lighter, a shade more urgent than the Du Pré/Barbirolli version, and in the Scherzo he finds more fun, just as he finds extra sparkle in the main theme of the finale. The key movement with Ma, as with Du Pré, is the Adagio, echoed later in the raptness of the slow epilogue, poised in its intensity. Warm, fully detailed recording, finely balanced, with understanding conducting from Previn. At mid price a splendid bargain.

The Finnish cellist, Arto Noras, like his Swedish colleague, Torleif Thedéen (on BIS 486) seems completely attuned to the Elgar sensibility and gives a moving account of this marvellous work, balancing vigour with a reticent serenity. He is very well accompanied and this bargain triptych is highly recommendable.

(i) Cello Concerto in E min., Op. 85; (ii; iii; v) Violin Concerto in B min., Op. 61; (iii; v) Cockaigne Overture, Op. 40; (iv; v) Enigma Variations, Op. 36.

(M) **(*) Decca (ADD/DDD) 473 085-2 (2). (i) Lloyd Webber, RPO, Y. Menuhin; (ii) Chung; (iii) LPO; (iv) Chicago SO; (v) Solti.

A useful if variable collection of some of Elgar's major works. The digital account of the *Cello Concerto* (originally Philips) features two artists inseparably associated with Elgar's music. The performance is both warmly expressive and an unusually faithful reading, the more satisfying for its fidelity to the score and the absence of exaggeration. The speeds – as in the flowing Moderato in the first movement – are never extreme, always well judged, and Lloyd Webber in his playing has never sounded warmer or more relaxed on record, well focused in the stereo spectrum.

Kyung-Wha Chung's 1977 account of the *Violin Concerto* also maintains its position as one of the finest available. It is an intense and deeply committed reading which rises to great heights in the heart-felt account of the slow movement – made the more affecting by its vein of melancholy – and the wide-ranging performance of the finale. At the start of that third movement Chung, at a fast tempo, finds a rare element of fantasy, a mercurial quality, and the great accompanied cadenza is commandingly done, ending on an achingly beautiful phrase from the third subject of the first movement. The first movement itself brings much beautiful playing too, but there are one or too tiny flaws of intonation, and here Solti's accompaniment does not have quite so firm a grasp, though the performance will undoubtedly be refreshing to any Elgarian.

Solti is back on top form in an exciting and sharply dramatic account of the *Cockaigne Overture* in vintage 1976 Decca sound, though his usually exhilarating approach to Elgar does not come off quite so well in the 1974 *Enigma Variations*. With Solti the variations become a dazzling showpiece, but if the charm of the work is given short measure, the structure emerges even more strongly. With the fast variations taken at breakneck speed, the Chicago orchestra is challenged to supreme virtuosity, but the main disappointment is *Nimrod* where, from a basic tempo faster than usual, Solti allows himself to get faster and faster still, in a style that misses the feeling of *nobilmente*. Still, the performance is anything other than dull, and with its three outstanding couplings, this set in Decca's 'British Collection' is still of considerable interest.

Violin Concerto in B min., Op. 61.

(B) *** CfP 575 1392. Kennedy, LPO, Handley.

(BB) (***) Dutton mono CDBP 9735. Sammons, Liverpool PO, Sargent – DELIUS: *Violin Concerto*. (***)

(BB) (**(*)) Naxos mono 8.110951. Sammons, Liverpool PO, Sargent – DELIUS: *Violin Concerto*. (**(*))

For many ears, Nigel Kennedy's earlier 1984 recording of the *Violin Concerto* has an even greater freshness than his later recording in Birmingham with Rattle (CDC5 56413-2 – see our main volume). It is certainly commanding, and with Vernon Handley as guide it is centrally Elgarian in its warm expressiveness, but its steady pacing also brings out more than usual the clear parallels with the Beethoven and Brahms concertos. This is particularly striking in the first movement and, both here and in his urgent account of the allegros in the finale, Kennedy shows that he has learnt more than any recorded rival from the example of the concerto's first great interpreter, Albert Sammons. Yet the influence of Yehudi Menuhin is also apparent, not least in the sweetness and repose of the slow movement and in the deep meditation of the accompanied cadenza which comes as epilogue. The recording, produced by Andrew Keener, with the soloist balanced more naturally than usual, not spotlit, is outstandingly faithful and atmospheric. The CfP reissue makes a remarkable bargain.

Kreisler, to whom the Elgar *Violin Concerto* was dedicated and who gave the first performance, never took it up, but it is difficult to imagine it being better played than it is in this inspired 1928 recording by Albert Sammons, who had recorded it in abridged form in the days of acoustic recording. Even the classic Menuhin – Elgar version made four years later, wonderful though it is, is in some ways outclassed. The HMV Treasury LP transfer by A. C. Griffith was very fine but collectors may now turn with confidence to these transfers. As is the case with the Delius, the Dutton is a clear first choice, smoother and more detailed as far as the orchestra is concerned, and it does better justice to Sammons' tone.

Enigma Variations (Variations on an Original Theme), Op. 36.

(M) *** EMI CDM5 67748-2 [567749]. LSO, Boult – HOLST: The Planets. ***

Boult's Enigma comes from the beginning of the 1970s, but the recording has lost some of its amplitude in its transfer to CD: the effect is fresh, but the violins sound thinner. The reading shows this conductor's long experience of the work, with each variation growing naturally and seamlessly out of the music that has gone before. Yet the livelier variations bring exciting orchestral bravura and there is an underlying intensity of feeling that carries the performance forward.

Enigma Variations; Introduction and Allegro for Strings, Op. 47; In the South (Alassio) Overture, Op. 50; Sospiri, Op. 70.

**(*) DG 463 265-2. VPO, Gardiner.

On the evidence of this disc John Eliot Gardiner is not an instinctive Elgarian. His reading of Enigma is very personal in its moulding of line, and while the VPO provide virtuosity and finely etched detail, they fail to get to the heart of the music, especially in Nimrod which is spacious and serene rather than heart-tugging. The Introduction and Allegro is again brilliantly played, but the great striding tune in the middle strings, which Barbirolli shapes so passionately, is here without real depth of expressive feeling and the final climax, too, falls short. But In the South is a different matter. It bursts vividly into life with a Straussian surge of ardour, the Roman Juggernaut sequence is almost overwhelming, with a balancing tenderness on the touching central section. The closing section carries all before it. The Vienna Philharmonic strings also bring a Mahlerian warmth to Sospiri which is very affecting. But Enigma is a disappointment – in spite of first-class recording.

Enigma Variations; Serenade for Strings, Op. 20.

(B) **(*) CfP 574 8802. LPO, Handley – VAUGHAN WILLIAMS: The Lark Ascending; Greensleeves & Tallis Fantasias. ***

Vernon Handley's generously full CfP disc is given brilliant, wide-ranging 1983 digital sound. The Elgar readings are in the Boult tradition and very well played. But Handley's strong personal identification with the music brings a consciously moulded style that tends to rob the Enigma Variations of its forward impulse. The Elgarian ebb and flow of tension and dynamics is continually underlined by a highly expressive manner and, although he uncovers much imaginative detail, there is a consequent loss of spontaneity. The performance of the Serenade is more direct, although the Larghetto again has a more personal idiosyncrasy.

Serenade for Strings in E min., Op. 20.

** Häns. 93.043. Stuttgart RSO, Norrington – HOLST: The Planets. **

Like Norrington's account of The Planets with which it is coupled, his version of Elgar's Serenade for Strings is beautifully played and brilliantly recorded, but lacks something in expressive warmth, a little stiff rather than idiomatic.

(i) Symphonies Nos. 1–2; Cockaigne Overture; (ii) Elegy, Op. 58; (ii; iii) Romance for Bassoon & Orchestra, Op. 62; (iii) Serenade for Strings, Op. 20.

(B) ** Sony (ADD) SB2K 89976. (i) LPO; (ii) ECO; both cond. Barenboim; (iii) with Gatt.

(i) Symphonies Nos. 1–2; (ii) Introduction and Allegro for Strings, Op. 47; (iii) Serenade in E min., Op. 20.

(M) *** Decca (ADD) 473 082-2 (2). (i) LPO, Solti; (ii) ECO, Britten; (iii) ASMF, Marriner.

Solti's accounts of the two Elgar Symphonies must be counted among his most successful recordings and certainly remain among the top choices for this repertoire several decades later. Before he recorded the First he made a searching study of Elgar's own 78 recording, and the modifications of detailed markings implicit in that account are reproduced here, not with a sense of calculation but with very much the same rich, committed qualities that mark out Elgar's performance. Solti seems freed from emotional inhibitions, with every climax superbly thrust home and the hushed intensity of the glorious slow movement captured magnificently on CD. The Second receives an equally incandescent reading, once again, closely modelled on Elgar's own surprisingly clipped and urgent performance, but benefiting from virtuoso playing and, as with the First, vintage Decca sound. Fast tempi bring searing concentration and an account of the finale that for once presents a true climax. Whilst no one can grumble at the couplings – Britten's full-blooded and distinctive account of the Introduction and Allegro and Marriner's Serenade for Strings (perhaps a little stiff in manner) – the original Solti/LPO couplings of the Cockaigne and In the South overtures were more logical. That said, this remains a useful reissue – another set in Decca's 'British Collection' series.

Barenboim, like Solti, studied Elgar's own recording before interpreting the First Symphony, and the results are certainly idiomatic, though in the long first movement Barenboim overdoes the fluctuations, so losing momentum. The other three movements are beautifully performed, with the Adagio almost as tender as Solti's reading with the same players. The Second Symphony was Barenboim's first exercise in Elgar recording, in 1972. Here he followed very much in the path set by Barbirolli, underlining and exaggerating the contrasts of tempi, pulling the music out to the expansive limit. Yet this is still a red-blooded, passionate performance, capable of convincing for the moment at least, and the only real snag with both symphonies is that the recording is not as full and opulent or well balanced as Elgar's orchestration really demands, and the same comment applies to *Cockaigne*. The well-played *Romance* is placed on the first disc, after the symphony and before the overture. The string pieces sound fuller and in the *Serenade* the *Larghetto* is touching. But in the *Elegy* Barenboim tends to dwell too affectionately on detail and the result is amost schmaltzy.

Symphony No. 1 in A flat, Op. 55.

(BB) *** LSO Live LSO 0017. LSO, C. Davis.

Symphony No. 1; In the South, Op. 50.

(***) Testament mono SBT 1229. LPO, Boult.

Symphony No. 1; Pomp and Circumstance Marches Nos. 1–5.

(B) *** CfP (ADD/DDD) 575 3052. LPO, Handley.

Vernon Handley directs a beautifully paced reading which can be counted in every way outstanding. The LPO has performed this symphony many times before but never with more poise and refinement than here. It is in the slow movement above all that Handley scores; his account is spacious and movingly expressive. The coupled *Marches* are exhilaratingly brilliant and if Nos. 2 and (especially) 3 strike some ears as too vigorously paced, comparison with the composer's own tempi reveals an authentic precedent. Certainly the popular *First* and *Fourth* have an attractive gutsy grandiloquence. With very good sound well transferred to CD this is highly recommendable indeed.

Recorded live at the Barbican in the autumn of 2001, Sir Colin Davis's version of the *First Symphony* is both spacious and refined, with an exceptionally measured account of the slow introduction, masterfully sustained. Reflecting the emotions of a live event, Davis's use of rubato and expressive hesitations is greater than it might have been in a studio performance, notably in the tender account of the slow movement, but the concentration of the playing is so intense that the results are magnetic, not self-conscious. The performance builds up to a thrilling account of the finale, which prompts wild applause. Excellent sound. A first-rate recommendation at super-bargain price, even if the reissue of Vernon Handley's CfP version offers not only a generous coupling as well but a performance a degree more idiomatic still.

The first wonder of this superb transfer of Boult's 1949 version of Elgar's *First Symphony* from Testament is the astonishing quality of the sound: mono only but full-bodied and finely detailed to give a keener sense of presence than EMI's less than ideal CD transfer of Boult's stereo version of 1976, with a surprisingly wide dynamic range. As to interpretation this mono version, beautifully paced, has far more thrust and tension than the later one, notably in the finale. Also, the heavenly *Adagio* has an extra meditative intensity in the way that Boult presents each of the great lyrical themes, pure and poignant in their

beauty. Nobility is the keynote of the whole interpretation, with speeds held more steadily than in Elgar's own wonderfully expressive, more freely emotional reading of 1931. Boult's recording of the overture, *In the South*, made in 1955, brings out his thrustful side even more strikingly, with urgent speeds giving way in the lovely *Canto popolare* section to a honeyed beauty, with George Alexander the superb viola soloist. Sadly, the 1955 sound is shallower than that of six years earlier for the *Symphony*.

Symphony No. 2 in E flat, Op. 63.

(BB) *** LSO Live LSO 0018. LSO, C. Davis.

Symphony No. 2; (i) Sea Pictures.

(B) *** CfP (DDD/ADD) 575 3062. LPO, Handley; (i) with Greevy.

Handley's remains the most satisfying modern version of a work which has latterly been much recorded. What Handley conveys superbly is the sense of Elgarian ebb and flow, building climaxes like a master and drawing excellent, spontaneous-sounding playing from an orchestra which, more than any other, has specialized in performing this symphony. The sound is warmly atmospheric and, at the peak of the finale, vividly conveys the added organ part in the bass (which Elgar himself suggested 'if available'): a tummy-wobbling effect. As a generous coupling Bernadette Greevy – in glorious voice – gives the performance of her recording career in *Sea Pictures*. Handley's sympathetic accompaniments are no less memorable, with the LPO players finding a wonderful rapport with the voice. In the last song Handley uses a telling *ad lib* organ part to underline the climaxes of each final stanza.

Recorded live in the autumn of 2001 as part of his Elgar series, Sir Colin Davis's account of No. 2 follows a similar pattern to No.1 in a spacious, refined reading that readily sustains speeds broader than usual, notably in the development section of the first movement and in the whole of the slow movement. Particularly for a live recording the dynamic range is remarkable with whispered *pianissimos* of breath-taking gentleness, set against ripe *fortissimos* with glorious brass sounds. Though in the finale Davis adopts a fast speed, his account of the lovely epilogue with its hushed reference back to the opening theme of the whole work is exceptionally spacious and tender, making a haunting close. But, as with No. 1, Handley remains the primary recommendation.

Symphony No. 3 (from the composer's sketches, realized by Anthony Payne).

(BB) *** LSO Live LSO 0019. LSO, C. Davis.

With each new recording of Anthony Payne's inspired realization of Elgar's sketches, so the finished piece seems ever more clearly a part of the true canon, not exactly what Elgar himself would have created, but valid and satisfying in its own right. It lets us clearly appreciate how the dying composer was on the verge of new and exciting developments, totally consistent with his earlier work but quite distinctive. The opening exposition section – the only part that Elgar completed himself with full orchestration – points to that new flavour, followed in Payne's working-out of the sketches. This Davis version, recorded live, comes into direct rivalry with Paul Daniel's superb Naxos disc with the Bournemouth Symphony, offering a performance just as powerful and concentrated, marked by refined string-playing, with *pianissimos* magically caught even if the weight of tuttis is not quite as great as in the more forwardly balanced Naxos recording. Davis's reading of the finale is particularly fine with its clear pointing of sections, leading up to Payne's imaginative treatment of the close, and indeed this can be recommended alongside Daniel's account.

Complete Works for Organ: *Sonatas Nos. 1–2; Cantique; Loughborough Memorial Chime; Vesper Voluntaries, Op. 14.*

*** HM HMU 907281. Butt (organ of King's College, Cambridge).

Here you have the American subsidiary of a French company promoting an excellent disc of rare Elgar, an issue with no direct rival. On the massive organ of King's College, Cambridge, John Butt, formerly an organ scholar there, brings out not only the sonic grandeur of the *Organ Sonata No. 1* – by far the most ambitious work here – but its gentle, lyrical beauty. If that work sounds like orchestral music transcribed, the *Organ Sonata No. 2* offers the opposite phenomenon; a work originally written for brass band under the title *Severn Suite*, it was transcribed for organ with the composer's approval by Ivor Atkins, most effectively in the second-movement *Toccata* with its echoes of Widor. The eight *Vesper Voluntaries* are attractive Elgarian fragments written early in his career, as is *Cantique*. The oddity is the piece Elgar wrote in 1923 for the opening of the Loughborough memorial carillon, with bell-sounds warmly translated.

ENESCU, Georges (1881–1955)

Symphonies Nos. 1–2; Roumanian Rhapsodies Nos. 1–2; Suites for Orchestra, Nos. 1–3; Concert Overture in A, Op. 32; Interméde.

(BB) Arte Nova 74321 49145-2 (4). George Enescu Bucharest PO, Mandeal.

Symphony No. 1 in E flat, Op. 13; Suite No. 1 for Orchestra, Op. 9; Intermède, Op. 12.

(BB) *** Arte Nova 74321 37314-2 George Enescu Bucharest PO, Mandeal.

Symphony No. 2 in A, Op. 17; Roumanian Rhapsody No. 2 in D, Op. 11.

(BB) *** Arte Nova 74321 34035-2 George Enescu Bucharest PO, Mandeal.

Symphony No. 3 in C, Op. 21; Concert Overture in A, Op. 32.

(BB) *** Arte Nova 74321 37863-2 George Enescu Bucharest PO, Mandeal.

Suites Nos. 2, Op. 20; 3 (Villlageoise), Op. 23; Roumanian Rhapsody No. 1 in A, Op. 11.

(BB) *** Arte Nova 74321 37855-2 George Enescu Bucharest PO, Mandeal.

The days when Enescu was represented only by the *Roumanian Rhapsodies* and perhaps the *First Symphony* are a thing of the past, and as readers who have taken the trouble to acquire *Oedipe* will know, he was a composer of vision and originality. His compositional gifts were overshadowed during his lifetime by his prowess as a violinist, finesse as a pianist, his authority as a conductor and wisdom as a teacher. The four CDs listed above, whether purchased as a box or individually, offer an inexpensive means of getting to know some of his finest orchestral music. Romanian orchestras are renowned for the quality of their strings and they are heard to excellent effect on these discs, which are superbly enginereed. They are not inferior to the many rivals that are to be found in the catalogue and are for the most part performances of quality. There is nothing bargain basement about them except the price. At first encounter one is reminded of other composers, especially in the early music where Strauss is the paramount influence, though one's mind can stray as widely afield as Rachmaninov, Szymanowski and Scriabin. There is much interesting music here, and if the recordings are not uniformly the equal of, say, Chandos, they are of a high standard.

Violin Sonatas Nos. 2, Op. 6; 3, Op. 25; Torso.

(B) *** Hyp. Helios CDH 55103. A. Oprean, J. Oprean.

Enescu's *Second Violin Sonata* is an early work written in 1899 when he was seventeen and still studying in Paris with Fauré. The *Third* (1926), together with the opera, *Oedipe*, is his masterpiece and shows an altogether different personality; the difference in stylistic development could hardly be more striking, comparable perhaps to the difference between Bartók's *First Suite for Orchestra* and the *Miraculous Mandarin*. Adelina Oprean, a Carl Flesch prize-winner, is thoroughly inside the idiom, as befits a Romanian, and deals with its subtle rubati and quarter-tones to the manner born. She exhibits excellent musical taste but her partner (and brother) is somewhat less scrupulous in his observance of dynamic nuance. The additional *Torso* is a sonata movement from 1911, which was published only in the 1980s.

ENNA, August (1859–1939)

The Little Match Girl (opera); The Shepherdess and the Chimney-sweep (ballet for orchestra and narrator).

** CPO 999 595-2. Bonde-Hansen, Sjöbergt, Helmuth, Danish Rad. Sinf., Zeilinger.

The Danish composer August Enna produced a steady stream of operas and operettas throughout his career that, thanks to his melodic gift and attractive orchestration, earned him considerable success. Alas, by the end of his life his music fell out of fashion, and he died poverty-stricken and disappointed. It is good that CPO has made available these two representative works, based on Hans Andersen fairytales, which have never fallen completely out of the Danish repertoire. There is nothing profound here, but *The Little Match Girl* of 1897 has some charming ideas, with the influence of Wagner felt in the style, though not in profundity. *The Shepherdess and the Chimney-sweep* has some engaging music, but the prominence (in volume and in quantity) of the narration will surely be too much for English-speaking listeners, although full texts and translations are offered. The performances are sympathetic, but the recording, though acceptable, lacks richness and depth.

FALLA, Manuel de (1876–1946)

(i; ii) *Harpsichord Concerto*; (iii; iv; v) *El amor brujo*; (iv, vi, vii) *Nights in the Gardens of Spain*; (viii) *The Three-Cornered Hat*; (xi) *La vida breve: Interlude and Dance*; (x) *Homenaje 'Le tombeau de Claude Debussy'*; (vii) *4 Spanish Pieces*; (xi) *7 Canciones populares españolas*; (ii; xii) *Psyché*.

✹ (B) *** Double Decca (ADD/DDD) 466 128-2 (2). (i) Constable; (ii) L. Sinf., Rattle; (iii) New PO; (iv) Frühbeck de Burgos; (v) Mistral; (vi); LPO; (vii) De Larrocha; (viii) Montreal SO, Dutoit; (ix) SRO, Ansermet; (x) Fernández; (xi) Horne, Katz; (xii) with Jennifer Smith.

A myriad of performances have been perceptively gathered together for this 'Essential Falla' compilation, which is surely rightly named. Dutoit's 1984 complete version of *The Three Cornered Hat* is wonderfully atmospheric as well as brilliantly played – one of the first Decca digital demonstration recordings, and still a top recommendation. Recorded in 1966, Frühbeck de Burgos's *El amor brujo* enjoys exceptionally vivid sound, yet with plenty of light and shade: the superbly graduated crescendo after the opening is immediately compelling, and the control of atmosphere in the quieter passages is masterly, while Nati Mistral has the vibrant open-throated production of a real flamenco singer.

Alicia de Larrocha's later digital version of *Nights in the Gardens of Spain* is unsurpassed among modern recordings: it has rich, lustrous sound and refined detail. The piano image is well forward, and this allows the listener to relish the freshness and brilliance of the soloist's articulation in the work's later sections. The playing has undoubted poetry and in the first movement there is a thoughtful improvisatory quality which captures the evocative feeling of the shimmering Andalusian night. Her playing of the *4 Spanish Pieces* glitters.

The other shorter works are equally worthwhile. Ansermet's *Interlude and Dance* from *La vida breve*,

with its melodramatic opening and lively dance section, is always enjoyable, and Marilyn Horne's *Spanish Folksongs* are vibrantly idiomatic. John Constable's crisply vivid account of the delightful *Harpsichord Concerto* (with Rattle) and the haunting rarity, *Psyché*, for voice – Jennifer Smith a fine soloist – and orchestra complete an extraordinarily generous survey. This Double Decca is the finest and most comprehensive Falla collection in the catalogue.

(i; ii) *Nights in the Gardens of Spain*; (iii) *El amor brujo: Ritual Fire Dance; The Magic Circle.*

** Arthaus **DVD** 100 034. (i) Barenboim (piano); Chicago SO; (ii) Domingo; (iii) cond. Barenboim – SIBELIUS: *Violin Concerto.* ** (*) (Producer: Bernd Hellthaler. V/D: Bob Coles.)

The Arthaus DVD offers a 1997 recording made while the Chicago Orchestra was in Germany. On the face of it this should have strong claims on the collector, a master-pianist as soloist and a great Spanish singer-now-conductor on the podium. Yet despite the latter, the performance is curiously wanting in mystery and atmosphere, and one remains untransported to the magical Sierra de Córdoba. Barenboim plays with customary aplomb and the video direction is expert and unobtrusive. The encores, the *Ritual Fire Dance* and *The Magic Circle* from *El amor brujo* come off well under Barenboim's baton.

FARNON, Robert (born 1917)

(i) *Canadian Caravan*; (ii) *Gateway to the West; High Street; How Beautiful is Night; Huckle-Buckle; In a Calm; Journey into Melody; Jumping Bean; Manhattan Playboy; Melody Fair; Mountain Grandeur; Ottawa Heights; Peanut Polka; Portrait of a Flirt; Sophistication Waltz; A Star is Born; State Occasion; String Time; Taj Mahal*; (i) *Willie the Whistler.*

(BB) (***) Naxos mono 8.110849. Orchestras conducted by (i) Williams; (ii) Composer.

Admirers of Robert Farnon's entertainingly light and tuneful art, not unlike that of Leroy Anderson, will already know the recent Marco Polo recording (8.223401), which was reviewed in the last main Penguin Guide. These recordings date mainly from the late 1940s and offer a ring of authenticity, which instantly takes one back to that era. The fleetness of the string playing in, for example, *Portrait of a Flirt*, is inimitable, while the use of subtle portamento is an art now all but lost. Elsewhere, one readily responds to the nostalgic atmosphere of these recordings, with the quiet *How Beautiful is Night* having a most haunting, even hypnotic quality. *State Occasion* could hardly sound more imperially British, and it is appropriate, if maybe not now politically correct, that the exotic *Taj Mahal* follows. Care has been taken over the remastering of these tracks, which comprise Decca and Chappell Library recordings. Unique, then, and well worth the very modest cost. The documentation is excellent, too.

FARRANCE, Louise (1804–75)

Piano Quintets Nos. 1 in A min., Op. 30; 2 in E, Op. 31.

*** ASV CD DCA 1122. London Schubert Ens.

Louise Farrance studied with Reicha, Hummel and Moscheles and became the only woman professor of the piano at the Paris Conservatoire during the nineteenth century. She composed prolifically for the piano, but her output includes three symphonies, which were given in Paris, Brussels, Geneva and Copenhagen during her lifetime, as well as a quantity of chamber music. She has fallen from view: the *Everyman Dictionary of Music* does not mention her, nor do Michael Kennedy's *Oxford Dictionary* and Alison Latham's newly published *Oxford Companion*. All the same, there does seem to be an upsurge of interest in her on CD: two of the symphonies have been recorded, as have the *Nonet*, the *Sextet for Wind and Piano* and two of her piano trios. The *Piano Quintet in A minor* comes from 1839 and was her first chamber work of any kind, its successor following a year later. Both are scored for the same forces as the Hummel *Quintet* and the Schubert *Trout*. Although her musical language owes much to Haydn and Hummel, there are elements of Weber, Spohr and Mendelssohn to be found, and there is considerable harmonic subtlety in her writing. Good playing from the London Schubert Ensemble and truthful recording.

FAURÉ, Gabriel (1845–1924)

Ballade for Piano & Orchestra, Op. 19; Berceuse for Violin & Orchestra, Op. 16; Caligula, Op. 52; Les Djinns (orchestral version), Op. 12; Elégie for Cello & Orchestra, Op. 24; Fantasie for Piano & Orchestra, Op. 111; Masques et bergamasques, Op. 112; Pelléas et Mélisande, Op. 80; Pénélope: Prélude; Shylock, Op. 57.

(B) *** EMI Double fforte CZS5 74840-2 (2). Collard, Y.-P. & P. Tortelier, Von Stade, Gedda, Bourbon Vocal Ens., Toulouse Capitole O, Plasson.

Although Fauré's most deeply characteristic thoughts are intimate rather than public, and his most natural outlets are the mélodie, chamber music and the piano, this set of his orchestral music contains much that is very rewarding indeed. It includes the delightful *Masques et bergamasques* and the *Pelléas et Mélisande* and *Shylock* music, as well as such rarities as *Les Djinns* and *Caligula*. The Orchestre du Capitole de Toulouse may lack the finesse and bloom of the finest ensembles, but Plasson gets an alert and spirited response, and the recordings are very good. Plasson shows a genuine feeling for the Fauréan sensibility, and the fine-spun lyricism of the Nocturne from *Shylock* is nicely conveyed. The two works for piano and orchestra are particularly valuable; Jean-

Philippe Collard gives a really distinguished account of both the early *Ballade* and the seldom heard *Fantasie*, Op. 111. Although the vocal items no longer have texts and translations, as on the original issues, the set is now offered at bargain price. Altogether this is a lovely collection in every way, offering many delights, and it cannot be too warmly recommended.

Masques et bergamasques; Pavane.

(B) *** CfP (ADD) 575 1382. LPO, Handley –
CANTELOUBE: *Chants d'Auvergne.* *** ●

These performances under Vernon Handley are very enjoyable, fresh and sympathetic, with excellent recording to add bloom to the fine playing. A fine bonus for the outstanding Canteloube coupling.

CHAMBER MUSIC

Cello Sonata No.1 in D min., Op. 109.

(BB) *** Warner Apex 0927 40599-2. Noras, Rigutto –
DEBUSSY, FRANCK: *Cello Sonatas.* ***

This is an eloquent performance on Warner Apex of the wonderful *D minor Sonata* by this aristocratic Finnish cellist, who plays with subtlety and finesse. If the couplings appeal, this makes an excellent bargain.

(i) Piano Quartets Nos. 1–2; (ii) Piano Quintets Nos. 1–2.

(B) *(*) Erato Ultima 8573 84251-2 (2). (i) Hubeau, Gallois-Montbrun, Lequien, Navarra; (ii) Hubeau, Via Nova Qt.

These performances originally appeared in the 1970s as part of a five-LP Erato set, which was subsequently issued on three CDs. They were displaced in the late 1970s by Jean-Philippe Collard's set with the Parennin Quartet, which is currently not available. Jean Hubeau was a distinguished professor at the Paris Conservatoire and recorded the complete Fauré piano music in the early 1970s. These accounts, though serviceable and reasonably priced, lack the sensitivity and finesse of their best modern rivals, Domus on Hyperion for the *Piano Quartets* (CDA 66166) and *Quintets* (CDA 66766), both of which have been awarded a ●, and Pascal Rogé and the Ysaÿe Quartet on Decca in all four pieces.

String Quartet in E min., Op. 121.

● (BB) *** Naxos 8.554722. Ad Libitum Qt. – RAVEL: *Quartet.* ***

The Ad Libitum Quartet are from Romania, all the members having been students of the Georges Enescu Academy in Iasi, and they came to wider notice when they won first prize at the Evian Competition in 1997. Their ensemble and intonation are perfect and their tone is silken, and they give a wonderfully expressive and beautifully characterized account of Fauré's elusive late *String Quartet* – one of the best we have ever heard and one of the best in the catalogue. It is recorded in the Moldava Philharmonic Hall in Iasi and is very natural and lifelike.

PIANO MUSIC

Ballade in F sharp, Op. 19; Barcarolle, No. 1, Op. 26; Impromptu No. 2, Op. 31; Improvisation (8 Pièces brèves), Op. 84/5; Nocturnes Nos. 1, Op. 33/1; 3, Op. 33/3; 6, Op. 63; 11, Op. 104/1; 13, Op. 119; Préludes, Op. 103, Nos. 2 & 7; Romance sans paroles, Op. 17/3.

*** Decca 470 246-2. Paik.

The Korean-born, Paris-based Kun-Woo Paik continues to impress as much in French music as he did in his recent Bach–Busoni recital (see our main Guide, p.63). This Fauré recital is the finest single-disc anthology of this great composer's music to have appeared for some time, since Pascal Rogé's 1989 recital in fact. Kun-Woo Paik is completely attuned to the outwardly gentle but powerful and subtle vein of feeling that Fauré exhibits and is completely inside his sensibility. Even if Fauré is well represented in your library, you should add this excellently recorded recital, which would make a fine introduction for those new to this repertoire.

Barcarolles Nos. 1–13 (complete); Theme and Variations in C sharp min., Op. 73.

(***) Testament mono SBT 1215. Thyssens-Valentin.

Nocturnes Nos. 1–13 (complete).

(***) Testament mono SBT 1262. Thyssens-Valentin.

Impromptus Nos. 1–5; Impromptu, Op. 86; 8 Pièces Brèves; Valses Caprices Nos. 1–4.

(***) Testament mono SBT 1263. Thyssens-Valentin.

These three Testament CDs, superbly transferred from Ducretet-Thomson discs in mono, offer Fauré interpretations that have rarely been matched for their poetry and natural spontaneity of expression, coupled with a flawless technique. The reason that this master-pianist, born in 1902, is not more widely known is that after early success in the 1920s she married and retired from the concert platform for twenty-five years, returning in the 1950s with little attempt to seek international fame. In France she became a cult figure, giving her last recital in Paris in 1983 at the age of 81. She died in 1987. These discs, recorded respectively in 1955, 1956 and 1959, consistently have one marvelling at the fluidity of Thyssen-Valentin's playing, which yet is combined with sparkling control, in a way that few rival versions can begin to match. It almost feels as though she herself is actually creating this music as she plays. Any lover of Fauré's subtly nuanced piano music should immediately investigate these magnetic, revelatory performances. For each disc the pianist's daughter, Jeannine Lançien, provides a fascinating account of her mother's idiosyncratic career, and Bryce Morrison, a lifelong devotee, adds a critical assessment.

VOCAL MUSIC

Requiem, Op. 48.

(*) HM HMC 901771. Zomer, Genz, La Chapelle Royale, Collegium Vocale Gent, O des Champs-Élysées, Herreweghe – FRANCK: *Symphony.* *

(*) Testament mono SBT 1240. Angelici, Noguéra, Duruflé, Chanteurs et O de Saint-Eustache, Cluytens – SAINT-SAENS: *Symphony No. 3.* (*)

Requiem, Op. 48; Cantique de Jean Racine, Op. 11; La naissance de Vénus, Op. 29.

*** Australian ABC Classics 472 045-2. Macliver, Tahu Rhodes, Cantillation, Sinf. Australis, Walker.

Fauré never published the original chamber version of his *Requiem*, and it underwent many forms before arriving at its well-known orchestral version. These Australian artists give a translucent, sensuous performance, and their well-blended sound and fine balance are enhanced by the singing of Cantillation, which is a relatively small choir. Teddy Tahu Rhodes is a bass-baritone with a slightly grainy finish to his voice, but an uncommon agility, whilst Sara Macliver's lovely *Pié Jesu* is effortless and pure. The performance of the *Cantique de Jean Racine* is very fine too. However, the special interest of this release is the inclusion of *La naissance de Vénus*. A rarity and a 'Prix de Rome' cantata, in essence a single-scene mythological opera, intended for the concert hall. Fauré considered it one of his best compositions, and it is an ambitious work which readily displays his distinctive vocal style and his sometimes undervalued skill in orchestration. Again Rhodes, in the role of the deity Jupiter, shows considerable agility, this time in a high baritone register. This is the only available recording of this work, except for an EMI version which used a piano reduction. Here we can enjoy the orchestral passages, depicting the miraculous transformation of the sea, for the first time. A worthwhile addition to the catalogue. Full texts and translations are included, with excellent documentation.

Some thirteen years after making his mould-breaking recording of the Fauré *Requiem*, using the original, spare-textured 1892 version of the score, Herreweghe here has followed it up with the full-orchestra version of 1901, again using period instruments and style. The surprise is to find that so many of the speeds, notably in the opening *Introit* and *Kyrie*, are very slow. The *Introit* (setting *Requiem aeternam*) is also repeated later as an introduction to the *Libera me*. With fine singing from soloists and choir, this is a distinctive account, fresh and refined, not a primary choice perhaps, but filling an obvious gap and offering a generous, apt and unique coupling in a period-instrument performance of the Franck *Symphony*.

André Cluytens recorded the *Requiem* in the Eglise Saint-Roch in 1950, and the excellent re-mastering by Paul Baily belies its date. At the time of its recording the famous Strasbourg set held sway. The singing of the Chanteurs de Saint-Eustache and the unnamed orchestra is not always distinguished, and the vocal tone is not always perfectly focused. The solo singers, Martha Angelici and Louis Noguéra, are more than acceptable but the performance as a whole does not begin to match the later recording Cluytens made with Victoria de los Angeles and Fischer-Dieskau a little over a decade later (EMI CDM 5 66894-2).

FAYRFAX, Robert (1464–1521)

Missa Albanus; Missa O bone Ihesu (with Elevation Motet: Anima Christi … Resurrexio Christi); Missa O quam glorifica; Missa Regali ex progenie; Missa Tecum principium.

(M) *** ASV CDGAX 353 (3). Cardinall's Musick, Carwood.

This fine mid-priced set gathers together all Fayrfax's known masses, as recorded in their previous series (discussed in our main volume), plus a bonus in the newly discovered and magnificent *O bone Ihesu* and an incomplete four-part setting of *Anima Christi* (an 'elevation motet' sung during the elevation of the host). The surviving text begins with '*Resurrexio*' and David Skinner, whose editions are used throughout, tells us in the notes that there is no doubt about the connection of this motet with the mass. The performances and recordings are of outstanding quality, and anyone who has not yet sampled this glorious music could do no better than start here.

FIELD, John (1782–1837)

Piano Concertos Nos. 5 (L'Incendie par l'orage); 6 in C.

(BB) *** Naxos 8.554221. Frith, Northern Sinf., Haslam.

John Field, the inventor of the nocturne, was a virtuoso pianist as well as a composer, writing a series of concertos for his own use, of which these are splendid examples, exhilaratingly performed by Benjamin Frith with the Northern Sinfonia. Though Field was much more adept at embroidering rather than developing the themes that bubble up through each work, the results are consistently attractive, with Frith's sparklingly clear articulation in rapid scales and figuration magnetising the attention in music that can easily seem just trivial. The title of the *Fifth Concerto*, *L'Incendie par l'orage* ('Fire from Lightning'), reflects a dramatic storm passage in the long and ambitious first movement, while the lovely slow movement of the *Sixth Concerto* is a nocturne in all but name, with the outer movements full of bright ideas.

FILS, Anton (1733–60)

Symphonies in A; C; D; E flat; G min.

*** CPO 999 778-2. Orfeo Bar. O, Gaigg.

Here is another composer emerging from eighteenth-century obscurity (this time from Bavaria), and with the opening of the *Symphony in C*, with its dramatic *crescendi*, it comes as no surprise to find that he was very much part of the Mannheim music scene. Interestingly, unlike many composers from this period, Fils's music came into fashion just after his death. Per-haps its freshness, with pleasing folk music elements, especially in some snappy rhythmic patterns, made it stand out. The minuets in general have a charmingly rustic dance quality, and the Prestissimo finale of the *A Major Symphony* interrupts its headlong rush with a very characteristic sequence, complete with bass-drone. The finale of the *D Major Symphony* displays the composer's ability to build up tension steadily, starting off with unison strings, and includes a particularly striking pedal point (on violas) lasting some twenty-six bars. The poignant oboe solo in the minuet of the *C major Symphony* is another highly attractive episode. Indeed all these symphonies are melodically appealing and lively, the *G minor Symphony* is particularly exhilarating. The Orfeo Barock-orchester, plays excellently under Michi Gaigg: the string ensemble is elegantly pointed, and the often piquant woodwind writing is delightfully brought out. The recording is both warm and vivid.

FINZI, Gerald (1901–56)

Cello Concerto.

*** Chan. 9949. Wallfisch, RLPO, Handley – LEIGHTON: *Cello Concerto*. ***

(i) Cello Concerto; (ii) Eclogue for Piano and Strings; Grand Fantasia & Toccata.

(BB) *** Naxos 8.555766. (i) Hugh; (ii) Donohoe; N. Sinf., Griffiths.

The *Cello Concerto* is arguably Finzi's greatest work, not just ambitious but deeply moving, written under the stress of knowing he was terminally ill. Marking the centenary of Finzi's birth, Chandos here reissues Raphael Wallfisch's richly romantic reading, still at full price but with a rather more generous coupling than on Naxos, the tautly argued *Cello Concerto* of Kenneth Leighton. Wallfisch finds all the dark eloquence of Finzi's central movement, and the performance over-all has splendid impetus, with Handley providing the most sympathetic backing. The Chandos recording has a very natural balance.

The Naxos version, with Tim Hugh a most sensitive soloist, has the advantage not only of bargain price but of a very apt coupling in two of Finzi's concertante works with piano, originally designed for a concerto. Peter Donohoe is the powerful soloist, not always as tender as he might be, but still very sympathetic. A good bargain alternative choice.

FORQUERAY, Antoine (1671–1745)

Pièces de clavecin: Harpsichord Suites Nos. 1–5.

*** Decca 466 976-2 (2). Rousset.
**(*) MDG 605 1101-2 (2). Meyerson.

Only one composite work survives from Forqueray's pen, the present suites, edited in 1747 by his son, Jean-Baptiste (1699–1782). They exist in two forms: for solo viola de gamba with a second gamba as continuo and for solo harpsichord. Forqueray was a colourful figure, who beat his wife and his son, committing the latter to prison for gambling, theft and consorting with *filles de mauvaise vie*. Forqueray *père*'s prowess as a gamba player was so impressive that he was engaged by the royal household as tutor to Louis XIV himself, but it has been suggested that Forqueray *fils*, who included three pieces of his own, may not have been entirely responsible for the arrangements. Be that as it may, the music is of much originality and considerable beauty and is given with great character by both players.

Christophe Rousset plays a harpsichord by Jean-Henri Hemsch of 1761 from the collection of the Musée de la Musique in Paris. Mitzi Meyerson uses a copy by Keith Hill of a 1769 instrument by Taskin from the Russell Collection in Edinburgh. Rousset benefits from a fine Decca recording, which gives his instrument presence and plenty of space around the sound. Unusually, as MDG has high standards in these matters, the excellent Mitzi Meyerson is closely balanced and the aural image is too upfront so that the ear tires. A pity, as the playing is very fine.

FRANÇAIX, Jean (born 1912)

Ouverture anacréontique; Pavane pour un Génie vivant; Scuola de Ballo; Sérénade; Symphony No. 3 in G.

*** Hyp. CDA 67323. Ulster O, Fischer.

Françaix did not number his symphonies but this amiable G major work is his *Third* (1953), composed light-heartedly in memory of Papa Haydn. The opening movement combines a jauntily genial theme with a lyrical secondary idea, although the buoyant mood predominates; the *Andante*, with its wistful oboe solo, has engaging textural delicacy; the Minuet is quirky, with a slinky Trio, and the finale a delectable moto perpetuo. What a happy work this is!

The *Serenade*, written twenty years earlier, is even more jocular, opening with fake rhythmic abrasiveness before a melancholy bassoon introduces the *Andantino*. But high spirits return in the chirping *Poco Allegretto* and dashingly ribald finale.

A touching calm then dominates the rather lovely opening of the *Ouverture anacréonique* (1978): the composer tells us he is trying to portray an imaginary world without conflict. But the music soon livens up vivaciously and reaches a confident, jazzy climax. The exquisite *Pavane pour un Génie vivant*, a homage to Ravel, is the most recent composition here (1987), and evoke's that composer's world idyllically. The programme then ends winningly with a pastiche *Scuola de ballo*, based on the music of Boccherini. It is in a direct line with Stravinsky's *Pulcinella*, although less corrosive, and Tomasini's *Good Humoured Ladies*, but wittier. Its finesse and elegance combine with vivacity to scintillating effect. The whole programme is played with warmth, polish and vitality in equal measure, the recording is first-class, and this is very highly recommended. We hope that the enormously sympathetic

Thierry Fischer will continue his exploration of Françaix's orchestral output.

FRANCK, César (1822–90)

(i) Symphonic Variations for Piano and Orchestra; Prélude choral et fugue.

(B) *** RCA 2CD (ADD) 74321 846062 (2). Rubinstein, Symphony of the Air, Wallenstein – CHABRIER: *Pièces pittoresques: Scherzo-valese*; DEBUSSY: *Estampes* etc.; FAURE: *Nocturne No. 3*; RAVEL: *Valses nobles et sentimentales* etc.; SAINT-SAENS: *Piano Concerto No. 2 in G min., Op. 22*. ***

Rubinstein's fine 1958 recording of the *Symphonic Variations* (the first in stereo) is also available differently coupled (see our main volume) but the present RCA Double is much more generous and includes his persuasive piano version of the *Prélude, choral et fugue*.

(i) Symphonic Variations for Piano and Orchestra; (ii) Symphony in D minor.

(*(*)) Testament mono SBT 1237. (i) Ciccolini, Paris Conservatoire O; (ii) French Nat. R. O; Cluytens – D'INDY: *Symphonie sur un chant montagnard français*. (**)

Both the *Symphony* and the *Variations symphoniques* were recorded in the Théâtre des Champs-Elysées in 1953, although the former is much better balanced. Cluytens gives a dignified and finely shaped account of the piece, which is well worth hearing, even if the Orchestre National de la Radiofusion Française does not always produce a refined tone and the sound is a bit two-dimensional. The *Variations symphoniques* are well played by Aldo Ciccolini, but unfortunately the sound is dryish and the piano is too forwardly balanced to do full justice to the soloist's tone.

Symphony in D min.

*** HM HMC 901771. O des Champs-Elysées, Herreweghe – FAURE: *Requiem*. **(*)
(***) Teldec mono 8573 83025-2. Concg. O, Mengelberg. – DVOŘÁK: *Symphony No. 9 (New World)*. (***)

Symphony in D min.; Les Eolides.

(BB) **(*) Warner Apex 0927 41372-2. NYPO, Masur.

Offered as an unusual but apt coupling for the Fauré *Requiem*, Herreweghe's reading of the Franck *Symphony* – written during the same period – is quite different in style. Generally urgent speeds add to the freshness and clarity brought by period instruments – the only version so far to use them – with sentimentality completely avoided. Clear, warm sound to match.

Masur creates a sound-world with the New York Philharmonic which is totally different from that achieved by his predecessor, Zubin Mehta. The wind phrasing is sensitive, the brass blend more subtle and the strings produce a far more cultured sonority. Moreover the recording, too, is more sophisticated, without the brash, overlit quality we have noted in the past. The performances of both *Les Eolides* and the

Symphony are very fine, sensitively shaped and with the architecture held together well. All the same, Masur's account of the *Symphony* does not generate quite the same excitement and blazing conviction that Monteux, Beecham or Bernstein brought to it, and does not displace existing recommendations. Moreover, even at bargain price, it offers rather less than top value with a playing time of only 48 minutes.

When Mengelberg took up his appointment at the Amsterdam Concertgebouw in 1895 both the Franck *Symphony* and the *New World* were new music, and although the Franck had been composed in 1888, it was not published until the mid-1890s, when it soon appeared at a Concertgebouw concert. Mengelberg conducted it with an enormous lyrical ardour and gets such responsive playing from his wartime orchestra that criticism is almost silenced. His Franck last appeared in the 1980s (Philips 416 214-2), although this was a broadcast from October 1940, a month before the present commercial recording was made. Bryan Crimp's transfer reveals a sound that is extraordinarily vivid and rich for its period. Of course, the same agogic mannerisms that are so characteristic of this conductor are in evidence, but we have to say that such are the dramatic fire and fervour of this playing that most listeners will surely be willing to take them in their stride.

Cello Sonata in A (trans. of Violin Sonata).

(BB) *** Warner Apex 0927 40599-2. Noras, Rigutto – DEBUSSY; FAURE: *Cello Sonatas.* ***

** DG 471 346-2. Maisky, Argerich – CHOPIN: *Cello Sonata; Polonaise brillante*; DEBUSSY: *Cello Sonata.* **

There have been numerous discs of the cello arrangement of the Franck *Violin Sonata in A major* (Isserlis, Cohen, Du Pré, Maisky, Mørk and others), and if you want it in this form, Arto Noras is as good as any, particularly at this competitive price. He is an elegant player of much finesse, and both the Debussy and Fauré sonatas come off well.

Recorded live in Japan, this account by Maisky and Argerich of the Franck *Sonata* in its cello transcription cannot compare with the same artists' studio version made in Geneva in 1981 for EMI. Though these two highly individual artists consistently strike sparks off each other, the pulling about of phrase and tempo is so extreme it is almost grotesque, with less dedication than before. Even in the dashing Scherzo the unsteadiness of tempo is distracting, and in the finale the result is almost scrappy, even though predictably they build up to an exciting climax.

ORGAN MUSIC

Cantabile; Chorals Nos. 1 in E; 2 in B min.; 3 in A min.; Fantaisies in A & C; Finale in B flat; Grande pièce symphonique; Pastorale; Pièce héroique; Prélude, fugue et variation; Prière.

(BB) *** Regis RRC 2054 (2). Bate (organ).

Jennifer Bate plays the Danion-Gonzalez organ at Beauvais Cathedral and is given the benifit of an excellent digital recording. The spacious acoustic contributes an excellent ambience to the aural image, and Miss Bate's brilliance is always put at the service of the composer. The *Pièce héroique* seems rather well suited to the massive sounds which the Beauvais organ can command and all the music chosen here – the content of three CDs, previously available on the Unicorn label – shows the instrument to good advantage. The only small criticism is that Bate rushes the opening of the *A minor Choral*, some of whose detail does not register in this acoustic at the speed. However, this is a splendid bargain issue by any standards.

FRANKEL, Benjamin (1916–71)

Film music from: *The Curse of the Werewolf; The Importance of Being Earnest; Footsteps in the Fog; The Night of the Iguana; Trottie True; The Years Between.*

**(*) CPO 999 809-2. Queensland SO, Albert.

Perhaps the most enjoyable music here is the lively opening and closing theme to the 1952 film of *The Importance of Being Earnest*, which instantly raises a smile. The slow section in the middle is not quite as memorable, and that reflects the main reservation of this disc: much of the music is rather slow, if often brooding, and there are few really striking melodies. Even so, the short *Pastoral* from *The Curse of the Werewolf* is (believe it or not) quite memorable, while *Trottie True* features frothy music in the best light music tradition. There are imaginative orchestral effects in the sombre score to *The Night of the Iguana*, which includes the wistful *Hanna and Shannon Theme*. That said, the performances and recording are very sympathetic, and the documentation is generous. But this CD will appeal mainly to admirers of film music rather than to those who appreciate the orchestral repertoire and powerfully conceived symphonies for which this composer is best known.

FROBERGER, Johann (1616–67)

Organ Music: *Capriccios: in A min., FbWV 502; in D min., FbWV 503; in G, FbWV 507; in G min., FbWV 508; Fantasia sopra Ut, Re, Mi, Fa, Sol, La, FbWV 201; Ricercari: in G min., FbWV 405; G min., FbWV 407a; Toccatas: in G, FbWV 197; C, FbWV 109; F, FbWV 110; A min., FbWV 112; Toccata da Sonarsi all Levatione in G min., FbWV 106.*

(BB) *** Arte Nova 74321 85322-2. Kelemen (Baumeister organ, Klosterkirche, Maihingen).

Froberger composed almost solely for keybord and published three major collections of pieces in 1646, 1656 and, towards the end of that decade, an undated Book of Capricci and Ricercari. The influence of his teacher, Frescobaldi, is apparent in the freedom of the writing, the *Toccatas* are often unpredictable and the *Capriccios* (each using a single theme) lively and spirited, with the exception of the *G minor* which is comparatively solemn – even the polyphony is melancholy. The *Ricercars* are also more thoughtful pieces, each with a similar melodic layout. Perhaps the most strikingly individual piece here is the evocative *Toccata da Sonarsi all Levatione*, using a tremulant registration, which was intended for use during the liturgy at the elevation of the host. The most impressive work structurally is the *Fantasia sopra Ut, Re, Mi, Fa, Sol, La*, where all seven sections are linked, like a set of variations, to the motive implicit in the title. Throughout, Froberger's inventive resource and Joseph Kelemen's fluent playing, which is full of life, ensure that the listener's attention is held, and indeed Kelemen's registration on this splendid organ always pleases the ear. He is excellently recorded and provides lucid, readily communicative notes about both the composer and his music. He even tells us about the organ itself, and the 'retrospective character of the instrument's design,' which makes it highly suitable for recording 'repertoire that is almost eighty years older than the organ itself'. This is a bargain CD of the highest calibre.

FRY, William Henry (1813–64)

The Breaking Heart; Niagara Symphony; Overture to Macbeth; Santa Claus (Christmas Symphony).

**(*) Naxos 8.559057. RSNO, Rowe.

William Henry Fry has a distinct place in the history of American music, for as an academic, critic and composer he was the first native-born American to write for a large symphony orchestra, and also the first to write a grand opera. His music is innocently tuneful, thought its roots are firmly in the European, rather than in native American soil. The longest work here is the *Santa Claus, Christmas Symphony*, written in 1853 and lasting just under 27 minutes. It is an ingenuous, episodic work, originally performed with a detailed programme of the Christmas story. The writing has a certain period charm and if it doesn't always hold the listener's full attention, there are some attractive episodes. The finale features a sleigh-ride, followed by shimmering strings ushering in *O Come Oh Ye Faithful*, which is thundered out at the end.

The *Niagara Symphony* brings some quite startling passages depicting the famous Falls, with strings scurrying about in watery cascades, and no fewer than eleven timpani to ram the effect home. This is real tempest music – and with a reflective chorale in the middle for contrast. *The Breaking Heart* is a rather sentimental 10-minute piece which includes a lilting waltz theme, while the melodramatic *Overture to Macbeth* seems to have borrowed some of *Niagara's* swirling strings at one point. The performances are enthusiastic, though there are signs that more rehearsal time would have been desirable. The recording is satisfactory, but this is hardly an indispensable issue.

FRYE, Walter (died 1475)

Tut a par moy.

*** ASV CDGAU 302. Clerks' Group, Wickam – JOSQUIN DESPREZ: *Motets; Missa Faisant regretz.* ***

We still know very little about the hugely influential English composer, Walter Frye. Yet it is fascinating to discover that this touching three-part rondeau, *Tut a part moy* ('Everything comes to me alone: in order not to see me as sad as I could possibly be') reached the ears of Josquin. He used a four-note motif from the song on which to bass his *Missa faisant regretz*. But the rondeau is memorable in its own right and is beautifully sung here.

GABRIELI, Giovanni (1557–1612)

Canzoni da sonare: I (La spiritata) a 4; I a 5 (1615); I toni a 10 (1597); II a 4 (1606); III a 6 (1615); VII a 7 (1615); XII toni a 10 (1597; 2 versions); XXIV a 8 (1608); XXVII a 8 (1608); Ricercar sopra 'Re fa me don' a 4.

(BB) *** Virgin VBD5 62028-2 (2). Hespérion XX, Savall – (with A. GABRIELI: *Canzon sopra 'Qui la dira'*. GUAMI: *Canzon: 'La Accorta' a 4; Canzon sopra 'La Battaglia' a 4; Canzon 'La Cromatica' a 4; Canzon 'La Guamina'; Canzon XXIV a 8; Canzon XXV a 8*); SCHEIN: *Banchetto musicale*; SCHEIDT: *Ludi Musici*. ***

A fine selection of Giovanni Gabrieli's *Canzonas*, together with half a dozen more by his contemporary Giuseppe Guami, which are in much the same style. Also included is a *Canzon sopra 'Qui la dira'* by Giovanni's uncle Andrea (with whom he studied), based on a song. This is played on the harpsichord and makes an attractive interlude. But Jordi Savall varies the scoring throughout, so that some works are for strings (including the solemn *Ricercar*), others include brass to splendid effect. Guami's *'La Accorta'* is melancholy, and his *'Battaglia'* is disappointingly low key, but many of the others are very jolly, notably Giovanni's dancing *Canzon VII a 7* and Guami's *Canzon XXV a 8*. This and Giovanni's florid closing *Canzon XII toni* in ten parts demand great bravura from all concerned. The performances are splendid, and so is the recording. This is one of the finest collections of Renaissance music in the catalogue.

'A Venetian Christmas'

*** DG 471 333-2. Gabrieli Consort and Players, McCreesh (with DE RORE: *Missa praeter rerum serie*).

In this disc entitled 'A Venetian Christmas' Paul McCreesh adds to his evocative series recreating great religious occasions with what might have been heard at Christmas in St Mark's in Venice around the year 1600. Punctuated by chant, a variety of pieces by Giovanni Gabrieli for choir, for organ and for brass ensemble, sets the central liturgy in context. Gabrieli characteristically exploits the wide-ranging antiphonal effects inspired by St Mark's, with the first motet, *Audite principes*, involving no fewer than sixteen parts divided into three separate groups, each led by a solo voice. Most striking is the setting of the mass chosen, dating from half a century earlier, a so-called parody mass by Cipriano de Rore in seven parts (one more than the complex motet by Josquin des Prez on which it is based), a magnificent example of polyphony superbly performed here.

GADE, Axel (1860–1921)

Violin Concerto No. 2 in F, Op. 10.

**(*) Danacord DACOCD 510. Astrand, Danish PO, South Jutland, Brown – NIELS GADE: *Capriccio; Overtures.* **(*)

Axel Gade was himself a gifted violinist who studied with Joachim and was leader or concertmaster of the Royal Danish Orchestra for many years. He was naturally overshadowed by his father, but his output includes an opera, *Venetian Night*, and a quantity of chamber music. The *Second Violin Concerto* (1899) is expertly crafted and the solo part is very well written. The idiom is post-romantic and the invention fluent. It is amiable and pleasing rather than memorable or personal. Christina Astrand plays with great conviction and is well supported by Iona Brown and the Sønderjylland (South Jutland) Orchestra.

GADE, Niels (1817–90)

(i) Capriccio in A min. for Violin and Orchestra (orch. Reinecke); Overtures: Echoes of Ossian, Op. 1; Hamlet, Op. 37; Mariotta.

**(*) Danacord DACOCD 510. (i) Astrand; Danish PO, South Jutland, Brown – AXEL GADE: *Violin Concerto No. 2.* **(*)

This is the second volume in the Danacord 'Harmonious Families' series, which couples music by Danish composers and their sons. Niels Gade exerted enormous influence on Danish musical life: in addition to his eight symphonies, he was an influential teacher, and although they were not strictly speaking pupils, both Grieg and Nielsen benefited from his guidance. This disc includes his well-known Op. 1, the *Overture, Echoes of Ossian* (1840), as well as two other overtures and a *Capriccio* for violin and orchestra, new to disc. As always, the mantle of Mendelssohn weighs heavily on Gade's muse. Good performances and decent recording.

Symphonies Nos. 4 in B flat, Op. 20; 7 in F, Op. 45; Concert Overture No. 3, Op. 14.

**(*) Chan. 9957. Danish Nat. RSO, Hogwood.

This is the second volume in Christopher Hogwood's fine and musicianly survey of the Gade symphonies with the Danish National Radio Symphony Orchestra. His record of the *Fourth* is actually a reissue and was originally coupled with an interesting rarity, a symphony by Johannes Frederik Frohlich. The *Seventh Symphony* was written in 1864, 14 years after the *Fourth*, although Gade's musical idiom never really changed or developed, and he never succeeded in making any significant escape from the orbit of Mendelssohn. But it has great geniality and charm, and is winningly played on this disc. The only reservation concerns the sound, which, though naturally balanced and with plenty of presence, places the listener far too close to the orchestra. Tutti passages are thick and oppressive, and one longs for more air round the aural image. Neeme Järvi's recordings of both symphonies with the Stockholm Sinfonietta (BIS) have the greater tonal finesse and transparency of texture, and sound much fresher. The *Concert Overture No. 3*, composed in 1846 between the *Second* and *Third* symphonies, is an appealing piece, a first recording and well worth having. Others may not be worried by the sound, and the disc can certainly be recommended for the spirited playing of the Danish Orchestra and the elegance of Hogwood's direction.

Octet, Op. 17; Sextet, Op. 44.

*** MDG 308 1102-2. Berlin Philharmonic String Octet.

Gade began the *Octet for Strings* not long after the death of Mendelssohn, whom he had succeeded at the Leipzig Gewandhaus Orchestra. He finished it in Copenhagen in 1848, when war broke out between Prussia and Denmark. The turbulence of the times does not disturb its sunny nature nor does it cast any shadow over the *Octet*, written when war clouds were again gathering for the 1864 conflict between the two countries. As always with Gade, the craftsmanship is impeccable and the musical architecture is finely balanced, but the musical ideas are heavily indebted to Mendelssohn. It is all very mellifluous, even if neither piece ever approaches Mendelssohn in quality of inspiration or distinction of mind. The playing of the Berlin ensemble is thoroughly dedicated and enthusiastic, and although the recording places us fairly far forwards in the recital room, there is plenty of air around the sound. Both are available in alternative recordings, but neither is superior to the present issue.

GALUPPI, Baldassare (1706–85)

(i) La Caduta di Adamo (oratorio); (ii) Harpsichord Concertos in G, C, F and C min.

(B) *** Erato Ultima (ADD/DDD) 0927 41393-2 (2). (i) Zampieri, Palacio, Rigacci, Schmiege; (ii) Farina, I Solisti Venici, Scimone.

Galuppi's oratorio *La Caduta di Adamo* (*The Fall of Adam*) was first performed in Rome in 1747. There are four singers (representing Adam, Eve, the Angel of Justice and the Angel of Mercy), and the string orchestra (with harpsichord or, sometimes, organ) is supplemented by two horns. The writing is very much in the operatic style of the period in its florid, *style galant* way, pointing to latter classical styles, although the influence of Vivaldi is certainly felt. Eminently tuneful and inventive, with each of the singers tested on their control of long legato lines as well as their vocal dexterity, it is highly enjoyable, especially as the performances from the soloists and orchestra are very sympathetic, and the digital recording is first class. As well as being a major force in the operatic world, Galuppi was also considered one of the most important keyboard composers of the century, and this set offers four very attractive harpsichord concertos by way of a fill up. Once again, there is some eminently tuneful *galant* writing, with the *C minor Concerto* adding greater depth. Although the 1977 recording is not quite as well focused as in the digital oratorio, it is more than acceptable. An excellent bargain, and congratulations are due to Erato for including texts and translations in this bargain Ultima set.

Il mondo alla roversa (opera: complete).

*** Chan. 0676 (2). Italian Swiss R Ch., I Barochisti, Fasolis.

Galuppi, working in collaboration with the playwright, Carlo Goldoni, might be counted the father of comic opera in Italy, finding much greater success with his comic works than with his formal operas. First seen in Venice in 1750, this delightful piece, *Il mondo alla roversa* ('The Topsy-Turvy World'), subtitled *Le donne che commandano* ('Women in Command'), helps to explain why, with its brisk sequence of short solo numbers and ensembles, punctuated by brief recitatives. The idea of an island where a council of women has taken over control from the men is lightly treated, and predictably in a non-feminist age leads to their final overthrow and their capitulation in love. The Italian studios of Swiss Radio have lately produced a number of impressive recordings of early music, and this fresh, lively account is no exception.

GANNE, Louis (1862–1923)

Les Saltimbanques (operetta: complete).

(BB) **(*) EMI (ADD) CZS5 74079-2 (2). Mesplé, Lublin, Amade, Calàs, Tirmont, Benoit, René Duclos Ch., LOP, Marty.

Louis Ganne is hardly a well-known figure now, but in his day he had quite a successful career in Paris, both as a conductor and as a composer of music theatre, operetta, salon pieces and songs. His best music is light and catchy, though it is mainly *Les Saltimbanques* ('The Travelling Entertainers') that now keeps his name alive and that also shows his particular facility for dance and march rhythms. Written in collaboration with Maurice Ordonneau in 1899, *Les Saltimbanques* quickly became a popular favourite throughout France. The story centres on Suzanne, a foundling taken in by a travelling circus, who, by the end of the work in true operetta fashion, discovers her noble origins and is free to marry the man she loves. The novel circus backdrop and romantic intrigue were constructed with elements of both *opéra comique* and operetta, and the result is a score of much charm. This 1968 performance is probably the only one we'll get, so it's just as well it's a good one. Mady Mesplé has exactly the right perky timbre

for the part of the heroine Suzanne, very French-sounding and characterful, while Claude Calàs as her tenor lover, André de Langeac, is light-voiced, but sensitive and convincing. The rest of the cast does not disappoint, especially the lively chorus. Jean-Pierre Marty conducts with enthusiasm, well contrasting the racy numbers with the gently lilting rhythms, and his Lamoureux orchestra, with its French-sounding brass, is good too. The recording is reasonably vivid and full for its period, although a little strident at times. The only real reservation about this bargain set is that it comes with no texts or translations.

GAY, John (1685–1732)

The Beggar's Opera (complete; arr. Britten).

(M) *** Decca 473 088-2 (2). Murray, Langridge, Kenny, Rawnsley, Lloyd, Collins, Aldeburgh Festival Ch. & O, Bedford.

There is much more Benjamin Britten than John Gay in this version of *The Beggar's Opera*, making it an extra Britten opera in effect – neglected on disc until this 1993 recording. What Britten has done is to take the simple melodies assembled by Gay and treat them to elaborate, very Britten-ish accompaniments and developments that go even further in individuality than his folksong settings. It becomes very much a twentieth-century piece, starting with an overture that is pure Britten, with Gay tunes woven in. *Fill Every Glass* is then no longer a simple drinking-song but a slow contrapuntal movement, and *The Modes of the Court*, to the tune of 'Lilliburlero', becomes another elaborate mosaic. Conversely, some nostalgic arias like *O What Pain it is to Part* are done briskly, even abrasively, almost as though Britten was determined to counter received ideas on any well-known number.

Both traditionalists and authenticists may well find the result perverse, but Britten's genius and imagination are what matter, together with his brilliant sense of instrumental colouring. Under Steuart Bedford this first recording is based on a staged presentation, given at The Maltings during the Aldeburgh Festival, with Declan Mulholland as an Irish beggar bluffly introducing the entertainment. Philip Langridge sings clearly and incisively as Macheath, portraying him very much as a gentleman, and Robert Lloyd is outstanding as Peachum, dark and resonant, a bluff Cockney. The team is a strong and characterful one, though neither Ann Murray as Polly Peachum nor Yvonne Kenny as Lucy Lockit is caught very sweetly. Britten's distinctive orchestration, one instrument per part, is well played by a distinguished group, including Jennifer Stinton on the flute, Nicholas Daniel on the oboe and Richard Watkins on the horn. Excellent sound, good direction of the well-edited spoken dialogue by Michael Geliot. Now offered at mid-price, it is far more than a curiosity.

GERSHWIN, George (1898–1937)

An American in Paris.

(M) ** DG (ADD) 463 665-2. Siegel-Schwall Band, San Francisco SO, Ozawa – RUSSO: *3 Pieces for Blues Band and Symphony Orchestra* etc.**

There is a softness of focus in Ozawa's 1976 account of the Gershwin work that takes away the necessary bite, and although the recording sounds fine in its new Originals transfer, this is far from a top choice. The rarer couplings are the main interest of this release.

An American in Paris; Piano Concerto in F; Cuban Overture; 'I Got Rhythm': Variations for Piano & Orchestra; Porgy and Bess: Symphonic Suite (arr. Robert Russell Bennett); *Rhapsody in Blue; 2nd Rhapsody for Orchestra with Piano; Songs: Girl Crazy; Strike up the Band* (both orch. Don Ross).

(M) *** Virgin VBD5 62056-2 (2) [CDVB 61922]. Marshall, Aalborg Symphony.

With this dazzling Gershwin programme Wayne Marshall both acts as soloist and directs the orchestra. *An American in Paris* and the *Cuban Overture* are full of character, with superbly idiomatic orchestral playing; and the orchestral soloists shine individually in Robert Russell Bennett's brilliant orchestrations of the music from *Porgy and Bess*, while the strings are gorgeously seductive in both tone and inflection. This is consistently exhilarating.

The performance of the *Rhapsody in Blue* in some ways outshines even Bernstein's famous New York account in its audacious glittering brilliance, although Bernstein still has a special place in the catalogue. But Marshall manages spontaneously to coalesce both the 'symphonic' and jazz character of the piece, with the accent on the latter (where with Bernstein the balance is more even). Here the players of the Aalborg Symphony produce a hell-for-leather 'bezaz' in the fast brass tuttis contrasting with a rapturous bluesy account of the the the big tune. The *'I Got Rhythm' Variations* are played with comparable bravura and panache, full of affection and witty touches.

Marshall opens the *Concerto* much faster than usual and this too is a peppy transatlantic reading, but one that relaxes wonderfully for the heart-touching trumpet blues theme of the slow movement, splendidly played here. The *Second Rhapsody* is almost as dazzling as the first, with the closing pages winningly brought off. *Girl Crazy* and *Strike up the Band* are lively pot-pourries, presumably following the outline of the orginal theatre overtures. The recording is first class, full of ambient atmosphere, while the violins have just the right degree of brightness and tonal body to add sumptuousness and bite where needed. In every way this set leads the field.

PIANO DUET

An American in Paris (original 2-piano version).

(BB) ** EMI Encore CDE5 75224-2. Katia & Marielle Labèque – GRAINGER: *Fantasy on Gershwin's 'Porgy and Bess'.* **

The Labèque sisters here present the first recording of the composer's own two-piano score of his famous overture, in which several brief passages are included that were later cut in the orchestral score. There is plenty of freshness and bite in the performance, if not much warmth, and the recording is to match: bright to the point of aggression. But the CD is now offered at budget price.

I Got Rhythm Variations; Second Rhapsody; 2 Waltzes. **Arrangements:** *Blue Monday; Embraceable You; Our Love is Here to Stay.*

(BB) ** EMI Encore CDE5 74729-2. K. and M. Labèque.

The Labèque sisters have prevously recorded piano duet versions of the *Piano Concerto* plus the *Rhapsody in Blue*, and these will probably follow the present collection on EMI's Encore label. Here their usual exuberant brashness of style is matched by bright, almost metallic piano timbre, and no one could complain of a lack of jazzy impetus – indeed the effect is often dazzling, although also a little wearing without the orchestral cushion in the two main works. The song arrangements (*Blue Monday* uses the same material that Gershwin features in *Lullaby for Strings*) have a less aggressive, more sophisticated charm that is highly communicative.

Porgy and Bess (opera; complete).

✪ *** EMI **DVD** 4 92496-9. White, Hayman, Blackwell, Baker, Clarey, Evans, Glydebourne Ch., LPO, Rattle.

After the huge success of the Glyndebourne production of *Porgy and Bess*, EMI took the whole cast to the Shepperton Studios, where it was produced for video by Trevor Nunn and Yves Baignere, using the giant stage to move the actions around freely as in a film. The result is stunningly successful, with Willard White as Porgy, Cynthia Hayman as Bess, Gregg Baker as Crown, and Damon Evans as Sporting Life all singing superbly and bringing the story to life with extraordinary vividness. This is one of the most creative of all such productions so far, fully worthy of Gershwin's masterly score.

GHEDINI, Giorgio Frederico

(1892–1965)

Violin Concerto (Il belprato); Musica da concerto for Viola, Viola d'amore and Strings.

*(*) Essay CD 1075. Tenenbaum, Pro Musica Prague, Kapp – SIBELIUS: *6 Humoresques.* *(*)

Giorgio Federico Ghedini belongs to the generation which came to the fore in Italy in the wake of Pizzetti and Malipiero. In the 1950s the *Concerto dell'Albatro* (1945), generally regarded as his finest work, was periodically broadcast but he has since fallen out of the repertory. His transcription of *Quattro pezzi* by Frescobaldi was once in the LP catalogue in the 1950s but his neglect has been pretty comprehensive. Yet he was a prolific composer: his output includes an opera on *Billy Budd* (1949) based on Melville with a libretto of Quasimodo – two years before Britten's opera of the same name. The *Concerto for Violin and Strings (Il belprato)* (1947) and the *Musica da concerto for Viola, Viola d'amore and Strings* (1953) are well worth getting to know, or would be if the performances had greater charm and were better recorded. The second movement of *Il belprato* is imaginative even if it is reminiscent of the slow movement of the Prokofiev *G minor Violin Concerto*. Mela Tenenbaum is not particularly well served by the engineers and does not seem to possess a particularly beautiful tone: the recording is close, dry and two-dimensional. This disc is useful as a reminder that apart from Ghedini, there is a lot of Italian repertoire waiting to be explored: Casella's *Violin Concerto*, Pizzetti's *Symphony in A* and the Petrassi *Piano Concerto*.

GLAZUNOV, Alexander

(1865–1936)

Violin Concerto in A min., Op. 82.

✿ *** RCA 74321 87454-2. Znaider, Bavarian RSO, Jansons – PROKOFIEV: *Violin Concerto No. 2*; TCHAIKOVSKY: *Méditation.* *** ✿

Nikolaj Znaider has collected golden opinions from all quarters and his coupling of the Glazunov and Prokofiev concertos has been greeted with ecstatic reviews in both the monthly and daily press. Rightly so! Born in Denmark of Polish-Israeli parents, Znaider studied in Copenhagen and Vienna, and at the Juilliard with Dorothy DeLay. He was the first prize-winner at the 1997 Queen Elisabeth of the Belgians Competition in Brussels where Menuhin hailed him as 'the successor of Ysaÿe'. His Glazunov reveals an artist who not only has commanding technical address but eloquence and taste. His approach is fresh and so he makes one fall for this glorious (and sometimes underrated) work all over again. Only the most exalted rivals come to mind, Vengerov and Heifetz among them, and he is given splendid support by Mariss Jansons and the excellent Orchester des Bayerischen Rundfunks. A special mention should be given to the recording engineer, Wolfgang Karreth, who gets the ideal balance between soloist and orchestra and a very natural and lifelike sound.

Symphony No. 2 in F sharp min., Op. 16; From Darkness to Light, Op. 53; Mazurka in G.

*** BIS CD 1308. BBC Nat. O of Wales, Otaka.

Tadaaki Otaka provides a very convincing account of the *Second Symphony*, mastering its rhetoric and revelling in its profusion of attractive, very Russian themes. He opens arrestingly and proceeds with plenty of impetus, the lyrical secondary material is warmly phrased and he builds towards an exciting coda. The sinuous woodwind and string writing in the *Andante* recalls Borodin and the playing here is very beguiling, as it is in the delicately scored Scherzo, always the finest movement in a Glazunov symphony. The finale opens seductively with lovely wind and string playing and Otaka maintains the concentration of the playing to the end rather more successfully than Polyansky on the competing Chandos recording of this same work (CHAN 9070). However, Polyansky's coupling is the *Coronation Cantata*, a rare and very attractive piece which is given an excellent performance.

The *Mazurka* on the BIS CD is rhythmically buoyant; perhaps its material is overstretched, but there is variety of mood which Otaka manipulates very convincingly. *From Darkness to Light* is an unsettled piece, as enigmatic as its title. It produces a rather striking lyrical theme, but the intervening episodes, with heavy brass and cymbals, are less convincing. However, it is very well played indeed, and the recording throughout is excellent, full-bodied and spacious with a resonant concert-hall acoustic. For the *Second Symphony* this is now probably a first choice.

Symphony No. 3 in D, Op. 33; Concert Waltzes Nos. 1-2.

**(*) Chan. 9658. Russian State SO, Polyansky.

The *Third Symphony* has an enticing opening with the principal theme soaring aloft over throbbing wind chords. Polyansky freely varies the music's forward impetus but keeps the tension fairly high, helped by a passionate response from his string section. At the close Glazunov brings the opening theme back again in brassy grandeur. The delectably scored Scherzo (in a sparkling 6/16 metre) glitters, and this movement is the highlight of the work.

The *Andante* has a melancholy flowing line; the central unexpected explosion of passion brings a piercing fortissimo trumpet solo which is over-strident, but then strings and woodwind conclude the movement wistfully. The finale then opens with a conventional Russian folk-dance theme, but is too extended for its material, in spite of the excellent, committed playing and plenty of momentum. The two *Concert Waltzes*, however, are most winning and they are played with affection and finesse. One cannot fault the performance of the *Symphony* either, but apart from the Scherzo, Polyansky does not convince us that it shows the composer at his most imaginative. The Chandos recording is excellent if resonant.

GLUCK, Christophe (1714–87)

Orfeo ed Euridice (complete).

(M) *** Decca 470 424-2 (2). Ragin, McNair, Sieden, Monteverdi Ch., E. Bar. Soloists, Gardiner.

(BB) *** Naxos 8.660064. Biel, Boog, Avemo, Drottningholm Theatre Ch. & O, Östman.

Gardiner's Philips – our first choice for this opera – has now been reissued at mid-price as part of Decca's

'Compact Opera Collection'. However there is no printed libretto, only a CD Rom facility which carries full text and translation (that can be printed out via a computer). The full-priced set remains available (Philips 434 093-2).

Using the original Italian text of the first Vienna version of 1762, Östman's Naxos version offers a refreshingly robust account using period forces, recorded live in the beautiful Drottningholm Theatre near Stockholm. Without any of the extra items that Gluck composed for Paris, the result fits neatly on a single CD, which, unlike most bargain opera issues, includes a complete libretto and translation. The performance has its uneven moments, but all three soloists have fresh, clear voices, with the warm mezzo, Ann-Christine Biel, sustaining the title role well, even if she is not specially characterful. Clear, undistracting sound. Not a first choice, which rests with Gardiner (DG 434 093-2) or Leppard's Glyndebourne production with Dame Janet Baker (Erato 2292 45864-2), but well worth having.

Italian arias from: *Antigono; La clemenza di Tito; La corona; Ezio; Il parnaso confuso; La Semiramide riconasciuta.*

*** Decca 467 248-2. Bartoli, Berlin Akademie fur alte Musik, Forck.

In this fine collection of eight formidable arias from Gluck's Italian operas, all to libretti by Metastasio and written early in his career before his 'reform' operas, Cecilia Bartoli reinforces her claims as a prima donna who delights in making new discoveries, bringing her magnetism and vitality to bear on music that would otherwise be forgotten. Her vocal range, spanning far more than the mezzo register, as well as her range of expression are astonishing. Bravura items like the opening aria from *La clemenza di Tito* are thrown off with flawless technique and obvious enjoyment, sharply contrasted with tender arias which draw out her expressive depth. Fascinatingly, one of the three items from *La clemenza* is an early version of one of the heroine's big arias from *Iphigenie en Tauride*. This formidable display of singing is splendidly supported by crisp, alert playing from the Berlin orchestra of period instruments. Clear, full recording. Decca attractively presents the disc in fascsimile-style book form.

Arias from *La clemenza di Tito; Paride e Elena.*

*** DG 471 334-2. Kozena, Prague Philh., Swierczewski – MOZART: Arias from *La clemenza di Tito, Le nozze di Figaro, Idomeneo, La finta giardiniera*; MYSLIVECEK: Arias from *Abramo ed Isacco; L'Olimpiade.*

An outstanding stylist in whatever she sings, Magdalena Kozena is seemingly untroubled by any of the formidable technical problems in this fine collection of arias, producing glorious tone from beginning to end. Well-coupled with familiar Mozart and rare Mysliveček, this fine Gluck group includes a fascinating aria from his version of *Clemenza di Tito*. Under Swierczewski the Prague Philharmonia equal the Czech Philharmonic in the refinement of their playing.

GODOWSKY, Leopold (1870–1938)

Piano Sonata in E min.; Passacaglia.

*** Hyp. CDA 67300. Hamelin.

Marc-Andre Hamelin has here had the idea of coupling for the first time Godowsky's two biggest piano works. First performed by the composer in 1911, his *E minor Sonata* is a massive 47-minute piece in five movements. It is framed by the two longest movements, both predominantly slow and intense, ending darkly with a sombre funeral march. It is a work which Hamelin, a Godowsky devotee, relates to such similarly massive masterpieces as Bach's *Goldberg Variations* and Beethoven's *Diabelli Variations*. That is a serious overestimate of a work which in places outstays its welcome. However Hamelin's intense commitment makes the most persuasive case for it, with brilliant pianistic effects never used for mere display. The *Passacaglia*, well under half the length, is far tauter, offering an impressive set of forty-four variations plus cadenza and fugue on the theme which opens Schubert's *Unfinished Symphony*. Again Hamelin, brilliant technician though he is, refuses to treat this closely argued piece as mere display. Fine sound, atmospheric and full of presence.

GÓRECKI, Henryk (born 1933)

(i) *Lerchenmusic, Op. 53*: 2nd movement only; (ii; iii) *Old Polish Music*; (iv) *Symphony No. 3: Finale*; (ii; v) *Totus Tuus*; (i) *Kleines Requiem für eine Polka, Op. 66*: 2nd and 3rd movements only.

(B) ** Decca 470 128-2. (i) Schoenberg Ens., de Leeuw; (ii) Nelson; (iii) Czech PO; (iv) Warsaw PO, Kord; (v) Prague Ph. Ch.

Here is a sampler obviously designed to tempt listeners to explore beyond the *Third Symphony* (originally issued by Philips), the popular third movement of which became such a hit. It is here coupled with other, generally more demanding works. Only the vigorous second movement and the infectiously jazzy finale of the *Little Requiem* are included and are well performed on this 1995 recording (again with a Philips source). *Totus Tuus* and the *Old Polish Music* emanate from a 1993 Argo CD. The latter work is perhaps the most striking, effectively contrasting both lullaby and medieval organum, while the a cappella *Totus Tuus* is a beautifully reflective piece of choral writing. The *Lerchenmusic* movement is quite effective in a quasi Bartókian way, if without that composer's individuality. A fair collection then, although fewer complete works would have been a better proposition for the serious collector. Excellent sound and performances.

Symphony No. 3 (Symphony of Sorrowful Songs), Op. 36.

*** Australian ABC Classics 472 040-2. Kenny, Adelaide SO, Yuasa.

Despite its several predecessors, this new recording of Górecki's *Third Symphony* finds new things to say. Where others tend to blend the differences between the movements, Yvonne Kenny treats the work almost like an opera, comprising three very distinct dramatic soliloquies: the sorrowful *Stabat mater* figure of the first movement, contrasting with the terrified imprisoned girl of the second, and the shattered, bereft mother of the last. Kenny is never given to melodrama, but her expressive warmth and intensity binds her portrayal together, and the result makes this symphony less abstract and, in a way, more powerful. Kenny's eloquent singing and her sense of drama are well supported by the Adelaide Symphony Orchestra. The CD is very well documented and full texts and translations are included. However there is no coupling, whereas the fine Naxos version includes also the *Three Pieces in the Olden Style* (8.550822).

GOSSEC, François-Joseph

(1734–1829)

Sinfonia a più stromenti in E flat, Op. 5/2; Symphonies: in E flat; in F, Op. 8/2; in G, Op. 12/2; Suite de dances (orch. Calmei); *Gavotte in D.*

**(*) ASV CDA 1124. Orchestre de Bretagne, Sanderling.

Gossec has been described as the 'father of the French symphony'. Those recorded here in F and G are in three-movement form: the *G major* has a delightfully graceful centre-piece, and an especially vivacious finale. The *F major*, with its haunting minor key introduction, then launches off into another lively allegro. The *Symphony in E flat* also begins with a slow section, and its five minutes are full of incident: pizzicato strings, expressive crescendi, swelling chords, solo staccato horns. The *Sinfonia a più stromenti* has both melody and rhythmic drive, often taking unexpected turns, showing the experimental side of the composer which emerged more fully in his later works. And it is easy to see why Gossec's *Gavotte in D* was so popular in its day: it is a charming lollipop which raises a smile and remains in the mind.

The *Suite de dances* offers more modern dress. It was orchestrated in 1964 and makes agreeable listening, never more so than in another *Gavotte* with a minor-keyed middle section. The Brittany orchestra, whilst not in the first rank, plays with enthusiasm and some flair, and they are warmly recorded.

GOUNOD, Charles (1818–93)

Faust: Ballet music.

(BB) **(*) EMI Encore (ADD) CDE5 75221-2. New Philh. O, Mackerras – DELIBES: *Coppélia; Sylvia* (excerpts); MESSAGER: *Les Deux Pigeons* (excerpts). **(*)

This lively and nicely pointed reading of the *Faust* ballet music from Mackerras, very well played indeed, forms part of an attractive collection of French music.

The 1969 recording is a little thin by modern standards but is certainly vivid enough.

GRAINGER, Percy (1882–1961)

(i) *Country Gardens;* (ii) *Green Bushes;* (i) *Handel in the Strand;* (iii) *Harvest Hymn;* (iv) *The Warriors;* (ii) *Irish Tune from County Derry;* (i) *The Immovable Do;* (ii) *Molly on the Shore;* (v) *Shepherd's Hey;* (vi) *Let's Dance Gay in Green Meadow* (for 2 pianos); (vii) *In Dohomey;* (viii) *Tribute to Foster;* Songs: (x) *Brigg Fair;* (xi) *The Sprig of Thyme Died for Love.*

(M) *** Decca (ADD/DDD) 470 126-2. (i) Eastman-Rochester Pop O, Fennell; (ii) ECO, Bedford; (iii) ASMF, Marriner; (iv) Philh. O, Gardiner; (v) ECO, Britten; (vi) Britten, Tunnard; (vii) Feinberg; (viii) Kazimierczuk, Higgins, Podger, Savage, Monteverdi Ch., E. Country O, Gardiner; (x) Pears, Linden Singers; (xi) Von Otter, Fosberg.

By raiding the Mercury, Philips, and DG as well as the Decca archives, Universal has assembled on Decca an excellent Grainger collection which fully justifies its 'World Of' heading. The Mercury recordings are famously bright and vivid, while the well-known Bedford and Britten items are beautifully recorded and superbly played. There is a good mix of Grainger's imaginative orchestrations interspersed with piano and vocal items, including Pears' famous *Brigg Fair* and Sofie von Otter's haunting *The Sprig of Thyme*.

The disc closes with one of Grainger's most flamboyant works, the extravagantly scored music to *The Warriors*. It was written between 1913 and 1916 for a ballet which never materialized, hence the work's subtitle: '*Music for an Imaginary Ballet*'. The *Tribute to Stephen Foster* comes from a particularly attractive collection of folksong arrangements selected and directed by John Eliot Gardiner and is an unexpected highlight.

Fantasy on Gershwin's Porgy and Bess (arr. for piano duet).

(BB) ** EMI Encore CDE5 75224-2. Katia & Marielle Labèque – GERSHWIN: *An American in Paris* (original 2-piano version). **

The Labèque sisters in their tough brilliance bring out the strong dramatic contrasts of Grainger's two-piano arrangement of passages from *Porgy and Bess*, a piece more obviously pianistic than the composer's own two-piano version of *An American in Paris*, with which it is coupled. A fair coupling, recorded with a brightness that threatens to become aggressive, with the occasional clattery quality still apparent in its new bargain incarnation.

GRANADOS, Enrique (1867–1916)

12 Danzas espanolas (orch. Ferrer).

(BB) *** Naxos 8.555956. Barcelona SO & Catalonia Nat. O, Brotons.

Granados claimed that his 12 *Danzas espanolas para piano* were written when he was 12 years old, though they were not performed in public until 1890, from which time they have enjoyed great popularity, with pianists such as Alicia de Larrocha bringing special insights to the music. This overtly nationalistic music, using original tunes, has encouraged various composers to orchestrate them, of which this set by Rafael Ferrer is colourful and effective. The flutes and oscillating strings in No. 2 have a haunting atmosphere, and the delicacy of writing in the central sections of No 5, flanked with its strong, brooding theme, is imaginative, too. If, in its orchestral format, this is hardly the most subtle music, it is all colourful and enjoyable. The recording is vivid and bright, matching the performance, and this inexpensive CD is worth its modest price.

GRAUPNER, Christoph

(1683–1760)

Double Flute Concerto in E min., GWV.321; Overtures in E flat, GWV.429; in E, GWV.439; Sinfonias in D, GWV.538; in G, GWV.578.

*** MDG 341 1121-2. Nova Stravaganza.

MDG has a knack of finding these previously forgotten baroque composers. German-born Graupner was prolific, writing 113 symphonies, 50 concertos, 80 suites (overtures), operas, cantatas, as well as a vast amount of chamber music. The works recorded here are typical, showing both imagination and individuality. The three-movement *Sinfonias* demonstrate the composer's adventurous spirit, with plentiful ideas: the *Sinfonia in D* has a charming flute duet in the central movement, whilst the finale is both vivacious and fresh. The *G major Sinfonia* uses its two horns to good effect in the first movement, rather like a hunting concerto, contrasting with its minor-keyed central movement and the elegant, if more formal, minuet finale. Again in the *Double Flute Concerto*, while there are with two quite substantial fast movements, the minor key ensures that the writing is not entirely frivolous, while the finale, with its interplay between the two soloists, is especially infectious. The *Overture/Suites* are in the late-baroque style, featuring dance movements but beginning with a more substantial introduction. They are agreeable enough, though not as striking as their companion works. Excellent performances and recording.

GRECHANINOV, Alexander

(1864–1956)

(i) *Cello Sonata in E min., Op. 113;* (ii) *Piano Trios Nos. 1 in C min., Op. 38; 2 in G, Op. 128.*

*** Hyp. CDA 67295. (i) Tsinman, Yampolsky; (ii) Moscow Rachmaninov Trio.

Grechaninov was born a year earlier than Sibelius and also predeceased him by one year. He was barely represented at all on LP in the late 1950s, and only his choral music kept his name alive. Now his symphonies are being recorded, and the remainder of his vast output is being explored. The *First Piano Trio* comes from 1906 and was dedicated to Sergei Taneyev; the *Second* comes from 1930, by which time he had left Russia and settled in Paris. Their musical language is highly conservative and rooted in Tchaikovsky, Brahms and Rachmaninov, though no really distinctive voice surfaces here and the ideas fall short of memorability. Like the two piano trios, the *Cello Sonata* of 1927 is strongly lyrical and beautifully fashioned and played with tremendous ardour and conviction by the cellist, Mikhail Tsinman, and pianist, Viktor Yampolsky, both of the splendid Moscow Rachmaninov Trio. First-class recorded sound.

GREENE, Maurice (1696–1755)

Hearken unto Me, ye Holy Children (motet).

*** Hyp. CDA 67298. Blaze, Daniels, Harvey, King's Consort Ch. & O, King – HANDEL: *The Choice of Hercules.* ***

Maurice Greene, Handel's contemporary and for many years his unfriendly rival, cannot compare with that master in originality of invention, but this extended motet makes an attractive and valuable fill-up for the rare Handel cantata, equally well performed by the King's Consort.

GRIEG, Edvard (1843–1907)

Cello Concerto (arr. from *Cello Sonata* by Horovitz & Wallfisch); *Elegiac Melodies: The Last Spring; Peer Gynt* (excerpts): *Solveig's Song; Ingrid's Lament* (arr. Wallfisch); *I Love but Thee; To Spring* (arr. Freyhan).

*** Black Box BBM 1170. Wallfisch, LPO, Handley.

No, Grieg did not write a cello concerto, but what Joseph Horovitz has brilliantly done here, abetted by Benjamin Wallfisch, is to orchestrate the magnificent Grieg *Cello Sonata*. Amazingly, with echoes of *Peer Gynt* and much else in the instrumentation, the result sounds more Grieg-like than the original, with Raphael Wallfisch as soloist giving a commanding performance, and with Vernon Handley drawing warmly committed playing from the LPO. Comparable cello arrangements of favourite Grieg pieces and songs make an ideal coupling.

Piano Concerto in A min., Op. 16.

(BB) (***) Dutton mono CDBP 9719. Lipatti, Philh. O, Galliera – SCHUMANN: *Piano Concerto.* ***

(B) (**(*)) EMI mono CDZ5 74802-2. Lipatti, Philh. O, Galliera – CHOPIN: *Piano Concerto No. 1.* (**)

(BB) * EMI Encore (ADD) CDE5 74732-2. Cziffra, New PO, Cziffra Jr. – RACHMANINOV: *Piano Concerto No. 2.* *

(i) *Piano Concerto in A min., Op. 16; 6 Lyric Pieces, Op. 65.*

(M) *** Virgin VM5 61996-2. Andsnes; (i) Bergen PO, Kitajenko – LISZT: *Piano Concerto No. 2.* ***

(i) *Piano Concerto in A min.;* (ii) *Peer Gynt Suites Nos. 1–2.*

(M) ** DG 445 604-2. (i) Zilberstein; Gothenburg SO, Järvi.

Virgin have now restored Andsnes's original coupling – an outstanding account of the Liszt *A major Concerto* – but have included Book VIII of the *Lyric Pieces* (Op. 65) with its touching *Melancholy* and lively *Wedding Day at Troldhaugen*, which Grieg later orchestrated. They are played with real imagination and finesse. In the *Concerto* Andsnes wears his brilliance lightly. There is no lack of bravura and display, but no ostentation either. Indeed, he has great poetic feeling and delicacy of colour, and Grieg's familiar warhorse comes up with great freshness.

Dinu Lipatti's classic version of the Grieg *Concerto*, intensely poetic, like the Schumann with which it is coupled, has been a staple of the catalogue from when it was made in the late 1940s, but here in the superb Dutton transfer the sound is fuller and clearer than ever before, preferable to the EMI remastering, with the additional advantage that the disc comes at bargain price.

The famous 1947 Lipatti performance remains eternally fresh, and while it has been effectively remastered by Simon Gibson, the Dutton transfer is even finer.

Lilya Silberstein is a commanding artist with firm fingers, a good feeling for architecture and fine musical intelligence. In the *Concerto*, flamboyance has to go hand in hand with poetic feeling, and she has that too, though not in such strong supply as her best rivals. Zilberstein gives what one might call a good narrative performance – she holds your attention from moment to moment. Her playing could never be called routine, but her view is quite conventional and is without fresh insight. Järvi's *Peer Gynt* suites use material from his recording of the complete incidental music, but replaces the vocal numbers with their purely orchestral equivalents, recorded at a later date. Compared to the original vocal numbers, such as *In The Hall of The Mountain King*, these newer, purely orchestral ones fail to generate quite the same excitement, but are enjoyable, nevertheless.

Cziffra's account of the Grieg from the early 1970s is singularly disappointing. There are moments of poetry here, but the too leisurely first movement does not hold the listener's attention and the performance overall fails to make a strong impression. The backward balance of the orchestra and the indifferent early 1970s sound, shallow and thin, does not help matters. There are too many outstanding versions of this concerto to make this worth considering, even at

its modest cost, especially as the coupling is hardly better.

Holberg Suite, Op. 40.

(M) *** Decca (ADD) 470 262-2. ASMF, Marriner – TCHAIKOVSKY: *Serenade* ***; DVORAK: *Serenade* **(*).

Marriner's richly lyrical account of the *Holberg Suite* is outstanding in every way: the *Air* has a pleasing graciousness and the *Rigaudon* plenty of sparkle. The 1970 (Argo) recording remains splendidly fresh.

Holberg Suite, Op. 40; Lyric Suite, Op. 54; Peer Gynt: Suites Nos. 1, Op. 46; 2, Op. 55; Sigurd Jorsalfar: Suite, Op. 56.

(B) ** Ph. (ADD) 468 201-2 (2). ECO, Leppard – SIBELIUS: *En Saga* etc. ***

Leppard's (1976) account of the *Peer Gynt* suites is beautifully recorded, the sound at once lively and spacious. The music-making is fresh and has an air of thoughtfulness that will appeal to many, especially as the orchestral playing is so good. However, occasionally there is just a lack of vitality: *In the Hall of the Mountain King*, for instance, opens slowly and atmospherically, then does not build up quite the head of steam one expects. Of the rest, the delightful *Lyric Suite* is the finest performance, freshly played and warmly recorded. The *Holberg Suite*, however, is rather bland, and although the *Sigurd Jorsalfar* items are reasonably vivid, they are not especially distinctive. The Sibelius couplings, however, are generally superb.

(i) *Cello Sonata in A min., Op. 36;* (ii) *String Quartet in G min., Op. 27.*

*** Virgin VC5 45502-2. (i) Mørk, Gimse; (ii) Sigerland, Sponberg, Tomter, Mørk.

Like Leif Ove Andsnes's recent set of *Lyric Pieces*, the *Cello Sonata* was recorded at Grieg's home, Troldhaugen, on his own piano. It is Truls Mørk's second recording (his earlier version was with Jean-Yves Thibaudet, also on Virgin), and he plays with characteristic sensitivity and refreshing ardour. Håvard Gimse is an impeccable partner: he has the keenest musical instincts and great keyboard finesse. This is arguably the best and most compelling account of the *Sonata* to be had. Apart from the *Ballade*, Op. 24, the *String Quartet*, also in G minor, is Grieg's most deeply felt instrumental piece, and it is more often than not coupled with the unfinished F major quartet of 1890, which Julius Röntgen completed after his death. The most recommendable are the Chilingirians (Hyperion CDA 67117) and, at bargain price, the New Helsinki Quartet (Finlandia Apex 0927 40601-2) or the Oslo Quartet (Naxos 8.550879). However, the four artists assembled for the excellent Virgin recording can hold their own with the best, and they bring an intensity, freshness and imagination to this fine score.

Lyric Pieces, Op. 12/1, 2, 3 & 6; Op. 18/6–8; Op. 47/1; Op. 54/3–4; Op. 57/2, 3 & 6; Op. 62/1, 4–6; Op. 65/6:

Wedding Day at Troldhaugen; Op. 68/3; Op. 71/2, 6–7.

⚫ *** EMI CDC5 57296-2. Andsnes.

Lyric Pieces, Opp. 43, 54, 65; 3 Poetic Tone-Pictures; Op. 3/4,–66; Agitato; Album Leaves, Op. 28/1 in A flat; 4 in C sharp min.

(B) *** HMV CDZ5 74363-2. Andsnes

The *Op. 65 Lyric Pieces* on the Andsnes bargain recital derive from the young Norwegian pianist's debut recordings of the Grieg A minor and Liszt A major concertos, while the remainder come from the following year when he was 22 years old. The playing has great freshness, and Andsnes almost succeeds in making listeners feel that they have not heard such oft-played pieces as *Butterfly, Solitary Wanderer, To Spring* or *Shepherd Boy* before. Andsnes commands great tonal subtlety and a wonderful range of keyboard colour, yet there is no pursuit of surface beauty at the expense of artistic truth. At its price, this is outstanding. But the later recital, performed on Grieg's own piano at the composer's villa in Troldhaugen, is very special indeed.

Lyric Pieces, Opp. 12/1, 38/1; 43/1, 2 & 6; 47/2–4; 54/1, 3–5; 57/6; 62/4 & 6; 65/5 & 6; 68/2, 3 & 5; 71/1–4, 6 & 7.

(BB) ** Regis RRC 1071. Austbø.

Born in Norway but now based in Amsterdam, Håkon Austbø enjoyed success in Paris, where he won the Ravel Competition, and in Royan, where he won the Messiaen Competition. He is best known for his advocacy of the French master as well as Scriabin, and his command of keyboard colour and his wide dynamic range are impressive. There is no lack of tonal sophistication here, although he is rather too forwardly balanced, but for all its unfailing accomplishment and sensitivity, he lacks the naturalness of utterance and freshness of vision that such rivals as Gilels, Andsnes and Pletnev bring to this repertoire. Theirs is the art that conceals art.

25 Norwegian Folk-Songs and Dances, Op. 17, Nos. 1, 5, 7, 8, 10, 12, 18, 19, 22, 24, 25; Norwegian Folk Dances, Op. 66, Nos. 1, 7, 8, 12, 14, 15, 18, 19; Norwegian Peasant Dances, Op. 72, Nos. 2, 7, 8, 14–16; Songs, Op. 41, Nos. 1, 4, 6; Op. 52, Nos. 1–3.

(B) *** Naim CD 059. Gimse.

Håvard Gimse is among the most impressive and imaginative of Norwegian pianists, and he offers an expertly chosen anthology of dances from the Op. 17 set of 1870 and a handful of pieces from the much later Op. 66 and Op. 72 collections from 1896 and 1902. He also gives us half a dozen of Grieg's own song transcriptions. The lifelike recording (if slightly closely balanced) is made on a well-regulated Steinway in the fine acoustic of the Sofienberg Church in Oslo, and this is a most distinguished and satisfying addition to the Grieg discography.

Peer Gynt: extended excerpts.

(B) *** Sony SBK 89898. Hendricks, Oslo PO Ch., Salonen.

Salonen offers some seventeen numbers in all, all those included in the suites plus various other shorter pieces. The orchestral playing is excellent, the style idiomatic and anyone investing in this inexpensive collection with Barbara Hendricks and the Oslo Philharmonic Chorus is unlikely to be disappointed. The recording is of very good quality.

GROFÉ, Ferde (1892–1972)

Grand Canyon Suite; Mississippi Suite; Nigara Falls Suite.

** Naxos **Audio DVD** 5.110002. Bournemouth SO, Stromberg.

These are well-played performances although they only emphasize that the music of the *Mississippi* and *Niagara Falls* suites does not match *Grand Canyon*, and the only hit here is *On the Trail*. The recording is good but has nothing like the spectacular quality of Previn's EMI Audio DVDs. The only illustrations on the screen are 'still' pictures (including during the Grand Canyon music what appears to be a picture of Monument Valley).

HADLEY, Henry Kimball (1871–1937)

The Culprit Fay (Rhapsody), Op. 62; The Ocean, Op. 99; Symphony No. 4 in D min., Op. 64.

(BB) **(*) Naxos 8.559064. Ukraine Nat. SO, McLaughlin Williams.

Another issue in Naxos's enterprising American Classics series. Hadley's music is very much in the European Romantic tradition, and the 1921 tone poem *The Ocean*, is full of melodrama, thundering timpani and sea effects (the poem on which it is based is included in the sleeve notes). Though this style of writing is not too far away from a Hollywood film score of the 1930s or 40s, it is not less effective for that, especially when it is so colourfully orchestrated. *The Culprit Fay*, wth its evocative string writing at the opening, portrays the magical, airy quality of Joseph Drake's poem depicting the adventures of a fairy. There is more attractive colouring in this delicate, animated score, and it sustains its 15 minutes remarkably well. The *Fourth Symphony* was composed for the Norfolk, Connecticut Festival and was first performed in 1911. It comes with a programme that portrays different parts of America (the four movements are entitled *North, South, East* and *West*), though, curiously, the second movement is described as an 'Oriental tone-picture' and is predictably exotic. If far from a masterpiece, it is entertaining and ingenuously tuneful. The performances here are enthusiastic, and the recording vivid, though the violins tend to sound a bit under-nourished above the stave.

HAHN, Reynaldo (1875–1947)

Piano Quintet in F sharp min.

*** Hyp. CDA 67258. Coombs, Chilingirian Qt. – VIERNE: *Piano Quintet in C min.* ***

Hahn's *Piano Quintet* makes a striking contrast to its companion on this disc. Apart from the finale, which is a bit manufactured, its invention is both compelling and fresh, although the debt to Fauré (not so much the later music but the Fauré of the *A major Sonata* and the *Piano Quartets*) is pervasive. Civilized discourse, though not as deeply felt as the Vierne. Stephen Coombs and the Chilingirians play with conviction and character, and are given the benefit of present and vivid recorded sound.

HALVORSEN, Johan (1864–1935)

Fossegrimen, Op. 21 (complete stage music); Norway's Greeting to Theodore Roosevelt, Op. 31.

*** Simax PSC 1027. Bergset (hardanger fiddle), Blunck, Vollestad, Refsdal, Ginnungagap Ch., Latvian Nat. SO, Mikkelsen.

Although he wrote in a variety of genres including the symphony, much of Halvorsen's output was for the theatre. Some of it is uneven, but there is much that is charming (even enchanting), with a freshness of melodic invention and orchestral colour. Sigurd Eldegard's *Fossegrimen*, a 'troll-play in four parts', is partly based on the story of Torgeir Augundsson, better known as *Myllarguten* ('The Miller's Son'), Norway's celebrated folk fiddler who learned his art from Fossegrimen, musical master of all the underworld creatures, and Faust-like 'pawned his soul' for his secrets. Halvorsen's music from 1904 has much charm and fluency, and is full of appealing folk-like ideas alongside some more conventional episodes. Some of it is so good that it seems curmudgeonly to say that, at over 50 minutes, it slightly outstays its welcome. The playing is very commited, particularly that of Arve Moen Bergset who not only handles the hardanger fiddle and the violin brilliantly but also contributes vocally. There are four other soloists including a boy soprano, and a mixed choir. Øivind Bergh recorded a 20-minute suite from it way back in the 1970s which left one wanting more; better compile one's own suites than play it all at one go. *Norway's Greeting to Theodore Roosevelt* was commissioned to mark the occasion of the former president's visit to Norway in 1910 to receive the Nobel Peace Prize and is occasional music. However, there is a lot here that rewards the enterprising listener.

HAMERIK, Asger (1843–1923)

(i) Concert Romance for Cello and Orchestra, Op. 27; Jødisk Trilogi, Op. 19.

**(*) Danacord DACOCD 526. (i) Steensgaard, Danish PO, South Jutland, Atzmon – EBBE HAMERIK: *Concerto molto breve; Cantus firmus V (Sinfonia breve).* **(*)

Another issue in the 'Harmonious Families' series that the Danish label Danacord has compiled. Asger Hamerik was a pupil of von Bülow, and was befriended by Berlioz in the 1860s. He spent many years directing the Peabody Institute in Baltimore. His Sixth *Symphony for strings* (*Symphonie spirituelle*) was occasionally heard in the 1950s, but the pieces here are new to the catalogue and worthwhile. The performances are persuasive, and the value of the disc is enhanced by the coupling devoted to his son, Ebbe.

Symphonies Nos. 5 in G min. (Sérieuse), Op. 36; 6 in G (Spirituelle), Op. 38.

*** dacapo 8.224161. Helsingborg SO, Dausgaard.

The *Symphonie spirituelle* was the first of Hamerik's symphonies to reach the gramophone, when Boyd Neel recorded it on four Decca 78rpm discs (AK 1420-3). This newcomer is every bit as fine as Johannes Goritski's CPO recording listed in our main volume, and it has the benefit of a richer string sonority. The *Fifth* (1889–91), subtitled *Sérieuse*, is new to the catalogue and was composed in Baltimore, as was its companion here. It is engaging, well crafted and very much in the Leipzig tradition, but it is well worth taking the trouble to know, being fresher than Gade and eminently well laid out for the orchestra. Thomas Dausgaard gets very lively performances, and there is fine recorded sound.

HAMERIK, Ebbe (1898–1951)

(i) Concerto molto breve for Oboe and Orchestra; Cantus firmus V (Sinfonia breve).

**(*) Danacord DACOCD 526. (i) Frederiksen; Danish PO, South Jutland, Atzmon – ASGER HAMERIK: *Jødisk Trilogi* etc. **(*)

In the 1950s visitors to Copenhagen would find Danish musicians speaking with some enthusiasm of Ebbe Hamerik and listening to his *Sinfonia breve*. One can see why. He had imagination and musical resource, and his almost complete disappearance from the scene is puzzling. There is a searching quality about this music and an individual voice. Well worth exploring.

HANDEL, George Frideric

(1685–1759)

Concerti grossi, Op. 6/1–12.

(BB) *(*) Arte Nova 74321 37326-2 (3). Hamburg Soloists, Klein.

The Arte Nova Klein set, dating from 1995, is a reissue, with a new catalogue number, of a set we orginally discussed in our 1999 Guide. It costs no more now, and has no more to recommend it. There is certainly no lack of sonority in the playing of the Hamburg Soloists, using modern instruments, but the music's progress is too often marked by a lack of resilience and sparkle. The soloists are very good and the orchestral playing itself is finished, but the rhythmic weightiness and sporadic lack of vitality are enervating. The plodding opening of Op. 5/6 is matched by the leaden account of the famous *Larghetto e piano* melody of the third movement of No. 12. First choice for Op. 6 lies with the Musici di Montréal on Chandos (9004/6).

Oboe Concertos Nos. 1 in B flat, HWV 301; 2, HWV 302a; 3, HWV 287; Sonatas for Oboe & Continuo in B flat, HWV 357; in F, HWV 363a; in G min., Op. 1/6, HWV 364a; in C min., Op. 1/8, HWV 366; Sonata in G min. for Oboe, Violins & Continuo, HWV 404.

(BB) *** Regis RRC 1106. Francis, L. Harpsichord Ens.

Sarah Francis is a superb baroque oboeist, at the same time directing the members of the London Harpsichord Ensemble with spirit and finesse. These performances are not only delightful, but a model of style. In the sonatas Handel's ever-engaging contrapuntal interplay is beautifully clear (the harpsichord comes through in perfect balance with the continuo), so that for sheer pleasure, these performances almost upstage the more familiar concertos. A collection that leads the field, not least for its excellent sound. At its new Regis price it is a remarkable bargain.

Organ Concertos, Op. 4/1–6; Op. 7/1–6; in F (The Cuckoo and the Nightingale), HVW 295; in A, HWV 296; in D min., HWV 304.

(BB) *** DG Trio 469 358-2 (3). Preston; Holliger (harp in Op. 4/6), E. Concert, Pinnock.

Simon Preston's set of the major organ concertos returns to the catalogue economically priced on a DG Archiv Trio. On the first CD, containing the six Op. 4 works, although the balance of the solo instrument is not perfect, the playing of both Preston and the English Concert is admirably fresh and lively. While, with alternative recordings of the *Harp Concerto*, Op. 4/6 available, many collectors might have preferred all the works to be played on the organ, Ursula Holliger's solo contribution on a baroque harp is memorable, for she creates some delicious sounds. The second and third discs contain the six Op. 7 works, plus *The Cuckoo and the Nightingale* and the *A major* and *D minor Concertos*. All but the *A major* were recorded using the organ at St John's, Armitage, in Staffordshire and are even more attractive for the warmth and assurance of the playing. The *A major* which completes the set was recorded earlier with Op. 4. For those wanting a complete coverage of these engaging works this should serve admirably, although we have

much admiration for Ton Koopman's recording of just Opp. 4 and 7 on a two-disc Erato Double (● 0630 17871-2 – see our main volume).

Music for the Royal Fireworks; Water Music (complete).

(*) EMI **Audio DVD DVC4 92400-9. LSO or Prague CO, Mackerras.

Music for the Royal Fireworks; Water Music (complete); (i) Il trionfo del Tempo e del Disinganno: Sonata.

(B) ** CfP (ADD) 574 8812. Virtuosi & Wind Virtuosi of England, Davison; (i) with Kynaston (organ).

Mackerras's 1977 EMI recording of the *Royal Fireworks Music* attempted to recreate the spectacle of his famous stereo Pye version of 1957 with an enormous wind band, including 26 oboes. Here on DVD the impact of that later recording is vividly and impressively caught, if without quite the visceral thrill of the early Pye version. For the *Water Music* Mackerras moved to Prague and secured some fine Czech wind and brass playing. But the result has a heavy quality in the string tone (hardly a question of recording) which too often weighs the music down and prevents it from sparkling. There are finer versions than this, and the present issue must be regarded as a merely a DVD stopgap.

The Classics for Pleasure reissue of the complete *Water Music* is not only less expensive than its Chandos competitor (see below), but is a great deal more generous. It not only includes the *Fireworks Music*, but throws in for good measure the Sonata which Handel wrote for his allegorical oratorio *Il trionfo del Tempo e del Disinganno* which is used to accompany Bellezza (who represents Beauty) when she is enticed into the Palace of Pleasure. It is an engaging miniature, with an obbligato organ part and is given a very spirited account here. Davison employs additional wind for his performance of the *Royal Fireworks Music* but the result rather lacks weight in the bass, although the playing is fresh and stylish and the recording crisply immediate. His authenticity of style is carried over into the *Water Music*, which is well played and recorded but cannot compare with Gibson's SCO in liveliness of personality.

Water Music: Suites Nos. 1–3 (complete).

(M) **(*) Chan. 6642. SCO, Gibson.

Water Music: Suites Nos. 1–3 (complete); Double Trumpet Concerto in D.

(M) (*) Westminster (ADD) 471 276-2. Vienna State Op. O (with soloists), Scherchen – VIVALDI: *Double Trumpet Concerto* (*); TORELLI: *Trumpet Concerto in D* *(*).

The Scottish Chamber Orchestra re-emerges on Chandos with its head held high, due not only to the sense of style and polish, but also to the vigour and sparkle of the playing. Gibson's pacing of the allegros is brisk and he points rhythms with infectious zest. There is fine lyrical playing too, notably from the principal oboe, and the horns are robust without being too emphatic. This combination of energy and warmth comes as a welcome relief after prolonged exposure to period instruments. The ample acoustic of Glasgow City Hall is most attractive and the sound has fine clarity and firmness of definition. But the measure is short, and without the *Fireworks Music*, even at mid price, this cannot carry a strong recommendation.

Scherchen's 1960 version of the *Water Music*, although it has a certain character, is a non-starter in today's market place; indeed it was fairly dated at the time of its initial release. With generally plodding speeds – the *Alla hornpipe* almost comically so – and some pretty tatty orchestral playing, it is outclassed in every way by current rival versions. While it must be admitted that there is character in the performance, it represents not much more than a curiosity value. Likewise, the sloppily played *Double Concerto*. Our recommendation for the combined *Fireworks* and *Water Music* is with the Orpheus Chamber Orchestra (❂ DG 435 390-2).

Flute Sonatas; Oboe Sonatas & Violin Sonatas; Recorder Sonatas; Trio Sonatas (complete).

(BB) **(*) CRD (ADD) CRD 5002 (6). L'Ecole d'Orphée.

The complete period-instrument recording by L'Ecole d'Orphée of Handel's chamber music involves outstanding artists like Stephen Preston (flute), David Reichenberg (oboe) and the string players are led by John Holloway. The playing is distinguished, the recording excellent, and the new bargain box is handsomely packaged (the full contents are listed on p. 559 of our main volume). The one great snag, carried over from the separate CD issues, is the absence of cues for individual movements, so these records are more difficult to delve into that the original LPs. They are very good value just the same, and the documention cannot be faulted.

Flute Sonatas: in E min., Op. 1/1–1a, HWV 359b & HWV 379; in G, Op. 1/5, HWV 363b; in B min., Op. 1/9, HWV 367b; Halle Sonatas Nos. 1-3, HWV 374–6; Sonata in D, HWV 378.

*** Hyp. CDA 67278. Beznosiuk, Tunnicliffe, Nicholson.

Flute Sonatas: in E min., Op. 1/1, HWV 359b; in G, Op. 1/5, HWV 363b; in B min., Op. 1/9, HWV 367b; in D, HWV 378; in E min., HWV 379.

** MDG 311 1078-2. Hünteler, Zipperling, Lohff.

Both the Hyperion and MDG CDs purport to contain Handel's 'Complete Flute Sonatas' but, as can be seen above, Konrad Hünteler omits the three so-called *Halle Sonatas* and includes HWV 379 in E minor, which is not authentic: it was intended by Handel for the violin. In any case the performances on MDG, while musical enough, lack the vitality and point of those on Hyperion, and are recorded amorphously in a too resonant acoustic.

On the other hand the playing of Lisa Beznosiuk (using an attractive period instrument), Richard Tunnicliffe and Paul Nicholson is delightful in every way,

freshly spontaneous, warmly responsive and always aptly paced. There are excellent, extensive notes by Stanley Sadie. As he points out, the poetic *Adagio* which opens the most recent addition to the canon (HWV 378), which comes last in the programme, shares the nobility of line of the more familiar melody in the Largo of Op. 1/1a. Both are beautifully played here, and the closing jig-like finale of the *D major Sonata* ends the concert with sparkling felicity. The Hyperion recording is naturally balanced in an ideal acoustic.

Violin Sonatas, Op. 1/3, 6, 10, 12–13; in G, HWV 358; D min., HWV 359a; Allegro in C min., HWV 408; Andante in A min., HWV 412.

*** HM HMU 907259. Manze, Egarr (harpsichord).

Anyone looking for a complete set of Handel's *Violin Sonatas* on period instruments need look no further. The performances are buoyant and full of life. They have undoubted panache and easy virtuosity, and the eloquence of Andrew Manze's lyrical phrasing is immediately demonstrated by the opening *Affetuoso* of the D major, Op.1/13 with which the programme begins. The period violin is vividly caught and the harpsichord is well placed in the attractively resonant sound picture. Highly recommended.

VOCAL MUSIC

Apollo e Dafne (cantata); The Alchemist (incidental music).

(BB) *** Naxos 8.555712. Pasichnyk, Pomakov, European Union Bar. O, Goodman.

Roy Goodman, an alert, stylish interpreter of Handel, draws from his baroque orchestra, with its team of international players, a lively reading of this dramatic cantata on a classical theme, written by Handel at the beginning of his career during his stay in Italy. The Overture used here is the Allegro from the *Concerto grosso* Op. 3 No. 1, with the brisk sequence of brief arias and duets culminating in the longest aria, *Cara pianta*, with its expansive phrases well-sustained by the young baritone, Robert Pomakov. As Dafne, Olga Pasichnyk sounds fresh and girlish. Voices are balanced forward with the orchestra cleanly focused behind, despite distantly distracting reverberation. But with the attractive suite of incidental music from *The Alchemist* thrown in for good measure this is a good Naxos bargain.

The Choice of Hercules (cantata).

*** Hyp. CDA 67298. Gritton, Coote, Blaze, King's Consort Ch. & O, King – GREENE: *Hearken unto Me.*
***

The Choice of Hercules is unique among Handel's works, a dramatic cantata to an English text in a single act lasting 50 minutes. It was in the summer of 1750, at the peak of his powers, that Handel decided to re-use material he had composed for a play by Smollett, never produced, on the subject of Alceste. He changed both the subject and the words in his customary way, and the result is a delightful sequence of two-dozen brief numbers crisply telling the story of Hercules (taken by a counter-tenor, here the excellent Robin Blaze) making his choice between Virtue (the rich, firm mezzo, Anna Coote) and Pleasure (Susan Gritton, equally radiant). Robert King in this work otherwise unavailable on disc brings out the unquenchable freshness of invention that Handel retained even in his last years, with the choir and players of the King's Consort consistently responsive and resilient. The extended anthem by Handel's contemporary and rival, Maurice Greene, makes a valuable extra.

Deborah (complete).

*** Hyp. CDA 66841/2. Kenny, Gritton, Denley, Bowman, George, New College Ch., Oxford, Salisbury Cathedral Ch., King's Consort, King.
(BB) **(*) Naxos 8.554785/87 (3). Scholl, Ducret, Zazzo, Wolak, Kantorei, Frankfurt Bar. O, Martini.

Handel's 1733 oratorio, Deborah, only the second which he wrote in English (after Esther) is a work which readily sustains its length in telling a Biblical story, despite Handel's extensive borrowing from earlier works. The Hyperion version is based on a performance first heard at a 1993 Promenade Concert, opening spectacularly with a fine trumpet overture, which borrows fom the Fireworks Music. The cast is strong with clear, bright singing from Yvonne Kenny in the name role and Susan Gritton as Jael. James Bowman as Barak and especially Michael George as Abinoam make impressive contributions and Catherine Denley is even more striking as Sisera. But what gives the set its distinction is the fine singing from the combined choristers of Salisbury Cathedral and the Choir of New College, Oxford, although the resonance does take some of the edge off the sound. Nevertheless, Robert King's direction is assured and stylish and this is most enjoyable.

Recorded live in May 1999 in a reverberant German church, the Naxos version also gets off to a big, bold start, again with trumpets and drums adding to the impact. While rhythms tend to be too square, the choral singing is fresh and lively, but the soloists make a variable team. Best is the countertenor, Lawrence Zazzo, clear-toned and stylish as Barak, leader of the army of Israel, but both Elisabeth Scholl in the title role and Natacha Ducret as Jael are edgy in tone and often not steady. The oratorio comes on three discs instead of the two for the rival Hyperion version, but there is the incidental advantage of having each of the three parts on a separate disc. That full-priced rival brings a much more sympathetic performance with soloists far finer. Even so, this Naxos set at super-budget price is valuable in spreading knowledge of a long-neglected work, and is worth its asking-price.

(i) Gloria in B flat; (ii) Dixit Dominus.

*** Ph. 462 697-2. (i) Keith; (ii) Kazimierczuk, Ross, Deam, Fugue, Humphries, Roberts, O'Connor, Burt, Clarkson, Monteverdi Ch., E. Bar. Sol., Gardiner – VIVALDI: Gloria. ***

Emma Kirkby made the dazzling debut recording of Handel's newly discovered Gloria, but her disc (BIS CD 1235) includes only the Dixit Dominus, whereas Gardiner offers the bonus of a splendid account of Vivaldi's most famous Gloria. Moreover Gillian Keith's refreshingly nimble account of the Handel Gloria also has great lyrical beauty and Gardiner's Dixit Dominus is superb in every way, with memorable contributions from the whole team of soloists. The richly combined sopranos in De torrente in via bibet sing most movingly, and the recording is altogether first class.

(i) Israel in Egypt: Lamentations of the Israelites for the Death of Joseph; (ii) The Ways of Zion do Mourn (funeral anthem).

(B) *** Erato Ultima (ADD) 0927 41394-2 (2). (i) Knibbs, Troth, Greene, Priday, Royall, Stafford, Gordon, Clarkson, Elliott, Kendall, Varcoe, Stewart; (ii) Burrowes, Brett, Hill, Varcoe; Monteverdi Ch. & O, Gardiner.

Using modern instruments, Gardiner made his Erato recording in 1978. His style here, crisply rhythmic, superbly sprung, with dozens of detailed insights in bringing out word-meaning, is very much what has since become his forte in period performances of Handel and others. The singing both of the chorus and of the twelve soloists chosen from its members is excellent, though, like all other modern recordings, this one slightly falls down in resonance on the most famous number, the duet for basses, The Lord is a Man of War. In almost every way Gardiner gains by presenting the Lamentations not as an introduction to the main oratorio, but as a supplement, with the same music given in its original form, with text unamended, as written for the funeral cantata for Queen Caroline. Excellent, full-bodied, analogue sound. This set (reviewed in our main Guide) is even more attractive at Ultima price.

Messiah (complete).

(B) **(*) Decca (ADD) 467 475-2 (2). Sutherland, Tourangeau, Krenn, Krause, Ambrosian Singers, ECO, Bonynge.
(B) ** Virgin VBD5 62004-2 (2). Kirkby, Van Evera, Cable, Bowman, Cornwell, Thomas, Taverner Ch. & Players, Parrott.
(M) ** Westminster (ADD) 471 232-2 (2). Alarie, Meriman, Simoneu, Standen, V. Ac. Chamber Ch., V. State Op. O, Scherchen.
(B) * Teldec Ultima 0630 18952-2 (2). Gale, Marjana, Lipovsěk, Werner Hollweg, Kennedy, Stockholm Chamber Ch., VCM, Harnoncourt.

Bonynge's 1970 recording of the Messiah contained much of the electricity which marked his live accounts in London's Festival Hall and Albert Hall at the time. This is an exuberant Messiah, more remarkable for its brilliance of colour than for any more meditative qualities. Tempi for the choruses are often very fast, and the overall result is most refreshing. The main area of controversy is in the choice of Huguette Tourangeau as contralto soloist, who has a striking voice for opera, but her distinct, fruity timbre will not be to all tastes here. Werner Krenn and Tom Krause sing neatly and enjoyably, matching the performance as a whole, whilst the piping tone of the trebles adds point to a number of passages. Sutherland here is far fresher than she was in her earlier version for Boult, and *I Know that my Redeemer Liveth*, rather surprisingly, is done with no trills at all – very different from last time. All in all, an individual and fresh account, brilliantly recorded, and at bargain price.

Parrott assembled a fine team of performers, as well as his own Taverner Choir and players, on his 1989 set. Emma Kirkby is even more responsive than she was on her earlier recording for Oiseau-Lyre; but for all its merits, the performance lacks the zest and the sense of live communication that mark out a version like Pinnock's, another period performance which also dares to adopt slow, expressive speeds for such arias as *He was despised* and *I know that my Redeemer liveth*. Even at bargain price this is not a strong contender.

Scherchen's version is fascinatingly eccentric, notable for his erratic choice of tempi, and it is a pity that (because of a playing time of well over three hours) it comes on three mid-priced CDs, for it is a real collector's item.

So we have *And the Glory of the Lord* slow and steady, while *And He Shall Purify* is so fast that it becomes a choral scramble, and *For Unto Us a Child is Born* and *All We Like Sheep* are similarly brisk and lightly articulated, attractively so, but severely straining the resources of the Vienna Academy Choir.

Scherchen has fine soloists, two of them outstanding. Beginning with a memorable *Ev'ry Valley*, Léopold Simoneau's tenor contribution is very fine indeed, and throughout there is some exquisite soprano singing from Pierette Alarie. *I Know that my Redeemer Liveth* is very slow but very pure and true, and wonderfully sustained, with the orchestral accompaniment partly restricted to soloists from the first desks. *Since by Man came Death*, which follows, sustains the rapt atmosphere, with a spurt of energy to follow, and Richard Standen's *Trumpet shall Sound* is full of robust vigour. Nan Merriman sings most sensitively too, but not all will take to her close vibrato in *He was Despised*.

But when Scherchen is slow he is usually very slow and while the effect is touching in *And with His Stripes we are Healed*, the adagio tempo for the closing *Amen* is grotesque, providing easily the longest performance on record – taking over eight minutes to reach its marmoreal conclusion. The 1959 recording made in the Mozartsaal of the Vienna Konzerthaus is excellent, spacious and well transferred, giving a natural bloom to the voices, a good overall balance and a warm-textured orchestral sound.

Harnoncourt's version was compiled from two public concerts in Stockholm in 1982, with ill-balanced sound that puts the choir at a distance, making it sound even duller than it is. With the exception of Elizabeth Gale, the soloists are poor, and Harnoncourt's direction lacks vigour. This cannot even begin to match Scherchen's version on Westminster, let alone the top recommendations. Pinnock still heads the list on DG (423 630-2) alongside Suzuki on BIS (❂ CD 891/2), with Christophers leading the bargain versions (Hyperion Dyad CDD 22019).

Messiah (sung in English): highlights.

(BB) **(*) EMI Encore CDE5 74733-2. Battle, Quivar, Aler, Ramey, Toronto Mendelssohn Ch. & SO, Davis.

Andrew Davis's 1987 performance of *Messiah* steps back a little in time to what was until recently considered a traditional style of performance; nevertheless his presentation follows current practice in using judicious decoration in da capo arias, and his tempi for choruses are lively, even though he uses a modern orchestra and a large amateur choral group. They are well trained and generally cope well with the demands he places on them. The special strength of this set of highlights lies in the soloists, a team without weakness, each of them getting a chance to shine, although the tenor only has the opening number, and the soprano gets the lion's share. Kathleen Battle's *I Know That My Redeemer Liveth* has mature expressive feeling and Florence Quivar's *He was Despised* is comparably eloquent. The sound is first-class, clear and well balanced and the selection runs for 75 minutes. Excellent value.

Nabal (compiled by **John Christopher Smith**).

(BB) **(*) Naxos 8.555276/77 (2). MacLeod, Boog, Schoch, Heijden, Perillo, Junge Kantorei, Frankfurt Bar. O, Martini.

Given just two performances in 1764, five years after Handel's death, *Nabal* is a pasticcio oratorio with material drawn from a wide range of the composer's works. It was compiled by John Christopher Smith, Handel's favourite copyist as well as a composer, using material left to him in Handel's will. The story is drawn from the Old Testament, the book of Samuel, where the young David defies the rich and churlish Nabal, who promptly dies and whose wife, Abigail, then becomes one of David's wives. The libretto was written by Thomas Morell, who had collaborated with Handel on at least four of his oratorios, including *Theodora* and *Jephtha*. Here he had to fit words to music already written, with fluent results. It makes an attractive curiosity in a generally well-sung, alert performance, recorded live with occasionally intrusive applause. All five soloists have fresh young voices, with all three sopranos first-rate and Knut Schoch as David clear and fluent. As Nabal, Stephan MacLeod is not weighty or old-sounding enough for a villainous role, but he sings well. The principal snag is that the chorus is dimly recorded, set behind the soloists and period orchestra. A valuable issue, just the same.

OPERA

Alcina (complete).

*** EMI CDS7 49771-2 (3). Augér, Jones, Kuhlmann, Harrhy, Kwella, Davies, Tomlinson, Opera Stage Ch., City of L. Bar. Sinfonia, Hickox.

* Arthaus **DVD** 100 338. Nagelstad, Coote, Schneidermann, Smith, Romei, Mahnke, Ebbecke, Gerger, Stuttgart Op. Ch. & O, Hacker. Producers: Wieler, Morabito; Video director: Darvas.

Alcina is thought to be among the finest of Handel's operas, and Hickox's CD set from 1987 has long been the yardstick by which others are judged. His recording is complete, comprising the entire original 1735 score as given by Handel himself at Covent Garden, with no cuts. It runs in all for 217 minutes and is, moreover, blessed with a superb cast.

The Arthaus DVD performance is cut and runs to 159 minutes. Its strong points are the musical direction of Alan Hacker, who has a real feeling for the Handelian style, and some of the singers, most notably the Bradamante of Helene Schneidermann and Alice Coote's vibrant Ruggiero. However, the production, which was recorded at Stuttgart in 2000, is appalling and shows scant respect for, or interest in, Handel and a predisposition for sensational stage tricks. The set is grotty, and the tone of the whole production can be discerned during the course of the overture when the camera shows us an array of shoes, Second World War tin helmets, an electric light bulb and a bowl of cherries! Those who have the patience to get further will find a great deal of intrusive and quite silly stage business, much tearing away at others' clothing and a generally anti-musical approach to Handel's score. Don't waste your time or money! Stick with Hickox on CD.

Alcina: highlights.

(M) *** Erato 8573 85356-2 (from complete recording with Fleming, Graham, Dessay, Les Arts Florissants, Christie).

An excellent and generous (78 minutes) set of highlights centring on Act II but with well chosen excerpts from the other two Acts and ending with the brief final chorus. This will suit those who already have the Hickox EMI set and want to sample Christie's splendid live version made at the Paris Opéra in 1999.

Hercules (complete).

*** DG 469 532-2 (3). Saks, Von Otter, Croft, Dawson, Daniels, Pujol, Ch. & Musiciens du Louvre, Minkowski.

Mark Minkowski conducts an urgently dramatic account of Handel's music-drama in English on a classical theme. It is a work strangely neglected, when it contains exceptionally fine and memorable inspirations, with two very striking central roles, not just Hercules but, even more deeply expressive, that of Dejanira, his wife. Anne-Sofie von Otter may not float her voice quite so smoothly and easily as she once did, but hers is still a vividly characterful performance which, with fine gradation of tone and expression, brings out the full range of emotion implied. She is specially moving at the end when she realizes that her jealousy has brought the death of her husband.

As Hercules, Gidon Saks sings with fine, clear focus, not as weighty as many a traditional Handel bass, but firm and dark. Excellent contributions too from Lynne Dawson as a bright, charming Iole, the countertenor, David Daniels, peerless as the herald, Lichas, and Richard Croft elegant in the music of Hyllus, Hercules's son. The French chorus is not quite as idiomatic as the Monteverdi Choir in the rival Gardiner version, which dates from the early eighties but still sounds well, and is more consistently paced. The new set brings fewer cuts in a work which presents textual problems that the composer failed to resolve. However, the earlier set (DG 447 689-2) is now offered at mid-price – see our main volume.

Julius Caesar (*Giulio Cesare*; complete in English).

(*) Arthaus **DVD 100 308. Baker, Masterson, Walker, Jones, Bowman, Tomlinson, ENO Ch. & O, Mackerras. (Director: John Copley. V/D: John Michael Phillips.)

Taken from Channel 4's TV presentation of the English National Opera production, the Arthaus DVD offers a studio performance with the original staging modified. Recorded in 1984, the same year as the audio recording was made at EMI's Abbey Road studio, it vividly captures the dramatic bite of John Copley's production, using Brian Trowell's fluent translation, with a cast of principals that would be hard to match. Dame Janet Baker sings and acts commandingly in the title role, with Valerie Masterson a sympathetic if hardly sensuous Cleopatra, and Sarah Walker as Pompey's widow, Cornelia, matching even Dame Janet in the intensity of her singing and acting. Della Jones as Sextus, James Bowman as the scheming Ptolemy and John Tomlinson as Achillas are all ideal in their roles, with Michael Stennett's sumptuous costumes adding to the success of the production. Sir Charles Mackerras paces the music masterfully, but sadly the orchestral sound on DVD is thinner than in the audio recording, with an edge to it. So the CDs remain first choice (Chandos 3019).

Tamerlano (complete).

*** Arthaus **DVD** 100 702 (2). Director Jonathan Miller. (CD version **(*) Avie AV 0001 (3)). Bacelli, Randle, Norberg-Schulz, Pushee, Bonitatibus, Abete, English Concert, Pinnock.

Written in 1724, just after *Giulio Cesare* and just before *Rodelinda*, *Tamerlano* comes from one of the most fruitful periods of Handel's career, full of compelling inspiration, yet it has been relatively neglected on disc. This Avie recording was made live at Sadler's Wells in London in collaboration with the BBC in June 2001, marking a welcome return to disc of Trevor Pinnock and the English Concert. The result is delicate on a smallish scale, less sharply focused than Pinnock's Archiv recordings, but with unerring judgment on style and pacing. This is an instance where the DVD, recorded live in the small and ideal Goethe theatre in BadLauchstädt, is greatly preferable to the

CDs, with solo voices naturally caught and strongly projected against the beautifully recorded and balanced orchestra. It is a strong team of soloists, with Monica Bacelli in the title role controlling her full, firm contralto well, the countertenor, Graham Pushee, light and free as Andronico and Anna Bonitatibus a charming Princess Irene. Thomas Randle gives a vigorously resonant account of the role of Bazajet, and Elizabeth Norberg-Schulz is most resonant as Bazajet's daughter, Asteria. The production is simple and very effective, and Judy Levine's vivid costumes create a colourful contrast. The DVD performance is totally gripping throughout, whereas on CD the stage noises tend to be obtrusive. The DVD set is splendidly documented, and includes a 'read the score' facility, with the action taking place behind the music – of course one can alternatively have the sur-titles. The additional features include a retrospective review of 50 years of the Handel Festivals, from which this comes, and rehearsal sequences of the present performance.

Arias from: _Acis and Galatea; Atalanta; Athalia; Esther; Jephtha; Judas Maccabaeus; Messiah; Ode for St Cecilia's Day; Ptolemy; Samson; Semele; Serse; Tamerlano; Il trionfo del Tempo e del Disinganno._

(*) Australian ABC Classics 472 151-2. Hobson, Cantillation, Sinf. Australis, Walker.

David Hobson's voice is suave if relatively light-timbred, but its reedy sound gives it more of a penetrating quality of the kind one more readily associated with French tenors rather than Australian ones, and his diction is crystal-clear. The coloratura is brilliant in such items as _Sound an Alarm_ (from _Judas Maccabaeus_) and _The Trumpet's Loud Clangor_ (from the _Ode for St. Cecilia's Day_), and although Walker's tempi are at breakneck speeds, the results are exciting. In the slower arias, such as _Tune your Harps_ (from _Esther_) and _Gentle Airs_ (from _Athalia_), he is winningly elegant, and able to produce a dark, grave timbre for slow arias like _Total Eclipse_ (from _Samson_) which is really quite doleful. The odd transcription is included here, such as the tender arioso _Care selve_ (from _Atalanta_). Although a modern orchestra and chorus are used, their approach acknowledges period-instrument manners, and they are certainly warmly recorded, with the voice emerging vividly. Full texts and translations are included, along with an interesting essay on the use of tenor voice in nineteenth-century England.

Arias from: _Belshazzar; Jephtha; Messiah; Saul; Semele; Theodora._

*** Virgin VC5 45497-2. Daniels, Ens. O de Paris, Nelson.

Even David Daniels has rarely matched the brilliance, beauty and expressive intensity of this superb collection of arias from Handel oratorios. If anyone has ever felt that the counter-tenor voice is lacking in variety, this disc counters that in its contrasts of tone and expression, starting with two arias from _Belshazzar_, the one exuberant in vigour, a display aria for Cyrus with trumpets and timpani, the other

noble and deeply felt for Daniel, _O Sacred Oracles of Truth._ Similarly a light and brilliant aria from _Semele_ is set against one in a poignant minor-key, while the four arias from _Theodora_, all for the character Didymus, similarly cover a wide range. Those from _Saul_ have David singing his lament for Jonathan set against a noble prayer, while Hamor's arias from _Jephtha_ lead to the noblest performance of all, _He was despised_ from _Messiah_, the most ambitious and original of all the arias. Daniels' combination of flawless technique and expressive depth makes for magnetic performances, with elaborate divisions effortlessly thrown off. John Nelson draws electric playing from his period orchestra, starting brilliantly on the first _Belshazzar_ aria.

HANSON, Howard (1896–1981)

Symphony No. 1 in E min. (Nordic); Merry Mount (suite); Pan and the Priest, Op. 26; Rhythmic Variations on Two Ancient Hymns.

(BB) **(*)** Naxos 8.559072. Nashville SO, Schermerhorn.

Schermerhorn gives a relaxed account of the _First Symphony_, notably slower than the composer's own thrusting Mercury account, but this warmer approach offers its own rewards, especially in some of the more lyrical passages. The two tone poems are rarities: _Pan and the Priest_, written during 1925–6, begins quite mournfully on a solo cor anglais, and is passionate and reflective in turn, with the orchestra (including a piano) used colourfully. The _Rhythmic Variations_ are melancholic and contemplative in nature, but appealing so, and the colourful _Merry Mount_ suite (one of Hanson's best works) is splendidly done. The Nashville SO play well for Schermerhorn, and the sound is warm and reasonably vivid. Good value.

HARRIS, Roy (1898–1979)

Symphonies Nos. 7; 9; Epilogue to Profiles in Courage – J.F.K.

(BB) **(*)** Naxos 8.559050. Nat. SO of Ukraine, Kuchar.

Roy Harris occupied so commanding a position in American music in the 1930s and 1940s, when the _Third Symphony_ in one movement became a repertory piece, that the subsequent collapse of interest in his work in the 1950s and '60s, both inside and outside America, came as a shock. True, the _Fifth_, _Sixth_ and _Seventh Symphonies_ were recorded, but only maintained a peripheral hold on the catalogue. It is a truism no doubt that the _Third_ sums up his achievement, encapsulates the essence of his symphonism and, with such other works as the _Piano Quintet_ and the _Third String Quartet_, most fully enshrines his always immediately recognizable musical personality.

Every commentator tactfully – or not, as the case may be – implies that succeeding symphonies (there are thirteen in all) are but a shadow of the *Third*; however, as it is difficult to track down recordings or scores, we have had to reserve judgment. Ormandy and the Philadelphia Orchestra recorded the *Seventh Symphony* (1955) in the days of the mono LP but the *Ninth* (1962) had to wait until 1998 for its première recording (see below).

Kuchar and the Ukraine orchestra offer powerfully idiomatic accounts of these two symphonies, and they are recorded vividly, though his upper strings are lacking real body and weight. The writing, open and strong, with antiphonal effects between massed strings and brass is recognizably from the same pen as the *Third*, well worth investigating. No. 7, like that celebrated work, is in a single 20-minute movement of contrasted sections, and builds up from a slowly monumental opening to a massive climax with powerful strings and brass, and relaxes at the end with tinkling percussion effects that are anything but monumental.

Commissioned for Philadelphia, No. 9 takes its inspiration from the American Constitution and is in three substantial movements, each with a quotation from the Constitution as a superscription. Surprisingly, the opening, '*We, the people*', brings a jolly waltz motif with whooping brass, and it is only in the second and third movements, much more extended, that the composer takes on a solemn mood, with the pavane-like second movement, leading to a strong finale with martial overtones. The *Epilogue* in memory of President Kennedy is elegiac, dignified without quite becoming a funeral march, gritty at times, leading to a meditative close. A valuable addition to the Naxos 'American Classics' series but collectors wanting to try the *Ninth* should turn to the much superior alternative listed below, even though it is more expensive. At present there is no alternative *Seventh*.

Symphonies Nos. (i) 8 (San Francisco Symphony) for Orchestra with Piano; 9; Memories of a Child's Sunday.

*** Albany Records TROY 350. Albany SO, Miller (i) with Feinberg.

The *Eighth* and *Ninth Symphonies* were written in close proximity and both completed in 1962, though the former, commissioned by the San Francisco Orchestra, echoes the 35-minute *Canticle of the Sun* – a setting of St Francis of Assisi for soprano and chamber ensemble Harris had written the previous year. Indeed the fourth section is an adaptation of some of the vocalise. It is a one-movement piece in five sections; although the melodic language and harmonic vocabulary are familar from the *Third* and *Seventh*, the scoring is different (apart from some inventive wind writing, Harris provides a virtuoso piano part, and tubular bells).

Dan Stehman speaks of the chorale-like slow movement of the *Ninth Symphony*, along with the slow movement of the *Fifth*, as being Harris's finest and 'one of the richest utterances of its kind in the American repertoire'. Its sound world is fresh and there is a Gallic transparency of texture. In listening

to this music, it is perhaps time to try and put the *Third Symphony* out of one's mind. A listener hearing either of these symphonies before encountering the *Third* would not fail to respond to their own strengths, instead of stressing the echoes of the earlier masterpiece. *Memories of a Child's Sunday* is a slight piece written much earlier, in 1945, for Rodzinski and the New York Philharmonic. The Albany Orchestra plays very well for David Alan Miller and in the *Ninth* they are to be preferred to their Ukrainian colleagues. The strings have greater weight and the orchestral performance overall has even greater conviction and eloquence. Very fine recorded sound.

HARTMANN, Emil (1836–98)

(i) Cello Concerto in D min., Op. 26; Hakon Jarl (symphonic poem); Hærmædene på Helgeland: Overture.

**(*) Danacord DACOCD 508. (i) Dinitzen; Danish PO, South Jutland, Wallez – J.P.E. HARTMANN: *Hakon Jarl: Overture; En efterårsjagt: Overture.* **(*)

Emil Hartmann was naturally overshadowed in Denmark by his father, Johann Peter Emilius, who, fearing accusations of nepotism, did virtually nothing to further his son's career. He studied first with his father in Copenhagen and then in Leipzig, subsequently becoming organist at the Christianborg Slotskirke (Palace Church). He made more of a name in Germany, particularly as a conductor, where three of his seven symphonies were performed. The *Cello Concerto* is a relatively short piece, perhaps reminiscent in style of Saint-Saëns. The disc also affords an opportunity of contrasting the two composer's approach to the overture: Emil's Overture to Ibsen's *Hærmædene på Helgeland* is probably the most successful here.

Piano Concerto in F min., Op. 47.

*(*) Danacord DACOCD 581. Marshev, Danish PO, South Jutland, Aescbacher – WINDING: *Piano Concerto; Concert allegro.* **(*)

Emil Hartmann's *Piano Concerto*, composed in 1889, is, perhaps, less interesting than the *Cello Concerto* (reviewed above) and is too strongly reminiscent of Weber and Schumann to speak with a strongly individual voice. However, the Russian-born Oleg Marshev plays with such ardour and authority (and is so well supported by the Danish Orchestra) that one is almost persuaded that it is better than it is. Three stars for the pianist but not the work, which comes with a concerto by his brother-in-law, August Winding.

HARTMANN, Johann Peter Emilius (1805–1900)

Overtures: En efterårsjagt, Op. 63b; Hakon Jarl, Op. 40.

**(*) Danacord DACOCD 508. Danish PO, South Jutland, Wallez – EMIL HARTMANN: *Cello Concerto* etc. **(*)

Though little played nowadays, J.P.E. Hartmann composed one fine opera, *Liden Kirsti,* and wrote excellently for the orchestra. He became Niels Gade's father-in-law in the 1850s, and one of his descendants, albeit remotely, was Niels Viggo Bentzon. These two concert overtures make an admirable introduction to his work as well as a useful foil to the *Cello Concerto* by his son, Emil.

HARTMANN, Karl Amadeus

(1905–63)

Concerto funèbre.

(BB) *** Warner Apex 0927 40812-2. Zehetmair, Deutsche Chamber Philharmonie – BERG: *Violin Concerto.* JANACEK: *Concerto.* ***

As one of the two couplings for a highly sensitive version of the Berg *Concerto,* Zehetmair offers this strong intense *Concerto funèbre* for violin and strings – very much reflecting in its dark moods the troubled period (1939) when it was written.

HAYDN, Josef (1732–1809)

Cello Concerto No. 1 in C, Hob VIIb/1.

(M) * DG Masters 445 608-2. Haimovitz, ECO, Davis – C. P. E. BACH: *Concerto in A;* BOCCHERINI: *Concerto in B flat.* *

There is an unrelieved emotional intensity about Matt Haimovitz's account of the *C major Concerto.* His playing is just that bit too overheated, and there are moments of inelegance. Having said that, this recording was made when he was still a student, and his fresh enthusiasm and good technique tell, but there are many strong contenders in this repertoire and this is not their equal.

Horn Concerto No. 3 in D, Hob VII/d3.

(BB) *** Teldec (ADD) 0630 12324-2. Baumann, Concerto Amsterdam, Schröder – DANZI; ROSETTI: *Concertos.* ***

Baumann's 1969 account has firm classical lines. The *Adagio* is rather sombre here, but brings some splendidly resonating low notes from the soloist and the finale is attractvely spirited. The recording has been attractively remastered and has more bloom than on its last appearance.

Horn Concertos Nos. 3 in D, Hob VII/d3; 4 in D, Hob VII/d4.

(BB) *** Warner Apex 0927 40825-2. Clevenger, Franz Liszt CO, Rólla – M. HAYDN: *Concertino.* ***

Dale Clevenger gives superb accounts of the two surviving *Horn Concertos* attributed to Haydn (the fourth is of doubtful lineage). He is especially good in slow movements, like Baumann a little solemn in No. 3, but eloquently so, with the Adagio of No. 4 given a gentle melancholy. The dotted main theme of the first movement, nicely pointed, is most engaging and the performance projects a galant charm of the kind we associate with Hummel. The accompaniments are supportive, polished and elegant. These performances have fine spirit and spontaneity and the recording, made in a nicely judged and warm acoustic approaches the demonstration class: when Clevenger plays his solo cadenzas, the tangibility of his presence is remarkable, yet the orchestra remains well in the picture.

Trumpet Concerto in E flat.

(B) *** Ph. Duo 464 028-2 (2). Hardenberger, ASMF, Marriner – HERTEL; HUMMEL; STAMITZ: *Concertos* ***; (with Concert: 'Famous Classical Trumpet Concertos' *** ❂).
(M) *** Sony SMK 89611. Marsalis, Nat PO, Leppard – HUMMEL: *Concerto* ***; (with Concert: *Trumpet Concertos.* *** ❂).

Both the Hardenberger and Wynton Marsalis performances have been reissued within well chosen collections, both worthy of their ❂ and it is difficult to make a choice between them. Couplings will surely dictate the collector's choice.

Hardenberger's playing of the noble line of the *Andante* is no less telling than his fireworks in the finale and with Marriner providing warm, elegant and polished accompaniments throughout this is outstanding in every way.

But Marsalis is splendid too, his bravura no less spectacular, with the finale a tour de force, yet never aggressive in its brilliance. His way with Haydn is eminently stylish, as is Leppard's lively and polished accompaniment.

SYMPHONIES

Symphonies: A in B flat; B in B flat; Nos. 1–104 **(complete).**

❂ (BB) *** Brilliant Classics 9925 (33). Austro-Hungarian Haydn O, Fischer.

This box of thirty-three discs covering all of Haydn's numbered symphonies, plus *A* and *B* (earlier thought to be string quartets) brings a welcome return to the catalogue of the series recorded for Nimbus over fourteen years in the Esterházy Palace where Haydn himself worked. The final box of twenty symphonies arrived just as the demise of that record company was announced, and by a sad irony it was the finest of all, a superb culmination to a great project, covering the *Symphonies Nos. 21–39* plus *A* and *B.* These were works written in the 1760s when Haydn was busy experimenting, and the performances are outstanding, taking full note of period practice while staying faithful to modern instruments.

The virtuosity of individual players in this orchestra of carefully selected Austrian and Hungarian musicians fully matches Haydn at his most demanding, with soloists challenged to the limit by fast speeds. So a movement like the variation finale of No. 31, the *Hornsignal*, features a sequence of brilliant soloists such as Haydn might have been writing for in his Esterházy orchestra – violin, cello, horn and so on, even double bass. It is a performance full of panache, with the four horns braying out superbly.

Other striking symphonies in the group include *No. 22 in E flat*, the *Philosopher*, with its extraordinary parts for two cor anglais. Also the *Alleluia Symphony*, *No. 30 in C*, with trumpets and drums dramatically added to the usual published scoring – according to H. C. Robbins Landon brought in later by Haydn as an option. The minor-key works in that batch, such as the *Lamentation*, *No. 26 in D minor*, and best of all, *No. 39 in G minor*, are fine examples of Haydn's *Sturm und Drang* manner, with Fischer heightening dynamic contrasts in biting attack. No. 39 brings a superb example of Fischer's mastery, when he enhances the tension of the nervily tentative opening, exaggerating the pauses, so that he is far more effective in that movement than Dorati in the long-established Decca series.

In the symphonies recorded at the beginning of the project (from 1987 to 1990) comparisons with the Decca series generally have the merits of each balanced fairly evenly, but the advantage tips in favour of Fischer as the project develops. In the *London Symphonies*, Nos. 93–104, the very first to be recorded, the Nimbus engineers produce rather washy sound, where the works recorded later benefit from a sharper focus. In those early recordings too the slow movements tend to be taken at the sort of broad speeds of tradition, with warmly expressive phrasing.

Over the fourteen years it took to complete the project Fischer, following period practice, increasingly opts for faster speeds for both slow movements and Minuets (which begin to acquire a scherzo-like flavour), giving him a clear advantage over Dorati. Also the string playing comes closer to period practice, with lighter phrasing and less marked use of vibrato. That development is noticeable as early as the recordings made in 1994 and 1995, when most of the *Sturm and Drang Symphonies* were covered – broadly those in the late 40s and early 50s in the regular Breitkopf numbering. Finales in particular, taken fast, have all the bite and wildness one could want, with pin-point attack.

Symphonies Nos. 1–20 were recorded early in the project between 1989 and 1991, with results that are more variable. The finale of No. 12, for example, marked presto, is taken surprisingly slowly, almost like a Minuet. In No. 13, very adventurously for that early period, Haydn uses four horns, yet because of the reverberant acoustic they do not bray out as prominently as those used in works like the *Hornsignal*, recorded later. Here Roy Goodman's Hyperion

series (also now being reissued at bargain price) clearly has the advantage.

Even in these early symphonies, recorded near the beginning of the project, the trios in Minuets have solo strings, and regularly the vigour and thrust of allegros is exhilarating, with rhythms lifted and admirably crisp ensemble.

Though the set of thirty-three discs comes at super-budget price, around £80 (or roughly half the cost of the rival Dorati series), it is sad that the notes fail to deal with the symphonies in any detail. Fischer himself contributes a substantial essay on Haydn's career, the history of the symphony leading up to Haydn and a broad survey of the cycle of his 104 works, as well as a very perceptive note on period performance and the Austro-Hungarian way of music-making. Yet with simple, attractive packaging, with cardboard sleeves contained in a neat box, this is a set guaranteed to encourage collectors to delve more into works which from first to last convey the joy in creation of this ever-rewarding master.

Symphonies Nos. 1–5.

(BB) *** Hyp. Helios CDH 55111. Hanover Band, Goodman.

Symphonies Nos. 6 (Le Matin); 7 (Le Midi); 8 (Le Soir).

(BB) *** Hyp. Helios. CDH 55112. Hanover Band, Goodman.

Symphonies Nos. 9–12.

(BB) *** Hyp. Helios. CDH 55113. Hanover Band, Goodman.

Symphonies Nos. 13 in D; 14 in A; 15 in D; 16 in B flat.

(BB) *** Hyp. Helios CDH 55114. Hanover Band, Goodman.

Symphonies Nos. 17 in F; 18 in G; 19 in D; 20 in C; 21 in A.

(BB) *** Hyp. Helios CDH 55115. Hanover Band, Goodman.

It is good that Hyperion have decided to reissue Roy Goodman's Hanover series of Haydn symphonies at budget price, where they are very competitive, indeed those wanting period performances of the early works need look no further. These accounts offer consistently alert and well-sprung readings, generally favouring fast Allegros and relatively spacious slow movements which, more than in most period performances, give expressive warmth to Haydn's melodies without overstepping the mark into romanticism. The performances of the linked Esterházy works (Nos. 6–8) are characteristically lively and fresh, bringing out the colour of all three works. Allegros never sound breathless and slow movements are relaxed enough to allow a winning expressiveness. The following four works are full of charm and imagination, fully realized by Goodman and his players. Excellent recording.

The chronology of these early Haydn symphonies is difficult to pin down. They were written between

1759 and 1764, but it is certain that the numbering here is only approximate in indicating the order of their composition, and it seems likely that Nos. 13–16 were in fact written in reverse numerical order. *No. 13 in D* is remarkably mature, being scored for four horns. Haydn uses them to fill out the rich sonority of the first movement, but they also state and restate in unison the very striking arpeggio main theme as well being featured in the Minuet and finale. The slow movement is an *Adagio cantabile* for solo cello (here sounding more like a gamba) and strings. The finale, more surprisingly still, anticipates the key four-note theme of the finale of Mozart's *Jupiter Symphony*.

The high horns return in No. 14, and Haydn introduces an oboe solo for the Trio of its Minuet. Nos. 15 and 16 are by no means predictable either, with the first movement of the former in the style of a French overture (slow–fast–slow) and the sprightly 6/8 finale of the latter wittily looking to the future.

The horns remain important in the first work on the second disc (No. 17) which has a gracious slow movement, and the opening *Andante* of No. 18 is even more stately, with a sparkling allegro to follow and a Minuet acting as finale. The *Andante* of No. 19, for strings alone, has a gentle melancholy offset by a vigorous closing movement, while the more festive No. 20 includes trumpets and drums, dating it to Haydn's pre-Esterházy years (for those forces were not available to the composer in his early Esterházy period); but again the wind are silent in the slow movement. No. 21 (which exists in an autograph score) dates from 1764. It has an eloquent opening *Adagio*, followed by a vigorously rhythmic following Presto, again bringing the horns to the fore, while the lively finale returns to the vibrant style of the second movement. Throughout both discs Goodman's performances are full of vitality and excellently recorded, and one is continually stimulated by Haydn's unflagging resourcefulness of invention.

Symphonies Nos. 22 in E flat (Philosopher); 23 in G; 24 in D; 25 in C.

(BB) *** Hyp. Helios CDH 55116. Hanover Band, Goodman.

Symphonies Nos. 22–4 date from 1764. Goodman's account of the *Philosopher*, with its pair of cor anglais, is predictably bold and rhythmic, with an exhilarating finale (superb horn triplets!) to cap what has gone before. Opening No. 23 with horn whoops, Haydn seems determined that its first movement should not fall flat after that famously spectacular work, and the four-note groups which dominate the finale have a similar rhythmic sharpness. The dramatic contrasts of the first movement of No. 24 are offset by a delicate Adagio with a cantabile flute solo. No. 25 has a briefly pensive introduction, but is most notable for its hectic final Presto. Again brilliant, highly persuasive performances and excellent recording.

Symphonies Nos. 82–87 (Paris Symphonies).

(B) ** Decca (ADD) 470 062-2 (2). SRO, Ansermet.
(M) ** Sony (ADD) SM2K 89566 (2). NYPO, Bernstein.

Both Ansermet and Bernstein offer traditional, pre-authentic yet certainly individual accounts of the six *Paris Symphonies*. Ansermet directs strong, direct readings, a touch cool, with the Minuets weightier than we expect today, but with the outer movement allegros robustly spirited. The Swiss conductor is always stimulating to hear in matters of detail and the performances have plenty of character, showing his commitment to the composer. Accepting that the SRO does not possess the finesse of the VPO, this set will reward the conductor's admirers (and perhaps surprise others), especially as the 1962 sound is warm and vivid and the price modest.

Bernstein offers equally characterful performances, full of life and zest, with greater warmth and more sophisticated orchestral playing than Ansermet's. Bernstein has greater dynamic nuance too, and again shows much attention to detail. The main snag is the recording which, though basically full and vivid, offers rather strident strings when under pressure, and the whole sound picture is not as ingratiating as the Decca set. At mid price, it is hardly a bargain, nor do Sony opt for the more convenient slim-line packaging.

Symphonies Nos. 82 (The Bear); 83 (The Hen); 85 (La Reine); 87 (Paris).

(BB) **(*) Ph. Eloquence (ADD) 468 192-2. ASMF, Marriner.

Fine, lively, polished modern-instrument performances from Marriner and the ASMF, aptly paced and naturally recorded. If they lack ultimate distinction – slow movements have charm but also a touch of blandness – they are warmly enjoyable with lively minuets and spirited outer movements. *The Hen* is a good example. Marriner's account is spruce and lively but Barbirolli's Hallé version has added grace and exuberance (BBCL 4038 – see our main volume).

Symphonies Nos. 92 (Oxford); 104 (London).

(BB) *** Regis RRC 1084. E. Sinfonia, Groves –
MOZART: *Symphony No. 31 (Paris).*

Sir Charles Groves's performances are robust yet elegant; both slow movements are beautifully shaped, with Haydn's characteristic contrasts unfolding spontaneously. In the last movement of the *Oxford* the dancing violins are a special delight in what is one of the composer's most infectious finales. Excellent recording, and this budget Regis reissue has an equally recommendable Mozart bonus.

Symphonies Nos. 93 in D; 94 in G (Surprise); 103 in E flat (Drum Roll).

(M) (***) Sony mono SMK 89890. RPO, Beecham.

Though Beecham was almost as devoted to Haydn as to his beloved Mozart, he had his firm favourites among the symphonies, concentrating almost exclusively on the last twelve, the *London Symphonies*, of which he recorded a complete cycle for EMI in 1957–8. Even among those he had his clear preferences, with Nos. 93 and 102 appearing on his concert programmes more than all the others, even the popular ones with nicknames, each receiving over seventy performances. These mono recordings from 1950–1 certainly deserve their place beside the EMI stereo versions. The ear quickly adjusts to the relative dryness of the mono sound, with good inner detail conveyed. The main Allegros in the first movements of each bring either triple or compound time, and it is there above all that Beecham's rare mixture of energy and charm comes over most distinctively, with slow movements and Minuets on the slow side by latterday standards but beautifully lifted rhythmically, and the finales bringing the most exuberant conclusion in each, giving the feeling of live performance.

Symphonies Nos. 94 (Surprise); 96 (Miracle); 104 (London).

(BB) **(*) RCA 74321 68003-2. Philh. O, Slatkin.

Leonard Slatkin's series of Haydn London Symphonies brings fresh, refined readings at speeds that never sound breathless. Indeed, there is a certain urbane quality about these readings, especially when compared with Sir Colin Davis on Philips, which sometimes puts polish and eighteenth-century elegance before an earthier gusto. There is wit from the Philharmonia woodwind and the string phrasing always gives pleasure (particularly as Slatkin likes to divide his first and second violins on either side of the spectrum). But Davis finds an added tension – No. 104, for instance, is a work that can readily sound too easy-going, and with Davis there is more bite. However, the Miracle is both robust and genial and if you want just these three symphonies this RCA disc is certainly worth its bargain price.

Symphony No. 104 in D (London).

(M) *** Decca (ADD) 470 256-2. VPO, Karajan – BEETHOVEN: Symphony No. 7. **(*)

A really noble account, powerful and forward-looking, of the London Symphony from Karajan and the Vienna Philharmonic on their finest form. At the time of its first issue Gramophone commented on the 'vigour and sense of proportion' of the interpretation. As in Karajan's later DG account, the first movement repeat is observed and detail is etched with loving care, the delicate passages perfectly balanced with the bold tuttis. The slow movement, without any self-conscious mannerisms, is shaped warmly and graciously, and the Minuet sparkles, taken at a brisk pace, while the outer movements have splendid life and impetus. The 1959 recording, produced by John Culshaw, is extremely fine for its period (indeed any period), and has been transferred to CD without loss of the ambient bloom of the Sofiensaal.

CHAMBER MUSIC

Piano Trios: in G, Hob XV/5; in A, Hob XV/18; B flat, Hob XV/19; B flat, Hob XV/20.

*** CPO 999 468-2. Trio 1790.

The Trio 1790, so called because that year is the midpoint of the repertoire they play, are currently engaged on a complete survey of the Haydn Piano Trios on original instruments. The four works recorded here were composed for English publishers (there was a much greater demand for this genre than in Vienna in the mid-1780s). Harald Hoeran uses a fortepiano built by Derek Adlam, a copy of an instrument by Matthäus Heilmann, the violinist, Susanne von Bausznern uses a Hopf from the mid-eighteenth century and Philipp Bosbach a copy of a South German instrument from about 1640. The performances sparkle; there is plenty of wit and character, and the Cologne Radio recordings are first-class.

Piano Trios in A, Hob XV/18; in C, Hob XV/21; Nos. 39 in G (Gypsy), Hob XV/25; in E flat, Hob XV/29.

(B) *** Erato Ultima 0927 41402-2 (2). Trio Fontenay – String Quartets Nos. 74 & 77. ***

These Teldec performances are polished, warm and spirited, and are beautifully recorded. The famous Gypsy Trio is included, with its sparkling closing rondo, where the pianist in the Fontenay group, Wolf Harden, proves his excellence as an ensemble player. This delightful collection (reviewed in our main volume) is made even more attractive by its Ultima reissue, where the Alban Berg's outstanding accounts of two of Haydn's most famous quartets are added.

String Quartets Nos. 15 in G, Op. 3/3; 16 in B flat, Op. 3/4; 17 in F (Serenade), Op. 3/5; 18 in A, Op. 3/6 – see under HOFFSTETTER.

String Quartets Nos. 63–5, Op. 64/1–3.

*** ASV CDDCA 1083. Lindsay Qt.

Op. 64 are splendidly played by the Lindsays and are well up to the standard of their outstanding cycle. The slow movements of the B minor and B flat major are particularly searching. First-class recording.

String Quartets Nos. 74 (Rider), Op. 74/3; 77 (Emperor), Op. 76/3.

(B) *** Erato Ultima 0927 41402-2 (2). Alban Berg Qt. – Piano Trios. ***

Back in the early 1970s the Alban Berg Quartet displayed admirable polish, but the end-result was without that hint of glossy perfection which poses a problem with some of their more recent, digital recordings. The playing here has wonderful resilience and sparkle. The famous slow movement of the Emperor Quartet has seldom been put on record with such warmth and eloquence, and the slow movement of No. 74 is even more beautiful. Indeed the performance of this Quartet is masterly, with the rhythmic figure in the first movement which gives the work its title admirably managed. The recording too is first-class, full and clear, and this is one of the most rewarding of all Haydn quartet couplings. The playing time is only 45 minutes, but every one of them is treasurable. Furthermore, this disc (reviewed in our main volume) now comes as part of an inexpensive Ultima Double, including outstanding performances of Haydn Piano Trios admirably played by the Trio Fontenay.

String Quartets Nos. 76 (Fifths); 77 (Emperor); 78 (Sunrise), Op. 76/2–4.

(BB) *** Warner Apex 0927 40824-2. Eder Qt.

The Eder is a Hungarian Quartet which came to the fore in the early to mid 1980s, when these recordings were made. The players command a refined and beautiful tone, with generally excellent ensemble and polish. These are elegant performances that are unlikely to disappoint even the most demanding listener, save perhaps in the finale of the *Emperor*, which they take a little too quickly. They are unfailingly thoughtful players whose internal balance and tonal blend are practically flawless. The recording is altogether excellent and this reissue is a bargain.

Piano Sonatas Nos. 1–62 (complete).

(BB) **(*) Arte Nova 74321 59202-2 (9). Piazzini.

Carmen Piazzini comes from Argentina where she studied before settling in Europe. She continued her studies with Hans Leygraf and was a protégé of Kempff. These recordings were made in the studios of Bayerischer Rundfunk in Munich over a period of six years (1992–8) and show a refined musicianship and a generally high level of artistic accomplishment, even if at times there is a slight touch of gentility. But if on occasion one could wish a little more sparkle (in the opening of the *D major, Hob XVI/4*) or dash (in the *G major, Hob XVI/40*) but overall, there is an unfailing musicality and finesse to this playing which gives pleasure. Ms Piazzini produces a beautiful sound throughout and is admirably served by the Munich engineers. Given its highly competitive price, it makes a useful alternative to John McCabe's long serving Decca survey (443 785-2), though the latter still sounds eminently fresh and the playing has just that greater authority and character. McCabe has written an excellent BBC Music Guide to the Haydn sonatas and his documentation is vastly more informative than the somewhat skimpy notes offered with this set.

Piano Sonatas Nos. 33 in C min, Hob XVI/20; 39 in D, Hob XVI/39; 40 in E flat, Hob XVI/25; 41 in A, Hob XVI/26.

*** BIS CD 1163. Brautigam (fortepiano).

Piano Sonatas Nos. 35 in A flat, Hob XVI/43; 36 in C, Hob XVI/21; 37 in E, Hob XVI/22; 38 in F, Hob XVI/23.

*** BIS CD 1095. Brautigam (fortepiano).

We have written with some enthusiasm about the earlier Brautigam series (see our main volume, p.614) and with the present pair he reaches the *Esterházy Sonatas* (Nos. 36–41) dating from 1773. They are so-called because when they were published, in February 1774, they bore the dedication 'Six Sonatas for Prince Nikolaus Esterházy'. The additional sonatas, *No. 33 in C minor* (Hob XVI/20) and *No. 35 in A flat* (Hob. XVI/43) come from 1771 and the period 1771–73 respectively, though doubt has been cast on the latter's authenticity. However both Christa Landon and Georg Feder think it genuine. As in the earlier issues Ronald Brautigam

uses a fortepiano by Paul McNulty based on an instrument by Anton Gabriel Walter of about 1795.

VOCAL MUSIC

The Creation (Die Schöpfung; in German).

(BB) **(*) EMI Double fforte CZD5 75163-2 (2). Bonney, Blochwitz, Rootering, Wiens, Bär, SW German R. Ch. & O, Stuttgart, Marriner.

What distinguishes Sir Neville Marriner's 1989 Stuttgart recording is the truly outstanding contribution of the soloists. Each in turn enters singing most beautifully, Hans Peter Blochwitz as Uriel, Jan Henrik Rootering as Raphael, and Barbara Bonney a radiant-voiced Gabriel, ravishing in *Nun beut die Fleur das fritsche Grün* and *Auf starkem Fittiche*. And how delightfully they combine in their Trios in Part II, *In holder Anmut* and especially, *Zu dir, O Herr, blickt alles auf*, the effect very like Mozartian opera in its felicity. In Part III Edith Wiens is a hardly less delightful Eve, and her duets with the warm-voiced Adam of Olaf Bär are similarly memorable. The chorus is comparatively lightweight in *Die Himmel erzälen*, but they sing with vigour and convinction and the finale of Part III, *Sing dem Herrn,* combined with the soloists, is exhilarating. Throughout the orchestral playing is first-rate, and the recording excellent. A splendid bargain version that can be ranked alongside the best, only let down by the absence of a translation and instead an inadequate synopsis. Most enjoyable, just the same.

Masses Nos. 2a: Sunt bona mixta malis; 3 in C: Missa cellensis in honorem Beatissima Virginis Mariae.

*** Chan. 0667. Gritton, Stephen, Padmore, Varcoe, Coll. Musicum 90, Hickox.

In his excellent series of Haydn masses for Chandos, Richard Hickox here tackles two of the earlier works, both problematic in their own way. The fragmentary *Missa sunt bona mixta malis*, discovered as recently as 1983 in a farmhouse in Northern Ireland, consists only of a brief setting of the *Kyrie* followed by a more expansive setting of the *Gloria* which is cut off after the *Gratias agimus tibi*. No orchestra is involved, just organ and string continuo in support of the choir. Dating from 1768, it has contrapuntal writing which presents Haydn at his most indivudal. It makes a fascinating supplement to Hickox's superb account of what is, by a fair margin, the longest setting of the liturgy that Haydn ever composed, dating from 1766, five years after Haydn joined the service of Prince Esterhazy.

The title, Missa Cellensis – referring to the small Austrian town of Mariazell – is misleading when there is another later mass also entitled *Cellensis*, although this one has generally been known as the *St Cecilia Mass*. Now known to date from 1766, it is a 'cantata-mass' with the liturgy of six main parts divided into 18 separate movements. Hickox's version gains over the fine Preston issue from the late 1970s in weight and warmth of expression, helped by warm Chandos recording which allows ample detail in the many splendid contrapuntal passages. Whereas in the Preston version, which does not include a fill-up, the boys' voices of the Christ Church Cathedral Choir have attractive freshness, the Collegium Musicum 90 choir has sopranos that are amply bright and boyish, while achieving crisper ensemble. The soloists, all associated with earlier issues in Hickox's series, make an outstanding, responsive team, a fair match for those on the rival version, which is part of a L'Oiseau-Lyre Double (455 712-2 – see our main volume).

Masses Nos. 4 in E flat: Missa in honorem Beatissimae Virginis Mariae (Great Organ Mass), Hob XXII/4; 8 in C (Mariazeller Messe), Hob XXII/8.

*** Chan. 0674. Gritton, Winter, Padmore, Varcoe, Watson, Collegium Musicum 90, Hickox.

The coupling of two of Haydn's more rarely recorded masses, Nos. 4 and 8, brings a superb culmination to Richard Hickox's outstanding series for Chandos, covering all fourteen of Haydn's masses. As in earlier issues, with full immediate sound, Hickox and his team consistently bring out the exuberance of Haydn's inspiration as well as the drama, with exhilarating singing and playing from chorus and orchestra alike, matched by warm-toned soloists. The *Great Organ Mass*, dating from 1768 to 1769, is unique among Haydn's earlier Masses, with a pair of cor anglais instead of oboes bringing a darkness to the textures, and with the organ adding delicate baroque tracery, beautifully played with light registration by Ian Watson. A devout catholic, Haydn's joy in the liturgy bubbles out, as in the wildly syncopated *Amen* at the end of the *Sanctus*.

The *Mariazeller Mass*, written in 1782, was the last mass setting that Haydn composed before the final six masterpieces, in many ways anticipating the stylistic development that they represent. As in those late masses, the *Kyrie* is in a compressed sonata form, with a slow introduction leading to a vigorous allegro, and with the *Christe eleison* as the development section. Clearly, Haydn was already thinking of mass settings in symphonic terms, as he did in the final six. Adventurous modulations of key also relate to Haydn's symphonic writing, leading to an exuberant setting of the final *Dona nobis pacem*, so syncopated it is almost jazzy. There and throughout, Hickox, with bouncing rhythms, inspires performances that convey the pure joy of Haydn.

Masses Nos. (i) 13 in B flat: Schöpfungsmesse (Creation Mass), Hob XXII/13; (ii) 14 in B flat (Harmoniemesse), Hob XXII/13.

(B) *** DG. 470 297-2 (2). (i) Ziesak, Fink, Pregardien, Widmer; (ii) Lunn, Mongardo, Lehtipuu, Sherratt; Monteverdi Ch., E. Bar. Sol., Gardiner.

This is one of three issues covering the six last and greatest of Haydn's masses, a supreme sequence written each year towards the end of the composer's long life for the name-day of the Princess Esterhazy, wife of Haydn's employer. DG offers a generous two-discs-

for-the-price-of-one package, and Gardiner adds to the attractions by choosing outstanding teams of soloists. Worthy of special note in the *Harmoniemesse* is the outstanding young British soprano, Joanne Lunn, with her fresh clear tone, at times almost boyish, nicely set against the creamy mezzo of Sara Mingardo. Gardiner takes a dramatic, incisive view of these last two of the masses, which in many ways can be said to carry on Haydn's symphonic sequence. So the *Harmoniemesse* begins the *Kyrie* with a weighty slow introduction that might have been devised for a symphony. Each mass characteristically ends with an exuberant setting at high speed of the final *Dona nobis pacem*, and it is notable in both masses, each involving an orchestra larger than usual, that in his call for peace he introduces martial music with trumpets and drums. Gardiner more than most seems to relate that military flavour to what Beethoven so dramatically, and much more specifically, developed in the *Dona nobis pacem* of the *Missa solemnis*.

Where Richard Hickox in his prize-winning rival versions on Chandos is warmer in his approach, with bouncing rhythms which bring out the joy of the old composer's inspiration, Gardiner is more incisive, with the Monteverdi Choir singing with pin-point attack and exceptionally clean textures, helped by the warm but relatively transparent recording quality. The Chandos sound for Hickox is a degree fuller and more immediate, so in each case the sound suits the performances. Gardiner also tends to favour speeds a shade quicker than Hickox, often challengingly so, with fast and furious speeds for the settings of *Et resurrexit*, though in such a slow movement as the *Sanctus* of the *Schöpfungsmesse* Gardiner takes a broader view, moulding the phrases.

The Seasons (Die Jahreszeiten): highlights (in German).

(BB) **(*) EMI Encore (ADD) CDE5 74977-2. Janowitz, Hollweg, Berry, Ch. of German Op., BPO, Karajan.

Karajan's 1973 reading of *The Seasons* offers a fine, polished performance of Haydn's last oratorio which is often very dramatic too. The characterization is vivid, and in Karajan's hands the exciting 'Hunting Chorus' of *Autumn* (*Hört! Hört! Hört das laute Getön*) with its lusty horns anticipates *Der Freischütz*. The remastered sound is drier than the original but is vividly wide in dynamic range. Choruses are still a little opaque, but the soloists are all well caught and are on good form; the overall balance is satisfactory.

Stabat mater.

*** Griffin GCCD 4029. Bern, Ager, Carwood, Underwood, Christ Church Cathedral Ch., L. Musici, Darlington, Goode (organ).

Haydn's *Stabat mater* was the first of his vocal works to establish his reputation internationally, an ambitious cantata written in 1767 soon after Haydn took over responsibility for Prince Esterhazy's church music. Even against strong competition, the Griffin issue finds a distinctive place. Like the Heltay version (available on a Double Decca with the *Theresien-messe* and *Salve Regina* – 458 373-2), it uses an orchestra of modern instruments but, far more than Heltay, Stephen Darlington takes note of period practice, lightening string textures and finding extra detail. He also tends to adopt fast speeds, at times challengingly so, as in the big tenor aria, *Vidit sum*, stylishly sung by Andrew Carwood. The other striking quality of this set, besides the use of a church choir with boy trebles, is the warmly atmospheric cathedral acoustic, which yet allows ample detail. The line-up of soloists may not be as starry as those on rival versions, but these are young singers with fresh, clear voices and, like Carwood, with keen experience of the choral repertory.

HAYDN, Michael (1737–1806)

Horn Concertino in D.

(BB) *** Warner Apex 0927 40825-2. Clevenger, Franz Liszt CO, Rólla – J. HAYDN: *Horn Concertos Nos. 3 & 4.* ***

Michael Haydn's *Concertino* is in the form of a French overture, beginning with a slow movement, followed by a fast one and closing with a Minuet and Trio where the soloist is only featured in the middle section. The music itself is attractive; the second-movement allegro is played in fine style by Dale Clevenger, whose articulation is a joy in itself. Rólla and his excellent orchestra clearly enjoy themselves in the Minuet, which they play with elegance and warmth, and in the absence of the soloist, the unnamed continuo player embroiders the texture gently and effectively. The recording, like the coupled *Concertos* of Josef Haydn, is very realistic, especially during the solo cadenzas which Clevenger provides for the first two movements. An outstanding bargain coupling.

HENZE, Hans Werner (born 1926)

(i) 3 Dithyramben; (ii) Ode to the Westwind; (iii) 5 Neapolitan Lieder.

(BB) ** Arte Nova 74321 89404-2. Saarbrücken RSO; (i) Wich; (ii) Rivinius, Saarbrücken RCO, Skrowaczewski; (iii) Hermann, Halffter.

Henze's music is not well served on bargain disc, so this issue should be welcome, even if the welcome must be qualified. The good news – in that it is not otherwise recorded and is also by far the best thing on the disc – is the *Drei Dithyramben* with its Italianate warmth and strong atmosphere. In the *Ode to the Westwind* the cellist is rather too far forward and in the *Neapolitanische Lieder*, one of Henze's most approachable and charming scores, Roland Hermann is less subtle and less varied in tonal colour than in the pioneering Fischer-Dieskau recording from the 1950s. The balance in all three pieces is less than ideal, and in the *Ode to the Westwind* the sound is opaque. Recommended at the price for the *Drei Dithyramben*.

HERBERT, Victor (1859–1924)

Cello Concerto No. 2 in E min., Op. 30.

**(*) Guild GMCD 7253. Kreger, Philh. O, Yu – DVORAK: *Cello Concerto; Silent Woods.* **(*)

James Kreger's dedication and artistry come across in this fine version of Victor Herbert's *Cello Concerto*, coupled with the Dvořák concerto, which it inspired. He comes into direct competition with Yo-Yo Ma with Kurt Masur and the New York Philharmonic (SK 67173; see our main volume), and although there is much to be said for Kreger's naturalness of expression, Masur provides stronger support than Djong Victorin Yu.

HÉROLD, Ferdinand (1791–1833)

La fille mal gardée (ballet; complete. Choreography: Frederick Ashton).

*** Warner NVC Arts **DVD** 0630 19395-2. Collier, Coleman, Shaw, L. Edwards, Grant, Royal Ballet, ROHCG O, Lanchbery. (Design: Osbert Lancaster. V/D: John Vernon.)

One of the jewels in the crown of the Royal Ballet, *La fille mal gardée*, with costumes and scenery by Osbert Lancaster, is a visual delight from beginning to end. Frederick Ashton's ever-inventive choreography is both witty and charming, and Lesley Collier and Michael Coleman are a most engaging pair of lovers and dance with nimble grace. Brian Shaw's Widow Simone is the perfect foil, with the famous *Clog Dance* a captivating highlight, and Garry Grant is by no means outshone as the goofy Alain: he remains in our affections when his inept wooing comes to naught.

The orchestra is conducted by John Lanchbery who has arranged this complex score so that it naturally follows every move of the dancers, while his constant drawing on familiar passages by Rossini adds to the listener's pleasure. The recording too (if not as fine as the Decca CDs) is excellent, and the slight touch of thinness on the violin timbre is not a problem when the overall sound is so rich and resonantly full. The imaginative production brings much to please the eye, including a spectacular storm which is a true *coup de théâtre*; and the ballet's closing visual flourish cannot but raise a smile with its ingenious parallel with the final moments of *Der Rosenkavalier*. A greatly entertaining DVD which wears well on repetition.

HERTEL, Johann (1727–89)

Trumpet Concerto in D.

(B) *** Ph. Duo 464 028-2 (2). Hardenberger, ASMF, Marriner – HAYDN; HUMMEL; STAMITZ: *Concertos.* ***; (with concert: 'Famous Classical Trumpet Concertos' *** ●).

Johann Hertel's *D major Trumpet Concerto* is typical of many works of the same kind written in the

Baroque era. Håken Hardenberger clearly relishes every bar and plays with great flair. This now comes as part of a Philips Duo compilation of trumpet concertos, which is outstanding value.

HINDEMITH, Paul (1895–1963)

(i) Horn Concerto; Concert Music for Brass and Strings.

(M) *** EMI mono CDM5 67782-2 [567783]. (i) Brain; Philh. O, Sawallisch – R. STRAUSS: *Horn Concertos Nos. 1-2.* (***) ❁.

The Hindemith *Horn Concerto* at first seems lyrically much less voluptuous than its Strauss couplings, but it is very atmospheric and has a brief but witty central Scherzo which Brain articulates very winningly. Towards the close of the haunting palindromic finale the soloist imaginatively declaims a short poem – written by the composer – in such a way that the horn's note values match the syllables of the words (which are not intended to be spoken). Brain's performance is incomparable, with splendid support from Sawallisch, a superb Straussian, who also directs a fine account of the *Concert Music for Brass and Strings.* Both were recorded in the Kingsway Hall in 1956 and the early stereo is clear and full.

Violin Concerto.

(M) *** Decca (ADD) 470 258-2 (2). D. Oistrakh, LSO, Composer – MOZART: *Sinfonia concertante* etc **(*); BRUCH: *Scottish Fantasia* ***.

Oistrakh's 1962 reading of the *Violin Concerto* is still first choice. It was a revelation on its release: the work has never before or since blossomed into such rewarding lyricism on record. The orchestral contribution, under the composer himself, is strikingly passionate, with the soloist providing many moments when the ear is ravished by the beauty of phrasing and inflection. The superb sound emerges freshly in the transfer and this is an ideal choice for reissue in Decca's 'Legends' series.

Mathis der Maler (symphony); Symphonic Metamorphosis on Themes by Weber; Neues vom Tage (News of the Day): Overture.

(B) ** Virgin VBD5 61922-2-2 [CDVB 61922]. Bamberg SO, Rickenbacher – MAHLER: *Blumine; Totenfeier* etc. **

Rickenbacher's are straightforwardly strong and very serious-minded performances, not helped by a recording which is well balanced but rather opaque. His lighter novelty is the brief overture to an early 'comic' opera, *Neues vom Tage*, which generates plenty of sardonic energy, introduces a melancholy lyrical theme, becomes more exotic, and ends rumbustiously, but heavily. The main interest of this reissue is the Mahler couplings.

Symphonic Metamorphoses on Themes by Carl Maria von Weber.

(M) *** Decca (ADD) 470 264-2. LSO, Abbado – JANACEK: *Sinfonietta*; PROKOFIEV: *Chout*. ***

Abbado's 1968 *Symphonic Metamorphoses* is second to none: it is brilliantly played and recorded, and has equally impressive couplings. Moreover this latest 'Legends' transfer is excellent.

CHAMBER MUSIC

Octet.

(BB) * Warner Apex 0927 44395-2. Berlin Soloists, Bashkirova – PROKOFIEV: *Overture on Hebrew Themes; Quintet, Op. 39.* *

Those unsympathetic to the composer will find Hindemith at his ugliest and most manufactured in the *Octet* (1957-8), and the close balance of the Warner recording provided for the excellent Berlin Soloists does not enhance its beauty.

HOFFMEISTER, Franz

(1754–1812)

Clarinet Quintets in A; B flat; D; E flat.

*** CPO 999 812-2. Klöcker, Vlach Qt., Prague (members).

Hoffmeister's *Clarinet Quintets* bubble on amiably for the duration of this 75-minute CD. There is nothing deep or profound here, but this is galant, light music of quality, well constructed, and brimming with geniality and melodic resource. The first three *Quintets* are in three movements, each with a fairly substantial first movement, a simple *Adagio*, and fizzing finales, either allegros or Minuets. The *Adagio* of the *D major Quintet* is one of the few places where a minor key is allowed in for any length of time and the *E flat Quintet* breaks tradition with five movements, but maintains the appeal of its companions. Performances are first-rate, with creamy-toned Dieter Klöcker taking all the virtuosity in his stride. The recording too, is warm and well-balanced.

HOFFSTETTER, Romanus

(1742–1815)

String Quartets Nos. 3 in G; 4 in B flat; 5 in F (Serenade); 6 in A (attrib. HAYDN, as Op. 3/3–6).

(BB) *** Naxos 8. 555704. Kodály Qt.

Romanus Hoffstetter, if it was he who composed these works, seems fated never to have his name on them, even though no less than H. C. Robbins Landon discovered that 'Signor Hoffstetter' was inscribed on the plates from the which the original parts were printed. The six quartets were published in Paris by Bajlleux in 1777 as being by Haydn – no doubt to boost potential sales – and Haydn never questioned their authenticity when Pleyel included them in the complete edition of his string quartets.

Little is known about Hoffstetter except that he was a priest as well as a composer and wrote a fair amount of instrumental music including concertos for the viola (which was perhaps his own instrument). But as Allan Radley suggests in the excellent notes which accompany this CD: 'In a sense the question of authorship is largely irrelevant, since the music has a life of its own. There is much to admire in these works, whoever the composer might have been. They are elegant, neatly composed works with lively outer movements, gentle, graceful slow movements and the kind of lilting, intoxicating minuets that are an integral part of Austrian music of this period'.

The Minuet of the *A major*, with its engaging pizzicatos, is a typical instance, and that same quartet has an appealing *Adagio*, and a charming *Scherzando* finale. The *B flat major* is unusual for the period in being in two movements only, opening with a Minuet; the *G major* is the quartet most like Haydn, with a witty finale. But it is the *F major* that is justly the most famous, for it not only has the unforgettable 'Serenade' for its *Andante cantabile*, but another *galant* lilting tune as the second subject of the opening movement, and another amiable *Scherzando* finale.

The Kodály Quartet's performances are in every way first-class, treating the music with all the finesse that is its due, and winningly acknowledging its vitality and charm. The recording is most real and vivid and this disc is fully worthy to stand alongside the best of their performances of the quartets that really are by Haydn.

HOLMBOE, Vagn (born 1909)

(i) Preludes for Sinfonietta Ensemble, Vol. 2: To a Pine Tree, Op. 164/1; To a Willow Tree, Op. 170/4; To the Seagulls and the Cormorants, Op. 174/6; To the Pollution of Nature, Op. 180/7; To the Calm Sea, Op.187/9. (ii; iii) Music with Horn, Op. 148; (iii; iv) Trombone Sonata, Op. 172a.

*** dacapo 8.224124. (i) Copenhagen Atlas Sinf., Bellincampi; (ii) Ekman; (iii) Steohr; (iv) Sørensen.

The *Ten Preludes* for chamber orchestra are the product of Holmboe's last years (1986-91) and the first five were listed in our main volume. This second issue includes the remainder together with two other pieces from the 1980s, the *Music with Horn* for piano, violin and horn (1981) and the *Trombone Sonata* (1987). There is something cleansing about Holmboe's late music and readers will find its rewards are rich. These are thoughts of a master who never sought the limelight or played to the gallery: his music goes its own way without any thought of ephemeral fashion. Very good playing and recording.

Requiem for Nietzsche, Op. 84.

✪ *** dacapo 8.224207. Rønning, Reuter, Danish Nat. Ch. & SO, Schønwandt.

The *Requiem for Nietzsche* is quite simply one of the most inspired choral works of the twentieth century. It speaks with the distinctive and original voice we know from the Holmboe symphonies, yet its language seems new and exploratory. Composed in 1963–4, it was a *succé d'estime* on its first performance and has only recently been revived. It is a work by which the composer set great store – and rightly so! Inspired by Torkhild Bjørnvig's sonnets on events in the life of Nietzsche, it has everything we recognize from the finest of the symphonies; vision, subtlety, concentration, power, and originality – particularly in the imaginative use of voices. We have long campaigned for a recording of this piece, though pleas fell on deaf ears in the shallow musical climate of the late 1960s–early 1970s, and it is good to welcome its appearance now in so eloquent and committed a performance. An exceptionally rewarding work and altogether excellent sound.

HOLST, Gustav (1874–1934)

(i; ii) Egdon Heath, Op. 47; (iii) A Fugal Concerto, Op. 40/2; (iv) A Moorside Suite; (i; ii) The Perfect Fool (ballet suite), Op. 39; (iii) St. Paul's Suite, Op. 29/2; (v; vi) Choral Hymns from the Rig Veda, Op. 26/3; (v) The Evening Watch, Op. 43/1; (vii; ii) The Hymn of Jesus, Op. 37; (v; viii) 7 Part Songs, Op. 44; (v; vii; i; ix) Savitri (opera; complete).

(M) *** Decca ADD/DDD 470 191-2 (2). (i) LPO, (ii) Boult; (iii) St. Paul CO, Hogwood; (iv) Grimethorpe Colliery Band, Howarth; (v) Purcell Singers, Imogen Holst. (vi) with Ellis; (vii) BBC Ch. & SO; (viii) ECO; (ix) with J. Baker, Tear, Hemsley.

A fine collection of Decca's classic Holst recordings. The mystical element of *The Planets* is very apparent in *The Hymn of Jesus*, and the fine 1962 recording adds remarkable atmosphere to Boult's distinguished performance. The bleak, sombre portrayal of *Egdon Heath* is just as hauntingly evocative, while the brilliantly played and recorded *Perfect Fool* music flashes with colour. There are few chamber operas so beautifully scaled as *Savitri*. The simple story is taken from a Sanskrit source – Savitri, a wood-cutter's wife, cleverly outwits Death, who has come to take her husband – and Holst, with beautiful feeling for atmosphere, sets it in the most restrained way. With light textures and many slow tempi, it is a work which can fall apart in an uncommitted performance, but Imogen Holst could hardly be more imaginative, and Janet Baker in particular produces some of her most intense and expressive singing. The *Rig Veda Choral Dances* are also from a Sanskrit source, and the composer suggested himself that the last of them could, if necessary, be used as a prelude to *Savitri*. The opening *Hymn to the Dawn* brings more echoes of *Neptune* from *The Planets*, and the fast and rhythmically fascinating *Hymn to the Waters* is even more attractive. The *7 Part Songs* are hardly less inventive and, like the other Imogen Holst performances, are equally sympathetic. The

Grimethorpe account of the *Moorside Suite* (in its original brass-band form) is first-class and given recording that approaches demonstration standard. Hogwood's digital *St. Paul's Suite* and *Fugal Concerto* are excellent. Only the lack of texts mars this highly recommendable release, which is marginally preferable to the companion Decca Double collection listed in our main volume (444 549-2).

The Planets (suite), Op. 32.

(M) *** EMI CDM5 67748-2 [567749]. Geoffrey Mitchell Ch., LPO, Boult – ELGAR: *Enigma Variations, Op. 36.* ***

(M) ** RCA 74321 68018-2. Philh. O, Slatkin – VAUGHAN WILLIAMS: *Fantasia on Greensleeves* etc. **(*)

** Häns. 93.043. Stuttgart RSO (with Ch.), Norrington – ELGAR: *Serenade for Strings* **.

(M) * Westminster (ADD) 471 240-2. V. State Op. O with Ac. Ch., Boult – VAUGHAN WILLIAMS: *Greensleves & Tallis Fantasias.* *(*)

(i) The Planets; Egdon Heath, Op. 47; The Perfect Fool (suite), Op. 39.

❂ *** EMI (ADD) **Audio DVD** DVC4 92399-9. LSO, Previn (i) with Amb. S.

Like others in EMI's first release of Audio DVDs, Previn's analogue Kingsway Hall recordings of 1973/4 were originally made in quadrophony. They have been newly remastered (with a choice – using either side of the disc – for surround sound or high resolution stereo) and the result is astonishing. *The Planets* was always of demonstration quality, now it sounds more spacious than ever, with greater depth in the bass, enhanced internal definition and the dynamics expanded. The result is thrilling (sample the brass in *Uranus*), and brings a remarkable sense of the concert hall. The performance is basically traditional, with plenty of ferocity in *Mars*, delicacy in *Mercury* and sparkle in *Jupiter*, and throughout there is an appealing freshness as if one were experiencing Holst's wonderful orchestral effects for the first time. The masterly Hardy tone poem, *Egdon Heath*, makes a superb coupling, here given a darkly intense performance, illuminatingly different from Boult's cooler approach and the rip-roaring ballet suite from *The Perfect Fool* presents a colourful contrast. Again outstanding sound.

Sir Adrian Boult with the LPO gives a performance at once intense and beautifully played, spacious and dramatic, rapt and pointed. The great melody of *Jupiter* is calculatedly less resonant and more flowing than previously but is still affecting, and *Uranus* as well as *Jupiter* has its measure of jollity. The spacious slow movements are finely poised and the recording, always excellent, has added presence and definition in its latest remastering, although it does not match the Previn Audio DVD.

Slatkin's recording dates from 1996 and has the benefit of first-class orchestral playing and recording. He brings out much of the beauty and detail of the

work if, ultimately, the reading does not convey the full magical qualities that the score possesses. *Mercury* is certainly fleet and light, but *Jupiter*, the 'Bringer of Jollity', feels a little earth-bound. *Saturn* and *Neptune*, too, seem just that bit too slow and uncelestial in Slatkin's hands, whereas in other accounts, Boult's, for example, the otherworldly qualities of the score are conveyed much more mystically.

Very well played and recorded, with complex textures clarified, Norrington's reading of *The Planets* is of interest as an example of a German orchestra tackling English music, but the result is literal rather than idiomatic. *Mars* is very slow and emphatic, leading to an account of *Venus* that is steady and meticulous rather than poetic. *Mercury* and *Jupiter* then sound a little cautious, with the big tune of *Jupiter* not as legato as usual, with detached phrasing. The other three movements at steady speeds are also too metrical to convey the evocative overtones that Holst requires, though the offstage chorus (unnamed) sings most beautifully in the final movement, *Neptune*.

Younger readers may not remember that Boult, after making his first mono LP of *The Planets* for Pye (subsequently PRT) with the so-called Philharmonic Promenade Orchestra, in 1959 went to Vienna to make his first stereo version. Boult's trips to Europe have often produced some unexpectedly good records – but not in this instance. The Viennese playing is barely acceptable. The orchestra sounds under-rehearsed: there are fluffs in the strings and a very clumsy principal horn solo at the beginning of *Venus*. In the big, bold tunes the players miss the breadth of the music and sound phlegmatic. Only in *Mars* does the Viennese brass add a characterful hint of Wagner, which was to be amplified in Karajan's inspired later version for Decca with the VPO. The recording is bright and fully acceptable, but this well-transferred CD can be regarded as no more than a curiosity, for the Vaughan Williams couplings are little better.

The Planets (suite; including MATTHEWS: Pluto); The Mystic Trumpeter.

(BB) *** Naxos 8.555776; also **Audio DVD** 5.11004. RSNO, Lloyd-Jones.

This fine Naxos issue follows up the pioneering disc from Mark Elder and the Hallé Orchestra on Hyperion (CDA 67270), which was the first to round off Holst's original suite with the extra movement by Colin Matthews, celebrating the outermost planet, Pluto, discovered only after Holst had written his seven movements. On balance David Lloyd-Jones's reading with the Royal Scottish National Orchestra is even finer than Elder's, more spontaneous-sounding if not always quite so polished. Where Lloyd-Jones scores is in bringing out the contrasted character of each movement, starting with an account of *Mars* which in its urgency and menace contrasts strongly with the strangely relaxed view of Elder. *Mercury* is lighter and wittier, *Jupiter* jollier and *Uranus* more full of flair. Where Elder has for coupling a rare late work, Lloyd-Jones and Matthews have unearthed a very early work of Holst's that was never performed, a Scena to a text by Walt Whitman, which may reveal little of Holst's mature style, but which is colourful and atmospheric and well worth hearing. Full, vivid sound. This is also available on Audio DVD with the additional possibility of Advanced Resolution Surround Sound, but this costs considerably more.

VOCAL MUSIC

A Choral Fantasia, Op. 51; Choral Symphony, Op. 41.

(B) **(*) Hyp. Helios CDH 55104. Dawson, Guildford Choral Society, RPO Davan Wetton.

Though the ensemble of the Guildford Choral Society is not ideally crisp, and one really wants more weight of sound, the originality of Holst's choral writing and the purposeful nature of the argument are never in doubt in this surprisingly rare coupling, with Lynne Dawson the radiantly beautiful soprano soloist in both works. Holst is nothing if not daring in using well-known texts by Keats in the *Choral Symphony*, adding a new dimension even to the 'Ode on a Grecian Urn'. This is well worth considering in its bargain-priced reissue.

HONEGGER, Arthur (1892–1955)

Chant de joie; Symphonic Movement No. 3; Pacific 231; Pastorale d'été; Rugby; La tempête: Prélude.

(M) *(*) Westminster mono 471 245-2. RPO, Scherchen – STRAVINSKY: *Petrushka.* *

Scherchen's *Pacific 231* is reasonably effective but pales next to Ansermet's Decca account of a few years later in both performance and recorded sound. For the rest of this well-transferred 1954 programme the conductor makes some interesting points here and there, and a certain character and vigour comes through, but the playing is really rather scrappy. Far better to pay a little extra for this repertoire with versions by Plasson (DG 435 438-2) or Martinon (EMI CDM7 63944-2) among others, all of whom offer greater subtlety of detail and much better playing. And while they all provide different programmes, none is coupled with Scherchen's flaccid *Petrushka*.

Symphony No. 2 for Strings & Trumpet.

(M) *** EMI (ADD) CDM5 67595-2 [567597]. O de Paris, Munch – RAVEL: *Boléro; Daphnis et Chloé: Suite No. 2; Rapsodie espagnole.* ***

Honegger's war-time *Second Symphony*, scored for strings, to which an obbligato trumpet is added at the very end of the work, must be numbered among the most compelling of his symphonies. It commands a genuine intensity of feeling with a strong and vital imagination. Munch conducted the work's French première and made the pioneering set of 78s. The present version, his fourth and last recording, was made in 1967, not long after the Orchestre de Paris was formed.

Apart from the very first, this is his finest account of this dark and haunting score, and he secures first-class playing from the strings of the Orchestre de Paris. When it was recorded in 1967 it was certainly the most persuasive and eloquent account of the work committed to disc, and although Karajan and the Berlin Philharmonic have since surpassed it (◉ DG 447 335-2), it surely deserves its place in the EMI annals of 'Great Recordings of the Century', for the naturally balanced recording is lively and has atmosphere as well as opulence, and it has been splendidly transferred to CD. The Ravel coupling is no less successful.

Symphony No. 4 (Deliciae Basilienses).

(BB) *** Arte Nova 74321 86236-2. Basle CO, Hogwood – MARTINU: *Toccata e due canzoni*; STRAVINSKY: *Concerto in D.* ***

All three works on the Arte Nova CD were given their première on 21 February 1947 by Paul Sacher, who had commissioned them to mark the twentieth anniversary of the Basle Orchestra. The balmy, sunny pastoral opening, with its bucolic humour and lively intelligence, and the gentle, reflective middle movement have an underlying melancholy and a keen sense of nostalgia that is unfailingly affecting. Christopher Hogwood is totally attuned to the symphony's sensibility and gets splendid results from his players, although the string tone is meagre by the side of some earlier rivals like Dutoit and Baudo. His reading more than holds its own against current competition, however, and is much to be preferred to Támás Vásáry on Chandos. It is well worth the modest outlay.

HOWELLS, Herbert (1892–1983)

Canticles for Morning and Evening Services, Vol. 1: Settings of Magnificat and Nunc dimittis: in G (1918); for Men's Voices and Organ (performed by women's voices, 1941); Collegium regale (1945); New College, Oxford (1949); Colllegium Sancti Johannis Cantabrigiense (1957); Sarum (1966); York (1973).

*** Priory PRCD 748. Collegiate Singers, Millinger, Moorhouse (organ).

Canticles for Morning and Evening Services, Vol. 2: Settings of Magnificat and Nunc dimittis: Gloucester (1946); Worcester (1951); Collegiate Church of Saint Peter in Westminster (1957); Chichester (1967); Magdalen College, Oxford (1970). Nunc dimmitis (only, for unaccompanied choir, 1914). Anthem: Behold O God our Defender; Hymn for St Cecilia; Salve Regina, Op. 9/4.

*** Priory PRCD 759. Collegiate Singers, Millinger, Moorhouse (organ).

Howells composed some twenty settings of the *Magnificat* and *Nunc dimittis* and while it is not difficult to pick one's favourites, the amazing consistency of inspiration shines out again and again through these two collections, making his contribution to the Anglican Matins and Evensong uniquely special. One of the earliest and most memorable unaccompanied settings of the *Nunc dimittis* alone (1914) immediately establishes the combination of serenity and passionate expressive feeling that is characteristic of Howells, so astonishing when one realizes that he was himself an agnostic. The familiar examples from the *Collegium regale*, using a tenor soloist in the *Nunc dimittis*, have a natural beauty and eloquence, while the *Sarum Magnificat* with its rich interplay of trebles, and the lyrically glowing male line in the *Nunc dimittis* which the upper voices then join resplendently, also stand out, as does the *York Magnificat* with its radiant opening, gleamingly anticipated by the organ.

The 1941 settings for men's voices and organ are here sung by women, with tonally lavish and at times radiantly ethereal effect. Similarly Howells's writing for the upper voices is richly harmonized for Oxford in 1970, showing that the composer's touch remained as sure as ever three decades later. Also included on the second CD is the brief, but memorable *Hymn for St Cecilia* and the luminous unaccompanied *Salve Regina* which is so poignant in its emotional pull, for all its underlying serenity. The performances here are splendidly sung by the Collegiate Singers who are based at Westminster Abbey, where they regularly deputize for the Abbey Choir. They have made a speciality of singing Howells's music and their deep involvment can be felt throughout these unvariably fine performances under Andrew Millinger, while Richard Moorhouse's organ contribution always makes its mark. The recording, made in Marlborough College Chapel, could hardly be bettered.

Magnificat and Nunc Dimittis; Office of Holy Communion; Preces & Responses I & II; Psalm 121 & 122; Psalm Prelude, Op. 32/2; Take Him, Earth, for Cherishing; Te Deum & Jubilate; Rhapsody for Organ, Op. 17/3.

⬤ (M) *** Decca 470 194-2. Moore, Williams, King's College, Cambridge, Ch., Cleobury, Barley (organ).

Here is an unmatchable collection of the settings inspired by the greatest of our collegiate choirs, King's College, Cambridge, in performances of heart-warming intensity given in 1989. The boy trebles in particular are among the brightest and fullest ever to have been recorded with this choir. The disc sensitively presents the music in what amounts to liturgical order, with the service settings aptly interspersed with responses, psalm-chants and anthems with organ introits and voluntaries all by Howells. Even those not normally attracted by Anglican church music should hear this – especially as it is now offered at mid price.

HUMMEL, Johann (1778–1837)

Piano Concerto in A flat, Op. 113; Concertino in G, Op. 73; Gesellschafts Rondo, Op.117.

*** Chan. 9558. Shelley, LMP.

The *Concertino* is an 1816 arrangement for piano and orchestra of the *Mandolin Concerto* of 1799. The music is slight and frothy but is played with elegance and virtuosity by Howard Shelley who directs from the keyboard. The *A flat major Concerto* comes from 1827 and was written for the composer's concert tours of 1828–30. As Hummel was uncertain of the rehearsal time and the quality of some of the orchestras with which he would be playing, his orchestration errs on the side of caution. All the same, it is well scored, and the solo part is brilliantly decorative. Some have found the final *Rondo alla Spagniola* prophetic of Chopin's *E minor Concerto*.

The *Gesellschafts Rondo (Society Rondo)* from 1829 is a 12-minute piece consisting of a slow introduction and a dashing vivace. It is all fresh and delightful, even if it plumbs no depths. Brilliant playing from Shelley, whose artistry tends to be taken all too much for granted in his homeland. The 1997 recording still sounds as fresh and present as we thought first time round.

Trumpet Concerto in E.

(B) *** Ph. Duo 464 028-2 (2). Hardenberger, ASMF, Marriner – HAYDN; HERTEL; STAMITZ: *Concertos* ***; (with concert:'*Famous Classical Trumpet Concertos*' *** ⬤).

Trumpet Concerto in E flat.

(M) *** Sony SMK 89611. Marsalis, Nat PO, Leppard – HAYDN: *Concerto* *** (with concert: *Trumpet Concertos.* *** ⬤).

Both the Hardenberger and Wynton Marsalis performances have been reissued within well chosen collections and both are worthy of their ⬤s. But here there is a distinct choice between the two accounts of Hummel's *Concerto*. This is usually heard in the familiar brass key of E flat (which is the way Marsalis plays it), but the brilliant Swedish trumpeter, Håken Hardenberger, uses the key of E, which makes it sound brighter and bolder than usual. Neither he nor Marsalis (and their respective accompanists) miss the genial lilt inherent in the dotted theme of the first movement, and the finale captivates the ear with its high spirits and breezy bravura.

Marsalis also gives a very fine account of this engaging work, but his approach is straighter, more classical, less galant. In matters of bravura, however, he matches Hardenberger at every turn: he relishes the sparkling finale.

IBERT, Jacques (1890–1962)

Concertino da camera (for saxophone and orchestra).

⬤ (BB) *** Arte Nova 74321 27786-2. Kelly, Ostrobothnian CO, Kangas – LARSSON: *Concerto*; MARTIN: *Ballade*. *** ⬤

John-Edward Kelly was born in San Francisco, where he studied philosophy as well as music. He also studied with Sigurd Raschèr, who premièred the Ibert

Concertino da camera in 1935. It is a delightful piece, long thought problematic since it made technical demands seemingly impossible in the 1930s. Kelly's virtuosity is dazzling and lightly worn, and he tackles the extreme treble (or perhaps one should say altissimo) passages without the slightest sense of effort. Quite brilliant and highly entertaining music, and the Ostrobothian Chamber Orchestra under Juha Kangas gives good support. An enterprising coupling and an inexpensive price make this a most desirable issue.

INDY, Vincent d' (1851–1931)

Symphonie sur un chant montagnard français (Symphonie cévenole).

(**) Testament mono SBT 1237. Ciccolini, Paris Conservatoire O, Cluytens – FRANCK: *Symphonic Variations; Symphony.* (*(*))

As with the Franck *Variations symphoniques*, d'Indy's *Symphonie sur un chant montagnard français* (sometimes known as the *Symphonie cévenole*) was recorded in the Théâtre des Champs-Elysées in 1953, and suffers from too forwardly balanced a soloist and a dryish acoustic. The playing of Aldo Ciccolini is sensitive, and André Cluytens is very supportive.

IPPOLITOV-IVANOV, Mikhail (1859–1935)

Caucasian Sketches (suite), *Op. 10.*

(M) (***) Westminster mono 471 267-2. RPO, Rodzinski – KODALY: *Dances from Galánta* etc. (***)

Ippolitov-Ivanov's once popular *Caucasian Sketches* make an enjoyable coupling for an excellent Kodály triptych. As in that programme, Rodzinski brings out plenty of colour in the score, although it is the *Procession of the Sadar* that of course remains the most memorable movement. The 1955 mono sound is vivid and exceptionally detailed for its period.

IRELAND, John (1879–1962)

(i) *A Comedy Overture;* (ii) *The Bells of San Marie;* (iii) *The Holy Boy;* (ii) *Sea Fever; The Vagabond.*

(M) **(*) Decca (ADD) 470 195-2. (i) Grimethorpe Colliery Band, Howarth; (ii) Terfel, Martineau; (iii) Ryde-Weller, Richardson, Bournemouth SO, Hill – RUBBRA: *Songs*; QUILTER: *Songs.* ***

Bryn Terfel brings plenty of life to these effective and tuneful folk-like songs, and he is superbly accompanied and recorded (by DG in 1995). Stephen Ryde-Weller and Nicholas Richardson are the boy trebles in Ireland's best known work, the beautiful *Holy Boy*, here with full symphony orchestra (it was written as a piano prelude on Christmas Day 1912; the words were provided by Ireland's neighbour and solicitor Herbert S. Brown). The

Grimethorpe Colliery Band change the mood with the *Comedy Overture*, although the performance and recording fall short of the first-rate. However these Ireland items make an acceptable bonus to classic accounts of the Quilter and Rubbra songs.

IVES, Charles (1874–1954)

'An American Journey': From the Steeples and the Mountains; Symphony No. 4: 3rd Movement: Fugue; Three Places in New England; The Unanswered Question. Choral: (i) *The Circus Band;* (i; ii) *General William Booth enters into Heaven;* (i) *The Pond (Remembrance); Psalm 100; They are There.* Songs: (ii) *Charlie Rutlage; In Flanders Fields* (orch. David Tredici); *Memories; Serenity* (orch. John Adams); *The Things our Fathers Loved; Tom Sails Away.*

✿ *** RCA 09026 63703-2. (i) San Francisco Girls' Ch.; (ii) Hampson; San Francisco Symphony, Tilson Thomas.

Michael Tilson Thomas follows up his superb CD of the three complete Copland ballets (✿ 09026 63511-2 – see our main volume), with this remarkable survey of the extraordinarily diverse music of Charles Ives. The programme opens with one of Ives's most succinct and evocative orchestral explosions of dissonant polyphony, *From the Steeples and the Mountains*, and ends with his most beautiful, enigmatic, and visionary work, *The Unanswered Question* (with a haunting trumpet obbligato from Glenn Fischthal, and wonderfully quiet strings).

Tilson Thomas places Ives's other out-and-out masterpiece, *Three Places in New England*, at the centre of a collection of vocal music. The choral items range from the mystically brief evocation of *The Pond* (subtitled *Remembrance*) for female voices, and a heartfelt setting of *Psalm 100*, to the rumbustiously syncopated *Circus Band*, and the enthusiastically patriotic but characteristically zany *They are There!*

The songs include rhythmically spirited folksy numbers like *Memories* and *Charlie Rutlage* contrasting with the touchingly nostalic *Serenity* (sensitively orchestrated by John Adams), and *Tom Sails Away*. Thomas Hampson is obviously in his element in this repertoire. But the vocal highlight is *General William Booth Enters into Heaven*, where soloist and the excellent choruses exultantly combine in Ives's glorious portrayal of Booth and his Salvation Army leading his assembly of converted drunks and floozies into heaven, to the discomforture of the angels. Not to be missed.

JACOB, Gordon (1895–1987)

Mini-Concerto for Clarinet & String Orchestra.

(B) *** Hyp. Helios CDH 55069. King, Northwest CO of Seattle, Francis – COOKE: *Concerto*; RAWSTHORNE: *Concerto.* ***

Gordon Jacob in his eighties wrote this miniature concerto for Thea King, totally charming in its compactness. She proves the most persuasive of dedicatees, splendidly accompanied by the orchestra from Seattle and treated to first-rate 1982 analogue sound, splendidly transferred. An enticing bargain reissue.

JANÁČEK, Leoš (1854–1928)

Violin Concerto (Pilgrimage of the Soul) (reconstructed Faltus and Stědrů)

(BB) *** Warner Apex 0927 40812-2. Zehetmair, Philh. O, Holliger – BERG: Violin Concerto; HARTMANN: Concerto funèbre. ***

(i) Violin Concerto (Pilgrimage of the Soul); (ii) Violin Sonata.

(B) *** Virgin 2 CD VBD5 62053-2 (2). Tetzlaff, (i) Philh. O, Pešek; (ii) Andsnes – BARTOK: Violin Concerto No. 2; Violin Sonata; WEILL: Concerto. ***

In his last year Janáček worked on his opera, From the House of the Dead, based on Dostoevsky, the autograph score of which contains sketches for a violin concerto he had planned to call Pilgrimage of the Soul. He used some of its ideas in the overture to the opera, but the concerto itself remained in fragmentary form. On his death, Janáček's pupil, Břetislav Bakala, who had also reorchestrated the opera for its first performance, prepared a performing version of the piece. It was premièred in 1988, and there are two rival accounts currently on the market (from Josef Suk on Supraphon and Christian Tetzlaff on Virgin). This is highly original music, with some delightful lyrical ideas, imaginatively scored, albeit also with moments of top-heavy orchestral writing, searing in its intensity – particularly as played here by Thomas Zehetmair and the Philharmonia under Heinz Holliger. Excellent recorded sound. This is a most rewarding triptych, well worth exploring at budget price.

Christian Tetzlaff also gives an outstandingly sympathetic account of the short reconstructed Violin Concerto, in essence a series of seven brief vignettes lasting about 11 minutes. He is most sensitively accompanied by Pešek. In the equally attractive Sonata he is joined by Leif Ove Andsnes and they play with commitment and dedication. Theirs is an eloquent – indeed at times inspired – performance and in both works the recording is excellent. A thoroughly recommendable collection.

(i) Idyll for String Orchestra; (ii) Mládi for Wind Sextet.

(BB) **(*) Warner Apex (ADD) 7559 79680-2. (i) LACO, Schwartz; (ii) LA Wind Ens.

Mládi ('Youth') is a work of Janáček's old age and the Idyll for strings is a product of his youth. The latter, written in 1878 when he was in his early twenties, springs from the tradition of Dvořák, though its thematic material lacks the spontaneity and freshness of that master. It is very persuasively played by the Los Angeles Chamber Orchestra under Gerard Schwartz who is mindful of dynamic nuances and shapes phrases with imagination, while the sound is very lifelike and clean. The wind players of the Los Angeles orchestra play marvellously in Mládi with altogether superb ensemble and blend. They show sensitivity, too, in the Andante sostenuto (particularly from fig. 6 onwards), though they are not quite as poignant and expressive as the players in the London Sinfonietta (now on a Double Decca set – 448 255-2) who enjoy the advantage of a more natural and distant balance. The Los Angeles team are placed very forward, though the acoustic is warm and the detail remarkably clean. However, lasting under 45 minutes, this disc is not quite the super-bargain it first appears.

Sinfonietta.

(B) *** Sony SBK 89903. LSO, Tilson Thomas – Glagolitic Mass. ***
(M) *** Decca (ADD) 470 264-2. LSO, Abbado – HINDEMITH: Symphonic Metamorphoses; PROKOFIEV: Chout. ***
**(*) Orfeo C 55201B. Bav. RSO, Kubelik – DVORAK: Symphony No. 6. **(*)

A bold and brassy performance from Michael Tilson Thomas with the LSO at their virtuoso best, helped by very full recorded sound, bright as well as weighty. This makes a fine bargain alternative coupling to Rattle (EMI CDM5 66980-2).

Abbado's splendid 1968 account of the Sinfonietta still ranks among the best, with the conductor evoking a highly sympathetic response from the LSO. His acute sensitivity to dynamic nuances and his care for detail are felt in every bar, in addition to which the recording balance allows the subtlest of colours to register while still having plenty of impact. Superb couplings too, in this new 'Legends' transfer.

Kubelik made the pioneering 78 rpm records of the Sinfonietta just after the war in 1946 with the newly founded Philharmonia Orchestra. That version, recently issued on Testament, has a special freshness and authority and sounds amazingly good for the period. His later (1970) recording with the Bavarian Orchestra, whose fortunes he directed throughout the 1960s and '70s, has the advantage of stereo and, like the present issue, the benefit of the fine acoustic of the Herkulesaal. The Orfeo broadcast is not quite as polished nor the recording as finely focused as the 1970 DG account which is coupled with Taras Bulba and the Concertino for piano.

(i) Mládi: Suite for Wind Quintet; (ii) Pohádka (Fairy Tale); (iii) String Quartet No. 2 (Intimate Letters); (iv) Adagio II for Organ; (iv; v) Otče náš (The Lord's Prayer); Zdrávas Maria (Hail Mary).

(M) *** ASV PLT 8509. (i) COE Wind Soloists; (ii) Gregor-Smith, Wrigley; (iii) Lindsay Qt; (iv) Webber; (v) Gonville and Caius College Choirs.

A rather enticing collection. The Lindsay Quartet have the right blend of sensitivity and intensity for Janáček, and this account of the Second Quartet from the early 1990s remains a strong recommendation, and it is recorded with great naturalness. In *Mládí*, exceptionally vivid sound and sharp performances, as one would expect from the soloists of the Chamber Orchestra of Europe. *Pohádka* for cello and piano is sensitively done, and if the piano seems a little too backwardly balanced, the music is appealing The main choral work here, *Otče náš*, was commissioned in 1901 by a women's home, and originally written for mixed choir, tenor solo, piano and harmonium. However, the composer revised it in 1906, changing the accompaniment to an organ and harp, the version recorded here, with the organ and harp adding much to the colour and enjoyment of this devotional work. There is much beauty in this score which lingers in the mind and, like the *Zdrávas Maria*, for tenor, strings and organ, shows the composer creating his own style whilst not forgetting Czech musical tradition. The performances are sympathetic and warmly recorded. The tenor soloist is not named.

(i; ii) The Diary of One who Disappeared (song cycle; with 2 extra settings); (ii) Moravian Folk Songs; Intimate Sketches; Vzominka.

*** EMI CDC5 57219. (i) Bostridge, Philogene; (ii) Adès.

Few composers can match Janáček in the extraordinary flowering of inspiration that overtook him late in life, prompted by his passionate, unrequited love for a young, married woman, Kamila Stosslova. The work which set this flood of new music going, exactly symbolizing what he was feeling, was the uniquely involving song-cycle, *The Diary of One who Disappeared*.

Janáček saw in a Brno newspaper a sequence of 22 poems in folk-style, purporting to be written by a farmer's son who had become obsessed by the mysterious gypsy girl he met in the woods. After much self-searching he leaves his family to live the gypsy life with his beloved. As recently as 1997 it was proved to be a literary hoax devised by an obscure Moravian poet, Ozef Kalda, but Janáček genuinely equated the gypsy girl with his own Kamila, and the wildness of the writing – spontaneous, electric, both for voice and piano – reflects the urgency of his inspiration, with a high tenor taking the central role, a mezzo-soprano as the gypsy girl and an off-stage chorus of three women singers.

EMI here offers a superb version with Ian Bostridge an ideal soloist, totally unfazed by the cruelly high tessitura of the vocal writing, with the two high Cs at the end ringing out superbly. This is a performance which fully exploits Bostridge's great gift of conveying nervily intense emotion, with neurotic tension here giving way to moments of ecstasy. The mezzo, Ruby Philogene, is also ideally cast, sensuously rich-toned in the relatively brief role of the Gypsy-girl, and the off-stage trio is most atmospherically caught.

Fascinatingly, as a supplement at the end of the disc, alternative versions are offered of two of the songs, both longer than Janáček's later, definitive reworkings. The composer Thomas Adès proves an inspired accompanist. For fill-up, instead of more songs, there is Janáček piano music with Adès magnetically bringing out the spontaneity of pieces often only a few seconds long, while the Moravian folk inspiration makes one appreciate more clearly the folk element in the *Diary*.

Glagolitic Mass.

(B) *** Sony SBK 89901. Beňačková, Palmer, Lakes, Kotcherga, LSO Ch., LSO, Tilson Thomas – *Sinfonietta*. ***

Tilson Thomas directs a powerful, virtuoso performance of the normal published score, superbly played and sung, and helped by full, weighty recorded sound. The soprano solos are both idiomatic and beautiful as sung by Beňačková, unsurpassed by any rival, and Gary Lakes, though not quite so idiomatic, uses his clean-cut, firm Heldentenor tone in the important tenor solos with no strain whatsoever. The London Symphony Chorus is magnificent and the LSO plays brilliantly in every department, not least in the woodwind and brass, with the brightness of the sound adding to the impact. An excellent alternative to Rattle on EMI and a real bargain.

(i) Glagolitic Mass; (ii) The Diary of One Who Disappeared (song-cycle).

(M) ** DG (ADD) 463 665-2. (i) Lear, Rössl-Majdan, Haefliger, Crass, Bav. R. Ch., Bav. RSO, Kubelik; (ii) Griffel, Haefliger, Kubelik (piano).

Kubelik's 1965 account of the *Mass* is in most respects impressive, but there are now many outstanding versions available, and this is not especially recommendable. Nor is the – admittedly enterprising – coupling of the song-cycle among the best we have heard (it can't hold a candle to the old mono Supraphon account by Beno Blachut). However, this performance is more than acceptable, and the work itself, a hauntingly immediate account of a farmer's son's love for a gypsy, is irresistible. The transfers are excellent, and full texts and translations are provided for this Originals release.

(i) Glagolitic Mass; (ii) The Cunning Little Vixen: Suite; Zárlivost: Overture.

(M) *** Decca (ADD) 470 263-2. (i) Kubiak, Collins, Tear, Schöne, Brighton Festival Ch., RPO, Kempe; (ii) VPO, Mackerras.

Kempe's 1973 *Glagolitic Mass* makes a welcome return to the catalogue on Decca's 'Legends' label. Written when the composer was over seventy, it is full of those strikingly fresh orchestral textures that make his music so distinctive. The text is taken from Croatian variations of the Latin, and indeed Janáček said that he had village services in mind when he wrote the work. Though Kempe's interpretation and the singing of the Brighton Festival Chorus do not always have the sharpness of character of some competing versions, this account has an advantage in having a recording of great realism and brilliance, and the playing of the RPO is wonderfully committed and vivid. First-rate solo singing, with Teresa Kubiak particularly impressive. Fine, colourful bonuses from Mackerras also in excellent sound.

The Cunning Little Vixen (complete).

(*) Arthaus **DVD 100 240. Allen, Jenis, Minutillo, Orchestre de Paris, Mackerras.

With Sir Charles Mackerras bringing out the characteristic sharpness of Janáček's writing in this fantasy opera, the power of the score as well as its charm comes over strongly in this production at the Châtelet Theatre in Paris with Nicholas Hytner as stage director. Central to the production's success are the designs of Bob Crowley, which take one into a toy-town world with stylized brightly coloured sets in angular shapes and costumes to match. Musically, the singing of Thomas Allen as the Forester focuses the whole performance, strong and sympathetic in conveying this character's devotion to the life of the forest. He is one of the few singers who dominates the orchestra in a recording which favours instruments against voices. The bright, penetrating voices of Eva Jenis as the Vixen and Hana Minutillo as the Fox also defy the recording balance. With Czech titles for individual tracks it is not always easy to identify which character is singing.

Jenůfa (complete).

*** Arthaus **DVD** 100 208. Alexander, Silja, Langridge, Mark Baker, Glyndebourne Ch., LPO, Andrew Davis. (V/D: Nikolaus Lehnhoff).

The impact of Nikolaus Lehnhoff's production of *Jenůfa* was always strong and positive, with the stark yet atmospheric designs of Tobias Hoheisel adding to the sharpness. On DVD, with close-ups in this television film of 1989 adding to the impact, the result is even more powerful. This visual treatment exactly matches the sharp originality of Janáček's score, with its often abrasive orchestration heightened by passages of surging beauty, superbly realized by Andrew Davis and the LPO.

Roberta Alexander makes a warm, slightly gawky Jenufa, with Philip Langridge as the frustrated lover, Laka, making this awkward character totally believable, an object for sympathy, finally fulfilled. Both sing superbly, and so do the rest of the cast, including Mark Baker as the wastrel, Steva, a tenor well contrasted with Langridge.

Yet dominating the cast is the Kostelnicka of Anja Silja. This was the production which brought this characterful soprano, veteran of many years of singing Wagner at Bayreuth, to Glyndebourne for the first time, where she has since added an Indian Summer to her long career singing this and other Janáček roles with enormous success.

The abrasiveness in her voice, which with Wagner heroines was often obtrusive, is here a positive asset, and her portrayal of this formidable character, positive and uncompromising yet ultimately an object of pity, is totally convincing in all its complexity. The way she delivers Kostelnicka's apprehensive cry at the end of Act II was 'as if death were peering into the house'. Full, vivid sound very well transferred, if with an edge that suits the music.

Káta Kabanová (complete).

*** Arthaus **DVD** 100 158. Gustafson, Palmer, Davies, McCauley, Graham-Hall, Winter, Glyndebourne Ch., LPO, Andrew Davis. (V/D: Nikolaus Lehnhoff.)
(**) TDK Mediactive **DVD** DV-OPKK. Denoke, Kuebler, Henschel, Smit, Delamboye, Trost, Peckova, Slovak Phil. Ch., Czech PO, Cambreling.

First seen at Glyndebourne in 1988, this Arthaus DVD offers the ground-breaking production by Nikolaus Lehnhoff with stark, striking designs by Tobias Hoheisel, which led to a whole sequence of memorable Janáček productions. It remains one of the most powerful, with Nancy Gustafson tenderly moving as the heroine starved of love, constantly frustrated by her implacable mother-in-law, the deeply unsympathetic Kabanicha, brilliantly portrayed and sung by Felicity Palmer, with a powerful cutting edge.

The production, too, is exactly suited to the distinctive idiom of Janáček, with its contrasts of abrasiveness and rich beauty. Strong contributions too from Ryland Davies as Tichon, Káta's husband, Barry McCauley as Boris, and John Graham-Hall as Kudrjas, with characterful contributions too from such a veteran as Donald Adams as Boris's father, Dikoj. Bright, forward sound adds to the impact.

Recorded live at the 1998 Salzburg Festival, the TDK DVD of *Káta Kabanová* offers a starkly updated production by Christoph Marthaler with a permanent set by Anna Viebrock which puts the whole opera in a courtyard surrounded completely by highrise apartment blocks. Such an urban setting may capture an appropriate feeling of claustrophobia, and the visual brutality chimes to a degree with the abrasiveness of the score, but, totally unatmospheric, it flies in the face of Ostrovsky's story in more than the period. So instead of throwing herself in the Volga at the end, Kata curls up among the tiny fountains dotted about a central flower-bed, and instead of gazing at the Volga in the opening scene Kudrjas is simply looking at a small painting.

This is the sort of production that makes one despair of present-day opera presentation, and the stiffly stylized acting adds to the feeling of alienation, all the more so when musically the performance with the Czech Philharmonic and a Slovakian Choir under Sylvain Cambreling is first-rate. The whole opera is presented without intervals, adding to its concentration, with the title role most movingly taken by Angela Denoke, singing with radiant, creamy tone. Among the others Jane Henschel stands out, characterful as the Kabanicha, looking less menacing than she might, with David Kuebler excellent as Káta's lover, Boris. However collectors would do better to stay with the excellent Decca CDs conducted by Mackerras, with Elisabeth Söderström superb as the tragic heroine (421 852-2).

JENNER, Gustave (1865–1920)

Piano Quartet in F; String Quartets Nos. 1-3; (i) Trio for Piano, Clarinet and Horn in E flat.

*** CPO 999 699-2. Mozart Piano Quartet (members); (i) with Pencz, Darbellay.

We don't know much about Gustave Jenner (born in Keitum on the Island of Sylt), though the insert notes are helpful. However, it is the music that matters, and this is another one of CPO's interesting discoveries. The *Piano Quartet* begins with a lovely sweeping figure and the secondary theme is no less beguiling. The slow movement quotes Schubert's *Piano Trio in B flat* and is most attractively decorated. The lively *scherzo* is then followed by a theme and variations with a diverting Hungarian sequence. The three *String Quartets* are very much in the tradition of Jenner's teacher and mentor, Brahms. They are quite spontaneous, with plenty of amiable ideas. Occasionally, too, there are darker Hungarian colourings, notably in the *G minor Quartet*. The *Third Quartet* has a particularly attractive finale, witty and energetic and lyrically quite seductive. Though not in the league of the Brahms *Horn Trio* (Brahms apparently did not care too much for it), Jenner's differently scored work is notable for the facility and vigour of the writing, rather than any deeper qualities. But this remains an enjoyable enough collection of chamber rarities, and the performances and vivid sound make the very most of the music's felicities.

JOEL, Billy (born 1949)

Fantasies and Delusions for Solo Piano: Air (Dublinesqe); Aria (Grand Canal); Fantasy (Film Noir); Invention in C minor; Reverie (Villa d'Este); Soliloquy (On a Separation); Suite; Waltzes 1-3.

*** Sony SK 86397. Joo.

Billy Joel is a talented composer in the world of 'pop' music but here, in the most cultivated manner, he turns to music of a more permanent kind. His brief but memorable *Invention* certainly turns our thoughts to Bach and Scarlatti, but although his skilful piano writing is thoroughly eclectic, Chopin is the predominating influence, especially in the *Third* of the three charming *Waltzes*, each quite different, and the *Aria* (subtitled *Grand Canal*) is like an extended nocturne. The closing, nostalgic *'Dublinesque' Air*, with its quirky mood changes, is also most winning. Richard Joo maintains a sense of improvisatory spontaneity throughout the recital – Joel could hardly have a more persuasive advocate, and the recording is excellent. What a pity the documentation consists of only photographs and titles.

JOSQUIN DESPREZ (died 1521)

Motetti de Passione … B (1503): Ave verum corpus; Christem ducem/Qui velatus; Domine, non secundum; O Domine Jesu Christe; Tu solus qui facis mirabilia. Missa faisant regretz.

✪ *** ASV CDGAU 302. Clerks' Group, Wickam – FRYE: *Tut a par moy.* ***

Josquin's compact, but characteristically fluent and appealing four-part mass setting *Faisant regretz* is based on a four note motif taken from Walter Frye's rondeau for three voices *Tut a par moy* which is also included on this CD. This dolorous song must have been very famous in its day and Josquin ingeniously weaves the very striking motto theme (always easy to recognize) into his vocal texture with great imaginative resource – right through to the *Agnus Dei*. In his notes Edward Wickham wittily describes this fascinating work as a 'masterpiece of minimalism'.

But even more striking in this outstanding collection is the cycle of five motets largely based on the readings in Petrucci, *Motetti de Passione … B* of 1503. They are arrestingly chordal in style, the opening declamatory *Tu solus, qui facis mirabilia*, with its bare harmonies, arrestingly so, the *Ave verum corpus* similarly simple and affecting, *Domine, non secundum* more elaborate, and with women's voices soaring celestially in *O Domine Jesu Christe*. The extended *Christem ducem/Qui velatus* (a setting of Passiontide hymns by St Bonaventure) which Wickham rightly places last, is the most movingly expressive of all. Superb performances, given an uncanny presence in an ideal acoustic.

Motets: *Inter natos mulierum; Pater noster/Ave Maria; Planxit autem David; Recordare, virgin mater.*

*** Hyp. CDA 67183. Binchois Consort, Kirkman (with: BAULDEWEYN: *Ave caro Christi cara.* CHAMPION (or JOSQUIN): *De Profundis.* FORESTIER (or JOSQUIN): *Veni sancte spiritus.* CRAEN: *Tota pulchra est.* WILLAERT: *Verbum bonum et suave*).

Entitled '*Josquin and his Contemporaries*', the Binchois Consort's excellent disc adds two formidable motets by Nicolaes Craen and Adrian Willaert to major items by Josquin himself, with the authenticity of three of them now questioned in favour of Noel Bauldewyn, Mathurin Forestier and Nicolas Champion. What the disc amply demonstrates is that though Josquin's fame and reputation is securely based (a supreme master of the period – witness the lovely *Recordare* for upper voices), there was much superb music being written by less celebrated composers from the early sixteenth-century. Willaert's six-part *Verbum bonum* is wonderfully inventive, and Forestier's *Veni sancte spiritus*, long thought to be by Josquin, is equally powerful. Under Andrew Kirkman the Binchois Consort sing with fine, beautifully matched ensemble, and are treated to finely balanced recording.

KÁLMÁN, Emmerich (1882–1953)

Countess Maritza: highlights (in English).

**(*) TER CDTER 1051. Hill-Smith, Remedios, Livingstone, Moyle, Rice, Martin, Barber, Bullock, New Sadler's Wells O, Wordsworth.

Set in the Hungarian countryside, *Countess Maritza* gave Kálmán plenty of chances to display his skill in writing memorable numbers with a Hungarian flavour. The plot is slight, but the nostalgic *Luck is a Golden Dream*, sung by Lynn Barber as a gipsy girl, sets the scene, followed by the delightful *How Do You Do* characterfully sung by Count Tassilo, the opera's hero, with children's chorus . But the score's highlight must be the evocative *Vienna mine*, one of the composer's most catchy melodies, although Remedios has not quite the easy smoothness of a Tauber to make it as captivating as it might be. Marilyn Hill-Smith as the Countess, singing with her customary style, is charming in the sentimental duet with the Count, *Be Mine, my Love*, as well as in the aria *Set the Gipsy Music Playing* – another popular hit. The opera ends with a swinging waltz. Barry Wordsworth conducts securely and catches the spirit of Kálmán's world with a fair degree of success. The recording, though perhaps not ideally atmospheric, is reasonably full and bright. The English translation works with varying degrees of success, but operetta fans should not be too disappointed.

Die Csárdásfürtin (The Csárdás Princess).

(BB) ****(*)** Arte Nova 74321 93588-2. Serafin, Bothmer, Grotrian, Eröd, Mörbisch Festival Ch. & O, Bible.

It is easy to see why *Die Csárdásfürtin* (dating from 1913–15) is generally regarded as Kálmán's finest operetta. The opening immediately launches into a delightfully Hungarian-sounding aria for the heroine, Sylvia, with an exhilarating *Csárdás* chorus. In fact, the melodies come thick and fast and the story, involving a cabaret singer and a prince, brings many opportunities for vivacious duets, cabaret arias, as well as some splendid waltzes, be they lively or pensive.

Kálmán has much in common with Lehár, although his style is more robust, with a touch of Offenbach thrown in. He is never more alluring than in such numbers as the waltz-duets *Heller Jubel* and *Tanzen möcht ich*. The grand finales of each act are very spirited, but the trace of melancholy which runs through parts of the score is said to be the result of the death of the composer's brother half way through the work's composition.

Martina Serafin proves a spirited Sylvia, and if at times she is a little shrill, the lively numbers such as *O jag dem Glück nicht nach*, are dispatched with spirit. Edwin Ronald makes an attractive Prince with his light but secure tenor, and the rest of the cast provides ebullient support. The recording is warm and well balanced, but it is a little confined in the upper register, failing to open out as it should. Only a German text is provided (the dialogue is omitted in this recording), but the CD is inexpensive.

KELLY, Bryan (born 1934)

(i) *Crucifixion; Missa brevis; Magnificat from the Emanuel Evening Service; Like as the Hart; O Clap your Hands; Praise his Name in the Dance; The Lovely Lady.*

*** Priory PRCD 755. (i) Manahan Thomas, Mulroy; Clare College, Cambridge, Ch., Brown, Reid (organ).

Bryan Kelly was born in Oxford, trained as a boy chorister ar Worcester Cathedral and later studied with Gordon Jacob, Herbert Howells and Nadia Boulanger, a heady mix of influences, well absorbed. He now lives in France.

It is good to have a *Crucifixion* setting so powerful and immediate in its appeal, completely removed from the Victorian heritage of Stainer, while still featuring simple sung chorales. The work's radiantly pungent choral opening is underpinned by highly individual organ writing, which is later to demand great bravura in describing the disciples' panic. The bold contrasts between soprano and tenor soloists are a strong feature of a work which intersperses biblical texts with poems by George Herbert, the librettist Anne Ridler and W. H. Auden's 'Shield of Achilles', and the touching solo dialogue, *A Ragged Urchin* makes a poignant interlude after Jesus's final cry of despair to God.

Kelly's *Missa brevis* is equally compelling, with another brilliant contribution from the organ in the *Gloria in excelsis*, with the chorus later joyfully moving into waltz tempo without a suggestion of triviality. But the *Agnus Dei* ends the work in serenity. The exuberant *Magnificat* is trumped in rhythmic energy by *Praise His Name in the Dance*, and while *O Clap your Hands* is more tranquil, the use of a 5/8 time signature gives the melodic lines a subtle lift. Neither the lovely medieval carol setting, *The Lovely Lady Sat and Sang* or the passionate closing *Like as the Hart* are in the least predictable, but both show the composer at his imaginative best. The Clare College Choir have a famous association with John Rutter, and under their current conductor, Timothy Brown, they are as naturally at home in this moving, highly communicative music, which they sing with great freshness, vigour and beauty, while the organist John Reid's contribution is in every way admirable. They are excellently recorded and those looking for choral music which tweaks the ear, but which remains melodic in the best sense, will find this a most rewarding collection.

KETÈLBEY, Albert (1875–1959)

(i) *Bells Across the Meadow; (i; v) A Dream of Christmas*. (i) *In a Fairy Realm: Suite; (ii; vi) In a Monastery Garden; (i) In a Persian Market; (iii; vii) In the Mystic Land of Egypt; (iv; vii) The Sacred Hour; (i; viii) Sanctuary of the Heart; (i; ix) Wedgwood Blue; (ix; x) Algerian Scene* (for violin

and piano). **Songs: (i; xi)** *Fairy Butterfly; King Cupid.*

(BB) (***) Naxos mono 8.110848. O cond. (i) Composer; (ii) Geehl; (iii) Prentice (iv) Dawson; with (v) Easton; (vi) Natzke; (vii) Noble; (viii) Walker; (ix) Composer (piano); (x) Sandler (violin); (xi) Smithson.

A fascinating disc. Albert Ketèlbey's picture-postcard music can be curiously haunting, and here one recalls Noël Coward's observation on the potency of cheap music, especially when there are such starry names on the cast list. These historic performances, largely under the direction of the composer, like the Eric Coates recordings above, are imbued with the atmosphere of pre-war England. Florence Smithson, a famously agile soprano notable for her incredibly high notes, flutters through the mists of time in the charming *Fairy Butterfly*, and both this and *King Cupid* are great fun to hear, though her final high notes defeat the 1917 acoustic recording. The rest of the items, from the late 1920s and early 1930s, bar the odd crumbly passage, sound much better, with presence and plenty of warmth and atmosphere. *In a Monastery Garden* is eloqently sung by Oscar Natzke, and the famously full and clear bass-baritone of Peter Dawson rings out in *The Sacred Hour*. One readily enters into *The Mystic Land of Egypt* (with Dennis Noble appearing from a distance and gradually getting nearer) or the exotic imagery of the anglicized *Persian Market*, the composer's most famous number. With the composer at the piano, the salon pieces *Wedgwood Blue* and *Algerian Scene* (with Albert Sandler, the 'King' of the Palm Court) have a distinct faded charm, glowingly sentimental like *A Dream of Christmas* and *In a Fairy Realm*. A nostalgic bargain on Naxos's excellent historical label.

KHACHATURIAN, Aram
(1903–78)

Cello Concerto in E min.; Concerto-Rhapsody for Cello & Orchestra in D min.

(BB) **(*) Regis (ADD) RRC 1094. Tarasova, Russian SO, Dudarova.

Marina Tarasova plays both works with great eloquence and expressive vehemence; she has a big tone and impeccable technique. The orchestral playing is gutsy and sturdy without, perhaps, the finesse that might have toned down some of the garishness of the orchestral colours. The recording is bright and breezy – not worth a three-star grading and nor is the orchestral contribution, though Tarasova certainly is.

(i) *Cello Concerto in E min.;* **(ii)** *Violin Concerto in D.*

*** Chan. 9866. (i) Wallfisch, LPO, Bryden Thomson; (ii) Mordkovich, RSNO, Järvi.

On the face of it it would seem a sensible idea to re-couple Raphael Wallfisch's sympathetic and committed account of the *Cello Concerto* with Lydia Mordkovich's

even more fiery account of the *Violin Concerto*, particularly as they both have outstandingly realistic Chandos recordings. However, the music itself is uneven – the work for violin is an underrated masterpiece of great vitality, but the work for cello cannot match it in melodic inspiration. None the less, admirers of the composer should be well satisfied.

Piano Concerto in D flat.

(B) (***) RCA Double mono 74321 845952 (2). Kapell, Boston SO, Koussevitzky – CHOPIN: *Sonata 2*; DEBUSSY: *Children's Corner;* PROKOFIEV: *Piano Concerto No. 3* (***); RACHMANINOV: *Rhapsody on a Theme of Paganini* (with SHOSTAKOVICH: *3 Preludes;* SCHUBERT: *Imprompu; Ländler; Moment musical; Waltzes* ***).

(BB) (***) Naxos mono 8.110673. Kapell, Boston SO, Koussevitzky – PROKOFIEV: *Piano Concerto No. 3* (***); SHOSTAKOVICH: *3 Preludes; Piano Concerto No. 3* (***).

There is not a great deal to choose between these two transfers of the legendary Kapell recording with Koussevitzky, although it is at least possible to read the notes with the Naxos. The RCA 'artwork' is dreadful and renders detail illegible: moreover, no recording dates are given. The performance is the greatest account of the Khachaturian – ever! Quite electrifying and inspiriting, although Koussevitzky's presence at the helm also has something to do with it. The same must also be said for the Prokofiev. The RCA transfer does not give us the Prokofiev but includes an extraordinary Rachmaninov *Paganini Rhapsody*.

Gayaneh: Suite.

(M) *(*) Westminster (ADD) 471 265-2. Vienna State Op. O, Scherchen – PROKOFIEV: *Lieutenant Kijé: Suite* etc. (*(*))

Reasonably well played, if tame, readings from Scherchen of the standard suite, dating from 1957, in quite full, early stereo sound, but they lack the brilliance and energy of Dorati (Mercury 434 323-2) or the composer's own readings on Decca (460 315-2), recorded in exceptionally brilliant sound and in the same price bracket on Decca Legends.

KJERULF, Halfdan (1815–68)

42 Selected Norwegian Folk Tunes; 25 Selected Norwegian Folk Dances; 34 Pieces; 4 Song Transcriptions.

*** Simax PSC 1228 (3). Steen-Nøkleberg.

Halfdan Kjerulf was the most important Norwegian composer before Grieg, and Einar Steen-Nøkleberg, who so successfuly recorded Grieg's complete piano music for Naxos, offers three CDs devoted to his keyboard output. Kjerulf's father came to Christiania (now Oslo) from Denmark in 1810 and stayed in Norway after the dissolution of the union between the two countries. Although he composed and played the piano as a boy, he studied law, but tuberculosis, from which he subsequently recovered, prevented him from qualifying. When he was in his early thirties he studied with Gade in Copenhagen and with E. F. Richter in Leipzig. His output is confined to piano music, songs and music for male choir. His idiom is steeped in Mendelssohn and Schumann: the *Scherzo* (CD1, track 5) recalls the *Scenes from Childhood*, as does the *Intermezzo* (track 9). Slowly, a more distinctively Norwegian voice surfaces, and some of the dances, such as the *Springdands* (track 10), anticipate some of the keyboard devices with which we are familiar in Grieg. Einar Steen-Nøkleberg is a highly intelligent and persuasive advocate, and the set, which has authoritative notes from Professor Nils Grinde, is beautifully recorded and elegantly presented.

4 Norwegian Folk Dances; 17 Norwegian Folk Tunes; 9 Pieces; 2 Song Transcriptions (from above).

*** Simax PSC 1225. Steen-Nøkleberg.

Not everyone will want to invest in the 105 pieces in the complete works for piano by Kjerulf and will doubtless content themselves with this generous anthology of some of the most interesting. Steen-Nøkleberg shows this music in the best possible light, and although no one would claim that these miniatures have the quality or individuality of Grieg or Svendsen, they are highly rewarding and unfailingly enjoyable.

KLENAU, Paul von (1883–1946)

Symphonies Nos. 1 in F min.; 5 (Triptikon); Paolo and Francesca (symphonic fantasy).

*** dacapo 8.224134. Odense SO, Wagner.

Paul von Klenau, the son of an insurance executive, was related on his mother's side to the composer Andreas Peter Berggreen (1801–80). After studies in Copenhagen, he went to Germany where he studied with Karl Halíř (who had given the première of Sibelius's *Violin Concerto* under Richard Strauss) and later with the composer-conductor Max von Schillings. He spent much of his time in Germany, travelling widely as a conductor, returning to Denmark in 1940. In the 1920s he directed the Wiener Konzerthaus Gesellschaft, and in Copenhagen he introduced works by Scriabin, Debussy and Delius as well as Schoenberg, with whom he briefly studied in the 1920s. He belonged among Alban Berg's circle of friends.

His *First Symphony* (1908) owes something to Bruckner and Strauss, although the orchestration is wonderfully transparent and has a Regerian delicacy. In his book *Music in the Third Reich* Erik Levi describes how Klenau vigorously responded to Nazi attacks on his opera *Michael Kohlhaas*, which included a tonally determined 12-note technique and escaped serious censure. The *Fifth Symphony* of 1939 is short and completely tonal, closer to Reger than to Schoenberg, and is often quite beautiful, although, as with the other pieces on this disc, the thematic material is not always memorable. Perhaps the most imaginative work here is *Paolo*

and Francesca, which is also more exploratory in idiom than the two symphonies. The favourable impression made by these pieces is in no small measure due to the sensitive and persuasive direction of Jan Wagner, who conjures up fine performances by the Odense Orchestra. A most interesting issue.

KNUSSEN, Oliver (born 1952)

(i) *Songs without Voices, Op. 26* (for 8 instruments); **(ii)** *Piano music: Sonya's Lullaby, Op. 16; Variations, Op. 24.* **(iii; i)** *Hums and Songs of Winnie the Pooh, Op. 6;* **(iii)** *4 Late Poems and Epigram of Robert Maria Rilke, Op. 23;* **(iv; i)** *Océan de terre, Op. 10;* **(iv; ii)** *Whitmann Settings, Op. 25.*

(B) *** EMI CDZ5 75296-2. (i) Chamber Music Soc. of Lincoln Center, composer; (ii) Serkin; (iii) Saffer; (iv) Shelton.

Some of Oliver Knussen's shorter works, all sharply characterful, here receive superb performances from Americam musicians, biting and committed, making light of the complexities of argument and texture. Peter Serkin, for whom the solo piano works were written, plays incisively, both warmly responsive and muscular, not just in those works but also as accompanist to Lucy Shelton in the angular Whitman settings. The *Pooh Songs*, with Lisa Saffer another bright, clear soprano, reflects Knussen's fascination with children's literature; but they are certainly not music for children, reflecting simply a mood of playfulness. The most complex work is the earliest, *Océan de terre*, but even that is clarified in such a performance as this. Good, well-focused sound.

KODÁLY, Zoltán (1882–1967)

Dances of Galánta; Dances of Marosszék; Háry János: suite.

(M) (***) Westminster mono 471 267-2. RPO, Rodzinski – IPPOLITOV-IVANOV: *Caucasian Sketches.* (***)

Rodzinski's Kodály triptych was recorded in 1955, and remains very impressive in this Westminster CD release with its exceptionally clear, vivid mono sound and very little tape hiss. The performances tingle with life: the *Dances of Galánta* are full of drama, yet the relaxed passages are beguilingly played. If neither set of *Dances* has the white-heat intensity of Fricsay's classic DG accounts from the same period, they are equally dramatic and bring out other qualities: the finale of the *Dances of Marosszék*, for example, which gets faster and faster, has more witty sparkle, especially in the brilliantly played woodwind parts. Similarly, *Háry János* has plenty of character: *Song* is even more atmospheric and haunting than usual, while the extrovert numbers, such as *The Battle and Defeat of Napoleon*, have much character and energy – the brass and percussion are most telling here – and one is impressed with the sheer detail of the mono sound. The *Intermezzo* –

one of Kodály's best tunes – is exhilaratingly done, and the *Entrance of the Emperor and His Court* has all the pomp and glitter one could hope for. With an attractive fill-up and excellent sleeve notes, this makes a genuine collector's item. However, Ivan Fischer with the Budapest Festival Orchestra (on Philips 462 824-2) remains first choice for this repertoire.

Psalmus hungaricus, Op. 13.

(M) *** Decca (ADD) 468 487-2 (2). Kozma, Brighton Festival Ch., Wandsworth School Boys' Ch., LSO, Kertész – DVORAK: *Requiem; Symphonic Variations.* ***

Kodály's *Psalmus hungaricus* is splendidly vibrant in the hands of Istvan Kertész, but there is no doubt that the training of the Brighton Festival Chorus by their Hungarian chorus master, László Heltay, has contributed much to the fluency of the outstanding performance, idiomatically presented in Hungarian, with Lajos Kozma an ideally chosen soloist. The vintage 1970 Kingsway Hall recording is excellent and here superbly transferred.

KORNGOLD, Erich (1897–1957)

Film scores: *Captain Blood; Elizabeth and Essex; The Prince and the Pauper The Sea Hawk* (all arr. Russ).

*** DG 471 347-2. LSO, Previn.

At a time when CDs of new film scores by composers like James Horner are high in the charts, it is good to welcome a disc of film music in spectacular sound which fully deserves the description classical. As Previn points out, Erich Korngold – called from Vienna by Max Reinhardt – used a style he had already established in his operas and symphonic works, so producing what was quickly recognized as the characteristic musical idiom for Hollywood epics. He thought of the ripely romantic film scores for these four swashbucklers starring Errol Flynn as 'operas without singing'. Considering how quickly he had to work, the complexity of the writing is astonishing, with Korngold closely supervising sumptuous orchestrations by associates such as Hugo Friedhofer and Milan Roder. The sequence culminates in *The Sea Hawk* of 1940, with over 100 minutes of music deftly compressed into a colourful 18-minute suite of highlights, the most substantial of the four here, each with scores reconstructed and reassembled by Patrick Russ. Such a haunting movement as *Sold into Slavery* from the *Captain Blood* suite fully matches anything Korngold ever wrote in originality. André Previn, nurtured in Hollywood and himself the winner of four Oscars for his film music, proves the ideal interpreter, with the LSO both brilliant and passionate.

KROMMER, Franz (KRAMAR, František) (1759–1831)

Octet-Partitas in B flat, Op. 76; in E flat, Op. 79.

(M) *** CRD (ADD) CRD 3410. Nash Ens. – DVORAK: *Serenade for Wind.* ***

The Nash Ensemble give excellent and lively accounts of both these attractive pieces. They are not great music, but they are highly agreeable (the main theme of the first movement of Op. 67 is engagingly ingenuous), and the Nash ensemble readily demonstrate their charms in a direct way, for which the bright recording is admirably suited.

LALO, Edouard (1823–92)

Symphonie espagnole (for violin and orchestra), Op. 21.

*** Claudio CB 5256-2. Jin, LSO, Wordsworth – SARASATE: *Carmen Fantasy* ***; PROKOFIEV: *Solo Violin Sonata* ***. (with KROLL: *Banjo and Fiddle.* orch. BRADBURY; TARREGA: *Recuerdos de la Alhambra*, arr. RICCI **(*).)

There is always room for a fresh view of Lalo's Spanish showpiece, and Min Jin's essentially delicate approach is very appealing. Born in South Korea, at the age of seven she was the youngest student ever to be accepted at London's Purcell Music School, and it was with this Lalo work that she made her debut at the age of twelve. Barry Wordsworth's spacious opening sets the mood for her warm, yet gently lyrical entry, and how delicately and seductively she introduces the secondary theme. The Scherzo is again lightly pointed, and in the *Intermezzo* she responds with an appealingly bouncy rhythmic touch.

The *Andante* then becomes the heart of the performance, with a noble breadth in the orchestral introduction and the soloist entering on an exquisite half-tone, managing the gentle rhythmic snaps very engagingly. Yet her playing is deeply felt, and the orchestra finds comparable intensity. The chirping woodwind opens the finale invitingly, and again she displays airily blithe phrasing in her lilting bowing.

If overall the Spanish flavour of the music is not as obvious as in some performances, the soloist's charm captivates the ear. The Abbey Road recording is very well-balanced and natural.

Among the encores the *Recuerdos* of Tárrega (arranged for solo violin by Min Jin's mentor, Ruggiero Ricci) is a distinct novelty, and bowed with exquisite fragility; but the transcription is not really convincing. Kroll's *Banjo and Fiddle* (with orchestra) is more successful, good-humoured, and played with warmth as well as virtuosity.

LANE, Philip (born 1950)

3 Christmas Pictures; Cotswold Dances; Diversions on a Theme of Paganini; Divertissement for Clarinet, Harp and Strings; London Salute; A Maritime Overture; 3 Nautical Miniatures for Strings; Prestbury Park.

*** Marco Polo 8.225185. Royal Ballet Sinf., G. Sutherland.

Philip Lane is best known for his valuable reconstructions of film scores. His own music is tuneful and entertaining, nostalgic and very much in the British light music tradition. He offers a new slant on the Paganini theme which has enticed so many composers before him, and the result is very enjoyable. His quietly charming set of *Cotswold Dances*, some delicately piquant writing in the *Divertissement for Clarinet, Harp and Strings*, and robust nautical writing interspersed with more melancholy sections in the *Maritime Overture*, all catch and hold the ear. The *Sleighbell Serenade*, the first of the *3 Christmas Pictures*, is his best-known work, but the central *Starlight Lullaby* is very attractive too, rather in the manner of film music. Gavin Sutherland has proved himself in this field before, and he does so again here, with the Royal Ballet Sinfonia showing an appropriately light touch. The recording and presentation are both excellent too.

LANGGAARD, Rued (1893–1953)

Fra Arild (Piano Concerto).

**(*) Danacord DACOCD 535. Marshev, Danish PO, South Jutland, Aeschbacher – SIEGFRIED LANGGAARD: *Piano Concerto No. 1.* **(*)

Rued Langgaard may well enjoy cult status at present, and at its best, such as in *The Music of the Spheres*, his music has real vision. At worst, he is a mere windbag, as in this mightily unrewarding concerto. Its genesis is somewhat complex: it draws on material by his father, Siegfried, who was working on a concerto before his death, and attempts to reproduce the feeling of the piece. Oleg Marshev despatches it with great brilliance and flair. Admirers of the composer should try it, of course, but its neglect (it has never been heard before) strikes us as unsurprising as it is desirable.

Symphonies Nos. 9 (From Queen Dagmar's City); 10 (Yon Hall of Thunder); 11 (Ixion).

** dacapo 8.224182. Danish National RSO, Dausgaard.

All three symphonies come from the war years and the Nazi occupation of Denmark. The *Ninth (From Queen Dagmar's City)* tells of the Bohemian princess who in 1211 married the Danish king, Woldemar, and her subsequent visit the following year to Ribe, where she died in childbirth. Langgaard, incidentally, had been appointed organist of Ribe Cathedral at the time of the invasion in 1940. It sounds rather Schumann-esque, although there are some queasy modulatory lurches that are vaguely Wagnerian. The Tenth, *Yon*

Hall of Thunder, was inspired by the Kullaberg peninsula in Skåne (Sweden), where Langgaard spent many summers. Again, there is a lot of regurgitated Wagner and Strauss, occasionally interrupted by some flashes of individuality. Scored for a large orchestra (there is a figure with three piccolos playing in unison and five clarinets that is quite striking), for the most part the invention is banal. Not as banal, however, as the *Eleventh Symphony* (1945), subtitled *Ixion*, the figure in Greek mythology who was fixed to an eternally rotating flaming wheel in punishment for offending the gods. Much of Langgaard's writing is awkward and unschooled, and the waltz theme, an idea of breathtaking mindlessness, is repeated no fewer than eleven times in the six long minutes this 'symphony' takes. Can you wonder that the Danish musical establishment of the day thought him a joke? Decent performances and acceptable recording.

LANGGAARD, Siegfried

(1852–1914)

Piano Concerto No. 1 in E minor.

**(*) Danacord DACOCD 535. Marshev, Danish PO, South Jutland, Aeschbacher – RUED LANGGAARD: *Fra Arild (Piano Concerto).* **(*)

Musical dynasties, so familiar a feature of the eighteenth century, are relatively rare in our own age but still flourished in nineteenth-century Denmark. This is another issue in the 'Harmonious Families' series that Danacord has compiled. Siegfried Langgaard was a pupil of Eduard Neupert, the pianist who premièred the concertos by Grieg, Gade and Liszt, no less. His *Piano Concerto* (1885), which Bernard Stavenhagen played to Liszt when the latter's eyesight was failing, has some effective writing, but there is much overblown, inflated Lisztian rhetoric, which Oleg Marshev despatches with astonishing aplomb.

LANNER, Joseph (1801–43)

Galops: Amazonen; Jägers Lust; Malapou. Ländler: Neue Wiener. Polonaise: Bankett. Polka: Cerrito. Waltzes: Marien-Walzer; Steyrische Tänze; Die Werber.

(BB) **(*) Naxos 8.555689. Vienna Tanzquartett – J. STRAUSS: *Pariser-Polka; Wiener Blut Walzer* etc. **(*)

Joseph Lanner may not have been quite the equal of the Strauss family, but his waltzes and polkas have considerable charm and grace. These arrangements, for string quartet, would have been heard all over Austria's coffee-houses and restaurants in the nineteenth century, and the Tanzquartett Wien easily evoke that period. This CD sensibly mixes some energetic polkas with the more leisurely waltzes and a single Ländler to make a good representative programme. The recording and performances are both good, if not quite in the superlative league.

LARSSON, Lars-Erik (1908–86)

Concerto for Saxophone and String Orchestra.

✪ (BB) *** Arte Nova 74321 27786-2. Kelly, Ostrobothnian CO, Kangas – IBERT: Concertino; MARTIN: Ballade. *** ✪

The Saxophone Concerto is one of Lars-Erik Larsson's finest works. Written in 1934, it was given its première by Sigurd Raschèr, who recorded it on 78rpm records. It is finely wrought, and its gravely beautiful, canonic slow movement is both striking and affecting. In his notes the soloist John-Edward Kelly says, 'when heard frequently the charm of Larsson's music becomes irresistible,' and he conveys it perfectly. Good support from the Ostrobothnian Chamber Orchestra under Juha Kangas and a good 1991 recording.

LASSUS, Orlandus (c. 1532–94)

Missa super 'Bell'Amfrit' alterna'.

(B) **(*) CfP 575 5602. St John's College, Cambridge, Ch., Guest – ALLEGRI: Miserere. **(*); PALESTRINA: Missa Veni sponsa Christi **(*).

Amphrite was not only the mythological goddess of the sea but also a nickname for Venice, and this Mass is almost certainly connected with the city rather than Poseidon's wife. It is a complex and varied piece of remarkable textural diversity, and it is finely sung here, although perhaps a little more Latin fervour would have been in order. The digital recording is first-class.

LAWES, William (1602–45)

Consort Setts a 5 Nos. 1–5; Consort Setts a 6, Nos. 1–5.

*** Allia Vox AV 9823 (2). Hespèrion XXI, Savall.

Consort Setts a 5 Nos. 1–5; Consort Setts a 6 Nos.1–5; 2 Airs for Lyra Viol; Airs for 3 Lyra Viols; 5 Dances for Lyra Viol.

(B) **(*) Virgin 2 CD VBD5 62001-2 (2). Fretwork, Nicholson (organ).

William Lawes was born in Salisbury in 1602. His older brother Henry was also a musician and both eventually found employment with Charles I, who referred to William affectionately as 'the father of music'. He was killed by a stray bullet at the siege of Chester and his music was forgotten when Purcell appeared. The Consort Setts reveal a distinct musical personality, not as strong as Purcell's, but with an individual lyrical gift, a propensity for moments of dissonance and the skill of a craftsman. Like Dowland, Lawes also had a penchant for melancholy.

The Consort Setts in five and six parts are in three movements, usually consisting of a pair of Fantazies and an Air, or sometimes a plaintive Paven. Scored for viols with an underlying organ continuo, they are through-composed – each of the movements draws on the same thematic material, and Lawes weaves his part writing to achieve the fullest possible sonorities. The Fantazies are searching, usually melancholy or sombre in feeling, while the Airs provide lighter contrast. Jordi Savall and Hespèrion XXI, give well-paced, expressive performances, often intense, and the balance of the viols with the organ avoids making the texture opaque. However, unlike Fretwork, they offer no bonus items which makes the Allia Vox issue less competitive, even though the Hespèrion performances would be a first choice for the complete set.

The Fretwork viols are closely balanced which reduces the dynamic range of the playing, while the organ integrates so well with the vibrato-less string texture that there seems a lack of contrast in colour, if not in feeling. The pieces for lyra bring a livelier 'country dance' feel, but when one turns to the Concordia collection below, the effect is undoubtedly fresher.

Consort Setts a 6 in B flat; in F; in D; Lyra Viol Trios in D; in D min.; Catches; Come my Lads, Hark Jolly Lads; Whither go Ye' The Wise Men were but Seven.

*** Metronome METCD 1045. Concordia, Levy.

Mark Levey and Concordia give stylish and appealing performances of these three well chosen Consort Setts in six parts. The playing is alert and sensitive, and the recording is very successful. It was made in Orford Church, Suffolk and the acoustics and microphone placing seem just right to bring a pleasing freshness of string texture (seventeenth-century viols are used), yet attractively underpinned by the organ. Incidentally they play the F major Fantasy with the four movements in a different order from Jordi Savall's version (Fantazy–Air–Fantazy-Air, instead of the other way about). The pacing here is exceptionally well judged to reveal the full character of all these works. It is good to have the Lyra Viol Trios: the D major, with its central movement entitled Humor and with a closing Saraband, is a striking little work. The catches, which act as interludes, are paired, in each case alternating slow and fast examples. The curious title of the collection 'Knock'd on the Head' refers to the composer's death; but as the 'knock' came from a bullet, it hardly seems an appropriate description, and the sobriquet could put some collectors off acquiring the disc, which is very recommendable.

LECOCQ, Alexandre (1832–1918)

La Fille de Madame Angot (opéra-comique): complete.

(BB) **(*) EMI (ADD) CSZ5 74082-2 (2). Mesplé, Stutzmann, Burles, Sinclair, Benoit, Roux, Paris Nat. Op. Ch. & l'Opéra-Comique O, Doussard.

Most music-lovers outside France know La Fille de Madame Angot through Gordon Jacob's scintillating arrangement of the score for the ballet Mam'zelle Angot, but the opera itself, La Fille de Madame Angot, is Lecocq's masterpiece. Its intriguing plot, with believable characters in a romantic setting, beautiful sets and costumes and, of course, Lecocq's sparkling and elegant score, led to its enormous success, running for 500 consecutive performances on its initial production in 1872. It overflows with memorable tunes, catchy arias, couplets and choruses, capped by the magnificent waltz-finale, *Tournez, tournez*. Doussard's 1973 recording captures much of the charm of the score, and with its excellent, largely French cast, led by the agile Mady Mesplé, the score's *opéra-comique* character projects well. The recording is reasonably clear and vivid, if occasionally a bit raucous. It is a pity that there are no texts or translations provided, but this pair of CDs is inexpensive.

LEHÁR, Franz (1870–1948)

Chinese Ballet Suite; Fata morgana; Korallenlippen; Marsch und Palótas; Ein Märchen aus 1001 Nacht; Peter and Paul in Cockaigne: Ballet Music; Preludium religioso; Resignation; Suite de danse; Zigeunerfest (ballet scene).

*** CPO 999 761-2. German (Berlin) RSO, Jurowski.

A delightful concoction of unfamiliar Lehár, most of it stemming from his stage works. It is all highly tuneful and vivacious in the Viennese manner, with splashes of local colour - such as the delightful *Chinese Ballet Suite* and the very Hungarian sounding *Fata morgana* – with lively orchestrations adding spice. Lehár's inventive ideas always engage the ear, helped by enthusiastic performances and a warm recording.

The Land of Smiles (Le Pays du sourire): sung in French.

(B) ** EMI (ADD) CZS5 74097-2 (2). Dens, Antoine, Sinclair, Paule, Guimay, René Duclos Ch., LOP, Leenart.

This intriguing French recording of Lehár's easily tuneful *The Land of Smiles* dates from 1970, and the sound, recorded in the ample acoustic of the Salle Wagram, is vivid and warm. Lehár sung in French works surprisingly well, and the atmosphere here is convincingly Gallic with its largely French cast. The performance is fresh enough, and even if the principals do not have the glamorous voices of some of their German counterparts, they are never less than agreeable. Bernadette Antoine as the heroine Lisa is light and agile, very much in the French manner, and if Michel Dens occasionally betrays some strain in the high notes, he is generally stylish, with his famous *You are My Heart's Delight* ('*Je t'ai donné mon coeur*') passionately done. The spoken dialogue, which is closely recorded, is characterful and lively, though the snag with this release, as with the others in this EMI operetta series, is that there are absolutely no texts or translations, nor any information about the opera in English at all.

The Merry Widow (La Veuve joyeuse): sung in French.

(B) *(*) EMI (ADD) CZS5 74094-2 (2). Dax, Dens, Lafaye, Mallabrera, Benoit, Grigoriou, Pruvost, René Duclos Ch., Paris Conservatoire O, Leenart.

With its Parisian setting, it might seem appropriate to sing *The Merry Widow (La Veuve joyeuse)* in French and with a largely French cast. But the recording, dating from 1967, inclines to harshness at times. It is vivid enough, the spoken dialogue – brightly delivered – comes over clearly, and the conducting is spirited, as is the performance. But much of the singing is less than ideal, especially that of the heroine, Micheline Dax, who sounds a rather faded widow, not at all ingratiating, which is a major flaw in this operetta. So the set is really of curiosity value only, especially as there are no texts or translations included; indeed, there is no documentation in English whatsoever.

Arias from: *Frasquita; Friederike; Giuditta; Die lustige Witwe; Paganini; Schön ist die Welt; Der Zarewitsch*. Overtures: *Das Land des Lächelns; Zigeunerliebe*. *Suite de dance*.

(**(*)) CPO mono 999 781-2. Pfahl, Wittrisch, Reichssender Saarbrücken O, composer.

This CD opens with a broadcast from German Radio introducing this June 1939 concert, designed to promote tuneful and edifying music to the German public girding up for war. At that time, Gustav Kneip was in charge of organizing such patriotic events, and it was he who was able to secure two of the most famous artists around to take part in the progamme recorded here, preserved on shellac disc and found, quite recently, in the recording archive of the Reich Radio Society. The performances ooze period nostalgia, with Lehár extracting a large helping of sentimentality from his orchestra, as well as plenty of robust energy in the lively passages, with the idiomatic use of portamenti adding to the period flavour. Margaret Pfahl was a popular coloratura soubrette, and although she is obviously not at her best here (there is an obtrusive vocal wobble), she sings with much character. Marcel Wittrisch's contribution has a style and energy often missing in operetta recitals today, but he is capable of singing softly too – the high cadence at the end of the *Zarewitsch* is a delight, and the tenderness of the *Friederike* aria is also most affecting. With the composer directing, the Overtures are enjoyable too, especially *Zigeunerliebe* with its Hungarian flavour, and the *Suite de dance* is an unexpected bonus. The transfers seem to be very satisfactory, being warm and reasonably vivid. The wonder is the discs survived at all!

LEIFS, Jón (1899–1968)

Baldr, Op. 34.

*** BIS CD 1230/1. Guôbjörnsson, Schola Cantorum, Iceland SO, Kropsu.

The Icelandic composer Jón Leifs studied in Germany and remained there with a Jewish wife and two daughters until he was able to take refuge in Sweden in 1944. *Baldr* is a 'choreographic drama in two acts' which draws on the *Prose Edda*, written in 1220 by Storri Sturluson. It relates the struggle between Baldr, the son of Odin and the fairest of the gods, and Loki, the personification of evil. Leifs began the score in 1943 when he was still in Nazi Germany (where Loki ruled) finishing it in 1947, the year in which Mt. Hekla erupted: the final movement is called *Volcanic Eruption and Atonement*. In *Baldr* Leifs goes even further than he did in earlier works: the wind section includes *lurs* (primitive horns), and to the percussion he adds anvils, cannons, rocks, metal chains and so on – not to mention organ and carillons! Disprins must have been in brisk demand in Reykjavik after this performance. Imposing though it is, Leifs's primitivism may strain the patience of some listeners: the brutal, repetitive pounding rhythms and the crude *fortissimos* prompt longing for some variety of pace and rhythm but at the same time there are many imaginative and even beautiful episodes that reward perseverance. Enough of his music is recorded to leave no doubt that Leifs is distinctive, a maverick no doubt but powerful nonetheless, and as unlike anyone else as the Icelandic landscape is unlike anywhere else! The present performance is totally committed and convincing while the recording is pretty amazing and of demonstration quality.

LEIGHTON, Kenneth (1929–88)

Cello Concerto.

*** Chan. 9949. Wallfisch, RSNO, Thomson – FINZI: *Cello Concerto.*

(i) *Cello Concerto;* (ii) *Symphony No. 3 (Laudes musicae).*

*** Chan. 8741. (i) Wallfisch; (ii) Mackie; SNO, Thomson.

Though not as powerful or deeply moving as the superb Finzi *Cello Concerto*, this Leighton work makes an excellent coupling, tautly argued and thoughtful. Raphael Wallfisch plays it as if his life depended on it. The work is also available alternatively coupled, but while the *Symphony* draws the same complete dedication from its performers, many will opt for the pairing with Finzi. The recording is very immediate and has splendid clarity and definition.

(i; iii) *Elegy for Cello and Piano, Op. 5;* (ii; iii) *Metamorphoses for Violin and Piano, Op. 48;* (ii; iii) *Partita for Cello and Piano, Op. 35;* (i–iii) *Piano Trio, Op. 46.*

(M) *** Dutton CDLX 7118. (i) Fuller; (ii) McAslan; (iii) Dussek.

With the exception of the *Elegy*, which was written in 1949 as the slow movement for a cello sonata, which the composer later abandoned, these pieces all come from the period 1959–65, when Leighton was in his early thirties. The *Piano Trio* (1965) is a work of real substance, which grows with repeated hearing. It has a powerfully argued, sinewy first movement and a brilliantly vital scherzo, which has the occasional echo of Petrassi (with whom he studied) and Shostakovich. There is an eloquent and highly individual slow movement to bring the work to an end. The *Partita for Cello and Piano* (1959) is another searching, thoughtful piece with an impassioned opening *Elegy* and an inventive scherzo. All three works are deeply felt and serious, concentrated in utterance, and all deserve to be more widely known. With the exception of the *Elegy*, Op. 5, they are new to the catalogue. There are committed and powerful performances from all three artists, who are completely inside this fine music, and the cellist, Andrew Fuller, provides the excellent and informative notes. This is not music that will be accessible to those prone to casual listening who are not prepared to give it their full concentration, but it will reward those who do. This is a first-rate recording, and the recorded sound is in the top flight.

LEO, Leonardo (1694–1744)

Judica me Deus; 3 Lamentations of Jeremiah; Misereris omnium; Reminiscrere miserationem; Salve Regina.

*** Decca 460 020-2. Piau, Sollied, Summers Les Talens Lyriques, Rousset.

Following in the footsteps of Alessandro Scarlatti, pioneer of the Neapolitan school, Leo, like his master, was writing church music on the cusp between the old and new styles, *stile antico* and *stile moderno*, paying tribute to each in turn. Though he was best known for his operatic music, notably comic operas, the dedication and originality of his religious writing comes over in each of these pieces inspired by Holy Week. The polyphonic mastery is formidable in the two Graduals which open this disc, each consisting of three short motets, while the setting of *Salve Regina* with soprano soloist – the superb Sandrine Piau – is a cantata in the full *stile moderno*, ranging wide in its emotional expression. The three *Lamentations* each involve a solo voice, soprano in the outer *Lamentations* (Anne-Lise Sollied and Piau), mezzo in the central one (Hilary Summers, rich and firm). The choral numbers are sung by solo voices too, fresh and clear, with Rousset sensitive and alert.

LEONIN (c. 1163–90)

Organa for Christmas: Ludea et Iherusalem; Descendit de celis; Easter: Et valde mane; Christus resurgens; Sedit angelus; Pentecost: Dum complerentur; Adventit ignis repleti sunt omnes; Benedictus Domino.

*** Hyp. CDA 67289. Red Byrd & Yorvox.

Red Byrd's first Hyperion disc of the music of Magister Leoninus (CDA 66944) was highly praised by us in our main volume. But this second Leonin collection, containing some of the very first music for Christmas, Easter and Pentecost to be written down, is even more compelling. The melismatic upper part of the plainsong weaves its way over the sustained pedal-like sonority below, never more passionately or floridly than in the Easter plainsong *Et valde mane* which tells of the discovery of Christ's empty tomb ('And very early in the morning, the first day of the week, they came to the sepulchre, the sun being now risen …'). A superb disc gloriously sung in an ideal acoustic.

LEWIS, Michael J. (born 1939)

Film Scores: *Julius Caesar; The Medusa Touch; The Naked Face; 92 in the Shade; North Sea Hijack; The Rose and the Jackal; Sphinx; The Stick Up; Theatre of Blood; The Unseen; Upon this Rock; The Madwoman of Chaillot; The Hound of the Baskervilles.*

*** Pen Dinas PD 951. Berlin RSO, Los Angeles Ens., composer.

Welsh born Michael J. Lewis (currently based in Los Angeles) first came to notice with his 1969 score for *The Madwoman of Chaillot*, the highlight of which is the romantic *Aurelia's Theme*, though the *Palais de Chaillot*, with its battery of percussion instruments, shows the composer's knack for vibrant, atmospheric writing. The brooding evocation of Dartmoor is well conveyed in *The Hound of the Baskervilles*, whilst the exotically perfumed score to *Sphinx* uses authentic eastern instruments alongside a full modern symphony orchestra. Lewis's ability to create an atmosphere of menace showed his mastery in the genre of horror films. *The Unseen*, a now largely forgotten B-movie, owes almost all its success to the background music. The simple yet affecting *Love Theme* and *Romance* are included here.

The *Medusa Touch* gets the full gothic treatment, and the dramatic *Destruction of Cathedral* (London's Westminster Cathedral, no less), with its driving rhythms and organ, is very effective. One of the most enjoyable items, however, is the score to *Theatre of Blood*, in which a Shakespearean actor (outrageously hammed up by Vincent Price) wreaks revenge on all his critics by dispatching them to gory deaths which correspond with the plays in which his performances were lambasted. The mixture of humour and horror is underlined in the score; the opening theme begins on a single mandolin but soon expands into a full-blooded, sweeping statement, whilst the fugal *Duel* (perhaps, uniquely, the only duel on film ever fought on a trampoline) is not meant to be taken too seriously. Lewis possesses a distinctive voice, and this CD, with excellent performances in good sound, will be savoured by film buffs and is worth exploring by anyone interested in film music in general.

LIADOV, Anatol (1855–1914)

Baba Yaga, Op. 56; Ballade, Op. 21b; The Enchanted Lake, Op. 62; From the Apocalypse, Op. 66; Intermezzo, Op. 8; Kikimora, Op. 63; Mazurka, Op 19; Nénie, Op 67; Polonaises Opp. 49 & 55.

(BB) **(*) Naxos 8.555242. Slovak PO, Gunzenhauser.

It is good that Gunzenhauser's comprehensive Liadov collection has been transferred from full price Marco-Polo to bargain price Naxos. They are well played and recorded versions of this colourful and imaginative music, and certainly worth the very modest cost. The new full-price Chandos version under Sinaisky, with slightly different programming, offers more sophisticated playing and outstandingly atmospheric recording (Chan. 9911) and is obviously preferable, though the Naxos has the brighter focus.

LILBURN, Douglas (born 1915)

Symphonies Nos. 1–3.

(BB) *** Naxos 8.555862. New Zealand SO, Judd.

Douglas Lilburn is one of New Zealand's leading composers and his music deserves to be better-known. He could not be better served than by this splendid Naxos disc which gathers together the three symphonies which are at the very kernel of his output. He is a true symphonist: his structures are not inflated, and the orchestral colouring is an integral part of the musical argument. Inspired by the spacious landscapes and mountain ranges of his homeland, the first two are heavily influenced by Sibelius; indeed the slow movement of No. 1 (1949) includes a direct quotation. Vaughan Williams (under whom the composer studied in England) makes his presence felt in the slow movement of No. 2 and perhaps also in the folksy flavour of the scherzos. In the the *Third Symphony* (1961) Lilburn finds an even more individual voice. Lighter textured than the others, often skittish, it is in one continuous movement that falls into five sections, all of which use a three-note rising motif heard at the very opening. Although there are aspects of serialism here, one would hardly guess, so spontaneously appealing is the writing. Indeed all three symphonies are splendid works, immediately drawing in the listener to their special world, and they could not have a more committed advocate. Judd's performances are vigorously alive, gripping, and splendidly played, and the Naxos recording is vividly detailed, with plenty of warmth and atmosphere.

LISZT, Franz (1811–86)

Piano Concertos Nos. 1 in E flat; 2 in A; 3 in E flat, Op. posth. (ed. Rosenblatt); Concerto pathétique (orch. Reuss).

*** Chan. 9918. Lortie, Hague Residentie O, Pehlivanian.

This is the third volume in Louis Lortie's fine series of Liszt's concertante music for piano and orchestra. The so-called *Third Concerto*, first given in 1990, and the *Concerto pathétique* are reconstructions and of interest to Lisztians rather than to the wider musical public. Lortie's accounts of the concertos with the Hague Residentie Orchestra under George Pehlivanian are very impressive and can hold their own with all but the very best (only the likes of Zimerman, Brendel and Richter remain unchallenged, and, in No. 1, Arrau and Argerich). They are better recorded than any of their rivals and bring poetic insights as well as virtuosity. Highly recommendable.

(i) *Piano Concertos Nos. 1–2; (ii) Hungarian Fantasia; Harmonies poétiques et religieuses, No. 7: Funérailles; Hungarian Rhapsody No. 12.*

(M) **(*) Decca stereo/mono 470 257-2. Katchen; (i) LPO, Argenta; (ii) LSO, Gamba.

Piano Concertos Nos. 1–2; Hungarian Fantasia; Totentanz.

(B) ** EMI Encore (ADD) CDE5 74736-2. Cziffra, O de Paris, Cziffra Jr.

(i) *Piano Concertos Nos. 1 in E flat; 2 in A, Piano Sonata in B min.*

(M) *(*) Sony SMK 89880. Ax; (i) Philh. O, Salonen.

It is right that Julius Katchen's exciting 1957 accounts of the Liszt *Piano Concertos* be granted 'legendary' status (unlike some recordings in Decca's 'Legends' series), and in this transfer – which is richer than in its Double Decca incarnation listed in our main Guide – they are exceptionally full and vivid, only occasionally hinting at their age. The vitality of the music-making is arresting, its success partly due to the fiery conducting of Ataulfo Argenta, though the reflective passages relax romantically. The substantial fill-ups are brilliantly done too: Katchen is joined in the *Hungarian Fantasia* by the bright, if short-lived star in Decca's early roster, Piero Gamba, who is at one with the soloist in the youthful vitality of the music-making. The mono sound lacks the spread of the stereo recordings of course, but is reasonably full, and the 1953 *Funérailles* is very immediate. Well worth investigating.

These father and son performances on EMI Encore (the father being the pianist) emanate from the early 1970s. The playing has some flair and character, but the recording in the concertos lets the side down – the sound is opaque and shallow, with the piano inclining to brittleness. Although the *Hungarian Fantasia* and *Totentanz* have greater vividness, they are still not ideal. EMI list 12 tracks in the booklet, but in reality we have only one track per piece.

Emanuel Ax and the Philharmonia Orchestra under Esa-Pekka Salonen combine to give a rumbustious and lyrically appealing account of the *First Concerto*, with plenty of brilliance from the soloist and full-blooded recording to match. They are less successful in creating atmosphere at the opening of No. 2 – which is always more elusive – although the

performance picks up tension as it continues. Ax's interpretation of the *Sonata*, however, is disappointingly melodramatic and artificially brillant, showing little feeling for its unique combination of romanticism and structural cohesion. The recording here does not flatter the piano.

Piano Concerto No. 2 in A.

(M) *** Virgin VM5 61996-2. Andsnes, Bergen PO, Kitajenko – GRIEG: *Piano Concerto; Lyric Pieces, Op. 65.* ***

This reissue reverts to the original Virgin coupling for the Grieg concerto and very fine it is. Leif Andsnes is a real musician who plays with great tenderness and poetic feeling as well as bravura. First class sound too, with a piano in perfect condition (not always the case on records) and an excellent balance.

Hungarian Rhapsodies Nos. 1–6; Hunnenschlacht; Mazeppa; Mephisto Waltz No. 1; Les préludes.

(M) ** Westminster (ADD) 471 237-2 (2). Vienna State Op. O, Scherchen.

Scherchen's recordings date from the late 1950s, but sound surprisingly full and refined for their age. They contain their fair share of the characteristically eccentric tempi for which this conductor is famous, but at times he coaxes surprisingly subtle detail from these scores, while the fast passages generate plenty of excitement. Not a top choice in this repertoire but a characterful and interesting one. A pity the disc isn't at bargain price.

PIANO MUSIC

Années de pèlerinage: Book 1, 1st Year: Swizerland; 2nd & 3rd Years: Italy; Supplement: Venezia e Napoli (complete).

(B) *** DG (ADD) 471 447-2 (3). Berman.

The *Années de pèlerinage* contain some of Liszt's finest inspirations, and Lazar Berman's 1977 recording is fully worthy of this complete survey. Berman's technique is fabulous, more than equal to the demands made by these twenty-six pieces. The playing is enormously authoritative and quite free of empty display and virtuoso flamboyance, even though its brilliance is never in question. Indeed Berman brings searching qualities to this music; much of the time he is thoughtful and inward-looking in pieces like *Angelus* and *Sunt lachrymae rerum*. The imaginative colour and flair he displays in *Les cloches de Genève* and the simple freshness of *Eglogue* are matched by the felicity of the watery evocations, *Au lac de Wallenstadt* and *Les jeux d'eaux á la Villa d'Este*, while the power of the *Dante sonata* is equalled by the coruscating glitter of his articulation of the *Tarantella* from the *Supplément: Venezia e Napoli*. The recording is firmly and faithfully transferred to CD and does full justice to Berman's range of colour and dynamics. Moreover this box is remarkably inexpensive and well documented.

Recital: *Années de pèlerinage: Au bord d'une source. Concert Studies 1–2: Waldesrauschen; Gnomenreigen. Concert Paraphrase: Les Patineurs (Illustration No. 2 from Meyerbeer's Le Prophète); Etudes de Concert: La leggierezza; Un sospiro; Paganini Etudes Nos. 2 in E flat, 3 (La campanella), 5 (La Chasse). Etudes d'exécution transcendante: Feux follets.*

(**) Pearl mono GEM 0148. Kentner – BARTOK: *Piano Concerto No. 3* etc. (*)

The Liszt performances come from 78rpm records made between 1937 and 1949 for the Columbia DX label. Louis Kentner was a Lisztian of great distinction, and these old discs testify to his finesse and sensitivity. Decent transfers, but the Bartók coupling is much less recommendable.

Collection: *12 Etudes d'exécution transcendante; Hungarian Rhapsodies Nos. 1–19; Rhapsodie espagnole; Sonata in B min. Recital: Années de pèlerinage: Les jeux d'eau à la Villa d'Este; Ballade No. 2; Etudes de concert: 1, Ronde des lutins; 2, Danse le bois; Grand études après Paganini: La campanella; La chasse; Grand galop chromatique; Harmonies poètiques et religieuse: Funérailles; 2 Légendes; Liebestraume No. 3; Mephisto Waltz; Polonaise No. 1; Valse-impromptu; Valse oubliée No. 1.*

(B) (***) EMI mono/stereo 7243 5 74512-2 (5). Cziffra.

This five-disc set gathers together the recordings made by the celebrated virtuoso, Georges Cziffra, over two decades between the mid-1950s and the mid-1980s. He began with a chimerically brilliant set of the *Etudes d'exécution transcéndante* and the equally legendary *Hungarian Rhapsodies*. Both were made in faithful if slightly restricted mono sound in the Hungaroton studio in Budapest in 1956. The result is strikingly fresh and the easy technical dexterity is astonishing. He was to re-record both sets in stereo, in 1959 and in 1974–5 respectively; later both appeared on CD, but certainly they do not dwarf the earlier achievement. Much of the rest of the repertoire appears for the first time. Cziffra remained at the height of his powers throughout, and the shorter bravura pieces, mostly recorded in stereo, display the same enormous technical command and delectably clean, light articulation as the earlier sessions, the playing volatile and charismatic, the recordings clear and forward. The two *Legends* (1985) are played with full romantic power, rather than being subtle performances of the kind we expect from say, Kempff, and the dashing account of the *Sonata* (1968) is flamboyantly romantic, although certainly not lacking delicacy of feeling or thoughtfulness in the gentler lyrical pages, with the closing section memorable. The recordings have been effectively remastered, the sound variable, often good, very good in the *Sonata*. But the panache of the playing triumphs over the early technology.

Collection: Disc 1: *6 Etudes d'exécution transcendante d'après Paganini; Années de pèlerinage; Au lac du Wallenstadt; Il penseroso; Les jeux d'eau à la Villa d'Este; Hungarian Rhapsody No. 13 in A min.*
Disc 2: *Piano Sonata in B min.; Bagatelle without Tonality; Concert Study in D flat (Un sospiro); En rêve; Etude d'exécution transcendante No. 10: Appassionata; Nuages gris; Schlaflos Frage und antwort; Valse oubliée No. 1.*

(B) *** EMI double fforte CZS5 74846-2 (2). André Watts.

This EMI double fforte reissue from 1986 combines two separate recitals, so we have listed them accordingly. On the first disc André Watts gives sensitively conceived, well-paced accounts of all these pieces, in which his virtuosity (sparkling vividly in the *Etudes d'exécution transcendante d'après Paganini*), though it can be taken for granted, does not dominate at the expense of sensibility. There are some minuscule miscalculations, which the artist, believing in the importance of truth and of the kind of playing one encounters in the concert hall, does not correct. These performances convey spontaneity and are well recorded.

On the second disc the performance of the *Sonata* has not the sheer dramatic power of such artists as Brendel, Bolet, or Pletnev, but it is still very fine and undoubtedly grips the listener, as does the varied remainder of his programme with *Un sospiro, Nuages gris* and the *Bagatelle sans tonalité* standing out in their different ways. *En rêve* too, is played with great delicacy. Again good recording, and this inexpensive set provides a well-planned survey of the composer's wide range of style, mood and colour.

Piano Sonata in B min.; Années de pèlerinage: Dante Sonata. Bagatelle without Tonality; Czárdás macabre; La lugubre gondola; Mephisto Waltz.

(BB) ** Regis (ADD) RRC 1020. Brendel.

Readers unfamiliar with these Vox recordings from the 1960s, originally issued in England on Turnabout, will be surprised at the impetuously volatile nature of the playing of the young Alfred Brendel in both sonatas. Of course, in the *B minor Sonata* he is obviously aware of the structural underlay, but here as in the other works his playing is more overtly emotional than it later became, indeed with an unexpected overflow of passionate bravura . The recording is a bit hard, but such is the interest of the playing and the imaginative programme, that this recital remains of considerable appeal.

LLOYD, George (1913–98)

(i) *Cello Concerto; The Serf (opera): Orchestral Suite No. 1.*

*** Albany TROY 458. (i) Ross; Albany SO, Miller.

Like the comparable work of Elgar, George Lloyd's poignant *Cello Concerto* was a late composition. It was completed in July 1997, a year before his death at the age of 85. The first page of the manuscript is inscribed 'Have you no pity for those you would destroy', and its ethos clearly reflects the composer's frustration at the rejection of his work by the musical establishment.

After what is undoubtedly a stabbing moment of anguish from the soloist, Lloyd creates a mood of deep nostalgia, of sadness for what might have been. The work is in seven continuing sections, all based on the opening lyrical theme. The variations which follow alternate fast, sometimes lighter-hearted writing, with deeply expressive, introspective slow sections. The penultimate movement, with its intense yearning, then moves into the closing 'epilogue' with a life-assertive surge, leading then to an air almost of resignation, followed by acceptance – a truly affecting coda.

Anthony Ross is clearly very commited to this highly emotional work and, with strong support from the Albany Symphony Orchestra under David Miller, he gives a performance of moving eloquence.

Lloyd's final task before he died was to gather together the music of his early opera, *The Serf*, and rework it into two orchestral suites. It is a colourful score, but its touches of melodrama are not wholly convincing, and the extended Love Duet is without a sufficiently memorable melodic line for its purpose. *Sicily* (which does not obviously relate to the opera's plot) is the most attractive movement, but this suite is not vintage Lloyd, although it is effectively played here. First-class recording throughout.

(i) *Requiem; Psalm 130.*

⊕ *** Albany TROY 450. (i) Wallace; Exon Singers, Owens.

The Requiem was George Lloyd's final work and it represents the composer's infinitely touching farewell to life, which he always celebrated with vigour in spite of his many disappointments. It is written for counter-tenor and small chorus, although the choral writing is as rich in melody and harmony as anything in the *Symphonic Mass*. Indeed at 50 minutes the *Requiem* is hardly less ambitious, and one does not sense a smaller scale. The pencil score was begun in 1997 and the final proofing was completed in January 1998, only two months before Lloyd's death. Because of his realization that he would not have enough time to complete a large orchestral score, Lloyd turned to the organ, and that proved one of the work's principal strengths, for the organ writing is often thrilling and always imaginatively resourceful. The *Confutatis*, for instance, brings a surging bravura organ passage and then the *Dies irae* (using the medieval chant) makes its thrillingly exuberant choral entry. But the work is predominently lyrical, and the serene mood of the opening of the *Kyrie* returns radiantly at the *Lacrimosa*. The jaunty, scalic *Hostias* and the following, comparably rhythmic *Sanctus* demonstrate that the vitality of Lloyd's inspiration was undiminished, and after a touching solo *Agnus Dei*, finely sung by Stephen Wallace, the work closes peacefully and opti-mistically with a seraphic *Lux eterna*, quoting the celestial rocking theme from the *Kyrie*. The work is splendidly sung and played (the organist, Jeffry Makinson, deserves his own ⊕). It is inspirational in feeling, with that special quality that almost always comes with a first recording. The simple *a cappella* setting of *Psalm 130*, written in 1995, makes an apt coupling. The recording itself, made in the Church of St Alban the Martyr, Holborn, is first-class, but black marks for the documentation which provides no translation of the Latin text of the *Requiem* and omits the words of the *Psalm* altogether.

ŁUTOSŁAWSKI, WITOLD (1916–94)

Dance Preludes (for clarinet and orchestra).

(BB) *** Hyp. Helios CDH 55068. King, ECO, Litton – BLAKE: *Clarinet Concerto;* SEIBER: *Concertino.* ***

Łutosławski's five folk-based vignettes are a delight in the hands of Thea King and Andrew Litton, who give sharply characterised performances thrown into bold relief by the bright, clear recording. An excellent bargain reissue.

LYAPUNOV, Sergei (1859–1924)

(i) *Piano Concerto No. 2 in E, Op. 38; Symphony No. 1 in B min., Op. 12; Polonaise in D, Op. 16.*

*** Chan. 9808. (i) Shelley; BBC PO, Sinaisky.

As far as the wider musical public is concerned, Lyapunov is remembered for the fiendishly demanding *Transcendental Studies*, modelled on Liszt, which Louis Kentner recorded so brilliantly after the war. Lyapunov was a pupil of Sergei Tanayev, and this shows in the exemplary craftsmanship that informs these pieces. The *First Symphony* comes from 1897 and belongs very much to the world of Glazunov, Tchaikovsky and Arensky, although Borodin is perhaps the most obvious model. Like Liadov and Rimsky-Korsakov he evokes a kind of fairy-tale world, and if, perhaps, the thematic substance is not particularly distinctive, it is highly attractive and the scoring has greater transparency than Glazunov. In the *Second Piano Concerto* of 1909, Liszt is again the model, though Lyapunov is very much his own man. David Brown's excellent notes speak of its opening as being 'especially ravishing [with] a touch of languor of a sort exploited especially by Lyapunov's idols, Balakirev and Borodin'. It is a short, one-movement work, like the Liszt *A major Concerto*, and highly engaging. Howard Shelley plays with impressive virtuosity, and the BBC Philharmonic respond to Vassily Sinaisky's direction with enthusiam. Rightly so, for this music is quite a find. At a time when Taneyev is gaining advocacy in the concert hall from Isserlis and friends, Lyapunov deserves to come in from the cold. The recording is in the best traditions of the house.

McCABE, John (born 1939)

Maze Dances; (i) Star Preludes.

*** Metier MSV CD 92029. Sheppard Skaerved; with (i) Honma – RAWSTHORNE: *Violin Sonata,* etc. ***

These two substantial works by McCabe make an ideal coupling for the two fine violin pieces by Rawsthorne, a fellow composer he has long championed. *Maze Dances* is a brilliant and varied fantasia for unaccompanied violin, inventive and ingenious in exploiting this limited medium, while *Star Preludes* for violin and piano, just as varied in expression, equally reveals the composer's deep understanding of string technique. Flawless performances, beautifully recorded.

McEWEN, John Blackwood

(1868–1948)

String Quartets Nos. 4; 7 (Threnody); 16 (Quartette provançale); 'Fantasia' for String Quartet, No. 17.

*** Chan. 9926. Chilingirian Qt.

John Blackwood McEwen, principal of the Royal Academy of Music in London from 1924 to 1936, yet remained true to his Scottish roots in marrying Scottish motifs into skilful quartet-writing which equally paid tribute to developments in Europe, whether Debussy and Ravel or more radically Bartók. By the time he died in 1948 he had written no fewer than seventeen quartets, from which this group of four, in superb, warmly expressive performances by the Chilingirian Quartet, provide an illuminating musical profile of a composer long neglected. The *Fourth Quartet* in its chromatic writing yet brings in a Scottish flavour, while No. 7 is a moving response to the tragedy of the First World War. No. 16 is openly evocative in its often Debussian response to the countryside of Provence, and the *Fantasia Quartet,* No. 17, his last, written the year before he died, in a single substantial movement of five linked sections, reaffirms his romantic allegiances with echoes of Dvořák in the meditative central section. Full, warm Chandos sound.

MacMILLAN, James (born 1959)

(i) Piano Sonata; Barncleupedie; Birthday Present; For Ian; (ii) Raising Sparks (cantata).

*** Black Box BBM 1067 (i) York; (ii) Rigby, Nash Ens., Brabbins.

The four piano works find the pianist, John York, just as dedicated as the Nash Ensemble in the coupled cantata. The *Piano Sonata* of 1985 in three movements is much the most demanding, far grittier than the rest, inspired by the extreme winter of that year and later the source of the *Second Symphony. For Ian,* then brings total release into pure tonality and lyricism, a strathspey full of Scottish-snap rhythms. *Birthday Present* seems a very sombre gift, musically striking

nonetheless, and the final *Barncleupedie* (1990) rounds things off light-heartedly with a piece which in slow barcarolle rhythm supports the melody, *Will ye No Come Back Again.*

The 35-minute cantata, *Raising Sparks,* is given a superb premiere recording by Martyn Brabbins and the Nash Ensemble. Like so much of MacMillan's music, *Raising Sparks* has a profoundly religious base, this time not from the Roman Catholic church, which has so influenced his life and work, but from a Jewish inspiration. The opening incantation by the mezzo-soprano soloist, low and sustained in the chest register with occasional ornamentation, immediately makes the Jewish associations clear enough, leading to a sequence of five songs setting poems by Michael Symmons Roberts on the theme of creation and redemption. The striking imagery, with one simile piled on another, inspired MacMillan to musical ideas, comparably varied, often onamatopoeic in direct illustration, which are striking and dramatic within a taut musical structure. The vocal line, though taxing, is more lyrical than in many new works, superbly sung by Jane Rigby, while the instrumental accompaniment is endlessly inventive, with the piano (the masterly Ian Brown) generally the central instrument in the ensemble. In the penultimate song, spare and recitative-like, the question is asked 'Was the diaspora for this – to look in places no one else has looked, to send the sun home piece by piece?'

MACONCHY, Elizabeth (1907–94)

Concertinos Nos. 1 (1945); 2 (1984).

(B) *** Hyp. Helios CDH 55060. King, ECO, Wordsworth – ARNOLD: *Clarinet Concertos Nos. 1–2; Scherzetto;* BRITTEN: *Clarinet Concerto Movement.*

The two Maconchy *Concertinos,* each in three movements and under ten minutes long, have a characteristic terseness, sharp and intense, that runs no risk whatever of seeming short-winded. Not only Thea King but the ECO under Barry Wordsworth bring out the warmth as well as the rhythmic drive, as in the other attractive works on this disc.

MADETOJA, Leevi (1887–1947)

Comedy Overture, Op. 53; Kullervo (symphonic poem), Op. 15; Symphony No. 2, Op. 35.

(BB) *** Finlandia Apex 0927 43074-2. Finnish RSO, Segerstam.

These performances are drawn from an Ultima set listed in our main volume. The *Comedy Overture* is very attractive, and the *Second Symphony* and *Kullervo* also deserve to be explored. But the Ultima set includes all three symphonies and other works too and is well worth the extra cost (8573 81971-2).

Songs, Op. 2; Dark-hued Leaves, Op. 9/1; Serenade, Op. 16/1; Folksongs from Northern Ostrobothnia, Op.

18; *Songs of Youth, Op. 20b; From Afar I Hear Them Singing, Op. 25/1–2, 4–5; I Would Build a Hut, Op. 26/3; Song at the Plough, Op. 44/1; 2 Songs, Op. 49/1–2; 2 Songs, Op. 60/2–3; Op. 71/1–2; Land in Our Song; Song of the Winter Wind.*

*** Ondine ODE 996-3. Suovanen, Djupsjöbacka

Madetoja composed fewer songs than did Sibelius, with whom he briefly studied, and far fewer than his contemporary, Yrjö Kilpinen. There are some sixty-five in all, the majority to Finnish texts, and in this respect he is unlike Sibelius who, in his solo songs, was primarily drawn to the lyric poets writing in Swedish. There are some in Danish (Opp. 44 and 58) including *Sang bag Ploven* ('Song at the Plough') set to the same poet, Ludvig Holstein, that Nielsen favoured. (Those using French texts will presumably follow in the next volume.) Only a few of his songs are currently available in recitals by Torju Valjukka and Yorma Hynninen, but it is evident right from the very first song that Madetoja had a strong lyrical talent with a good feeling for the atmosphere of the poem. Many have a distinct feeling for nature, for example *Winter Morning* and *The Starry Sky* (Op. 2/3–4). Although none of the songs here are as inspired as the best Sibelius or as concentrated in feeling or poetic insight as the finest Kilpinen, Madetoja is obviously a talent to reckon with. Gabriel Suovanen is a fine and persuasive artist, though he rarely gives us much *pianissimo*, and Gustav Djupsjöbacka gives good support.

MAHLER, Gustav (1860–1911)

Symphonic movements: *Blumine; Totenfeier; Symphony No. 10: Adagio.*

(B) ** Virgin VBD5 61922-2 [CDVB 61922]. Bamberg SO, Rickenbacher – HINDEMITH: *Mathis der Maler; Symphonic Metamorphosis; Neues vom Tage Overture.* **

Blumine is comparatively well known as the movement Mahler intended for his *First Symphony* and then omitted. *Totenfeier* ('Funeral Rites'), written in 1888, was an amalgam of symphonic poem and funeral march which gestated into the first movement of the *Second, Resurrection Symphony*, without being greatly altered, except in detail. The Bamberg Orchestra under Karl Anton Rickenbacher give sympathetic performances of these two movements and an eloquent account of the well known Adagio from the *Tenth*. They are well recorded, but this seems to be a reissue for dedicated Mahlerians rather than the general collector.

(i) *Symphonies Nos. 1–10; 6 Early Songs; Kindertotenlieder;* (ii) *Das Lied von der Erde;* (i) *Lieder eines fahrenden Gesellen; Das Klagende Lied.*

(BB) **(*) DG 471 451-2 (15). Studer, Meier, Goldberg, Allen, Fassbaender, Plowright, Schwartz, Keikl, Gruberova, Terfel, Vermillion, Lewis; (i) Philh. O; (ii) Dresden Staatskapelle; all cond. Sinopoli.

Giuseppe Sinopoli began his Mahler symphony cycle with the Philharmonia in January 1981, when he recorded the *Fifth*, and rounded it off six years later with No. 4. If the orchestra initially found it hard to respond to the subtleties of expression demanded by the conductor – more under the tight rehearsal schedules for London concerts than in recording sessions – there is no sign of it here. These are individual, sometimes wilful readings of Mahler, but ones which with full-blooded recording bring out the warmth as well as the power. One is never in doubt of the greatness of the music, and the dedication with which the conductor approaches each work. Just occasionally Sinopoli chooses a tempo that is not just wilful but perverse – as in the snail-pace for the second Nachtmusik of No. 7, and he generally favours speeds on the broad side, but magnetism is a consistent quality, and so it is in the other Mahler works which make up this 15-disc set. *Das Klagende Lied* – with a starry quartet of soloists – is taken from a live concert which the Philharmonia gave in Tokyo in November 1990, while the song-cycles were recorded as adjuncts to the symphonies. *Das Lied von der Erde* is the odd one out, recorded in Dresden with the Staatskapelle five years after the rest had been completed, but just as persuasive in its Mahlerian manners, with Iris Vermillion and Keith Lewis strong and reliable soloists, if not as characterful as some.

The brilliantly extrovert Solti (Decca 430 804-2) or the more refined Haitink (Philips 442 050-2) are a safer recommendation for the nine symphonies.

Symphony No. 1 in D (Titan).

(B) *** Sony SBK 89783. VPO, Maazel.

(BB) **(*) EMI CDE5 74963-2. Phd. O, Muti.

With superb playing and refined recording, Maazel's account of the *First* has an authentic Viennese glow. Though there are other versions which point detail more sharply, this performance has a ripeness and an easy lyricism that places it among the most sympathetic bargain versions. The sound too is full and atmospheric as well as brilliant. A fine bargain alternative to Solti (Decca 459 622-2 – see our main Guide).

Muti's 1984 version was the first recording made in the Philadelphia Orchestra's (then new) Memorial Hall venue, which did convey the richness of timbre typical of this orchestra. Muti, like other conductors prone to fierceness, manages to relax most persuasively for the gentler *Wunderhorn* inventions, contrasted sharply against extrovert outbursts, with rhythms crisply pointed and solo playing exceptionally fine. This is not the greatest performance of Mahler's *First Symphony* available, but at its new budget price it is certainly worth considering.

Symphonies (i) Nos. 1 in D (Titan); (ii) 10 (Adagio).

(M) (*) Westminster mono 471 246-2. (i) RPO; (ii) Vienna State Op. O, Scherchen.

The first movement of Scherchen's account of Mahler's *First* is ponderous without any special magnetism, and when he speeds up dramatically at the end of the movement, the effect sounds contrived, almost comic. The rustic second movement is also very briskly paced, though the middle section relaxes. The final two movements are the most successful, but frankly this is not a performance to return to. The 1955 recording is vivid enough, but the strings are rather edgy and the playing sometimes scrappy. The account of the *Tenth* is slow without the tension to make one accept the thinly disagreeable 1952 string tone. With so many superb stereo performances of these works available, this CD is for Scherchen enthusiasts only.

Symphony No. 2 in C min. (Resurrection).

(B) ** Sony SB2K 89784 (2). Marton, Norman, V. State Op. Konzertvereinigung, VPO, Maazel.

Symphony No.2 in C min. (Resurrection); Totenfeier.

*** Decca 470 283-2 (2). Diener, Lang, Prague Phil. Ch., Concg. O, Chailly.

Beauty and refinement are the mark of Chailly's reading of the *Resurrection Symphony*. Until the choral finale, with its vision of Judgment Day, the performance has a degree of restraint, but then, with massed forces superbly recorded, it is rounded off as dramatically as one could want. It also has the unique merit of offering *Totenfeier* as a coupling, Mahler's first working of what later became the first movement of the *Symphony*. The differences between the two versions – mainly in the long development section – are fascinating, but would have been made even clearer to the curious listener had that fill-up been placed before the *Symphony* on the same disc as the first movement. Petra Lang is the warm-toned soloist in *Urlicht*, and both soloists and chorus sing superbly in the great finale. A fine alternative to Rattle's excellent version (❂ EMI CDS7 47962-8).

With full recording, clear and atmospheric, and no lack of presence, Maazel's mid-1980s Vienna version brings impressively weighty accounts of the vocal passages in the last part of the symphony, the vision of Judgement Day. But even there Maazel's preference for a very steady pulse, varied hardly at all by rubato and tenuto, married to exceptionally slow speeds, undermines the keen intensity of the performance. Rhythmically the first movement becomes leaden and, paradoxically with this orchestra, the Viennese element in Mahler is minimized.

Symphony No. 3 in D min.

*** DG 471 502-2. Larsson, LSO Ch., CBSO Youth Ch., BPO, Abbado.

(i) Symphony No. 3. Kindertotenlieder.

(B) ** Sony SB2K 89893 (2). Baltsa, VPO, Maazel; (i) with V. Boys' Ch.; V. State Op. Ch.

In a live recording made at the Royal Festival Hall in London in October 1999, Abbado and the Berlin Philharmonic with British choruses give a reading of the *Third Symphony* significantly different from his earlier version from the early 1980s with the Vienna

Philharmonic (DG 410 715-2). Where that studio recording offers a finely polished, thoughtful account of this most massive of the symphonies, the live version, at speeds faster than before, markedly so in the slow finale, is even more expressive and spontaneous in phrasing, with freer, more persuasive rubato. The result is richer and warmer, yet with ensemble still admirably polished. The dance-like elements come over more clearly, with the *Wunderhorn* atmosphere brought out more in the Scherzando third movement, with its evocative off-stage posthorn. Anna Larsson, the contralto soloist may not be as powerful as Jessye Norman before, but the extra tenderness is most moving, while the *Bell Chorus* is even jollier and the slow finale more songful, less monumental if still noble. A fine alternative version, demonstrating the conductor's development towards warmer, more involved expression, very well recorded for radio by BBC engineers.

As in his other Mahler recordings with the Vienna Philharmonic, Maazel draws beautiful, refined playing from the orchestra; however at a time when a spacious approach to this symphony has become the norm, he outdoes others in his insistence of slow speeds until the very measured gait for the finale comes to sound self-conscious, lacking a natural forward pulse. His soloist, Agnes Baltsa, adds to the appeal of this bargain reissue by the heartfelt simplicity of her approach to the *Kindertotenlieder*, where Maazel's accompaniment is again sympathetic and warmly supportive. However for the Symphony Rattle remains first choice (EMI CDS5 56657-2).

Symphony No. 4 in G.

(B) ** CfP (ADD) 574 8822 [574882]. M. Price, LPO, Horenstein.

Horenstein's many admirers will probably be tempted by the CfP reissue of his 1970 recording with the LPO and Margaret Price. Yet his characteristic simplicity of approach here seems too deliberate (the rhythms of the second movement, for instance, are curiously precise) and even the great slow movement sounds didactic, though it is not without atmosphere. The solo singing in the finale is beautiful but cool, in line with the rest of the interpretation. The recording, made in Barking Town Hall (produced by John Boydon) is forwardly balanced, so the CD transfer reveals excellent detail and certainly the sound is vivid, full and rich. Szell remains first choice for the *Fourth Symphony* (Sony SBK 46535).

(i; ii) Symphony No. 4 in G; (iii) Kindertotenlieder; (i; iv) Das Lied von der Erde.

(B) **(*) RCA (stereo/mono) 74321 845992-2. (i) Chicago SO, Reiner; (ii) with Della Casa; (iii) Anderson, San Francisco SO, Monteux; (iv) with Forrester, Lewis.

Reiner's version of the *Fourth Symphony* dates from 1958, though it is exceptionally vivid and bright, its detailed sound naturally glowing from within Chicago's Orchestra Hall, even if in the present transfer it lacks the fullest amplitude. The performance is wayward, but lovingly so, and everything Reiner does sounds spontaneous. There is a mercurial quality in the first movement and plenty of drama, too; the second movement is engagingly pointed but with a balancing warmth, and the Viennese influence is strong. The slow movement has striking intensity, with its rapt closing pages leading on gently to the finale, where Lisa Della Casa, in ravishing voice, matches Reiner's mood.

Reiner's approach to *Das Lied von der Erde* is cooler, but he follows the letter of the score exactly. For instance, at the climatic point of the closing *Abschied* Reiner and Maureen Forrester create considerable tension with their gentle tenderness, and if the whispered murmurs of 'Ewig' at the close have not the heart-searching intensity that others have found, their deliberate understatement may be nearer to the meaning of the poem. Forrester is on top form throughout, and if Richard Lewis is not quite her match, he is imaginative and musicianly. The recording has the same qualities as the symphony. *Kindertotenlieder* dates from 1950, and while the mono recording is exceptionally clear and vivid, its up-front perspective is rather unyielding, with some of the woodwinds glaringly forward – the oboist in *Wenn dein mütterlei*, for instance, sounds as if he is performing a concerto. The performance, with Marian Anderson's rich contralto instantly conveying the emotional intensity of the poems, is one of much character. Monteux is sensitive, too, though once again the bright recording vividly robs the reading of some of its atmospheric beauty. No texts are provided for this release.

(i; ii) *Symphony No. 4 in G*; (iii) *Das Lied von der Erde*; (i; iv) *Rückert Lieder*.

(B) **(*) DG (ADD/DDD) 469 304-2 (2). (i) BPO, Karajan; (ii) Mathis; (iii) Fassbaender, Araiza, BPO, Giulini; (iv) Ludwig.

With playing of incomparable refinement – no feeling of rusticity here – Karajan directs a performance of compelling poise and purity, not least in the slow movement, with its pulse very steady indeed, most remarkably at the very end. Karajan's view of the finale is gentle, wistful, almost ruminative, with the final stanzas very slow and legato, beautifully so when Edith Mathis's poised singing of the solo is finely matched. Not that this quest for refinement means in any way that joy has been lost in this performance, and the 1979 recording is excellent. Karajan is no less sensitive in his 1975 recording of the *Rückert Lieder*, and his accompaniment is perfectly matched with Christa Ludwig's beautiful singing in these fine, positive performances.

Giulini's 1984 performance of *Das Lied von der Erde* is a characteristically restrained and refined reading. With Francisco Araiza a heady-toned tenor rather than a powerful one, the line 'Dunkel ist das Leben' in the first song becomes unusually tender and gentle, with rapture and wistfulness the keynote emotions. In the second song Brigitte Fassbaender gives lightness

and poignancy rather than dark tragedy to the words '*Mein Herz ist müde*'; and even the final *Abschied* is rapt rather than tragic, following the text of the poem. Not that Giulini fails to convey the breadth and intensity of Mahler's magnificent concept, and the playing of the Berlin Philharmonic could hardly be more beautiful. The only snag to this Panorama release is the absence of texts, but it is an inexpensive way to acquire some wonderful Mahler performances.

Symphony No. 5 in C sharp min.

(BB) **(*) RCA (ADD) 74321 68011-2. Phd. O, Levine.

(M) * Westminster mono 471 268-2. Vienna State Op. O, Scherchen.

Apart from a self-consciously slow account of the famous *Adagietto*, Levine directs a deeply perceptive and compelling performance, bringing out the glories of the Philadelphia Orchestra. The outer movements are beautifully paced and the 1977 recording has been very successfully transferred to CD, so this remains a distinctly recommendable budget version.

Scherchen was a great champion of Mahler and, when this immensely vivid 1952 recording was made, Mahler was a rarity and so the LP set served a purpose. But the explosion of Mahler recordings from the 1960s onwards has led us to expect very high standards in this repertoire, and this release does not supply them. It does, admittedly, have character and some excitement alongside less than exact orchestral playing, but this release is for Scherchen admirers only. Others can choose between Chailly (Decca 458 860-2), Abbado (DG 437 789-2) and Barbirolli (● EMI CDM5 66910-2).

Symphony No. 5 in C sharp min.; (i) Das Lied von der Erde.

(B) ** EMI Double fforte (ADD/DDD) CZS5 74849-2 (2). LPO, Tennstedt; with (i) Baltsa, König.

Tennstedt takes a ripe and measured view of Mahler's *Fifth* (recorded in 1978), and though his account of the lovely Adagietto lacks the fullest tenderness (starting with an intrusive balance for the harp), this is an outstanding interpretation, thoughtful on the one hand, impassioned and expressive on the other. The recording is warm and full. The coupling of *Das Lied von der Erde* is less successful. Though Tennstedt's interpretative insight is never in doubt, the tension behind the performance is relatively low, not helped by the recorded sound, which is lacking in bass and with a relatively narrow dynamic range. The moments of hushed intensity, of which there are many, notably in the long final *Abschied*, fail to create the necessary heart-stilling effect. In that the choice of Agnes Baltsa as mezzo soloist is in good measure to blame. Not only is her tone often made impure with pronounced vibrato, words are so heavily inflected that the oriental detachment implied in the poems is completely missing. For all the expressive weight of the mezzo songs, the singing should be poised if the full emotion is to be conveyed. Klaus König is a clear-toned Heldentenor, strained at times at the top but always well focused, though he too misses the Mahlerian magic. No texts are provided.

Symphony No. 6 in A min.

(M) * Orfeo d'Or (ADD) C 554011B. Bav. RSO, Leinsdorf.

Erich Leinsdorf's performance of what is arguably Mahler's greatest symphony was recorded with the Bavarian Radio Orchestra at a concert in the Herkulesaal in 1983. Leinsdorf made the first stereo recording of the symphony with the Boston Orchestra in 1965 and, although that did not get completely to the heart of the work, it is a good deal better than this lustreless Munich account. The orchestra shows little interest in the proceedings, and the sound is not what one expects from this venue. Karajan's version is the one to have (DG 457 716-2).

Symphony No. 7 in E min.

(B) **(*) Sony SB2K 89785 (2). VPO, Maazel.

(M) * Westminster mono 471 263-2. Vienna State Op. O, Scherchen.

Maazel's account comes from his Mahler cycle of the early 1990s. He always works well with the Vienna Philharmonic and this performance, very well played and spacious in conception, is no exception. The recording too is very good. However the effect is rather studio bound and there is not the spontaneous feeling of a live occasion.

Like Scherchen's recording of the *Fifth Symphony*, this 1953 performance of the *Seventh* is outclassed in every way by most modern stereo accounts. The mono sound is vivid and has been very well transferred, but Mahler needs really decent orchestral playing to do the music full justice. For Scherchen fans only. Solti is first choice otherwise (Decca 425 041-2).

Symphony No. 9 in D min.

*** DG 471 624-2. BPO, Abbado.

(B) **(*) Sony SB2K 89786 (2). VPO, Maazel.

Symphony No. 9; Symphony No. 10: Adagio.

(B) *** EMI double fforte (ADD) CZS5 75169-2 (2) LPO, Tennstedt.

Recorded live in the Berlin Philharmonie in September 1999, Abbado's single-disc version of No. 9 brings an incandescent performance to compare in its dedication and intensity with Herbert von Karajan's live account, also with the Berlin Philharmonic (430 924-2), which crowned the reign of the orchestra's music director. Yet where Karajan and others have underlined the elegiac quality of this last completed Mahler symphony, Abbado finds joy in the inspiration of all four movements. That is so not just in the bluff rhythms of the middle two movements, with the folk element brought out, but in the concentrated expansiveness of the outer movements. Even the final *Adagio* conveys warmth and tenderness in its lyrical progress rather than impending tragedy, helped by sumptuous Berlin string-tone, with the *pianissimo* coda poignant as a farewell to pure beauty. Abbado's preference for steady speeds adds to the inexorable

power of the whole, a great occasion caught on the wing. This is now a primary recommendation, alongside Karajan.

Tennstedt's *Ninth* is a performance of warmth and distinction, underlining nobility rather than any neurotic tension, so that the outer movements, spaciously drawn, have architectural grandeur. The second movement is gently done, and the third, crisp and alert, lacks just a little in adrenalin. The playing is excellent and the 1979 Abbey Road recording is full and well focused, with good detail. The *Adagio* from the *Tenth* makes an acceptable fill-up, although here the sound is slightly less sharply detailed. However, Tennstedt's admirers will surely count this good value.

On its original full-priced issue Maazel's superbly controlled Vienna version was coupled with a comparably powerful reading of the opening Adagio of the *Tenth*. Without it the second of the two discs only plays for just over 25 minutes, which all but negates the bargain aspect of this reissue! However, those prepared to accept this short measure will find the *Ninth* very impresssive. Maazel may not have quite the gravity and supreme control that mark the very finest versions - Karajan's for example - but with glorious playing from the Vienna strings and unexaggerated speeds it is hard to fault him on any point. He steers a masterly course between the perils of either being too plain or too mannered. Though some may miss an element of temperament, this is one of the more satisfying of his mid-1980s Mahler series. It is very well recorded, although the transfer of the spectacular sound quality to CD does bring a feeling in the climaxes that the microphones were very near the orchestra.

Symphony No. 10 in F sharp (revised performing edition by Deryck Cooke).

*** EMI **Audio DVD** DVC4 92394-9. BPO, Rattle.

A direct comparison with Rattle's superb CD version of this fine recording (CDC5 56972-2) shows little appreciable difference in sound quality. Collectors can therefore rest content with the CDs, unless they have facilities for surround sound, where the ambient effect is enhanced.

Symphony No. 10 in F sharp (revised performing edition by Joe Wheeler).

(BB) **(*) Naxos 8.554811. Polish National RSO, Olsen

Simultaneously with Deryck Cooke, Joe Wheeler in the 1950s was producing his performing edition of Mahler's unfinished *Tenth Symphony*. He uses simpler, sparer scoring, which – so it is argued – is closer to Mahler's practice in his last works. Whatever the arguments, this recording demonstrates that the result sounds far less like genuine Mahler than the Cooke version, though the rugged strength of the full five-movement structure is convincingly brought out in this well-rehearsed and warmly recorded account.

VOCAL MUSIC

Kindertotenlieder; Lieder eines fahrenden Gesellen.

(M) ✱✱ Decca (ADD) 468 486-2. Flagstad, VPO, Boult –
WAGNER: *Wesendonck Lieder* etc. ✱✱✱

Flagstad sings masterfully in these two most appealing of Mahler's orchestral cycles, but she was unable
to relax into the deeper, more intimate expressiveness
that the works really require. The voice is magnificent,
the approach always firmly musical (helped by Sir
Adrian's splendid accompaniment), but this recording is recommendable for the singer rather than for
the way the music is presented. The coupled *Wesendonck Lieder*, however, offers repertoire far more suited
to her special artistry. The recording (late-1950s vintage) re-emerges with remarkable freshness.

**(i) *Kindertotenlieder*; (ii) *Lieder eines fahrenden
Gesellen*; (iii) *Des Knaben Wunderhorn: Das irdisch
Leben; Wo die schönen Trumpeten blasen; Rückert
Lieder: Ich atmet' einen linden Duft; Ich bin der Welt
abhanden gekommen; Um Mitternacht*.**

(BB) ✱✱✱ EMI Encore (ADD) CDE5 74738-2. Ludwig,
Philh. O; (i) Vandernoot; (ii) Boult; (iii) Klemperer.

This disc was issued just as we were going to press with
our main volume and, regrettably, the contents were
there wrongly listed, with the items conducted by
Klemperer (the three Rückert songs and *Knaben
Wunderhorn* excerpts) omitted. Here Ludwig's singing
is intensely poetic and the Kingsway Hall recording
gloriously atmospheric. In the two cycles, dating from
1958, her voice is in its early prime and equally rich.
Other versions may find a deper response to the
words, but the freshness of the singing here gives
much pleasure. It is a pity texts and translations are
omitted, but this disc is well worth its modest price.

Das Lied von der Erde.

✱✱✱ Audite 95.491. Baker, Kemntt, Bavarian RSO, Kubelik.

(M) (✱) Sony (ADD) SMK 89567. Ludwig, Kollo, Israel
PO, Bernstein.

**(i; ii) *Das Lied von der Erde*; (i) *Rückert Lieder: Ich
bin der Welt abhanden gekommen; Symphony No. 5
in C sharp min.: Adagietto*.**

(BB) (✱✱) Naxos mono 8.110850. VPO, Walter; with (i)
Thorborg; (ii) Kullman.

**(i) *Das Lied von der Erde; Symphony No. 5:
Adagietto*; *Lieder: Ich bin der Welt abhanden
gekommen; Ich atmet' einen linden Duft*.**

(BB) ✱✱(✱) Dutton mono CDBP 9722. (i) Thorborg,
Kullmay; VPO, Walter.

Recorded live for radio in February 1970, Kubelik's
version on the Audite label offers a magnetic reading
which reveals both the conductor and the mezzo soloist, Dame Janet Baker, at their peak. Fine and fresh as
Waldemar Kemntt's account of the tenor songs is,
with positive characterization and no sense of strain,
it is Baker's performance which sets the seal on the
performance. The tonal range which she uses is magical, velvety down to finely shaded *pianissimos*, vividly
responding to the words. With subtlety and warmth
concentrated over the full span, the long *Abschied* cul-

minates in Baker's heartfelt account of the final coda
with its murmurs of 'ewig', ever tear-laden but with
no hint of sentimentality, kept fresh by Kubelik. First-
rate radio sound. However, Baker's earlier version
with James King and the Concertgebouw Orchestra
under Haitink still stands supreme (Philips 432 279-2;
or on a Philips Duo coupled with Mahler's three other
key song cycles, 454 014-2 – see our main volume).

Bruno Walter's 1936 recording of Mahler's *Das Lied
von der Erde* was made live, with fine soloists, even if
they do not quite match Kathleen Ferrier and Julius
Patzak on Walter's later Decca recording. Warmly idiomatic, it atmospherically captures the feeling of a
great occasion in this new transfer.

The Naxos disc of Bruno Walter's pre-war Mahler
recordings from Vienna duplicates the Dutton issue
of the same live recordings, but the transfers give less
body to the orchestral sound. It also lacks some of the
clarity and immediacy of the Dutton issue and has
higher background hiss. In addition the Dutton offers
an extra item, one of the other *Rückert Lieder, Ich
atmet' einen Linden duft*, recorded by Charles Kullman in London with Sargent conducting, using an
English translation.

Bernstein, Ludwig and Kollo have all appeared earlier in other versions of *Das Lied von der Erde*, but the
conjunction of the three in this 1972 Israeli performance did not produce extra illumination – rather the
reverse. The recording, idiosyncratically balanced and
put together from a series of live performances, didn't
rival the best performances then, and it doesn't now.

MALIPIERO, Gianfrancesco

(1882–1973)

***I capricci di Callot* (opera; complete).**

✱✱ CPO 999 830-2 (2). Winter, Müller, Kjellevold,
Valentin, Ulrich, Sabrowski, Kiel PO, Marschik.

Malipiero wrote some twenty-three operas and it is
surprising that, with the exception of the trilogy
L'Orfeide, none has been previously recorded. The
eclectic writing we know from the composer's
orchestral music is found in this score of 1941–2. The
story concerns Giacinta, a seamstress who, when
putting on the dress she is making, is transformed –
in her mind at least – into a princess. In her fantasy-
state, she meets a real prince disguised as a charlatan,
and a poet who has written a play about another
prince and a princess. Meanwhile, her poor actor
lover, Giglio, would like only too much to exchange
his identity for that of a Royal. Described as a 'comedy', the opera is rather deeper than that, and might
be described as bitter-sweet. Much of its narrative
spell comes from the blurring of fantasy and reality,
with the dull dressmaker's room contrasting with the
colourful back-drop of palaces and carnivals in
Rome. The story provided Malipiero with plenty of
opportunity to use his imaginative orchestral palette,
notably in the haunting 'Funeral dance' in Act III, as

well as writing some fine if not memorably tuneful lyrical music for the voices. There are some striking moments, including Giacinta's 'Mad scene', where she imagines herself waiting for an imaginary prince in a glittering palace.

Martina Winter is securely sympathetic in the role of Giacinta, firm throughout her registers, while her lover, Giglio, is ably sung by Markus Müller, a light tenor whose line is only occasionally marred by a wobble. The rest of the cast is generally more than acceptable. This live performance captures the atmosphere of the opera well enough although the recording is a bit dry and closely miked (the strings sound a little pinched in the upper register). With full texts and translations and excellent essays, curious collectors might find this worth exploring.

MARENZIO, Luca (1553–99)

Madrigals (1580): Book I: Così moriro i fortunato amanti; Deh rinforzate il vostro pianto; Dolorosi martir, fieri tormenti; Freno Tirsi il desio; Liquide perle Amor da gl'occhi sparse; Per duo coralli ardenti; Tirsi morir volea. Book II: La dove sono i pargoletti Amori; E s'io mi doglio, Amor; Fuggi speme mia, fuggi; Vaghi e lieti fanciulli. Book IV: Caro Aminta pur vuoi; Donne il celeste lume; Nè fero sdegno mai donna mi mosse; Non puo filli più. Book V: Basciami mille volte; Consumando mi vo di piaggia in piaggio. Book VI: O verdi selv'o dolci fonti o rivi; Udite lagrimosi. Book VII: Cruda Amarilli; Ma grideran pur me le piagge. Book IX: Così nel mio parlar; Et ella ancide, e non val c'huom si chiuda. (with PHILIPS: Tirsi morir vola. TERZI: Intavolatura di liuto, libro primo: Liquide perle Amor, da gl'occhi sparse).

*** Opus 111 OP 30245. Concerto italiano, Alessandrini.

Rinaldo Alessandrini in a whole series of fine recordings has signalled a new generation of choral singers in Italy, at once scholarly yet with voices rooted in the authentic Italian tradition. Here he demonstrates the claims as a madrigalist of Luca Marenzio, born fourteen years before Monteverdi, concentrating in his choice on the madrigals Marenzio wrote early in his life in a fresh, open style that attracted listeners with its sweetness. A good selection from those written later in the composer's brief career complete the picture. Very well-paced, with structures clearly presented, they make a superb sequence in these beautifully recorded, finely detailed performances. Adding to the variety, Alessandrini adds discreet instrumental continuo to many of the items.

MARTIN, Frank (1890–1974)

Ballade for Alto Saxophone and Orchestra.

✿ (BB) *** Arte Nova 74321 27786-2. Kelly, Ostrobothnian CO, Kangas – IBERT: Concertino; LARSSON: Concerto. *** ✿

John-Edward Kelly studied with Sigurd Raschèr who premièred the Ibert Concertino da camera in 1935 and commissioned the coupled Larsson work. Martin's Ballade is an emotionally searching as well as a technically demanding work. In his notes John-Edward Kelly writes: 'Behind a basically serious façade Frank Martin's music unfolds an artistic world of prodigious wealth, of great inner depth and warmth.' Kelly and his Ostrobothnian partners have the measure of this extraordinary piece. An enterprising coupling and an inexpensive price make this a strongly desirable issue.

Concerto for Seven Wind Instruments, Timpani, Percussion and String Orchestra (i) Petite Symphonie concertante; (ii) 6 Monologues from Jedermann.

*** Cascavelle VEL 3026. (i) Guibentif, Jaccottet, Riuttimann; (ii) Cachemaille; SRO, Jordan.

The Petite symphonie concertante was the first of Martin's works to reach LP, and Ansermet's pioneering account was a demonstration record in its day – 1951! The Chandos Martin series under Matthias Bamert has not included it except in the transcription for full orchestra, when it is simply known as the Symphonie concertante, coupled with the wonderful and unaccountably neglected Symphony of 1937. Strangely enough, there are relatively few rivals, although Frank Martin's own version, taken from a 1970 broadcast, is of special interest despite the primitive Swiss Radio recording, for it confirms suspicions that most performances are too fast. Armin Jordan has atmosphere and an unhurried sense of pace, and the soloists and orchestra are very well balanced. The wind players of the Orchestre de la Suisse Romande are not in the same league as the Concertgebouw, which has recorded the Concerto for Seven Wind Instruments for Decca. The Netherlands was Martin's adopted homeland in his later years, and the virtuosic wind players of the Dutch orchestra do him proud. The Six Monologues from Hofmannsthal's Everyman, written at the height of the Second World War, are subtle and profound. Their concentration of mood is well conveyed by Gilles Cachemaille, and the orchestral detail is well captured. Eminently recommendable.

(i) 3 Chants de Noël; 3 Minnelieder; (ii) 6 Monologues from 'Jederman' (Everyman); (iii) Poèmes de la mort.

*(*) Cantate C 58013. (i) Thomas-Martin, Kroupa; (ii) Arendts, Kroupa; (iii) Arendts, Schildt & various artists.

The Six Everyman Monologues are among Frank Martin's finest works, and indeed among the greatest song cycles of the twentieth century. They are heard here in their monochrome form (voice and piano) rather than in the composer's wonderful orchestration, and derive from a 1998 Sender Freies Berlin broadcast. The performance, too, is a bit monochrome and not to be preferred to José van Dam (Virgin VM5 61850-2) or David Wilson-Johnson (Chandos 9411), who are much more imaginative (alongside Fischer-Dieskau, whose

DG disc is deleted). The post-war *Trois chants de Noël* for soprano, flute and piano have charm, though the *Drei Minnelider*, written in the wake of the *Mystère de la Nativité*, have more depth. The *Poèmes de la mort* are composed for three male voices and the unusual combination of three electric guitars. The sonority is highly distinctive in Martin's hands and the songs are of both originality and quality. Decent broadcast performances but, at 48 minutes, very short measure.

Golgotha (oratorio; complete).

*** Cascavelle VEL 3004. Locher, Graf, Dami, Fink, Brodard, Baghdassarian, Antoniotti, Ens. Voc. de Lausanne & Sinfonietta, Corboz.

At the end of the war Martin saw Rembrandt's *The Three Crosses* and it was this painting that inspired *Golgotha*, the oratorio that occupied him for the next three years (1945–8). Although it is one of his major works, of greater emotional power than *Le vin herbé*, it has suffered complete neglect in this country. It is the first Passion by a major composer since Bach, but unlike the Bach Passions, the narrative moves between the various soloists and the body of the choir. If Bach was a lifelong source of inspiration, so were Monteverdi and, in matters of declamation, Mussorgsky and Debussy. As always in Martin's most characteristic work, there is a keen affinity with the world of *Pelléas*, which surfaces most readily in the last section, *La Résurrection. Golgotha* is both inspired and inspiring, its invention seamless, and its nobility, dignity and eloquence everywhere in evidence. The performance is magnificent, admirably paced by Michel Corboz, and with some fine solo singing. Elisabeth Graf in the *Méditation* that opens the second half sings with much feeling though it is almost invidious to single out any of the fine soloists. The recording made in Lausanne Cathedral in 1994 has greater presence and depth than its Erato predecessor, and there is plenty of space around the aural image. There are two Cascavelle booklets, one reproducing the text and the other the notes that Harry Halbreich wrote for the original Erato LPs, made under the artistic supervision of Martin himself, and included in the CD transfer: indeed it even reproduces the note on the *Mass for Double Choir* which Erato used as a fill-up and which is not, of course, included here. A powerful work and a masterpiece which should be as widely known and celebrated as any of the great choral works of our times.

MARTINŮ, Bohuslav (1890–1959)

Toccata e due canzoni.

(BB) *** Arte Nova 74321 86236-2. Basle CO, Hogwood – HONEGGER: *Symphony No. 4;* STRAVINSKY: *Concerto in D.* ***

Hogwood has previously recorded the Martinů *Toccata* with the St Paul Orchestra, coupling it, as have other artists with the *Sinfonietta La Jolla*, and adding for good measure both *La revue de cuisine* and *Tre ricercari*. There is no doubt that Hogwood is com-

pletely inside the idiom, though the recorded balance is not ideally focused. The acoustic is a shade reverberant here and the excellent pianist, Florian Hölscher, a bit too forward, but otherwise this is a highly desirable issue.

MASCAGNI, Pietro (1863–1945)

Le maschere (complete).

(M) * Warner Fonit 0927 43298-2 (2) Felle, Gallego, La Scola, Sabbatini, Dara, Chausson, Teatro Comunale di Bologna Ch. & O, Gelmetti.

Over ten years before Strauss brought *commedia dell'arte* characters on to the operatic stage in *Ariadne auf Naxos*, Mascagni attempted a more direct approach in a full *commedia dell'arte* presentation, complete with Prologue as introduction. *Le maschere* appeared in January 1900, the same month as Puccini's *Tosca*. Such was Mascagni's fame after *Cavalleria rusticana*, that no fewer than six world premières were organized on the same night in the principal Italian opera-houses. Except in Rome, where Mascagni was himself conducting to a polite reception, the performances were all fiascos, with audiences rowdily unsympathetic, even in Milan with Toscanini conducting and Caruso singing.

This live recording, made in 1988, helps to explain why. The score is skilfully written, with light textures and tripping rhythms, as one would anticipate with such a subject, but without the luscious tunes and big emotional moments that audiences had come to expect of Mascagni. One can understand audiences growing impatient, even if the total and immediate condemnation suggests some plotting.

Under Gelmetti the Bologna performance is competent enough, with a reasonable provincial cast, but what seriously minimises enjoyment is the balance of the voices. Most of the time they are so distanced, the characters seem to be off-stage. Recommended only to Mascagni devotees.

MASSENET, Jules (1842–1912)

Cendrillon: Suite; Esclarmonde: Suite; Suite No. 1, Op. 13.

(BB) *(*) Naxos 8.555986. Hong Kong PO, Jean.

This CD, originally released in the early 1990s on full-price Marco Polo, is worthwhile for including the only recordings of the *Esclarmonde* and *Cendrillon Suites*, both attractive and colourful works in the best Massenet style. However, the performances and recording are pretty ordinary and the music fails to sparkle as it should. The *Suite No. 1* is better served on a newer Naxos recording, along with Massenet's other more famous suites for orchestra, better played and recorded (Naxos 8.553124).

Manon (ballet; complete, arr. Lucas).

(B) *** Double Decca 470 525-2 (2). ROHCGO, Bonynge.

This confection of Massenet lollipops – with the famous *Elégie* (surely one of the composer's most haunting tunes) returning as an idée fixe – is the work of Leighton Lucas. With characteristically lively and colourful playing from the Covent Garden Orchestra under Richard Bonynge, this makes a delightful reissue, the more attractive when the Decca engineers deliver sound of spectacular quality. It is wonderfully played and simply crammed full of memorable tunes.

Manon (complete).

*** EMI CDS5 57005-2 (2). Gheorghiu, Alagna, Patriarco, Van Dam, La Monnaie Op. Ch. & O, Pappano.

The starry husband-and-wife team of Angela Gheorghiu and Roberto Alagna are ideally cast in Massenet's *Manon*, a favourite opera that in comparison with *Werther* has been neglected on disc. In Act I Gheorghiu instantly establishes the heroine as a vivacious, wilful character with a great sense of fun, and her singing is both imaginative and technically flawless. The aria, *Adieu, notre petite table*, is tenderly affecting, shaded down to a breath-taking *pianissimo* at the end. A fine actress, she develops the character too, while Alagna, always at his happiest in French-language opera, portrays Des Grieux as full of eager innocence as well as passion, impulsive in his responses before disillusion teaches him new lessons. The other La Monnaie soloists make a splendid team under Antonio Pappano, with José van Dam impressively cast as Des Grieux's father. Pappano himself is as understanding an interpreter of Massenet as he is of Puccini, drawing warmly committed playing and singing from the whole company. Well-balanced recording to match.

Thaïs (complete).

*** Decca 466 766-2 (2). Fleming, Hampson, Sabbatini, Bordeaux Op. Ch. & O, Abel.

The character of Thaïs in Massenet's opera, developing as she does from one moral extreme to another, is one of his most complex, and finds an ideal interpreter in Renée Fleming, a fine actress. The technical demands of the role too are comparably great, and again Fleming is ideal from first to last, at once powerful and delicate, with trills and other decorations meticulously placed in phrases of sweeping warmth. After making the heroine's unlikely conversion to virtue totally convincing, she crowns her performance with a deeply affecting account of her death scene, ending with a ravishing *pianissimo* top A. No soprano in a complete set has come near to matching her achievement, and though Thomas Hampson as Athanael, a character working just as improbably in the opposite direction, cannot quite equal her in such total conviction he is vocally ideal. The others are well cast too, notably Giuseppe Sabbatini as Nicias, and though the Bordeaux Opera Orchestra is not quite as refined as some, Yves Abel draws warmly sympathetic playing from them throughout, with the young French virtuoso, Renaud Capuchon, luxuriously cast in the big violin solo of the *Méditation*. Excellent

sound. A clear first choice, even finer than the EMI set with Gheorghiu and Alagna under Pappano.

MENDELSSOHN, Felix

(1809–47)

Violin Concertos in D min. (for Violin & Strings); in E min., Op. 64.

(BB) *(*) EMI Encore CDE5 74739-2. Zimmermann, Berlin RSO, Albrecht.

Though it makes an apt and attractive coupling to have Mendelssohn's great *E minor Violin Concerto* coupled with his youthful essay in the genre, Zimmermann's disc has to be approached with caution. It is in the major work that he falls short. Not helped by a close balance which exaggerates the soloist's tonal idiosyncrasies, the violin sound has a distinct edge, with the melodic line often gulpingly uneven. The second subject then gives respite, but the slow movement is ungainly, and only in the finale does the playing sound happy and relaxed – though even there Zimmermann does not compare with the finest versions. Though in the youthful concerto the slow movement is delightfully persuasive, the outer movements fail to sparkle as they should. Apart from the distractingly close balance of the soloist, the sound is full and firm.

Violin Concerto in E min., Op. 64.

(M) *** CRD (ADD) CRD 3369, R. Thomas, Bournemouth SO – BEETHOVEN: *Romances Nos. 1–2*; SCHUBERT: *Konzertstück*. ***

**(*) Sony SK 89505. Bell, Camerata Salzburg, Norrington – BEETHOVEN: *Violin Concerto*. **(*)

(B) *(*) CfP 574 8782. Huggett, OAE, Mackerras – BEETHOVEN: *Violin Concerto*. *(*)

(i) Violin Concerto in E min., Op. 64; (ii) Song without Words: May Breezes, Op. 62/1.

(BB) (***) Naxos mono 8.110909. Kreisler; (i) Berlin State Op. O, Blech; (ii) Sàndor (piano) – BEETHOVEN: *Violin Concerto* (***). (with BACH: *Unaccompanied Violin Sonata No. 1, BWV 1001: Adagio* (***)).

Ronald Thomas's account is in many ways the opposite of a dashing virtuoso approach, yet his apt, unforced choice of speeds, his glowing purity of intonation and the fine co-ordination with the orchestra he leads (an amazing achievement in this often complex, fast-flowing music) put this among the most satisfying versions available. It is intensely refreshing from first to last, and is helped by excellent recording and fine couplings.

Kreisler's Mendelssohn is hardly less cherishable than the Beethoven coupling: richly lyrical, full of charm and with an unforgettably songful account of the Andante, with an exquisite coda and a beautifully-judged transition to the sparkling, delectably articulated finale. Leo Blech accompanies persuasively and the orchestral ensemble follows the soloist impressively. The orchestral sound is backward, but

Kreisler's violin is vividly present in Mark Obert-Thorn's first-class transfer. The *Song without Words*, played very simply, comes before the *Concerto*, following the Bach *Adagio*.

As in the Beethoven concerto with which it is coupled, Bell in the Mendelssohn uses his own cadenza in the first movement, controversial when one is provided in the published score. Bell claims authority for his departure by suggesting that the published cadenza was mainly by Mendelssohn's friend, Ferdinand David, not the composer himself. As in the Beethoven, he seems to revel in exploiting the material. Perhaps more controversial is the coolness of the slow movement, very simple, pure and direct, totally avoiding sentimentality, though missing some of the warmth Bell brought to this movement in his earlier Decca version of this work, a reading a shade more expansive in all three movements. The finale this time is very fast indeed, light and sparkling, but with plenty of detail, again in a performance relatively small in scale in reflection of the chamber accompaniment. A strong, distinctive reading, but hardly a first choice among many others.

Monica Huggett's 'authentic' version is a disappointment. Without a memorably lyrical slow movement, any recording of this concerto is a non-starter.

(i) Violin Concerto in E min., Op. 64; (ii) Piano Quartet No. 2 in F min., Op. 2; (iii) String Quartet No. 1 in E flat, Op. 12.

(M) **(*) ASV PLT 8513. (i) Xue-Wei, LPO, Bolton; (ii) Schubert Ens.; (iii) Vellinger Qt.

Xue-Wei's 1990 version of the *Violin Concerto* is clean and fresh, if a little emotionally reticent. There are more strongly characterized readings than this but, with its pastel-shaded lyricism, this is undoubtedly enjoyable, helped by first-rate recording. The Vellinger Quartet's account of the *String Quartet No. 1* is new to the catalogue: it is a relaxed, unforced reading and well recorded. The *F minor Piano Quartet* was the product of a 14-year-old, yet there is no sign of immaturity: the *Adagio* is a song without words, the *Intermezzo* a delightful interlude before the slightly garrulous finale. The Schubert Ensemble's account is fresh, direct and spontaneous, and William Howard's piano playing is musicianly and expert. Excellent recording, too.

2 Concert Pieces for Clarinet & Basset Horn: in F min., Op. 113; in D min., Op. 114.

*** EMI CDC5 57359-2. S. Meyer, W. Meyer, ASMF, Sillito – BAERMANN: *Clarinet Quintet No. 3;* WEBER: *Clarinet Quintet.* ***

*** Sup. SU 3554-2. Peterkova, Prague Philh. O, Bělohlávek – BRUCH: *Double Concerto;* ROSSINI: *Introduction, Theme and Variations; Variations in C.* ***

These two delightful pieces for clarinet and bassett horn are miniature concertos in all but name, each in three tiny movements. The story has often been told of Mendelssohn being challenged by his friend, the clarinettist, Heinrich Baermann and his son to write a piece for them while they cooked one of his favourite dishes, a cheese strudel. Mendelssohn followed that up almost immediately with the second of the two pieces, just as freely spontaneous in its inspiration. They are perfect vehicles for the brother-and-sister team of Sabine and Wolfgang Meyer, here opting for string orchestra accompaniment rather than the original piano. The perfect coupling for the Weber and Baermann *Quintets,* very well recorded.

In her outstanding disc of rare clarinet music Ludmila Peterkova also brings out the charm of these two miniature concertos as well as the wit, with Jiri B

lohlávek and the Prague Philharmonia sensitive partners. Excellent, full-bodied sound.

(i) Overtures: *Calm Sea and Prosperous Voyage; The Hebrides (Fingal's Cave); Ruy Blas;* (ii) *A Midsummer Night's Dream: Overture and Incidental Music: Scherzo; Intermezzo; Notturno; Wedding March.*

(BB) (*) Naxos 8.554433. Slovak PO; (i) Bramall; (ii) Dohnányi.

Leaden performances, with no magic, flair or sparkle, with a recording to match.

Symphonies Nos. 1 in C min., Op. 11; (i) 2 in B flat, Op. 52 (Hymn of Praise); 3 in A min., (Scottish), Op. 56; 4 in A (Italian), Op. 91; 5 in D min., (Reformation), Op. 107.

(B) *** Decca Trio 470 946-2 (3) (i) Banse, Rubens, Cole, Berlin R. Ch.; Deutsches SO, Berlin, Ashkenazy.

Symphonies Nos. 1–5; Overtures: *Fair Melusina; The Hebrides; Meeresstille un glückliche Fahrt; A Midsummer Night's Dream; Ruy Blas; Trumpet Overture; Overture for Wind Instruments; Octet, Op. 20: Scherzo.*

(B) *** DG 471 467-2 (4). LSO, Abbado.

Abbado's is an outstanding set with which to brush cobwebs off an attractive symphonic corner; in the lesser-known symphonies it is his gift to distract you from any weaknesses of structure or thematic invention with the brightness and directness of his manner. In the *First Symphony,* the toughness of the piece makes one marvel that Mendelssohn ever substituted the third movement with the Scherzo of the *Octet* (as he did in London), but Abbado helpfully includes that extra Scherzo, so that on CD, with a programming device, you can readily make the substitution yourself. This set is now available at bargain price in DG's handsome Collector's Edition, with some extra overtures included which, like the symphonies, are superbly played and recorded. This set takes its place at the top of the list, irrespective of price.

The alternative tastefully presented Trio box collects Ashkenazy's Decca Mendelssohn symphonies, recorded at various times between 1993 and 1997 with the Deutsches Sympohonie-Orchester, Berlin (the reborn Radio Symphony Orchestra). The set has a great deal going for it particularly at this attractive price with characterfully shaped phrasing and vital playing. Ashkenazy is unfailingly musical and fresh in his approach and both the playing of this fine orchestra and the Decca recording are first-rate. Although Karajan and Abbado remain a first choice in this price range (and Peter Maag's account of the *Scottish* still holds a special place in our affections), this Trio set is eminently satisfying, very well recorded, and represents good value for money.

Symphonies Nos. 3 (Scottish); 4 (Italian).

(BB) ** EMI Encore CDE5 74965-2. LPO, Welser-Möst.

Welser-Möst's are light, consciously controlled readings, very well paced, fresh and unsentimental. He brings out the finesse of the playing of the LPO, of which he had recently become music director, helped by slightly distant recording. The strings lead the ensemble in refinement, with the splendid LPO horns cutting through the texture well, though the big horn whoops in the coda of the *Scottish* are disappointingly thin and uninvolving. Elsewhere, too, Welser-Möst's concern for refinement means that in places the performances fail to lift in the way they would in a concert hall. He observes the exposition repeat in the first movement of the *Italian*, but not in the *Scottish*. Even in the bargain range this is not really competitive.

Symphony No. 4 (Italian).

(M) *** Cala CACD 0531. Nat. PO, Stokowski – BRAHMS: *Symphony No. 2*. ***

(B) (***) EMI mono CDZ5 74801-2. Philh. O, Cantelli – SCHUBERT: *Symphony No. 8*; SCHUMANN: *Symphony No. 4*. (***)

Like the coupled Brahms this was one of the last recordings Stokowski made, with a first-class orchestra of London's top musicians. The result is a fizzingly brilliant acount of the *Italian Symphony*, exhilarating, yet with never any sense of the music being rushed. Stokowski observes the all-important first movement exposition repeat, and the elegant *Andante* and the colourful Minuet, with delightful playing from the horns in the Trio, show him at his most beguiling. The new transfer of the 1978 recording is splendidly done.

A strong welcome for EMI's bargain reissue of Cantelli's finely characterized 1955 recording of the *Italian Symphony*. It has only rarely been equalled and even more rarely surpassed.

Symphony No. 4 (Italian); A Midsummer Night's Dream: Overture; Incidental Music: Scherzo; Over Hill and Dale; Allegro vivace; Intermezzo; Nocturne; Dance of the Clowns; Wedding March.

(M) *** Virgin VM5 61975-2. OAE, Mackerras.

(i) Symphony No. 4 (Italian); (ii) A Midsummer's Night Dream: Overture, Op. 21; Incidental Music, Op. 61: Scherzo, You Spotted Snakes, Intermezzo, Nocturne, Wedding March & Finale.

(M) ** DG 445 605-2. (i) BPO; (ii) Blegen, Quivar, Chicago Ch. & SO; Levine

Mackerras directs fresh, resilient, 'authentic'-style performances of both the *Symphony* and the *Midsummer Night's Dream Overture*. The middle two movements of the *Symphony* are marginally faster than usual but they gain in elegance and transparency, beautifully played here, as is the *Midsummer Night's Dream* music. It is particularly good to have an ophicleide instead of a tuba for Bottom's music in the *Overture*, and the boxwood flute in the Scherzo is a delight.

Levine's version of the *Italian* brings characteristically polished playing from the BPO, with fine detail of expression and texture brought out by the rather close-up recording, which lacks something in bloom on the violins. Speeds are unexceptional, and fine though this performance is, it lacks the sparkle and freshness of the finest performances. Levine also offers the *Overture* and six main items from *A Midsummer's Night Dream*, all well done with excellent singing from the soloists and chorus. If the last ounce of charm is missing, the playing is first-class. However, first choice for this coupling lies with Klemperer (EMI CDM5 67038) or Bernstein/Kubelik (DG 439 411-2).

CHAMBER MUSIC

Octet in E flat, Op. 20.

(B) **(*) DG 469 766-2. Brandis and Westphal Quartets – BEETHOVEN: *Septet*. **(*)

A fresh, well-recorded account from the Brandis and Westphal Quartets; the finale is especially vivacious, and if other accounts have shown an extra degree of polish, this performance is worth its modest cost. The early digital recording is good, if a touch astringent at times.

Piano Trio No. 1 in D min., Op. 49.

(BB) (***) Naxos mono 8.110185. Thibaud, Casals, Cortot – SCHUMANN: *Piano Trio No. 1*. (***)

The partnership of Jacques Thibaud, Pablo Casals and Alfred Cortot was perhaps the most celebrated of its kind – and certainly the most famous pre-war trio. The Trio was formed in 1925 and made this set two years later so that the actual sound is wanting the body and colour of later recordings. For those growing up in the 1940s, this was *the* Mendelssohn Trio, so completely did the three masters seem attuned to its spirit. They are technically immaculate, supremely lyrical and their apparent spontaneity of feeling is born of firm musical discipline. Ward Marston's transfer gives this exalted performance, with its miraculously characterized scherzo, a new lease of life.

Piano Trios Nos. 1 in D min., Op. 49; 2 in C min., Op. 66.

(BB) *** Naxos 8.555063. Gould Piano Trio.

Mendelssohn's two *Piano Trios*, warm, lyrical works with songs without words for slow movements and fairy-like scherzos, make an ideal coupling. The young players of the Gould Trio give performances as fine as any on disc. Not just the violinist, Lucy Gould, but the cellist, Martin Storey, and above all the pianist, Benjamin Frith prove to be inspired recording artists, offering passage-work of sparkling evenness and clarity. Written in 1839, when the composer was 30, the *First Trio* with its haunting melodies for the cello in the first movement is the more striking of the two, full of the freshness which marks Mendelssohn's early music. Dating from just two years before his untimely death, the *Second Trio* follows a similar pattern, at once structurally strong and charming. At Naxos price an outstanding bargain.

String Quartets Nos. 1 in E flat, Op. 12; 2 in A min., Op. 13.

*** MDG 307 1055-2. Leipzig Qt.
*** EMI CDC5 57167-2. Alban Berg Qt.

String Quartets Nos. 1–2; Fugue in E flat, Op. 81/4.

(BB) *** ASV CDQS 6236. Vellinger Qt.

In what is described as Volume I the excellent Leipzig Quartet, with their warm, richly blended tone and natural finesse, give superbly polished acccount of these delightful works. Their lightness of touch and elegance in the *Canzonetta* of the *E flat Quartet* and the equally charming *Intermezzo* of the *A minor* is balanced by great (but not exaggerated) depth of feeling in both slow movements; the *Adagio* of Op. 13 is particularly memorable. They are beautifully recorded and even if there is no bonus item this new series looks set to be a firm first recommendation.

The Vellinger also give excellent, spontaneous performances, with clean ensemble and genuine warmth in the slow movements. They play the *Intermezzo* of the *A minor* with engaging delicacy, with the crispest ensemble in the central *Allegro di molto*. The finale too has splendid opening attack. They have not quite the fullness of tone of the Leipzig group but are not far behind, and they not only have a considerable price advantage, but include also the *Fugue* from the *4 Pieces*, Op. 81, and play it very well indeed. Excellent, truthful recording makes this a very viable bargain alternative.

The Alban Berg versions are concert performances, recorded in the Mozartsaal in the Konzerthaus, Vienna, in 1999 and the Grosser Sendesaal of the Funkhaus, Hanover, in 2000. As with all this ensemble's performances, there is immaculate technical address and ensemble, but there is also greater spontaneity than we have had in some of their recent records. There is much delicacy of tone, even if the opening of the finale of the A minor is unduly aggressive. There is minimal audience noise, although applause is included.

Violin Sonatas: in F (1820); in F min., Op. 4 (1823); in F (1938). Allegro in C; Andante in D min.; Fugues: in C min.; in D min.; Movement in G min.

(BB) *** Naxos 8.554725. Nomus Duo.

Two of these *Sonatas* date from Mendelssohn's early years, but are attractively crafted. The mature work dates from the year after the composer's marriage and is notable for its brilliant *vivace* finale in which the Nomos Duo (Nicholas Milton and Nina-Margret Grimsdóttir) really let rip. Some may feel that a little more poise here would have been welcome, but that is the only reservation. They are a fine team and make a good case for the earliest work (more of a *Sonatina*) especially the closing moto perpetuo *Presto* which is neatly paced. The shorter pieces come from a book of exercises, but are rather pleasing miniatures. Excellent recording in a friendly acoustic.

A Midsummer Night's Dream: Overture, Op. 21; Incidental Music, Op. 61 (complete).

(BB) *** EMI Encore (ADD) CDE5 74981-2. Watson, Wallis, Finchley Children's Music Group, LSO, Previn.
(B) *** CfP 575 1422. Wiens, Walker, LPO Ch. & O, Litton
– GRIEG: *Peer Gynt*: excerpts; cond. Pritchard. **

On EMI Previn offers a wonderfully refreshing account of the complete score; the veiled pianissimo of the violins at the beginning of the *Overture* and the delicious woodwind detail in the *Scherzo* certainly bring Mendelssohn's fairies to life. Even the little melodramas which come between the main items sound spontaneous here, and the contribution of the soloists and chorus is first class. The *Nocturne* (taken slowly) is serenely romantic and the *Wedding March* resplendent. The recording is naturally balanced and has much refinement of detail. This is one of the very finest bargains on EMI's new budget Encore label.

Andrew Litton also includes the melodramas and, like Previn, he uses them most effectively as links, making them seem an essential part of the structure. He too has very good soloists; in the *Overture* and *Scherzo* he displays an engagingly light touch, securing very fine wind and string playing from the LPO. The wide dynamic range of the recording brings an element of drama to offset the fairy music. Both the *Nocturne*, with a fine horn solo, and the temperamental *Intermezzo* are good examples of the spontaneity of feeling that permeates this performance throughout and makes this disc another bargain. However Sir John Pritchard's account of the excerpts from *Peer Gynt*, although well played, is rather matter-of-fact.

A Midsummer Night's Dream (ballet; complete. Choreography by George Balanchine).

*** BBC Opus Arte **DVD** OA 0810D. Pacific Northwest Ballet, BBC Concert O, Steven Kershaw. Producer: Francia Russell. (V/D: Nigel Shepherd.)

Balanchine's 1962 ballet was created for the New York City Ballet, and based not only on the inspired score to Shakespeare's play of Mendelssohn's *A Midsummer Night's Dream* but other Mendelssohn scores, including the overtures *Athalia*, *Die schöne Melusine* and *Son and Stranger*, plus two movements of the *Ninth* of his early symphonies for strings.

This performance was recorded in 1999 at the then newly reopened Sadler's Wells Theatre while the Pacific Northwest Ballet were on tour. It is a fine company with an enviable reputation and some altogether excellent principal dancers: Lisa Apple's Helena and Julie Tobiason's Hernia are particularly fine, and the scene between Titania and Bottom is quite touching. The fairy scenes are imaginatively handled and staged.

Mendelssohn's music is well served by the ever underrated BBC Concert Orchestra, who always excel when given a chance to play repertoire of quality – and Mendelssohn's score is always a source of wonder! The acoustic of the new Sadler's Wells does not have much warmth or space, but the engineers get a very good and well-defined sound. The camerawork and the quality of colour are very high. An enchanting ninety minutes.

MENOTTI, Gian-Carlo (born 1911)

(i) *Violin Concerto*; Cantatas: (ii) *The Death of Orpheus*; (iii) *Muero porque no muero*; (iv) *Oh llama de amor viva.*

*** Chan. 9979. (i) Koh; (ii) MacDougall; (iii) Melinek; (iv) Roberts. Spoleto Ch. & O, Hickox

This new version of Gian-Carlo Menotti's lyrical *Violin Concerto* of 1952, one of his most popular instrumental works, comes neatly coupled with première recordings of three cantatas written in his seventies and eighties. Richard Hickox draws from his fine Spoleto team warmly persuasive readings of eclectic works which are powerfully convincing in committed performances like these. The young American violinist, Jennifer Koh, is the excellent soloist in the *Concerto*, originally written for the great violinist and teacher, Efrem Zimbalist, the long-time principal of the Curtis Institute in Philadelphia where both Menotti and Koh studied. The first movement with its sequence of flowing melodies might easily seem to meander, but Koh and Hickox between them give it a clear shape, with each new idea emerging seductively. The slow movement, played with hushed dedication, has a tender poignancy, while the vigorous finale with its jaunty main theme predictably ends with virtuoso fireworks.

The two cantatas, using Spanish texts by the mystics St Teresa of Avila and St John of the Cross, offer sensuous music closer to Puccini's opera, *Suor Angelica*, than to any religious model. The chorus in each dramatically enhances the meditative solos representing each saint. Julia Melinek is the vibrant soloist in the St Teresa cantata, though Stephen Roberts is sadly unsteady in the St John of the Cross setting. *The Death of Orpheus*, to an English text by Menotti himself, is similarly dramatic, based on the legend of Orpheus being killed by Thracian women in a Bacchanalian frenzy (represented in a violent opening chorus) with his severed head finally being borne down river, still singing. Orpheus's song emerges as a broad diatonic melody, with choral writing of Delian sensuousness. Jamie MacDougall is the expressive soloist, with the chorus fresh and incisive in all three cantatas.

The Saint of Bleecker Street (opera; complete).

*** Chan. 9971 (2). Melinek, Richards, Stephen, Bindel, Zeltzer, Farrugia, Howard, Rozynko, Spoleto Festival Ch. & O, Hickox.

Overlook the melodramatic plot, even forget the variable casting of solo singers – not Italianate enough with too many wobblers – for this pioneering recording of Gian-Carlo Menotti's opera, *The Saint of Bleecker Street*, demonstrates that this is one of the composer's most powerful scores, colourful, atmospheric and tuneful, with telling dramatic effects, often involving genuine Italian tunes. Set in New York's Little Italy, it revolves round the dying Annina, a would-be nun with a gift for faith-healing and her boorish agnostic brother, Michele. For Menotti, a Catholic who lost his faith, the story aims to symbolize the clash between faith and doubt. In this performance, recorded live, the red-blooded feelings involved are passionately brought out by Richard Hickox, with talented young performers from the Festival Choir and Orchestra of Menotti's summer music festival at Spoleto. Full, brilliant sound.

MESSAGER, André (1853–1929)

Les Deux Pigeons (ballet: excerpts).

(BB) **(*) EMI Encore (ADD) CDE5 75221-2. ROHCG O, Mackerras – DELIBES: *Coppélia*; *Sylvia* (excerpts); GOUNOD: *Faust: ballet music.* **(*)

This delightful 20-minute suite from the ballet *Les Deux Pigeons* was recorded in stereo as early as 1956 and, despite a certain thinness, is remarkably vivid. The performance is stylishly enjoyable, with Messager's melodic inspiration at his most felicitous. The numbers that employ 'local colour', such as the *Danse Hongroise*, are particularly piquant, as is the charming *Pas des deux pigeons*.

Véronique (opera: complete).

(BB) **(*) EMI (ADD) CZS5 74073-2 (2). Mesplé, Guiot, Benoit, Dens, Dunand, Pruvost, René Duclops Ch., LOP, Hartemann.

Messager's gentle charms are well displayed in his 1898 opera *Véronique*. The story of Hélène de Solanges, who works in disguise in a Parisian florist's in the 1840s under the assumed name Véronique, produces plenty of romantic complications, which are all sorted out by the end. There are several numbers that understandably became Edwardian favourites, including the two duets from Act I: the 'Donkey duet' (*De ci, de l'*) and the 'Swing duet' (*Poussez, poussez, l'escarpolette*). The Act I quartet with the refrain 'Charmant, charmant' is another highlight of the utmost piquancy. The performance here is excellent, Mady Mesplé again showing her supremacy in this repertoire, while the rest of the cast and the conductor understand Messager's idiom perfectly. The 1969 recording has transferred very well to CD, with the voices clear and vivid. But as ever in this bargain operetta series, no texts and translations are provided, which will be a distinct drawback for many collectors.

MESSIAEN, Olivier (1908–92)

Turangalîla Symphony.

*** EMI (ADD) **Audio DVD** DVC4 92398-9. Béroff, Loriod, LSO, Previn.

(B) **(*) Sony SBK 89900. Crossley, Murail, Philh. O, Salonen.

Messiaen's *Turangalîla Symphony* is of epic scale, seeking to embrace almost the totality of human experience. *Turanga* is Time and also implies rhythmic movement; *Lîla* is love and, with a strong inspiration from the Tristan and Isolde legend, Messiaen's love-music dominates his conception of human existence. The actual love-sequences feature the ondes martenot with its 'velvety glissandi'. The piano obbligato is also a strong feature of the score. Previn's vividly direct approach, helped by spectacular recording, has much electricity. He is at his best in the work's more robust moments, for instance the jazzy fifth movement, and he catches the wit at the beginning of the *Chant d'amour No. 2.* The idyllic *Garden of the Sleep of Love* is both serene and poetically sensuous, and the apotheosis of the love theme in the closing pages is jubilant and life-affirming. Previn's recording is also available less expensively on a pair of CDs coupled with outstanding versions of two of Poulenc's finest concertos. The Audio DVD, like the others in the EMI series, is available in multi-channel surround sound or (by turning the disc over) in high resolution stereo, in each case with enhanced dynamic range and definition. Because the sound balance of the 1977 Abbey Road recording is comparatively unexpansive in the bass, the improvement in amplitude is less striking here than with some other Audio DVDs, yet the sound is still remarkably vivid and present.

Esa-Pekka Salonen directs a performance in sharp focus. Relatively this is an account which minimizes atmospheric beauty and sensuousness, instead underlining the elements which look forward to later composers. This is emphasized by the close balance of the piano and ondes martenot, which stand out instead of emerging as part of the rich orchestral texture. So the passagework for piano, beautifully played by Paul Crossley, sounds angular in a very modern way rather than evoking birdsong. Significantly, the syncopated rhythms of the energetic fifth movement are pressed home very literally at a speed faster than usual, with little or no echo of jazz. The Philharmonia play brilliantly and the recording accentuates the sharp focus of the readings, while giving ample atmosphere.

Complete piano music

Disc 1: *Catalogue d'oiseaux, Books 1–3* (RRC 1108).

Disc 2: *Catalogue d'oiseaux, Books 4–6* (RRC 1109).

Disc 3: *Catalogue d'oiseaux, Book 7; Supplement: La fauvette des jardins; Petites esquisses d'oiseaux* (RRC 1110).

Disc 4: *Vingt regardes sur L'enfant-Jésus* (RRC 2055 (2)).

Disc 5: *Cantéyodjaya; 4 Etudes de rhythme; Fantaisie burlesque; Pièce pour le tombeau de Paul Dukas; Préludes; Rondeau;* (i) *Visions de l'amen* (RRC 2056 (2)).

(BB) *** Regis RRC 7001 (7). Hill; (i) with Frith.

Peter Hill made his outstanding collection of Messiaen's piano music between 1986 and 1992 for Unicorn. Those recordings now appear at bargain price on the Regis label, admirably documented. They come complete in a slip case, but are available separately as listed above.

Hill began his survey in 1986 with the vast *Catalogue d'oiseaux* which derive their inspiration from Messiaen's beloved birdsong. Little of the piano writing is conventional, but there is no question as to the composer's imaginative flair, and the music is vivid and colourful to match the plumage of the creatures which Messiaen depicts so strikingly. Peter Hill prepared this music in Paris with the composer himself and thus has his imprimatur. He has great sensitivity to colour and atmosphere and evokes the wildlife pictured in this extraordinary music to splendid effect.

The *Oiseaux* sessions were completed in 1988–9 with *La fauvette des jardins*, another half-hour of music, composed in the summer of 1970, which the producer, Anthony Pople, describes as the perfect paregon to the cycle. The recording (by Bob Auger) was made in Rosslyn Hill Unitarian Chapel with the utmost clarity and definition.

The *Petites esquisses d'oiseaux*, written in 1985, formed a belated postlude to the series. Yvonne Loriod tells how she enticed her husband back to work with a commission for a miniature describing a robin. This led to the *Six esquisses*, with the first, third and fifth describing the robin, surrounded by the blackbird, song thrush, and skylark, the latter particularly vividly represented. Again, Hill plays with total dedication and understanding; the recording was made much later in 1992 at Brandon Hill, Bristol.

However the *Préludes* and shorter pieces were recorded at Rosslyn Hill in 1984 and 1985, where Peter Hill chose to use a Bösendorfer. With his inherent feeling for the colour and atmosphere of Messiaen's sound world he makes an excellent case for all this repertoire, save perhaps for the somewhat repetitive *Fantaisie burlesque* of 1932 which outstays its welcome. His playing is consistently sensitive and has great finesse, with the *Cantéyodjaya* (1948) particularly refined.

For the *Vingt regards sur L'enfant-Jésus*, recorded in 1991 in St Paul's Southgate, Peter Hill chose a Fazioli and his interpretation is surely enhanced by the special tonal qualities of the instrument, for he seeks to reveal the music's inner essence and colouring, its tranquil, unruffled moments of spiritual inspiration and subtlety of detail, rather than emphasise its inherent drama. In his hands it is the contemplative lyrical writing that one remerbers, the moments of calm, rather than the vibrant climaxes. Which is not to say that the playing is not vividly alive, but rather that bravura is never the first consideration even though the pianism shows complete mastery. The composer himself has spoken with great warmth of the artist and he has every reason too. Bob Auger's recordings, too, are a splendid memento of one of Britain's most musically perceptive sound engineers.

Complete organ music

Complete organ music (including unpublished works): *Monodie; Prélude; Offrande au Saint Sacrement.*

*** DG 471 480-2 (6). Latry (organ of Notre-Dame de Paris).

Disc 1: *Apparition de l'église éternelle; Le banquet céleste; La Nativité du Seigneur (9 Méditations)* (RRC 1086).

Disc 2: *L'ascension (4 Méditations); Les corps glorieux (7 Visions de la vie des ressuscités)* (RRC 1087).

Discs 3–4: *Livre d'orgue* (1951); *9 Méditations sur le mystère de la Sainte Trinité; Messe de la Pentecôte* (RRC 2051) (2).

Discs 5–6: *Diptyque (Essai sur la vie terrestre); (i) Livre du Saint Sacrement; Verset pour la fête de la dedicace* (RRC 2052) (2).

⊕ (B) *** Regis RRC 6001 (6). Bate (organ of Cathedral of Saint Pierre, Beauvais or (i) L'Église de la Saint-Trinité, Paris).

'C'est vraiment parfait!' said Messiaen after hearing Jennifer Bate's recording of *La nativité du Seigneur*, one of his most extended, most beautiful and most moving works, with the nine movements each hypnotically compelling in their atmospheric commentaries on the Nativity story. But the composer also gave his imprimatur to every one of these recordings, all but one of which were made between 1979 and 1981 on the Beauvais organ, endorsing the performances with great enthusiasm. He then sent Jennifer Bate the manuscript of his last masterpiece, *Livre du Saint Sacrement*, which she premiered at Westminster Cathedral in 1986 and went on to record at Saint-Trinité in 1987. Of the other pieces, *La banquet céleste* and *Diptyque* are both early works, the former already intense in its religious feeling, the latter dedicated to Messiaen's teachers, Dukas and Dupré.

While much of this music is meditative, imbued with mysticism, *L'apparition* builds directly to a great central climax, then recedes, while *L'ascension* is in four movements specifically inspired by religious texts, joyfully proclaiming, in turn, the majesty of Christ amd the serenity of heaven. The *Messe de la Pentecôte* brings together most tellingly the three principal elements of Messiaen's style – plainsong, birdsong and his own rich brand of harmony – in a particularly satisfying combination. The recordings were superbly engineered by the late Bob Auger and are all in the demonstraion bracket, but the final disc is perhaps the most spectacular of all. Jennifer Bate is

completely at home in Messiaen's sound world and readily identifies with the religious experience which has inspired all of the composer's organ music. In every way this inexpensive reissue of recordings originally made by Unicorn is definitive, marking the tenth anniversary of the composer's death. At the moment RRC 1086 and RRC 2052 are the only CDs available separately.

Olivier Latry's survey is also distinguished and is very well recorded indeed in Notre-Dame. The result has great atmosphere, especially effective in conveying the composer's spiritual mysticism which is at the heart of Latry's essentially thoughtful interpretations. Jennifer Bate is more vividly extrovert and this is clear when comparing the two accounts of *La Nativité du Seigneur*, which also demonstrates the special suitability of the Beauvais organ. Both approaches are valid, of course, and the DG set has the advantage of offering some more unpublished items. But it is offered on six full-priced CDs, whereas Bate's Regis reissue is in the budget range.

MIASKOVSKY, Nikolay

(1881–1950)

Symphonies Nos. 1 in C min., Op. 3; 25 in D flat, Op. 69.

*** Olympia OCD 731. Russian Fed. Ac. SO, Svetlanov.

Evgeny Svetlanov was particularly close to the Miaskovsky symphonies, and before his death in early 2002, he was able to hear the first issues in the complete cycle he recorded in the 1990s in digital sound. And so collectors will, for the most part, no longer have to return to their Melodiya LPs, which so often sounded as if they were pressed on dog biscuits. Miaskovsky was brought up in a military family and had become a lieutenant in the engineers when in 1906 he enrolled in the St Petersburg Conservatoire as a pupil of Liadov and Rimsky-Korsakov. The *First Symphony* comes from 1908, when he was still a student, and is very much in the received tradition. It was first performed in 1914 when Glazunov, then director of the Conservatoire, awarded him a scholarship. In 1921, after the war, during which Miaskovsky served on the front line and suffered shell-shock, he returned to the score, revising the outer movements. This performance displaces Rozhdestvensky's account on Russian Disc (coupled with *Symphony No. 19*). The *Twenty-Fifth Symphony in D flat* comes from the other end of Miaskovsky's career; it was composed in 1946, the same year as the *Cello Concerto*. Its opening *Adagio* has something of the same all-pervasive melancholy of the concerto and includes some of the most touching music that he penned. Svetlanov takes it more slowly than it was in the earlier LP version. There is some less than polished playing but there is an authentic feel to it, and the recording is eminently serviceable.

Symphonies Nos. 2 in C sharp min., Op. 11; 18 in C, Op. 42.

*** Olympia OCD 732. Russian Fed. Ac. SO, Svetlanov.

The *Second Symphony* comes from 1911, the year of the composer's graduation from the Conservatoire. In the three years that separate it from the *First Symphony*, Miaskovksy had written a number of smaller pieces and the tone poem *Silence*. Per Skans, the excellent Swedish annotator of the whole series, speaks of echoes of Rachmaninov's *Isle of the Dead* in the middle movement and quotes Miaskovsky's own verdict on the work as 'sugared water with sighs of Rachmaninov and Tchaikovsky'. This hardly does justice to the melancholy and pessimisim that surfaces in the first movement. The whole piece breathes much the same air as Scriabin, Glière and Rachmaninov and is larger in scale even than the *First Symphony*. Svetlanov's reading is well held together, and generally to be preferred to Gottfried Rabl and the Austrian Radio forces on Orfeo. The much shorter, and often attractive, *Eighteenth Symphony* was composed in 1937, the year of the Terror, and it enjoyed such popularity that arrangements were made of it for brass band. (When Miaskovsky heard one of them, he decided to write his next symphony for that medium.)

Symphonies No. 3 in A min., Op. 15; 13 in B flat min., Op. 36.

*** Olympia DDD/ADD OCD 733. Russian Fed. Ac. SO, Svetlanov.

For the *Third Symphony*, with its overtones of Scriabin's of *Le Poème divin*, this project to record a complete Miaskovsky symphony cycle turns to the recording Svetlanov made in 1965, which appeared on a Melodiya LP and subsequently (in 1987) on Olympia OCD 117, where it was coupled with the charming *Lyric Concertino in G major*. The performance was inadvertently ascribed on the sleeve (but not the label) to Vladimir Verbitsky. Miaskovsky himself spoke of the *Third*, composed in 1914, as bearing 'the mark of deep pessimism', and underlying the two powerful movements is a dark and melancholic fervour. It belongs among the finest and most concentrated in feeling of the early symphonies. But the discovery here is the one-movement *Thirteenth Symphony* of 1933, a much shorter piece, merely 20 minutes long as opposed to 46. It is exploratory in idiom and enigmatic in character, with angular melodic lines, and it could not be further removed from the familiar and endearingly old-fashioned Nos. 21 and 27. It was premièred in Moscow and almost at the same time in Chicago, although the performance Miaskovsky's friend, Prokofiev, had hoped for in Paris fell through. Its language is austere and uncompromising, and the contrapuntal writing is inventive and dark. Though never overtly atonal, it contains passages of indeterminate tonality: it is richer harmonically and quite haunting. It has not been recorded before and proves to be a work of absorbing interest whose enigmatic and pensive ending shows this master in an entirely new light.

Symphonies Nos. 4 in E min., Op. 17; 11 in B flat min., Op. 34.

*** Olympia OCD 734. Russian Fed. Ac. SO, Svetlanov.

After the October Revolution and the Treaty of Brest-Litovsk, Miaskovsky spent some time in Tallinn, where he began his *Fourth Symphony*. He was later transferred to the general staff of the fleet and spent the winter of 1918 in Petrograd, composing during his time as duty officer, on night watch in the unheated rooms of the Admiralty. Here he completed not only this symphony but the *Fifth* as well. The *Fourth* will be new to all but a few specialists (this is its première on records). Its opening is bleak, and its mood reflects the tragic events of the times, as does the second movement. This is an imposing and generally dark piece, powerful in feeling and full of breadth. Those who warm to Rachmaninov and Glière should feel at home here. The *Eleventh Symphony* was composed in 1931, four years after the *Tenth*, an unusually long time in the composer's symphonic activity, and it was dedicated to Maximilian Steinberg, the son-in-law of Rimsky-Korsakov, two of whose symphonies have been recorded recently on DG. It is somewhat lighter in spirit and colouring than its companion, but as always crafted with great mastery. Svetlanov takes a more expansive view of it than did Veronika Dudarova and the Moscow Symphony Orchestra (now no longer available). Highly recommended.

Symphonies Nos. 5 in D, Op. 18; 12 in G min., Op. 35.

*** Olympia OCD 735. Russian Fed. Ac. SO, Svetlanov.

The first sketches for the *Fifth Symphony* were made as early as 1914, but the work was not completed until the end of the war. Miaskovsky spoke of it as his 'quiet' symphony, and its international success was remarkable. After its première in Moscow under Nikolai Malko in 1920, it was given in Prague, Madrid, Vienna, Chicago and Philadelphia. When Stokowski conducted it in New York the demand for tickets was so great that such eminent musicians as Prokofiev, Siloti, Szigeti and Casella had to content themselves with standing places. It is lyrical and pastoral in feeling with a strong sense of nostalgia. Like the whole series so far, this is a labour of love. Svetlanov directs the score with total dedication. It is a broader, far more expansive reading than Konstantin Ivanov with the USSR Radio Symphony Orchestra from the 1960s, though those who have that version will not necessarily find their allegiance shaken. The *Twelfth Symphony* (1931–2) comes from the period when Soviet artistic policy was taking a turn for the worse, and the climate turned against any kind of experimentation. Its programme portrays Russian village life before and after the revolution, and much of its material is folk-like. However, this is not in the least a propaganda score, in spite of its dedication 'to the fifteenth anniversary of the October Revolution', and there is some music of real substance and poetry here. Its first performance in Moscow was under the baton of Albert Coates in 1932. Good performances and decent recording.

MILHAUD, Darius (1892–1974)

(i; ii) *Le Carnaval d'Aix;* (ii) *Suite Provençale; Suite Française;* (iii) *Le Bal Martiniquais;* (i; iii; iv) *Paris;* (iii) *Scaramouche.*

(BB) **(*) EMI Encore (ADD). CDE5 74740-2. (i) Béroff; (ii) Monte Carlo PO, Prêtre; (iii) Ivaldi & Lee; (iv) with Collard.

It is difficult to understand why Milhaud's *Le Carnaval d'Aix* does not enjoy greater popularity. It has immense charm and an engaging easy-going Mediterranean sense of gaiety that never ceases to captivate. However, the present account proves something of a disappointment. Béroff rattles off the solo part without a trace of charm and without the tenderness that is at times called for. It comes here with the endearing *Suite Provençale* and *Suite Française* as companions, but the orchestral playing under Prêtre is fairly brash too, and the digital sound does not help very much either: it is inclined to be dry and close.

We regret that this enticingly inexpensive collection was given a wrong catalogue number in our main Guide. The listing is corrected above and and although performances and recording are uneven, there is no lack of sparkle in the well-known *Scaramouche,* the less familiar, but charming, *Bal Martiniquais,* and *Paris* (for four pianos!), all of which are very well played indeed.

La Création du monde.

(B) *** Virgin 2 CD VBD5 62050-2 (2). Lausanne CO, Zedda – DEBUSSY: *Danse; Sarabande*; PROKOFIEV: *Symphony No. 1 (Classical)* ***; SHOSTAKOVICH: *Chamber Symphony; Symphony No. 14* **.

Milhaud's ballet, with its mixture of yearning melancholy and jazzy high spirits, comes off splendidly in Alberto Zedda's highly spontaneous account, its witty syncopations and brassy exuberance bringing an unbridled effervescence to offset the restrained blues feeling of the main lyrical theme. The performance does not miss the Gershwin affinities, and the very vivid recording makes a bold dynamic contrast between the work's tender and abrasive moments. It is a pity that this CD was not reissued separately instead of in harness with Shostakovich.

String Quartet No. 12.

(B) (***) EMI mono CDZ5 74792-2. Italian Qt. – DEBUSSY: *String Quartet in G min.* (**(*)); RAVEL: *String Quartet in F* (**(*)).

This 1954 performance originally appeared in harness with the Debussy (on Columbia 33CX 1155). The piece has that sunny, relaxed Provençal charm that distinguishes so much of Milhaud's output, and the Quartetto Italiano play it with characteristic elegance. The sound is amazingly fresh.

MOERAN, Ernest J. (1894–1950)

Symphony in G min.; Sinfonietta.

(BB) *** Naxos 8.555837. Bournemouth SO, Lloyd Jones.

Built confidently on strikingly memorable ideas, Moeran's *G minor Symphony,* first heard in 1937, is among the most attractive British symphonies of the period. The Naxos version, warmly and idiomatically conducted by David Lloyd Jones, could hardly be more persuasive, well played by the Bournemouth Orchestra and treated to a full-range recording, with transparent textures bringing out the fine detail of the orchestration. The jolly, vigorous *Sinfonietta,* equally well played, makes an apt coupling. In the *Symphony* Handley (Chandos 7106) might be marginally more bitingly powerful, but this new version has a considerable price advantage and is certainly not second best.

MOMPOU, Federico (1893–1987)

Musica callada, Books I–IV; El pont; Muntanya (Dansa).

(BB) **(*) Naxos 8.554727. Masó.

Jordi Masó's survey of Mompou's piano music continues with the *Musica callada* – twenty-eight pieces which appeared in four volumes between 1959 and 1967. The title comes from the *Cántico espiritual* and means 'music without sound' although this is complemented with the additional description *Soledad sonora* ('insistent solitude'). The very first piece, *Angelico,* creates the work's atmosphere and other pieces are called *Placid, Tranquillo – trè calme, Luminoso* and so on. The problem for the performer is that almost all this music is slow and reflective (the Lento marking reappears frequently), and it has to be said that this is not entirely solved here. Jordi Masó is by no means insensitive, but although he is well recorded, the colouring remains monochrome. The two impressionistic pieces which close the recital are *El pont* ('The Bridge') and *Muntanya* ('Mountain'). They have not been recorded before and make successful encores.

MONTEMEZZI, Italo (1875–1952)

L'amore dei tre re (complete).

(M) (**(*)) Warner Fonit mono 8573 87487-2 (2). Bruscantini, Petrella, Berdini, Capecchi, RAI Ch. & O of Milan, Basile.

Recorded for Cetra in Milan in 1950 in collaboration with Italian Radio, this mono recording of Montemezzi's one operatic success brings a red-blooded, idiomatic account of a piece cherished in America as well as Italy, largely through the initial advocacy of Toscanini. It says much for the conductor, Arturo Basile, that he drives the piece so strongly through a tale of such improbable blood and thunder, helped by a strong cast. Central to the success of the performance is the singing of Sesto Bruscantini as the barbarian king, Archibaldo, who forces his daughter, Fiora, to marry the unfortunate Manfredo, before malevolently rooting out her passionate affair with her true love, Avito, with widespread carnage at the end. Bruscantini, only thirty-one at the time, sings with commanding power in this villainous role, cutting a very different figure from his classic Figaro which became such a favourite at Glyndebourne. Clara Petrella sings sensitively as Fiora, well-matched against her lover, Avito, sung by Amedeo Berdini, with the young Renato Capecchi making Manfredo into a believable character. The mono recording is very limited, but catches voices well. Though the later stereo version with Moffo and Domingo (RCA 74321 50166-2) must take priority, this one from a company of singers and players familiar with the music is both convincing and enjoyable in putting over such outrageous hokum. An Italian libretto is provided but no translation, only multi-lingual synopses.

MONTEVERDI, Claudio

(1567–1643)

Madrigals (duets and solos): *Chiome d'oro, bel thesoro; Il son pur vezzosetta pastorella; Non è gentil core; O come sei gentile, caro augellino; Ohimé dov'é il mio ben?; Se pur destina e vole il cielo, partenza amorosa.* Sacred music: *Cantate Domino; Exulta, filia Sion; Iste confessoe II; Laudate Dominum in sanctis eius; O bone Jesu, o piissime Jesu; Sancta Maria, succurre miseris; Venite, siccientes ad aquas Domini.* Opera: *Il ritorno d'Ulisse in patria: Di misera regina (Penelope's Lament).*

(BB) *** Regis 1060. Kirkby, Tubb, Consort of Musicke, Rooley.

Admirers of Emma Kirkby will surely revel in this collection, mostly of duets, in which she is joined by Evelyn Tubb. The two voices are admirably matched and both artists ornament their lines attractively and judiciously. Evelyn Tubb is given a solo opportunity in Penelope's lament from *Il ritorno d'Ulisse*, which she sings dramatically and touchingly. Anthony Rooley's simple accompaniments with members of the Consort of Musicke are also imaginatively stylish. We are pleased to report that this inexpensive reissue has been properly documented.

Selva morale e spirituale (complete).

*** HM HMC 901718/20 (3). Cantus Cölln, Concerto Palatino, Konrad Junghändl.

Many of the 40 or so pieces which make up the *Selva morale e spirituale* – his last publication, a collection of sacred pieces, following up his eight books of madrigals – have often been recorded, but it is especially valuable that Junghändl and his talented performers have recorded the complete collection. These are performances marked by keen perception as well as energy. In his presentation Junghändl effectively solves one of the main problems of the whole: the very variety of the pieces, which range widely in their styles from pure polyphony to the latest developments of the mid seventeenth century, plainly drawn from all periods of Monteverdi's career. The original publication also had them in higgledy-piggledy order, and Junghändl has perceptively reordered them to present the first and third of the three CDs roughly as *Vespers* collections, with miscellaneous items on the second disc. It works well, with the 12 singers of Cantus Cölln, led by the superb soprano Johanna Koslowsky, offering ample variety of colour and expression to keep concentration. A superb achievement helped by fine atmospheric recording.

L'incoronazione di Poppea (opera; complete).

*** Arthaus DVD 100 108. Schumann, Croft, Kuhlmann, Gall, Peeters, Brooks, Concerto Köln, Jacobs. (Director: Michael Hampe. V/D: José Montes-Baquer.)

The best *L'incoronazione di Poppea* so far on video/LaserDisc has been the Ponelle Zurich Opera production with Yakar as Poppea, and conducted by Harnoncourt from 1986 (Decca 071 406-1/3). (That occupied no fewer than four LaserDisc sides as opposed to the one DVD.) This newcomer from the 1993 Schwetzingen Festival is far more severe, both artistically and as a visual experience, and better conducted too.

It suffers from a less than ideal Poppea in Patricia Schumann but both Kuhlmann's Ottavia and Darla Brooks's Drusilla are expressive and intelligent singers, and the Seneca of Harry Peeters is exemplary. The performance as a whole is more compelling than the old Zurich alternative, which will presumably find its way on to DVD in the fullness of time. Subtitles are in English, French, German and Spanish.

MOSCHELES, Ignaz (1794–1870)

Piano Concertos Nos. 2 in E flat, Op. 56; 3 in G min., Op. 58; Anticipations of Scotland (Grand Fantasia), Op. 75.

*** Hyp. CDA 67276. Shelley, Tasmanian SO.

Where the concertos of Hummel have been well-treated on disc, those of his younger contemporary, Ignaz Moscheles, have been seriously neglected, and this excellent disc in Hyperion's 'Romantic Piano Concerto' series provides the first CD of the *Third Concerto*. Moscheles, a close friend of Mendelssohn and similarly from a Jewish background, provides a stylistic link between Mozart and Chopin, with a touch of Mendelssohn too. Both these piano concertos appeared in 1825. *No. 2 in E flat* is particularly attractive, with one striking idea after another bubbling up in the substantial outer movements – the finale a Chopin-like Polacca – and with a deeply meditative central Adagio. Though the thematic material of *No. 3 in G minor* is not so memorable, with passage-work that involves note-spinning reminiscent of a study by Czerny, the finale makes amends with a jolly Rondo in a galloping 6/8 time. *Anticipations of Scotland*, as the title suggests, was written before Moscheles ever visited the country. Scottish songs were freely available to him, however, and in this fantasia he uses three in particular, with characteristic Scottish snap-rhythms – *Kelvin Grove, Auld Robin Gray* and *Lord Moira's Strathspey* – for a sequence of variations. Again this is a piece full of conventional passage-work, this time helped by the underlying melodies. Moscheles' writing is always winningly fluent, so that even when the writing is at its most predictable, it sparkles away in the hands of a fine pianist like Howard Shelley, who draws lively playing from the Tasmanian Orchestra, with vivid, immediate recording.

MOSZKOWSKI, Moritz

(1854–1925)

Piano music: *Air de ballet, Op. 36/5; Albumblatt, Op. 2; Au crépuscule, Op. 68/3; Barcarolle from Offenbach's Contes d'Hoffmann; Chanson bohème from Bizet's Carmen; Danse russe, Op. 6/4; En automne, Op. 36/4; Expansion, Op. 36/3; La Jongleuse, Op. 52/4; Minuetto, Op. 68/2; Nocturne, Op. 68/1; Poème de Mai, Op. 67/1; Près de berceau, Op. 58/3; Rêverie, Op. 36/2; Serenata, Op. 15/1; Tarantella, Op. 27/2; Valse mignonne.*

(BB) **(*) Hyp. Helios CDH 55141. Tanyel.

The composer/pianist once came to London to conduct his *Spanish Dances* at a Henry Wood Promenade Concert. Famous in their day, they are seldom heard now, and his once popular piano music has also faded from view. Pieces like *Au crépuscule* have a certain sub-Lisztian charm, and *La Jongleuse* is an engaging moto perpetuo, while *Près de berceu* is the epitome of a salon piece. Setya Tanyel characterizes the music sympathetically, but she is hard put to sustain interest through a 69-minute recording of genre pieces that are heard most effectively as encores at the end of a more substantial programme. The *Air de ballet* is an ideal example with its brilliant filigree at the close which sparkles readily in her hands. Truthful recording.

MOYZES, Alexander (1906–84)

Down the River Vah, Suite for Large Orchestra, Op. 26; Germer Dances, Suite for Large Orchestra, Op. 51; Pohronie Dances, Suite for Large Orchestra, Op. 43.

*(*) Marco Polo 8.223278. CSR SO (Bratislava), Lenard.

This disc contains some attractive dances and colourful (not over-extended) tone poems, which, although not great music, are yet not unappealing. Their Slavonic flavour and vivid orchestration, with considerable rhythmic interest, helps to hold the listener's attention. The performances are enthusiastic, but the orchestral playing and especially the 1989 sound (which produces a scrawny effect at times) are

not very inviting. At Naxos price this would be worth considering for the rare repertoire, but its full-price tag gives one pause.

Symphonies Nos. 11, Op. 79; 12, Op. 83.

** Marco 8.225093. Slovak RSO, Slovák.

Moyzes established himself as a pioneer of Slovak national music, and both these works mix Slovakian elements into the Western Romantic tradition. Nothing is remotely atonal: it is all approachable, melodic and boldly coloured. The *Eleventh Symphony* dates from 1978 and begins ominously with repeated timpani strokes, but, from the *Allegro* onwards, the composer's penchant for lively folk material soon emerges. There is no lack of energy. The *Twelfth Symphony* was the composer's last work, and follows the conventional pattern of its predecessor. The opening movement (after a slow introduction) is a kind of *moto perpetuo*, which the composer suggested represented 'contemporary living – with everyone running and hurrying, always on the move'. The central slow movement is powerfully reflective, and the finale has plenty of robust vitality. The performances are excellent, and if neither the orchestral playing nor the sound is first class, they are more than satisfactory.

MOZART, Wolfgang Amadeus

(1756–91)

(i; ii; iii) *Andante for Flute and Orchestra;* (iii; iv; v) *Bassoon Concerto, K.191;* (vi; vii) *Clarinet Concerto in A, K.622;* (i; vii; viii) *Flute and Harp Concerto, K.299;* (i; ii; iii) *Flute Concerto No. 1, K.313;* (iii; v) *Sinfonia concertante, K.297b.*

(B) ** Erato Ultima (ADD) 3984 27000-2 (2). (i) Rampal; (ii) Vienna SO; (iii) Guschlbauer; (iv) Hongne; (v) Bamberg SO; (vi) Lancelot; (vii) Jean-François Paillard CO, Paillard; (viii) Laskine.

These are all fresh, unpretentious accounts from the 1960s, not as distinguished as the very finest performance and recordings of today, but lively, polished music-making none the less to which one makes a ready response. Jean-Pierre Rampal is the obvious star whose contribution sparkles characteristically. This Ultima reissue is inexpensive, and the transfers are more refined than the LP originals.

(i) *Bassoon Concerto, K.191;* (ii) *Clarinet Concerto, K.622;* (iii) *Flute Concerto No. 1, K.313; Andante, K.315;* (iii; iv) *Flute and Harp Concerto, K.299;* (v) *Horn Concertos 1–4;* (vi) *Oboe Concerto, K.314. Divertimenti Nos. 2 in D, K.131; 11 in D, K.251; 12 in E flat, K.252; 14 in B flat, K.270; A Musical Joke, K.522; Serenades Nos. 6 (Serenata notturna); 10 in B flat, K.388; 12 in C min., K.388; 13 (Eine kleine Nachtmusik); Sinfonia concertante in E flat, K.197b.*

(B) *** DG 471 435-2 (7). (i) Morelli; (ii) Neidich; (iii) Palma; (iv) Allen; (v) Jolley or Purvis; (vi) Wolfgang; Orpheus CO.

The first three CDs containing the concertos were initially reissued together and were highly praised by us. Frank Morelli chortles his way engagingly through the outer movements of the *Bassoon Concerto* and is contrastingly doleful in the Andante; Charles Neidich uses a basset clarinet in K.622 and his timbre is very appealing; Randall Wolfgang's plaintive, slightly reedy tone is especially telling in the Adagio of the *Oboe Concerto* and he plays the finale with the lightest possible touch, as does Susan Palma the charming Minuet which closes the *Flute Concerto*. The *Sinfonia concertante* for wind has three new soloists (Stephen Taylor, David Singer and Steven Dibner) plus William Purvis, and is pleasingly fresh; the players match their timbres beautifully in the Adagio, and again the last movement is delightful with its buoyant rhythmic spirit.

The *Divertimenti* and *Serenades* also bring highly admirable performances. Alert, crisply rhythmic allegros show consistent resilience, strong, yet without a touch of heaviness, while slow movements are warmly phrased, with much finesse and imaginative use of light and shade. *Eine kleine Nachtmusik* is wonderfully light-hearted and fresh, and among the finest of record; the *Serenata notturna*, which can easily sound bland, has a fine sparkle here, while the B flat *Wind Divertimento*, K.270 is notable for some felicitous oboe playing.

Impeccable in ensemble, this splendid playing has no sense of anonymity of character or style. All the works are given excellent recordings, and this is a very persuasive collection indeed, probably a 'best buy' for all wanting this music in a digital format.

(i) *Bassoon Concerto in B flat, K.191;* (ii) *Clarinet Concerto in A, K.622;* (iii) *Flute Concerto No. 1 in G, K.313; Andante in C, K.315;* (iii;iv) *Flute and Harp Concerto in C, K.299;* (v) *Horn Concertos Nos. 1–4;* (vi) *Oboe Concerto in C, K.314; Sinfonia Concertante in E flat, K.197b.*

(B) *** DG Trio 469 362-2 (3). (i) Morelli; (ii) Neidlich; (iii) Palma; (iv) Allen; (v) Jolley or Purvis; (vi) Wolfgang; Orpheus CO.

Randall Wolfgang's plaintive, slightly reedy timbre is especially telling in the *Oboe Concerto* and he plays with the lightest possible touch, as does Susan Palmer in the charming Minuet which closes the *Flute Concerto*. The *Sinfonia Concertante* for wind has three new soloists (Stephen Taylor, David Singer and Steven Dibner) plus William Purvis, and is pleasingly fresh; the players match their timbres beautifully in the *Adagio*, and again the last movement is delightful with its buoyant rhythmic spirit. All three works are given excellent modern recordings, and as a bargain-priced Trio this is a very persuasive collection, probably a 'best buy' for those wanting all the music in a digital format.

(i) *Clarinet Concerto, K.622;* (ii) *Clarinet Quintet, K.581;* (iii) *Exsultate, Jubilate, K.165.*

(M) *** ASV Platinum PLT 8514. (i) Johnson, ECO, Leppard; (ii) Hilton, Lindsay Qt; (iii) Lott, LMP, Glover.

This collection fascinatingly contrasts the styles of two young British clarinettists. Emma Johnson recorded her version of the *Clarinet Concerto* soon after winning the BBC's Young Musician of the Year in 1984. The result lacks some of the technical finesse of rival versions by more mature clarinettists, but it has a sense of spontaneity, of natural magnetism which traps the ear from first to last. There may be some rawness of tone in places, but that only adds to the range of expression, which breathes the air of a live performance – whether in the sparkle and flair of the outer movements, or the inner intensity of the central slow movement, in which Emma Johnson plays magically in the delightfully embellished lead-back into the main theme. Leppard and the ECO are in bouncing form, and the recording is first rate.

Janet Hilton then gives a disarmingly unaffected account of the *Clarinet Quintet* and gets excellent support from the Lindsays. The recording is forward, but well balanced and vivid. There are many delights in Felicity Lotts's *Exsultate, Jubilate*: her clean and stylish singing is well supported by Jane Glover's sympathetic conducting, which elicits poised playing from the LMP. Beautiful, if slightly distant, recording.

(i; iv; v) *Flute Concerto No. 1 in G, K.313;* (i; ii; iv; vi) *Flute and Harp Concerto in C, K.314;* (iii; iv; v) *Oboe Concerto in C, K.314.*

(B) **(*) CfP 575 1442. (i) Snowden; (ii) C. Thomas; (ii) Hunt; (iv) LPO; (v) Mackerras; (vi) Litton.

Jonathan Snowden's account of the *Flute Concerto* is attractive, sprightly, stylish and polished (though some might not take to his comparatively elaborate cadenzas). The performance of the *Flute and Harp Concerto* is even more winning. Where Gordon Hunt in the *Oboe Concerto* seems a natural concerto soloist, Snowden, in collaboration with Caryl Thomas on the harp, is both sparkling and sensitive, regularly imaginative in his individual phrasing. The recording is lifelike and this is good value although, in the final analysis, not a first choice.

Flute & Harp Concerto in C, K.299.

(M) *** DG (ADD) 463 648-2. Zöller, Zabaleta, BPO, Märzendorfer – REINECKE: *Harp Concerto;* RODRIGO: *Concierto serenata.* *** ◉

We regret that this very attractive CD was given the wrong catalogue number in our main Guide. It is corrected above. Karlheinz Zöller is a most sensitive flautist, his phrasing a constant source of pleasure, while Zabaleta's contribution is equally distinguished. Märzendorfer conducts with both warmth and lightness; the outer movements have an attractive rhythmic buoyancy. The 1963 recording is clear and clean, if not quite so rich as we would expect today. This performance is also available coupled with the solo flute concertos (see above).

Horn Concertos Nos. 1–4; Concert Rondo, K.371 (ed. Tuckwell); Fragment in E flat, K.494a.

(BB) *** EMI Encore (ADD) CDE5 74967-2. Tuckwell, ASMF, Marriner.

Barry Tuckwell was a fine artist and brilliant player and his 1971 set of Mozart *Horn Concertos* offers strong, warm performances which have stood the test of time. If they do not quite have the magic of Dennis Brain's classic mono accounts, they are still highly enjoyable, especially with Marriner's beautifully managed accompaniments. At bargain price, with the two short fill-ups (the performance of the *Fragment* ends where Mozart left it at bar 91), this CD is well worth its modest price.

Piano concertos

Piano Concertos Nos: (i) 9 in E flat (Jeunehomme), K.271; (ii) 12 in A, K.414; (i) 17 in G, K.453; (ii) 19 in F, K.459; Rondos: in D, K.382; A min., K.511.

(B) *** Erato (ADD) 0927 41397-2 (2). Pires, with (i) Gulbenkian Foundation O, Guschlbauer (ii) Lausanne CO, Jordan.

Piano Concertos Nos. 13 in C, K.415; 14 in E flat, K.449; 21 in C, K.467; 23 in A, K.488; 26 in D (Coronation), K.537; Rondo in A, K.386.

(B) Erato (ADD) 0927-41396-2 (2). Pires, Gulbenkian Foundation O, Guschlbauer.

Maria João Pires recorded these Mozart concertos in the 1970s, before fame had overtaken her. They are refreshingly musical and full of character, and no allowances need be made for the sound. Readers wanting bargain accounts of these concertos can rest assured that these are far more than serviceable – indeed, they have style as well as the accomplished musicianship one expects from her. Eminently recommendable.

Piano Concertos Nos. 9, K.271; 21, K.467.

(B) ** CfP 575 145-2. Hough, Hallé O, Thomson.

On one of his early recordings (1987) Stephen Hough plays with fine freshness, point and clarity, but he tends to prettify two of Mozart's strongest concertos, minimizing their greatness. This delicate, Dresden-china treatment would have been more acceptable half a century ago, but it leaves out too much that is essential. Excellent playing and recording.

(i) Piano Concertos Nos. 12 in A, K.414; 14 in E flat, K.449; 20 in D min., K.466; (ii; iii) Sinfonia concertante in E flat, K.364; (iii) Symphony No. 41 (Jupiter); (iv) Requiem Mass.

(M) *** Andante 4993/5 (3). VPO; with (i) Pollini (piano & cond.); (ii) I. & D. Oistrakh; (iii) D. Oistrakh (cond.); (iv) Popp, Lilowa, Dermota, Berry, Wiener Singakademie, Krips.

This three-disc collection of historic recordings, made in Vienna by Austrian Radio, brings a winning celebration of Mozart as played by the Vienna Philharmonic. The most revealing disc of the three has Maurizio Pollini directing the orchestra from the keyboard in three contrasted Mozart piano concertos. Here, in repertory that he has largely ignored on disc, you have Pollini magnetically spontaneous-sounding, playing with a freedom that as a rule in his studio recordings he rarely matches.

Recorded in 1981 in the Konzerthaus in Vienna, a relatively intimate space, the Vienna Philharmonic sound is on a more aptly Mozartian scale than on the other two discs, with the tuttis immediately revealing the sort of detailed artistry that seems to come naturally to these players. Pollini at the piano draws a clear distinction between the three works: K.414, one of the lightest of all, K.459, weightier with its contrapuntal finale, and K.466, almost Beethovenian in its minor-key drama. By today's standards Pollini's speeds for slow movements are very measured, but the refinement and elegance make them anything but sentimental.

It is good too to have Josef Krips's account of the Mozart *Requiem*, given in the Musikverein in December 1973, his last public concert before he died less than a year later. The performance is irresistible, bitingly fresh from first to last and often brisk, with the chorus full-bodied and with a superb, characterful quartet of soloists. The third disc, with David Oistrakh's reading of the *Jupiter Symphony* in coupling with the *Sinfonia concertante* is more variable, with sound less full-bodied.

The father-and-son duo, Igor on violin and David on viola, recorded the *Sinfonia concertante* a number of times, and there is a winning spontaneity about this reading, as there is in the *Symphony*, with the outer movements forthright and incisive, though it is a pity that Oistrakh does not observe the repeats in either half of the great finale. The slow movement is taken at a spacious speed, but again the purity and refinement of the playing make it most persuasive, and the Minuet brings a delectable Ländler-like spring to the dance-rhythms. The quality of the original Austrian Radio recordings has here been faithfully captured on the French-made CD transfers.

Piano Concerto No. 13 in C, K.415

✪ *** TDK **DVD** DV-VERSA. Barenboim, BPO – with CONCERT ***. (see below)

This outstanding DVD brings a captivating account of this early concerto, greatly enhanced in video, with the empathy between pianist/conductor and his players communcating directly and magically to the viewer. The other works in the programme are Ravel's *Le tombeau de Couperin* and Beethoven's *Eroica Symphony*, also very finely played.

Piano Concerto No. 15 in B flat, K.450.

(BB) (*) EMI Encore mono CDE5 75230-2. Michelangeli, Orchestra Sinfonica da Camera dell'Ente dei Pomeriggi

Musicali' di Milano, Gracis – BACH/BUSONI: *Partita No. 2: Chaconne.* BRAHMS: *Paganini Variations* (**(*)).

The 1952 recording for Michelangeli is indifferent with thin, papery violins and poor focus developing towards the end of the slow movement. It is a cool, yet bold, classical reading, with Michelangeli at his best in the finale, although the sound takes some getting used to.

Piano Concertos Nos. (i) 15 in B flat, K.450; (ii) 23 in A, K.488; 24 in C min., K.491.

✹ (***) Testament mono SBT 1222. Solomon, Philh. O, (i) Ackermann, (ii) Menges.

All three concertos were recorded in 1955, not long before this great pianist suffered the cruel stroke that silenced him. This is quite exceptional Mozart playing: it has depth and serenity, impeccable grace and wit, and an incomparable sense of style. Almost half a century has passed since these recordings were made, and they have been out of circulation most of that time. They are in a class of their own: only Perahia has come remotely close to them. Remarkably good sound.

Piano Concertos Nos. 18, K.456; 20, K.466.

(BB) **(*) Arte Nova 74321 80784-2. Kirschnereit, Bamberg SO, Beerman.

Matthias Kirschnereit will be a new name to most collectors. This coupling of the *B flat* and *D minor Concertos* shows him to be a Mozartian of no mean order. Well worth the money, though not a first choice.

Piano Concerto No. 19, K.459; 21, K.467.

(BB) **(*) Arte Nova 74321 8714702. Kirschnereit, Bamberg SO, Beermann.

Sprightly performances. Even in a competitive environment, Matthias Kirschnereit can hold his head high, though, given the distinction of so many rival versions, his cannot be a primary recommendation, but those who do invest in it will not be disappointed.

Piano Concerto No. 20, K.466.

(M) (***) Westminster mono 471 214-2. Haskil, Winterthur SO, Swoboda – D. SCARLATTI: *Sonatas.* (**)

The Westminster Legacy series that DG is now issuing is not specific on this occasion in giving recording details, apart from the year. This fine 1951 performance is not to be confused with the slightly later recording Haskil made with Bernhard Paumgartner and the Wiener Symphoniker in 1954, both in mono, which was included in the Philips 'Clara Haskil Legacy'. Although the Winterthur Orchestra was not the equal of the Vienna Orchestra, it plays very well for Henry Swoboda, and the technical refurbishment here is really rather impressive. The sound naturally lacks the transparency of detail you find in early stereo, but it is very much more vivid than we remember.

Piano Concertos Nos. 20, K.466; 21, K.467.

(BB) ** EMI Encore CDE5 74741-2. Zacharias, Bav. RSO, Zinman.

Christian Zacharias is a much admired Mozartian in Germany. He is an artist of strong classical instinct, although less impressive in the variety and subtlety of keyboard colour he has at his command. These performances are thoroughly acceptable, but neither account challenges existing recommendations.

(i) Piano Concertos Nos. 20, K.466; 21, K.467; (ii) 22, K.482; 23, K.488.

(B) ** Teldec Ultima 0630 18956-2 (2). Barenboim, BPO.

Barenboim has turned to the Berlin Philharmonic Orchestra for his digital re-recordings of the key Mozart concertos. He directs them from the keyboard and they play most expressively for him; but the result is weighty in a way which sometimes makes the music look forward to Beethoven. This would not matter were the effect seemingly spontaneous, but in that respect these performances do not match his earlier EMI series with the ECO, and the portentous opening of the *D minor Concerto* seems overdramatized. The famous slow movement of K.467 generates a languor that misses the simplicity of Mozart's ethereal inspiration, and similarly the lovely Adagio of the *A major*, K.488, again very leisured, is self-conscious. Of course there is much fine pianism throughout the series, even if at times Barenboim's articulation seems over precise, and the very fast tempo he chooses for the finale of K.466 loses much of the music's poise. On the whole, the *Concerto in E flat*, K.482, is the most rewarding performance, the *Andante* obviously deeply felt, and the finale, in which Barenboim chooses to play an abridged version of a cadenza by Edwin Fischer, is agreeably light-hearted. The recordings are very well balanced.

(i) Piano Concertos Nos. 20 in D min., K.466; (ii) 23 in A, K.488; 24 in C min., K.491; 26 in D (Coronation), K.537; (i) 27 in B flat, K.595.

(M) *** Decca (ADD) 468 491-2 (2). Curzon, ECO, Britten or LSO, Kertész.

As Cyrus Meher-Homji's excellent notes for this reissue make abundantly clear, Curzon's recordings of the late Mozart concertos for Decca, made between 1967 and 1970, were fraught with issue problems. Always a perfectionist and especially so in Mozart, the great pianist was seldom satisfied with his performances, always feeling he could do better. Initially only K.466 and K.491 were approved by the soloist for release, yet K.595 was hardly less distinguished, and this is currently coupled with K.466 (417 288-2) and as such received a ✹ from us in our main volume. K.488 and 491 were eventually released together (452 888-2). Even if they are slightly less fine and as such bear out Curzon's doubts, by any normal standards this is pianism of distinction. The attraction of the present set is the inclusion of K.537 (hitherto unavailable on

CD) where Curzon is completely seductive in the *Larghetto*, and sparkles happily in the finale. Strong support from the LSO although Kertész perhaps proved a rather less imaginative accompanist than Britten. The recordings, made in the Kingsway Hall or the Maltings, are up to Decca's highest standards and reservations must be swept aside, for this 'Legendary' reissue is certainly treasurable.

Piano Concertos Nos. 21, K.467; 23, K.488; Rondos for Piano & Orchestra Nos. 1 in D, K.382; 2 in A, K.386.

(M) *** Sony (DDD/ADD) SMK 89876. Perahia, ECO.

Both concertos capture Perahia's very special Mozartian sensibility and are beautifully recorded. The *C major*, K.467, is given delicacy and charm, rather than strength in the way of Brendel or Kovacevich, but the opposite is true of the exquisite slow movement (with very beautiful orchestral playing) and spirited finale. The slow movement of K.488 has an elevation of spirit that reaffirms one's conviction that this is indeed a classic recording. The finale, however, has a robust quality, with lively but controlled spontaneity. The digital recording is particularly fresh and natural. This very generous collection is completed with the two *Concert Rondos* which, when recorded in 1983, incorporated for the first time on record the closing bars newly rediscovered by Professor Alan Tyson.

Piano Concertos Nos. 21, K.467; 24, K.491.

(BB) *** Regis RRC 1067. Shelley, City of L. Sinf.
**(*) Virgin VC5 45504-2. Anderszewski, Sinfonia Varsovie.

Unfortunately we allotted a wrong catalogue number in our main Guide to Howard Shelley's delightfully fresh and characterful readings of these fine concertos. The correct number is above and it is outstanding value at budget price.

The Polish pianist Piotr Anderszewski came to attention some years back by walking out of the Leeds Competition in dissatisfaction at his own playing and more recently by giving an impressive account of the *Diabelli Variations* in London and on record (VC5 45468-2; see our main volume). His playing and direction of his Warsaw orchestra are fastidious, keenly felt, highly musical and very intelligent, and the disc should be heard by all Mozarteans. He is obviously a pianist of quality. At the same time, for all its insights, a recommendation must be qualified, for in the very keenness of his responses, there is a self-awareness that does not wear well. His entry in the first movement of K.491 is very self-conscious, and after a while one yearns for the simple, unadorned but never plain speech of the finest performances on record. These include those by Howard Shelley these same two concertos (Regis RRC 1066), which at budget price are highly recommendable.

(i) Piano Concerto Nos. 21, K.467; (ii) 27, K.595; (iii) Piano Sonata No. 15 in C, K.545; (iv) Die Zauberflöte: highlights.

(B) **(*) DG (ADD) 469 307-2 (2). (i) Anda, Salzburg Mozarteum Camerata; (ii) Gilels, VPO, Boehm; (iii) Eschenbach; (iv) from complete recording with Lear, Peters, Wunderlich, Fischer-Dieskau, Crass, Hotter, Lenz, BPO, Boehm.

A curiously random Mozart collection. Outstanding is Gilels's 1974 account of the *B flat Concerto*; his Mozart is in a class of its own, the pacing totally unhurried and superbly controlled. In short, this is playing of the highest artistic integrity and poetic insight, while Boehm and the VPO provide excellent support. Anda's unfussy and thoroughly musical account of the *C major Concerto* from the early 1960s has stood the test of time, and if Eschenbach's (1971) contribution of the well-known *C major Sonata* is rather cool, it is elegantly played and without any distracting mannerisms. The recordings are generally excellent, only K.467 slightly betraying its age. The excerpts from *Die Zauberflöte* are not obviously directed to bringing out its special qualities. One would have liked more of Wunderlich's Tamino, one of the great glories of the set. However, the key arias are included and the sound is fresh and full. Texts and translations are not included.

Piano Concertos Nos. 24 in C min., K.491; 25 in C, K.503; 26 in D (Coronation), K.537; 27 in B flat, K.595.

(B) ** Teldec Ultima 3984 21037-2 (2). Barenboim, BPO.

The second of Barenboim's two Ultima collections of late Mozart concertos opens disappointingly. The 1988 performances of the *C minor* and *C major Concertos* refuse to take off until the playful finale of K.503 displays a lightness of touch that is missing elsewhere. Both opening movements are over-weighted and the actual orchestral sound is curiously unrefined. The two final concertos were recorded the following year and they show Barenboim approaching his old form. Although the orchestral tuttis remain very fully textured, the BPO playing is elegant and both performances are agreeably spontaneous. Slow movements are appealing (though there are idiosyncratic touches in the *Andante* of K.503 that some might find self-conscious), but finales sparkle and the sound too is good. We hope this enjoyable disc can be reissued separately, for it is well recorded, provided once accepts the resonance.

Piano Concertos Nos. (i) 24, K.491; (ii) 27, K.595.

(M) (**) Orfeo (mono) C 536001B. Casadesus, VPO, with (i) Mitropoulos; (ii) Schuricht.

Any reminder of Casadesus's artistry is to be welcomed: his stature as a Mozartian was unquestioned, and his concerto recordings with Georg Szell were legendary in their day. The value of the present issue is somewhat diminished, however, by the inferior quality of the Austrian Radio recordings. The *C minor*, K.491, with Mitropoulos at the helm of the Vienna Philharmonic, comes from a Salzburg Festival performance in 1956 but sounds thin and shallow, almost as if it had been made on a domestic tape recorder. The *B flat*, K.595, made in 1961 with Schuricht, is better but only marginally so. Casadesus is on characteristically good form in both works, but the disc's sonic limitations call for much tolerance.

Violin Concerto No. 4, K.218.

(BB) (***) Naxos mono 8.110946. Szigeti, LPO, Beecham – BEETHOVEN: *Violin Concerto*. (***)

Szigeti's account of this Mozart concerto has appeared many times before, most recently in harness with the Prokofiev *D major*, which he recorded at much the same time. Now it comes in harness with his memorable Beethoven with Bruno Walter. Szigeti was at his prime when this was made, and his individuality shines through.

Violin Concerto No. 5 in A (Turkish), K.219.

(***) Testament mono SBT 1228. Kogan, Conservatoire O., Vandernoot – BEETHOVEN: *Violin Concerto*. (***)

Matching the outstanding account of the Beethoven *Concerto* with which it is coupled, this 1957 version of Mozart, recorded later in the same month, is comparably strong and purposeful in the first movement, positive in the expressive contrasts. The slow movement is sweet and tender, poetic without self-indulgence, and the finale sparkles in its contrasting sections. Excellent transfer to make one forget the absence of stereo.

Double Concerto for Violin, Piano and Orchestra, K.315f; (i) Sinfonia concertante in E flat, K.364.

*** Sony SK 89488. Midori, North German RSO, Eschenbach (piano & cond.); (i) with Imai (viola).

The Mozart scholar, Alfred Einstein, described the 120 bars that have survived of Mozart's *Double Concerto for Piano, Violin and Orchestra* as 'a magnificent torso', the most promising of starts to a work. The mystery is what happened to the rest. The reconstruction recorded here stems from the detective work of Philip Wilby, who has deduced that the *Violin Sonata in D*, K.306, grander in scale and manner than its fellow sonatas, was a reworking of the concerto.

The première recording with Iona Brown and Howard Shelley as soloists was issued as part of Volume 8 of the Philips Complete Mozart Edition, an excellent account, also coupled with K.364, as well as another reconstructed sinfonia concertante movement. In sound the Sony version is marginally fuller, with a more airy acoustic, while interpretively Midori takes a more freely expressive, even romantic view, notably in the central *Andantino* of the *Double Concerto*, which is two minutes longer than the Brown/Shelley performance. The contrasts are similar in the familiar masterpiece, K.364, with Nobuko Imai magnificent in both versions, at once individual and classically pure. This is well worth exploring for those collectors without the Mozart Edition.

Divertimentos in B flat, K.Anh.227 (K.196f); 12 in E flat, K.252; 13 in F, K.253; Serenade No. 12 in C min., K.388.

(BB) *** Naxos 8.555943. Oslo PO Wind Ens.

These 1997 performances show the Oslo Philharmonic wind on top form. They give the two Salzburg divertimentos with finesse and grace, and bring great intensity to the *C minor Serenade*. The recording, made at the Lommedalen Church at Baerun, has splendid presence and bloom. An outstanding bargain.

Overtures: Bastien und Bastienne; La clemenza di Tito; Così fan tutte; Don Giovanni; Die Entführung aus dem Serial; La finta giardiniera; Idomeneo; Il rè pastore; Lucio Silla; Le nozze di Figaro; Der Schauspieldirektor; Die Zauberflöte.

(BB) *** RCA 74321 68004-2. Dresden State O, Davis.

A self-recommending set of Mozart overtures from Colin Davis. They are thoroughly musical and have both drama and warmth, with much felicitousness of orchestral detail emerging from the superb Dresden orchestra throughout the programme. Davis perfectly balances the full weight of the dramatic moments with the sparkle of the lighter ones, and the dynamic contrasts are very well judged. The recording is good. If occasionally the tuttis can seem a little bass heavy because of the resonant Dresden acoustic, this is not a serious problem, and anyone wanting a budget collection of Mozart overtures on modern instruments in digital sound cannot go far wrong here.

Serenades Nos. 1 in D, K.100; 10 in B flat for 13 Wind Instruments (Gran Partita), K.361.

*** BIS CD 1010. Tapiola Sinf., Kantorow.

The Tapiola Sinfonietta under Jean-Jacques Kantorow gives a finely paced and splendidly phrased account of the great *Wind Serenade* and a delightfully vital account of the *D major Serenade*, K.100, lightly accented and full of character and wit. They make more of this piece than many of their rivals, and they get superb recording from the BIS team. Very recommendable.

(i) Serenade No. 7 in D (Haffner), K.250; (ii) Divertimento for Winds in B flat, K.186.

(B) ** DG Eloquence (ADD) 469 755-2. (i) Berlin PO, Boehm; (ii) VPO Wind Ens.

The Berlin orchestra plays with such polish and refinement of tone in the *Haffner Serenade* and the (1972) recording is so perfectly balanced that one is inclined to overlook a certain dourness on the part of Boehm – he is a shade wanting in sparkle and sense of enjoyment. The coupling with the slight but charming wind *Divertimento* rather shows up the weakness of Boehm's performance: the former is a delectably stylish performance, full of sparkle and wit, and is well recorded.

Serenade No. 10 for 13 Wind Instruments, K.361.

(BB) **(*) Hyp. Helios CDH 55093. Albion Ens.

Serenade No. 10 in B flat (Gran Partita), K.361; Adagio in B flat for 2 Clarinets and 3 Bassett Horns, K.484a.

*** MDG 301 1077-2. Consortium Classicum.

The Consortium Classicum continues to enhance its reputation as a group outstanding in musicianship and sensitivity, and their performance of the *Gran Partita* is among the finest on disc. The CD begins with a rarity, the *Adagio in B flat for Two Clarinets and Three Bassett Horns*, K.484a, which Mozart probably wrote at the end of the 1785 for Masonic friends, Anton David and Vincent Springer – and the Stadler brothers. K.361 is a serenade with a difference. The 12 wind instruments, including bassett horns, plus double-bass would not have been easy to assemble outside Vienna, and Franz Gleissner (1759–1818) arranged it for more conventional forces renaming it 'Sinfonie concertante pour deux violins, flûte, deux hautbois, deux clarinettes, deux bassons, deux Cors, Alto & basso arrangé d'après une grande Sérénade pour les instruments à vent de Mozart'. The title obviously indicates that as far as Gleissner was concerned the work was much more than a Serenade. There are unusual touches: the first trio of the second movement and the theme in the variation movement are for strings alone. They are very well recorded, too. Most readers would not want to hear this very often, but it is well worth investigating.

The Albion Ensemble give a most enjoyable account of Mozart's large scale *Serenade*, finely blended and polished and with the outer movements enjoyably robust and spirited. There is some very fine oboe playing, and Andrew Marriner's clarinet is noticeably elegant in the penultimate *Theme and Variations*. Elsewhere there are moments when the mellifluous playing has rather less character, although it never becomes bland. Marriner's ASMF version remains first choice in this work (Philips 412 726-2), but that is at full price, so the present disc is certainly competitive on the Helios budget label.

Serenades Nos. 11, K.375; 12, K.388; Overtures: Le nozze di Figaro (arr. Vent); Don Giovanni (arr. Triebensee); Die Zauberflöte (arr. Heidenreich).

(BB) *** Hyp. Helios CDH 55092. E. Concert Winds.

Hyperion have now reissued on their budget Helios label one of the most enjoyable CDs of Mozart's wind music to have appeared in the last decade (the recording date was 1996). Both *Serenades* are among the finest on disc and the *Overtures* are great fun. Fresh spirited playing throughout, firmly focused and well-blended sound, both from the players and from the engineers. A delight.

(i) Sinfonia concertante in E flat, K.364; (ii) Duo for Violin and Viola in G, K.423.

(M) **(*) Decca (ADD) 470 258-2 (2). D. Oistrakh; (i) Moscow PO, Kondrashin; (ii) I. Oistrakh – BRUCH: *Scottish Fantasia*; HINDEMITH: *Violin Concerto*. ***

The performance by the Oistrakh duo is not notable for its relaxed manner. Everything is shaped most musically, but sometimes the listener might feel that the performers in their care for detail and concern for the balance are less involved in the music itself. However, with solo playing of a high calibre the music-making is still rewarding, and the 1963 recording sounds well in this new Legends transfer.

SYMPHONIES

Symphonies Nos. 1 in E flat, K.16; in F, K.19a; 5 in B flat, K.22; in G, K.45a; 6 in F, K.43; 7 in D, K.45; 8 in D, K.48; 9 in C, K.73; in F, K.76; in B flat, K.45b; in D, K.81; in D, K.97; in D, K.95; 10 in G, K.74; 11 in D, K.84; in B flat, K. Anh. 214; in F, K.75; in C, K.96; 12 in G, K.110; 13 in F, K.112; 14 in A, K.114; 15 in G, K.124; 16 in C, K.128; 17 in G, K.129; 18 in F, K.130; 19 in E flat, K.132; 20 in D, K.133; 21 in A, K.134; 22 in C, K.162; 23 in D, K.181; 24 in B flat, K.182; 25 in G min., K.183l 26 in E flat, K.184; 27 in G, K.199; 28 in C, K.200; 29 in A, K.201; 31 in D (Paris), K.297; 32 in G, K.318; 33 in B flat, K.319; 34 in C, K.338; 35 in D, K.385 (Haffner); 36 in C (Linz), K. 425; 38 in D (Prague), K.504; 39 in E flat, K.543; 40 in G min., K. 550; 41 in C (Jupiter), K. 551.

(B) *** DG 471 666-2 (7). E. Concert, Pinnock.

This is repertoire that Hogwood pioneered on original instruments in a most arresting way. But Pinnock's Mozartian enterprise has the advantage of some years' experience of authentic performance, and certain exaggerated elements have been absorbed into a smoother, but not less vital, playing style. Moreover, players have accommodated themselves to 'authentic' manners, and intonation improved considerably. So in these early 1990s performances we have greater polish, smoother and less edgy violins, and even a hint of vibrato. Slow movements have more lyrical feeling. The early symphonies show the remarkable advance from the childhood works, which are often rather engaging, to those symphonies written at the beginning of the 1770s when a recognizable Mozartian personality was formed. The invigorating later 'Salzburg' Symphonies which Pinnock recorded next (Nos. 16–29) were a splendid follow-up. The playing has polish and sophistication, fine intonation, spontaneity and great vitality, balanced by warm, lyrical feeling in the slow movements. Indeed, the account of No. 29 in A is amongst the finest available and the earlier *A major* work (No. 21) is very impressive too, as is the *G minor*, K.183, and the very 'operatic' No. 23 in D. In the later symphonies, Pinnock's performances stand out from other period performances, and the masterpieces from the *Paris* to the *Jupiter* can be warmly recommended, and not only to period enthusiasts. It is the joy and exhilaration in Mozart's inspiration that consistently bubble out from these accounts, even from the dark *G minor* or the weighty *Jupiter*. The rhythmic lift which Pinnock consistently finds is infectious throughout, magnetizing the ear from the start of every movement, and few period performances are as naturally and easily expressive as these. Allegros are regularly on the fast side but never hectically so, and it is a measure of Pinnock's mastery that when in a slow movement such as that of the *Prague* he chooses an unusually slow speed, there is no feeling of dragging. Where Gardiner in these same works exaggerates the dynamic contrasts, Pinnock keeps them firmly in the the eighteenth-century tradition, with textural contrasts more clearly integrated. These performances are billed as being 'directed from the harpsichord', but that continuo instrument is never obtrusive, and one can only register surprise that such subtlety and exuberance have been achieved without a regular conductor. Clear, well-balanced sound throught the series (though in some the orchestra placed more distantly than others), which is an obvious primary recommendation for those wanting period-instrument performances, especially at its new bargain price.

Symphony No. 29 in A, K. 201.

(**(*)) Testament mono SBT 2242 (2). Royal Danish O, Klemperer – BEETHOVEN: *Symphony No. 3; Leonore No. 3*; BRAHMS: *Symphony No. 4* (**(*)).

In Klemperer's live recording of No. 29 with the Royal Danish Orchestra, made in 1954, the opening Allegro moderato is characteristically slow and square, heavy despite the thin orchestral sound. But the last three movements are quite different, with the Andante refined and beautifully moulded at a flowing tempo, the Minuet light and tripping and the finale exhilarating in its energy. However, as in the other two items from the same concert on the first of the discs in this set, the coughing of the audience is distracting.

Symphony No. 31 in D (Paris), K.297.

(BB) *** Regis RRC 1084. E. Sinfonia, Groves – HAYDN: *Symphonies Nos. 92 (Oxford); 104 (London).* ***

Sir Charles Groves's account of the *Paris Symphony* is mellow and relaxed, with a beautifully played slow movement and finely observed detail. The playing is alert, but the unhurried pacing brings out the music's breadth. The Abbey Road recording is excellent: warm yet clear.

Symphonies Nos. 31 in D, (Paris) K.297; 34 in C, (Salzburg) K.338; 35 in D, (Haffner) K.385; 36 in C, (Linz) K.425; 38 in D, (Prague) K.504; 41 in C, (Jupiter) K.551.

(B) **(*) Erato Ultima 8573 85667-2 (2). Amsterdam Bar. O, Koopman.

Koopman's somewhat arbitrary 1992 collection of six of Mozart's middle and late symphonies is certainly bracing, with his lively orchestral playing and telling period detail in the timpani and brass. It is all generally invigorating, with the sound vivid, yet warm and well-balanced. Only in the *Jupiter Symphony* is there a feeling that in this authentic approach the music is robbed of some of its greatness. The clipped rhythms,

too, may take a while for some to get used to, but most will find there is more to enjoy than criticize.

Symphonies Nos. 33 in B flat, K.319; 35 in D (Haffner), K.385.

(M) *** Hänssler CD 94.003. ASMF, Brown.

These are spirited, sparkling performances, full of life and warmth. They were recorded in the Henry Wood Hall in 1997, and Andrew Keener has succeeded in getting a very good, natural and well-balanced sound. This CD delights, though it is short measure at 40 minutes even at mid-price. There are no liner notes.

Symphony No. 35 (Haffner).

(M) *** BBC Legends BBCL 4076-2. Hallé O, Barbirolli – BEETHOVEN: *Symphony No.7* ***; WAGNER: *Siegfried Idyll* (***).

Barbirolli's view of the *Haffner Symphony* is just as characterful as the Beethoven *Seventh* with which it is coupled on this BBC Legends issue. Recorded at the Royal Albert Hall during the Prom season, the sound is rather thick and dull, due in part to the string section being larger than we might expect today. Even so, Barbirolli's characteristic pointing of phrase and rhythm remains very compelling, leading to an effervescent account of the finale. The Wagner item also adds to this striking portrait of the conductor.

Symphonies Nos. 35 in D (Haffner), K.385; 38 in D (Prague), K.504; 39 in E flat, K.543; 40 in G min., K.550; 41 in C (Jupiter), K.551.

(B) *** Ph. Duo 470 540-2 (2). Dresden State O, Colin Davis.

These performances date from 1981 (39 and 41) and 1988 (35, 38 and 40). Though Colin Davis favours big-scaled Mozart he opts for fastish allegros, and the refinement of the playing helps to make up for the bass-heavy thickness of the Dresden sound as recorded by engineers. The dramatic opening of the *Haffner* is made very weighty indeed. In the slow movements of both the *Haffner* and *Prague*, Davis is less detached than he sometimes used to be in Mozart, more obviously affectionate, yet without sentimentality. Davis has recorded the *Jupiter* more than once and this version is all one would expect: alert, sensitive, perceptive and played with vitality and finesse by the Dresden Orchestra. The *E flat Symphony* was one of the finest on the market at the time of its release, and there is no reason to modify that view. If the *G minor* may seem a little weighty to some, its relaxed manner and the superbly refined and elegant playing ensure the full power of the work is fully conveyed. The warm, reverberant (though detailed) Dresden acoustic throughout suits Davis's conception of this music.

Symphonies Nos. 38 (Prague); 39; 40; 41 (Jupiter).

(B) ** Virgin 2 CD VBD5 62010-2. L. Classical Players, Norrington.

Norrington's readings have many individual points of detail, which – even if not all are convincing – bring the sense of a fresh approach, and his players are certainly at one with him. Exposition repeats are included throughout, and after a strong, grave introduction the first movement of the *Prague* is taken at a lively but not exaggerated pace, and if tuttis are somewhat fierce the second subject has warmth and elegance. The *Andante* too flows agreeably and the finale has plenty of energy and bite. *No. 40 in G minor* opens briskly, but is so lightly articulated that there is no sense of hurry until the slow movement, which is surely not relaxed enough. The Minuet is curiously mellow and unpointed, but the finale combines neatness with energy.

However, on the second disc the measured introduction to No. 39 is so fast that it is barely recognizable. The result is again refreshingly different, but totally misses the grandeur which is implicit in the piece. Other speeds are disconcertingly fast too, although the central movements of the *Jupiter* flow agreeably and the finale, if explosive, certainly has weight. Those who want period performances of these masterpieces that are characterful rather than purely tasteful will find Norrington's way specific, but less eccentric than say, Harnoncourt. He is very well recorded. However, collectors wanting outstanding versions of Mozart's late symphonies (35, 36, 38 and 39–41) should turn to Virgin's 5-disc super-bargain box where Menuhin's performances with the Sinfonia Varviso are outstanding in every way. (VBD5 61678-2 – see our main volume, p.854).

CHAMBER MUSIC

(i) *Clarinet Quartet in B flat* (trans. of *Violin Sonata, K.327d*); (ii) *Oboe Quartet in F, K.370*; *String Quartet No. 21 in D, K.575*.

(BB) **(*) HM Classical Express HCX 3957 107. (i) Hoeprich; (ii) Marc Schachman; Artaria Qt.

The transcription of the *Violin Sonata*, K.327d into a *Clarinet Quartet* is a surprising success, and the work sounds for all the world as if it was written for the present combination, particularly in the jocular finale. The more so as the clarinettist, Erich Hoeprich, is a most personable and musical player. Marc Schachman's creamy yet nicely pointed oboe playing is also just right for the *Oboe Quartet*, a most spirited, expressive performance that is among the best on record. Without soloists the Artaria Quartet give an accomplished account of the *First Prussian Quartet*, enjoyable if not distinctive. But the recording is first-class, and the other two works make this disc well worth investigating at bargain price

Clarinet Quintet in A, K.581.

(BB) *** Warner Apex 0927 44350-2. Leister, Berlin Soloists – BRAHMS: *Clarinet Quintet*. ***

Simplicity is the keynote of Karl Leister's 1988 performance, but in the lovely slow movement he finds a gentle reflective serenity that creates a mood of elysian rapture with his string group supporting him most sensitively. The Minuet makes a strong rhythmic contrast so that the final variations can again charm the ear with their combination of lyricism and high spirits. The coda is then presented as a light-hearted culmination. Very good recording and a modest price make this coupling, with an equally fine account of the Brahms, very recommendable indeed.

Divertimento in E flat for String Trio, K.563; Duo for Violin and Viola in B flat, K.424.

*** Hyp. CDA 67246. Leopold String Trio.

Here is a completely natural performance of Mozart's *E flat Divertimento* and the first for some years that can come close to approaching the celebrated Grumiaux Trio version, which has served us so well for the past three decades. Marianne Thorsen and Scott Dickinson give a first rate account of the *B flat Duo*, K.424. Very lifelike recording, totally at the service of Mozart and the musicians.

Divertimento No. 17 in D, K.334 (Chamber version).

(**) Pearl mono GEMD 129. Vienna Octet (members) – SCHUBERT: *Piano Quintet (Trout)*. (**)

In the 1955 edition *The Record Guide* gave both the recordings on the Pearl disc two stars, their highest accolade. The Mozart appeared in one of Decca's earliest LP supplements at the end of 1950. The second repeat of the Trio in the minuet is not observed and there are two cuts in the finale, one of them substantial and both unwelcome. But those who recall the Vienna Octet's broadcasts and records of this period will relish the elegance and grace of their playing. Roger Beardsley has gone to great trouble in his remastering to do justice to these performances. He claims that now for the first time they can be heard to far better effect than in the early 1950s and to those who recall hearing them will recognise a great improvement.

Flute Quartets Nos. 1–4; Rondo in G, K.494 (arr. Bearb).

(M) ** DG 445 606-2. Wincenc, Emerson Qt.

The Emersons' 1991 recording of the *Flute Quartets* is musical and immaculately performed, with a consistently rich tone from both the flautist, Carol Wincenc, and the strings. However, there is a distinct feeling of glossiness here: the rich, plush recorded sound is almost too much of a good thing, and the overall effect is a little cloying. The short but pleasing bonus is an arrangement of a solo piano piece, but first choice for the *Flute Quartets* rests with Emmanuel Pahud, who gives inspired performances in which he is joined by fellow members of the Berlin Philharmonic (EMI CDC5 56829-2).

Horn Quintet, K.407; Oboe Quartet, K.370; Piano and Wind Quintet, K.452; Quintet Movement, K.580b.

*** Hyp. CDA 67277. Gaudier Ens.

With superb soloists drawn from leading orchestras, notably the Chamber Orchestra of Europe, the Gaudier Ensemble here offers an ideal Mozart coupling of four wind-based chamber works. The oboist, Douglas Boyd, brings out the depth in the D minor slow movement of the *Oboe Quartet* as well as the fun of the outer movements, while Jonathan Williams is brilliant in the *Horn Quintet*, with the more ambitious *Piano and Wind Quintet*, in which Susan Tomes is the outstanding pianist, providing the anchor point. The rarity is the *Quintet Movement* for the unusual grouping of clarinet, basset horn and string trio, a magnificent piece, left unfinished at Mozart's death and here completed by Duncan Druce.

(i) Horn Quintet; String Quartet No. 19 in C (Dissonance), K.465; (ii) String Quintet No. 4 in G min., K.516.

(BB) (***) Dutton mono CDBP 9717. (i) Brain; (ii) Gilbert (viola); Griller Qt.

This further outstanding disc of Mozart chamber music from the Griller Quartet offered in the Dutton bargain series, superbly transferred, demonstrates again the strength and refinement of this leading quartet of the post-war period, largely neglected by record companies during the age of the LP. The *G minor Quintet* is outstanding, with excellent sound, while it is also good to have the *Horn Quintet* in another vintage performance with Dennis Brain as soloist.

Piano Quartets Nos. 1 in G min., K.478; 2 in E flat, K.493.

(M) *** Sony SMK 89794. Ax, Stern, Laredo, Ma.

The grouping of star names by Sony offers performances of keen imagination and insight, with the line-up of three string soloists bringing extra individuality compared with members of a string quartet. Speeds are beautifully chosen and in both works the performances consistently convey a sense of happy spontaneity. It is striking that Emanuel Ax, in the many passages in which the piano is set against the strings, establishes the sort of primacy required, pointing rhythms and moulding phrases persuasively. The recording, made in the Manhattan Center, New York, in 1994, is a degree drier than in many previous versions, suggesting a small rather than a reverberant hall. This has now been reissued at mid price which increases its claims to be considered a front runner among several other excellent accounts.

Piano Trios Nos. 1 in B flat, K.254; 2 in G, K.496; 3 in B flat, K.502.

(BB) **(*) HM Classical Express HCX 3957033. Mozartean Players.

Fresh, unaffected performances from the Mozartean Players, an American period-instrument group from the New York State University at Purchase. Steven Lubin leads attractively on a copy of a Viennese fortepiano of 1785 and the balance is excellent. Undoubtedly enjoyable but not especially individual.

String Quartets Nos. 14–19 (Haydn Quartets); 20 (Hoffmeister), K.499; 21–23 (Prussian Nos. 1-3).

(BB) *** CRD (ADD) CRD 5005 (5). Chilingirian Qt.

These splendid Chilingirian recordings on modern instruments have long been praised by us and rank among the freshest and most spontaneous performances in the catalogue. They are still second to none among versions using modern instruments, and at budget price this well-documented box is very highly recommendable.

String Quartets Nos. 14–19 (Haydn Quartets).

**(*) DG 471 024-2 (3). Hagen Qt.

The Hagens' set of the six Mozart *Quartets* dedicated to Haydn has been highly praised in the record press, understandably so, in the sense that their ensemble playing is impeccable and the level of accomplishment in terms of tonal blend and beauty of sound is second to none. But not everyone will feel at home with them: they are *very* self-conscious and overstate every dynamic shading whether marked or superimposed; the accents in the second movement of the *G major*, K.387 are exaggerated. Throughout one finds one's attention drawn to the artists and not Mozart. Other respected critics have derived much more pleasure from them, and the recordings made at various times between 1995 and 2000 are certainly exemplary and the balance expertly judged (as one would expect from Wolfgang Mitlehner). They cannot but inspire admiration but their sensibility is at variance with Mozart's naturalness of utterance. The Chilingirians or the Leipzig Quartet are to be preferred.

String Quartets Nos. 17 (Hunt); 19 (Dissonance).

✪ (BB) *** Warner Apex (ADD) 0927 40828-2. Alban Berg Qt.

*** MDG 307 1107-2. Leipzig Qt.

The Alban Berg Quartet recorded the *Hunt* in 1979 and it still ranks among the very finest accounts on disc. It has much greater polish and freshness even than the *Italian Quartet*, and well withstands all the competition that has come since. The *Dissonance* is of similar vintage. It, too, is first-class with a wonderfully expressive account of the slow movement. Although dynamic graduations are steep, there is no sense of exaggeration – on the contrary, there is only a sense of total dedication about these wholly excellent performances which are recommended with enthusiasm. No reservations about the transfers either, and this Apex reissue is a marvellous bargain.

The Leipzig Quartet continue their excellent performances of Mozart's Haydn Quartets by pairing the two most famous works. As with their equally fine coupling of Nos. 14 and 15 (MDG 307 1035-2 – see our main Guide), these are most musicianly performances, strikingly fresh and free from the slightest trace of affectation and full of vital musical feeling. This series ranks alongside the finest modern instrument performances, for the recording although fairly close, is naturally balanced.

String Quartets Nos. 20 in D (Hoffmeister), K.499; 22 in B flat, K.589.

(BB) *** Hyp. Helios CDH 55094. Salomon String Qt.

The Salomon Quartet have impeccable ensemble and a real sense of style; they use vibrato judiciously and with taste. There is no lack of finesse or vitality, and if you want period-instrument performances of these two works, the present inexpensive CD could be a good choice. The recording is real and shows the transparency of texture these instrumentalists achieve, while blending beautifully together.

(i) String Quintets Nos. 1–6; Divertimento for String Trio in E flat, K. 563.

(B) *** Ph. Trio (ADD) 470 950-2 (3). Grumiaux Trio; (i) with Gérecz, Lesueur.

String Quintets Nos. 1 in B flat, K.174; 6 in E flat, K.614.

*** MDG 304 1031-2. Ensemble Villa Musica.

String Quintets Nos. 2 in C min., K.406; 3 in C, K.515.

*** MDG 304 1032-2. Ensemble Villa Musica.

String Quintets Nos. 4 in G min., K.516; 5 in D, K.593.

*** MDG 304 1106-2. Ensemble Villa Musica.

On this bargain-priced Trio, Grumiaux's distinguished 1973 set of the String Quintets is coupled with his unsurpassed 1967 version of the rather less well-known but equally inspired Divertimento for String Trio – an ideal linking. The remastering of these fine analogue recordings is outstandingly natural – a tribute to the Philips engineers, for the bloom on the original LPs remains on CD, yet detail is enhanced.

A fine new modern-instrument set of the Mozart Quintets comes from the Ensemble Villa Musica, led by Rainer Kussmaul, each disc available separately. The first, with the B flat and E flat Quintets, is particularly fine; the second is very nearly as good with the outer movements of K.515 standing out and the finale of K.406 equally felicitous (as indeed are the lightly played finales of all six works). The third includes a very impressive account of the G minor. For those wanting modern-instrument performances of these works in excellent digital recordings this can be recommended. The recording is real and present, although the balance lets Kussmaul's principal violin rather dominate the proceedings. The older recordings by the Grumiaux ensemble (see above) and the Talich (CAL 3231/3) are not surpassed.

Solo piano music

Adagio in B min., K.540; Eine kleine Gigue, K.574; Fantasy Fragment in D min., K.397; Klavierstücke in F, K.33b; Kleiner Trauermarsch, K.453a; Modulation Prelude in F/E min., KV 6 Deest; Overture, K.399; Prelude in C, K.284a; Prelude and Fugue in C, K.394; Rondos, K.485 & K.511; Variations, K.24; K.25; K.180; K.264; K.265; K.352; K.353; K.354; K.398; K.455; K.457; K.460; K.573 K.613.

(B) *** BIS CD 1266/676 (4). Brautigan (fortepiano).

Ronald Brautigan's set is extraordinarily refreshing. It is bursting with life and intelligence. He uses a 1992 copy (made in his native Amsterdam) of a fortepiano by Anton Gabriel Walter from about 1795. It is a very good instrument and he is a very good player. Dip in anywhere in this set and you will be rewarded with playing of great imagination and sensitivity - not to mention sureness and agility of mind and fingers. At every turn he commands both delicacy and vitality, and he is completely inside the Mozartian sensibility of the period. Even if you prefer Mozart's keyboard music on the piano, you should investigate this set without delay. It brings Mozart to life in a way that almost no other period-instrument predecessor has done. It starts off very well from the early C major Sonata, K.279, with playing that sparkles and delights, and continues as it has begun. This series has given great pleasure as it has emerged over the last couple of years and it is beautifully recorded too. It could not be more recommendable now that the four CDs have reappeared offered for the price of two in a box, and very well documented.

Piano Sonatas Nos. 10 in C, K. 330; 11 in A, K.331; 12 in F, K. 332.

(BB) **(*) EMI Encore CDE5 74983-2. Zacharias.

EMI have chosen well from Christian Zacharias's series of the Mozart sonatas, for all three works here show him in very good form. Even if at times he is a shade self-aware, both K.331 (with its sparkling Alla Turca Finale) and the F major, K.332, are played with real character. This gifted artist is an intelligent, cultured player with an immaculate technique and he is most naturally recorded.

Piano sonatas Nos. 12 in F, K.332; 13 in B flat, K.333; Adagio in B min., K. 540; Theme & 5 Variations in C min., K.457.

** Ph. 488 048-2. Brendel.

Superbly recorded piano tone from the Philips engineers, but curiously didactic and studied playing from this great pianist, which is completely uninvolving.

VOCAL MUSIC

Concert arias: Alma grande e nobil core, K.578; Ch'io mi scordi di te?, K.505; Nehmt meinen Dank, K.383;

Vado, ma dove?, K.583. **Lieder:** *Abendempfindung; Als Luise die Briefe; Die Alte; An Chloë; Dans un bois solitaire; Im Frühlingsanfang; Das Kinderspiel; Die kleine Spinnerin; Das Lied der Trennung; Oiseaux, si tous les ans; Ridente la calma; Sehnsucht nach dem Frühling; Das Trumbild; Das Veilchen; Der Zauberer; Die Zuhfriedenheit.*

(M) *** EMI mono/stereo CDZ5 74803-2. Schwarzkopf, Gieseking, Brendel, LSO, Szell.

A very welcome reissue on EMI's References label of Schwarzkopf's classic recital of the Mozart songs with Gieseking, recorded in 1955, and including the famous *Das Veilchen*. With such inspired performances, one hardly worries about the mono sound, which remains fully acceptable in this transfer. The coupling includes Schwarzkopf's much later recordings (1968) of four concert arias with Szell conducting – including the most taxing of all, *Ch'io mi scordi di te*. Though the voice is not quite so fresh here, the artistry and imagination are supreme, and the stereo recording helps to add bloom. Thankfully, full texts and translations are included in this mid-price release.

OPERA

La clemenza di Tito (complete).

*(**) Arthaus **DVD** 100 406. Langridge, Putnam, Montague, Mahe, Szmytka, Rose, Glyndebourne Festival Ch., LPO, A. Davis. (Producer: Nicholas Hytner.)

Recorded at Glyndebourne during the 1991 festival, this Arthaus DVD version of Mozart's last opera is superbly sung by an outstanding cast, with conducting by Andrew Davis that brings out the charm as well as the power of this *opera seria*. Among the soloists there is no weak link. The singing is consistently firm, clear and stylish, with Philip Langridge masterly in the title role, Ashley Putnam superb as Vitellia and Diana Montague most moving as Sesto. In place of the usual recitatives (not by Mozart) new ones have been provided by Stephen Oliver, though some of them seem very long, notably the five-minute stretch immediately after the overture and before the first duet between Sesto and Vitellia.

However, as so often with modern opera productions, Nicholas Hytner's staging, with stylized geometric sets by David Fielding, will not be to all tastes, and the flat backdrops, often decorated with torn wallpaper effects, have their bizarre side. The Roman costumes are relatively conventional, even if the long swirling skirts for male characters sung by women are very questionable. Excellent sound, but this can only be recommended with considerable visual reservations.

Don Giovanni (complete).

(B) **(*) Double Decca 470 059-2 (2). Hågegard, Cachemaille, Augér, Terfel, Bonney, Jones, Sigmundsson, Drottningholm Court Theatre Ch. & O, Ostman.

(*) Sony **DVD SVD 46383. Ramey, Tomowa-Sintow, Varady, Battle, Winbergh, Furlanetto, Malta, Burchuladze; V. St. Op. Ch., VPO, Karajan. (Director: Michael Hampe. V/D: Claus Viller.)

(M) ** Decca (ADD) 470 427-2 (3). Weikl, M. Price, Burrows, Sass, Bacquier, Popp, Sramek, Moll, London Op. Ch., LPO, Solti.

Ostman followed up his earlier recordings of *Così fan tutte* and *Le nozze di Figaro* with this (originally Oiseau-Lyre) period performance of *Don Giovanni*. This time, with a far darker score, he modified his stance. Though speeds are still often fast, this time they rarely seem breathless. Håkan Hågegard as Giovanni could be sweeter-toned, but his lightness and spontaneity, particularly in exchanges with the vividly alive Leporello of Gilles Cachemaille, are most winning, with recitative often barely vocalized. Arleen Augér is a radiant Donna Anna, while Della Jones is a full-toned Elvira and Bryn Terfel a resonant Masetto. Understandably, the original Prague text is used and the bonus arias (Ottavio's *Dalla sua pace* and Elvira's *Mi tradi*) are included on this bargain Double Decca release on a pair of CDs.

The Sony DVD offers one of Karajan's final productions at Salzburg and was recorded during a performance at the 1987 Festival. It first appeared on video and on LaserDisc, where it occupied three sides as opposed to a single double-sided DVD here. There are some impressive things. The Donna Anna of Anna Tomowa-Sintow and the Donna Elvira of Julia Varady are splendidly matched and both vocally and dramatically commanding: it is probably worth having solely for them. The Leporello of Ferruccio Furlanetto is vivacious, and has a dramatic flair that seems to elude Samuel Ramey's Don.

Kathleen Battle's Zerlina is better sung than acted but for the most part this is a satisfying performance, certainly superior to the *Don* that Karajan recorded in Berlin for DG two years earlier with an almost identical cast (save for the Elvira, who was Baltsa). Some have found Karajan a little stiff, but there is no question as to the tonal splendour of the Vienna Philharmonic or the dignity and spaciousness of his reading. The visual presentation is excellent, as indeed is the well-balanced sound. There are subtitles in English, German and French.

Solti's is a crisp, incisive account, with generally fast tempi and very well-directed recitatives. If it shows no special signs of affection, it contains one glorious performance in Margaret Price's Anna, pure in tone and line but powerfully dramatic too, always beautiful. Next to her, Sylvia Sass, as a somewhat gusty Elvira, sounds rather miscast, characterful though her singing is. The two baritones, Bernd Weikl and Gabriel Bacquier, are clearly contrasted as Giovanni and Leporello respectively, though the microphones are not kind to either. The recording is brilliant, achieving realistic clarity. This has now been reissued at mid-price as part of Decca's 'Compact Opera Collection'. However, there is no printed libretto, only a CD-

ROM facility which carries full text and translation (which can be printed out via a computer), and in any case the set is hardly a front runner.

The Abduction from the Seraglio (Die Entführung aus dem Serail; complete in English).

❂ (M) *** Chan. 3081 (2). Dodds, Eddy, Gedda, Fryatt, Mangin, Kelsey, Amb. S., Bath Festival O., Y. Menuhin.

Menuhin's set of The Abduction from the Seraglio in English is one of the most enjoyable of all the Opera in English series promoted by the Peter Moores Foundation. Recorded originally by EMI in 1967, it stemmed directly from a staged production at the Bath Festival, of which Menuhin was then the musical director. He makes the performance sparkle from first to last, favouring brisk, well-lifted allegros, so that the fun of the piece comes over vividly. Crowning this, you have Wendy Toye's lively production, using witty spoken dialogue by Hugh Mills with helpful sound-effects, to make an overwhelming case for Mozart opera in English.

The acting of the principal singers is exceptionally fine too, with Noel Mangin superb as Osmin, commandingly comic yet believable too, not least when in duo with John Fryatt, an outstanding Pedrillo. Their drinking duet is hilarious as well as musically sparkling. Mangin sings magnificently, firm and dark over the widest register, while Fryatt crowns his performance with a wonderful, mock-heroic account of his big 'battle' aria, with fine, true attack. Nicolai Gedda, brought in as an international star, fully lives up to expectation, giving one of his finest Mozart performances, poised and stylish, his English accent flawless.

The American soprano, Mattiwilda Dobbs, similarly brought in as a star, uses her bright, agile coloratura brilliantly, not least in the second of her two big arias, Tortures Unrelenting (Martern aller Arten). The first of the two is deeply expressive, even if the voice does not quite soften as it should. Jennifer Eddy makes an enchanting Blonda, perfect as a defiant English girl, and again the dialogue helps. It is sad that illness brought a premature end to this lovely Australian soprano's career.

When it comes to style, it is the Menuhin touch which makes all the difference. With his own orchestra and a smaller band of strings than was usual in Mozart opera recordings at the time, his pointing of the music is equivalently subtle and refined, besides anticipating the scale of later period performances. There is a generous – but not too generous – allocation of dialogue, and as it is separately banded on CD it can be dispensed with if one wants the music alone; for the score is absolutely complete, with all Belmont's arias included (and the full text given in the booklet). What completes this as wonderful entertainment is the quality of the 1967 recording, as full and vivid as if it was recorded yesterday, the soundstage cleanly and atmospherically focused.

Idomeneo (complete).

*** EMI CDS5 57260-2 (3). Bostridge, Hunt Lieberson, Milne, Frittoli, Johnson, SCO, Mackerras.

Ian Bostridge with his heady tenor may seem too light a choice of singer for the title role in Mozart's great opera seria, but with his ever-illuminating feeling for words and his sensitive response to each phrase he brings the character vividly to life, with never a hint of strain. It is a magnetic performance, helped by the stylish and perceptive conducting of Sir Charles Mackerras, who contributes a highly informative note on his reading in the booklet. As he explains, in this recording he has opted for 'all of Mozart's original inspirations before he made any cuts or changes'. That gives a very full text, even if, unlike Gardiner on his DG Archiv version, he does not give alternatives in an appendix. It works very well indeed, with Mackerras's choice of speeds always excellent, and for the cadenzas and ornamentation he has used as his model cadenzas that Mozart wrote for arias by J. C. Bach. The secco recitatives are played by cello and harpsichord, and the result is a performance, strong, dramatic and expressive, which brings out the originality of instrumentation, a point that Mackerras highlights. The others in the cast are first rate, with Lorraine Hunt Lieberson a bright, strong Idamenta and Lisa Milne a charming, sweet-voiced Ilia and Barbara Frittoli a powerful Elettra. It is good too to have Anthony Rolfe Johnson, who takes the title role in the Gardiner version, singing very stylishly as Arbace, here given both his arias, often cut. This new set is probably a marginal primary recommendation, especially for those preferring modern instruments, but the Gardiner version must be enthusiastically recommended alongside it (❂ DG 431 674-2).

Le nozze di Figaro (complete).

*** DG DVD 073 018-9. Terfel, Hagley, Gilfry, Martinpelto, Monteverdi Ch., E. Bar. Sol., Gardiner.
(B) *** Warner NVC DVD 0630-14013-2. Finley, Hagley, Fleming, Schmidt, LPO, Haitink. (Producer: Stephen Medcalf; V/D: Derek Bailey.)
(BB) **(*) Arte Nova 74321 92759-2 (3). Youn, Steinberger, Schörg, Schmeckenbecher, Donose, Muraro, Vienna RSO and Ch., Bertrand de Billy.
(BB) *(*) Arte Nova 74321 77071-2 (3). Miliani, Antonucci, Frittoli, Dohmen, Minarelli, Facini, Macerata Fest. Ch., Marchigiana PO, Kuhn.
(BB) (**(*)) Naxos mono 8.110206/7. Mildmay, Helletsgruber, Rautavaara, Domgraf-Fassbänder, Henderson, Nash, Glyndebourne Fest. Ch. & O., Busch.
* TDK DVD DV-OPNDF (2). Gilfry, Mei, Rey, Chausson, Nikiteanu, Von Magnus, Holl, Vogel, Larsson, Zurich Op. House Ch. & O., Harnoncourt. (Producer: Jurgen Flimm.)

Like John Eliot Gardiner's CD version with the same forces, this DG DVD was recorded for video live, although at a different venue. Where the CDs were recorded at the Queen Elizabeth Hall in London, this staged version was made at the Théâtre du Châtelet in Paris, with economical but evocative sets. Simple screens illustrating each scene are dropped in front of a panoramic backcloth with trees and the Almaviva Palace in black silhouette against blue. Props as well as scenery are minimal but succeed in pointing the humour without distracting. The performance follows the splendid pattern of the CD version, with Terfel superb in the title role, already at his peak in 1993, leading a young and consistently attractive cast. As on CD the revised Moberly/Raeburn order of numbers for Act III is observed, and Gardiner's scholarly note arguing for an order reflecting key-relationships is also repeated from the CD set. Regrettably, no doubt for reasons of length, Marcellina's and Basolio's arias are omitted from Act IV, but otherwise this makes for an outstanding, consistently exhilarating presentation of the Mozart/Da Ponte masterpiece.

This Warner version must be one of the great bargains of DVD. At the time of writing it retails at £19.99, and you would not find it easy to get a CD version of any distinction at the price. And this *is* a performance of distinction, wonderfully conducted by Bernard Haitink and with four first-class principals. Gerald Finley's Figaro is expertly characterized and beautifully sung, and the same goes for both Renée Fleming's Countess and Alison Hagley's Susanna. The sets and staging are admirable in every way. It was with this production that the Glyndebourne Opera House reopened in May 1994 after its successful renovation. The three hours nine minutes are accommodated on one double-sided DVD, which accommodates two acts per side. There are subtitles in English, French and German, together with cast and character screens. The quality of the colour and the sharpness of focus are in the demonstration bracket and so, too, is the vivid, well-balanced sound. A most musically satisfying set and one of the handful of DVDs that should be in every serious collection.

Recorded in collaboration with Austrian Radio in August 2001, Arte Nova's second attempt at recording *Nozze di Figaro* in almost every way improves on the first. Though there are no star names in the cast, these young singers form an excellent team with no seriously weak link. Standing out is the characterful Figaro of the Korean, Kwangchoul Youn, resonant and full of fun but with a hint of menace in the voice. Like the others he responds well to the decision of the conductor, Bertrand de Billy – chief conductor of the Austrian Radio Orchestra in Vienna – to encourage extra elaborations and ornamentation in arias. So even *Non più andrai* includes little cadenzas, thrown off as though spontaneously, a pattern followed throughout the performance. As Susanna, Birgit Steinberger has an edge to the voice, but generally manages to control it convincingly, and Regina Schörg as the Countess similarly controls her rapid vibrato to produce tender accounts of her key numbers, not least her two big arias, taken at aptly flowing speeds. Schmeckenbecher's Count of Jochen is rather gruff, but the Cherubino of Ruxandra Donose is excellent, with the ornamentation on her arias crisp and stylish. De Billy keeps the music moving, even

refusing to relax in the Countess's crucial entry in the finale of Act IV, a rare misjudgement. A fortepiano is used for continuo instead of a harpsichord, and the studio recording is full and well balanced. With both Marcellina's and Basilio's arias included in Act IV, the third of the three discs is devoted entirely to that final Act. Unlike the earlier Arte Nova version this one offers full libretto and translations.

Recorded live at the Macerata Festival in Italy in 1993, but not issued till much more recently, Gustav Kuhn's alternative version of *Figaro* for Arte Nova promisingly offers two fine singers in the roles of Count and Countess, Albert Dohmen and Barbara Frittoli, but the vagaries of live recording, with voices set at a distance and inevitable slips, prevent even those leading singers from having the impact they should. The others make a disappointing team, with Stefano Milano wooden and faceless as Figaro and Paola Antonucci a shrill Susanna. Kuhn's speeds are often on the sluggish side – as in the Countess's *Porgi amor* in Act II – and with a simple synopsis in place of a libretto it is completely supplanted by the later Arte Nova version.

At the beginning of June 1934, only a few weeks after the very first Glyndebourne Festival, work was started on this pioneering recording of *Figaro*. It was recorded and later issued by HMV on short-playing 78 discs in batches, arias separate from ensembles, and surprisingly the finished set omitted secco recitatives. Even so, with a classic cast the performance is well worth hearing, for, though in the Naxos transfer the orchestra is relatively dim, the voices come over well. Willi Domgraf-Fassbänder, father of Brigitte, is the most characterful Figaro, a dominant personality, even if his Italian is idiosyncratic. Audrey Mildmay, wife of John Christie, founder of Glyndebourne, is a charming, refined Susanna, nicely contrasted with Aulikki Rautawaara as the Countess. It is good too to have Heddle Nash in the comic role of Basilio, not a side of his work generally heard on disc, and Roy Henderson is characterful too as the Count, if a little stiff, stressed as he is by the high tessitura of his big aria, and, like the others, by the often hectic speeds demanded from the overture onwards by the inspired Fritz Busch. A historic document well worth investigating at Naxos price.

Dating from 1996, this TDK version on two DVDs offers a live recording of *Figaro* from the Zurich Opera House with Nikolaus Harnoncourt proving surprisingly expansive, not what one expects of a conductor who initially worked in the field of period performance. Not only are his speeds slow from the overture onwards, with the Countess's *Porgi amor* depressingly so, the recitatives are so pauseful that the action often fails to catch fire. It does not help that the staging by Jurgen Flimm is so bizarre, updated to the nineteenth century with bald and ugly sets by Erich Wonder. So Susanna (Isabel Rey) pours tea over the very young-looking Marcellina (Elisabeth von Magnus) in their duet of insults, and instead of having a chair in Act I Cherubino and the Count hide on and under a bare bedstead. The garden scene of Act IV is then dotted inconsequently with modern deckchairs and garden furniture. The television direction by Felix Breisach compounds the problem by using more distance shots of the stage than usual. The singing and acting are variable too. Rodney Gilfry makes an upstanding Count, as he does for John Eliot Gardiner, but Eva Mei is an undistinguished Countess, too often tremulous, and Isabel Rey a shrill Susanna, with Carlos Chausson a stiffly unfunny Figaro. The only advantage of the two-disc format is that it allows the arias of Marcellina and Basilio in Act IV, often omitted, to be included. The recorded sound puts an edge on all the women's voices. Not recommended.

Le nozze di Figaro: highlights.

(BB) ** EMI Encore CDE5 74745-2. (from complete recording with Allen, Battle, Price, Hynninen, Murray, V. State Op. Ch., VPO, Muti).

Recorded in 1986, the Muti Vienna selection is disappointing for the cloudiness of the recording and the singing, from a starry line-up of soloists, is very variable. Commanding as Thomas Allen is as Figaro, this is not a comic figure, dark rather, and less than winning. Kathleen Battle is a sparkling Susanna, but Margaret Price's Countess is not as nobly distinctive as she might be, and Ann Murray makes a somewhat edgy Cherubino. Muti's pacing is sometimes too fast to convey a feeling for the comedy. This 70-minute selection gives a good idea of the character of the set, but the sparse synopsis is barely adequate.

Die Zauberflöte (complete).

(B) **(*) Decca 470 056-2 (2). Bonney, Jo, Streit, Cachemaille, Sigmundsson, Drottningholm Court Theatre Ch. & O, Ostman.
**(*) Arthaus DVD 100 188. Sonntag, Frei, Van der Walt, Mohr, Hauptmann, Connors (speaker), Ludwigsburg Festival Ch. & O, Gönnenwein. (Director: Axel Manthey. V/D: Ruth Kärch.)
**(*) DG DVD 073 003-9. Battle, Serra, Araiza, Hemm, Moll, Schmidt (speaker), Met. Op. Ch. & O., Levine. (Producers: Guus Mostart/John Cox; (V/D: Brian Large).

In contrast with his earlier Drottningholm recordings of Mozart operas, often rushed and brittle, Ostman (in his originally Oiseau-Lyre series) offers a far more sympathetic set of Die Zauberflöte. It may lack weight but it rarely sounds rushed, for Ostman consistently gives a spring to the rhythms and there is no weak link in the cast: Barbera Bonney is a charming Pamina, Kurt Streit a free-toned Tamino, and Gilles Cachemaille as Papageno is finely focused and full of fun. Sumi Jo is a bright, clear Queen of the Night and, though the Sarastro of Kristian Sigmundsson is lightweight, that matches the overall approach. It is now offered (without texts) at Double Decca price.

The cast is less starry and the production less glamorous on the Arthaus DVD than the DG discussed below, but it has a good deal more style and gives more pleasure. None of the singers with the exception

of Andrea Frei's Queen of the Night, who is inclined to be a little squally, falls seriously short of the highest standards and some are touched by considerable distinction – notably Ulrike Sonntag's Pamina and the Tamino of Deon van der Walt.

Musically there is not much wrong and a great deal right about this performance, which is well paced and sensitively conducted by Wolfgang Gönnenwein. It comes from the Ludwigsburger Festival of 1992. The staging has great simplicity and the sets and costumes are all in bright primary colours. And no production detail gets in the way of Mozart. Subtitles are in English, French and the original German.

The DG Zauberflöte is also pretty impressive. It derives from the Met's Mozart Bicentennial celebrations in 1991, and was issued on both video and LaserDisc but not on CD. It is not in the same league as the performances under Marriner, Gardiner, Boehm, Fricsay, Beecham and Karajan, under whom Araiza sang Tamino.

The best performances, however, are Kathleen Battle's Pamina, Manfred Hemm's Papageno and Kurt Moll's magisterial Sarastro. David Hockney's sets are an absolute delight, and though Levine does not always get a light or transparent texture from his players, there is still a lot of pleasure to be had.

Guus Mostart's adaptation of John Cox's production is pleasingly unobtrusive and Brian Large's visual direction up to his usual high standard. Though the quality of the picture does not match the definition and clarity of the BBC DVD of Coppélia or the Glyndebourne Figaro, it is still very impressive. Subtitles are in German, English, French and Mandarin.

Die Zauberflöte: highlights.

(BB) *** EMI Encore CDE5 74770-2. (from complete recording with Popp, Jerusalem, Gruberová, Lindner, Brendel, Bracht; cond. Haitink).

The selection from the Haitink set makes a fine bargain on the Encore label, including many favourites. The gravitas of Haitink's approach does not miss the work's charm and the quality of the singing is matched by outstanding, wide-ranging digital sound.

Arias from La clemenza di Tito; Le nozze di Figaro; Idomeneo; La finta giardiniera.

*** DG 471 334-2. Kozena, Prague Philh. O, Swierczewski – GLUCK: Arias from La clemenza di Tito; Paride e Elena; MYSLIVECEK: Arias from Abramo ed Isacco; L'Olimpiade. ***

The Czech mezzo, Magdalena Kozena, glamorous of voice as well as of appearance, is an outstanding stylist in whatever she sings, seemingly untroubled by any of the formidable technical challenges in this fascinating collection of arias. The familiar Mozart arias are superbly done, all made to sound fresh and new, even Cherubino's aria from Figaro. An outstanding disc with the valuable coupling of arias by Gluck and the underappreciated Mysliveček. Under Swierczewski the Prague Philharmonia equals the Czech Philharmonic in the refinement of their playing.

MUFFAT, Georg (1653–1704)

Concerti Grossi Nos. 1 in D min. (Good News); 2 in A (Watchful Heart); 3 in B (Convalescence); 4 in G min. (Sweet Sleep); 5 in D (The World); 6 in A min. (Who is This?).

(BB) ** Naxos 8.555096. Musica Aeterna Bratislava, Zajíček.

Concerti Grossi Nos. 7 in E (Delight of Kings); 8 in F (Noble Coronation); 9 in C min. (Sad Victory); 10 in G (Perseverance); 11 in E min. (Madness of Love); 12 in G (Propitious Constellations).

(BB) ** Naxos 8.555743. Musica Aeterna Bratislava, Zajíček.

The twelve *Concerti grossi* of Muffat are inventive works, in which the influences of both Corelli and Lully are much in evidence. There is plenty to enjoy in these pieces, written for court entertainment, which are melodic and well contrasted, with a few unexpected quirks of harmony and rhythm adding spice. The performances are good ones, stylish and lively, with attractive embellishments, but the recording is rather strident, with the strings not very ingratiating – the effect becomes a little tiring after a while. However, this pair of CDs come at a modest price and the repertoire is certainly worth exploring. Incidentally, the intriguing titles have little to do with the actual music, but refer to the occasions of their first performances.

MUSSORGSKY, Modest

(1839–81)

Night on the Bare Mountain (orch. Rimsky-Korsakov).

(BB) **(*) EMI Encore (ADD) CDE5 74763-2. Philh. O, Cluytens – RIMSKY-KORSAKOV: *Capriccio espagnol* etc.; BORODIN: *In the Steppes of Central Asia.* **(*)

An impressively dramatic performance from Cluytens, full of imaginative touches, dating from 1958 yet sounding astonishingly well in this transfer; only a touch of thinness by modern standards betrays its age, but the sound is beautifully balanced. Part of a highly attractive budget CD of Russian showpieces.

Night on the Bare Mountain; Khovanshchina: Prelude (both orch. Rimsky-Korsakov); *Pictures at an Exhibition.*

(B) ** EMI double fforte CZS5 75172-2 (2). Oslo PO, Jansons – RIMSKY-KORSAKOV: *Scheherazade; Capriccio espagnol.* **(*)

The highlight of Jansons' recording is the haunting *Khovanshchina Prelude* which is played most beauti-

fully, yet produces a passionate climax. *Night on the Bare Mountain* is diabolically pungent, but here, as in the *Pictures*, the fiercely brilliant EMI recording, with its dry bass and lack of sumptuousness, brings dramatic bite and sharply etched detail, but less in the way of expansiveness. The dark brass sonorities are well captured in *Catacombes* and the final climax is powerfully wrought and certainly spectacular as sound, but sonically this is less appealing than the finest versions.

Pictures at an Exhibition (orch. Ravel).

(B) ** CfP 575 5642. LPO, Pritchard – PROKOFIEV: *Romeo and Juliet* (ballet): highlights. **

(BB) (**(*)) Naxos mono 8.110154. Boston SO, Koussevitzky – RAVEL: *Boléro; Ma Mère l'Oye; Rapsodie espagnole.* (**)

** RCA 74321 72788-2. NDR SO, Wand – DEBUSSY: *Le Martyre de Saint Sébastien.* **

A well characterized account under Pritchard in which the personality of the orchestra comes over strongly, the players obviously enjoying themselves and their own virtuosity. The well-detailed 1970 recording, made in Barking Town Hall, makes every detail of the orchestration clear against a pleasing ambience, and the building up of *The Great Gate of Kiev* sequence provides an impressive finale. However, first choice remains with Karajan (DG 447 426-2).

Naxos offers the very first recording of Ravel's transcription of *Pictures at an Exhibition* under the baton of its 'onlie begetter'. Koussevitzky commissioned Ravel's score, and his reading has obvious authority and imaginative intensity. The 1930 recording is not ideal: the lustrous Boston strings sound a little hard and climaxes are at times congested, but Mark Obert-Thorn has improved on earlier transfers.

Pictures at an Exhibition (orch. Ravel); *Khovanshchina: Prelude to Act I* (arr. Shostakovich); *Night on the Bare Mountain* (arr. Rimsky-Korsakov); *Sorochinsky Fair: Gopak* (orch. Liadov).

**(*) Ph. 468 526-2. VPO, Gergiev.

This is a larger than life reading of Mussorgsky's *Pictures*, with the subtleties of colouring introduced by Ravel underplayed in favour of more earthy Russian flavours. Also, the coupling is an all-Mussorgsky programme, surprisingly rare with this much-recorded work. Recorded live in the Musikvereinsaal in Vienna, it brings brilliant playing, with the speeds in fast movements bringing an edge-of-the-seat feeling of perils just avoided. The opening *Promenade*, taken squarely, establishes the monumental Russian quality, enhanced by the immediacy of the sound. Even *The Hut on Fowls' Legs* seems larger than life, and the whole culminates in an account of *The Great Gate of Kiev* shattering in its weight and thrust. The regular Rimsky version of *Night on the Bare Mountain*, though not recorded live, brings a performance to compare in power with *Pictures*, with very weighty brass, and Shostakovich's orchestration of the

Khovanschina Prelude, though less evocative than it can be, is warm and refined, with the *Gopak* added as a lively encore.

(i) *Pictures at an Exhibition* (orch. Ravel); (ii) *Pictures at an Exhibition* (original piano version).

(M) *** Sony SMK 89615. (i) BPO, Giulini; (ii) Bronfman.

This is easily the finest coupling available of Ravel's inspired orchestration of Mussorgsky's picture gallery and the original piano version. Giulini's account of the orchestral score can be considered among the best accounts of the 1990s. Recorded in the Jesus Christus Kirche, Berlin, the sound is rich and spacious, the orchestral playing superb. The reading has a pervading sense of nostalgia which haunts the delicate portrayal of *The Old Castle* and even makes the wheedling interchange between the two Polish Jews more sympathetic than usual. In the lighter pieces the scherzando element brings a sparkling contrast, with the unhatched chicks cheeping piquantly, and there is sonorous solemnity for the *Catacombs* sequence. A powerful and weighty *Baba-Yaga*, yet with the bizarre element retained in the subtle rhythmic pointing in the middle section, leads naturally to a majestic finale, with the Berlin brass full-bloodedly resplendent, and the tam-tam flashing vividly at the climax.

Yefim Bronfman's account of the original piano score then matches Giulini's approach surprisingly closely. *The Old Castle*, beautifully graduated, is most poignant, there is strong characterization throughout and plenty of picaresque detail. Bronfman finds an added sense of fantasy in *Baba-Yaga* and the massive closing spectacle of *The Great Gate at Kiev* is viscerally thrilling, to give a genuine frisson when the piano recording is so full-bodied, and the playing so grand and powerful.

Songs and Dances of Death (orch. Shostakovich).

(B) *** EMI double fforte CZS5 75178-2. Lloyd, Phd. O, Jansons – SHOSTAKOVICH: *Piano Concerto No. 1; Symphonies Nos. 1 & 10.* **(*)**

Robert Lloyd gives a commanding and sonorous account of the Shostakovich transcription of Mussorgsky's gripping song cycle. But this is a fill-up for three Shostakovich performances, only one of which (an intense and powerful reading of the *Tenth Symphony*) is of a similar calibre.

Boris Godunov (1872 version).

✪ *** Ph. **DVD** 075 089-9 (2). Lloyd, Borodina, Steblianko, Leiferkus, Morosov, Ognovenko, Diadkova, Kirov Op. Ch. & O, Gergiev.

In 1990 the Covent Garden production of *Boris Godunov* directed by the Russian, Andre Tarkovsky, and rehearsed by Stephen Lawless, was adopted by the Mariinsky Theatre in St Petersburg. This two-disc DVD offers the resulting film, originally shown on BBC television, a magnificent presentation of the opera in the edition prepared by David Lloyd Jones using the original 1872 version of the score. Valery Gergiev conducts an outstanding Kirov Opera cast, joined in the title role by Robert Lloyd from Covent Garden, giving one of his greatest performances ever, strong and resonant and movingly acted. It is astonishing how the different incidental parts are cast from strength with star singers, each rising superbly to the challenge of a major scene – Pimen, Varlaam, Rangoni and the Simpleton (who sings his pathetic solo twice – in the first scene of Act IV and at the end). Olga Borodina is magnificent as Marina in the Polish scenes opposite the powerful Grigory of Alexei Steblianko, and even such a small part as Feodor, Boris's young son, is taken with passionate intensity by a then-rising star, Larissa Diadkova. Musically it would be hard to imagine a finer performance, even though recording balance sometimes has voices too distant and unrelated to close-up pictures. Visually it is superb too with the complex, episodic story told with extraordinary clarity, set on a simple but very grand stage, with a floor in false perspective, adding to the grandeur. Costumes are authentic and often colourful, with Tarkovsky's often stylized production bringing unforgettable moments, as when Rangoni comes and sits centre-stage at the end of the love scene between Marina and Grigory, and turns to give the most sinister stare as the curtain falls.

MYSLIVEČEK, Josef (1737–81)

Arias from: *Abramo ed Isacco; L'Olimpiade*.

*** DG 471 334-2. Kozena, Prague Philh. O, Swierczewski – GLUCK: Arias from *La clemenza di Tito; Paride e Elena*. MOZART: Arias from *La clemenza di Tito; Le nozze di Figaro; Idomeneo; La finta giardiniera*.

The Czech mezzo, Magdalena Kozena, an outstanding artist in every way, boldly offers four nicely contrasted arias by Myslivecek as a welcome fill-up for her disc of Mozart and Gluck arias. One of the most talented as well as most seriously neglected of Mozart's contemporaries, Myslivecek writes with consistent alertness and imagination, with Swierczewski and the Prague Philharmonia sensitive accompanists.

NABOKOV, Nicolas (1903–78)

(i) *Ode: Méditations sur la majesté de Dieu; Union Pacific*.

*** Chan. 9768. (i) Shaguch, Kisselev, Russian State Symphonic Cappella; Residentie O, The Hague, Polyansky.

Nicolas Nabokov studied with Vladimir Rebikov, leaving Russia in 1919 to continue working with Paul Juon and Busoni in Berlin. He moved to Paris in 1923 where he came into contact with Prokofiev, Stravinsky and Diaghilev, and the *Ode* was one of the great successes of Diaghilev's last season. It consists of ten loosely related movements and two interludes, much in the manner of Stravinsky's *Symphony of Psalms*, and was choreographed by Massine. But in spirit it is much closer to *Les Noces*, though it does not have the inventiveness or character of Stravinsky. *Union Pacific* was commissioned for Massine and the Ballets Russes to take to America, and although it enjoyed much success at the time, it disappeared from the repertoire, and it was only with difficulty that the composer traced the score. It is on the whole attractive, diatonic music influenced by 'Les Six', Prokofiev and the spirit of the 1920s. In its use of American popular music it is reminiscent of Berners' *Triumph of Neptune*.

Nicolas Nabokov is related to the novelist and poet Vladimir Nabokov, whose *Lolita* caused such a stir in the early 1960s. (When the composer announced himself at the foyer of Broadcasting House to a startled receptionist, he immediately reassured her, 'No, I am not the pornographer but his cousin, the uncle of Lolita!') The soloists Marina Shaguch and Alexander Kisselev, are first rate, as are the Russian State Symphonic Cappella. The Hague Residentie Orchestra respond well to Polyansky's direction, and the recording is in the finest traditions of the house, with well-focused detail and totally truthful.

NIELSEN, Carl (1865–1931)

(i) *Commotio, Op. 48*; (ii) *Violin Sonata No. 2 in G min., Op. 35*; (i) 7 Early Songs (all orch. Holten).

*(*) Danacord DACOCD 588. (i) Hansen, (ii) Bonde-Hansen; Odense SO, Holten.

These three works come from different periods of Nielsen's life. The early songs have a touching and artless simplicity that is quite special and that is lost in these orchestrations. At times *Æbleblomst (Appleblossom)*, which has great purity and tenderness, acquires a Mahlerian lushness that changes its character. So, too, does *I Seraillets Have (In the Garden of the Seraglio)*. Nor is the scoring always that expert: *Irmelin Rose* sounds crude. Bo Holten's orchestration of *Commotio* (1931) completely transforms its character. Instead of enhancing its majesty and splendour, it thickens Nielsen's textures; the overall effect sounds cumbersome, laboured and overblown, completely at variance with the clarity and grandeur of the original. The *G minor Violin Sonata* of 1912 is one of the composer's strangest and most haunting pieces, but its essential inwardness and feel of strangeness are lost. The character of the opening of the finale is changed beyond recognition. It all serves to show that Nielsen's thinking was keenly attuned to the medium in which it sought expression. Decent performances and recording but not really recommendable.

(i) *Violin Concerto, Op. 33*; (ii) *Symphony No. 1, Op. 7*.

(BB) **(*) Warner Apex 0927 40622-2. (i) Hannisdal; Norwegian RO, Rasilainen, or (ii) Mikkelsen.

The Norwegian Radio Orchestra is very good indeed, even if their strings do not match the excellence of the Oslo Philharmonic, nor for that matter do the wind and brass. Under their Finnish conductor, however, they turn in a very natural and unaffected account of the *First Symphony* and a hardly less appealing version of the *Violin Concerto*. Henrik Hannisdal was once the leader or concertmaster and his playing gives consistent pleasure, particularly when the recorded sound is so well balanced. If you want the pairing this is worth considering on this bargain reissue, but neither of these performances displaces the top recommendations with other couplings.

Symphonies Nos. 1–6.

(BB) **(*) Regis (ADD) RRC 3002. LSO, Schmidt.

Ole Schmidt's survey of the Nielsen symphonies was the first one-man overview of the canon and it generated quite a stir when it first appeared in 1976. It had the benefit of a first-rate orchestra, even if it was less familiar with this repertoire than it would be now, and in Ole Schmidt it had an intuitive interpreter. Musically these performances remain strong and, though the orchestral playing is not free from blemish, Schmidt has a keen authenticity of spirit. The *Fifth* is very impressive and the *Sixth (Sinfonia semplice)* remains the most searching of the set. The *First* and *Second Symphonies* would be better if their unforced and unaffected lyricism was allowed to speak for itself but they still have much going for them. The original sound was far from ideal and there is a limit to what remastering can accomplish. Some trouble has been taken over these transfers, even if there is still not enough air around the aural image and the horns and brass are still too prominent. Yet the sound is certainly better focused now, and it is good to have these spirited and likeable performances back so inexpensively, even if Blomstedt has the benefit of better balanced recording and a finer orchestral response. His recording of the complete cycle, plus other music is available on a pair of Double Deccas (460 985-2 and 460 988-2).

Symphonies Nos. 1 in G min., Op. 7; 2 in B min. (The 4 Temperaments), Op. 16.

*(*) Finlandia 8573 85574-2. Finnish RSO, Saraste.

There is some very good playing from the Finnish Radio Orchestra, and Saraste is generally attentive to detail and free from any kind of interpretative point making. At the same time it makes a less strong impression than his powerful accounts of the *Fourth* and *Fifth Symphonies*. Tempi are generally well chosen (even if some may find Saraste fractionally on the fast side in the third movement of No. 1 and distinctly so in the finale of No. 2). Elsewhere, as in the finale of No. 1, he sets off at exactly the right stride. But the first movement of *The Four Temperaments* is coarse rather than choleric and its second theme wanting in nobility, as is the slow movement. The phlegmatic movement is a bit short on charm. Competition in both works is pretty stiff and readers will find more recommendable versions listed in our main volume.

Symphonies Nos. 1; 6 *(Sinfonia semplice)*.

*** BIS CD 1079. BBC Scottish SO, Vänskä.

Osmo Vänskä comes fresh from his impressive Sibelius cycle and is now the latest to embark on the Nielsen symphonies. Vänskä never fails to provoke thought or to offer insights, and there is no trace of routine about his music-making. The *First Symphony* comes up fresh, though some expressive point-making does inhibit the onward flow in the first movement. The slow movement, perhaps, needs to move forward a little more: memories of Thomas Jensen's pioneering LP are not dislodged. The *Sixth Symphony* has a great deal going for it and, in intensity and freshness of approach, makes a real challenge to the recent Schønwandt, which made so strong an impression (dacapo 8.224169; see our main Guide, p.937). The BBC Scottish Symphony Orchestra give keenly responsive playing in all departments, even if they do not match the Gothenburg Orchestra for Järvi, the Danish Radio or the San Francisco orchestras. Recommended, though not in preference to Blomstedt or (in No. 6) to Schønwandt.

NORDHEIM, Arne (born 1931)

(i) *Violin Concerto. Duplex; Partita für Paul*.

*** BIS CD 1212. (i) Herresthal; Stavanger SO, Aadland.

Arne Nordheim was the pioneer of electronic music in Norway. Two of the works on this CD, the *Duplex for Violin and Viola* (1991) and the *Partita für Paul* (1985), have been recorded previously, but these new versions replace them. The Paul of the latter, incidentally, is Klee, five of whose paintings inspire these short pieces. In the last two, the player is recorded and plays, as it were, in concert with himself to quite imaginative effect. The *Duplex* is the 1999 revision of an earlier score for violin and cello. The main piece is the *Violin Concerto* of 1996, written for (and expertly played by) Peter Herresthal, who displays much virtuosity throughout. Nordheim is an eclectic with a sophisticated aural imagination and a lively musical intelligence, but the concerto itself is more arresting than satisfying: there is some beauty of incident and some striking sonorities, but the whole does not constitute the sum of the parts. Others may find more substance to this work than we do, and there is no question as to the quality of the performance or the superb recording, which can safely be recommended to Nordheim's admirers.

NØRGÅRD, Per (born 1932)

Symphony No. 6 *(At the End of the Day)*; *Terrains vagues*.

*** Chan. CHAN 9904. Danish Nat. SO, Dausgaard.

Written in 1998–9 to celebrate the millennium in the Danish Orchestra's first concert in January 2000, Nørgård's *Sixth Symphony* is a powerful and violent piece that makes no compromises. One takes it on trust even at a first hearing that, as the composer claims, it is tautly structured, for from the opening onwards it demonstrates a vivid feeling for orchestral colour presented with an energy too often missing in new music of the late twentieth century. Nørgård has said that this is to be the last of his symphonies, and the hushed close suggests something valedictory, but the vitality of invention not just in the symphony but in the substantial orchestral work with which it is coupled, written even more recently, suggests that he may change his mind. Neither work makes for easy listening, but in a superbly engineered recording the power of the writing comes over most persuasively, demanding attention.

NYMAN, Michael (born 1948)

String Quartets Nos. 1–3.

(M) **(*) Decca 473 091-2. Balanescu Qt.

Michael Nyman's three *String Quartets* make much use of his musical trademark, repeated rhythmic patterns, and the results can be quite hypnotic. His music is agreeable without being tuneful or, in the last resort, especially memorable. But there are plenty of effective passages in these scores: the driving rhythmic patterns in the first movement of the *First Quartet* interspersed with more folksy-sounding music in a different pulse, while the *String Quartet No. 3* has a nostalgic atmosphere which would not seem out of place in a period film drama. However, those not in tune to his style may find his repeated sequences a little wearing. The performances and recordings are excellent, and the composer supplies some detailed and informative sleeve-notes.

OFFENBACH, Jacques (1819–80)

La Belle Hélène: complete.

*** TDK DVD DV-OPLBH. Stage director: Laurent Pelly. (Audio recording *** Virgin VCD5 45477-2 (2)). Lott, Beuron, Sénéchal, Le Roux, Naouri, Todorovitch, Ch. & Musiciens du Louvre, Grenoble, Minkowski.

**(*) Arthaus DVD 100 086. Kasarova, Van der Walt, Chausson, Vogel, Widmer, Zurich Op. Ch. & O, Harnoncourt. (Producer: Helmut Lohner. V/D: Hartmut Schottler.)

(B) ** EMI (ADD) CZS5 74085-2 (2). Millet, Burles, Benoit, Dens, LOP Ch., Marty.

It is some fifteen years since EMI issued their fine set of *La Belle Hélène* with Jessye Norman as Hélène, John Aler as Paris, Charles Burles as Menelaus and Gabriel Bacquier as Agamemnon with the Toulouse Orchestra under the sparkling direction of Michel Plasson. Strange that such a masterpiece should have attracted so little attention in recent years. Not all the assumptions that Meilhac, Halévy and Offenbach made about their audience in 1864 can still apply, and modern audiences less familiar with classical legends are also not shocked by the irreverence of the operetta.

Favouring brisk speeds and light textures, using the period instruments of Les Musiciens du Louvre, Mark Minkowski gives a winning sparkle to this operetta with its delectable send-up of the classical story. He also has the benefit of offering a more complete, more authentic text than any predecessor. It was recorded after a highly successful stage production at the Châtelet Theatre in Paris in September 2000, when Felicity Lott was hailed as an outstanding star in the role of Helen. That is true, even if vocally there are moments when her voice is not at its sweetest, not as rounded as it might be, but her feeling for the idiom and her characterization are unerring. Outstanding in the cast is the seductively honeyed tenor of Yann Beuron as Paris. His 'Judgment of Paris' solo in Act I has rarely been matched, with exquisite *pianissimo* singing in the final stanza, enhanced by Minkowski's persuasive rubato. An excellent supporting cast including such stalwarts of the repertory as Michel Sénéchal and François Le Roux. But although the CDs are in every way recommendable, the live performance on DVD is sheer delight, adding an extra dimension to Offenbach's scintillating score.

The new production staged by Laurent Pelly, with costumes by Chantal Thomas, retains all the mythological characters, but they appear to Helen as in a dream – of being the most beautiful woman in the world and falling in love with the virile young Paris. Her double bed, to which she retires at the beginning, becomes the focus of the action until Act III, which takes place on the beach at Naples, from which she finally sails away with Paris. The whole production fizzes and has touches of romantic naughtiness which only the French can bring off with real style. There is an additional 'Behind the Scenes' sequence narrating the background to this brilliantly succesful production.

Musically *La Belle Hélène* offers special challenges and those who discovered it through René Leibowitz's pioneering Nixa mono recording with Janine Linda as Hélène will have found its pace, sense of style and sophistication hard to match let alone surpass in subsequent recordings.

However, the roster in this 1997 Arthaus production at the Zurich Opera is a strong one and Kasarova makes a positive impression here, as for that matter do the remainder of the cast. Harnoncourt gets lively results from his players but crisper and more lightly accented rhythms would have been welcome. He is a touch heavy-handed. The production is inventive and flows smoothly and the evening is thoroughly enjoyable: this can certainly be recommended, particularly for Vessalina Kasarova's Hélène. The French of the principals is wonderfully clear. Subtitles are in English and German.

Jean-Pierre Marty's 1970 recording is fair value at its bargain price, although no texts are provided. He has the advantage of a largely French cast, who generally sing their parts well enough and with character, but Danièle Millet is not the equal of either Norman or Lott in the other available sets. The recording is acceptable and would be recommendable enough were it not for the Plasson and Minkowski versions, which outclass it in every way and are well worth the extra outlay.

Les Contes d'Hoffmann (The Tales of Hoffmann: complete).

(M) **(*) Westminster (ADD) 471 247-2 (2). Sills, Burrows, Treigle, Marsee, Castel, John Aldis Ch., LSO, Rudel.

It says much for Beverly Sills's masterly technique that she is convincing not just in the role for which her bright, flexible soprano is well-suited, the doll, Olympia, in the Coppélius Act, but in the other very different roles. Both as Giulietta in the Venice Act and as Antonia in the Crespel Act she copes well with the lyrical music, with ample weight and projection, even if dramatic outbursts find her too shrill and bright. Stuart Burrows is a splendid Hoffmann, singing with heady tone, though in places he is stressed by the high tessitura, and Norman Treigle is outstanding in the villainous roles, consistently firm and dark. Susanne Marsee is clear and reliable if not very characterful as Nicklausse, while Raimund Herinx is a wonderfully convincing Schlemil, relishing his solo, *Scintille, diamant*. This was a set primarily intended for the American market, and Julius Rudel generally paces the music well, even if in the Septet of the Venice Act the speed he sets is too heavy and slow. The traditional text is followed, which works well enough, even if it leaves the epilogue very skimpy. The 1972 recording is full and vivid – using a top EMI recording team – but it is set in an open, reverberant acoustic inappropriate for any but the Venice Act.

The Tales of Hoffman (fairly complete; sung in English).

(M) (***) Somm mono 13-2 (2). (Recording made for the soundtrack of the Michael Powell and Emeric Pressburger film with Rounseville, Bond, Grandi, Ayars, Dargavel, Sinclair, Brannigan, Clifford, Sadler's Wells Ch., RPO, Beecham.) (Includes Beecham at the piano, playing and singing through the score.)

The idea of Sir Thomas Beecham's name – after all his years with HMV – appearing on the Decca label, was anathema to the great man, and he went to enormous trouble to contest Decca's right to publish their soundtrack recording of *Tales of Hoffman* on disc. But he failed and now Somm in turn have aquired the rights, not just to the recording of the opera, but also to excerpts from Beecham's fascinating private introduction of the music to Michael Powell and Emeric Presburger before the film was made. This was accomplished at an informal session with Beecham sitting at the piano, playing through the whole score and providing the vocalizations himself with passionate and sometimes bizarre enthusiasm. When asked later by the press to comment on the film, he demurred, but added 'All I know is that the musical performance is first class'.

And so it is, richer and grander than usual, worth the money to hear his handling of the great Trio in the last Act. None of the singers were famous, but all justified his confidence in them, and this new transfer brings plenty of bloom to their voices. Robert Rounseville is a warmly lyrical Hoffman and, as one would expect, Monica Sinclair a superb Niklaus, while Dorothy Bond makes a charmingly petite Olympia. Margherita Grandi may be a bit over the top in her sultry portrayal of Giulietta, but Ann Ayes is fully equal to the role of Antonia in the demanding final Act. The smaller parts are all characterfully sung, with Grahame Clifford excellent as both Spalanzani and Franz, and Owen Brannigan ready to change roles as Schemil, Crespel and Hermann. But the surprise choice was Beecham's own discovery, Bruce Dargavel. He takes the three villanous roles, Coppelius, Dapertutto and Dr Miracle, and his richly resonant bass-baritone is wonderfully caught by the microphone in the celebrated *So Gleam with Desire* and of course in the finale. Franz's sole aria, *Day and Night I am Always Slaving*, included here, was cut from the film when the last Act was in danger of longeurs.

Most productions of Offenbach's finest opera are too long, but this performance is if anything too short. It is not for those expecting French finesse, but with Beecham in charge there is much to be said for British lustiness and the orchestral playing is splendid, especially in the *Barcarolle*. In short this is very enjoyable indeed, for the words are crystal clear, and we hope that Lady Beecham can be persuaded to organize the release of the film as a DVD, using the present remastering of the soundtrack.

Orphée aux enfers (complete).

*** EMI CDS5 56725-2 (2). Dessay, Beuron, Naouri, Fouchécourt, Lyon Nat. Op. O, Grenoble Chamber O, Minkowski.

(*) Arthaus **DVD 100 402. Badea, Vidal, Duesing, Macias, Jung, Quaille, Callatat, Théâtre de la Monnaie Ch. & O, Davin. (Producer: Herbert Wernicke.)

The EMI version of Offenbach's first great success is based on the original 1858 version, with additions from the expanded 1874 score (used in Plasson's recording), including much of the delightful ballet music and some character arias, and the result is most winning. Both the 'earthly' leads are superb: Natalie Dessay's secure, clear coloratura is well employed as the nagging wife, Eurydice, and one genuinely feels sorry for her hapless husband, Orphée, amiably characterized by Yann Beuron. Eurydice's contempt for her husband's new composition in the concerto duet (one of Offenbach's most attractive inventions) and her mimicking of her doomed lover, John Styx, is cruelly hilarious. Jean Paul Fouchécourt as Pluto oozes deceptive charm in his pastoral aria, though his true devilish character is revealed in some grotesque falsetto at the end, and Cupid's kissing song is charmingly sung by Patricia Petibon. From the opening

bars, Minkowski's authentic approach is apparent in the sparkling, crystal-clear textures, which bring out more than any other recording of this work the full zest of the score, and he propels the opera along at a tremendous pace and with a bouncing rhythmic bite, matched by the exceptionally lively cast, who turn the recording into a genuinely theatrical experience. The recording is superbly vivid and clear and adds to the immediacy of the drama. Offenbach devotees will want the rival Plasson set for the complete 1874 version: it is a weightier performance, the recording not so sharply focused, but it still has a great deal to recommend it. However, the sheer energy of this Minkowski account will tip the balance for many.

Although the Arthaus DVD performance, recorded in the Brussels Théâtre de la Monnaie in 1997, has been updated to the twentieth century, the setting of Mount Olympus in the famous *fin de siècle* café La Mort Subite, with the Gods wearing evening dress, ensures that there is less of a visual jolt of the kind which often affects modern productions of Offenbach. There are a few curiosities here which may slightly irritate the DVD collector, notably the use of a honky-tonk piano in the finale of the Act I *Can-can*. However, the ensuing journey down to Hell, conveyed spectacularly by a steam train plummeting through the surface of Heaven into the Underworld, with great whooshes of steam, is considerable compensation.

The cast is a good one: Alexandru Badea is a younger, more ardent Orpheus than might be expected, but his well-focused tenor and convincing acting is certainly engaging, whilst his coquettish wife, Eurdice, is well characterized by Elizabeth Vidal, though her voice is less well caught by the microphones and is a little harsh at times. Both Dale Duesing and Reinaldo Macias in the roguish roles of Jupiter and Pluto sing with plenty of character. André Jung's drunken John Styx is amusing to watch – though it would be less of a pleasure just to hear – and most of the incidental parts are well done. The conducting is efficient rather than inspired: Minkowski's new EMI recording shows how much heady effervescence there is in Offenbach's music. However, there is plenty to enjoy here and a good deal more so than in many recent productions of this work.

Orpheus in the Underworld: highlights in English.

** TER CDTER 1134. Kale, Watson, Angas, Squires, Bottone, Pope, ENO Ch. & O, Elder.

After listening to Minkowski's recording of *Orphée*, this version, based on ENO's production of the mid-1980s, now seems rather flat and dated, with Public Opinion obviously based on the then current prime minister. Those who saw and enjoyed the show will get more out of this than those who did not, for while there is plenty of knock-about British humour, little of Offenbach's French champagne comes through here. Indeed, this kind of performance, when even Bonaventura Bottone's hilariously camp portrait of prancing Mercury is not nearly so much fun when simply heard, ideally needs a DVD.

ONSLOW, Georges (1784–1853)

Symphonies Nos. 2 in D min., Op. 42; 4 in G, Op. 71.

*** CPO 999 738-2. Hannover Rad. PO, Goritzki.

Georges Onslow, an Englishman who following a scandal was forced to live in France, is best remembered for his *'Bullet' Quartet*, written after he was shot in the head whilst out hunting by a bullet destined for a wild boar. He wrote four symphonies between 1831 and 1846, though the two recorded here had limited success at the time. It is hard not to respond to the *Second Symphony*, which launches into its opening *Allegro* with tremendous gusto and one is swept away by the momentum. The second movement has a graceful charm, the *Minuetto* is energetic, more of a Beethovian *Scherzo*, whilst the finale is an enjoyably lively *Presto*.

The *Fourth Symphony* has a rather dramatic *Largo* introduction before being propelled into another vital *Allegro* which has both wit and energy. A vigorous *Scherzo* follows, with plenty of dash (even a hint of Berlioz is felt here), whilst the slow movement has a more dramatic minor-keyed central section flanked by cantabile writing. The finale, subtitled 'Souvenir de Rhim' brings trills and scurrying, chromatic glissandi alternating between the strings and woodwind. Whilst these are hardly profound works, they are thoroughly entertaining, and well worth investigating by anyone interested in rare symphonies. The recordings and performances are excellent, and the sleeve notes are copious and fascinating.

ORFF, Carl (1895-1982)

Carmina Burana.

*** RCA **DVD** 74321 852859. Popp, Van Kesteren, Prey, Bavarian R. Ch., Munich R. O, Eichhorn. (Video Producer: Jean-Pierre Ponnelle.)

(BB) **(*) Teldec Apex 0927 41377-2. Jo, Kowalski, Skovhus, L. Philh. Ch. & O, Southend Boys' Ch., Mehta.

(BB) **(*) EMI Encore (ADD) CDE5 74747-2. Popp, Unger, Wolansky, New Philh. Ch. & O, Frühbeck de Burgos – STRAVINSKY: *Circus Polka; Fireworks.* **(*)

(BB) ** CfP (ADD) 575 1462. Armstrong, Hall, Cook, Hallé Ch. & O, Handford (with FAURÉ: *Pavane*; FRANCK: *Panis Angelicus*).

This fine RCA recording of *Carmina Burana*, conducted by Kurt Eichhorn with outstanding soloists in 1975, has been issued previously on CD, and here is treated to an imaginative staging for DVD by Jean-Pierre Ponnelle. The main background set is a ruined church against which the singers are seen in medieval costume, with action, sometimes surreal, invented to illustrate each section of the work, a technique which seems to anticipate the virtual reality of our digital age.

So the roasted swan episode is introduced by a drunken monk, with a large swan in the background actually being roasted on a spit, and Lucia Popp in a medieval wimple looking and sounding enchanting. Hermann Prey is a superb baritone soloist, taking the main burden, and the choir is bright and lively. Not a first choice sonically, although the recording is very impressive, but there is an added dimension here. As a supplementary item comes a long interview with Orff himself – in German with English subtitles – in which he talks animatedly about key childhood experiences and how he came to write *Carmina Burana*, with many dozens of illuminating photographs and illustrations.

Mehta's 1992 Teldec recording is often enjoyably vigorous, it has good soloists and an excellent choral response, with the Southend boys thrusting throatily, enjoying their pubescent spree. Sumi Jo is a seductive if rather knowing Girl in the Red Shift who submits willingly, rising nimbly up her ascending scale to a spectacularly floated pianissimo. But Boje Skovhus makes a strongly vibrant rather than subtle contribution. The recording, made at The Maltings, Snape, is resonantly spectacular, but the quieter choral passages are a little recessive. Mehta's direction is not as imaginative or as spontaneously exuberant as that of his finest competitors, but this is excellent value at budget price.

Unfortunately the Frühbeck de Burgos version, with Lucia Popp outstanding among the soloists combined with choral singing of considerable gusto, was given a wrong catalogue number in our main Guide. This is corrected above and it remains a strong contender on EMI's super-bargain Encore label as the Stravinsky pieces are very well played too.

Once principal horn of the Hallé Orchestra, Maurice Handford later took up conducting, but his career seemed to be relatively short-lived. His *Carmina Burana* dates from 1982 and is notable for its excellent soloists, with Sheila Armstrong coming close to matching her supremely lovely performance for Previn. The men of the Hallé Choir provide some rough singing at times, but the women are much better, and the performance gathers energy and incisiveness as it proceeds, although there is some fall-off in tension at the very end. The analogue recording has transferred well to CD but this is hardly a primary choice, even at bargain price, although some may be tempted by the two choral encores. First CD choice, however, rests with Plasson (EMI CDC5 55392-2) or Blomstedt (Decca 430 509-2) although Ormandy's bargain version is also irresistible (● Sony SBK 47668).

PALESTRINA, Giovanni Pierluigi da (1525–94)

Canticum canticorum Salomonis (**fourth book of motets for 5 voices from the *Song of Songs***).

(BB) *** Hyp. Helios CDH 55095. Pro Cantione Antiqua, Turner.

The *Canticum canticorum Salomonis* is one of Palestrina's most sublime and expressive works, possibly wider in its range than anything else he composed, and certainly as deeply felt. His disclaimer in the dedication to Pope Gregory XIII, which Bruno Turner quotes at the beginning of his notes ('There are far too many poems with no other subject than love of a kind quite alien to the Christian faith'), cannot disguise the fervour which he poured into these twenty-nine motets. The ten members of the Pro Cantione Antiqua under Turner bring an appropriate eloquence and ardour, tempered by restraint. They are accorded an excellently balanced and natural-sounding recording. Now reissued in the budget range, this can be recommended even more highly.

Missa Assumpta est Maria (including Gregorian Chant Proper for the Feast of the Assumption); Missa Papae Marcelli.

(BB) *** Regis RRC 1025. Pro Cantione Antiqua, Brown

Mark Brown and his Pro Cantione Antiqua made a series of Palestrina recordings (which last appeared on Carlton), and for this reissue Regis have re-coupled two of the finest. They give accounts of these celebrated pieces that aspire to total authenticity in that the forces used are those Palestrina himself would have known: no boys' voices, no women, and just one-to-a-part, with the mass sections interspersed with plainchant. The Pro Cantione Antiqua sing with eloquence and power against the background of a resonant acoustic. The mid-1980s recording is splendidly balanced. Whatever other versions you might have of either work, this has special claims, and its outward severity does not preclude depth of feeling – rather the reverse.

Missa Veni sponsa Christi (with Motet).

(B) **(*) CfP 575 5602. St John's College, Cambridge Ch., Guest – ALLEGRI: *Miserere*; LASSUS: *Missa super 'Bell'Amfrit' alterna'*. **(*)

Every section of the *Veni sponsa Christi Mass* is introduced by the same idea with much subtle variation, and this impressive work ends with two *Agnus Dei* settings, the second with an additional tenor part. It receives an eloquent, imaginatively detailed and finely shaped performance here, and the relative restraint of the Anglican choral tradition suits Palestrina's flowing counterpoint better than it does the Lassus Venetian coupling.

Music for Holy Saturday: Lamentations and Responsories; Book 3, Nos. 1–3; Benedictus for Holy Week; Sicut cervus; Stabat Mater.

*** Chan. 0679. Musica Contetexta, Simon Ravens.

In his perceptive note Simon Ravens points out that Holy Saturday has inevitably tended to be overshadowed in the church calendar by the days immediately before and after Good Friday and Easter Day. Yet in this fine collection, superbly performed by his group, Musica Contexta, and vividy recorded, he demonstrates what inspired music Palestrina wrote for this in-between occasion. Like the other sets of *Lamentations*, this third of the four has the first two motets using Hebrew letters as an introduction, leading on in the third to a magnificent setting of the Prayer of Jeremiah. More than usual, Palestrina's polyphony here has a biting edge, beautifully achieved in this performance. The *Stabat Mater* for double choir, one of Palestrina's best-loved works, follows up in its dedication, leading to the *Benedictus for Easter Saturday* and finally to the motet *Sicut cervus*, which prepares the way as a concluding liturgical act for the celebrations of the following day. Using texts transcribed from early editions, Ravens draws direct and dedicated performances from his fine group of singers.

PANUFNIK, Andrzej (1914–91)

Symphony No. 8 (Sinfonia votiva).

(BB) *** Hyp. Helios CDH 55100. Boston SO, Ozawa – SESSIONS: *Concerto for Orchestra*. ***

The *Sinfonia votiva* has a strongly formalistic structure, but its message is primarily emotional. Though Panufnik's melodic writing may as a rule reflect the formalism of his thought rather than tapping a vein of natural lyricism, the result is most impressive, particularly in a performance of such sharp clarity and definition as Ozawa's. Very well recorded, and excellent value.

PARRY, Hubert (1848–1918)

(i) *Blest Pair of Sirens; I Was Glad; Judith: Long Since in Egypt's Plenteous Land; Jerusalem;* (ii) *Songs of Farewell: My Soul, There is a Country.* (iii) *English Lyrics: And Yet I Love Her; Blow, Blow, thou Winter Wind; Bright Star; From a City Window; Looking Backward; Love is a Babel; Marion; No Longer Mourn for Me; O Mistress Mine; On a Time the Amorous Silvy; Take, O Take those Lips Away; There; There Be None of Beauty's Daughters; Thine Eyes Still Shine for Me; Weep You no More; A Welsh Lullaby; When Comes my Gwen; When Icicles Hang by the Wall; When Lovers Meet Again; When We Two Parted.*

(M) **(*) Decca (ADD/DDD) 470378-2. (i) Winchester Cathedral Ch., Waynflete Singers, Bournemouth SO, Hill; (ii) Canterbury Cathedral Ch., Wicks; (iii) Tear, Ledger.

The bulk of this CD is drawn from Robert Tear's 1979 (Argo) LP of Parry songs. The music is of fine quality, showing judicious use of texts, all distinctively set, and offering variety of mood, from the jaunty *Love is a Babel*, to the haunting, even a touch unnerving, *From a City Window*. Tear is on good form; if very occasionally he seems just a bit too stylized, his diction is superb, and the accompaniments are excellent, though the piano timbre is not as rich and full as the voice. The splendid David Hill performances of the popular anthems provide strong contrast to the songs and are strikingly full and resonant in sound. *I was*

Glad, in Gordon Jacob's colourful orchestration, is almost overwhelming at its final climax. Elgar's orchestration of *Jerusalem*, with it sweeping strings after the words 'arrow of desire' is thrilling. Another excellent mid-price CD in Decca's 'British Collection', and although no texts are provided, you barely need them when Tear's diction is so clear.

PERGOLESI, Giovanni (1710–36)

La morte de San Giuseppe (oratorio).

(M) * Warner Fonit 0927 43308 (2). Farruggia, Manca di Nissa, Angeles Peters, Pace, Naples Alessandro Scarlatti R & TV O, Panni.

The autograph score of Pergolesi's oratorio has only recently come to light in the New York Pierpont Library, which acquired it from a European dealer. It is a splendid work, but the present recording will not do. The singing of Maria Angeles Peters in the role of San Michelle is insecure to say the least and suffers from poor intonation. A delightful aria like *Appena spira aura soave* ('As soon as the gentle breeze blows') needs a voice like Emma Kirkby's. The contralto, Bernadette Manca di Nissa, who takes the part of Maria Santissima is much stronger, but Patrizia Pace in the demanding coloratura role of Amor is not always accurate either, and Michele Farruggia as San Giuseppe is only adequate. Panni gets a lively and stylish response from the excellent orchestra and the digital recording is excellent, but this can only serve as a stopgap until something better comes along.

PETRASSI, Goffredo (born 1904)

Concerti for Orchestra Nos. (i) 1 & 2; (ii) 3 (Récréation concertante); 4 for Strings; (iii) 5 & 6 (Invenzione concertato); (i) 7 & 8.

(M) **(*) Warner Fonit 8573 83274-2. (i) BBC SO; (ii) Philh. Hungarica; (iii) SO di Milano della RAI, Peskó.

Petrassi is scantily represented on disc, and this is the only version of his eight *Concertos for Orchestra*. The *Primo Concerto* comes from 1934 and was the only one of the eight to have been recorded before on a mono Decca LP (by Fernando Previtali and the Orchestra of the Accademia di Santa Cecilia in Rome, of which Petrassi was long director). The influences are neo-Classical, namely Casella, Hindemith and Stravinsky, and it is a work that wears well, particularly its strongly atmospheric slow movement. The *Secondo Concerto* (1951) and the *Récréation concertante* (No. 3) (1952–3) continue the same line. They have a strong sense of forward movement and of musical purpose that impresses. In a way, they can be compared with the kind of writing favoured by Vagn Holmboe or Hilding Rosenberg further north. The *Quattro Concerto per orchestra d'archi* (1954) is closer to Bartók than its companions but again serious and purposeful – and also beautiful. The *Quinto Concerto* (1955), commissioned by the Boston Symphony Orchestra, is

imaginative and thoughtful; its opening has its roots in Bartók but is suffused with Italian light. The *Sesto Concerto* (1956–7) (*Invenzione concertato*) was one of the works commissioned by the BBC to commemorate the foundation of the Third Programme (others were Tippett's *Second Symphony* and Holmboe's *Epitaph for Orchestra*); it is eventful and holds the listener. The *Settimo Concerto* (1964) and *Ottavo Concerto* (1972), the latter written for the Chicago Symphony, are tougher nuts to crack but, like everything this composer has done, are worth taking trouble with.

The performances were all recorded in the 1970s, Nos. 1 and 8 in the BBC Maida Vale studios, 2 and 7 in the more ample acoustic of St Pancras Town Hall; the former have the more opaque string quality and less transparent orchestral detail. Nos. 3 and 4 were recorded in Hungary, and Nos. 5 and 6 in the Milan Conservatory in 1979. Two LPs were issued on the Fonit Cetra label but not released in the UK. This is an important and rewarding set that goes some way at least in redressing the neglect this composer has suffered in recent years. It would be good if we had new recordings of the pre-war *Partita* that put him on the map and the fine *Piano Concerto*, which Pietro Scarpini and Nino Sanzogno introduced to Britain in the late 1950s.

PFITZNER, Hans (1869–1949)

Cello Sonata in F sharp min., Op. 1.

(BB) *** Arte Nova 74321 87072-2. Schiefen, Dressler – RICHARD STRAUSS: *Sonata.* ***

The *Cello Sonata in F sharp minor* (1890) was one of the first Pfitzner works, apart from the *Three Preludes* to *Palestrina* and the *Symphony in C*, to reach the gramophone. It is very well fashioned but rather Brahmsian in style, although it perhaps outstays its welcome. This performance is vital and sensitive: these fine artists make up in quality for what they may lack in 'celebrity', and the recording, made in the studios of Bayerischer Rundfunk, is superbly balanced and very lifelike.

PICKARD, John (born 1963)

String Quartets, Nos. 2–4.

(M) *** Dutton CDLX 7117. Sorrel Qt.

John Pickard, born in 1963, has combined his composing with academic positions, yet there is nothing dry or uninvolved about his music, as represented here in three formidable quartets. These are warmly expressive works in a vigorous post-Bartókian idiom, played with passion by the Sorrel Quartet, to whom No. 4 is dedicated. No. 2, written in 1993, is a single, extended movement in three distinct sections, at once establishing Pickard's gift for exploiting weighty quartet textures, with a richly lyrical 'second subject' on the viola leading to the long central slow section, also warmly expressive, and on to an urgent final section. In No. 3, written in 1994, the first movement starts abrasively with scrunching discords, leading an energetic first movement, a middle movement marked *intensivo* and a finale, also predominantly slow, which maintains a meditative mood. No. 4 was written for the Sorrel Quartet in 1997–8, the vigorous, positive first movement is entitled *Sinfonia*, almost a symphonic allegro, leading to a middle movement which brings four concertante sections, one for each quartet instrument starting with the viola and ending with a scurrying gallop in which the first violin finally is allowed to lead the pack. The third movement, marked *Fantasia of Four Parts*, brings a conscious reflection of the great string fantasias of Gibbons and Purcell, with a deeply felt slow first half leading to a fast, sharply syncopated final section. The Sorrel Quartet bring out the powerful emotional thrust of this closely organized music to the full, almost as though they are composing it on the spot, and are superbly recorded.

PICKER, Tobias (born 1954)

Thérèse Raquin (complete opera).

*** Chan. 9659 (2). Soviero, Fulgoni, Gietz, Bernstein, Woods, Andrasy, Kazaras, Dallas Op. O, Jenkins.

The idea of turning Emile Zola's melodramatic novel *Thérèse Raquin* into an opera came to the American composer Tobias Picker from his sister, who had accidentally knocked a copy of the book off a library shelf. This is his third opera, and in two Acts, each just under an hour, with Gene Sdcheer as librettist, he confidently compresses the story. The first Act in three scenes leads to the murder by drowning of Camille, Thérèse's husband, by her lover, Laurent, ending on an orchestral coda in which 'Psycho'-style chopping sounds mark the dramatic moment. The second Act, picturing the rising guilt and bitter quarrels of Thérèse and Laurent, ends with the deaths of both; Thérèse stabbing herself, Laurent drinking the poison he had prepared for her. The eight brief scenes accelerate the gathering tensions of the story. Picker's style is broadly lyrical if often abrasive, with heightened passages to mark emotional climaxes, and with ensembles playing an important part in punctuating the drama, a device too often avoided by modern composers. The orchestral writing is colourful and positive, and Graeme Jenkins, music director of the Dallas Opera, formerly of Glyndebourne Touring Opera, draws warmly committed playing and singing from the whole company. Outstanding among the singers is the fine British mezzo Sara Fulgoni in the title role, who following the composer's wishes inspires more sympathy for Thérèse as victim than the novel may have intended. One oddity is that Picker defies convention in his allocation of voices, with Laurent, Thérèse's lover, a bass baritone, and Camille, her husband, a tenor (Richard Bernstein and Gordon Gietz respectively, both with fresh, clear voices). The role of Camille's sinister mother, who

after her stroke cannot reveal the truth to her friends, is also allotted not to a mezzo as one might expect, but to a soprano, the characterful Diana Soviero. The live recording is a composite of four performances in December 2001, the world premiere, with atmospheric sound. The trilingual booklet provides not just the libretto but helpful essays and an analysis with musical illustrations.

PLANQUETTE, Robert (1848–1903)

Les Cloches de Corneville (operetta): complete.

(B) **(*) EMI (ADD) CSZ5 74091-2. Mesplé, Sinclair, Stutzmann, Burles, Giraudeau, Benoit, Paris Opéra-Comique Ch. & O, Doussard.

Les Cloches de Corneville was undoubtedly Planquette's most successful work. The plot (a cross between *La Dame Blanche* and *Martha*), with its action eerily set in an old, supposedly haunted castle, is agreeable enough, but it is the strongly melodic music that has made the work so durable. So much so that in 1877, when the original Paris production at the Théâtre des Folies-Dramatiques ran for 461 performances, the management made the unprecedented gesture of serving every member of the audience with free rolls and beer!

The operetta is crammed with good tunes, and not just the famous '*Legende des cloches*' and the simple but very charming '*Chanson du mousse*' (a lovely rondeau-valse), but also plenty of jolly choruses, comic numbers and rustic songs. This flavourful performance dates from 1973, with Mady Mesplé's agile French soprano ideally suited to the role of the heroine, Germaine. The only drawback for non-French speakers is the high proportion of dialogue, which is delivered with panache but without any supporting texts or translations. The recording is vivid if a touch raucous, but this set remains strongly recommendable at its modest cost.

PLEYEL, Ignaz (1757–1831)

(i) Symphony concertante in F, B.115; Symphony in D, Op. 3/1; Symphony Périodique in F, B.140.

**(*) CPO 999 759-2. Zurich Chamber O, Griffiths, with (i) Dzialak, Bobino.

Pleyel's elegantly attractive if relatively conventional symphonies are given first rate performances here. There is an infectious bounce to the playing, the minuets are nicely pointed, and the finales have plenty of vitality. The *Symphony concertante*, with piano and violin soloists, brings many attractive episodes and the finale is irrepressibly jolly. The only real criticism of this CD is the recording, which lacks expansive richness, with the orchestra rather too backwardly balanced, but not enough to seriously diminish the wit of the music.

POULENC, Francis (1899–1963)

(i) *Concert Champêtre* (for harpsichord); (ii) *Concerto in G min. for Organ*; (iii) *Piano Concerto*.

(M) ** (*) Virgin VM5 61979-2. (i) Cole; (ii) Weir; (iii) Pommier; City of L. Sinf., Hickox.

The *Piano Concerto* receives rather laid-back treatment at the hands of Jean-Bernard Pommier, who misses the *gamin*-like charm of the opening. The instrument is also a bit backward and has a slightly resonant halo. The *Concert Champêtre* is charming, though the perspective is not good. The harpsichord occupies an appropriately small space, but the wind and, more particularly, the percussion are far too prominent. Maggie Cole and the City of London Sinfonia produce a splendidly idiomatic performance, as does Gillian Weir in the *Organ Concerto*. Duchable is to be preferred in the *Piano Concerto*, but otherwise there are good things here.

(i) *Suite Française*; (ii) *Cello Sonata*; (iii) *3 Mouvements Perpétuels*; (iv) *Ave verum; Exsultate Deo; 4 Motets pour le temps de Noël; 4 Petites Prières de Saint François d'Assise; Salve Regina*.

(M) ** ASV Platinum PLT 8515. (i) London Wind O; (ii) Wallfisch, York; (iii) Bennett, Wynberg; (iv) Joyful Company of Singers.

Raphael Wallfisch's account of the *Cello Sonata* was recorded as recently as 2000 and, as you would expect, he turns in a good performance. But next to Fournier's EMI version, this newcomer sounds more efficient than inspired. Perhaps the effect is exacerbated by the recording which tends to iron out the dynamic range, and the piano tone is not especially rich. The choral items, too, are quite well done, but there is also plenty of competition here (see our main volume), and in terms of ensemble, chording and tonal blend, they do not match other recommendations. The *Suite Française* is admirably fresh, and the familiar *Mouvements Perpétuels* are beautifully played and recorded. But this collection is not especially enticing.

3 Mouvements Perpétuels; Napoli: Suite.

(B) *** Decca Eloquence 467 471-2. Rogé – SAINT-SAENS: *Piano Concertos Nos. 2 & 4.* ***

The *Mouvements Perpétuelles* are among Poulenc's most seductive piano miniatures and the *Napoli Suite* also has much charm. These pieces could hardly be better played or recorded and this makes an attractive bonus for two favourite Saint-Saëns *Piano Concertos*.

***Dialogue des Carmélites* (complete).**

✪ *** Arthaus DVD 100 004. Schmidt, Fassbender, Petibon, Henry, Dale, Chœurs de l'Opéra du Rhin, Strausbourg PO, Latham-Koenig.

Poulenc set great store by this opera and it was superbly served in the early days of LP by Pierre Dervaux with the incomparable Denise Duval as Blanche. (This is still available in the boxed set EMI issued to mark the Poulenc centenary year in 1999.) This DVD is a remarkably gripping and wholly convincing production which may well serve to persuade those who have not seen the light about this piece.

In Anne-Sophie Schmidt it has a Blanche who looks as good as she sounds, and a cast which has no weak member. The production conveys the period to striking effect and the claustrophobic atmosphere of the nunnery. The camerawork is imaginative without ever being intrusive and the production so well managed that the *longueurs* that normally afflict the closing scene in the opera house pass unnoticed. Of the other roles Hedwig Fassbender (Mère Marie de l'Incarnation), Patricia Petibon (Sœur Constance), Didier Henry (Le Marquis de la Force) and Laurence Dale (as the Chevalier de la Force) are exemplary both as singers and as interpreters.

This production is excellent dramatically – and *looks* good. The stage director is Marthe Keller, who was the eponymous heroine of Honegger's *Jeanne d'Arc au bûcher* on DG. The Strasbourg Orchestra play well for Jan Latham-Koenig and, even apart from its compelling visual presence, it has the strongest musical claims as well. Subtitles are in English, German and Flemish.

PREVIN, André (born 1929)

A Streetcar Named Desire (opera; complete).

*** Arthaus DVD 100 138. Fleming, Futral, Forst, Gilfry, Griffey, San Francisco Op. O, Composer. (V/D: Colin Graham.)

André Previn's ambitious project to turn Tennessee Williams's ground-breaking play into an opera has resulted in one of the richest, most moving American works in the repertory. The approach may be more conventional in operatic terms than the operas of leading American minimalists, and Colin Graham's richly evocative production with ingenious sets by Michael Yeargan follows that approach, yet the power of the result is undeniable.

Previn himself draws passionate playing from the orchestra of the San Francisco Opera, leading an exceptionally strong cast of soloists, each establishing a distinctive character as laid down in the play.

Central to the opera's success is the moving and powerful assumption of the central role of Blanche by Renée Fleming, relishing music that was specially tailored for her. The big melody of her solo '*I can smell the sea air*' inspires her to producing ravishing sounds, leading to the final scene, where she is led away to the asylum, which is made the more poignant by the sheer beauty of her singing.

Rodney Gilfry admirably copes with the problem of singing freshly and clearly, while making Stanley necessarily a slob. This DVD offers a video recording of the world première, a historic occasion, even more vivid when seen as well as heard.

'The Kindness of Strangers': A Portrait by Tony Palmer.

*** Arthaus **DVD** 100 150.

Tony Palmer, second to none in portraying great musicians, made this film in 1988 to coincide with the world premiere of Previn's opera, *A Streetcar Named Desire*. Starting with that as a news item, together with a tempting sample of Renée Fleming in the central role of Blanche, the film offers a wide-ranging survey of Previn's achievements, covering his career since boyhood.

It is a measure of his breadth of achievement, not just as a classical conductor, composer and pianist but as a jazz performer and an Oscar-winning Hollywood film composer, that the 90 minutes is crammed with so much rich material. That includes early and rare archive film, not just of Previn himself, but of clips of his early film-successes, *On an Island with You* and *The Sun Comes Out*.

Previn himself is the most engaging of musicians, full of sharp remarks, as when he turned down the idea of an opera as suggested by a German company: 'I can't write an opera where everyone's wearing a toga.' Or on gymnastic conducting: 'An orchestra does not play any louder if you jump, so why jump?' A film full of treasurable material about a fascinating and engaging musician.

PRIN, Yves (born 1933)

(i) Dioscures (Concerto Grosso for Flute, Violin, Clarinet and Chamber Orchestra); (ii) Ephémères (Capriccio for Violin and Chamber Orchestra); (iii) Le Souffle d'Iris (Concerto for Flute and Orchestra).

(BB) *** Naxos 8.555347. (i) Post; (i; ii) Graffin; (i; iii) Artaud; French RPO, Farrandis.

Yves Prin is probably new to most music-lovers outside France. He is new to the catalogues and is not to be found in *Grove VI*, Michael Kennedy's *Oxford Dictionary* or any of the usual dictionaries. He studied piano with Yves Nat and conducting with Louis Fourestier, becoming director of the Orchestre Philharmonique des Pays de la Loire and, for a time, the Nouvel Orchestre Philharmonique de Radio France in the early 1980s. Although *Ephémères* has its origins in a solo piece composed in 1974, it has undergone several revisions, most recently in 1992; it is a beautiful and inventively scored work. *Le Souffle d'Iris*, a concerto for flute and orchestra, comes from the mid-1980s and was also revised in 1992. All three pieces on this disc are inventive and full of original sonorities, which spring from a rich imagination. Structurally they do not always convince, but the music mostly proceeds purposefully.

PROKOFIEV, Serge (1891–1953)

Chout (ballet): Suite.

(M) *** Decca (ADD) 470 264-2. LSO, Abbado – HINDEMITH: *Symphonic Metamorphoses*; JANACEK: *Sinfonietta*. ***

Abbado's 1966 *Chout* is still the best way to explore this score, as no one has yet surpassed his combination of energy, precision of ensemble and brilliant recording. Just listen to the sparkling playing in the *Dance of the Buffoon's Daughter*, or the ironic *Dance of the Wives*, and also the way he builds up the *Final Dance* to a frenzy. The score is marvellously inventive and shows Prokofiev's considerable melodic and harmonic resources at their best. This should be as popular as any of his ballet scores, and this disc is a fine addition to Decca's 'Legend' series.

Piano Concerto No. 3 in C, Op. 26.

(BB) (***) Naxos mono 8.110673. Kapell, Dallas SO, Dorati – KHACHATURIAN: *Piano Concerto* (***); SHOSTAKOVICH: *3 Preludes; Piano Concerto No. 3* (***).

(B) (***) RCA Double mono 74321 845952 (2). Kapell, Dallas SO, Dorati – BEETHOVEN: *Piano Concerto No. 2*; CHOPIN: *Piano Sonata No. 2*; DEBUSSY: *Children's Corner*; KHACHATURIAN: *Piano Concerto*; RACHMANINOV: *Rhapsody on a Theme of Paganini* (with SHOSTAKOVICH: *3 Preludes*; SCHUBERT: *Impromptu; Ländler; Moment musical; Waltzes*) (***).

(i) Piano Concerto No. 3, Conte de la vieille grand-mère, Op. 31/2–3; Etude, Op. 52; Gavotte, Op. 32/3; Paysage, Op. 59/2; Sonata No. 4, Op. 29: Andante assai. Sonatine pastorale, Op. 59/3; Suggestion diabolique, Op. 4/4; Visions fugitives, Op. 22/3, 5–6, 9, 10–11, 16–18.

(BB) *** Naxos mono 8.110670. Composer; (i) with LSO, Coppola.

Kapell's fabulously played and electrifying account of the Prokofiev concerto is a *must*. He outstrips even the composer himself – and most others who came after him. Not to be missed. Choice will depend on coupling, but the difficult-to-read sleeve material counts against the RCA version. Naxos promises a complete Kapell, and that may well be the best version to choose.

Pearl issued this coupling of the Prokofiev *Third Concerto* plus the recordings of piano music the composer made in the 1930s some years ago, and the present transfer is a useful and cheaper alternative. However, readers should remember that last year Dutton issued the concerto in an impeccable transfer, coupled with Koussevitzky's unsurpassed account of the *Fifth Symphony*.

Violin Concertos Nos. 1, Op. 19; 2, Op. 63.

(*) Ph. 462 592-2. Josefowicz, Montreal SO, Dutoit – TCHAIKOVSKY: *Sérénade mélancolique*. *

(i) Violin Concertos Nos. 1, Op. 19; 2, Op. 63. (ii) Overture on Hebrew Themes; March, Op. 99.

(M) *** DG 445 607-2. (i) Mintz, Chicago SO; (ii) COE; both cond. Abbado.

Mintz's performances are as fine as almost any: he phrases with imagination and individuality and there is an attractive combination of freshness and lyrical finesse. He has the advantage of Abbado's sensitive and finely judged accompaniments and this partnership casts the strongest spell over the listener. The modern digital recording is another plus point, as is the inclusion of the underrated *Overture on Hebrew Themes*, finely played by the Chamber Orchestra of Europe, which makes for a considerable bonus, while the encore, the *March, Op. 99*, is a genuine novelty.

Leila Josefowicz made a strong impression with her Dvořák/Janáček recital some years ago and her coupling of the two Prokofiev concertos present a strong challenge to existing versions. She is an intelligent interpreter and gives strongly characterized and individual accounts, carefully thought out and expertly executed. In this respect hers is probably a more appealing set than Gil Shaham, though she is less well served by the engineers who put the spotlight on her and give a less transparent orchestral texture. Compared with the great naturals like Cho-Liang Lin and Kyung-Wha Chung, she may seem a bit self-aware even without this. The CD is well worth hearing but is not a first choice, in spite of its positive features and personality, and of course its appealing coupling.

Violin Concerto No. 2 in G min., Op. 63.

✪ *** BMG 74321 87454-2. Znaider, Bavarian RSO, Jansons – GLAZUNOV: *Violin Concerto;*
TCHAIKOVSKY: *Méditation, Op. 42/1.* *** ✪
(***) Testament mono SBT 1224. Kogan, LSO, Cameron – TCHAIKOVSKY: *Violin Concerto etc.* (***)

Nikolaj Znaider's account of the *Second Prokofiev Concerto* reveals an artist not only of effortless and commanding technique but a natural eloquence and taste. His approach is strongly lyrical and though his slow movement is just slightly too sweet, his playing throughout is highly imaginative with a wide range of tone colour and refined, sensitive phrasing. As with the Glazunov only the most exalted rivals come to mind, and he gets superb backing from Mariss Jansons and the Munich Orchestra. The recording is superbly balanced and the overall sound very natural and lifelike.

Leonid Kogan's mono recording from 1955 first appeared in harness with the Mozart *G major concerto*. A fine reading, it has never been reissued on CD and its reappearance here gives us a welcome chance to reassess it. No doubt some will find it cooler than Oistrakh (EMI CZS5 69331-2), but Kogan is very aristocratic and has tremendous grip and energy. Basil Cameron, who did sterling service at the Proms during the 1940s and 50s but made few records, proves how supportive an accompanist he could be.

Lieutenant Kijé: Suite; Scythian Suite, Op. 20.

(M) (*(*)) Westminster mono 471 265-2. Vienna SO, Scherchen – KHACHATURIAN: *Gayaneh: Suite.* *(*).

The mono sound for Scherchen's 1951 Prokofiev recordings is vivid for its day, though, of course, a little thin by modern standards. These performances are quite characterful in their way, though next to Dorati's brilliant Mercury version of a few years later

(432 753-2), this performance lacks sheer guts and brilliance. Scherchen makes a few interesting points here and there: his slow tempi in the lento section of *The Adoration of Veless and Ala* has a hypnotic quality, and he brings out some of the subtle details of the score. Much the same can be said of the *The Lieutenant Kijé Suite*: there are effective moments in the brass, but generally the performance is pretty heavy going. First choice for Kijé is with Szell (Sony SBK 89287), but if you want this coupling, the Mercury disc is still the one to go for.

Romeo and Juliet (ballet; complete. Choreography and staging Rudolf Nureyev).

*** Warner NVC Arts **DVD** 0630 15154-2. Legris, Loudières, Jude, Delanoe, Carbonnel, Martinez, Paris Opéra O, Pähn. (Director: Alexandre Tarta. Producers: François Duplet and Damien Mathieu.)

Rudolf Nureyev famously created the role of Romeo for the Royal Ballet in 1965 with Margot Fonteyn as Juliet. In 1977 he revised the choreography for his own London Festival Ballet production, and in 1984 reworked the entire ballet for the Paris Opéra Ballet. The present live performance dates from 1995, with Manuel Legris dancing the role of Romeo with great distinction and Monique Loudières a delightful, elegantly graceful, and passionate Juliet. Their love scenes together, at first romantic and finally erotically ardent, are among the ballet's highlights. But so too are the scenes with Tybalt (Charles Jude) and Mercutio (Lionel Delanoe) on whom Nureyev's choreography places special emphasis as 'champions' of the younger generation of the two rival families.

The confrontations between Mercutio and Tybalt are thrillingly visceral, the choreography for the electrifying dual with Romeo and the death of Tybalt a *coup de theâtre*, well matched by Prokofiev's vibrant music. The earlier panorama, with spectacularly spacious set designs by Ezio Frigerio, presents a brilliant, large-scale fresco of a turbulent Verona, full of colour and movement. Yet the simpler background for Friar Lawrence's chapel is equally memorable. Mauro Pagano's vivid costume designs give a vivid survey of the Italian Quattrocento, borrowing from paintings by Uccello, Piero Della Francesca, Pisanello and others.

In short, the production offers an ideal backcloth for superb dancing from the principals and a totally gripping projection of the narrative. At the anguished climax, Romeo's angry despatch of Paris is more like murder than a duel. But by the ballet's close, which is not protracted, 'all are punished'. There is some intrusive audience applause, notably in Acts I and III, but it is a price well worth paying for the electricity of a live performance, and there are plenty of entry points on the DVD (which has an excellent booklet). The orchestra plays Prokofiev's infinitely inspired score very well indeed, and the recording, too, is very good (it seems to gain range and impact as the ballet proceeds). But it is not up to the superb demonstration quality provided by Decca for Maazel's riveting Cleveland audio recording, which, on a Double Decca (452 970-2), is surely an essential supplement to the DVD.

Romeo and Juliet (ballet), Op. 64: highlights.

(B) *** Sony SBK 89740. BPO, Salonen.

(B) ** CfP 575 5642. LPO, Pritchard – MUSSORGSKY: *Pictures at an Exhibition.* **

With magnificent playing from the Berlin Philharmonic Orchestra, Esa-Pekka Salonen's set of excerpts – now reissued at bargain price – is probably a 'best-buy' for those wanting a single disc of highlights from Prokofiev's masterly score. The orchestral playing has an enormous intensity and a refined felicity in the score's more delicate evocations. One is touched and deeply moved by this music-making, while the selection admirably parallels the ballet's narrative. The recording, made in the Philharmonie, matches sumptuousness with a potent clarity of projection, and the dynamic range is dramatically wide.

Pritchard's selection is not always predictable in its content, but follows the narrative until the fight between Tybalt and Mercutio, then moves straight to the *Death of Juliet*. He is rhythmically positive, yet most effective in the gentler lyrical music, as is shown by his sensitive rubato in the atmopheric introduction, and his picture of *Juliet as a Young Girl* delicately evoked. The LPO play with colour and commitment, although the passion of the lovers has been depicted with even greater intensity in other selections. The 1975 recording made in Barking Town Hall is certainly vivid.

Romeo and Juliet (ballet): Suites Nos. 1 & 2, Op. 64.

(BB) ** EMI Encore CDE5 75227-2. Oslo PO, Jansons.

Jansons secures playing of alert sensibility, discipline and refinement from the Oslo Philharmonic and has the advantage of a naturally balanced and vividly present recording, but the performance as a whole is wanting in a sense of the theatre. The best buy for this music remains Salonen on Sony.

Sinfonia concertante for Cello and Orchestra, Op. 125.

(M) **(*) Ph. 470 250-2 (2). Schiff, LAPO, Previn – DVORAK: *Cello Concerto;* SCHUMANN: *Cello Concerto;* R. STRAUSS: *Don Quixote.* **(*)

No grumbles about Heinrich Schiff's playing in the *Sinfonia concertante* (or *Symphony-Concerto*, as it is sometimes called) which Prokofiev composed for (and with) Rostropovich. The composer had originally planned to call it 'Cello Concerto No. 2', but it is so closely related to the thematic material of his pre-war *Cello Concerto* as to be a re-working. Schiff's is an impassioned, red-blooded and eminently well-recorded account which will give pleasure. Previn gets good results from the orchestra but this is not a first choice – that rests with Truls Mørk (Virgin VC5 45310-2) or Maisky and Pletnev (DG 449 821-2).

SYMPHONIES

Symphony No. 1 in D (Classical), Op. 25.

(B) *** Virgin 2 CD VBD5 62050-2 (2). Lausanne CO, Zedda – DEBUSSY: *Danse; Sarabande ***;* MILHAUD: *La création du monde ***;* SHOSTAKOVICH: *Chamber Symphony; Symphony No. 14.* **

Zedda's account of the *Classical Symphony* is highly persuasive, the violins exquisitely gentle at their poised entry in the Larghetto and the outer movements spirited, with the finale mercurial in its zestful progress. The fairly resonant sound, with the orchestra slightly recessed, adds to the feeling of warmth without blunting the orchestral articulation.

(i) Symphonies Nos. 1 (Classical) in D, Op. 25; (ii) 5 in B flat, Op. 100; (iii) 6 in E flat min., Op. 111; 7 in C sharp min., Op. 131; (i) Autumnal, Op. 8; (iv) Overture on Hebrew Themes, Op. 34.

(B) ** Double Decca (ADD/DDD) 470 527-2 (2). (i) LSO; (ii) Concg. O; (iii) Cleveland O; (iv) Puddy, Gabrieli Qt; all cond. Ashkenazy.

Ashkenazy gives us an exhilaratingly vivacious account of the *Classical Symphony* which hasn't been available for many years. The LSO players are pressed to the extreme, but there is plenty of character and delightful woodwind detail. The much darker *Autumnal* is an early work but well worth having, and the quirky *Overture on Hebrew Themes* (Ashkenazy as pianist) is excellently done too. All these performances are captured in Decca's best 1970s sound. On to the digital era, where the *Fifth Symphony* receives a superlative recording which captures the hardly less remarkable playing of the Concertgebouw Orchestra, with every strand of the texture audible yet in the right perspective – the sound has marvellous presence and range. The same can be said, recording-wise, about Ashkenazy's Cleveland accounts of the *Sixth* and *Seventh Symphonies*. But here, the performances are less remarkable. In the *Sixth Symphony* he sometimes loses the vital current that flows through the first movement, relaxing the tension a little too much. On the other hand, the *Largo* is really too fast to make the requisite contrast with the *Allegro*, and the opening of the finale is far too fast. The beginning of the *Seventh Symphony* is phrased rather fussily, though further into the first movement the music is allowed to adopt its natural flow. Generally speaking, these Cleveland recordings were not quite the artistic successes one had every reason to expect.

CHAMBER MUSIC

Overture on Hebrew Themes (for clarinet, piano & string quartet), Op. 34; Quintet (for oboe, clarinet, violin, viola & cello), Op. 39.

(BB) * Warner Apex 0927 44395-2. Berlin Soloists, Bashkirova – HINDEMITH: *Octet.* *

On the Apex CD the recording really is too close for enjoyable listening, which is a pity as the performances are excellent.

String Quartets Nos. 1 in B min., Op. 50; 2 in F (Kabarda), Op. 92; (i) Overture on Hebrew Themes, Op. 34.

(B) **(*) Hyp. Helios Dig. CDH 55032. Coull String Qt.; with (i) Malsbury, Pettit.

String Quartets Nos. 1 in B min., Op. 50; 2 in F (Kabarda), Op. 92; (i) Overture on Hebrew Themes, Op. 34; (ii) Quintet in G min., Op. 39.

(BB) *** Arte Nova 74321 65427-2. Russian Qt.; with (i) Federov, Khakhlov; (ii) Kotenok, Tantsov, Goloubev.

The Russian Quartet gives first-class accounts of both quartets and scores over the Hyperion bargain issue both artistically and in offering the imaginative and rarely played *Quintet* for oboe, clarinet, violin, viola and double-bass, originally called *Trapeze*. As an inexpensive introduction to Prokofiev's chamber music, it can be strongly recommended, although the American Quartet on Olympia (OCD 340) remains a first choice for the two quartets in the higher price range.

The eminently serviceable performances on Helios give pleasure, though the ensemble, ultimately, lacks the zest and authority of some of its rivals, though the Coull produce a clean, well-blended sonority. The nickname of No. 2 derives from Kabarda in the Caucasus whose musical folklore Prokofiev had encountered when he was evacuated there during the Second World War.

Violin Sonata (for solo violin), Op. 115.

*** Claudio CB 5256-2. Jin – LALO: *Symphonie espagnole*. SARASATE: *Carmen Fantasy, Op. 25.* *** (with KROLL: *Banjo and Fiddle*, orch. Bradbury; TARREGA: *Recuerdos de la Alhambra*, arr. Ricci **(*)).

Min Jin's disarmingly direct approach to the *Solo Sonata* is most appealing, crisply so in the opening *Moderato*, seductively simple in the *Tema con variazioni*, buoyantly rhythmic and certainly *Con brio* in the closing *Allegro precipitato*, where she brings out the lyrical underlay. She is truthfully recorded and not balanced too closely. An unexpected but welcome coupling for an equally fresh approach to Lalo's *Symphonie espagnole*.

PIANO MUSIC

Piano Sonatas Nos. 1 in F min., Op. 1; 3 in A min., Op. 28; 4 in C min., Op. 29; 10 Pieces from Romeo and Juliet, Op. 75.

(BB) **(*) Naxos 8.554270. Glemser.

This is more than serviceable, both for performances and recordings, for those with limited budgets and makes a good individual collection, but it makes no real challenge to the rival series now on offer (Berman on Chandos, Chiu on Harmonia Mundi).

Piano Sonatas Nos. 6 in A, Op. 82; 8 in B flat, Op. 84.

*** Naive V 4898. Guy.

The young French pianist François-Frédéric Guy studied at the Paris Conservatoire with Dominique Merlet and Christian Ivaldi. He made a great impression on his visit to London in 2002, and he has already appeared with many leading orchestras both on the continent and in Britain. Prokofiev's wartime trilogy of piano sonatas comprises Nos. 6 through to 8, and it is a pity that the present disc does not include No. 7. Be that as it may, these are electrifying performances of virtuosity and great musical intelligence. This ranks among the best Prokofiev sonata discs in the current catalogues along with the likes of Richter (within a recital collection), Pollini and Pletnev.

Piano Sonata No. 7 in B flat, Op. 83.

(BB) *(*) Warner Apex 0927 40830-2. Sultanov – RACHMANINOV: *Piano Sonata No. 2* *(*); SCRIABIN: *Piano Sonata No. 5* *(*).

A strongly muscular and powerful account of the *Seventh Sonata* comes from Alexei Sultanov, although it is too crude and aggressive to disturb allegiance to such recommendations as Argerich, Pollini and Pletnev.

Piano Sonatas Nos. 7 in B flat, Op. 83; 8 in B flat, Op. 84; Romeo and Juliet: Romeo and Juliet before Parting; Masks.

(M) *** Decca (ADD) 468 497-2. Ashkenazy – LISZT: *Impromtu (Nocturne); Mephisto Waltz No. 1.* ***

Ashkenazy's commanding performances of these two sonatas, recorded in 1967, have great authority and conviction, and in our original review we hoped 'that Decca may one day persuade him to record the complete cycle'. This came about in the course of time, but the present recordings are rather special. The rhapsodical excerpts from *Romeo and Juliet* are also memorable and the Liszt couplings are hardly less impressive, the *Mephisto Waltz* is predictably dazzling.

Piano Sonatas Nos. 8 in B flat, Op. 84; 9 in C, Op. 103; Toccata, Op. 11.

(BB) ** Arte Nova 74321 85291-2. Dimitriev.

Peter Dimitriev is now in his mid-twenties and has a distinguished musical pedigree. He was first prize-winner at the Tokyo Piano Competition in 1995. He possesses a first-class technique and has an evident feeling for Prokofiev, but the recording rather lets him down: it is not ideally focused, and there is some unwelcome resonance. However, he is an artist to watch and we hope that subsequent recordings will be better.

OPERA

L'Amour des trois oranges (The Love for Three Oranges) (sung in French).

*** Arthaus **DVD** 100 404. Bacquier, Viala, Perraguin, le Texier, Gautier, Henry, Reinhart, Lagrange, Caroli, Fournier, Dubosc, Bastin, Uria-Monzon, Lyon Opéra Ch. & O, Nagano. (Producer: Erlo; V/P: Jung.)

There are two fine versions on CD, Kent Nagano with the cast listed above (in French) and Valéry Gergiev's Kirov version, recorded in Russian in a concert performance at the Concertgebouw, Amsterdam (Philips 462 913-2). Although it contains some of Prokofiev's most popular orchestral interludes, the opera is in some ways less successful than its companions. As in *The Gambler* and *The Fiery Angel*, there are no set-pieces for the singers and there is scant thematic development. Indeed, the familiar orchestral *March* and *Scherzo* are practically the only elements that reappear. There is, however, no want of invention and exuberance, and the opera is ideal for DVD as it is very visual. The cast here is identical with the Virgin set, and the video recording was made during the 1989 production run. It initially appeared on a two-sided Pioneer LaserDisc but without subtitles and in inferior sound: when the scoring was heavy, the sonority was strident and coarse. The present transfer is much finer in this respect and, of course, offers subtitles in English, German, Italian, Spanish and the French in which it is sung. Recommended.

Ivan the Terrible, Parts I and II (complete).

(***) Eureka **DVD** EKA 40018 (2). Cherkassov, Tselikovskaya, Birman. (Film director: Sergei Eisenstein.)

When Sergei Eisenstein sought to follow up the brilliant success of his film *Alexander Nevsky* with an even more ambitious epic, *Ivan the Terrible*, he naturally turned again to Prokofiev to provide the music, whose score for *Nevsky* is uniquely memorable.

The subject of Ivan the Terrible equally inspired Prokofiev to write a powerful and distinctive score, which can stand on its own as a concert work. Yet over two films (94 and 85 minutes respectively) the result is necessarily more diffuse.

Eisenstein's astonishingly striking and beautiful images in black and white have remarkable impact on DVD, based on an excellent copy of the original film, but sadly, the soundtrack is depressingly crumbly and ill-focused. Though it makes it hard to enjoy Prokofiev's music, its power is still very clear, enhancing the heavyweight treatment of history.

Olivier's *Henry V* with Walton's music was made at exactly the same period, but offers infinitely finer sound than this. It is a pity that it was not possible to superimpose a modern recording of the music, as has been effectively done in live concert-showings of the film.

PUCCINI, Giacomo (1858–1924)

Messa di gloria; Crisantemi; Prelude sinfonico.

(BB) *** Naxos 8.555304. Palombi, Lundberg, Hungarian R Ch. & Op. O, Morandi.

Written in his early twenties but not unearthed till the 1950s, Puccini's *Messa di gloria* already points forward to his operatic style in colour and dramatic force. As the title suggests, the centrepiece is the extended setting of the *Gloria* in five clearly defined sections, starting with a jaunty march, and ending with an elaborate double fugue, and including a setting of *Gratias agimus tibi* for tenor solo, freshly sung here by Antonello Palombi. The *Credo*, even

more dramatic, leads from a dedicated male-voice setting of *Crucifixus* into a striking *Et resurrexit* in a minor key. The final *Agnus Dei*, with tenor and baritone soloists, was later adapted as the madrigal in Act 2 of *Manon Lescaut*.

The Naxos recording from Budapest brings bright, urgent singing and playing under Pier Morandi, fully matching previous versions, although Pappano's EMI version with Alagna and Hampson (CDC5 57159-2) remains a first choice. The early orchestral works (*Crisantemi* also provided material for *Manon Lescaut*) make an attractive bonus. An outstanding bargain.

OPERA

La Bohème (complete).

(M) *** Decca (ADD) 470 431-2 (2). Tebaldi, Bergonzi, Bastianini, Siepi, Corena, D'Angelo, St. Cecilia Ac., Rome, Ch. & O, Serafin.

(*) DG **DVD 073-027-9. Freni, Martino, Raimondi, Panerai, La Scala Ch. & O, Karajan (Director: Franco Zeffirelli).

(*) Warner **DVD 4509 99222-2. Cotrubas, Shicoff, Allen, Zschau, Howell, Rawnsley, ROHCG Ch. & O, Gardelli. (Producer: John Copley. V/D: Brian Large.)

(BB) (**) Naxos mono 8.110072/3. Albanese, Gigli, Menotti, Poli, Baronti, Baracchi, La Scala Milan Ch. & O, Berrettoni.

The famous Tebaldi/Bergonzi set has also now been reissued at mid-price as part of Decca's 'Compact Opera Collection'. However, there is no printed libretto, only a CD-ROM facility which carries full text and translation which can be printed out via a computer. The set remains available as a Decca Double (with synopsis) which many will feel is preferable (448 725-2).

Based on Zeffirelli's spectacular 1963 production at La Scala, Milan, this Karajan DVD version of *La Bohème* gives no idea of stage limitations. Indeed by completely avoiding shots of the full stage, Acts II and III give the illusion of being out of doors. One snag is that with the singers miming to recorded voices, often distant, there is sometimes little relationship between what one hears and what one sees in close-up. Nonetheless, with Karajan second to none as a Puccini interpreter, pointing the great emotional climaxes unerringly, and with Freni a meltingly beautiful Mimi, the combination of vividly atmospheric settings and a high-powered performance have one forgiving any discrepancies. Gianni Raimondi is a forthright Rodolfo with his ringing, unstrained tenor, while Panerai is an outstanding Marcello, and Adriana Martino a spunky Musetta.

Recorded for television in February 1982 with Brian Large directing, the alternative Warner DVD gives a vivid idea of John Copley's classic production of *La Bohème* at Covent Garden when it was new, with its evocative sets by Julia Trevelyan Oman. Traditionally realistic, the stage pictures are yet imaginatively fresh, at once grand to suit the opera-house, yet true to life.

Though Lamberto Gardelli's conducting is relatively relaxed, veering towards expansive speeds, the results are keenly idiomatic with an excellent cast of soloists. With voices balanced relatively close, Neil Shicoff may be too loud at times, but this is yet a warmly sympathetic portrayal, never coarse, and Ileana Cotrubas at the peak of her career makes a charming Mimi, if at times with a beat in her voice. Thomas Allen, at his full maturity, is superb as Marcello, commanding in every way, but, for all her vivacity, the Musetta of Marilyn Zschau, suffering from a very slow speed in the *Waltz Song*, is often too tremulous. Excellent singing and acting from Gwynne Howell and John Rawnsley as the other two Bohemians. Altogether this is another most recommendable DVD *Bohème*.

Gigli was always at his most winning in the role of Rodolfo in *La Bohème*, and here opposite Licia Albanese he is the central focus of a warmly enjoyable version, recorded in 1938 at La Scala. Gigli indulges at times in his cooing manner, but it is a powerful as well as a charming assumption, with humour well caught. In the next decade Albanese was Toscanini's choice for Mimi, and she went on singing the role at the Met. in New York until the mid-sixties, a role she made her own. The others are reliable if not comparably characterful, with Umberto Berrettoni as conductor. First-rate transfers from 78s.

La Bohème: highlights.

(BB) ** EMI Encore (ADD) 7243 5 74984 2 5. Scotto, Kraus, Milnes, Neblett, Plishka, Manuguerra, Amb. Op. Ch., Trinity Boys' Ch., Nat. PO, Levine.

With Levine's 1979 complete set currently unavailable, collectors might consider this highlights disc, even though the singing is flawed. Alfredo Kraus's relatively light tenor is no longer as sweet as it was and Scotto is not flatteringly recorded here. Milnes make a a a powerful Marcello and Neblett a strong Musetta, but Levine could be more persuasive in the big melodies.

La fanciulla del West (The Girl of the Golden West; complete).

(M) (*(*)) Warner Fonit mono 8573 87488-2 (2). Gavazzi, Campagnano, Savarese, Caselli, RAI Ch. & O of Milan, Basile.

Recorded in 1950 for Cetra in collaboration with Italian Radio, this Warner Fonit set was the first ever commercial recording of *La fanciulla del West*, an opera for long unfairly ignored outside Italy. It yields to later versions both in recorded sound – limited mono with clear voices but dim orchestra – and in the casting, which features a team of singers from a generation that built up opera in Italy after the war without making an impact outside. All the principals have powerful voices, but as recorded their singing is fluttery, maybe in part a question of recording balance. What makes the performance convincing nonetheless is the conducting of Arturo Basile, totally idiomatic, pressing home the great lyrical and dramatic moments with a conviction born of familiarity. An Italian libretto is provided but no translation. A his-

toric document rather than a serious contender. First choice among stereo versions still rests with the Decca Tebaldi set (421 595-2), which itself might almost be regarded as historic were not the Decca recording so spectacular, denying its age.

Madama Butterfly (complete).

(M) *** Decca (ADD) 470 577-2 (2). Tebaldi, Bergonzi, Cossotto, Sordello, St. Cecilia Ac., Rome, Ch. & O, Serafin.

(*) Decca **DVD 071 404-9. Freni, Ludwig, Domingo, Kerns, Senechal, Vienna PO, Karajan (Director: Jean-Pierre Ponnelle).

** Warner **DVD** 4509-99220-2. Kabaivanska, Antinori, Jankovic, Saccomani, Arena di Verona Ch. & O, Arena (Director Giulio Chazalettes; Video Director: Brian Large).

(M) (*) Warner Fonit mono 0927 43551-2 (2). Petrella, Tagliavini, Taddei, Cetra Ch., RAI SO of Turin, Questa.

As with *La Bohème* above, the famous Tebaldi/Bergonzi/Cossotto set has also now been reissued at mid-price as part of Decca's 'Compact Opera Collection'. However, there is no printed libretto, only a CD-ROM facility which again carries full text and translation via a computer. The set remains available as a Decca Double (with synopsis) which many will feel is preferable (452 594-2).

Recorded for television in 1974 in the same period as he recorded the opera for audio disc, Karajan's DVD of *Butterfly* is similarly magical in its evocation of Puccini's most atmospheric score. As on CD the title role is taken by Mirella Freni, as tenderly appealing to see as to hear, but where for audio the role of Pinkerton was taken by Luciano Pavarotti, here you have the much more telegenic Placido Domingo, singing with similar fervour, responding to the inspired stage direction of Jean-Pierre Ponnelle to make this cad of a hero more complex than usual. Butterfly's house is set in fields on a misty hill-top, in period around 1900, though Pinkerton is initially seen off-duty wearing a modern-looking T-shirt, and Butterfly demonstrates her American status in Act II by abandoning her kimono for blouse and skirt, before she returns to traditional dress at the end of the act. She uses no telescope to identify the 'Abramo Lincoln' entering Nagasaki harbour, but otherwise the setting is conventional and effective, with a comic portrait of Goro given by Michel Sénéchal, politically incorrect in its Japanese send-up, and the Bonze rather like a caricature from *Turandot*. The sound is full and atmospheric, though there is a curious pitch-problem in the middle of the *Flower Duet*, one of the few flaws in a fine issue.

The Warner issue offers an atmospheric evocation of a performance, directed for video by Brian Large at the open-air Arena di Verona, complete with shots of the crowd outside beforehand and with curtain-calls at the end of each act. In such a setting the performance is lusty rather than subtle, with voices amplified reasonably well, but with the principals tending to belt things out, notably the tenor, Nazzareno Antinori. Raina Kabaivanska is more responsive, though her acting is rather stiff. In *Un bel dì* she looks rather like a schoolmistress, implacable rather than tender, not helped by her likeness to Dame Maggie Smith in imperious mood.

Recorded in 1954, the old Cetra set of *Butterfly*, now reissued on Warner Fonit, brings perfunctory conducting from Angelo Questa and a flawed cast. Ferruccio Tagliavini as Pinkerton sets out loud and hectoring in the opening scene, only to be transformed by the sight of Butterfly, becoming from then on seductively honey-toned. Giuseppe Taddei is an impressive Sharpless, while Clara Petrella is an idiomatic if hardly distinctive Butterfly. Not a viable set with its limited mono sound, with voices balanced so close that even Goro sounds loud.

Madam Butterfly (complete; in English).

(M) **(*) Chan. 3070 (2). Barker, Clarke, Rigby, Yurisich, Kale, Geoffrey Mitchell Ch., Philh. O, Abel.

With Cheryl Barker a warm, fresh heroine, bringing out the girlish shyness at the beginning, and singing with radiant tone, this set of *Butterfly* in English, sponsored by the Peter Moores Foundation, fills an important gap (as do many other operas in English). Cheryl Barker as a pupil of Dame Joan Hammond, for long celebrated in this role, has plainly learnt from that experience, and she is helped by the expressive conducting of Yves Abel which consistently brings out the beauty of Puccini's orchestration, helped by full-bodied Chandos sound. As Pinkerton, the tenor, Paul Charles Clarke, is a disappointment with his gritty, tight tone, penetrating and un-Italianate, but he characterizes sensitively, and Gregory Yurisich is a splendid Sharpless and Jean Rigby a fine Suzuki. The old Elkins translation is used with a few necessary modifications.

Tosca (complete).

✪ (M) *** EMI (ADD) CMS5 67756-2 [567759] (2). Callas, Di Stefano, Gobbi, Calabrese, La Scala Milan Ch. & O, De Sabata.

*** EMI CDC5 57173-2 (2). Gheorghiu, Alagna, Raimondi, ROHCG Ch. & O, Pappano.

(BB) (**) Naxos (mono) 8.110096-97 (2). Caniglia, Gigli, Borgioli, Dominici, Tomei, Rome Opera Ch. & O, Fabritiis.

(M) (**) Warner Fonit mono 8573 87479-2 (2). Frazzoni, Tagliavini, Guelfi, RAI Ch. & O of Turin, Basile.

There has never been a finer recorded performance of *Tosca* than Callas's first, with Victor de Sabata conducting and Tito Gobbi as Scarpia. Gobbi makes the unbelievably villainous police chief into a genuinely three-dimensional character, and Di Stefano, as the hero Cavaradossi, was at his finest. The conducting of De Sabata is spaciously lyrical as well as sharply dramatic, and the mono recording is superbly balanced in Walter Legge's fine production. The recording now rightly takes its place as one of EMI's 'Great Recordings of the Century' and the new transfer brings enhanced sound that could almost be stereo, with the voices caught gloriously.

With all three principals the clarity of words adds to the power of this Pappano performance, most strikingly with Gheorghiu, who constantly sheds new light on one phrase after another. When Cavaradossi attempts to explain the black eyes of the Madonna he is painting, Gheorghiu, responding in the half-tone phrase '*Ah, quegli occhi*' ('Ah, those eyes') conveys her doubt with heart-stopping intensity. In Act II, when Scarpia is all-dominant, Gheorghiu, instead of being defiant from the outset is plainly frightened out of her wits, so that we then movingly witness the build-up of resolve that will lead to murder, punctuated by an account of the aria *Vissi d'arte* of velvet beauty. Gheorghiu's is a great performance, significantly expanding on what we already know of her, as magnetic as Callas's, rich and beautiful as well as dramatic. The EMI sound is superb, full, clear and atmospheric, making this a classic among the many versions of this opera.

It is rare for a recording of *Tosca* to centre round the tenor taking the role of Cavaradossi, rather than round the Scarpia or Tosca herself, yet here Gigli at the height of his fame in 1938 is manifestly the main focus. He does not disappoint, making the hero a more rounded, more human character than is common, with fun and playfulness well caught as well as pathos. Maria Caniglia was a last-minute choice when Iva Pacetti proved unavailable, and though it is not a searching portrayal of the jealous opera-singer, it is a vocally strong and purposeful one with the occasional edge on the voice apt enough. Armando Borgioli as Scarpia is reliable vocally rather than characterful, with Oliviero de Fabritiis pacing the score well in a full, red-blooded reading. Excellent CD transfers mastered by Ward Marston, with voices very well caught indeed. The two discs include a 50-minute supplement taken from a version of *Tosca* recorded in French in 1931, an abridged version on seven 78 discs chiefly valuable for the enchanting portrayal of Tosca by Nino Vallin, very feminine and seductive. The others are no match for her – Enrico de Mazzei self-indulgent as Cavaradossi and Paul Payan as Scarpia not remotely sinister. One does not regret that the hero's two big arias are both omitted from this supplement.

Though this historic mono recording from Warner Fonit is uncompetitive in a crowded field, it is worth hearing for the mellifluous Cavaradossi of Ferruccio Tagliavini, at his peak in 1956 when the recording was made. Also for the stentorian Scarpia of Gian Giacomo Guelfi, dark and powerful rather than convincingly villainous. It was recorded for Cetra by Italian Radio, which accounts for the absence of stereo in a 1956 recording, but the voices are well caught. The Tosca of Gigliola Frazzoni is totally idiomatic but not very distinctive.

Tosca: highlights.

*** EMI CDC5 57634-2. (from complete set with Gheorghiu, Alagna, Raimondi, ROHCG Ch. & O, Pappano).

This EMI highlights follows the progress of the opera over a generous 78 minutes of excerpts well covered by the detailed synopsis.

Turandot (complete).

(*) Arthaus **DVD 100 088. Marton, Sylver, Mazzaria, Langan, San Francisco Op. Ch. & O, Runnicles. (Production/Design: David Hockney; Director: Peter McClintock, V/D: Brian Large).

This comes from a 1994 San Francisco production and has Eva Marton in the title role, which she has, of course, sung in Vienna under Maazel for Sony (1983), Roberto Abbado (RCA) and James Levine (DG). Thus the merits and shortcomings of her Turandot are well known: hers is a big, dramatic voice, but with far too little expressive variation in tone and she is content to sing loudly and leave it at that. However, there are other things in its favour: a decent Calaf in Michael Sylver, a good Ping (Theodore Baerg), Pang (Dennis Peterson) and Pong (Craig Estep). We have heard more moving accounts of Liù than Lucia Mazzaria's, but generally speaking the cast are more than acceptable. The orchestral and choral forces are very well harnessed by Donald Runnicles, who fires on all cylinders and visually the designs by David Hockney are vivid and bold (some might think them garish, and have had a dismissive press) but they will strike most readers as effective. The sound is rather forward and bright, and detail is very well captured by the engineers. Brian Large, as always, makes sure that the camera is where you would want it to be, and although there are more subtle Turandots to be found than Marton, the performance is thoroughly gripping. (There are sub-titles in English, French, Dutch and German.)

PURCELL, Henry (1659–95)

The Fairy Queen (complete).

*** Arthaus **DVD** 100 200. Kenny, Randle, Rice, van Allan, ENO Ch. & O, Kok. (Director: David Pountney.)
(M) **(*) Virgin VMD5 61955 2 (2). Bickley, Hunt, Pierard, Crook, Padmore, Wilson-Johnson, Wistreich, L. Schütz Ch., L. Classical Players, Norrington.

Recorded live at the Coliseum in London in 1995, this ENO production of *The Fairy Queen*, conducted by Nicholas Kok, turns an entertainment which can, under modern conditions, seem cumbersome into a sparkling fantasy, thanks to the brilliant stage direction of David Pountney and choreography of Quinny Sacks. The sequence of masques are treated as a series of circus turns, and thanks also to the fantastic costumes of Dunya Ramicova the atmosphere of the circus is never far away, helping to hold together an episodic sequence of scenes, originally designed to back up a garbled version of Shakespeare's *A Midsummer Night's Dream*.

The result is as much a surreal ballet as an opera, with Nicholas Kok drawing stylish playing from the ENO Orchestra, echoing period practice, using a realization prepared by Clifford Bartlett. So the scene of the Drunken Poet proves genuinely funny, with Jonathan Best (identified only in the final credits on film) doing a jolly imitation of a 1950s poet with scruffy sports jacket and pullover.

By contrast Titania - Yvonne Kenny at her finest - and Oberon - the exotic Thomas Randle - stand out the more sharply as otherworldly figures thanks to their glamorous costumes. More equivocal is the presentation of Puck by Simon Rice, lively as he is. A fun entertainment, as unstuffy a presentation of Purcell's problematic masterpiece as could be, vividly filmed and recorded.

Roger Norrington recorded *The Fairy Queen* following a 'Purcell Experience' weekend, which culminated in a concert performance of this inspired but disjointed semi-opera. There is a refinement and polish about the solo singing and the ensemble which reflects the intensive preparation. Where William Christie's earthier reading with Les Arts Florissants (HMC 901308/9) reflects the experience of a stage production – bold, jolly and intense – Norrington's wears its polished manners in a crisp, lightly rhythmic way, helped by the finely honed playing of the London Classical Players. Speeds are often brisk, with rhythms lightly sprung, and the impressive line-up of soloists brings distinctive characterization from such singers as David Wilson-Johnson as the Drunken Poet, Mark Padmore in the tenor songs of Act IV and Lorraine Hunt in *Hark! The echo'ing air*, which is taken very fast and lightly. There is less fun and less dramatic bite here than in Christie's or Gardiner's versions, but recorded in a spacious acoustic, Norrington's light, clean approach never diminishes Purcell's bubbling inspiration.

QUILTER, Roger (1877–1953)

(i) *Slumber Song; Where go the Boats.* Songs: (ii) *Down by the Sally Gardens; Drink to Me Only; The Fair House of Joy;* (ii/iii) *Now Sleeps the Crimson Petal;* (iv) *Love's Philosophy;* (i) *Over the Mountain; To Daisies;* (v) *Weep You no More;* (ii) *Ye Banks and Braes.*

(M) *** Decca mono/stereo 470 195-2. (i) Lloyd Webber, Lenehan; (ii) Ferrier, Spurr; (iii) Luxon, Willison; (iv) Vyvyan, Lush; (v) Ameling, Jansen – IRELAND: *Songs* **(*); RUBBRA: *Songs* ***.

It is good to see a group of Roger Quilter's most famous songs appearing together on record in really fine performances. After Julian Lloyd Webber's affectionate accounts of the two cello pieces, we have a short anthology of recordings, from the 1950s to the 1970s. Kathleen Ferrier was especially suited to this repertoire, and the other singers provide telling contrast. Elly Ameling is most touching in *Weep You no More*, and it is fascinating to hear *Now Sleeps the Crimson Petal* in two quite different versions by Ferrier and Luxon. Excellent recordings, be they mono or stereo, with Ferrier as transferred here uncannily present.

RACHMANINOV, Sergei

(1873–1943)

Piano Concertos Nos 1–4; Rhapsody on a Theme of Paganini.

(M) **(*) Danacord DACOCD 582-583 (3). Marshev, Aarhus SO, Loughran.

Oleg Marshev, born in Baku, a Russian-trained virtuoso who earlier recorded a whole series of adventurous discs for Danacord – Emil von Sauer, Strauss, Rinstein as well as Prokofiev and Liszt – here goes on to central, much-duplicated repertory, emerging as a formidable contender if hardly an outright winner. These are broad-brush readings in many senses. The speeds are generally broader than usual – with No. 2 taking over five minutes longer than in some vintage versions – but with his weight and power Marshev sustains broad tempi well, only occasionally letting the music run the risk of sounding plodding, as in the slow movement of No. 2 and at the start of the *Third Concerto*. Yet the thrust and intensity of his performances consistently carries one along, with full, forward recording balance adding to the power. It also allows one to appreciate Marshev's clarity of articulation in Rachmaninov's brilliant passagework. The downside is that the weight of the recording in heavy-textured passages tends to obscure inner detail. It also tends to downplay the poetic side of these heartfelt warhorses. Marshev's control of rubato is always fluent and idiomatic, conveying spontaneity of feeling, but others are even freer, and the absence of a true pianissimo makes the slow movements in particular sound a little heavy-handed in comparison with the finest versions. Loughran draws comparably powerful playing from the excellent Aarhus Symphony Orchestra, with a fine sheen on the strings, its most outstanding section. The broad speeds mean that the set has had to spread to three discs, but they come at mid-price. However, first choice for the four concertos still remains with Ashkenazy and Previn (Double Decca 444 839-2).

(i) Piano Concertos Nos. 1 in F sharp min., Op. 1; (ii; iii) 2 in C min., Op. 18; (ii; iv) Rhapsody on a Theme of Paginini.

(BB) (***) Naxos (mono) 8.110676. Moiseiwitsch, with (i) Philh O, Sargent; (ii) RLPO; cond (iii) Goehr; or (iv) Cameron.

Rachmaninov used to say that his friend Moiseiwitsch was an even finer interpreter of some of his works than himself, and from this vintage collection one can understand why. Moiseiwitsch recorded No. 2 in 1937 for HMV on four budget-label 78s, undercutting the composer's classic version by half in price, yet the performance is if anything more electrifying. The sound is limited, with the piano close, but in Ward Marston's masterly transfer one quickly forgets the limitations, as one does in the other pre-war recording of the *Rhapsody on a Theme of Paganini*, a sparkling performance, again urgent in its expression, with the celebrated

eighteenth variation all the warmer for going at a flowing speed. The rarity is the post-war, 1948 account of No. 1, in which the sound is full and clear with Moiseiwitsch still at the peak of his form, both passionate and sparkling, powerful and poetic.

Piano Concerto No. 2 in C min., Op. 18.

(BB) ** Warner Apex 0927 40835-2. Sultanov, LSO, Shostakovich – TCHAIKOVSKY: *Piano Concerto No. 1.* **

(**) BBCL mono 4074-2. Moiseiwitsch, BBC SO, Sargent – BEETHOVEN: *Piano Concerto No. 5.* (***)

(B) * EMI (ADD) CDE5 74732-2. Cziffra, New Philh. O, Cziffra Jr – GRIEG: *Piano Concerto.* *

Sultanov's recording was made in the immediate aftermath of his success at the eighth Van Cliburn Competition. There is plenty of exuberance and brilliance and an impressive range of tonal colour. Whatever reservations one may have, this is an eminently serviceable account, even if this would hardly be a first choice. The balance places the soloist too far forward, and the recording does not do justice to the LSO strings, which sound lustreless.

Rachmaninov thought Moiseiwitsch one of his finest interpreters, and this performance from a 1956 Prom serves as a reminder of his stature. Moiseiwitsch was seventeen years younger than the composer and grew up in his shadow. He is certainly steeped in both his spiritual and sound world, even if, in the heat of live performance, he was prone to the odd split note. But by this time, when he was in his sixties, he unaccountably appeared less in the concert hall than he had during the 1940s, and this inevitably took its toll. There are plenty of insights into this piece that the gladiatorial virtuosi of the present day do not bring, and he is given excellent support from Sir Malcolm Sargent, a fine concerto accompanist. Unfortunately, the sound is wanting in transparency and range and comes close to distortion in climaxes. All the same, this is an invaluable musical document, which all who care about the piano should investigate.

Though not entirely lacking poetic feeling, Cziffra's early 1970s account brings a general lack of passion and brilliance (mainly the fault of the conductor), though the finale does catch fire in the right places. The sound is below 1970s standards, with the orchestra sounding scrawny at times. Not recommended, even at budget price, with so much white-hot competition.

(i) Piano Concerto No. 2; (ii) Rhapsody on a Theme of Paganini.

(M) * Sony (ADD) SMK 89568. Graffman, NYPO, Bernstein.

(i) Piano Concerto No. 2 in C min., Op. 18; (ii) Rhapsody on a Theme of Paganini, Op. 43. Prelude in C sharp min., Op. 3/2.

(BB) (***) Naxos mono 8.110692. Kapell, Robin Hood Dell O, Philadelphia, (i) Steinberg or (ii) Reiner.

This collection of recordings by William Kapell, killed in an aircraft crash at the age of 33, presents his art at its most compelling. These are exceptionally urgent readings, notably in No. 2, where the first movement gets you off to an electrifying start, pressing on at a far faster speed than usual. Yet there is nothing perfunctory about Kapell's fast speeds, just a demonstration of mastery, both in the *Concerto* and in the *Variations*. Significantly, each of the 'takes' in the many 78 sides involved was the first, with no retakes needed, demonstrating the spontaneous, white-hot quality of Kapell's playing, which yet did not rule out poetry. The Ward Marston transfers are vivid and full, both in the *Concerto* (1950) and in the *Rhapsody* (1951). The *Prelude*, recorded in 1945, is dimmer, and curiously the recording of that relatively simple piece comes from the fifth retake.

The Graffman/Bernstein performances date from 1964 and are not a success. Graffman's playing is without feeling for the winding Rachmaninov phrase, and the slow movement fails to relax in the right way. The *Rhapsody*, played with considerable brilliance, is more enjoyable – the sound is quite vivid and rather better than some recordings from this source. However, there are too many outstanding bargain versions of this repertoire to consider this, and first choice still rests with Ashkenazy and Previn (Decca 460 632-2).

(i) *Piano Concertos Nos. 2 in C min., Op. 18; 3 in D min., Op. 30;* (ii) *Symphony No. 2 in E min., Op. 27; Vocalise, Op. 34/14.*

(B) **(*) Warner Ultima 0630 18958-2 (2). (i) Berezovsky, Philh. O, Inbal; (ii) Bolshoi SO, Lazarev.

The best things here are the two concertos, which are played with much eloquence and assurance by Boris Berezovsky, and we hope these may be reissued separately later on Apex. The *Second Symphony* is good without being special, but the performance is idiomatic and enjoyable, and at the price this set is worth having for Berezovsky.

(i) *Piano Concerto No. 4 in G min., Op. 40;* (ii) *The Isle of the Dead; The Rock, Op. 7; Symphonic Dances, Op. 45;* (iii; iv) *Cello Sonata in G min., Op. 19;* (iii; v) *Vocalise* (arr. Rose).

(B) ** Warner Ultima 8573 81967-2 (2). (i) Lubimov, Toronto SO, Saraste; (ii) Royal Stockholm PO, Davis; (iii) Noras; (iv) Heinonen; (v) Valsta.

This compilation includes more than serviceable accounts of the *Symphonic Dances*, *The Isle of the Dead* and *The Rock* from Andrew Davis and the Royal Stockholm Philharmonic. Vladimir Lubimov is a fluent soloist in the *Fourth Piano Concerto*, although he does not displace Ashkenazy, let alone Michelangeli, both modestly priced. Arto Noras is a refined and eloquent player, but his pianist pulls the second group of the *Cello Sonata*'s first movement horribly out of shape, and we would find it difficult to live with this on repetition.

(i) *Rhapsody on a Theme of Paganini, Op. 43.*

(B) (***) RCA Double mono 74321 845952 (2). Kapell, Robin Hood Dell O, Reiner – BEETHOVEN: *Piano*

Concerto No. 2 (***); CHOPIN: *Piano Sonata No. 2*; DEBUSSY: *Children's Corner*; PROKOFIEV: *Piano Concerto No. 3* (***); KHACHATURIAN: *Piano Concerto* (***) (with SHOSTAKOVICH: *3 Preludes*; SCHUBERT: *Impromptu; Ländler; Moment musical; Waltzes* ***).

One of the supreme performances of the *Paganini Rhapsody* and ample testimony to Kapell's stature. Some allowances have to be made for the sound, but the sheer high voltage and poetic feeling of the solo playing carry all before it. Fine support from Reiner and the Robin Hood Dell Orchestra.

Symphonies Nos. 1–3.

(B) *** Virgin VBD5 62037-2 (2). RPO, Litton.

Andrew Litton's mid-priced box is highly competitive alongside the Previn set, especially as all three symphonies are encompassed by a pair of CDs. They offer first-class digital sound with a beauty of orchestral texture ideal for Rachmaninov, and in this respect are superior to Previn, although the comparable Decca set (448 116-2), if not quite as rich in its violin textures, remains very competitive sonically, with the Concertgebouw acoustic providing full and atmospheric ambience.

In No. 1, Litton is most persuasive in his free use of rubato and his performance combines power and ripeness of romantic feeling with tenderness, bringing out the refinement of Rachmaninov's scoring. In the *Second Symphony* he readily sustains the observance of the exposition repeat in the first movement, making it a very long movement indeed at just over 23 minutes. But the moments of special magic are those where, as in his lightly pointed account of the Scherzo or, most of all, the lovely clarinet melody of the slow movement, subtlety of expression gives Rachmaninov's romanticism an extra poignancy.

In the *Third Symphony*, the gentleness of his treatment of the great second subject melody means that the transparent beauty of Rachmaninov's scoring is brought out luminously, and though the opening of the finale may not sound urgent enough, it is crisply pointed and leads on to a superbly brisk, tense conclusion.

Symphony No. 1, Op. 13; 5 Etudes-tableaux (orch. Respighi).

*** Chan. 9822. Russian State SO, Polyansky.

Good playing and particularly good recording make Polyansky's Chandos CD a competitive issue, even though neither Jansons nor Pletnev, both coupled with *The Isle of the Dead*, is challenged artistically. A worthwhile addition to the catalogue, particularly in view of the Respighi transcription of the *Etudes-tableaux*.

Symphony No. 2 in E min., Op. 27.

**(*) BIS CD 1279. RSNO, Arwel Hughes.
(B) **(*) CfP (ADD) 575 5652. Hallé O, Loughran – TCHAIKOVSKY: *Romeo and Juliet*. **(*)

Owain Arwel Hughes on BIS offers an exceptionally expansive reading of Rachmaninov's *Second Symphony*. It is expansive not only in the tempos he chooses and in his expressive style, but in his decision to observe the rarely performed exposition repeat in the first movement. So it is that the first movement alone lasts just over 25 minutes. Inevitably the tensions and thrust are markedly less than in the finest rival versions, a point brought out the more when the BIS recording balance sets the orchestra at a slight distance. With fine discipline from the Royal Scottish National Orchestra the result is refined and thoughtful rather than fervently passionate, emphasizing the beauty of sound. This is a reading for those who prefer to meditate over the beauty of this Rachmaninov masterpiece rather than to be swept away by its redblooded romanticism. But for most readers Previn (EMI CDM5 66982-2) will prove a better choice, while Kurt Sanderling's mono recording with the Leningrad Philharmonic is hardly less voluptuous and altogether more inspired (● DG 449 767-2).

Although Loughran's performance takes a little while to warm up, the reading does not lack intensity, with a fine slow movement, and the orchestral playing is excellent. He plays the work uncut (something that could not be taken for granted in 1973 when the record was made). The recording is vivid and refined in detail and the equally impressive coupling gives this bargain disc a playing time of 79 minutes.

Symphony No. 3 in A min., Op. 44.

(M) **(*) Decca (ADD) 468 490-2. LPO, Boult –
VAUGHAN WILLIAMS: Symphony No. 8. ***

Sir Adrian Boult's early stereo (1956) recording of the Third Symphony would appear to be a strange choice for reissue in Decca's 'Legends' series. Yet the Walthamstow recording has come up vividly – it is remarkably well detailed, the stereo warm-toned and colourful. A greater breadth of tone from the higher strings would have been welcome, but the LPO play passionately for him and create a touching mood of very Russian nostalgia in the Adagio, particularly at the close, which is is very haunting. The original Gramophone review mentioned Boult's 'splendid sense of movement', and this is very striking in the scherzo section of the central movement, which is very successful and in the lively finale. It is overall a most sympathetic performance. Boult does not let his own personality intrude, but he captures the idiom with conviction, and the remastered sound is certainly impressive. The coupling with Vaughan Williams is unexpected but works well.

Symphony No. 3 in A min, Op. 44. Symphony in D min. (Youth); Vocalise.

*** BIS CD 1299. RSNO, Arwel Hughes.

Owain Arwel Hughes, following up his thoughtful reading of Rachmaninov's Second Symphony, draws from the Scottish National Orchestra a comparably well-played account of the Third, also brilliantly recorded with textures exceptionally clear. Again speeds are on the broad side in a reading less redbloodedly emotional than most, with the BIS sound again slightly distanced. Yet while in the Second Symphony that brought a lessening of emotional thrust, the degree of restraint in the Third Symphony brings advantages. That is especially so in the central Adagio, where the lovely horn solo at the start and the sweet solo violin entry at a full pianissimo have a tenderness that is most moving. Though in the finale the treatment is exceptionally expansive, Hughes holds the structure together well to bring an exciting close with its wildly syncopated rhythms in the coda.

The symphonic movement in D minor, written in 1891, Rachmaninov's Youth Symphony, may merely hint at his mature style, but it makes an attractive coupling, while Vocalise brings a touchingly refined and restrained reading of a popular piece that has often prompted much heavier-handed accounts.

CHAMBER MUSIC

Cello Sonata in G min., Op. 19.

(M) *** Somm SOMMCD 026. Walton, Owen –
CHOPIN: Cello Sonata. ***

(B) **(*) RCA 2-CD 74321 84598-2 (2). Starker, Neriki –
BRAHMS: Cello Sonatas Nos. 1-2; in D (arr. of Violin Sonata, Op. 78) **(*); SCHUMANN: Adagio and Allegro; Fantasiestücke. ***

A first-class account from Jamie Walton and Charles Owen – warm, passionate and refined, with fine lyrical impetus in the finale. A good recording balance too, although the otherwise attractive acoustic does not offer the clearest separation.

In the warmly full-blooded Starker/Neriki account, the piano part is always to the fore, and not just because of the recording balance. Shigeo Neriki is a natural Rachmaninovian, playing brilliantly and following the rich lyrical ebb and flow of the melodic lines. Starker certainly responds with ardour, and the finale is particularly successful, but it is Neriki who dominates throughout. The recording is vividly realistic.

Trios Elégiaques Nos. 1 in G min., Op. 8; 2 in D min., Op. 9.

*** Tavros EPT 4516. Koo, Sakharova, Arnadóttir.

An outstanding new coupling of the paired Rachmaninov Trios Elégiaques from this impressive group of young musicians – Korean pianist Yung Wook Koo, Russian violinist Julia Sakharova, with the warm-toned Icelandic cellist, Margarét Arnadóttir. They make a fine team and give performances that are as passionate as they are lyrically spontaneous. The long elliptical first movement of Op. 8 is admirably shaped, and the pianist emerges with special distinction in the following even more extended set of variations. The D minor Trio is an elegy for Tchaikovsky and its atmosphere of Russian melancholy (the composer's marking is lento lugubre) is richly caught, notably by the cellist. The recording is vividly up front – on one occasion the bass end of the piano is made to seem right on top of the listener – but the performances are so committedly vivid and alive that this debut CD must be welcomed with enthusiasm. (The disc is available from Tavros

Records, 1187 Coast Village Road, 1-288, Santa Barbara, California 93108, USA. Fax: 00-1-805-969-5749. E-mail: info@tavrosrecords.com)

Trios Elégiaques Nos. 1 & 2, Opp. 8–9; 2 Pieces for Cello & Piano, Op. 2; 2 Pieces for Violin & Piano, Op. 6.

*** Hyp. CDA 67178. Moscow Rachmaninov Trio.

Apart from two incomplete string quartets and the *Cello Sonata, Op. 19*, the four works here comprise Rachmaninov's complete chamber output. The two piano trios are both called *Trio élégiaque*; the *First in G minor*, dating from 1892, was not published until 1947, four years after Rachmaninov's death, and is a short one-movement piece. The *Second in D minor, Op. 9*, was composed in memory of Tchaikovsky who had been a staunch champion and friend (it includes variations on a theme from *The Rock*) and was completed within a few months of Tchaikovsky's death. Rachmaninov himself took part in its first performance together with the Opp. 2 and 6 pieces. The Moscow Rachmaninov Trio (Viktor Yampolsky, Mikhail Tsinman and Natalia Savinova) are superb artists and play this music with feeling and sensitivity. This can be strongly recommended alongside the Tavros issue from the Koo/Sakharova/Arnadottir Trio, although the former has the advantage of including much more music.

PIANO MUSIC

Piano duet

Suites Nos. 1–2; Symphonic Dances.

** Sony SK 61767. Ax, Bronfman.

As long as Ashkenazy and Previn's 1979 Double Decca recording of this coupling remains in circulation (444 845-2), there is little need to look further. Emanuel Ax and Yefim Bronfman have impressive technical address, but they are curiously unresponsive to the atmosphere engendered by these glorious pieces. These artists relish the bright surfaces without penetrating much further.

Solo piano music

Etudes-tableaux, Opp. 33 & 39; 3 Nocturnes (1887–8); 23 Preludes, Op. 23/1–10, Op. 32/1–13 Nos. 1–24; Piano Sonatas Nos. 1–2, Opp. 28 & 36; Variations on a theme of Corelli, Op. 42.

(M) ** CMS5 67938-2 [ZDMC 67938] (3). John Ogdon.

Previously unpublished, this wide-ranging survey of Rachmaninov's piano music was recorded in 1988, the year before John Ogdon died tragically young at the age of 52. In the 1980s he had bravely returned to the concert platform having suffered for years after a severe mental breakdown. Though the playing here may have nothing like the diamond precision of his earlier recordings, the weight, warmth and concentration over long spans are very typical, demonstrating

Ogdon's natural sympathy for the Russian idiom and his joy in the pianist-composer's virtuoso demands. The booklet includes an excellent account of Ogdon's life and career, as well as a note on the John Ogdon Foundation, which promotes scholarships for young pianists and performances of his compositions.

Etudes-tableaux, Opp. 33 & 39; 6 Preludes, Op. 23/1–2, 4–5, 7–8; 7 Preludes, Op. 32/1–2, 6–7, 9–10,12.

(BB) *** Regis (DDD/ADD) RRC 1022. Richter.

Although he played them in public, Sviatoslav Richter did not record all the *Preludes*, only the ones he liked best. Those here were recorded in 1971 but the *Etudes-tableaux* are later digital recordings. The playing is of a rare order of mastery and leaves strong and powerful resonances. Richter's conception goes far beyond the abundant virtuosity this music calls for and the characterization is very strong and searching. The sound quality is less than ideal, a bit hard and two-dimensional, but fully acceptable when the playing is so riveting. This reissue (of the original Olympia CD) is unique and not to be missed.

Moments Musicaux, Op. 16; Preludes, Op. 3/2; Op. 23/1–10.

*** Erato 8573 85770-2. Lugansky.

Nikolai Lugansky belongs to the same generation as Andsnes and Kissin, and those who acquired his Chopin *Etudes* on Erato will know that he is an artist of impeccable technique and taste. He was a protégé of Tatiana Nikolayeva and won the Tchaikovsky Prize, whose winners have included Pletnev (under whose baton he appeared in London). His musicianship in this repertoire is no less impressive; there is plenty of virtuosity but none of his playing is too ostentatious. As impressive an account of this repertoire as we have had since Ashkenazy and Shelley, and warmly recommended.

Morceaux de fantaisie, Op. 3; Sonata No. 2 in B flat min., Op. 36; Variations on a Theme of Chopin, Op. 22.

✿ *** Elan 82248. Rodriguez.

Préludes, Op. 32/1–13 ; Sonata No. 1 in D min., Op. 28.

✿ *** Elan 82244. Rodriguez.

This is some Rachmaninov playing! Santiago Rodriguez is the real thing. For a moment one imagines that Rachmaninov himself is at the keyboard. He has something of Pletnev about him: wonderful authority and immaculate technical control, tremendous electricity as well as great poetic feeling. Outstanding in every way.

24 Preludes, Op. 23/1–10; Op. 32/1–13; in D min. Mélodie; 6 Moments musicaux, Op. 16; Morceaux de fantaisie, Op. 3; Oriental Sketch; Song transcriptions: Daisies; Lilacs.

(B) *** Virgin 2 x 1 VBD5 61624 (2). Alexeev.

Dmitri Alexeev's 1989 two-CD set of the *Preludes* and various other works brings us formidable and powerful pianism. His mastery is evident throughout, and although there are occasions, such as in the *B minor Prelude*, Op. 32, No. 10, where one misses the depth and poetic feeling of some rivals, the recital is a satisfying one and value for money.

Piano Sonata No. 2 in B flat min., Op. 36.

(BB) *(*) Warner Apex 0927 40830-2. Sultanov – PROKOFIEV: *Piano Sonata No. 7*; SCRIABIN: *Piano Sonata No. 5*. *(*)

Even at its modest price, Sultanov's Apex CD is of questionable value. There is no want of virtuosity, but it is of the designed-to-dazzle variety. Alexei Sultanov gives a pretty aggressive account of the sonata, very brightly lit and fiery. Some readers may respond more warmly to his showmanship than others, but he is essentially brilliant but brash and no challenge to the top recommendations.

VOCAL MUSIC

(i) The Bells, Op. 35; The Rock, Op. 7.

(BB) ** Naxos 8.550805. Nat. SO of Ireland, Anissimov; (i) with Field, Choupenitch, Meinikov, RTE Philharmonic Ch.

A far from negligible account of *The Bells* from this Russo-Irish partnership on Naxos, and *The Rock* is well played too. But at bargain price Previn and the LSO are better value (coupled with Prokofiev on EMI double fforte CZS5 73353-2). However, Pletnev's DG account on *The Bells* is well worth the extra outlay (✪ DG 471 029-2), and this has an enticing coupling in Taneyev's *John of Damascus*.

OPERA

Francesca da Rimini (complete).

*** DG 453 455-2. Guleghina, Larin, Leiferkus, Aleksashkin, Levinsky, Gothenburg Op. Ch. & SO, Järvi.

DG recorded all three of Rachmaninov's operas in 1996, issuing them in a box. Now, all of them have been made available separately. *Aleko*, a graduation exercise of striking quality is discussed in our main volume. *Francesca da Rimini* comes from 1906 and, like *The Miserly Knight*, shows something of the effect Bayreuth had on him. The opera is encumbered by an unsatisfactory libretto by Modest Tchaikovsky, but there is some glorious music and some fine singing from Maria Guleghina as Francesca and Sergei Leiferkus as Lanciotto Malatesta, the jealous husband. Sergei Larin makes a convincing Paolo, and the Gothenburg Orchestra and Chorus respond magnificently to Neeme Järvi. The recording quality is quite outstanding.

The Miserly Knight (complete).

*** DG 453 454-2. Aleksashkin, Larin, Chernov, Caley, Gothenburg SO, Järvi.

The Miserly Knight, to a Pushkin text, contrasts the old knight, whose devotion to gold is total, and his son, who eyes his father's fortune enviously. The famous soliloquy, arguably Rachmaninov's finest dramatic scena, is powerfully done by Sergei Aleksashkin, who succeeds in winning us over to the Knight. Sergei Larin is hardly less convincing as his son, Albert. The outstanding recording and the fine orchestral playing make this a most desirable set.

RAFF, Joachim (1822–82)

Symphony No. 1 in D (An das Vaterland), Op. 96.

(BB) ** Naxos 8.555411. Rhenish PO, Friedman.

As we commented in our main Guide, Raff's *First Symphony (An das Vaterland)* takes itself very seriously and its 70-minute duration invites longueurs. However, now it has been reissued at Naxos price admirers of this uneven composer might feel it is worth trying. It is well enough played and recorded.

RAUTAVAARA, Einojuhani

(born 1928)

(i) Harp Concerto. Symphony No. 8.

*** Ondine ODE 978-2. (i) Nordmann; Helsinki PO, Segerstam.

Both works are hot off the press: the *Harp Concerto* was completed as recently as 2001 for the Minnesota Orchestra, and the *Symphony* in 1999. The new concerto is predominantly reflective and highly imaginative in its use of texture. In addition to the soloist, Rautavaara adds two harps in the orchestra in order, as he puts it, to create 'a really full and lush harp sound when needed'. The whole piece takes 23 minutes, all three movements are slow, and our only problem is with the somewhat amorphous finale. The French soloist, Marielle Nordmann, a pupil of Lily Laskine, gives a performance of great distinction and subtlety. The *Eighth Symphony* was commissioned by the Philadelphia Orchestra, which premièred it in April 2000 under Sawallisch. Rautavaara speaks of its musical growth as characterized by slow transformation, a strong narrative element and 'the generation of new, different aspects and perspectives from the same premises, the transformation of light and colour'. As always with this composer there is a strong feeling for nature. Perhaps the most haunting movement is the third, whose quiet radiance stays with the listener. Excellent playing from the Helsinki Philharmonic under Leif Segerstam and state-of-the-art recording.

RAVEL, Maurice (1875–1937)

Alborada del gracioso; Une Barque sur l'ocean; Boléro; (i) Daphnis et Chloé (complete ballet); L'Eventail de Jeunne (Fanfare); Ma Mère l'Oye;

Menuet Antique; Pavane pour une infante défunte; Rapsodie Espagnole; Shéhérazade: Overture de fèerie; Le Tombeau de Couperin; La Valse; Valses Nobles et sentimentales.

(B) **(*) DG Trio 469 354-2 (3). LSO, Abbado; (i) with LSO Ch.

Much of this collection is already available on a DG Double (459 439-2 – see our main volume). But by using three CDs (offered for the cost of a pair of mid-priced discs) *Ma Mère l'Oye* has now been included plus the complete *Daphnis et Chloé*. Here the brilliant playing of the LSO is helpd by an exceptionally analytical DG recording which has the widest possible dynamic range – so that the *pianissimo* at the very opening is barely audible for almost 30 seconds. For all the refinement and virtuosity this is a performance to admire rather than love, lacking the atmosphere of the rest of the programme which is altogether more evocative, beautifully played and recorded without dynamic exaggeration. So the DG Double mentioned above is preferable, unless *Ma Mère l'Oye* is essential.

(i) *Alborada del gracioso; Boléro; Daphnis et Chloé: Suite No. 2; La Valse; (ii) Ma Mère l'Oye* (complete); *Pavane pour une infante défunte; Le Tombeau de Couperin* – DEBUSSY (orch. RAVEL): *Danse (Tarantelle Styrienne); Sarabande.*

(B) ** Teldec Ultima 0630 18959-2 (2). (i) Cleveland O (with Ch.), Dohnányi; (ii) St Paul CO, Hugh Wolf.

As so often with paired CDs using different performers, the results here are uneven. On the first CD, the Teldec recording for Dohnányi is in the demonstration bracket and the playing of the Cleveland Orchestra is virtuosity itself. But there is no magic here, no sense of mystery or atmosphere in *Daphnis*, and little sense of the intoxication one encounters in Karajan, Ormandy, or in such Ravel conductors as Reiner or Munch. Nor does *La Valse* fare better, and the *Alborada del gracioso* emerges as just a display piece. As sound, this is worth a three-star rating, but as a musical experience Ravel lovers will not want it. The performances from the St Paul Chamber Orchestra under Hugh Wolf are a different matter. They too are very well recorded, but the concert-hall effect is more natural. The playing is polished and musical, and *Le Tombeau de Couperin* is both elegant and stylish. The two orchestrations of Debussy are pleasing and the *Tarantelle Danse* is spirited and has delicacy of feeling, with a neatly rhythmic horn solo. The horn playing in the *Pavane* is quite beautiful.

Alborada del gracioso; Boléro; Ma Mère l'Oye; (i) Piano Concerto in G; Piano Concerto for Left Hand; (ii) Tzigane; La Valse; (iii) Shéhérazade.

(B) ** Warner Ultima 8573 84255-2 (2). SRO, Jordan; with (i) Duchable; (ii) Amoyal; (iii) Yakar.

There are good things in this unique Ravel compilation, although René-François Duchable's account of the *G major Concerto* is not strong on charm, particularly in the slow movement. The performances are far from routine but far from flawless, and none

would be a first choice given the abundance of *richesses* on offer, unless this combination of works is especially wanted.

Alborada del gracioso; Boléro; Rapsodie Espagnole; Le Tombeau de Couperin; La Valse.

(BB) *** RCA 7461 68015-2. Dallas SO, Mata.

In the late 1970s Eduarda Mata helped to build the Dallas orchestra into a splendid band, and their excellence and his stylish conducting (helped by the splendid acoustics of the Dallas auditorium) was demonstrated by a series of outstanding Ravel recordings made in the early 1980s. The *Alborada* flashes, the *Rapsodie Espagnole* shimmers and there is a balmy underlying patina of sensuous colour. Mata and his players are at their most impressive in *Le Tombeau de Couperin*, which has pleasing elegance and finesse and the expansive climaxes of *Boléro* and *La Valse* are very compelling. The recording has the most spectacular dynamic range and at bargain price this collection is most recommendable, standing up well to all the competition.

Alborada del gracioso; (i) Daphnis et Chloé: Suites Nos. 1 & 2; Une Barque sur l'océan. Menuet Antique.

(**(*)) Testament mono SBT 1238. French Nat. RO, Cluytens; (i) with ch. – BIZET: *La Jolie Fille de Perth* **(*); ROUSSEL: *Le Festin de l'araignée* ***.

Cluytens' recording of these Ravel pieces is thoroughly idiomatic even if his later stereo versions sound better and are arguably superior artistically. The earlier versions come from 1953 and the *Daphnis* suites are unusual for that period in including the chorus. *Une Barque sur l'océan* sounds eminently fresh though the later Conservatoire Orchestra version has the benefit of stereo. The coupling brings *Le Festin de l'araignée*, a magical account of Roussel's inspired score which has never been surpassed.

Boléro; (i) Daphnis et Chloé (ballet: complete); La Valse.

❂ *** EMI **Audio DVD** DVC4 92395-9. O de Paris, Martinon; (i) with Ch.

Martinon's complete *Daphnis et Chloé*, recorded in the Salle Wagram, Paris in 1974, was the most sensuous and magical to have appeared on disc since Munch's celebrated RCA Boston account, and in some ways it even surpasses it. Its intoxicating atmosphere, sense of ecstasy and Dionysian abandon are altogether captivating. *La Valse* is very fine too, though Cluytens's 1963 performance is every bit as good. *Boléro* is impressively graduated and stands alongside Karajan's BPO account on DG. Altogether this DVD is outstanding in every way, the sound wonderfully atmospheric, yet clearly defined, the dynamic range and amplitude enhanced, with an expansive lower range. As usual with this series, there is a choice between multi-channel surround sound (here remixed) or high-resolution stereo on alternate sides of the disc. The results are spectacular in either instance.

Boléro; Daphnis et Chloé: Suite No. 2; Rapsodie Espagnole.

(M) *** EMI (ADD) CDM5 67595-2 [567597]. O de Paris, Munch – HONEGGER: *Symphony No. 2.* ***

Munch recorded these Ravel pieces in 1968, shortly before his death on tour with the newly founded Orchestre de Paris. They bear the hallmark of his personality, intensity of expression and wonderful finesse. Apart from the excellence of the Ravel, the disc is of particular value in bringing his final thoughts on the Honegger symphony, of which he had made pioneering records in the war and with which he had a life-long association. Excellent sound.

Boléro; Ma Mère l'Oye; Rapsodie Espagnole.

(BB) (**) Naxos mono 8.110154. Boston SO, Koussevitzky – MUSSORGSKY: *Pictures at an Exhibition.* (**(*))

Koussevitzky's feeling for Ravel is second to none and we wish Naxos had included his magical post-war account of the second suite from *Daphnis et Chloë*. There is a certain want of enchantment in the first two movements of *Ma Mère l'Oye*, but for the most part criticism is silenced.

(i) Piano Concerto in G; Piano Concerto in D for the Left Hand. Jeux; Gaspard de la nuit; Pavane pour un enfante défunte.

(BB) **(*) Ph. Eloquence (ADD) 468 199-2. Haas; (i) Monte Carlo Opéra O, Galliera.

It is good to welcome Werner Haas back to the catalogue both in the music of Debussy (see above) and Ravel, for he had a special feeling for both composers. When his coupling of the *Piano Concertos* was issued at the end of the 1960s, we thought that with good analogue recording these refined, satisfying performances were the most recommendable versions on LP. Haas was perhaps a little straight-faced, but Galliera's persuasive accompaniments add to the authenticity of the performances. Now with some impressive solo piano music added (recorded a few years earlier), this is excellent value on the budget Eloquence label.

Daphnis et Chloé (ballet; complete); Ma Mère l'Oye: suite.

*(*) Testament mono SBT 1264 O. French Nat. RO, Ingelbrecht.

Ingelbrecht's complete *Daphnis* was recorded in 1953 not long after Ansermet's pioneering LP and a year or so year before Münch's famous Boston Symphony disc. It does not withstand comparison with them either in terms of conception or execution. The playing of the French Radio Orchestra is at times scruffy, and there is none of the distinctive authority that can be discerned in other records by this (rightly) admired conductor. The Testament transfer does its best for a recording that fell far below those the French engineers gave André Cluytens. Most, if not all, of Testament's reissues from this period in the French catalogue are self-recommending but this is an exception.

Ma Mère l'Oye: Suite; La Valse

*** MDG 337 1099-2. Orchester der Beethovenhalle, Bonn, Soustrot – DEBUSSY: *Le Martyre de Saint-Sébastien.* ***

Soustrot gives a simple, dedicated reading of *Ma Mère l'Oye*, with the tender delicacy of Ravel's score glowingly revealed by the warm sensitivity of the players. The opening of *La Valse*, too, has an almost ethereal quality, but there is no lack of drama later. Indeed, Soustrot's approach, with careful attention to detail, allows the dramatic elements of the score to emerge without the exaggerated point-making one sometimes encounters in this score. The recording is beautifully balanced, with the natural concert-hall acoustic combining clarity with a warm ambience.

Le Tombeau de Couperin; Valses nobles et sentimentales.

** Testament mono SBT 1236. French Nat. RO, Cluytens – DEBUSSY: *La boîte à joujoux; Children's Corner.* **(*)

Cluytens's performance and recording of *Le Tombeau de Couperin* are less satisfactory than his 1962 account with the Conservatoire Orchestra which Testament reissued on vinyl some while back. The recording was made in the Théâtre des Champs-Elysées in 1953, a year before its companions on this disc. Like the Debussy, the *Valses nobles et sentimentales* were recorded in the Salle de la Mutualité and have slightly more air around the aural image. This is well worth having all the same: Cluytens never re-recorded *La Boîte à joujoux*, which has great charm, and the sound is very good for the period.

(i) Le Tombeau de Couperin; (ii) String Quartet in F; (iii) Introduction and Allegro for Harp, Flute, Clarinet & Strings; (iv) Valses nobles et sentimentales.

(M) **(*) ASV Platinum PLT 8517. (i) ASMF, Marriner; (ii) Lindsay Qt; (iii) Prometheus Ens.; (iv) Fergus-Thompson.

Marriner's *Le Tombeau de Couperin* is, as one would expect, extremely well played and recorded, and there is plenty to enjoy on the way. But next to the classic French accounts of Cluytens, Paray and others, it lacks that last ounce of character which would put it amongst the very best. The Lindsays give a highly accomplished and finely etched performance of the *Quartet*, played with their usual aplomb and panache. There are splendid things here, notably the youthful fire of the opening movement and the vivid finale, but they do not always catch all the work's delicate poetic feeling. However, this is far from a negligible account and it is well recorded. Gordon Fergus-Thompson's performance of *Valses nobles et sentimentales* cannot be faulted while the *Introduction and Allegro* is an atmospheric, sensitive account, not quite in the league of the classic Decca Melos Quartet recording, but a good deal more than serviceable.

CHAMBER MUSIC

Piano Trio in A min.; Violin Sonata in G; Violin Sonata posth.; Sonata for Violin & Cello.

*** Virgin VC5 45492-2. R. & G. Capuçon, Braley.

The cover of this Virgin issue spells the pianist Frank, but everywhere else he is referred to as Franck. Both the string players, the Capuçon brothers, are first-rate players, and the pianist, too, is excellent – very sensitive in pianissimos, though once or twice a little too overpowering in louder passages. However, this does not detract from what are by any standards first-class readings, splendidly characterized and imaginative performances from all three artists, which can hold their own with any in the current catalogue. The Nash performance of the *Trio* remains a first choice (also Virgin – VBD5 61427-2; see our main Guide), and Tetzlaff and Andsnes are first rate in the *Violin Sonata in G* (VC5 45122-2). On this newer CD the characterization of these brilliant performers is just a shade exaggerated, but such is the quality and accomplishment of this playing that criticism should be silenced – or very nearly so! This is brilliantly thought out and executed playing, and readers wanting all these pieces, including the rare *Sonata posthume*, on one CD will not be disappointed.

String Quartet in F.

(BB) *** Naxos 8.554722. Ad Libitum Qt. – FAURE: *Quartet.* *** ✹

(B) (**(*)) EMI mono CDZ5 74792-2. Italian Qt. – DEBUSSY: *String Quartet in G min.* (**(*)); MILHAUD: *String Quartet No. 12* (***).

(M) (**(*)) BBC mono BBCL 4063-2. Borodin Qt – BORODIN: *Quartet No. 2* (**(*)); SHOSTAKOVICH: *Quartet No. 8.* **(*)

'In the name of God,' Debussy is reported to have said on first reading Ravel's score, 'I implore you not to change a note of your quartet.' It is one of the most beautifully written (and beautiful) works in the quartet repertory, formally perfect and beautifully proportioned. The ensemble and intonation of the Romanian Ad Libitum Quartet are perfect, and their tone is silken. They couple the quartet with the late *E minor Quartet* by Ravel's teacher, Gabriel Fauré, one of the most persuasive and most haunting accounts in the catalogue and given a ✹ by us. Their Ravel is also refined and sophisticated (some may find it just a shade over-characterized, perhaps at times beautified, and not entirely free from exaggerated dynamic shadings), but all the same, this is most distinguished playing and can be confidently recommended given the excellence of the recorded sound, which is natural and lifelike, and the appeal of the coupling.

The Quartetto Italiano's (Columbia) account of the Ravel *Quartet* comes from 1959 and originally appeared in Britain in 1961 coupled with the Mozart *G major*, K.156. It is a lovely performance, and although they re-recorded it even more satisfyingly a few years later for Philips (464 699-2), this is wonderfully fresh and the sound fully acceptable.

The sheer tonal finesse and subtlety of colouring that the Borodin Quartet bring to the score serve to make it a performance to remember. It is not quite as polished as their later studio version (currently withdrawn), but it is eminently fresh and the 1962 sound is well balanced.

Tzigane **(for violin and piano).**

(BB) (***) Dutton mono CDBP 9710. G. & J. Neveau – BRAHMS: *Violin Concerto in D, Op. 77*; SUK: *4 Pieces; Encores.* (***)

Ginette Neveu's account of the *Tzigane* is full of gypsy temperament and fire, with some dazzling pyrotechnics at the close. She dominates the proceedings, although her brother, Jean, accompanies supportively. Also offered are some delectable encores including Chopin's *Nocturne in C sharp minor*, its cantilena sounding for all the world like a violin piece, and dazzling versions of Falla's *Spanish Dance* from *La vida breve* and Dinicu's gutsy *Hora Staccato*. The transfers of these 1946 Abbey Road sessions are vividly realistic.

PIANO MUSIC

Piano duet

(i) *Entre cloches; Frontispiece; Introduction and Allegro; Ma Mère l'Oye; Rapsodie Espagnole; Shéhérazade: Ouverture de féerie; La Valse.*

(M) *** Somm SOMMCD 025. Miscallef, Inanga, (i) with Sterling.

When Ravel was such a brilliant orchestrator, it is surprising that he wrote so many of his orchestral works with a two-piano version either completed beforehand or conceived alongside the full orchestral score. That gives an extra validity to this fine collection, particularly when the young, prize-winning duo of Miscallef and Inanga is so warmly responsive, so naturally in sympathy with the idiom. They consistently demonstrate in each of these works that, while piano-tone is inevitably more limited than orchestral, Ravel was at least as much in love with the keyboard and its colourings as with the orchestra. The collection starts with the work which in many ways is the least appropriate for two-piano arrangement, the *Introduction and Allegro*, in which one piano has a transcription of the central harp part, and the other fills in the rest.

Miscallef and Inanga quickly make one appreciate the merits of these alternative versions. Their subtle and persuasive use of rubato comes out very clearly, as in the *Malaguena* from *Rapsodie Espagnole*, a piece written earlier than the other three movements. That work was originally coupled with the much squarer *Entre cloches* (also included here) under the title, *Sites Auriculaires*. Bell-sounds appear again in the fragment *Frontispiece*, written in 1918 as the introduction to a collection of war-poems. Lasting barely more than a minute, it brings some extraordinary polytonal writing, totally un-Ravelian. The other major item, *Shéhérazade*, should not be confused with the song-cycle of that name. Ravel described it as a fairy-overture, originally designed, like the cycle, for a projected opera that he never completed. In this two-piano version with hard keyboard textures it is less evocative than tough, sounding more modern than the orchestral version. Best of all is *La Valse*, a brilliant transcription already a favourite with two-piano duos. Miscallef and Inanga, instead of emerging from formless clouds of notes at the start, at once establish hints of the waltz rhythm, and go from strength to strength.

Solo piano music

A la manière de Borodine; A la manière de Chabrier; Gaspard de la nuit; Jeux d'eau; Menuet Antique; Menuet sur le nom de Haydn; Miroirs; Pavane pour une infante défunte; Prélude; Sérénade Grotesque; Sonatine; Le Tombeau de Couperin; Valses nobles et sentimentales.

*** Hyp. CDA 67341/2. Hewitt.

A la manière de ... Borodine; A la manière de ... Chabrier; Gaspard de la nuit; Jeux d'eau; Menuet Antique; Menuet sur le nom d'Haydn; Miroirs; Pavane pour un infante défunte; Prélude; Sonatine; Le Tombeau de Couperin; Valses nobles et sentimentales.

(B) (***) EMI mono CZS5 74793-2 (2). Gieseking.

Ravel's solo piano music has been well served in the last couple of decades – Louis Lortie, Jean-Philippe Collard, Paul Crossley, Pascal Rogé and Jean-Yves Thibaudet – but this newcomer from Hyperion is second to none and will now probably be a first choice for most collectors. We associate Angela Hewitt with Bach, but the clarity she brought to that repertoire serves to illumine Ravel's textures without ever entailing any loss of atmosphere.

Her performances are characteristically full of the searchingly imaginative approach she takes to everything she plays. The playing is impeccable, in both technique and taste. While the gleamingly crisp and fresh *Menuet Antique*, which opens the programme, and the elegantly played *Le Tombeau de Couperin* are models of neo-classical style, her performance of the *Sonatine*, pastel shaded, is poetically flexible and free. This applies even more to her wide range of tempi and use of rubati in the highly individual *Valses nobles et sentimentales*. The *Pavane* has a restrained melancholy nobility, *Jeux d'eaux* is wonderfully translucent, and the magical triptych that makes up *Gaspard* is particularly haunting and atmospheric, helped by the superbly balanced Hyperion recording, so that the gentle tolling bell of *Le Gibet* can seem far away and the opening crescendo of *Scarbo* makes its fullest effect. *Miroirs*, too, is full of luminous evocation: *Noc-*

tuelles and *Oiseaux tristes* have great delicacy, the *Alborada* glitters with colour, and the closing *La Vallée des cloches* has a magical, glowing languor. Altogether this is a fascinating new look at these inspired pieces, so perfect in their detail, and one continually has the sense of coming to this music afresh.

Gieseking's classic recordings were made in 1954, with Walter Legge and Geraint Jones acting as producers. Gieseking's special affinity for this repertoire shines through, and no one with a serious interest in the French master should neglect these readings. Of course, the age of stereo has brought impressive modern successors, but nearly half a century on these performances speak with a specially idiomatic accent. Here are a pianist with a limpid, translucent tone and a piano with no hammers.

Valses nobles et sentimentales (complete); *Le tombeau de Couperin; Forlane; Miroirs; La Vallée des cloches.*

(B) *** RCA 2CD (ADD) 74321 846062. Rubinstein – CHABRIER: *Pièces Pittoresques: Scherzo-Valse*; DEBUSSY: *Estampes*, etc.; FAURE: *Nocturne No. 3*; FRANCK: *Symphonic Variations for Piano and Orchestra; Prélude choral et fugue*; SAINT-SAENS: *Piano Concerto No. 2*. ***

These pieces (including the Fauré and Chabrier) appear to derive from an LP called 'A French Programme' which appeared in mono in the mid-1960s, and later in stereo. The playing is eminently aristocratic, and the sound greatly improved in these new transfers. Rubinstein could be a magician in French music just as he was in Chopin. A reissue of distinction.

RAWSTHORNE, Alan (1905–71)

Clarinet Concerto.

(B) *** Hyp. Helios CDH 55069. King, Northwest CO of Seattle, Francis – COOKE: *Concerto*; JACOB: *Mini-Concerto*. ***

Though the *Clarinet Concerto* is an early work of Rawsthorne's it already establishes the authentic flavour of his writing, the more obviously so in a performance as persuasive as this from soloist and orchestra alike. Excellent recording, and very good value.

(i; ii) *Violin Sonata*; (i; iii) *Theme and Variations for two Violins.*

*** Metier MSV CD 92029. (i) Skaerved; (ii) Honma; (iii) Sohn – MCCABE: *Maze Dances*, etc. ***

Alan Rawsthorne's *Theme and Variations for Two Violins*, one of his earliest works, stands among the finest pieces ever written for this daunting medium, with the interplay between the two instruments bringing a kaleidoscopic sequence of ideas, sharply defined. The *Violin Sonata* of over 20 years later is tougher in its idiom with the four movements tautly argued within a compressed span, not a note wasted. Peter Sheppard Skaerved gives flawless performances, very well-matched by Christine Sohn in the

Variations and Tamami Honma in the *Sonata*. Clear, immediate sound.

REINECKE, Carl (1824–1910)

Harp Concerto in E min., Op. 182.

(M) *** DG (ADD) 463 648-2. Zöller, Zabaleta, BPO, Märzendorfer – MOZART: *Flute & Harp Concerto in C, K. 299* ***; RODRIGO: *Concierto serenata.*** ✪

We regret that this very appealing CD was given the wrong catalogue number in our main Guide. It is corrected above. This is an attractive work, Zabaleta's performance is an outstanding one, and it is truthfully recorded. If the couplings are suitable this is a highly recommendable disc.

Symphonies No. 2 in C min., Op. 134; No. 3 in G min., Op. 227.

*** Chan 9893. Tasmanian SO, Shelley

Few forgotten 19th-century composers so richly deserve revival as Carl Reinecke, in his time a leading teacher as well as a successful composer. Almost ten years older than his friend Brahms, he lived on until 1910, prolific into his eighties. His style is conservative but never bland, like a cross between Mendelssohn and Brahms, with memorable themes strongly developed, and with refined orchestration regularly revealing his Brahmsian love of the horn and oboe. *Symphony No. 2* is the more relaxed, leading to a warmly Mendelssohnian finale, while *No. 3 in G minor* is sharper and more dramatic, vigorously belying the idea that this was by a composer in his mid-seventies. You could hardly find more persuasive advocates than Howard Shelley and the brilliant Tasmanian Symphony Orchestra, vividly recorded.

RESPIGHI, Ottorino (1879–1936)

Belkis, Queen of Sheba: Suite; Dance of the Gnomes; The Pines of Rome.

*** Reference RR 965CD. Minnesota O, Oué.

The Minnesota (formerly Minneapolis) Orchestra celebrates its latest music director with colourful performances of three Respighi showpieces, two of them rarities. Even by Respighi's standards the suite from the full-length ballet, *Belkis, Queen of Sheba*, is brazen to the point of vulgarity, with maximum decibels allied to minimal argument. The *Dance of the Gnomes* (1920) is a set of four pieces inspired by a deeply unpleasant poem of Carlo Clausetti, involving Amazon-like gnomes who first torture their newly acquired husbands and then kill them. The orchestral writing – with the shrieks of the victims illustrated – is yet subtler and more atmospheric than in *Belkis*, with a fascinating trial-run for the opening of *The Pines of Rome* (1924) at the start. Oué draws playing at once powerful and refined from his orchestra, and refinement is one of the elements in his reading of *The Pines of Rome*, generally light and transparent in its textures.

Feste romane; The Fountains of Rome; The Pines of Rome (symphonic poems).

*** Delos DE 2387. Oregon SO, DePreist.

The first great merit of the Delos version from Oregon is the spectacular sound which has a sensuously velvety, wraparound quality that is both warmly atmospheric and finely detailed. The sharp terracing of textures also enhances the sound, making it both immediate and vividly realistic. DePreist, over the years since he became music director of the Oregon Orchestra in 1980, has shaped it into a virtuoso band more than capable of holding its own in any international company, and these showpieces are presented with just the sort of panache that they need. Often they gain from the extra weight of the bass response, as in the second movement of *The Fountains, The Triton Fountain in the Morning*, when the pedal-notes from the organ have the tummy-wobbling quality usually experienced only in live performance.

REYNOLDS, Alfred (1884–1969)

Alice Through the Looking Glass: suite. The Duenna: suite of Five Dances. Festival March; Marriage à la mode: suite. Overture for a Comedy; 3 Pieces for Theatre; The Sirens of Southend; The Swiss Family Robinson: Swiss Lullaby and Ballet. The Taming of the Shrew: Overture. 1066 and All That: suite (inc. Ballet of the Roses). The Toy Cart: suite.

**(*) Marco Polo 8.225184. Royal Ballet Sinf., Sutherland.

Born in Liverpool, the son of waxwork museum proprietors, Alfred Reynolds studied music in Liverpool, Heidelberg, and then six years in Berlin under the guidance of Humperdinck. His name is largely associated with the stage, with much of the music here written as incidental for plays. It is all spontaneously tuneful in the best British light music tradition, occasionally more substantial, but never attempting profundity. The more substantial overtures are highly enjoyable: the *Overture for a Comedy* has some diverting episodes and, like the rest of the programme, makes one nostalgic for the past. *Alice Through the Looking Glass* features some nice, piquant numbers (especially the *Jabberwocky* and *March of the Drums*), and Reynolds' interest in eighteenth-century music is felt sporadically throughout the programme, including the *Entr'acte* from *The Critic* (*Three Pieces for Theatre*), a charming minuet with a gentle hint of pomposity. The excerpts from his most famous work, *1066 and All That*, are highly enjoyable, as is the splendidly rousing *Festival March*. Dance rhythms make up a fair proportion of the music – a lively tarantella here, a nostalgic waltz there, plus a rustic jig and a Spanish fandango. Gavin Sutherland is as reliable as ever in securing the right style from his orchestra, though occasionally the sound isn't as sweet as it might be. Lovers of light music should consider this CD, as Alfred Reynolds deserves to be remembered.

RIMSKY-KORSAKOV,
Nikolay (1844–1908)

(i) Capriccio espagnol, Op. 34; (ii) Russian Easter Festival Overture, Op. 36; Tsar Sultan: The Flight of the Bumble Bee.

(BB) **(*) EMI Encore (ADD) CDE5 74763-2. (i) Philh. O; (ii) Paris Conservatoire O; Cluytens – MUSSORGSKY: *Night on the Bare Mountain*; BORODIN: *In the Steppes of Central Asia*. **(*)

Cluytens imbues his *Capriccio espagnol* with more of a sultry atmosphere than is often the case, rather than simply treating the work as a brilliant show-piece. Not that excitement is lacking: it is a splendid performance and the recording is excellent for its period (1958), if a little thin by modern standards. Cluytens coaxes more sensitive playing from the Paris orchestra as well as drama (and a jet-propelled bumble bee) although the distinctive French sound (in particular, the vibrato on the brass) may not be to all tastes. Still, this is worth investigating at the price.

Le Coq d'or: Suite.

(M) (***) BBC Legends mono BBCL 4084-2. RPO, Beecham – BALAKIREV: *Symphony No. 1*; BORODIN: *Polovtsian Dances*. (***)

This live broadcast performance has all the swagger and panache that one would expect of Beecham in this music, compensating for the lack of stereo. A welcome fill-up for the outstanding account of the Balakirev *Symphony No. 1*.

Scheherazade (symphonic suite), Op. 35.

(M) *(*) Westminster (ADD) 471 215-2. Vienna State Op. O, Scherchen – TCHAIKOVSKY: *1812 Overture*. **

Scheherazade; Capriccio espagnol, Op. 34.

(B) **(*) EMI double fforte CZS5 75172-2 (2). LPO, Jansons – MUSSORGSKY: *Night on the Bare Mountain*; *Khovanshchina: Prelude*; *Pictures at an Exhibition*. **

Scheherazade; Russian Easter Festival Overture.

(BB) **(*) RCA 74321 68014-2. NYPO, Temirkanov.

Jansons gives us a very well-played and warmly characterful account with much to recommend it. What distinguishes this from other versions is the way he points rhythms in all four movements – lilting, bouncy and affectionate – before bringing a satisfying resolution at the great climax towards the end of the finale, with Joakim Svenheden a warmly expressive soloist. The *Capriccio espagnol* brings a similar combination of warmth and exuberance. This is now reissued in EMI's bargain double fforte series coupled with Mussorgsky.

The highlight of the Temirkanov account lies in the richly languorous slow movement, with the warmest, most sensuous string playing at the opening and a delightfully wistful, almost elegiac close. The work opens boldly, with the brass heavily enunciating the Sultan's powerful theme, and the leader of the NYPO, Glenn Dicterov, portrays Scheherazade sinuously, helped by a lifelike balance. But the spacious opening movement lacks real tension, and the colourful events of the second movement are also very relaxed. The finale brings alert playing and vivid detail with an explosively climatic shipwreck, where the bold tam-tam stroke is followed by a hammering nemesis from the timpani. But overall this cannot compete with the finest bargain versions. The *Russian Easter Festival Overture*, too, takes a while to warm up properly, though again the climax is impressive. The recording was made in New York's Manhattan Center and is spacious and wide ranging, if not quite as spectacular as Mackerras's Telarc CD which remains first choice (❂ CD 80208).

Scherchen's 1957 *Scheherazade* (DG engineered) comes up well enough in this transfer, if lacking the full dynamic range this score ideally needs. It is hardly a general recommendation: the usual eccentricities of tempi abound, indeed some of the slow music almost grinds to a halt, but it is not completely without tension and the finale is lively enough. The performance is for Scherchen devotees only.

(i) Scheherazade; (ii) Capriccio Espagnol; Le Coq d'Or: Suite; May Night Overture; Russian Easter Festival Overture; The Tsar's Bride: Overture; (iii) Tsar Sultan: The Flight of the Bumble Bee.

(B) ** Erato Ultima 8573 85668-2 (2). (i) Monte Carlo PO, Foster; (ii) Bolshoi SO, Lazarev; (iii) SCO, Leppard.

Lawrence Foster directs a spontaneous account of *Scheherazade*, and even if it is not among the most memorable versions – the Monte Carlo strings fail to create the necessary richness of texture – it is still enjoyable, especially in the lively finale. Alexander Lazarev is quite imaginative in the rest of the main programme, drawing much vivid colouring from his orchestra, though not all will take to the traditional Russian edge on the brass. In short these are all highly musical performances with drama as well as atmosphere. If the programme appeals, this is fair value.

Scheherazade (symphonic suite), Op. 35; Symphony No. 2 (Antar).

(M) **(*) Decca (ADD) 470 253-2. SRO, Ansermet.

This is something of an historic CD as Ansermet's *Antar* was Decca's first stereo recording. Taped in June 1954, the booklet gives a fascinating account of the circumstances in which it was recorded, with Ansermet proclaiming elatedly at the end of the session: 'This is utterly magnificent. It is wonderful. It's just as if I was standing at my desk'. To modern ears the rather tubby sound now seems a bit dated, but it remains a tribute to the skill of the Decca engineers that their first stereo recording still sounds so acceptable today. Decca subsequently made swift progress technically and by the time *Scheherazade* was recorded in 1960 the sound was altogether more brilliant as well as warm – with a clarity which made Ansermet's Victoria Hall recordings legendary.

Both performances have plenty of character, even if the Swiss orchestra is never the most refined of ensembles. *Scheherazade* has plenty of drama in the outer movements, aided and abetted by Decca's vivid sound picture, with its impressive percussion, especially the bass drum in the finale. This CD will certainly interest collectors and Ansermet admirers alike, though his *Scheherazade* is also available on an even more attractive Double Decca CD, which has some of Rimsky's most glittering and luminous music including the delightful *Christmas Eve Suite* (443 464-2 – see our main volume).

VOCAL MUSIC

Cantatas: (i) *Inz Gomera, Op. 60; The Song of Alexis, Man of God, Op. 20;* (ii) *The Song of Oleg the Wise, Op. 58;* (iii) *Switsezianka (or The Girl in the Lake), Op. 44.*

⍟ *** Chant de Monde RUS 288175. (i) Fedotova, Sizova; (ii) Didenko; (ii; iii) Kortchak; (iii) Mitrakova, Moscow Academy Ch., Moscow SO, Ziva.

These splendid secular choral cantatas are a real find, and show an endearing new facet to Rimsky's genius. Try the opening *Song of Alexis, Man of God*, superbly sung by a fine Russian chorus, and you will surely immediately be hooked. The composer re-uses music written to accompany pilgrims in *The Maid of Pskov*, to evoke the legend of Saint Alexis, who renounced marriage with a princess in order to lead a hermit's life. Its noble melody is based on a Russian folk song. *The Song of Olga the Wise*, to a poem by Pushkin, for tenor (who tells the story) and bass (Oleg) is melodramatically operatic, and *Inz Gomera*, based on Homer, even more so with its powerful orchestral *Prelude* depicting Poseidon's tempest, before the luminously seductive writing for the female voices.

Switsezianka (set to a poem by Lev May) is the familiar folk tale of the watery nymph who captivates her young swain and insists on his fidelity, with a dire penalty if he forgets her. She then returns in an even more beautiful form to test his faithfulness and 'as she spoke the wind disturbed her rainment, uncovering her milk-white breast'. Needless to say, he immediately forgets his vows, succumbs to temptation, realizing only too late that 'the young girl was none other than his former beloved', and he is swallowed up by the frothing waters of the lake. Rimsky's highly atmospheric scena, using soprano and tenor soloists, climax as a splended quartet of performances, with fine Russian singers throughout. The recording is first class and so is the documentation, with full translations included, which are easy to follow even without the original Russian.

RODGERS, Richard (1902–79)

Ballet scores: *Ghost Town; On Your Toes: La Princess Zenobia; Slaughter on Tenth Avenue.*

*** TER CDTER 1114. O, Mauceri.

Richard Rodgers often wrote quite extensive ballets for his Broadway output, the best known being *Slaughter on Tenth Avenue*, first heard in the 1936 musical *On Your Toes*, which also presented *La Princess Zenobia* for the first time. However, *Ghost Town*, an American folk ballet about the Gold Rush, was commissioned by the Ballet Russe de Monte Carlo in 1939 and produced at the Metropolitan Opera that year. All three ballets have their fair share of good tunes – *Slaughter on Tenth Avenue*, easily the best of them, has three superb melodies (among Rodgers's finest) – and there is no doubting that the colourful orchestrations of Hans Spialek go a large way towards making these scores as sparkling as they are. The performances under John Mauceri are first rate, as is the vivid and bright recording, which admirably catches the Hollywoodesque orchestrations. The fine orchestra is presumably a pick-up ensemble, as, curiously, it is not credited with a name.

RODRIGO, Joaquín (1902–99)

(i) *Concierto de Aranjuez; Invocación y danza, Homage à Falla.*

(M) *** Sony (ADD) SMK 89753. John Williams, ECO, Barenboim – CASTELNUOVO-TEDESCO: *Guitar Concerto No. 1;* VILLA-LOBOS: *Concerto.* ***

What makes John Williams's 1974 recording of the *Concierto* particularly enticing is his bravura performance of Rodrigo's solo *Invocación y danza, Homage à Falla* which opens the programme. Williams's style is not strikingly Spanish in its evocation, but the performance is full of charisma and the closing section brings electrifying virtuosity: indeed his digital dexterity is astonishingly clear and clean. The performance of the *Concierto* is superior to his earlier version with Ormandy. The playing again has marvellous point, the Adagio played with poetic spontaneity.

Concierto serenata (for harp and orchestra).

⍟(M) *** DG (ADD) 463 648-2. Zöller, Zabaleta, BPO, Märzendorfer – MOZART: *Flute & Harp Concerto in C, K.299;* REINECKE: *Harp Concerto.***

We regret that this very attractive CD was given the wrong catalogue number in our main Guide. It is corrected above. We have always had a special regard for Zabaleta's pioneering version of Rodrigo's *Concierto serenata*, which has an unforgettable piquancy and charm both in its invention and in its felicity of scoring. The performance has great virtuosity and flair, and our ⍟ is carried over from the original LP. It is excellently recorded, with the delicate yet colourful orchestral palette tickling the ear in charming contrast to the beautifully-focused timbre of the harp. A worthy addition to DG's series of legendary 'Originals'.

Soleriana (ballet, arr. from Soler's keyboard music); *5 Piezas infantiles; Zarabanda lejana y villancico.*

(BB) **(*) Naxos 8.555844. Asturias SO, Valdés.

Valdés includes Rodrigo's delightful eighteenth-century picture of Spain in his ballet *Soleriana*, which is based on the keyboard works of Antonio Soler and consists of eight dances lasting some 40 minutes in all. The *Pastoral* has a lovely melancholy beauty, though most of the movements are relatively lively and well portray a picturesque, rococo image of eighteenth-century Spain in music of great charm and piquancy. The *Zarabanda lejana* ('Distant Sarabande') is a haunting work, its two movements displaying some lovely string writing, and the highly engaging *Cinco piezas infantiles* are characteristically brightly coloured. The performances are good, if perhaps not quite so imaginative as Bátiz on EMI (see our main volume), who also benefited from more vivid sound. Here, the massed strings sound a bit thin above the stave (especially noticeable in the *Zarabanda lejana*), but the overall sound-picture is very acceptable, and this disc is well worth its modest price.

Complete Solo Piano Music

Air de ballet sur le nom d'une jeune fille; Album de Cecilia; A l'ombre de Torre Bermeja; Bagatela; 2 Berceuses; Canción y danza; Danza de la Amapola; 3 Danzas de España; 4 Estampas Andaluzas; 3 Evocaciones; Pastoral; 4 Piezas; 5 Piezas del sieglo XVI; Preludio de Añoranza; Preludio al alla mañanero; Serenata española; Sonata de adiós (Homage To Paul Dukas); 5 Sonatas de Castilla con Toccata a modo de Pregón; Suite; Zarabanda Lejana.

*** Sony S2K 89828 (2). Marianovich.

Sara Marianovich knew Rodrigo personally and played for him, learning a great deal, so that her performances received his imprimatur. She is indeed completely at home in this attractive repertoire, the early works with their distinct gallic flavour (Ravel, Debussy, even Poulenc), the comparable influence from Scarlatti, and the later interpolation of glittering Andalusian dance rhythms. The *Cuatro Estampas Andaluzas* and the engaging *Danzade de la Amapola* are brilliantly played, while the *Trez evocaciones*, which reach out towards Granados and Falla, are hardly less dazzling. The music is attractively arranged, as far as possible in order of composition, and ends nostalgically with Rodrigo's last piano work, the *Preludio de Añoranza* of 1987. But besides her ready bravura and feeling for the Spanish as well as the French pianistic palette, Sara Marianovich is also at her finest in the simpler pieces, the charming early *Suite*, the *Pastoral* (a captivating siciliana), the pair of *Berceuses*, the touching 'Adios' to Paul Dukas, the children's album, written for the composer's daughter, Cecilia, and the 'Five Pieces from the 16th Century' – transcriptions of Spanish renaissance miniatures. Also included is an impressive first recording of the rare *Canción y danza* of 1925 which opens musingly, but slowly becomes more passionate. This does not appear in the previous outstanding 'complete' coverage of this repertoire by Gregory Allen (Bridge BCD 9027A/B) discussed in our main

Guide. However, joined by Anton Nel, he *does* include the repertoire for two pianos, which the Sony set omits. So that probably remains a primary choice. But Sara Marianovich's playing is so compellingly persuasive that her new set must also receive the strongest possible advocacy. She is vividly and truthfully recorded, and this highly rewarding music is undeservedly neglected.

ROMBERG, Sigmund (1887–1951)

The Student Prince (musical play/operetta): complete.

*** TER CDTER 1172 (2). Bailey, Smith, Montague, Rendall, Ambrosian Ch., Philh. O, Edwards.

The *Student Prince* (orchestrated by Emil Gerstenberger) is Romberg's most famous score and was first performed in New York in 1924. The story of a young prince who falls in love with a barmaid but is forced to give her up for the sake of duty gives it a bitter-sweet quality, though Romberg's music all but redeems its sentimentality. The melodic invention is very strong indeed, with colourful orchestrations adding to the impact, and this (1990) recording presents the music complete for the first time on CD. John Owen Edwards directs an enthusiastic, yet polished performance, and with a fair sprinkling of star performers, notably Marilyn Hill Smith as the heroine Kathy – completely at home in this repertoire – and David Rendall as her lover, the result is most enjoyable. There are excellent contributions, too, from Norman Bailey and Diana Montague, and the heady if somewhat dated atmosphere of the operetta-musical play style of the 1920s is vividly conveyed.

ROSETTI, Antonio (*c.* 1750–1792)

Horn Concerto in E, K.3:42.

(BB) *** Teldec (ADD) 0630 12324-2. Baumann, Concerto Amsterdam, Schröder – DANZI; HAYDN: *Concertos*. ***

The Bohemian composer, born Franz Anton Rössler, who adopted an Italian version of his name, wrote prolifically for the horn. This *Concerto*, galant in style, is characteristic of the taxing melodic lines he provides for the soloist, with lyrical upper tessitura contrasting with florid arpeggios. He was especially good at jolly rondo finales and the present work shows him at his melodically most exuberant. Baumann plays with elegance and aplomb and is well accompanied. The remastered recording now sounds warmer with more ambience than on its last appearance, and altogether this is a very pleasing triptych.

ROSSINI, Gioachino (1792–1868)

La Boutique fantasque (ballet: complete; arr. Respighi).

⚫ (M) *** Somm mono SOMMCD 027. LSO, Ansermet – STRAVINSKY: *Petrushka*. (***).

Ansermet's classic 'complete' version (there are some fairly minor cuts) of *La Boutique fantasque* was outstanding among early LPs. It was recorded in the Kingsway Hall in 1950, which lends its ambient richness to the proceedings, and was one of the rare occasions on which Ansermet conducted the LSO. They play wonderfully for him, especially the woodwind, and in particular the distinguished principal oboe, whose phrasing and tone are exquisite. The whole orchestra are clearly on their toes and the exhilarating can-can and brilliantly executed finale have tremendous vivacity. But the disc is especially famous for its magical opening which has an extraordinary aura, with the gentle pizzicatos of the lower strings answered by glowing horn chords. There is a crescendo and decrescendo which Ansermet graduates perfectly, and the disc is worth having for this section alone. Fortunately, David Henning's digital remastering miraculously reflects the outstanding quality of those early Decca LXTs (before the recording was re-cut and given horridly thin violin timbre for its Ace of Clubs reissue). As it now stands the sound has fine range and bloom, almost like stereo at times. This is one of Ansermet's finest ballet records, if not the finest of all. What a pity he made so few recordings with the London orchestra.

Introduction, Theme & Variations in B flat; Variations in C (for clarinet and orchestra).

*** Sup. SU 3554-2. Peterkova, Prague Philh., Bělohlávek – BRUCH: *Double Concerto*. MENDELSSOHN: 2 *Concert Pieces*. ***

The Czech clarinettist Ludmila Peterkova is an artist who is not only warmly expressive, but sparkles in everything she plays, bringing out the pure fun of the two sets of Rossini variations, warmly accompanied by Bělohlávek and the Prague Philharmonia. A delightful fill-up for an outstanding disc of rare clarinet pieces.

String Sonatas Nos. 1–5 (arr. for wind quartet by Berr).

(BB) ** Naxos 8.554098. Michael Thompson Wind Qt.

The considerable charm of Rossini's delightful early *String Sonatas* is the more remarkable when one realizes that they are the work of a 12 year old: their invention is consistently on the highest level and their bubbling humour is infectious. This wind arrangement adds another dimension to these works and is highly enjoyable, with the quartet of soloists (horn, flute, clarinet and flute) providing felicitous interplay, and it shows considerable resource of colour with only four instruments. The performances here are spontaneous, stylish and lively with plenty of sparkle. Alas, the very forward recording is set in a too dry and un-atmospheric acoustic, and the effect is rather unyielding after a while, with a lack of bloom and an inadequate ambience.

Overtures: Il barbiere di Siviglia; La Cenerentola; L'italiana in Algeri; La scala di seta; Il Signor Bruschino; Tancredi; William Tell; (i) Il barbiere di Siviglia: excerpts.

(B) (*) EMI Encore CDE5 74752-2. Stuttgart RSO, Gelmetti; (i) with Hampson, Mentzer.

Gelmetti races off with the opening string flourish of *La scala di seta*, the effect unpleasingly gabbled. The rest of the performance is fast and hard pressed, with little of the wit allowed to bubble to the surface (and with some disagreeable stresses on the violin phrase around 3'40"). A similar pattern emerges with the rest of the programme, with generally charmless playing. *Il barbiere* sounds really quite brutal, and the elegant string opening of *Il Signor Bruschino* is also rushed. The famous galop in *William Tell* is curiously four square and has nothing of the exhilarating verve which, for example, Marriner (Philips) and Abbado (DG) generate. The recording is vivid, but this disc is a non-starter – even with three celebrated *Il barbiere* thrown in.

Overtures: Elisabetta, Regina d'Inghilterra; La scala di seta; Semiramide; Tancredi; Il Turco in Italia; William Tell.

(BB) *** RCA 74321 68012-2. LSO, Abbado – VERDI: *Overtures*. ***

The *Overture Elisabetta, Regina d'Inghilterra* is in fact our familiar friend, *The Barber of Seville Overture*, and is listed as such on this reissued CD. But there is a subtle change here which surely implies the use of the proper title – a triplet in the first theme of the Allegro which is repeated each time the theme reappears. This adds a touch of novelty to these zestful performances from Abbado, with exhilaratingly fast tempi, the LSO players kept constantly on their toes and obviously enjoying themselves. The effect is more genial than on Abbado's earlier DG collection with the same orchestra (419 869-2). The exuberance comes to the fore especially in *Tancredi* – there is even a brief clarinet glissando – heard in a revised version by Philip Gosset. But some might feel that *La scala di seta* would be more effective if a fraction more relaxed and poised. *William Tell* opens with elegant cellos, then offers an unashamedly over-the-top storm sequence and a final galop taken at breakneck speed. The remastered recording is vividly bright, but it matches Abbado's approach and has plenty of supporting weight and a concert hall ambience.

OPERA

Il barbiere di Siviglia (complete).

(M) *** EMI CMS5 67762-2 [567765] (2). De los Angeles, Alva, Cava, Wallace, Bruscantini, Glyndebourne Festival Ch., RPO, Gui.

(M) *** Decca 470 434-2 (2). Baltsa, Allen, Araiza, Trimarchi, Lloyd, Amb. Op. Ch., ASMF, Marriner.

(*) Arthaus **DVD 100 090. Bartoli, Quilico, Kuebler, Feller, Lloyd, Cologne City Op. Ch., Stuttgart RSO, Ferro. (Director: Michael Hampe.)

Gui's 1962 Glydebourne production has been remastered for EMI's 'Great Recordings of the Century', and the bloom on voices and orchestra is even more apparent. The charm of de los Angeles' Rosina matches the unforced geniality of the production as a whole, strongly cast and easy to enjoy. Good documentation too. Not perhaps a first choice against competition like Bartoli (Decca 425 520-2), but that involves three full-priced CDs, making this a good mid-priced recommendation.

Marriner's sparkling Philips set with Araiza, Agnes Baltsa, and Thomas Allen as Figaro has also now been reissued at mid-price as part of Decca's 'Compact Opera Collection'. However, there is no printed libretto, only a CD-ROM facility which carries full text and translation, printable via a computer. The set remains available at full price with a normal libretto (Philips 446 448-2).

Recorded live at the Schwetzingen Festival in a very pretty theatre in 1988, this DVD version of *Il barbiere* centres around the superb performances of the two principals, Cecilia Bartoli, already dominant, with voice and technique fully developed even before she became a superstar, and Gino Quilico as Figaro, wonderfully winning in his acting with voice magnificently firm.

David Kuebler with his rather gritty tenor is far from winning as the Count, Robert Lloyd is an imposing Basolio and Carlos Feller a characterful Bartolo. Gabriele Ferro springs the rhythms persuasively, and Michael Hampe's production works well using realistic sets by Ezio Frigerio and costumes by Mauro Pagano. Excellent, cleanly separated sound.

La Cenerentola (complete).

*** Decca **DVD** 071 444-9. Bartoli, Dara, Giménez, Corbelli, Pertusi, Houston Grand Op. Ch. & Symphony, Campanella.(V/D Brian Large.)
*** Arthaus **DVD** 100 214. Murray, Berry, Araiza, Quilico, Schöne, V. St. Op.Ch., VPO, Chailey. (Director: Michael Hampe. V/D: Claus Viller.)

Few Rossini operas have such fizz as Decca's Houston Opera production of *La Cenerentola*, a part Cecilia Bartoli was born to play. The rest of the cast is the same as the CD set, except that Raúl Giménez takes the part of Don Ramiro. Bruno Campanella conducts very spiritedly. Visually the production could not be more winning, and the camera placing is a great credit to Brian Large.

Riccardo Chailly (who directed the Decca CDs) conducts the alternative version, which comes from the 1982 Salzburg Festival, and had the Bartoli set not been available it would have been a very strong recommendation, for Ann Murray is delightful in the principal role and the rest of the cast is excellent. If in Act I Don Magnifico's castle looks run down and needing a coat of paint, the glamour of the Palace more than compensates. The recording is bright and sparking but has plenty of bloom and the camerawork is always well managed. Most enjoyable, with a dazzling *Non più mesta* and a particularly infectious finale. But Chailly is at his finest throughout and so are the chorus and orchestra.

L'equivoco stravagante (complete opera).

(BB) **(*) Naxos 8.660087/8 (2). Petrova, Felice, Vinco, Schmunck, Minarelli, Santamaria, Czech Chamber Ch. & Chamber Soloists, Zedda.

L'equivoco stravagante ('The Bizarre Deception'), is one of Rossini's earliest operas, written when he was only 19. Already the Rossini fingerprints are firmly in place, with the music regularly sparkling from the overture, with its brilliant horn triplets, onwards. The story of this *dramma giocoso* involves a scheming servant, Frontino, who deceives the stupid suitor, Buralichio, into believing that the girl he is wooing, the heroine, Ernestina, is in fact male and whose *nouveau riche* father, Gamberotto, has had 'him' castrated so that he could become a high-earning opera-singer. The complications are many, until Ernestina is safely united with Ermanno, the impecunious tutor whom she loves. After three performances in 1811 the piece was banned for being too licentious. Rossini cut his losses, using material from it in his subsequent operas. It makes an attractive rarity, generally well sung and very well conducted in this live recording by the Rossini scholar Alberto Zedda – if unhelpfully punctuated by tepid applause.

Guglielmo Tell (William Tell; abridged in Italian).

(M) (*) Warner Fonit mono 8573 87489-2 (3). Taddei, Carteri, Sciutti, Filippeschi, Tozzi, Corena, RAI Ch. & O of Turin, Rossi.

Where most of the 1950s Cetra recordings in collaboration with Italian Radio were made in the studio like other commercial issues, this one of Rossini's last and longest opera, recorded in a single day, seems to have been a one-off studio performance, with all the flaws that entailed. Beginning with an excruciating cello solo, the celebrated overture brings the most rough and ready playing, even if the out-of-tuneness may in part be a result of 'wow' on the tape. While the whole performance has energy, it remains too rough for comfort, though several individual performances stand out, notably the magnificent singing of Giuseppe Taddei in the title role, rich and firm, heroic in every way. The young Graziella Sciutti in the *travesti* role of Tell's son, Jemmy, is also impressive, powerful in the scene in Act III, following the celebrated archery test. Giorgio Tozzi and Fernando Corena are also singers who stand out and Mario Filippeschi, in the principal tenor role of Arnoldo, sings incisively with cleanly focused tone, even if under strain at times. Sadly, Rosanna Carteri, one of the principal Italian sopranos of the day, sounds too unsteady for comfort. The text is the much-cut version in general use in Italy. The voices come off best in the limited recording. As with others in this series, a libretto is provided but not a translation.

L'Italiana in Algeri (complete).

** Arthaus **DVD** 100 120. Soffel, Gambill, Von Kannen, Bulgarian Male Ch. Stuttgart Radio SO, Weikert.

This production from the 1987 Schwetzingen Festival was available in the early 1990s on a Pioneer LaserDisc and looks even better on this DVD with its sharper, steadier focus and good colour – and subtitles in English, French and German.

Doris Soffel is a vivacious Isabella and the Mustafà of Günter von Kannen is characterized with great zest. Michael Hampe's direction is witty and well paced, and the set design and costumes of Mauro Pagano colourful.

The stage is small (as is the theatre itself) and despite the merits of the singing and playing leaves the impression of being cramped and provincial with little sense of back-to-front perspective. But there is a lot to enjoy here, particularly the final ensemble of the first Act, and much that is of quality. The Südwestfunk Orchestra plays well for Ralf Weikert and the sound is well balanced and has good presence.

COLLECTIONS

Arias from: *Il barbiere di Siviglia; La Cenerentola; La donna del lago; La gazza ladra; L'Italiana in Algeri; Otello; Semiramide; Zelmira.*

*** Decca 470 024-2. Floréz, Verdi O Sinfonica di Milano, Chailly.

Even in a generation that has thrown up some remarkable Rossini tenors, the Peruvian, Juan Diego Floréz, stands out with his clean-cut, wonderfully flexible voice, with not a suspicion of an intrusive aitch in the extraordinarily elaborate divisions of these challenging arias and with top Cs thrown off with consistent ease. The authority is never in doubt, and it is good to have such brilliant performances mainly of little-known arias, yet one hopes that Floréz will develop a gentler touch in hushed passages, with half-tones and a diamond bright timbre regularly dominating. Yet there are few recent discs of Rossini's tenor arias that begin to match this in excitement, with Chailly and the Milan Orchestra the most understanding partners. Full, clear sound.

ROTA, Nino (1911–79)

(i) *Castel del Monte (Ballad for Horn & Orchestra);* **(ii)** *Bassoon Concerto;* **(iii)** *Harp Concerto;* **(iv)** *Trombone Concerto.*

*** Chan. 9954 (i) Corti; (ii) Carlini; (iii) Prandina; (iv) A. Conti; I Virtuosi Italiani, M. Conti.

This is a delightful disc in every way, a collection of three concertos and one concertante work for horn demonstrating the unforced mastery of Rota, a composer remembered almost entirely for his film scores. Born in 1911, he joined the staff of the Bari conservatory in 1939 and stayed there until he retired in 1977, two years before his death. He remained a conservative in style, but one whose freshness of invention in each of these works brings out the colourful possibilities of instruments too rarely used in concertos. Both in the *Harp Concerto* of 1947 and the three other works from much later in his career the outer movements regularly display a sparkle more often associated with French composers of the inter-war period, with chattering ostinato rhythms supporting jaunty melodies, and slow movements striking deeper, darker moods. In each Rota gives important solos to rival instruments, varying textures. This is fun music in the best sense, regularly concealing the ingenuity of the writing in the overall light-heartedness. The *Trombone Concerto* – the only one of the four works to have been recorded before – has exuberant outer movements framing a much longer *Lento* movement with a powerful climax. The *Bassoon Concerto* is the most original in structure, while the *Ballad for Horn and Orchestra, Castel del Monte* (a title taken from a medieval castle built by the Emperor Frederick II) builds up passionately over sharply contrasted sections. With brilliant playing from all the Italian soloists as well as the orchestra this is a celebratory disc to parade the gifts of a long-neglected but warmly approachable composer, helped by full, well-balanced sound.

Film music: *Il gattopardo; Guerra e pace; La strada; Waterloo.*

(BB) *** EMI Encore CDE5 74987-2. Monte Carlo PO, Gelmetti.

Nino Rota's film music is arranged here into four entertaining orchestral suites. His late-romantic style is appealing and interesting enough to stand on its own. The brooding drama of *Il gattopardo* is rather telling, as is the often quirky music to *La strada*, which includes among its eight diverse numbers a lively *Rhumba* and a circus sequence with a 'madman's violin'. The finale, *Zampano Alone in Tears*, brings some particularly vivid writing, and when the solo trumpet enters the effect is quite haunting, while the opening of *Zampano's Anger* sounds curiously like *The Rite of Spring*. *La Rosa di Novgorod* from *Guerra e pace* has an attractive, melancholy beauty, and the lilting waltz from *Waterloo* is another highlight. The performances and recordings are first class, and this inexpensive CD is tempting enough for those wanting to explore this composer's film music.

ROUSSEL, Albert (1869–1937)

Bacchus et Ariane: Suite No. 2; Sinfonietta for Strings, Op. 52; Symphonies Nos. 3 in G min., Op. 42; 4 in A, Op. 53.

*** Testament SBT 1239. Paris Conservatoire O, Cluytens.

These recordings from the mid 1960s still sound very good and in some ways remain unchallenged. The sound is reverberant but detail emerges clearly. Cluytens has a splendid grasp of the energy and character of both symphonies, and in *Bacchus et Ariane* is scarcely less impressive than in his magical *Le Festin de l'araignée* reviewed below. Strongly recommended – for many this will be a first choice.

Le Festin de l'araignée (The Spider's Feast), Op. 17.

*** Testament SBT 1238. Paris Conservatoire O, Cluytens – BIZET: *La Jolie Fille de Perth*; RAVEL: *Daphnis*, etc. ****(*)**

Cluytens's 1963 recording of *Le Festin de l'araignée* remains in a class of its own: it has never been surpassed. There is tremendous atmosphere and delicacy of feeling. The recording was made in the rather reverberant Salle Wagram, but every strand is beautifully transparent and the orchestral texture expertly balanced with a lifelike perspective. This magical score strikes a strong spell, and this is one of Cluytens's finest recordings.

RUBBRA, Edmund (1901–86)

Piano Concerto in G, Op. 85.

(B) *** EMI CDZ5 74781-2. Matthews, BBC SO, Sargent – BRITTEN: *Piano Concerto; Prelude and fugue for strings.* ******

Edmund Rubbra's magnificent and original score was recorded a few months after its première by these same artists in March 1956. As often with Rubbra, it is immediately evident that it tells of deep and serious things. This music has a profound serenity: it was inspired by (and is dedicated to) the great Indian sarod player Ali Akbar Khan, and the thoughtful, meditative character of the central *Corymbus* movement and the spacious unforced eloquence of its first movement mark it off from the usual run of virtuoso concertos. (Malcolm Binns gave a searching and eloquent account of it with Vernon Handley and the LSO, recorded in the presence of the composer as part of the BBC's celebrations marking his seventy-fifth birthday in 1976, which is still listed as being in circulation. But there has been no commercial recording since this originally appeared.) Perhaps Chandos, who have done so much for Rubbra, will invite Howard Shelley to record it. Denis Matthews plays with eloquence and sympathy, and the sound is amazingly fresh considering its age. Andrew Walters's transfers are eminently faithful.

(i) Sinfonia concertante, Op. 38; A Tribute, Op. 56; (ii) The Morning Watch; (ii) Ode to the Queen, Op. 55.

*** Chan. 9966. BBC Nat. O of Wales, Hickox; with (i) Shelley; (ii) BBC Nat. Ch. of Wales; (iii) Bickley.

Originally issued in harness with the *First Symphony*, the *Sinfonia concertante* was composed just before it, though the form in which we know it is the revision Rubbra made in the 1940s. Its beautiful opening almost anticipates the *Piano Concerto in G major*, but it is the searching and thoughtful finale, a prelude and fugue dedicated to the memory of Rubbra's teacher Gustav Holst who had died in 1934, which makes the strongest impression. Howard Shelley is a superb advocate and it is difficult to imagine a better performance. *The Morning Watch* is Rubbra at his most inspired. The text comes from the seventeenth-century metaphysical poet Henry Vaughan, and the music matches its profundity and eloquence. It dates from 1946, and so comes roughly half way between the *Fourth* and *Fifth Symphonies*. (It originally appeared in harness with the *Ninth*.

The *Tribute* is to Vaughan Williams, one of three commissions (the others were Constant Lambert's *Aubade* and *One Morning in Spring* by Patrick Hadley), and the *Ode to the Queen* was commissioned by the BBC to celebrate the Coronation of the present Queen and is Rubbra's only song cycle with full orchestra. He set three poems on regal themes by Richard Crashaw, Sir William d'Avenant and Thomas Campian, in which inspiration runs high. Susan Bickley is the excellent soloist and Hickox is as always a dedicated interpreter of music that obviously means much to him.

(i) Festival Gloria, Op. 94; Magnificat and Nunc Dimittis in A flat, Op. 65; Missa in honorem Sancti Dominici, Op. 66; Salutation, Op. 82; Tenebrae, Op. 72.

**(*) Paraclete Press Gloria Dei Cantores GDCD 024. Gloria Dei Cantores, Patterson with; (i) Jordan (organ). Available from: www.paraclete-press.com

It is good to see Rubbra's sacred music receiving the advocacy of an American choir and a very good one, too. Gloria Dei Cantores ('Singers to the Glory of God') come from Cape Cod, Massachusetts, and have already given us an outstanding CD of the music of William Mathias (GCD 026). With the exception of the *Salutation*, Op. 82, written for the Queen's accession, and the *Festival Gloria*, Op. 94, the repertoire is duplicated on the Naxos disc from St John's College, Cambridge under Christopher Robinson (8.555255) reviewed in our main volume.

However, Gloria Dei Cantores offer dedicated, well-prepared performances, although the sopranos do not have the accuracy and tonal purity of the boys' voices of St John's, nor their breadth of dynamic range and colour. Good though the *Missa in honorem Sancti Dominici* is (it has a mystical dedication that is impressive), it is outclassed by the Cambridge Choir, not only in the security of the soprano lines but also in the quality of tonal blend. In the *Magnificat and Nunc Dimittis in A flat* it is rather overpowering. The balance, which is mostly excellent, compares unfavourably with the more discrete relationship between singers and organ in Cambridge. But both the *Salutation* and the *Festival Gloria* are of great beauty, and the disc is worth acquiring for these works alone. But for those wanting the glorious *Tenebrae* and the *Dominican Mass*, the St John's College, Cambridge, CD is the one to have; for a third of the price the collector also has the bonus of the *Missa Cantuariensis*.

Psalm 6: O Lord, Rebuke Me Not; Psalm 23: The Lord is My Shepherd; Psalm 150: Praise Ye The Lord.

(M) (***) Decca mono 470 195-2. Ferrier, Lush –
IRELAND: *Songs* ** (*); QUILTER: *Songs.* (***)

These short but haunting songs are persuasively sung by Kathleen Ferrier and the 1953 mono recording, a few crackles aside, has warmth and presence – this is atmospheric music-making of rare quality.

RUBINSTEIN, Anton (1829–94)

Symphony No. 3 in A, Op. 56; Eroica Fantasia, Op. 110.

(BB) * Naxos 8.555590. Slovak RSO, Stankovsky.

The *Third Symphony* is not endowed with ideas of interest or even with personality, and although it is not entirely without merit it is mostly predictable stuff. The playing by the Bratislava Radio Orchestra is fairly routine and Robert Stankovsky brings few insights to the score. The *Eroica Fantasia*, as its high opus number suggests, is a later and if anything less inspired work.

Symphony No. 4 in D min. (Dramatic), Op. 95.

(BB) * Naxos 8.555979. Slovak PO, Stankovsky.

The Rubinstein Symphonies, originally issued on Marco Polo, are now reappearing on Naxos and are perhaps more enticing on a budget label. The *Fourth*, the *Dramatic* of 1874, runs to some 65 minutes and is not a stong work. Its thematic substance is pretty thin and, despite its epic proportions, there is little sense of sweep or consistency of inspiration. The performance is acceptable but no more, as is the recording.

RUSSO, William (born 1928)

3 Pieces for Blues Band and Symphony Orchestra; Street Music, Op. 65.

(M) ** DG (ADD) 463 665-2. Siegel-Schwall Band, San Francisco SO, Ozawa – GERSHWIN: *An American in Paris.* **

William Russo has been an assiduous advocate of mixing jazz and blues traditions with the symphony orchestra, and *Street Music* has its attractive side. But despite the presence of Corky Siegel on harmonica, it is no more successful at achieving genuine integration than other pieces of its kind, and its half-hour span is far too long for the material it contains. The 1976 recording is excellent, though the close focus for the harmonica makes for some unattractive sound from Mr Siegel. *Three Pieces for Blues Band* represents another vigorous attempt at barrier-leaping and will appeal to those who like such mixtures. To others it is likely to seem both over-sweet and over-aggressive (rather like the 1972 sound, which is both rich and fierce). Still, this is rare repertoire, although a curious choice for DG's Originals label.

RUTTER, John (born 1943)

Christmas carols: *Angels' Carol; Candelight Carol; Carol of the Children; Christmas Lullaby; Donkey Carol; Dormi Jesu; Jesus Child; Love Came Down at Christmas; Mary's Lullaby; Nativity Carol; Sans Day Carol; Second Amen; Shepherd's Pipe Carol; Star Carol; There is a Flower; The Very Best Time of Year; What Sweeter Music; Wild Wood Carol.*
Arrangements: *Angel Tidings; Away in a Manger; I Wonder as I Wander; Silent Night.*

*** Hyp. CDA 67245. Polyphony, City of L. Sinf., Layton.

John Rutter's larger-scale choral works, including the *Gloria*, *Requiem* and *Te Deum*, are among the most performed (by amateur choral societies throughout Britain and in America too) of any vocal works by a living British composer; but it is for his delightful carols that the composer will be especially remembered. 'They were my calling cards,' he says, 'you have to remember that the Christmas carol is one of the very few musical forms which allows classically trained musicians to feel it's permissible to write tunes!' And, as is shown again and again here, Rutter never had difficulty in coming up with a memorable melodic line, whether it be the *Shepherd's Pipe Carol*, with its characteristic flute writing, which opens the programme, or the deliciously perky *Donkey Carol*, with its catchy 5/8 syncopated rhythm, which closes it.

The twenty-two carols included here were composed in a steady stream over a period of three decades, with the charming *Dormi Jesu* dating from as recently as 1999. Rutter's writing is notable not only for its tunefulness and winning use of choral textures, but also for his always engaging orchestrations. I.M. has been playing Rutter's own Clare College recordings every Christmas since the 1970s, yet the present collection is the most comprehensive on record, and it is beautifully sung, played and recorded. But they were not written to be heard in a continuous sequence, rather to be juxtaposed with other carols; so to enjoy them at their best one needs to play them in small groups, or their melodic sweetness may tend to cloy. (Even so this is perfect background music for Christmas Eve.)

SAINT-SAËNS, Camille

(1835–1921)

(iii) *Carnival of the Animals; (ii) Piano Concerto No. 2; (iii) Violin Concerto No. 3 in B min.; (iv) Danse macabre; (ii) Havanaise, Op. 83; Introduction and Rondo capriccioso, Op. 28; (iv) Symphony No. 3 in C min. (Organ), Op. 78.*

(B) ** Erato Ultima (ADD/DDD) 0630 18971-2 (2). (i) Postnikova & Soloists, Rozhdestvensky; (ii) Duchable, Strasbourg PO, Lombard; (ii) Amoyal, New Philh. O, Handley; (iv) French Nat. RO, Martinon.

Rozhdestvensky's chamber forces in the *Carnival of the Animals* are recorded in clear and vivid digital sound. The performance is certainly lively and enjoyable, if ultimately missing a certain gallic insouciance. However, with the piano forwardly balanced, Duchable's bold assertiveness brings the wrong sort of approach to the outer movements of the *Second Piano Concerto*, which at times sounds aggressive, and generally lacks charm. In the *Violin Concerto* too, the soloist is placed rather too forward. Yet all Amoyal's performances are sympathetic, if not especially distinctive, and they are supported by good orchestral playing throughout, although the 1977 sound is not top drawer. The highlight of the set is Martinon's splendidly idiomatic 1966 account of the *Organ Symphony*, which has stood the test of time, the first movement sparkling and alert, the *Poco adagio* warmly romantic, with a touch of nobility at the close. The organ entry in the finale is massively buoyant, yet the balance allows detail to register fully, so that in the Scherzo the rippling piano figurations are clearer than usual. In fact, the recording, with its ambient glow, is almost ideally balanced. The same conductor's *Danse macabre* is no less persuasively played in its extrovert way. But overall this is rather a mixed bag.

(i) *Carnival of the Animals* (chamber version); (ii) *Piano Concerto No. 2 in G min.*; (iii; iv) *Danse Macabre*; (v) *Havanaise*; *Introduction et rondo capriccioso*; (vi) *Le Rouet d'Omphale*; (vii; viii; iv) *Symphony No. 3 in C min.*; *Samson et Dalila*: (vi; iv) *Bacchanale* & (ix) *Mon coeur s'ouvre à ta voix.*

(B) **(*) DG Panorama (ADD/DDD) 469 310-2 (2). (i) Argerich, Freire, Kremer, Keulen, Maisky et al; (ii) Rogé, RPO, Dutoit; (iii) O de Paris; (iv) Barenboim; (v) Perlman, NYPO, Mehta; (vi) O Nat. de France, Bernstein; (vii) Litaize; (viii) Chicago SO; (ix) Bumbry, Berlin RSO, Kulka.

A generally excellent DG Panorama collection of Saint-Saëns's most famous works. Barenboim's inspirational 1976 performance of the *Third Symphony* glows with warmth from beginning to end, even if the strings have lost some of their expansive quality in the CD re-mastering. Rogé's natural elegance brings out the warmth and sparkle of the *Second Piano Concerto* – which 'starts off like Bach, and ends like Offenbach' – in this (Decca) 1981 performance, and the tone-poems are also highly successful. The reservations concern the chamber performance of the *Carnival of the Animals*: the combination of Martha Argerich and Nelson Freire playing the piano duo ensures plenty of character and sparkle, as well as some extreme tempi, but overall this account is rather short on charm and is not helped by the dry sound, which at times is aggressive. However, at the price, this collection is certainly worth considering, and the rest of the recordings give no cause for complaint.

Cello Concerto No. 1 in A min., Op. 33.

(M) ** EMI CDM5 67593-2 [567594]. Rostropovich, LPO, Giulini – DVORAK: *Cello Concerto.* *(*)

Rostropovich's 1977 recording serves as a pairing for the Dvořák concerto and is more successful than its coupling, though not as successful as his earlier version (currently withdrawn). There is less rhetorical intensity here than in the Dvořák, and the performance is warmly and atmospherically recorded, with an impresssive CD transfer.

(i) *Cello Concerto No. 1*; (ii) *Piano Concerto No. 2*; (iii) *Violin Concerto No. 3.*

✪ (M) *** Sony SMK 89873. (i) Ma, O Nat. de France, Maazel; (ii) Licad, LPO, Previn; (iii) Lin, Philh. O, Tilson Thomas.

Three outstanding performances from the early 1980s are admirably linked together in this highly desirable CBS mid-price reissue. Yo-Yo Ma's performance of the *Cello Concerto* is distinguished by fine sensitivity and beautiful tone, while Cécile Licad and the LPO under Previn turn in an eminently satisfactory reading of the *G minor Piano Concerto* that has the requisite delicacy in the Scherzo and seriousness elsewhere. Cho-Liang Lin's account of the *B minor Violin Concerto* with the Philharmonia Orchestra and Michael Tilson Thomas is exhilarating and thrilling. Indeed, this is the kind of performance that prompts one to burst into applause – his version is arguably the finest to have appeared for years.

Piano Concertos Nos. 1 in D, Op. 17; 2 in G min., Op. 22; 3 in E flat, Op. 29; 4 in C min., Op. 44; 5 in F ('Egyptian'), Op. 103.

(B) * Sony (ADD) SB2K 89977 (2). Entremont, O du Capitole Toulouse, Plasson.

Piano Concertos Nos. 1–5; Africa, Op. 39; Allegro appassionato, Op. 70; Rapsodie d'Auvergne, Op. 71; Wedding Cake, Op. 76.

(BB) *** ASV CDQS 262 (2). Brownridge, Hallé Orchestra, Murphy.

Angela Brownridge's set of these fine concertos, plus four highly engaging encores, is consistently enjoyable, admirably fresh and with a genuine sense of style. She gets excellent support from Pat Murphy and the Hallé players, with the Hallé strings in particularly good form. This can be recommended in its own right and is splendid value for money, for the recording too is excellent. It would be churlish to give less than three stars for performances that are so spirited. But it has to be said that the full-priced Hyperion set from Stephen Hough with the CBSO under Oramo is finer on almost all counts, and offers demonstration sound quality. It is well worth its extra cost (Hyperion CDA 67331/2).

Entremont is a vigorously persuasive interpreter of French music, but here he is let down by the recording. As with other reissues in the 'Essential Classics' series Sony is coy about the recording date, but '1989' is given on the disc itself and '2002' on the back of the insert listing. However, in reality the recording dates from the late 1970s and did less than justice to the soloist's gentler qualities, with the forward balance reducing the dynamic range. The CD remastering has made matters worse, with orchestral tuttis sounding crude and fierce and no bloom given to the piano, which becomes clattery and aggressive under pressure.

Piano Concerto No. 2 in G min., Op. 22.

(B) *** RCA 2CD (ADD) 74321 846062 (2). Rubinstein, Phd. O, Ormandy – CHABRIER: *Pièces pittoresques;* DEBUSSY: *Estampes* etc.; FAURÉ: *Nocturne No.3;* FRANCK: *Symphonic Variations; Prelude choral et fugue;* RAVEL: *Valses nobles et sentimentales etc.* ***

The Saint-Saëns *Second Concerto* was a great favourite with Rubinstein. This 1969 version with Ormandy is most enjoyable and very effectively remastered. The couplings too are more generous than the single disc listed in our main volume and this RCA Double is highly recommendable.

Piano Concertos Nos. 2 in G min.; 4, Op. 44.

(B) *** Decca Eloquence (ADD) 467 471-2. Rogé, RPO or Philh. O, Dutoit – POULENC: *Mouvements perpétuels; Napoli.* ***

These have long been the two favourite Saint-Saëns piano concertos, often coupled together on LP, and they are most persuasively presented by Pascal Rogé in partnership with Dutoit. No. 4 with its indelible main theme is particularly attractive, and the Decca recording is first-class. A bargain – but one can get all five concertos played by these artists on a Double Decca (443 865-2).

Morceau de concert, Op. 154.

(B) *** DG Eloquence (ADD) 469 689-2. Zabaleta, French Nat. R. O, Martinon – BIZET: *Symphony in C; Jeux d'enfants; Suite bohémiennes* ***; DEBUSSY *Danse sacrée et danse profane.* ***

A charming account of the *Morceau de concert, Op. 154 for Harp and Orchestra*, which dates from 1919. Zabaleta's recording with the French National Radio Orchestra under Jean Martinon, made in 1970, sounds very fresh and is yet to be surpassed.

Symphony No. 3 in C min., Op. 78.

(*) Testament mono SBT 1240. Roget, Paris Conservatoire O, Cluytens – FAURÉ: *Requiem.* (*)

André Cluytens recorded Saint-Saëns's *Third Symphony* at the Salle de la Mutualité in 1955 – and, of course, in mono. Cluytens gives a generally well-paced and finely conceived account of it, although the playing of the Paris Conservatoire Orchestra falls short of distinction.

Samson et Dalila (opera): complete.

*** Arthaus **DVD** 100 202. Domingo, Verrett, Wolfgang Brendel, San Francisco Opera Ch. & O, Rudel. (Director: Nicolas Joel. V/D: Kirk Browning.)

(M) ** EMI (ADD) CDM5 67598-2 [567602] (2). Gorr, Vickers, Blanc, Diakov, René Duclos Ch., Paris Nat. Op. O, Prêtre.

Recorded in 1981 at the San Francisco Opera House, this DVD of Saint-Saëns's biblical opera offers a heavily traditional production with realistic sets and costumes like those in a Hollywood epic. Sporting a vast bouffant wig like a tea-cosy (ripe for Dalila's shears in Act 2), Placido Domingo is in magnificent, heroic voice, with Shirley Verrett also at her peak as Dalila, at once seductive and sinister. Other principals are first-rate too, and the chorus, so vital in this opera, sings with incandescent tone in a riproaring performance under Julius Rudel, culminating in a spectacular presentation of the fall of the Temple of Dagon. Most enjoyable.

Jon Vickers and Rita Gorr are in commanding voice, both recorded at their vocal peak. Ernest Blanc characterises well as the High Priest, but the other soloists are undistinguished. The main snag is the conducting of Prêtre, which presents the big moments of high drama effectively enough, but is coarse-grained at too many points. The recording is basically atmospheric and vivid, but from the very opening the choral focus is far from sharp, and the new transfer still brings the occasional touch of distortion on vocal peaks. The overall effect is certainly red-blooded and the set is perhaps more enticing at mid price, but is hardly an apt candidate for EMI's 'Great Recordings of the Century'.

SARASATE, Pablo (1844–1908)

Carmen Fantasy, Op. 25.

*** Claudio CB 5256-2. Jin, LSO, Wordsworth – LALO: *Symphonie espagnole.* PROKOFIEV: *Solo Violin Sonata.* *** (with KROLL: *Banjo and Fiddle,* orch. Bradbury; TARREGA: *Recuerdos de la Alhambra,* arr. Ricci **(*)).

Min Jin does not quite have Perlman's flamboyant panache in Saraste's brilliant arrangement of Bizet, but her airily fragile approach is equally spontaneous and refreshingly different. Against a strong backing from Barry Wordsworth and the LSO, the solo playing is still dazzling, but never uses effect for its own sake. Just sample her delicate harmonic slides (1'06" and 2'12") – and how seductive she is in the delicate *Habañera,* while throughout she clearly relishes Bizet's wonderful tunes. Very good recording much more naturally balanced with Perlman.

SATIE, Erik (1866–1925)

Piano 4 hands: *La belle excentrique; Chapitres tournés en tous sens; En habit de cheval; 3 Morceaux en forme de poire; 3 Petites pièces montées.* Solo piano music: *Aperçus désagréables; Avant dernières pensées; Carnet d'esquisses et de croquis; Croquis et agaceries d'un gros bonhomme en bois; Descriptions automatiques; Danses gothiques; Embroyens desséchés; Enfantillages pittoresques; La fils des étoiles; 3 Gnossiennes* (2 sets); *3 Gymnopédies; Heures séculaires et instananées; Jack in the Box; Menus propos enfantins; Musiques intimes et secrètes; 2 Nocturnes; 3 Nocturnes; Ogives; Pages mystiques; Les pantins dansent; Passacaille; Peccadilles importunes; 12 Petites chorals; Petite ouverture à danser; 6 Pièces de la période 1906-1913; Pièces froides & Nouvellles pièces froides; Le piège de Méduse; Poudre d'or; Première menuet; Première pensée de la Rose + Croix & Sonneries de la Rose + Croix; 4 Préludes; Préludes flasques (pour un chien); Prélude et tapisserie; Rêveries de l'enfance de Pantagruel; 2 Rêveries nocturnes; 3 Sarabandes; Sonatine bureaucratique; Sports et divertissements; 3 Valses du précieux dégoûté; Véritable préludes flasques (pour un chien); Vieux sequins et viellies cuiresses.*

(BB) **(*) EMI (ADD) CZS5 74534-2 (5) Ciccolini.

Recorded between 1967 and 1971, Aldo Ciccolini's 5-CD survey of Satie's piano music is now the most comprehensive available, including a number of novelties and many works in revisions by Robert Cadby. Ciccolini's playing is certainly sympathetic and idiomatic, and he manages the four-handed pieces by pre-recording and playing in duet with himself. The currrent remastering by EMI France has improved the realism of the piano image – it is firm, full and clear, just a bit hard at times, but fully acceptable. The notes, however, are sparse and only in French without translation. Those not wanting such an extensive coverage, inexpensive as it is, might turn to a single CD recorded during the 1980s where in the piano duet pieces Ciccolini is joined by Gabriel Tacchino, to even greater effect (CDM5 67230-2 [567260] – see our main volume). Though hardly a 'Great Recording of the Century' as suggested by French EMI, it is a distinctive collection.

(i) *Chapitres tournés en tous sens; Croquis et agaceries d'un gros bonhomme en bois; Le fils des étoiles (Act II Prélude); Gnossiennes Nos. 2 & 4; 3 Gymnopédies; Heures séculaires et instantanées; Nocturnes Nos. 2 & 4; Nouvelles pièces froides; Piège de Méduse; Passacaile; Sonata bureaucratique; (ii) Embryons desséchés; Fantaisie et divertissements Nos. 11, 13 & 15-21; Gnossiennes Nos. 1 & 3; Je te veux; Le Piccadilly (La Transatlantique); Valse-ballet.*

(B) ** CfP (ADD/DDD) 575 147-2. (i) Peter Lawson; (ii) Angela Brownridge.

This Classics for Pleasure CD draws on two LPs, Peter Lawson's from 1979 (all of it included) and around half of Angela Brownridge's compilation from 1985 (digital). Lawson's recital opens with the famous *Gymnopédies*, played coolly but not ineffectively. The highlight is a perceptive and articulate characterization of *Le piège de Médusa* – seven epigrammatic *morceaux de concert*. Elsewhere his account is quietly tasteful, and though he catches comething of Satie's gentle and wayward poetry, he is less successful in revealing the underlying sense of fantasy. Angela Brownridge's playing is bright and stylish, sensitively reflecting the sharply changing moods and lacking only the last touch of poetry.

SCARLATTI, Alessandro

(1660–1725)

Sedecia (oratorio; complete)

*** Virgin VC5 45452-2 (2). Lesne, Pochon, Jaroussky, Harvey, Padmore, Il Seminario Musicale, Lesne.

Alessandro Scarlatti's oratorios, some 30 of them, have been shockingly neglected, even in our age of baroque rediscovery. This superb premiere recording of *Sedecia, re di Gerusalemme* reveals a vital masterpiece written for Rome in 1705, where oratorio regularly took the place of secular opera. The most important of Scarlatti's oratorios on an Old Testament theme, *Sedecia* tells the story of the last king of Jerusalem and the punishment meted out to him at the hands of Nebuchadnezzar. Though it was dismissed as 'extremely tedious' by Edward J. Dent in his biography of the composer, that shallow judgement is absurd. The fast-moving sequence of 54 generally compact numbers, arias and recitatives, punctuated by the occasional duet and rounded off with a chorus, broadly follow the pattern later developed by Handel in his English oratorios, with a flexibility, energy and variety of invention found only in the finest religious music of the period. Gerard Lesne, himself taking the counter-tenor role of the king, directs a performance which with an excellent cast carries the listener foward – through the preparation of Part One, to a most moving climax in Part Two, with one deeply expressive aria after another. The work culminates in a duet marked by scrunching suspensions, where the blinded Sedecia bids farewell to his wife, Anna. Following Lesne's own example, each of the principals sings with clear, fresh tone and superb technique. Clear, well-balanced recording to match. Not to be missed.

SCARLATTI, Domenico

(1685–1757)

Keyboard Sonatas, Kk. 2, 35, 87, 132, 193, 247, 322, 388, 437, 515, 519.

(M) (**) Westminster mono 471 214-2. Haskil – MOZART: *Piano Concerto No. 20.* (***)

The best of these Scarlatti sonatas, such as the *F minor*, Kk.386, and its successor on this disc, Kk.519, are outstanding in Haskil's hands, full of life and character, though the monochrome, slightly tubby sound does not flatter them all. They were recorded in 1951, and three – Kk.87, 193 and 386 – were included in the Philips 'Clara Haskil Legacy' published in 1994. Haskil began her career as early as 1902, but it was not until these 1951 recordings that she really came into her own.

Keyboard Sonatas, Kk. 9, 27, 33, 69, 87, 96, 159, 193, 247, 427, 492, 531; Fugue in G min., Kk. 30.

(BB) *** Warner (ADD) Apex 0927 44353-2. Queffélec (piano).

Anne Queffélec employs a modern Steinway with great character and aplomb. She immediately captures the listener in the dashing opening of the *D major Sonata*, Kk.96, with its lively fanfares and, in the gentler *B minor*, Kk.27, her rippling passage-work is Bach-like in its simplicity. She alternates reflective works with those sonatas calling for sparkling bravura and her choice is unerringly effective: the recital closes with the *Fugue* which unfolds with calm inevitability. The 1970 recording is first class; the piano is naturally focused and has plenty of space without any resonant blurring.

Keyboard Sonatas: Kk.20, 32, 39, 79, 109, 124–5, 128, 342, 381, 394, 425, 454, 470, 491, 495, 547, 551.

(BB) *** EMI Encore CDE5 74969-2. Tipo.

Maria Tipo's 18 Scarlatti sonatas first appeared in 1989 and sound every bit as good now as they did then. Tipo has not gained the wider recognition for which her artistry entitles her, but this recital shows her in the best possible light. Her range of keyboard colour is wide and her sense of dynamic contrast strong, but she never uses them simply to make effect. No fewer than seven of her sonatas are in G major and only three are in minor keys. There is a spontaneity and a sense of discovery here that is delightful, and the EMI sound is very faithful. She is not the equal of Horowitz or Pletnev in this repertoire, but she has undoubted grace and sparkle, and this record is an unmissable bargain.

SCHEIDT, Samuel (1587–1654)

Ludi musici (Hamburg, 1621): excerpts.

(BB) *** Virgin VBD5 62028-2 (2). Hespérion XX, Savall – G. GABRIELI: *Canzoni da sonare;* SCHEIN: *Banchetto musicale.* ***

Although he studied briefly under Sweelinck in Amsterdam in 1608/9, Samuel Scheidt spent his life in Halle, both as organist and for five years as Kapellmeister. He published four collections of instrumental music between 1621 and 1624 under the title *Ludi musici*, but only the First Book survives and all these pieces are drawn from it. For all its good nature, his music has a melancholy streak. This is immediately striking in the touchingly expressive extended opening of the *Paduan a 4* (from Cantus IV) with its gentle, lyrical flow and passing dissonances. The later *Paduan* (from Cantus V) is also very touching and has much in common with Dowland's *Lachrimae*. Scheidt actually draws on Dowland in his spirited *Battle Galliard*, so characteristic of its time. Other English tunes are featured in his canzons, notably the delightful five-part *Canzon* (from Cantus XXVI). All this music is played with characteristic finesse, nicely judged espressivo and plenty of vitality by the superb Hespérion XX under Jordi Savall, and the viol sound is smooth and pleasingly natural with none of that scratchiness which comes from too close microphones. The coupling with the music of Johann Schein could not be

more apt and this reissue is topped off with *Canzoni* by Giovanni Gabrieli and his contemporaries to make altogether a sumptuous Rennaisance feast.

SCHEIN, Johann Hermann

(1586–1630)

Banchetto musicale (1617): Suites a 5 Nos. 2, 6, 16, 20, 36, Canzon in A (Collarium).

(BB) *** Virgin VBD5 62028-2 (2). Hespérion XX, Savall – G. GABRIELI: *Canzoni da sonare;* SCHEIDT: *Ludi musici.* ***

Johann Hermann Schein's instrumental music has much in common with that of his Italian contemporary Giovanni Gabrieli, although the interplay between various groups, usually brass and strings (or recorder), is much less spectacular. The *Canzon in A (Collarium)*, however, is a more ambitious piece, very much in the contrapuntal Gabrieli manner. The *Banchetto musicale* is intended as a background for meals, although the sonorous brass writing with occasional bravura roulades suggests that the banqueting hall would have needed to be very spacious. However, the very pleasing expressive music (especially the *Padouanas*) invites lower dynamic levels. The *Intradas* open the feast with a drumbeat suggesting the musicians marching in. The performances here are stylish and pleasing, responding well to the music's dolorousness. Perhaps they could have been more robust, but the result is very suitable for domestic listening and is very well recorded. The coupling with music by Schein's contemporary Samuel Scheidt is most appropriate, bringing the attention of the collector to a pair of talented early seventeenth-century composers, each with an individual musical personality.

SCHOENBERG, Arnold

(1874–1951)

Chamber Symphonies Nos. 1-2, Opp. 9 & 38; Verklaerte Nacht, Op. 4.

(BB) *** Warner Apex 0927 44399-2. COE, Holliger.

Schoenberg's *Chamber Symphonies* are superbly performed by the COE, played with both warmth and thrust, with complex textual problems masterfully solved. *Verklärte Nacht* in its orchestral version receives one of its most passionate performances on disc, reflecting 'the glow of inmost warmth' in the Richard Dehmel poem which inspired it. This new coupling makes an excellent bargain on the Apex label, and the sound is first-rate.

Concerto for String Quartet & Orchestra after Handel's Concerto Grosso, Op. 6/7.

(BB) *** Warner Apex 7559 79675-2. American Qt., NYCO, Schwarz – R. STRAUSS: *Divertimento (after Couperin).* ***

Schoenberg virtually recomposed Handel's Op. 6/7 for string quartet and orchestra, offering a rich spicing of dissonance. The result, inflated to nearly twice the size of the original, is at times grotesque, but always aurally fascinating and entertaining. The performance by the excellent American Quartet with the New York Chamber Orchestra under Gerard Schwarz is spirited and given bright, lively sound. The coupling too is particularly desirable, and the price will surely tempt the collector to explore this excellent CD.

Verklaerte Nacht.

*** ECM 465 778-2. Camerata Bern, Zehetmair – BARTOK: *Divertimento*; VERESS: *4 Transylvanian Dances.****

Thomas Zehetmair and the Camerata Bern recorded this account of *Verklaerte Nacht* in 1995, four years earlier than the Bartók and Sándor Veress couplings but in an equally good acoustic. Eloquent playing and very present and lifelike recording make this, while not necessarily a first choice, a highly recommendable version.

CHAMBER MUSIC

Chamber Symphony No. 1 (arr. Webern for piano quintet); (i) *Concerto for String Quartet and Orchestra (after Handel's Concerto grosso, Op. 6/7)*; (ii) *Ode to Napoleon, Op. 41; Phantasy for violin and piano, Op. 47; String Quartet in D; String Quartets Nos. 1–4; String Trio, Op. 45; Wind Quintet, Op. 26; 6 Little Piano Pieces, Op. 19* (both arr. Guittart for strings); *Verklaerte Nacht.*

*** Chan. 9939 (5). Schoenberg Qt with Narucki, Grotenhuis, (i) Arnhem PO, Benzi; (ii) Grandage.

This ambitious five-disc set brilliantly brings together all of Schoenberg's chamber music for strings, including several arrangements. What is so persuasive is the expressive warmth of the Schoenberg Quartet. Even when the atonal Schoenberg is at his most abrasively intellectual, as in the *String Trio* of 1946, one is made to appreciate that this is music with an emotional core. So it is, too, in the four *String Quartets*, which form a central core to the collection, a splendid cycle stretching from the post-romantic No. 1 of 1904–5 through the mould-breaking No. 2 of 1907–8 with its evocative use of a soprano soloist in the third and fourth movements to the severity of Nos. 3 and 4, both commissioned by Mrs Sprague Coolidge, a great musical patron. The portrait of the composer is made all the more persuasive by having such a wide range of works including not just the early *Verklaerte Nacht*, wonderfully evocative, but the unnumbered string quartet of 1897. It is good, too, to find him relaxing in the *Concerto for String Quartet and Orchestra* of 1933, which he freely transcribed from Handel's *Concerto grosso* Op. 6, No. 7, which he wrote in France as a relaxation immediately after fleeing from Germany in 1933. One also welcomes the inclusion of the *Napoloen Bonaparte Ode* in its version for reciter and piano

quintet. The recordings made in Holland are first-rate, warm and atmospheric.

Gurrelieder.

*** EMI CDS5 57303-2 (2). Mattila, Von Otter, Moser, Langridge, Quasthoff, Berlin R. Ch., Leipzig R. Ch., Ernest Senff Ch., BPO, Rattle.

Drawn from live performances given in the Philharmonie in Berlin in September 2001, Rattle's version of Schoenberg's opulent score is the most refined yet in its beauty, warmly spontaneous from first to last, sweeping you away with its richness and magnetism up to the final choral climax. Though the sound is not as sharply focused as some, the dramatic contrasts are superb, with elaborate textures over the widest range magically caught. The soloists and massed choruses are all first-rate, with Karita Mattila as Tove consistently warm and tenderly responsive, opposite Thomas Moser in the key role of Waldemar, here more firmly focused than usual, stronger than on Sinopoli's Teldec version (4509 98424-2). As in Abbado's Vienna version on DG (439 944-2) Philip Langridge is outstanding as Klaus-Narr and though Anne Sofie von Otter sings with grainy tone in the *Song of the Wood Dove*, her performance is both dramatic and moving, while Thomas Quasthoff is superb both as the Woodsman (Bauer) and in the difficult role of the Speaker in the melodrama of the final section, sounding younger and fresher than immediate rivals.

N.B. In our main Guide we have the Abbado DG version incorrectly sited in the Berlin Philharmonie with the BPO. In fact it is with the Vienna PO in the Musikverein.

SCHREKER, Franz (1878–1934)

Ekkehard Overture; Fantastic Overture; Die Gezeichneten: Prelude. Der Schatzgräber, Act III: Interlude. Das Spielwerk: Prelude.

(BB) ** Naxos 8.555246. Slovak PO, Seipenbusch.

Prelude to Memnon; Romantic Suite.

(BB) ** Naxos 8.555107. NOe. Tonkünstler O, Vienna, Mund.

Both these issues first appeared on Marco Polo in the late 1980s, when Schreker's representation in the catalogue was relatively meagre. It is, of course, useful to have these (on the whole) adequate performances at bargain price, but it would be idle to pretend that they are of the highest order. Neither the Slovak Philharmonic under Edgar Seipenbusch nor the NOe. (Lower Austrian) Tonkünstler Orchestra with Uwe Mund are the equal of the BBC Philharmonic, nor do the recordings approach the Chandos Schreker series. On the Slovak disc neither the *Ekkehard Overture* nor the *Fantastic Overture* is the best Schreker; they are, in fact, less than distinguished. The Prelude to *Die Gezeichneten* is another matter, although the playing is more guts than finesse. The Chandos account of the *Romantic Suite* under Valery Sinaisky knocks spots off the Viennese rival and is altogether richer and more enjoyable. Incidentally the *Prelude to Memnon* is identical to the *Prelude to a Drama* on Chan. 9797.

Prelude to a Grand Opera (Vorspiel zu einer grossen Oper).

(B) *** EMI double fforte CZS5 75157-2 (2). Cologne PO, Conlon – BRUCH: *Symphonies Nos. 1–3.* ***

Schreker's *Prelude to a Grand Opera*, a late work written in 1933, is quite a find, in essence an expansive (22-minute) and colourful symphonic poem presenting the opera in chrysallis. The planned work, which was never completed, was *Memnon* (in Greek mythology he was the son of Eos and nephew of King Priam). It is vividly scored and makes an impressive entity in its own right, with a sinuous and ear-catching oriental atmosphere in its lyrical melodic lines. It is very well played indeed and the recording is very good too, even if fortissimos are just a little fierce.

Prelude to a Grand Opera; Prelude to Das Spielwerk; Romantic Suite, Op. 14. (i) 5 Gesäng.

*** Chan. 9951 (i) Katarina Karnéus; BBC PO, Sinaisky.

The *Romantic Suite* comes from 1903, when Schreker was in his mid-twenties though its third movement began life independently as an *Intermezzo for strings* a year earlier. It is a rather beautiful piece as, for that matter, is the opening *Idylle*, written at much the same time as he was making the first sketches for *Der ferne klang*. There is a lot of Strauss here and in the mercurial Scherzo, Reger – the latter is a highly inventive movement. Only the finale, *Tanz* is routine. The *Five Songs*, imaginatively sung by the Swedish mezzo, Katarina Karnéus, are later; they were written in 1909, the year before the opera was finished, but were not scored until the early 1920s. They have plenty of atmosphere and mystery, and are well worth getting to know. The opening song, *Ich frag' nach dir jedwede Morgonsonne*, has a touch of Szymanowski about it, and certain moments elsewhere call the Chamber Symphony to mind. The disc covers the whole of Schreker's career: the Prelude to *Das Spielwerk* is a wartime piece while the *Vorspiel zu einer groâen Oper* comes from the last months of his life. This was after he had been hounded from his teaching post in Berlin by the Nazis, a trauma which is said to have induced the stroke which eventually killed him in March 1934. It is an ambitious piece, some twenty-four minutes in length and draws on material that he had intended for the opera, *Memnon* whose libretto he had completed in 1918 but which he never managed to complete. It is darker than his earlier pieces but despite its expert orchestration remains somewhat overblown. The playing of the BBC Philharmonic under Sinaisky is superb and the recording is in the demonstration class. Intelligent liner notes.

SCHUBERT, Franz (1797–1828)

Konzertstück for violin and Orchestra in D, D.345.

(M) *** CRD (ADD) CRD 3369, R. Thomas, Bournemouth SO – BEETHOVEN: *Romances Nos. 1–2;* MENDELSSOHN: *Violin Concerto.* ***

Schubert's *Konzertstück* is slight, but Ronald Thomas's refreshing playing and direction make it well worth having on disc, along with the excellent Beethoven and Mendelssohn. The recording is first class.

Rosamunde: Overture (Die Zauberharfe), D.644, and incidental music (complete), D.797.

(M) *** Decca (ADD) 470 261-2. VPO, Münchinger – WEBER: *Preciosa Overture;* SCHUMANN: *Genoveva: Overture.* ***

It is right that these beautifully played and recorded performances are released on Decca's Legends series. This delightful music glows with affectionate warmth and understanding which places it as one of Münchinger's very best records, and the 1974 sound emerges fresher than ever in this new transfer. The two overtures, taken from a long-forgotten 'Romantic Overtures' LP are similarly also beautifully played and recorded. Strongly recommended.

Symphonies Nos. 1–6; 8–9; Rosamunde: Overture (Die Zauberharfe); Ballet Music 1–2.

(B) ** EMI CZS5 74808-2 (4). VPO, Muti.

Symphonies Nos. 1–6; 8 (Unfinished); 9 (Great); Rosamunde: Ballet Music Nos. 1–2; Entr'acte No. 3 in B flat.

(M) *** RCA (ADD/DDD) 09026 63940-2 (5); also Nos. 1 & 2 (09026 63941-2); 3 & 6 (09026 63942-2); 4 & 8 (*Unfinished*) (09026 63943-2); 5 & *Rosamunde* (09026 63944-2); 9 (09026 63945-2). Cologne RSO, Wand.

Günter Wand's complete cycle with the Cologne Orchestra was made over a period of eight years, beginning with the *Great C Major* in 1977, and ending with No. 5 in 1984. Nos. 3, 5 and 6 as well as the *Rosamunde* music are digital, but the current remastering ensures that the recordings – made by the West German Radio – all sound excellent; even if in No. 2 the violins have less body than elsewhere, there is more overall fullness than previously.

The freshness and bluff honesty of Wand's interpretations shine through all the performances, with plenty of warmth in slow movements. Note that Boehm on DG takes only four discs (against Wand's five), but does not include *Rosamunde* and is less generous with repeats.

Wand's accounts of the first two boyhood works set the seal on his approach: strong and direct, but the natural way he presents these sunny inspirations, bringing out the youthful energy, is consistently winning. On the second CD, Nos. 3 and 6 are no less exuberant and joyful. The only controversial point is the comparatively fast, though well pointed, speed for the second-movement *Allegretto* of No. 3. But Wand's touch is light, and in the finales, which find Schubert at his most effervescent, Wand draws finely sprung, resilient playing from the Cologne orchestra – not the most refined in Germany, but one which vividly responds to the natural spontaneous-sounding energy of the veteran conductor.

Aptly, among these early symphonies, Wand gives greater weight to No. 4, the *Tragic*, in keeping with the C minor intensity which prompted the work's title. The slow movement is on the fast side but easily lyrical, and the finale electrically intense, helped by the immediate, vivid recording. This is coupled with an inspired performance of the *Unfinished*, which brings out the sunny elements; but in Wand's strong, bluff way contrasting that lighter character in both movements with Schubert's darker inspiration to make this disc – available separately – one of the finest of the set.

No. 5 is freshly attractive and spontaneous, the first movement light and bouncing, the *Andante* warm and gracious, the *Scherzo* with a winning lift. The coupled *Rosamunde* ballet music, too, has charm but is never made to sound trivial.

What is striking about the *Ninth* is the ease with which Wand moves from tempo to tempo in the opening movement (exposition repeat included) and especially the culminating section. The *Andante*, with an exquisite oboe solo, is lyrically sustained, yet with plenty of light and shade. The *Scherzo* has plenty of genial vigour and again the move to the slower speed for the Trio is naturally achieved, while the finale has a strong, energetic forward pulse, convincingly sustained.

Muti's set is a disappointment: his robust approach is not endearingly Schubertian, even with the VPO at his disposal. The playing is rather routine, despite the conductor's natural electricity and preference for urgent speeds, and there is little to set the blood tingling or to charm the ear. With a relatively mannered if spacious account of the *Ninth* this set cannot compare with the Abbado or Boehm sets in either natural zest or warmth. The recording is no help. Moreover the clumsy layout, on four discs, splits the *Great C major Symphony* after the first movement.

(i) *Symphony No. 3 in D*; (ii) *Rosamunde: Overture (Doe Zauberharfe); Act II Entr'acte; Ballet*; (iii) *Piano Trio in B flat, D.898*; (iv) *4 Impromptus, D.899; Piano Sonata in B flat, D.960*.

(B) **(*) DG Panorama (ADD/DDD) 469 313-2 (2). (i) VPO, Kleiber; (ii) COE, Abbado; (iii) Beaux Arts; Kempff.

Carlos Kleiber is nothing if not unpredictable, and sometimes his imaginative flair goes too far towards quirkiness, and that is certainly so in the slow movement of the *Third Symphony*, which is rattled through jauntily and at breakneck speed. The effect is bizarre, even for an *Allegretto*, if not lacking charm. The Minuet, too, becomes a full-blooded scherzo, and there is little repose in the outer movements. There are no such problems in Abbado's fresh-sounding (digital) excerpts from *Rosamunde*, and in the impeccably played performance of the *Piano Trio* with the Beaux

Arts, where Menahem Pressler is a sharply imaginative pianist. And it is a tribute to Kempff's artistry that with most relaxed tempi he conveys such consistent, compelling intensity in the *B flat major Sonata*, recorded in 1967. Hearing the opening one might feel that this is going to be a lightweight account, but in fact the long-breathed expansiveness is hypnotic, so that here, quite as much as in the *Great C major Symphony*, one is bound by the spell of heavenly length. Rightly, Kempff repeats the first-movement exposition with the important nine bars of lead-back, and although the overall manner is less obviously dramatic than is common, the range of tone-colour is magical, with sharp terracing of dynamics to plot the geography of each movement. The *Impromptus* also evoke predictably fine playing, though here the magic comes more unevenly than usual. However, by any standards, they are beautifully done and well-characterized. The recordings and transfers are excellent in this DG Panorama release.

Symphony No. 4 in C min. (Tragic), D.417.

(M) *** BBC (ADD) BBCL 4093-2 (2). New Philh. O, Giulini – BEETHOVEN: *Missa solemnis.* **(*)

Recorded at the Edinburgh Festival in 1968, Giulini's reading of Schubert's *Tragic Symphony* brings a bitingly intense reading, more than usual making this early work live up to its nickname. It makes an attractive fill-up to Giulini's monumental reading of Beethoven's *Missa solemnis* recorded earlier in that year.

(i) *Symphonies Nos. 4 in C min.; 5 in B flat; (ii) 8 in B min. (Unfinished); (i) 9 in C (Great). Rosamunde: Entr'acte No. 3 & ballet music, Nos. 1 & 2*.

(B) *** RCA (ADD/DDD) 74321 846 072 (2). (i) N. German RSO, Wand; (ii) Chicago SO, Reiner.

The freshness and robust, spirited vigour of Gunter Wand's Schubert shines through all of his performances and cannot fail to give pleasure. The recordings are excellent (the *Fourth* is analogue; nos. 5 and 9, plus the engaging *Rosamunde* excerpts, are digital). Reiner's *Unfinished*, however, dates from the early days of stereo (RCA is coy about its date) but hardly betrays its age. The performance is atmospheric and dramatic, especially so in the impulsive first movement, the second is richly lyrical. Good value if the programme suits.

Symphony No. 8 in B min. (Unfinished), D.759.

(B) (***) EMI mono CDZ5 74801-2. Philh. O, Cantelli – MENDELSSOHN: *Symphony No. 4;* SCHUMANN: *Symphony No. 4.* (***)

It is good to see Cantelli's beautifully shaped reading from the mid-1950s back in circulation, not that it has ever been long out of the catalogue. The *Unfinished* is one of the classic accounts of the symphony and, with its couplings, is among the finest performances ever committed to disc.

Symphonies Nos. 8 (Unfinished); 9 in C (Great).

(B) *** CfP (ADD) 574 8852. LPO, Pritchard.

(BB) **(*) RCA (ADD) 74321 68007-2. Cologne RSO, Wand.

Pritchard's reading of the *Unfinished* is magnetic, unusually direct, establishing the first movement as a genuine symphonic allegro but with no feeling of breathlessness, even in the melting lyricism of the incomparable second subject. The high dramatic contrasts – as in the development – are fearlessly presented with fine intensity, and the second movement, too, brings purity and freshness. The *Great C major* is as vital as it is refreshing. The opening brings a slightly square account of the introductory horn theme, but after that the resilience of the LPO playing is consistent, with the players often keenly challenged by the fast tempo and later able to relax into the lyricism of the beautiful slow movement.

As in the *Unfinished*, Pritchard's manner is direct and presses forward strongly, but there is never any feeling of rushing. It is always significant when one welcomes repeats observed in this already long symphony, and at the time he made these recordings (1975), Pritchard observed repeats more than anyone else on record. Only the exposition repeat in the finale is omitted – which is a pity when the repeat in the first movement adds so effectively to the scale of the argument. Both recordings have the advantage of a warm ambience (Watford Town Hall) and are naturally balanced.

More of Wand's immensely sure-footed Schubert recordings are offered on RCA at budget price. The *Great C major* was recorded in 1977 yet is similar in conception to his later digital recording with the North German Radio Symphony Orchestra (see above), the earlier version having marginally faster tempi and a recording that is brighter in the treble, but it is still good by any standards, even if the strings do not always have quite as much bloom. However, there is little to choose between the performances, both of which are excellently conceived and balanced. Wand's *Unfinished* from 1980 is a beautifully relaxed and satisfying reading, though it has not quite the theatrical impetus of Reiner's dramatic account on RCA (see also above), which includes Wand's later, digital account of the *Great C major*.

Symphony No. 9 in C (Great), D.944.

**(*) BBC stereo/mono BBCL 4072-2. BBC SO, Boult (with CHERUBINI: *Anacréon Overture*; CORNELIUS: *Barber of Baghdad Overture*).

Sir Adrian recorded the *Great C major* as early as 1934 and, for the last time (after some agitation in the press), in 1972 with the LPO. The present version with the BBC Symphony Orchestra, which, of course, he founded, comes from a 1969 Prom. It has a grandeur and sense of space that compel admiration, not for Boult but for Schubert. Sir Adrian observes pretty well every repeat, including the second time expositions in the scherzo, so that his performance runs to 55 minutes and offers plenty of opportunities to relish Schubert's 'heavenly lengths'. It is a supremely classi-

cal performance, with what one critic, speaking of the 1972 account called 'a restrained eloquence'. In some ways it is more gripping than the studio performance, but the recording is not always ideally transparent; in fact, it is at times distinctly murky (the oboe is very reticently balanced in the opening of the second movement), and the Prom audience is unusually noisy and takes time to settle down at the beginning of every movement. The *Anacréon Overture* comes from a Royal Festival Hall Concert with the RPO from 1963, while the Cornelius *Barber of Baghdad Overture* is much earlier, a mono recording taken from one of the many enterprising studio concerts he conducted in the 1950s.

CHAMBER MUSIC

Octet in F, D.803.

(BB) *** HM Classical Express HCX 3957049. Music from Aston Magna.

A wholly delightful account from the Aston Magna American group using period instruments with great finesse and affectionate warmth. Indeed, the music-making is pervaded with an American-styled geniality throughout, although the allegro of the first movement, like the jocular finale, is agreebly brisk and vivacious. All the playing is very personable, but the star of the occasion is the clarinettist, Eric Hoeprich, whose timbre is utterly seductive. He uses a pair of instruments, including a C clarinet in the fourth movement *Andante con variazioni*. The recording is first class and this is a real bargain.

Piano Quintet in A (Trout), D.667.

(**) Pearl mono GEMD 129. Walter Panhofer, Vienna Octet (members) – MOZART: *Divertimento No. 17 in D, K.334.* (**)

(i) Piano Quintet in A (Trout); (ii) String Quartet No. 14 (Death and the Maiden).

(B) **(*) CfP (ADD) 574 8862 [5748862]. (i) Lympany, LSO Principals; (ii) Gabrieli Qt.

Dame Moura Lympany's performance of the *Trout* sets off in a brisk manner, the playing lively and fresh. In the second movement the interpretation relaxes and the variations are attractively done. The matter-of-fact approach is enhanced by the overall spontaneity of the music-making. The balance, however, is less than perfect, favouring the piano and not ideally sympathetic to the first violin (John Brown) with less body to his tone as recorded than the lower strings, while in his decorations of the 'Trout' theme he is too distant. But in most respects this is an enjoyable performance, if not a primary choice. For a coupling the Gabrielis give a sensitive and polished accout of Schubert's great *D minor Quartet*, not wearing their hearts on their sleeves, but genuinely touching in the slow movement. The recording here, made three years earlier than the *Trout*, is first class and has been smoothly transferred to CD.

The Record Guide gave the early Decca mono recording on the Pearl disc two stars, in those days the Guide listed only two versions! The *Trout* was reissued on Decca's Ace of Clubs economy label, in the early 1960s by which time Curzon's set with the same artists had supplanted it. Curzon brings greater subtlety and tonal refinement to the piano part, though Panhofer has undeniable sparkle and style. The original sounded wiry and unpleasing (particularly in its ACL format), but Roger Beardsley has gone to great trouble to find a stylus that would do justice to these performances. The sound is far richer and better defined. An affecting reminder of performance style fifty years back and well worth hearing fifty years on!

Piano Trios Nos. 1–2; Adagio in E flat ('Notturno') (for piano trio), D.897; Sonata in B flat (for piano trio), D.28.

(BB) *** Arte Nova 74321 79424-2. (2) Trio Opus 8.

Arte Nova offer both trios at the most competitive of prices – less than the Hyperion accounts of the two Trios alone. No quarrels with the playing or recording. Neither of the Trio performances is touched by routine, though at the same time neither quite attains the level of distinction of the Florestan Trio. If one bought a ticket for a concert one would feel very satisfied at this playing, and the present issue is well worth the money and well recorded too.

Piano Trio No. 1 in B flat, D.898; Sonata in B flat (for piano trio), D.28; Notturno, D.897.

*** Hyp. CDA 67273. Florestan Trio.

The Florestan Trio are the latest to tackle the Schubert *B flat Piano Trio* and are among the finest on disc. This is highly musical playing, whose value is enhanced by the contributions of that fine pianist Susan Tomes. They have the benefit of excellent recording. A strong recommendation and arguably a first choice.

Piano Trio No. 2 in E flat, D.929 (includes both first and second versions of finale).

*** Hyp. CDA 67347. Florestan Trio.

The Florestan Trio follow up their outstanding account of Schubert's *B flat major Trio* with another memorable performance of the more profound, yet still often light-hearted, *E flat Trio*, written in the same month (November) in which Schubert completed *Winterreise*. We are instantly reminded of this in their aptly paced account of the C minor *Andante con moto*, with what Richard Wigmore describes as its 'stoical trudging gait'. Its wistfulness is gently caught in a reading which is searching yet full of spontaneity, and elsewhere has much Schubertian bonhomie. If once again the playing of the pianist, Susan Tomes, stands out, the cellist's (Richard Lester's) contribution is hardly less memorable. As before, the recording is completely lifelike and very well balanced, catching the widest range of dynamic with naturalness and fidelity. This, like its companion, is now a primary recommendation.

As a bonus we are additionally offered Schubert's original finale, nearly two minutes longer without the two cuts in the development made by the composer, totalling 98 bars. There may be a case for the original extra 'heavenly' length, but the finale normally heard seems to be just right. However, with the benefit of CD you can make your own choice.

Piano Trio No. 2 in E flat, D.929; Sonatensatz, D.28.

(BB) *** Virgin x 2 VBD5 62007-2 (2). Castle Trio – BEETHOVEN: *Piano Trio No. 7 (Archduke); 10 (Variations) & 11 (Variations).* ***

Anyone seeking Schubert's *E flat Piano Trio* on period instruments will find it difficult to better this performance by the Castle Trio. Led by the nimble-fingered Lambert Orkis, playing a modern copy of a 1824 Graf fortepiano, the transparency of texture is a joy as is the playing itself, full of life, with bold dynamic contrasts. The *Andante* is particularly fine, with a memorably refined contributon from the cellist, Kenneth Slovak, while the sparkling Scherzo and finale (full of rhythmic character) show the mettle of both Orkis, with crisply incisive articulation and his fortepiano never sounding clattery, and the violinist, Marilyn McDonald. The early *Sonatensatz* too has charming naivité and simplicity, and is presented with consummate style and freshness.

String Quartets Nos. 10 in E flat, D.87; 12 (Quartettsatz), D.703; 13 in A min., D.804.

(M) *** Virgin VM5 61995-2. Borodin Qt.

These Virgin recordings of the silken-toned Borodins playing Schubert come from 1991 and offer cultured performances that will give much pleasure. They are unforced readings, which are free from any interpretative point-making and are content to leave the music to speak for itself. Some might feel that the *E flat Quartet* could be more strongly characterized, but the *Quartettsatz* is as powerfully dramatic a reading as any in the catalogue. Though in the *A minor Quartet* they are not necessarily to be preferred to the Lindsays (ASV CDDCA 593), the New Leipzig (in their MDG series), or the Quartetto Italiano on a Philips Duo, also offering the *Quartettsatz* plus the *Death and the Maiden Quartet* (446 163-2), they can certainly be recommended alongside them.

PIANO MUSIC

Fantasia in C (Wanderer Fantasy), D.760; Piano Sonata No. 19 in G, D.894.

(BB) *(*) Warner Apex 0927 40831-2. Leonskaja.

Even at budget price Elisabeth Leonskaja's account of the *Wanderer Fantasy* and the *G major Sonata*, D.894, would not be a strong recommendation. There is something four-square about her playing, and she does not fully convey the vulnerability and tenderness of Schubert's art. The Teldec recording is a bit hard, which does not help.

Impromptus Nos. 1–4, D.899; 5–8; D.935; Moments musicaux, D.780/3–6.

(BB) *** Regis (ADD) RRC 1019. Brendel.

This is the finest of Brendel's Vox (Turnabout) recordings made in the 1960s so far reissued on the Regis budget label. His playing has an unaffected simplicity that is utterly disarming, and the lightness of his articulation is a pleasure in itself. The fresh, natural eloquence is also very striking in the four favourite *Moments musicaux* which are offered here as a bonus (the disc has a playing time of 71¢). The recording, too, is suprisingly good. While his Philips Duo, which includes the later Philips analogue recordings of both complete sets, plus the *Klavierstücke*, D.946, and some delightful *German Dances,* remains very special (❂ 456 061-2), this Regis CD is well worth having at its very modest price.

Piano Sonatas: Nos. 1 in E, D.157; 15 in G (Rélique), D.894.

*** Sony SK 89647. Volodos. (with LISZT: *Concert paraphrase: Der Müller und der Bach*.)

Arcadi Volodos's reputation as a dazzling virtuoso is now enhanced by his natural lyricism and keen musical insight. This Schubert recital has been greeted with well-deserved acclaim and shows this Russian artist as a real musician not just a brilliant showman. Sony offer very good recorded sound and this CD is highly recommended.

Piano Sonatas Nos. 7 in E, D.568; 16 in A min., D.845.

(BB) *(*) Naxos 8.553099. Jandó.

These are decent performances from Jenö Jandó but ultimately plain and unmemorable. Not a patch on Schiff, Kempff or Lupu.

Piano Sonatas Nos. 9 in B, D.575; 16 in A min., D.845.

*** Ph. 462 596-2. Uchida.

Mitsuko Uchida is beautifully recorded, and collectors who have admired the other issues in her Schubert recordings (discussed in our main guide) need not hesitate. Some may find her tendency to beautify this music a little intrusive, so this is not for every Schubertian, but this is still imaginative and distinguished playing.

Piano Sonatas Nos. 13 in A, D.664; 20 in A, D.959.

(BB) ** Warner Apex 0927 40832-2. Leonskaja.

The two A major Sonatas coupled here find Elisabeth Leonskaja much more attuned to the Schubertian sensibility, though in neither would her performances be a first choice. Were this on the shelf alongside the likes of Lupu, Brendel or Kempff, it would be to them rather than Leonskaja that you would turn.

VOCAL MUSIC

Lieder: Abschied; Abenstern; Der Alpenjäger; Antigone und Oedip; Atys; Auf der Donau; Auflösung; Der entsühnte Orest; Der Fahrt zum Hades; Fragment aus dem Aeschylus; Freiwillges

Versinken; Gondelfahrer; Lied eines Schiffers an die Dioskuren; Memnon; Nach einen Gewitter; Nachtstück; Nachtviolen; Philoktet; Der Schiffer; Der Sieg; Die Sternennächte; Wie Ulfru fischt; Der zürnendeden Diana.

**(*) Teldec 8573 85556-2. Prégardien, Staier (fortepiano).

As on his previous discs of Lieder Christoph Prégardien opts for accompaniment by a fortepiano rather than a modern grand, presenting the songs on a scale such as the composer might have expected. This collection to lyrics by Mayrhofer finds him and his accompanist, Andreas Staier, unfailingly responsive to the words, even if the singer too often attacks notes from below, with intonation questionable at times. Moreover, the sound of a fortepiano is an acquired taste in such repertory.

Song-cycles

Die schöne Müllerin, D.795; Winterreise, D.911.

(B) *** EMI double fforte CZS5 74855-2 (2). Bär, Parsons.

Die schöne Müllerin was the first of the cycles which Olaf Bär recorded in 1986 in Dresden, with the voice fresher and more velvety than later, especially when the digital recording is so flattering to Bär's warmly beautiful lyrical flow. In *Winterreise*, recorded two years later, again with Geoffrey Parsons a masterful accompanist, Bär finds a winning beauty of line and tone in singing which is both deeply reflective and strongly dramatic. If without quite the power of Fischer-Dieskau's poetic projection, or the sheer intensity of Britten and Pears, these are most rewarding performances in their own right.

Winterreise, D.911.

*** Warner NVC Arts **DVD** 8573 83780-2. Bostridge, Drake. (Producer: Gordon Baskerville. V/D: David Alden.)
(*) Arthaus **DVD 100 258. Hynninen, Gothoni. (V/D: Julie Didier.)
(BB) *** EMI Encore CDE5 74989-2. Fassbaender, Reimann.

These two admirably sung video recordings of Schubert's *Winterreise* demonstrate only too well the difficulties of 'staging' an extended song cycle, however imaginative the producer and director. Ian Bostridge's revelatory way with Schubert is already familiar in an outstanding collection of favourite Lieder on EMI (CDC5 56347-2), and his youthfully radiant and eagerly detailed performance of *Die schöne Müllerin* is a key issue in Graham Johnson's Schubert Lieder Collection on Hyperion (CDJ 33025). His account of *Winterreise*, with a hardly less fine partner in Julius Drake, brings the same beautiful voice and even greater imaginative detail. The performance also has an extraordinarily powerful atmosphere – it is imbued with an air of desolation which we can see in his gaunt face as well as hear in his voice. David Alden's setting is an empty room, within which Bostridge, in his dark coat, can freely move about. There are occasional bursts of visual histrionics, which not all will take to, but on the whole the production works well, and the performance itself is gripping throughout, especially as the recording is so vivid. An additional documentary, rather facetiously titled 'Over the Top with Franz', details the background to the recording and filming and the artistic conflicts generated.

Jorma Hynninen and Ralf Gothoni recorded their fine account of *Winterreise* in 1994 at the Särestöniemi Museum in Finnish Lapland. The artist Reidar Särestöniemi (1925–81) designed the building so that he could draw inspiration in both winter and summer from the beauties of the Finnish countryside. The performance takes place before a small audience, and apart from the two artists themselves, we see some of Särestöniemi's impressions of Finnish landscape as well as nature itself. The visual side of the production is handled with both taste and imagination, and the musical balance is well focused and natural. Hynninen and his admirable partner convey the poignancy of this music to splendid effect, although some may well find that the pauses between each song could have been fractionally longer.

The effect, with Jorma Hynninen's warm baritone, is less bleak than with Bostridge (his richly resonant voice is especially telling in *Der Lindenbaum*), and it is anger, rather than desolation that registers so vividly in Hynninen's eyes and facial muscles. He is very well accompanied by Ralf Gothoni and the two artists give a moving performance, but are in the last resort less affecting than Bostridge and Drake, who leave an unforgettable impression with their deeply touching reading of that haunting final portrait of *Der Leiermann*.

Brigitte Fassbaender gives a fresh, boyishly eager reading of *Winterreise*, marked by a vivid and wide range of expression; she demonstrates triumphantly why a woman's voice can bring special illumination to this cycle, sympathetically underlining the drama behind the tragic poet's journey rather than the more meditative qualities. Reimann, at times a wilful accompanist, is nevertheless spontaneous-sounding, matching the singer. A remarkable bargain Encore reissue.

OPERA

Fierrabras (complete).

(M) *** DG 459 503-2 (2). Protschka, Mattila, Studer, Gambill, Hampson, Holl, Polgár, Schoenberg Ch., COE, Abbado.

Schubert may have often let his musical imagination blossom without considering the dramatic effect, but there are jewels in plenty in this score. Many solos and duets develop into delightful ensembles, and the influence of Beethoven's *Fidelio* is very striking, with spoken melodrama and offstage fanfares bringing obvious echoes. A recording is the ideal medium for such buried treasure, and Abbado directs an electrifying

performance. Both tenors, Robert Gambill and Josef Protschka, are on the strenuous side, but have a fine feeling for Schubertian melody. Cheryl Studer and Karita Mattila sing ravishingly, and Thomas Hampson gives a noble performance as the knight, Roland. Only Robert Holl as King Karl (Charlemagne) is unsteady at times. The sound is comfortably atmospheric, outstanding for a live recording. Now reissued at mid price this is even more attractive.

SCHUMANN, Clara (1819–96)

Graham Johnson Lieder Edition

Lieder Edition, Vol. 6: *6 Lieder from Jucunde.*

*** Hyp. CDJ 133106. McGreevy, Johnson – R. SCHUMANN: *Lieder*. ***

6 Lieder from Jucunde, Op. 23; 6 Lieder, Op. 13; Lieder, Op. 12: Er ist gekommen; Liebst du um Schönheit; Warum willst du. Lieder: *Der Abendstern; Walzer; Am Strande; Beim Abschied; Die gute Nacht; Ihr Bildnis; Lorelei; Mein Stern; Oh weh des Schiedens; Sie lieben sich beide; Das Veilchen; Volkslied; Der Wanderer; Der Wanderer in der Sägemühle.*

*** Hyp. CDA 67249. Gritton, Loges, Asti.

Clara Schumann wrote almost all her songs during her marriage to Robert, often inspired by special occasions such as birthdays and Christmases. When he died she wrote no more, which is greatly to be regretted when these charming inspirations have so many delightful qualities, generally light-hearted and lyrical. Her Rückert setting, *Liebst du um Schonheit*, in its folk-like innocence contrasts nicely with the well-known Mahler setting of the same words, and in addition to the mature songs from her married years it is good to have a group that date from her early girlhood, with *Der Wanderer* written when she was only 12, and thought until recently to have been composed by her father. Another of her early songs, *Der Wanderer in der Sägemühle* ('The Wanderer at the Sawmill'), has unexpected harmonic twists, rather in the manner of Schubert, as do many of her songs. Susan Gritton is a charming soloist in the *Jucunde* songs, also included in Graham Johnson's Schumann series, freer in expression than Geraldine McGreevy, if stylistically less pure. She and Stephan Loges are the excellent soloists in the whole programme, given inspired accompaniment by Eugene Asti, often more volatile than his former teacher, Graham Johnson.

Lieder: *An einem lichten Morgen; Geheimes Flüstern hier und dort; Liebst du um Schönheit; O Lust, o Lust; Sie liebten sich beide; Die stille Lotosblum.*

*** Ph. 462 610-2. Holzmair, Cooper – ROBERT SCHUMANN: *Lieder*. ***

These seven songs by Clara Schumann illuminatingly supplement the main collection of songs by her husband in ideally sensitive performances from the well-established partnership of Holzmair and Cooper, the one honey-toned, the other in support consistently subtle in her expressive shading of tone. It is fascinating to hear Clara Schumann's rendering of the Rückert poem *Liebst du um Schönheit*, set very differently by Mahler much later.

SCHUMANN, Robert (1810–56)

Cello Concerto in A min., Op. 129.

(M) **(*) Ph. 470 250-2 (2). Schiff, BPO, Haitink – DVORAK: *Cello Concerto;* PROKOFIEV: *Sinfonia concertante;* R. STRAUSS: *Don Quixote.* **(*)

Schiff's is a forthright reading, yet warm and sensitive and there are points of detail in his performance where, by comparison, Ma on Sony is made to sound a little self-conscious. Schiff's richly expressive style certainly brings greater spontaneity, particularly in the finale which dances along joyfully, the rhythmic sharpness and Hungarian vigour of the soloist well matched by Haitink and the Berlin players. The only drawback is the balance, with the cello very close, so that the delicate cello pianissimos are not fully projected. Nevertheless this is still very enjoyable.

(i; iii) Cello Concerto; (ii; iii) Piano Concerto; (ii) Etudes symphoniques, Op. 13.

(M) *** Sony SMK 89716. (i) Ma; (ii) Perahia; (iii) Bav. RSO., C. Davis.

The two concerto performances on Sony make a recommendable mid-priced coupling and this disc is undoubtedly good value. In the *Cello Concerto* Yo-Yo Ma's playing is characteristically refined, but keenly affectionate too, although at times he carries tonal sophistication to excess and suddenly drops into *sotto voce* tone and near inaudibility. But both he and Sir Colin Davis are thoroughly attuned to the sensibility of this composer and the recording balance is excellent. Similarly Davis makes a fine partner for Perahia, who in the *Piano Concerto* enjoys displaying his ardour and virtuosity, as well as his ability to invest a phrase with poetry and magic. The recording is live, but is full and spacious. The *Symphonic Etudes* are equally fine although here the balance is rather close.

Piano Concerto in A min., Op. 54.

(BB) (***) Dutton CDEP 9719. Lipatti, Philh. O, Karajan – GRIEG: *Concerto.* (***)

Dinu Lipatti's classic version of the Schumann *Concerto*, a staple of the catalogue from when it was recorded in the late 1940s, now comes in this Dutton bargain issue with the sound fuller and clearer than ever before, and superior to the newest EMI transfer.

Symphonies Nos. 1–4.

(B) **(*) Virgin VBD5 61884-2 (2). Bamberg SO, Eschenbach.

We were very taken with Christoph Eschenbach's excellent survey of the Schumann symphonies with the NordDeutscher Rundfunk Symphony Orchestra

(on RCA 74321 61820-2), which appeared two years ago and proved among the most satisfying sets of the last decade. The present survey with the Bamberg Symfoniker is somewhat earlier, recorded in 1990. Eschenbach's conception is not much different but the well-recorded Bamberg set does not boast playing of quite such finesse as the RCA set, which can be recommended alongside the classic Karajan and Sawallisch sets (DG 429 672-2 and EMI CMS7 64815-2 respectively).

Symphonies Nos. 1 in B flat, Op. 38 (Spring); 4 in D min., Op. 120.

*(*) DG 469 700-2. Philh O, Thielemann.

As with earlier issues in Thielemann's Schumann cycle, this much and rightly admired conductor proves too intrusive and self-conscious to be a realistic recommendation. He gets splendid playing from the Philharmonia and receives a fine DG recording but readers are advised to save money and stick with Karajan in this coupling (DG 445 718-2).

Symphony No. 4 in D min., Op. 120.

(B) (***) EMI mono CDZ5 74801-2. Philh. O, Cantelli – MENDELSSOHN: *Symphony No. 4;* SCHUBERT: *Symphony No. 8.* (***)

Along with Furtwängler's recording, also made in 1953 (DG ❂ 457 722-2), Cantelli's is one of the really great accounts of Schumann's *Fourth Symphony*. It sounds first class in this excellent transfer and serves as yet another reminder of the loss music suffered by his untimely death. Everything is beautifully proportioned and feeling is finely controlled.

CHAMBER MUSIC

(i) Adagio and Allegro, Op. 70; (ii) Fantasiestücke, Op. 73 (both for cello & piano).

(B) *** RCA 2-CD 74321 84598-2 (2). Starker; (i) Buchbinder; (ii) Neriki – BRAHMS: *Cello Sonatas Nos. 1 –2; in D* (arr. of *Violin Sonata, Op. 78*). RACHMANINOV: *Cello Sonata.* **(*)

Adagio & Allegro in A flat, Op. 70; Fantasiestücke, Op. 73; 5 Stücke im Volkston, Op. 102 (all for cello & piano).

**(*) BIS CD 1076. Thedéen, Pöntinen – CHOPIN: *Cello Sonata.* **(*)

Starker and Neriki give a quite splendid account of the three pieces which make up the *Fantasiestücke* and are very well recorded (in 1990). The *Adagio and Allegro* is also very fine – producing a passionate flow of ardour, but here (two years later) Starker's tone is less ripely captured. However, this is still very recommendable if the couplings are suitable.

The rather reverberant acoustic of the former Academy of Music, Stockholm, at Nybrokajen, does not help these fine artists, either here or in the Chopin *Sonata*. Torleif Thedéen and Roland Pöntinen are sympathetic exponents of this repertoire even if in the

Fünf Stücke im Volkston they are just a bit too earnest and lacking in charm. Maria Kliegel and Kristin Merscher (on Naxos 8.550654) are fresher and more appealing and they couple these works successfully with the Schubert *Arpeggione Sonata*.

Adagio and Allegro, Op. 70; 3 Fantasiestücke, Op. 73; 3 Romanzen; Marchenbilder; (i) Marchenerzahlungen, Op. 132.

*** Zig-Zag Territoires ZZT 010401. Beranger, Gastaldi; (i) with Heau.

This is above all a celebration of the viola in Schumann's chamber music, with the young French viola-player Vinciane Beranger fresh, incisive and full-toned in all five works. Schumann was always accommodating about the instrumentation of these pieces, with the viola regularly interchanged with the clarinet. This has no doubt led Beranger to also take on the *Fantasiestücke* and the *Romanzen*, where Schumann suggests clarinet and violin as options but not the viola. The *Adagio and Allegro*, originally with horn or cello, works beautifully here, and the two later 'fairy-tale' works, *Marchenbilder* and *Marchenerzahlungen*, are among the glories of the viola repertoire. It is only in the latter work that the clarinettist Florent Heau appears, another sensitive artist.

Piano Quintet, Op. 44; Andante & Variations for 2 Pianos, 2 Cellos & Horn, Op. 46 ; Fantasiestücke for Cello and Piano, Op. 73; Märchenbilder for Viola & Piano, Op. 113.

*** EMI CDC5 57308-2. Argerich, Rabinovitch, Hall, Imai, Gutman, Maisky, Neunecker.

A very distinguished line-up. In our main volume (p.1196) we described the performance of the *Piano Quintet*, recorded at the Concertgebouw, Nijmegen, in 1994 as 'among the most vibrant on record'. We also spoke of the informality of the music-making, which had 'the enthusiasm and intimate inspiration of a house-party'. EMI has now detached it from the two-CD set issued in 1995 (CDS5 55484-2), albeit without a reduction in price, but nonetheless giving it another lease of life. The other items are also finely done.

(i; ii) Piano Quintet in E flat, Op. 44; (ii) String Quartet No. 1 in A min, Op. 41/1; (i) Arabeske, Op. 18; Blumenstück, Op. 19.

*** Linn CKD132. (i) d'Ascoli; (ii) Schidlof Qt.

The pianist, Bernard d'Ascoli, is an inspirational artist whose playing on disc is regularly marked by a winning spontaneity. This Linn programme makes an attractive mixture, with two of the major Schumann chamber works from the magic year, 1842, linked to two shorter piano works. In the *Piano Quintet* it is d'Ascoli who leads the ensemble, maybe controversially in the first movement, when he unashamedly encourages marked changes of tempo – persuasively so, thanks to the feeling of spontaneity. The freshness and ease of the interchanges between players gives the performance a relaxed warmth, not least in the finale, which is not overdriven. There are similar qualities in

d'Ascoli's performances of the *Arabeske* and *Blumenstück*, with textures fresh and clean.

The *String Quartet* brings another refined performance with plenty of light and shade, starting with a slow introduction that brings out the mystery of the writing, echoing late Beethoven. The recording, made in the Blackheath Concert Halls, is finely focused within a helpful acoustic.

(i) Piano Quintet in E flat, Op. 44; String Quartets Nos. 1 in A min.; 2 in F; 3 in A, Op. 41/1–3.

(B) *** EMI double fforte CZS5 75175-2 (2). Cherubini Qt, with (i) Zacharias.

A vital and intelligent account of the *Piano Quintet*, not perhaps as fine as some presently available – most notably the Beaux Arts (see our main volume) – but very acceptable given the competitive price and the couplings. The *Quartets* are not generously represented in the current catalogues and some of the finest recordings (the Vogler Quartet on RCA and the Quartetto Italiano on Philips) are not currently in circulation. The present recordings were first issued as part of a series coupling Schumann and Mendelssohn, and the performances date from 1989–91. They are finely paced and well shaped, and as persuasive as any now before the public – so this double fforte reissue is well worth considering.

Piano Trio No. 1 in D min., Op. 63.

(BB) (***) Naxos mono 8.110185. Cortot, Thibaud, Casals – MENDELSSOHN: *Piano Trio No. 1*. (***)

The partnership of Jacques Thibaud, Pablo Casals and Alfred Cortot was the most celebrated piano trio of the pre-war years though their repertoire was relatively small and they recorded relatively little. They were formed in 1925 and made their recording of the *D minor Piano Trio* in 1928, so the sound is wanting the body and colour of later recordings. Coming to this set afresh one wonders if it has ever been surpassed in musical insight even by such an exalted ensemble as the Beaux Arts. They are immaculate, wonderfully singing in their phrasing and their apparent spontaneity of feeling is born of a firm musical grip. Ward Marston's transfer is first rate.

PIANO MUSIC

Carnaval, Op. 9; Davidsbündlertänze, Op. 6; Papillons, Op. 2.

(BB) **(*) DG Eloquence (ADD) 469 765-2. Kempff.

The comparatively extrovert style of *Carnaval* does not seem to suit Kempff too well: there is no special degree of illumination here such as we expect from this artist in his performance, which even seems to lack absolute technical assurance. However, in *Papillons* and the *Davidsbündlertänze* he is back on top form. Good recordings from the 1960s and 1970s.

Carnaval, Op. 9; Fantasiestücke, Op. 12; Papillons, Op. 2.

(M) ** Somm SOMMCD 024. Lazaridis

George-Emmanuel Lazaridis was perhaps unwise to choose this very demanding Schumann programme for his debut CD. The moments of gentle poetry show that he has a feeling for the composer, even if his tempi and phrasing are somewhat indulgent, especially in *Papillons*. But for the most part his impulsive tendency to press ahead, seeking to convey a spontaneous forward impulse, serves Schumann less well. Even in *Carnaval*, the most successful performance here, one sometimes feels the piano hammers being applied too percussively, although the playing has plenty of spirit. Fine recording, its brightness partly accounted for by Lazaridis's bold articulation.

Davidsbündlertänze, Op. 6; Fantasiestücke, Op. 12; Papillons, Op. 2.

(M) *** Sony (ADD) SMK 89714. Perahia.

Perahia has a magic touch and his electric spontaneity is naturally caught in the studio. In the works of Schumann, which can splinter apart, this quality of concentration is enormously valuable, and the results could hardly be more powerfully convincing, despite recording quality which lacks something in bloom and refinement. The *Papillons*, added for this reissue, are unlikely to be surpassed, and it is a pity that the close balance robs the piano timbre of some of its allure.

Davidsbündlertänze, Op. 6; Sonata No. 2 in G min., Op. 22; Toccata, Op. 7.

(B) *** Warner Apex 0927 40834-2. Berezovsky.

These performances, discussed in our main volume, are of the highest calibre. The *Davidsbündlertänze* is particularly charismatic and this bargain reissue cannot be too strongly recommended, alongside his companion Apex reissue of the Chopin *Etudes* (8573 89083-2).

Fantasy in C, Op. 17; Faschingsschwank aus Wien (Carnival Jest from Vienna), Op. 26; Papillons, Op. 2.

(BB) *** EMI Encore (ADD) CDE5 75233-2. Richter.

Richter's 1961 account of the *C major Fantasy* is a wonderfully poetic performance. His phrasing, his magnificent control of dynamics, his gift for seeing a large-scale work as a whole – all these contribute to the impression of unmatchable strength and vision. The recording is faithful, with genuine presence. The other two works included on this CD were recorded live during Richter's Italian concert tour a year later. Inevitably, the piano sound is somewhat less sonorous, shallower at fortissimo level, but fully acceptable. The account of *Papillons* is beguilingly subtle in its control of colour. Reissued at budget price, this is an unmissable bargain.

Humoreske, Op. 20; Nachtstücke, Op. 23; 8 Novelletten, Op. 21; Sonata in F sharp min., Op. 14.

*** ECM 472 119-2 (2). Schiff.

András Schiff has moved on from Decca to ECM label and makes an impressive debut with this live 1999 Schumann recital which communicates strongly. His playing is refreshingly light-textured with much deli-

cacy of colour plus a natural response to the music's mood swings. This especially applies to the eight *Novelletten*, by no means easy works to bring off for they can easily seem inflated. The *Sonata* too is finely played, never hectoring, and imaginatively detailed, the *Variations on Clara's Andantino* especially so, followed by a brilliantly articulated finale. The closing encore, the *Nachtstücke*, is quite magical. The recording is excellent, the piano image clear and realistic.

VOCAL MUSIC

The Graham Johnson Lieder Edition

Lieder, Vol. 6: Spanishes Liebespiel, Op. 74; Spanische Liebeslieder, Op. 138; 5 Lieder, Op. 40.

*** Hyp. CDJ 133106. McGreevy, Doufexis, Thompson, Loges, Johnson, Hough – C. SCHUMANN: *6 Lieder from Jucunde.*

This sixth instalment in Graham Johnson's splendid Schumann Lieder series brings together two neglected Spanish-inspired cycles, important for having prompted Brahms to write his *Liebeslieder Waltzes*. Op. 138 offers an almost exact model when, like those popular Brahms pieces, it has piano-duet accompaniment, here with Stephen Hough as Johnson's partner. It was Schumann who in these colourful cycles pioneered the idea of treating a group of soloists in a quasi-operatic way, coupling this with his fondness for 'armchair travelling', so popular in the mid-nineteenth century. They involve not just solo songs but duets, trios and quartets too, generally lightweight inspirations made the more winning by a characterful team of soloists. The baritone of the group, Stephan Loges, also tackles the five Op. 40 songs, four of them settings of Hans Andersen poems in German translations by Adalbert von Chamisso, poet of *Frauenliebe und Leben*. As a coupling come six songs by Clara Schumann setting poems contained in Hermann Rollett's novel, *Jucunde*, fresh and lyrical, beautifully sung here by Geraldine McGreevy. As with other issues in this and Johnson's Schubert series, the detailed notes are endlessly illuminating.

Frauenliebe und Leben, Op. 42. Liederalbum für die Jugend, Op. 79 (excerpts): Der Abendstern; Frülings Ankunft; Frühlingsbotschaft; Frülingsgruss; Hinaus ins Frele; Käuzlein; Kinderwacht; Des knaben Berglied; Marienwürmchen; Der Sandmann; Schmetterling; Sonntag; Vom Schlaraflenland; Die Walse. Lieder und Gesäng aus Wilhelm Meister, Op. 98a (excerpts): Lied der Mignon I–III; Lied der Philine; Mignons Gesang. Myrten, Op. 25 (excerpts): Hochländlisches Wiegenlied; Die Hochländer-Witwe; Im westen; Jemand; Lied der Suleika; Weit, weit.

(BB) *** DG Eloquence (ADD) 469 767-2. Mathis, Eschenbach.

It is good to have these recordings (which once formed part of a 3 LP set), made in the early 1980s, available again. With her fresh tone and delicately poised manner, Edith Mathis brings out the girlish feelings implied by the *Frauenliebe* songs. If her voice inevitably lacks a little weight in the last song of bereavement, there is no lack of intensity. The rest of the programme brings equally sensitive and imaginative singing with fine support from her accompanist. Texts are not included, but the CD is inexpensive.

Gedichte (Kerner Lieder),Op. 35; Gedichte aus Liebesfrühling; Der Himmel hat ein Trane geweint; Ich hab' in mich gesogen. Myrthen, Op. 25: (excerpts); Widmung; Freisinn; Der Nussbaum; Lied aus dem Schenkenbuch im Divan; Venetian Lied I & II; Zum Schluss.

*** Ph. 462 610-2. Holzmair, Cooper – CLARA SCHUMANN: *Lieder*. ***

The ever-perceptive duo of Wolfgang Holzmair and Imogen Cooper offers readings of this wide-ranging collection of Schumann Lieder which are not just beautiful and sensitively phrased but deeply expressive in their response to the German words. The central set of twelve settings of Kerner are well supplemented by a well-chosen collection of songs to words by Rückert, Goethe, Geibel and others. Performances like these have one eager to listen on from one item to the next, the more so when the main collection is so illuminatingly supplemented by the seven Lieder by Clara Schumann. Ideally balanced sound.

Das Paradies und die Peri, Op. 50.

(BB) ** Arte Nova 74321 87817-2 (2). Kernes, Wollitz, Paulsen, Dewald, Fernández, Schulte, Cechova, Zabala, Europa ChorAkademie, Pforzheim Wind Ens., SW German CO, Daus.

(i) *Das Paradies und die Peri, Op. 50;* (ii) *Requiem für Mignon, Op. 98b; Nachtlied (for chorus & orchestra), Op. 108.*

*** DG 457 660-2 (2). (i) Bonney, Coku, Fink, Prégardien, Archer, Finley, Hauptman; (ii) Dazeley; Monteverdi Ch., ORR, Gardiner.

It takes a conductor as perceptive and persuasive as Sir John Eliot Gardiner to transform *Das Paradies und die Peri* into something like a masterpiece. That he does with his period forces in this fine version on DG Archiv. For good measure he adds two other much shorter neglected works, and similarly presents them in their full originality. Clara Schumann may have claimed *Das Paradies* as the most beautiful of her husband's works, and it seems to have been his first major piece to establish his international reputation; yet this secular oratorio on a Persian legend from Thomas Moore's oriental epic *Lalla Rookh* is by latterday standards sentimental, telling the story of the Peri who is refused entry into Paradise, having been the child of a fallen angel and a mortal.

With his period forces Gardiner brings out the clarity and subtlety of the choral and orchestral writing, moulding phrases warmly but with none of the syrupy sweetness that gave the piece a bad name. In such a

performance the fairy choruses have a sparkle to match Mendelssohn. Barbara Bonney, pure and tender, is ideally cast as the Peri and she is well matched by the rest of the team, with the mezzo, Bernarda Fink, and the two tenors, Christoph Prégardien and Neill Archer, all outstanding. Yet most brilliant of all is the Monteverdi Choir, singing with freshness and clarity.

With William Dazeley as soloist, and with four trebles from the Hanover Boys Choir in key solo roles, the *Requiem für Mignon* is also most atmospherically done with wonderfully varied textures. To words by Hebbel, the *Nachtlied*, too, is revealed as more buried treasure. Refined, beautifully balanced recording made at the Watford Colosseum.

Recorded live at performances in Wiesbaden and Bremen, Joshard Daus's version of Schumann's secular oratorio offers a serviceable version at super-budget price, generally well recorded and with Simone Kermes sweet-toned as the Peri, only occasionally overstressed. As a more traditional, heavier-handed reading than Gardiner's on DG Archiv, it cannot match that full-price version. It comes with the German text but no translation.

SCRIABIN, Alexander (1872–1915)

Allegro Appassionato, Op. 4; Canon in D min.; Etude in D sharp min.; Fugue in E min.; Muzurkas in: B min. & F; Nocturnes in F sharp min., Op. 5/1; A, Op. 5/2; D flat, Op. 9/2; A flat. Prelude in C sharp min., Op. 9/1; Sonata in E flat min.; Sonate-fantaisie; Variations on a Theme by Mlle. Egorova; Waltz in F min., Op. 1; Waltzes in G sharp min. & D flat.

*** Hyp. CDA 67149. Coombs.

Stephen Coombs concentrates on Scriabin's early period, when he had yet to escape from Chopin's magnetic field, which has received less attention than the late sonatas. The earliest piece here, a *Canon in D minor*, was written when he was only 11 years old, but many of these Chopinesque pieces are of real quality and do not deserve to be so completely overshadowed. Coombs has a genuine feel for this repertoire and is very well served by the recording team.

Piano Sonata No. 5 in F sharp, Op. 53.

(BB) *(*) Warner Apex 0927 40830-2. Sultanov – PROKOFIEV: *Piano Sonata No. 7* *(*); RACHMANINOV: *Piano Sonata No. 2.* *(*)

Alexei Sultanov has great brilliance and a formidable technical address, which is heard to considerable effect here. But the concentration is largely on virtuosity, dazzle and gloss.

SEIBER, Mátyás (1905–60)

Clarinet Concertino.

(BB) *** Hyp. Helios CDH 55068. King, ECO, Litton – BLAKE: *Clarinet Concerto*; LUTOSLAWSKI: *Dance Preludes.* ***

Mátyás Seiber's highly engaging *Concertino* was sketched during a train journey in 1926 (before the days of seamless rails) and certainly the opening *Toccata* has the jumpy, rhythmic feeling of railway line joints and points. Yet the haunting slow movement has a touch of the ethereal, while the Scherzo has a witty jazz element. Thea King has the measure of the piece; she is accompanied well by Andrew Litton, and very well recorded. On Hyperion's budget Helios label, this reissue is well worth seeking out.

SESSIONS, Roger (1896–1985)

Concerto for Orchestra.

(BB) *** Hyp. Helios CDH 55100. Boston SO, Ozawa – PANUFNIK: *Symphony No. 8.* ***

Sessions's *Concerto for Orchestra* finds him at his thorniest and most uncompromising, with lyricism limited to fleeting fragments of melody; but the playful opening leads one on finally to a valedictory close, sharply defined. Ozawa makes a powerful advocate, helped by superb playing from the Boston orchestra.

SHCHEDRIN, Rodion (born 1933)

Carmen (ballet, arr. from Bizet: complete); Concertos for Orchestra Nos. 1 (Naughty Limericks) and 2 (The Chimes).

*** DG 471 136-2. Russian Nat. O, Pletnev.

Shchedrin's brilliantly original *Carmen* ballet has never sounded more dramatically vivid than in this new Pletnev recording, which is now top choice for this piece. The *Concerto for Orchestra No. 1 (Naughty Limericks)*, is a vibrant scherzo, a fun piece, brightly scored and full of character in this performance. The *Second Concerto (The Chimes)* (referring to the historical significance of bells in Russia) could hardly be more contrasted. It begins broodingly with tremolo strings, which leads on to an array of orchestral effects and, of course, quite a few bells (18 tubular bells are used). It is not especially inspired but has its moments. Superlative playing and recording throughout.

SHOSTAKOVICH, Dmitri

(1906–75)

The Bolt: Suite; Jazz Suites Nos. 1 & 2; Tahiti Trot.

(BB) **(*) Naxos 8.555949. Russian State SO, Yablonsky.

The *Jazz Suites* show a light-hearted Shostakovich at his witty best, with some delightful melodies, colourfully orchestrated, with the composer's ironic tang adding a piquant spice. Likewise, the dances from *The Bolt*, not quite so inconsequential, but just as enjoyable, have an edge, which makes Shostakovich in popular mode so enticing. Yablonsky directs enjoyable, straightforward accounts of these works.

Chailly's account of *The Bolt Suite* on Decca is obviously superior, but, that said, this CD is still good value, especially at its super-bargain price, and the inclusion of Shostakovich's arrangement of 'Tea for Two' as the *Tahiti Trot* is a real bonus.

Chamber Symphony No. 1, Op. 110a; Symphony for Strings, Op. 118a; (i) Suite on Finnish Themes.

*** BIS CD 1256. (i) Komsi, Nyman; Ostrobothian CO, Kangas.

The *Suite on Finnish Themes* was written in 1939 in the immediate wake of the *Sixth Symphony* (indeed Shostakovich had to miss the Moscow première of the symphony in order to finish the piece) in response to a commission from the Leningrad Military District. This was of course the year of the first Winter War between the Soviet Union and Finland. It is slight (lasting less than twelve minutes) and yet often very characteristic, and is scored for soprano, tenor, flute, oboe, clarinet, trumpet, triangle, tambourine, side-drum, piano and strings. For some reason it was never performed at the time (Shostakovich did not add the words himself) and the score has only recently come to light in a private collection in St Petersburg. It comes with two of the so-called *Chamber Symphonies*, transcriptions for full strings of the *Eighth* and *Tenth Quartets* by Rudolf Barshai and was made with the approval of the composer. Dedicated playing and exemplary recording.

Chamber Symphony No. 1, Op. 110; (i) Symphony No. 14 in G min., Op. 135.

(B) ** Virgin 2 CD VBD5 62050-2 (2). Kastrashvili, Krutikov, Lausanne CO, Lazarev – DEBUSSY: *Danse; Sarabande;* MILHAUD: *La création du monde;* PROKOFIEV: *Symphony No. 1 (Classical).* ***

In the *Chamber Symphony* Lazarev gets off to a sluggish start from which the performance never fully recovers, though it is very well played. He is obviously at home in the *Symphony*, creating a powerful atmosphere, but the contribution of his very Russian soloists is uneven. The rich-toned Makvala Kastrashvili, although she sings with much intensity of feeling (and is especially moving in *The Suicide*) has a troublesome vibrato and moments of squalliness, notably in *The Death of a Poet*. The bass, Mikhail Krutikov, is very impressive and *In the Santé Prison* is really memorable. But in this symphony one badly needs texts and translations, which are not forthcoming. The recording is excellent.

Cello Concertos Nos. 1–2.

(BB) *** Warner Apex 0927 40604-2. Noras, Norwegian R.O, Rasilainen (with R. STRAUSS: *Romanze.* ***)

(i) Cello Concertos Nos. 1-2; (ii) Piano Concerto No. 1 for Piano, Trumpet and Strings; (iii) Cello Sonata, Op. 40; (iv) Piano Trio No. 1, Op. 8; (v) String Quartet No. 3, op. 73.

(BB) *** Warner Ultima 8573 81969-2 (2). (i) Noras, Norwegian R.O, Rasilainen; (ii) Lagerspetz, Harjanne, Tapiola Sinf., Lamminmäki; (iii) Noras, Valsta; (iv) Finnico Trio; (v) Sibelius Academy Qt.

Arto Noras is an aristocratic artist with a beautiful tone, and his playing is wonderfully flexible with intelligent phrasing and an instinctive feel for this repertoire. He never plays to the gallery, and his performances are all the more effective as a result. Although Rostropovich is doubtless to be preferred in both concertos, this is a very good set, for Noras gives a very fine account of the *Cello Sonata*. Juhani Lagerspetz, too, gives a generally well-characterized account of the *Concerto for Piano, Trumpet and Strings* and has in Jouko Harjanne an excellent trumpeter. (The disc originally appeared in the early 1990s coupled with the Jolivet *Concertino for Trumpet, Piano and Strings* and the Prokofievian *Second Concerto* by Uuno Klami.) Decent performances too of the early Op. 8 *Trio* and the *Third Quartet*. Not first choices, then, but eminently recommendable in terms of value for money.

(i) Cello Concerto No. 1; Piano Concertos Nos. (ii) 1, Op. 35; (iii) 2, Op. 102.

(M) *** Sony (DDD/ADD) SMK 89752. (i) Ma, Phd. O, Ormandy; (ii) Previn, Vacchiano, NYPO, Bernstein; (iii) Bernstein (piano & cond.), NYPO

Yo-Yo Ma plays with an intensity that compels the listener, the Philadelphia Orchestra give eloquent support, and the digital recording is excellent. This couples aptly with the shrewd, much earlier pairing of Bernstein's radiant account of the *Second Piano Concerto* with Previn's equally striking reading of No. 1. If these recordings are far from recent they are transferred most vividly.

Cello Concerto No. 2, Op. 126.

(M) (**(*)) BBC mono BBCL 4073-2. Rostropovich, LSO, Hurst (with KHACHATURIAN: *Concerto Rhapsody*; TCHAIKOVSKY: *Rococo Variations*. **(*))

The BBC recording of the Shostakovich *Second Cello Concerto* was made at the Festival Hall in October 1966 not long after its Soviet première in Moscow, with Colin Davis conducting. The sound has less transparency than in the much later DG studio version but against that there is, of course, the intensity of a première performance and the consequent excitement. The Khachaturian *Concerto Rhapsody* of 1963 is also captured at its première with the LSO and George Hurst, and the 1964 *Rococo variations*, again with Colin Davis but at the Albert Hall, is a performance of no mean mastery. All in all, well worth having as a document of both the master cellist and two new works to which he is so deeply committed.

(i; ii) Piano Concerto No. 1 for Piano, Trumpet and Strings: Symphonies Nos. (ii) 1 in F min.; (iii) 10 in E min.

(B) **(*) EMI double fforte CZS5 75178-2. (i) Rudy, cond. Antonsen; (ii) BPO; (iii) Phd. O; Jansons – MUSSORGSKY: *Songs and Dances of Death.* ***

This EMI double fforte reissue is something of a mixed offering. In Mikhail Rudy's hands the *Concerto for Piano, Trumpet and Strings* starts off very slowly for an *Allegro moderato*, and the effect is ponderous, although he does proceed at a more normal tempo at the second *Più mosso* marking. In the slow movement Jansons is also a shade slower than most rivals, but he draws ravishing sound from the Berlin Philharmonic strings. Ole Edvard Antonsen plays the trumpet part with impeccable musicianship and taste. Altogether a well thought-out but not wholly convincing performance and much the same verdict must be returned on the *First Symphony*. Wonderful playing from the Berliners, but the overall impression is a little studied, something wanting in spontaneity.

The *Tenth Symphony* is another matter and is highly recommendable. Jansons draws a splendid response from the Philadelphia Orchestra and the playing has tremendous fervour. Karajan's interpretation (DG 429 036-2) remains pre-eminent, but the EMI sound is generally preferable. The Mussorgsky coupling is also well worth having, so this collection is by no means to be dismissed.

Piano Concerto No. 2 in F, Op. 102.

(BB) *** EMI Encore (ADD) CDE5 74991-2. John Ogdon, RPO, Foster – BARTOK: *Piano Concerto No. 3, etc.* **(*)

John Ogdon, at the height of his powers, gives a splendidly idiomatic account of this concerto written originally for Shostakovich's son, Maxim. The playing is full of character, the outer movements striking for their wit and dash, and the beautiful slow movement richly romantic without being sentimentalized. This remains one of the finest versions available and the 1971 sound is excellent.

Symphonies

Symphonies Nos. 1; 6 in B min., Op. 54.

(M) **(*) Sony (ADD) SMK 89572. NYPO, Bernstein.

Shostakovich's admiration for Bernstein's conducting is well known: his 1959 performance of the *Fifth* is said to have moved the composer to tears. This coupling brings a very fine account of the *First* (not, perhaps the equal of Ormandy's classic 1960 account but not far off), together with his finely-paced *Sixth*. Here the first movement is not quite as intense as the pioneering sets by Stokowski and Reiner and the performance as a whole is not quite as memorable as his *Fifth*. All the same this is well worth considering and the transfer engineers do their best with the less than ample sound produced by the 1960s CBS recording.

Symphony No. 4 in C min., Op. 43.

*** DG 447 759-2. Phd. O, Chung.

The *Fourth Symphony* has been well served by the gramophone ever since its appearance in the early

1960s with Kondrashin's pioneering LP. In fact, it is difficult to think of any version that has fallen short of excellence. This fine new recording from Myung-Whun Chung and the Philadelphia Orchestra will surely take its place alongside the classic Shostakovich symphony recordings. It has vision and intensity – and, of course, wonderful orchestral playing. Moreover, the state-of-the-art recording reproduces the widest dynamic range and greatest transparency. Chung's producer is Lennart Dehn, who achieved such spectacular results with the Gothenburg Orchestra, and this is a demonstration record among demonstration records. There is also a thought-provoking and insightful sleeve note from David Brown. Recommended with enthusiasm.

Symphonies Nos. 5 in D min., Op. 47; 6 in B min., Op. 54.

(BB) *** Regis RRC 1075. Cologne RSO, Barshai.

Rudolf Barshai's coupling comes from concert performances in the Cologne Philharmonie in 1995–6. (It was apparently included in a complete cycle issued on the super-economy Brilliant label but until now has not enjoyed wide currency in Britain.) Barshai's credentials in this repertoire are well known. He conducted the first recording of the *Fourteenth Symphony* and has, of course, arranged the *Fourth, Eighth* and *Tenth Quartets* for full strings with the composer's blessing. These are very well-prepared and expertly played accounts, which may not equal the likes of Haitink, Mariss Janssons (or Järvi in No. 6) but are finely shaped and felt. At the price, and given the clarity of the recording, these can certainly be recommended.

(i) Symphonies Nos. 5 in D min., Op. 47; (ii) 10 in E min., Op. 93.

(BB) ** Warner Ultima 8573 85237-2 (2). (i) Nat. SO, Washington; (ii) LSO, Rostropovich.

Rostropovich brings great feeling and intensity to this music, and he is well served by both the Washington Orchestra in the *Fifth Symphony* and the LSO in the *Tenth*. At the same time there is something hectoring in his interpretations. Gestures are overemphatic, and he leaves the listener exhausted rather than exalted.

Symphony No. 6, Op. 54; (i) The Execution of Stepan Razin, Op. 119.

** Chan. 9813. Russian State SO, Polyansky; (i) with Lochak, Russian State Symphonic Capella.

Valéry Polyansky has given us some splendid things, but his account of the *Sixth Symphony* does neither him nor Shostakovich full justice. The performance is touched by routine. *The Execution of Stepan Razin* is given with much greater character and Polyansky has greater conviction than in the symphony, but although Anatoly Lochak is a fine soloist, memories of Vitaly Gromadsky with Kondrashin in 1966 are not banished.

Symphony No. 7 in C (Leningrad), Op. 60.

(BB) *** Regis RRC 1074. Cologne RSO, Barshai.

(B) **(*) Sony (ADD) SBK 89904. NYPO, Bernstein.

(B) *(*) Warner Apex 0927 41409-2. Nat. SO (of Washington), Rostropovich.

Barshai's recording comes from a concert performance in the Cologne Philharmonie in 1992. EMI also issued a very fine *Eighth Symphony* with the Bournemouth Orchestra in the late 1980s, but this newly released Cologne version of the *Leningrad* has a great deal going for it. There is no bombast, yet the understatement does not entail loss of character and impact, and the sound quality is very good indeed, thanks to the excellent Cologne acoustic. An eminently viable choice and not only in this price bracket.

Bernstein brings a certain panache and fervour to his reading, particularly in the inspired slow movement, so that one is tempted to look indulgently at its occasional overstatements. The up-front recording is rich and weighty, flattering the strings, but the steadily built climax of the opening movement lacks the fullest range of dynamic in the sound, if not in the playing itself.

Rostropovich's account is eminently well prepared and springs from undoubted feeling, but he is often a bit heavy-handed, rarely letting the music speak for itself and the overall effect is studied. The engineers provide him with a recording of impressive dynamic range. However there is a literal feeling here – all i's are dotted and t's crossed.

Symphony No. 10 in E min., Op. 93.

(M) (***) DG mono 463 666-2. Czech PO, Ančerl – STRAVINSKY *Violin Concerto* ***.

Though recorded in 1955, Karel Ančerl's DG recording still makes a very considerable impact, as it did on its original release. The sense of brooding atmosphere in the opening movement is superbly caught, and it carries a sense of momentum that is utterly compelling. The ensuing *allegro* is fast and furious, rather clipped, but extremely exciting and provides striking contrast with the succeeding *Allegretto*; throughout the tension is superbly maintained. The finale is electrifying, bursting through all the limitations of the mono sound. The transfer is excellent, and so too is the coupling. Karajan may reign supreme among stereo recordings of this work (DG 439 036-2) but this Czech version is also unforgettable.

CHAMBER MUSIC

Adagio and Allegretto for String Quartet; (i) Piano Quintet, Op. 57; (ii) 2 Pieces for String Octet, Op. 1/1; (i) 5 Pieces for 2 Violins and Piano (arr. Atovmian).

*** Challenge CC 72093. Brodsky Qt (members), with (i) Blackshaw; (ii) Shave, Theaker, Atkins, Baillie. (available from www.challengeclassics.com)

A superb collection. Like the Brodsky's equally recommended coupling of string quartets by Britten and Tchaikovsky, the sense of spontaneous, live music-making inhabits every bar here. The range of mood is remarkably wide. The early *Pieces for String Octet*, Op. 1 are as wild and uninhibited as the delightful *Pieces for Two Violins and Piano* are elegantly tuneful. The deeply expressive *Adagio* and quirky *Allegretto* are arrangements of Katerina's aria from *Lady Macbeth of the Mtsensk District* and the famously witty *Polka* from *The Golden Age* ballet. But the key work here is the *Piano Quintet*, a marvellously concentrated performance. The second movement *Fugue-Adagio* and the *Intermezzo* both open with a rapt pianissimo framing the bold, jaunty central *Scherzo* and leading on to the puissant finale. Excellent recording throughout, although some might think the acoustic for the quintet gives the piano a rather too resonant image.

String Quartet No. 8, Op. 110.

(M) (**(*)) BBC mono BBCL 4063-2. Borodin Qt.
BORODIN: *Quartet No. 2;* RAVEL: *Quartet* (**(*)).

Written at white heat, while his thoughts were very much on death, Shostakovich described how his tears flowed when he was composing Op. 110. And when the Borodin Quartet, after preparing the work with scrupulous attention, played the piece through to him, hoping for detailed criticism, he was again moved to tears and turned away. They went on to record the Shostakovich and Borodin quartets at the Decca studios (now on 425 541-2). This performance is not quite as fine, but it is still well worth having and sounds very good for its age. The Borodins recorded the Shostakovich on three further occasions after 1962, as part of their complete cycles in 1974 and 1978 and again in 1990. In the very opening bars, their tempo is fractionally brisker here than in their 1978 recording, and the vibrato is more intense. A well worthwhile momento of an important musical event.

OPERA

Lady Macbeth of Mtsensk (complete).

✪ (M) *** EMI (ADD) CMS5 67776-2 [567779] (2).
Vishnevskaya, Gedda, Petkov, Finnilä, Krenn, Tear, Malta, Valjakka, Amb. Op. Ch., LPO, Rostropovich.

Rostropovich, in his finest recording ever, proves with thrilling conviction that this first version of Shostakovich's greatest work for the stage is among the most original operas of the century. Vishnevskaya is inspired to give an outstanding performance and provides moments of great beauty alongside aptly coarser singing; Gedda matches her well, totally idiomatic. As the sadistic father-in-law, Petkov is magnificent, particularly in his ghostly return, and there are fine contributions from Robert Tear, Werner Krenn, Birgit Finnilä and Alexander Malta. With an enhanced transfer this now rightly takes its place as one of EMI's 'Great Recordings of the Century'.

SIBELIUS, Jean (1865–1957)

(i) Andante festivo; (ii) En Saga; (iii) Pohjola's Daughter; (iv) Rakastava; Impromptu.

(***) Ondine mono/stereo ODE 992-2. (i) Finnish RSO, Composer; (ii) Swedish RSO, Franck; (iii) Tampere PO, Ollila; (iv) Virtuosi di Kuhmo, Czaba. (with: KAJANUS: Aino. ***.)

Though, unlike Svendsen and Nielsen, Sibelius was not a conductor by profession, he was a highly effective interpreter of his own music. The *Andante festivo* is the only surviving recording of him conducting and he draws playing of great intensity. (An earlier account attributed to him was in fact a recording of a rehearsal under Tauno Hannikainen.) Mikko Franck's version of *En Saga* is both concentrated and atmospheric. There is a more than serviceable account of *Pohjola's Daughter* and an affecting *Rakastava*, while the *Impromptu* is an arrangement for strings of two early piano pieces, Op. 5. The bonus is a rarity, the 1991 recording under Jorma Panula of *Aino* by Sibelius's great champion, Robert Kajanus, which was the spark that kindled the flame that led to Sibelius's *Kullervo Symphony*.

The Bard; Dance-Intermezzo; The Dryad; En saga; Legend: Night Ride and Sunrise; The Oceanides; Pohjola's Daughter.

**(*) BIS CD 1225. Lahti SO, Vänskä.

Osmo Vänskä has already recorded *The Wood-Nymph*, *Tapiola* and the 1892 version of *En saga*. This CD brings the remaining tone poems – with the exception of *Pan and Echo*. This conductor, much and rightly admired in this repertoire, is unfailingly sure of instinct. In *En saga* phrasing is so natural and unforced, though the *pianissimo sul ponticello* string passage (18 bars before M: track 1, 8:14 mins) is exaggerated to the point of inaudibility. *Pohjola's Daughter* is very impressive though the affected dynamic exaggerations (the *piano-pianissimi* at 7:30 mins and again at the very end) are irritating. In *Night Ride and Sunrise* pacing is superb and the final sunrise is magnificent and beautifully sustained. But ultimately in both *The Oceanides* and *Night Ride* the LSO and Sir Colin Davis remain unchallenged, and among very recent issues we liked Oramo and the CBSO, who give very convincing accounts of *The Bard* and *Pohjola's Daughter*.

The Bard; Four Legends, Op. 22; Pohjola's Daughter, Op. 49.

**(*) RCA 74321 68945-2 LSO, Colin Davis

Sir Colin Davis is one of the finest living Sibelians; few have explored this composer's spiritual landscape with such understanding and authority or are so totally attuned to his sensibility. But though he has recorded the symphonies twice, these are his very first recording of the complete set of the *Legends* and *The Bard*.

The first *Legend* is finely paced and one feels, as with any great conductor, that there is always something left in reserve. But at almost twelve minutes Sir Colin's *Swan* is excessively ruminative: his Boston version was just over nine! Moreover while the sense of menace in *Lemminkäinen in Tuonela* is very striking, and it is enormously atmospheric it is *far* too slow. In *Lemminkäinen's Homeward Journey*, Davis is not as headlong as Beecham or Vänskä. Their hero is altogether rougher and in very much of a hurry while Davis's is a more thoughtful chap. *The Bard* is magical, every bit as mysterious and inward-looking as the recent CBSO version under Oramo. Sir Colin recorded *Pohjola's Daughter* with the Boston Orchestra way back in 1981, though it was never transferred to CD. Though they actually differ by only a few seconds, this newcomer feels even slower: many collectors will find it far too measured. Vänskä offers the earlier 1896 versions of Nos. 1 & 4 and the alternative 1897 ending of No. 4, and Mikko Franck on Ondine has *En Saga*. Mike Hatch produces exceptionally fine recorded sound for Davis, but this collection, which we overpraised in our main volume, must be approached with a degree of caution.

Belshazzar's Feast, Op. 64; Scènes historiques I & II; Swanwhite.

*** Finlandia 0927 41935-2. Norwegian RO, Rasilainen.

These are performances of quality. Everything here derives from the stage, except the second set of *Scènes historiques*. Both *Belshazzar's Feast* and *Swanwhite* are among Sibelius's most atmospheric scores, and they can be easily spoilt by unimaginative playing. But Ari Rasilainen captures their often elusive poetry, and both *Night Music* and *Khadra's Dance* from *Belshazzar* are beautifully shaped. Rasilainen is completely attuned to this music and gets dedicated playing from his fine musicians. There is the occasional oddity of balance: the supportive chords on horns and brass, the accompaniment, swamp the strings in *The Prince Alone* in *Swanwhite*. The first set of the *Scènes historiques* comes from the music Sibelius wrote for the patriotic Press Celebrations pageant in 1899, but the second set, written in 1912, is completely unrelated to it. The performances have a freshness and sense of pleasure. An enjoyable disc, notwithstanding the odd lapse in the record balance.

Violin Concerto in D min., Op. 47.

(*) Arthaus **DVD 100 034. Vengerov, Chicago SO, Barenboim – FALLA: *Nights in the Gardens of Spain.* ** (Producer: Bernd Hellthaler. V/D: Bob Coles.)

(i;ii) Violin Concerto in D min., Op. 47; (iii) En saga, Op. 9; Finlandia, Op. 26; Karelia Suite, Op. 11.

(BB) ** CfP (ADD) 575 5662. (i) Sarbu; (ii) Hallé O, Schmidt; (iii) RSNO, Gibson.

Violin Concerto in D min., Op. 47; Humoreske No. 5 in E flat, Op. 89/3; 2 Serenades, Op. 69.

(BB) **(*) EMI Encore (ADD) CDE5 75236-2. Haendel, Bournemouth SO, Berglund.

Maxim Vengerov's 1997 recording made while the Chicago Orchestra was in Germany. Pretty stunning virtuosity and much *zigeuner* brilliance though less of the silvery aristocratic restraint that is called for in the slow movement. But if you warm to this player – and he has a strong following – this DVD can be recommended, although the Falla coupling is lacking in atmosphere. Barenboim accompanies sensitively and Vengerov dashes off the Bach *Sarabande* from the *D minor Partita* and the *Third Solo Sonata (Ballade)* of Ysaÿe as encores.

Ida Haendel brings great attack to the *Violin Concerto*, and there is a refreshing want of egocentricity to her interpretation. She plays with dash and authority, though others have brought to it greater poetic refinement (Kyung-Wha Chung, for example). Bergland accompanies sympathetically, although the finale could go with greater panache. The two *Serenades* are marvellously atmospheric, and Miss Haendel does them proud in this, their première recording. The 1975 sound is good for its period and has been well transferred; had Berglund created greater atmosphere in the *Violin Concerto*, this would be one of the top recommendations. As it is, it remains a richly enjoyable performance, as Ida Haendel's tone and phrasing have memorable warmth and eloquence. Good value at its bargain Encore price.

Eugene Sarbu is a Romanian artist who made his recording of the Sibelius *Concerto* in 1980, when he was in his early thirties. His vibrato is a little wide and intonation is not always impeccable though he has plenty of dash and power. He makes the most of every expressive point and underlines romantic fervour rather than spirituality. His is a *zigeuner*-like approach without the purity and refinement of tone which are ideal – and which emerge in Cho-Liang Lin and Kyung-Wha Chung. There is a nobility in this music which Sarbu does not always convey. But he is well supported by the Hallé who give Ole Schimdt sensitive and responsive playing, and they are heard to great effect in the *Karelia* and *Finlandia* couplings. Gibson's atmospheric RSNO *En saga* (recorded in 1974) has been added as a makeweight for this reissue. Sarbu is a formidable artist and this vibrant collection is good value.

(i) En Saga, Op. 9; Finlandia, Op. 26; Karelia Suite, Op. 11; (ii) Legend: The Swan of Tuonela.

(B) *** Ph. 468 201-2 (2). Philh O, Ashkenazy; (ii) ASMF, Marriner – GRIEG: *Holberg Suite* etc. **

Ashkenazy's superb (Decca) Sibelius recordings – a fresh-sounding yet exciting *Finlandia*, an impressively evocative *En Saga* and an enjoyably vivid *Karelia Suite* – remain top choices, and the early digital recordings are superb in every way. Marriner's *Swan of Tuonela* is most sensitive, with the cor anglais solo beautifully played by Barry Griffiths. However, the Grieg couplings are not quite so recommendable.

Six Humoresques, Opp. 87 & 89.

*(*) Essay CD 1075. Tenenbaum, Pro Musica Prague, Kapp – GHEDINI: *Violin Concerto; Musica da concerto for viola & viola d'amore.* **

Sibelius was toying with the idea of a second violin concerto in 1915 and it is not too fanciful to imagine that some of its ideas could have found their way into the two sets of *Humoresques.* They are rarely heard in the concert hall, thanks partly to their dimensions and the technical demands they make. Mela Tenenbaum is no match for the likes of Dong-Suk Kang (BIS CD 472), Aaron Rosand or Accardo (now deleted). She inserts all sorts of little expressive hesitations and does not produce a particularly beautiful sound, though to be fair the close balance and unglamorous studio acoustic does not help her. The liner notes are uninformed on matters Sibelian and marred by factual errors. Nor are they well written: we learn at one point that Sibelius at the time of the *Humoresques* 'found himself prematurely obsolesced'!

Symphonies No. 1–7; (i) *Kullervo; En Saga; Rakastava.*

(B) *** RCA 74321 54034-2 (5). LSO, C. Davis; (i) with Martinpelto, Frederiksson, LSO Ch.

Capped with a superb account of *Kullervo,* Sir Colin Davis's set of the Sibelius *Symphonies* rather sweeps the board. The excellence of the LSO playing is matched by the consistently fine RCA recording which sets the seal on a totally authoritative and triumphant survey, including equally fine performances of *En Saga* and *Rakastava* for good measure.

Symphonies Nos. 1 in E min., Op. 39; 3 in C, Op. 52; *Finlandia, Op. 26.*

**(*) Warner 0927 43500-2. CBSO, Oramo.

Sakari Oramo's earlier Sibelius symphonies with the Birmingham Orchestra have been highly successful. He is thoughtful and perceptive, and completely inside the mind of his great countryman. Of the present two symphonies, the *First* is particularly fine, with well-judged tempi and playing that is full of spirit and feeling. The *Third,* too, has a good deal going for it, though in Oramo's hands the first movement is more allegro than moderato. Momentum is well sustained, however, without the result being as headlong as in Anthony Collins's pioneering LP. The slow movement, though only a few seconds longer than Kajanus, feels slower, and although the atmosphere is finely conveyed, Oramo allows the tension to sag. The wind are not as impeccably tuned and blended as they might be, and in the finale the balance gives the horns rather too much prominence, and they sound blustery. But there are many sensitive touches, although Sir Colin Davis (09026 61963-2) and Ashkenazy (455 405-2) are to be preferred. The claims of another Sakari (Petri Sakari and the Iceland Orchestra on Naxos) should not be passed over. He is totally unselfconscious and has an air of authenticity.

Symphonies Nos. 1 in E min., Op. 39; 4 in A min., Op. 63; 5 in E flat, Op. 82; 6 in D min., Op. 104; *Karelia Suite, Op. 11.*

(B) *** EMI Double fforte (ADD) CZS5 74858-2 (2). Berlin PO, Karajan.

In the *First Symphony,* Karajan, a great Tchaikovsky interpreter, identifies with the work's inheritance. But there is a sense of grandeur and vision here, and the opulence and virtuosity of the Berliners helps to project the heroic dimensions of Karajan's performance. The early digital recording (1981) is not top-drawer; the bass is over-weighted, but the full upper strings sing our gloriously with the richest amplitude in the finale which has an electrifying climax and the brass is comparably rich and resonant.

In Karajan's second recording of the *Fourth* (1976), he courts controversy in his spacious tempi, especially in the first and third movements – much slower than his earlier DG version – but it is all highly atmospheric. He conveys eloquently the haunting quality of the landscape in the third movement, and the first undoubtedly has great mystery and power. Again, in the *Fifth,* recorded the same year, the opening movement is broader than in his earlier DG account, achieving a remarkable sense of strength and majesty. The transition in to the scherzo is slightly more abrupt than in the 1965 recording, and indeed tempi in the first half of the work are generally rather more extreme in this version. The variety of tone-colour and, above all, the weight of sonority that the Berlin Philharmonic have at their command is remarkable; the bassoon lament in the development section finds the Berlin strings reduced to a mere whisper. Both the slow movement and finale are glorious, demonstrating real vision, and the recording is excellent.

The 1980 recording of the *Sixth* brings to life the other-worldly qualities of this score, in particular the long white nights of the northern summer and their 'fragile melancholy' conjured by the slow movement (or, for that matter, the opening polyphony). While this is a spacious account (though actually marginally quicker than his 1967 DG performance), we are always aware of the sense of forward movement. In short, this is Karajan at his finest, and this inexpensive Double fforte reissue can be very strongly recommended, especially with a strong, weighty performance of the *Karelia Suite* included too.

Symphonies Nos. 1 in E min.; 7 in C, Op. 105.

(M) **(*) Sony (ADD) SMK 89576. NYPO, Bernstein.

Bernstein's 1967 account of No. 1 is impassioned and strong as well as reasonably free from mannerisms. It has greater fire than Berglund and the power and eloquence of the string playing (especially in the finale) are most satisfying. The recording of No. 7 was begun in 1960 but not completed until five years later. However the reading holds together as an impressive entity, and is certainly deeply felt. The recording, although full-bodied, could be more refined.

Symphony No. 5; The Bard; Karelia Suite; The Bard; Pohjola's Daughter.

**(*) Teldec 8573 85822-2 CBSO, Oramo.

Symphony No. 5 in E flat, Op. 82; Karelia Suite.

(M) ** Decca (ADD) 468 488-2. LSO, Gibson – CONCERTS. **(*)

Symphonies Nos. 5 in E flat, Op. 82; 6 in D min., Op. 104; Tapiola.

(B) **(*) Ph. Eloquence 468 198-2. Boston SO, C. Davis.

Now that the 1915 version of the *Fifth Symphony* is in the public domain we know something of the struggles Sibelius had with its gestation, though his diaries and correspondence show the extraordinary changes it underwent even after that – he toyed with the notion of dropping the last two movements altogether! As the recent disc of the *Second* and *Fourth* symphonies showed, Sakari Oramo is a Sibelian of sound instinct. He conveys the awe and majesty of the symphony's opening paragraphs to perfection as well as the sense of mystery of the development. In fact this is highly impressive, even if in the scherzo section he is a fraction headlong. The slow movement and finale are well paced and the Birmingham Orchestra give him excellent support. Of the remaining works *Pohjola's Daughter* is taut and highly charged, miles removed from Sir Colin Davis on RCA, *The Bard*, one of Sibelius's most concentrated and profound utterances, is wonderfully atmospheric; indeed it is among the very finest accounts ever recorded (not forgetting Beecham). The recording is state-of-the-art – spacious, well defined and transparent. But for the symphony, this is not a first choice.

Sir Colin Davis's mid-1970s account of the *Fifth* is already available coupled with his Boston *Seventh* as one of the Philips '50 Great Recordings' (464 740-2). This Eloquence re-coupling is a more attractive proposition apart from its greater economy. The recording still sounds extremely good and the performance, if without quite the resplendence of his later LSO version for RCA, is still compelling and very well-played (as is *Tapiola*). The account of the *Sixth* is very fine indeed, so this is excellent value, if the coupling is wanted.

Gibson's account may be, to quote the orginal *Gramophone* review, 'a vivid and wholly succesful performance' but it is hardly the stuff of which Legends are made, and it is a pity Decca could not find other repertoire to add to the concert (originally entitled '*Witch's Brew*') with which these Gibson Sibelius performances are coupled. The reading of the *Symphony* is certainly capable and sometimes exciting, but Gibson does not show a complete grasp of the structure as a whole: there is a lack of tautness in the moments where the emotional tension lies beneath the surface. The LSO play beautifully and there is much – almost too much – evidence of careful rehearsal. The *Karelia* pieces are even more disappointing, particularly the unimaginative and half-hearted approach to the delightful *Ballade*. No

complaints about the Kingsway Hall recording, produced by Erik Smith and Christopher Raeburn as early as 1957, but still sounding very impressive.

CHAMBER MUSIC

(i) **Music for Cello and and Piano:** *Canzonetta, Op. 62a. King Christian II: Elegie. Malinconia, Op. 20; 2 Pieces, Op. 77; 4 Pieces, Op. 78; Romance for strings in C, Op. 42; Rondino Op. 81/2; Valse romantique, Op. 62b; Valse triste, Op. 44/1.* (ii) **Music for Violin & Piano:** *Sonatina in E, Op. 80;* (iii) *Berceuse. Op. 79/6; Danse charactéristique, Op. 116/1 & 2. 4 Pieces, Op. 78; 4 Pieces, Op. 81; 4 Pieces, Op. 115; Scène de danse.*

(B) ** Finlandia 0927 41355-2 (2) (i) Raimo Sariola, Hui-Ying Liu; (ii) Yoshiko Arai, Izumi Tateno; (iii) Yuval Yaron, Rena Sharon.

Sibelius was of course an accomplished violinist in his youth and never lost his feeling for the instrument. The two CDs here collect performances made in 1976-77 (the first CD) and 1985 in the case of the the second. Most of the violin pieces with the exception of Opp. 115 & 116, come from the war years when Sibelius was cut off from the great European orchestras and from his livelihood, namely his royalties from Breitkopf in Leipzig. He wrote a large number of instrumental pieces to generate the income his isolation cost him. In the first decade of the century Breitkopf also published arrangements of some of his smaller orchestral scores (the *Elégie* from *King Christian II* was made by the conductor, Georg Schnéevoigt). Most of the pieces on the second CD played by Raimo Sariola were composed for violin and piano or violin or cello and piano, and some can be heard in both forms. Although most of these pieces are slight, they are (for the most part) of quality and are presented as such.

PIANO MUSIC

Complete Youthful Production of music for the Piano I.

*** BIS CD 1067. Folke Gräsbeck.

This first Volume is discussed in our main Guide.

Complete Youthful Production of music for the Piano II.

*** BIS CD 1202 Folke Gräsbeck

Since Sibelius forbade performances of such fine pieces as the A minor quartet and its successor, the B flat, Op. 4, and discouraged interest in *Kullervo*, his views about the appearance of the juvenilia on this disc can only be imagined. All the same, perspectives change and there is a natural curiosity about the kind of music he was composing as a student in Helsinki and Berlin, though recording his 1889 student exercises for Albert Becker is carrying reverence too far. Some of the pieces, such as the *Moderato – Presto in D minor* (1888) are worth hearing, but none can be said to be remotely characteristic. Some are fragments only, a few seconds in duration; some have no title. Two of the scraps he composed while studying in Vienna under Goldmark and Robert Fuchs are only 20 seconds. None are in print and the performances are based on the autograph material held in the Helsinki University Library. All, with the exception of the *Florestan Suite* of 1889, are first recordings. Folke Gräsbeck plays them with the fluent grace that characterised his earlier disc in this series and the BIS recording and documentation are exemplary.

VOCAL MUSIC

Belshazzar's Feast; Den judiska flickans sång (The Jewish Girl's Song); 6 Songs, Op. 36: Svarta Rosor (Black Roses); Men min fågel märks dock icke (But my Bird is Long in Homing); Bollspelet vid Trianon (Tennis at Trianon) Säv, säv, susa (Sigh, Sedges, Sigh); Marssnön (The March Snow); Demanten på marssnön (The Diamond on the March Snow). 5 Songs, Op. 37: Den första kyssen (The First Kiss); Lasse liten (Little Lasse); Soluppgång (Sunrise); Var det en dröm? (Was it a dream?); Flickan kom ifrån sin älsklings möte (The Tryst). 6 Songs, Op. 50: Lenzgesang (Spring Song); Sehnsucht (Loneliness); Im Feld ein Mädchen singt (In the Field a Maiden Sings); Aus banger Brust (From anxious heart); Die stille Stadt (The Silent Town); Rosenlied (Rose Song). Illale (To Evening); Jag är ett träd (I am a Tree), Op 57/5; Näcken (The Watersprite or The Elf King), Op 57/8; Under strandens granar (Beneath the Fir Trees), Op 13/1; Våren flyktar hastigt (Spring is Flying) Op 13/4; Norden (The North), Op 90/1; Vem styrde hit din väg? (Who Brought you Here?), Op 90/6.

*** Hyp. CDA 67318. Karnéus, Drake.

Decca's splendid survey of the complete songs with Elisabeth Söderström and Tom Krause has never appeared on CD in the UK, although it has appeared in Japan. However, this important strand in Sibelius's output is decently represented on CD by Anne Sofie von Otter and Bengt Forsberg on BIS CD 457 and 757 and a handful of other discs, although masterpieces like *Jubal* and *Teodora* are not well represented.

Of his hundred or so songs, all but a handful are to texts by Swedish poets, a quarter of them are to settings of Runeberg. The only Finnish song here is *Illale (To Evening)*, among the most lyrical and affecting of his songs. Katarina Karnéus offers the Op. 36 and Op. 37 sets, which include some of the best loved (and best) songs like *Säv, säv susa* and *Men min fågel märks dock icke*, and one of the subtlest, *Bollspelet vid Trianon*. She also includes the German settings, Op. 50, written in 1906. It was natural that at a time when the composer's music was beginning to find a welcome in Germany that he should turn to a major language (Sibelius spoke little French or English). Two of them, *Im Feld ein Mädchen (In the Field a Maiden Sings)* and *Die stille Stadt (The Silent Town)* are among his greatest songs.

Karnéus possesses a glorious voice and sings with real interpretative insight, and in these inspired performances she and Julius Drake find new dimensions in these jewels of songs, performances that sharply bring out the contrasts of mood, the range of emotion and the sense of drama, as in the overpowering tragic climax of *The Tryst*. The eerie originality of such a song as *Näcken (The Watersprite)* is perfectly caught, with Drake at the piano drawing out the beauty of sound, just as Karnéus does in the vocal line. It is a magical partnership, giving fresh insights in every item. Those who have yet to explore Sibelius's songs should start right here. And no one should miss the orchestral songs on BIS CD 270 discussed in our main volume.

(i) *The Maiden in the Tower* (opera; complete); *Pelléas et Mélisande* (incidental music), Op. 46; *Kuolema: Valse Triste.*

*** Virgin VC5 45493-2. (i) Kringelborn, Jonsson, Passikivi, Magee, Estonian Girls' Ch. & Nat. Male Ch.; Estonian NSO, Järvi.

Sibelius toyed with operatic plans for much of his life. Even his first major tone poems, the Op. 22 *Lemminkäinen Legends*, contained material from the opera *Veneen luominen (The Building of the Boat)* to his own libretto. In 1896 he returned to the genre with what was to be his only opera, *Jungrun i tornet (The Maiden in the Tower)*. It was first staged in Helsinki in the same year but was never revived in the composer's lifetime. Indeed, it is unlikely that he would have approved of its revival in 1981 and subsequent recording. The libretto does not rise much above Victorian melodrama, and the layout of the opera (eight short scenes not lasting for much more than 35 minutes) does not really work dramatically. There is a lot of pretty routine Nordic nationalism, but the orchestral interlude between the first two scenes is real Sibelius, the *Maiden's Prayer* in Scene 2 is impressive, and there are occasional echoes of Wagner. The portrayal of the coming of spring is quite captivating, and much of the music resonates in the mind afterwards. Obviously, it is not top-drawer Sibelius and the composer never revised it. The present issue is more generously filled than the rival version from Gothenburg and Neeme Järvi and comes with the *Pelléas* suite, which was composed a decade later. Jorma Hynninen is an imposing villain in the Gothenburg version, and of the two heroines, Margareta Häggander is perhaps the more convincing. This is a useful alternative to the BIS account, even if it does not completely displace it.

SILLÉN, Josef Otto af (1859–1951)

(i) *Violin Concerto in E min.; Symphony No. 3 in E min.*

** Sterling CDS 1044-2 (i) Christian Bergqvist; Gävle SO, Göran W. Nilson

Josef Otto af Sillén is a very minor figure and is not listed in Grove or Bakers, or even in Sohlman, their Swedish equivalent. As a young man he pursued a military career and then turned to insurance, while at the same time being active in the Philharmonic Society: he was briefly in charge of the Stockholm Opera, and held a court appointment as a royal chamberlain. He composed for much of his life, though performances were not always under his own name as he felt his aristocratic name might work to his disadvantage. His *Violin Concerto* probably dates from the early 1920s and he wrote the *Third Symphony* in his late seventies (it was premièred in 1937). A musician of culture rather than originality, he conveys little feeling of real mastery. The *Violin Concerto*, dedicated to his daughter, Greta af Sillén Roos, an Auer pupil but who, alas, never played it, opens like Bruch and in the symphony there is a lot of Tchaikovsky: the scherzo is Mendelssohnian, albeit somewhat heavy-handed. There are moments here and there which are rather endearing. Christian Bergqvist is the persuasive soloist in the concerto and the performance and recording are perfectly acceptable. Of interest for its curiosity value.

SINDING, Christian (1856–1941)

Symphonies Nos. 1 in D min., Op. 21; 2 in D, Op. 83.

*** CPO 999 502-2. Hanover NDR PO, Thomas Dausgaard

Most Norwegian composers after Grieg and Svendsen are steeped in their rich storehouse of folk song but an exception is Christian Sinding of *Rustle of Spring* fame. He was a year older than Elgar, and his musical language has its roots in Wagner, Liszt and Strauss – particularly Wagner. There is scant evidence of interest in the Norwegian folk tradition, even if his music is still recognisably Nordic. Though he dominated the scene in the early part of the century, his pro-German sentiments affected his popularity in post-war Norway. He began the First of his four symphonies in 1887 though it did not reach its final form until the mid-1890s, while the Second followed a decade later. At the beginning of the last century Sinding along with Grieg and Svendsen symbolised Norwegian music for the rest of Europe but no one listening to either of these symphonies would suggest that he possesses more than a fraction of their inventive quality. One of his professors at the Leipzig conservatory suggested that his 'talent for music is only of a very limited nature' and he was not far off target. Both symphonies are both well crafted though the scoring is often opaque. Thomas Dausgaard is a persuasive a

cate and gets good playing from the excellent Hanover Orchestra. On balance this is to be preferred to the rival Norwegian Radio accounts under Ari Rasilainen.

SMETANA, Bedřich (1824–84)

***Má Vlast* (complete).**

(B) **(*) Sony SBK 89776. Israel PO, Mehta.

It would be easy to undervalue Mehta's Israel performance, for he clearly enjoys the music and so do the Israeli players; the recording is fuller and somewhat more atmospheric than we often experience in Tel Aviv, although it is at times unrefined and string detail is husky. Mehta's tempi are close to Järvi's in the first three symphonic poems, rather more expansive in the second triptych. *Vyšehrad* comes off quite effectively. But after an attractively delicate opening, the great string-tune of *Vltava* fails really to take off, and the climax needs a more expansive acoustic. The opening of *Tábor* isn't very arresting either, and both here and in *Blaník*, although the adrenalin runs freely, there is an element of bombast (the comparatively dry acoustic does not help) and Mehta seldom displays the imaginative flair of his competitors.

Piano Trio in G min., Op. 15.

(BB) *** Warner Apex 7559 79679-2. Boston Symphony Chamber Players – DVORAK: *String Sextet in A.* ***

This 1983 Boston performance on Warner Apex brings a distinguished line-up, Joseph Silverstein, the cellist Jules Eskine and the pianist Gilbert Kalisch. This sensitive and vital account ranks among the most competitive of Smetana's *Piano Trio*, particularly given its price bracket. It comes with a warm and affectionate account of the Dvořák *Sextet*.

SPOHR, Ludwig (1784–1859)

String Quintets Nos. 1 in E flat; 2 in G, Op. 3/1–2.

(BB) *** Naxos 8.555965. Augmented Danubius Qt.

Spohr's *String Quintets* feature a second viola, which gives them a characteristically full, slightly bland texture. But the suave opening theme of the *E flat major Quartet* is deceptive, for it is strong enough to influence the two following movements including the near-melancholy *Larghetto* and the attractive Minuet and Trio. In the *G major* work a similarly mild opening theme is to dominate. Both quintets are warmly and sympathetically played by the Danubius Quartet, augmented by Sándor Papp, and smoothly and pleasingly recorded. Originally on Marco Polo, this reissue is eminently competitive at its new Naxos price.

STAINER, John (1840–1901)

(i) *The Crucifixion; Come Thou Long Expected Jesus* (hymn); *I saw the Lord* (anthem); (ii) *Love Divine, all Loves Excelling* (hymn).

(M) *** Decca (ADD/DDD) 470 379-2. (i) Lewis, Brannigan, St John's College, Cambridge Ch., Guest; (ii) King's College, Cambridge Ch., Cleobury.

All five hymns in which the congregation is invited to join are included on the Decca (originally Argo) record. Owen Brannigan is splendidly dramatic and his voice makes a good foil for Richard Lewis in the duets. The choral singing is first-class and the 1961 recording is of Argo's best vintage, even finer than its CfP competitor. Moreover the latest Decca reissue includes three bonuses: a fine eight-part anthem, *I Saw the Lord*, and two hymns, one of which is a favourite, sung by King's College Choir.

STAMITZ, Johann (1717–57)

Trumpet Concerto in D (arr. Boustead).

(B) *** Ph. Duo 464 028-2 (2). Hardenberger, ASMF, Marriner – HAYDN; HERTEL; HUMMEL: *Concertos.* *** (with concert: *'Famous Classical Trumpet Concertos'* *** ✪).

This *Concerto* was written either by Stamitz or by a composer called J. G. Holzbogen. The writing lies consistently up in the instrument's stratosphere and includes some awkward leaps. It is quite inventive, however, notably the finale, which is exhilarating on the lips of Håken Hardenberger. There is no lack of panache here and Marriner accompanies expertly. Good if reverberant recording, with the trumpet given great presence. This now comes as part of a Duo anthology, which is very highly recommendable.

STANFORD, Charles (1852–1924)

(i) *Agnus Dei*; (ii) *Beata Quorum Via, Op. 38/3; The Bluebird*; (ii) *The Fairy Lough*; (iv or v) *Magnificat; Nunc Dimittis*; (vi) *O Praise God In His Holiness; O Sing Unto the Lord a New Song*; (iii) *A Soft Day*; (vii) *Songs of the Sea, Op. 91*; (iv) *Te Deum Laudamus*.

(M) *** Decca (ADD/DDD) 470 384-2. (i) Royal School of Church Music Ch., Dakers; (ii) New College Oxford Ch., Higginbotton; (iii) Ferrier, Stone; (iv) Winchester Cathedral Ch., Bournemouth SO, Hill; (v) King's College Cambridge Ch., Ord; (vi) St. John's College Ch., Guest; (vii) Allen, LPO Ch. & O, Norrington.

John Allen is excellent in this 1996 recording of the superbly briny *Songs of the Sea*, beautiful and commanding, with fine support from the LPO chorus and orchestra, and a first-rate Decca recording. David Hill's 1990 performances with his Bournemouth forces are similarly enjoyable – these enormously attractive works are very exciting in their full symphonic form (they were originally for, and usually recorded with voices and organ), especially in the swelling climaxes of the music. The choral works are well executed, and the Ferrier items make an attractive bonus. Good value in Decca's British Music Collection.

STENHAMMAR, Wilhelm (1871–1927)

Serenade for Orchestra, Op. 31.

✪ (BB) *** Warner Apex 0927 43075-2. Royal Stockholm PO, Davis (with GRIEG: *Holberg Suite* (Helsinki Strings, Szilvay); NIELSEN: *Little Suite* (Norwegian RO, Rasilainen). ***)

The Stenhammar was recorded in 1998 and originally coupled with the Brahms *D major Serenade* (Stenhammar was a notable exponent of the Brahms piano concertos), and in this full-price format it received a ✪ in our main volume. We can only reiterate our wonder at this glorious work; its invention is rich and its harmonies subtle. Nothing more perfectly enshrines the spirit of the Swedish summer night than its *Notturno*, but throughout the level of inspiration is uniformly high. Andrew Davis shapes the score with scrupulous attention to detail and evident sensitivity and feeling. In this bargain-basement refurbishment it is coupled with fine performances of the Grieg *Holberg Suite* from Helsinki and the enchanting Nielsen *Little Suite* from Norway. A terrific bargain.

STOJOWSKI, Zygmunt (1870–1946)

Piano Concertos Nos. 1 in F sharp min., Op. 3; 2 in A flat (Prelude, Scherzo & Variations), Op. 32.

*** Hyp. CDA 67276. Plowright, BBC Scottish SO, Brabbins.

The Polish-born, pianist and composer, Zygmunt Stojowski, emigrated to the United States in 1905 where, despite early success, he found his unashamedly romantic style irrevocably overtaken and submerged. Even in Poland he is almost entirely forgotten, but this charming disc of his first two piano concertos demonstrates that such easily fluent, lyrical music has much to offer even today. It is true that none of his thematic material can quite match that of a contemporary like Rachmaninov, whose late-romantic style is similar, but the tunes are there and in brilliant performances like those given by Jonathan Plowright, with warmly committed accompaniment from the BBC Scottish Orchestra, both works are well worth hearing. The structure of the *First Concerto*, written in 1890, is relatively conventional with a delightful central Andante in which the cello and cor anglais are given solo roles alongside the piano, and a '*Dance of Death*' finale. The *Second Concerto*, dating from between 1909 and 1910, is unconventional in its structure – a Prologue, Scherzo and Variations in which the model of Liszt is more striking than in No. 1. The most memorable section is the *Presto Scherzo*, with echoes of Litolff and Saint-Saëns in its galloping rhythms, but until the substantial closing section the final set of variations is rather too full of stopping and starting. Nevertheless this is most enjoyable. Warm, well-balanced recording.

THE STRAUSS FAMILY

Strauss, Johann Sr (1804–49)

Strauss, Johann Jr (1825–99)

Strauss, Josef (1827–70)

Strauss, Eduard (1835–1916)

(all music listed is by Johann Strauss Jr unless otherwise stated)

Arranged ballets

Le beau Danube (ballet; arr. Désormière); *Cinderella (Ashenbrodel)* ballet, revised and edited. Gamley; complete); *Ritter Pásmán* (ballet music).

(B) *** Double Decca (ADD/DDD) 470 522-2 (2). Nat. PO, Bonynge.

Johann Strauss did not live to finish his full-length ballet, *Ashenbrodel*. Most of Act I was completed, but the rest was pieced together and scored by Joseph Bayer; this version has been further revised and edited by Douglas Gamley. Although no masterpiece has been discovered, there is a fair sprinkling of good, if not especially memorable, tunes, felicitously scored, though the most memorable moment is when the *Blue Danube* is quoted as a barrel organ effect, sounding piquantly like an ocarina. The Decca sound is superb and Bonynge does the utmost to engage the listener with stylish, elegant playing.

The *Ritter Pásmán* ballet music has rather more memorable themes, the *Czárdás* especially so. But the best thing here is Désormière's sparklingly entertaining ballet *Le beau Danube* which, apart from that famous waltz, offers less well-known music, all eminently tuneful and brightly scored, and ending in exhilarating fashion. The orchestra plays with enthusiasm and the 1974 sound is strikingly vivid.

New Year Concerts

'New Year's Day concert in Vienna (1979)'. Polkas: *Auf der Jagd* (with encore); *Bitte schön! Leichtes Blut; Pizzicato* (with Josef); *Tik-Tak.* Waltzes: *An der schönen blauen Donau; Bei uns zu Haus; Loreley-Rheine-Klänge; Wein, Weib und Gesang.* JOSEF STRAUSS: *Mouliniet Polka; Die Emanzipierte Polka-Mazurka; Rudolfsheimer-Polka; Sphärenklänge Waltz.* JOHANN STRAUSS SR: *Radetzky March.* E. STRAUSS: *Ohne Bremse Polka.* ZIEHRER: *Herreinspaziert! Waltz.* SUPPE: *Die schöne Galathée Overture.*

(M) *** Decca 468 489-2. VPO, Boskovsky.

Decca chose to record Boskovsky's 1979 New Year's Day concert in Vienna for their very first digital issue on LP. The clarity, immediacy and natural separation of detail are very striking throughout, and the strings

of the Vienna Philharmonic are brightly lit. There is some loss of bloom and not quite the degree of sweetness one would expect today on a record made in the Musikvereinsaal, but the ear soon adjusts. The music-making itself is another matter. It gains much from the spontaneity of the occasion, reaching its peak when the side-drum thunders out the introduction to the closing *Radetzky March*, a frisson-creating moment which, with the audience participation, is quite electrifying. The whole concert is now fitted onto a single mid-priced CD playing for five seconds over 81 minutes.

'1989 New Year Concert in Vienna': Overture: *Die Fledermaus; Ritter Pásmán: Czárdás.* Polkas: *Bauern; Eljen a Magyar; Im Krapfenwald'l; Pizzicato* (with Josef). Waltzes: *Accelerationen; An der schönen blauen Donau (Blue Danube); Bei uns z'Haus; Frühlingsstimmen; Künsterleben.* JOSEF STRAUSS: Polkas: *Jockey; Die Libelle; Moulinet; Plappemäulchen.* JOHANN STRAUSS SR.: *Radetzky March.*

**(*) DG DVD 073 024-9. VPO, Kleiber. (Producer: Horst Bosch. V/D: Brian Large.)

Carlos Kleiber's pursuit of knife-edged precision prevents the results here from sounding quite relaxed enough, although the advantage of the DVD is that being able to watch his flexible and often graceful arm-movements makes his rather precise style with Viennese rhythms easier to accept. Moreover he does relent and produce a meltingly seductive string passage just before the close of the fine but little known waltz, *Bei uns z'Haus* (which had to be omitted on the single-CD version). In the delicious polka, *Im Krapfenwald'l* the cheeky cuckoo-calls which comically punctuate the main theme are made to sound beautiful rather than rustic, and fun is muted elsewhere too. But in one or two numbers Kleiber really lets rip, as in the Hungarian polka, *Eljen a Magyar* and in the *Ritter Pásmán Czárdás.* With well-judged camera-work the viewer is made to feel closely involved with the orchestra's music-making, making this an enjoyably spontaneous concert. The recording is both vivid and warmly atmospheric, although the violin timbre is brightly lit to match Kleiber's style.

'2000 New Year Concert': Csárdás from *Ritter Pásmán:* Csárdás; March: *Persischer.* Polkas: *Albion; Eljen a Magyar; Hellenen; Process; Vom Donaustrande.* Waltzes: *An der schönen blauen Donau; Lagunen; Liebeslieder; Wein; Weib und Gesang.* EDUARD STRAUSS: Polkas: *Mit Extrapost; Gruss an Prag.* JOSEF STRAUSS: Polkas: *Die Libelle; Künstler-Gruss.* Waltz: *Marien-Klänge.* JOHANN STRAUSS SR: *Radetzky March.*

*** EMI **DVD** DVB4 92361-9 (CD version on CDC5 67323-2). VPO, Muti (with SUPPE: Overture: *Morning, Noon and Night in Vienna*).

Like Lorin Maazel before him, Riccardo Muti loses any prickly qualities, concentrating on charm rather than bite, as is obvious from the very opening number in the 2000 concert. The *Lagunen Waltz* of Johann Strauss Jr makes the gentlest possible start, leading to a couple of sparkling novelties, never heard at these concerts before, the brisk *Hellenen Polka* and the feather-light *Albion Polka*, dedicated to Prince Albert. That sets the pattern for the whole programme. For all the brilliance of the playing, it is the subtlety of the Viennese lilt (as in Josef Strauss's *Marien-Klänge*, another novelty) that one remembers, or the breath-taking delicacy of the *pianissimo* which opens the first of the encores, the *Blue Danube*, perfectly caught by the EMI engineers. For its Millennium concert the Vienna Philharmonic could not be more seductive. The two-disc format at mid-price, with the first half shorter than the second, allows the whole programme to be included without cuts.

The performance of Suppé's *Overture: Morning, Noon and Night in Vienna*, played with great spirit, makes an attractive bonus, but it is with the music of the Strauss family that Muti shows himself a true master, and this DVD is one of the most enjoyable of all the recent New Year Concerts. The video opens with a long shot of the Grosse Saal of the Musikverein and then we are soon with Muti and his players who are obviously enjoying themselves, readily sharing this music with the Viennese audience and with us. Two tracks, the *Ritter Pásmán Csárdás* and Josef's *Marien-Klänge Waltz* have optional, fairly unimagi-native ballet sequences provided by members of the Vienna State Opera Ballet, but one can stay with Muti. During the splendid performance of the *Blue Danube*, we are taken on a visual tour of the building, inside and out, and there are other shots of Vienna plus an introduction to those famous Viennese white horses. Muti's New Year speech (in English) is brief and simple and he controls his audience firmly and adeptly in the closing *Radetzky March*.

Einzugsmarsch; Perpetuum mobile; Polka Eljen a Magyar. **Waltzes:** *Accelerationen; An der schönen blauen Donau; Freue euch des Lebens; Frühlingsstimmen; Geschichten aus dem Wienerwald; Kaiser; Künstlerleben; Liebeslieder; Mörgenblätter; Rosen aus dem Süden; Schatzwalzer; Wiener Blut; Wiener Bonbons; Wo die Citronen blüh'n.*

(B) **(*) Erato/Teldec Ultima 3984 21091-2 (2). Vienna Op. O, with Michalski, Falk or Scholz.

These performances date from the late 1980s, though the CD does not tell us who is conducting what. If the collection doesn't boast the luxurious distinction of Boskovsky or Karajan, it has a genuine Viennese spirit, as you would expect from this source. There is a good mixture of familiar and little-known waltzes, enjoyably interspersed with one or two of Strauss's delightful marches and polkas. The acoustic is fairly dry and closely balanced, but it suits these intimate, smaller scale readings, perhaps closer to the original

spirit of the composer's conception. An entertaining and inexpensive collection.

Overtures: *Cagliostro in Wien; Carnival in Rom'; Das Spitentuch der Königin.* **Polkas:** *Banditen; Episode; Explosionen; Express; Grüss aus Osterreich; I-Tipferl; Karnevalotschafter; Karnevalsbilder; Kreuzfidel!; Maskenzug; Im Sturmschritt; Unter Donner und Blitz; Vom Donaustrande.* **Waltzes:** *Accelerationen; An den schönen Blauen Donau; Donauweibchen; Du und Du; Feuilleton; Flugschriften; Gedankenpflug; Geschichten aus dem Wienerwald; Kaiser; Künsterleben; Küss; Lagunen; Leichtes Blut; Die Leitartikel; Morgenblätter; Rosen aus dem Süden; Schatz; Wein, Weib und Gesang; Wiener Blut; Wiener Frauen; Frühlingsstimmen.* EDUARD STRAUSS *Polkas: Alpenrose; Ausser Rand und Band; Faschingsbrief; Mit Vergnügen; Reiselust; Unter der Enns; Wo man Lacht und lebt.*

(B) **(*) EMI CZS 5 74528-2 (5). Johann Strauss O of Vienna, Boskovsky – JOSEF STRAUSS: *Polkas and Waltzes.* ***

Willi Boskovsky's digital re-recordings of many of the best-known Strauss waltzes and polkas were made between 1982 and 1987 with a pick-up orchestra in a Viennese studio, but one with a warmly attractive ambi-ence. The performances are affectionate, lively, idiomatic and well played. With good sound this gener-ous and inexpensive anthology is certainly enjoyable, if for the most part without quite the distinction and sheer character of the conductor's earlier Decca record-ings. There are some attractve novelties too. Why for instance are the three shrewdly chosen novelty waltzes on the fourth disc, *Flugschriften, Gedankenpflug,* and *Die Lietartikel* not better known? Virtually all the Josef Strauss items are on the fifth disc in the box – see below.

Polka: *Pariser.* **Waltz:** *Wiener Blut.* J. STRAUSS SR: **Polkas:** *Eisele und Beisele-Sprünge; Salon.* **Waltz:** *Kettenbrücke;* JOSEPH STRAUSS: **Polka:** *Sehnsucht.*

(BB) **(*) Naxos 8.555689. Vienna Tanzquartett – LANNER: *Polkas & waltzes.* **(*)

The waltzes and polkas of the Strauss family, usually recorded in their full-blown orchestral versions, were more often heard in their day in the countless coffee-houses, restaurants and beer-halls throughout Austria in much smaller arrangements, as recorded here for a string quartet. These are sympathetic performances, which readily evoke nineteenth-century Austria. The waltzes are well contrasted with the polkas (the minor-keyed *Sehnsucht Polka*, a sentimental and charming piece, is a highlight). Perhaps the string tone, alongside the highest standards, isn't as sophis-ticated as it might be, but most importantly, the right style is conveyed. Not perhaps a disc to listen to all in one go, but ideal back-ground or late-night listening. The recording is essentially good, with the slight thin-ness of tone not a serious fault.

Waltzes: *An der schönen blauen Donau; Frühlingstimmem; Geschichten aus dem Wiener Wald; Kaiser; Künsterleben Roses aus dem Süden; Wiener Blut.*

(BB) *** EMI Encore CDE5 75239-2. Vienna Strauss O, Boskovsky.

This 1982 compilation was Boskovsky's most impressive Strauss collection since his Decca era. From the very opening of the *Blue Danube* the playing balances an evocative Viennese warmth with vigour and sparkle. Each performance is freshly minted, rhythmic nuances are flexibly stylish, and the spontaneity is enjoyably obvious. The digital sound is agreeably rich – there is no digital edge on top – yet detail is realistic, within the resonant acoustic. Highly recommendable at its new budget price.

Waltz transcriptions: *Kaiser; Rosen aus dem Süden* (both trans. Schoenberg); ***Schatz Waltz*** (from ***Der Zigeunerbaron;*** trans. Webern); ***Wein, Weib und Gesang*** (trans. Berg).

(M) **(*) DG (ADD) 463 667-2. Boston SO Chamber Players – STRAVINSKY: *Octet for Wind Instruments; Pastorale etc.* ***

A fascinating curiosity. Schoenberg, Berg and Webern made these transcriptions for informal private performances. Schoenberg's arrangements of the *Emperor* and *Roses from the South* are the most striking, though Berg's *Wine, Woman and Song* is sweetly appealing with its scoring for harmonium. As might be expected, Webern's *Schatz Waltz* is aptly refined. With the Boston Chamber Players taking rather too literal a view and missing some of the fun, the lumpishness of some of the writing is evident enough, but the very incongruity and the obvious love of these three severe atonalists for music with which one does not associate them is endearing. The recording and balance are excellent, and remains so in this transfer with its new Stravinsky couplings.

OPERA AND OPERETTA

Die Fledermaus (complete).

(BB) (***) Naxos mono 8.110180/181 (2). Gueden, Lipp, Patzak, Dermota, Poell, Wagner, Preger, Vienna State Op. Ch., VPO, Krauss.
(*) DG **DVD 073 007-9. Coburn, Perry, Fassbaender, Waechter, Brendel, Hopferwieser, Bavarian St Op. Ch. & O, Kleiber. (Director: Otto Schenk.)

Die Fledermaus was one of the first Decca mono sets to show us what operatic treats the LP was to bring, and signalled a breakthrough in the recording of both opera and operetta, freed from the tyranny of the short-playing 78 side. It also demonstrated the extraordinary quality of the Vienna State Opera company in that post-war period, and many would claim that this version of *Fledermaus* has never since been matched, let alone bettered. Clemens Krauss conducts an irresistibly sparkling account of the score

with the starry cast forming a wonderfully co-ordinated ensemble. Hilde Gueden with her golden tones makes a deliciously minxish Roselinde, with a naughty, provocative smile implied, and Julius Patzak as a tenor Eisenstein has never been surpassed, totally idiomatic, well-contrasted with the equally fine Alfred of Anton Dermota. Add to that Wilma Lipp's bright, agile Adele and the firm, clear if very feminine Orlofsky of Sieglinde Wagner. The original snag was the thin violin timbre which became even more 'whistly' in the old Ace of Clubs reissue. Unlike the later CD transfer on Decca's historic label, which still put an unpleasant glassiness on the violins, in the latest Naxos transfer the voices are very well caught, set very much in front of the orchestra and Davis Lennick's remastering tames the sound, even if the violins remain a little fizzy. The Overture is acceptable now (a most vivacious performance) and the voices have striking immediacy, even if a degree of peakiness remains. A treasurable reissue, nevertheless. This is a gramophone classic by any standards.

Recorded live at the Bavarian State Opera in 1987, Carlos Kleiber's film version of *Die Fledermaus* is preferable to his audio recording, also for DG, in fair measure because of the superb assumption of the role of Prince Orlofsky by Brigitte Fassbaender, a fire-eater who makes the most positive host in the party scene of Act 2, singing superbly, where the audio recording has a feeble falsettist. Though Janet Perry's soprano is shallow and bright, she has the agility and sparkle for the role of Adele, with Patricia Coburn as a warm, positive Rosalinde, whooping away persuasively in the waltz numbers, and entering into the spirit of the part, despite a violently unconvincing red wig. Eberhard Waechter sounds too old and unsteady as Eisenstein, and Josef Hopferwieser is also unconvincingly old as the philandering tenor, Alfred, both shown up by the dark firm Alfres Brendel as Falke. As on CD, Kleiber directs a taut performance, which yet has plenty of sparkle, helped by full-bodied sound.

Die Fledermaus (complete, in English).

*** Arthaus **DVD** 100 134 (2). Gustafson, Howarth, Kowalski, Otey, Michaels-Moore, Bottone, ROHCG Ch. & O, Bonynge. (Director: John Cox.)

Lasting well over three and a quarter hours, this version of *Die Fledermaus*, in an English version by John Mortimer, stretches to two DVDs, largely because in this gala performance at Covent Garden on New Year's Eve 1989/90 a half-hour of performances by the 'surprise guests' is included in the party scene: Luciano Pavarotti, Marilyn Horne and – making her farewell to the opera-stage – Dame Joan Sutherland. For Sutherland devotees it is an essential item, with the two duets specially cherishable, the *Semiramide* duet with Horne and *Parigi o cara* from *La Traviata* with Pavarotti.

Under Richard Bonynge's light, beautifully sprung direction, the gala fizzes splendidly with a first-rate cast, even though at the start of Act 2 Falke (Michaels-Moore) unwittingly loses his monocle. The countertenor, Jochen Kowalski, makes a characterful, distinctive Orlofsky with baritone speaking voice contrasted with his singing. Nancy Gustafson is a warm Rosalinde and Judith Howarth a sweet Adele, and the others all sing well, despite the pressure of the occasion.

Valses de Vienne (operetta, arr. Korngold, Bittner & Cools): complete.

(B) ** EMI (ADD) CZS5 74103-2 (2). Mesplé, Sinclair, Stutzmann, Verlen, Gaudin, Loreau, René Duclos Ch., Opéra-Comique Nat. Theatre O, Doussard.

Valses de Vienne is not, of course, an original operetta by Johann Strauss but an arrangement of his music by Erich Korngold, Julius Bittner and others, set to a libretto that is a loosely biographical study of the Strausses, father and son. It was a hit in 1931 and spawned a Hollywood film in 1938 (*The Great Waltz*) as well as a British film by Alfred Hitchcock (*Waltzes from Vienna*). As a confection of the Strauss's music, it works well enough, and its novelty is to present familiar music in unfamiliar settings. This performance is quite a good one, including French operetta stalwarts such as Mady Mesplé. Bernard Sinclair as Johann Strauss Jr shows some strain under pressure, but the rest of the cast is generally rather good. The conducting is sympathetic, and the 1971 recording is fully acceptable, if lacking depth and richness. The voices are clearly recorded. The main snag of this release is that, as usual in this EMI series, there are no texts or translations, nor any documentation in English at all.

STRAUSS, Josef (1827–70)

Josef Strauss: The Complete Edition (continued)

Vol. 21: *Andressy-Marsch* (arr. Pollock). Ländler: *Waldbleamin*. Polkas: *Buchstaben; Flora; Immergrün; Lebensgeister; Steeple Chase.* Quadrilles: *Stegreif; La Périchole.* Waltzes: *Günstige Prognosen; Die Vorgeiger.* Arr. of MENDELSSOHN: *Song without Words No. 1.*

** Marco Polo 8.223 623. Slovak State PO, Dittrich.

Michael Dittrich conducted Volumes 13 and 14 of the Marco Polo Josef Strauss series and he shows here, as he did then, that he is happiest in the polkas – which dominate the present collection – but less imaginative with the waltzes. There are only two of them, neither especially memorable as presented here: *Die Vorgeiger* ('The Leading Violinists') and the appropriately mellow *Favourable Prognosis*, written in 1863 for a medical ball attended by the male students at the University of Vienna (females were not admitted until nearly the turn of the century). Apart from the lively if unsubtle potpourri of tunes from Offenbach's *La Périchole*, the highlights here are the delightful Ländler, *Waldb-*

leamin ('Forest Flowers'), which deserve to be rescued from oblivion, and Josef's charming arrangement of an unidentified *Song without Words* of Mendelssohn.

Vol. 22: *Einzugs-Marsch*. Polkas: *Elfen; Die Kosende; Lock; Patti.* Quadrilles: *Rendezvous; Sofien.* Waltzes: *Flimserin; Die Sonderlinge; Die Veteranen; Die Zufälligen.*

*** Marco Polo 8.223 624. Slovak State PO, Geyer.

There are four fine waltzes here and *Die Veteranen* was dedicated to Field Marshall Count Radetzky, for whom Johann Senior wrote his most famous march. The brassy two-in-a-bar opening is appropriate, and indeed *Die Sonderlinge* and *Die Zufälligen* also have lively introductions not in waltz time. They are both attractive, but the most pleasing of all, *Die Flinserin* ('Sequins'), opens most delicately and has a seductive principal melody. As we have already discovered in Volume 18, Geyer is a much more persuasive exponent of these pieces than many of his colleagues, and each of these waltzes has an agreeable rhythmic lift and lilt, while the polkas and quadrilles also have plenty of life. One of the best discs in the series.

Vol. 23: *Fest-Marsch*. Polkas: *Aus dem Wienerwald; Cabriole; Concordia; Vergissmeinennicht.* Quadrilles: *Crispine; Kadi.* Waltzes: *Heiden-Gedichte; Neue Welt-Bürger; Zeitbilder.*

** Marco Polo 8.223625. Slovak State PO (Košice), Müssauer.

Manfred Müssauer is a promising newcomer, and he directs Volume 23 spiritedly. All three quick-waltzes are fresh and lively, but none is a masterpiece. *Heiden-Gedichte* ('Heroes' Poems') originally had a ceremonial connection, and opens with robust fanfares. Müssauer makes the most of it and provides an effective accelerando at the end. He also brings out the striking contribution of the horns in *Zeitbilder* and we would like to hear him conduct some more seductive waltzes. The opening *Cabriole Polka* is vivacious but here it is the *Quadrilles* which contain the most engaging music. Good playing and recording but none of these pieces show Josef at his best.

Polkas: *Auf Ferienreisen; Buchstaben; Feuerfest; Frauenherz; Im Fluge; Jockey; Ohn Sorgen; Sport; Vorwärts; Die Schwätzerin.* Waltzes: *Aquarellen; Delirien; Dorfschwalben aus Osterreich; Dynamiden; Jockey; Mein Lebenslauf is Lieb' und Lust.*

(B) *** EMI CZS 5 74528-2 (5). Johann Strauss O of Vienna, Boskovsky – JOHANN STRAUSS JNR: *Overtures, Polkas and Waltzes.* **(*)

As always orchestras respond to the lesser-known music of Josef, which at its best can easily match Johann in melodic distinction. All six waltzes included here are delightful and presented with much spirit, finesse and affection, with *Delirien, Dorfschwalben aus Osterreich* and *Dynamiden* standing out. This is the most attractive of the five CDs in EMI's reissued Strauss box and it ought to be available separately.

STRAUSS, Richard (1864–1949)

An Alpine Symphony, Op. 64; Also sprach Zarathustra, Op. 64.

*** EMI (ADD) **Audio DVD** DVC4 92396-9. Dresden State O, Kempe.

The *Alpine Symphony* has all the rhetoric, confidence and opulence of the great Strauss tone poems, and if its melodic invention is not up to the best of them, its visual imagination more than compensates when the performance and recording are as good as this. Kempe brings a glowing warmth and humanity to the score and there is no doubt that in his hands it sounds a greater work than it is. He moulds each phrase with great sensitivity and life, observing all the pictorial detail yet retaining a strong sense of forward movement. The Dresden Orchestra is a magnificent body here at its finest and producing a rich, cultured yet essentially vital playing throughout. The 1971 EMI recording was made in quadraphony and is sensational in this Audio DVD transfer, offered either in high resolution stereo or multi-channel surround sound. There is remarkable depth and splendid detail; although the upper strings date the sound just a little, the horns and heavy brass are superb and the concert hall illusion is remarkable.

Also sprach Zarathustra is transferred at a somewhat lower level, no doubt to encompass the huge expansion of dynamic at the opening, with the organ pedal becoming almost overwhelming. The contrasting gentle string passage that follows is wonderfully mellow yet radiant. Kempe's performance is always convincingly paced, and the strings produce a sumptuous tone throughout. The work's climax, with its tolling bell, expands magnificently. A superb reissue in every way.

An Alpine Symphony; Don Juan; Der Rosenkavalier Waltzes.

✪ (BB) (***) Dutton CDBP 9720. Bav. State O, Composer

When in the past Richard Strauss's own recording of *An Alpine Symphony*, made in Munich in 1941, has appeared on disc, the sound has been scrubby and barely tolerable. This transfer in the Dutton bargain series is quite different, bringing out the sensuousness of this evocative score, so that one can wallow in its beauty and richness just as one would with the latest digital recording. This opulent piece is presented unapologetically with an unmatched fervour that bears witness to what many have said, that Strauss was not just a great composer but one of the outstanding conductors of his time. The sumptuousness, with glorious horns and trombones standing out, even makes one wonder how far he observed his often-quoted instruction to would-be conductors that you must never look at the brass, as it would encourage them!

Also sprach Zarathustra – see also under *Four Last Songs.*

Horn Concertos Nos. 1 in E flat, Op. 11; 2 in E flat.

✪ (M) (***) EMI mono CDM5 67782-2 [Angel 5 67782 2 o]. Brain, Philh. O, Sawallisch – HINDEMITH: *Horn Concerto; Concert Music.* ***

Dennis Brain's performances are incomparable and almost certainly will never be surpassed. Sawallisch gives him admirable support, and fortunately the latest EMI CD transfer captures the full quality of the 1956 mono recording. This coupling certainly deserves a place among EMI's 'Great Recordings of the Century' and for the reissue an extra Hindemith work has been added.

Divertimento (after Couperin) for Small Orchestra, Op. 86.

(BB) *** Warner Apex 7559 79675-2. NYCO, Schwarz – SCHOENBERG: *Concerto for String Quartet & Orchestra after Handel.* ***

Strauss's *Divertimento* draws on sixteen of the keyboard pieces of François Couperin and scores them for small orchestra. The result is expressive, witty and tangy by turns in this very spirited account by the New York Chamber Orchestra under Gerard Schwarz. With vivid recordings and an unexpectedly entertaining Schoenberg/Handel coupling, this is well worth exploring.

Don Quixote.

(M) **(*) Ph. 470 250-2 (2). Schiff, Leipzig Gewandhaus O, Masur – DVORAK: *Cello Concerto;* PROKOFIEV: *Sinfonia concertante;* SCHUMANN: *Cello Concerto.* **(*)

Beautifully recorded in the glowing Leipzig acoustic, the Schiff/Masur account has much going for it, with superb orchestral playing to match the dedication and care for detail from Schiff himself. But yet his portrayal of the Don, eloquent as it is, has a missing dimension, a lack of passion, no feeling of recklessness. Even so there is much to enjoy, both from soloist and the orchestra, but this would not be a primary recommendation.

Till Eulenspiegel (Rehearsal).

*(*) Arthaus **DVD** 100 286 Israel PO, Mehta (rehearsal only)

Here is Zubin Mehta rehearsing (but not performing) Strauss's *Till* with the Israel Philharmonic who have – incredibly – not played it since the war for political reasons. Strauss's political record during the war is well documented (see Michael Kennedy's masterly biography – OUP, 1999) when the composer had to protect his Jewish daughter-in-law and his two half-Jewish grandsons. But so often judgements rest on prejudice rather than knowledge and reason as Barenboim discovered when he tried to conduct the *Prelude to Tristan* in Israel. Mehta takes the players through this wonderful score which is (naturally enough) unfamiliar to them as orchestral musicians, and virtually teaches them. Mehta has both tact and charm, and gets a good response even when the players show boredom (the clarinet impatiently watches the time). Generally speaking Mehta tells you nothing you don't already know and the 55 minutes of rehearsal does not lead to a performance. Were we observing a great orchestra unfamiliar with this classic, going through their paces in a complete performance it would be another matter, but as it is there seems little point in this exercise. The camera work is perfectly well managed as indeed is the sound.

CHAMBER MUSIC

Cello Sonata in F, Op. 6; Romance in F.

(BB) *** Arte Nova 74321 87072-2. Guido Schiefen, Olaf Dressler – PFITZNER: Sonata. ***

The Strauss Cello Sonata in F, Op. 6 is well represented on CD though the Romance, which did not appear in print until 1987, exists in only one alternative disc. Even if there were many, this performance would be difficult to beat. These fine artists play with sensitivity and musicianship. Neither are well known outside Germany but perhaps this welcome issue will help to do so. The recording made in the studios of Bayerischer Rundfunk is superbly balanced and very lifelike.

VOCAL MUSIC

(i) Four Last Songs. Orchestral Lieder: Befreit; Morgen; Muttertändelei; Ruhe meine Seele; Wiegenlied; Zueignung. (ii) Also sprach Zarathustra.

(M) **(*) Sony SMK 89881. (i) Kanawa; LSO, A. Davis; (ii) Tilson Thomas.

Dame Kiri Te Kanawa gives an open-hearted, warmly expressive reading of the Four Last Songs. If she misses the sort of detail that Schwarzkopf uniquely brought, her commitment is never in doubt. Her tone is consistently beautiful, but might have seemed even more so if the voice had not been placed rather too close in relation to the orchestra. The orchestral arrangements of the other songs make an excellent coupling and Andrew Davis directs most sympathetically. No complaints about the balance in Also sprach Zarathustra which has a fine concert hall layout producing lustrous strings and sonorous brass. The LSO again plays very well indeed and this makes a generous (if hardly apt) bonus, even if the performance does not quite maintain the intensity of the Kempe and Karajan versions.

OPERA

Arabella (complete).

*** DG DVD 073 005-9. Te Kanawa, Wolfgang Brendel, McLaughlin, Dessay, Kuebler, Dernesch, McIntyre, Met.

Op. Ch. and O, Thielemann. (Producer: Otto Schenk. V/D: Brian Large.)

It would be hard to think of a starrier line-up of soloists for Arabella than in this live account, recorded at the Met in New York in November 1994. One of the great strengths of the production is the conducting of Christian Thielemann, who was then just emerging as a new star among Strauss conductors. He is at once thrustful and emotional, drawing ripe sounds from the orchestra.

Dame Kiri Te Kanawa gives a convincing dramatic account of the title role and is in glorious voice, producing ravishing sounds in her big numbers, even more charming when observed in close-up. She obviously relishes the sumptuous production, which is as traditional as could be, with grandly realistic sets by Gunther Schneider-Siemssen. The stage direction is by Otto Schenk, who shows appropriate respect for Hoffmansthal and Strauss's wishes, and the intelligence of the public.

The Mandryka of Wolfgang Brendel carries conviction even if he looks somewhat older than he should (mid-thirties). His voice is strong, firm and unstrained in a rather intimidating yet ultimately vulnerable characterization, and Marie McLaughlin is poignantly convincing as Zdenka, the younger sister forced to adopt the role of boy. Donald McIntyre and Helga Dernesch are vivldy characterful as Arabella's parents, and in the second act Natalie Dessay as the Fiakermilli is full of character, and she makes much of her brief appearance at the ball, bright and brilliant in her showpiece.

The balance favours the voices and not all the wealth of orchestral detail registers, but the recording is aptly rich and full-bodied. The visual side of the production is first rate (and a great improvement on the Laserdisc). As usual Brian Large's camera is pointing exactly where one wants it to point. On the videotape there were no subtitles at all, and on the LaserDisc there were English subtitles which could not be removed. Here not only are there subtitles in English, French and Mandarin, but the original Hofmannsthal text is also accessible. Strongly recommended.

Ariadne auf Naxos (complete).

*** DG 471 323-2 (2). Voigt, Dessay, Von Otter, Heppner, Dohmen, Dresden State O, Sinopoli.

(BB) *** Arte Nova 74321 77073-2 (2). Wachutka, Woodrow, Komlosi, Kutan, San Carlo, Naples O, Kuhn.

(***) Arthaus DVD 100 170. Susan Anthony, Martinez, Koch, Villars. Junge, Adam, Semper Oper Ch., Dresden State O, C. Davis. (Producer: Marco Arturo Marelli. V/D: Felix Breisach.)

It is good to have a really outstanding new set of Ariadne auf Naxos. While the Schwarzkopf/Karajan version reigns supreme for those willing to accept less expansive mono recording (EMI CMS5 67077-2), Sinopoli now offers a strong alternative with modern digital sound. Recorded in the warm acoustic of the Lukaskirche in Dresden, Sinopoli's version offers an opulent view of this most delicate of the Strauss operas. The full-bodied sound goes with an outstandingly strong and characterful cast with no weak link. In the *Prologue* Anne Sofie von Otter is at once tender and vulnerable as the Composer. Encouraged by Sinopoli she brings out an urgently volatile element in the character, leading up to the passionate outburst of the closing solo glorifying this *heilige Kunst*, 'the Holy Art of music'. Deborah Voigt brings power as well as warmth and flexibility to the role of Ariadne, and Natalie Dessay as Zerbinetta is similarly commanding and characterful, even if both of them have their moments of edginess. Ben Heppner is a superb Bacchus, both pure and heroic with no hint of strain, and one big benefit of a studio recording is that the harlequinade ensembles are so light and crisp.

However, the modestly priced Arte Nova version can also be strongly recommended, offering a warmly enjoyable live recording made at the San Carlo operahouse in Naples in February 2000. With Gustav Kuhn an urgent Straussian, this is a passionate and persuasive reading, very well recorded, if with occasional stage noises. The cast is a strong one, with Elisabeth-Marie Wachutka outstanding as Ariadne, sweet and pure over the widest range, and bringing girlish passion to the role, culminating in a heartwarming account of Ariadne's final solo in response to Bacchus, the excellent clear-voiced Alan Woodrow. Aline Kutan is a similarly impressive Zerbinetta, matching more starry rivals, brilliant in coloratura with a winning sparkle. Though the harlequinade characters are inevitably less polished in their ensembles than in a studio recording, the fun of the piece comes over well, as well as the atmospheric beauty of the Naiads' music. The one snag is the miscasting of Ildiko Komlosi as the Composer. It is a rich, warm contralto rather than a mezzo, satisfying enough vocally except under pressure, but too feminine for this trouser role. Yet the thrust of a live performance makes this a highly competitive version at super-budget price. The German libretto is included but, alas, no translation.

We are at odds about the Arthaus Ariadne auf Naxos, recorded live at the Semper Oper in Dresden. R.L. feels that for most collectors it will be a complete turn-off. The setting is in a present-day museum of modern art whose visitors wander in an out of the gallery throughout the whole opera to mightily distracting effect. It contributes nothing to an opera whose creators knew what they were doing. They were masters of their art and in no need of 'interpretation' from an attention-seeking director.

The performance is not particularly distinguished vocally either, save for Sophie Koch's Composer. The best of the others are John Villars's Bacchus and Theo Adam's Music Master, and the orchestra make a pretty sumptuous sound under Sir Colin Davis. The intrusive silliness of the production makes it difficult to sit through this performance once, let alone a second time!

E.G. on the other hand feels that Sir Colin Davis, at his most inspired, directs a glowing performance with a cast of young singers who respond superbly, both to the conducting and to the imaginative stage direction of Marco Arturo Marelli. The Prologue, updated to the twentieth century, takes you behind the scenes of an impromptu theatre, with a piano centre-stage and with a washroom half visible behind.

The costumes, also designed by Marelli, add to the atmosphere of fantasy. The Composer, characterfully sung by Sophie Koch, heartfelt in the final solo, rightly provides the central focus, with his new passion for Zerbinetta well established. The main opera follows without an interval. The scene is neatly changed before our eyes to a picture gallery during a private view.

The composer (silent in this half) again provides a focus, with Ariadne and the others performing the opera as an impromptu charade. Central to the performance's success is the radiant singing of Susan Anthony as Ariadne with her firm, creamily beautiful voice. The sparky Zerbinetta of Iride Martinez, vivaciously Spanish-looking, unashamedly shows off in her big aria, both vocally in her dazzling coloratura and in her acting.

Jon Villars is a powerful, unstrained Bacchus in the final scene, with the commedia dell'arte characters all very well taken too. Though this is not as starry a cast as some, it is unusually satisfying, with no weak link. Clear, full-bodied sound, and, as in other Arthaus operas, a helpful booklet is provided.

Your Editor had not better enter the fray, as he hates almost all modern opera productions which make a time-change, and do not follow the original intentions of the composer and librettist. Readers can make up their own minds as to whose side they are on.

Elektra (complete).

*** Arthaus **DVD** 100 048. Marton, Fassbaender, Studer, King, Grundheber, V. St. Op. Ch. & O, Abbado.

Eva Marton recorded *Elektra* with Wolfgang Sawallisch in 1990, but the present account comes from a Vienna performance of the preceding year with Abbado conducting. It appeared on laser disc on the Pioneer label in 1993 and now makes a welcome appearance on DVD. A direct comparison between LD and DVD is definitely in the latter's favour: although the sound is equally good in both, the aural image is just that bit firmer and more finely focused even than on LD.

The performance has enormous intensity: both Marton's Elektra and Fassbaender's Klytemnestra stay long in the memory, and all the remaining characters are triumphantly realized, not least Franz Grundheber's blood-thirsty Orest. Marton makes the most of the intent, obsessive, powerfully demonic Elektra and has enormous dramatic presence.

Harry Kupfer's production is gripping. The setting is dark though not quite as dismal as Götz Friedrich's 1981 production with Rysanek and Varnay under Boehm on a Decca LD. Musically, this is an exciting and concentrated account, and the camera is musically handled by Brian Large. He has an unerring feel for directing our attention where it needs to be. Unlike the unsubtitled LD, the present issue offers subtitles in English and French as well as the original German, and many collectors will feel that this is an essential acquisition, alongside the Sinopoli CD set (DG 453 429-2; see our main volume).

Friedenstag (complete).

*** DG 464 494-2. Voigt, Dohmen, Reiter, Martinsen, Dresden State Op. Ch. & State O, Sinopoli.

The great merit of the DG version of this impractical but richly moving one-Acter is the passionate conducting of Giuseppe Sinopoli, helped by opulent sound to bring out the glories of the orchestral writing for an outsize band. The chorus plays a vital part too, and the performance builds up to a deeply satisfying account of the big final ensemble. The solo singing may not quite match that on Sawallisch's EMI version, which remains first choice (CDC5 56850-2), but the team is a strong one, with Deborah Voigt commanding as Maria, the Commandant's wife, readily dominant when she needs to be, even if the voice goes sour at times. Albert Dohmen is strong and thoughtful as her husband, and the others make a good team, if none is outstanding, adding up to a richly enjoyable experience.

Der Rosenkavalier: complete.

☀ *** DG DVD 073 008-9 (2). Lott, Von Otter, Bonney, Moll, Hornik, V. St. Op. Ch. & O, Kleiber. (Producer: Otto Schenck. V/D: Horant Hohlfeld.)

(M) ** DG (ADD) 463 668-2 (3). Schech, Seefried, Streich, Böhme, Fischer-Dieskau, Unger, Wagner, Dresden State Op. Ch., Saxon State O, Dresden, Boehm.

This celebrated DG DVD production, recorded in Vienna in March 1994, appeared on videotape and laser disc the following year. Carlos Kleiber has spoken of Felicity Lott as his ideal Marschallin, and she is probably currently as unrivalled in this role as was Schwarzkopf in the 1950s. She does not wear her heart on her sleeve, and her reticence makes her all the more telling and memorable.

The other roles are hardly less distinguished, with Anne Sofie von Otter's Octavian splendidly characterized and boyish, while Barbara Bonney's Sophie floats her top notes in the Presentation of the Rose scene with great poise and impressive accuracy. Kurt Moll's Ochs, a splendidly three-dimensional and subtle reading, is one of the highlights of the performance.

Otto Schenck's production deserves the praises that have been lavished on it, and Rudolf Heinrich's sets are handsome. Carlos Kleiber gets some ravishing sounds from the Vienna Philharmonic, and his reading of the score is as Straussian and as perfect as you are likely to encounter in this world. It is even finer than the version he did in Munich in 1979 with Dame Gwyneth Jones as the Marschallin, Fassbaender as Octavian and Popp, which was issued on video and laser disc and which will presumably find its way onto DVD in the fullness of time.

The sound is very natural and lifelike, not too forward, and with a good perspective. On the video there were no subtitles, although they were on laser disc. Things look up here, as not only are subtitles given in English, French and Mandarin but Hofmannsthal's original is also available.

There is much that is very good indeed about the Boehm Dresden performance. Yet here is undoubtedly a set that elusively fails to add up to the sum of its parts. It is partly Boehm's inability to generate the sort of power and emotional tension that are so overwhelming in the Karajan/Schwarzkopf set on EMI. More importantly, the Feldmarschallin of Marianne Schech is decidedly below the level set by Seefried as Octavian and Streich as Sophie. Schech just does not have the strength of personality that is needed if the opera's dramatic point is to strike home. We cannot feel the full depth of emotion involved in her great renunciation from the performance here. Kurt Böhme is a fine Ochs and the recording is appropriately rich, but in almost every way the EMI set provides a more convincing experience – and how fine that is.

STRAVINSKY, Igor (1882–1971)

Apollo (ballet; complete); (i) *Capriccio for Piano and Orchestra; Le chant de rossignol; Circus Polka;* (ii) *Concerto for Piano and Wind;* (iii) *Violin Concerto. Petrushka* (complete; original (1911) ballet); *Symphony in E flat, Op 1; Symphony in C; Symphony in Three Movements;* (iv) *Symphony of Psalms;* (iv; v) *Oedipus Rex.*

(B) ** Chan. 6654 (5). SRO, Järvi, with (i) Tozer: (ii) Berman; (iii) Mordkovitch; (iv) Chamber Ch., Lausanne Pro Art Ch., Société Ch. de Brassus; (v) Schnaut, Svensson, Amoretti, Grundheber, Kannen, Rosen, Plat.

Neeme Järvi offers typically red-blooded readings in his five-disc collection of symphonies, concertos and ballets, plus *Oedipus Rex.* His performances do not always have the refinement and sharpness of focus that one ideally wants, but the thrust of the music comes over convincingly, even if some of the slow movements – as in the *Symphony in Three Movements* – grow curiously stodgy rhythmically at relatively slow speeds. However, the *Violin Concerto* is beautifully played by the warm-toned Lydia Mordkovitch, with the romantic expressiveness of the two central *Arias* an apt counterpart to the vigour and panache of the outer movements. The string playing in *Apollo* has plenty of warmth, and Järvi's vivid *Petrushka* is particularly winning. Using the 1911 score he finds an attractive sparkle at the opening and in the *Shrovetide Fair,* with the *Russian Dance* given a superb bounce. Some of the subtlety of Stravinsky's scoring in the central tableaux may be missing, but such characterful playing is most attractive, both here and in the *Circus Polka* on the same disc. Generally speaking the symphonies and concertos are all very successful in their outer movements and disappointing in their slow ones, and both Geoffrey Tozer and Boris Berman are convincingly muscular soloists in the two concertante works with piano. The performance of the youthful *Symphony*, Op. 1 is particularly convincing in its warmth and thrust. *Oedipus Rex*, with a good narrator in Jean Piat, receives the same sort of full-blooded approach, but the cast is uneven, with Gabriele Schnaut wobbly and shrill as Jocasta and with pianissimos sadly lacking, partly a question of recording balance. The sound throughout the five discs is generally warm and full, although the resonance means that inner detail often lacks sharpness of focus, and in the *Symphony of Psalms* the chorus is rather backwardly balanced. The texts for the vocal items are not included, but these CDs remain individually available at mid-price (including texts where applicable).

(i) Apollo; Dumbarton Oaks Concerto; Concerto in D; (ii) Le chant de rossignol; Symphony in C; Symphony in Three Movements.

(BB) *(*) Virgin VBD5 62022-2 (2). Saraste with (i) Scottish CO; (ii) Finnish Rad. SO.

There is nothing really wrong with the Scottish performances but, on the other hand, there is nothing especially brilliant about them either. The Scottish Chamber Orchestra offer some impressive and sometimes beautiful playing in *Apollo*, but in some of the slow sections of the score the tension is not well maintained. The neo-classical *Concertos* are quite lively, but their effect is dampened down by the rather over reverberant acoustic. *Le chant de rossignol*, which opens the Finnish CD, is played with considerable finesse, but here the sound is undistinguished with a limited dynamic range, the bright orchestral colours blunted by the flat, under-recorded sound. The two *Symphonies* suffer much the same fate.

Violin Concerto in D.

(M) *** DG (ADD) 463 666-2. Schneiderhan, Czech PO, Ančerl – SHOSTAKOVICH: *Symphony No. 10 in E min., Op. 93* (***).

*** Sony SK 89649. Hahn, ASMF, Marriner – BRAHMS: *Violin Concerto*. ***

Schneiderhan is just the man to bring out the work's neo-classicism and his sprightly playing in the outer movement is contrasted with a touch of restraint in the cantilena of the central *Arias*, which are nevertheless shaped most sensitively. The performance, dating from 1962, projects splendidly in this new Originals transfer, which is both warm and full, and the excellent support the soloist receives from Ančerl is an important factor. The coupling – the main work on this CD – is quite superb.

The opening of Hilary Hahn's reading of the Stravinsky *Concerto* is the more striking in its power because of the close balance of the violin, intensifying the impact of the very fast tempo she adopts. Her playing is phenomenal in its precision, but anyone used to more conventional readings such as Mullova's or, in particular, Chung's, will find it sounding very hectic, rather lacking in the rhythmic bounce which

can so readily warm this neoclassical writing. Hahn's reading of the finale brings a similarly urgent speed, again intensifying the power of the work, but with little of its geniality conveyed. It is certainly a valid view, but will not please everyone used to other readings. Hahn, needless to say, in the two arias brings out the full meditative depth of the music. The result is to underline the toughness of the work, making it more clearly an apt coupling for the epic Brahms *Concerto*, plainly as she intends.

Concerto for Strings in D.

(B) *** Arte Nova 74321 86236-2 Basle CO, Hogwood – HONEGGER: *Symphony No. 4*; MARTINU: *Toccata e due canzoni*. ***

Sir John Barbirolli and the Hallé Orchestra premiered the Stravinsky *Concerto* almost immediately after it first appeared on two HMV plum-label 78 rpm discs (now available on Dutton Laboratories CDSJB 1999). The Basle Orchestra is splendidly alert and vital, and though the Concerto is well served on CD, theirs is a very lively and satisfying version and the balance is excellently judged. Well worth the modest outlay involved.

Complete ballets: The Firebird; Petrushka; The Rite of Spring; Fireworks; Scherzo fantastique.

(B) * Erato/Teldec Ultima 0630 18964-2 (2). Philh. O, Inbal.

This Ultima CD is a non-starter. With the three main ballets generating a very low voltage, and smooth rather than vivid sound, there is little drama and excitement to be found here. Imbal's very metrical view of the *Rite* may be valid in principle, but the music sounds too safe in practice. Not recommended.

(i)The Firebird; (ii) Pulcinella (complete ballets).

** Arthaus DVD 100 130 (i) Hønningen, Jeppesen, Damsgaard, Royal Danish Ballet; Royal Danish O, Jørgensen, Glen Tetley, Choreography, Dir. Grimm. (ii) Scapino Ballet, NOS choreography, Christe, Berganza, Davies, Shirley-Quirk, LSO, Abbado. Dir. Hullscher.

The performance of *Firebird* comes from a production mounted in Copenhagen in 1982, the centenary of Stravinsky's birthday, with choreography by Glen Tetley. The principals and in particular the Firebird of Mette Hønningen are excellent, as are the *corps de ballet* and the excellent Royal Danish Orchestra under Poul Jørgensen give a good account of the score. Glen Tetley's choreography will interest his many admirers and is undoubtedly inventive. Others may find it wanting in atmosphere and the fact that the Firebird herself is on stage at the very beginning makes a nonsense of her entry. The *Pulcinella* comes from a 1988 Dutch TV broadcast which uses Abbado's commercial record with the LSO and not live musicians. All the same this is colourful and entertaining, and offers some fine dancing from the company. Nils Christe worked for many years with the celebrated Nederlands Dans Theater before becoming a director of the Scapino Ballet of Rotterdam. Of the two, he comes closer to the spirit of the score. As far as *Firebird* is concerned, Arthaus has announced (as we go to press) that they are releasing the Royal Ballet's version coupled with *Les noces* with Nijinska's original choreography, together with attractive bonuses: Stravinsky himself conducting the *Firebird Suite* with the BBC Symphony Orchestra at the Festival Hall and rehearsal material from the Royal Ballet.

Petrushka (1911 original version)

(M) (***) Somm mono SOMMCD 027. SRO, Ansermet – ROSSINI: *La boutique fantasque.* *** ◐

(M) * Westminster mono 471 245-2. RPO, Scherchen – HONNEGER: *Chant de joie; Pacific 231, etc.* *(*)

In November 1949, when Ansermet's ffrr Decca recording of *Petrushka* was made, the Suisse Romande Orchestra was in better shape than when he made his stereo Stravinsky discs in the later 1950s. It was among the first LPs IM and EG acquired and was much admired at the time. Listening to it again in David Henning's excellent new transfer, one rediscovers why it was long considered a classic recording. Overall the performance, besides being better played, is more gutsy than Ansermet's later stereo version. Its strikingly vivid quality and sense of the dramatic is brought about by everthing being sharply focused in strong primary colours, a tribute to the engineering as well as the performance. The second tableau, with its trumpet and drum duet, glitters with colour and it is only the inherent thinness in the upper range of the violins that gives cause for complaint.

With a sprinkling of Scherchen eccentricities to remind one who is at the helm, it is hard to recommend his otherwise rather flaccid 1954 account to the general collector with so many excellent and less idiosyncratic performances available.

(i) Petrushka (1911 score): complete; (ii) The Rite of Spring.

(BB) ** RCA 74321 68020-2. RPO, Temirkanov.

There is nothing intrinsically wrong with Yuri Temirkanov's 1988 readings of these two masterful scores – they are well played and well recorded – but there is nothing especially outstanding about them either. *Petrushka* lacks the character of the best performances, and although there is some nice detail in *The Rite*, it lacks the sheer overwhelming impact that the score should generate.

Symphony in 3 Movements.

*(*) Arthaus DVD 100 320. Bavarian RSO, Solti – BRUCKNER: *Symphony No. 3.* *(*)

In this Bavarian Radio recording on DVD of the Stravinsky *Symphony in Three Movements* there is nothing light or witty in Solti's approach to this neoclassical work. The first movement is heavy and chunky, made to seem unremitting and abrasive, with jagged rhythms underlined. Even in the central Andante, again on the slow side, Solti is too heavy, and in the finale, again jagged and relentless, there is

none of the tongue-in-cheek quality which lead the composer to end on a jazz chord. Textures are clear, with the important piano and harp parts – the players credited – brought out both aurally and visually. What cannot be denied is the power of Solti's reading and the brilliance of the orchestral playing.

CHAMBER MUSIC

Concertino for 12 Instruments; Octet for Wind Instruments; Pastorale for Violin & Wind Quartet; Ragtime for 11 Instruments.

(M) *** DG (ADD) 463 667-2. Boston SO Chamber Players – J. STRAUSS: *Waltz Transcriptions.* **(*)

The *Pastorale*, a vocalise for voice and piano, is an early piece, written in 1907, which Stravinsky arranged for Samuel Dushkin in 1934. All these pieces are musically rewarding and full of Stravinsky's wit and intelligence, and they are given exemplary performances by this distinguished group. The recording too, lively and well-detailed, comes up well in its new Originals transfer.

OPERA

The Rake's Progress (complete).

Arthaus DVD 100 254. Upshaw, Hadley, Pederson, Henschel, Banks, Ormison, Best, Tuff, V. State Op. Ch., Camerata Academica, Cambreling. Producer: Mussbach; Video producer: Large.

In addition to the composer's own version (Sony SM2K 46299), there are two recommendable *Rakes* on CD, the Kent Nagano version on Erato (0630 12715-2) with Dawn Upshaw and Jerry Hadley, who appear in this 1996 production staged at the Salzburg Festival, and the recent Gardiner set on DG (459 648-2). The present production is highly intrusive and more concerned with presenting the 'ideas' of Peter Mussbach than offering a straightforward account of Stravinsky's score. Nick Shadow has a checker board painted on one side of his face, is dressed in jeans and the other accoutrements of the modern-day lout. Shadow arrives in a cardboard aeroplane which remains on stage – and so on! There is some good playing from the pit and the singers do their best, but, as so often with going to the opera these days, you are far better off with any of the CDs and the theatre of the imagination. Not recommended and no stars!

SUK, Josef (1874–1935)

4 Pieces for Violin and Piano, Op.17.

(BB) (***) Dutton mono CDBP 9710. G. Neveu, J. Neveau – BRAHMS: *Violin Concerto in D, Op. 77;* RAVEL: *Tzigane; Encores.* (***)

Ginette Neveu's fiery temperament is shown at its most compelling in these lively genre pieces by Josef Suk with the closing moto perpetuo *Burleska* scintillating on her nimble bow. Her brother Jean accompanies attentively and the recording sounds most real and present in this first-class Dutton transfer.

About Mother (O matince), Op. 28; Moods (Nálady), Op. 18; 6 Pieces, Op. 7.

(BB) **(*) Naxos 8.553762. Lauriala.

Although we associate Suk more with large-scale orchestral canvases, like *Asrael* and *A Fairy-Tale*, his piano music is also of the highest quality, as readers who have sampled the two-CD set made by Margaret Fingerhut on Chandos, which includes Op. 7 and Op. 28, will know. The Finnish pianist Risto Lauriala has a strong affinity with this music and gives a sympathetic account of the five pictures, Op. 28, *O matince (About Mother)*, composed for Suk's son in 1907, two years after Otilie's death. The recording is generally well balanced if a little close, so that there is a touch of glare in fortissimo passages.

SULLIVAN, Arthur (1842–1900)

Overtures: (i; iii) *The Gondoliers*; (ii) *HMS Pinafore*; (i; iii) *Iolanthe*; (i; iv) *Patience*; (i; iii) *The Mikado*; *The Pirates of Penzance*; (i; iv) *Princess Ida*; (ii) *Ruddigore* (2 versions); (i; iii) *The Yeomen of the Guard*; *Di Ballo*.

**(*) TER CDVIR 8316. (i) D'Oyly Carte Op.; (ii) New Sadler's Wells Op. O, Phipps; (iii) Pryce-Jones; (iv) Edwards.

The majority of Sullivan's overtures are not original compositions, but arrangements by the hands of others, though are all enjoyable pots-pourris of Sullivan's splendid tunes. These recordings are taken from TER's excellent complete opera recordings, and in that context they are enjoyable and offer very good sound. However, collected together in this way, with some of the tempi on the slow side, they sometimes lack the sparkle that brings out the full exhilaration of the music; *Di Ballo* is rather heavy going here too. The orchestral playing is very good. However, those who must have everything of Sullivan available will enjoy two versions of the *Ruddigore* overture.

ORATORIO

The Golden Legend.

**(*) Hyp. 2 x 1 CDA 67280 (2). Watson, Rigby, Wilde, Brown, Black, L. Ch., New L. O, Corp.

Following up his earlier successes in reviving Victorian and Edwardian favourites, Ronald Corp here tackles what was once Sullivan's most popular choral work. Appearing in 1886, *The Golden Legend*, based on a Longfellow poem, promptly overtook *Elijah* as the second most popular oratorio in Britain, with only Handel's *Messiah* clocking up more performances. Certainly the opening is most striking, quite

unlike what one would expect of the composer of the Savoy operettas, with unaccompanied chimes that anticipate the opening of Puccini's *Suor Angelica*, leading almost at once into storm music that owes much to Wagner's *Flying Dutchman*.

The prologue finds Lucifer and his minions at the height of the storm seeking to tear down the cross from Strasburg Cathedral, but then the bold musical gestures evaporate, with the writing for chorus surprisingly tame, punctuating the plot with set-piece anthems like the evening hymn, *O Gladsome Light*, sung unaccompanied. By contrast the orchestral writing is bright, colourful and imaginative. Sullivan's portrayal of the fiendish Lucifer is then relatively mild; he introduces him over tripping rhythms closer to Wagner's music for the Apprentices in *Meistersinger* than to anything devilish. Nonetheless, the free lyricism of the writing carries one along very agreeably, even if one misses the sort of tunes the composer so consistently provided for his operettas. Whatever its shortcomings, *The Golden Legend* will delight anyone wanting to get to know the Sullivan outside the operettas. The Victorian soppiness of the story remains a barrier, with Elsie's prayer glutinous in its sentiment, as she prepares to sacrifice her life for that of the Prince. She even likens herself, almost blasphemously, to Christ, aiming to 'more nearly dying thus, resemble Thee'.

Ronald Corp draws alert playing and singing from the chorus and orchestra, but sadly, in the casting of soloists there is a serious flaw. Jeffrey Black's portrayal of Lucifer – the only soloist in the Prologue – brings strained and ill-focused singing, with the very pitch in doubt. Things improve in the less sustained writing, but one longs to hear a good, firm, dark-toned baritone in this music. Happily, the other principals are all first-rate, not just Janice Watson as the heroine, Elsie and Jean Rigby as Ursula, her mother, but Mark Wilde as Prince Henry, with his clear, unforced, distinctive tenor.

OPERA

The Gondoliers (complete; without dialogue).

(BB) (***) Naxos mono 8.110196/7. Green, Osborn, Styler, Mitchell, Harding, Dean, Wright, Goodier, Watson, Halman, D'Oyly Carte Op. Ch., New Promenade O, Godfrey.

This vintage *Gondoliers* from the D'Oyly Carte Decca mono era was recorded in 1950, the same year as the similarly excellent *Mikado*. Although originally issued on shellac, both were to be highlights of the early LP catalogue. Even though Decca only gave him a small orchestra, noticeably thin on strings, Godfrey conducts with verve throughout, and he has a splendid cast. Apart from the inimitable Martyn Green as the recalcitrant Duke of Plaza Toro, admirably partnered by Ella Halman as the Duchess, there is a strong Don Alhambra in Richard Watson.

The two Gondolieri, Leonard Osborn and Alan Styler, are perfectly cast and if Osborn (as usual at this period) sounds a bit strained in his higher register, his 'Sparkling Eyes' is still very spirited. The younger women are uniformly good. Margaret Mitchell is a strong Casilda, and Tessa's *When a merry maiden marries*, nicely sung by Yvonne Dean, is as charming as Gianetta's *Kind Sir, you cannot have a heart*, with Muriel Harding in particularly sweet voice. Henry Goodier is not the strongest Luiz, but his meeting duet in Act I with Casilda comes off well. Throughout, the vigorous ensembles have plenty of life, and the *Cachucha* sparkles under Godfrey in a way that it never did with Sargent. The quartet *In a contemplative fashion* is delightfully sung. All-in-all a most entertaining set, cleanly transferred with clear words, even if the orchestra is less full-bodied than one would wish.

HMS Pinafore (complete with dialogue).

*** TER CDTER 1259 (2). Sandison, McVeigh, Boe, Barclay, McCafferty, Wilding, D'Oyly Carte Op. Ch. & O, Edwards.

The recent series of D'Oyly Carte stage revivals at London's Savoy Theatre, the natural home of G. & S., have brought a breath of fresh air into the company's traditional style of performance, with an imaginative new approach to production values.

This production of *HMS Pinafore* first appeared during the company's 1994–5 season, but scored a great critical and public success when it was revived at the Savoy Theatre in February 2000 to celebrate the Sullivan centenary. The set changed to that of an early steamship, looking more like the deck of a cruise-ship than a navy frigate, and this lighter touch to the proceedings is helped by Frances McCafferty's engagingly individual Scottish Buttercup.

Gordon Sandison here moved on from his casting as Captain Corcoran in the 1987 Sadler's Wells production to an avuncular, less aristocratic portrayal of Sir Joseph, an infectiously spirited characterization which is vivaciously caught in this recording. Tom McVeigh's crisply enunciated portrayal of the Captain makes an excellent foil. The two lovers are vocally perfectly matched, with Alfred Boe's pleasingly ardent tenor paired with the simplicity of Yvonne Barclay's delighfully sweet-voiced Josephine. In short, it is difficult to imagine this opera being more effectively cast, while with John Owen Edwards at the helm, the sheer zip of the briny choruses in Act I is matched by the vibrant ensembles which close both Acts.

At first one has minor doubts about the inclusion of the dialogue, but the interchanges between the principal characters are increasingly engaging, especially Buttercup and the Captain, while Dick Deadeye's colloquial accent underlines the common sense of his observations about the navy's class-consciousness, without losing the gruffness. An interesting novelty is the reinstatement of Hebe's dialogue (cut, for reasons explained in the booklet, just before the opera's original premiere) and a section of abandoned recitative for the principals in the finale. Also included is a reconstructed duet, *Reflect My Child*, between the Captain and Josephine in Act I. All-in-all this sparkling set cannot be too highly praised and the vivid recording projects the voices with such clarity that every word is clear.

HMS Pinafore (complete without dialogue).

*** TER CDTER2 1150 (2). Grace, Sandison, Gillett, Ritchie, Ormiston, Lawlor, New Sadler's Wells Op. Ch. & O, Phipps.

As with the new generation of D'Oyly Carte recordings, the 1987 Sadler's Wells set has a fine theatrical atmosphere. It is consistently well cast, with Linda Ormiston a pleasing Buttercup, if not so individual as Frances McCafferty, and Nickolas Grace making a traditionally aristocratic Sir Joseph Porter. The lovers sing well together and the choral numbers of Act I have plenty of zest. Simon Phipps paces the music fluently, if without quite the unerring timing of Godfrey or the sheer zest of John Owen Edwards, and this is very likeable from first to last, especially if no dialogue is required. While the famous Godfrey set (Decca 414 283-2) is not upstaged, nor the more recent D'Oyly Carte version, this is still very enjoyable. Moreover it offers three fascinatingly different endings (separately cued), so that listeners can choose their own. One includes Arne's *Rule Brittania* as used for Queen Victoria's Jubilee celebrations.

The Mikado (complete without dialogue).

**(*) TER CDTER 1178 (2). Ducarel, Roberts, Bottone, Rees, Rivers, Gordon, D'Oyley Carte Op. Ch. & O, Pryce Jones.

The newest D'Oyly Carte *Mikado* dates from 1989 so it is a comparatively distant relative of the very successful 2001 production at the Savoy, revived in 2002. What is common to both is the superb choral and orchestral contibutions (the latter with its arresting opening bass drum and splendidly regal trumpets to announce the Lord High Executioner). The cast is uniformly strong, with Bonaventura Bottone a fine Nanki-Poo and Deborah Rees a pleasing if not memorable Yum-Yum. Eric Roberts is a fairly traditional Ko-Ko, though his extended 'little list' now sounds very dated. Alas, additional lyrics for this famous number seldom match Gilbert's wit, and their topicality soon evaporates. Moreover Roberts's darker baritone has less charm than, say, Martyn Green, when he woos Katisha with *On a Tree by a River*.

Michael Durcarel is an authoritative Mikado, but his repeated gutteral laugh (following in the Fancourt tradition) rather goes over the top, especially second time round. However John Pryce Jones paces the ensembles admirably and directs the whole proceedings with vigour and aplomb. The drama of both Act finales, with Susan Gorton, a splendidly venemous Katisha, leading both ensembles very powerfully, is indeed memorable. A fine performance then, with excellent teamwork, very well recorded with a real theatrical atmosphere; but overall the cast shows rather less induality than in the other recent D'Oyly Carte recordings.

The Mikado (slightly abridged).

**(*) TER CDTER 1121. Angus, Idle, Bottone, Garrett, Van Allan, Palmer, ENO Ch. & O, Roinson.

This selection from the 1986 ENO production includes all the important numbers. As is normal, the performance is dominated by Ko-Ko and Eric Idle takes the role effectively enough, although his 'little list' is, understandbly even more dated than Eric Robert's additions in the newest D'Oyly Cart version. Bonaventura Bottone is a rather stylized Nanki-Poo, but Lesley Garrett anticipates her later fame with her charming portrait of Yum-Yum. There are some memorable moments here, and the recording is vivid, but this will appeal primarily to those wanting a memento of the Engligh National Opera production.

The Pirates of Penzance (complete without dialogue).

*** TER CDTER2 1177 (2). Roberts, Creasy, Hill Smith, Rivers, Gorton, Jones, D'Oyly Carte Op. Ch. & O, Pryce Jones.

This D'Oyly Carte production, like the companion set of The Mikado, dates back to 1989, but its verve and panache recognizably carried through to the much more recent revival at the Sayoy. It is splendidly paced and could hardly be better cast. Even Samuel (Gareth Jones), who opens the show with Pour, Oh Pour the Pirate Sherry, is strong-voiced enough to take a more leading role, and Susan Gordon immediately shows her versalility as a very personable Ruth, with fine characterization and crisp diction. She is partnered by Malcolm Rivers's commanding Pirate King, while the lovers, Philip Creasy as Frederic and the charming Marilyn Hill Smith, are equally well matched (especially in the lovely Oh Leave me Not to Pine Alone). Eric Roberts's bold portrayal of the Major General will disappoint no one, and in Act II Simon Masterton Smith makes a winningly colloquial Sergeant of Police. The whole of the second Act has tremendous pace and gusto, with the choral numbers from both Pirates and Police superbly sung, given an exhilarating lift by the conductor. The recording is first class and altogether this might be counted the most vividly theatrical Pirates on record. One returns to it with unalloyed pleasure.

(i; ii) The Pirates of Penzance (complete without dialogue); (ii; iii) Trial by Jury.

(BB) (**) Naxos mono 8.110196/7. (i) Green, Fancourt, Halman; (ii) Harding, Osborn; Watson; (ii) Rands, Flyn; D'Oyly Carte Op. Ch. & O, Godfrey.

Alas, this 1949 Decca Pirates, which appeared first on 78s and later on LP, is lack-lustre, with even Godfrey not as sprightly as usual. None of the principals are at their best, and Murial Harding is below form as Mabel. Of course Martyn Green and Darrell Fancourt have their moments, and the performance picks up and becomes more spirited in Act II, with Richard Watson an excellent Sergeant of the Police. It is he who, as the Learned Judge, is at the centre of Trial by Jury which shows all concerned in a far better light. Fine singing all round, especially from the chorus, makes this very enjoyable, and the recording too has transferred most vividly. But overall this set is primarily of historical interest.

The Yeomen of the Guard (complete without dialogue).

*** TER CDTER2 1195 (2). Maxwell, Pert, Gray, Echo Ross, Roebuck, Fieldsend, Montaine, D'Oyly Carte Op. Ch. & O, Edwards.

This 1992 D'Oyly Carte production of The Yeomen of the Guard is outstanding in every way, with the splendidly authoritative and formidable Dame Carruthers (Jill Pert) dominating the action by the force of her vocal personality. Her nobly sung When our Gallant Norman Foes is a sombre highlight of Act I, and she gets excellent support from Terence Sharpe's Sergeant Meryll. The consistently vibrant choral singing, from men and women alike, is often viscerally thrilling, and gives splendid weight and bite to the finales of both Acts, admirably paced by John Owen Edwards. And how beautifully the women sing the lovely melody which opens the second act, Night has Spread her Pall.

There is no weak link in the cast. Janine Roebuck is a most appealing Phoebe, even if perhaps she could have found more wit in Were I thy Bride, Lesley Echo Ross rises to her big moments as a sympathetic Elsie Maynard, and the pleasingly-voiced David Fieldsend is a convincingly gallant Colonel Fairfax. It was an excellent idea to include the spirited snatch of dialogue with which Jack Point (Fenton Gray) and Elsie make their entry, and Point not only delivers his patter songs with aplomb but the comic duets he shares with Wilfred Shadbolt (Gary Montaine) are the more telling by being sung colloquially. But above all it is the superb theatrical atmosphere of the recording which tells, after a spacious account of the Overture played by an expanded orchestra, with the strings again sounding richly full-bodied at the Introducion to Act II.

There are bonuses too, including an additional verse for the third and fourth Yeomen in the Act I finale, and as an appendix, extra numbers for Sergeant Meryll and Wilfred Shadbolt (A Joyous Torment) and an earlier version of Fairfax's Is Life a Boon? Highly recommended.

Arias from: The Beauty Stone; The Chieftain; The Emerald Isle; Haddon Hall; Ivanhoe; The Martyr of Antioch; The Rose of Persia.

**(*) TER CDTER 1248. Davies, Jones, Knight, Masterson, McCafferty, Suart, Nat. SO, Steadman.

While Sullivan's most successful works are undoubtedly found in his collaboration with W. S. Gilbert, their ten-year-quarrel of 1890 led the composer to use other collaborators and to venture into more 'serious' works. The arias on this disc date from that period, and, as recent performances of the complete works have shown, they contain music of much quality and fine invention, if less consistency. This disc gathers some of the best numbers. *In Days of Old* (from *Haddon Hall*), *The Gay Hussar* (from *The Chieftain*), and *I Care Not if the Cup I Hold* (from *The Rose of Persia*) are all rollicking, lively songs in the best Sullivan manner, while there is characteristic lyrical appeal in such arias as *O Moon Art Thou Clad* (from *Ivanhoe*).

If You Wish to Appear as an Irish Type (from *The Emerald Isle*) is a patter-song and would fit easily into any of the Savoy operas, while *Since it Dwelt in That Rock* (from *The Beauty Stone*) is another first-class melody, embellished with piquant detail. *Ah, Oui, J'étais une pensionnaire* (from *The Chieftain*) is sung in both French and English, to charming effect, as if the ghost of André Messager had suddenly taken over its composition. There are some splendid choruses too: the opening *Now Glory to the God Who Breaks* (from *The Martyr of Antioch*) sounds almost like Weber with its flurry of brass. With some typically enjoyable ensembles, such as *On the Heights of Glentaun* (another item from *The Emerald Isle*), the programme is varied and well designed. The performances are generally of quality, though occasionally an obtrusive vibrato mars the singing, notably Gillian Knight's acccount of *Io Paean* (from *The Martyr of Antioch*), but with such G. & S. stalwarts as Valerie Masterson, the character of the music is well captured. The recording is very good and full texts are included.

SVENDSEN, Johann Severin

(1840–1911)

Symphonies Nos. 1 in D, Op. 4; 2 in B flat, Op. 23; Polonaise, Op. 28.

*** Chan. 9932 Danish Nat. R SO, Thomas Dausgaard.

The Svendsen symphonies were staple diet in the pre- and post-war years as far as broadcasting was concerned though they were not strongly represented on records. There was an early account of the *Second Symphony* under Øivin Fjeldstad on Mercury and a later stereo version also by the same conductor. The *First* was also recorded by Fjeldstad on Philips and later by Miltiades Caridis. However they were for the most part neglected. Svendsen barely maintained a toehold on the catalogue in the 1960s and 70s, and in one year (1971) not one work of his was available. Neeme Järvi's 1988 coupling with the Gothenburg Orchestra and Mariss Jansons's Oslo version the following year put them back on the map though no British or American orchestra recorded them until the Bournemouth Orchestra made them for Naxos with a gifted Norwegian conductor, an excellent bargain disc (8.553898 – see our main volume).

The freshness, polish and sheer inventive resource of the *D major Symphony* is little short of amazing. It was written while Svendsen was still studying at Leip-

zig, and has a natural feeling for form and a mastery of the orchestra that Grieg never really commanded. Thomas Dausgaard and the Danish Radio Orchestra capture the youthful exuberance of the one and the warmth and generosity of spirit of the other. This is captivating music and the Danes, among whom Svendsen spent so much of his life, respond with enthusiasm. Tempi are well judged though the scherzo of the D major would benefit from being brisker . The *Polonaise* of 1881 is not the equal of the famous *Fest-Polonaise*. Recommended alongside though not necessarily in preference to Järvi.

SWEELINCK, Jan (1562–1621)

Keyboard music (complete).

(M) *** DG 468 417-2 (4). Koopman (harpsichord, organ or virginals).

Sweelinck was the greatest Dutch composer of his day (he belonged to the generation after Byrd though he died in the same year as the English master). He spent his working life in Amsterdam where he was organist at the Oude Kerk. Although he visited Antwerp and other Dutch cities he never travelled outside the Netherlands, but musically he was influenced by both the English virginalists and the Venetians. Not one of Sweelinck's instrumental pieces survives in his own hand and his output survives thanks to the copies made by pupils. Nor is there any indication of the actual instrument for which the music was intended, though it is nearly always possible to determine. This modestly priced set assembles his keyboard output on four CDs: in these recordings Ton Koopman uses two organs including the Compenius at Frederiksborg Castle, Denmark, three harpsichords including a 1637 Ruckers at Nürnburg and three different sets of virginals including a 1580 double virginal by Martinus van der Biest also at Nürnburg. The playing is impeccable and lively as are the 1981 analogue recordings. Not all of Sweelinck's music is of equal interest (some of it is boring) but the bulk of it is worth the attention of any serious collector. A bargain.

TALLIS, Thomas (c. 1505–85)

Complete music, Vol. 5: Music for the Divine Office II: Audivi vocem de coelo; Candidi facti sunt; Honor virtus et potestas; Homo quidam fecit coenam; Te lucis ante terminum (2 settings). Liturgical Organ Music: Alleluia per te Dei genitrix; Clarifa me pater I, II, & III; Ecce tempus idoneum; Ex more docti mistico; Felix namque (II); Gloria tibi trinitas; Jam lucis orto sidere; Natus est nobis hodie; Veni redemptor genitum.

*** Signum SIGCD 016. Du Roy, Dixon; Benson-Wilson (organ of the Chapel, Knole House, Sevenoaks, Kent).

Volume 5 of Alistair Dixon's invaluable survey continues the music that Tallis wrote for the Divine Office begun in Volume 4. There are some particularly beautiful examples, notably the opening responsory for All Saints Day, *Audivi vocem de coelo* (set for three trebles and an alto), the following, even richer *Candidi facti sunt* and the even more imaginative *Honor virtus et potestas*, all gloriously sung here.

But the special interest of this CD is the inclusion of the organ music, simply written and based on plainchant melismas. Tallis generally used the organ as a substitute for voices, interchanging instrumental with sung text. In this aurally appealing alternation, the organist played the odd-numbered verses, usually providing – as in *Veni redemptor genitum* – a piquant introduction to contrast with the sonorous vocal entry. The organ prelude for *Ex more docti mistico* is most engagingly light-hearted: the mood then deepens for the plainchant entry. The final item *Felix namque* (II) is non-liturgical, an extended postlude for organ alone. The organ used for the recordings, in the private chapel at Knole, is the oldest playable organ in England, so its choice seems admirable, and Andrew Benson-Wilson's contribution to the success of this CD is considerable, since all the organ music is most appealing.

Audivi vocem de Caelo; Honor virtus et Postestas; O sacrum convivium; Salvator mundi; Sancte Deus.

(M) *** CRD 3372, Ch. of New College, Oxford, Higginbottom – TAVERNER: *Western Wynde etc.* ***

This collection of votive antiphons, motets and responds makes up an attractive group and the Choir of New College, Oxford produces a clean and well-blended sound. Given the attractions of the coupling this disc has a strong appeal.

TAVENER, John (born 1944)

'Choral Ikons': Annunciation; As One who has Slept; The Hymn of the Unwaning Light; A Hymn to the Mother of God; The Lamb; The Lord's Prayer; Magnificat and Nunc Dimittis; A Parting Gift for Tom Farrow; Song for Athene; The Tyger.

*** BBC Opus Arte **DVD** OS 0854 D. The Choir, Whitbourn.

This collection of some of John Tavener's most attractive choral pieces is not only beautifully sung by The Choir, a professional group founded in 1999, but imaginatively presented. Using virtual-reality techniques, the fourteen singers, recorded in a Dutch television studio in Hilversum, are placed against the background of Hagia Sophia in Istanbul, (what was in medieval times the church of St Sophia). With heavy reverberation added, some of the items suggest a far bigger choir, as in the longest item, *The Hymn of the Unwaning Light*, marred slightly by the wobbly contributions of the baritone soloist. The hypnotically repetitious *Song for Athene* has become popular thanks to its use at the end of Princess Diana's funeral service and the two Blake settings, *The Lamb* and *The Tyger*, are widely heard too,

but the dedication behind all the pieces is very clear, each of them introduced visually by an ikon or an ikon-like illustration. A fine DVD premiere for Tavener's music. As supplementary items the disc offers a long and illuminating interview with the composer, who provides a spoken commentary on each piece (not the most convenient method of providing programme notes), and a Dutch expert talking about the sources of ikon painting.

TAVERNER, John (c. 1495–1545)

Missa Corona Spinea; Responsory: Audivi vocem de caelo.

*** Proud Sound PROUCD 1149. Ch. of King's College, London, Trendell – BYRD: *Laetentur caeli; Tristitia et anxietas* ***.

The 28 young singers in this choir from King's College, London, tackle a formidable programme of polyphonic music, centred on the magnificent setting of the Mass which Taverner wrote for Cardinal College, Oxford, to which he had been appointed choirmaster in 1526. The 16 sopranos with their fresh tone confidently tackle the exuberant writing for trebles in its wonderfully varied contrasts of timbre, even if their matching is not always as polished as it might be. Like Christ Church Cathedral Choir on the rival ASV version they establish this as yet another long-buried masterpiece of early Tudor polyphony. The responsory, *Audivi*, using a similar combination of high voices, provides an apt tail-piece for a programme also celebrating the mastery of William Byrd in two superb motets. Warmly atmospheric recording.

Mass: The Western Wynde. Mater Christi.

(M) *** CRD 3372, Ch. of New College, Oxford, Edward Higginbottom – TALLIS *Audivi vocem de Caelo etc.* ***

This CRD version of Taverner's *Mass* was the first to appear after the King's College, Cambridge recording of 1962. Since then there have been others, but it was a worthy successor and the acoustic of New College, Oxford is, if anything superior to King's producing greater clarity and definition. Higginbottom's choir sings with great feeling but with restraint and splendid control, both of line and ensemble.

TCHAIKOVSKY, Peter (1840–93)

Capriccio italien, Op. 45; Nutcracker Suite, Op. 71a; Sleeping Beauty: Suite, Op. 66a; Swan Lake: Suite, Op. 20; Eugene Onegin: Polonaise and Waltz.

(B) **(*) Erato Ultima 0630-18965-2 (2). Bolshoi SO, Lazarev.

There are finer accounts of all this music available, but Lazarev has this repertoire in his bones and a first-rate Russian orchestra at his disposal. He generally favours ballet tempi for the ballet suites; some may find certain dances a bit slow (especially the *Pano-*

rama from the *Sleeping Beauty*), but there is no lack of excitement or inner tension, with some dances, such as the *Spanish Dance* from *Swan Lake*, rather faster than usual. *Capriccio italien* begins with almost classical restraint, but the allegro is crisply vigorous. The *Eugene Onegin* excerpts are most enjoyable, especially in the *Waltz* where the theme in the gentler middle section is played with rare delicacy, providing more contrast than usual. There are plenty of similar individual touches throughout this set, and with excellent 1992 sound (highlighting the Russian-sounding brass), this is certainly good value.

Piano Concerto No. 1 in B flat min., Op. 23.

🌐 (BB) (✲✲✲) Naxos mono 8.110671. Horowitz, NBC O, Toscanini – BRAHMS: *Piano Concerto No. 2*. (✲✲)

(BB) ✲✲ Warner Apex 0927 40835-2. Sultanov, LSO, Shostakovich – RACHMANINOV: *Piano Concerto No. 2*. ✲✲

✲✲ Sony **DVD** SVD 45986. Kissin, BPO, Karajan (with PROKOFIEV: *Classical Symphony.* ✲✲(✲))

Horowitz's famous wartime Carnegie Hall recording of the *B flat minor Concerto* has since remained the yardstick by which all subsequent versions have been judged. Somehow the alchemy of the occasion was unique and the result is unforgettable. In spite of the Carnegie Hall ambience the recording is confined and lacking bass, but the transfer engineer, Mark Obert-Thorn, has achieved impressive results from a single post-war set of 78s in mint condition. Such is the magnetism of the playing, however that the ear forgets the sonic limitations within moments. Toscanini's accompaniment is remarkable not only for matching the adrenalin of his soloist (particularly in the visceral thrill of the finale's climax), but for the tenderness he finds for the lyrical passages of the first movement. The powerful cadenza becomes its apex, with one passage in which there seem to be two pianists in duet, rather than just one pair of human hands.

Toscanini's moments of delicacy extend to the *Andantino*, which is truly *simplice*, even when accompanying the coruscating pianistic fireworks of the central section. The finale carries all before it, with Horowitz's riveting octaves leading to a tremendously exciting statement of the big tune before storming off furiously to the coda.

There is some fiery playing from Alexei Sultanov, which testifies to a considerable technique; but compare his handling of the prestissimo episode in the slow movement with someone like Argerich and he emerges as rather coarse-grained, and the second group of the finale is crudely handled. However, there is much more that excites admiration, and it is only the indifferent accompanying and the less than ideal recording balance that inhibit a strong recommendation, even at bargain price.

Both works on the Sony DVD were recorded at a New Year's Eve concert at the end of 1988, and the concerto was issued on DG 427 485-2 as well as on video. Kissin was 16 at the time of this performance, though he looks even younger, and the whole occasion must have been rather an awesome experience for him. His playing has great elegance and tremendous poise – his pianissimo tone is quite ravishing – but he tends not to let himself go, and there is just a slight feeling that he is playing safe, particularly in the finale. The performance as a whole, for all its finesse, lacks abandon.

The strings in the DVD of Prokofiev's *Classical Symphony* have the characteristic Berlin sheen, and the slow movement has great tonal sweetness. The *Scherzo* is a bit heavy-handed, but it is offset by an altogether captivating finale, perfectly judged in pace and character. The camera work is unobtrusive, and although the piano is rather forward, the balance is well judged, though the overall sound is a shade dry.

Violin Concerto in D, Op. 35.

✲✲✲ DG 471 428-2. Garrett, Russian Nat. O, Pletnev – CONUS: *Violin Concerto*. ✲✲✲

(i) Violin Concerto in D, Op. 35; (ii) Méditation, Op. 42/1; (iii) Sérénade mélancolique, Op. 26.

(✲✲✲) Testament mono/stereo SBT 1224. Kogan; (i; ii) Paris Conservatoire O, (i) Vandernoot; (ii) Silvestri; (iii) Philh. O, Kondrashin – PROKOFIEV: *Violin Concerto No. 2*. ✲✲✲

David Garrett was still only seventeen when he recorded this fluent and sweet-toned account of the Tchaikovsky with Mikhail Pletnev and the Russian National Orchestra for DG. Beautifully balanced it is too, with the violin in an ideal relationship with the orchestra. His technique is immaculate and so too (one or two expressive emphases in the cadenzas apart) is his taste. In the slow movement his playing has great feeling and a high emotional temperature that is at the same time restrained. Mikhail Pletnev gives finely judged and sympathetic support. Undoubtedly one of the most enjoyable modern accounts of this masterly score in which new things are always to be discovered. Don't be put off by the gushing autobiographical notes by the young soloist.

Kogan's account of the Tchaikovsky concerto was made in Paris in 1956, three years before his better-known (and generally speaking better) version with Constantin Silvestri conducting the same orchestra. (He had also recorded a version in 1950 with Vassily Nebolsin, which was briefly available in the U.K. on the short-lived Saga label.) However any performance by this aristocrat of violinists is worth having and his effortless virtuosity and purity of tone is heard to excellent effect in this well balanced mono recording. The *Sérénade mélancolique* and the *Méditation*, both recorded in 1959, are in stereo and among the finest performances of the piece on disc.

1812 Overture, Op. 49.

(M) ✲✲ Westminster (ADD) 471 215-2. Vienna State Op. O, Scherchen – RIMSKY-KORSAKOV: *Scheherazade*. ✲(✲)

Scherchen's account takes a little while to warm up, but soon gets underway in his distinctive manner, with the slow music played very slowly, and the fast music very fast. Eccentrically enjoyable after its fashion, and the 1957 (DG) sound has come up well.

(i) 1812 Overture; Francesca da Rimini; Marche Slave; Romeo and Juliet (Fantasy Overture); (ii) Eugene Onegin: Tatiana's Letter Scene.

(B) *** CfP 575 5672. (i) RLPO, (ii) LPO, Edwards; (ii) with Hannan.

An outstanding re-issue, which shows Sian Edwards as an instinctive Tchaikovskian. In *Romeo and Juliet* the love-theme is ushered in very naturally and blossoms with the fullest ardour, while the combination of the feud music with the Friar Lawrence theme reaches a very dramatic climax. *Marche Slave*, resplendently high-spirited and exhilarating, makes a splendid foil. The emotional ebb and flow of *Francesca da Rimini* is persuasively managed, and this performance is the highlight of the disc. Francesca's clarinet solo is melting, and the work's middle section has a Beechamesque feeling for woodwind colour. The passionate climax could hardly be more eloquent, while the spectacular recording gives great impact to the closing whirlwind sequence and despair-laden final chords, where the tam-tam makes its presence felt very pungently.

The inclusion of *Tatiana's Letter Scene*, Tchaikovsky's greatest inspiration for soprano – originally coupled with the *Fifth Symphony* – was a capital idea. This is freshly and dramatically sung in a convincingly girlish impersonation by the Australian, Eileen Hannan. *1812*, which closes the concert, is also very enjoyable indeed. Full of vigour and flair, it has a majestic final sequence, with superbly resounding cannon.

Hamlet (fantasy overture); Romeo and Juliet (fantasy overture); The Tempest, Op. 18.

*** BIS CD 1073. Bamberg SO, Serebrier.

José Serebrier follows up the first impressive disc in his Tchaikovsky series for BIS (*Francesca da Rimini* and the *Fourth Symphony*) with this fine Shakespeare triptych, and what a good idea it was to couple Tchaikovsky's three fantasy overtures inspired by Shakespeare. Serebrier himself writes an illuminating note on the genesis of each of the three, together with an analysis of their structure, pointing out that after establishing his concept of the fantasy overture in the first version of *Romeo and Juliet* in 1869 – slow introduction leading to alternating fast and slow sections, with slow coda – Tchaikovsky used it again in both the *1812 Overture* and *Hamlet*. *The Tempest* (1873), based on a programme suggested by the art historian, Vladimir Stasov, has similarly contrasting sections, but begins and ends with a gently evocative seascape, with shimmering arpeggios from strings divided in thirteen parts followed by a haunting theme on the horns. It is typical of Serebrier's performance that he makes that effect sound so fresh and original, and one wonders for the first time whether it gave Sibelius the

idea for the opening of *En saga*. In many ways, early as it is, this is stylistically the most radical of the three overtures here, with sharp echoes of Berlioz in some of the woodwind effects. The clarity of Serebrier's performance, both in texture and in structure, helped by brilliant BIS recording both warm and analytical, brings that out. *Hamlet*, dating from much later, is treated to a similarly fresh and dramatic reading, with Serebrier bringing out the yearningly Russian flavour of the lovely oboe theme representing Ophelia. He may not quite match the thrusting power of his mentor, Stokowski, but he is not far short, and brings out far more detail, bearing out that maestro's remark about his pupil being 'a master of orchestral balance'.

Serebrier is also meticulous in seeking to observe the dynamic markings in each score. Those in *The Tempest* are nothing if not extravagant – up to a fortissimo of five f's in the final statement of the love theme – yet Serebrier graduates the extremes with great care. In *Romeo and Juliet*, like Abbado but unlike Dorati, he is just as careful over observing Tchaikovsky's relatively modest markings, so that the central development section, built on the conflict music, is rightly restrained, mainly *mezzo forte* but down to *pp* for the violins in places. This is the opposite of a 'wham-it-home' approach like Dorati's, with fortissimos coming far too easily, yet the playing of the Bamberg Orchestra, incisive as in the earlier BIS disc, both wonderfully drilled and warmly committed, with outstanding solos from wind and brass, ensures that there is no lack of power. It is good to welcome so refreshing a Tchaikovsky compilation.

Méditation, Op. 42/1.

✪ *** RCA 74321 87454-2. Znaider, Bav. Rad. SO, Jansons – GLAZUNOV: *Violin Concerto*; PROKOFIEV: *Violin Concerto No. 2*. *** ✪

This piece comes from the *Souvenir d'un lieu cher* for violin and piano which Tchaikovsky composed while staying on the estate of his patroness, Madame von Meck. It had originally been planned as the slow movement of the *Violin Concerto* and it fell to Glazunov to put it into orchestral form. It is beautifully played and comes here as a fill-up to Nikolaj Znaider's outstanding set of the Glazunov and Prokofiev concertos.

The Nutcracker (ballet; complete), Op. 71.

✪ *** Warner NIVC Arts DVD 0630 19394-2. Collier, Dowell, Coleman, Rose, Niblett, Royal Ballet, ROHCG O, Rozhdestvensky. (Producer: Peter Wright. Video Director John Vernon, in association with Peter Wright. Choreography Lev Ivanov and Peter Wright.)

(B) *** Sony SB2K 89778 (2). Philh. O & Ch., Thomas.

Lesley Collier has already enchanted us in *La fille mal gardée*, and here, in this superb 1985 Royal Ballet production from Covent Garden, she is ideally cast as the Sugar Plum Fairy, dancing delectably in Act II to one of Tchaikovsky's most famous numbers – in which he introduced the celesta into the orchestra.

Her romantic partner in the earlier ballet, Michael Coleman, now takes a more dramatic role, to dominate E.T.A. Hoffman's fantasy tale, in the role of Herr Drosselmeyer. This curiously sinister creator of mechanical toys, whose nephew – before the ballet begins – has been transformed into a grotesque Nutcracker Doll, does not dance; but in Peter Wright's production he is always in the background of the narrative to remind us that his aim is to break the spell and have his nephew return to human form. It is a formidably astute and compelling characterization, that at times recalls the art of Robert Helpmann: no praise could be higher.

The heroine, Clara, who is charmingly and unwittingly at the centre of the action, is also a non-dancing role. Fortunately she finds the ungainly Nutcracker (Guy Niblett) endearing, and helps him defeat and slay the Mouse King in battle to provide a happy ending for the story. But first there is a family Christmas party – full of colour and bustling incident, in which Herr Drosslmeyer arrives as magician to entertain the children and take the opportunity to give Clara the toy Nutcracker, which her clumsy brother subsequently breaks, but Drosslmeyer repairs.

Later that night Clara comes down to retrieve her toy, and at the hour of midnight the magic begins and the Christmas tree grows to dominate the stage. After the battle sequence, Clara and the transformed Nutracker journey together in a sleigh, through the Pine Forest and among the waltzing Snowflakes, to the Land of Snow – against a musical background of two of Tchaikovsky's finest melodic inspirations – and on to the Kingdom of Sweets.

Here, in the great Act II Divertissement, come the enchanting characteristic dances (familiar in the suite), capped by *Waltz of the Flowers*, the passionate *Pas de deux*, the bravura solo numbers for the Sugar Plum Fairy and her Prince (splendidly danced by Anthony Dowell) and the *Waltz* finale. It is a miraculously inspired score, and here, under Rozhdestvensky's persuasive baton, the Covent Garden Orchestra realizes its eternal freshness. Peter Wright's production is gloriously traditional, brilliantly choreographed, lavishly spectacular, while Julia Oman's costumes (especially for the battling Mice) are no less imaginative. The camera is always in the right place – one is hardly aware of it – and the orchestral recording is wonderfully vivid, full, and immediate. In short this DVD is treasurable in every way.

Michael Tilson Thomas has the advantage of fine Philharmonia playing, recorded in an attractive acoustic. The Sony balance is very good too, and this account lies between Previn and Mackerras, with a touch more spectacle than the former. The clock striking midnight makes for quite a sinister effect after a feeling of skilfully created tension. The party scene before this has been pressed on strongly, but there is a pleasing relaxation after the battle, and the *Waltz of the Snowflakes* has real radiance. Tempi are generally a fraction brisk, but the brighter rhythmic feeling often pays dividends. If this would not be a first choice it is excellent value, although the documentation is meagre.

The Nutcracker (complete ballet); Symphony No. 4 in F min., Op. 36.

(M) **(*) (ADD) Westminster 471 228-2 (2). RPO, Rodzinski.

Rodzinski's RPO *Nutcracker* is full of character and vitality, and if his approach isn't always balletic in terms of tempi, it is certainly theatrical and often exciting. The 1956 stereo recording is strikingly vivid for its vintage, rather up front in the Mercury manner, though telling in its impact and in delineation of instruments, especially the woodwind. Only a certain dryness on top, which particularly effects the strings, betrays its age. The performance of the *Fourth Symphony* has the same characteristics in terms of drama and character, but its structural strength is not undervalued. This is one of the most stimulating of these Westminster reissues and, with attractive packaging, this 2 CD set is an undoubted collector's item.

Romeo and Juliet (fantasy overture).

(BB) **(*) EMI Encore (ADD) CDE5 749641-2. Philh. O, Muti – DVORAK: *Symphony No. 9 (New World).* **
(B) **(*) CfP 575 5652. Hallé O, Kamu – RACHMANINOV: *Symphony No. 2 in E min., Op. 27.* **(*)

In his Philharmonia period Muti was an outstanding Tchaikovskian and his 1977 *Romeo and Juliet* is a very fine performance, full of imaginative touches. The opening has just the right degree of atmospheric restraint and immediately creates a sense of anticipation; the great romantic climax is noble in contour yet there is no lack of passion, while the main allegro is crisply and dramatically pointed. The repeated figure on the timpani at the coda is made to suggest a tolling bell and the expressive woodwind which follows gently underlines the feeling of tragedy. The recording is good although rather light in the bass and it is a pity that the coupling is not a performance of distinction.

Okko Kamu's account of *Romeo and Juliet* is impressive, well paced and exciting. There is no lack of thrust, although there is a curious momentary broadening – it barely lasts a bar – at the climax of the love theme which some might find intrusive on repetition. But the sombre opening and closing sections evoke a powerful and very Russian melancholy.

Serenade for Strings in C, Op. 48.

(M) *** Decca (ADD) 470 262-2. ASMF, Marriner – GRIEG: *Holberg Suite* ***; DVORAK: *Serenade.* **(*)

Marriner's classic 1968 version holds its place among the best. Although Tchaikovsky asked for as big a body of strings as possible in his delectable *Serenade*, there is much to be said, in these days of increased string resonance and clever microphone placing, for having a more modest band like the Academy of St. Martin's-in-the-Field. However, one does notice the lack of sheer tonal weight that a larger group would afford. Marriner's performance compensates with expressive phrasing (most striking in the slow movement), imaginative and fresh playing from the Academy, and the finest pointing and precision of ensemble. The original coupling of the *Souvenir de Florence* now lives on a Double Decca CD with the *String Quartets* (452 614-2), but the couplings here are excellent. A fine transfer, too, in this Legends reissue.

The Sleeping Beauty (ballet), Op. 66 (complete).

✪ (M) *** BBC (ADD) BBCL 4091-2 (2). BBC SO, Rozhdestvensky.

Rozhdestvensky's recording, made in the Royal Festival Hall in 1979, was part of the BBC Symphony Orchestra's fiftieth anniversary celebrations and is fully worthy of the occasion. The great Russian conductor (using the original Russian score which is absolutely complete) shows just how to hold Tchaikovsky's ballet together as a symphonic entity by creating a consistent narrative pulse. Yet his pacing can never be faulted: this always remains music to be danced to. It could not be entrusted to more caring or sensitive direction, and the ear is continually amazed by the quality of Tchaikovsky's invention. Rozhdestvensky's loving attention to detail and his response to the vivid colouring are matched by his feeling for the narrative drama. He is masterly in building his climaxes, while his lyrical phrasing brings flowing rubato beautifully controlled, so that the wonderful *Panorama* floats elegantly over its rocking bass while the Entracte, *Sommeil*, brings real atmospheric magic.

The first *Pas de quatre* of Act III leads to Tchaikovsky's inspired series of characteristic dances in which the conductor's light rhythmic touch and delicacy of feeling draws a wonderfully refined yet vividly coloured response from the BBC players. The ballet ends majestically, and the BBC recording has plenty of amplitude, warm strings, glowing woodwind, and a natural concert hall balance. Climaxes have brilliance and full dynamic impact, and this is every bit as enjoyable as Pletnev's DG studio recording, with the additional magnetism of live music-making. We gave this recording a ✪ when it first appeared on LP and it sounds even better on CD. Highly recommended.

Swan Lake (ballet; complete), Op. 20.

*** Arthaus **DVD** 100 001. Scherzer, Matz, Händler, Ballet of the Deutsche Oper, Berlin, Berlin St. O, Barenboim. (Choreography: Patrice Bart).
(BB) *** Decca Eloquence (ADD) 467 490-2 (3). Nat. PO, Bonynge.
(B) ** Sony SB2K 89735 (2). LSO, Thomas.

Barenboim's *Swan Lake* was recorded in performance at the Deutsche Staatsoper, Berlin, with the soloists and corps of the Lindenoper (which takes its name from Unter den Linden, where the Opera is based). Patrice Bart has been with the Paris Opéra since 1990, and his keenly inventive choreography brings fresh air into the Marius Petipa–Lev Ivanov original.

All the principals are fine dancers: Steffi Scherzer's Odette/Odile is strikingly characterized – she has been prima ballerina with the company since 1987 –

and Oliver Matz makes an elegant Prince Siegfried. Bart recasts the four acts as two, and his choreography also gives much scope to the part of Rotbart, danced brilliantly by Torsten Händler.

Apart from the excellence of the dancing, what a good ballet conductor Barenboim is! He has obviously thought long and deeply about this inexhaustible score, which emerges with eloquence and radiance in his hands. The camera work is natural and unobtrusive, and the colour is gloriously vivid. Watching the performance lifts the spirits and makes one realize yet again what wonderful music this is.

Bonynge's approach is grippingly strong and vigorous, holding the listener from the first bar with his striking forward impulse. Yet when the famous Waltz arrives it is by no means over-driven. In short this is consistently alive music-making full of adrenalin. The recording has been splendidly remastered and if the string tone is comparatively leonine, it is by no means thin, the woodwind playing is full of colour, the brass sounds are open and vibrant, and the hall ambience attractive. The balance too is managed well, although the violin solos (very well played by Mincho Minchev) sound rather larger than life. With the accent on brilliance rather than ripeness this may not appeal to all ears, but there is a consistent freshness here and the moments of spectacle make a thrilling impact. Reissued on Eloquence this is a sure bargain.

Unlike his splendid version of the *Nutcracker*, there is a slight wanting of character in Tilson Thomas's Sony recording, and the performance does not feel especially theatrical in impact. The opening lacks the atmosphere that implies a great romantic drama to follow and the music is not sustained at the highest level of tension. There is little to complain of in terms of the orchestral playing and recorded sound, but the end result is disappointing.

SYMPHONIES

Symphonies Nos. 4–6 (Pathétique).

(B) *(*) Teldec Ultima 0630 18966-2 (2). Leipzig Gewandhaus O, Masur.

Symphonies Nos. 4–6; Hamlet (Fantasy Overture), Op. 67.

(BB) **(*) Double Decca (ADD) 470 065-2 (2). VPO, Maazel.

This Double Decca is the second volume of Maazel's Tchaikovsky cycle (the first complete cycle on LP), vividly transferred. The three Symphonies (and especially No. 4) all receive gripping, spontaneous performances which, helped by the freshness of the VPO, sound newly minted. The strength of the reading of the *Fourth* is its basic simplicity and lack of personal mannerism. The dramatic and emotional power of the writing emerges in consequence with great effect; in the first movement, the appearance of the relatively gentle second subject is not over-romanticized, and the contrast which Tchaikovsky intended is underlined by this lack of emphasis. The slow movement is played most beautifully, and the scherzo is not too fast. The finale explodes just as it should and is superbly recorded. Perhaps the *Fifth* lacks the fullest expansive qualities, and is at times a little cool, but it is very well recorded with some excellent playing from the VPO, including a beautifully phrased horn solo in the *Andante*. The *Sixth* is a good, straight-forward account, though the somewhat deadpan account of the second movement and the restrained finale, which lacks emotional depth, are slight draw-backs. However, this direct, unmannered playing offers its own rewards, and there are few more effective accounts of the March/Scherzo. The *Hamlet Overture* is brilliantly done, perhaps too hard driven, but very exciting. But the first recommendation for the three symphonies lies with Karajan on a DG Double (453 088-2) or Ashkenazy on a Double Decca (443 844-2).

Masur and the Leipzig Gewandhaus Orchestra give rich and refined readings which reflect the German tradition rather than anything Russian, which cer-tainly does not suit the slavonic intensity of the *Fourth Symphony*. Looking at Tchaikovsky without a hint of hysteria emphasizes the symphonic strength, as it did with both Klemperer and Boehm, but unlike those German predecessors, Masur's account is warm and smooth rather than rugged, accentuated by the rounded, bass-heavy recording. His reading of the *Fifth* is spacious in many of the speeds as well as in the characteristically distanced recording, well blended with woodwind behind the strings. A major snag is the ponderousness of the slow introductions to outer movements. The *Pathétique* is well laid out but with a very low level of tension despite consistently fine play-ing from the Leipzig orchestra. The recording is again rich and natural, but the Leipzig acoustics do not pro-vide the necessary brilliance and projection, and this Ultima reissue is difficult to recommend, even at its modest cost.

Symphony No. 4 in F min.; Francesca da Rimini.

*** BIS CD 1273. Bamberg SO, Serebrier.

On the Swedish BIS label, surprisingly for a company best-known for rarities, comes this impressive foray into mainstream repertory, with the *Fourth Symphony* superbly played and recorded. Consistently textures are clarified, helped by the thoughtful, finely-judged reading of José Serebrier. The Bamberg Orchestra boasts an exceptional line-up of refined wind soloists, phrasing subtly. Not that in this concern for detail there is any lack of excitement, for the incisive attack and Serebrier's preference for steady speeds brings a structural strength roo rarely achieved in Tchaiko-vsky. *Francesca da Rimini*, inspired by Dante, makes an apt coupling, a work written in very much the same period as the *Symphony*. Again with full, clear sound, the orchestral outbursts have biting impact, with the Bamberg wind soloists once more phrasing seductively in the love music. While Szell (● Decca

460 655-2) and Jansons (Chan. 8361) still hold their place, this can be ranked alongside them.

Symphony No. 4; Romeo and Juliet (fantasy overture).

(BB) * Naxos 8555714. Colorado SO, Alsop.

After her excitingly committed recordings of Samuel Barber's music for Naxos, Marin Alsop's first Tchaiko-vsky CD is a great disappointment. Although the Colorado Orchestra plays very well indeed and is meticulously rehearsed, the performance of the *Fourth Symphony* is passionless and entirely without flair. The feeling of routine persists throughout but especially in the slow movement, and while the finale cannot help but make an impact when the recording is so vivid and the acoustic of the Denver Boetcher Hall so suitable, the only movement which really springs to life is the Scherzo, which is by far the highlight of the perform-ance. The opening of *Romeo and Juliet,* too, is totally unatmospheric and lacking tension and the appear-ance of the great love theme is entirely without magic. By the side of Karajan's superb VPO performance on Decca, which has great evocation and passion, this is very lack-lustre. Szell's account of the *Symphony* with the LSO on the same Decca reissue (460 655-2) has all the thrilling emotional power and surging thrust which is missing in Colorado, and the Decca recording is even more spectacular.

(i) Symphony No. 5; (ii) Variations on a Rococo Theme for Cello and Orchestra.

(M) **(*) Sony SMK 89795. (i) Chicago SO, Abbado; (ii) Ma, Pittsburgh SO, Maazel.

Abbado's Chicago *Fifth* is admirably fresh and superbly played. All Tchaikovsky's markings are scru-pulously yet imaginatively observed and the reading is full of contrast. Thus, in the second subject group of the first movement, the firmly articulated crotchet/quaver motif is the more striking in its emphasis, leading as it does to the lyrical legato of the *Molto più tranquillo*. Other versions of the slow move-ment have more extrovert passion, but Abbado shows that the climaxes can be involving without being his-trionic. After an elegant Waltz, with the orchestra in sparkling form, the finale has fine energy and momen-tum. If it does not have quite the gripping excitement of Jansons or Gergiev, the moment of the composer's self-doubt, before the *Poco più animato*, is the more effectively characterized. The recording is made in a convincingly resonant acoustic: if inner detail is not always sharply defined, the balance is very good with full strings and a supporting weight in the bass, but it is less rich than the Philips and Chandos versions.

As an encore Yo-Yo Ma's *Rococo Variations* are characteristically refined, and although his playing is at times just a little mannered (and one longs for the full-timbred Rostropovich approach), Ma always engages the listener's sympathy by his delicacy and grace. Maazel's less than inspired accompaniment does, however, diminish the appeal of the performance, which is again very well recorded.

CHAMBER MUSIC

(i) *Souvenir de Florence*, (string sextet). *Op. 70.*

*(**) EMI CDC5 57243-2. Chang, Hartog, W. Christ, T. Christ, Faust, Maninger – DVORAK: *String Sextet.* *(**).

Sarah Chang and her starry team of string-players drawn from the Berlin Philharmonic, past and present, give the most joyfully exuberant performance of one of Tchaikovsky's happiest works, perfectly coupled with another great sextet by a Slavonic composer. The opening movement's bouncy rhythms in compound time set the pattern, with the second subject hauntingly seductive in its winning relaxation. Chang's individuality is matched throughout by her partners, each challenging the others, yet in a manner plainly developed from orchestral work keeping the ensemble perfectly crisp and polished, so that inner textures are beautifully clear. The *Adagio cantabile* second movement is tenderly beautiful, with the central section sharply contrasted, and the folk-dance rhythms of the last two movements are sprung with sparkling lightness. The snag is the recording, which in tuttis has a fierce treble response unsupported by a full, expansive bass, so necessary in Tchaikovsky. On some reproducers the sound is tiring to the ears.

String Quartet No. 1 in D, Op. 11.

✪ *** Challenge Classics CC 72106. Brodsky Qt – BRITTEN: *String Quartet No. 1; Divertimenti.* ✪ ***

The Brodsky Quartet seem to find an affinity between the gently lyrical opening theme of Tchaikovsky's *D major Quartet* and the luminous magic at the beginning of the coupled Britten work in the same key; in both there is an elliptical reprise, but although Britten ends his movement hauntingly, Tchaikovsky characteristically provides a dashing coda. The Brodskys are completely at home in both works, and after a superb account of Tchaikovsky's opening movement, passionate yet full of dynamic contrast and delicately observed detail, they provide a ravishingly tender *Andante cantabile*. The vigorous bite of the Scherzo is followed by a bustling, joyous, yet always essentially rhythmic finale, with its elated lyrical theme carrying all before it in an exhilarating close. The performance has all the spontaneity of live music-making and the Brodskys are given a superb presence by the recording, made at The Maltings.

PIANO MUSIC

Capriccioso in B flat, Op. 19/5; Chanson triste, Op. 40/2; L'Espiègle, Op. 72/12; Humoresque in G, Op. 10/2; Méditation, Op. 72/5; Menuetto-scherzoso, Op. 51/3; Nocturne in F, Op. 10/1; Rêverie du soir, Op. 19/1; Romances: in F min., Op. 5; in F, Op. 51/5; The

Seasons: May (White Nights), June (Barcarolle), November (Troika), January (By the fireplace); Un poco di Chopin, Op. 72/15; Valse de salon, Op. 51/2; Waltz in A flat, Op. 40/8; Waltz-scherzo in A min., Op. 7.

(BB) *** Regis (ADD) RRC 1093. S. Richter.

It is good to hear Richter (recorded in 1993 by Ariola-Eurodisc) given first-class, modern, digital sound and on top technical form, showing that he had lost none of his flair. These miniatures are invested with enormous character in playing of consistent poetry; there is never a whiff of the salon. The opening *Nocturne in F major*, the charming neo-pastiche called *Un poco di Chopin* and the haunting *Rêverie du soir* readily demonstrate Richter's imaginative thoughtfulness, while the apparently simple *Capriccioso in B flat* produces a thrilling burst of bravura at its centre-piece. They are all captivating, and the bolder *Menuetto-scherzoso* also shows Tchaikovsky at his most attractively inventive. With its very truthful sound-picture, this is a first recommendation for anyone wanting a single CD of Tchaikovsky's piano music.

OPERA

Eugene Onegin (complete).

*** Decca **DVD** 071 124-9. Kubiak, Weikl, Burrows, Reynolds, Ghiaurov, Hamari, Hartle, Sénéchal, Van Allan, Mason, John Alldis Ch., ROHCG O, Solti. Stage/Video Director: Petr Weigl.

** Arthaus **DVD** 100 126. Boylan, Gluschak, König, Burford, Schelomianski, EU Opera Ch. & O, Rozhdestvensky. (Producer: Nikolaus Lehnhoff.)

This is a fascinating DVD experiment by Decca, and may represent the future process by which an outstanding older audio recording can be laminated onto a newer production, acted out visually. In the present instance, the brilliant Czech director, Petr Weigl, has in his 1988 film illustrated the familiar Decca audio recording, conducted by Sir Georg Solti, with the most evocative visual realization of the narrative. Actors mime to the words in settings as nearly as possible those of the original Pushkin story, whether in the Russian countryside or in St Petersburg. The result is all the more moving, when the agonizing of the young Tatiana or of the disillusioned Onegin is presented by actors who so accurately look the part, as do all the authentically-costumed cast. The contrast between the country ball of Act 2 with the grand ball of Act 3 set in a St Petersburg palace is brought out in a way that could never be achieved on stage, and the chill of the duel scene is all the more involving when the scene is of genuine snow in a genuine forest. Musically, the oddity is that the Prelude and first scene (the Tatiana-Olga duet) are presented in audio recording only, for Weigl starts his film most atmospherically with the peasants' chorus which opens the second scene of Act 1, with the reapers observed from afar wending their way in the mist down a winding country path.

But because the action is filmed in various locations including the open air, with actors miming the singers, the Kingsway Hall acoustic in which Decca recorded the original in the mid-1970s does not quite match up with what we see, and though the direction and the sets are always imaginative, the free-ranging camera does not (and cannot) match the evidence of the ear, so that the acoustic disparity is obvious.

Weigl was the original producer at Covent Garden and ideally should have filmed his Covent Garden production. But he didn't, and this is what he has designed in its place. The cast are handsome and mime for the most part successfully. But some collectors, like RL, may be unable to sustain the suspension of disbelief, and will find the result here ultimately unconvincing. RL feels that here is a case where the collector is better served by the original CD set (still available on CD – 417 413-2), which sounds splendid.

But both E.G. and I.M. find the DVD totally compelling and convincing, and are only too delighted that the recording was made in such an attractive acoustic ambience, with the disparity soon forgotten. With the surtitles so easy to follow, the viewer/listener can be totally caught up in the action and at the same time enjoy not only the glorious singing, but also the inspired orchestral detail of Solti's accompaniment through which Tchaikovsky is conveying the emotions of the characters as one watches them. The sound itself is superb. So while R.L. has his doubts, for E.G. and I.M. this set is a triumph.

Rozhdestvensky's performance, which was staged at the 1998 Baden-Baden Festival, has the advantage of an excellent Onegin in Vladimir Glushchak, the cast is but otherwise not wholly convincing. (Ineke Vlogtman's Larina looks far too young to be a mother, let alone the mother of Orla Boylan and Anna Burford!) There are good things, of course, among which the conducting ranks high. But there is little sense of period, and the chorus certainly don't sound Russian, despite the presence of a Russian conductor. Above all, there is little sense of atmosphere, and the bright, overlit opening scene, with its abundance of kites, hardly induces confidence.

The Queen of Spades (Pique Dame; complete).

*** DVD Ph. 070 434-9. Grigorian, Gulehgina, Leiferkus, Gergalov, Filatova, Borodina, Kirov Op. Ch. & O, Gergiev. (Producer: Temirkanov; V/D: Brian Large.)

**(*) DVD Arthaus 100 272-2. Marusin, Gustafson, Leiferkus, Khartinov, Palmer, Todorovich, Glyndebourne Fest. Ch., LPO, A. Davis. (Producer: Vick; V/D: Peter Maniura.)

Pushkin's dark story of a the gambler's growing obsession with discovering the secret that will bring him riches is taut and concentrated. It unfolds with a gripping psychological intensity, all the more powerful for its understatement. Modest Tchaikovsky's libretto differs in many respects from Pushkin's story. In the opera Lisa becomes a romantic figure who meets a melodramatic end; in the original she is the downtrodden ward of the Countess, not her granddaughter, whose ideas are conditioned by romantic novelettes and who fastens on Herman as a deliverer. There is no fiancé: the figure of Prince Yeletsky was written into the plot by Modest. Lisa's fate, too, is very different, for in the original she marries a pleasant enough young man, a civil servant with a comfortable income. Herman, for whom Tchaikovsky felt such compassion, ends his days in an asylum and is an altogether colder figure than in the opera, where his love for Lisa is genuine and only gradually subsumed in his obsession.

Dating from 1992, the Philips DVD, with the conductor, Valery Gergiev, looking very young, is a live recording of the Kirov Company's grandly traditional production. It is handsome to look at and very well staged, a joy to watch as well as listen to. Yuri Temirkanov (Gergiev's predecessor at the Kirov) produces and does not lose sight of the rococo component in this wonderful opera. Yet it is a straightforward and clean-cut presentation, deftly using massive choruses to match the opulent costumes and scenery, and nearly all the cast is first-rate. Incidentally, this cast differs from the CDs reviewed in our main volume (Ph. 438 141-2), with Irina Arkhipova's Countess being replaced by Ludmila Filatova and Nikolai Putilin giving way to Leiferkus as Tomsky, who appeared in the Ozawa set on RCA and also in the Glyndebourne production reviewed below.

Gegam Grigorian's Herman makes an unromantic figure, a predator rather than an ardent lover. He is a little stiff to start with and rarely sings below *forte*, but he improves as the opera unfolds and his performance acquires intensity, the characterization deepens, and he sings powerfully and cleanly. Maria Gulegina is superb as the heroine, Liza, impressively dramatic and vocally powerful. The others are first-rate with the sad exception of Ludmila Filatova as the Countess, with a voice that is too thin and tremulous even to be acceptable in that aged role. This shortcoming is serious in her big scenes, which should be the climax of the whole drama, though she is certainly affecting, and makes up for it in vocal characterization.

Leiferkus is the soul of elegance, both vocally and as an actor. Nor should Olga Borodina's outstanding Pauline go unmentioned. Above all the hero is Gergiev himself who paces this marvellous score with depth and passion, and Brian Large's visual direction is superb. The eyes are directed to where the action and sound naturally dictate. The video recording was made after the CD and without the audience.

After the Gergiev–Temirkanov, Graham Vick's Glyndebourne production is a distinctly lesser pleasure, albeit a pleasure nonetheless. The smaller stage (this was recorded in 1992 before the renovation) naturally imposes constraints and the set, a slanted black box whose walls are daubed with paint, are a self-imposed limitation. Vick changes the angle of his box to reflect Herman's psychological state. Since Tchaikovsky so eloquently shows this is in the music, this is supererogatory. (How right the late Hans Keller was to describe the opera producer as 'one of music's unnecessary professions'.) Yuri Masurin's Herman is if anything more impressive than Grigorian's; he is the part from beginning to end. Nancy Gustafson is an expressive Liza, who conveys her bewilderment and anguish with much artistry and the cast in general is first-rate. Felicity Palmer's Countess is particularly fine. Andrew Davis holds all the threads together magnificently and gets an impressive response from his singers and the LPO. Gergiev perhaps gets the greater sweep and depth of tone and has of course the most sumptuous and authentic staging.

Vocal Collection

Prelude: The Battle of Poltava. **Arias from:** *Eugene Onegin; The Maid of Orleans* (with *Prelude*); *Mazeppa* (with *Gopak*) ; *The Queen of Spades; The Sorceress; Yolanta.*

** Orfeo C540 011 A. Varady, Munich Radio O., Kofman

Julia Varady gives commanding performances of this wide-ranging collection of Tchaikovsky arias, even if the voice sounds very mature for the young Tatiana in the *Letter Scene* of *Eugene Onegin*. What sadly undermines the impact of the performances is that the recording, made in collaboration with Bavarian Radio, lacks the warmth and fullness usually associated with this source, with Varady's voice lacking its characteristic bloom. The three orchestral pieces make a useful supplement.

TELEMANN, Georg Philipp

(1681–1767)

Double Concerto for Flute and Recorder in E min.; Oboe Concerto in E min.; Viola Concerto in G; Violin Concerto in A min.; Concerto (Sonata) for 4 Solo Violins in D; (Overture) Suite (Don Quichotte).

(BB) ** Arte Nova 74321 34028-2. Borsch, Guttman, Tavernara, Langgarner, Sigl, Cis Collegium Mozarteum, Salzburg, Geise.

As with the Naxos disc of *Recorder Concertos*, these works are unidentified with catalogue numbers but the *Double Concerto for Flute and Recorder*, the *Sonata for Four Solo Violins* and the *Viola Concerto* are all included on other CDs listed below. Comparison with the Arte Nova collection is not to Geise's advantage. The playing of both soloists and orchestra has less personality in Salzburg and this is an agreeable but not distinctive collection. Moreover there is more character in Telemann's *Don Quichotte* portrait than the Cis Collegium Orchestra reveals.

Oboe Concertos: in C min. (2); *D (Concerto grazioso); D min.; E; E flat; F; F min.; Oboe d'amore Concertos: E; E min.; G;* (i) *Triple Concerto for Oboe d'amore, Flute & Viola d'amore.*

(BB) *** Regis RRC 2057 (2). Francis, L. Harpsichord Ens.; (i) with Mayer, Watson.

Sarah Francis's survey of Telemann's *Oboe* and *Oboe d'amore Concertos* brings modern-instrument performances, which are a model of style. The *G major Oboe d'amore Concerto* on the first disc is most gracious (with colouring dark-timbred like a cor anglais in the *soave* first movement). The *Concerto grazioso*, too, is aptly named. The *C minor Oboe Concerto* begins with a *Grave*, then the main Allegro brings a witty dialogue between soloist and violins, with the theme tossed backwards and forwards like a shuttle-cock. But it is the works for oboe d'amore that are again so striking. Most imaginative of all is the *Triple Concerto* with its sustained opening *Andante* (rather like a Handel aria) and *Siciliano* third movement with the melody alternating between oboe d'amore and viola d'amore, and nicely decorated by flute triplets. The performances are full of joy and sparkle as well as expressive. They are beautifully recorded and make a very good case for playing this repertoire on modern instruments. Now reissued as a budget Double on Regis they are even more highly recommended.

Oboe d'amore Concerto in E min., TWV 51:E2; Double Horn Concerto in F, TWV 52:F4; Viola Concerto in G, TV 51:G9; Double Viola Concerto in G, TWV 52:G3; Violin Concertos: in A (Die Relinge); TWV 51:A4; in G, TWV51:G6; Double Violin Concerto in B flat, TWV 52:B2; Concerto for 2 Violins and 2 Horns in D, TWV 52:D4.

🏵 *** EMI CDC5 57232-2. Mayer, Christ, Kussmaul, Dohr, Schreckenberger, Berlin Baroque Soloists

This compilation is described as 'unknown works', but that does not apply to the *Viola Concerto*, which Wolfgang Christ plays so beautifully. These are period instrument performances but the Berlin Soloists have a particularly light, graceful style of playing and the dainty articulation of their oboist, Albrecht Mayer, is captivating. The *Violin Concerto* nicknamed *Die Relinge* pictures pond frogs, but their croaking here is engagingly delicate. The first movement of the *Concerto for 2 violas* is a Minuet marked *Douceur*, the second *Gay*, and these superb players catch both moods delightfully, while the *Double Violin Concerto* is hardly less felicitous. The works including horns are obviously more robust, but the Vivace finale of TWV52:F4 is wonderfully lighthearted and polished. Indeed all the performances have an unusual elegance, the solo playing of the very highest calibre. With splendidly natural recording and a concert hall balance, this is one of the very finest of all Telemann collections.

Recorder Concertos: in C & E major; Double Concerto for Recorder and Flute; Suite in A min. for Recorder and Strings.

(BB) *** Naxos 8.554018. Rothert, Umbach, Cologue CO, Müller-Brühl.

It is a pity that Naxos do not provide TWV identification as do EMI and DG Archiv, but the *Suite in A minor* is an irresistible masterpiece if ever there was one, and is easily identified. It is played here as winningly and stylishly as anywhere else on disc. The two named soloists share the *Double concerto* (which has a delightful *Largo* that starts off like Handel's 'Where'er you walk'), but it is not clear who plays elsewhere. However it is of no moment; all the solo playing here is expert and personable, and there is some delicious virtuoso piping in the second movement of the *E major Concerto*. Indeed all four works show Telemann on top form, Helmut Müller-Brühl's accompaniments are polished and equally stylish, and the recording is first class.

(i) *Recorder Concertos in C; in F*; (ii) *Suite in A min. for Recorder & Strings*; (i) *Sinfonia in F.*

(B) **(*) Hyp. Helios CDH 55091. (i) Holtslag, Parley of Instruments; (ii) cond. Goodman.

The three solo concertos here are a delight. Peter Holtslag's piping treble recorder is truthfully balanced, in proper scale with the authentic accompaniments, which are neat, polished, sympathetic and animated. The *Sinfonia* is curiously scored, for recorder, oboe, solo bass viol, strings, cornett, three trombones and an organ, with doubling of wind and string parts. Even with Roy Goodman balancing everything expertly the effect is slightly bizarre. About the great *Suite in A minor* there are some reservations: it is played with much nimble bravura and sympathy on the part of the soloist, but the orchestral texture sounds rather thin. However, at budget price this remains an attractive proposition.

(i–iii) *Double Concerto in E min. for Recorder & Transverse Flute*; (iv) *Viola Concerto in G*; (i; v) *Suite in A min. for Flute & Strings*; (iii) *Overture des nations anciens et modernes in G.*

(BB) *** Warner Apex (ADD) 0927 40843-2. (i) Brüggen; (ii) Vester; (iii) Amsterdam CO, Rieu; (iv) Doctor, Concerto Amsterdam, Brüggen; (v) Southwest German CO, Tilegant.

All these works show Telemann as an original and often inspired craftsman. His use of contrasting timbres in the *Double Concerto* has considerable charm; the *Overture des nations anciens et modernes* is slighter but is consistently and agreeably inventive, and the *Suite in A minor*, one of his best-known works, is worthy of Handel or Bach. Frans Brüggen and Franz Vester are expert soloists and Brüggen shows himself equally impressive on the conductor's podium accompanying Paul Doctor, the rich-timbred soloist in the engaging *Viola Concerto*. The 1960s sound, splendidly remastered, is still superb, with excellent body and presence, and this Apex reissue is a fine bargain.

(i) *Violin Concerto in A (Die Relinge), TWV 51:A4; Concerto in A for 4 Violins and Strings, TWV 54:A1; Overture (Suite) in D for viola da gamba concertata, TWV 55:D6; Sinfonia spiritosa in D, TWV 44:1; Symphony in D, TWV Anh. 50:1. Sonatas for 4 Solo Violins in C, G & D, TWV 40:201/3.*

**(*) DG 461 492-2. Soloists, Musica Antiqua Köln, Goebel.

Reinhard Goebel's Musica Antiqua Köln's bold rhythmic style is less charming, more abrasive than that of the Berlin Baroque Soloists, as is obvious at the very opening of the *Sinfonia spiritosa*, and the *Symphony in D* (written for Hamburg's jubilee celebration) is similarly bold and robust. Yet their playing is full of character and in *Die Relinge* their frogs croak with robust realism. They are at their finest in the two outstanding unaccompanied works for four violins, where Telemann's invention is strikingly innovative. The solo playing here is superb and all the composer's individual figurations, including a *moto perpetuo* in the *D major* and a striking *Largo e staccato* in the *C major*, are realized with playing of the very highest calibre. But at times elsewhere one wishes the tuttis were not quite so gruff and especially so in the colourful *Overture with viola da gamba concertata*.

(i) *Violin Concerto in A (Les Rainettes). Overtures (Suites) in B flat (Les Nations); in D TWV 55; in G (La Bizarre).*

*** HM HMC 901744. (i) Seiler; Berlin Akademie for Alte Musik.

The bluff good humour of Telemann and his fondness for a musical joke are splendidly illustrated in this delightful disc of three of his *Overture/Suites* and a *Violin Concerto* equally spirited with its joky imitation of frogs ('rainettes' in French), which the note suggests might be a take-off of Vivaldi. The *B flat Overture* with its sequence of brief movements celebrating different nations is well enough known, but the jolliest work of all here is the one nicknamed *La Bizarre*, with its deliberate rule-breaking in the fugue of the opening movement. The players of the Berlin Academy of Early Music bring out the fun all the more effectively with the brilliance, precision and energy of their playing, vividly recorded.

Darmstadt Overtures (Suites), TWV 55/C6 (complete).

(B) *** Teldec Ultima (ADD) 0927 41403-2 (2) VCM, Harnoncourt.

These overtures or suites originate from Telemann's period in Frankfurt, and were almost certainly composed for the Darmstadt Court. The Harnoncourt performances (see our main volume) are comprehensive, light in touch, and can be recommended with even more enthusiasm now that they have been reissued as an Ultima Double.

CHAMBER MUSIC

Overtures (Suites) for 2 Oboes, 2 Horns, Bassoon and Double Bass in F (La Joie); (La Fortune); (La Chasse), TWV 55:F5; F8; F9; in F TWV 55:F15 & F18.

*** MDG 301 1109-2. Consortium Classicum.

Telemann wrote many works for wind ensemble but only ten Overture/Suites have survived, five of which are offered here. They are all essentially in the same pattern of five or six movements although the dances vary between them. One would have expected the work nicknamed *La Chasse* to have the most spectacular horn parts, but in the event *La Fortune* and *La Joie* are the most impressive in this respect and the two works without nicknames are just as inventive as those with a sobriquet, with TWV 55: F18 the most attractive of all. The playing here is expert and full of life, but with similar sonorities throughout and all the works in the key of F, this is a CD to dip into rather than play right through. Excellent recording.

Sonata Metodiche Nos. 1–6 (1728); 7–12 (1732).

** MDG 311 1110-2 (2). Hünteler, Zipperling, Lohff.

There is already a fine set of these Sonatas on Accent ACC 94104/5D by the Kuijkens, and we are inclined to prefer their performances to the new set from Konrad Hünteler. He plays well enough but his early flute seems to offer performance problems, for there are just occasionally moments when the intonation is slightly insecure.

THOMPSON, Randall (1899–1984)

Alleluia; Choose something like a Star; The best of Rooms; The Eternal Dove; Felices ter.

*** ASV CDDCA 1125. Harvard University Ch., Somerville; Erica Johnson (organ) – BEACH: *Choral Music.* ***

Commissioned by Koussevitzky in 1940 for the opening of the Tanglewood Music Center, Randall Thompson's *Alleluia* is for choral societies the American vocal equivalent of Barber's *Adagio* for string orchestras. Built on that single word it rises to a climax of comparable intensity, never losing its grip on the listener during its imaginative forward progress. *The Eternal Dove* and *Choose something like a Star* are much later works and in many ways equally fine, and almost as memorable. Thompson is an individual writer and all these works are very rewarding when so committedly sung.

TIPPETT, Michael (1905–98)

(i) Concerto for Double String Orchestra; (ii) Concerto for Orchestra; (ii; iii) Concerto for Violin, Viola, Cello and Orchestra; (i) Fantasia concertante on a Theme of Corelli; (iv) Byzantium; (v) Fanfare for Brass; (i) Little Music for String Orchestra; (vi) Dance, Clarion Air.

(M) *** Decca (ADD/DDD) 470 196-2. (i) ASMF, Marriner; (ii) LSO, Davis; (iii) Pauk, Imai, Kirshbaum; (iv) Robinson, Chicago SO, Solti; (v) Philip Jones Brass Ens., Snell; (vi) Kelly, Eckersley, Cave, Cann, Schola Cantorum of Oxford, Cleobury.

This double CD is an ideal way to begin an exploration of Tippett's music. The *Triple Concerto* was recorded (by Philips) in 1981, and was nominated 'Record of the Year' by *Gramophone* magazine. This beautiful recording presents a near-ideal performance of one of Tippett's later works, its new more exuberantly lyrical style representing an important development for the composer when the work was first heard in 1979, with these same artists.

The *Concerto for Double String Orchestra* is surely one of the finest twentieth-century works for strings. With utter commitment Marriner and his colleagues allow the jazz inflections of the outer movements to have their lightening effect on the rhythm, and in the heavenly slow movement the slowish tempo and hushed manner display the full romanticism of the music without ever slipping over the edge into sentimentality. The *Corelli Fantasy*, a similarly sumptuous work but without the same lyrical felicity, and the *Little Music* are both equally well done, and the early 1970s sound remains excellent.

The *Concerto for Orchestra* was a by-product of the opera *King Priam* and, even more successfully than the opera, exploited Tippett's thorny style; tough and sinewy, hardly at all lyrical in the manner of the composer's early work. To study such a work on CD is very rewarding, and the performance is excellent. This 1964 (Philips) recording remains warm and vivid, though with a little tape hiss.

Byzantium was written to celebrate Solti's 30-year association with the Chicago Symphony Orchestra and is an extended setting for soprano of the Yeats poem of the same name. This is Tippett at his most exotic, responding vividly to the words, and the live 1991 recording can hardly be faulted. Faye Robinson, taking over from Jessye Norman at the last minute, gives a radiant performance, triumphantly breasting the problems of the often stratospheric and angular vocal line. Equally, Solti draws brilliant, responsive playing from the orchestra. With the vibrant *Fanfare* and the striking choral work *Dance, Clarion Air* included, this British Collection CD is not to be missed.

(i) Symphonies Nos. 1–2; (i; ii) 3; (iii) Suite in D for the Birthday of Prince Charles.

(M) *** Decca (ADD/DDD) 473 092-2 (2). (i) LSO, Davis; (ii) with Harper; (iii) Chicago SO, Solti.

Sir Colin Davis's pioneering versions of Tippett's first three symphonies, recorded in 1968 (No. 2), 1973 (No. 3) and 1975 (No. 1), are here restored to circulation in excellent transfers as a highlight of Decca's 'British Collection'.

When it first appeared, in 1945, Tippett's *First Symphony* was regarded as a hard nut to crack, in spite of its relatively accessible idiom. In a way it is the most concentrated of the three symphonies here and certainly the most organically conceived. This is a work of substance whose eloquence does not lie on the surface. In this 1975 recording, Colin Davis and the LSO do justice to its grit and intellectual power (it originally received a ✪ in the 1977 Guide) and the vivid and warm recording still sounds good in its CD transfer.

The *Second Symphony*, a superb work, bears constant repetition and like Tippett's *Piano Concerto* offers a wealth of interesting ideas to the listener. The composer began work on it in the mid-1950s and completed it in response to a commission from the BBC to mark the tenth anniversary of the Third Programme. When one first encounters it, the proliferation of ideas seems almost to undermine the sense of forward direction, and the detail attracts attention to itself before dissolving into another idea of almost equal interest. But a closer acquaintance shows this to be misleading: the parts fit into an integrated and logical whole. The slow movement in particular has an atmosphere of striking imaginative quality: it explores the 'magical side' of Tippett's personality and deserves a place among his finest inspirations. The first movement opens with pounding C's, suggested to the composer when listening to some Vivaldi, and the music that flows from this has enormous vitality and complexity. Again the LSO under Davis rise to the occasion and give a performance of great confidence and brilliance, and the sound quality is excellent.

Tippett describes his ambitious *Third* as a hybrid symphony, and consciously follows the example of Beethoven's *Ninth Symphony* in the transition to the final vocal sections in which the soprano sings three blues numbers and a dramatic scena to words by the composer. The first half consists of a powerful first section in Tippett's brand of sonata form and a deeply intense second section which exploits total stillness in a fascinating variety of textures. Before the blues conclusion the second half is introduced by a busy scherzo. The pity is that the first half is far more cogent than the second and the two halves do not really match up to each other. In this fine performance, Davis is as persuasive as any conductor could be, while Heather Harper almost manages to mute the crudities of Tippett's text. Solti's digital account of the *Suite for the Birthday of Prince Charles* makes a charming, if lightweight, fill-up.

TOCH, Ernst (1887–1964)

String Quartets Nos. 8 in D flat, Op. 18; 9 in C, Op. 26.

*** CPO 999 680-2. Verdi Qt.

One of the casualties of the 1930s, Toch's music is receiving welcome attention from the CPO label. Widely played in the 1920s, Toch lost no time in emigrating when the Nazis seized power and spent the rest of his life writing for Hollywood and teaching in the University of Southern California. (Incidentally, his pupils in Berlin included the young Vagn Holmboe.) Toch was largely an auto didact, copying out the expositions of Mozart quartet movements and then trying to complete them. He was drawn early on to the quartet medium and the two works recorded here are in the Strauss Reger tradition: the *Eighth Quartet* comes from 1909 just after he had won the Mozart Prize in Vienna,

and the *Ninth* was composed in 1920, and though indebted to Strauss is more radical in language. As the post-war symphonies show, Toch was a composer of real substance and these two quartets reward acquaintance. Good performances and decent recording.

TORELLI, Giuseppe (1658–1709)

Trumpet Concerto in D.

(M) *(*) Westminster (ADD) 471 276–2. Vienna State Op. O, Scherchen – HANDEL: *Water Music* etc. (*); VIVALDI: *Double Trumpet Concerto* (*).

Scherchen's account of Torelli's attractive concerto is the best performance on this CD; at least it has some life in it, though it could hardly be described as a 'brilliant rendition'.

TVEITT, Geirr (1908–81)

A Hundred Hardangar Tunes, Op. 151: Suites Nos. 1, Nos 1–15; 4 (Nuptials) Nos 46–60.

(BB) *** Naxos 8.555078. RSNO, Bjarte Engeset.

If Tveitt's musical schooling was cosmopolitan (he studied with Honegger, Wellesz, Florent Schmitt and Villa-Lobos), his musical outlook was steeped in the Hardangar music of western Norway. Even though almost eighty percent of his output was destroyed in a fire, he can almost rival Milhaud, Niels Viggo Bentzon or Villa-Lobos in fecundity. The *Fourth Suite of Hardangar Tunes* was the first Tveitt work to be recorded on LP, way back in the 1960s, albeit in a much less complete form than it is here. Try '*So stilt dei ror på glitre-fjord*' (*How silently they row on the glittering fjord*), and you will understand why Tveitt enjoyed such an enviable reputation as an orchestrator. His sound world is highly original and imaginative, and unfailingly inventive. Each of these suites comprises fifteen numbers which some may find too much of a good thing, and there is something to be said for making one's own shorter compilations. The Royal Scottish National Orchestra play with evident enthusiasm for Bjarte Engeset who has collated the various different sources in preparing his edition. Nearly all these pieces are delightful and many are quite captivating.

A Hundred Hardanger Tunes: Suites Nos. 2: 15 Mountain Songs (Nos. 16–30); 5: Troll Tunes (61–75).

(BB) *** Naxos 8.555770. RSNO, Engeset.

Readers who have sampled Bjarte Engeset's earlier CD of Tveitt's *Hardanger Tunes Suites* will find much to delight them here. What an inventive orchestrator and arranger he is! Small wonder that the Norwegian Radio employed him as their official orchestrator. These are every bit as imaginative and colourful as the earlier sets. Something of a find.

VARNEY, Louis (1844–1908)

Les Mousquetaires au couvent (operetta): complete.
**(*) EMI (ADD) CZS5 74076-2 (2). Mesplé, Command, Trempont, Bastin, Burles, Monnaie Theatre Ch., RTBF SO, Doneux.

Although Louis Varney was a prolific composer of operetta, his name is kept alive (in France, at least) only by *Les Mousquetaires au couvent* of 1880, mainly because of the amusing libretto. Varney's music owes much to the spirit of Offenbach, and this excellent performance makes a good case for its revival. There are plenty of good tunes and attractive ensembles to keep the listener entertained. The lively cast are all stalwarts of the French operetta tradition, and they receive excellent support from Edgard Doneux, who conducts with plenty of verve. The 1979 recording is clear and vivid, and this recording fills an important gap in the French operetta catalogue. As usual in this otherwise enterprising EMI series, there are no texts and translations, but praise be for small mercies: there is both a synopsis of the story and something about the work and composer in English.

VAUGHAN WILLIAMS, Ralph (1872–1958)

(i; ii) *Concerto Grosso*; (iii; iv) *Fantasia on a Theme by Thomas Tallis*; (i; ii; v) *The Lark Ascending*; (i; ii) *Partita*; (vi; iv) *Romance in D flat*; (i; ii; vii; viii) *Dona nobis pacem*; (i; ii; vii; ix) *Fantasia on the Old 104th Psalm Tune*; (x) *Magnificat*; (i; ii; vii; viii) *Toward the Unknown Region*.

(B) **(*) EMI mono/stereo CDZ5 74782-2 (2). (i) LPO; (ii) Boult; (iii) Philh. O; (iv) Sargent; (v) with Pougnet; (vi) Adler, Gritton, BBC SO; (vii) LPO Ch.; (viii) Armstrong, Carol Case; (ix) Katin; (x) Watts, Amb. S., O Nova of London, Davies.

This self-recommending Vaughan Williams anthology includes some unexpected items, notably the atmospheric *Romance*, beautifully performed by the late Larry Adler, its dedicatee, in 1952. Boult's affinity with this composer is well known, and it is good to hear again just how well he presents the powerful and sustained climax in the *Dona nobis pacem*. As for the *Fantasia on the Old 104th* (for piano, chorus and orchestra) – far from the composer's greatest work – Boult's team (with Peter Katin as the pianist) makes it sound better than it really is. The *Partita* and *Concerto Grosso* are beautifully done, and *Toward the Unknown Region* is similarly impressive. The *Lark Ascending* is the only Boult item not dating from the 1970s: it was recorded (in mono) with Jean Pougnet as the soloist in 1952 and makes its CD debut here. It's a good performance, though some allowances have to made for the sound. Also, it was a pity that Boult's 1970s version of the *Tallis Fantasia* was not chosen; Sargent doesn't

quite produce the spiritual quality this work ideally needs, despite the beautiful playing and good 1959 sound. The Holstian *Magnificat* is performed with sympathy and imagination by Meredith Davies's team, and the 1970 recording has transferred well. This set is well worth considering, even though no texts are offered.

(i) *English Folksongs Suite*; (ii) *Fantasia on a Theme by Thomas Tallis*; *The Lark Ascending*; (iii) *Partita for Double String Orchestra*; (iv; v) *6 Studies in English Folk Song*; (iv; vi) *3 Vocalises for Soprano and Clarinet*.

(M) **(*) ASV Platinum (DDD/ADD) PLT 8520. (i) London Wind O; (ii) ASMF, Marriner; with Brown (iii) London Fest. O, Pople; (iv) Johnson; (v) Martineau; (vi) Howarth.

The London Wind Orchestra's 1980 account of the *English Folk Suite* is the only analogue recording here, but the sound is extremely bright and vivid, and the *Suite* is given a comparably zestful performance. If the slow movement might have been played more reflectively, the bounce of *Seventeen Come Sunday* is irresistible. Iona Brown has recorded *The Lark Ascending* before with Marriner and the ASMF on Argo (now Decca), but this newer digital version is both eloquent and evocative although the great clarity of the recording does rob it of a little atmosphere. However, Marriner's ASV version of the *Tallis Fantasia*, though beautifully played, is relatively bland beside his classic Argo account (now on a Double Decca). Ross Pople's fresh yet relaxed reading of the *Partita* is a very good one indeed, even if it can't match the sheer beauty of sound of the ASMF. The *6 Studies in English Folk Song* are excellently played and recorded and are delightful, as are the brief *3 Vocalises*, a curiously haunting work.

Fantasia on Greensleeves; *Fantasia on a Theme of Thomas Tallis*.

(BB) **(*) RCA 74321 68018-2. Philh. O, Slatkin – HOLST: *The Planets*. **
(M) * Westminster 471 240-2. V. State Op. O, Boult – HOLST: *The Planets*. *

Beautifully played and very well-recorded accounts of the two *Fantasias* from Slatkin, with the contrasts between the main string group and the smaller 'concertino' in the *Tallis Fantasia* well brought out. If not in the Barbirolli league, these performances are still enjoyable. Unfortunately, the main work on this disc, Holst's *Planets*, is less recommendable.

Recorded in 1959, the players of the Vienna State Opera Orchestra find hardly more affinity with the music of Vaughan Williams than they do with Holst, although the ensemble is better. Despite Boult's special efforts, the solo string quartet in the *Tallis Fantasia* fail to respond to the hushed, ethereal quality of the writing (especially the cellist, whose phrasing is awkwardly angular). *Greensleeves*, too, is comparatively graceless.

Job (A Masque for Dancing).

(BB) *** Warner Apex 0927 444 394-2. BBC SO, Davis – WALTON: *Belshazzar's Feast.* ***

Job (A Masque for Dancing); Fantasia on a Theme by Thomas Tallis; 5 Variants on Dives and Lazarus.

(B) *** CfP (ADD/DDD) 575 3142. LPO, Handley.

Handley's performance of *Job* is outstandingly fine. His dedicated approach shows the composer's inspiration at its most deeply characteristic and at its most consistently noble. The breath of dynamic of the EMI analogue recording is used to enormous effect to increase the drama: the organ entry representing Satan enthroned in heaven has great presence and is overwhelming in impact. Comparably the ravishingly luminous espressivo playing in the work's quieter lyrical pages is movingly beautiful, with the music's evocative feeling memorably captured. The other works also show Handley at his best, especially *Dives and Lazarus.*

It was an imaginative idea to re-couple Vaughan Williams's early 1910 ballet score (intended for Diaghilev, but rejected as being 'too English') with Andrew Davis's fine recording of *Belshazzar's Feast* taken from the last night of the 1994 Promenade Concerts – both the '*Masque for Dancing*' (as the composer described it) and Walton's famous choral work vividly depict Bible narratives. The BBC Symphony Orchestra plays *Job* splendidly, and the recording is spacious.

As in Davis's other Vaughan Williams records, the orchestra is set back and some of their power is lost. However no one could say that the spectacular organ entry (recorded earlier by Andrew Davis in King's College Chapel, Cambridge, and effectively dubbed in) does not make a huge impact, while *Job's* comforters are strongly characterized and the serene closing music, including the lovely *Pavane of the Sons of the Morning*, is radiantly presented.

(i) *The Lark Ascending;* (ii) *Fantasia on Greensleeves; Fantasia on a Theme by Thomas Tallis.*

(B) **(*) CfP 574 8802 [574880]. (i) Nolan, LPO, Handley; (ii) RLPO, Handley – ELGAR: *Enigma Variations; Serenade for Strings.* ***

Handley gives an essentially rhapsodic account of the *Tallis Fantasia*, relaxing in its central section and then creating an accelerando to the climax. The inner string group creates radiantly ethereal textures, but ideally the recording needs a little more resonance – the work was written to be performed in Gloucester Cathedral – although it is rich-textured and truthful.

The immediacy of the recording allows no mistiness in *The Lark Ascending*, but it still a warm, understanding performance.

(i) *The Lark Ascending; The Wasps: Overture and Aristophanic Suite; Prelude and Fugue in C min.*

(B) *** CfP (ADD/DDD) 575 3162. (i) Nolan; LPO, Handley – DELIUS: *Collection.* ***

This attractive pairing of favourites items by Vaughan Williams and Delius is aptly entitled '*A Lark and a Cuckoo*'. David Nolan gives a warm, understanding performance of *The Lark Ascending*, projected in clear yet atmospheric digital sound. Then the *Wasps Overture* buzzes in lively fashion. It is spaciously conceived, and leads to charming, colourful accounts of the other four pieces which make up the suite, among which the engaging *March Past of the Kitchen Utensils* stands out. The spectacular *Prelude and Fugue* is an orchestral arrangement of an organ piece (made by the composer) for the Three Choirs Festival, Hereford, in 1930: its style has something in common with *Job*.

SYMPHONIES

A Sea Symphony (No. 1).

(B) *** CfP 575 3082. Rodgers, Shimell, RLPO & Ch., Handley.

Vernon Handley conducts a warmly idiomatic performance, which sustains relatively slow speeds masterfully. The reading is crowned by Handley's rapt account of the slow movement, *On the Beach at Night Alone*, as well as by the long duet in the finale, leading on through the exciting final ensemble, *Sail Forth*, to a deeply satisfying culmination in *O my Brave Soul!* Joan Rodgers makes an outstandingly beautiful soprano soloist, with William Shimell drier-toned but expressive. The recording, full and warm, has an extreme dynamic range, placing the two soloists rather distantly.

A London Symphony (No. 2); Symphony No. 8 in E min.

(B) *** CfP 575 3092. RLPO, Handley.

Vernon Handley gives a beautifully paced and wellsprung reading of the *London Symphony*, although not as crisp in ensemble as some and with sound diffused rather than sharply focused. The result is warmly sympathetic and can be strongly recommended if the generous coupling of the *Eighth Symphony*, an underestimated work, is preferred.

A Pastoral Symphony (No. 3); Symphony No. 4 in F min.; English Folk Songs Suite.

(B) *** CfP 575 3102. RLPO, Handley.

Although Vernon Handley's speeds are relatively fast – as those of his mentor, Boult, tended to be – he has the benefit of refined modern digital recording to help bring out the element of mystery in the *Pastoral Symphony*. Handley's approach to the *Fourth Symphony* is relatively light and not at all violent, and makes a good case for this alternative approach. The engaging *Folk Songs Suite* now makes a lovely encore.

Symphony No. 4; Fantasia on Greensleeves; Fantasia on a Theme by Thomas Tallis; (i) Serenade to Music.

(B) **(*) Sony SBK 89779. NYPO, Bernstein; (i) with vocal soloists.

Symphony No. 4 in F min.; (i) Mass in G min.; (ii) Six Choral Songs to be Sung in Time of War.

✪ *** Chan. 9984. (i) Hickox Singers; (ii) LSO Ch.; LSO, Hickox.

Richard Hickox builds on the brilliant success of his prize-winning account of the *London Symphony* in its original version, with this searing reading of the *Fourth Symphony*, matching and even outshining in its fury the premiere recording conducted by the composer in 1937. What Vaughan Williams brought out more than anyone until this Hickox recording is the fierce urgency of the writing, above all in the first movement. Hickox even manages to match the very fast speed RVW set, angry to the very last bar. The intensity of the LSO's playing, brilliant from first to last, has one magnetized in all four movements, chill in the slow movement with its eerie polytonal writing, and unrelenting even in the skipping rhythms of the scherzo and the oompah sequences of the finale. Like the composer, Hickox never relaxes into mere jauntiness, but does not sound rigid either, moulding the great melodies which in defiance of the overall mood surge up in each movement. This work, written in 1935 and designed by Vaughan Williams to shock his contemporaries and possibly even himself, emerges fresher than ever. The *Mass in G minor* makes a fine and unusual coupling, here given sharper focus than usual, with dramatic contrasts underlined, and with the precision of ensemble compensating for having women's rather than boy's voices in the upper parts. The six unison *Songs to be Sung in Time of War*, which come as a unique supplement, were written at the outbreak of war in 1939 to texts by Shelley, miniatures that in their natural lyrical intensity rise beyond the limits of scale. Superb Chandos sound in both the symphony and the choral works.

Bernstein's account of the *Fourth Symphony* is strangely impressive. His first movement is slower than usual but very well controlled; he captures the flavour and intensity of the score as well as the brooding quality of the slow movement. The New York orchestra plays extremely well and the 1965 recording is full and vivid. The *Serenade to Music* is less successful: the solo singers are too forwardly balanced and the sound in general is unimpressive, though the performance itself is not without interest. The two *Fantasias* are expansively done (American performances of *Greensleeves* are always slow), and the *Tallis* certainly has plenty of tension. Well worth trying at bargain price.

Symphony No. 5 in D; (i) Oboe Concerto; (ii) Flos campi.

✪ (B) *** CfP 575 3112. (i) Small; (ii) Balmer, RLPO Ch.; RLPO, Handley.

Vernon Handley's disc is outstanding in every way, a spacious yet concentrated reading, superbly played and recorded, which masterfully holds the broad structure of this symphony together, building to massive climaxes. The warmth and poetry of the work are also beautifully caught. The rare and evocative *Flos campi*, inspired by the Song of Solomon, makes a generous and attractive coupling, equally well played if rather closely balanced. The sound is outstandingly full, giving fine clarity of texture. For this reissue Jonathan Small adds a delectable account of the charmingly lyrical *Oboe Concerto*.

Symphonies Nos. 6 in E min.; 9 in E min.; Fantasia on Greensleeves.

(B) *** CfP 575 3122-2. RLPO, Handley.

Handley, with rich, full recording, gives warm-hearted readings of Nos. 6 and 9. The two works can be seen as related not only by key, but also in their layout – both end on measured, visionary slow movements. Next to Previn's now withdrawn recording in the same coupling, Handley lacks some of the darker, sharper qualities implied. Though his speeds are consistently faster, his is a more comfortable reading, and the recording adds to that impression. Handley's approach is a valid one as the slow pianissimo finale, here presented as mysterious rather than desolate, was inspired not by a world laid waste by nuclear war (as was once thought), but by Prospero's 'cloud-capp'd towers' in Shakespeare's *The Tempest*. The *Greensleeves Fantasia* is now added as a contrasting encore.

(i) Sinfonia Antartica (No. 7); (ii) Serenade to Music (choral version); Partita for Double String Orchestra.

(B) *** CfP (ADD) 573 3132. (i) Hargan; (ii) RLPO Ch.; RLPO, Handley.

Handley shows a natural feeling for expressive rubato and draws refined playing from the Liverpool orchestra. At the end of the epilogue Alison Hargan makes a notable first appearance on disc, a soprano with an exceptionally sweet and pure voice. In well-balanced digital sound it makes an outstanding bargain, particularly when it offers an excellent fill-up, the *Serenade to Music* (though in this lovely score a chorus never sounds as characterful as a group of well-chosen soloists). Also added for this latest reissue is the rare *Partita*, very well-played and sonorously recorded.

Symphony No. 8 in D min.

(M) *** Decca (ADD) 468 490-2. LPO, Boult – RACHMANINOV: *Symphony No. 3*. **(*)

This was the only Vaughan Williams symphony that Boult recorded in stereo for Decca – in the Kingsway Hall in 1956. Its quality in this Legends reissue is excellent, vivid and fresh, just like the performance, with the LPO responding with committment, especially in the pastoral slow movement which is scored for strings alone. The coupling is unexpected but surprisingly successful.

VERDI, Giuseppe (1813–1901)

Overtures: *Aida* **(reconstructed and arr. Spada);** *La forza del destino; I vespri siciliani.*

(BB) *** RCA 74321 68012-2. LSO, Abbado – ROSSINI: *Overtures.* ***

The novelty here is the *Overture* which Verdi originally wrote for the first Italian performance of *Aida* and subsequently rejected in favour of the well-known brief Prelude. It is a considerably extended piece in Spada's reconstruction and one can hear why the composer decided against anticipating effects in instrumental terms far more telling in the full operatic setting. But heard independently it is most entertaining and deftly scored. Together with the other two familiar overtures it is given a strong and brilliant performance with the conductors's magnetism felt not only in the pianissimo string playing but especially in the exciting account of *La forza del destino.* The sound is bright, but has supporting weight and a concert hall resonance.

Requiem Mass.

*** EMI **DVD** DVB4 92693-9. Gheorghiu, Barcellona, Alagna, Konstantinov, Swedish Radio Ch., Eric Ericson Chamber Ch., BPO, Abbado.

*** EMI CDC5 57168-2 (2). Gheorghiu, Barcellona, Alagna, Konstantinov, Swedish R Ch., BPO, Abbado.

(*) Arthaus **DVD 100 146. Price, Norman, Carreras, Raimondi, Edinburgh Fest. Ch., LSO, Abbado.

(M) ** Sony (ADD) SM2K 89579 (2). Arroyo, Veasey, Domingo, Raimondi, LSO Ch. & O., Bernstein.

The EMI DVD offers the video version, very well-presented, of Abbado's superb live recording of the Verdi *Requiem* made at the Philharmonie in Berlin in January 2001 to commemorate the 100th anniversary of the composer's death. The visual element adds significantly to the impact with the chorus full-toned and weighty, and with the four soloists an outstanding team of singers, all still young. The power and beauty of Gheorghiu's singing in the final *Libera me* are even more striking when one can see as well as hear the vibrant intensity with which she attacks that key section.

On CD Claudio Abbado's new version of the Verdi *Requiem*, recorded live in Berlin in January 2001, completely replaces his earlier studio version for DG. Abbado is at his most powerful, helped by full, weighty sound. The Swedish Radio Chorus and the Berlin Philharmonic, challenged by the drama of a live event, add to a performance of electric intensity. Among the soloists, Angela Gheorghiu stands out in a reading which repeatedly brings new revelation, as in her high, floating entry in the *Offertorio*, leading finally to an account of the concluding *Libera me* – where the soprano reigns supreme – which is at once tender and commanding, conveying to the full the disturbing emotions of the liturgy. The other soloists are excellent too, not just Alagna, but a rich-toned young mezzo in Daniela Barcellona and a characterfully Slavonic bass in Julian Konstantinov. With no fill-up, this comes as a two-discs-for-the-price-of-one package. An outstanding version in every way.

As a performance, Abbado's earlier live DVD recording, made for television at the Edinburgh Festival in 1982, outshines his regular audio recordings of the *Requiem*, not least thanks to the extraordinary line-up of soloists, with Jessye Norman taking the mezzo role against Margaret Price as the soprano.

All four soloists are in superb voice, with Ruggiero Raimondi almost sinister in *Mors stupebit* when viewed in close-up, his villainous expressions projected, quite apart from the power and precision of his singing. Similarly, José Carreras has never sounded more powerful, with the big solo *Ingemisco* flawlessly delivered. Jessye Norman sings gloriously too, in such solos as the *Liber scriptus* and the *Recordare*, and she makes a fine match with Margaret Price in their duetting, equally firm and secure, distinct yet blended.

Yet it is Margaret Price who crowns the whole performance in the final *Libera me*, deeply moving and keenly dramatic, the more so when seen in close-up. The Edinburgh Festival Chorus sing as though possessed, and Abbado draws passionate playing from the LSO, with none of the coolness that can mark this conductor's work in the studio. The sound cannot match the finest modern recordings, and it is not helped by the dryness of the Usher Hall, where the performance was recorded, but, as transferred to DVD, the result is still full and vivid, with powerful impact.

Bernstein's 1970 *Requiem* was recorded in the Royal Albert Hall. By rights, the daring of the decision should have paid off, but with close balancing of microphones the result is not as full and free as one would expect. Bernstein's interpretation remains persuasive in its drama, exaggerated at times, maybe, but red-blooded in a way that is hard to resist. The quartet of soloists is particularly strong. At mid price, with no coupling, many may feel this is a bit expensive these days.

4 Sacred Pieces (Quattro pezzi sacri).

(M) ** Sony SMK 89619. Sweet, Ernest Senff Ch., BPO, Giulini – VIVALDI: *Credo, RV 591* (revised Malipiero). *(*)

Giulini's Berlin account of the *Quattro pezzi sacri*, mystical and serene, is beautiful in its way. Tempi are leisurely, and the distanced chorus in a warm acoustic yet provides the widest dynamic contrast at the opening of the *Te Deum*, moving from *pianopianissimo* to a *fortefortissimo* at the *Sanctus*. Yet the performance overall sadly lacks vitality and does not compare in intensity with his earlier EMI recording.

OPERA

Aida (complete).

*** DG **DVD** 073 001-9. Millo, Domingo, Zajick, Milnes, Burchuladza, Kavrakos, Met. Op. Ch. & O., Levine.

Recorded live at the Metropolitan in New York in October 1988, James Levine's powerful and starrily cast reading of *Aida* brings a grandly traditional staging. The sets and costumes are so lavish that the unveiling of the same scene in Act II prompts enthusiastic applause. In that same scene Plácido Domingo is encumbered not only with his golden armour but with a ridiculously tall egg-shaped head-dress. Yet he still manages to sing superbly throughout, a believable hero, and though Aprile Millo has her edgy moments, her poise as well as her power are impressive, not least in the Nile Scene. Dolora Zajick is a vibrant, powerful Amneris and Sherrill Milnes, only just past his peak, a magnificent Amonasro. Luxury casting brings Paata Burchuladze in as Ramfis, though Dimitri Kavrakos is less impressive as the King. Levine is in his element drawing warm and dramatic playing and singing from his formidable team at the Met. Good, bright sound.

Aida (complete; in English).

(M) **(*) Chan. 3074 (2). Eaglen, Plowright, O'Neill, Yurisich, Rose, Alistair, Miles, Geoffrey Mitchell Ch., Philh. O, Parry.

Though this account of Aida in English starts unpromisingly with Dennis O'Neill over-stressed in Radames' opening aria (in Edmund Tracey's translation 'Goddess Aida Fair as a Vision'), this is overall a strong and dramatic reading. Central to the set's success is the formidable assumption of the title role by Jane Eaglen, here sounding more comfortable singing in English than she often has in international original-language recordings. The voice is rich and warm, better focused than it often has been, with fearless attack above the stave, and fine poise in reflective moments. After his strenuous start O'Neill sings most sensitively, so that even by the end of his first aria he achieves a quiet top B flat such as Verdi wanted, and sustains it impressively using a head-voice. Rosalind Plowright, gravitating down to the mezzo register, makes a suitably fruity and vehement Amneris, not quite steady enough, with Gregory Yurisich an incisive Amonasro, and Peter Rose and Alastair Miles strongly cast as Pharaoh and Ramfis respectively. Though David Parry does not always keep dramatic tensions as taut as they might be, the rich and vividly atmospheric Chandos sound regularly compensates.

Aroldo (complete).

*** Ph. 462 512-2 (2). Shicoff, Vaness, Michaels-Moore, Scandiuzzi, Maggio Musicale Fiorentino Ch. & O, Luisi.

Aroldo, Verdi's drastic reworking of Stiffelio, is just as flawed as that earlier failure, in many ways less convincing dramatically thanks to the transfer from nineteenth-century Austria to thirteenth-century Kent, with Aroldo a knight recently returned from the Crusades. Many of the points that have made Stiffelio a latter-day success on stage are missing here, and in the revision some fine passages have been excised. But equally there is much new material that for the Verdian is essential listening, notably in the entirely new Act IV, which may be muddled dramatically but contains a series of superb ensembles. The Philips set is most welcome, when the only previous version was little more than a stopgap, despite the excellent contribution of Montserrat Caballé as the heroine, Mina. Carol Vaness, though with a less pure vocal production, is more dra-

matic in the new set, and Neil Shicoff, rarely singing softly, yet gives life to the title-role. Outstanding is Anthony Michaels-Moore as Egberto, the heroine's father, sensitively sung and acted, while Fabio Luisi draws strong and warmly expressive performances from his whole company, helped by excellent Philips recording.

Don Carlos (complete).

*** Warner DVD 0630 16318-2. Alagna, Hampson, Van Dam, Mattila, Meyer, Halfvarson, Théâtre du Châtelet Ch., O de Paris, Pappano.

This fine issue provides one of the clearest instances where DVD scores on almost every level over the equivalent CD set. Here you have a full three and half hours of music on a single disc, as against the three-CD set from EMI. That also offers a live recording made in the Théâtre du Châtelet in Paris with an identical cast of principals. The sound on DVD may be marginally less full than on CD, but it would take someone with an exceptional ear to feel short-changed. The chorus is rather less crisply disciplined in places, but rises splendidly to the big challenge of the Auto da fe scene of Act III. And where too many DVDs skimp on the number of index points, this one follows the normal CD practice of having them at every crucial point.

All that plus the advantage of having a visual presentation of Luc Bondy's production. Though the sets are simple and stylized, the production never gets in the way of the music, with the costumes of Moidele Bickel (coloured, black, white or crimson) close enough to seventeenth century fashion not to distract from the drama. The score is tautly and warmly presented, as on CD, by Antonio Pappano and the principals are as fine a team as have ever been assembled for this opera on disc – here using the original French text and the full five-act score complete with Fontainebleau scene. Karita Mattila gives the most masterly performance as the Queen, with one inspired passage after another culminating in a supreme account of her Act V aria. Roberto Alagna is in superb voice too, firm and heroic, well-matched against Thomas Hampson, noble as Rodrigo. José van Dam may not have the deep bass normal for the role of Philip II, but having a more lyrical voice brings compensating assets, and he contrasts well with the Grand Inquisitor of Eric Halfvarson. One of the few controversial points in the production is the way that the Grand Inquisitor's entry prompts a few fiery flashes of lightning round him. Otherwise the simple sets add to the speed of the production, with the gantry used in the garden scene of Act III, quickly opening out before one's eyes to make a gallery for the chorus in the Auto da fe scene. An outstanding issue.

Falstaff (complete).

*** DG 471 194-2 (2). Terfel, Pieczonka, Diadkova, Hampson, Röschmann, Shtoda, Berlin R. Ch., BPO, Abbado

(*) BBC Opus Arte **DVD** OA 0812D. Terfel, Frittoli, Rancatore, Manca di Nissa, Montague, Frontali, Tarver, Leggate, Howell, ROHCG Ch. & O, Haitink.

Abbado's is a big-scale view of *Falstaff*, helped by the weighty recorded sound and upfront balance of voices, matching the larger-than-life characterization of the fat knight by the charismatic Bryn Terfel. Terfel gives a vital, three-dimensional reading as one might expect, but uses tone-colours that do not generally have you picturing a fat character, a point that also applies to the classic portrayal by Tito Gobbi in the first Karajan recording on EMI. The darkness of the Falstaff's Act III monologue after his ducking is as intense as you will ever hear it, while the final fugue at a very fast tempo is thrillingly precise, thanks to a team of leading singers who respond brilliantly to Abbado's strong, thoughtful direction. Adrianna Pieczonka is a superb Alice, full-toned and character-ful, and Dorothea Röschmann a charming Nannetta with Larissa Diadkova a fruity Mrs Quickly. The male characters are well contrasted too, and though Tho-mas Hampson's velvety baritone hardly conveys the meanness of Ford, the sensitive detail in his character-ization is magnetic. For most collectors this will now be the primary recommendation, although Giulini's famous version is not eclipsed (DG 410 503-2).

Graham Vick's provocative production with crudely-coloured toy-town sets by Paul Brown was the opening attraction in the newly refurbished Covent Garden opera-house. It is powerfully conducted by Bernard Haitink as Music Director who, in a brief interview, rightly suggests that this is a score with not a superfluous note. The production's principal asset is the strong, characterful Falstaff of Bryn Terfel, musi-cally and dramatically most satisfying despite his grotesquely exaggerated costume and pot-belly. In the tradition of the finest Falstaffs he is at once comic and dignified and ultimately moving, while the voice is in splendid form. Barbara Frittoli also makes an excellent Alice, and the rest of the cast is consistently fine. The problem lies in the sets with their aggressive primary colours and simplistic lines, though the false perspec-tives have a vaguely medieval look.

The costumes, although equally garish, are in Eliza-bethan style, and Vick allows Falstaff to be tipped into the Thames in a genuine laundry basket, but he removes all magic from the final Windsor Forest scene, with a tower of bodies (intrepid members of the chorus) taking the place of Herne's Oak. In an interview (one of the extra features) Vick explains that he wanted to bring out the physicality of the piece, emphasizing that this is an Italian opera, not a Shakespeare play. The interview with Terfel is not helped by the questioner who is rather too pleased with himself, but the singer's warm personality over-rides that drawback. There is also a 10-minute tour backstage of the newly-refurbished opera-house, and an illustrated synopsis of the opera. Unlike many operas on DVD this one has ample index points, with 31 chapters or tracks.

Falstaff (complete; in English).

(M) ******* Chan. 3079 (2). Shore, Kenny, Gritton, Holland, Banks, Kale, De Pont, Davies, Coote, ENO Ch. & O, Daniel.

Taken straight from the ENO stage at the Coliseum to the recording studio, Paul Daniel's brilliant version of *Falstaff* is among the finest of the Opera in English series sponsored by the Peter Moores Foundation. Ensemble is consistently crisp and pointed, yet the feeling of a live experience is vividly caught, with sound-production creating an illusion of a staged per-formance, so getting the best of both worlds. The role of Falstaff is a speciality of Andrew Shore, and he deliv-ers a vivid portrait, at once comic and weighty, but with lightness and sparkle part of the mixture, and with the Act III monologue of disillusion after his ducking ('*Your World is Crumbling*' in the excellent translation of Amanda Holden) a high point. The voice grows rough in places, but Shore is unfazed by the high-lying passages, which come over well. There is no weak link in the rest of the cast, with Yvonne Kenny as Alice and Susan Gritton as Nannetta both outstanding. Yet above all, it is the taut and finely paced conducting of Paul Daniel and the playing of the orchestra, superbly recorded, which make set this musically com-petitive with the finest versions in Italian. As they sing in the final fugue, '*Life is a burst of laughter*'.

La forza del destino (1862 version): complete.

*** Arthaus **DVD** 100 078. Gorchakova, Putilin, Grigorian, Tarasova, Kirov Ch. & O, Gergiev. (Producer: Elijah Moshinsky. V/D: Brian Large.)

The DVD production of the 1862 version of *La forza* comes from St Petersburg, where the opera had its première. In discussing the differences between the 1862 and 1869 versions of the opera itself, Julian Bud-den says that there is 'not a change in the revision which is not an improvement,' but all the same it is good to have Verdi's first thoughts together with some music that is unfamiliar.

In 1862 the overture was replaced by a short prelude, but otherwise the changes concern the final scenes of Act III, where the duo between Don Alvaro and Don Carlo follows rather than precedes the encampment scene. The finale is also different: the Alvaro–Carlo duel takes place on stage and Alvaro does not survive, but takes his own life. Of particular interest is the fact that the Kirov repro-duce the original sets, which look quite handsome, even if the staging is at times a bit hyperactive.

The performance is much stronger than in the ver-sion that the Kirov brought to Covent Garden in the summer of 2001, and Valéry Gergiev here proves a more idiomatic Verdi conductor than he was during the Lon-don season. The cast is strong, with Gorchakova in good form as Lenora singing with great dramatic eloquence.

Philips have recorded it under Gergiev on three CDs (446 951-2) with substantially the same cast, the major changes being Marianna Tarasova (instead of Olga Borodina) as Preziosilla and Sergei Alexashin (instead of Mikhail Kit) as the Padre Guardiano. Otherwise the main characters are the same.

Gegam Grigorian is an impressively confident Alvaro, and Nikolai Putilin's Don Carlo is every bit as good as on CD. Tarasova's Preziosilla does not disappoint, and Sergei Alexashin's Guardiano is better focused than Mikhail Kit in the 1996 CD. The opera looks very good – and sounds very good: the audio balance is first class. Brian Large's video direction is first class, too, and although Moshinsky's direction is busy, it is for the most part effective. Subtitles are in English, German, French and Dutch.

Macbeth (complete).

(*) Arthaus **DVD 100 140. Bruson, Zampieri, Morris, O'Neill, Deutsche Op. Ch. & O, Sinopoli. (Director: Luca Ronconi.)

In his second recording on DVD, made at the Deutsche Oper in Berlin in 1987, Giuseppe Sinopoli conducts a dramatic reading of Macbeth, dominated by the fine Macbeth of Renato Bruson, his self-searching the more compelling in close-up on DVD, and the powerful, if sometimes hooty, Lady Macbeth of Mara Zampieri, perfectly looking the part, young and handsome still.

She points the drinking-song well, and although she avoids the final top note of the sleep-walking scene, it is still a magnetic performance. The rest of the cast is strong too, with Dennis O'Neill as Macduff and James Morris as Banquo. The chorus sings splendidly, with a line-up of dozens of witches in the opening scene, gathered behind the long table that dominates a fair proportion of scenes in Luca Ronconi's bare production, with sets and costumes by Luciano Damiani. Excellent, well-separated sound.

Otello (complete).

(*) DG **DVD 073-006-9. Vickers, Freni, Glossop, Malagu, Bottion, Senechal, Van Dam, Deutsche Op. Ch., BPO, Karajan.

On DVD, as well as conducting, Karajan himself directed this glamorous film version of Otello, presenting it in spectacular settings, with effects going far beyond what is possible on stage, as in the opening storm scene. The singers mime their parts to an audio recording, with mouth-movements not always well-synchronized.

That is a small price to pay for a fine, bitingly dramatic performance, characterfully cast and beautifully sung. Jon Vickers was still at his peak when the recording was made in 1974, thrilling in the title role with not a hint of strain and backed up by powerful acting. Similarly, Peter Glossop has never been finer on disc, whether in his singing or his acting, a plausible yet uncompromising Iago, and Mirella Freni gives a radiant performance as Desdemona, rising superbly to the challenge of the final scene, both sweet and powerful.

The balance of the voices frequently follows the closeness or distancing of the camerawork, which can be distracting, but this is an involving presentation of the Verdi masterpiece, intelligently re-thought for the camera. The sound is good, though not as vivid as in the latest fully digital recordings.

Otello (complete; in English).

(M) **(*) Chan. 3068 (2). Craig, Plowright, Howlett, Bottone, ENO Ch. & O, Elder.

Recorded live at the London Coliseum in 1983 and now reissued on Chandos, the ENO version of Otello is flawed both vocally and in the sound; but those who seek records of opera in English need not hesitate, for almost every word of Andrew Porter's translation is audible, despite the very variable balances inevitable in recording a live stage production. Less acceptable is the level of stage noise, with the thud and ramble of wandering feet all the more noticeable on CD. The performance itself is most enjoyable, with dramatic tension building up compellingly. Charles Craig's Otello is most moving, the character's inner pain brought out vividly, though top notes are fallible. Neil Howlett as Iago may not have the most distinctive baritone, but finely controlled vocal colouring adds to a deeply perceptive performance. Rosalind Plowright makes a superb Desdemona, singing with rich, dramatic weight but also with poise and purity. The Death scene reveals her at her finest, radiant of tone, with flawless attack.

Rigoletto (complete).

(M) *** Decca 470 437-2 (2). Bruson, Gruberová, Shicoff, Fassbaender, Lloyd, St. Cecilia Ac., Rome, Ch. & O, Sinopoli.

(*) BBC Opus Arte **DVD OA 0829D. Gavanelli, Schafer, Alvarez, Halfvarson, ROHCG Ch. & O, Downes.

The Philips set with Bruson, Gruberová and Shicoff has also now been reissued at mid-price as part of Decca's 'Compact Opera Collection'. However there is no printed libretto, only a CD Rom facility which carries full text and translation to be printed out via a computer. The set remains available as a Philips Duo (with synopsis) which many will feel is preferable (462 158-2).

David McVicar's Covent Garden production of Rigoletto was one of the offerings leading towards the Verdi centenary in January 2001, strongly cast with Paolo Gavanelli firm and powerful in the title role. As McVicar explains in an interview (one of the extra DVD features) he perceives the piece as a concentrated howl of pain, evoking the atmosphere of the once-banned play, Le roi s'amuse by Victor Hugo, on which Verdi and his librettist, Piave, based the opera. McVicar incidentally points out that the opera dates from the period of Marx and the Communist Manifesto, though the menace in the production has as much to do with sado-masochistic violence as politics, helped by Tanya McCallin's costumes (with a leather clown costume making Rigoletto into a gnome-like figure and the Duke's leather outfit when he meets Gilda underlining his role as predator). The setting is rough too in what looks like an old junkyard with much wire-netting and corrugated iron sheets. However, this twentieth-century touch hardly gets in the way of the drama, with the costumes broadly traditional in period.

The casting is first-rate, with Gavanelli well-matched by the girlish Gilda of Christine Schafer (not previously known as a coloratura but admirably flexible) and the menacingly seductive Duke of Marcelo Alvarez. Edward Downes as ever is a masterly Verdi interpreter, pacing the drama strongly and purposefully. The extra features include a BBC documentary celebrating the Verdi centenary, with atmospheric shots of Busseto, doing for Verdi what Salzburg has done for Mozart.

La traviata (complete).

⚙ *** Decca DVD 071 431-9. Gheorghiu, Lopardo, Nucci, ROHCG Ch. & O, Solti. (Director: Richard Eyre. V/D: Humphrey Burton & Peter Maniura.)

*** Warner NVC DVD 4509 92409-2. Gruberová, Shicoff, Zancanaro, La Fenice Ch. & O, Rizzi.

(M) **(*) Decca (ADD) 470 440-2 (2). Sutherland, Bergonzi, Merrill, Ch. & O of Maggio Musicale Fiorentino, Pritchard.

As the DVD rightly claims, this famous Solti performance of *La traviata* captures one of the most sensational debuts in recent operatic history. Singing Violetta for the first time, Angela Gheorghiu made the part entirely her own. But the DVD can also claim a special plaudit for the magical opening, when the camera focuses closely on Solti while he conducts the *Prelude*, with every movement of his hands and the concentration in his eyes creating the music in front of us.

He holds the tension at the highest level throughout, with the strings playing marvellously, and recorded with absolute realism. Then the curtain goes up and Bob Crowley's superb stage spectacle spreads out in front of our eyes. The singing is glorious, and this is one of the DVDs that should be a cornerstone in any collection.

Recorded in December 1992 in the beautiful theatre of La Fenice in Venice before the disastrous fire, the alternative Warner DVD offers a moving performance, well cast and with sympathetic conducting from Carlo Rizzi, despite an excessively slow opening prelude. Though Neil Shicoff as Alfredo is made to look like a Victorian bank-clerk, hardly a romantic figure in metal-framed spectacles, the production is traditional, with colourful costumes and evocative sets. Romantic or not, Shicoff is in splendid voice, phrasing and shaping his big set-pieces sensitively, and Edita Gruberová makes a moving Violetta, jolly and vivacious in Act I, taking to the coloratura like a bird before gradually transforming into the haggard tragic figure of Act IV, crowning her performance with the most tender singing. Just as Giorgio Zancanaro as a strong, forthright Germont sings both verses of *Di Provenza al mar* in Act II, Gruberová sings both verses of the *Addio del passato*, surpassing herself in the whispered half-tone, perfectly controlled, of the second

stanza. Though this must come second to the superb Decca Solti DVD, it is still very much worth having.

Sutherland's earlier 1963 recording of the opera has now been reissued at mid-price as part of Decca's 'Compact Opera Collection'. However, there is no libretto, only a CD Rom facility which can print out the full text and translation via a computer. The set remains available as a Decca Double with a cued synopsis and 'listening guide' and many will feel that this is preferable (460 759-2).

La traviata: highlights.

(BB) ** EMI Encore (ADD) CDE5 74760-2. (from complete recording with Sills, Gedda, Panerai, John Alldis Ch., RPO, Ceccato).

Beverly Sills makes an affecting Violetta, producing much lovely singing, although when she is pressed, her voice grows shrill and unfocused. The character of an older woman knowing what suffering is to come remains firm, however, and with a fine Alfredo in Gedda this is a very acceptable set of highlights, when Panerai is a strong-voiced, if not subtle Germont and Aldo Ceccato proves an alert and colourful conductor. The RPO play well for him and the closely miked recording is almost too vivid in its CD transfer. It is a pity that the selection (only 59 minutes) is not more generous, and the synopsis sparsely inadequate.

Il trovatore (complete).

*** EMI CDC5 57360-2 (2). Gheorghiu, Alagna, Hampson, Diadkova, d'Arcangelo, L. Voices, LSO, Pappano.

**(*) Arthaus DVD 100 276. Sutherland, Collins, Summers, Elms, Shanks, Australian Op. Ch., Elizabethan Sydney O., Bonynge. Director Elijah Moshinsky.

(BB) (***) Naxos mono 8.110162.63 (2). Scacciati, Molinari, Zinetti, Merli, Zambelli, La Scala Co. & O, Molajoli.

** DG DVD 073 002-9. Marton, Zajick, Pavarotti, Milnes, Met. Ch. & O, Levine.

(*) Sony S2K 89533 (2). Frittoli, Licitras, Urmana, Nucci, La Scala Ch. & O, Muti.

As in Puccini and Massenet, Antonio Pappano here masterfully draws out the individual artistry of the starry husband-and-wife team of Angela Gheorghiu and Roberto Alagna, pacing the music to bring out not just the drama but the expressive, often atmospheric warmth of the score. The problem for the two principals here is rather greater than in their previous recordings with Pappano, when their lyric voices might not seem weighty enough for the roles of Leonora and of Manrico. Angela Gheorghiu characteristically capitalizes on the problem, bringing a rare tenderness to her big arias, floating her top notes ravishingly, and exploiting her formidable coloratura powers in cabalettas, always stylish in ornamentation. This is a portrait of a heroine younger and more ardently girlish in her love than we are used to, and the drama is the more intense for it. Only in the bravura aria *Tu vedrai che amore in terra* and the final scenes does she press the voice, so that it flickers in emotion. Though in the heroic outburst of *Di quella pira* Alagna tends to force his tone, holding on provocatively to his final top C, that is rather the exception, and generally this is a performance marked, like Gheorghiu's, by individual phrasing to bring out the warmth of emotion along with the meaning of the words. Thomas Hampson as di Luna is at once sinister and ardently sincere in his love for Leonora, giving a warmly involved performance, while Larissa Diadkova with a Slavonic tang in her mezzo tone is a formidable and moving Azucena. Ripely atmospheric recording beautifully balanced, with fine playing and singing from the LSO and London Voices. This is now a pretty clear first choice though the mid-priced RCA set (74321 39504-2) is still very strongly recommendable. Domingo is a superb Manrico, and Fiorenza Cossotto's fiery Azucena unforgettable, while some may prefer the more voluptuous Verdian line of Leontyne Price, although Gheoghiu is quite ravishing in her own way.

Recorded live in July 1983, the Australian Opera DVD presentation of *Il trovatore* offers a bravura display from Dame Joan Sutherland as Leonora, bringing the rarest combination of weight and flexibility to the role, surpassing in mastery her Decca studio recording of six years earlier, gloriously free over the widest range. Though the rest of the cast may not be so starry, they all sing with firmness and clarity to make it an exceptionally satisfying performance, with Richard Bonynge persuasively idiomatic in his conducting. Kenneth Collins is far more sensitive than many more celebrated Manricos – even though he is made to look like a Sicilian bandit – and Jonathan Summers is a strong, handsome di Luna, with Lauris Elms as Azucena making one wonder why she was never used as she should have been in recordings. Elijah Moshinsky's production updates the story to the time of Verdi, with characterful backcloths by Sydney Nolan colourful if not always helpful to the story. The sound on DVD has an edge to it which does not help the voices, but the magnetism of the occasion has one forgetting that.

Recorded by Columbia in 1930, the Naxos issue offers a lustily red-blooded reading typical of Italian performances at that period dominated by verismo. As Leonora Bianca Scacciati has a distinctive timbre, slightly throaty. She is occasionally gusty in her production, but technically secure beyond what one can expect in latterday recordings. Similarly Francesco Merli, a tenor much-admired by Toscanini, with his baritonal timbre is a strong and satisfying Manrico. Enrico Molinari is a reliable Count, sounding a little old at times, and Giuseppina Zinetti is a fruitily resonant Azucena, rich and firm throughout her register, making one appreciate how at that period few leading singers had the sort of wobbles so common today. The performance under Lorenzo Molajoli is lusty and red-blooded to match, and is exceptionally well-transferred by Ward Marston, marrying 78 pressings from different sources. The usual cuts of the period are observed,

which leaves room for a supplement of fine recordings by Scacciati, four of the five with Merli as well, including rare items from Marchetti's *Ruy Blas*, Gomes's *Guarany* and Catalani's *Loreley*, as well as the Trio from Verdi's *I Lombardi*, all very well sung.

Recorded in October 1988 at the Metropolitan in New York, this DG DVD offers an effective presentation of the production by Fabrizio Melano with typically grand, traditional sets by Ezio Frigerio and costumes by Franca Squarciapino. This will please those who resist modern trendy 'concept' productions, but sadly the singing, even with a starry cast of principals, is flawed. Luciano Pavarotti as the Duke is in ringing voice, giving a gloriously full-throated performance with words sharply focused, but the others are disappointing. Sherrill Milnes is sadly past his best, with the voice no longer as rock-steady as in his earlier career, yet he cuts a splendid figure as the Count. Dolora Zajick as Azucena is not as steady as she can be either, with a flutter in the voice, but the principal drawback is the casting of Eva Marton as Leonora, not a singer one would have expected in this role which requires velvet legato and bright flexibility rather than sheer power. She controls the voice better than in Wagner, but too often the focus of such a fruity, gusty soprano is approximate, with pitching vague, disastrously so in coloratura. James Levine directs a typically thrustful, dramatic reading of score.

When there are many fine versions of this opera, it seems a waste to have a live recording from Muti and Scala forces which might just pass muster in a radio broadcast, but which is far too flawed for repeated listening. Even Barbara Frittoli is well below form as Leonora, not as steady as usual, and though Salvatore Licitra as Manrico has a ringing tenor, he uses it with little subtlety, while Leo Nucci is a mere shadow of his former self, singing coarsely throughout, too often failing to pitch notes at all, resorting to a sort of sing-speech. By far the best soloist is Violeta Urmana as Azucena, even if she sounds too young for the role. Muti is at his least sympathetic, forcing the pace so as to make the music sound breathless and brutal, and though five performances were edited together for the recording, the musical imprecisions and stage noises counterbalance any of the advantages of a live event. The sound too has little bloom on it.

Choruses from: *Aida; La battaglia di Legnano; Don Carlos; I Lombardi; Macbeth; Nabucco; Otello; Il trovatore.*

(BB) ✱✱ Warner Apex 0927 40836-2. Saint Cecilia Ch. & O, Rizzi.

These are certainly very well-sung accounts of Verdi's most popular choruses, but Rizzi concentrates on refinement rather than on drama. The result lacks the raw energy that can make these war-horses so exciting. Compared with Decca's rival 1960s recording with the same orchestra under Franci (now on Opera Gala 458 237-2), these digital performances feel a little anaemic. Side-by-side, the ubiquitous *Anvil Chorus*, and *Grand March* from *Aida* sound tame compared to the Decca set, which has more character and excitement. Even if there is some tape hiss, the Decca sound is palpably more vivid and theatrical too, and if it costs a little more, there is almost 15 minutes extra music, and full texts and translations are provided.

Arias: *Aida; Ernani; La forza del destino; Otello; Il trovatore; I vespri siciliani.*

(B) (***) Naxos mono 8.110728. Ponselle (with various partners and accompanists including Martinelli, Pinza and Stracciari).

This splendid disc celebrating the glories of Rosa Ponselle's unique voice and interpretative powers brings excellent CD transfers of her most celebrated electrical recordings made for RCA in 1928, including the heroine's big aria from *Ernani*, spectacularly well done, and the sequence of *Forza* recordings with Martinelli and Pinza – as well as Columbia recordings from the pre-electric period, made between 1918 and 1924 – all chosen by Ward Marston as being the finest Ponselle versions of each item. The result is a wonderful gallery of perfection, beautifully transferred with the voice vividly caught.

VERESS, Sándor (1907–92)

4 Transylvanian Dances.

*** ECM 465 778-2. Camerata Bern, Zehetmair –
SCHOENBERG: *Verklaerte Nacht*; BARTOK: *Divertimento.****

Unlike Bartók, whose colleague he was, Sándor Veress remained in Budapest during the years of the pro-Nazi Horthy régime, succeeding Kodály at the Budapest Academy in 1943, when three of these *Transylvanian Dances* were written. Not long after Rákosi seized power in 1948 he settled in Switzerland where he added the much darker *Lejtös* movement. These are first-rate pieces, strongly Bartókian in feeling, but nonetheless distinctive. RL remembers being much impressed by a broadcast of a highly imaginative Violin Concerto in the early 1950s. Let us hope that these excellently played and vividly recorded pieces will presage more of his music on CD.

VIERNE, Louis (1870–1937)

Piano Quintet in C minor.

*** Hyp. CDA 67258. Stephen Coombs, Chilingirian Qt.
– HAHN: *Piano Quintet in F sharp minor.* ***

An interesting coupling: both Hahn and Vierne turned to the piano quintet within a few years of each other though we associate Hahn mostly with song and Vierne with the organ. Vierne composed his piano quintet in 1917 after the death of his second son, killed in action at only seventeen during the Great War. It is finely structured and its slow movement is particularly searching and thoughtful. The sleeve note draws a parallel with Frank Bridge, and its dark chromaticism is bleak and its world altogether harsher than the more familiar organ. Its centrepiece is the haunting and powerful *Andante*, the emotional core of the work. Stephen Coombs and the Chilingirians play with conviction and character, and are given the benefit of excellently vivid recorded sound. If you enjoy the Franck *F minor Piano Quintet* or the Chausson *Concert*, you will feel very much at home here.

VIEUXTEMPS, Henri (1820–81)

Violin Concertos Nos. 4 in D min., Op. 31; 5 in A min., Op. 37. (ii) Ballade et Polonaise, Op. 38.

(BB) ** Ph. Eloquence 468 204-2. Grumiaux, LAP, Rosenthal.

Grumiaux did much to pioneer these two concertos (separately) on LP in the mid-1960s and although this romantic virtuoso repertoire is perhaps less suited to him than the music of Bach and Mozart, he is fully equal to the bravura, sparkling in the Scherzo of the *D minor Concerto* and the brief finale of the *A major*, and offering a rapturously lyrical line whenever called on to do so (and especially in the secondary themes of the finale of Op. 31 and the first movement of Op. 37). Although the Paris Lamoureux Orchestra is not one of Europe's finest, especially in the brass section, they provide strong accompaniments under Manuel Rosenthal (with some nice woodwind contributions). The recording balance, which is in favour of the soloist without really flattering him, sounds somewhat dated, but it frames Grumiaux well enough. The rare *Ballade et Polonaise* for violin and piano makes a lively encore. Good value, although Perlman is first choice in the concerto coupling, offering Ravel's *Tzigane* and Saint-Saëns's *Havanaise* for good measure. (EMI CDM5 66058-2).

VILLA-LOBOS, Heitor
(1887–1959)

Chôros Nos. 8; 9.

(BB) *** Naxos 8.555241. Hong Kong PO, Schermerhorn.

The *Chôros No. 8* (1925) is what we think of as quintessential Villa-Lobos, exotic, full of colour and superbly evocative insect, bird and forest sounds, all effectively conveyed by the Hong Kong Orchestra under Kenneth Schermerhorn. Villa-Lobos himself spoke of the *Chôros* as 'representing a new form of musical composition synthesizing different kinds of Brazilian Indian and folk-music, having as their principal elements rhythm and all kinds of typical folk melody that appear accidentally from time to time, always transformed by the personality of the composer'. Like No. 8, the *Chôros No. 9* (1929) calls for a huge orchestra, including Brazilian percussion instruments. There is an exuberance, exoticism and an abundance of musical ideas clamouring for attention. The recordings were made in the 1980s and are very good indeed.

Guitar Concerto.

(M) *** Sony (ADD) SMK 89753. Williams, ECO, Barenboim – CASTELNUOVO–TEDESCO: *Concerto*; RODRIGO: *Concierto de Aranjuez; Invocación y danza.* ***

John Williams's compulsive performance makes the very most of the finer points of Villa-Lobos's comparatively slight concerto, and especially the rhapsodic quality of the Andantino. The recording is bright and fresh, the soloist characteristically close, but the effect is vividly present.

Symphonies Nos. 6 (Sobre a linha das montanhas do Brasil); 8; Suite for Strings.

*** CPO 999 517-2. SWR RSO Stuttgart, St Clair.

In all, Villa-Lobos composed 12 symphonies, the first in 1916 and the last two years before his death. The composer himself recorded the *Fourth* and conducted the premières of most of the others, including Nos. 6 and 8. The *Sixth Symphony* (1944) is subtitled *Sobre a linha das montanhas de Brasil (On the Profiles of the Mountains of Brazil)*, and after its première in 1950 Villa-Lobos took it on tour to the Vienna Philharmonic, to the Buffalo Philharmonia and to Havana. The most memorable of its four movements is arguably the lush, atmospheric slow movement with its imaginative orchestration, reminiscent of Ravel and Respighi. The outer movements are over-scored. The *Eighth Symphony* (1950) was also composed in Rio de Janeiro and was dedicated to Olin Downes, the New York critic who championed Sibelius in the 1930s and 1940s. Villa-Lobos conducted its première at a Carnegie Hall concert with the Philadelphia Orchestra in 1955 before taking it on to Paris. It is all exuberant, colourful stuff, wanting the concentration of the genuine symphony no doubt but worth hearing all the same. The slow movement is beautifully laid out for the orchestra and the scherzo, too, shows Villa-Lobos as the resourceful orchestrator he was. The fill-up is an early, albeit, not particularly original but attractive *Suite for Strings* from 1913. Very good playing from the Südwestrundfunk Orchestra of Stuttgart under Carl St Clair and well-balanced recording.

VIVALDI, Antonio (1675–1741)

The Trial between Harmony and Invention (12 Concertos), Op. 8.

(B) *** Sony (ADD) SB2K 89980 (2). Zukerman, Black, ECO, Ledger (continuo).

(B) ** Erato Ultima (ADD) 0630 18968-2 (2). Toso, Pierlot, I Sol. Ven., Scimone.

Sony have now restored Pinchas Zukerman's complete set of Op. 8 to the catalogue. Concertos Nos. 5–12 are still available squeezed onto a single CD (SBK 53513 – see our main volume), but here six concertos are allotted to each of the two discs. Those not wanting Zukerman's *Four Seasons* can choose that single CD, but here the performances of those celebrated works bring out all the drama, and their expressive qualities are in no doubt, with the solo movements offering playing that is both thoughful and searching. Concerto No. 9 on the second CD is allotted to the oboe, and admirably played by Neil Black. The ECO provide alert and resilient accompaniments and the early 1970s recording is full and lively, with a close balance for the soloists.

Scimone directs energetic readings of the twelve concertos, including the *Four Seasons*, with the 1971 recording (actually made in Italy) nicely balanced except for a backward continuo. But stylish as these performances are for their period, with Piero Toso an excellent soloist, they are not quite as fine as other versions listed in our main Guide. Good value but not a top choice.

The Four Seasons, Op. 8/1-4.

(B) **(*) CfP 574 8872 [5748872]. Sillito, Virtuosi of E., Davison – ALBINONI: *Concerti a cinque, Op. 7/3 & 6.* **(*)

** EMI **DVD** 4 92498-9. Kennedy, ECO.

** Sony **DVD** SVD 46380. Mutter, BPO, Karajan.

(i) The Four Seasons, Op. 8/1-4; (i; ii) L'estro armonico: Concerto for 2 Violins & Cello in D min., Op. 3/11, RV 565; (iii) Double Oboe Concerto in D min., RV 535. Concerto for Strings in A, RV 158.

(BB) *** RCA 74321 68001-2. (i) Spivakov; (ii) Futer & Milman; (iii) Utkin & Evstigneev; Moscow Virtuosi.

Vladimir Spivakov's highly enjoyable 1988 account of Vivaldi's *Four Seasons* comes high on the list of bargain recommendations, and is made the more attractive by the inclusion of three other appealing and varied concertos. The first is for strings alone, the second (from *L'estro armonico*), brings a delicate central *Largo e spiccato* in the form of a wistful siciliano, and has a moto perpetuo finale. The *Double Oboe Concerto* has Alexei Utkin and Mikhail Evstigneev as most engaging soloists, again displaying delicacy and charm in the slow movement. Indeed all three concertos are played with much sophistication and grace, as is the more famous main work which like its companions, is given an essentially chamber-scaled account; the very opposite of a larger-than life full orchestral version and yet not lacking in robust moments.

Spring is tinglingly fresh, with much use made of light and shade, and Spivakov's sweet, classically focused timbre is particularly melting in the sleepy sentience of the gentle episode of the first movement of *Autumn* and in the beguiling somnambulance of the central Adagio. *Winter* opens in suitably frosty style and the rain falls in the Largo with a soft quality that any Irishman would recognize. There is plenty of vigour for the summer storms, and altogether this is highly refreshing, with the recording vivid and well balanced within the attractive background ambience of L'Église du Liban, Paris.

The performance by Kenneth Sillito with the Virtuosi of England stands out for its bold, clear sound, well focused and full of presence. Indeed the soloist is a shade too present, and this detracts a little from the gentler expressiveness. Yet Sillito's playing is both poetic and assured and, with such vivid projection, is full of personality. The same comments apply to the Albinoni concertos now offered as a fill-up.

No one could say that Kennedy's DVD of *The Four Seasons* is dull; the only snag is that he talks a lot about it, not very illuminatingly, in his special kind of vernacular, and then introduces each movement as well. The performance itself is certainly spectacular in conveying the picturesque imagery (except for the viola's barking shepherd's dog, which is rather feeble).

Autumn brings a degree of controversy in that there are weird special effects, including glissando harmonics in the slow movement and percussive applications of the wooden part of the bow to add to the rhythmic pungency of the finale. Kennedy also likes to stomp about a bit. The ECO's playing is always responsive to match the brilliant bravura of its soloist. The total running time, including all the documentary bits, is still only 48 minutes.

Karajan sits and directs from the harpsichord for Mutter, but, beautifully as she plays, the result is plushy and in the last resort rather bland.

6 Flute Concertos, Op. 10.

(BB) *** Regis RRC 1077. Hall, Divertimenti of L., Barritt.

Judith Hall's record of the Op. 10 *Flute Concertos* is fresh and brightly recorded, and she plays with great virtuosity and fine taste. The Divertimenti of London is a modern-instrument group and the players are both sensitive and alert. At budget price this is distinctly competitive.

Flute Concertos Op. 10/1-6; Flute Concertos in: A min., P.80; G, P.118; E min., P.139; G, P.140; G, P.141; E min., P.142; D, P.203; D, P.205; C min., P.440; Concerto for Flute & 2 Violins in A min.; Double Flute Concerto, P.76; Piccolo Concertos in C, P.78 & P.79.

(B) **(*) Sony (ADD) SB2K 89981 (2). Rampal, I Solisti Veneti, Scimone.

Jean-Pierre Rampal is without a doubt the aristocrat of the modern flute, with a silvery timbre which sets him apart. His art is much in evidence in these performances in which his vitality and superb sense of style is matched by Vivaldi's seemingly inexhaustible invention. The Op. 10 set of flute concertos is self-recommending, but there is always fresh delight in exploring the less well-known works. Especially enjoyable are the minor key concertos – and just sample the *Double concerto* for sheer effervescence (Sony do not reveal the other player's identity), or the short, cheerful one-movement of the *G major Concerto*, P.141. The principal reservation on this release is the variable quality of the sound: the flute tone is generally truthful, but the string quality is not particularly

ingratiating, rather glassy and unyielding, which is a bit wearing after a while. This is a pity as Scimone secures some lively playing from I Solisti Veneti. Sony are also coy about the recording dates, but it is assumed that they emanate from the 1960s.

Double Trumpet Concerto in C, RV 537.

(M) (*) Westminster (ADD) 471 276-2. Vienna State Op. O, Scherchen – HANDEL: *Water Music, etc.* (*); TORELLI: *Concerto for Two Trumpets*. *(*)

A plodding, dull performance of Vivaldi's popular double concerto.

Violin Concertos, in C, RV 187; in D, RV 209.

(BB) *** RCA 74321 68002-2. Zukerman, ECO – BACH: *Violin Concertos, BWV 1041–2, BWV 1056; Double Violin Concerto*. ***

Two of Vivaldi's most attractive concertos played with great vitality and warmth, make a splendid coupling for Bach, particularly as the finale of the *C major* recalls the *Third Brandenburg Concerto*. Excellently vivid sound too.

VOCAL MUSIC

Credo, RV 591 (revised Malipiero).

(M) *(*) Sony SMK 89619. Ernest Senff Ch., BPO, Giulini – VERDI: *4 Sacred Pieces*. *(*)

Giulini presents Vivaldi's four-section *Credo* in a late nineteenth-century arrangement by Malipiero. It is lovely music richly sung, and beautifully recorded but as with the Verdi coupling the performance lacks vitality, notably so in the closing *Et resurrexit*.

Dixit Dominus in D, RV 594; Gloria in D, RV 589; Magnificat in G min., RV 610.

**(*) EMI CDC5 57265-2. Fox, Norman, Chance, Gilchrist, Lemalu, King's College Cambridge Ch, AAM, Cleobury.

These are fine performances, with an excellent team of soloists (and a most sensitive oboe solo in the *Domine Deus* of the *Gloria*). The King's College Choir are on fine form too, but in the last resort the performances, though committed and musical, are a shade lacking in the spontaneous feel of live music-making. In the *Gloria*, too, one would have liked a brighter sound from the period violins. Otherwise the recording is spacious and well balanced.

Gloria in D, RV 589.

*** Ph. 462 697-2. Fugue, Ballard, Cameron, Carter, Monteverdi Ch., E. Bar. Sol., Gardiner – HANDEL: *Gloria*. ***

Gardiner's account of Vivaldi's most famous setting of the *Gloria* goes easily to the top of the list. Incisive string playing and choral singing combined with apt tempi are balanced by some lovely lyrical contributions from the soloists, notably the mezzo/soprano duet,

Laudamus te. With its equally memorable Handel couplings this is one of Gardiner's finest recent discs.

Juditha triumphans (oratorio; complete).

*** Opus 111 OP 30324 (3). Kozĕna, Trullu, Comparato, Herrman, Carraro, Santa Cecilia Academy, Chamber Ch., Academia Montis Regalis, De Marchi.

Juditha triumphans, Vivaldi's only surviving oratorio, has been recorded a number of times, and this Italian version, recorded in Mondovi in Italy in October 2000, offers a vigorous and scholarly account, meticulously prepared. With fair justification De Marchi has transposed the tenor and bass parts of the chorus up an octave, as Vivaldi is believed to have done with his female chorus at the Ospedale della Pieta in Venice. The result is fresh and brilliant, and the team of female soloists, two sopranos and three mezzos, adds to that impression, except that the recording balance sets them at a slight distance, seriously reducing their impact. Even so, the brilliant and rich-toned Slovakian soprano stands out in the title role, with the mezzo, Maria Jose Trullo bringing variety to the role of her adversary, Holofernes.

Longe mala, umbrae, terrores, RV 629; Nisi Dominus (Psalm 126), RV 608; Stabat Mater, RV 621.

*** Virgin VC5 45474-2. Daniels, Europe Galante, Bondi.

A superb triptych. David Daniels has not made a finer solo record than this, and he receives splendid support from Fabio Bondi and Europe Galante. The warmth of expressive feeling from singer and accompaniment alike is apparent from the very opening of the *Stabat Mater,* which is superbly sung, and the performance of *Nisi Dominus* is both dramatic and moving. How beautiful is the *Beatus vir,* sung seraphically over the continuo accompaniment, while there is splendid bravura in *Sidcut erat* without any loss of lyrical feeling. The motet *Longe mala* ('Long-standing ills, shadows, terrors') opens very dramatically, with more virtuosity demanded and relished, while the closing section *Descende o coeli vox* ('Descend O voice of heaven') again makes warm lyrical contrast; then the piece ends with an excitingly florid *Alleluia.*

Il Giustino (dramma per musica; abridged).

*** Virgin VCD5 45518-2 (2). Labelle, Comparato, Provvisionato, McGreevy, De Lisi, Cherici, Il Complesso Barocco, Curtis.

Written for Rome in 1724, Vivaldi's *Il Giustino* is based on a libretto that had already been set by Domenico Scarlatti and Albinoni, while twelve years later in London Handel also used it with modifications. Taking his cue from some of the simplifications made by the composer, Alan Curtis has introduced judicious cuts, preserving what he regards as the most inspired numbers. The result in this live recording made in Rotterdam is a sparkling entertainment, with one brief number after another advancing the involved plot about the Emperor Justinian with winning speed. The mood is consistently light, fresh and lively, with

Curtis an inspired director. He consistently relishes the instrumental colouring, as in the ceremonial trumpets and timpani, as well as the occasional reference to music we know, as in the quotation from the *Four Seasons* in the *Sinfonia* introducing the fifth scene of Act I. Among the most striking numbers are a pastoral aria for Giustino in Act I, an extended minor-key aria for Anastasia full of side-slipping chromatic harmonies and a magnificent aria for Arianna ending Act I. The bird-song aria for Arianna in Act II is also remarkable, with Curtis introducing various eighteenth-century bird whistles, which, as he says, are played with great enthusiasm by the group's oboe and recorder players. The casting is strong, with fresh, clear voices in all the parts except one, and that sadly the title role of Giustino, in which the mezzo, Francesca Provvisionato, sings with a distracting judder. Despite that blemish, this is a set to transform one's ideas of Vivaldi and his mastery as an opera-composer, so long ignored. Light, transparent sound.

'Viva Vivaldi': Arias: (i) Agitata da due venti La Griselda, RV 718. Gloria in D, RV 589: Domine Deus. Opera arias: Bajazet (Il Tamerlano): Anch'il mar par che sommerga. Farnace: Gelido in ogni vedo. La fida Ninfa: Dite, Oimè. Giustino: Sventurata Navicelli. Juditha Triumphans: Armatae face et Angibus. L'Olimpiade, Tra la follie divers ... Siam navi all'onde algenti. Ottone in villa, Gelosia, tu già rendi l'alma mia. Teuzzone: Di due rai languir costante; Zeffiretti che sussurrate. Tito Manlio: Non ti lusinghi la crudeltae. Concertos in C for flautino, RV 443; in D for lute, RV 93.

*** Arthaus **DVD** 100 128. (i) Bartoli; Il Giardino Armonico, Antonini. (V/D: Brian Large.)

Although Vivaldi is known to have composed 90 operas, only 20 have survived. For this programme Cecilia Bartoli has drawn on autograph material in the Turin Library and has come up with some valuable additions to the repertory. The recital was recorded in September 2000 at the Théâtre des Champs-Elysées and is presented very unobtrusively, albeit with a limited repertoire of shots.

In the two concertos, the Domine Deus and a couple of the arias, the score is available, though it must be said that its superimposition all but obliterates the visual image. As in her handsomely presented Decca set *The Vivaldi Album* (Decca 466 569-2), Bartoli sings effortlessly and magnificently – and she duplicates one or two arias here.

Il Giordano Armonico are full of virtuosity and delicacy, and the presence of Brian Large prevents the kind of ostentatious visual 'cleverness' that wrecked their recital listed below. The music is left to speak for itself, and the presence of Bartoli's Decca producer, Christopher Raeburn, ensures an excellent and musical balance. It is a tribute to Vivaldi's spectacular fund of invention that there is so much of quality yet to be discovered. The CD is entitled *'Viva Vivaldi',* and that is what he does in this enjoyable and brilliant set. Sub-titles of the aria texts are in German, French, English and Spanish, and are also available in the original Italian.

VOLANS, Kevin (born 1949)

String Quartets Nos.1 (White man sleeps); 2 (Hunting-Gathering); & 6.

Black Box BBM 1069. Duke Quartet.

Born in South Africa, Kevin Volans in his *First Quartet* (*White Man Sleeps*), dating from 1982, ingeniously uses fragments of African music, translating it with its different scales into Western terms in a sequence of five dance-movements. In his *Second Quartet* (*Hunting-Gathering*, dating from 1987, the debt to African music is much more incidental, yet the use of the medium is just as striking and original, a collage of contrasted ideas over two extended movements and a brief third movement of summary. The *Sixth Quartet* of 2000 is much tougher and more severe, using no African material at all, and points forward to further developments in his highly original use of a traditional genre. The Duke Quartet, very well recorded, give totally committed performances which bring out the underlying emotional intensity behind Volans' inspiration.

WAGNER, Richard (1813–83)

(i) *Die Feen: Overture; Grosser Festmarsch (American Centennial March); Huldigungsmarsch; Kaisermarsch; Das Liebesverbot: Overture.*(ii) *Lohengrin: Preludes to Acts I & III. Die Meistersinger: Preludes to Acts I & III; Dance of the Apprentices; Finale.Tannhäuser: Overture. Tristan und Isolde: Prelude.*

(BB) ** Virgin (ADD/DDD) VBD5 62034-2 (2). (i) Radio France PO or (ii) LSO, Janowski.

This two-CD compilation combines two unequal Wagner collections. One CD contains a not terribly distinguished group of operatic preludes and orchestral excerpts, but they generate no real excitement or tension, and the digital recording is disappointing. But the paired CD, recorded by EMI in 1972, makes this collection worth considering. It consists of early, rarely heard works and occasional pieces, none of them great music, all of them at the very least interesting. Indeed, it is quite a surprise to hear Wagner's music sounding not too different from Offenbach, as in the racy gallop – complete with glittering castanets – which opens the *Overture Das Liebesverbot* (a failed Wagner operetta, dating from 1836). Elsewhere, the marches such as the *Huldigungsmarsch (Homage March)* and the *Grand Festival* march (written to celebrate the centenary of American independence in 1876) have a pomp more associated with Meyerbeer, whilst *Die Feen* resides in the world of Weber. It is all eminently enjoyable and enthusiastically played by the LSO, with the 1972 EMI analogue recording much more vivid than its digital companion.

Siegfried Idyll.

(M) (***) BBC Legends mono BBCL 4076-2. Hallé O, Barbirolli – BEETHOVEN: *Symphony No. 7*; MOZART: *Symphony No.35.* ***

(M) * Decca (ADD) 470 254-2. VPO, Knappertsbusch – BRAHMS: *Academic Festival Overture, etc.* *

Barbirolli's account of the *Siegfried Idyll*, recorded in the BBC's Manchester studios, comes in mono sound only, with obvious limitations. The use of reduced strings means that the woodwind solos come over very clearly, with a glorious horn outburst at the climax (track 9, 11¢30ð), and though the tempo for the central episode is on the slow side, with Barbirolli letting it get slower still in ecstasy, the magic of this birthday gift to Cosima Wagner comes over superbly, with thrilling climaxes. With the Beethoven and Mozart symphonies as coupling, one welcomes a splendid portrait of this ever-characterful conductor.

Nothing special at all about Knappertsbusch's 1955 mono *Siegfried Idyll*, either in the playing or the sound, which is below Decca's best efforts. This reissue does nothing at all for its famous conductor's reputation.

ORCHESTRAL EXCERPTS AND PRELUDES FROM THE OPERAS

Overtures: Der fliegende Holländer; Die Meistersinger; Lohengrin: Preludes to Acts I & III; (i) Tannhäuser: Overture and Venusberg Music; Tristan und Isolde: Prelude and Liebestod.

*** EMI (ADD) **Audio DVD** DVC4 92397-9. BPO, Karajan; (i) with German Op. Ch.

Anyone looking for a single-disc collection of Wagnerian overtures and preludes could hardly beat this. Karajan was at his finest, and these 1974 performances are in a class of their own. The body of tone produced by the Berlin Philharmonic gives a breath-taking amplitude to the climaxes. That of the *Lohengrin Act I Prelude* is superbly graduated and there is plenty of contrasting brilliance and gusto when the brass blaze into the Prelude to Act III. There is urgency and edge in *The Flying Dutchman* and in the *Tristan Liebestod* the orgasmic culmination is quite overwhelming.

Karajan's same superb sense of timing and spaciousness is again felt in the *Tannhäuser Overture and Venusberg Music*, while *Die Meistersinger Prelude* has a similar imposing breadth. As with the other EMI Audio DVDs the recording was originally made in quadrophony, and there is a choice between multichannel surround sound or high-resolution stereo. The results are spectacular with greater depth, a wider dyamic range and a remarkable sense of the ambience of the Berlin Philharmonie.

Der fliegende Holländer: Overture. Gotterdämmerung: Funeral Music; Siegfried's Rhine Journey. Lohengrin: Act I Prelude. Die Meistersinger: Overture; Dance of the Apprentices; Entry of the Masters. Parsifal: Good Friday Music.

(M) (***) Sony mono SMK 89889. RPO, Beecham.

The 1954 recordings here – *Der fliegende Holländer*, the *Meistersinger* excerpts (the three items linked together) and *Siegfried's Rhine Journey* – come in fuller and weightier sound than Beecham generally enjoyed at that final period of mono recording with CBS, with splendid brass but an occasional edge on strings. The swagger and panache of Beecham in Wagner comes out superbly, and though the other recordings are not quite so full, with edginess more obtrusive, they too are most enjoyable. In the manner of the time concert endings are provided where necessary.

(i) *Der fliegende Holländer: Overture*. (ii) *Götterdämmerung: Dawn; Siegfried's Rhine Journey & Funeral March*. (i) *Lohengrin: Prelude to Act III*. *Die Meistersinger: Preludes to Acts I & III*. *Tannhäuser: Overture and Venusberg Music. Die Walküre: Ride of the Valkyries*.

(B) ** CfP (DDD/ADD) 575 5682. LPO, (i) Elder; (ii) Rickenbacher.

Most of the excerpts here are conducted by Mark Elder who provides well-played but unmemorable performances, brightly but not particularly richly recorded. The *Ride of the Valkyries* comes off best, but it seems a curious plan to include the *Venusberg music* from *Tannhäuser* without the chorus. The *Götterdämmerung* excerpts conducted by Karl Anton Rickenbacher, added as a makeweight, are altogether superior, and it was a pity that EMI did not choose to reissue the complete collection from which they derive, instead of the Elder disc.

VOCAL MUSIC

Wesendonck Lieder; Lohengrin: Einsam in trüben Tagen; Parsifal: Ich sah das Kind seiner Mutter Brust; Die Walküre: Du bist der Lenz.

(M) *** Decca (ADD) 468 486-2. Flagstad, VPO, Knappertsbusch – MAHLER: *Kindertotenlieder; Lieder eines fahrenden Gesellen*. **

Flagstad's glorious voice remained perfectly suited to the rich inspiration of the *Wesendonck Lieder* right towards the end of her recording career. *Im Treibhaus* is particularly beautiful here. The excerpts from three of her most famous Wagner roles were recorded at the same time, with equal success. Fine accompaniments under Knappertsbusch. However the coupled Mahler Lieder are rather lesss successful. The Wagner recordings, made in the Sofiensaal in 1956, are still a tribute to the Decca engineering of the time.

OPERA

Solti Wagner Edition:

Der fliegende Holländer.

(M) **(*) Decca (ADD) 470 792-2 (2). Bailey, Martin, Talvela, Kollo, Krenn, Isola Jones, Chicago Ch. & O, Solti.

Lohengrin.

(M) *** Decca 470 795-2 (4). Domingo, Norman, Nimsgern, Randová, Sotin, Fischer-Dieskau, V. State Op. Concerto Ch., VPO, Solti.

Die Meistersinger von Nürnberg.

(M) *** Decca 470 800-2 (4). Van Dam, Heppner, Mattila, Opie, Lippert, Vermillion, Pape, Chicago SO Ch. & O, Solti.

Parsifal.

(M) *** Decca (ADD) 470 805-2 (4). Kollo, Ludwig, Fischer-Dieskau, Hotter, Kelemen, Frick, V. Boys' Ch., V. State Op. Ch., VPO, Solti.

Tannhäuser (Paris version).

(M) *** Decca (ADD) 470 810-2 (3). Kollo, Dernesch, Ludwig, Sotin, Braun, Hollweg, V. State Op. Ch., VPO, Solti.

Tristan und Isolde.

(M) *** Decca (ADD) 470 814-2 (4). Uhl, Nilsson, Resnik, Van Mill, Krause, VPO, Solti.

Solti Wagner Edition (complete).

(M) *** Decca (ADD/DDD) 470 600-2 (21).

Following on after the box containing Solti's unsurpassed *Ring Cycle* (455 555-2), Decca have handsomely repackaged his other Wagner recordings, which are now available separately at mid-price for the first time, or together, in a slip case, at a further reduced price. Those who invest in the Complete Edition receive a free bonus CD comprising rehearsal sequences from the *Tristan* recording, which was included in the original LP set. Many of these recordings remain amongst the top recommendations, and have the advantage of Decca's finest vintage opera sound. With the exception of the digital recordings they have been remastered for this release.

Amongst the highlights must be the 1972 *Parsifal* which is, by any standards, a magnificent recording, with universally excellent singing and Solti sustaining the right sort of tension throughout the performance. Hardly less impressive is *Tannhäuser*, with superlative playing from the VPO, and Christa Ludwig as Venus outshining all rivals. The 1971 sound remains impressive. Solti is less flexible in the 1960 *Tristan*, but he does relax in the more expansive passages, and he generates superb thrust in the exciting moments, such as the end of Act I, and the opening of the Love Duet, which has knife-edged dramatic tension.

The digital 1986 *Lohengrin* finds Domingo on magnificent form, and if Jessye Norman is not ideally suited to the role of Elsa, she is always commandingly intense, full of character. The rest of the cast and the VPO is superb. Throughout these recordings, Decca employ, almost always successfully, plenty of Culshaw-like production effects, but curiously, in the 1976 *Der fliegende Holländer*, there are none, so that characters 'halloo' at one another when they are obviously standing elbow to elbow. However, the cast on this recording is generally impressive, and though Kollo is a little coarse as Erik, it is an illuminating portrayal.

Decca rightly chose Solti's later (digital) recording of *Die Meistersinger* where the conductor's characteristic urgency is counterbalanced by a great warmth, and the cast is generally outstanding – a fine conclusion to an impressive achievement. This is now a clear first recommendation. Collectors might like also to be reminded that our primary recommendations for the other operas lie as follows: *Die fliegende Höllander* (Sinopoli – DG 457 778-2); *Lohengrin* (Abbado – DG 437 808-2); *Parsifal* (Karajan – DG 413 347-2); *Tannhäuser* (Sinopoli – DG 427 625-2); *Tristan und Isolde* (Karajan – EMI CMS7 69319-2).

Götterdämmerung (complete).

(BB) *** Arte Nova 74321 80775-2 (4). Woodrow, Silberbauer, Del Monte, Adami, Ottenthal, Wolak, Martin, Tyrol Fest Ch. & O, Kuhn

Recorded live at the 2000 Tyrol Festival in Erl, this is the finest of the four *Ring* recordings made by Gustav Kuhn over successive years, with a more consistent cast than *Rheingold* and *Die Walküre*. Alan Woodrow, excellent in the title-role of Siegfried, here excels himself – his death scene is most moving – while in the role of Brünnhilde Eva Silberbauer sings with warmth and absence of strain, unlike her two rivals in *Die Walküre* and *Siegfried*. A young singer, she yet finds ample power in what is evidently a relatively intimate setting, helped by full, immediate recording. Duccio del Monte, overparted as Wotan in *Die Walküre*, here makes a strong, firm Hagen, while the roles of Gunther and Gutrune are well-taken by Herbert Adami and Gertrud Ottenthal, and Andrea Martin is excellent as Alberich, as he is in both *Rheingold* and *Siegfried*. It is a pity that the other three sections of Kuhn's *Ring* cycle do not measure up to this, which can be strongly recommended in the budget range.

Die Meistersinger von Nürnberg (complete).

**(*) Arthaus DVD 100 152 (2). Johansson, Brendel, Winbergh, von Halem, Schulte, Peper, Walther, Deutsche Oper Ch. & O, Frühbeck de Burgos (Director: Gotz Friedrich; TV Director: Brian Large).

Updated to the early 20th century, Gotz Friedrich's production of *Meistersinger* for the Deutsche Oper in Berlin is introduced by shots of a toy-town Nuremberg with houses set at rakish angles, and to the designs of Peter Sykora;the final scene is backed by the toytown city set in an upended semicircle. Otherwise this is a relatively straightforward presentation of Wagner's warmest opera, well-produced on video by Brian Large, and enjoyable despite detailed flaws in the singing. Wolfgang Brendel, made up to look like the Polish leader, Lech Walesa, with a big moustache, is not always steady enough as Hans Sachs, but char-acterizes well, and is at his finest in the concluding monologue. Eva Johansson is a buxom Eva, sometimes squally under pressure, but rising beautifully to the challenge of the big Quintet in Act III. Gösta Winbergh, while not a conventional Heldentenor, sings the role of Walther with no strain, even though he is given to unstylish sliding up to notes. Beckmesser is presented by Eike Wilm Schulte as a pompous little shrimp, singing impressively despite the clowning, and Uwe Peper as David, also singing well, plays the role as a comic part, exaggerating archly. Finest of the Masters is Victor von Halem as Pogner, imposing in every way. The chorus sings well, but it is a pity that the younger Apprentices look so very feminine, not even attempting to seem boyish. Frühbeck is a sympathetic Wagnerian, never letting the music drag.

Der Ring des Nibelungen (complete).

(BB) *(*) Arte Nova 74321 87075-2 (13). Various artists incuding: Martin, Woodrow, Oesch, Silberbauer, Wachicha, Comotti, Ottenthal, Del Monte, Dohmen, Tyrol Festival Ch. & O, Kuhn.

Recorded out of sequence in four consecutive years at the Tyrol Festival, 1998-2001, Kuhn's version of the *Ring* cycle is disconcertingly inconsistent. Where *Siegfried* and *Götterdämmerung* bring performances that convey the electricity of a great drama, *Rheingold* and *Die Walküre* bring low-key performances, using casts less consistent than in the later operas. It is perhaps significant that three different singers were used in the role of Wotan (Wanderer) and also three in that of Brünnhilde. Andrea Martin as Alberich is one of the few constants throughout, and it is good to find Julia Oesch in various roles, Fricka, Erda and First Norn, always impressive. For bargain versions of the *Ring* cycle those of Sawallisch (on EMI CZS 72731 2) and Janowski (on RCA 74321 45417-2) are far more consistent.

Siegfried (complete).

(BB) (***) Naxos mono 8.110211 (3). Melchior, Flagstad, Thorborg, Schorr, List, Habich. Met. Op. O, Bodanzky.

Taken from a radio transmission from the Metropolitan in New York on 30 January 1937, this Naxos Historical Met. issue offers an astonishingly vivid view of a classic occasion with a cast unlikely ever to be equalled. Both Lauritz Melchior and Kirsten Flagstad were at their peak, and the firmness, clarity and absence of strain of their singing offers a lesson to all latter-day exponents of this music. Melchior is a Heldentenor without a hint of roughness in his tone, freely confident, while the noble Flagstad brings not only a comparable power to the role of Brünnhilde, but an element of tenderness that may surprise some. Kirsten Thorborg makes for luxury casting in the role of Erda, and Friedrich Schorr as the Wanderer sings with comparable firmness and clarity, virile rather than elderly. Artur Bodansky, the Met's chief conductor at the time in the German repertory, is a brisk but understanding Wagnerian, and though there are statutory cuts, as was customary at the time, it means that each act is contained on a single CD. All the voices are superbly caught, but the orchestra is much dimmer, not helped by variable surface-noise which is yet intrusive only occasionally, mainly in *pianissimo* passages. The voices are what matter, and they sound glorious, thanks to the excellent transfers of Ward Marston. An astonishing bargain.

Tannhäuser (Dresden version; complete).

** Teldec 8573 88064-2 (3). Seiffert, Eaglen, Meyer, Hampson, Meyer, Deutsche Op. Ch., Berlin State O, Barenboim

This is a set which does not add up to the sum of its parts. Though the casting is starry, arguably as fine a team as could be assembled today, and Barenboim's credentials as a Wagnerian have long been tested at Bayreuth and elsewhere, the performance lacks the dramatic thrust needed to bring together one of the more problematic of Wagner's operas. For many it will be in the set's favour that the text used is the original Dresden form with the more elaborate version of Act I Scene 2, the big duet between *Tannhäuser* and Venus, taken from the much later Paris version. It does not help that Barenboim's speeds tend to be on the slow side, yet with little of the hushed tension that marks his finest Wagner performances, while occasionally by contrast he will choose a frenetic speed. The impression is of a carefully prepared studio run-through, and indeed the solo singing is beautifully controlled as though for a concert, so when Thomas Hampson as Wolfram sings his song to the evening star the emphasis is on beauty of tone and phrase. In the title role Peter Seiffert sings with clean, firm projection with no sign of strain, yet the sound is hardly beautiful and his vocal acting is unconvincing. Waltraud Meyer is a formidable Venus, but again the sound as recorded is unrelenting rather than sensuous. Jane Eaglen as Elisabeth controls her massive soprano well, but one really wants a more tender, lyrical sound. The recording, faithful enough, tends to confirm the feeling of a concert performance.

Tristan und Isolde (complete).

(M) (***) EMI mono CMS5 67621-2 [567626] (4). Flagstad, Suthaus, Fischer-Dieskau, Thebom, Philh., Furtwängler.

Though Wilhelm Furtwängler hated working in the recording studio, he was persuaded in 1952, just two years before his death, to conduct the Philharmonia in this classic version of *Tristan* with Kirsten Flagstad a commanding Isolde. It stands among his finest memorials, still unsurpassed by later versions in its spacious concentration and intensity. Now reissued in EMI's 'Great Recordings of the Century' series, the mono sound in a superb transfer is astonishingly vivid, fuller than before with wonderful immediacy, often giving the illusion of stereo. The rest of the cast, including Ludwig Suthaus as an unstrained Tristan and the youthful Fischer-Dieskau as Kurwenal, gives strong support to the dominant Flagstad. At mid-price the set comes with lavish packaging and notes.

Die Walküre (complete).

*** DG DVD 073 011-9 (2). Behrens, Norman, Ludwig, Lakes, Morris, Moll, Met. Op. O, Levine. (Director: Otto Schenk.)
(M) ** Decca (ADD) 470 443-2 (3). Vickers, Brouwenstijn, Ward, Gorr, Nilsson, London, LSO, Leinsdorf.
(BB) * Arte Nova 74321 90068-2 (3). Brunsdon, Ottenthal, Del Monte, Hay, Comotti, Oesch, Tyrol Festival O, Kuhn

Recorded live at the Metropolitan in New York in April 1989, two years after the DG audio recording with the same personnel, the DVD film offers an even more compelling experience, with James Levine more thrustfully dramatic and drawing more spontaneous-sounding performances from his team. To have the gloriously voiced Jessye Norman as Sieglinde is luxury casting. She is totally secure and consistently intense and so commanding you feel that, far from being afraid, this Sieglinde could eat any of the Valkyries alive, including the Brünnhilde of Hildegard Behrens.

Powerfully projected and deeply expressive, Behrens's performance is none the less compelling. Gary Lakes makes a firm, secure Siegmund to match his Sieglinde, and the dark-voiced Kurt Moll is an ideal, sinister Hunding, with James Morris a noble Wotan, his presence even more imposing than his voice. Christa Ludwig as Fricka sounds hardly less fresh than she did in the famous Solti *Ring* on Decca.

Thanks to Levine, this is above all a powerful reading, with the heavy brass superbly caught in the full-ranging recording. The traditonal production of Otto Schenk, with heavily realistic sets by Gunther Schneider-Siemssen, enhanced by evocative back-projections, may have disappointed some critics, yet with well-planned close-ups it works splendidly on DVD. Nor does the production or the direction for the camera disappoint. The former is generally straightforward and refreshingly free from the kind of egocentric attention-seeking 'creativity' that is so normal in the opera house these days. It is good to watch, and the only real reservation lies in the orchestral sonority (the opening storm and Hunding's entry sound pretty crude).

The Metropolitan is a fine orchestra, and much that they do gives pleasure but ultimately one misses the nobility and eloquence one finds in so many of the sound-only versions from Boehm, Solti, Karajan and Furtwängler.

Leinsdorf's 1961 version of *Die Walküre* has now been reissued at mid-price as part of Decca's 'Compact Opera Collection'. Although hardly matching what Solti was to achieve later, the recording quality is outstanding for its period. Leinsdorf is vigorous and thrustful and the LSO playing is first class.The result is always exciting but lacks repose where necessary, and this affects the singers. Jon Vickers is too strenuous in the spring greeting, although most of his performance is superbly rich and heroic. Gré Brouwenstijn is even finer as Sieglinde; her vibrant voice is radiant. David Ward is a resonant Hunding, Rita Gorr a strong Frick and this is still a set to be reckoned with. However, there is no printed libretto, only a CD Rom facility which carries full text and translation to be printed out via a computer.

Die Walküre, the last of the *Ring* operas to be recorded in Kuhn's Tyrol Festival cycle, proves a serious disappointment, not just because of variable casting but because of the feeling of slackness which too often afflicts the performance, this live recording, made in 2001, so much less tense than that of *Götterdämmerung*, made a year earlier. The low-key reading of Act I brings a curiously casual-sounding account of *Winterstürme* from Andrew Brunsdon as Siegmund, even if he focuses better in the concluding moments of the Act, with Gertrud Ottenthal also shaking off her earlier lethargy. Neither singer is helped by the relatively dry, close acoustic, and the same applies for Duccio del Monte as Wotan, overparted, seriously overstressed in the Farewell of Act III. Elena Comotti is bright rather than weighty as Brünnhilde, a young singer not suited to the role, and it is a relief to find Julia Oesch as Fricka singing with firmness and warmth. Yet most damaging of all is the lack of bite in the orchestral playing, with rhythms too often plodding, quite different from how the orchestra sounds in *Siegfried* and *Götterdämmerung*.

VOCAL COLLECTIONS

Der fliegende Holländer: Overture; Die Frist ist um.
Die Meistersinger: Wahn! Wahn!; Fliedermonolog.
Parsifal: Amfortas's Monologues. Tannhäuser: O du
mein holder Abendstern. Die Walküre: Wotan's
Farewell.

*** DG 471 348-2. Terfel, BPO, Abbado.

The challenge of Wagner plainly suits Bryn Terfel to perfection both musically and dramatically. Though when he made these recordings in Berlin he had yet to sing the roles on stage (with the exception of the least demanding, Wolfram in *Tannhäuser*) the impression of fully-formed characterisations is irresistible, with none of the run-through quality of too many recital discs. This is helped by the generosity of the settings, with the feeling of 'bleeding chunks' avoided, while Abbado and the orchestra are plainly inspired by their soloist to give incandescent performances, full and intense. *The Flying Dutchman Overture* and the Dutchman's monologue were recorded live, and arguably the latter is on the slow side, but the illumination of words is as revelatory here as elsewhere on the disc. All of the items are vividly realized, making one long to see Terfel in these roles on stage, notably the two Hans Sachs monologues from *Meistersinger* and the wonderfully expressive portrait of Wotan in the *Walküre* monologue. This final item brings the most daring half-tone phrases from Terfel as he kisses Brünnhilde's godhead away, the culminating moment of the whole opera, here with the agony intensified by the intimacy of expression. The sound is among the richest from this source, with brass gloriously full and rich.

Götterdämmerung: (i) Prelude: Dawn; (i) Love Duet;
Siegfried's Rhine Journey; Siegfried's Monologue
and Funeral March. Siegfried: (ii) Forging Scene;
Forest Murmurs; (iii) Closing Scene with Woodbird.

*** EMI CDC5 57242-2. Domingo, ROHCGO, Pappano;
(i) with Urmana; (ii) Cangelosi; (iii) Dessay.

This superb issue follows up Placido Domingo's earlier prize-winning Wagner disc with Deborah Voigt, Antonio Pappano and the Covent Garden Orchestra in duets from *Tristan* and *Siegfried* (EMI CDC5 57004-2 – see our main volume). Here he amplifies his portrait of Siegfried in powerfully heroic singing in these substantial sections of *Siegfried* and *Götterdämmerung*. It is astonishing that a tenor now 60 should retain a voice at once so full and sharply focused. As a Heldentenor he may not produce such honeyed sounds as in Italian opera, but there is never a suspicion of the ugly barking that disfigures so much Wagner singing, with pitching clear and firm. As on the earlier disc Pappano proves a sympathetic partner, drawing from the orchestra playing at once rich and powerful, helped by the warm acoustic of the Colosseum, Watford. Urmana as Brünnhilde and David Cangelosi as Mime make excellent foils for the hero, though Natalie Dessay is less well-cast as the Woodbird, not as fresh and bright as one really wants. The items are very well presented, with generous orchestral sections helping to avoid any suspicion of this as a collection of 'bleeding chunks'.

WALLACE, William Vincent
(1812–65)

Celtic Fantasies: Annie Laurie; Auld Lang Syne and
The Highland Laddie; The Bard's Legacy; Charlie is
my Darling and The Cambells are coming; Coolun,
Gary Owen and St Patrick's Day; Homage to Burns:
Impromptu on Somebody and O for Ane and Twenty
Tam; Kate Kearney and Tow, row. row; The Keel
Row; The Last Rose of Summer; The Meeting of the
Walters and Eveleen's Bower; Melodie Irlandaise;
The Minstrel Boy and Rory O'More; My Love is like a
Red Red Rose and Come o'er the Stream Charlie;
Comin' through the Rye; Robin Adair; Roslin Castle
and A Highland Lad my Love was Born;Ye Banks
and Braes.

(M) ** Cala CACD 88042. Tuck.

William Wallace was born in Waterford, Ireland and began his career as a bandmaster, later concentrating on the violin, leading the Adelphi Theatre Orchestra in Dublin. In 1829 he heard Paganini and was so mesmerized that he 'stayed up all night' practising that composer's more dashing pieces. When he went to Tasmania (for his health) in 1836, his virtuosity caused a sensation, and moving on to Sydney, he was dubbed the 'Australian Paganini'. He subsequently travelled the world; in New Orleans he met and befriended Gottschalk, and in the early 1840s his playing was to be acclaimed in New York, Boston and Philadelphia. But when he returned to London in 1845 he made his name not with his fiddling, but with his first opera, *Maritana*, the work by which he is now chiefly remembered, although his ballads and songs also became very popular. His *Celtic Fantasias* for piano, based on traditional melodies, are little more than eloborate arrangements, with bravura embellishments which add little except surface gloss. Rosemary Tuck plays them with accomplished sympathy, but cannot make them more than showpieces: the tunes are far more indelible than Wallace's embellishments. She is well recorded.

WALTON, William (1902–83)

'At the Haunted End of the Day' Television Profile directed by Tony Palmer

*** Decca **DVD** 074 150-9.

Tony Palmer's Italia Prize-winning television profile of William Walton, is among the most moving ever made of a composer. The approach is both direct and evocative, starting with Walton himself nearing 80 and plainly rather frail, musing at the keyboard of the piano in his work room as he composes the solo cello *Passacaglia* for Rostropovich, one of his very last works. This moment brings several of his wrily humorous obiter dicta with which the film is delightfully dotted. He admits to composing at the piano, but being no pianist, he finds 'has rather boogered the whole thing oop' (resorting to the Lancashire accent he promptly dropped when as a boy treble he joined the choir of Christ Church Cathedral, Oxford).

The story of his career with its extraordinary sequence of lucky breaks, with one protector or helper after another coming along, is then told for the most part chronologically. We see the house where he was born, by Oldham standards relatively grand, (although as he points out, with an outside loo), and evocative shots follow of Oldham (including the 'very rough' board school he attended and his church), Oxford and later London and Amalfi in Italy. The impact of *Belshazzar's Feast* is fully brought out, not least thanks to Simon Rattle's conducting.

Later, Rattle also directs the passages from the *First Symphony*, which comes into the story not in its proper place in the 1930s, but in a sequence on the loves of Walton's life, when he is safely married to Susana and living comfortably on the isle of Ischia. The film was made within a couple of years of the composer's death in 1983 and has a vein of melancholy running through it, explaining Palmer's title, 'At the Haunted End of the Day', taken from one of the most striking of the arias in the opera *Troilus and Cressida*.

Even so, the impact of the film is anything but depressing, with the effervescent personality of Susana taking over towards the end. A unique career, vividly re-created.

(i) *Capriccio burlesco;* (ii; iii) *Violin Concerto;* (i) *Johannesburg Festival Overture;* (iv) *Partita;*

Symphony No.2; Variations on a Theme by Hindemith; (iii; v) *Belshazzar's Feast.*

(B) *** Sony (ADD) SB2K 89934 (2). (i) NYPO, Kostelanetz; (ii) Francescatti; (iii) Phd. O, Ormandy; (iv) Cleveland O, Szell; (v) with Cassel, Rutgers University Ch.

Sony's celebration for the Walton Centenary in 2002 brings together an outstanding batch of high-powered American performances such as no other British composer has ever received. Well-transferred in typical CBS up-front sound in recordings dating as far back as 1959, they come at bargain price in the Essential Classics series. The three performances with Szell and the Cleveland Orchestra of the *Symphony No. 2*, the *Hindemith Variations* and the *Partita* are all stunning in every way, not just brilliant and powerful but passionately intense too, while Ormandy is a warmly persuasive conductor with the Philadelphia Orchestra in both *Belshazzar's Feast* (with the Rutgers University Choir and baritone soloist, Walter Cassel) and in the *Violin Concerto* with Zino Francescatti the flamboyant soloist. Andre Kostalanetz conducts the New York Philharmonic in comparably brilliant performances both of the *Johannesburg Festival Overture* and the work he was the first to conduct, the *Capriccio burlesco*, a comedy overture in all but name.

'Centenary Edition': (i) *Cello Concerto;* (ii) *Viola Concerto;* (iii) *Violin Concerto; Scapino;* Coronation Marches: *Crown Imperial; Orb and Sceptre; Façade Suites Nos. 1 & 2; Henry V: Suite; Symphonies Nos. 1 & 2; Variations on a Theme of Hindemith;* (iv) *Coronation Te Deum; Belshazzar's Feast.*

(M) *** Decca 470 508-2 (4). (i) Cohen; (ii) Neubauer; (iii) Little, (iv) Terfel; L'inviti, Wayneflete Singers, Winchester Cathedral Ch., Bournemouth Ch. & SO, Litton or Hill.

Decca's four-disc Walton Edition offers consistently fine versions of all of the composer's most important orchestral works, some of them unsurpassed among rival versions, with Andrew Litton an idiomatic Waltonian with a natural feeling for the jazzy syncopations. This brings together the three Litton discs previously issued by Decca but with important additions. The third of the four discs, never originally issued along with the others, contains outstanding versions of the *Viola Concerto* and *Hindemith Variations* plus the two *Façade Suites*.

Where most latter-day interpreters of the *Viola Concerto* have taken a very expansive view of the lyrical first movement, *Andante comodo*, Paul Neubauer comes nearer than anyone to following the example of the original interpreters on disc, Frederick Riddle and William Primrose, in adopting a flowing tempo, encouraged by the composer. It makes Neubauer's and Litton's far more persuasive than other modern versions with no expressive self-indulgence, and with the brisker passages in this movement also taken faster than has become usual. Neubauer's tone is taut and firm to match, clean rather than fruity, with the central Scherzo taken excitingly fast and the finale again kept moving but without losing a spring in the jaunty rhythm of the main theme. He then relaxes beautifully for the hauntingly lovely epilogue, ending on a whispered pianissimo. Litton also encourages wide dynamic contrasts with the big tuttis bringing an element of wildness in brassy syncopations.

The *Hindemith Variations* also delivers a performance with contrasts heightened, not just of dynamic but of speed, extreme in both directions. This goes with an exceptional transparency in the orchestral textures, well-caught in the recording and bringing out the refinement of Walton's orchestration. *Façade*, predictably, is a fun performance, although the warm acoustic runs the danger of taking some edge off these witty parodies.

Two of the other discs are the same as before, with Tasmin Little's heartfelt reading of the *Violin Concerto* very well coupled with Litton's outstanding account of the *Second Symphony* and *Scapino*, and Robert Cohen's thoughtful reading of the *Cello Concerto* in coupling with the *First Symphony*. Litton's powerful account of *Belshazzar's Feast* with Bryn Terfel as the most dramatic of baritone soloists, brings fresh, cleanly focused choral sound that, with the help of keenly atmospheric recording, points up more clearly than usual the terracing between the different groupings of voices. This disc also includes the two coronation marches, the *Coronation Te Deum* and the *Henry V Suite*, with David Hill, chorus-master in *Belshazzar*, ably standing in for Litton in *Orb and Sceptre* and the *Te Deum*.

Cello Concerto.

(M) *** Sony SMK 89712. Ma, LSO, Previn – ELGAR: *Cello Concerto.* ***

Yo-Yo Ma and Previn give a sensuously beautiful performance. With speeds markedly slower than usual in the outer movements, the meditation is intensified to bring a mood of ecstasy, quite distinct from other Walton, with the central allegro becoming the symphonic kernel of the work, far more than just a scherzo. In the excellent CBS recording, the soloist is less forward and more faithfully balanced than is common.

(i) *Cello Concerto;* (ii;iii) *Viola Concerto;* (iv) *Violin Concerto;* (v) *Sinfonia concertante;* (iii) *Symphony No. 1.*

(B) *** RCA Double (mono/stereo) 74321 92575-2 (2). (i) Piatigorsky, Boston SO, Munch; (ii) Bashmet; (iii) LSO, Previn; (iv) Heifetz, Philh. O, composer; (v) Stott, RPO, Handley

The RCA two-disc collection includes the premiere recording of the *Cello Concerto* with Piatigorsky, who commissioned the work, as the soloist. He plays it with a gripping combination of full-blooded eloquence and subtlety of feeling, readily capturing the bitter-sweet melancholy of its flowing lyrical lines. The closing pages of the final variations are particularly haunting.

Munch provides a totally understanding accompaniment with the strings of the Boston Symphony finding the lyrical ecstasy which is such a distinctive part of this concerto. They are given up-front recording which for 1957 is commendably full and open.

Similarly, Heifetz as the virtuoso who commissioned the *Violin Concerto* remains in his way supreme as an interpreter, urgent beyond any rival, here with the composer conducting the Philharmonia Orchestra. The 1950 mono recording has been opened up to put more air round the sound.

The other two concertante works come in modern digital versions – Kathryn Stott, in a recording made for Conifer, performs the original more elaborate version of the *Sinfonia concertante*, and Yuri Bashmet brings his yearningly Slavonic temperament and masterly virtuosity to the *Viola Concerto*. With his opulent viola tone he warmly embraces the work's ripe romanticism as well as the high-voltage electricity of the jazz-based writing, and opts for a daringly spacious tempo for the haunting opening melody, relishing the bravura of the contrasting sections. The central scherzo brings another dazzling display with the fun of the scherzando passages well brought out there and in the finale. He ends with another daringly slow speed for the wistful epilogue, again superbly sustained.

Bashmet's partners are the ideal combination of Previn and the LSO, and it is Previn's vintage version of the *First Symphony* with the LSO of an earlier generation that sets the seal on the whole package, a reading that has never been matched let alone surpassed. What is also remarkable here is the clarity, definition and sense of presence of the 1966 recording, with the stereo spectrum even more sharply focused than in the later digital recordings. For IM this bargain-priced RCA Double stands out among the special offerings for the Walton Centennial.

(i; ii) *Cello Concerto;* (iii) *Façade suites* (excerpts): *Old Sir Faulk; Popular Song; Tango-pasodoble; Tarantella Sevillana;* (iii) *Variations on a Theme on Hindemith;* (iv) *Coronation Te Deum;* (iv; v) *The Twelve.*

(M) (***) BBC mono/stereo BBCL 4098-2. (i) Fournier, (ii) RPO; (iii) BBC SO; (iv) LPO Ch., LPO, (v) with Dowdall, Minty, Tear, Wakeham; all cond. composer.

This BBC Legends disc is specially valuable in giving us the composer's recordings of live performances of works which Walton did not otherwise record in the studio, filling in important gaps. It is good too to have a mono recording of Pierre Fournier as soloist in a 1959 Edinburgh Festival performance of the *Cello Concerto*, a work he did not otherwise record. Though sadly in the opening section he has an uncharacteristic lapse in intonation, it is a fine reading, sensitive and brilliant, with the soloist going along with the conductor in a far more flowing treatment than usual of the predominantly slow variations of the finale, shaving over two minutes off the regular timing, making it a much tauter conclusion. The *Hindemith Variations*, also with the RPO, come from a Festival Hall performance of 1963, antedating George Szell's studio recording. Walton's own reading has a keener sense of fun in scherzando variations, and is a degree more warmly expressive in lyrical passages, even if the ensemble is not quite so polished. The four favourite movements from *Façade* come from a Prom at the Royal Albert Hall in 1968, and also surprisingly are mono recordings, but show Walton as a supreme master of witty pointing, bringing out the fun of these delectable parodies. In some ways the greatest revelation comes in the two choral works, recorded in Westminster Abbey in 1966, with the BBC engineers skilfully getting round the problem of heavy reverberation to produce glowingly atmospheric sound with ample weight for the chorus. The *Coronation Te Deum* was of course written for the Abbey, and is made all the more ripely dramatic with antiphonal brass. Yet best of all is *The Twelve*, which in its usual form with organ accompaniment can sound bitty, whereas here with massive forces this 'Anthem for the Feast of Any Apostle' to words by Auden relates directly to the major Walton choral works including *Belshazzar*, weighty and dramatic.

(i; ii) *Violin Concerto: Andante tranquillo*; (ii) *Crown Imperial*; (iii) *Façade* (excerpts); (ii) *Henry V: Charge and Battle Music*; (iv) *Portsmouth Point Overture*; (v) *Symphony No. 2: Passacaglia*; (vi) *5 Bagatelles for Guitar*; (vii) *Belshazzar's Feast* (excerpts); (viii) *Set Me as a Seal upon thine Heart*.

(B) *(*) Decca (ADD/DDD) 470 127-2. (i) Little (ii) Bournemouth SO, Litton; (iii) Ashcroft, Irons, L. Sinf., Chailly; (iv) LPO, Boult; (v) RPO, Ashkenazy; (vi) Nicola Hall; (vii) LPO Ch. & O, Solti; (viii) Moule, Kendall, Winchester Cathedral Ch., Wayneflete Singers, Hill.

This ill-advised collection in Decca's 'World Of' composer anthologies is much too piecemeal to be satisfying. Boult's mono *Portsmouth Point Overture*; an early 1954 recording, is an obvious piece for inclusion, and the Litton items are well performed in digital sound. The *Façade* excerpts are acceptable, but hardly compare with the Collins/Sitwell complete version. The guitar *Bagatelles* are very well played but it is frustrating that we are offered only one movement from Tasmin Little's fine performance of the *Violin Concerto*. The programme ends with excerpts from Solti's lively 1977 *Belshazzar's Feast*, which should tempt any listener to explore the complete work. But this is not really the way to approach Walton's music.

Hamlet (film score).

** Carlton **DVD** 37115 00183. Olivier, Herlie, Sydney, Simmons, Aylmer, Philh. O, Mathieson. (Director: Laurence Olivier.)

Although Laurence Olivier's film of *Hamlet* was made in 1948, four years after *Henry V*, the sound of Walton's evocative film score, as transferred to DVD, is far inferior to that in the earlier film, with far less body and less sense of space. Though it is not nearly as crumbly as the soundtrack of Eisenstein's *Ivan the*

Terrible, it is not even as full-bodied as the sound on the VHS equivalent and, like that, offers only a truncated version of the most substantial section of the score, the final *Funeral March*. Muir Mathieson again conducted, but this time with the newly founded Philharmonia Orchestra. Needless to say, for all the lack of focus in the sound, the evocative camerawork in black and white, with swirling mists around the castle of Elsinore, is beautifully caught in sharp focus, and Olivier's truncated version of Shakespeare works very well as film.

Henry V (film score).

** Carlton **DVD** 37115 00193. Olivier, Newton, Banks, Asherson, LSO, Mathieson. (Director: Laurence Olivier.)

Walton's music for Laurence Olivier's film of *Henry V* has never been surpassed in the way it adds so vividly both to the dramatic impact and to the atmospheric beauty. The very opening, with a play-bill fluttering to a flute figure and a panoramic view of Elizabethan London to a haunting off-stage chorus, sets the pattern even before the drama starts. Although the sound from a mono soundtrack is necessarily limited, it has been beautifully cleaned up for DVD, so that such effects are vividly atmospheric, giving a satisfying sense of space.

Much of Walton's music is well known in concert form, but the film brings home just how much more there is than that and how it is even more effective in its original context. Even the Agincourt charge music, a uniquely effective set-piece, is more effective still when seen as well as heard.

Olivier's concept, with the film moving from the Globe Theatre at the start to an idealized setting in France, with medieval false perspectives, remains masterly. An extraordinarily starry line-up of leading British actors of the time brings a whole gallery of characterful portrayals, not least from Olivier himself, unforgettable in the title role.

The Quest (complete ballet; original score); *The Wise Virgins* (ballet suite); *Siesta*.

(BB) *** Naxos 8.555868. English Northern Philh. O, Lloyd-Jones

In 1943, at the height of the war, Walton was commissioned to write a full-length ballet for the Sadler's Wells Company to the choreography of Frederick Ashton. The 40-minute score of *The Quest* had to be completed while Ashton was on five week's leave from the RAF, forcing Walton to abandon his usual meticulous mode of working. Despite a starry cast, including Margot Fonteyn, Moira Shearer and Robert Helpman, and beautiful sets by John Piper (one of which is reproduced on the cover of the disc) the ballet was a failure, largely because of the confusing allegorical plot derived from Spenser's *Faerie Queene* about St George fighting the forces of evil.

The ballet was never revived and the score lost for many years, only to be brought out for a recording for the Chandos Walton Edition in 1990 with Bryden

Thomson conducting. That used elaborated scoring by Christopher Palmer designed to counter the composer's feeling that the original spare orchestration, the result of wartime limitations, could be improved. What Lloyd-Jones has done with this fine Naxos version is to go back to Walton's original with only modest expansion of forces, and the result in his brilliant performance, helped by refined recording, is greater transparency, and far from seeming thin the impact is sharper than in the earlier, more opulent version. This is vintage Walton, consistently fresh, defying any unevenness of invention, culminating in a radiant *Passacaglia*. One hopes the success of the disc will encourage the revival of the original ballet with its Piper sets.

Like Thomson, Lloyd-Jones couples *The Quest* with the suite from a ballet which Walton wrote earlier in the war, *The Wise Virgins*, orchestrating movements from Bach cantatas, including *Sheep May Safely Graze*. Again Lloyd-Jones's performance, at faster speeds, more effectively brings out the sharpness of orchestration which, so far from being inflated, gives off electric sparks. The brief interlude for strings, *Siesta*, one of Walton's earliest orchestral pieces, makes an attractive supplement.

Symphonies Nos. 1–2. Siesta.

(B) *** CfP 575 5692. LPO or LSO, Mackerras.

Sir Charles Mackerras, in coupling Walton's two symphonies in 1989, made a particularly strong case for No. 2 with the LSO sharply incisive, helping to bring out both its consistency with No. 1 and a new sensuousness of expression. Mackerras, like Previn before him, firmly established the work's distinction in its control of argument, its brilliant use of a very large orchestra, and above all its lyrical warmth. Mackerras's reading of No. 1, using the LPO, adopts broader speeds than usual. It may not be as bitingly dramatic as the very finest versions, but the richness and strength of the symphony come over powerfully. Warm, full recording in both works, with *Siesta* now making an attractive interlude between them.

Symphony No. 1 in B flat min.; (i) Belshazzar's Feast.

(M) (***) BBC mono/stereo BBCL 4097-2. (i) RPO; (ii) McIntyre, BBC Ch. & Choral Soc, Christchurch Harmonic Ch., BBC SO, composer.

Though Walton recorded both these major works in the studio for EMI, these live radio recordings are invaluable in amplifying his interpretative ideas. Neither performance replaces the studio version, when the sound in each is more limited, but the vitality of a live occasion in each case gives an extra dramatic thrust to the readings. The *First Symphony* was recorded in mono at the Usher Hall at the 1959 Edinburgh Festival, and inevitably suffers from the dryness of the acoustic, as well as from a restless audience. The finale was clearly less well-rehearsed than the rest, but there as in the earlier movements Walton on a live occasion consistently gives a lift to the jazzy syncopations,

encouraging a degree of freedom that stamps them as totally idiomatic. Speeds are a shade faster than in the studio, and the grinding dissonances at the climax of the slow movement bite even harder, while the elegiac trumpet solo just before the final coda in the finale is more tender as well as more spacious.

Belshazzar's Feast comes in a stereo recording of 1965 from the Royal Festival Hall, with the chorus more backwardly balanced and less clear than in the studio version. One clear gain is the choice of soloist, with Donald McIntyre more bitingly dramatic than Donald Bell, and the points where the live account scores over the studio version include the description of the writing on the wall, more sinister in its pausefulness, and the lovely passage for semi-chorus in the finale, 'The Trumpeters and pipers are silent'.

Symphony No. 2; Overtures: Portsmouth Point; Scapino; (i) Belshazzar's Feast.

*** EMI **Audio DVD** DVC4 92402-9. LSO, Previn; (i) with Shirley-Quirk, LSO Ch.

If Walton's *Second Symphony* prompted George Szell to direct the Cleveland Orchestra in one of his most spectacular performances on record, André Previn and the LSO give another brilliant performance which in some ways gets closer to the heart of the music, with its overtones of the romantic opera, *Troilus and Cressida*. Previn is less literal than Szell, more sparkling in the outer movements, more warmly romantic in the central slow movement of this still under-rated symphony. In the two Overtures Previn, the shrewdest and most perceptive of Waltonians, finds more light and shade than usual. *Portsmouth Point* is attractively spirited, and *Scapino* affectionately light-hearted as well as brilliantly played. The recording from the early 1970s is outstandingly fine, enhanced further in this DVD remastering and this applies even more strikingly in the choral work.

Previn's 1972 Kingsway Hall *Belshazzar's Feast* on EMI still remains among the most spectacular yet recorded. The digital remastering has not lost the body and atmosphere of the sound and now the DVD transfer further increases its impact and range. The splendid performance was recorded with Walton present on his seventieth birthday and, though Previn's tempi are slower than those set by Walton himself in his two recordings, the authenticity is clear, with consistently sharp attack and with dynamic markings meticulously observed down to the tiniest hairpin markings. Chorus and orchestra are challenged to their finest standards, and John Shirley-Quirk proves a characterful and imaginative soloist, with every word clear. To sample the demonstration standard of the CD transfer try track 5: *Praise Ye the God of Gold*. The DVD offers alternative two-speaker stereo and surround sound versions of the recordings, one on each side of the disc.

CHAMBER MUSIC

5 Bagatelles for Guitar and Chamber Orchestra.

*** Chan. 9963. Ogden, Northern Sinf. Hickox –
ARNOLD: *Guitar Concerto; Serenade;* BERKELEY:
Guitar Concerto. ***

It was the bright idea of Patrick Russ to mix together
the set of *Five Bagatelles for Solo Guitar* which Walton
wrote for Julian Bream and his very last work, *Varii
capricci*, a brilliant orchestration of those same five
pieces. The result is a guitar concerto which in many
ways – rather surprisingly – transcends those two
original sources, creating a work as effective as the
fine guitar concertos of Sir Malcolm Arnold and Sir
Lennox Berkeley.

What Russ has done is to retain as far as possible
the substance of the solo guitar part of the *Bagatelles*,
and use Walton's orchestral version mainly for comment, with the strands often alternating rather than
playing together. This has involved a modest expansion of the fast outer movements, a positive gain
when, without altering their character, it gives them
added weight. The three genre pieces in between, all
briefer and more relaxed, then together take on the
role of a conventional slow movement. The composite work seems less lightweight than either the solo
Bagatelles or *Varii capricci*, a genuine concerto rather
than a suite of miniatures. Craig Ogden is a brilliant,
persuasive advocate, warmly supported by Hickox
and the Northern Sinfonia.

String Quartet in A min; String Quartet No. 1.

*** Black Box BBM 1035. Emperor Qt.

The young members of the Emperor Quartet give brilliant, incisive performances of both of Walton's string
quartets, not just the *A minor* from his high maturity in
1947, but the very early work which after a handful of
performances in the early 1920s he suppressed but did
not destroy. For that early work – which points forward
to an atonal style very different from later Walton – the
Emperor Quartet have had access to extra material
involving editing and cuts, observing those that plainly
were the composer's own. In addition to those minor
differences of text, the Emperor Quartet's speeds are
consistently faster than those of the Gabrieli Quartet
on the rival version in the Chandos Walton Edition
(Chan. 8944), notably in the fugal finale of the 1922
work, which here more clearly echoes Beethoven's
Grosse Fuge, helped by drier recording.

CHORAL MUSIC

Antiphon; Cantico del sole; 4 Carols; Coronation Te Deum; Jubilate; A Litany (3 versions); Magnificat and Nunc dimittis; Missa brevis; A Queen's Fanfare; Set Me as a Seal; The Twelve; Where does the Uttered Music Go?.

*** Hyp. CDA 67330. Polyphony, Wallace Collection,
Layton; Vivian (organ).

This collection of Walton's shorter choral pieces from
Polyphony brings important advantages which all
Walton admirers will value. The inclusion of the Wallace Collection in the ensemble brings an immediate
advantage in the first choral item, the *Coronation Te
Deum*, when the extra bite of brass adds greatly to the
power of a piece originally designed for far bigger
forces in Westminster Abbey. That is preceded dramatically by the *Fanfare for the Queen* from 1959, and
the use of brass also adds to the impact of the final
item, *Antiphon*, one of Walton's very last works, setting George Herbert's hymn, *Let all the World in Every
Corner Sing*. The other big advantage of this new disc
is that it offers three contrasted versions of *A Litany*,
the motet setting of Phineas Fletcher, which Walton
wrote at Christ Church in his early teens. The original, conceived in 1916 when the boy was only 14, was
for four treble voices and pitched a minor third
higher than the definitive version, while the second
version, made in 1917, introduced a full range of
voices and was pitched slightly lower. What comes out
from the three performances on this disc is the growing complexity of the writing, though from the start
the young Walton obviously relished scrunching discords. Also included here are the *Four Carols*, making
this as comprehensive a collection of Walton's shorter
choral pieces as could be imagined. The fine professional group, Polyphony, with sopranos very boyish,
sound very like a cathedral choir, set in an ecclesiastical atmosphere, though the acoustic of Hereford
Cathedral is rather washy, with balance favouring the
organ and brass.

Antiphon; Cantico del sole; Coronation Te Deum; Jubilate Deo; Magnificat & Nunc dimittis; A Litany; Missa brevis; Set Me as a Seal Upon thine Heart; The Twelve; Where Does the Uttered Music Go? Organ solos: Henry V: Touch her Soft Lips and Part; Passacaglia: Death of Falstaff.

(BB) *** Naxos 8.55579. St John's College Ch., Robinson.

This disc of Walton's church music and smaller choral
pieces is another in Naxos's superb series of English
choral music from St John's College, Cambridge. It
gains over rival collections of these pieces not just in
price but in using boys' rather than women's voices.
With Walton himself trained as a boy chorister at
Christ Church Cathedral, Oxford, his writing gains
positively from that brighter, fresher sound, not just in
the liturgical pieces. Even the *Coronation Te Deum* of
1953, designed for a big choir on the grandest of ceremonial occasions, benefits from the extra sharpness of
focus, revealing not just a brilliant compression of a
long text, but a taut musical structure. The pieces
stretch over the widest span of Walton's career, from
the setting of Phineas Fletcher in *A Litany*, the amazing
inspiration of a 14-year-old but, anticipating the
mature Walton, to *Antiphon*, one of his last works, a

stirring setting of George Herbert's hymn, *Let All the World in Every Corner Sing.*

Belshazzar's Feast.

(BB) *** Warner Apex 0927 444 394-2. Terfel, BBC Singers, BBC Ch. & SO, A. Davis – VAUGHAN WILLIAMS: *Job.* ***

In Andrew Davis's dramatically eloquent account of *Belshazzar's Feast,* taken from the last night of the 1994 Promenade Concerts, the glorious choral contribution demonstrates how perfectly suited Walton's masterly oratorio is to the Royal Albert Hall's famous and sometimes intractable acoustics. From the powerful trombone opening and the riveting '*Thus spake Isaiah*' from the BBC Singers and Chorus, the listener is held under the music's spell, and Bryn Terfel's resonant '*If I forget thee*' is as compelling as his cry '*Babylon is a great City*', while the choral responses to '*Praise ye*' are as thrilling as the 'writing hand' sequence is creepily sinister. The apt coupling with *Job,* another biblical work, makes this a most desirable reissue.

WARLOCK, Peter (1894–1930)

(i) *Capriol Suite; Serenade for Strings;* (ii) *Lullaby My Jesus.* Songs: (iii) *After Two Years; As Ever I Saw; The Bayley Berith of Bell Away; The Birds; The Cricketers of Hambledon; The Droll Lover; Eloré Lo; Fair and True; The Fox; The Frostbound Wood; Ha'nacker Mill; Julian of Berry; My Own Country; 12 Oxen; Passing By; Pretty Ring Time; Robin Goodfellow; Roister Doister; Romance; Sigh No More, Ladies; Sleep; There is a Lady Sweet and Kind; To the Memory of a Great Singer; Whenas the Rye Reach to the Chin; Yarmouth Fair; Youth.*

(M) **(*) Decca (ADD/DDD) 470 199-2. (i) ASMF, Marriner; (ii) Winchester Cathedral Ch., Hill; (iii) Bailey, Parsons.

This collection of over two dozen of Warlock's songs displays his art as a miniaturist, whether in the brisk items with their crisp pay-offs (not always so lightly pointed here as they should be) or in such intense songs as *The Frostbound Wood.* Though Norman Bailey is consistently thoughtful in his singing, charm is not one of his great qualities, and the vocal tone is somewhat lacking in variety. But with superb accompaniments and an effective five-voiced chorus joining in for two numbers (originally the ends of each LP side) this is a valuable and attractive anthology. Marriner's stylish and polished accounts of the orchestral items are always a joy to hear, and the sound throughout is of Decca's best late-1970s quality (the pleasing *Lullaby My Jesus* is digital).

WEBER, Carl Maria von (1786–1826)

Clarinet Concertos Nos. 1 in F min., Op. 73; 2 in E flat, Op. 74; Clarinet Concertino.

**(*) Chan. 8305. Hilton, CBSO, Järvi.

Stylish and understanding performances of both concertos from Janet Hilton, spirited and rhythmic (particularly in No. 1), but erring a little on the side of caution next to her finest virtuoso rivals. The *Concertino,* however, is very successful and with full, well-balanced recording and nice matching between soloist and orchestra, this is certainly recommendable for its sound quality. But the original recordings date from 1982 and this should have been reissued at mid-price. Emma Johnson holds her own as a primary recommendation in this repertoire and for the same cost as this she includes also the *Grand duo concertante* (❂ ASV CDDCA 747).

Clarinet Quintet, Op. 34 (arr. for clarinet and string orch)

*** EMI CDC5 57359-2. Meyer, ASMF, Sillito – BAERMANN: *Clarinet Quintet No.3 in E flat, Op. 23;* MENDELSSOHN: *2 Concert Pieces for Clarinet & Basset Horn.* ***

Weber, inspired by the playing of his friend, Heinrich Baermann, began writing his *Clarinet Quintet* while on holiday in Switzerland in 1811, completing it the following year, a labour of love following the two concertos and concertino he had earlier written for Baermann. It is just as inspired and just as demanding technically, which makes it an ideal candidate to be translated, as here, into a full concerto for clarinet and strings. Sabine Meyer is at her most inspired, combining wit and warmth in the ambitious first movement and producing honeyed pianissimos in the *Fantasia* slow movement. The exuberance of the writing in the *Menuetto capriccio* and the *Allegro giocoso* finale is matched by the joy of her playing, with every technical difficulty relished to the full. Warm, well-balanced recording.

Der Freischütz (complete).

**(*) DHM 05472 77536-2 (2). Schnitzer, Stojkovic, Prégardien, Zeppenfeld, Röhlig, John (narrator), Capella Coloniensis & WDRO of Cologne, Weil.

(B) ** Double Decca (ADD) 460 194-2 (2). Behrens, Donath, Kollo, Moll, Brendel, Meven, Bav. Rad. Ch. & SO, Kubelik.

Bruno Weil conducts a recording of *Der Freischütz* with a difference. Not only does he bring his experience of period performance to the score, clarifying textures in a reading less grandly romantic than usual, often at crisply moving speeds, he uses in place of the usual spoken dialogue linking passages written by Steffen Kopetzy and spoken by an actor, Markus John, taking the role of Samiel. These are comments on the action rather than conventional narrations telling the story, and they work well in eliminating what has generally been regarded as the weakness of the usual dialogue. They are all brief and are optional, being separately banded. For the non-German-speaker that may be less important, but the freshness of the whole production is reinforced, using an excellent cast of mainly young singers, with only Christoph Prégardien a star already established. As Max he is first-rate, but so is Petra-Maria Schnitzer a fresh and girlish Agathe. As Annchen Johanna Stojkovic's soprano, less soubrettish than usual in this role, provides less contrast with the heroine, but hers too is a fresh, winning performance, with Georg Zeppenfeld excellent in Kaspar's drinking song. The climax of the Wolf's Glen scene at the end of Act 2 is splendidly biting in Weil's reading, but with cleancut recording less atmospheric than it can be. However Harnoncourt's electrifying and refreshing Teldec version remains first choice among modern recordings (4509 97758-2) and Keiberth's mid-priced analogue EMI set with Gümmer, Otto, Schock and Prey is splendidly sung and the Wolf Glen's scene here has never been surpassed in its malignant drama (CMS7 69342-2).

Kubelik takes a direct view of Weber's high romanticism. The result has freshness but lacks something of dramatic bite and atmosphere. There is far less tension than in the finest versions, not least in the Wolf's Glen scene, which in spite of the full-ranging 1979 recording seems rather tame. The singing is generally good, René Kollo as Max giving one of his best performances on record, but Hilde Behrens, superbly dramatic in later German operas, here as Agathe seems clumsy in music that often requires a pure lyrical line. Still, the bargain price (without texts) makes the set reasonable value.

WEILL, Kurt (1900–50)

Concerto for Violin & Winds, Op. 12.

(B) *** Virgin 2 CD VBD5 62053-2 (2). Tetzlaff, Deutsche Kammerphilharmonie Wind – BARTOK: Violin Concerto No. 2; Violin Sonata. JANACEK: Violin Concerto; Sonata. ***

Weill's Concerto for Violin and Winds has a seriousness of purpose and an originality that are persuasive, no doubt much helped by the highly sensitive and imaginative performance given by Christian Tetzlaff and the winds of the Deutsche Kammerphilharmonie; it is coupled with most interesting repertoire. It will surely convert any who doubt the quality of this work.

Street Scene (opera; complete).

* Arthaus DVD 100 098. Putnam, Wellbee, Handen, Wilborn, Rheinland-Pfalz State Philh, Holmes.

This video version of Kurt Weill's 'American Opera' was recorded in Ludwigshafen in 1995, with a German orchestra and chorus but with the cast and production translated from an earlier presentation by the Houston Grand Opera company, directed by Francesca Zambello. The result is strong and idiomatic, with realistic sets by Adrianne Lobel, and with Ashley Putnam warmly sympathetic in the central role of Mrs Maurant. Unfortunately, there is no synopsis provided in the booklet, and no identification of which character is performing at what point. The 4 x 3 format also cuts off the sides of what was originally a wide-screen production, and the sound is abrasively loud.

WELLESZ, Egon (1885–1974)

Die Bakchantinnen.

*** Orfeo Musica Rediviva C136012H (2). Mohr, Burt, Stamm, Alexander, Barainsky, Breedt, Aschenbach, Gottschick, Berlin R. Ch., Deutsches SO, Albrecht.

During the 1920s and 1930s Wellesz was better known as an operatic musicologist than as a composer. In England, to which he came at the time of the Anschluss, it was his eminence as a scholar in the field of early Christian and Byzantine hymnology and as an historian of opera that overshadowed his creative work. It was for his research on Giuseppe Bonno (a contemporary of Gluck), Cavalli and Venetian opera, Antonio Cesti and the development of opera and oratorio in Vienna that his reputation rested. True, Oxford put on his charming opera Incognita in a student performance under Sir Jack Westrup in 1951, but otherwise, apart from the rare broadcast from Austria, his operas remain unknown. His symphonies remain unrecorded, and Die Bakchantinnen is the first of his operas to reach CD.

He wrote five operas between 1921 and 1931, and Die Bakchantinnen, for which he supplied his own libretto in 1930, was his last. Premièred in Vienna under Clemens Krauss the following year, it leaves no doubts about his mastery of dramatic pacing and momentum nor about the quality of his musical imagination. Wellesz's musical language is tonal and direct in appeal, and though he was close to the Schoenberg–Berg–Webern circle (he was Schoenberg's first biographer), he is very different from them. He is a master of the orchestra and writes effectively for the voice, as in Agave's exchanges with Ino in Act II. Almost the most impressive thing is the extensive (and often high-lying) choral writing. The choir plays a prominent rôle throughout, and Wellesz's choral writing is consistently powerful. What impresses – more than the dramatic characterization – is the sense of line, which is so much stronger than in Schreker, whose refined palette and exotic scoring is far removed from his world. Unlike Schreker Wellesz never set great store by pure harmonic effect. Melodic lines are often angular but always move purposefully, and there is atmosphere and a strong responsiveness to dramatic mood. The cast is strong, in particular Roberta Alexander's Agave, even if Thomas Mohr's Dionysos shows the occasional sign of strain. The chorus and orchestra give a good account of themselves under Gerd Albrecht. The recording balance is well judged and the overall sound is very good. The notes are in German and English, but not in French, and the libretto is not offered in translation. Let us hope that Orfeo will go on to record Alkestis and the often enchanting Incognita.

WEYSE, Christoph Ernst Friedrich (1774–1842)

Sovedrikken (The Sleeping Draught)

**(*) dacapo 8.224149-2. Soloists, Sokkelund Ch., Danish R. Sinf., Giordano Bellincampi.

In the days of LP, Christoph Friedrich Emil Weyse, the 'Father of Danish song' was very little known outside his homeland. Even as late as 1980 he was unrepresented in the British catalogues. Aksel Schiøtz's recordings of some of the songs were fleetingly available but the exploration of the symphonic and instrumental output has been of relatively recent provenance. True, one aria from the present work, *Skøn jomfru! Luk dit vindue op (Fair maiden! Throw your window wide)* was recorded by Schiøtz with the composer Hermann D Koppel at the piano in 1938 and later on with orchestra, Weyse, however, composed half-a-dozen operas, of which the singspiel or 'Syngespil', *Sovedrikken (The Sleeping Draught)* is the first and best known. It was begun in 1800 with the encouragement of Kunzen, who had by this time returned to Copenhagen, and would have been finished earlier had his poet, Oehlenschlager been quicker to start work on the libretto (he put it on one side for eighteen months). The argument or plot line comes from Christoph Friedrich Bretzner, the same Bretzner whose *Belmont und Constanze* had served as the basis for *Die Entführung*. For a variety of reasons Weyse lost his appetite for the opera, and it was only after Kunzen had mounted *Don Giovanni* in Copenhagen in 1807, that his enthusiasm for his own project was rekindled. *The Sleeping Draught* was mounted in 1809 to great acclaim: the present issue is its first recording and indeed the first of any of Weyse's operas. The action is not easily summarised and calls for nine characters, who are all pretty two-dimensional. There is scant opportunity for characterisation and perhaps the most impressive things are the multi-movement finales: that of the first Act runs for some nineteen minutes. The cast is generally very good and the singing never falls below a decent level of accomplishment and the sole aria (a kind of catalogue aria) of the baritone Guido Paëvatalu gives much pleasure. The Danish Radio Sinfonietta under Giordano Bellincampi are lively and enthusiastic, and the recording is eminently well balanced and warm. It comes with extensive and authoritative essays by Jørgen Hansen on the historical background and the development of the singspiel in Denmark as well as Weyse himself. *Sovedrikke* is a fresh and pleasing entertainment for which few would make great claims but which has a lot of charm and is well worth hearing.

WILLIAMS, John (born 1932)

(i) Violin Concerto; Schindler's List: 3 Pieces; Tree Song.

**(*) DG 471 326-2. (i) Shaham, Boston SO, Composer.

Anyone who knows John Williams's film scores, from his wittily tuneful *Guide for the Married Man* to the epic *Star Wars* spectaculars and the haunting *Schindler's List* theme (beautifully played here), will know just how diversely inventive this composer can be. Yet the *Violin Concerto* is disappointing. It dates from 1974 but was revised into its present from in 1998, and is dedicated to the composer's late wife, the actress Barbera Ruick Williams. The world of film music is again never too far away and there is some effective writing, some of it quite striking, but, surprisingly, it lacks memorable basic themes. *Tree Song* dates from 2000 and shows Williams's skill in orchestration, but again the material is not especially strong. It is hard to imagine these performances being bettered, or their recordings.

WINDING, August (1835–99)

Piano Concerto in A minor, Op. 19; Concert Allegro in C minor, Op. 29.

**(*) Danacord DACOCD 581. Oleg Marshev, Danish PO, South Jutland, Matthias Aeschbacher – EMIL HARTMANN: *Piano Concerto*. *(*)

August Winding belonged to Grieg's circle of Copenhagen friends (Grieg introduced his *Overture to a Norwegian Tragedy* to Christiania as Oslo was then known). He studied with Gade, Reinecke and Dreyschock and had a flourishing but short career as a virtuoso pianist before a nervous complaint in his arm forced him to give up concert work. His *Piano Concerto* shares the same key but not the same opus number as the Grieg. The concerto is small talk, very derivative and much indebted to Gade and Mendelssohn. It has a certain charm even if the ideas are pretty unmemorable. The *Concert Allegro* is eminently Schumannesque, but is so brilliantly played by the Russian virtuoso Oleg Marshev and the Danish Orchestra that one is almost tempted to believe that it is better than it is. Winding shares the disc with his brother-in-law, Emil Hartmann.

WOLF, Hugo (1860–1903)

Spanisches Liederbuch (complete).

(B) *** EMI double fforte CZS5 75181-2 (2). Von Otter, Bär, Parsons.

Completed barely six months before Geoffrey Parsons's untimely death, the EMI set of the *Spanish Songbook* makes a superb memorial to that great accompanist, here working with two of the most searching and stylish Lieder singers of the present generation. They opt for an order of the songs quite different from the original published order, seeking to find 'a dramatic shape that worked in the atmosphere of a concert'. Quite apart from Parsons' superb contribution, the performances of both soloists vie with those on the classic DG set with Schwarzkopf and

Fischer-Dieskau. For the lighter songs von Otter uses a much brighter tonal range than elsewhere, though in such a song as *In dem Schatten meiner Locken* she remains more intimate than Schwarzkopf, pointing the words and phrases with comparable character. The double fforte reissue is a fine bargain, though no texts and translations are included.

WOLF-FERRARI, Ermanno

(1876–1948)

L'amore medico: Overture & Intermezzo; Il Campiello: Intermezzo; Ritornello; La dama bomba: Overture; I gioielli della Madonna: Suite; I quattro rusteghi: Prelude & Intermezzo; Il segreto di Susanna: Overture & Intermezzo.

(B) *** EMI double fforte CZS5 75160-2 (2). ASMF, Marriner – CHERUBINI: *Overtures.* ***

Wolf-Ferrari's overtures and (especially) his intermezzi have long been relished for their ready tunefulness and charm. Marriner and the Academy are only marginally below their finest form here, and this concert makes a delightful entertainment with everything elegantly played and warmly (if resonantly) recorded. In the concertante *Intermezzo* from *L'amore medico*, Stephen Orton takes the cello solo most winningly.

WOOD, Charles (1866–1926)

Anthems and Hymn Anthems: Ascension Hymn; The Earth trembled; Expectans expectavi; God omnipotent reigneth; Haec dies; I am risen; I will call upon God; Jesu the very thought is sweet; O King most high; O Lord rebuke me not; O Lord that seest from yon starry Heights; O Most Merciful; O Thou sweetest source; Sunlight all golden; This is the Day; 'Tis the Day of Resurrection; True love's the gift. (i) (Organ) *Preludes: Martyrs; Old 104th; Old 132nd; Old 136th; Psalm 23; York Tune.*

*** Priory PRCD 754. Gonville & Caius College, Cambridge Ch., Webber; Roberts; (i) Unglow (organ).

The career of the Anglo-Irish composer Charles Wood ran parallel with that of his better-known colleague, Stanford, whom he succeeded as Professor of Composition at the Royal College of Music. Wood's music is less flamboyant, less innovatory than Stanford's but his anthems and hymn-anthems form a rich part of the fabric of Anglican church music. If the opening *O thou sweetest source* is impressive in its very simplicity, the gleaming brightness of *Sunlight all golden* does not belie its title, and *God omnipotent reigneth*, underpinned by the organ, is boldly arresting. Yet one of the most memorable items, the unaccompanied *Jesu, the very thought is sweet* is quite brief, eloquently setting a melody from the *Piae Cantiones* of 1582. If Wood's harmonic language is not forward-looking, his music is of quality and often individual, as in his Latin settings, the

jubilant *Haec dies* and the very touching *Expectans expectavi*, written in memory of his son, killed in the First World War. The Organ Preludes draw on old church melodies and are comparatively conventional in style, but very well played, and here used effectively as interludes. Indeed the presentation could hardly be bettered, the choir singing with fervour and rich tonal blending. The recording is excellent.

WOOD, Hugh (born 1932)

Symphony; (i) *Scenes from Comus.*

*** NMC NMCD 070. BBC SO, Davis; (i) with McGreevy, Norman.

Hugh Wood's powerful *Symphony*, written in the late 1970s and early 1980s, is a major addition to British symphonic repertoire, in a direct line from Walton's *First*. If not so immediately approachable, it readily responds to repeated listening, for it is cogently argued and gripping from the first note to the last. Drama of a semi-theatrical nature is the composer's springboard and the opening *Tempesta* is violently histrionic, yet has an underlying dark lyricism directly related to Wagner's *Die Walküre* and the passion of Siegmund and Sieglinde. Their love motif is quoted to make the derivation clear and the long *Elegia* slow movement is headed by a classical Greek quotation which draws a connection with Siegmund's *Todesverkündigung*. Later there is an unexpected fragment from Mozart: the flute-and-drum 'ordeal' sequence in *Die Zauberflöte*. The throbbing Scherzo draws on the work's basic ideas, but fragmented into a powerful *con fuoco*. The energy subsides and with delicate colouring from horns, piccolo flute and glockenspiel we are led to the disconsolate calm of the opening of the passacaglia finale, which is finally to end the work with a passionate, triumphantly positive acclamation.

The *Scenes from Comus* are not incidental music for Milton's masque, but a highly atmospheric symphonic narrative in eight sections with vocalizations, confidently sung by Daniel Norman (Comus) and Geraldine McGreevy. As the 'Lady' of the narrative, she is enchanted by the son of Circe after being abducted in *The Wild Wood*, where in Wood's setting she responds willingly to the following orgiastic dances. The finale duet *Sabrina Fair* brings a mood of ecstatic serenity and this remarkably imaginative work ends with a peaceful epilogue. Sir Andrew Davis conducts throughout with mastery and a total identification with the music of both works, each of which resonates in the memory, but especially the symphony. The recording is splendid.

YOST, Michél (1754–86)

Clarinet Concertos Nos. 7 in B flat; 8 in E flat; 9 in B flat; 11 in B flat.

*** MDG 301 0718-2. Klöcker, Prague CO.

Not many collectors will have heard of Yost before discovering this CD. But here are four delightfully bubbly concertos, brimming with excellent tunes and plenty of wit, with any moments of drama soon pushed away with sunny abandon. Like the more substantial, but no less effervescent concertos of Cartellieri on the same label, this is a delightful CD and it is hard to imagine better performances or recordings.

ZELENKA, Jan (1679–1745)

Lamentations Jeremiae Prophete (Lamentations for Maundy Thursday, Good Friday and Easter Eve).

(BB) *** Hyp. Helios CDH 55106. Chance, Ainsley, George, Chandos Bar. Players.

These solo settings of the six *Lamentations* for the days leading up to Easter reinforce Zelenka's claims as one of the most original composers of his time. The spacious melodic lines and chromatic twists in the harmonic progressions are often very Bachian, but the free-flowing alternation of arioso and recitative is totally distinctive, as is the melismatic obbligato writing for oboes and recorders. The fine Deutsche Harmonia Mundi under René Jacobs has now been withdrawn, but fortunately Hyperion have reissued this hardly less moving account on their bargain Helios label. Here, too, all three soloists are excellent: Michael Chance singing with great beauty in the setting for Maundy Thursday and in the closing music, the bass Michael George distinguishing himself on Good Friday, and the tenor John Mark Ainsley equally impressive in the music for Easter Eve. The continuo is aurally beguiling, placed in an atmospheric acoustic, and the relaxed pacing very diverting.

ZEMLINSKY, Alexander von

(1871–1942)

(i) *Cymbeline* (incidental music): *Suite; Die Seejungfrau; Sinfonietta, Op. 23; Ein Tanzpoem*; (ii) *Frühlingsbegräbnis* (cantata).

✿ (B) *** EMI double fforte CZS5 75184-2 (2). (i) Kuebler; (ii) Voigt, Albert, Düsseldorf State Musikverein Ch.; Gürzenich O or Cologne PO, Conlon

James Conlon, a devotee of Zemlinsky's music, here conducts an admirable cross-section of his output. Apart from the comparatively familiar *Lyrische Symphonie* his best-known work is *Die Seejungfrau*, a ripely sensuous symphonic poem based on Hans Chrstian Andersen's fairy-tale about the mermaid. Conlon's reading is tender and poetic. At speeds rather more expansive than those in Chailly's brilliant and finely detailed Concertgebouw version (now withdrawn), he brings out the evocative beauty with a more affectionate manner. The recording (as throughout the set) is atmospheric rather than sharply focused again giving warmth to the sensuous writing in the much later *Sinfonietta* of 1934.

This was written just after the composer was forced to leave Germany for Switzerland, following the rise of the Nazis. With neoclassicism framing what is still essentially a late-Romantic work, it has a linking motif and opens with a wild scherzo, a malevolent burlesque mixed with hope and despair. The central *Ballade* is both questing and ironic, rising more than once to a passionate entreaty but ending in resignation. The Rondo finale returns to and amplifies the nightmare burlesque of the first movement, but at the last minute produces a positive closing flourish.

Ein Tanzpoem and the suite from the incidental music for *Cymbeline* are altogether lighter in feeling and more diverting. Both are imaginatively scored, with luminous textures and colourful use of trumpets and horns as well as strings and woodwind. The central movement of *Cymbeline* is an attractive setting of 'Horch, horch! Die Lerche' winningly sung by David Kuebler.

Ein Tanzpoem is an ambitious one-act ballet based on an aborted larger-scale mime drama of 1901, planned by Hofmannsthal, called *Der Triumph der Zeit* ('The Triumph of Time'). Although the writing is more luscious, Zemlinsky's music has more than a little in common with Glazunov's *The Seasons*, but with its four sections evoking the changing moods of the hours of the day. It is hardly less spontaneous and tuneful and played here with much grace and a natural feeling for its seductive dance rhythms.

Frühlingsbegräbnis ('The Burial of Spring') is a fantasy cantata in seven brief movements, each richly memorable. Using soprano and baritone soloists, and with succulent choral writing, Zemlinsky's scenario involves a funeral procession of fairies and animals, a handsome youth struck down by the brightness of the dawn light, a preaching woodpecker, and a thunderstorm. It is admirably sung and played here. Indeed all this music could hardly be presented with more dedication or more flatteringly recorded, and this is one of the most worthwhile and stimulating of all EMI's double fforte reissues. Don't miss it.

String Quartets Nos. 1–4; 2 Movements for String Quartet; Malblumen blühten überall.

*** Chan. 9772 (2). Schoenberg Qt.

This set of the four Zemlinsky quartets is very good indeed and the Dutch-based Schoenberg Quartet have the measure of this strange music. They convey the darker world of the *Adagio misterioso* of the *Two Movements* and the *Fourth Quartet*, composed two years before the Anschluss, as well as the post-Brahmsian gestures of the *First*. The *Malblumen blühten überall* is a setting for soprano and string sextet of Dehmel which the Schoenberg Quartet premièred (together with the *Two Movements*). Very good recordings on which much care has been lavished and altogether warmer than the long-serving set by the LaSalle Quartet on DG.

COLLECTIONS

CONCERTS OF ORCHESTRAL AND CONCERTANTE MUSIC

The Art of Conducting

'*The Art of Conducting*': Video: '*Great conductors of the past*' (Barbirolli, Beecham, Bernstein, Busch, Furtwängler, Karajan, Klemperer, Koussevitzky, Nikisch, Reiner, Stokowski, Richard Strauss, Szell, Toscanini, Walter, Weingartner): BRUCKNER: *Symphony No. 7* (rehearsal) (Hallé O, Barbirolli). GOUNOD: *Faust: ballet music* (with rehearsal) (RPO, Beecham). Silent film (BPO, Nikisch). Richard STRAUSS: *Till Eulenspiegel* (VPO, Richard Strauss). WEBER: *Der Freischütz overture* (Paris SO, Felix Weingartner). WAGNER: *Tannhäuser overture* (Dresden State O, Fritz Busch). MOZART: *Symphony No. 40* (BPO, Bruno Walter). BRAHMS: *Symphony No. 2* (rehearsal) (Vancouver Festival O, Bruno Walter). BEETHOVEN: *Egmont overture; Symphony No. 9* (Philh. O, Klemperer). WAGNER: *Die Meistersinger overture*. SCHUBERT: *Symphony No. 8* (Unfinished). BRAHMS: *Symphony No. 4* (both rehearsals) (BPO, Furtwängler). VERDI: *La forza del destino overture; La Traviata: Coro di zingarelle*. RESPIGHI: *The Pines of Rome* (NBC SO, Toscanini). PURCELL (arr. Stokowski): *Dido and Aeneas: Dido's lament*. RESPIGHI: *The Pines of Rome* (BBC SO). TCHAIKOVSKY: *Symphony No. 5* (NYPO) (both cond. Stokowski). BEETHOVEN: *Egmont overture* (Boston SO, Koussevitzky). TCHAIKOVSKY: *Violin concerto* (Heifetz, NYPO, Reiner). BEETHOVEN: *Symphony No. 7* (Chicago SO, Reiner). BRAHMS: *Academic festival overture*. BEETHOVEN: *Symphony No. 5* (Cleveland O, Szell). BEETHOVEN: *Symphony No. 5*. DEBUSSY: *La Mer* (BPO, Karajan). SHOSTAKOVICH: *Symphony No. 5* (rehearsal and performance) (LSO). MAHLER: *Symphony No. 4* (VPO) (both cond. Bernstein). BEETHOVEN: *Symphony No. 9* (Philh. O, Klemperer).

(Commentary by John Eliot Gardiner, Isaac Stern, Jack Brymer, Beecham, Menuhin, Oliver Knussen, Suvi Raj Grubb, Szell, Walter, Klemperer, Hugh Bean, Werner Thärichen, Richard Mohr, Stokowski, Julius Baker, Karajan).

⚙ *** Teldec VHS 4509 95038-3.

This extraordinary video offers a series of electrifying performances by the great conductors of our century, all seen and heard at their very finest. Enormous care has been taken over the sound, even in the earliest recordings, for it is remarkably full-bodied and believable. But most of all it is to watch conductors weaving their magic spell over the orchestra which is so fascinating. And sometimes they do it imperceptibly, like Richard Strauss conducting *Till Eulenspiegel* with apparent nonchalance, yet making music with the utmost aural vividness; Fritz Busch creating great tension in Wagner; Bruno Walter wonderfully mellow in Brahms; Klemperer in Beethoven hardly moving his baton and yet completely in control; Furtwängler rehearsing the finale of Brahms's *Fourth Symphony* with a tremendous flow of adrenalin; Toscanini the martinet in Verdi; Stokowski moulding gloriously beautiful sound with flowing movements of his hands and arms; and, most riveting of all, Bernstein creating enormous passion with the LSO in Shostakovich's *Fifth Symphony*.

Of the many commentaries from other artists and various musicians, the experience of Werner Thärichen stands out. He was participating in a Berlin performance when he suddenly realized that the sound around him had changed: it had become uncannily more beautiful. Not understanding why, he looked to the back of the hall ... and saw that Furtwängler had just walked in. The great Nikisch is seen conducting (on silent film) but not heard – and no one knows what the music was!

Barbirolli, Sir John

ELGAR: *Enigma Variations.* RAVEL: *Ma Mère l'oye* (suite) (both with Hallé O). WAGNER: *Die Meistersinger: Prelude* (with LSO). MAHLER: *Symphony No. 2 (Resurrection)* (with Donath, Finnila, Stuttgart Rad. Ch. S.O). PUCCINI: *Madama Butterfly: Love Duet* (with Scotto, Bergonzi, Rome Opera O).

(M)(***) EMI (mono/stereo) CZS5 75100-2 (2).

This valuable set brings out of limbo Barbirolli's 1956 Pye version of Elgar's *Enigma Variations* – his first in stereo but largely forgotten thanks to the excellence of his later EMI recording of six years later – and offers for the first time a radio recording from Stuttgart of a Mahler symphony Barbirolli never otherwise put on disc, No. 2, the *Resurrection*. This radio recording of the Mahler dates from April 1970, the year Barbirolli died, and although dynamic contrasts tend to be ironed out a little, the warmth and concentration of Barbirolli in Mahler come over from first to last, leading up to a thrilling account of the choral finale, with the re-creation of Judgement Day thrillingly caught. The acoustic seems to open up the moment the voices enter, with the excellent soloists, Helen Donath and Birgit Finnila, and the massed chorus all sounding full and vivid. The *Meistersinger Prelude*, recorded by EMI the previous year with the LSO, brings a weighty reading at broad speeds. After that the Pye recordings both of *Enigma* and of the Ravel *Mother Goose Suite* are more limited in different ways. The Ravel brings up-front sound with good, bright reproduction of percussion. In the Elgar the playing may not be as refined as in the much-loved EMI stereo version of 1962, but the Hallé with Barbirolli somehow convey an extra emotional tug, whether in *Nimrod* or the passionate climax of the finale. As a welcome supplement comes the heart-warming extract from Barbirolli's Rome recording for EMI of Puccini's *Madama Butterfly* with Renata Scotto and Carlo Bergonzi, as loving an account of the Act 1 duet as you will ever hear.

Busch, Fritz

BEETHOVEN: *Leonora Overture No. 2*; BRAHMS: *Tragic Overture; Symphony No. 2.* HAYDN: *Sinfonia concertante in B flat.* MENDELSSOHN: *Symphony No. 4 in A (Italian).* MOZART: *Symphony No. 36 in C (Linz).* WEBER: *Overture, Der Freischütz* (all with Danish State RSO). R. STRAUSS: *Don Juan* (with LPO).

(B) (***) EMI mono CZS5 75103-2 (2).

It is a revelation that Fritz Busch, the musical founder of Glyndebourne and normally regarded as just a Mozartian, conveys such authority in this wide range of works. They are superbly played, consistently reflecting the joy that the players had in renewing their relationship with a conductor who, from 1933, when he was sacked by the Nazis from his post in Dresden, was their great orchestral trainer in the classical and romantic repertory.

With the exception of the Strauss *Don Juan*, which was made in 1936 with the LPO, all these performances come from 1947–51, the heyday of the Danish State Radio Symphony Orchestra, which Busch brought to a level unrivalled in the other Scandinavian countries. They had greater personality as well as greater virtuosity and finesse than the Stockholm and Oslo orchestras of the day, as witness the 1949 *Linz Symphony* (the 78s were treasurable and still are) and the superb Brahms *Second Symphony*, which is also available on the Dutton anthology issued to mark the orchestra's 75th anniversary; the Dutton transfer is in every way superior. This is also valuable for the first reissue of the Haydn *Sinfonia concertante in B flat*, which features their celebrated oboist, Waldemar Wolsing, and three other first-desk players. The *Leonora No. 2 Overture* and the *Italian Symphony* are new to the catalogue and come from a 1950 concert in Copenhagen.

Cluytens, André

BIZET: *Symphony in C.* BERLIOZ: *Symphonie fantastique* (with French RO). DEBUSSY: *Images* (with Paris Conservatoire O). MUSSORGSKY: *Boris Godunov: Coronation Scene* (with Christoff, Sofia Opera Ch.) RAVEL: *La valse* (with Philh. O). SCHUMANN: *Manfred Overture.* WAGNER: *Lohengrin, Act III: Prelude* (with Berlin Philh. O).

(B) *** EMI (ADD) CZS5 75106-2 (2).

As far as British and American audiences are concerned, André Cluytens (pronounced Klwee-tunss) came to prominence only in the early 1950s: he accompanied Solomon in the Second and Fourth Beethoven concertos in 1952, but he made few appearances in England, although he was the first Belgian conductor to appear at Bayreuth (in 1955). Bizet was one of the first composers he recorded, and his 1953 account of the *Symphony in C* with the Orchestre National de la Radiodiffusion Française was highly thought of in its time – and rightly so. There is a straightforward quality about it, totally unconcerned with effect. It is also available in Testament's Bizet anthology. Also included here is the Coronation Scene from Mussorgsky's *Boris Godunov* with Boris Christoff in the title rôle – naturally in Rimsky-Korsakov's opulent scoring and a relatively little known account of *La Valse* with the Philharmonia Orchestra from 1958, which is more polished than his later recording, although the warmer acoustic of the Salle Pleyel shows the Parisians to better advantage.

The highlights of the set are the atmospheric accounts of the Debussy *Images*, quite unjustly overshadowed at the time by the Monteux (though that was admittedly better played) and the *Symphonie fantastique*, a different account from that issued on Testament. This was recorded at a 1964 concert in Tokyo while the Conservatoire Orchestra was on tour, and is new to the catalogue. A strongly narrative performance, it grips and holds the listener, not so much through its virtuosity but through its sense of forward movement and line. Cluytens knew what this music was all about, and though it lacks the polish of the very finest versions, there is a splendid sense of involvement. A most valuable issue, which gives a good picture of a much underrated maestro.

Golovanov, Nikolai

GLAZUNOV: *Symphony No. 6.* LISZT: *Symphonic Poems: Festklänge; Héroïde funèbre; Mazeppa; Orpheus; Prometheus.* MENDELSSOHN: *A Midsummer Night's Dream: Overture; Scherzo.* TCHAIKOVSKY: *1812 Overture* (all with Moscow RSO).

(B) (*) EMI mono CZS5 75112-2 (2).

Nikolai Golovanov, an exact contemporary of Prokofiev, brought the Moscow Radio Orchestra to a high pitch in the difficult post-war years. He gets playing of much sensitivity and vitality from the strings in Glazunov's endearing *Sixth Symphony* – a very spirited account. In the Liszt tone poems the playing is handicapped by ill-tuned, raw wind tone and blowsy horns. He sets a very fast tempo for the Mendelssohn *Scherzo*, and the results sound scrambled. The recording quality ranges from the just acceptable to the rough.

Kleiber, Erich

BEETHOVEN: *Symphony No. 6 (Pastoral), Op. 68* (with Czech Philharmonic Orchestra). DVORAK: *Carnaval Overture.* MOZART: *Symphony No. 40 in G min., K. 550.* JOSEF STRAUSS: *Waltz: Spharenklänge.* JOHANN STRAUS JR: *Der Zigeunerbaron Overture* (all with London Philharmonic Orchestra); *Du und Du Waltz* (with Vienna Philharmonic Orchestra). SCHUBERT: *Symphony No. 5 in B flat.* R. STRAUSS: *Till Eulenspiegel* (with North German Radio Orchestra).

(B) (***) EMI mono CZS5 75115-2 (2).

Often the most valuable items on the two-disc sets so far issued in this EMI 'Great Conductors' series are radio recordings never previously published. In the superb set representing the work of Erich Kleiber (father of the elusive Carlos Kleiber, and many would say even greater), the most exciting performances are indeed those on radio recordings. The recording he made with the Czech Philharmonic in Prague in 1955 (less than a year before his death) of Beethoven's *Pastoral Symphony* is at once glowingly incandescent and refined, with radiant string tone and rollicking Czech wind and horn playing in the Scherzo. Kleiber's readings for North German Radio of Schubert's *Fifth Symphony* and Strauss's *Till Eulenspiegel* are also outstanding, the Schubert sunny and full of character, the Strauss racily exciting. Though the transfer engineers have not tamed the fierce string sound of the Decca recordings included here, it is good to have from that source Kleiber's powerful, dramatic reading of Mozart's *G minor Symphony*, No. 40, and engaging trifles by the other Strausses, presented with warmth and a degree of indulgence.

Koussevitzky, Serge

BEETHOVEN: *Symphony No. 5 in C minor* (with the London Philharmonic Orchestra). SIBELIUS: *Symphony No. 7* (with BBC Symphony Orchestra). HARRIS: *Symphony No. 3.* TCHAIKOVSKY: *Symphony No. 5 in E min.* RACHMANINOV: *The Isle of the Dead* (all with Boston Symphony Orchestra)..

(B) **(*) EMI mono CZS5 75118-2 (2).

The two discs devoted to Serge Koussevitzky are variable in content, but among the treasures is the revelatory first recording, made live with the BBC Symphony in 1933, of Sibelius's *Seventh Symphony*. By comparison his 1934 studio recording of Beethoven's *Fifth* with the LPO is disappointingly heavy, while all the rest, recorded later with his own Boston Symphony Orchestra, bring superb playing, not least in Roy Harris's powerful, single-movement *Third Symphony*. This account of Rachmaninov's *Isle of the Dead*, never issued in Europe in the 78 era, even rivals the composer's classic account.

Malko, Nicolai

BORODIN: *Symphony No. 2.* DVORAK: *Symphony No. 9 (New World).* GLINKA: *Ruslan and Ludmilla – Overture.* PROKOFIEV: *Symphony No 7.* RIMSKY-KORSAKOV: *Tsar Sultan: Dance of the Tumblers.* SUPPE: *Poet and Peasant: Overture.* TCHAIKOVSKY: *Nutcracker:* excerpts. (all with Philh. O). HAYDN: *Symphony No. 92.* (with Royal Danish O). NIELSEN: *Maskarade: Overture* (with Danish State RO).

(B) (***) EMI mono/stereo CZS5 75121-2 (2).

Nicolai Malko conducted the première of Shostakovich's *First Symphony* in 1926 and was an eminent teacher, numbering Evgeni Mravinsky among his pupils. But when Soviet policy towards the Arts became less liberal, he decided to emigrate and take his chance as a freelance conductor. His recording career began in the days of shellac, and the present compilation ranges from Nielsen's *Maskarade Overture* (1947), thoroughly idiomatic and vital, through to Prokofiev's *Seventh Symphony* (1955) and Glinka's *Ruslan Overture* (1956), a spirited account but not breathless and headlong. He is at his best in Borodin's *Second Symphony* (the second of his two recordings) and the Prokofiev *Seventh Symphony*, whose first British performance he gave. Both have great clarity of texture and momentum, and in charm and finesse the *Seventh* has rarely been equalled. His Haydn with the Royal Danish Orchestra ('Det Kongelige') has great lightness of touch and, in the finale, wit. There is not the slightest trace of affectation, and the same goes for the *New World Symphony*, which is not a great performance, perhaps, but is lively and enjoyable. Malko was not a charismatic conductor, but he was always at the service of the composer and not his own ego. The sound is consistently good for its period.

Markevitch, Igor

CHABRIER: *España* (with Spanish Rad. & TV SO). DEBUSSY: *La Mer*. GLINKA: *A Life for the Tsar: Overture and 3 Dances* (with Lamoureux O of Paris). RAVEL: *Daphnis et Chloë: Suite No. 2* (with Hamburg NDR O). R. STRAUSS: *Till Eulenspiegel* (with French Nat. RO). TCHAIKOVSKY: *Manfred Symphony* (with LSO). VERDI: *La forza del destino: Overture* (with New Philh. O).

(B) ** EMI (ADD) CZS5 75000-2 (2).

An enormously gifted man and a composer of substance, Igor Markevitch gave us relatively few great recordings. His first *Rite of Spring* was certainly one, and his Berwald symphonies with the Berlin Philharmonic were very fine, too. None of the performances here falls below a certain standard, but nearly all have been surpassed elsewhere: his somewhat cool *Manfred Symphony* is not a patch on the electrifying Toscanini, Jansons or Pletnev accounts, and his *Daphnis* is no match for the likes of Ormandy or Karajan. As is the case with other issues in this series, the performances derive not only from commercial recordings but from broadcasts. Trouble has been taken over the transfers, so Markevitch's admirers need not hesitate on that score.

Ormandy, Eugene

BRAHMS: *Symphony No. 4*. RACHMANINOV: *Symphony No. 2*. SIBELIUS: *Legend: Lemminkäinen's Homeward Journey, Op. 22/4*. WEBERN: *Im Sommerwind* (all with Phd. O). KABALEVSKY: *Colas Breugnon: Overture*. R. STRAUSS: *Don Juan* (both with Bavarian RSO).

(B) *** EMI (ADD) CZS5 75127-2 (2).

All these recordings, except for the brilliantly played Kabalevsky *Colas Breugnon Overture* and Strauss's *Don Juan*, are with the Philadelphia Orchestra, over whose fortunes Ormandy presided for the best part of half a century. Since theirs was one of the most prolific recording partnerships, selection must have presented a problem, although it is natural that Rachmaninov, with whom Ormandy was so closely associated, should feature. He recorded that composer's *Second Symphony* four times, and it is the fourth version, in which he opened out all the old traditional cuts, that is offered here. The 1973 performance sails forth with consistent ardour, but for all the splendour of the rich, massed Philadelphia strings, the continuous intense expressiveness, with relatively little light and shade, almost overwhelms the listener. What a pity the 1956 CBS version was not chosen, cuts and all, for that is much fresher and more spontaneous sounding.

The performance of Brahms's *Fourth Symphony*, another work that Ormandy recorded more than once, brings a similar problem. The performance has great forward thrust, and the passionate progress of the music certainly holds the listener, but at the end one is left emotionally spent, craving more subtle detail and greater dynamic contrast.

Ormandy's recordings of Shostakovich's *First* or *Fifteenth*, both peerless, his wonderful Prokofiev *Fifth* or either of his magical accounts of the *Daphnis et Chloë Suite No. 2* would have done his art greater justice.

Undoubtedly the highlight of the first disc is Webern's rarely heard early work, *Im Sommerwind*, an evocation of a summer day spent in the countryside. Its vivid impressionism obviously fired Ormandy, and he conducted its première in 1962. The recording followed a year later, and like most first recordings the performance has constant freshness and is most stimulating and enjoyable. Fortunately, the second disc closes with an excerpt from the *Lemminkäinen Legends* of Sibelius, one of Ormandy's finest late recordings for EMI, dating from 1978. Throughout these Philadelphia sessions the sheer orchestral opulence and dazzling virtuosity of the players and the control exercised by this great conductor (whose powers were so often taken for granted in his lifetime) still put one under his spell, and the sound is certainly full blooded.

For the brashly exciting Kabalevsky overture and Strauss's *Don Juan* Ormandy turned to the Bavarian Radio Symphony Orchestra, and in an exciting live recording of Strauss's tone poem they provide a balance between passion and strong characterization.

Schuricht, Carl

BEETHOVEN: *Symphony No. 1 in C* (with Paris Conservatoire O). BRUCKNER: *Symphony No. 8 in C min.* MENDELSSOHN: *Overture: The Hebrides*. MOZART: *Symphony No. 35 in D (Haffner)*. SCHUBERT: *Symphony No. 8 (Unfinished)* (all with VPO).

(B) *** EMI CZS5 75130-2 (2).

Carl Schuricht was a conductor of the old school, a wholly dedicated and thoughtful musician, unconcerned with image or publicity. Although Testament reissued his glorious Bruckner *Ninth* with the Vienna Philharmonic some years back (in a special vinyl pressing), his *Eighth* (in the Haas Edition) with the same orchestra has not been available since the 1960s. It never received its proper due at the time, but it is every bit as glorious a performance, finely proportioned and noble, and sounds pretty sumptuous in this splendidly restored 1963 recording. It can challenge many of its more celebrated rivals. Yet, starting with an account of Mendelssohn's *Hebrides Overture* that is thrusting and not at all atmospheric, there is a penny-plain element in Schuricht's approach to these masterpieces that makes one hanker after more idiosyncratic touches. In Schubert's *Unfinished Symphony*, recorded for Decca in 1956, there is none of the magic one finds, for example, in the earlier Decca mono version from Josef Krips and the Vienna Philharmonic. As in the Mendelssohn, Schuricht is strong and rugged with no attempt at charm, and it is much the same in both Mozart's *Haffner Symphony* and Beethoven's *First*; there is no lingering by the wayside. That comes closer to latterday taste than the more romantically expressive manner often favoured at the time, with the slow movement of the Beethoven crisp and clean with relatively little moulding. When Schuricht varies tempo, it tends to be towards an accelerando rather than an easing up, with the fundamental impression being one of ruggedness, with textures clarified. Except for the Beethoven, all these performances are with the Vienna Philharmonic.

Walter, Bruno

BEETHOVEN: *Symphony No. 6 in F (Pastoral).*
MAHLER: *Symphony No. 5: Adagietto.*
Kindertotenlieder: Nun vill de Sonn' so hell aufgeh'n
(with Ferrier) (all with VPO). BRAHMS: *Symphony No. 2 in D* (with New York Philh. O). HAYDN: *Symphony No. 92 in G (Oxford).* J. STRAUSS: *Die Fledermaus: Overture* (both with Paris Conservatoire O). MOZART: *Le nozze di Figaro: Overture.* WAGNER: *Die Meistersinger: Overture; Die Walküre: Act 2, Scene 5* (with Lehmann, Melchior & soloists) (both with British SO).

(B) (***) EMI mono CZS5 75133-2 (2).

The value of this Bruno Walter set lies in its pre-war rarities: his 1936 account of the Beethoven *Pastoral*, which has great freshness and warmth, and one of the Haydn symphonies he recorded in 1938 during his days with the Paris Conservatoire, a performance of great elegance, treasured by all who have them in their shellac form. The radiance of the *Adagietto* from Mahler's *Fifth Symphony* is richly caught in a reading that is by no means slow – it had to fit on two 78rpm sides! – yet because of the expansive phrasing, it still sounds relaxed, and the recording is remarkably warm and spacious.

Walter's partnership with Kathleen Ferrier was certainly worth remembering, and she is in superb voice in this finely transferred excerpt from the *Kindertotenlieder*. Walter also championed Wagner on his regular London visits, and his *Meistersinger* overture, where the sound is less flattering, comes from 1930, as does the *Figaro* overture, brilliantly done by the British Symphony Orchestra. The excerpt from *Die Walküre* with Lotte Lehmann and Lauritz Melchior among others is almost worth the price of the whole disc. The only post-war recording is a fine New York Brahms *Second* from 1946 – once again given a first-class transfer. Definitely worth having, not least for the sake of the *Pastoral*, which he never surpassed.

Other Concerts

Academy of Ancient Music, Christopher Hogwood

PACHELBEL: *Canon & Gigue.* HANDEL: *Water music: Air. Berenice: Overture; Minuet; Gigue.* VIVALDI: *Flute concerto in G min. (La notte), Op. 10/2.* BACH: *Christmas oratorio, BWV 248: Sinfonia. Quadruple harpsichord concerto in A min., BWV 1065.* CORELLI: *Concerto grosso (Christmas concerto), Op. 6/8.* A. MARCELLO: *Oboe concerto in D min.*

(M) **(*) O-L ADD/DDD 443 201-2.

It seems a curious idea to play popular baroque repertoire in a severe manner; Pachelbel's *Canon* here sounds rather abrasive and lacking in charm. But those who combine a taste for these pieces with a desire for authenticity should be satisfied. The selection for this reissue has been expanded and altered. Handel's *Queen of Sheba* no longer arrives – and she is not missed (for she was much more seductive in Beecham's hands) – and the highlight of the original, full-priced compilation (a pair of Gluck dances) is no longer present! Instead, we get several new items taken from another Academy of Ancient Music compilation of baroque music associated with Christmas, notably Corelli's splendid Op. 6/8, in which the playing has a suitably light touch, and Vivaldi's engaging *La notte Flute concerto*, while Bach's *Quadruple harpsichord concerto* substitutes for the famous Vivaldi work for four violins (Op. 3/10). On the whole an enjoyable mix. The new playing time is 67 minutes.

Academy of St Martin-in-the-Fields, Sir Neville Marriner

'*Fantasia on Greensleeves*': VAUGHAN WILLIAMS: *Fantasia on Greensleeves; The Lark ascending* (with Iona Brown); *English folksongs suite.* WARLOCK: *Serenade; Capriol suite.* GEORGE BUTTERWORTH: *A Shropshire lad; Two English idylls; The Banks of green willow.* DELIUS: *A Village Romeo and Juliet: The walk to the Paradise Garden. Hassan: Intermezzo and serenade. A song before sunrise; On hearing the first cuckoo in spring; Summer night on the river; La Calinda.* ELGAR: *Serenade for strings, Op. 20; Sospiri for strings, harp and organ; Elegy for strings, Op. 58; The Spanish Lady (suite); Introduction and allegro, Op. 47.*

(B) *** Double Decca (ADD) 452 707-2 (2).

This exceptionally generous programme, mainly of English pastoral evocations but including Iona Brown's Elysian account of *The Lark ascending* and Elgar's two string masterpieces in not wholly idiomatic but very characterful performances, is self-recommending, for the Academy are thoroughly at home here and play with consistent warmth and finesse, while the vintage Decca sound never disappoints. Marvellous value for money.

'*English Classics*': VAUGHAN WILLIAMS: *Fantasia on Greensleeves; English folk song suite* (trans. Gordon Jacob). ELGAR: *Serenade for strings, Op. 20.* BUTTERWORTH: *The Banks of Green Willow.* WARLOCK: *Capriol suite.* DELIUS: *On hearing the first cuckoo in Spring; The walk to the Paradise Garden.*

(B) *** Decca Penguin Classics (ADD) 460 637. ASMF, Marriner.

These recordings are rarely out of the catalogue, and rightly so. They are lovely performances and show the Academy on vintage form; there is much subtlety of detail here as well as striking commitment and depth of feeling, and although the recordings range from 1967-81, they are all rich and full. Reissued on the Penguin Classics label, they come with a personal appraisal by Jim Crace. However the fuller selection on the Decca Double above is an even more attractive proposition.

American masterpieces

'*American masterpieces*' (with (i) Cleveland O, Louis Lane; (ii) Phd. O, Eugene Ormandy; (iii) NYPO, André Kostelanetz): (i) BERNSTEIN: *Candide overture.* (ii) IVES: *Variations on 'America'.* (iii) William SCHUMAN: *New England triptych.* (ii) BARBER: *Adagio for strings.* GOULD: *American salute.* (iii) GRIFFES: *The pleasure dome of Kubla Khan.* (ii) MACDOWELL: *Woodland sketches: To a wild rose.* (iii) GERSHWIN: *Promenade.* (ii) GOTTSCHALK: *Cakewalk: Grand walkaround* (arr. Hershy Kay). (i) BENJAMIN: *Jamaican rumba.* RODGERS: *On Your Toes: Slaughter on 10th Avenue.* Virgil THOMSON: *Louisiana story* (film score): *Arcadian songs and dances.*

(B) **(*) Sony (ADD) SBK 63034.

Not everything here is a masterpiece, and Arthur Benjamin, who makes the wittiest contribution, was an Australian! But there are some obvious favourites included and one or two novelties, among them the attractively folksy *Arcadian songs and dances* of Virgil Thomson, affectionately directed in Cleveland by Louis Lane. He is well recorded, and so, on the whole, is

Ormandy, who presents the Ives *Variations* with charm as well as panache, while the Philadelphia strings are powerfully eloquent in Barber's *Adagio* and warmly persuasive in MacDowell's engaging *To a wild rose*. Kostelanetz conducts with plenty of personality and zest and is at his best in the Gershwin *Promenade* and the touching central movement of Schuman's *New England triptych*. But here the up-front recording of the NYPO is overlit and the climaxes of the otherwise atmospheric *Kubla Khan* sound aggressive. A stimulating programme, just the same.

André, Maurice (trumpet)

Trumpet concertos (with BPO, Karajan): HUMMEL: *Concerto in E flat.* Leopold MOZART: *Concerto in D.* TELEMANN: *Concerto in D.* VIVALDI: *Concerto in A flat* (ed. Thilde).

(M) **(*) EMI (ADD) CDM5 66909-2 [CDM 66961].

A key collection of trumpet concertos, brilliantly played by André. His security in the upper register in the work by Leopold Mozart and the fine Telemann concerto is impressive, with Karajan and the BPO wonderfully serene and gracious in the opening *Adagio* and the *Grave* slow movement of the latter. The jaunty quality of the Hummel is not missed, and the finale of this work, taken at breakneck pace, is certainly exhilarating, while the cantilena of the *Andante* is nobly contoured.

The Vivaldi work is arranged from the Sonata in F major for violin and continuo, RV 20, and makes a very effective display piece. The 1974 recording has generally been well transferred to CD. Although the trumpet timbre is very bright and the violins are not absolutely clean in focus, there is plenty of ambience. However, this reissue has a playing time of only 47 minutes and hardly seems an apt choice for EMI's 'Great Recordings of the Century' series.

'Trumpet concertos' (with ASMF, Marriner): STOLZEL: *Concerto in D.* TELEMANN: *Concerto in C min; Concerto in D for trumpet, 2 oboes and strings* (with Nicklin and Miller). VIVALDI: *Double trumpet concerto in C, RV 537* (with Soustrot); *Double concerto in B flat for trumpet and violin, RV 548* (with I. Brown).

(B) *** EMI Red Line (ADD) CDR 569874.

Maurice André is peerless in this kind of repertoire and the accompaniments under Marriner are attractively alert and stylish. The Academy provides expert soloists to match André on the concertante works by Telemann (in D) and Vivaldi (RV 548) which come together towards the end and offer much the most interesting invention. The concerto by Stölzel is conventional, but has a fine slow movement. Throughout, André's smooth, rich timbre and highly musical phrasing give pleasure. The recording is first class, with the CD adding extra definition and presence.

Music for trumpet and organ (with Jane Parker-Smith or Alfred Mitterhofer): CHARPENTIER: *Te Deum: Fanfare.* ALBINONI: *Adagio* (arr. Giazotto). BACH: *Violin Partita in E: Gavotte & Rondeau. Orchestral suite No. 3: Air. Cello suite No. 4: Bourrée. Cantata No. 147: Chorale: Jesu joy of man's desiring.* CLARKE: *Trumpet voluntary.* SENAILLE: *Allegro spiritoso.* STANLEY: *Trumpet tune.* BACH/GOUNOD: *Ave Maria.* MOZART: *Exsultate jubilate: Alleluja.* PURCELL: *The Queen's dolour* (aria). Music for trumpet and orchestra: HANDEL: *Concerto in D min.* (arr. Thilde from *Flute sonata in B min.*). ALBINONI: *Concertos: in B flat and D, Op. 7/3 & 6* (arr. of Oboe concertos). TELEMANN: *Concerto in D for trumpet and oboe* (all with ECO, Mackerras). HERTEL: *Concerto in E flat.* HAYDN: *Concerto in E flat.* TELEMANN: *Concerto in F min.* (arr. of Oboe concerto). ALBINONI: *Concerto in D min.* (arr. of *Chamber sonata for violin and continuo, Op. 6/4*). ALESSANDRO MARCELLO: *Concerto in C* (originally for oboe) (all with LPO, Jesús López-Cobos).

(B) *** EMI Double fforte (ADD) CZS5 73374-2 (2).

Both these discs open with a series of famous tunes arranged for trumpet and organ, which for baroque repertoire works well enough. Played with rich tone, cultured phrasing, and when needed, dazzling bravura, they are sumptuously presented, if you don't mind an excess of resonance. The programme begins with a larger-than-life account of the famous Charpentier *Te Deum*, and includes Clarke's famous *Voluntary* and the comparable trumpet piece by Stanley.

But otherwise the repertoire ranges wide, encompassing music originally written for other, very different instruments. These include pieces by Bach for solo violin and cello, by Albinoni and others for oboe, a famous bassoon encore by Senaillé and even (in the case of Mozart) a display-piece for the soprano voice. But André's presentation is so assured that one could be forgiven at times for thinking that they were actually conceived for the trumpet. Indeed the Bach *Gavotte* and *Rondeau* are most attractive on the trumpet.

Much the same applies to the concertos. The first group, vivaciously conducted by Mackerras, includes an ingenious Handel concoction, which even brings a brief reminder of the *Water music*, and the Telemann multiple concerto is also very diverting. Then André negotiates the Hertel concerto, with its high tessitura, with breathtaking ease.

The second group, also given lively accompaniments, by the LPO under López-Cobos, are particularly successful, with the famous Haydn concerto most elegantly played, and in the transcriptions of works by Albinoni and Marcello slow movements are warmly phrased and André's stylishness and easy execution ensure the listener's enjoyment. Throughout, the analogue recording from the mid to late 1970s is of high quality and very well transferred to CD. It is a pity that room was not found for the Hummel concerto, but this is undoubtedly excellent value.

Argerich, Martha (piano), with other artists

Martha Argerich Collection.

(M) **(*) DG ADD/DDD 453 566-2 (11).

Volume I: Concertos: BEETHOVEN: *Piano concertos Nos. 1 in C, Op. 15; 2 in B flat, Op. 19* (with Philh. O, Sinopoli). CHOPIN: *Piano concertos Nos. 1 in E min., Op. 11* (with LSO, Abbado); *2 in F min., Op. 21.* SCHUMANN: *Piano concerto in A min., Op. 54* (both with Nat. SO, Rostropovich). TCHAIKOVSKY: *Piano concerto No. 1 in B flat min., Op. 23* (with RPO, Dutoit). LISZT: *Piano concerto No. 1 in E flat* (with LSO). PROKOFIEV: *Piano concerto No. 3 in C, Op. 26.* RAVEL: *Piano concerto in G* (with BPO) (both cond. Abbado).

(M) **(*) DG ADD/DDD 453 567-2 (4).

The chimerical volatility of Martha Argerich's musical personality comes out again and again in this impressive survey of her recorded repertory. Her ability in concertos to strike sparks in a musical partnership with the right conductor (Giuseppe Sinopoli in Beethoven and Abbado in Chopin's *First Concerto*) brings characteristically spontaneous music-making, bursting with inner life.

If Chopin's *F minor Concerto*, recorded ten years later in 1978, is rather less successful, she is back on form again in Tchaikovsky (with Dutoit), to produce a performance which has a genuine sense of scale and which balances poetry with excitement. Her temperament takes less readily to the Schumann *Concerto* (here with Rostropovich), a performance which has dynamism, vigour and colour, and delicacy in the slow movement, but which does not quite capture the work's more refined romantic feeling in the outer movements.

Yet her Liszt *E flat Concerto* is surprisingly restrained, gripping without any barnstorming. She is perhaps at her very finest in Prokofiev's *Third Concerto* and hardly less impressive in the Ravel *G major*, a performance full of subtlety, but vigorous and outgoing too. Abbado was again her partner in the three last-mentioned works and together they found a rare musical symbiosis. DG have generally given Argerich's concertos excellent recording, and there is nothing here which will not provide stimulating repeated listening. All these performances (except the Chopin *Second Concerto*) are discussed in greater depth under their composer entries in our main Volume.

Volume II: Chopin and Bach: CHOPIN: *Piano sonatas Nos. 2 in B flat min., Op. 35; 3 in B min., Op. 58; Barcarolle in F sharp, Op. 60; Scherzos Nos. 2 in B flat min., Op. 31; 3 in C sharp min., Op. 39; 24 Preludes, Op. 28; Preludes in C sharp min., Op. 45; in A flat, Op. posth.; Andante spianato & Grande polonaise brillante, Op. 22; Polonaise No. 6 in A flat, Op. 53; Polonaise-Fantaisie in A flat, Op. 61; 3 Mazurkas, Op. 59.* BACH: *Toccata in C min., BWV 911; Partita No. 2 in C min., BWV 826; English suite No. 2 in A min., BWV 807.*

(M) **(*) DG (ADD) 453 572-2 (3).

Argerich's accounts of the two Chopin Sonatas are fiery, impetuous and brilliant, with no want of poetic vision to discommend them. Both, however, have a highly strung quality that will not be to all tastes. The *Preludes* show Argerich at her finest, full of individual insights. The *Scherzo No. 3* and *Barcarolle* are taken from her remarkable début LP recital of 1961 and are very impetuous indeed, and are also less easy to live with. She seems not to want to provide a firm musical control, but is carried away on a breath of wind. Many of the other pieces are played splendidly, with the *Scherzo No. 2* impressively demonstrating her technical command. Her Bach, too, is lively but well conceived. The digital remastering gives the piano-image striking presence, and the recording is resonant and full in timbre, although at fortissimo levels the timbre becomes hard.

Volume III: Music for piano solo and duo: SCHUMANN: *Kinderszenen, Op. 15; Kreisleriana, Op. 16; Piano sonata No. 2 in G min., Op. 22.* LISZT: *Piano sonata in B min.; Hungarian rhapsody No. 6.* BRAHMS: *Rhapsodies, Op. 79/1-2.* PROKOFIEV: *Toccata, Op. 11.* RAVEL: *Gaspard de la nuit; Jeux d'eau; Sonatine; Valses nobles et sentimentales. Ma Mère l'Oye; Rapsodie espagnole* (arr. 2 pianos & percussion). BARTOK: *Sonata for 2 pianos & percussion* (with Freire, Sadlo, Guggeis). TCHAIKOVSKY: *Nutcracker suite, Op. 71a* (arr. 2 pianos). RACHMANINOV: *Symphonic dances for 2 pianos, Op. 45* (with Economou).

(M) **(*) DG ADD/DDD 453 576-2 (4)

The third box contains much of interest. There is no doubting the instinctive flair or her intuitive feeling for Schumann. However, she is let down by an unpleasingly close recording of *Kinderszenen* and *Kreisleriana*. Her Ravel again shows her playing at its most subtle and perceptive, yet with a vivid palette, even if at times a little more poise would be welcome. Taken from her début recital of 1961, the Brahms *First Rhapsody* is explosively fast; then suddenly she puts the brakes on and provides most poetic playing in the central section. Such a barnstorming approach is more readily at home in the Prokofiev *Toccata*, and she goes over the top in the Liszt *Hungarian rhapsody* with a certain panache.

In the Liszt *Sonata*, although the playing demonstrates an impressively responsive temperament, the work's lyrical feeling is all but submerged by the brilliantly impulsive virtuosity. The Ravel arrangements (with percussion!) are done with eminently good taste, restraint and musical imagination but, all the same, is there a need for them at all? They are more interesting to hear once or twice than to repeat.

The Bartók, though, has tremendous fire and intensity. The aural image is very good and discreetly balanced. The Tchaikovsky *Nutcracker* arrangement of Nicolas Economou works well. The playing is of a very high order. The Rachmaninov *Dances* are played with great temperament, and everything is marvellously alive and well thought out. There is much sensitivity and a lively sense of enjoyment in evidence, as well as great virtuosity. The recording is good.

Ashton, Graham (trumpet)

CD I: (with Irish Chamber Orchestra) PURCELL: *Trumpet Sonata in D*. CORELLI: *Trumpet Sonata in D*. VIVALDI: *Double Trumpet Concerto* (with Ruddock). TELEMANN: *Trumpet Concerto in D*. ALBINONI: *Trumpet Sonatas Nos. 1 in C; 2 in D*. STRADELLA: *Sinfonia 'Il Barcheggio' in D*. TORELLI: *Sonata No. 5 for Trumpet and Strings in D*. HANDEL: *Suite for Trumpet and Strings in D*. **CD 2: (with John Lenehan (piano)** MAXWELL DAVIES: *Trumpet Sonata*. JOLIVET: *Heptade for Piano and Percussion* (with Gregory Knowles, percussion). NYMAN: *Flugal Horn & Piano Sonata*. HENZE: *Sonatina for Solo Trumpet*. BERIO: *Sequenza X for Solo Trumpet*. FENTON: *Five Parts of the Dance*.

(BB) ** Virgin VBD5 62031-2 (2).

This inexpensive set combines two recital CDs, one devoted to baroque trumpet repertoire, the other to more contemporary works. The baroque items are well enough played by the soloist but his orchestral support is indifferent, and the reverberant recording is poorly detailed. The avant garde works on the second CD are altogether more sharply performed and are given better sound. Maxwell Davies's *Trumpet Sonata* echoes the layout of the baroque concertos, though the harmonic language is of an entirely different world. Jolivet's *Heptade* has a battery of percussion instruments to support the myriad effects the soloist achieves on his instrument, and after this generally spiky work, Michael Nyman's lyrical writing is welcome. The longest piece here is Berio's *Sequenza*. It is everything one expects of this composer, and if there is no melody to speak of, the effects are aurally fascinating, even if some may feel that twenty minutes of them is too much of a good thing. Fenton's *Five Parts of the Dance* begins rather hauntingly, with the trumpet placed in the distance, and the ensuing movements, with piano and percussion are quite imaginative. This set will be of greatest appeal to those interested in the contemporary items (which would be better off on a separate issue and with more helpful documentation).

Ballet Music

'Ballet gala' (with (i) ROHCG O; (ii) BPO; (iii) L. Symphony Ch., LSO; (iv) Israel PO, cond. Sir Georg Solti): (i) PONCHIELLI: *La Gioconda: Dance of the hours*. GOUNOD: *Faust: ballet music*. OFFENBACH (arr. Rosenthal): *Gaîté parisienne ballet music*. GLUCK: *Orfeo ed Euridice: Dance of the Furies; Dance of the Blessed Spirits*. (ii) MUSSORGSKY: *Khovanshchina: Dance of the Persian slaves*. (iii) BORODIN: *Prince Igor: Polovtsian dances* (both ed.

Rimsky-Korsakov). (iv) ROSSINI-RESPIGHI: *La Boutique fantasque* (complete ballet).

(B) **(*) Double Decca (ADD) 448 942-2 (2).

Scintillating performances of high polish and prodigious vitality, recorded with great brilliance, mostly in the late 1950s. At times one might feel that the strings are overlit, although there is glowing woodwind colour and plenty of ambience, even if the Israel recording of *La Boutique fantasque* is drier than the rest. Yet they play very well, the strings are on very good form indeed, there are moments of affectionate charm, and this is easy to enjoy.

The bright, intense Solti style suits the *Faust ballet music* less well (compared, say, with Beecham's affectionate coaxing) but the sparkle is in no doubt. Solti drives Offenbach's *Gaîté parisienne ballet music* hard, with strongly accented rhythms. But the Covent Garden Orchestra respond vivaciously (as they do in Ponchielli's *Dance of the hours*) and give a virtuoso performance: their bravura is certainly infectious, if sometimes a little breathless.

Solti seldom recorded with the Berlin Philharmonic, and this great orchestra seems to have had a slight softening effect on his vibrant musical nature: the sensuously sinuous playing in the Mussorgsky/Rimsky-Korsakov *Dance of the Persian slaves* is certainly seductive. This derives from a 1959 concert called 'Romantic Russia' which is now reissued in Decca's Legend series. The characterful Gluck dances come from the complete set of a decade later. Overall this programme is highly stimulating – Solti couldn't be dull even if he tried.

'Fête du Ballet' (played by the ECO, LSO, New Philh. O, ROHCG O, Bonynge): ROSSINI: *Matinées musicales; Soirées musicales; William Tell: ballet music*. CHOPIN: *Les Sylphides*. STRAUSS (arr. Desormière): *Le Beau Danube*. SAINT-SAENS: *The Swan*. TCHAIKOVSKY: *Pas de deux* from *The Black Swan, Sleeping Beauty* and *Swan Lake; Melody; December*. RUBINSTEIN: *Danses des fiancées de Cachemir*. CZIBULKA: *Love's Dream after the Ball*. KREISLER: *The Dragonfly*. ASAFYEV: *Papillon*. LINCKE: *Gavotte Pavlova*. DELIBES: *Naïla: Intermezzo*. CATALANI: *Loreley: Danza delle ondine*. KUPRINSKI: *Polish Wedding*. TRAD: *Bolero, 1830; Mazurka*. DRIGO: *Le Flûte magique: Pas de trois; Le Réveil de Flore; Pas de deux* from *Le Corsaire, Diane et Actéon* and *La Esmeralda*. MINKUS: *Pas de deux* from *La Bayadère, Paquita* (including *Grand pas*) and *Don Quixote*. ADAM: *Giselle* (excerpts). LOVENSKJOLD: *La Sylphide: Pas de deux*. PUGNI: *Pas de quatre*. HALSTED: *Flower Festival at Genzano: Pas de deux*. MASSENET: *Le Cid: ballet music; La Cigale: Valse très lente; Le Roi de Lahore: Entr'acte (Act V)* and *Waltz (Act III); Meditation de Thaïs; Cendrillon; Scènes alsaciennes; Scènes dramatiques*. MEYERBEER: *Les Patineurs*. LUIGINI: *Ballet égyptien*. AUBER: *Pas classique; Marco Spada; Les Rendez-vous*. THOMAS: *Françoise de Rimini*. SCARLATTI: *The Good-humoured Ladies*.

DONIZETTI: *La Favorite: ballet music.* BERLIOZ: *Les Troyens: ballet music.* LECOCQ (arr. Jacob): *Mam'zelle Angot.* OFFENBACH: *La Papillon: Suite.* BURGMÜLLER: *La Péri.*

✿ (BB) *** Decca (ADD/DDD) 468 578-2 (10).

This set is a perfect and well-conceived tribute to Richard Bonynge's indefatigable quest to resurrect forgotten treasures: it's a feast of some of the most delightful and piquant ballet music of the (mainly) nineteenth century. It includes two major ballets not released on CD before: Auber's *Marco Spada*, which is full of the catchy tunes we know from his overtures, and Burgmüller's *La Péri*, a work seeped in the romantic ballet tradition. Other highlights include Lecocq's deliciously witty *Mam'zelle Angot*; the rarely heard and effervescent *Le Beau Danube*; Luigini's *Ballet égyptien* (still the only available recording of the complete work and originally part of a two LP set 'Homage to Pavlova', of which all the charming vignettes are included here); the only recordings of Auber's *Pas classique* and *Les Rendez-vous*; plus a string of vivacious and colourful *pas de deux*. Other unexpected delights are the perky *Bolero, 1830*; the once-popular coupling of *Le Cid* and *Les Patineurs* ballet music (here in exceptionally vivid sound); the luscious *Waltz* from Massenet's *Le Roi de Lahore*; the same composer's *Scènes dramatiques* (first time on CD) and *Scènes alsaciennes*, along with the sparkling *March of the Princes* from *Cendrillon*. Bonynge's supremacy in this repertoire is obvious: through his well-sprung rhythms and elegant pointing of the melodic line, the music glows. With excellent sleeve notes and vintage Decca sound, this set is highly recommended.

'Bonynge Ballet festival' (played by the LSO or National Philharmonic Orchestra):

Volume 1: WEBER (orch. Berlioz): *Invitation to the dance.* CHOPIN (arr. Douglas): *Les Sylphides.* J. STRAUSS JR (arr. Gamley): *Bal de Vienne.* LUIGINI: *Ballet égyptien.*

Volume 2: TRAD. (arr. O'Turner): *Bolero 1830.* PUGNI: *Pas de quatre.* MINKUS: *La Bayadère* (excerpts). DRIGO: *Pas de trois.* ADAM: *Giselle* (excerpts). LOVENSKJOLD: *La Sylphide* (excerpts).

Volume 3: 'Homage to Pavlova': SAINT-SAENS: *The Swan.* TCHAIKOVSKY: *Melody; Noël.* RUBINSTEIN: *Danses des fiancées de Cachemir.* CZIBULKA: *Love's dream after the ball.* KREISLER: *The Dragonfly* (Schön Rosmarin). ASSAFIEFF: *Papillons.* LINCKE: *Gavotte Pavlova* (Glow worm idyll). DELIBES: *Naïla: Intermezzo.* CATALANI: *Danza delle Ondine.* KRUPINSKI: *Mazurka* (Polish Wedding).

Volume 4: 'Pas de deux': AUBER: *Pas classique.* MINKUS: *Don Quixote: Pas de deux; Paquita: Pas de deux.* TCHAIKOVSKY: *The Nutcracker: Pas de deux. Sleeping beauty: Pas de deux.* DRIGO: *Le Corsaire: Pas de deux ; La Esmeralda; Pas de deux.* HELSTED: *Flower festival at Genzano.*

Volume 5: 'Ballet music from opera': ROSSINI: *William Tell.* DONIZETTI: *La Favorita.* GOUNOD: *Faust; La Reine de Saba (waltz).* MASSENET: *Ariane; Le Roi de Lahore.* BERLIOZ: *Les Troyens.*

*** Australian Decca (ADD/DDD) 452 767-2 (5). With the NPO or LSO.

This less comprehensive set of Richard Bonynge's ballet recordings also includes much music not otherwise available. Volume 1 has two rarities: *Bal de Vienne* – a particularly felicitous arrangement of Johann Strauss's lesser-known works, with an exhilarating finale, and (surprisingly) the only complete recordings of Luigini's delightful *Ballet Egyptien* (Fistoulari only recorded the four-movement suite).

Volume 2 draws from Bonynge's 'The art of the Prima Ballerina' set: each of the rarities by Minkus, Drigo and Pugni has at least one striking melody, and all are vivacious and colourfully orchestrated; the *Bolero 1830* is short but piquant.

Volume 3, 'Homage to Pavlova' is more reflectively nostalgic and has delightful rarities: many are just salon pieces, but show their worth when played so beautifully on a full orchestra.

Volume 4's collection of *Pas de deux* is both elegantly and robustly enjoyable, with the Auber, Minkus and Drigo numbers especially lively and memorable.

Volume 5 comprises generally better known ballet music from operas. It includes the lovely Massenet ballet music from *Le Roi de Lahore*, which starts off ominously in a minor key, before a theme, magically introduced on the saxophone, builds up into a magnificent full orchestral waltz swirling around the whole orchestra. *The Dance of the Gypsy* from Saint-Saëns's *Henry VIII* is another gem: it begins sinuously, but ends in a jolly *valse macabre*.

This is music in which Bonynge excels: he has exactly the right feel for it and produces an infectious lift throughout. The recordings are in Decca's best analogue tradition – vivid, warm and full (though a few are from equally fine digital sources), and all sound pristinely fresh in these transfers. With full sleeve-notes included, this is a splendid bargain collection of highly entertaining music well worth seeking out.

Baltimore Symphony Orchestra, David Zinman

'Russian sketches': GLINKA: *Overture: Ruslan and Ludmilla.* IPPOLITOV-IVANOV: *Caucasian sketches.* RIMSKY-KORSAKOV: *Russian Easter Festival overture.* TCHAIKOVSKY: *Francesca da Rimini, Op. 32. Eugene Onegin: Polonaise.*

**(*) Telarc CD 80378.

Opening with a fizzingly zestful performance of Glinka's *Ruslan and Ludmilla overture*, with impressively clean articulation from the violins, this remarkably well-recorded concert of Russian music readily demonstrates the excellence of the Baltimore Symphony in every department.

The *Caucasian sketches* are a disappointment, but only because Zinman's conception of the evocative first three movements (*In the Mountain Pass, In the Village* and *In the Mosque*) is too refined, not Russian enough in feeling; but the famous *Procession of the Sardar* has plenty of piquant colour and impetus. *Francesca da Rimini* brings the most brilliant playing and the middle section, with its rich, Tchaikovskian woodwind palette, is glowingly beautiful.

However, the impact of the closing pages here depends more on the spectacular Telarc engineering than on the conductor, who does not generate the necessary degree of passionate despair in the work's great climax. Rimsky-Korsakov's *Russian Easter Festival overture* is a different matter, generating considerable excitement. It is superbly done, with lustrous colours from every section of the orchestra and a memorable solo contribution from the trombones (who are also very impressive in *Francesca*). The recording here is very much in the demonstration bracket and shows Telarc engineering at its most realistic, thrilling in its breadth and body of orchestral tone, with excellent detail and a convincing presence in a natural concert-hall acoustic.

Barbirolli, Sir John (cello), and conducting various orchestras

'*Glorious John*': Barbirolli centenary collection (1911-69): Disc 1: (1911-47): VAN BIENE: *The broken melody* (Barbirolli, cello). MOZART: *String quartet in E flat, K.428: Minuet* (with Kutcher Qt). MASCAGNI: *Cavalleria rusticana: Santuzza's aria* (with Lilian Stiles-Allen). VERDI: *Otello: Niun me tema* (with Renato Zanelli). PUCCINI: *Tosca: Tre sbirri, una carozza* (with Giovanni Inghilleri). JOHANN STRAUSS JR: *Die Fledermaus: Brother dear and sister dear.* SAINT-SAENS: *Valse-caprice, Op. 76* (with Yvonne Arnaud, piano). BALFE: *The Bohemian girl overture* (with Symphony Orchestra). COLLINS: *Overture.* WEINBERGER: *Christmas* (with New York Philharmonic Orchestra). WEBER: *Euryanthe overture.* DELIUS: *Walk to the Paradise Garden* (with Vienna Philharmonic Orchestra).

Disc 2: (1948-64) (all with Hallé Orchestra): STRAVINSKY: *Concerto in D.* MOZART: *Cassation in G, K.63: Andante; Divertimento No. 11 in D, K.251: Minuet.* GRIEG, arr. Barbirolli: *Secret.* VILLA-LOBOS: *Bachianas brasileiras No. 4.* FALLA: *Seguidilla murciana* (with Marina de Gabarain). LEHAR: *Gold and silver waltz.* BACH, arr. Barbirolli: *Sheep may safely graze.* BERLIOZ: *Damnation of Faust: rehearsal sequence.* Interview: Barbirolli and R. Kinloch Anderson.

(B) (***) Dutton mono/stereo CDSJB 1999 (2).

It was Vaughan Williams who referred to Barbirolli as 'Glorious John', hence the title of this budget-priced compilation to celebrate the great conductor's centenary: twenty historic items, five of them previously unpublished, plus a rehearsal sequence and an interview full of reminiscences. From 1911 you have the eleven-year-old Giovanni Barbirolli playing the cello, swoopy but perfect in intonation.

As a budding conductor he accompanies star soloists, including Yvonne Arnaud in Saint-Saëns's charming *Valse-caprice*, while items from his underprized New York period include a delightful Weinberger piece, otherwise unavailable, *Christmas*. Also unexpected is Barbirolli's pioneering account with the Hallé of Stravinsky's *Concerto in D*, recorded in 1948, two years after the work first appeared. And how revealing to have the Vienna Philharmonic heartfelt in Delius's *Walk to the Paradise Garden*!

The rehearsal of the *Dance of the Sylphs* dates from 1957, and in many ways most endearing of all is the 1964 conversation between the gravel-voiced Barbirolli and his recording producer Roland Kinloch Anderson, covering such subjects as Mahler, the Berlin Philharmonic and Elgar – a splendid portrait.

Baroque music

'*Music of the Baroque*' (played by: (i) Orpheus CO; (ii) Simon Standage; (iii) David Reichenberg; (iv) Trevor Pinnock (harpsichord); (v) English Concert Ch.; (vi) English Concert, Trevor Pinnock; (vii) Söllscher (guitar), Camerata Bern, Füri; (viii) Hannes, Wolfgang & Bernhard Läubin, Simon Preston, Norbert Schmitt): (i) HANDEL: *Solomon: Arrival of the Queen of Sheba.* (vi) *Water music: Allegro – Andante; Air; Bourrée; Hornpipe.* (i) *Xerxes: Largo.* (v, vi) *Messiah: Hallelujah chorus.* (vi) *Music for the royal fireworks: La Réjouissance.* (iii; iv; vi) *Oboe concerto No. 1 (Adagio; Allegro).* (vi) *Concerto grosso, Op. 6/12 in B min. (Aria; Larghetto e piano).* (i) PACHELBEL: *Canon in D.* (viii) MOURET: *Rondeau.* J. S. BACH: (i) *Jesu, joy of man's desiring.* (vi) *Brandenburg concerto No. 3 in G (Allegro).* PURCELL: *Sound the trumpet, sound.* (ii; vi) VIVALDI: *The Four seasons: Winter (Largo).* (vii) *Lute concerto in D (Largo).* (i) ALBINONI (arr. GIAZOTTO): *Adagio in G min.* CORELLI: *Christmas concerto, Op. 6/8 (Allegro; Pastorale; Largo).* (iv) DAQUIN: *Le Coucou.*

(B) *** DG 449 842-2.

This 75-minute concert draws on various digital recordings made during the 1980s to make a most agreeable entertainment. The various items have all been issued previously, and their performance pedigrees, on either modern or original instruments, cannot be gainsaid. The opening *Arrival of the Queen of Sheba* and the elegantly played Pachelbel *Canon* feature the Orpheus Chamber Orchestra, but Pinnock's suite from the Handel *Water music* is equally persuasive in demonstrating the advantages of period instruments in baroque repertoire. Such contrasts are aurally stimulating and, with plenty of favourite items included, this makes a very successful bargain sampler, when all the music is consistently well played and recorded. However, the lack of proper documentation is a drawback: the two excellent vocal soloists in Purcell's *Sound the trumpet* are unnamed.

BBC Philharmonic Orchestra, Matthias Bamert

'*Stokowski encores*': HANDEL: *Overture in D min.* GABRIELI: *Sonata piano e forte.* CLARKE: *Trumpet Prelude.* MATTHESON: *Air.* MOZART: *Rondo alla turca.* BEETHOVEN: *Adagio from Moonlight sonata.* SCHUBERT: *Serenade.* FRANCK: *Panis Angelicus.* CHOPIN: *Funeral march.* DEBUSSY: *The Girl with the flaxen hair.* IPPOLITOV-IVANOV: *In the manger.* SHOSTAKOVICH: *United Nations march.* TCHAIKOVSKY: *Andante cantabile.* ALBENIZ: *Festival in Seville.* SOUSA: *The Stars and Stripes forever.* (all arr. Leopold Stokowski).

*** Chan. 9349.

However outrageous it may seem to take a tiny harpsichord piece by a contemporary of Bach and Handel, Johann Mattheson, and inflate it on full strings, the result caresses the ear, and the Chandos engineers come up with recording to match. Amazingly, Mozart's *Rondo alla turca* becomes a sparkling moto perpetuo, Paganini-like, with Stokowski following Mozart himself in using 'Turkish' percussion, *Entführung*-style.

The opening *Adagio* of Beethoven's *Moonlight sonata* with lush orchestration then echoes Rachmaninov's *Isle of the Dead*, with menace in the music. Stokowski's arrangement of the Handel *Overture in D minor* (taken from the *Chandos anthem No. 2*) is quite different from Elgar's transcription of the same piece, opulent in a different way, with timbres antiphonally contrasted.

If Bamert cannot match the panache of Stokowski in the final Sousa march, *The Stars and Stripes forever*, that is in part due to the recording balance, which fails to bring out the percussion, including xylophone. The least attractive item is Schubert's *Serenade*, given full Hollywood treatment not just with soupy strings but with quadruple woodwind trilling above. Hollywood treatment of a different kind comes in the *United Nations march* of Shostakovich, in 1942 used as the victory finale of an MGM wartime musical, *Thousands Cheer*. Stokowski promptly cashed in with his own, non-vocal arrangement. A disc for anyone who likes to wallow in opulent sound.

BBC Philharmonic Orchestra, Yan Pascal Tortelier

'*French bonbons*': Overtures: ADAM: *Si j'étais roi.* AUBER: *Le cheval de bronze (The bronze horse).* HEROLD: *Zampa.* MAILLART: *Les dragons de Villars.* THOMAS: *Mignon: Gavotte.* OFFENBACH: *La Belle*

Hélène (arr. Haensch); *Contes d'Hoffmann: Entr'acte & Barcarolle.* CHABRIER: *Habanera; Joyeuse marche.* GOUNOD: *Marche funèbre d'une marionette.* MASSENET: *Thaïs: Méditation* (with Yuri Torchinsky, violin; both with Royal Liverpool PO Choir). *Mélodie: Elégie* (with Peter Dixon, cello); *Les erinnes: Tristesse du soir. La Vierge: Le dernier sommeil de la Vierge.*

*** Chan. 9765.

As Sir Thomas Beecham well knew there is something special about French orchestral lollipops and this is a superb collection, beautifully played and given demonstration standard recording – just sample the brass evocation of Maillart's Dragoons, and in *La Belle Hélène*, which is played with much warmth and style. Gounod's whimsical *Funeral march of a marionette*, which Hitchcock has made famous, is delightfully done, and the other bandstand overtures have plenty of sparkle and zest, yet are not driven too hard – the galop which climaxes *The Bronze Horse* is exhilaratingly jaunty. Highly recommended.

BBC Symphony Orchestra, Sir Adrian Boult

'*Boult's BBC years*': BEETHOVEN: *Symphony No. 8 in F, Op. 93.* HUMPERDINCK: *Overture Hansel and Gretel.* TCHAIKOVSKY: *Capriccio italien, Op. 45; Serenade for strings, Op. 48.*

(***) Beulah mono 1PD12.

These recordings return to the catalogue for the first time since the days of shellac and will almost certainly be new to the majority of younger collectors. The Beethoven is a strong, sturdy performance which gives a good idea of the excellence of the BBC Symphony Orchestra in the early days of its existence. It comes from 1932 and the strings produce an opulent, weighty sound without having the opaque quality they developed in the post-war years. The recording is not at all bad for the period, and the transfer does it justice. The Tchaikovsky *Serenade* was recorded five years later in the same Abbey Road studio but with the acoustic sounding much drier. A patrician account with no nonsense about it that may since have been surpassed by many other great partnerships but which will give pleasure to those old enough to remember Sir Adrian's pre-war and wartime broadcasts. The Colston Hall, Bristol, in which the orchestra recorded the *Capriccio italien* in 1940, has the richer acoustic, and the performance combines dignity and freshness.

BBC Symphony Orchestra & Chorus, Sir Andrew Davis

'*Last Night of the Proms 2000*'

BACH: *Fantasia and Fugue in C min., BWV 537.* MOZART: *Violin Concerto No. 4 in D, K.218* (with

Hahn, violin). RICHARD STRAUSS: *Salome: Dance of the Seven Veils Final Scene* (with Eaglen, soprano). SHOSTAKOVICH: (orch. McBurney) *Jazz Suite No. 2.* GRAINGER: *Tribute to Foster* (with Watson, Murray, Spence, Tear, Davies). DELIUS: *A Village Romeo and Juliet: Walk to the Paradise Garden.* ELGAR: *Pomp & Circumstance March No. 1.* WOOD: *Fantasia on British Sea Songs.* ARNE: *Rule Britannia!* (with Eaglen). PARRY orch. (Elgar:) *Jerusalem. National Anthem* (with Introductions, Interviews with Soloists, Laying of the Wreath; Speech by Sir Andrew Davis and presentation by Nicholas Kenyon. Producer: Peter Maniura).

*** BBC **DVD** WMDVD 8001-9.

Watching an old Last Night of the Proms programme on DVD might seem like eating half-warmed-up soup, but the year 2000 had some special claims – not just marking the Millennium but also in celebrating Sir Andrew Davis. He said goodbye after eleven consecutive Last Nights, as well as giving his final concert as Chief Conductor of the BBC Symphony Orchestra. The programme itself reflects Davis's own preferences, when, as he explains in an interview, three of his favourite composers are represented: Elgar, with his sumptuous arrangement of Bach organ music, the *Fantasia and Fugue in C minor*; Mozart, with the *Violin Concerto No. 4 in D* featuring the brilliant young American, Hilary Hahn, as soloist; and Richard Strauss, with the *Dance of the Seven Veils* and the final scene from *Salome*, in which Jane Eaglen is the soprano, producing the most opulent tone, a commanding figure in every way.

Special facilities on the DVD consist of options on subtitles and an ability to limit the playing to music only, without introductions. What is infuriating and pure sloppiness over the transfer, however, is that tracking is so limited, so that the Mozart violin concerto, 25 minutes long, is on a single track, with no separation of movements.

BBC Symphony Orchestra & Chorus, Sir Andrew Davis
(with other artists)

'Prom at the Palace': The Queen's Golden Jubilee Concert: WALTON: *Anniversary Fanfare.* HANDEL: *Music for the Royal Fireworks*: Excerpts (both with Band of Royal Marines, Col. Richard Waterer). *Coronation Anthem: Zadok the Priest.* BIZET: *Carmen: Micaëla's Aria.* GERSHWIN: *Porgy and Bess: Summertime* (Dame Kiri Te Kanawa). TRAD. Arr. BURTON: *2 Spirituals* (London Advent Chorale, Ken Burton). MESSAGER: *Solo de Concours for clarinet and piano* (Julian Bliss, Ashley Wass). HOLST: *The Planets: Jupiter.* TCHAIKOVSKY: *Swan Lake; Black Swan pas de deux* (Danced by Roberto Bolle & Zenaida Yanowsky). ROSSINI: *Il Barbiere di Siviglia: Largo al factotum.* GERMAN: *Merrie England: The Yeomen of England* (Sir Thomas Allen). ARNOLD: *Irish Dance; 2 Scottish Dances; Welsh Dance.* VILLA-LOBOS: *Bachianas Brasileiras No. 1* (Rostropovich & Cellos of LSO). PUCCINI: *Tosca: Vissi d'arte; 'E lucevan le stelle.* VERDI: *La Traviata: Brindisi* (Angela Gheorghiu & Roberto Alagna). ELGAR: *Pomp and Circumstance March No. 1.* ARNE: *God Save the Queen.* (DVD introduced by Michael Parkinson. TV Producer: Ben Weston; Director: Bob Coles. DVD Producer: James Whitbourn.)

*** BBC Opus Arte **DVD** OA 0844 D. CD: VTCDX 42.

The DVD offers a straight repeat of the BBC's television relay of the concert in the grounds of Buckingham Palace, celebrating the Queen's Golden Jubilee in June 2002. Introduced by Michael Parkinson, it offers a sequence of short items, not all of them predictable, performed by an excellent choice of artists, with none of the media-boosted, middle-of-the-road performers who in too many so-called classical events represent a degrading of standards. Gheorghiu and Alagna may have been glamorized, but in musical terms they are outstanding, and here offer arias from Puccini's *Tosca* and the *Brindisi* duet from Verdi's *La Traviata.* Sir Thomas Allen, as well as singing Figaro's aria from Rossini's *Barbiere*, gives the *Yeomen of England* from Edward German's *Merrie England*, nowadays a rarity, and as an encore to Micaëla's aria from Bizet's *Carmen* Dame Kiri Te Kanawa sings *Summertime* from Gershwin's *Porgy and Bess.* A charming interlude has the 13-year-old clarinettist Julian Bliss performing a *Solo de Concours* by Messager (an item that specially delighted the Queen) and Rostropovich with the cellos of the LSO plays the *Prelude* from Villa-Lobos's *Bachianas Brasileiras No. 1*, not on the outdoor stage but more intimately in the Music Room of Buckingham Palace. In the Ballroom of the Palace, the dancers Roberto Bolle and Zenaida Yanowsky perform the *Black Swan Pas de Deux* from Tchaikovsky's *Swan Lake*, and Sir Andrew Davis and the BBC Symphony Orchestra crown their many contributions with Handel's *Fireworks Music*, joined by the Royal Marines Band and prompting a cracking firework display in *La Rejouissance* just as dusk gives way to night. The concert ends in true Proms-style with *Land of Hope and Glory* and the *National Anthem.* Though the amplified sound is aggressive at times, the wonder is that it comes over so well.

The CD version simply includes most of the musical items with the Parkinson introductions omitted as well as the *Fireworks Music.*

Belgian Radio & TV Philharmonic Orchestra, Brussels, Alexander Rahbari

Romantic symphonic music from Antwerp: MORTELMANS: *Spring idyll.* ALPAERTS: *Pallieter: Wedding feast.* VAN HOOF: *1st Symphonic suite.*

BLOCKX: *Milenka: Flemish Fair.* STERNFIELD: *Song and dance at the court of Mary from Burgundy.*

(BB) ** Koch/Discover DICD 920100.

Flemish rhapsodies: BRUSSELMANS: *Flemish rhapsody.* SCHOEMAKER: *Flemish rhapsody.* DE JONG: *Flemish rhapsody.* ABSILL: *Flemish rhapsody.* ROUSSEL: *Flemish rhapsody.* DE BOECK: *Flemish rhapsody.*

(BB) **(*) Koch/Discover DICD 920101.

This is all unknown repertoire – easy-going late nineteenth- or twentieth-century music from Belgium. On the first CD, Mortelmans' *Spring idyll* is lyrically appealing but perhaps a shade extended for its thematic content, the Jef Van Hoof and Jan Blockx *suites* agreeably inventive but innocuous. By far the most attractive music comes in the suite of *Song and dance from Burgundy*, nicely scored and piquantly harmonized dances by Susato and his sixteenth-century contemporaries, somewhat comparable with Respighi's *Ancient airs and dances*.

The *Flemish rhapsodies* all use folk material very effectively, although Brusselmans employs themes of his own invention, written in folk style. All these works are colourfully orchestrated and make agreeable listening, using jolly tunes which in flavour are often like Christmas carols. By far the most striking is the work by the Frenchman Albert Roussel, which has a characteristic touch of harmonic astringency to tickle the ear. The playing of the Brussels orchestra under Rahbari is enthusiastic yet does not lack finesse, and the recording has an attractive concert-hall ambience and balance. It is not always too sharply defined in some of the more elaborately scored climaxes of the rhapsodies, but the effect is natural. The documentation is excellent.

Berlin Philharmonic Orchestra, Claudio Abbado

'New Year's Gala 1997'. BIZET: *Carmen:* excerpts (with Von Otter, Alagna, Terfel); BRAHMS: *Hungarian Dance No. 5 in G min.;* FALLA: *El amor brujo; Ritual Fire Dance;* RACHMANINOV: *Rhapsody on a Theme of Paganini* (with Pletnev); RAVEL: *Rhapsodie espagnole;* SARASATE: *Carmen Fantasy, Op. 25* (with Shaham).

*** Arthaus **DVD** 100 026.

A concert that takes Bizet's *Carmen* as a theme, or point of departure. The sound is very good indeed and naturally balanced, and the camerawork discreet and unobtrusive. The excerpts from the opera come off very well, but easily the best thing on the disc is the *Paganini Rhapsody*, played effortlessly by Mikhail Pletnev. Rachmaninov-playing does not come better than this. It is every bit as strongly characterized and brilliant in execution as his CD recording and must be numbered among the very finest on disc. The individual variations do not have access points. Gil Shaham's

performance of the Sarasate *Fantasy* is also played with virtuosity and panache. A rather strangely designed programme, but well worth having purely for the sake of Pletnev's dazzling Rachmaninov.

'New Year's Gala Concert' (with Swedish Radio Chorus): BRAHMS: *Hungarian Dances Nos. 1, 5, 7, 10, 17, 21; Gypsy Songs, Op.103; Liebesliederwalzer Nos. 1, 2, 4, 5, 6, 8, 9, 11; Es tont ein voller, Op.17.* BERLIOZ: *Hungarian March.* RAVEL: *Tzigane* (with Maxim Vengerov); *La valse.*

*** Arthaus **DVD** 100 042.

The Berlin Philharmonic in this 'New Year's Gala' puts up a direct challenge to Vienna, using Brahms pieces very much as the Vienna Philharmonic uses Johann Strauss, concentrating on the *Hungarian Dances* and the *Liebesliederwalzer*, with a delightful addition in *Es tont ein voller* for women's choir with horn and harp accompaniment, one of the four in his Opus 17. As in Vienna it makes for a fun occasion with Abbado at his most relaxed, smiling as he conducts. The theme of dances and gypsy tunes then extends to Ravel in two major items, *Tzigane* and *La valse*, while Berlioz is finally brought in with the *Hungarian March* from the *Damnation of Faust* as an obvious equivalent of Vienna's *Radetsky March*, though happily no one in the Berlin audience dares to clap to it.

One great bonus of this programme is the inclusion of Maxim Vengerov as a masterly soloist in the *Tzigane*, as well as in Brahms's *Hungarian Dance No. 7*, which comes as his encore. Just as striking is the contribution of the Swedish Radio Chorus, not just visually with the ladies sporting velvet stoles over their black dresses in brightly contrasted primary colours, but in their obvious affection for Brahms. The *Liebeslieder Waltzes* are charmingly done, as is the lovely song for women's chorus with horn and harp accompaniment, *Es tont ein voller*, though one is sorry not to have the other three songs in that Opus 17 group. The only extra item is a brief tourist sequence on Berlin and its attractions, Kunst und Genuss ('Arts and Delights').

Berlin Philharmonic Orchestra, Daniel Barenboim

'1997 European Concert at the Opéra Royal de Château de Versailles': RAVEL: *Le tombeau de Couperin.* ◉ MOZART: *Piano Concerto No. 13 in C, K. 415* (with Barenboim, piano). BEETHOVEN: *Symphony No. 3 in E flat (Eroica).*

*** TDK **DVD** DV-VERSA.

An oustanding example of the way DVD video can enhance one's enjoyment of a live concert. All the performances here are of the highest calibre, and although the cameras are at times restless, and the back-of-the-hall perspective is too distant, the close-ups of the conductor and players communicate the music visually as well as aurally, with members of the orchestra projecting as individual personalities.

Ravel's *Le tombeau* is played with engaging freshness and luminous beauty, and one identifies especially here with the principal oboe.

One turns the disc over for Barenboim's *Eroica*, which is very strong indeed, the climaxes gripping, the Funeral March powerfully moving. In the Scherzo the horns dominate visually, as they should, and the finale, with its visually fascinating variations and fugue, ends the work with an explosion of joy.

But the highlight of the concert is the captivating account of the early Mozart *Concerto*, when Barenboim, like the composer before him, directs from the keyboard. Here the empathy between soloist and players is magical and this communicates to the viewer, raptly so in the concentration of the lovely slow movement and the light-hearted finale, with its intriguing changes of tempo and mood. The recording throughout is first-class, very naturally balanced with a dramatic but not exaggerated dynamic range, and a full, clean bass response. The piano too is naturally focused. This is a DVD to return to and it is enhanced by the glorious visual backcloth of the Opéra Royal de Château de Versailles.

'1998 Concert at the Berlin State Opera, Unter den Linden': BEETHOVEN: *Symphony No. 8 in F.* SCHUMANN: *Konzertstück in F for 4 Horns & Orchestra, Op. 86* (with Dale Clevenger, Stefan Dohr, Ignacio Garcia, George Schreckenberger, horns). LISZT: *Les préludes.* WAGNER: *Die Walküre: Ride of the Valkyries.*

*(*) TDK **DVD** DV-LINDE.

After Barenboim's 1997 Berlin Philharmonic Concert at the Opéra Royal de Château de Versailles this is a great let-down. It opens with a comparatively routine account of Beethoven's *Eighth Symphony*, while Liszt's *Les préludes* is lacking in flamboyance and adrenalin, though in both the Berlin Philharmonic playing cannot be faulted for poor tone or ensemble. The great highlight of the concert is the superb performance of the Schumann *Konzertstück for Four Horns*. This work is not only technically very demanding, but lies very high in the horn register, with continually repeated passages where the soloists are taken up into the stratosphere, which is very tiring on the horn-player's lip muscles, something Schumann did not seem to understand. With fine players a studio recording is feasible as the work can be recorded in sections. But this is a live performance by a superb quartet led by Dale Clevenger, one of America's most distinguished orchestral principals, and the spirited bravura of all four players (to say nothing of their stamina) throughout the work's 21 minutes is as exhilarating as it is astonishing, while Barenboim accompanies zestfully. The horn quartet returns for the final item in the programme and lines up behind the orchestra as the extras in Wagner's *Ride of the Valkyries*. But that performance, well played as it is, only serves to emphasize the other drawback to the audio recording throughout this DVD – its very limited dynamic range. This has a damping down effect in both the Beethoven and Liszt, and when the extra brass is visibly seen to enter in Wagner's famous galloping showpiece and the music fails to increase in volume, the effect is bizarre.

Berlin Philharmonic Orchestra, Plácido Domingo

'Spanish Night': CHABRIER: *España.* LINCKE: *Berliner Luft.* LUNA: *Cancion Espanola.* SERRANO: *Romanza.* TORROBA: *La Petenara* (all with Ana Maria Martinez). MASSENET: *Thaïs: Méditation.* SARASATE: *Carmen Fantasy; Zigeunerweisen* (all with Sarah Chang). MONCAYO: *Huapango.* RIMSKY-KORSAKOV: *Capriccio espagnol.* J. STRAUSS JNR: *Spanish March.* VIVES: *Fandango.*

*** TDK Euro Arts **DVD** 10 5123 9.

The Waldbuhne (Woodland Stage) in Berlin where the open-air concert on this DVD took place in July 2001 is like a cross between the concert venue at Kenwood in north London and the Hollywood Bowl. With an audience of 22,000 this performance rounded off the orchestra's season and, following tradition, ended with Lincke's rousing Prussian song, *Berliner Luft*, with Domingo finally persuaded to sing as well as conduct, and with the audience flashing lights and waving sparklers. The focus of the whole event this time was Spanish, with Plácido Domingo as conductor putting together a delightful sequence of Spanish-inspired pieces, including three songs from his favourite genre of the distinctive Spanish form of operetta, the zarzuela, in which Martinez's warm, throaty soprano is ideal.

Sarah Chang makes just as glamorous a figure, playing with masterly point in the two Sarasate works, *Zigeunerweisen* and the *Carmen Fantasy*, as well as sweetly and tenderly in the *Méditation* from Massenet's *Thaïs*. Besides the purely Spanish items, such orchestral show-pieces as Chabrier's *España* and Rimsky-Korsakov's *Capriccio espagnol* are self-recommending, and loyally Domingo includes a colourful piece, *Huapango*, by the Mexican composer, Moncayo, well worth hearing. Of particular interest is the rarity by Johann Strauss, the *Spanish March*, with its sharply varied sections. One of the 'Special Features' of the disc is an interview session with both Chang and Domingo. Considering how dry the sound can be in the open air, the quality here is first-rate, no doubt helped by the canopy over the orchestra resembling an extended crusaders' tent.

Berlin Philharmonic Orchestra, Wilhelm Furtwängler

Wartime Concerts 1942–4

Vol 1: BEETHOVEN: *Coriolan Overture, Op. 62; Symphonies Nos. 4, 5 & 7; Violin Concerto* (with Röhn). HANDEL: *Concerto grosso in D min., Op. 6/10.* MOZART: *Symphony No. 39 in E flat, K.543.*

SCHUBERT: *Symphony No. 9 in C (Great).* WEBER: *Der Freischütz: Overture.*

(B) (***) DG mono 471 289-2 (4).

Vol 2: BRAHMS: *Piano Concerto No. 2 in B flat, Op. 83* (with Fischer). BRUCKNER: *Symphony No. 5 in B flat.* RAVEL: *Daphnis et Chloë: Suite No. 2.* SCHUMANN: *Cello Concerto in A min., Op. 129* (with de Machula); *Piano Concerto in A min., Op. 56* (with Gieseking). SIBELIUS: *En saga.* RICHARD STRAUSS: *Don Juan, Op. 20; Till eulenspiegel, Op. 28; Symphonia domestica, Op. 53.*

(B) (***) DG mono 471 294-2 (5).

Hans Werner Henze once recalled how during the war he came to associate music-making with danger, having played chamber music with some Jewish friends who were in continual fear of discovery and arrest. And there is certainly a heightened intensity and an urgent, emotional charge about performances given in wartime conditions, as we can hear in the astonishing recordings Furtwängler made with the Berlin Philharmonic 1942–4, which DG have just repackaged. British Intelligence was puzzled by the sheer quality of wartime German broadcast concerts, which were technically far ahead of their time, thanks to the excellence of the recordings, which were made on 14-inch reels of iron-oxide tape running at 30 inches per second. There are performances of great stature in these inexpensive boxes, including a Brahms *Second Piano Concerto* with Edwin Fischer, and an imposing Mozart *Symphony No. 39 in E flat*, as well as repertoire that one does not associate with Furtwängler: Sibelius's *En saga*, full of atmosphere and mystery, and a magical account of the Second Suite from Ravel's *Daphnis et Chloë*. Strauss's *Symphonia domestica*, Furtwängler's only recording of a longer Strauss tone-poem, is superbly shaped and vividly characterized: it comes from the last concert before the Philharmonie was destroyed by Allied bombs. The other work in the same 1944 concert was the Beethoven *Violin Concerto*, seraphically played by the Berlin Philharmonic's leader, Erich Röhn – a very special performance indeed. Not everything is inspired (Gieseking's Schumann concerto is curiously prosaic by his standards), but there is much that is, including an incandescent and noble Bruckner *Fifth Symphony*, and some powerful Beethoven.

Berlin Philharmonic Orchestra, Herbert von Karajan

Overtures and Intermezzi: JOHANN STRAUSS JR: *Overture Zigeunerbaron.* MASSENET: *Thaïs: Méditation* (with Anne-Sophie Mutter, violin). CHERUBINI: *Overture Anacréon.* WEBER: *Overture: Der Freischütz.* SCHMIDT: *Notre Dame: Intermezzo.* PUCCINI: *Suor Angelica: Intermezzo; Manon Lescaut: Intermezzo.* MASCAGNI: *L'amico Fritz: Intermezzo.* HUMPERDINCK: *Overture Hänsel und Gretel.* MENDELSSOHN: *Overture The Hebrides (Fingal's Cave).*

(BB) ** EMI Encore (ADD/DDD) CDE5 74764-2.

A curiously planned programme. It opens with a brilliantly played and indulgently seductive account of the *Gypsy Baron Overture*; then comes the *Méditation* from *Thaïs* (a young Anne-Sophie Mutter the gentle soloist) played very romantically, immediately followed by Cherubini's *Anacréon Overture*. The performances of the Weber and Humperdinck overtures are disappointing, the first lacking electricity, the second charm. Best are the intermezzi, played with the utmost passion. The digital recording here is very brightly lit and there is a fierce sheen on the strings, but the closing *Fingal's Cave Overture* is played most beautifully, generating plenty of excitement, its effect enhanced by the resonantly spacious acoustic.

CHOPIN: *Les Sylphides* (orch. Roy Douglas). DELIBES: *Coppélia: ballet suite.* GOUNOD: *Faust: ballet music and Waltz.* OFFENBACH: *Gaîté parisienne* (ballet, arr. ROSENTHAL): extended excerpts. TCHAIKOVSKY: *Sleeping Beauty: suite.* PONCHIELLI: *La Gioconda: Dance of the hours.*

✪ *** DG (ADD) 459 445-2 (2).

This scintillating collection of ballet music is superbly played, and every item shows Karajan and his great orchestra at their finest. The very beautiful performance of Roy Douglas's exquisite arrangement of *Les Sylphides* – with its ravishing string playing, and glowingly delicate woodwind solos – has never been matched on record. It is also available on a single bargain disc together with the exhilaratingly racy *Gaîté parisienne* selection (which includes most of the ballet), and the *Coppélia suite*; but the latter is cut.

The missing movements are restored here and sound marvellous, as does the vivacious *Faust ballet music* and *Waltz*, the latter played with irresistible panache. Another riveting moment comes in the thrilling crescendo at the climax of the *Introduction* to the *Sleeping Beauty ballet suite*, yet there is much elegance and delicacy of colour to follow. The closing *Dance of the hours* – so affectionately phrased – also sparkles as do few other recorded performances, and throughout, these excellent CD transfers demonstrate DG's finest analogue quality from the 1960s and 1970s.

Berlin Philharmonic Orchestra, Georges Prêtre

'*Concert at the Waldbühne*': BERLIOZ: *Overture Le carnaval romain.* BIZET: *Carmen Suite; L'Arlésienne: Farandole.* DEBUSSY: *Prélude à l'après-midi d'un faune.* RAVEL: *Concerto for piano left hand* (with Leon Fleischer). *Boléro.* JOHANN STRAUSS SNR: *Radetzky March.* (Director & Video Director: Hans-Peter Birke-Malzer.)

*** TDK **DVD** DV-WBFRN.

This is a 1992 outdoor concert recorded at the Waldbühne in Berlin with the Berlin Philharmonic in splendid form under the vivacious Georges Prêtre. The Berlioz *Carnaval romain* is wonderfully spirited and there seems to be an excellent rapport between the Berliners and their French guest. The DVD is worth acquiring for the rare opportunity of seeing and hearing Leon Fleischer play the Ravel *Left Hand Concerto* with impressive authority. The camera work is unobtrusive and expert.

Berlin Philharmonic and Israel Philharmonic Orchestra; Zubin Mehta

'Joint Concert, Tel Aviv (1990)': BEN-HAIM: *Symphony No. 1, 2nd Movement: Psalm;* SAINT-SAENS: *Introduction & Rondo capriccio, Op. 28* (with Hagner, violin); WEBER: *Clarinet Concertino in E flat, Op. 67* (with Kam, clarinet); RAVEL: *La Valse;* BEETHOVEN: *Symphony No. 5.*

*(*) Arthaus **DVD** 100 068.

The visit of the Berlin Philharmonic had been keenly awaited in Tel Aviv, and this joint concert in the Mann Auditorium should have been an electrifying occasion. The two soloists are very good, and there is some excellent orchestral playing, with the two orchestras combined in the *Psalm* and the Beethoven and sounding pretty splendid in the Ravel, in spite of the less than ideal acoustics. However, the account of Beethoven's *Fifth* simply fails to spark into life until the finale and even then it is hardly earth-shaking. Certainly the DVD gives one a sense of being there, but the concert remains a disappointment.

Berlin State Opera Orchestra, Daniel Barenboim

'Berliner Luft' (Gala Concert from the State Opera, Unter den Linden): NICOLAI: *Overture: The Merry Wives of Windsor.* MOZART: *Don Giovanni: La ci darem la mano* (with Pape, Röschmann). SAINT-SAENS: *Introduction & Rondo capriccioso, Op. 28* (with Christ, violin). TCHAIKOVSKY: *Swan Lake: Dance of the Little Swans* (with ballet); *Waltz.* SHOSTAKOVICH: *Tahiti Trot.* WEILL: *Berlin im Licht* (Gruber, Barenboim, piano). KOLLO: *Untern Linden* (Vocal Ens.). LINCKE: *Glow-Worm Idyll* (Nold); *Berliner Luft.* J. STRAUSS JR: *Unter Donner und Blitz.*

*** Arthaus **DVD** 100 094.

This is obviously the Berliners' equivalent of the Last Night of the Proms and the well-dressed audience clearly have a wonderful evening. The DVD has tremendous spirit and atmosphere, Barenboim and the Orchestra are obviously enjoying themselves and there are even magicians doing party tricks to add to the revels. Everyone joins in the closing popular numbers, and although it is not as uninhibited as at the Proms (the audience is much older for one thing), it is still very infectious and enjoyable. The recording obviously came from a broadcast, for it is compressed here and there, but it does not affect the sense of spectacle. One could criticize the cameras for being too volatile in moving around the orchestra, but it suits the occasion, especially in the delightful account of Shostakovich's *Tahiti Trot* (based on Vincent Youmans's *Tea for Two*).

Boskovsky Ensemble, Willi Boskovsky

'Viennese bonbons': J. STRAUSS SR: *Chinese galop; Kettenbrücke Waltz; Eisele und Beisele Sprünge; Cachucha galop.* J. STRAUSS JR: *Weine Gemüths waltz; Champagne galop; Salon polka.* LANNER: *Styrian dances; Die Werber & Marien waltzes; Bruder halt galop.* MOZART: *3 Contredanses, K.462; 4 German dances, K.600/1 & 3; K.605/1; K.611.* SCHUBERT: *8 Waltzes & Ländler.*

(M) *** Van. (ADD) 8.8015.71 [OVC 8015].

This is a captivating selection of the most delightful musical confectionery imaginable. The ensemble is a small chamber group, similar to that led by the Strausses, and the playing has an appropriately intimate Viennese atmosphere. The transfer is impeccable and the recording from the early 1960s, made in the Baumgarten Hall, Vienna, is fresh, smooth and clear, with a nice bloom on sound which is never too inflated.

Boston Symphony Orchestra, Serge Koussevitzky

COPLAND: *El salón México.* FOOTE: *Suite in E min., Op. 63.* HARRIS: *Symphony (1933); Symphony No. 3.* MCDONALD: *San Juan Capistrano - Two Evening Pictures.*

(M) (***) Pearl mono GEMMCD 9492.

Koussevitzky's performance of the Roy Harris *Third Symphony* has never been equalled in intensity and fire – even by Toscanini or Bernstein – and Copland himself never produced as exhilarating an *El salón México.* The Arthur Foote *Suite* is unpretentious and has great charm. Sonic limitations are soon forgotten, for these performances have exceptional power and should not be missed.

PROKOFIEV: *Symphony No. 1 in D (Classical), Op. 25; Chout, Op. 21 bis: Danse finale.* SHOSTAKOVICH: *Symphony No. 9 in E flat, Op. 70.* TCHAIKOVSKY: *Francesca da Rimini, Op. 32.*

(***) Biddulph mono WHL 058.

Koussevitzky is in a class of his own. His premier recordings have great freshness and authority. His Shostakovich *Ninth Symphony*, recorded in 1946–7, was a rarity and never appeared in Britain in the days of shellac. The pre-war set of the Prokofiev *Classical Symphony* has even greater sparkle than the 1947 version included here, but this will do very nicely too! An electrifying *Francesca da Rimini*. Very good notes by David Gutman and decent transfers by Mark Obert-Thorn.

Bournemouth Sinfonietta, Richard Studt

English string music: BRITTEN: *Variations on a theme of Frank Bridge, Op. 10.* HOLST: *St Paul's suite, Op. 29/1.* DELIUS: *2 Aquarelles.* VAUGHAN WILLIAMS: *5 Variants of Dives and Lazarus.* WARLOCK: *Capriol suite.*

(BB) *** Naxos 8.550823.

This is the finest of the concerts of string music recorded for Naxos by Richard Studt and the excellent Bournemouth Sinfonietta. The Britten *Frank Bridge variations* is particularly memorable, showing easy virtuosity yet often achieving the lightest touch, so that the Vienna waltz movement sparkles in its delicacy. The *Funeral march* may not be so desperately intense as Karajan's famous mono version with the Philharmonia, but it is still very touching; and the following *Chant* is ethereal in its bleakly refined atmosphere.

The sprightly Holst *St Paul's suite* and Warlock's *Capriol*, agreeably robust, could hardly be better played, while Vaughan Williams's *Dives and Lazarus* is especially fresh and conveys the famous biblical story of the rich man and the beggar most evocatively, especially in the very beautiful closing section, when Lazarus finds himself in heaven. The recording, made in St Peter's Church, Parkstone, is full-bodied, immediate and real – very much in the demonstration bracket.

20th-century string music: BARTOK: *Divertimento.* BRITTEN: *Simple Symphony, Op. 4.* WALTON: *2 Pieces from Henry V: Death of Falstaff (Passacaglia); Touch her soft lips and part.* STRAVINSKY: *Concerto in D.*

(BB) ** Naxos 8.550979.

This is the least successful of the three concerts of string music recorded by Naxos in Bournemouth. The Sinfonietta players do not sound completely at ease in the shifting moods of the Bartók *Divertimento* and their ensemble could be crisper in the Stravinsky *Concerto*. The *Simple Symphony* comes off brightly, with a gently nostalgic *Sentimental sarabande* and a brisk, alert finale, but the *Playful pizzicato* could be more exuberant, especially in its famous trio which the composer wrote so joyously. The two Walton pieces are warmly atmospheric, and there are no complaints about the sound.

Scandinavian string music: GRIEG: *Holberg suite.* DAG WIREN: *Serenade, Op. 11.* SVENDSEN: *2 Icelandic melodies; Norwegian folksong; 2 Swedish folksongs, Op. 27.* NIELSEN: *Little suite in A min., Op. 1.*

(BB) *** Naxos 8.553106.

The liltingly spontaneous account of the Dag Wirén *Serenade* ensures a welcome for this enjoyable collection of Scandinavian music. The performance of Grieg's perennially fresh *Holberg* suite is hardly less successful in its combination of energy and polish, folksy charm and touching serenity in the famous *Air*. Nielsen's *Little suite* also has plenty of style and impetus, the changing moods of the finale neatly encompassed. The Svendsen folksong arrangements belong to the 1870s. The two *Icelandic melodies* are melodically robust but the *Norwegian folksong* is gentler and quite lovely. Yet it is the second of the two *Swedish folksongs* that most reminds the listener of Grieg. All are played with a natural expressive feeling, and the recording, made in the Winter Gardens, Bournemouth, has a fine, full sonority to balance its natural brilliance.

Brain, Dennis (horn)

BEETHOVEN: *Horn sonata in F, Op. 17* (with Denis Matthews). MOZART: *Horn concertos Nos. 2 in E flat, K.417* (with Philharmonia Orchestra, Susskind); *4 in E flat, K.495* (with Hallé Orchestra); *Horn quintet in E flat, K.407* (with Griller Quartet). RICHARD STRAUSS: *Horn concerto No. 1 in E flat, Op. 11* (with Philharmonia Orchestra, Galliera).

(M) (**(*)) Pearl mono GEM 0026.

Dennis Brain recorded the Beethoven *Sonata* with Denis Matthews in February 1944 on a simple, valved Boosey and Hawkes French horn (which legend has it cost £12). Because of its valve system, this was a more flexible instrument than the Viennese hand-horns used in Mozart's own time, but also a more imperfect one, with a few insecure upper harmonics. Brain's timbre is unique, his articulation is endearingly musical, his technique phenomenal, but never showy; even so there is the occasional slightly insecure note. Yet the passagework in both Beethoven and Mozart is full of imaginative touches. In the Beethoven *Sonata* Denis Matthews provides an elegant Mozartean-styled partnership, his lightness of touch balances nicely with Brain's elegance. How beautifully they exchange the question and answer of the briefly melancholy *Andante* and then launch into the robust finale so spiritedly!

The programme opens with the lovely Mozart *Quintet* (recorded eight months later). The Grillers play very sweetly and adroitly for the dominating horn, and the finale sparkles, but remains elegant. The two Mozart concertos followed. K.495 came first in 1943 (with the Hallé Orchestra – the strings in rather indifferent form, conducted by their leader, Laurence Turner), K.417 (with the Philharmonia under Susskind) in 1946. In both Brain's phrasing, of the lovely slow movement melodies is Elysian and the jaunty finale of K.417 remains unforgettable. When he came to re-record the Mozart *Horn concertos* with Karajan in 1953 (reissued in EMI's 'Great Recordings of the Century' series – CDM5 66898-2) he had adopted the wide-bore German double horn, which has a fatter, more spreading sound, not a timbre Mozart would have recognized. So there is a case for preferring Brain's earlier performances because Mozart simply sounds better on the narrower bore instrument, and that is not to disparage the marvellous playing on the Karajan disc.

It is not certain which instrument Brain used for the present 1947 recording of the Richard Strauss, but the playing is wonderfully ebullient and crisply articulated, all difficulties swept aside: it sounds like a French rather than a German horn. The effect is to echo the work's Mozartean inspiration and in the great soaring romantic theme at the centre of the slow movement – here, unfortunately affected by intrusive, uneven scratchy surface noise – the lyrical surge is thrilling, but not inflated, and this is one of his very finest solo performances on record. The Pearl transfers are faithful and agreeable (there is no edginess on the strings). But it surely ought to have been possible to diminish the background surface noise.

Brass Partout

'Playgrounds for angels': GRIEG: Sorgemarsj over Rikard Nordraak. NYSTEDT: Pia Memoria. RAUTAVAARA: A Requiem in our time; Playgrounds for angels. SIBELIUS: Overture in F minor; Allegro; Andantino and Menuett; Förspel (Preludium); Tiera.

*** BIS CD 1054.

Brass Partout (or rather brass partout, all fashionably lower case), is a virtuoso group of brass and percussion players, drawn from the Berlin Philharmonic, and other major German orchestras. The disc takes its title from the ingenious piece the Finnish composer Einojuhani Rautavaara composed for the Philip Jones Brass Ensemble. The Requiem in our time put Rautavaara on the map in 1953, and is only available in one other version.

All the Sibelius rarities are from 1889, before Kullervo, except only Tiera (1899).They fill in our picture of his growth during those formative years, though none is a masterpiece. The splendid Pia Memoria, a requiem for nine brass instruments, by the Norwegian, Knut Nystedt, has nobility and dignity. So, too, does Grieg's Sorgemarsj over Rikard Nordraak to whose strains the composer himself was buried. The playing is pretty stunning and so, too, is the superb BIS recording.

Brendel, Alfred (piano)

Alfred Brendel in Portrait: Documentary – Man and Mask. Produced by Emma Chrichton-Miller & Mark Kidel. Profile, conversation with Sir Simon Rattle, poetry-reading and recital: HAYDN: Piano Sonata in E flat, Hob XVI/49. MOZART: Piano Sonata in C min., K.457. SCHUBERT: Impromptu No. 3 in G flat, D.899.

*** BBC Opus Arte DVD OA 0811D (2).

This 70-minute portrait of Brendel, directed for television by Mark Kidel, takes the great pianist to many of the haunts of his early life, as well as showing him relaxing at home in Hampstead. As he wrily observes at the very start, he had none of the assets usually needed for a great musical career: he was not a child prodigy, he was not Jewish, he was not East European, his parents were unmusical, and he is not a good sightreader. He speaks of his parents, life in Vienna as a student, his love of art and the world of ideas. His geniality, culture and sophistication shine through, together with an engaging, self-deprecating humour – 'I was not a good sightreader, nor a virtuoso – in fact I don't know how I made it.'

One of his earliest musical memories is of playing records of Jan Kiepura in operetta on a wind-up gramophone to entertain the guests at the hotel his father managed. Later in Zagreb, where Alfred lived between the ages of five and thirteen, his father was the manager of a cinema, which took him in other directions than music, towards painting, among other things.

His first recital, in Graz in 1948, received glowing notices, when he concentrated on works with fugues, including a sonata of his own that boasted a double-fugue. Such revelations are amplified by the separate half-hour conversation Brendel has with Sir Simon Rattle on the subject of the Beethoven piano concertos, offering fascinating revelations from both pianist and conductor. We hear him accompanying Matthias Goerne in Schubert, playing Schubert, talking about primitive art from New Guinea and rehearsing a Mozart piano quartet with his son, Adrian. He also reads some of his own poetry in German, which strike a rather grim note of humour, while on the second disc comes a recital recorded at the Snape Maltings, crowning this revealing issue with masterly performances of three of Brendel's favourite works. In short, an unobtrusively shot film that brings us closer to a notoriously (or should one not say, famously) private person, a joy to look at and to listen to!

'The Art of Alfred Brendel' (complete)

(B) *** Ph. ADD/DDD 446 920-2 (25) (includes bonus CD).

'The Art of Alfred Brendel', Volume 1: HAYDN: Andante con variazione in F min., Hob. XVII/6; Piano sonatas in E flat, Hob. XVI/49; in C, Hob. XVI/50; Sonata in E flat, Hob. XVI/52. MOZART: Piano concertos Nos. 14 in E flat, K.449; 15 in B flat, K.450; 19 in F, K.459; 21 in C, K.467; 26 in D (Coronation), K.537; 27 in B flat, K.595; Double piano concerto in E flat, K.365 (with ASMF, Marriner; K.365 with Imogen Cooper). Adagio in B min., K.540; Piano sonatas Nos. 8 in A min., K.310; 11 in A, K.331; 13 in B flat, K.333; 14 in C min., K.457; Fantasia in C min., K.475; Rondo in A min., K.511.

(M) *** Ph. (IMS) ADD/DDD 446 921-2 (5).

Volume 2: BEETHOVEN: *Piano concertos Nos. 4 in G, Op. 58; 5 in E flat (Emperor), Op. 73* (with Chicago SO, Levine). *Andante in F (Andante favori), WoO 57; Bagatelle in A min. (Für Elise), WoO 59; 6 Bagatelles, Op. 126; 6 Ecossaises, WoO 83; Piano sonatas Nos. 3 in C, Op. 2/3; 11 in B flat, Op. 22; 18 in E flat, Op. 31/3; 23 in F min. (Appassionata), Op. 57; 24 in F sharp, Op. 78; 29 in B flat (Hammerklavier), Op. 106; 30 in E, Op. 109; 5 Variations on 'Rule, Britannia', WoO 79; 6 Variations in F, Op. 34; 15 Variations and fugue on a theme of Prometheus (Eroica), Op. 35; 33 Variations on a waltz by Diabelli, Op. 120.*

(M) **(*) Ph. (IMS) DDD/ADD 446 922-2 (5).

Volume 3: SCHUBERT: *Sonatas Nos. 4 in A min., D.537; 13 in A, D.664; 14 in A min., D.784; 15 in C (Relique), D.840; 16 in A min., D.845; 19 in C min., D.958; 20 in A, D.959; 21 in B flat, D.960; Allegretto in C min., D.915; 11 Ecossaises, D.781; Fantasy in C (Wanderer), D.760; 12 German dances, D.790; 16 German dances, D.783; Hungarian melody in B min., D.817; 6 Moments musicaux, D.780.*

(M) *** Ph. (IMS) ADD/DDD 446 923-2 (5).

Volume 4: LISZT: *Piano concertos Nos. 1-2; Totentanz (paraphrase on the Dies irae)* (with LPO, Haitink); *Années de pèlerinage: Book 1: 1st year: Italy; Book 2: 2nd & 3rd years: Italy; Sonata in B min.* Concert paraphrase: WAGNER: *Tristan: Isoldes Liebestod. Csárdás macabre; En rêve (Nocturne); Harmonies poétiques et religieuses: Invocations; Bénédiction de Dieu dans la solitude; Pensée des morts; Funérailles. Klavierstück in F sharp; Légendes; La lugubre gondola Nos. 1-2; Mosonyis Grabgeleit; RW (Venezia); Schlaflos! Frage und Antwort; Trübe Wolken (Nuages gris); Unstern: Sinistre; Valse oubliée No. 1; Vexilla regis prodeunt; Weihnachtsbaum (Christmas tree/Arbre de Noël) suite (excerpts); Weinen, Klagen, Sorgen Zagen.*

(M) *** Ph. (IMS) ADD/DDD 446 924-2 (5).

Volume 5: BRAHMS: *Piano concertos Nos. 1-2* (with BPO, Abbado). *4 Ballades, Op. 10; Theme and variations in D min.* (from *String sextet, Op. 18*). SCHUMANN: *Piano concerto in A min., Op. 54* (with LSO, Abbado). *Abendlied, Op. 85/12; Adagio and Allegro in A flat, Op. 70; Fantasiestücke, Op. 73; 3 Romances, Op. 94; 5 Stücke im Volkston, Op. 102* (all with Heinz Holliger). *Etudes symphoniques, Op. 13; Fantasia in C, Op. 17; Fantasiestücke, Op. 12; Kinderszenen, Op. 15; Kreisleriana, Op. 16.*

(M) *** Ph. (IMS) ADD/DDD 446 925-2 (5).

Weihnachtsbaum (A Christmas tree) (suite).

(***) Ph. mono 454 140-2 (bonus disc).

'The Art of Alfred Brendel' subdivides into five boxes, each of five CDs, and we have surveyed them in some depth under their composer entries in our main volume. Brendel aficionados will have to decide whether to invest in the complete set (with the five individual

boxes in a slip-case), which offers some saving in cost, or to pick and choose.

Brendel's overall achievement in a wide breadth of repertoire is quite remarkable, as indeed is the consistency of the Philips engineering: few (if any) artists have enjoyed such reliably truthful recording. However, while the Haydn/Mozart, the Liszt and the Schubert boxes can be recommended almost without serious reservation, the Beethoven collection is slightly marred by the inclusion of Brendel's digital recordings of the *Fourth* and *Emperor Piano concertos*, which are considerably inferior on almost all counts to his earlier, analogue versions.

The problem with the Brahms collection is again the inclusion of Brendel's recent digital versions of both concertos, but here for the opposite reason, since they are outstandingly fine and thus will probably have already found their way into the collections of most of his admirers! The choice for Volume 4 of his most recent, 1991 recording of the Liszt *Sonata* is also difficult to fathom when, by general consensus, both his earlier versions are superior in almost all respects. But the rest of the Liszt package is very impressive indeed, as is the Schubert box, which offers many of his analogue recordings not otherwise available.

With the complete set comes a bonus disc of Liszt's *Christmas tree suite*, a mono recording from 1951-2. While it is unique, its appeal is limited by its poor technical quality: a blurred focus at higher dynamic levels, and moments of distortion. The music itself, written by Liszt for his granddaughter to play, is of relatively limited interest. Only the complete set is available in the USA.

British light music

'*British light music*' (with (i) **Light Music Society O, Sir Vivian Dunn;** (ii) **Pro Arte O, George Weldon;** (iii) **Studio Two Concert O, Reginald Kilbey;** (iv) **Eric Coates and his O**): (i) DUNCAN: *Little suite: March.* CURZON: *The Boulevardier.* BINGE: *The Watermill.* DOCKER: *Tabarinage.* HOPE: *The Ring of Kerry suite: The jaunting car.* (ii) COATES: *Springtime suite: Dance in the twilight.* COLLINS: *Vanity Fair.* CURZON: *Punchinello: miniature overture.* TOMLINSON: *Little serenade.* BINGE: *Miss Melanie.* Alan LANGFORD: *Waltz.* BAYCO: *Elizabethan masque.* DEXTER: *Siciliano.* Haydn WOOD: *Moods suite: Joyousness.* (iii) *Paris suite: Montmartre.* BINGE: *Elizabethan serenade.* VINTER: *Portuguese party.* OSBORNE: *Lullaby for Penelope.* FARNON: *Portrait of a flirt.* HARTLEY: *Rouge et noir.* (iv) COATES: *Impression of a Princess; Wood nymphs; The Dam Busters march.*

(M) *** EMI stereo/mono CDM5 66537-2.

Obviously inspired by the great success of the programmes of British light music recorded (at premium price) by Ronald Corp for Hyperion, EMI have delved into their archives and brought out this equally attractive selection, drawing on four different sources, all of the highest quality. Moreover this EMI CD is offered at mid-price and includes 76 minutes of ear-catching melody. The obvious favourites are here, from Ronald Binge's famous *Elizabethan serenade* to his delectable vignette evoking *The Watermill*, Anthony Collins's *Vanity Fair* (the popularity of which he valued above his fame as a conductor) and Robert Farnon's witty *Portrait of a flirt*.

But also included are many more novelties of equal charm: Bayco's winning pastiche, *Elizabethan masque*, Binge's wistful portrait of *Miss Melanie*, Alan Langford's pastel-shaded *Waltz*, Harry Dexter's lilting *Siciliano*, Leslie Osborne's gently touching *Lullaby for Penelope*, and the delicious Irish whimsy of Peter Hope's *Jaunting car*. To bring lively contrast come Robert Docker's roisterous *Tabarinage* and Gilbert Vinter's equally vivacious *Portuguese party*. The stereo recordings, made at Abbey Road between 1963 and 1970, are excellent and very pleasingly transferred. Appropriately, the programme opens and closes with the music of Eric Coates, and the last three items are conducted by the composer, ending with a vigorous account of *The Dam Busters march*. These are mono recordings, but of high quality.

'British light music' (played by the Slovak or Czecho-Slovak Radio Symphony Orchestra, Andrew Penny, Adrian Leaper (with male chorus), Ludovit Raijter or Ernest Tomlinson; BBC Concert Orchestra, Kenneth Alwyn; Dublin RTE Concert Orchestra, Ernest Tomlinson or Proinnsias O Duinn):

Volume 1: COATES: *By the sleepy lagoon*. QUILTER: *Children's overture*. ADDINSELL: *Film music: Tom Brown's Schooldays*. CURZON: *Robin Hood suite*. Haydn WOOD: *Sketch of a dandy*. DUNCAN: *Little suite*. COLLINS: *Vanity Fair*. KETELBEY: *Suite romantique*. (8.554709).

Volume 2: KETELBEY: *In a monastery garden*. FARNON: *Colditz march*. GERMAN: *Gypsy suite*. Haydn WOOD: *Roses of Picardy; Serenade to youth*. DUNCAN: *Enchanted April*. CURZON: *La Pienneta*. QUILTER: *Rosmé waltz*. ELLIS: *Coronation Scot*. (8.554710).

Volume 3: ADDINSELL: *Film music: Goodbye Mr Chips*. GERMAN: *Romeo and Juliet* (incidental music): *suite*. DUNCAN: *20th-century express*. Haydn WOOD: *The Seafarer*. FARNON: *Pictures in the fire*. COATES: *The selfish giant*. QUILTER: *As you like it: suite*. BENJAMIN: *Jamaican rumba*. KETELBEY: *Bells across the meadow*. (8.554711).

Volume 4: ADDINSELL (arr. Roy Douglas): *Warsaw concerto*. BATH: *Cornish rhapsody*. Richard Rodney BENNETT: *Murder on the Orient Express: Theme and waltz*. Charles WILLIAMS: *Dream of Olwen* (with Philip Fowke). FARNON: *Lake in the woods; Westminster waltz*. DUNCAN: *Girl from Corsica; Visionaries' grand march*. CURZON: *Bravada: Paso*

doble. Haydn WOOD: *Evening song*. TOMLINSON: *Little serenade*. (8.554712).

Volume 5: COATES: *Dam Busters march*. ADDINSELL: *Film music: Fire over England*. GERMAN: *Nell Gwynn: 3 dances; Tom Jones: Waltz*. KETELBEY: *In the moonlight*. BINGE: *Elizabethan serenade*. FARNON: *Peanut polka*. QUILTER: *3 English dances*. HAYDN WOOD: *May-Day overture*. MAYERL: *Marigold*. KETELBEY: *In a Persian market*. (8.554713).

(BB) *** Naxos 8.505147 (5).

Unlike the set of 'British orchestral masterpieces' below, in which five existing CDs are offered in a slipcase, 'The Best of British light music' has been specially compiled, with items selected from a number of Naxos CDs. It offers a wide selection, well over five hours of music, so is less selective than the full-priced Hyperion CDs of the New London Orchestra under Ronald Corp. The NLO are also rather more characterful and even better recorded (see below) but the Naxos set remains excellent value. Although Kenneth Alwyn directs most of the film music, much of the rest is played, surprisingly idiomatically, by the Slovak Radio Symphony Orchestra, usually conducted by the erstwhile Adrian Leaper, although Ernest Tomlinson directs his own music (including his delicate lollipop, *Little serenade*). The highlights include Roger Quilter's lovely *Children's overture*, Anthony Collins's *Vanity Fair* (which he greatly prized), Binge's *Elizabethan serenade* and *Sailing by*, Benjamin's *Jamaican rumba* and mostly familiar items by Eric Coates. Robert Farnon is well represented by *Colditz*, his charming *Westminster waltz* and the catchy *Peanut polka*, as well as two rather effective tone pictures, *Lake in the woods* and *Pictures in the fire*, and there are other obvious hits like Vivian Ellis's *Coronation Scot* and of course the 'film concertos'. Not everything else is quite so memorable, but Edward German, Haydn Wood and Ketèlbey are all well represented and everything is brightly played and well recorded. The five records come for the price of four, and all are quite well documented.

'British orchestral masterpieces'

'British orchestral masterpieces' (played by (i) RSNO; (ii) E. Northern Philh. O; (iii) David Lloyd-Jones; (iv) Paul Daniel; (v) with Tim Hugh (cello): (i; iii) BAX: *Symphony No. 1; The garden of Fand; In the faery hills*. (ii; iii) BLISS: (v) *Cello concerto. Music for strings, Op. 54; 2 Studies, Op. 16*. ELGAR: *Falstaff, Op. 68; Elegy, Op. 58; The Sanguine fan (ballet), Op. 81*. (i; iii) HOLST: *Beni Mora; Egdon Heath; Fugal overture; Hammersmith*; (v) *Invocation for cello and orchestra. Somerset rhapsody*. (ii; iv) WALTON: *Symphony No. 1; Partita*.

(BB) *** Naxos 8.505154 (5).

With the five CDs offered for the price of four, this is an exceptionally successful anthology and a self-recommending bargain of the highest order. All these discs have been reviewed before. The Bax collection is the only one about which there are any reservations and these are minor, mostly concerning the recording, which is not as full and forward as usual from this source, with the solo cello rather backwardly balanced in the *Concerto*. Hugh's reading is reflective to match. Poetry rather than power is the keynote, centring on the *Larghetto* slow movement. In the Bax, David Lloyd-Jones draws warmly sympathetic performances from the RSNO, most impressively recorded, and the RSNO play extremely well for him. Tim Hugh is again a most responsive soloist in the rare Holst *Invocation*, with the rest of the Holst items hardly less distinguished. Lloyd-Jones's account of *Falstaff* brings tinglingly brisk tempi tempered with a highly idiomatic ebb and flow of rubato and *The Sanguine fan* is equally persuasive, alongside a touching account of the Elgarian *Elegy*. To cap the set comes Paul Daniel's outstanding version of the Walton *Symphony*, as bitingly intense as almost any in the catalogue, with the joyful *Partita* hardly less stimulating.

Brymer, Jack; David Glazer; Joza Ostrack (clarinet)

'*Clarinet concertos*': KROMMER: *Concerto in E flat*. WAGNER (Baermann): *Adagio for clarinet and strings*. DEBUSSY: *Première rapsodie*. (Jack Brymer, Vienna State Opera Orchestra, Felix Prohaska). WEBER: *Clarinet concerto No. 1 in F min.; Clarinet concertino, Op. 26*. STAMITZ: *Concerto No. 3* (David Glazer, Württemberg CO, Faerber). MOZART: *Clarinet concerto in A, K.622* (Joza Ostrack, Mozart Festival Orchestra, Lizzio).

(M) *** Vanguard (ADD) 08.9176.72 (2).

Jack Brymer's performance of the Krommer *Concerto* with its melting Adagio and delightful, chortling finale is a joy, while the Baermann *Adagio* (once attributed to Wagner) and the Debussy *Rapsodie* are also superbly poised. David Glazer's Weber (the *First Concerto* and the engaging *Concertino*) is most elegant, with the slow movement of the concerto beautifully phrased and both finales winningly jocular – the close of the *Concertino* chirrups just as it should. The Stamitz is plainer but still very agreeable. Joza Ostrack's performance of the greatest work of all, by Mozart, agreeably combines warmth and finesse; so altogether this makes a worthwhile anthology. Accompaniments are well managed and the recordings are all fully acceptable, if not absolutely refined; but the interest of the repertoire – so conveniently gathered together – more than compensates. No recording dates are given.

Camden, Anthony (oboe)

Italian oboe concertos (with City of London Sinfonia, Nicolas Ward): CIMAROSA, arr. Arthur BENJAMIN: *Concerto in C*. BELLINI: *Concerto in E flat*. RIGHINI: *Concerto in C*. FIORILLO: *Sinfonia concertante in F* (with Julia Girdwood). CORELLI, arr. BARBIROLLI: *Concerto in A*. PERGOLESI/BARBIROLLI: *Concerto in C min*.

(BB) **(*) Naxos 8.553433.

This collection recalls the series of outstanding recordings made by Evelyn Rothwell for Pye/PRT with her husband, Sir John Barbirolli, conducting. He specially arranged the highly engaging pastiche works of Corelli and Pergolesi for her to play and put his signature firmly on the *Sarabanda* of the Corelli *Concerto*, which he scored as a duet for oboe and cello, his own instrument. Lady Barbirolli's recordings have just been restored to the catalogue but at full price.

Meanwhile these sympathetic and stylishly played performances from Anthony Camden will suffice admirably, particularly at Naxos price. He has a most attractive timbre, and Nicholas Ward's accompaniments are impeccable. There are two very small reservations. The Fiorillo *Sinfonia concertante*, which features a pair of oboes (the second part is neatly managed by Julia Girdwood), although nicely written for the two soloists, is very conventional in its material and the first movement is a shade too long. The other point concerns the delightful five-note opening phrase of Arthur Benjamin's delicious Cimarosa confection, which Camden plays curiously lethargically, echoed by Ward. It is a small point, but Lady Barbirolli's account still lingers in the memory. The Naxos recording is excellently balanced and truthful.

'*The art of the oboe*' (with (i) London Virtuosi, John Georgiadis; (ii) City of L. Sinfonia, Nicholas Ward): (i) ALBINONI: *Oboe concertos in C, Op. 7/12; in D min., Op. 9/2; in C, Op. 9/5*. (ii) HANDEL: *Concerto No. 3 in G min.; Rondo in G; Rigaudon*. RIGHINI: *Idomeneus concerto*. CORELLI: *Concerto*. CIMAROSA: *Concerto in C min*. BELLINI: *Concerto in E flat*.

(BB) *** Naxos 8.553991.

This collection again has something in common with Evelyn Rothwell, Lady Barbirolli's collection of oboe concertos with her husband directing, but has the advantage of modern digital sound of high quality. Anthony Camden is a first-class soloist and these are vividly played performances, stylishly accompanied by both groups. Camden's tempi are not always quite so apt as his predecessor, but slow movements are always sensitive and finales sparkle. Most enjoyable.

Capella Istropolitana, Adrian Leaper

'*English string festival*': DOWLAND: *Galliard a 5*. ELGAR: *Elegy, Op. 58; Introduction and allegro, Op. 47; Serenade, Op. 20*. BRIDGE: *Lament*. PARRY: *An English suite; Lady Radnor's suite*.

(BB) **(*) Naxos 8.550331.

It is fascinating and rewarding to hear these excellent Slovak players turn their attention to essentially English repertoire, and with a considerable degree of success. The brief Dowland *Galliard* makes a strong introduction, and the attractive pair of neo-Baroque Parry suites of dance movements, played with warmth, finesse and spirit, are given bright and lively sound. In the Elgar *Introduction and allegro* the violins above the stave have their upper partials over-brilliantly lit by the digital recording, the focus not quite sharp; but otherwise the sound is full, with plenty of resonant ambience. The playing is strongly felt, but the fugue is a bit too measured, and the great striding theme, played in unison on the G string, could also do with more pace, especially when it returns. Otherwise this is persuasive, and the *Serenade* is presented simply, combining warmth and finish. At super-bargain price, this is worth exploring.

Capuçon, Renaud (violin)

'Le Boeuf sur le toit' (with Bremen Deutsche Kammerphilharmonie, Harding): BERLIOZ: *Rêverie et caprice.* MASSENET: *Thaïs: Méditation.* MILHAUD: *Le Boeuf sur le toit, Op.58.* RAVEL: *Tzigane.* SAINT-SAENS: *Danse Macabre; Havanaise; Introduction and Rondo capriccioso; Etudes, Op. 52* (arr. YSAYE): *En forme de valse.*

*** Virgin VC5 45482-2.

This is a violin and orchestra recital with an attractive theme that fills a neat gap. Featuring the brilliant young French virtuoso, Renaud Capuçon, masterly throughout, this collection of short concertante pieces by French composers offers such predictable items as the Massenet *Méditation*, the Ravel *Tzigane* and the Saint-Saëns *Havanaise* and *Introduction and Rondo capriccioso*, but also includes the less well-known Berlioz piece and other related items. *Danse Macabre* makes an obvious extra, although it features the solo violin more as an orchestral leader than a main soloist, while the fourth Saint-Saëns item, described as *Valse-caprice* on the disc, is an arrangement made by Ysaÿe of the most popular of Saint-Saëns's piano études.

Most intriguing is the longest item, which provides the title for the whole disc, *Le boeuf sur le toit*. This is one of two current versions of the arrangement which Milhaud himself made for the violinist, René Benedetti, of his Brazilian-inspired 'cinema-fantasy'. He characteristically takes the opportunity to emphasize the bizarre character of this suite of jazzy dances with its rondo theme inspired by Charlie Chaplin, making the solo violin the prime mover in bringing out the comic 'wrong-note' writing and clashing polytonality. Capuçon and Harding together make a strong case for this alternative version, relishing to the full the wit of the piece.

Casals, Pablo (conductor & cello)

Casals Edition (orchestral and concertante recordings)

BACH (with Prades Festival O): *Brandenburg concerto No. 5 in D, BWV 1050* (with Eugene Istomin, Joseph Szigeti, John Wummer); *Piano concerto in F min., BWV 1056* (with Clara Haskil); *Violin concerto in A min., BWV 1041* (with Isaac Stern); *Violin and oboe concerto in C min., BWV 1061* (with Isaac Stern, Marcel Tabuteau).

(M) (**(*)) Sony mono SMK 58982.

All these recordings come from the early 1950s, when Casals directed festivals at Prades and Perpignan and assembled some of the greatest artists of the day for these summer nights of music-making. This Bach disc comes from Prades and all the performances date from the first festival, in 1950. The *Brandenburg concerto No. 5* with Istomin as pianist, Szigeti and the flautist John Wummer is a rarity – and, if Sony's publicity is to be believed, has not appeared before. It is let down by Szigeti's (at times) scrawny tone, and the orchestral playing is a bit heavy-footed.

Clara Haskil's playing in the *F minor Concerto, BWV 1056* is as eloquent and sensitive as one would expect, and Isaac Stern's account of the A minor Violin concerto is hardly less impressive. Perhaps the most moving thing on the disc is the slow movement of the *C minor Violin and oboe concerto,* where the oboist is the legendary Marcel Tabuteau. Music-making from another age.

MOZART (with Perpignan Festival O): *Violin concerto No. 5 in A (Turkish), K.219* (with Erica Morini); *Sinfonia concertante in E flat, K.364* (with Isaac Stern, William Primrose).

(M) (**(*)) Sony mono SMK 58983.

The Mozart performances come from Perpignan and July 1951. The *A major Violin concerto, K.219* is played superbly by Erica Morini. Her Mozart playing is classically lithe and free from any striving after effect. The *Sinfonia concertante* (with Stern and Primrose) is also fine but is rather measured, and really needs to be a little lighter in touch.

MOZART (with Perpignan Festival O): *Piano concertos Nos. 14 in E flat, K.449* (with Eugene Istomin); *27 in B flat, K.595* (with Mieczyslaw Horszowski); *Concert aria: Ch'io mi scordi di te?* (with Jennie Tourel).

(M) (**) Sony mono SMK 58984.

Horszowski's playing in the *B flat Concerto, K.595,* is a model of style and elegance, though Casals gives him robust rather than discreet support. But neither the Istomin account of the *E flat, K.449* nor the Mozart *Ch'io mi scordi* with Jennie Tourel is well served by the engineers - though nor, for that matter, is Horszowski.

SCHUBERT (with Prades Festival O): *Symphony No. 5 in B flat. String quintet in C, Op. 163, D.956* (with Isaac Stern, Alexander Schneider, Milton Katims, Paul Tortelier).

(M) (***) Sony mono SMK 58992 [id.].

The Schubert *Fifth Symphony*, recorded in 1953, omits the first-movement exposition repeat but, as with everything this great musician does, is full of musical interest. It has not been issued in the UK before, eclipsed by the later (and perhaps even finer) performance by the 1970 Marlboro Orchestra in stereo. However, this earlier account boasts a particularly eloquent reading of the slow movement. The Casals account of the sublime Schubert C major String quintet has rarely been absent from the catalogue: it first appeared on Philips and then CBS, and is too familiar to require detailed comment. Recorded in 1952, it sounds as marvellous as ever. This coupling is surely a must for all Casals admirers.

SCHUMANN (with Prades Festival O, Ormandy): *Cello concerto in A min., Op. 129. Piano trio in D min., Op. 63* (with Mieczyslaw Horszowski, Alexander Schneider). *5 Stücke im Volkston* (with Leopold Mannes).

(M) (**(*)) Sony mono SMK 58993.

The Schumann *Cello concerto* was recorded in Prades in 1953 with Ormandy conducting the Prades Festival Orchestra, while the Op. 63 Trio and the *Fünf Stücke im Volkston* date from the previous year. Although one leading magazine claimed that the *Trio* had not appeared in the UK before, it was in fact released in a CBS commemorative box. The sound naturally calls for tolerance but that should be enthusiastically extended. Casals once said that 'In Schumann ... every note is so much from the heart.' Casals plays it for all it is worth, and some might wish for slightly more subdued and restrained emotions. Casals recorded the *D minor Trio* for HMV with Thibaud and Cortot in 1928, and this 1952 Prades performance with Schneider and Horszowski is, if anything, even finer. A performance of stature, with less of the heart-on-sleeve approach which distinguishes the *Concerto*, this was again listed in one source as 'new to the UK', but it has appeared both on LP and on CD. The sensitive and imaginative phrasing is a model of its kind. Whatever reservations one might have, these are all performances to be reckoned with.

Chang, Sarah (violin), Berlin Philharmonic Orchestra, Plácido Domingo

'Fire and Ice': BACH: *Orchestral Suite No. 3 in D, BWV 1068: Air.* BEETHOVEN: *Romance No. 2 in F, Op. 50.* DVORAK: *Romance in F min., Op. 11.* MASSENET: *Thaïs: Méditation.* RAVEL: *Tzigane.* SARASATE: *Concert Fantasy on Carmen, Op. 25; Zigeunerweisen, Op. 20.*

*** EMI CDC5 57220-2.

Don't be put off by the silly title of the disc – 'Fire and Ice'! We have here a collection of rightly popular violin virtuoso pieces played with terrific panache and splendid style by this still young player. It is only ten years since Chang's last record of the Sarasate, although it was made some years earlier (when she was nine) and played on a smaller-sized instrument. Since then she has gone on record concertos by Paganini, Tchaikovsky, Sibelius and Vieuxtemps, all of which have been acclaimed. In the early 1990s Miss Chang was hailed by Menuhin as 'the most ideal violinist I have ever heard', and now, ten years later, her prowess and virtuosity are never in doubt here. Those attracted to this repertoire can be assured that the playing from all concerned is pretty dazzling, and there are no reservations about the quality of the recording made in the Philharmonie, Berlin. The balance is very acceptable and places the soloist firmly in the spotlight without in any way allowing her to mask the orchestral detail.

Chicago Symphony Orchestra

Historic telecasts, Volume 1 (1954):

Fritz Reiner

BEETHOVEN: *Symphony No. 7 in A, Op. 92; Egmont overture, Op. 84.* HANDEL: *Solomon: Arrival of the Queen of Sheba.*

(***) VAI Video VAI 69601.

Historic telecasts, Volume 2 (1961):

Georg Szell

MUSSORGSKY: *Prelude to Khovanshchina.* BEETHOVEN: *Symphony No. 5 in C min., Op. 67.* BERLIOZ: *Le carnaval romain overture, Op. 9.*

(***) VAI Video VAI 69602.

Historic telecasts, Volume 3 (1962):

Leopold Stokowski

BACH, arr. Stokowski: *Toccata and fugue in D min.* BRAHMS: *Variations on a theme of Haydn* (St Anthony chorale). RIMSKY-KORSAKOV: *Capriccio espagnol, Op. 34.*

(***) VAI Video VAI 60603.

Historic telecasts, Volume 4 (1961):

Pierre Monteux

BEETHOVEN: *Symphony No. 8 in F, Op. 93.* WAGNER: *Die Meistersinger: Prelude to Act III.* BERLIOZ: *Le carnaval romain overture, Op. 9.*

(***) VAI Video VAI 60604.

The above four videos are even more valuable than the wider but more piecemeal coverage of the 'Art of conducting' above. They offer us four great conductors at the height of their powers directing a great orchestra, and every performance is memorable. We even have a chance to compare Szell's and Monteux's interpretations of Berlioz's supreme orchestral masterpiece, *Le carnaval romain*, Szell the more electrifying, Monteux the more colourful.

These telecasts are part of a series inaugurated in Chicago in 1951 (under Kubelik). But when Reiner took over the orchestra in 1953 the programmes were extended to 45 minutes, broadcast first on Sunday afternoons, and subsequently (in 1959) at 8 p.m. on Sunday evenings, with Deems Taylor as initial host. The list of guest conductors who joined the series is wide-reaching, including Barbirolli, Beecham, Copland, Hindemith, Martinon, Munch and Previn. Announcements and commentaries are omitted from the published videos and the music is presented without introductions.

It was right that Reiner should carry on the series, at a live concert in Symphony Hall in 1954. With the bold swathe of his strong, clear up-and-down beat, a serious mien, and frowning gaze, he establishes total control of the orchestra. Although the early recording quality brings the usual sound-track discoloration of woodwind upper partials, with moments of distortion in the wide amplitude of string sound, the warmth of the playing projects readily, as does its spontaneous feeling (after the single hour-long run-through rehearsal, which was standard for the series).

It is a pity that no Richard Strauss was included, but the Beethoven performances generate enormous electricity. The camera work is fairly primitive, and it is interesting that the producer misses the dominating role of the horns in the thrilling furioso close of the outer movements of the *Seventh Symphony* and focuses instead on the woodwind, whereas in *Egmont* the horn section is portrayed at the key moments. Reiner, stiff and unrelenting in manner throughout, permits himself a half smile to acknowledge the applause, and even gives the oboes a bow – after the Queen of Sheba has arrived and departed rather fiercely.

Szell's clear beat is hardly less concentrated, achieving extraordinary precision and powerful clipped rhythms in Beethoven's *Fifth*; but he uses his left hand much more subtly than Reiner. It is a great performance, creating and gathering intensity in a formidable progress to its gripping finale. The first movement repeat is observed (as it is later by Monteux in the *Eighth*) and the strings flowingly decorate the main theme of the slow movement with appealing warmth. Before that has come the evocatively detailed Mussorgsky *Khovanshchina Prelude*, with the delectable Rimsky-Korsakov orchestration glowing in the coda, and the following Berlioz overture is quite riveting in its orchestral bravura, almost upstaging the symphony in sheer adrenalin.

Reiner, Monteux and Szell conduct from memory, but Stokowski uses scores throughout, even in his famous Bach arrangement. Here the remarkably imaginative orchestration is made to seem the more vivid by camera close-ups which even feature the glockenspiel and show the great horn entry at the climax of the fugue, before the thrilling upward rushes of strings. Where his colleagues favour batons,

Stokowski uses his ever-supple hands to shape the music. This means slightly less precision of ensemble in the Bach (where he is concerned with the range of sonority and colour), but not the Brahms, a richly idiomatic account, in no way idiosyncratic, although the lyrical warmth of the string writing is brought out in the closing variations. Rimsky's *Capriccio* is then played with enormous virtuosity (especially at the close) and the camera relishes the opportunity to portray each of the orchestral soloists in turn. As with the Szell concert, this is a studio recording, with a much drier acoustic, but the middle strings still glow as Stokowski coaxes their phrasing affectionately.

For the Monteux concert we return to Symphony Hall, with an audience, and this tape offers the best sound of the four – warm and well-detailed. Monteux's dapper, genial manner is deceptive, yet it brings the most relaxed atmosphere of all and at one endearing moment the camera catches one of the violin players on the back desks turning to his companion and smiling. The performance of Beethoven's *Eighth* is superb, polished, wonderfully detailed, and with a perfectly judged forward flow. When Monteux wants to be forceful he clenches his left fist, and the result catches the music's full intensity without fierceness. The glorious horn playing (on which the camera dwells indulgently) gives great warmth and nobility to the following Wagner *Prelude*, and the Berlioz overture ends the programme with a fizzing burst of energy at its very close.

Historic telecasts, Volume 5 (1963):

Charles Munch

RAMEAU/D'INDY: *Dardanus suite.* BERLIOZ: *Les Troyens: Royal hunt and storm.* RAVEL: *Valses nobles et sentimentales; La valse.*

(***) VAI Video VAI 69605.

Historic telecasts, Volume 6 (1963):

Paul Hindemith

HINDEMITH: *Concert music for strings and brass.* BRUCKNER: *Symphony No. 7: first movement* (only). BRAHMS: *Academic festival overture.*

❀ (***) VAI Video VAI 69606.

Historic telecasts, Volume 7 (1961):

George Szell

MOZART: *Overture: Le nozze di Figaro; Violin concerto No. 5 in A (Turkish), K.219* (with Erica Morini). BEETHOVEN: *Overture: Leonora No. 3.*

(***) VAI Video VAI 60607.

This second batch of videos includes the most valuable of all, a video of Paul Hindemith conducting 'live' in Chicago's Orchestra Hall, where understandably the privileged audience give him an hero's welcome. With his lips pursed seriously throughout, and using a clear, purposeful stick technique, he directs an electrifying account of his own *Concert music for strings and brass*, with the Chicago strings and brass responding with the most glorious sounds. One might even use the adjective voluptuous in relation to the strings, except that rich though the textures are, Hindemith's lyricism remains sinewy – for that is its strength. The fugato (nicely observed by the camera) also has splendid bite. He also conducts a superbly paced account of the first movement of Bruckner's *Seventh*, full of humanity. This follows a brief filmed interview when he is suitably articulate on the music's universality to a not very imaginative TV interviewer. The closing Overture, spaciously and exciting, is richly Brahmsian. The sound really is remarkably good.

By the side of this, Munch's concert is just a shade disappointing. The Rameau/D'Indy suite is elegant enough, but lacking the incandescence of a Beecham touch, sounds anachronistic, and the *Royal hunt and storm*, beautifully played as it is, takes a little while to warm up. However, the climax when it comes does not disappoint (with the camerawork among the brass adding a great deal to the visual effect), and the closing horn solo is poetically atmospheric. The Ravel performances are warmly idiomatic, but here the sound lacks enough transparency to bring out the lustrous detail.

Szell, after a brilliant, if ungenial *Nozze di Figaro* overture, has the advantage of a very stylish soloist, Erica Morini, in Mozart's most popular violin concerto. She plays with beautful tone, splendid assurance, and a disarming simplicity of line, and only the three cadenzas (rather too much of a good thing) give any cause for criticism. *Leonora No. 3* makes a meticulously detailed but exciting finale. Good sound, with the solo violin well caught, although balanced very forwardly.

Chicago Symphony Orchestra, Daniel Barenboim or Pierre Boulez

'*Musik Triennale Cologne 2000*'

DVD 1: (cond. Pierre Boulez): BERG: *Lulu Suite.* DEBUSSY: *Le jet d'eau; 3 Ballades de Françoise Villon* (with Christine Schäfer). STRAVINSKY: *The Firebird* (ballet; complete).

*** **DVD** TDK DV-MTKBO.

DVD 2: (cond. Daniel Barenboim). BOULEZ: *Notations I–IV.* CARLI: *El firulete.* DEBUSSY: *La mer.* FALLA: *El sombrero de tres picos (The Three-Cornered Hat* (ballet; complete; with Elisabete Matos).

*** **DVD** TDK DV-MTKBA.

In April 2000 the Chicago Symphony Orchestra visited the Cologne Triennial Music Festival of 20th-century music, with these two concerts conducted respectively by Pierre Boulez and Daniel Barenboim. On each DVD comes a ten-minute excerpt, one following from the other, of a conversation between the two conductors,

both of them worthwhile supplements. The music-making in both concerts is persuasive, brilliant and warm, the more compelling when seen as well as heard.

It is Barenboim who conducts the Boulez work, the one example of music from after the Second World War. Not that these four *Notations* are typical of Boulez when they are basically orchestrations, made in maturity with revisions and development, of early piano pieces he wrote as a student of René Leibowitz. The first, with its evocative orchestral writing, here sumptuously performed, has one thinking of Debussy, while the energetic fourth piece brings echoes of *The Rite of Spring*, with Barenboim momentarily echoing Boulez's crisp 'tic-tac' style of conducting. The Barenboim programme then goes on to a sensuous account of Debussy's *La mer* and a vigorously dramatic one of the complete Falla ballet, with the Chicago players warmly idiomatic in the Spanish dance rhythms. Elisabete Matos is the fine mezzo soloist in the vocal introduction, with the members of the orchestra enthusiastically clapping and shouting '*Ole!*' They equally let their hair down when, at the end of the concert, Barenboim concedes an encore, a jolly dance by José Carli, *El firulete*, a frill or bit of nonsense.

The Boulez offering is even more striking, when Christine Schäfer is such an inspired soloist both in Berg's *Lulu Suite* and in the Debussy songs with orchestral accompaniment. Schäfer not only sings Lulu's Song in the second movement but the lament of Countess Geschwitz after Lulu's murder in the final movement, though she does not attempt a scream at the moment prescribed. When heard live, Schäfer's voice may seem relatively small, but as balanced here it is full, firm and sensous, ideal both for Berg in such a warm performance and for Debussy in the subtleties of the *Villon* songs with their echoes of early music. A pity though that the camera often takes you so close to her you practically see down to her tonsils. The orchestral sound is full-bodied on both discs, with solo instruments brought forward in reflection of the camera-work. An auspicious introduction to 20th-century music on DVD.

Chicago Symphony Orchestra, Sir Thomas Beecham

HAYDN: *Symphony No. 102 in B flat.* MOZART: *Symphony No. 38 in D (Prague), K.504.*

** NCV Arts Video 8573 84095-3.

DELIUS: *Florida Suite: By the River.* HANDEL arr. BEECHAM: *Love in Bath* (Suite). MENDELSSOHN: *Hebrides Overture.* SAINT-SAENS: *Le Rouet d'Omphale.*

** NCV Arts Video 8573 84096-3.

Beecham is not generously represented on film, and these performances given in Chicago in March 1960 are the only colour images to survive. The colour is admittedly not very good; nor, for that matter, is the sound. Moreover, the dynamic range is not as wide as we are accustomed to in Beecham's commercial recordings, so the rapt magical *pianissimo* tone is less in evidence. Of course, there are moments when the Beecham magic works, but they surface only intermittently. The camera work is rather stiff and wooden, with none of the flexibility you would expect from a BBC telecast of the period. We often focus on lines of string players, and Beecham himself gets far less attention from the camera than one might expect. Recommended, then, but with only modified rapture.

Chicago Symphony Orchestra, Fritz Reiner

ROSSINI: *Overture: La gazza ladra.* HAYDN: *Symphony No. 88 in G.* BEETHOVEN: *Symphony No. 7 in A, Op. 92.* WEBER: *Invitation to the Dance.* J. STRAUSS JR: *Emperor Waltz.* LISZT: *Mephisto Waltz No. 1.* R. STRAUSS: *Don Juan.* RAVEL: *Rapsodie espagnole.* BARTOK: *Hungarian Sketches.*

(B) *** RCA (ADD) 74321 84219-2 (2).

An ideal compilation for those wish to explore Fritz Reiner's Chicago recordings from the early stereo era, many of which remain top recommendations. Here we have a glittering *Rapsodie espagnole*, a dashing *Don Juan* and a powerful Beethoven *Seventh*. Reiner was also master of the lighter repertoire, and his Strauss waltzes and Rossini overtures are always a joy to hear; his Haydn is full of character, too. Indeed, all these performances have this conductor's magnetism stamped on them, and new listeners will understand why he has a cult following. The recordings all have the vivid Chicago ambience, though in these new transfers some can be bit aggressive under pressure. Notes about the music and conductor are included.

Chicago Symphony Orchestra, Frederick Stock

WAGNER: *Die Meistersinger overture.* BRAHMS: *Hungarian dances Nos. 17-21.* GOLDMARK: *In the springtime overture.* SUK: *Fairy tales: Folkdance (polka).* GLAZUNOV: *Les ruses d'amour: Introduction and waltz.* TCHAIKOVSKY: *Symphony No. 5 in E min.* PAGANINI: *Moto perpetuo, Op. 11 (orch. Stock).* WALTON: *Scapino: comedy overture.* DOHNÁNYI: *Suite for orchestra, Op. 19.* R. STRAUSS: *Also sprach Zarathustra.* STOCK: *Symphonic waltz. Op. 8.*

✪ (M) (***) Biddulph mono WHL 021/22.

Frederick Stock, born in Germany in 1872, studied composition and violin at the Cologne Conservatoire; among his teachers was Humperdinck, and Mengelberg was a fellow student. He began his career as an orchestral violinist, and in 1895 he emigrated to America to join the ranks of the Chicago Symphony

as a viola player. The orchestra was then four years old. In 1905 he was hired on a temporary basis as its musical director; but he stayed on for nearly forty years until he died in October 1942.

He built the orchestra into the splendid ensemble which Fritz Reiner was eventually to inherit and established its world reputation, especially for its brass playing, although (on the evidence of these recordings) the strings were equally impressive. Like Reiner, he had the advantage of the marvellous acoustics of Chicago's Symphony Hall in which to make his records, which, alongside Stokowski's Philadelphia recordings, are technically among the finest to come out of America in the late 1920s. Indeed, the sound in Tchaikovsky's *Fifth* (1927) is so warm and full-bodied that in no time at all one forgets one is listening to an old recording and simply revels in the rich string patina and fine woodwind colours (heard at their finest in the elegantly played waltz movement). The brass come fully into their own in the finale.

Stock's interpretation is endearingly wilful, very like Mengelberg's more famous reading, which was made only six months later. Stock pulls back at the entry of the secondary group in the first movement. The effect is emphasized because of a side change but is consistent in the recapitulation. The slow movement is very much *con alcuna licenza* (Tchaikovsky's marking) and the horn soloist must have needed great nerve to sustain his great solo at the chosen spacious tempo. But Stock has that supreme gift of being able to create the feeling of a live performance while making a recording, and this *Fifth*, for all its eccentricities, is very enjoyable. The finale has the traditional cut which was so often observed at that time, but the effect is seamless and the final brass peroration has only ever been topped by Stokowski's 78-r.p.m. Philadelphia set.

The programme opens with a thrillingly sonorous account of *Die Meistersinger overture* (1926), with the tension held right to the end, in spite of the big rallentando at the majestic reprise of the introductory 'fanfare'. The Brahms dances, played with virtuosity and considerable panache, were recorded in 1925 but never issued, and both the Suk Polka (1926) and the charming Glazunov *Waltz* (1929) show the colourful palette of Stock's Chicago woodwind section, while Goldmark's *In the springtime overture* sounds uncommonly fresh in this early (1925) performance. The Dohnányi suite too (1928) is stylishly and pleasingly done, with nice touches of wit and plenty of lilt in the waltz featured in the closing movement, where Stock handles the tempo changes with affectionate sophistication. But here for some reason the recording is very closely miked and dry; was it actually recorded in Symphony Hall, one wonders, for there is little ambient effect?

Stock's most famous record is of Walton's *Scapino overture*, which he commissioned for the orchestra's fiftieth anniversary celebrations. It is played here with fizzing virtuosity and much élan and is particularly valuable in being the only existing recording of Walton's original score before the composer made his revisions. This and an equally brilliant account of

Paganini's *Moto perpetuo*, deftly played in unison by the orchestral violins, were recorded in 1941, the sound brightly lit (the violins are closely miked in the Paganini) but retaining underlying warmth.

The set ends appropriately with a work indelibly associated with Chicago because of Reiner's superb, later, stereo version: Strauss's *Also sprach Zarathustra*. But Stock's account certainly does not come under its shadow. The spectacular opening is remarkably well caught and the passion of the violins is thrilling. This was made in 1940, and here the Columbia engineers made a compromise between brilliance and richness of timbre, with the hall ambience adding a natural breadth.

The range of dynamic is striking, and Stock's reading must be placed among the finest, for it is seemingly completely spontaneous, yet splendidly controlled and shaped. The orchestral concentration is held at the highest level throughout, and particularly so during the darkly dormant section of the score on the lower strings associated with '*Science*' and the later passage on the high violins; Stock then follows with an exciting accelerando to reach the spectacular climax in '*The Convalescent*'. He maintains this thrust through to the closing pages, with the tolling bell coming through plangently, and the coda very touching. Then for an encore the conductor provides a charmingly tuneful *Symphonic waltz* of his own composition, endearingly inflated but not boring when presented with such zest, and sumptuously recorded in 1930. Yet there is nothing 'historic' about live music-making of this calibre, and this fascinating set is very highly recommended. It certainly does Stock's reputation full justice.

(i) Chicago Symphony Orchestra, Frederick Stock; (ii) Cincinnati SO, Eugene Goossens

English music: (i) BENJAMIN: *Overture to an Italian comedy.* ELGAR: *Pomp and circumstance march No. 1.* (ii) VAUGHAN WILLIAMS: *A London Symphony* (No. 2 original version); WALTON: *Violin concerto* (with Jascha Heifetz (violin))

(***) Biddulph mono WHL 016.

This superbly transferred Biddulph issue celebrates the fact that some of the very finest recordings of British music have come from America. Heifetz's historic first recording of the Walton *Violin concerto* is imaginatively coupled with the only recording ever made (also by Goossens and the Cincinnati Orchestra, immediately following the Walton sessions in 1941) of the 1920 version of Vaughan Williams's *London Symphony*. As welcome fill-ups come Elgar's *Pomp and circumstance No. 1* and Arthur Benjamin's *Overture to an Italian comedy*, brilliantly played by the Chicago orchestra under Frederick Stock.

Chung, Kyung Wha (violin)

'*The great violin concertos*': MENDELSSOHN: *Concerto in E min., Op. 64* (with Montreal SO, Dutoit). BEETHOVEN: *Concerto in D, Op. 61* (with VPO, Kondrashin). TCHAIKOVSKY: *Concerto in D, Op. 35.* SIBELIUS: *Concerto in D min., Op. 47* (both with LSO, Previn).

(B) **(*) Double Decca ADD/DDD 452 325-2 (2).

This Double Decca begs comparison with Grumiaux's Philips Duo called, more sensibly, '*Favourite violin concertos*' (see below). Grumiaux offers Brahms instead of Sibelius and concentrates on repertoire in which his refined, poetic style produces satisfying results in all four works. Chung only scores three out of four. Her collection is let down by the 1979 account of the Beethoven which, measured and thoughtful, lacks the compulsion one would have predicted, due largely to the often prosaic conducting of Kondrashin. There is poetry in individual movements - the minorkey episode of the finale, for example, which alone justifies the unusually slow tempo - but, with too little of the soloist's natural electricity conveyed and none of her volatile imagination, it must be counted a disappointment, despite the first-class digital sound.

The Mendelssohn, made two years later, could not be more different. Chung favours speeds faster than usual in all three movements and the result is sparkling and happy, with the lovely slow movement fresh and songful, not at all sentimental. With warmly sympathetic accompaniment from Dutoit and the Montreal orchestra, amply recorded, the result was one of her happiest recordings.

The Sibelius/Tchaikovsky pairing (from 1970) is highly praised in our main volume. She brings an equally sympathetic and idiomatic response to both concertos, and Previn's accompaniments are of the highest order. The latter is a much better investment than the latest format, unless the Mendelssohn is essential.

Cincinnati Pops Orchestra, Erich Kunzel

'*Favourite overtures*': SUPPE: *Light cavalry; Poet and peasant.* AUBER: *Fra Diavolo.* HEROLD: *Zampa.* REZNICEK: *Donna Diana.* OFFENBACH: *Orpheus in the Underworld.* ROSSINI: *William Tell.*

*** Telarc CD 80116.

In this spectacularly recorded (1985) collection of favourite bandstand overtures the playing has fine exuberance and gusto (only the galop from William Tell could perhaps have had greater impetus) and the resonant ambience of Cincinnati's Music Hall lends itself to Telarc's wide-ranging engineering, with the bass drum nicely caught. Perhaps the opening of *Fra Diavolo* would have benefited from a more transparent sound, but for the most part the opulence suits the vigorous style of the music-making, with *Zampa* and the Suppé overtures particularly successful.

'Pomp and Pizazz': J. WILLIAMS: *Olympic fanfare.* SUK: *Towards a new life.* ELGAR: *Pomp and circumstance march No. 1.* IRELAND: *Epic march.* TCHAIKOVSKY: *Coronation march.* BERLIOZ: *Damnation de Faust: Hungarian march.* J. F. WAGNER: *Under the Double Eagle.* FUCIK: *Entry of the gladiators.* SOUSA: *The Stars and Stripes forever.* HAYMAN: *March medley.*

*** Telarc CD 80122.

As enjoyable a march collection as any available, with characteristically spectacular and naturally balanced Telarc recording, with its crisp transients and wide amplitude. The performances have comparable flair and sparkle. The inclusion of John Ireland's comparatively restrained *Epic march* and the Tchaikovsky *Coronation march*, with its piquant trio and characteristic references to the Tsarist national anthem, makes for attractive contrast, while the Hayman medley (including *Strike up the band, 76 Trombones, South Rampart Street Parade* and *When the Saints go marching in*) makes an exuberant, peppy closing section. By comparison the Berlioz *Rákóczy march* is quite dignified. The sound is in the demonstration class. Most entertaining.

'Symphonic spectacular': SHOSTAKOVICH: *Festival overture, Op. 96.* WAGNER: *Die Walküre: Ride of the Valkyries.* FALLA: *El amor brujo: Ritual fire dance.* BIZET: *L'Arlésienne: Farandole.* JARNEFELT: *Praeludium.* CHABRIER: *España.* TCHAIKOVSKY: *Marche slave, Op. 31.* HALVORSEN: *Entry of the Boyars.* ENESCU: *Rumanian rhapsody No. 1, Op. 11.* KHACHATURIAN: *Gayaneh: Sabre dance.*

*** Telarc CD 80170.

With spectacular recording, well up to Telarc's best standards, this is a highly attractive collection of orchestral lollipops. Everything is played with the special flair which this orchestra and conductor have made their own in this kind of repertoire. Most entertaining, and technically of demonstration standard.

'The Fantastic Leopold Stokowski' (transcriptions for orchestra): BACH: *Toccata & fugue in D min., BWV 565; Little fugue in G min., BWV 578.* BOCCHERINI: *Quintet in E flat: Minuet.* BEETHOVEN: *Moonlight sonata: adagio sostenuto.* BRAHMS: *Hungarian dance No. 6.* DEBUSSY: *Suite bergamasque: Clair de lune. Prélude: La cathédrale engloutie.* ALBENIZ: *Fête-Dieu à Seville.* RACHMANINOV: *Prelude in C sharp min., Op. 3/2.* MUSSORGSKY: *Night on the bare mountain; Pictures at an exhibition: The Great Gate of Kiev.*

✪ *** Telarc CD-80338.

Stokowski began his conducting career in Cincinnati in 1909, moving on to Philadelphia three years later; so a collection of his orchestral transcriptions from his first orchestra is appropriate, particularly when the playing is so committed and polished and the recording so sumptuous. Indeed, none of Stokowski's own recordings can match this Telarc disc in sheer glamour of sound. The arrangement of *La cathédrale engloutie* is very free and melodramatically telling. Most interesting is *Night on the bare mountain*, which has a grandiloquent brass chorale added as a coda. Any admirer of Stokowski should regard this superbly engineered CD as an essential purchase. It is now reissued with two extra items added, the Brahms *Hungarian dance No. 6* and Stokowski's extraordinary transcription of *The Great Gate of Kiev* from Mussorgsky's *Pictures at an exhibition*. Kunzel has the advantage of Telarc's bass-drum recording, and at the very close there is a highly imaginative added touch as the old magician introduces an evocation of Moscow cathedral bells.

City of Prague Philharmonic Orchestra, Gavin Sutherland

Music from the 'Carry On' films: *Carry on Camping; Carry on Suite* (music from *Carry on Sergeant, Teacher* and *Nurse*); *Carry on Cabby; Carry on Cleo; Carry on Jack; Carry on Behind; Raising the Wind; Carry on at your Convenience; Carry on up the Khyber; Carry on Doctor again.*

(M) *** ASV CDWHL 2119.

Some readers may raise a quizzical eyebrow at the inclusion of this collection, for the famous 'Carry On' series of films is the epitome of British vulgarity. Yet their incidental music shows the British light music tradition at its best. The early scores were written by Bruce Montgomery (*Carry on Teacher, Nurse, Cabby*, etc.) where a flavour of the late 1950s is evoked: the main 'Carry On' theme is unashamedly jazzy, yet has a central countertheme which is delightfully nostalgic and totally British. For the later films, Eric Rogers took over – he peppered the films with quotes from famous classical pieces, whilst his own melodies are distinctly appealing, reflecting the 'swinging sixties'. The *Carry on Camping* and *Carry on Doctor* suites are perhaps the best, not just for their vivaciousness, but also for the remarkably piquant and deft orchestration throughout. *Carry on at your Convenience* evokes the production line of a toilet-bowl factory, and the Prague orchestra respond with enthusiasm (the timpani are especially impressive); then there is an unexpectedly charming romantic passage which is quite touching, before the riotous ending. The imperial opening music of *Carry on up the Khyber* (perhaps the wittiest of the series) is strongly characterized, and the *Carry on Cleo* suite, with a Hollywood-style opening march à la Rosza, is also effective. Altogether the invention is surprisingly varied. The orchestra perform as though they have played it all their lives, no doubt a tribute to the conductor, Gavin Sutherland, and the producer, Philip Lane. The recording is also superb. Thoroughly recommended for those on the 'Carry On' wavelength, and for other lovers of this musical genre who are simply curious.

Cleveland Symphonic Winds, Fennell

'Stars and stripes': ARNAUD: *3 Fanfares.* BARBER: *Commando march.* LEEMANS: *Belgian Paratroopers.* FUCIK: *Florentine march, Op. 214.* KING: *Barnum and Bailey's favourite.* ZIMMERMAN: *Anchors aweigh.* J. STRAUSS Sr: *Radetzky march.* VAUGHAN WILLIAMS: *Sea songs; Folksongs suite.* SOUSA: *The Stars and Stripes forever.* GRAINGER: *Lincolnshire posy.*

*** Telarc CD 80099.

This vintage collection from Frederick Fennell and his superb Cleveland wind and brass group is one of the finest of its kind ever made. Severance Hall, Cleveland, has ideal acoustics for this programme and the playing has wonderful virtuosity and panache. Add to all this digital engineering of Telarc's highest calibre, and you have a very special issue.

Concertgebouw Orchestra, Eduard van Beinum

The Radio Recordings: ANDRIESSEN: *Miroir de Peine* (with Kolassi); *Symphony No. 4.* BACH: *Cantata No. 56* (with Harrell); *Clavier Concerto in D min., BWV 1052* (with Lipatti); *Double Concerto in C min., BWV 1060* (with van Beinum, den Hertog). BADINGS: *Cello Concerto No. 2* (with Leeuwen Boomkamp). BARTOK: *Concerto for Orchestra.* BEETHOVEN: *Egmont Overture, Op. 84; Piano Concerto No. 3 in C min., Op. 37* (with Solomon); *Violin Concerto in D, Op. 61* (with Francescatti). BRAHMS: *Symphony No. 1 in C min., Op. 67.* DEBUSSY: *La Mer; Images pour orchestre; Printemps.* DIEPENBROCK: *Te Deum* (with Spoorenberg, Merriman, Haefliger, Bogtman; Toonkunstkoor Amsterdam). ESCHER: *Musique pour l'esprit en deuil.* FRANCK: *Psyché* (excerpts); *Symphonic Variations* (with Hengeveld). HENKEMANS: *Viola Concerto* (with Boon). LISZT: *Piano Concerto No. 2 in A* (with Pembauer). RUDOLF MENGELBERG: *Salve Regina* (with van der Sluys). MOZART: *Violin Concerto No. 4 in D, K.218* (with Menuhin). PIJPER: *Symphony No. 3.* RAVEL: *Daphnis et Chloë: Suite No. 2; Piano Concerto in G* (with de Groot). REGER: *Eine Ballet Suite, Op. 130.* RESPIGHI: *Fountains of Rome.* SCHOENBERG: *5 Orchestral Pieces, Op. 16.* SCHUBERT: *Der Hirt auf dem Heisen* (with Vincent). STEPHAN: *Musik für Geige und Orchester* (with Kulenkampff). STRAVINSKY: *Firebird Suite.* TCHAIKOVSKY: *Romeo and Juliet (Fantasy Overture); Symphony No. 4 in F min.* VERDI: *Don Carlos: Dormirò sol nel manto mio regal* (with Christoff).

DVD: BEETHOVEN: *Symphony No. 3 in E flat (Eroica).*

(**(*)) One for You Q-Disc (mono) 97015 (11 CDs + 1 DVD).

Eduard van Beinum presided over the Concertgebouw Orchestra in the post-war years when Willem Mengelberg was in disgrace because of his collaboration with the Nazis. He was a most civilized and selfless artist, who never enjoyed the renown of some of his contemporaries but who, like Sir Adrian Boult in England, put the cause of the composer above all else. Although the Dutton label has brought us transfers of the *Symphonie fantastique*, the Brahms *First Symphony* and his amazing Bartók *Concerto for Orchestra*, this 11-CD set enables a generation for whom he is only a name to assess the quality of his contribution to Dutch musical life. Enterprising collectors will welcome the opportunity of having such rarities as Willem Pijper's *Third Symphony*, the *Fourth* of Hendrik Andriessen and the *Viola Concerto* of Hans Henkemans, all of which are rewarding scores (neither the Pijper nor the Henkemans is otherwise available). Van Beinum was a conductor of classical instinct, whose performances are perfectly straight yet infused with poetic feeling. Of particular interest are the concerto appearances of Solomon and Dinu Lipatti and, in the Bach *C minor Concerto* for two pianos, van Beinum himself. What a fine Debussy conductor he was too. This valuable set also comes with a black-and-white DVD of the *Eroica Symphony*, gripping and exhilarating, recorded from a TV broadcast in May 1957, which gives a rare glimpse of his technique and mastery. Naturally, the quality of these radio recordings, which come from the late 1940s and early 1950s, is variable although generally much better than you might reasonably expect. Well worth investigating and with an admirably annotated 150-page booklet in five languages.

Concertgebouw Orchestra, Bruno Walter

MAHLER: *Symphony No. 4 in G* (with Schwarzkopf). BRAHMS: *Symphony No. 4 in E min., Op. 98.* MOZART *Symphony No. 40 in G min., K.550.* STRAUSS *Don Juan.*

(**) Music & Arts mono CD 1090.

Music & Arts offers the whole of a 1952 Bruno Walter/ Concertgebouw concert with Elisabeth Schwarzkopf. Egon Wellesz, who often heard Mahler conducting in the first decade of the last century, spoke of the composer as having 'the fire and electricity of Toscanini and the warmth of Bruno Walter', and it was Walter he thought of as being, as it were, the keeper of the seal. Even now, when there is a superabundance of CDs of the *Fourth Symphony*, Walter's Mahler is still something special and carries an authenticity of feeling that comes across half a century. The sound is not up to the standard of commercial recordings of the 1950s but is perfectly adequate.

Concerto Copenhagen, Andrew Manze

'*Swedish rococo concertos*' (with soloists): AGRELL: *Flute concerto in B minor* (with Maria Bania); *Oboe concerto in B flat* (with Lars Henriksson). Heinrich Philip JOHNSEN: *Double bassoon concerto in F* (with Mats Klingfors & Christian Beuse). Ferdinand ZELLBELL: *Bassoon Concerto in A minor: Allegro.* (with Mats Klingfors). (v) *Cello Concerto in D* (with Åse Åkerberg).

*** Musica Sveciae Dig. MSCD 411.

These composers inhabit the outer fringes of the catalogue. None is represented by more than one work. Heinrich Philip Johnsen (1717–79) was born in Northern Germany and came to Stockholm with his princely employer, Adolf Frederik of Holstein-Gottorp, who was elected to the Swedish throne. Johan Agrell (1701–65) was born in Sweden but spent the bulk of his life in Germany, and of the three only Ferdinand Zellbell (1719–80) was born, bred and died in Sweden.

With the exception of the Handelian *Oboe concerto* of Agrell, all these pieces are in manuscript. The *F major Concerto for two bassoons* by Heinrich Philip Johnsen is rather delightful. It is fresh and entertaining, and played with polish and elegance. (Johnsen enjoys the distinction of having written an opera, *The Bartered Bride.*)

Zellbell was a pupil of Roman and went to Hamburg where he studied with Telemann, and to Hanover, where in 1741 he composed this cello concerto. He spent the bulk of his life in Stockholm where he succeeded to his father's position as organist of the Storkyrkan (cathedral) but he was unpaid for many years and died heavily in debt. The movement from his *A minor Concerto* is a witty piece, and the *Cello Concerto* is an inventive and at times touching. Andrew Manze and the Concerto Copenhagen give first-class support to the talented soloists and the aural perspective is eminently truthful. Impeccable scholarly notes by Martin Tegén.

Curzon, Clifford (piano)

BRAHMS: *Piano concerto No. 2 in B flat, Op. 83* (with VPO, Knappertsbusch). GRIEG: *Piano concerto in A min., Op. 16* (with LSO, Fjeldstad). RACHMANINOV: *Piano concerto No. 2 in C min., Op. 18* (with LPO, Boult). TCHAIKOVSKY: *Piano concerto No. 1 in B flat min., Op. 23* (with VPO, Solti).

(B) *(**) Double Decca stereo/mono 460 994-2 (2).

Any student of fine piano playing would surely want to experience Curzon's performances, and here we have four great concertos at bargain price, with the Grieg a classic. Recorded in 1959, it has remained at or near the top of the list ever since, notable as much for its freshness and power as for its lyrical tenderness. It is available with different couplings on Decca's 'Classic Sound' and 'Legends' labels. The partnership between Solti and Curzon in the Tchaikovsky may seem unlikely, but works well. If, like the recording, it is not quite in the same league as the Grieg, it is still very exciting.

Curzon's 1957 Rachmaninov would be better known had it been recorded in stereo as this technical advance rather eclipsed it – as it did Katchen's more extrovert Decca recordings at that time. However, Curzon's comparatively classical approach is both individual and telling and the recording is very good for its time. In the 1955 Brahms No. 2, Knappertsbusch is inclined to linger over much, but with these two imposing artists, a certain integrity comes over. The mono recording is a bit dry and close, but tolerable. All in all, this is a thoroughly worthwhile set.

Czech Philharmonic Orchestra, Gerd Albrecht

HAAS: *Studies for string orchestra.* SCHULHOF: *Symphony No. 2.* ULLMANN: *Symphony No. 2.* KLEIN: *Partita for strings.*

*** Orfeo C 337941 A.

Like the issues in Decca's *Entartete Musik* series, this Orfeo disc features music dismissed by the Nazis as decadent, all here by Jewish composers from Czechoslovakia slaughtered in the Holocaust. Pavel Haas, often counted as Janáček's most important pupil, wrote his *Studies* in Theresienstadt, the prison camp where the Nazis assembled Jewish intellectuals, later to be killed in death camps. Tautly argued in four sections lasting eight minutes, it was given its first performance in the camp under one of the then inmates who happily managed to survive, Karel Ančerl, later the conductor of the Czech Philharmonic. Albrecht and today's Czech Philharmonic bring out the vitality of the writing, with no hint in it of self-indulgence or self-pity. This is a composer writing in sight of death simply because he has to, relishing a last opportunity.

The *Symphony No. 2* of Erwin Schulhof was written in 1932, long before the Germans invaded Czechoslovakia, a work very much of its period with a charming *Scherzo alla Jazz* influenced by Stravinsky's *Soldier's tale.* The *Symphony No. 2* of Viktor Ullmann, also in four crisp movements, was one of no fewer than twenty-five works that he wrote in Theresienstadt, including the opera *The Emperor of Atlantis*, also on disc. Though he was a pupil of Schoenberg, he here returned to tonality, communicating directly.

The youngest of the four, Gideon Klein from Moravia, more specifically drew inspiration from folk roots, very much in the way that Bartók did in Hungary. His *Partita for strings*, like the Pavel Haas *Studies*, has darkness in it, notably in the central variation movement, but here too the piece culminates in a mood of energetic optimism, a heart-warming expression of defiance. Very well played and recorded, the four works are the more moving for giving only momentary hints of what the composers were going through. First-rate sound.

Damiens, Alain (clarinet), Ensemble InterContemporain, David Robertson

'*American clarinet*': ELLIOTT CARTER: *Concerto; Gra for solo clarinet.* STEVE REICH: *New York counterpoint for clarinet and tape.* HOWARD SANDCROFT: *Tephillah for clarinet and electronics.* ADAMS: *Gnarly buttons for clarinet and small orchestra* (with André Troutlet, clarinet).

*** Virgin VC5 45351-2.

Elliott Carter's Concerto is written in six sections, for different instrumental groups (percussion, strings, woodwind and so on). In a live performance the soloist moves among them. The music is characteristically complex and unpredictable, yet has a strong lyrical core. The solo *Gra* is more fragmented. Reich's *New York counterpoint* is written in eleven clarinet parts, only one of which is live. The soloist plays with his own recordings which are held in endless ostinato loops. There are three movements, and the last has syncopated jazz inflections. The composer demands a performance 'without charm', but the end result is very diverting. Sandcroft's *Tephillah* is based on Hebrew chant, although its fragmentation means that you might not guess it! The soloist is 'electronically' shadowed. By the side of these works John Adams's *Gnarly buttons* is positively traditional, readily communicative, with a central *Hoe down*, and the lyrical finale melodically haunting, with the soloist providing a burst of virtuosity to dominate a surge of energy near the close. The vivid performances throughout this anthology certainly illustrate the pluralism of twentieth-century American music.

Daniel, Nicholas (oboe), Peterborough String Orchestra

Italian oboe concertos: VIVALDI: *Concerto in C, RV 44.* ALBINONI: *Concerto in D min., Op. 9/2.* BELLINI: *Concertino in E flat.* MARCELLO: *Concerto in D min.* CIMAROSA: *Concerto in C* (arr. Arthur Benjamin).

(B) **(*) Hyp. Helios CDH 55034.

All the music here is tunefully undemanding, with the minor-key concertos adding a touch of expressive gravitas. Arthur Benjamin's arrangement of the delightful Cimarosa concerto is always a delight, and the lovely Bellini *Concertino* sounds like one of his operatic arias arranged for oboe – complete with cabaletta finale. Nicholas Daniel is closely miked, but he is a stylish performer and draws lively support

from the Peterborough orchestra. The disc plays for just under 55 minutes, but is offered at bargain-price.

Danish State Radio Symphony Orchestra

'*75th Anniversary Concert*': BRAHMS: *Symphony No. 2* (cond. Busch). HAYDN: *Symphony No. 91 in E flat; 12 German Dances* (cond. Wöldike). BEETHOVEN: *Funeral March.* NIELSEN: *Overture Maskarade.* DEBUSSY: *Prélude à l'après-midi d'un faune.* SÆVERUD: *Galdreslåtten.* STRAVINSKY: *Suite No. 2* (cond. Malko). GLINKA: *Ruslan and Ludmilla: Overture* (cond. Dobrowen). LUMBYE: *Dream Pictures.* NIELSEN: *At the Bier of a Young Artist* (cond. Grøndahl). RIISAGER: *Trumpet Concertino* (with Eskdale; cond. Jensen). NIELSEN: *Little Suite for Strings* (cond. Tuxen). MOZART: *Divertimento No. 12 in E flat, K.252* (orchestral wind soloists).

✪ (B) (***) Dutton mono 2CDEA 5027 (2).

Issued to celebrate the splendid Danish orchestra's 75th anniversary, these excellent recordings, mainly from the late 1940s, demonstrate what a superb band had developed in Copenhagen during and just after the Second World War. The late 1940s and early 1950s were the heyday of the orchestra, and the acoustic of the Concert Hall of the Radio House was, before its later refurbishment, altogether superb, bright yet warm and full bodied.

Nikolai Malko's account of the Stravinsky *Suite No. 2* and Sæverud's *Galdreslåtten* were demonstration 78rpm discs in their day, and this early 1950s account of Brahms's *Second Symphony*, urgent and direct under Fritz Busch's direction, was a revelation (particularly its thrilling finale), at a time when choice was limited to Beecham, Weingartner or Stokowski. In his admirable note Lyndon Jenkins calls it 'civilized, exhilarating, yet full of humanity'. The sound, as transferred by Dutton, is still vivid, as it is in all these varied items.

Mogens Wöldike's wonderfully spritely and stylish recording of Haydn's *Symphony No. 91 in E flat* is its first and arguably best recording, not even forgetting Jochum's glorious version with the Bavarian Radio Orchestra from 1958, while the little Riisager *Trumpet Concertino* is a delight, as is Nielsen's vigorous *Overture to Maskarade*. The *Deutsche Tänze* are absolutely captivating.

The *Funeral March* is, incidentally, a transcription and transposition Beethoven made of the first movement of the *Sonata in A flat, Op. 26*, for the play, *Leonora Prohaska*. As far as we know, neither the Haydn nor the Brahms symphonies was ever transferred to LP and make their first appearance since the 1950s. The same goes for most of the other material.

The original sound is so good that collectors will be amazed at its quality and presence. The transfers are really excellent with no trace of surface noise, although with a fractional loss of the body compared with the originals, which were probably bottom-heavy. A very special set, which for those who do not know these performances will bring unexpected musical rewards and which deserves the widest currency.

Davies, Philippa (flute), Thelma Owen (harp)

'The Romance of the Flute and Harp': HASSELMAN: La source, Op. 44; Feuilles d'automne. GODARD: Suite, Op. 16: Allegretto. GODEFROID: Etude de concert. FAURE: Berceuse, Op. 16; Impromptu, Op. 86. DOPPLER: Mazurka. MENDELSSOHN: Spring Song, Op. 62/3. THOMAS: Watching the Wheat. SAINT-SAENS: Carnival of the Animals: The Swan. BIZET: Fair Maid of Perth: Intermezzo. PARISH-ALVARS: Serenade. DEBUSSY: Syrinx; Suite bergamasque: Clair de lune.

(BB) *** Regis RRC 1085.

An unexpectedly successful collection which effectively intersperses harp solos with music in which the flute takes the leading role. The playing is most sensitive and the recording is very realistic indeed. The programme, too, is well chosen and attractively laid out and is fairly generous in playing time (59 minutes). Highly recommended for a pleasant summer evening.

Detroit Symphony Orchestra, Neeme Järvi

'Favourite Encores': CHABRIER: Fête polonaise. GLINKA: Kamarinskaya; Valse fantaisie. SIBELIUS: Andante festivo for strings. BOLZONI: Minuet. DVORAK: Humoresque. DARZINS: Valse mélancolique. ELLINGTON: Solitude (trans. for strings). SHOSTAKOVICH: The Gadfly: Romance. MUSSORGSKY: Gopak. DEBUSSY: Suite bergamasque: Clair de lune. SCHUMANN: Abendlied, Op. 107/6. MEDINS: Aria. GERSHWIN: Promenade: Walking the Dog. SOUSA: The Stars and Stripes Forever.

(M) **(*) Chan. 6648.

The acoustics of Detroit's Orchestra Hall, made famous by the Mercury engineers at the end of the 1950s, remain impressive and the Detroit orchestra is flattered here by opulently glowing sound, which especially suits the Glinka pieces and the lovely Sibelius Andante festivo. The rest of the programme is rather slight, consisting entirely of lollipops, some well-known, plus a few engaging novelties. All are presented with Järvi's customary flair and are very well played. If you enjoy this kind of concert, there is no need to hesitate, for the programme is generous at 73 minutes.

Detroit Symphony Orchestra, Paul Paray

'French opera highlights': HEROLD: Overture: Zampa. AUBER: Overture: The Crown diamonds. GOUNOD: Faust: ballet suite; Waltz (from Act II). SAINT-SAENS: Samson et Dalila: Bacchanale. BIZET: Carmen: Danse bohème. BERLIOZ: Les Troyens: Royal hunt and storm. MASSENET: Phèdre overture. THOMAS: Mignon: Gavotte.

(M) *** [Mercury (ADD) 432 014-2].

Paul Paray's reign at Detroit tempted the Mercury producers to record a good deal of French music under his baton, and here is a good example of the Gallic verve and sparkle that were achieved. The only disappointment is the unslurred horn phrasing at the magical opening and close of the Royal hunt and storm. This and its companion CD are not now available in the UK.

'Marches and overtures à la française': MEYERBEER: Le Prophète: Coronation march. GOUNOD: Funeral march for a marionette. SAINT-SAENS: Marche militaire française; Marche héroïque. DE LISLE: La Marseillaise. Overtures: ADAM: Si j'étais roi. BOIELDIEU: La Dame blanche. ROSSINI: William Tell. OFFENBACH: La belle Hélène; Orpheus in the Underworld. Contes d'Hoffmann: Barcarolle etc.

(M) **(*) Mercury (ADD) [434 332-2].

A generous and flavourful Gallic concert, recorded in three different Detroit venues, with acoustics not entirely flattering to the orchestra, who nevertheless always play splendidly. The Adam and Boieldieu overtures need the glow of Kingsway Hall: here the resonance of Cass Technical High School slightly clouds detail. The marches and the Offenbach items were recorded in 1959 in Old Orchestral Hall, and the sound is more expansive. The most memorable pieces are the wittily engaging Gounod (always to be remembered as Alfred Hitchcock's TV signature-tune) and the spirited Belle Hélène overture, not put together by the composer, but none the worse for that. Throughout, the élan of the playing always brings enjoyment, and the virtuosity of the fiddles in the William Tell galop is exhilarating.

Dichter, Misha (piano), Philharmonia Orchestra, Sir Neville Marriner

Concertante works: ADDINSELL: Warsaw concerto. GERSHWIN: Rhapsody in blue. LITOLFF: Concerto symphonique, Op. 102: Scherzo. CHOPIN: Fantasia on Polish airs, Op. 13. LISZT: Polonaise brillante (arr. of WEBER: Polacca brillante, Op. 72).

(B) *** Ph. Virtuoso 411 123-2.

Never before has the orchestral detail of Addinsell's indelible pastiche emerged so beguilingly on record as it does here under Marriner; he and Misha Dichter combine to give the music genuine romantic memorability, within a warmly sympathetic acoustic. Gershwin's famous *Rhapsody* is hardly less successful, the performance spirited yet glowing. To make a foil, the Litolff *Scherzo* is taken at a sparkingly brisk tempo and projected with great flair. The Chopin *Fantasia* has a lower voltage, but the closing Liszt arrangement of Weber glitters admirably. The sound is first rate and is very believable in its CD format.

Driessche, André van (horn), Belgian Radio & TV Orchestra, Rahbari

'Flemish romantic horn concertos' by MEULEMANS; DE JONG. HERBERIGS: *Cyrano de Bergerac.* EECHAUTE: *Night poem.*

(BB) *** Koch Discover DICD 920299.

Four Flemish composers, very little known outside Belgium, here offer a series of richly enjoyable works, very well recorded, all with solo horn brilliantly played by André van Driessche. The most striking is the Straussian symphonic poem, *Cyrano de Bergerac*, by Robert Herberigs, inspired by Rostand's play, with heroic outer sections and love music in the middle. The *Horn concertos* of Arthur Meulemans and Marinus de Jong, each in three compact movements, also have ripe Straussian echoes, as well as anticipations of Hollywood film music, while Prosper van Eechaute's *Night poem* brings the most sensuous music of all. At super-bargain price, this is well worth investigating.

Du Pré, Jacqueline (cello)

'The Art of Jacqueline du Pré' (with (i) LSO, Sir John Barbirolli; (ii) RPO, Sir Malcolm Sargent; (iii) New Philh. O; (iv) Chicago SO; (v) ECO; (vi) Daniel Barenboim; (vii) Valda Aveling; (viii) Gerald Moore; (ix) Ernest Lush; (x) Steven Bishop): (i) ELGAR: *Cello concerto in E min., Op. 85.* (ii) DELIUS: *Cello concerto.* (iii; vi) SAINT-SAENS: *Cello concerto No. 1 in A min., Op. 33.* (iv; vi) DVORAK: *Cello concerto in B min., Op. 104; Waldesruhe, Op. 68.* (iii; vi) SCHUMANN: *Cello concerto in A min., Op. 129.* (i; vii) MONN: *Cello concerto in G min.* HAYDN: *Cello concertos in* (i) *C and* (v; vi) *D, Hob VIIb/1-2.* (vi) CHOPIN: *Cello sonata in G min., Op. 65.* (vi) FRANCK: *Cello sonata in A.* (viii) FAURE: *Elégie in C min., Op. 24.* (viii) BRUCH: *Kol Nidrei, Op. 47.* BACH: *(Unaccompanied) Cello suites Nos. 1-2, BWV 1007/8.* (ix) HANDEL: *Cello sonata in G min.* BEETHOVEN: (vi) *Variations in G min. on Judas Maccabaeus: See the conqu'ring hero comes, WoO 45;* (x) *Cello sonatas Nos. 3, in A, Op. 69; 5 in D, Op. 102/2.* (vi) *Variations on themes from 'The Magic Flute': 7 variations in D, WoO 46 (Bei Männern, welche Liebe fühlen); 12 variations in F, 66 (Ein Mädchen oder Weibchen).*

(B) *** EMI (ADD) CZS5 68132-2 (8).

Admirers of this remarkably gifted artist, whose career ended so tragically, will welcome this survey of her major recordings, made over the incredibly brief period of a single decade. Her first recordings (1961) have a BBC source and her last (the Chopin and Franck *Sonatas*) were made at Abbey Road in 1971. But of course she made her real breakthrough in 1965 with the justly famous Kingsway Hall recording of the Elgar *Concerto* with Barbirolli. Some items included here are not otherwise currently available and, with excellent transfers, this set is an admirable and economical way of exploring her art. There are good if brief notes and some heart-rending photographs showing this young prodigy playing with characteristic concentration and joyously in conversation with her equally young husband, Daniel Barenboim.

Cello concertos: BOCCHERINI: *Concerto in B flat* (arr. GRUTZMACHER). HAYDN: *Concertos in C & D, Hob VIIb/1-2* (with ECO, Barenboim or LSO, Barbirolli). SCHUMANN: *Concerto in A min., Op. 129.* SAINT-SAENS: *Concerto No. 1 in A min., Op. 33* (with New Philh. O., Barenboim). DVORAK: *Concerto in B min., Op. 104; Silent woods, Op. 68/5* (with Chicago SO, Barenboim). DELIUS: *Concerto* (with RPO, Sargent). MONN: *Concerto in G min.* ELGAR: *Cello concerto in E min., Op. 85* (both with LSO, Barbirolli). RICHARD STRAUSS: *Don Quixote, Op. 35* (with New Philh. O, Boult).

(B) *** EMI (ADD) CZS5 67341-2 (6).

Those not wanting the chamber music on the above eight-disc coverage of the 'Art of Jacqueline du Pré', will find that this six-disc set is no less desirable, adding as it does the Boccherini/Grützmacher *Concerto*, most endearingly played, plus the recently remastered 1968 *Don Quixote* (with Boult), which is particularly fine. Fine transfers and excellent value.

'A Lasting inspiration' (with Daniel Barenboim, cond. or piano): BOCCHERINI: *Cello concerto in B flat* (arr. GRUTZMACHER). DVORAK: *Cello concerto (Adagio); Silent woods, Op. 68/5.* HAYDN: *Cello concerto in C.* BEETHOVEN: *Piano trio No. 5 in D (Ghost), Op. 70/1; 7 Variations on 'Bei Männern'* (both with Pinchas Zukerman). BRAHMS: *Cello sonata No. 1 in E min., Op. 38.* FRANCK: *Sonata in A* (arr. DELSART) *(Allegro ben moderato).*

(M) **(*) EMI (ADD) CMS5 66350-2 (2).

A medium-priced anthology that is self-recommending if the more comprehensive programme is of appeal. The chamber-music performances have the same qualities of spontaneity and inspiration that have made Du Pré's account with Barbirolli of Elgar's *Cello concerto* come to be treasured above all others. Any tendency to self-indulgence, plus a certain leaning towards romantic expressiveness, is counterbalanced by the urgency and intensity of the playing. In the Brahms *Sonata* it is hard to accept the blatant change of tempo between first and second subjects, but here too there is warmth and flair. If some find Du Pré's approach to Haydn too romantic, it is nevertheless difficult to resist in its ready warmth. The Beethoven *Ghost Trio* is comparably individual and inspirational. The sound-quality is fairly consistent, for all the remastered transfers are successful.

Eastman-Rochester Orchestra, Howard Hanson

American orchestral music: BARBER: *Capricorn concerto, Op. 21* (with Joseph Mariano (flute), Robert Sprenkle (oboe), Sidney Mear (trumpet)). PISTON: *The Incredible flutist* (ballet suite). GRIFFES: *Poem for flute and orchestra.* KENNAN: *3 Pieces.* MCCAULEY: *5 Miniatures for flute and strings* (all with Joseph Mariano (flute)). BERGSMA: *Gold and the Señor Commandante* (ballet suite).

(M) *** Mercury (ADD) [434 307-2].

A first-rate concert of pioneering recordings, made between 1957 and 1963. The collection is worth having for Barber's *Capricorn concerto* alone, a less characteristic work than, say, any of the Essays for orchestra, or the solo concertos. Walter Piston's ballet *The Incredible flutist* comes from 1938 and the suite is one of the most refreshing and imaginative of all American scores.

Griffes' *Poem* with its gentle, shimmering textures is French in feeling but is thoroughly worthwhile in its own right. Joseph Mariano is an excellent soloist as he is in the more simplistic but engaging *Miniatures* of the Canadian William McCauley (born 1917). Kent Kennan's *Three Pieces* are clearly influenced by the ballet music of Stravinsky. Bergsma's ballet is rather noisy at times, and fails to be memorable, though brightly scored. Excellent performances throughout and typically vivid Eastman-Rochester sound.

American orchestral music II: MCPHEE: *Tabuh-Tabuhan (Toccata for orchestra).* SESSIONS: *The Black maskers (suite).* Virgil THOMSON: *Symphony on a hymn tune; The Feast of love* (with David Clatworthy).

(M) *** Mercury (ADD) [434 310-2].

McPhee's *Tabuh-Tabuhan*, written in 1936, uses Balinese music for its main colouring and rhythmic background. Roger Sessions' *Black maskers suite* was written as incidental music for a play by Andreyev about devil worship and the Black Mass, but it is not in the same class as, say, Prokofiev's *Scythian suite*. This is no fault of the performance or recording. The Virgil Thomson *Symphony*, although based on hymn-like material, is attractively quirky (reflecting the composer's Parisian years, the influence of Les Six, and Satie in particular). The cantata *The Feast of love* could hardly be more contrasted in its warmly flowing lyricism, a heady setting of an anonymous Latin love poem. The poet revels in the erotic joys of love, and the composer and his excellent soloist are obviously delighted by the voluptuous feeling of the words. As always the vintage Mercury sound is vivid with colour.

American music: MOORE: *Pageant of P. T. Barnum.* CARPENTER: *Adventures in a perambulator.* Bernard ROGERS: *Once upon a time (5 Fairy tales).* Burrill PHILLIPS: *Selection from McGuffey's Reader.*

(M) *** Mercury (ADD) [434 319-2].

John Alden Carpenter's suite was a favourite of American audiences before the Second World War and is diverting and often charming. The idiom is amiably innocuous but surprisingly seductive, not least the closing number, *Dreams*. Douglas Moore's *Pageant of P. T. Barnum* is hardly less accessible, with its engaging portraits of Jenny Lind, General and Mrs Tom Thumb and Joice Heth, a negress who was supposedly 160 years old!

Bernard Rogers's set of *Five Fairy tales* is scored with whimsical charm. William Holmes McGuffey's *Readers* formed the staple textbook diet of schoolchildren in mid-nineteenth-century America. The gently nostalgic second movement of Burrill Phillips's *Selection* pictures John Alden and Priscilla (who sailed on the Mayflower), and the noisy finale depicts Paul Revere's midnight ride. If this is perhaps the least memorable of the four works included here, its composer sums up rather succinctly the ethos of the whole programme. The performances are affectionate and committed throughout and the early stereo (1956–8) remarkably truthful. The above three CDs are now withdrawn in the UK.

Eastman-Rochester Orchestra or Philharmonia, Howard Hanson

'Music for quiet listening' : John LA MONTAINE: *Birds of paradise, Op. 34* (with the Composer, piano). GRIEG: *Elegiac melody: The last spring.* LIADOV: *The enchanted lake; Kikimora.* Charles Martin LOEFFLER: *2 Rhapsodies: L'Etang (The pool); La Cornemuse (The bagpipe)* (with Robert Sprenkle, oboe; Francis Tursi, viola, Armand Basile, piano). HANSON: *Fantasy variations on a theme of youth* (with David Burge, piano).

(M) *** Mercury (ADD) [434 390-2].

Under a rather deceptive title, Wilma Cozart-Fine, the Mercury producer, has gathered together an exceptionally imaginative compilation which is considerably more than the sum of its individual musical components. John La Montaine's *Birds of paradise* is eclectic but ear-tickling, and it is recorded with that glittering sharpness of focus and bold colouring for which the Mercury engineers were justly famous. With the composer at the (concertante) piano, its opening evokes Messiaen and its close Debussy. Prefaced by a quotation from Wilfred Owen, it is artfully crafted and imaginatively scored, and not too long.

A particularly eloquent account of Grieg's most beautiful *Elegiac melody* is then followed by vividly atmospheric accounts of two of Liadov's most memorable orchestral miniatures. The orchestra then stays silent while Robert Sprenkle (a piquant-timbred oboist), Francis Tursi and Armand Basile present Charles Martin Loeffler's engaging – indeed haunting – pair of rhapsodic miniatures.

Loeffler was concertmaster of the Boston Symphony but resigned from his first desk in 1903 to devote himself to composition. (He was born in Alsace and before his Boston appointment had played as a member of the court orchestra of a Russian nobleman, wintering in Nice and spending the summers at Lake Lugano!) His elegantly fastidious style is undoubtedly Gallic, and these two pieces are more subtly written and offer a far wider range of invention than their titles suggest.

The programme ends with a set of variations for piano and orchestra by Howard Hanson, full of lyrical warmth and imbued with that strongly personal, nostalgically Nordic melodic imprint which makes this splendid composer's music so striking. It is gloriously played and richly recorded.

(i) Eastman-Rochester Pops Orchestra, or (ii) Eastman Wind Ensemble, Frederick Fennell

'*Fabulous marches*': WALTON: *Orb and sceptre.* BEETHOVEN: *The ruins of Athens: Turkish march.* SIBELIUS: *Karelia suite: Alla marcia.* BORODIN: *Prince Igor: March.* SCHUBERT: *Marche militaire.* GRIEG: *Siguard Jorsalfar: Homage march.* WAGNER: *Tannhäuser: Grand march;* (ii) *Rienzi: overture. Parsifal: Good Friday music.*

(M) *** Mercury (ADD) 434 394-2.

An invigoratingly robust collection. It begins with a stirring account of Walton's *Orb and sceptre*, made all the more exciting by the brilliant Mercury sound, and the piquant little Beethoven march which follows is toe-tappingly catchy. If the *Karelia suite march* takes a little while to warm up, the following Borodin piece grips from the word go (it sounds a bit sinister too) with well-pointed vibrant strings.

Schubert's *Marche militaire* is briskly done, and the Grieg and Wagner marches are most enjoyable. Two Wagner pieces, very effectively arranged for wind band, have been added to the original LP collection, and make an excellently played and unusual bonus. The 1959/60 recording is spectacular in the Mercury manner, closely miked, a bit dry, a bit of tape hiss, but remarkable even by modern standards. If the programme appeals, go ahead.

(i) Eastman-Rochester Pops Orchestra, or (ii) London Pops Orchestra, Frederick Fennell

'*Popovers II*': (i) RACHMANINOV: *Prelude in G min.* GLIERE: *Russian Sailors' dance.* WEINBERGER: *Schwanda: Polka and Fugue.* (ii) RODGERS: *Carousel waltz.* MASSENET: *Le Cid: Aubade; Aragonaise.* BOLZONI: *Minuet.* GERMAN: *Henry VIII: Dances.* BENJAMIN: *Cotillon Suite.* ROSSINI: *William Tell: Passo a sei.* RIMSKY-KORSAKOV: *Dance of the Tumblers; Procession of the Nobles.*

(M) ** (ADD) Mercury [434 356-2].

A good collection of sweetmeats, made all the more enjoyable by the inclusion of rarities: Arthur Benjamin's *Cotillon suite* is a collection of eighteenth-century airs and ballads in modern orchestral dress, and is charmingly rustic. German's once-popular *Henry VIII dances* conjure up a similarly rural scene, whilst Bolzoni's *Minuet* is neatly elegant. Fennell's direction is vivacious throughout (though not always producing perfection in ensemble, especially in the Eastman-Rochester recordings), notably in the spectacular numbers of Rimsky-Korsakov, Glière, and Weinberger.

The two excerpts from the *Le Cid* ballet music leave one hankering after the complete suite. The one great snag to this disc is the quality of the recording - it is vivid and bright in the Mercury manner, but doesn't allow for any real pianissimos, with the upper strings inclining to shrillness in high registers, especially in the earlier 1959 American recordings (the London ones date from 1965). An enjoyable collection all the same. But like most of the Eastman discs above, this has been withdrawn in the UK.

Eastman Wind Ensemble, Frederick Fennell

American wind band music: MORTON GOULD: *West Point (Symphony for band).* GIANNINI: *Symphony No. 3.* HOVHANESS: *Symphony No. 4, Op. 165* (cond. A. Clyde Roller).

(M) ** Mercury (ADD) [434 320-2].

Fine playing, but the music here is often too inflated to give pleasure on repetition. Gould's *West Point Symphony* is in two movements, *Epitaphs* (which at 11 minutes 55 seconds is far too long) and *Marches*. The *Symphony No. 3* of Vittorio Giannini improves as it proceeds: the Scherzo and finale are the most interesting movements and the most attractively scored. Best by far is the Hovhaness *Symphony No. 4* (admirably directed by A. Clyde Roller) with its bold, rich, brass sonorities in the slower outer movements contrasting with marimba, vibraphone and other tuned percussion instruments in the central *Allegro*. Splendid sound, too.

Music from ballet and opera:
SULLIVAN/MACKERRAS: *Pineapple Poll: suite* (arr. DUTHOIT). ROSSINI/RESPIGHI: *La boutique fantasque: suite* (arr. Dan GODFREY). GOUNOD: *Faust: ballet suite* (arr. WINTERBOTTOM). WAGNER: *Lohengrin: Prelude to Act III; Bridal chorus* (arr. WINTERBOTTOM); *Elsa's procession* (arr. CAILLIET). *Das Rheingold* (arr. Dan GODFREY).

(M) ** Mercury (ADD) [434 322-2].

Although played with characteristic Eastman verve, this is essentially a programme for admirers of wind band transcriptions – here mostly traditional scorings by prominent British military band arrangers. Little of this music gains from its loss of string textures, and the famous Rossini/Respighi *Boutique fantasque* lacks sumptuousness. All this would be entertaining on the bandstand, but at home the ear craves the full orchestra.

'Hands across the sea – Marches from around the world': SOUSA: *Hands across the sea; The US Field Artillery; The Thunderer; Washington Post; King Cotton; El Capitan; The Stars and Stripes forever.* GANNE: *Father of victory (Père de la victoire).* Mariano SAN MIGUEL: *The golden ear.* TIEKE: *Old comrades.* PROKOFIEV: *March, Op. 99.* HANSSEN: *Valdres march.* Davide DELLE CESE: *Inglesina.* COATES: *Knightsbridge.* MEACHAM: *American patrol.* GOLDMAN: *On the Mall.* MCCOY: *Lights out.* KING: *Barnum and Bailey's favourite.* ALFORD: *Colonel Bogey.* KLOHR: *The Billboard.*

(M) *** Mercury (IMS) (ADD) 434 334-2.

March records don't come any better than this, and nor does military/concert-band recording. The sparkling transients at the opening of *Hands across the sea* and the peppy spirit of the playing (as with all the Sousa items, and especially *The Stars and Stripes forever*) give the listener a real lift, while the French *Father of victory* and German *Old comrades* are just as full of character. The Prokofiev is as witty as you like, and Fennell shows he understands the more relaxed swagger of the British way in *Colonel Bogey*. First rate – but, with a 65-minute programme, this needs to be taken a march or two at a time, unless you want to fall out with the neighbours – this is not a CD to reproduce gently!

'Spirit of '76': Music for fifes and drums based upon the field music of the U.S. Army: *Drum solo* (2 versions); *The camp duty; Marching tunes* (6 versions); *Service calls; Traditional fife and drum duets.* 'Ruffles and Flourishes': Music for field trumpets and drums based upon the field music of the U.S. Armed Forces: *Music for rendering honours* (3 versions); *Marching tunes and inspection pieces* (15 versions); *Drum solo; Bugle Calls for the U.S. Army* (excerpts).

(M) *** Mercury (ADD) [434 386-2].

The sound quality of this CD is remarkably vivid, often startling, as though the cavalry is just about to burst into your sitting room; it was recorded in 1956 and it a wonderful tribute to the engineering of Mercury at that time. The sixty-six tracks cover American military music from the time of the Revolutionary War to the Civil War; the first half is fife and drum music, and the second group is for trumpets and drums. This is certainly not a disc to be played all in one go, with its lack of instrumental variety and brevity of duration (one piece lasts eight seconds!).

Some collectors might feel that it is not a disc to play at all! It is, none the less, a fascinating project. Frederick Fennell takes you through the music in a detailed booklet essay and generates plenty of electricity throughout the programme with his battery of percussion instruments. An eccentrically enjoyable disc then, but for whatever reason you buy it, it is hoped that you have tolerant neighbours. As most American readers will probably know, a similar 2CD collection called '*The Civil War*' is also available is the USA [Mercury 432 591-2], which is just as startling, and has one of the most detailed booklets in the history of the Compact Disc. If the above disc appeals, then so will that.

Ehnes, James (violin), Orchestre Symphonique de Québec, Yoav Talmi

'French Showpieces: Concert Français': SAINT-SAENS: *Introduction and Rondo Capriccioso.* BERLIOZ: *Le Corsaire: Overture; Rêverie et Caprice.* CHAUSSON: *Poème.* DEBUSSY: *Tarantelle Styrienne.* MILHAUD: *Le boeuf sur le toit (cinéma fantasie).* MASSENET: *Thaïs: Méditation.*

*** Analekta Fleur de Lys FL 2 3151.

By a remarkable coincidence James Ehnes and the Quebec Symphony Orchestra under Yoave Talmi have recorded a very similar programme to the young French virtuoso, Renaud Capuçon with the Bremen Chamber Philharmonique (see above) featuring *Le boeuf sur le toit* in the weird but ear-tweaking jazzy arrangement of this Brazilian-inspired 'cinema-fantasy' which Milhaud himself made for the violinist, René Benedetti. James Eines plays the solo part with much dash and relish and the Quebec orchestra obviously enjoy its more outlandish elements and witty polytonal acerbity.

Ehnes is also a memorable soloist in the two Saint-Saëns showpieces, with dazzlingly brilliant articulation of the pyrotechnics and a seductive response to the lyrical melodies, a response which he also extends to an all but voluptuous account of Chausson's *Poème*. For all his extrovert bravura he is above all a very stylish player, which shows in the Berlioz and Massenet pieces. His timbre is not as expansive as some, but perfectly formed and nicely coloured, with a wide range of dynamic: his intonation is impeccable, his playing involved and involving, the result is very appealing indeed. The orchestra also show their paces not only in the lively accompaniments but in a wildly uninhibited account of Berlioz's *Le Corsaire Overture* and are no less exhilarating in the Debussy *Danse*.

Elizabethan serenade

'*Elizabethan serenade*' (played by (i) Slovak RSO, Andrew Penny; (ii) Czecho-Slovak RSO, Adrian Leaper; (iii) RTE Concert O or Czecho-Slovak or Slovak RSO, Ernest Tomlinson; (iv) Slovak RSO, Gary Carpenter): (i) COATES: *By the sleepy lagoon;* (ii) *London suite: Knightsbridge march. Dam Busters march.* CURZON: *Robin Hood suite: March of the bowmen.* KETELBEY: *Bells across the meadows; In a monastery garden; In a Persian market* (both with chorus). (iii) ELLIS: *Coronation Scot.* (ii) Haydn WOOD: *Sketch of a dandy;* (iii) *Roses of Picardy.* (ii) FARNON: *Westminster waltz.* (i) DUNCAN: *Little suite: March.* (iii) BINGE: *Sailing by; Elizabethan serenade.* BENJAMIN: *Jamaican rumba.* TOMLINSON: *Little serenade.* WHITE: *Puffin' Billy.* (ii) GERMAN: *Tom Jones: Waltz.* (iii) COLLINS: *Vanity Fair.* (iv) MAYERL: *Marigold.*

(BB) *** Naxos 8.553515.

This Naxos collection is in effect a super-bargain sampler for a worthwhile (full-priced) Marco Polo Light Music composer series, and it inexpensively duplicates a great deal of the repertoire included on other, similar programmes by various orchestras (see above and below). Our allegiance to their excellence remains, but the strong appeal of the present collection is obvious. The performances are a little more variable but are always very good, and those conducted by Ernest Tomlinson, who includes his own delightful *Little serenade*, are excellent, notably Edward White's *Puffin' Billy*, Arthur Benjamin's *Jamaican rumba* and the morceau by Anthony Collins. There are no complaints about the recording either. Excellent value.

English Chamber Orchestra, Daniel Barenboim

English music (with (i) Neil Black; (ii) Pinchas Zukerman): DELIUS: *On hearing the first cuckoo in spring; Summer night on the river; 2 Aquarelles; Fennimore and Gerda: Intermezzo.* VAUGHAN WILLIAMS: *Fantasia on Greensleeves;* (i) *Oboe concerto;* (ii) *The Lark ascending.* WALTON: *Henry V* (film incidental music): *Passacaglia; The death of Falstaff; Touch her soft lips and part.*

(M) *** DG (ADD) 439 529-2.

We have always had a soft spot for Barenboim's warmly evocative ECO collection of atmospheric English music. Even if the effect is not always totally idiomatic, the recordings have a warmth and allure that are wholly seductive.

English Chamber Orchestra, Richard Bonynge

'*Handel overtures and Overtures of the 18th century*': HANDEL (ed. Bonynge): *Solomon: Overture and Arrival of the Queen of Sheba. Overtures: Berenice; Teseo; Ariodante; Jephtha (Sinfonia); Esther; Rinaldo* (with *March and Battle); Sosarme; Faramondo; Judas Maccabaeus; Radamisto; Arminio; Deidamia; Scipio; Belshazzar (Sinfonia); Julius Caesar* (with Act I *Minuet); Semele: Sinfonia* (Act II). 18th-century overtures: J. M. KRAUSS: *Olympia.* Florian GASSMANN: *L'amore artigiano.* BOIELDIEU: *Zoraime et Zulnar.* Ferdinando PAER: *Sargino.* GRETRY: *Le Magnifique.* SACCHINI: *La Contadina in Corte (Sinfonia).* HAYDN: *Orlando Paladino.* SALIERI: *La fiera di Venezie.*

*** Double Decca (ADD) 466 434-2 (2).

This remarkably generous Double (150 minutes) covers the contents of three LPs from 1968–71. The Handel collection may include the *Arrival of the Queen of Sheba*, but much of the rest has been left unheard, and all credit to Bonynge for resurrecting it with such vigour. Handel's cosmopolitan qualities give such music the benefit of all the traditions of the time – French finesse, Italian elaboration, English plainspokenness. Bonynge uses his scholarship to produce results that are the very opposite of the dry-as-dust approach which can affect hard-line authenticists.

He may use double-dotting, notes inégales and added appoggiaturas beyond what other scholars would allow, but the baroque elaboration is justified in the exuberance of the end result. The rarities included here are all delightful and if the English Chamber Orchestra fields a larger body of strings than we expect today, the playing is splendidly alert, and the recording is exceptionally vivid.

The overtures by lesser names are much less inspired, but they undoubtedly have an aural fascination. *Olympia* is like Gluck without the inspiration, and *L'amore artigiano* is conventional, if with an attractive middle section. *Zoraime et Zulnar*, an early work of Boieldieu, shows something of the wit and melodic flair of the better-known overtures. But *Sargino* is altogether more striking, offering more in the way of memorable tunes, and a distinct flavour of Rossini.

Grétry's *Le Magnifique*, if somewhat optimistically titled, is also quite memorable. Unexpectedly opening with a side-drum like Auber's *Fra Diavolo*, it gradually builds up to its middle section, a hauntingly serene and rather beautiful minor-keyed passage, before concluding as it began in military style. The Salieri piece, too, is pleasingly fresh, helped like the rest by first-class advocacy from conductor, orchestra and recording engineers alike. The CD transfers are excellent.

English Chamber Orchestra, Benjamin Britten

'*Britten at the Aldeburgh festival*': BEETHOVEN: *Coriolan overture.* DEBUSSY: *Prélude à l'après-midi d'un faune.* HAYDN: *Symphony No. 95 in C min.* MENDELSSOHN: *Overture Fingal's Cave.* MOZART: *Symphony No. 35 in D (Haffner).*

(M) **(*) BBC Music (ADD) BBCB 8008-2.

Though this is a strange mixture, Britten as conductor brings to each item a striking freshness, giving a vivid idea of the electricity he conveyed in his performances at the Aldeburgh Festival. Mendelssohn's *Hebrides overture* – the item which opens the sequence – is urgent and vigorous, giving a storm-tossed view of the Hebrides, while bringing out the strength of the musical structure. That and the Beethoven overture, given a similarly alert and dramatic reading in a 1966 performance at Blythburgh church, are especially valuable, as Britten otherwise made no commercial recordings of either composer's music.

The Debussy too is wonderfully fresh, with Richard Adeney's mistily cool flute solo at the start, presenting the whole score with a rare transparency, leading to a passionate climax. The recording, also made at Blythburgh, is a degree more immediate, less atmospheric than those from the Maltings, but the extra impact is an advantage – as it is in Britten's account of the Haydn symphony, which in its C minor angularity at the start has the biting toughness of *Sturm und Drang.* Mozart's *Haffner Symphony*, recorded in the Maltings in 1972, brings sound rather less focused than on the rest of the disc, but it is an amiable performance, energetic in the outer movements, warmly affectionate in the slow movement.

English Chamber Orchestra, Raymond Leppard

'*Music of the Baroque*': Marc-Antoine CHARPENTIER: *Te Deum in D: Introduction.* ALBINONI (arr. GIAZOTTO): *Adagio in G min.* (played by La Grand Ecurie et la Chambre du Roy, Jean-Claude Malgoire). PACHELBEL: *Canon and Gigue in D.* HANDEL: *Solomon: Arrival of the Queen of Sheba. Berenice: Minuet.* GLUCK: *Orfeo ed Euridice: Dance of the Blessed Spirits.* BACH: *Orchestral suites: No. 2 in B min., BWV 1067: Badinerie; No. 3 in D, BWV 1068: Air. Cantata No. 78: Wir eilen mit schwachen* (duet; arr. Leppard). MARCELLO: *Oboe concerto in D min.: Adagio.* VIVALDI: *L'Estro armonico: Violin concerto in D, Op. 3/9: Larghetto* (with José-Luis Garcia). PURCELL: *Abdelazar: orchestral suite. The Old Bachelor: suite.*

(M) *** Sony (ADD) SMK 60161.

Although it contains a number of favourite baroque lollipops which are presented by the ECO with characteristic elegance and finish, the major items here are two suites of Purcell's theatre music. The writing is consistently inventive, and *Abdelazar* includes the tune (a Rondeau) – taken briskly here – which Britten made famous in his variations. Leppard ensures that rhythms are keenly resilient and the expressive playing is nicely judged.

The elaborately decorated account of Pachelbel's *Canon* is also very attractive, opening and closing gently but with a fine central climax, while Leppard's arrangement of the jolly *Duetto* from Bach's cantata *Jesu der du meine Seele* is equally winning. William Bennett is the highly musical flute soloist in Gluck's *Dance of the Blessed Spirits.*

The forward balance and resonant acoustic produce agreeably warm sound-quality, but this may seem too well upholstered to ears used to the Academy of Ancient Music, with the harpsichord artificially balanced and only just audible in the quieter lyrical music. However, the bright violin timbre more than compensates. The programme opens with Charpentier's fanfare *Introduction* for his *Te Deum* which is instantly familiar as the signature tune of European television. La Grand Ecurie et la Chambre du Roy, directed by Jean-Claude Malgoire, ends the 74-minute concert with a memorably fresh version of the Albinoni/Giazotto *Adagio.* Altogether this is a superior collection of its kind.

English Northern Philharmonia, David Lloyd-Jones

'*Victorian Concert Overtures*': MACFARREN: *Chevy Chase.* PIERSON: *Romeo and Juliet, Op. 86.* SULLIVAN: *Macbeth.* CORDER: *Prospero.* ELGAR: *Froissart, Op. 19.* PARRY: *Overture to an Unwritten Tragedy.* MACKENZIE: *Britannia, a Nautical Overture, Op. 52.*

(B) *** Hyp. Helios CDH 55088.

Sir George (Alexander) Macfarren (1813–87) was an English composer of Scottish descent who taught at and eventually became Principal of the Royal Academy of Music. His music was very successful in its day; he was a distinguished early editor of Purcell's *Dido and Aeneas* and of major stage works of Handel. Many of his own operas were produced in London, including one based on the story of Robin Hood.

A CD showing us a wider range of his music is overdue, meanwhile he makes a strong contribution to this collection of Victorian concert overtures with *Chevy Chase*, a spirited, tuneful piece that was admired by Mendelssohn. Pierson's *Romeo and Juliet* hardly explores its theme with any substance but Frederick Corder's *Prospero* has a certain flamboyant gravitas. Mackenzie's *Britannia* is a pot-boiler featuring a borrowed tune now famous at the Proms. Against all this and more, Elgar's *Froissart* stands out as the early masterpiece it was. The whole concert is persuasively performed by the excellent Northern Philharmonia under the versatile David Lloyd-Jones, and this reissue is even more tempting at budget price.

European Community Chamber Orchestra, Eivind Aadland

'*Concertos for the Kingdom of the Two Sicilies*': A. SCARLATTI: *Concerto No. 6 in E* (for strings). *Sinfonia di concerto grosso No. 12 in C min.* PERGOLESI: *Flute concerto in G* (both with Giulio Viscardi). PORPORA: *Cello concerto in G* (with Giovanni Sollima). DURANTE: *Concerto per quartetto No. 1 in F min.*

(B) *** Hyp. Helios CDH 55005.

This most engaging and beautifully recorded collection is centred on Naples, the musical focus of the so-called 'Two Sicilies', which once embraced Southern Italy. The programme is lightweight but played – on modern instruments – with an airy lightness. Whereas Scarlatti's E major work is a concerto grosso, the *Sinfonia di concerto* features a solo flute and matches the concerto attributed to Pergolesi in charm, when the flute playing is so nimble. In Porpora's *Cello concerto* (again with an impressive soloist) exuberantly vivacious *Allegros* frame an eloquent central *Largo*. Durante's splendid little concerto grosso has a sombre introduction and is comparatively serious in mood; even the *Amoroso* third movement, using the solo quartet, is touching rather than romantic, but the tension lifts in the gay, rhythmically pointed finale.

European Union Chamber Orchestra, Dmitri Demetriades

'*The concerto in Europe*': PAISIELLO: *Harp concerto in D.* GRETRY: *Flute concerto in C.* GARTH: *Cello concerto No. 2 in B flat.* STAMITZ: *Viola concerto in D, Op. 1.*

(B) **(*) Hyp. Helios CDH 55035.

A collection of quietly attractive and tuneful, rarely heard concertos. The Paisiello *Harp concerto*, originally a keyboard work, is graceful and elegant, with a touching central movement and a jolly, if brief, finale. Grétry's operatic leaning is felt at the opening of his *Flute concerto*, and at intervals throughout; the central movement flirts with minor keys, but it is generally a sunny work. The English are represented by a cello concerto by John Garth: it is an interesting piece with some robust cello writing, stylistically a bit earlier than the other concertos (more baroque in flavour) but no less enjoyable for that. Stamitz's *Viola concerto* is the most substantial work with some nice ideas, especially in the slow movement, and has secured a place in the viola concerto repertoire. The performances and recordings are good, though at

times a hint of blandness creeps in. The CD, which plays for just under an hour, is worth considering if the programme appeals.

Fernández, Eduardo (guitar), English Chamber Orchestra

Guitar concertos: RODRIGO: *Concierto de Aranjuez.* CASTELNUOVO-TEDESCO: *Concerto No. 1 in D, Op. 99* (both cond. Miguel Gómez Martinez). GIULIANI: *Concerto in A, Op. 30.* VIVALDI: *Concerto in D, RV 93* (both cond. George Malcolm). PONCE: *Concierto del sur.* VILLA-LOBOS: *Concerto* (both cond. Enrique Garcia Asensio). ARNOLD: *Concerto.*

(B) **(*) Double Decca 455 364-2 (2).

There are few guitar concertos to match the effectiveness of the jazz-inflected piece by Malcolm Arnold. Fernández is in his element in this work, making the haunting melody of the first movement's second subject warm and not sentimental, echoed by the glowing ECO strings, while the full depth of the blues-inspired slow movement is also movingly conveyed. Yet outer movements are fizzingly vital, the playing spikily incisive in bringing out the jazz overtones.

As we have said elsewhere, Fernández is a musician's guitarist whose playing is consistently refined and sensitive, and he is again at his most inspired in the concertos by Ponce and Villa-Lobos, creating magical evocation in the atmospheric slow movements, where Enrique Garcia Asensio is a persuasive partner.

The Giuliani and Castelnuovo-Tedesco concertos are presented with warm, refined elegance; the *Andantino* of the latter is made to sound charmingly ingenuous, and the Vivaldi too brings refinement rather than extrovert brilliance. It is in the most famous concerto of all, the Rodrigo *Concierto de Aranjuez*, that some listeners may feel Fernández falls short in his total unwillingness to treat the music as a vehicle for extrovert display. The beautiful *Adagio* is unusually ruminative, but the outer movements, too, are comparatively laid back, delicate in feeling, yet by no means lacking in vitality. We found all the music-making here most refreshing, and certainly the Decca digital recording is consistently well balanced and of the highest quality.

Flute concertos

MOZART: *Flute concertos Nos. 1 in G, K.313; 2 in D, K.314* (with William Bennett, ECO, Malcolm). VIVALDI: *Flute concerto in C min., RV 441;* J. S. BACH: *Flute concerto in G min, from BWV 1056* (with William Bennett). attrib. GRETRY: *Flute concerto in C* (with Claude Monteux) (both with ASMF, Marriner). CIMAROSA: *Concerto in G for 2 flutes* (with Aurèle & Christiane Nicolet); C. P. E. BACH: *Flute concerto in D min., Wq. 22* (with Aurèle Nicolet) (both with Stuttgart CO, Münchinger).

SALIERI: *Concerto for flute and oboe in C* (with Richard Adeney, James Brown, ECO, Bonynge).

(B) *** Double Decca (ADD) 460 302-2 (2).

William Bennett's recordings of the two Mozart concertos are second to none, and the recordings which Marriner accompanies so stylishly (Vivaldi, Bach and Grétry) are equally enjoyable. The double concertos, by Cimarosa and Salieri, bring a fair amount of elegant chatter, but there is nothing here which fails to please, and the recording is consistently of Decca's vintage analogue standard.

Foundation Philharmonic Orchestra, David Snell

WILLIAMS: *Tuba Concerto* (with Easler).
TAILLEFERRE: *Harp Concerto* (with Dall'olio).
TOMASI: *Saxophone Concerto* (with Ashby).
MAYUZUMI: *Xylophone Concertino* (with May).
**(*) ASV DCA 1126.

An enterprising, if uneven, disc of twentieth-century concertos. There cannot be too many xylophone concertos; that by the Japanese composer Toshirô Mayuzumi dates from 1965, and although no masterpiece, it has its entertaining moments, if inevitably it sounds a bit 'Tom and Jerryish' at times. John Williams wrote his *Tuba Concerto* in 1985. His attractive film-music style provides a backcloth for his unusual soloist, though the piece is musically pretty thin, especially the slow middle section, which goes on for too long. Henri Tomasi's *Saxophone Concerto* of 1949 is more substantial; its full, colourful orchestration has atmosphere and imagination, suggesting at times a score for a *film noir* of the 1940s. But perhaps the best concerto here is Germaine Tailleferre's unpretentious work for harp of 1928, a piece that mixes impressionistic and classical influences with much charm. The performances cannot be faulted, the recording is good, and if the strings occasionally sound a little undernourished, the actual balance is well judged.

François, Samson (piano)

LISZT: *Piano Concertos Nos. 1 in E flat; 2 in A* (with Philh. O, Silvestri). PROKOFIEV: *Piano Concertos Nos. 3 in C, Op. 26; 5 in G, Op. 55* (with Philh. O, Rowicki); *Piano Sonata No. 7 in B flat, Op. 83.* SCHUMANN: *Piano Concerto in A min. Op. 54* (with French Nat. R. O, Kletzki).

(N) (B) *(*) EMI (ADD) CZS5 74324-2 (2).

Samson François enjoyed legendary status in his native France, although his undoubted talents were offset by a tendency to disregard dynamic markings under piano and sometimes under forte, which made for unsubtle results. The Schumann, recorded in 1958, conveys little of the freshness or delicacy of this masterpiece. We have no recollection of either the Liszt or the Prokofiev *Fifth Concerto*, recorded in 1960 and 1963

respectively, appearing in the UK. Muscular and decently recorded performances, but there were much finer accounts of all these pieces in the catalogue at the time. Recommendable only to admirers of François.

(i) French Radio Orchestra, (ii) Philharmonia Orchestra, Igor Markevitch

PROKOFIEV: (i) *Love for 3 Oranges (suite), Op. 33;* (ii) *Le pas d'acier (suite), Op. 41;* (i) *Scythian suite, Op. 20.* STRAVINSKY: (i) *Le baiser de la fée (Divertimento);* (ii) *Petrushka: suite;* (i) *Pulcinella (suite);* (ii) *The Rite of spring.*

(B) (**(*)) EMI mono/stereo CZS5 69674-2 (2).

Igor Markevitch was the last and most unusual of Diaghilev's protégés and married the daughter of his first, Nijinsky. Markevitch's career initally took off as a composer and pianist. However, after the end of the Second World War, during which he served in the Italian resistance, he gave up composition to concentrate on conducting full time. He was an excellent ballet conductor whose cool elegance can be readily observed in these recordings. His mono (1952) account of *Le Sacre* with the Philharmonia Orchestra caused quite a stir in its day, but this 1959 stereo re-make, undertaken at very short notice when Klemperer was taken ill, has much to recommend it, even if the former has perhaps the greater atmosphere.

Markevitch gets good results from the Philharmonia Orchestra throughout and a very professional response from the French Radio Orchestra, which was in better shape than the Conservatoire Orchestra at this period. *Le pas d'acier* is a rarity these days and is hardly ever encountered in the concert hall; it sounds to excellent effect here. The Paris recordings come from 1954–5 and the Philharmonia *Petrushka* and *Pas d'acier* from 1954. Only the 1959 *Le Sacre* is in stereo.

Fröst, Martin (clarinet), Malmö Symphony Orchestra, Lan Shui

Clarinet concertos: ARNOLD: *Concerto No. 2, Op. 112.* COPLAND: *Concerto for clarinet and string orchestra, with harp and piano.* HINDEMITH: *Concerto.*

*** BIS CD 893.

Three first-class performances of three outstanding twentieth-century concertos, all originally written for Benny Goodman. Fröst is an eloquently spontaneous soloist, stealing in gently against a magical orchestral pianopianissimo at the opening of the Copland; and he is equally at home in Hindemith's more sinewy lyricism. Both he and the persuasive conductor, Lan Shui, obviously relish the verve and energy of the Malcolm Arnold concerto and they play the slow movement very seductively, before romping away into the rooty-tooty finale, with its audacious orchestral whoops, the kind of music to bring the house down at a Promenade concert. The recording is splendid in every way and this can receive the strongest recommendation.

Galway, James (flute)

'*Pachelbel's Canon and other Baroque favourites*' (with various orchestras & conductors): VIVALDI: *Concerto in D (Il Gardellino), Op. 10/3: 1st & 2nd movts. Four Seasons: Spring* (arr. GALWAY). TELEMANN: *Suite for strings in A min.: Réjouissance; Polonaise.* PACHELBEL: *Canon.* HANDEL: *Sonatas in A min., Op. 1/4: 4th movt; in F, Op. 1/11: Siciliana; Allegro* (both with Sarah Cunningham, Philip Moll). *Solomon: Arrival of the Queen of Sheba* (arr. GERHARDT). *Messiah: Pifa (Pastoral Symphony). Xerxes: Largo.* BACH: *Suites Nos. 2 in B min., BWV 1067: Minuet & Badinerie; 3 in D, BWV 1068: Air. Trio sonata No. 2 in G, BWV 1039: 4th movt* (with Kyung Wha Chung, Moll, Welsh); *Flute sonatas Nos. 2 in E flat, BWV 1031: Siciliano* (with Maria Graf, harp); *4 in C, BWV 1033: 2nd movt* (arr. GERHARDT for flute & O). *Concerto in E min., BWV 1059/35* (ed. Radeke): *3rd movt.* ALBINONI: *Adagio.* QUANTZ: *Concerto in C: Finale.* MARAIS: *Le Basque* (arr. GALWAY/GERHARDT).

*** BMG/RCA DDD/ADD 09026 61928-2.

If the famous Bach *Air* from BWV 1068 is spun out somewhat romantically and the *Siciliano* from BWV 1031 (with harp accompaniment) is too solemn, Handel's famous *Largo* is gloriously managed, completely vocal in feeling. Galway certainly dominates Pachelbel's *Canon* in a way not intended by the composer, but his elegant line and simple divisions on the lovely theme are very agreeable.

Any of the composers included here would surely have been amazed at the beauty of his tone and the amazing technical facility, always turned to musical effect. He is a wonderful goldfinch in Vivaldi's Op. 10/3, while Gerhardt's arrangement of Handel's *Arrival of the Queen of Sheba*, which exchanges oboes for flutes, is ear-tickling. The engaging Quantz concerto movement is as sprightly in the strings (of the Württemberg Chamber Orchestra) as it is in the felicitously decorated solo part. The Bach and Handel sonata excerpts are refreshing and the (Handel) Siciliana from Op. 1/11 is matched in pastoral charm by the beautiful account of the *Pifa* from *Messiah*, but is not more engaging than the lollipop of the whole concert: the delicious *Le Basque* of Marais, one of Galway's most endearing arrangements. The recording naturally balances the soloist forward, but the sound is first class throughout. This is a full-price record but it includes 68 minutes of entertainment, perfect for a fine summer evening.

'*Dances for flute*' (with Nat. PO, Gerhardt or Mancini; I Solisti di Zagreb, Scimone; The Chieftains; RPO, Myung-Whun Chung; and other

artists): GODARD: *Waltz.* CHOPIN: *Minute waltz in D flat, Op. 64/1.* DEBUSSY: *La plus que lente; Petite suite: Ballet.* J. S. BACH: *Suite No. 2, BWV 1067: Polonaise; Menuet; Badinerie.* TRAD.: *Crowley's reel; Brian Boru's march; Belfast hornpipe.* KHACHATURIAN: *Waltz; Sabre dance.* MERCADANTE: *Concerto in D: Polacca.* MANCINI: *Pie in the face polka; Pennywhistle jig.* RODRIGO: *Fantasia para un gentilhombre: Canario.* BENJAMIN: *Jamaican rhumba.* MOZART: *Divertimento in D, K.334: Menuetto.* VIVALDI: *Concerto in D (Il Gardellino): Cantabile.* DINICU: *Hora staccato.* GOSSEC: *Tambourin.* KREISLER: *Schön Rosmarin.*

*** BMG/RCA (ADD) 09026 60917-2.

Galway can certainly make his flute dance – often in scintillating fashion. This collection is essentially for the sweet-toothed, but its consummate artistry is remarkable: just sample the delicious opening Godard *Waltz*. The traditional pieces are especially enjoyable, and two real lollipops are the Mercadante *Polacca* (from a virtually forgotten concerto) and the (Beechamesque) Gossec *Tambourin*. We also have a soft spot for Mancini's *Pennywhistle jig*. Good sound and 64 minutes of music.

'*Music for my Little Friends*' (with London Mozart Players, & Phillip Moll, piano): MOZART: *Piano Sonata in A, K.331: Finale: Rondo alla Turca* (arr. for flute & orchestra). COULTER: *Lament for the Wild Geese.* IBERT: *The Little White Donkey.* SAINT-SAENS: *Carnival of the Animals: The Swan; Romance.* FAURE: *Pavane, Op. 50; Pelléas et Mélisande: Sicilienne; Dolly: Berceuse.* ROTA: *5 Easy Pieces.* GAUBERT: *Madrigal.* RAVEL: *Pièce en forme de habañera.* TRAD.: *Londonderry Air.* GLUCK: *Orfeo ed Euridice: Dance of the Blessed Spirits.* DEBUSSY: *Mandoline.*

*** RCA 09026 63725-2.

James Galway phrases so musically and stylishly that surely no musical child could fail to respond to this programme, especially the engaging French items by Ibert (neatly arranged), Fauré, Gaubert (a charming *Madrigal*), Debussy and Ravel. In the latter's *Pièce en forme de habañera* and the Saint-Saëns *Romance* Philip Moll accompanies sensitively on the piano, as he does in the *Five Easy* (Children's) *Pieces* of Nino Rota, with which his intended audience will surely identify, especially the portrait of *La chiocca* ('The Mother hen'). The *Londonderry Air*, appropriately, has a harp accompaniment, the rest of the programme features the orchestra, and only in the Mozart *Alla Turca* does one feel that the arranged tuttis are a little coarse alongside the felicitous fluting. But on the whole this programme serves its purpose admirably.

Il Giardino Armonico, Giovanni Antonini

'The Italian Bach in Vienna': J. S. BACH: Double Clavier Concerto in C, BWV 1061; Triple Clavier Concerto in D min., BWV 1061 (both with Katia and Marielle Labèque, fortepianos; BWV 1061 also with Ottavio Danone, harpsichord). C. P. E. BACH: Sinfonia in G, Wq.182/1. VIVALDI: Il cimento dell'armonia e dell'inventione: Violin Concerto in D min., Op. 8/7, RV.242 (with Enrico Onofri, violin).

**(*) TDK DVD DV-BACON.

The Musikverein provides at attractive backcloth and an appealing ambience for this programme which centres on the music of Bach and Vivaldi. The novelty here is the performance of Bach's Triple Keyboard Concerto on a pair of fortepianos plus a harpsichord, which works surprisingly well. With a microphone given to each soloist, the engineers are able to achieve a satisfactory balance, but the snag in the Double Concerto, with such a close balance and the two keyboards side-by-side, is that the movement of Bach's solo line from one fortepiano to another is achieved electronically, and the effect is curiously unnatural. Moreover the close balance reveals an obbligato vocalise from one of the soloists, very audible in the Adagio of BWV 1061. The performances are certainly brilliant, with both finales very lively indeed. Enrico Onofri (the orchestra's leader) also plays with much bravura in the Vivaldi Concerto especially in his first movement cadenza, but his performance is without charm.

Il Giardino Armonico and its young and dynamic conductor, Giovanni Antonini, have made their name by a bravura period-instrument style, and that is very much to the fore in the G major Sinfonia of C. P. E. Bach, visually overflowing with energy, with sharply articulated, very brisk outer movements, and staccato articulation in the Poco Adagio. But their ensemble cannot be faulted and no one could suggest their music-making was lacking in spirit.

CASTELLO: Sonata concertante, Op. 2, Nos. 4 & 10. MARINI: Sonata, 'Sopra la Monica'. MERULA: Ciaconna. SPADI: Dominuziono; SOPRA: Anchor che co'l partire. VIVALDI: Lute Concertos in D, RV 93; in D (Il giardellino), Op. 10/3. Recorder Concerto in G min. (La notte), RV 104.

* Arthaus DVD 100 010.

Il Giardino Armonico is a brilliant group which performs this repertoire with stunning virtuosity and imagination. Musically, there are no quarrels here except, perhaps, for the over-bright sound. Moreover, the DVD facilities offer the scores, though when they are superimposed the visual image is masked – indeed, it virtually disappears. The text in the Vivaldi is, of course, the Ricordi short score. Although the performances are expert enough, though very brightly recorded, the visual direction is irritatingly hyperac-

tive. The musicians are superimposed on all sorts of Sicilian backdrops but never for more than a few seconds at a time. The empty 'cleverness' of the director, who cannot leave anything to speak for itself, is very tiresome to start with and insufferable after a few minutes. Two stars for the brilliant if exhibitionist music-making, but none for the distracting visual antics.

Glennie, Evelyn (percussion)

'Rebounds' (with Scottish CO, Paul Daniel): MILHAUD: Concerto pour batterie et petite orchestre. RICHARD RODNEY BENNETT: Concerto for solo percussion and chamber orchestra. ROSAURO: Concierto para marimba e orquesta de cordas. MIYOSHI: Concerto for marimba and strings.

*** BMG/RCA 09026 61277-2.

Here is a chance for Glennie to show what she can do with more ambitious concert music – although, of course, there are popular influences and jazz rhythms in the works by both Richard Rodney Bennett and Rosauro. Bennett even offers an aleatory element for the percussionist. But his concerto is imaginatively thought out and has plenty of atmosphere and colour. The Milhaud concerto (its title sounds so much more inviting in French) is a most spontaneous piece, without fireworks but very effectively written.

Other than that, the most enjoyable work here is the tuneful four-movement concerto by the Brazilian Ney Rosauro, with a haunting Lament for the slow movement, an engaging Dança, followed by an imaginative finale. The Miyoshi Marimba concerto is in a kaleidoscopic single movement. All these works are brilliantly played and the collection is much more diverse and entertaining than one might expect. The recording engineers have a field day yet they do not try to create exaggerated effects.

Gould, Glenn (piano)

Glenn Gould Edition

BACH: Harpsichord concertos Nos. 1-5; 7, BWV 1052-6 & BWV 1058 (with Columbia SO, Bernstein (No. 1) or Golschmann).

(M) (**) Sony mono (No. 1)/stereo SM2K 52591 (2).

BACH: Fugues, BWV 953 & BWV 961; Fughettas, BWV 961 & BWV 902; 6 Little Preludes, BWV 933-8; 6 Partitas, BWV 825-30; Preludes, BWV 902 & 902/1a; Prelude and fugue, BWV 895; 2 Preludes & fughettas, BWV 899-900.

(M) (**) Sony (ADD) SM2K 52597 (2).

BACH: Goldberg variations, BWV 988; Three-part Inventions, BWV 788-801.

(M) (**) Sony (ADD) SMK 52685 (live recordings from Salzburg and Moscow).

BACH: *Goldberg variations, BWV 988; Well-tempered Clavier: Fugues in E, BWV 878; F sharp min., BWV 883.*

(M) (**(*)) Sony mono SMK 52594 (1955 recording).
(M) (**) Sony SMK 52619.

BACH: *15 Two-part Inventions; 15 Three-part Inventions, BWV 772-801.*

(M) (**) Sony (ADD) SMK 52596.

BACH: *Well-tempered Clavier, Book I, Preludes and fugues Nos. 1-24, BWV 846-69.*

(M) (**) Sony (ADD) SM2K 52600 (2).

BACH: *Well-tempered Clavier, Book II, Preludes and Fugues Nos. 25-48, BWV 870-93.*

(M) (**) Sony (ADD) SM2K 52603 (2).

BACH: *Well-tempered Clavier: Preludes and fugues in E, BWV 878; in F sharp min., BWV 883.* HANDEL: *Harpsichord suites Nos. 1-4, HWV 426-9.*

(M) (**) Sony mono/stereo SMK 52590.

BACH: *Sonata for violin and harpsichord No. 4 in C min., BWV 1017.* BEETHOVEN: *Violin sonata No. 10 in G, Op. 96.* SCHOENBERG: *Phantasy for violin and piano, Op. 47* (all with Yehudi Menuhin).

(M) (**) Sony mono SMK 52688.

BEETHOVEN: *Piano concertos Nos. 1-5* (with Columbia SO, Golschmann (No.1); Columbia SO, Bernstein (Nos. 2-3); NYPO, Bernstein (No. 4); America SO, Stokowski (No. 5)).

(M) (***) Sony (ADD) SM3K 52632 (3).

BEETHOVEN: *7 Bagatelles, Op. 33; 6 Bagatelles, Op. 126; 6 Variations in F, Op. 34; 15 Variations with fugue in E flat (Eroica), Op. 35; 32 Variations on an original theme in C min., WoO 80.*

(M) (**) Sony (ADD) SM2K 52646 (2).

BEETHOVEN: *Piano sonatas Nos. 24 in F sharp, Op. 78; 29 in B flat (Hammerklavier).*

(M) (**) Sony (ADD) SMK 52645.

BIZET: *Nocturne No. 1 in F; Variations chromatiques.* GRIEG: *Piano sonata in E min., Op. 7.* SIBELIUS: *Kyllikki (3 Lyric pieces), Op. 41; Sonatinas Nos. 1-3, Op. 67/1-3.*

(M) (**(*)) Sony (ADD) SM2K 52654 (2).

BRAHMS: (i) *Piano quintet in F min., Op. 34.* SCHUMANN: (ii) *Piano quartet in E flat, Op. 47* (with (i) Montreal Qt; (ii) Juilliard Qt (members)).

(M) (**) Sony (ADD) SMK 52684.

BRAHMS: *4 Ballades, Op. 10; Intermezzi, Op. 76/6-7; Op. 116/4; Op. 117/1-3; Op. 118/1, 2 & 6; Op. 119/1; 2 Rhapsodies, Op. 79.*

(M) (**) Sony ADD/DDD SM2K 52651 (2).

HAYDN: *Piano sonata in E flat, Hob XVI:49.*
MOZART: *Piano concerto No. 24 in C min., K.491* (with CBC SO, Walter Susskind); *Fantasia (Prelude) and fugue in C, K.394; Sonata in C, K.330.*

(M) (**) Sony (ADD) SMK 52626.

HINDEMITH: (i) *Alto horn sonata in E flat;* (ii) *Bass tuba sonata;* (i) *Horn sonata;* (iii) *Trombone sonata;* (iv) *Trumpet sonata* (with (i) Mason Jones; (ii) Abe Torchinsky; (iii) Henry Charles Smith; (iv) Gilbert Johnson).

(M) (**) Sony (ADD) SM2K 52671 (2).

HINDEMITH: *Piano sonatas Nos. 1-3.*

(M) (**(*)) Sony (ADD) SMK 52670.

LISZT: *Concert paraphrases of Beethoven's Symphonies Nos. 5 in C min.; 6 in F (Pastoral): 1st movt.*

(M) (**) Sony (ADD) SMK 52636.

LISZT: *Concert paraphrase of Beethoven's Symphony No. 6 in F (Pastoral).*

(M) (ᴬ) Sony (ADD) SMK 52637.

RICHARD STRAUSS: *Piano sonata in B min., Op. 5; Enoch Arden, Op. 38; 5 Pieces, Op. 3;* (i) *Ophelia Lieder, Op. 67* ((i) with Elisabeth Schwarzkopf).

(M) (**(*)) Sony DDD/ADD SM2K 52657 (2).

Contemporary music: MORAWETZ: *Fantasy in D min.* ANHALT: *Fantasia.* HETU: *Variations, Op. 8.* PENTLAND: *Ombres.* VALEN: *Piano sonata No. 2.*

(M) (**) Sony (ADD) SMK 52677.

Consort music: BYRD: *1st Pavane & Galliard.* GIBBONS: *Fantasy in C min.; Allemande; Lord Salisbury's pavane & galliard.* BYRD: *Hugh Ashton's ground; 6th Pavane & galliard; A Voluntary; Selliger's round.* SWEELINCK: *Fantasia in D (Fantasia cromatica).*

(M) (**) Sony stereo/mono SMK 52589.

GOULD: *Lieberson madrigal; So you want to write a fugue* (McFadden, Keller, Fouchécourt, Van Kamp, Naoumoff, Ens., Rivvenq); *String quartet No. 1* (Monsaingeon, Apap, Caussé, Meunier); *2 Pieces for piano; Piano sonata* (unfinished) (Naoumoff); *Sonata for bassoon and piano* (Marchese, Naoumoff).

(M) (**) Sony SMK 47814.

Glenn Gould is an artist who excites such strong passions that guidance is almost superfluous. For his host of admirers these discs are self-recommending; those who do not respond to his pianism will not be greatly interested in this edition. For long he enjoyed cult status, enhanced rather than diminished by his absence from the concert hall. There is too much that is wilful and eccentric in these performances for any of them to rank as a sole first recommendation. Yet if for his devotees virtually all his recordings are indispensable, for the unconverted a judicious approach is called for.

Generally speaking, his earlier recordings are to be recommended to those who are sceptical as to his gifts. There is nothing eccentric about the early recordings. His 1957 performances of the Beethoven *Second Piano concerto* with Ladislav Slovák in Leningrad and Bernstein in New York are first rate in every respect. He leaves everything to his fingers rather than his head, and his performance is eminently sensitive. We have commented on these individually and on the set of Beethoven concertos, made with Golschmann, Bernstein and Stokowski. (The *C major Concerto*, with Vladimir Golschmann, is particularly exhilarating, and both this and the C minor with Bernstein command admiration.) There is no questioning Gould's keyboard wizardry or his miraculous control of part-writing in Bach, for which he had much intuitive feeling. The majority of his Bach discs evidence strong personality and commitment throughout, even though the tiresome vocalise (which became an increasing source of frustration, particularly later in his recording career) is a strain. The famous 1955 38-minute repeatless mono recording of the *Goldberg* sounds more of a curiosity nowadays, but it is nothing if not a remarkable feat of digital prestidigitation.

Gould possessed a fine and inquiring mind and both a sharp and an original intellect, as readers of his strongly recommended collection of his writings on music, *The Glenn Gould Reader*, will know. (Judging from the sampler Sony CD, widely available also on videocassette and laserdisc and containing *So you want to write a fugue* and some of his CBC television appearances, his sense of humour was less sophisticated, in fact pretty cringe-making.) His enterprise and intellectual curiosity, however, inspire respect. Everything he does is the result of artistic conviction, whether it is championing Bizet's *Nocturne* and *Variations chromatiques* ('a giddy mix of Chopin and Chabrier') or Schoenberg. He had great feeling for Hindemith and championed this composer at a time when he had become comparatively unfashionable, and likewise *Kyllikki* and the three *Sonatinas* of Sibelius. In fact his tastes are always unpredictable: Strauss's *Enoch Arden*, Grieg's early *Sonata*, and the *Second Piano sonata* of the Norwegian 12-note master, Fartein Valen. And who, nowadays, would dare to play Byrd and Gibbons on the piano?

Sony deserve congratulations on this formidable enterprise, and collectors will note that the sound-quality of the originals has in the main been much improved - as indeed it needed to be. However, the sound generally has insufficient freshness and bloom, and the eccentricity (some might say egocentricity) of some of Gould's readings and the accompanying vocalise are often quite insupportable.

Grafin, Philippe (violin), Ulster Orchestra, Thierry Fischer

'*Rare French Works for Violin and Orchestra*': FAURE: *Violin Concerto in D min., Op. 14.* SAINT-SAENS: *Morceau de concert, Op. 62.* LALO: *Fantaisie norvégienne.* GUIRAUD: *Caprice.* LALO: *Guitarre, Op. 28.* CANTELOUBE: *Poème.*

*** Hyp. CDA 67294.

This attractive compilation is worth having for the Fauré *Concerto* alone, which the composer never completed. The existing two movements are full of delightful ideas and Philippe Grafin is a most sympathetic exponent. The Saint-Saëns *Morceau* is a working of the *Caprice brillant* for violin and piano and shows all the composer's tuneful facility and flair. Lalo's *Fantaisie norvègienne* uses what he thought was a folksong, but was in fact a melody of Grieg's – and a very delightful one too. *Guitarre* is essentially an instrumental piece, engaging enough, and orchestrated by Pierné for his own use as an encore. It recalls the *Symphonie espagnole*, but is altogether slighter. The surprise here is the two movement *Caprice* of Ernest Guiraud, who we remember as the composer of recitatives for Bizet's *Carmen*. The gently seductive *Andante* is followed by a sparkling *Allegro appassionato*, after the fashion of the Saint-Saëns' *Introduction and Rondo Capriccioso*. The Canteloube *Poème* is passionately laguorous, richly orchestrated: its composer was afraid his scoring was too opulent and would drown its soloist, but that is not a problem here and one revels in its sumptuousess and orchestral colour. Altogether a most worthwhile collection, very well played and recorded.

Grumiaux, Arthur (violin)

'*Favourite violin concertos*' (with (i) Concg. O; (ii) New Philh. O; (iii) Sir Colin Davis; (iv) Bernard Haitink; (v) Jan Krenz): BEETHOVEN: (i; iii) *Concerto in D*; (i; iv) *Romance No. 2 in F*. (ii; iii) BRAHMS: *Concerto in D*. (ii; v) MENDELSSOHN: *Concerto in E min.* TCHAIKOVSKY: *Concerto in D*.

⭐ (B) *** Ph. Duo (ADD) 442 287-2 (2).

Another extraordinary Duo bargain set from Philips, containing some of the great Belgian violinist's very finest performances. He recorded the Beethoven twice for Philips, and this is the later account from the mid-1970s with Sir Colin Davis. Grumiaux imbues this glorious concerto with a spirit of classical serenity and receives outstanding support from Davis. If we remember correctly, the earlier account with Galliera had slightly more of a sense of repose and spontaneous magic in the slow movement, but the balance of advantage between the two versions is very difficult to resolve as the Concertgebouw recording is fuller and richer and (even if there is not absolute orchestral clarity) there is less background noise.

The performance of the Brahms, it goes without saying, is full of insight and lyrical eloquence, and again Sir Colin Davis lends his soloist the most sympathetic support. The (1973) account of the Mendelssohn is characteristically polished and refined, and Grumiaux, even if he does not wear his heart on his sleeve, plays very beautifully throughout: the pure poetry of the playing not only lights up the *Andante* but is heard at its most magical in the key moment of the downward arpeggio which introduces the second subject of the first movement.

Similarly in the Tchaikovsky his playing – if less overtly emotional than some – has the usual aristocratic refinement and purity of tone to recommend it. His reading is beautifully paced and has a particularly fine slow movement; both here and in the brilliant finale he shows superb aplomb and taste. With excellent accompaniments in both works from Krenz, this adds to the attractions of the set, for the 1970s recording has a wide range and is firmly focused in its CD format.

Concert (with Lamoureux Orchestra of Paris, Manuel Rosenthal): LALO: *Symphonie espagnole, Op. 21.* SAINT-SAENS: *Introduction et rondo capriccioso, Op. 28; Havanaise, Op. 83.* CHAUSSON: *Poème, Op. 25.* RAVEL: *Tzigane.*

**(*) Australian Ph. Eloquence (ADD) 462 579-2.

A worthwhile collection of French music. Grumiaux's playing is always individual, not showy or extrovert, but with plenty of colour and relaxed bravura. The orchestral support is lively and sympathetic, and lets the soloist dominate in the right way. The Lamoureux Orchestra is not the most refined of instruments, but is reasonably stylish, with a French timbre which is nice to hear in these conformist times. The recording is a little thin sounding (it dates form the mid 1960s), but is acceptable and well balanced.

Gutman, Michael (violin), Royal Philharmonic Orchestra, José Serebrier

'Four seasons': MILHAUD: *Spring concertino.* RODRIGO: *Concierto d'estio (Summer concerto).* CHAMINADE **(orch. Paul Ut):** *Autumn.* SEREBRIER: *Winter concerto.*

**(*) ASV CDDCA 855.

This is a well-conceived anthology that went a bit awry. Milhaud's *Spring concertino* is a fresh one-movement piece with a whiff of jazz *à la française*, and Rodrigo's *Concierto de estio*, conceived in the manner of Vivaldi, is the composer's own favourite among his many concertos; the central movement is an engaging *Sicilienne* with variations. Chaminade's *Autumn* is the composer's arrangement for violin and piano of her most successful lollipop, which another hand has subsequently orchestrated. The snag is that the conductor here, José Serebrier, has produced an undistinguished

and rather wild concerto for *Winter*, even quoting themes associated with that season from Haydn, Glazunov and Tchaikovsky: the result is a bit of a hotch-potch. Performances and recording do not let the side down, but ASV need to reissue this with a further winter appendix – there is plenty of room, for the CD plays for only around 54 minutes.

Hallé Orchestra, Sir John Barbirolli

BAX: *Oboe Quintet* **(arr. Barbirolli; with Evelyn Rothwell).** VAUGHAN WILLIAMS: *Symphony No.8 in D min.* DELIUS: *On hearing the First Cuckoo in Spring.* RAWSTHORNE: *Street Corner Overture.* WALTON: *Coronation March: Crown Imperial.* ELGAR: *Land of Hope and Glory* **(with Kathleen Ferrier & Hallé Choir).** *National Anthem* **(with Trumpeters & Band of Royal Military School of Music, Kneller Hall).**

(M) (***) BBC mono/stereo BBCL 4100-2.

On the BBC Legends label these radio recordings of British music, all but one from the late 1960s, offer a delightful selection of Barbirolli favourites, including his own arrangement of Bax's *Oboe Quintet* for oboe and strings, with his wife Evelyn Rothwell as the expressive soloist. Written for Rothwell's teacher, Leon Goossens, it originally involved writing for the string quartet that Barbirolli found awkward with its double-stopping, something that his arrangement clarifies. Vaughan Williams's *Eighth Symphony*, dedicated to him as 'Glorious John', was always a work he specially enjoyed, and this live performance from a 1967 Prom is both broader and warmer than his studio recording, if not quite so clean of texture. That and Rawsthorne's rumbustious *Overture, Street Corner*, are the only stereo recordings here. Walton's *Crown Imperial* is also given with plenty of panache, and Delius's *First Cuckoo* could not be more warmly done. The National Anthem, recorded at the same Royal Albert Hall concert, is an oddity with voices inaudible, and *Land of Hope and Glory*, also taken very slowly, is a much older recording, taken from a severely damaged shellac disc, with Kathleen Ferrier the radiant soloist. This was recorded at the opening of the rebuilt Free Trade Hall in Manchester in 1951.

BEETHOVEN: *Symphony No. 7 in A, Op. 92.* MOZART: *Symphony No. 35 in D (Haffner);* WAGNER: *Siegfried Idyll.*

(M) (**(*)) BBC Legends stereo/mono BBCL 4076-2

Barbirolli never made a commercial recording of Beethoven's *Seventh Symphony* (in fact he recorded only Nos. 1, 3, 5 and 8), so this Festival Hall account is more than welcome. One senses straight away that there is a strong personality in command, and one that is wholly dedicated to Beethoven. In this mighty work Sir John is totally straightforward and unfussy, yet attentive to every detail of phrasing, and there is a fine sense of momentum. The only slight reservation lies in the finale, which is not quite headlong enough. But this is a performance of stature, and the sound is remarkably good for its period and venue: the balance is excellently judged with every detail coming across, even if tuttis sound a bit fierce. The Mozart symphony has plenty of spirit and warmth; tempi are brisk but the phrasing is always alive. The Albert Hall sound, though not as finely detailed or as present as in the Beethoven, is more than acceptable. Sir John also never recorded the *Haffner Symphony* for his record companies, nor did he commit the *Siegfried Idyll* to disc. As you would expect, he shapes it beautifully, though the playing is generally less polished than in either of the symphonies. The strings sound vinegary at times although their quality and timbre were not flattered by the acoustic of the BBC Manchester Studios. The mono recording is less rich and detail less transparent. All the same, this set is a valuable addition to the Barbirolli discography.

'Barbirolli at the opera': RICHARD STRAUSS: *Die Liebe der Danae* (symphonic fragments; arr. Clemens Krauss); *Der Rosenkavalier: suite.* WEBER: *Der Freischütz; Euryanthe: overtures.* VERDI: *La Traviata: Preludes to Acts I & III.* MOZART: *Le nozze di Figaro overture.* WAGNER: *Lohengrin: Preludes to Acts I & III.*

(M) (***) Dutton Lab. mono CDSJB 1004.

Hearing these glowing performances, full of Barbirollian expressiveness and panache, brings it home how sad it is that he recorded so few complete operas in the studio. It is tantalizing to realize what a great interpreter of *Rosenkavalier* he would have been, when his account of the much-maligned suite is so warm and persuasive, a première recording of 1946. Every item demonstrates the quality of the Hallé as trained by Barbirolli in the immediate post-war period, notably the strings. The Dutton transfers are first rate, though the original recordings used here were obviously more limited than those on some earlier Barbirolli Society issues, and this collection is too highly priced.

'Hallé favourites – 2': SUPPE: *Overture The Beautiful Galatea.* TURINA: *Danzas fantásticas.* CHABRIER: *España.* LEHAR: *Gold and silver waltz.* SIBELIUS: *Valse triste.* WALDTEUFEL: *The Skaters' waltz.* GRIEG: *Two Elegiac melodies; Peer Gynt suite No. 1.*

(M) (***) Dutton Lab. mono/stereo CDSJB 1013.

Some of the recordings here have an EMI mono source from the 1950s; the rest, including the Sibelius and Grieg items (which are particularly warmly played), were early stereo with a Pye source. All the transfers are up to Dutton standard and Chabrier's *España* and the two waltzes have plenty of lilt and sparkle. It is a pity that - as it is sponsored by the Barbirolli Society - this disc is comparatively expensive.

'Barbirolli's English Music Album': BARBIROLLI: *An Elizabethan Suite.* BAX: *The Garden of Fand.*

BUTTERWORTH: *A Shropshire Lad.* ELGAR: *Three Bavarian Dances: Lullaby; Enigma Variations.* IRELAND: *The Forgotten Rite; Mai-Dun; These Things Shall Be* (with Parry Jones, tenor, Hallé Choir). PURCELL (arr. BARBIROLLI): *Suite for Strings.* VAUGHAN WILLIAMS: *Fantasia on Greensleeves; Fantasia on a Theme by Thomas Tallis.*

(M) (***) Dutton mono CDSJB 1022 (2).

The long-buried treasure here is Barbirolli's very first recording of Elgar's *Enigma Variations*, never previously issued. As Michael Kennedy's authoritative note explains, it was recorded in Manchester in May 1947, only months before he went on to make his first published recording in October of that year, an inexplicable duplication, when if anything this earliest version is even finer than the published one, certainly more spontaneously expressive at key points such as *Nimrod* and the finale variation, while the opening statement of the theme is more flowing and less emphatic.

There is much else to cherish on the two discs for any devotee of English music, let alone Barbirolli enthusiasts. The two Vaughan Williams items, the *Tallis Fantasia* dating from 1946 and *Greensleeves* from 1948, both recorded in Houldsworth Hall, Manchester, have never previously appeared on CD, and both are very welcome. In mono sound they may be less rich-textured than Barbirolli's stereo remakes, but the *Tallis Fantasia*, featuring a vintage quartet of Hallé principals, separates the quartet more clearly from the main body than the version with the Sinfonia of London, and again is more warmly expressive. The extra lightness of *Greensleeves* too sounds more easily spontaneous.

Those performances are contained on the second of the two discs, with the shorter works of Bax, Butterworth and Ireland on the first. The exotic orchestration of Bax's *The Garden of Fand* is well-detailed, as are the evocative textures of the Butterworth orchestral rhapsody, recorded for Pye like Barbirolli's own *Elizabethan Suite*, all of them stereo recordings. The EMI mono recordings of the two Ireland orchestral pieces, dating from earlier, have comparable weight. In the Ireland choral work, *These Things Shall Be*, the dynamic range is again wider than one expects in mono recordings of this vintage. The performances all have a passionate thrust typical of Barbirolli, with the tenor, Parry Jones, and the Hallé Chorus matching the orchestra in their commitment. The two suites devised by Barbirolli himself emerge as curiosities in an age devoted to period practice. It is striking that Purcell survives the romanticizing involved rather better than Byrd, Farnaby and Bull.

Hälsingborg Symphony Orchestra, Okko Kamu

'Swedish orchestral favourites': SODERMAN: *Swedish festival music.* STENHAMMAR: *The Song (cantata): Interlude.* LARSSON: *Pastoral suite; A Winter's Tale: Epilogue.* PETERSON-BERGER: *Frösöblomster: 4*

Pieces. ALFVEN: *Roslagspolka; Midsummer vigil; Gustavus Adolphus II suite.* WIREN: *Serenade for strings: Marcia.*

(BB) *** Naxos 8.553115.

A useful anthology of popular favourites from the Swedish repertory, nicely played by the Hälsingborg orchestra and Okko Kamu, which should have wide appeal, not only in but outside Sweden. The playing is lively, the performances of the Alfvén and Lars-Erik Larsson pieces are as good as any in the catalogue, the recording is excellent and the price is right.

Hanover Band, Graham Lea-Cox

18th Century British Symphonies: ABEL: *Symphony in E, Op. 10/1.* ARNE: *Symphony No. 4 in C min.* COLLETT: *Symphony in E flat, Op 2/5.* ERSKINE: *Periodical Overture No. 17 in E flat.* MARSH: *A Conversation Symphony in E flat.* SMETHERGELL: *Symphony in B flat, Op. 5/2.*

✪ *** ASV CDGAU 218.

This collection of six British symphonies dating from the late eighteenth century could not be more refreshing, brilliantly played and recorded. Hardly anything is known of John Collett, not even his dates, but his four-movement *Symphony in E flat.* Op. 5/2, published in 1767, is a delight, its eager energy echoing the new Mannheim school, with brazen horn writing. His patron, Thomas Erskine, the Earl of Kelly, studied for years in Mannheim, but his *Periodical Overture No. 17,* briefer and bluffer, is less striking. It is in three movements only, as are all the rest, including John Marsh's elegant *Conversation Sinfonie* for two orchestras from 1778, which was influenced by J. C. Bach. With such bright, carefree inspiration running through all these works, the old idea that Handel stifled British composers needs revising.

Hanslip, Chloé (violin)

'Chloé' (with LSO, Mann): PAGANINI (arr. KREISLER): *La Campanella.* BLOCH: *Nigun.* GADE: *Capriccio.* J. WILLIAMS: *Theme from Schindler's List.* MUSSORGSKY (arr. Rachmaninov & Ingman): *Gopak;* BRUCH: *Adagio appassionato.* GLAZUNOV: *Meditation.* TCHAIKOVSKY: *Valse-scherzo.* SHOSTAKOVICH: *The Gadfly: Romance.* SARASATE: *Romanza andaluza.* WAXMAN: *Carmen Fantasy.*

*** Warner 8573 88655-2.

Chloé Hanslip was 13 years old when she recorded this impressive recital disc. Although there is only limited evidence of distinctive artistry, it makes a formidable display, very well recorded. Chloé Hanslip, born and brought up in Surrey, gives formidably mature performances of all 11 pieces here, marked by dazzling virtuosity, flawless intonation, phenomenal attack in virtuoso showpieces like the Sarasate, and, above all, a genuine depth of expression that is sensitively matched to the style of each piece. So in Bloch's *Nigun,* with its subtitle of improvisation, she is uninhibitedly free in her warm phrasing, freer than in the Shostakovich, where the haunting melody is played with tender restraint. What are especially welcome are the rarities. Bruch's *Adagio appassionato,* written in 1891, the same year as the third violin concerto, is a violin equivalent of *Kol Nidrei.* Niels Gade's *Capriccio,* too, which was written in his sixties and has rarely appeared on disc, is here played with all the sparkle that is slightly lacking from the brilliant but literal account of the opening item, Kreisler's arrangement of the Paganini *Campanella* study, which is a little too metrical. By contrast, Tchaikovsky's *Valse-scherzo,* another rarity, sounds a little unsteady, with tenutos not quite spontaneous sounding.

Hardenberger, Håkan (trumpet)

'Famous classical trumpet concertos': HUMMEL: *Concerto in E.* HERTEL: *Concerto Nos. 1 in E flat.* STAMITZ: *Concerto in D.* HAYDN: *Concerto in E flat* (all with ASMF, Marriner). RICHTER: *Concerto in D.* Leopold MOZART: *Concerto in D.* MOLTER: *Concerto No. 1 in D.* Michael HAYDN: *Concerto No. 2 in C* (all with LPO, Howarth). CORELLI: *Sonata for trumpet, 2 violins and continuo.* ALBINONI: *Concerto in B flat, Op. 7/3* (with I Musici). ALBINONI/GIAZOTTO: *Adagio in G min.* CLARKE: *Trumpet Tune* (attr. PURCELL). BACH: *3 Chorale preludes.* BACH/GOUNOD: *Ave Maria* (all with Simon Preston, organ).

✪ (B) *** Ph. Duo 464 028-2 (2).

This is simply the finest collection of concertante music for trumpet in the catalogue. Hardenberger's playing in the famous Haydn concerto, with his noble line in the *Andante,* no less telling than his sparkling bravura in the finale, is matched by his account of the Hummel which he plays in E, rather than the expected key of E flat, which makes it sound brighter than usual. Neither he nor Marriner miss the galant lilt inherent in the dotted rhythm of the first movement, while the slow movement cantilena soars beautifully over its jogging pizzicato accompaniment, and the finale captivates the ear with its high spirits and easy virtuosity. The Stamitz concerto is a comparatively recent discovery. The writing lies consistently up in the instrument's stratosphere and includes some awkward leaps. It is inventive, however, notably in the exhilarating finale. There is no lack of panache here or in the lesser concerto by Hertel, and throughout Marriner's accompaniments are consistently elegant and polished. Apart from these obvious highlights there is much to enjoy in the lesser works too. The wealth of melody is apparent, and if not all the music here is in the masterpiece league, it is played as if it were. Hardenberger is as brilliant in the fast movements as he is sensitive in the slow ones, and his phrasing and tone are superb in both. In the two attractive baroque concertos by Albinoni and Marcello he plays with similar flair and gleaming tone, and he is a dab hand at embellishment, without overdoing thingas. The recordings and accompaniments are comparably fine, and it is difficult to imagine a better programme of this kind at any price.

Harle, John (saxophone), Academy of St Martin-in-the-Fields, Sir Neville Marriner

DEBUSSY: *Rapsodie for alto saxophone and orchestra.* IBERT: *Concertino da camera.* GLAZUNOV: *Concerto.* Richard Rodney BENNETT: *Concerto.* HEATH: *Out of the cool.* VILLA-LOBOS: *Fantasia.*

(B) *** EMI Red Line CDR5 72109.

A first-class disc in every way. These are all attractive and well written for their instrument, and John Harle is its master. The Debussy, Ibert and Glazunov are all works well worth getting to know. The recording is excellent.

Harp concertos

Harp concertos (played by: (i) Marisa Robles; (ii) ASMF, Iona Brown; (iii) Osian Ellis, LSO, Bonynge; (iv) Werner Tripp, Hubert Jellinek, VPO, Münchinger; (v) Philh. O, Dutoit): (i; ii) BOIELDIEU: *Harp concerto in C.* DITTERSDORF: *Harp concerto in A* (arr. PILLEY). (iii) GLIERE: *Harp concerto, Op. 74.* (i; ii) HANDEL: *Harp concerto, Op. 4/6.* (iv) MOZART: *Flute and harp concerto in C, K.299.* (i; v) RODRIGO: *Concierto de Aranjuez.*

(B) *** Double Decca (ADD) 452 585-2 (2).

Boieldieu's *Harp concerto* has been recorded elsewhere but never more attractively. The (originally Argo) recording is still in the demonstration class and very sweet on the ear. Dittersdorf's *Harp concerto* is a transcription of an unfinished keyboard concerto with additional wind parts. It is an elegant piece, thematically not quite as memorable as Boieldieu's, but captivating when played with such style. Glière's is an unpretentious and tuneful work, with Osian Ellis performing brilliantly. Excellent (1968) Kingsway Hall recording. Handel's Op. 4/6 is well known in both organ and harp versions.

Marisa Robles and Iona Brown make an unforgettable case for the latter by creating the most delightful textures while never letting the work sound insubstantial. The ASMF accompaniment, so stylish and beautifully balanced, is a treat in itself, and the recording is well-nigh perfect. The much earlier, Vienna recording of Mozart's *Flute and harp concerto* is played stylishly and has stood the test of time, the recording smooth, full, nicely reverberant and with good detail. Refinement and beauty of tone and phrase are a hallmark throughout, and Münchinger provides most sensitive accompaniments.

The glowing acoustic of St Barnabas's Church, London, creates an attractively romantic aura for Marisa Robles's magnetic and highly atmospheric account of the composer's own arrangement for harp of his *Concierto de Aranjuez*. Robles is so convincing an advocate that for the moment the guitar original is all but forgotten, particularly when, with inspirational freedom, she makes the beautiful slow movement sound like a rhapsodic improvisation. It is a haunting performance, and the digital sound is first rate. Altogether an excellent anthology; however, the Boieldieu, Dittersdorf and Handel concertos on the first disc are also available separately at mid-price, and we gave a Rosette to this disc in our main volume (Decca 425 723-2).

Haskil, Clara (piano)

Clara Haskil: The Legacy (Volume 2: Concertos)

(for Volumes 1 & 3, see below under Instrumental Recitals)

BEETHOVEN: *Piano concerto No. 3 in C min., Op. 37.* CHOPIN: *Piano concerto No. 2 in F min., Op. 21.* FALLA: *Nights in the gardens of Spain* (all with LOP, Markevitch). MOZART: *Piano concertos Nos. 9 in E flat (Jeunehomme), K.271; 23 in A, K.488; Concert rondo in A, K.386* (with VSO, Sacher or Paumgartner); *Piano concertos Nos. 20 in D min., K.466* (two versions, with VSO, Paumgartner or LOP, Markevitch); *24 in C min., K.491* (with LOP, Markevitch). SCHUMANN: *Piano concerto in A min., Op. 54* (with Hague PO, van Otterloo).

(M) **(*) Ph. (IMS) mono/stereo 442 631-2 (4).

This second box of recordings, issued in the Philips 12-disc 'Clara Haskil Legacy', is of concertante works. The earliest of Haskil's concerto records is the Schumann (1951) and is not quite as poetic as that of her compatriot, Lipatti (Haskil was born in Bucharest), though there are some wonderful things, such as the reposeful development section of the first movement and the slow movement. The Hague orchestra's oboe has a surprisingly wide vibrato. Haskil's refinement and grace are to be heard at their best in the Mozart concertos (K.466 and K.491 were recorded in the month before her death), and her fire and temperament, albeit beautifully controlled, in the Falla *Nights in the gardens of Spain*. Her family had originally come from Spain. One snag about the set is that the Beethoven is split over two CDs.

Hauk, Franz, Ingolstadt Philharmonic, Alfredo Ibarra

Music for organ and orchestra (Klais organ in Liebfrauenmünster Ingolstadt): WIDOR: *Symphony No. 3 for organ and grand orchestra, Op. 42.* JONGEN: *Alleluja, Op. 112; Hymne, Op. 78 (both for organ and orchestra). PARKER: *Organ concerto in E flat, Op. 55.*

**(*) Guild GMCD 7182.

In terms of sheer hyperbole Widor does this better than almost anyone. His *G minor concertante Symphony* is made up from two solo organ symphonies: the spectacular outer movements, including the brilliant closing *Toccata*, well laced with brass, are drawn from the *Sixth*, Op. 42/2, and the central *Andante* from the *Second*, Op. 13/2, composed ten years earlier.

The Jongen works are both lyrically colourful. The nobilement *Alleluja* was composed to inaugurate a new organ in the concert hall of Belgian Radio in 1940, and with its closing fanfares sounds rather like wartime film music. The *Hymne* (for organ and strings) is a threnody of some character, well sustained and making a welcome contrast with the surrounding flamboyance.

The American Horatio Parker earned the contempt of his pupil Charles Ives for 'imposing second-hand German romanticism on the patriots of New England'. But his readily tuneful if at times overblown edifice is endearing for its somewhat sentimental romantic feeling, symbolized by the violin and horn solos in the *Andante*. The work was modelled on a concerto of Rheinberger, and its third movement *Allegretto* is also lightly scored and has charm. The finale includes a fugato, a vigorous pedal cadenza, a bit like a recitative, and a resounding close to bring the house down. Here the finale cadence echoes away in the long reverberation period of the Liebfrauenmünster. The organ itself is a maginficent beast and is played with great bravura and expressive flair by Franz Hauk; the orchestra accompany with spirit and enthusiasm even if at times they are all but drowned in the resonant wash of sound. The recording copes remarkably well, although it is hardly refined.

'*Triumphal music for organ and orchestra*':
GOUNOD: *Fantaisie on the Russian national hymne; Suite concertante.* DUBOIS: *Fantaisie triomphale.* GUILMANT: *Adoration.* GIGOUT: *Grand choeur dialogue.*

*** Guild GMCD 7185.

Gounod's *Fantaisie* on the Tsarist anthem is imposing enough, if a bit repetitive.the Dubois Fantaisie suitably grand and pontifical, to be followed by Guilmant's very romantic *Adoration*, a rather beautiful soliloquy for organ and strings. After more pomp from Gigout, we return to Gounod, and an amiably attractive four-movement suite, with hunting horns setting off the jolly scherzo, followed by a songful *Andante* (nicely registered here). But, not surprisingly, it is the catchy vivace finale that steals the show: a bouncy tune that could become a hit if it got more exposure. It is most winningly played and completes an attractive concertante programme that does not rely on decibels for its main appeal. The performances are excellent and here the very reverberant acoustic seems for the most part under control

Heifetz, Jascha (violin)

'*Centenary Memorial Edition*' (1901–2001):
BEETHOVEN: *Concerto* (with NBC SO, Toscanini). BRAHMS: *Concerto.* PROKOFIEV: *Concerto No. 2, Op. 63* (both with Boston SO, Koussevitzky). SIBELIUS: *Concerto* (with LPO, Beecham). GLAZUNOV: *Concerto.* TCHAIKOVSKY: *Concerto.* WIENIAWSKI: *Concerto No. 2.* VIEUXTEMPS: *Concertos Nos. 4, Op. 31; Op. 37.* ELGAR: *Concerto* (both with LSO, Sargent). SAINT-SAENS: *Introduction & Rondo Capriccioso* (all with LPO, Barbirolli). *Havanaise.* SARASATE: *Zigeunerweisen* (both with LSO, Barbirolli). WALTON: *Concerto* (original version; with Cincinnati SO, Goossens). BRAHMS: *Double Concerto for Violin & Cello* (with Feuermann, O, Ormandy). BRUCH: *Scottish Fantasia* (with RCA Victor SO, Steinberg). MENDELSSOHN: *Concerto, Op. 64.* MOZART: *Concertos Nos. 4, K.218* (both with RPO, Beecham); *5 (Turkish), K.219* (with LPO, Barbirolli). GRUENBERG: *Concerto, Op. 47* (with San Francisco SO, Monteux). WAXMAN: *Carmen Fantasy* (with RCA Victor O, Voorhees).

(BB) (***) Naxos mono 8.107001 (7).

The seven Naxos discs of Heifetz's mono recordings of concertos are available in a boxed set as above, as well as separately. The transfers are of a good standard, mellower than the RCA originals, although the EMI alternative re-mastering is rather more sophisticated, and the EMI separate discs have less background hiss. They are also far more expensive. This Naxos box is certainly highly recommendable in its own right.

'*The Unpublished Recordings*': BEETHOVEN: *Romances Nos. 1 and 2.* LALO: *Symphonie espagnole* (both with Philh. O, Susskind). CHAUSSON: *Poème* (with San Francisco SO, Monteux).

(***) Testament mono SBT 1216.

It seems astonishing that any recordings by Heifetz, let alone performances as fine as these, should have slipped through the net and never been issued. The Lalo and Beethoven were recorded at EMI's Abbey Road studios in June 1950, just at the time when the long-time alliance between EMI in Britain and RCA Victor in America was slackening. Heifetz went on to record both the *Romances* and the Lalo again for RCA in America the following year, but the EMI sound is warmer and more helpful to the violin. In both (with the central *Intermezzo* of the Lalo omitted, as was then the custom) Heifetz also sounds more flexibly spontaneous. The Chausson, with Monteux and the San Francisco Orchestra, was recorded by RCA five years earlier, in 1945, with limited sound and a dry, unhelpful acoustic, making even Heifetz's violin tone sound rather fizzy at the start, and with the orchestra backwardly placed. The performance itself is magnificent, warmly expressive with the structure tautly held together.

'*Heifetz the supreme*': BACH: **(Unaccompanied)** *Violin Partita No. 2, BWV 1004: Chaconne.* BRAHMS: *Violin concerto in D, Op. 77.* TCHAIKOVSKY: *Violin concerto in D, Op. 35* (with **Chicago SO, Fritz Reiner**). BRUCH: *Scottish fantasy, Op. 46* (with **New SO of London, Sir Malcolm Sargent**). SIBELIUS: *Violin concerto, Op. 47* (with **Chicago SO, Walter Hendl**). GLAZUNOV: *Violin concerto, Op. 82* (with **RCA Victor SO, Walter Hendl**). GERSHWIN **(transcribed Heifetz):** *3 Preludes* (with **Brooks Smith, piano**).

(M) *** RCA (ADD) 74321 63470-2 (2).

For once the hyperbole of a record company's title is not exaggerated: truly Heifetz is the supreme virtuoso among violinists, and this generously compiled two-disc set shows him at his very finest. The performance of the great Bach *Chaconne* is not only technically phenomenal, it has an extraordinary range of feeling and dynamic, while Heifetz exerts a compelling grip over the structure. The performances of the five concertante works (discussed more fully in our main volume) are not only inspired and full of insights, they show how well Heifetz chose his accompanists, notably Fritz Reiner in Brahms and Tchaikovsky. Sargent too gives most sensitive support in the Bruch *Scottish fantasy* – the atmospheric opening is most evocative. Finally come the dazzling and touching Gershwin showpieces, showing that quicksilver bow arm at its most chimerical, even if here the recording is much too closely observed.

(i) Hilversum Radio PO or (ii) London Symphony Orchestra, Leopold Stokowski

(i) FRANCK: *Symphony in D min.* RAVEL: *L'eventail de Jeanne.* (ii) CHOPIN: *Mazurka in A min., Op. 17/4* (orch. Stokowski). MESSIAEN: *L'Ascension.* DUPARC: *Extase* (orch. Stokowski).

(M) ** Cala CACD 0526.

These recordings were made in the early 1970s in Decca's hi-fi-conscious Phase-Four system, and the exaggerated sound goes with the flamboyance of Stokowski's interpretations. The Franck *Symphony* is the most controversial reading on this disc. The conviction with which Stokowski moulds a romantic symphony like this is always striking. But here, by underlining the vulgarities in this score which most conductors seek to conceal, the overall balance of the work is disturbed, and the reading is less than satisfying. Of course, it has its moments, but Stokowski too often ventures perilously close to the cliff edge. The Hilversum orchestra does not have the virtuosity of the LSO in the companion pieces, but plays with energy as well as warmth. The rest of the programme is much more successful. After the Ravel *Fanfare* which is startling in its vividness, the following Chopin and Duparc pieces are richly atmospheric and

show Stokowski at his most magical. Messiaen's *L'Ascension* is an early work, written first for organ but then orchestrated in 1935 with a different third movement. Stokowski is characteristically persuasive in developing the smooth flow of the music, though some will object to the opulence of the sound he (and the engineers) favour in the sweet meditation for strings alone, *Prayer of Christ ascending to the Father.*

Hofmann, Josef (piano)

'*The Complete Josef Hofmann*', Vol. 2 (with **Curtis Institute Student O, cond. Reiner or Hilsberg**): BRAHMS: *Academic festival overture.* RUBINSTEIN: *Piano concerto No. 4 in D min.* CHOPIN: *Ballade No. 1 in G min., Op. 23; Nocturne in E flat, Op. 9/2; Waltz in A flat, Op. 42; Andante spianato et Grande polonaise brillante in E flat, Op. 22* (2 versions); *Nocturne in F sharp, Op. 15/2; Waltz in D flat, Op. 64/1; Etude in G flat, Op. 25/9; Berceuse in B flat, Op. 57; Nocturne in C min., Op. 48/1; Mazurka in C, Op. 33/3; Waltz in A flat, Op. 34/1.* HOFMANN: *Chromaticon for piano & orchestra* (2 versions). MENDELSSOHN: *Spinning song in C, Op. 67/4.* RACHMANINOV: *Prelude in G min., Op. 23/5.* BEETHOVEN-RUBINSTEIN: *Turkish march.* MOSZKOWSKI: *Caprice espagnole, Op. 37.*

✪ (***) Vai Audio mono VAIA/IPA 1020 (2).

Josef Hofmann's amazing 1937 performance of Rubinstein's *Fourth Piano concerto* has long been a much-sought-after item in its LP format, and those who possess it have treasured it. The performance was attended by practically every pianist around, including Rachmaninov and Godowsky. (It was the latter who once said to a youngster who had mentioned a fingerslip in one of Hofmann's recitals, 'Why look for the spots on the sun!') In no other pianist's hands has this music made such sense: Hofmann plays his master's best-known concerto with a delicacy and poetic imagination that are altogether peerless.

Olin Downes spoke of his 'power and delicacy, lightning virtuosity and the capacity to make the keyboard sing, the richness of tone colouring and incorruptible taste'. The 1937 concert included the Brahms overture, a speech by Walter Damrosch, the incomparable performance of the Rubinstein concerto and, after the interval, a Chopin group. One is tempted to say that the *G minor Ballade* has never been surpassed. The second CD includes four later items, recorded in 1945. Once again – and it can't be said too often – the Rubinstein is phenomenal.

Hungarian State Orchestra, Mátyás Antal

'*Hungarian festival*': KODALY: *Háry János: suite.* LISZT: *Hungarian rhapsodies for orchestra Nos. 1, 2 & 6* (arr. DOEPPLER). HUBAY: *Hejre Kati* (with

Ferenc Balogh). BERLIOZ: *Damnation de Faust: Rákóczy march.*

(BB) *** Naxos 8.550142.

The Hungarian State Orchestra are in their element in this programme of colourful music for which they have a natural affinity. There are few more characterful versions of the *Háry János suite* and Hubay's concertante violin piece, with its gypsy flair, is similarly successful, even if the violin soloist is not a particularly strong personality. The special interest of the Liszt *Hungarian rhapsodies* lies in the use of the Doeppler orchestrations, which are comparatively earthy, with greater use of brass solos than the more sophisticated scoring most often used in the West. The performances are suitably robust and certainly have plenty of charisma. The brilliant digital recording is strong on primary colours but has atmosphere too, and produces plenty of spectacle in the Berlioz *Rákóczy march.*

Jensen, Thomas

(conducting various orchestras)

'Scandanavian Classics' (with (i) Copenhagen PO, (ii) Royal Danish O; (iii) Tivoli Concert Hall O; (iv) Eskdale; (v) Danish State R. O; (vi) Andersen): (i) GADE: *Echoes of Ossian Overture, Op. 1.* J. P. E. HARTMANN: *Triumphal March of the Nordic Gods.* HENRIQUES: *Voelund the Smith: Prelude.)* HOFFDING: *Det er ganske vist (Once upon a time).* LANGE-MULLER: *Prelude to Renaissance.* NIELSEN: (ii) *Little Suite for Strings, Op. 1; Helios Overture, Op. 17;* (iii) *Saul & David, Act 2 Prelude.* RIISAGER: *Little Overture for Strings;* (iv; v) *Concertino for Trumpet and Strings;* (ii) *Slaraffenland (Fools' Paradise).* (iii) SIBELIUS: *Finlandia, Op. 26; Valse triste, Op. 44/1; Valse lyrique, Op. 96a.* (v; vi) SVENDSEN: *Romance for Violin and Orchestra, Op. 26.* TARP: *Mosaik Suite.*

(***) Danacord mono DACOCD 523/524 (2).

Thomas Jensen's post-war Nielsen LPs are well represented on CD. This generously filled 2-CD set collects some of his pre-vinyl records from the late 1930s and 1940s, including Nielsen's *Little Suite for Strings, Op. 1,* eloquently played by the Royal Danish Orchestra, and the *Helios Overture.* Jensen himself played under Nielsen and also heard Sibelius conduct *Finlandia* and *Valse triste* when he visited Copenhagen in 1925 to give the first Danish performance of the *Seventh Symphony.* His pioneering 1939 account of Svendsen's *Romance* with Carlo Andersen, leader of the Royal Orchestra, as soloist – recorded, incidentally, the day before the German invasion of Poland – is refreshingly free from cloying sentiment. It is a measure of the popularity of Riisager's *Slaraffenland (Fools' Paradise)* in the 1940s that there were two versions of it on 78s. *Slaraffenland* inhabits the vaudeville world of Satie or *Les Six* and was perhaps an echo of the days Riisager spent in

Paris in the 1920s. (Jensen's 1937 recording omits three movements.) George Eskdale, whose Haydn concerto was one of the mainstays of the shellac catalogue, recorded Riisager's *Concertino for Trumpet and Strings* in 1949, and it was not seriously challenged until Håkon Hardenberger came along. Finn Høffding, whose pupils, incidentally, included Vagn Holmboe, lived to be 98 and is best known by his short tone poem, *Det er ganske vist,* a brilliant orchestral show piece, which, in a just world, would be a well-known repertory piece. Not everything here is of interest: the *Prelude* to *Vølund Smed* by Fini Henriques is pretty thin stuff, and the same goes for the Lange-Müller and J. P. E. Hartmann pieces. A very welcome issue all the same, with admirably straightforward, no-nonsense transfers.

Johnson, Emma (clarinet)

Disc 1: *Concertos* (with the ECO): MOZART: *Concerto in A, K.488* (cond. Raymond Leppard). CRUSELL: *Concerto No. 2 in F min., Op. 5.* BAERMANN (attrib. WAGNER): *Adagio in D* (both cond. Sir Charles Groves). Malcolm ARNOLD: *Concerto No. 2, Op. 115* (cond. Ivor Bolton).

Disc 2: *Recital:* READE: *The Victorian kitchen garden (suite)* (with Skaila Kanga, harp). RIMSKY-KORSAKOV: *Flight of the bumblebee.* RACHMANINOV: *Vocalise, Op. 34/12.* MILHAUD: *Scaramouche.* SATIE: *Gymnopédie No. 1.* GERSHWIN (arr. COHN): *3 Preludes.* MACDOWELL (arr. ISAAC): *To a wild rose.* BLAKE: *The Snowman: Walking in the air.* BENJAMIN: *Jamaican rumba.* (all with Julian Drake, piano). SCHUMANN: *Fantasiestücke, Op. 73.* DEBUSSY: *La fille aux cheveux de lin.* RAVEL: *Pavane pour une infante défunte* (with Gordon Black, piano). FINZI: *5 Bagatelles, Op. 23* (with Malcolm Martineau, piano).

(M) *** ASV CDDCS 238 (2).

Emma Johnson's recording of Bernhard Crusell's *Second Concerto* made her a star and earned a Rosette for the original disc (ASV CDDCA 559) coupled with Baermann's rather beautiful *Adagio* (once attributed to Wagner) and music of Rossini and Weber. In return she put Crusell's engagingly lightweight piece firmly on the map, and later went on to record its two companion works (ASV CDDCA 784 – see our main volume). Here it comes coupled with Malcolm Arnold and her magnetic performance of the greatest clarinet concerto of all, by Mozart.

The solo pieces on the second CD derive from several compilations recorded over the last decade, two of which are listed below under Instrumental Recitals. But many will find the present collection works well as an ongoing recital, as it covers such a wide range. Highlights include her heartfelt account of the Schumann *Fantasy pieces,* and the 5 *Bagatelles* of Gerald Finzi. The charming – almost Ravelian – douceur of Paul Reade's *Victorian kitchen garden suite* is matched by the simplicity of MacDowell's *To a wild rose* and the famous *Snowman* theme is hauntingly presented. There is plenty of virtuosity too – *Scaramouche* is uninhibitedly scatty – the rhythmic sparkle here and in the *Jamaica rumba* is delightful, and Rimsky's *Bumblebee* is almost jet-propelled. The various pianists all accompany helpfully and the recording is excellent.

Kam, Sharon (clarinet)

'American Classics' (with London Symphony Orchestra, Gregor Buhl): BERNSTEIN: *Prelude, Fugue and Riffs.* COPLAND: *Clarinet Concerto.* GERSHWIN: *Summertime; They all Laughed; The Man I Love; I Got Rhythm.* GOULD: *Derivations for Clarinet and Band.* ARTIE SHAW: *Clarinet Concerto.*

(*) Teldec 8573 88482-2.

This unique collection of American works involving the clarinet is brilliantly performed, but the recording is so unrelentingly aggressive that it makes you feel you are shut up in a matchbox with a group of very loud and persistent performers. The acoustic of the Olympic Studios in London is close and dry, which may suit jazz, the music which inspires all these items, but they are works which demand more subtlety, with light and shade and a dynamic more varied than perpetual fortissimo. For all the virtuosity and understanding of idiom from Sharon Kam, it is hard to enjoy these performances. Even in the wonderfully smoochy melody which opens the *Clarinet Concerto*, written by Copland for Benny Goodman, Kam's playing is made to sound sour and unpleasant, with any sort of expressiveness undermined. The LSO strings equally are made to sound thin and dry. The Bernstein *Prelude, Fugue and Riffs* is certainly energetic, but misses any finer qualities. The second of the four movements of Morton Gould's *Derivations* is a 'slowly moving contrapuntal blues', but it is made to sound neither warm nor moving but depressingly arid. Rhythmic control in the fast music here and throughout the disc cannot be faulted, but how wearing it all is. A pity when not only the Gould but a work like Artie Shaw's *Clarinet Concerto* – conventional in its style but a skilful mix of jazz and classical procedures – are rarities in the classical catalogue.

Karajan Edition (EMI)

The Berlin years

BEETHOVEN: *Piano concertos Nos. 3 in C min., Op. 37; 5 in E flat (Emperor), Op. 73.*
Alexis Weissenberg BPO ((ADD) CDM5 66091-2).

BEETHOVEN: (i) *Piano concerto No. 4 in G, Op. 58;* (ii) *Triple concerto in C, Op. 56.* (i) Alexis Weissenberg; (ii) David Oistrakh, Rostropovich, Richter; BPO ((ADD) CDM5 66092-2).

BRAHMS: *Variations on a theme of Haydn, Op. 56a;* (i) *Piano concerto No. 2 in B flat, Op. 83.* BPO; (i) with Hans Richter-Haaser ((ADD) CDM5 66093-2).

BRUCKNER: *Symphony No. 7 in E.*
BPO ((ADD) CDM5 66095-2).

MOZART: *Symphonies Nos. 38 (Prague); 39; 40; 41 (Jupiter). Rehearsal extracts.*
BPO available separately: Nos. 38 & 39 (with rehearsal extracts) ((ADD) CDM5 66099-2); Nos. 40 & 41 (with rehearsal extracts) ((ADD) CDM5 66100-2).

R. STRAUSS: *Ein Heldenleben, Op. 40.* WAGNER: *Der fliegende Holländer: Overture. Parsifal: Preludes to Acts I & III.*
BPO ((ADD) CDM5 66108-2).

Karajan's period with EMI, after he had left Decca, was less consistently successful than his later, DG era, when he probably reached the peak of his recording career. Some collectors will resist the sumptuous orchestral sound he was given in the works of Mozart, where we are now accustomed to more transparent textures. In the Beethoven concertos he was not well partnered by Weissenberg, but in the Brahms B flat Concerto it was surely Karajan, rather than his soloist, Hans Richter-Haaser, who was responsible for the waywardness of the interpretation. Not surprisingly, he is heard at his finest in the music of Richard Strauss and Wagner. All these recordings are separate issues and rate between two and three stars.

King, Thea (clarinet)

'The clarinet in concert': BRUCH: *Double concerto in E min. for clarinet, viola and orchestra, Op. 88* (with Nobuko Imai). MENDELSSOHN: *2 Concert pieces for clarinet and basset horn in F min., Op. 113; in D min., Op. 114* (with Georgina Dobrée). CRUSELL: *Introduction and variations on a Swedish air, Op. 12* (all 4 works with LSO, Alun Francis). SPOHR: *Variations in B flat for clarinet and orchestra in a theme from Alruna.* RIETZ: *Clarinet concerto in G min., Op. 29.* SOLERE: *Sinfonie concertante in F for 2 clarinets* (with Georgina Dobrée). HEINZE: *Konzertstück in F* (all with ECO, James Judd or Andrew Litton).

(B) *** Hyp. Dyad CDD 22017 (2).

A thoroughly engaging programme of little-known music (the Bruch is not even listed in the *New Grove*), all played with skill and real charm, and excellently recorded. The Bruch *Double concerto* is particularly individual, but the two attractive Mendelssohn concert pieces (each in three brief movements) and the quixotic Crusell *Variations* are by no means insubstantial. They are discussed more fully under their composer entries in our main volume. The novelties on the second disc are slighter but no less entertaining: the jaunty Spohr *Variations* followed by the galant concerto by

Julius Rietz (1812–77) with its engaging lyrical flow. In Etienne Solère's *Sinfonie concertante*, one cannot help but smile at the garrulous chatter between the two solo instruments, which evokes the clinking of tea-cups, while Gustav Heinze's warmly tuneful *Konzertstück* has a jocular, Hummelian finale to match the bouncing closing Rondeau of the Solère. The playing brings many chortling roulades and a seductive timbre from the ever-stylish Thea King, and Georgina Dobrée is a nimble partner in the *Sinfonie concertante*. The accompaniments are excellent too, while the recording has fine range and presence.

Koussevitzky, Serge (double-bass and conductor), see also under Boston Symphony Orchestra

Collection (with (i) Pierre Luboshutz; (ii) Boston SO; (iii) Bernard Zighera, Pierre Luboshutz):
BEETHOVEN: (i) *Minuet in G* (arr. Koussevitzky) (ii) *Symphony No. 6 in F (Pastoral).* (iii) ECCLES: *Largo.* (i) LASKA: *Wiegenlied.* (ii) KOUSSEVITZKY: *Concerto, Op. 3: Andante; Valse miniature.* JOHANN STRAUSS JR: *Wiener Blut; Frühlingsstimmen.*

(M) (***) Biddulph mono WHL 019.

In his youth and before he was established as a conductor of international celebrity, Koussevitzky was regarded as the greatest double-bass virtuoso of the age. In 1928–9, in his mid-fifties, he was enticed into the New York Studios to record the above with the pianist Bernard Zighera, but he then re-recorded everything with Pierre Luboshutz the following year. These performances confirm that he brought to the double-bass the same lyrical intensity and feeling for line and sonority that distinguished his conducting.

Judging from the two concerto movements included here, he was no great composer, but the 1928 recording of the *Pastoral Symphony* with the Boston Symphony Orchestra is little short of a revelation. As an interpretation it feels just right; generally speaking, it is brisk but totally unhurried, each phrase wonderfully shaped. Given the fact that he never lingers, the paradox is that this performance seems strangely spacious. One young and knowledgeable collector to whom we played this thought it quite simply 'among the best *Pastorals* ever'; moreover the recorded sound is remarkable for its age and comes up very freshly. This disc, though comparatively expensive, is worth it.

Kraggerud, Henning (violin), Razumovsky Symphony Orchestra, Bjarte Engeset

'Norwegian violin favourites': Ole BULL: *The herd-girl's Sunday; La Mélancholie* (arr. Kraggerud); *Concerto in E min.: Adagio.* SINDING: *Suite im alten Stil, Op. 10.* SVENSEN: *Romance in G, Op. 26.*

HALVORSEN: *Norwegian dances 1-2; Maiden's song; The old Fisherman's song; Wedding march; Andante religioso.* GRIEG: *I love thee* (arr. Kraggerud); *Elegiac melody: The last spring.*

(BB) *** Naxos 8.554497.

Ole Bull, born in Bergen in 1810, was a virtuoso of the traditional Norwegian 'Hardanger' fiddle, which he took to Europe, where he achieved a considerable success in Paris. He was one of the first gatherers of Norwegian folk tunes, which he used in his own music. The opening piece here, *The herd-girl's Sunday*, with its charming melancholy, is characteristic, but the touching *Adagio* from his *Violin concerto* shows that he also used his folk material more ambitiously and his influence remained. The best-known piece here, Svensen's disarmingly memorable *Romance*, although more sophisticated in construction is in a similar melodic vein. Johan Halvorsen continued this tradition and his miniatures are equally attractive, as is the Sinding *Suite*. Henning Kraggerud plays a modern violin, and invests all these pieces with a simplicity of style and a beauty of tone that gives great pleasure, ending with two Grieg favourites including a transcription of his most famous song. With excellent accompaniments and a most natural sound balance this collection gives much pleasure.

Lawson, Colin (clarinet or basset horn), Parley of Instruments, Peter Holman

'English classical clarinet concertos': JOHN MAHON: *Concerto No. 2 in F; Duets Nos. 1 & 4 in B flat for 2 basset horns* (with Michael Harris). J. C. BACH: *Concerted symphony in E flat.* JAMES HOOK: *Concerto in E flat.*

** Hyp. CDA 66869.

The clarinet (invented around 1700) did not achieve a strong solo profile until well into the eighteenth century, and even then it was not favoured by amateurs. Mozart remains the only composer of that period to have written really great music for it. Thus, even more than in his companion disc of violin concertos (listed under Wallfisch), Peter Holman has had to scrape the barrel a bit and even include a *Concerted symphony* by J. C. Bach, which in the event is the most enterprising work here, but features (besides a pair of clarinets) two oboes, a bassoon and two horns. It has a very striking first movement and a touching *Larghetto*, which opens with a bassoon solo; the flute then takes over, and the clarinets enter much later. The most unusual scoring is in the closing Minuet, where in the Trio the woodwind take over entirely.

John Mahon's *Duos* for basset horns are agreeable but sub-Mozart. His *Concerto*, however, goes even further than the contemporary violin concertos (see below), by using a complete Scottish folksong for his ingenious *Andante* and another popular tune (*The wanton God*) for the Rondo finale. James Hook's *Concerto* has little that is individual to say in its conventional and rather long opening movement, yet it includes the prettiest roulades for the clarinet soloist. However, the composer reserves the real fireworks for the final Rondo, especially in the spectacular closing episode, introduced by the horns, where the clarinet ripples hectically up and down its register in a quite abandoned manner. Colin Lawson is fully equal to such bravura and he plays with fine style throughout. Holman provides excellent accompaniments, but it is a pity that the music itself is so uneven.

Leningrad Philharmonic Orchestra, Evgeni Mravinsky

'Mravinsky in Prague': BARTOK: *Music for Strings, Percussion and Celesta.* SHOSTAKOVICH: *Symphonies Nos. 5 in D min., Op. 47; 6 in B min., Op. 54; 11 in G min. (The Year 1905), Op. 103; 12 (The Year 1917), Op. 112; Violin Concerto No. 1 in A min., Op. 77* (with Czech PO & Oistrakh). PROKOFIEV: *Symphony No. 6 in E flat min., Op. 111.*

(***) (M) HM/Praga mono/stereo PR 256016/19 (4).

The performances in this set have been issued previously in various combinations and formats. The first disc couples the Bartók and the Shostakovich *Fifth* in 1967 performances recorded at the Prague Spring Festival. The *Music for Strings, Percussion and Celesta* has suitable intensity, although not as much as that in the Shostakovich *Eleventh Symphony* recorded in the same year, which occupies the third CD. This is one of the finest performances Mravinsky gave on disc, and it is played flat out with such electricity that criticism is silenced. The second CD brings a 1955 performance of the *Sixth Symphony*, a work he did with extraordinary concentration. It is not the equal of his Melodiya version from the 1960s and, quite apart from the limited mono sound, suffers from intrusive audience noise. The *Twelfth Symphony* comes from 1962, the same year as his Melodiya recording, and he gives it with 500 per cent conviction and frenetic but wonderfully controlled energy. The Shostakovich *First Violin Concerto* with David Oistrakh comes fresh from the press as it were, in 1957, when the piece was being introduced to the world, and, like its pioneering accounts under Mitropoulos and Mravinsky himself, is in mono. His first mono version of the Prokofiev *Sixth* was a classic of the LP catalogue, and this 1967 version, though not perhaps as intense, is still one of the most impressive on CD. The sound is of variable quality throughout, but the playing is mostly in a class of its own.

Leonhardt, Gustav ((i) harpsichord (ii) cond.), Orchestra of the Age of Enlightenment

'Portrait': BACH: (i) *English suite No. 3, BWV 808; Partita No. 1, BWV 825;* (ii) *Double harpsichord concerto No. 2 in C, BWV 1061* (with Bob van Asperen, Melante Amsterdam). C. P. E. BACH: *Hamburg Sinfonia, Wq. 183/2.* PURCELL: *Ode for Queen Mary: Love's goddess sure was blind* (with Julia Gooding, James Bowman, Christopher Robson, David Wilson-Johnson and OAE Chorus).

(M) **(*) Virgin VM5 61400-2.

Leonhardt opens ebulliently with the *G minor English suite* and he is also at his thoughtful best in the *B flat Partita*. The *Double harpsichord concerto* is lively too, although here the resonant acoustic means that the overall sound-picture is less than ideally clear in focus. The other highlight is the lively C. P. E. Bach *Sinfonia*, with its remarkably colourful, though brief, central *Adagio*. The single vocal item, the Purcell *Ode*, brings distinguished solo singing and refined detail, but could ideally be more robust in feeling. Readers wanting to sample Leonhardt's special contribution to the world of baroque music would do better to choose from his own Teldec Edition below, under Instrumental Recitals.

Lindberg, Christian (trombone), BBC National Orchestra of Wales, Grant Llewellyn

American trombone concertos: CHAVEZ: *Concerto.* ROUSE: *Concerto in memory of Leonard Bernstein.* Augusta Read THOMAS: *Meditation.*

(***) BIS CD 788.

By the time he started writing his concerto, Chavez was already in the terminal stages of cancer and his wife had just died. The work opens with an extended morose soliloquy in which the orchestra provides dissonantly pungent support; at times the pacing quickens, but the disconsolate atmosphere remains and, though some percussive intrusions towards the end provide more lively contrast, this music undoubtedly brings longueurs and is essentially depressing.

The *Meditation* by Augusta Read Thomas opens much more positively, with the soloist proceeding over a series of lively orchestral interjections. Bell effects (echoed by the strings) and a percussive spicing add variety, and there is a final eruption of energy. But the meagre musical invention is unenticing.

Easily the finest work here is the concerto by Rouse, which, though darkly atmospheric, readily holds the listener most compellingly. The music climbs up from the lower depths (the opening evocation rather like that at the beginning of the Ravel *Left-hand Piano concerto*). After an exciting climax the soloist has a ruminative cadenza before dashing off in a dazzling Scherzo (superb bravura from Lindberg), with the orchestra just about managing to keep up, yet doing so with some panache. There is a series of hair-raising orchestral explosions, followed by a mêlée of urgently volatile brass figurations which then die away slowly, leading to the touching finale, marked *Elegiaco, lugubre*.

This is designated by Rouse as a memorial to Leonard Bernstein and quotes what is described as the 'Credo' theme from Bernstein's *Third (Kaddish) Symphony*. The movement has an unrelenting thrust and the central orchestral declamation of grief makes a powerful statement, before the soloist steals in with his own gentle and moving valedictory lament. Then, Orpheus-like, he returns into the depths. Superb solo playing throughout this disc, and very fine recording. But the Rouse is the only piece here of real memorability, and it badly needs new couplings.

Lipatti, Dinu (piano)

'*The Legacy of Dinu Lipatti*' with Nadia Boulanger; Philh. O, Zürich Tonhalle O, Lucerne Festival O; Galliera, Ackermann, Karajan): BACH: *Chorale, Jesu, joy of man's desiring* (arr. HESS, from BWV 147); *Chorale preludes, BWV 599 & 639* (both arr. BUSONI); *Partita No. 1, BWV 825; Siciliana* (arr. KEMPFF, from BWV 1031). D. SCARLATTI: *Sonatas, Kk. 9 & 380.* MOZART: *Piano concerto No. 21 in C, K.467; Piano sonata No. 8 in A min., K.310.* SCHUBERT: *Impromptus Nos. 2–3, D.899/2 & 3.* SCHUMANN: *Piano concerto in A min., Op. 54.* GRIEG: *Piano concerto in A min., Op. 16.* CHOPIN: *Piano concerto No. 1 in E min., Op. 11; Barcarolle, Op. 60; Etudes, Op. 10/5 & 25/5; Mazurka No. 32, Op. 50/3; Nocturne No. 8, Op. 27/2; Piano sonata No. 3 in B min., Op. 58; Waltzes Nos. 11–4.* LISZT: *Années de pèlerinage, 2nd Year: Sonetto 104 del Petrarca.* RAVEL: *Alborada del gracioso.* BRAHMS: *Waltzes (4 hands), Op. 39/1–2, 5–6, 10, 14–15.* ENESCU: *Piano sonata No. 3 in D, Op. 25.*

⊕ (M) (***) EMI mono CZS7 67163-2 (5).

This set represents Lipatti's major recording achievements. Whether in Bach (*Jesu, joy of man's desiring* is unforgettable) or Chopin – his *Waltzes* seem to have grown in wisdom and subtlety over the years – Scarlatti or Mozart, these performances are very special indeed. The remastering is done well, and this is a must for anyone with an interest in the piano.

Lloyd Webber, Julian (cello)

'*Favourite cello concertos*': DVORAK: *Concerto in B min., Op. 104* (with Czech PO, Neumann). TCHAIKOVSKY: *Variations on a rococo theme* (original version), *Op. 33* (with RPO, Cleobury). FAURE: *Elégie, Op. 24.* SAINT-SAENS: *Concerto No. 1 in A min., Op. 33; Allegro appassionato, Op. 43* (with ECO, Yan Pascal Tortelier). *Carnaval des animaux: Le cygne* (with ECO, Cleobury). ELGAR: *Concerto in E min., Op. 68* (with RPO, Lord Menuhin); *Romance in D min., Op. 62* (with ASMF, Marriner); *Idylle, Op. 4/1* (arr. for cello and organ). ALBINONI: *Adagio* (arr. GIAZOTTO). SCHUMANN: *Kinderszenen: Träumerei* (arr. PARKER). BACH: *Cantata No. 147: Jesu, joy of man's desiring.* RIMSKY-KORSAKOV: *Flight of the Bumblebee.* BACH/GOUNOD: *Ave Maria* (all with ECO, or RPO, Cleobury). Julian LLOYD WEBBER: *Jackie's song.*

(M) *** Ph. (ADD) 462 505-2 (2).

Lloyd Webber is at his finest in the Elgar concerto. Nor is there any lack of intensity in the Dvořák, a strong and warmly sympathetic reading. He has the advantage of Menuhin to direct the RPO most idiomatically in the former, and the Dvořák specialist, Neumann, with the Czech Philharmonic to accompany him in the latter. The Czech orchestral attack has fine bite and the clipped style of articulation brings out the folk element. The horn soloist plays the great second subject melody with a degree of vibrato but he is a fine artist, and Lloyd Webber's playing is marked by a ripe, rich tone. Intonation is excellent, but the soloist's occasional easing of tempi may not appeal to some listeners.

Both Saint-Saëns works are played with considerable virtuosity and again there is the advantage of a first-class accompaniment, from Yan-Pascal Tortelier and the ECO. Tchaikovsky's original score is used for the *Rococo variations*, which is presented affectionately and elegantly. All in all, if the various encores also appeal, this is an attractive enough package, very well recorded in Philips's most natural manner. *Jackie's song*, Lloyd Webber's catchy little tribute to Jacqueline du Pré, is added as an ardent postscript.

'*Cello moods*' (with Royal Philharmonic Orchestra, James Judd): FRANCK: *Panis angelicus.* ELGAR: *Chanson de matin; Salut d'amour.* Julian LLOYD WEBBER: *Jackie's song.* DEBUSSY: *Rêverie. BACH: Suite No 3: Air.* MASSENET: *Thaïs: Méditation.* CACCINI: *Ave Maria.* BORODIN: *Nocturne.* GLAZUNOV: *Mélodie, Op. 20/1.* CHOPIN: *Nocturne, Op. 9/2.* BOCCHERINI: *Cello concerto: Adagio.* RHEINBERGER: *Cantilena.* BRUCH: *Kol Nidrei.*

*** Ph. 462 588-2.

Decorated with extraordinary artwork by Jane Powell, which shows an unclothed cellist, covered only with shadowy music staves (the cello hiding any suggestion of immodesty), this collection of lollipops is obviously aimed at the crossover market. The playing is of high quality, with none of these famous tunes sentimentalized. Franck's *Panis angelicus* and Massenet's *Méditation* here sound almost noble on the cello. The other highlights are the charming Glazunov *Mélodie*, the Rheinberger *Cantilena*, and the very eloquent Max Bruch *Kol Nidrei*. If you enjoy this kind of programme it couldn't be better played or recorded.

London Gabrieli Brass Ensemble

'*The splendour of baroque brass*': SUSATO: *La Danserye: suite.* G. GABRIELI: *Canzona per sonare a 4: La Spiritata.* SCHEIDT: *Suite.* PEZEL: *Ceremonial brass music.* BACH: *The Art of fugue: Contrapunctus IX.* CHARPENTIER: *Te Deum: Prelude in D.* arr. JAMES: *An Elizabethan suite.* CLARKE: *The Prince of Denmark's march.* HOLBORNE: *5 Dances.* STANLEY: *Trumpet tune.* LOCKE: *Music for His Majesty's sackbutts and cornetts.* PURCELL: *Trumpet tune and ayre. Music for the funeral of Queen Mary* (with Chorus).

✱ (BB) *** ASV CDQS 6013.

This is one of the really outstanding brass anthologies, and the digitally remastered analogue recording is very realistic. The brass group is comparatively small: two trumpets, two trombones, horn and tuba; and that brings internal clarity, while the ambience adds fine sonority. The opening Susato *Danserye* is splendid music, and the Scheidt *Suite* is similarly inventive. Pezel's *Ceremonial brass music* is also in effect a suite – it includes a particularly memorable *Sarabande*; while Matthew Locke's *Music for His Majesty's sackbutts and cornetts* opens with a very striking *Air* and offers six diverse movements overall.

With the Gabrieli *Canzona*, Purcell's *Trumpet tune and ayre* and the Jeremiah Clarke *Prince of Denmark's march* (better known as the Trumpet voluntary) all familiar, this makes a superb entertainment to be dipped into at will. The closing *Music for the funeral of Queen Mary* brings an eloquent choral contribution. Introduced by solemn drum-beats, it is one of Purcell's finest short works and the performance here is very moving. The arrangements throughout the concert (usually made by Crispian Steele-Perkins, who leads the group both sensitively and resplendently) are felicitous and the documentation is excellent. This is a very real bargain.

London Gabrieli Brass Ensemble, Christopher Larkin

Original 19th-century music for brass: BEETHOVEN: *3 Equales for 4 trombones.* CHERUBINI: *Trois pas redoublés et la première marche; Trois pas redoublés et la seconde marche.* DAVID: *Nonetto in C min.* DVORAK: *Fanfare.* LACHNER: *Nonet in F.* RIMSKY-KORSAKOV: *Notturno for 4 horns.* SIBELIUS: *Overture in F min.: Allegro; Andantino; Menuetto; Praeludium.*

*** Hyp. CDA 66470.

'From the steeples and the mountains': IVES: *From the steeples and the mountains; Let there be light.* BARBER: *Mutations from Bach.* HARRIS: *Chorale for organ and brass.* Virgil THOMSON: *Family portrait.* COWELL: *Grinnell fanfare; Tall tale; Hymn and fuguing tune No. 12; Rondo.* GLASS: *Brass sextet.* RUGGLES: *Angels.* CARTER: *A Fantasy upon Purcell's Fantasia about one note.*

(B) *** Hyp. Helios CDH 55018.

It is difficult to decide which of these two programmes is the more enterprising and the more rewarding. If you are responsive to brass sonorities and you acquire one of them, you will surely want its companion. Beethoven's *Equales* were used at the composer's funeral. They are brief, but noble and dignified. The Sibelius suite is folksy, uncharacteristic writing, but has genuine charm.

The second concert opens and closes with the always stimulating music of Charles Ives. *From the steeples and the mountains* is scored for four sets of bells, trumpet and trombones, and its effect is clangorously wild! Elliott Carter's Purcell arrangement also has tolling bells, and is quite haunting. Of the other pieces the most striking is the Barber *Mutations*, which draws on the chorale *Christe du Lamm Gottes* with highly individual effect. Most passionate of all is Ruggles's pungently compressed, muted brass *Angels*, yet the piece is marked 'Serene'! The brass playing throughout the two discs is as communicative as it is expert and the recording is splendidly realistic and present.

London Philharmonic Orchestra, Sir Thomas Beecham

'*Beecham favourites*': BIZET: *L'Arlésienne: suite No. 1: Prélude; Minuet; Adagietto; suite No. 2: Minuet* (from *The Fair Maid of Perth*); *Farandole.* GRIEG: *Peer Gynt: suite No. 1, Op. 46.* TCHAIKOVSKY: *Francesca da Rimini, Op. 32.* GRETRY: *Zémire et Azor: Air de ballet.* CHABRIER: *España (rhapsody).*

✱ (B) (***) Dutton Lab. mono CDEA 5017.

Beecham re-recorded both the *L'Arlésienne* and *Peer Gynt* suites with the RPO in stereo, but he did not surpass these earlier, LPO performances, recorded for the Columbia label in the late 1930s. The sound was remarkably good for its time, but in these fine Dutton transfers it is better than ever, glowing and warm yet with plenty of brightness for the violins, so that the earthily rumbustious *In the Hall of the Mountain King* unleashes a thrilling climax. But (even if the upper woodwind harmonics are not absolutely clean) it is perhaps the gentler evocations which remain most firmly in the memory and it is the oboist, Leon Goossens, who makes *Morning* from *Peer Gynt* unforgettable and who points the delicate rhythm of the famous Grétry *Air de ballet* so exquisitely.

The Bizet and Grieg suites were recorded at Abbey Road, except for the *Death of Aase*, for which Beecham chose Kingsway Hall, with warmly ravishing results, especially at the moving closing section; and Anitra has never danced with more alluring delicacy. Kingsway Hall was also used for *Francesca da Rimini* and *España*. In *Francesca*, Bernard Walton's clarinet solo which introduces the heroine in the middle section is delectably seductive and (in the words of Neville Cardus) Beecham's baton seems 'to bring the hell-fire outer sections of the work visually before us'. The closing pages have great ferocity, with a superb final burst from the timpani which all but drowns the tam-tam.

España was perhaps the most famous of all Beecham's 78s and was cherished by all three of the authors of this book. It always sounded marvellous, and so it does here. Beecham's combination of swagger and *joie de vivre* is balanced by Gallic elegance. He recorded the two 78 sides at two separate sessions, three weeks apart, but one would never guess that this sparkling performance was not played continuously. This CD offers one Beecham anthology that no admirer of this greatest of English conductors should miss. It has splendid notes by Lyndon Jenkins, and it is ridiculously inexpensive.

HANDEL, arr. Beecham: *The Great elopement* (ballet). HAYDN: *Symphony No. 97 in C.* MOZART: *Serenade (Eine kleine Nachtmusik); La clemenza di Tito: Overture.*

(**) Biddulph mono WHL 041.

BEETHOVEN: *Symphony No. 4 in B flat, Op. 60.* MOZART: *Die Entführung aus dem Serail: Overture.* SCHUBERT: *Symphony No. 6 in C, D.589.*

(**) Biddulph mono WHL 042.

BERLIOZ: *Les Troyens: Royal hunt and storm; Trojan march.* BORODIN: *Prince Igor: Overture.* MENDELSSOHN: *Symphony No. 5 in D min. (Reformation), Op. 107.* RIMSKY-KORSAKOV: *May night: Overture.* TCHAIKOVSKY: *Eugene Onegin: Waltz; Polonaise.*

(**) Biddulph mono WHL 043.

These three discs are most welcome for filling in the least-known period of Beecham's recording activities, towards the end of the Second World War, working with the newly self-governing LPO, before he founded the RPO. These recordings had a sadly brief period in the catalogue, and unlike Beecham's pre-war recordings have remained in limbo ever since.

The second of the three discs, coupling Mozart, Beethoven and Schubert, is the most substantial Beecham's account of Beethoven's *Fourth Symphony* – a work he never returned to on record – has great flair and vitality, with fierceness set alongside elegance. The *Entführung* overture here is very similar to the one in his classic recording of the complete opera, but with a concert ending.

This 1944 version of Schubert's *Sixth* was a first recording, differing from his RPO remake in that the outer movements are faster, and the middle two broader, notably the *Andante*. On the first disc, the finale of *Eine kleine Nachtmusik* in this 1945 version is more an *Allegretto* than an *Allegro*, idiosyncratically slow but deliciously sprung. In the *Clemenza overture*, originally issued by Victor not HMV, Beecham takes a

lightweight view, as though this is early Mozart, but the Haydn *97th Symphony* comes in a typically alert reading, with fierceness and elegance set in contrast, rather as in the Beethoven. The Biddulph transfers here lack sufficient body to sustain the top emphasis. That is very evident when one compares this transfer of the Handel–Beecham *Great Elopement* recording with the Dutton version.

On the third disc the sound for the Beecham lollipops – delectably done – is still thin, but the 1945 version of Mendelssohn's *Reformation Symphony* is generally better, with the brass full, bright and well separated, and with gentle string pianissimos (as in the '*Dresden Amen*') beautifully caught. A valuable trio of discs, which should be considered by Beecham devotees despite the reservations over the transfers and the fact that they are not inexpensive.

(i) London Philharmonic Orchestra or (ii) BBC Symphony Orchestra, Sir Thomas Beecham

(i) RIMSKY-KORSAKOV: *May Night Overture.* BERLIOZ: *The Trojans: Royal Hunt and Storm; Trojan March.* MENDELSSOHN: *Symphony No. 5 in D min. (Reformation), Op. 107.* BORODIN: *Prince Igor: Overture.* (ii) SIBELIUS: *Karelia Suite, Op. 11.* REZNICEK: *Donna Diana: Overture.*

(B) (***) Dutton Lab mono CDEA 5508.

All these excellent transfers come from 1945, before Beecham had formed the RPO. The *Royal Hunt and Storm* from the *The Trojans* and Rimsky-Korsakov's *May Night Overture* are characteristic of Beecham, and his guest appearances with the BBC Symphony Orchestra produced excellent accounts of the *Intermezzo* and *Alla marcia* from the *Karelia Suite* and the delightful *Donna Diana Overture* of Rezniček, which has not appeared before. Was its release delayed because, a year or so later, Karajan recorded it with the Vienna Philharmonic for Columbia? Sir Thomas's account of the *Reformation Symphony* does not, however, show him at his very best (the *Allegro vivace* movement is just a bit too fast). Excellent transfers.

London Philharmonic Orchestra, Sir Adrian Boult

'The Boult historic collection'

George BUTTERWORTH: *A Shropshire lad* (rhapsody); *The Banks of green willow* (idyll). BAX: *Tintagel* (tone-poem). HOLST: *The perfect fool* (ballet suite). VAUGHAN WILLIAMS: *Old King Cole* (ballet). ELGAR: *Chanson de nuit; Chanson de matin, Op. 15/1-2.*

(BB) (***) Belart mono 461 354-2.

Butterworth's two beautiful evocations of the English countryside have wonderful delicacy of texture and feeling, while Bax's *Tintagel* is both evocative and passionately full-blooded at its climax. Holst's *Perfect fool* ballet suite sounds remarkably fresh and vivid, and Vaughan Williams's *Old King Cole* (taken from another ballet, of 1923) is both jolly and boisterous, as befits the image of that famous nursery-rhyme monarch. Elgar's paired miniatures of morning and night have characteristically affectionate warmth, and here the full ambience of the recording might almost be mistaken for stereo.

London Symphony Orchestra, Albert Coates

'*Russian favourites*': GLINKA: *Ruslan and Ludmilla: Overture; Kamarinskaya.* BORODIN: *In the Steppes of Central Asia; Prince Igor: Polovtsian march.* LIADOV: *8 Russian folksongs, Op. 58.* MUSSORGSKY: *Sorochintsy Fair: Gopak.* TCHAIKOVSKY: *Marche slave.* RIMSKY-KORSAKOV: *May night overture; Dubinushka; Maid of Pskov: Storm music; Mlada: Procession of the Nobles; Snow Maiden: Danse des bouffons.* STRAVINSKY: *The Firebird: The princesses' game; Infernal dance.*

(***) Koch mono 37700-2.

On the Koch Historic label comes a collection of Coates's recordings with the LSO of Russian lollipops, vividly transferred by H. Ward Marston. Made between 1928 and 1930, they sound astonishingly fresh, with brass bright and forward. *The Procession of the Nobles* from Rimsky-Korsakov's *Mlada* has never been recorded with such flair and excitement, and consistently these performances reflect the natural understanding of a musician of British parentage born in Russia. As well as four other Rimsky items, the disc also has nine favourite pieces by Glinka, Borodin (a famous version of *In the Steppes of Central Asia*), Liadov, Mussorgsky, Tchaikovsky and Stravinsky.

London Symphony Orchestra, Antal Dorati

ENESCU: *Romanian rhapsody No. 2.* BRAHMS: *Hungarian dances Nos. 1–7; 10–12; 15; 17–21; Variations on a theme of Haydn, Op. 56a.*

(M) ** Mercury (ADD) [434 326-2].

Dorati is completely at home in the Enescu *Second Rhapsody* (played passionately – but, as music, not nearly as memorable as No. 1) and the Brahms *Hungarian dances*, where he captures a true Hungarian spirit. When he takes a piece faster than expected, one does not feel he is being wilful or intent on showing off, but simply that he and his players are enjoying themselves. If the delicious rubato in No. 7 does not spell enjoyment, one would be very surprised. The

recording, made at either Watford or Wembley, sounds firmer and cleaner than on LP. The *Variations* are enjoyable but not distinctive.

London Symphony Orchestra, Skitch Henderson

'*Children's Classics*' PROKOFIEV: *Peter and the wolf, Op. 67* (narrative revised). SAINT-SAENS: *Carnival of the animals* (with verses by Ogden Nash, and animals from the London Zoo; both with Beatrice Lillie). trad. (arr. Sharples) '*Uncle Ken's Nursery Rhymes*' (with Kenneth McKellar, and orchestral accompaniment directed by Robert Sharples).

**(*) Australian Decca Eloquence (ADD) 466 673-2. Beatrice Lillie (narrator), LSO, Henderson.

This collection includes a fascinating early LP version of *Peter and the Wolf* involving a 'cabaret act' by Beatrice Lillie to words by 'Bidrum Vabish' (a pseudonym for John Culshaw), full of asides and additions like 'the cat climbed up the tree *before you could say Prokofiev*'. The original LP was most notable for the correspondence it provoked (after the record's review in *The Gramophone*) between Mr Culshaw Vabish and Vetrov Hayver (Guess who?). Curious older readers are referred to the issues of November and December 1960.

The orchestral part of the performance is rather less than distinguished, but the conductor adopts a determined and unflagging pace, and after all it is Miss Lillie's record, and its enjoyment depends on whether or not you take to her rather arch contribution and the new text which she undoubtedly points up in lively fashion, as she does with the words (by Ogden Nash) which are a superfluous addition to Saint-Saëns's witty menagerie.

The grafted-on animal noises which set the scene for the *Carnival* were recorded at London Zoo: the lion's roar at the beginning is startling to say the least! What also makes this disc of interest is that Julius Katchen and Gary Graffman, no less, are the pianists, and the Decca sound from the early 1960s, which is remarkably vivid. The fill-up is a charming medley of the A–Z of nursery rhymes, inimitably sung by Kenneth McKellar, with nicely detailed orchestral accompaniments by Robert Sharples – it will appeal to children of all ages. A collectors' item.

London Symphony Orchestra, Sir Georg Solti

'*Romantic Russia*': GLINKA: *Ruslan and Ludmilla overture.* MUSSORGSKY: *Khovanshchina: Prelude; Night on the bare mountain* (arr. RIMSKY-KORSAKOV). BORODIN: *Prince Igor: Overture and Polovtsian dances* (with LSO Chorus). TCHAIKOVSKY: *Symphony No. 2 (Little Russian), Op. 17* (with Paris Conservatoire Orchestra).

☻ (M) *** Decca Legends (ADD) 460 977-2.

This was a demonstration record in its day and the analogue recording remains of Decca's vintage quality with marvellous detail and a warm ambience. The account of the *Ruslan and Ludmilla overture* is justly famous for its sheer brio, and Solti's *Polovtsian dances* are as exciting as any in the catalogue with a splendid contribution from the LSO Chorus. The *Prince Igor overture* is warmly romantic, yet has plenty of fire and spontaneity, and a lovely horn solo. *Night on the bare mountain* makes a forceful impact, but brings a tender closing section.

Solti also recorded the evocative *Khovanshchina Prelude* with the Berlin Philharmonic Orchestra around the same time, and that had marginally more lustre, but the LSO create plenty of atmospheric tension. The performance of Tchaikovsky's *Little Russian Symphony* has been added for this reissue. It dates from the late 1950s and the recording is noticeably less opulent. After a commanding opening, there is no lack of vitality, and the delightful slow movement is affectionately shaped. The Scherzo lacks something in elegance and charm, partly the fault of the French orchestral playing, but the finale certainly does not lack adrenalin. Overall this is surprisingly memorable and makes a splendid addition to Decca's 'Legends' series.

(i) London Symphony Orchestra; (ii) Royal Philharmonic Orchestra;, (iii) Anatole Fistourlari; (iv) Gaston Poulet

'*French favourites*': (i; iii) POULENC: *Les Biches (ballet suite)*. (ii-iii) *Aubade* (choreographic concerto for piano and 18 instruments). DEBUSSY: *Fantaisie for piano and orchestra* (both with Fabienne Jacquinot, piano). (i; iv) RAVEL: *Alborada del gracioso; Une barque sur l'océan.*

(B) *** Dutton Lab. mono CDEA 5501.

Here are some more splendidly fresh performances from the early-1950s Parlophone label. Expert and attractive accounts of *Alborada del gracioso* and *Une barque sur l'océan* from the LSO under Gaston Poulet are coupled with two Poulenc works: a sparkling and vivacious *Les Biches* from Fistoulari and the same orchestra, and a captivating *Aubade* with Fabienne Jacquinot. She is hardly less persuasive in Debussy's neglected *Fantaisie*, both with the RPO (billed on the LP at the time, as older collectors will remember, as the Westminster Symphony Orchestra for contractual reasons). In any event, these are thoroughly delightful performances and few allowances need be made, for the recorded sound is little short of amazing.

Long Beach Symphony Orchestra, JoAnn Falletta

'*Impressions of the sea*': MENDELSSOHN: *The Hebrides overture (Fingal's Cave).* DEBUSSY: *La Mer.* LIADOV: *The enchanted lake.* BRIDGE: *The Sea (suite).* DEBUSSY: *Prélude: La cathédrale engloutie* (arr. BUSSER).

*** LBSO 6698-1.

It is good to find an orchestra of this calibre, under the excellent JoAnn Falletta, producing playing of such high quality, especially in an often thrilling and certainly evocative account of *La Mer* where the body of orchestral tone is most impressive. Liadov's *Enchanted lake* is also atmospherically evoked, but best of all is Frank Bridge's *Suite* with the opening *Seascape* and penultimate *Moonlight* scenes pictured with memorable vividness of colour. Finally comes Henri Büsser's orchestration of Debussy's *La cathédrale engloutie*, not as outrageously original as the celebrated Stokowski version, but still imaginative, and richly sonorous in its scoring. The recording is excellent, spacious and well detailed. The CD is available from the orchestra direct, whose website is www.lbso.org

Los Angeles Philharmonic Orchestra, Zubin Mehta

'*Spectacular orchestral showpieces*': HOLST: *The Planets.* RICHARD STRAUSS: *Also sprach Zarathustra.* JOHN WILLIAMS: Film scores: *Close Encounters of the Third Kind (suite); Star Wars (suite).*

(B) **(*) Double Decca (ADD) 452 910-2 (2).

Zubin Mehta's set of *Planets* ranks high in stellar splendour and has been a demonstration record since it was first issued on LP in 1971. The performance is strongly characterized and splendidly played. It is discussed more fully under its composer entry in our companion volume, where it is paired with Holst's *Perfect fool* suite. However, hi-fi buffs will surely think this Double Decca set well worth considering with such appropriate couplings. In the never-to-be-forgotten opening of *Also sprach Zarathustra* Mehta has the distinction of stretching those famous first pages longer than any rival. From the start, this 1969 recording was also plainly intended for demonstration with its extrovert sonic brilliance, and as such it succeeds well; but other versions are more interesting interpretatively.

Mehta is a good, even a passionate Straussian, but he is a forceful rather than an affectionate one. The two John Williams film scores were recorded later, in 1977, and again offer a spectacular sound-stage. However eclectic the inspiration, both scores are undeniably attractive and each draws considerable appeal from the imaginative orchestration. The music from *Star Wars* forms a definite suite of six movements; the shorter piece from *Close Encounters* is continuous and essentially atmospheric. Both are very well played in Los Angeles and, if Mehta's approach has an element of hyperbole, in *Star Wars* the Hollywoodian theme picturing Princess Leia includes a horn solo which is played quite gorgeously, while the closing section has an appropriate swagger.

Los Angeles Philharmonic Orchestra or Chamber Orchestra, Zubin Mehta

'*Concertos in contrast*' (with soloists): HAYDN: *Trumpet concerto in E flat*. VIVALDI: *Piccolo concerto in A min., P.83*. WEBER: *Concertino for clarinet and orchestra, Op. 26*. WIENIAWSKI: *Polonaise de concert, Op. 4; Scherzo-Tarentelle, Op. 16*. BLOCH: *Schelomo* (with Janos Starker (cello), Israel Philharmonic Orchestra).

**(*) Australian Decca Eloquence (ADD) 466 683-2.

Contrasting concertos indeed – but the programme works. All are played with polish and sparkle, with the soloists (except in *Schelomo*) principals of the Los Angeles orchestra. The Wieniawski showpieces are brilliant rarities, and the delightful Weber piece has all the melodic freshness of his better-known concertos. The famous Haydn and Vivaldi concertos receive beefy performances, but not at all heavy, and it is a pleasure to hear them in such a rich sound. The recordings throughout are particularly full, though the Israeli strings in *Schelomo* cannot quite match those of the American orchestra. But the performance with Starker is very fine indeed.

Lympany, Moura (piano)

'*The Decca recordings*': KHACHATURIAN: *Piano concerto* (with LSO, Fistoulari). BALAKIREV: *Islamey*. POULENC: *Novelette No. 1*. DOHNANYI: *Capriccio in F min.* MENDELSSOHN: *Capriccio brillant in B min., Op. 22* (with Nat. SO, Boyd Neel); *Rondo brillante in E flat, Op. 29* (with LSO, Royalton Kisch).

(B) (***) Dutton Lab. mono CDEA 5506.

Moura Lympany's 1945 *ffrr* recording of the Khachaturian concerto, a work she had premièred, has a dash and sparkle which have never been matched on record since, while Khachaturian's Armenian melodies are given their full character under Fistoulari's baton. The Dutton transfer is well up to standard. Lympany cannot quite match Katchen in *Islamey*, although it is still brilliant playing, and there is plenty of charm and character in the Mendelssohn concertante pieces and the other solo items. But it is for the Khachaturian that this reissue will primarily be valued.

Ma, Yo-Yo (cello)

'*Great cello concertos*': HAYDN: *Concerto in D, Hob VIIb/2* (with ECO, Garcia). SAINT-SAENS: *Concerto No. 1, Op. 33* (with O Nat. de France, Maazel). SCHUMANN: *Concerto in A min., Op. 129* (with Bav. RSO, Colin Davis). DVORAK: *Concerto in B min., Op. 104* (with BPO, Maazel). ELGAR: *Concerto in E min., Op. 85* (with LSO, Previn).

(M) *** Sony DDD/ADD M2K 44562 (2).

An enticing mid-priced package, offering at least two of the greatest of all cello concertos, in Yo-Yo Ma's characteristic and imaginatively refined manner. Only the performance of the Haydn gives cause for reservations and these are slight; many will enjoy Ma's elegance here. He is also lucky in his accompanists, and the CBS sound gives no reasons for complaint.

Marches

'*40 Famous marches*' (played by various ensembles, including the Philip Jones Brass, Vienna Philharmonic Orchestra, Boskovsky and Knappertsbusch, Carlo Curley, organ): ALFORD: *Colonel Bogey*. C. P. E. BACH: *March*. BEETHOVEN: *Turkish march*. BERLIOZ: *Damnation de Faust: Hungarian march*. BIZET: *Carmen: March des contrebandiers*. BLISS: *Things to come: March*. CHABRIER: *March joyeuse*. CLARKE: *Trumpet voluntary*. COATES: *The Dambusters march*. ELGAR: *Pomp and Circumstance marches Nos 1 and 4 in D*. FUCIK: *Entry of the gladiators*. GOUNOD: *Funeral march of a marionette*. HANDEL: *Occasional Oratorio: March. Rinaldo: March. Saul: Dead march*. KARG-ELERT: *March triomphale*. MENDELSSOHN: *Athalie: War march of the priests. Midsummer night's dream: Wedding march*. MEYERBEER: *Coronation march*. NIELSEN: *Oriental festive march*. PROKOFIEV: *The Love for 3 Oranges: March*. PURCELL: *Funeral march*. RIMSKY-KORSAKOV: *The procession of the nobles; The Tale of Tsar Saltan: March*. SCHUBERT: *March militaire*. SIBELIUS: *Karelia Suite: All marcia*. SOUSA: *Stars and stripes forever; Washington Post*. J. STRAUSS JR: *Egyptian march; Jubel march; Napoleon march; Persian march; Russian march; Spanish march*. J. STRAUSS SR: *Radetzky march*. TCHAIKOVSKY: *The Nutcracker: March miniature*. VERDI: *Aida: Grand march*. WAGNER: *Tannhäuser: Grand march*. WALTON: *Crown Imperial (Coronation march)*.

(B) *** Double Decca (ADD) 466 241-2 (2).

Most of the obvious marches are here, but this splendid collection is made all more interesting by a shrewd choice of imaginative repertoire and performance, often in unexpected arrangements – the Philip Jones Brass Ensemble in the *Aida* and *Tannhäuser* marches (played with considerable brilliance), Carlo Curley's organ arrangement of Beethoven's *Turkish march*, and so on. Highlights include a string of J. Strauss's most exotic marches (*Egyptian, Persian, Russian* and *Spanish*) under Boskovsky, a crisply executed example from *The Tale of Tsar Saltan* by Martinon. Ansermet's hi-fi demonstration version of Chabrier's *March joyeuse*, a simple but striking march by C. P. E. Bach, arranged by the late Philip Jones, and many others. The Nielsen march is another unexpected choice, and no Decca collection of marches would be complete without Knappertsbusch's noble account of the *March militaire*. This is one of the best collection of its kind, and with recordings ranging from good to spectacular: it will not fail to lift the spirits.

Marsalis, Wynton (trumpet)

Trumpet Concertos (with English Chamber Orchestra or National Philharmonic Orchestra, Raymond Leppard): PURCELL: *The Indian Queen: Trumpet Overture.* HAYDN: *Concerto in E flat.* HUMMEL: *Concerto in E.* FASCH: *Concerto in D for Trumpet and 2 Oboes.* MOLTER: *Concerto No. 2 in D.* TORELLI: *2 Sonatas à 5 for Trumpet and Strings in D, t.v. 3 & 7.*

✿ (M) *** Sony SMK 89611.

The brilliant American trumpeter, Wynton Marsalis, recorded the Haydn, Fasch and Hummel concertos with the ECO over a period of a week in 1993 at St Giles Church, Cripplegate, in London. The playing is as expert and stylish as we have come to expect from this remarkable player. His approach is just a little cool, but none the worse for that, for there is also admirable poise, and in the finale of the Hummel he lets himself go with the most infectious bravura. Incidentally, there is no improvising in cadenzas: 'I don't feel comfortable enough to improvise in music of this period', Marsalis told us in the notes with the original full-priced issue.

The other recordings date from a year later with the Purcell *Trumpet Overture* from *The Indian Queen* used to open the programme arrestingly. So often in a trumpet anthology the ear wearies of the timbre, but never here. Marsalis scales down his tone superbly to match the oboes in the delightful Fasch *Concerto* (especially as they are backwardly balanced) and he plays the *Sonatas* of Torelli with winning finesse. The recording gives him a striking (but not too exaggerated) presence in relation to the orchestra, making the trumpet very tangible, especially in the upper tesitura of the Molter *Concerto*, where the solo playing makes the hairs at the nape of one's neck tingle.

Mewton-Wood, Noel (piano)

BEETHOVEN: *Piano Concerto No. 4 in G, Op. 58* (with Utrecht SO, Goehr); *Violin Sonata No. 8 in G, Op. 30/3.* ALBENIZ (arr. Kreisler): *Malagueña* (both with Haendel). CHOPIN: *Tarantelle in A flat, Op. 43.* WEBER: *Piano Sonata No. 1 in C, Op. 24.* LISZT: *Années de pèlerinage: Petrarch Sonnets Nos. 44 &*

104. TCHAIKOVSKY: *Piano Concerto No. 2 in G, Op. 44* (with Winterthur SO, Goehr). SHOSTAKOVICH: *Concerto No. 1 for Piano, Trumpet & Strings, Op. 35* (with Sevenstern, Concert Hall SO, Goehr). SCHUMANN: *Kinderszenen, Op. 15.* BUSONI: *Violin Sonata No. 2 in E min., Op. 36a* (with Rostal). TIPPETT: *Songs: Boyhood's End; The Heart's Assurance* (with Pears).

✿ *** Australian Universal Heritage ABC Classic mono 461 900-2 (3).

An invaluable re-issue, impressively produced and presented, this three-CD set forms one of three in the launch of the Australian Heritage Series. No effort has been spared in presentation, and the set pays tribute to an almost forgotten but outstanding artist, Noel Mewton-Wood. Born in Melbourne, Australia, he had a highly successful career in England, favoured by, among others, Beecham, Sargent, Henry Wood and Britten. His recordings have long been sought after by collectors, and this anthology presents him in solo and concertante repertoire. Several performances are especially worth pointing out: his sleight of hand in one of the silveriest performances of the Beethoven *G major Violin Sonata* on record, with a 13-year old Ida Haendel; a magnificent Beethoven *Fourth Concerto*; a corruscating Shostakovich concerto (the finale is electrifying); two searing Liszt *Petrarch Sonnets*; and a memorable recording of *Kinderszenen* (though with some surface noise) never before issued. The two Tippett song-cycles were the first recordings of any of the composer's vocal works (originally issued on Argo) with Peter Pears sounding admirably fresh and Mewton-Wood's accompaniments full of insight. His playing is consistently suffused with vitality and warmth, ranging from the imperceptibly delicate to overwhelmingly powerful. Tchaikovsky's *Second Concerto*, brought off with enormous aplomb, is highly charged emotionally and remains among the finest versions available. The sound ranges from acceptable to good, but this set is indispensable and well worth seeking out.

Meyer, Sabine or Wolfgang Meyer (clarinet)

'*A Tribute to Benny Goodman*' (with Bamberg SO or Bamberg SO Big Band, Ingo Metzmacher): ARNOLD: *Clarinet concerto No. 2.* COPLAND: *Clarinet concerto.* STRAVINSKY: *Ebony concerto.* BERNSTEIN: *Prelude, Fugue and Riffs.* PAGANINI: *Caprice, etc.*

*** EMI CDC5 56652-2.

Starting with a dazzling account of Sir Malcolm Arnold's *Second Concerto*, the one written for Benny Goodman, this is not just a tribute to the great polymath among clarinettists but a most attractive collection of music which is middle-of-the-road in the best sense, echoing the achievement of Goodman himself in crossing barriers. Only one of the longer works, the *Ebony Concerto*, and one of the shorter ones, the Paganini Caprice in jazzed-up form, feature Sabine Meyer, though four of the Big Band arrangements feature them both in duet.

It is not hard to deduce that the brother is the prime mover behind this whole programme, when in his flamboyant way he plays with an extra freedom and panache compared with his sister. Where he revels in the extrovert show of such a movement as the pre-Goodman Rag which closes the Arnold *Concerto*, Sabine Meyer is more reticent. Crisp accompaniment from the Bamberg Orchestra, though the Big Band conveys the fun behind this music even more winningly in the jazz arrangements. First-rate recording.

Minimalism

'The World of Minimalism': GLASS: 'Heroes' *Symphony: V2 Schneider* (with American Composers Orchestra, Davies). REICH: *Drumming*: excerpts (with Steve Reich and Musicians). MORAN: *Points of Departure* (with Baltimore SO, Zinman). FITKIN: *Frame* (Fitkin and Sutherland). ADAMS: *Shaker Loops: Shaking and Trembling* (with San Francisco SO, de Waart). NYMAN: *The Cook, the Thief, his Wife and her Lover: Memorial* (Michael Nyman Band). RILEY: *In C* (with Davidson-Kelly, Harris, Heath, Richter, Strawson, Wood).

(M) *(**) Decca (ADD/DDD) 470 125-2.

Minimalist music has a small yet sturdy following, but some of the music here will test all but its most devoted advocates. The excerpts from Steve Reich's *Drumming* falls into the 'stuck in groove' category, which may be hypnotic to some but is undoubtedly monotonous to others. Fitkin's *Frame*, played on two keyboards, merely grates from the first note. Repetition is taken to extreme in Riley's infamous *In C* – a 20-minute composition, based on the repeated playing of the octave C, for concert grand and upright piano, Rhodes piano, two harpsichords and vibraphone. Moran's mythical ballet *Points of Departure* offers far more attractive and colourful symphonic scoring and, like Glass's *V2 Schneider*, sounds not unlike many contemporary American film scores. Nyman's *Memorial* is perhaps the most approachable work here, with an easy listening quality that has made his film music so successful. However, it is John Adams who shines as the strongest and most original composer in this collection. Superb recordings and, as far as one can tell, performances.

Minneapolis Symphony Orchestra, Antal Dorati

Concert: GERSHWIN: *An American in Paris*. COPLAND: *Rodeo (4 Dance episodes)*. SCHULLER: 7 *Studies on themes of Paul Klee*. BLOCH: *Sinfonia breve*.

(M) ** Mercury (ADD) [434 329-2].

This is a disappointing collection, a rare occurrence for this label. Dorati's *Rodeo* lacks the incandescent vitality of Bernstein's electrifying New York version, and Gershwin's *American in Paris* doesn't suit the Hungarian conductor too well either (try the big blues tune at its trumpet entry). The almost over-detailed recording does not help, either here or in Bloch's rather dry *Sinfonia breve*, which needs richer string textures. It is highly suitable for Schuller's sharply etched *Seven studies on themes of Paul Klee* but, brilliantly though this is played, the music itself does not live up to the promise of titles like *The twittering machine* and *Little blue devil*.

ALBENIZ: *Iberia* (suite, orch. Arbós). FALLA: *La Vida breve: Interlude and dance*. MUSSORGSKY: *Khovanshchina: Prelude; Dance of the Persian slaves*. SMETANA: *The Bartered Bride: Overture and 3 Dances*.

(M) ** Mercury (ADD) [434 388-2].

The Northrop Auditorium in Minnesota never proved an ideal venue acoustically for the Mercury recording team. Although the sound is not without warmth and the woodwind have bloom, there is an underlying acoustic dryness. Using the favoured M56 Telefunken microphones, closely placed, this produced an unattractive glare, even a fierceness in fortissimos, an artificial brilliance likely to appeal only to hi-fi buffs. Of course, the somewhat brash Arbós scoring in *Iberia* does not help, and certainly Dorati catches the sinuous Spanishry of this music. He is equally vital in the rest of the programme, which is all brilliantly played; but easily the highlight here is Mussorgsky's highly atmospheric *Khovanshchina Prelude*. With its orchestration expertly touched in by Rimsky-Korsakov, it magically pictures the sun rising over the Kremlin. Although the timbre of the orchestra's principal oboe is not opulent, this is one of the most evocative accounts in the CD catalogue, and here the recording cannot be faulted.

Minnesota Orchestra, Eije Oue

'Orchestral fireworks': KABALEVSKY: *Overture Colas Breugnon*. Deems TAYLOR: *Through the Looking glass: Looking glass insects*. RIMSKY-KORSAKOV: *Tsar Sultan: Flight of the bumblebee*. LISZT: *Les Préludes*. BRAHMS: *Hungarian dance No. 3 in F*. DINICU: *Hora staccato*. DVORAK: *Slavonic dance, Op. 71/2*. JARNEFELT: *Praeludium*. BERLIOZ: *Damnation de Faust: Danse des sylphes*. KLEMPERER: *Merry waltz*. CHABRIER: *Habanera*. RAVEL: *Boléro*.

*** Reference Dig. RR-92 CD.

From the evidence of this enjoyable concert the Minneapolis Orchestra is in excellent shape under its new conductor, Eije Oue, and they play with refinement as well as virtuosity. *Les Préludes*, for instance, is a particularly impressive performance, entirely without vulgarity, with a dignified opening, yet the closing pages generate much excitement and the final peroration is really powerful. The slightly bass-heavy recording adds to the weight of the piece. And how warmly and elegantly does the orchestra play the Brahms and Dvořák dances, while the slinky Chabrier *Habanera* is very seductive. A attractive novelty here is the Deems Taylor scherzo, reminiscent of early Stravinsky, but very colourful in its own right.

Hora staccato and Rimsky's *Bumblebee* are both played with the lightest touch, the orchestral virtuosity sparkling throughout, while it is good to welcome the charming Jarnefelt *Praeludium*. But the surprise is the Klemperer *Waltz*, turned into a real lollipop, and more persuasive here than the conductor/composer's own version. *Boléro* is very well played indeed (the opening woodwind solos especially so), but it is also very relaxed until a sudden burst of adrenalin at the close. The recording is spacious and full, with warn, pleasing string quality, but the bass is at times a trifle boomy.

Molnar, Jozsef (alphorn)

Alphorn Concertos (with Capella Istropolitana or Slovak Philharmonic Orchestra, Urs Schneider): LEOPOLD MOZART: *Sinfonia Pastorella.* JEAN DAETWYLER: *Dialogue avec la Nature; Concerto.* FERENC FARKAS: *Concertino Rustico.*

(BB) *** Naxos 8. 555978.

The Alphorn (pictured on the front of the CD) has a fine fat timbre, but its natural harmonics only produce a basic range of five notes. Leopold Mozart uses them robustly in various permutations and most successfully in his ingenuously jolly rondo finale. But a good deal of the melodic action goes on in the orchestra, and the *Andante* omits the soloist altogether. For all its naiveté the result is rather endearing.

The *Concerto Rustico* of Ferenc Farkas is much more ingenious in using and extending the instrument's range. The slow movement, *Rubato, a piacere*, is surprisingly successful in its doleful *espressivo*, unashamedly featuring the instrument's out-of-tune harmonics, and in the finale the alphorn almost manages a tune rather like a garbled version of '*Poor Jennie is a weeping*'.

The Swiss composer, Jean Daetwyler, gets round the minimalistic problem even more enterprisingly by adding in a piccolo to portray the birds in his *Dialogue avec la Nature*, while his orchestral scoring is rich in atmosphere and colour. The alphorn and piccolo duet together piquantly in the charming rondo finale, which is not too extended.

Daetwyler's four-movement *Concerto* is much more ambitious, opening with a soliloquy taking his soloist up to his highest harmonics and, like Farkas, not shunning those notes that are inherently out of tune. Again the tangy orchestral colouring makes a rich backcloth for the soloist, especially in the razzle-dazzle *Scherzo* and the *Misterioso Pastorale*. The *Furioso* finale makes even more virtuoso demands, which Jozsef Molner clearly relishes. Indeed his playing throughout is astonishingly secure and full of character. The accompaniments are supportive and the recording excellent. This is a collection which would have been a doubtful recommendation at its original Marco Polo premium price, but on Naxos it is well worth trying – although not all at once!

Musica da Camera, Robert King

Baroque chamber works: BACH: *Cantata No. 42: Sinfonia.* CORELLI: *Concerto grosso in G min. (Christmas), Op. 6/8.* PACHELBEL: *Canon and Gigue.* HANDEL: *Concerto grosso in B flat, Op. 3/2.* VIVALDI: *L'Estro armonico: Concerto in D min., Op. 3/11.* ALBINONI, arr. GIAZOTTO: *Adagio for organ and strings.*

*** Linn CKD 012.

An exceptionally successful concert of baroque music, with a very well-chosen programme, presented on an authentic scale, with what appears to be one instrument to a part. Phrasing is thoroughly musical and the intimacy and transparency of sound are achieved without loss of sonority or disagreeable squeezing of phrases. The familiar *Largo* of the Corelli *Christmas concerto* is particularly fresh, and the opening of the famous Pachelbel Canon on a sombre solo bass-line is very telling. The colour of the lively Bach and Handel works (using wind as well as strings) is attractively realized. Excellent, realistic recording.

'Música española'

'Música española': Spanish music by foreign composers: GLINKA: *Jota aragonesa.* RAVEL: *Rapsodie espagnole; Pavane pour une infante défunte; Alborada del gracioso; Boléro* (SRO, Ansermet). LALO: *Symphonie espagnole* (with Ricci). RIMSKY-KORSAKOV: *Capriccio espagnol.* MOSZKOWSKI: *Danzas españolas: Book 1.* CHABRIER: *España* (LSO, Argenta). DEBUSSY: *Images: Iberia* (SRO, Argenta).

(B) **(*) Double Decca (ADD) (IMS) 433 911-2 (2).

These are all vintage performances from Decca's early stereo catalogue. Argenta's *Capriccio espagnol, España* and the Moszkowski *Spanish dances* are splendidly played by the LSO, and Ansermet's classic Ravel performances have real magnetism, re-emerging with remarkable freshness, even if the SRO playing is not always ideally polished. Of course, they are helped by the remarkable Decca recording from the late 1950s and early 1960s. *Boléro* remains in the demonstration class, its climax superbly graduated.

I Musici

ALBINONI: *Adagio in G min.* (arr. GIAZOTTO). BEETHOVEN: *Minuet in G, WoO 10/2.* BOCCHERINI: *Quintet in E, Op. 11/5: Minuet.* HAYDN (attrib.): *Quartet, Op. 3/5; Serenade.* MOZART: *Serenade No. 13* in G (*Eine kleine Nachtmusik*), *K.525.* PACHELBEL: *Canon.*

*** Ph. (IMS) 410 606-2.

A very enjoyable concert, recorded with remarkable naturalness and realism. The effect is very believable indeed. The playing combines warmth and freshness, and the oft-played Mozart *Night music* has no suggestion whatsoever of routine: it combines elegance, warmth and sparkle. The Boccherini *Minuet* and (especially) the Hoffstetter (attrib. Haydn) *Serenade* have an engaging lightness of touch.

Mutter, Anne-Sophie (violin)

MOZART: *Violin concertos Nos. 2 in D, K.211; 4 in D, K.218* (with Philharmonia O, Muti). BACH: *Concertos Nos. 1 in A min., BWV 1041; 2 in E, BWV 1042; Double violin concerto in D min., BWV 1043* (with ECO, Accardo). LALO: *Symphonie espagnole, Op. 21.* SARASATE: *Zigeunerweisen, Op. 20* (with O Nat. de France, Ozawa).

(M) *** EMI CMS5 65538-2 (3).

Anne-Sophie Mutter followed up her celebrated early coupling of Mozart's *G major*, K.216 and *A major*, K.219 *Violin concertos* (now reissued as a DG Original – see under the Composer entry in our main volume) with the two *D major Concertos* on HMV, and a different orchestra and conductor. The results are hardly less successful. Her variety of timbre as well as the imagination of her playing is extremely compelling, and while the degree of romantic warmth she adopts in her Bach playing is at odds with today's 'authentic school', her performance of the slow movement of the *E major Concerto* is finer than almost any other version except Grumiaux's, with marvellous shading within a range of hushed tone.

Accardo's accompaniment here (as throughout the collection) is splendidly stylish and alert. In principle the slow movement of the *Double concerto* – where Accardo takes up his bow to become a solo partner, scaling down his timbre – is too slow, but the result could hardly be more beautiful, helped by EMI recording which gives body to the small ECO string band. The account of Lalo's Spanish show-piece makes an excellent foil, with its dazzling display of bravura offset by Mutter's delicacy of phrasing, although there is no lack of passionate eloquence in the central movements. Here the balance is a shade too forward, and the digital recording brings a touch of digital edge to the sound. The Sarasate offers more violinistic fireworks, but some may find that Mutter's playing of the famous principal lyrical melody a little chaste. Overall, however, this makes a fine showcase for a splendid artist.

'Carmen-fantasie' (with Vienna Philharmonic Orchestra, James Levine): SARASATE: *Zigeunerweisen; Carmen fantasy.* WIENIAWSKI: *Légende.* TARTINI: *Sonata in G min. (Devil's trill).*

RAVEL: *Tzigane.* MASSENET: *Thaïs: Méditation.* FAURE: *Berceuse.*

*** DG 437 544-2.

This is an unashamedly fun record, with Mutter playing with freedom and warmth and obviously enjoying herself. Comparing the *Carmen fantasy* of Sarasate with Perlman shows Mutter as equally sharp in characterization, yet Perlman's easy style is in the end the more beguiling. But Mutter's Ravel *Tzigane* is made stunningly Hungarian in its fiery accelerando at the end, while Tartini's famous *Devil's trill sonata* is played as a virtuoso piece, rather than placed back in the eighteenth century – no harm in that in the present context. The recording is vividly close.

'Modern': STRAVINSKY: *Violin concerto in D* (with Philh. O, Sacher). LUTOSLAWSKI: *Partita for Anne-Sophie Mutter* (with Philip Moll, piano); *Chain II* (with BBC SO, composer). BARTOK: *Violin concerto No. 2.* MORET: *En rêve* (with Boston SO, Ozawa). BERG: *Violin concerto.* RIHM: *Time chant* (with Chicago SO, Levine).

(M) *** DG (IMS) 445 487-2 (3).

Here is an unexpected portrait of an outstanding young artist linked with the attractions of inexpensively cutting one's teeth on twentieth-century violin repertoire, offered in brilliant, modern, digital recordings. The Stravinsky *Concerto* makes a splendid opener: there is no more recommendable version, with wit and feeling nicely balanced, and excellent, sharply defined sound. The Berg is hardly less successful. Mutter opens with the most delicate pianissimo and her reading is intensely passionate.

Her Bartók is more controversial, played with stunning virtuosity and brilliance but at times over-characterized, even glossy in its brilliance, and in the scherzando section of the second movement she is much faster than the metronome marking; indeed, the performance tends to sensationalize the concerto, although the playing is not unfelt and the bravura is astonishing. The Lutoslawski pieces are among the best of his recent compositions and evoke a powerful response from their dedicatee. The Moret is a slight but enticing piece with plenty of shimmering sonorities and a dazzling solo part. The finale erupts suddenly but the introspective musing of the earlier writing returns with sporadic bursts of energy from the soloist which bring the piece to a lively conclusion. The Rihm concerto is a rhapsodical, meditative piece, its effect heightened by the orchestral backing. It is played with superb concentration.

Nakariakov, Sergei (trumpet)

Concertos (with Lausanne Chamber Orchestra, López-Cobos): JOLIVET: *Concertino for trumpet, piano and strings* (with Alexander Markovich, piano). HUMMEL: *Concerto in E flat.* HAYDN: *Concerto in E flat.* TOMASI: *Concerto in D.*

*** Teldec 4509 90846-2.

The very gifted young Russian trumpeter makes a brilliant contribution to the Jolivet *Double concerto*. His partner, the pianist Alexander Markovich, plays very well too, but the balance is less than ideal. Yet, at under ten minutes, the work does not outstay its welcome and it has a catchy, angular main theme. The Tomasi solo concerto is more kaleidoscopic, with lyrical and rhythmic elements alternating and a whiff of jazz in the melodic style.

In the Haydn and Hummel *Concertos* Nakariakov does not quite match the famous Hardenberger performances, and the orchestral playing in Lausanne is serviceable rather than outstanding. Nakariakov plays the Hummel in the key of E flat, rather than the brighter E major favoured by Hardenberger, but both this and the Haydn bring a superb solo contribution from the young Russian virtuoso, and the lovely *Andante* of the latter work is memorably warm and graceful before a sparkling finale which matches that of the Hummel in high spirits.

'No limit' (playing trumpet and flugel horn, with Philharmonia Orchestra, Vladimir Ashkenazy; arrangements by Mikhail Nakariakov & Timothy Dokshitser) of: SAINT-SAENS: **Trumpet: *Introduction and rondo capriccio*.** GERSHWIN: ***Rhapsody in blue*. Flugel-horn:** TCHAIKOVSKY: ***Andante cantabile; Variations on a rococo theme*.** BRUCH: ***Canzone*.** MASSENET: ***Thaïs: Méditation*.**

(***) Teldec 8573 80651-2.

Sergei Nakariakov's tone is so beautiful, his phrasing so naturally musical, his virtuosity so effortless and dazzling, that he almost reconciles one to these arrangements. Certainly the Saint-Saëns display-piece is presented with great flair – and Nakariakov's breathtakingly fast tonguing at the close is extraordinary.

But Tchaikovsky's *Andante cantabile*, on the flugel horn instead of the cello, just will not do. For all the warmth of line and tasteful vibrato, the atmosphere of the bandstand remains. The *Rococo Variations* works rather better, played very stylishly, with the melodic line here often lying higher up. But again it sounds far better on a cello.

Max Bruch's *Canzona* and Massenet's '*Méditation*' are effective enough, and undoubtedly Nakariakov is a natural in Gershwin, where he returns to the trumpet. It is a brilliant performance, with a strong jazzy inflection. The instrument's middle and lower range is used to good effect, and there is a touch of humour when the bassoon makes a solo entry. The big tune is introduced delicately and played with a cup mute; but in the following string climax the saxes fail to come through (if they are there). Throughout Ashkenazy provides good support, although the balance makes his contribution no more than an accompaniment. But that Gershwin opening should have been left to the clarinet.

NBC Symphony Orchestra, Arturo Toscanini

'The Immortal Toscanini' WAGNER: *Lohengrin: Preludes to Acts 1 & 3. Siegfried: Forest Murmurs. Tristan und Isolde: Vorspiel und Liebestod. Die Walküre: The Ride of the Valkryies.* BRAHMS: *Variations on a Theme by Haydn.* R. STRAUSS: *Till Eulenspiegel.* TCHAIKOVSKY: *Nutcracker Suite, Op. 71a.* MUSSORGSKY: *Pictures at an Exhibition.* DUKAS: *L'apprenti sorcier.* ROSSINI: *William Tell: Overture.*

(B) (**(*)) RCA mono 74321 84220-2 (2).

These 1950s performances give an excellent idea of Toscanini's legendary, often electrifying style, as well as RCA's notoriously dry Studio 8-H acoustics. The Wagner items display his special brand of electricity, especially the *Lohengrin Preludes* and the soaringly intense *Tristan Liebestod*, and although the dynamic range is compressed the sound is surprisingly good. In his view of the Mussorgsky–Ravel score he is at his least sympathetic in the statement of the opening *Promenade*, not only rigidly metrical but made the coarser by the cornet-like trumpet tone. Otherwise the orchestral playing has virtuoso brilliance and many of the individual movements are done with greater understanding – for example, the *Ballet of the Unhatched Chicks* – but too often Toscanini's lack of warmth undermines the character of this rich score. However he is on top form for the *Sorcerer's Apprentice*, creating memorably translucent textures at the opening and then setting off with great dash at the entry of the main theme – in that respect the performance is unique. The *William Tell Overture* was recorded in Carnegie Hall, and although closely miked the acoustic has obvious ambient advantage, and the performance is undoubtedly exciting, with a tautly exciting final gallop. The *Nutcracker Suite* receives a bright, crisp performance, even if the *Sugar Plum Fairy* might have danced with more lightness and grace. The straightforward account of the Brahms *Variations* has more drive than charm, though it is undoubtedly exciting. So is *Till Eulenspiegel*, which receives a well characterized and sharply dramatic performance – the maestro on top form. The transfers are generally excellent.

'Great symphonies': MOZART: *Symphony No. 40 in G min., K.550.* HAYDN: *Symphony No. 94 in G (Surprise).* CHERUBINI: *Symphony in D.* SCHUMANN: *Symphony No. 3 in E flat (Rhenish), Op. 97.* DVORAK: *Symphony No. 9 (New World), Op. 95.*

(B) (**(*)) RCA mono Twofer 74321 59481 (2).

This may be a mixed bag of symphonies, classical and romantic, but each one demonstrates the electrical intensity of Toscanini's conducting. Even in the new transfers the Haydn and Mozart sound rather thin as well as harsh, and the Cherubini, one of his most celebrated records, is only a little better. The two romantic symphonies on the other hand benefit greatly, with a sense of space and full-bodied sound, notably in the 1949 recording of Schumann, the earliest here.

Baroque music (with Mischa Mischkoff, Edwin Bachmann, Frank Miller, Yella Pessl): BACH: *Suite No. 3 in D; Passacaglia and fugue in C min.* (arr. RESPIGHI); HANDEL: *Concerto grosso in B min. Op. 6 No. 12*; VIVALDI: *Violin concerto in B flat, RV 370.*

(BB) (**(*)) Naxos mono 8.110835.

Toscanini demonstrates his devotion to this baroque repertory at the very start of this programme of 1947, when he sings along enthusiastically with the orchestra in the opening of the Bach *D major Suite*. Speeds are fast and rhythms crisply articulated, while the celebrated *Air* at a flowing speed avoids all sentimentality. This may be very different from period style, but it is also very different from the ponderousness of most Bach performances at that time.

The Handel is freshly done too, with the slow movement given a noble performance, set against hectic *Allegros*. The Vivaldi also, one of the rarer violin concertos, is chiefly remarkable for the lovely central slow movement. The Respighi arrangement finds Toscanini back on home ground, with high dynamic contrasts brought out, prompting wild applause at the end. A refreshingly different slant on Toscanini. The transfers give the dry sound more body than most from this source, though scratchiness develops on high violins after the Bach suite.

Neveu, Ginette (violin)

Concert: BRAHMS: *Violin Concerto* (with Philh O, Dobrowen). CHOPIN: *Nocturne No. 12 in C sharp min.* FALLA: *Danse espagnole.* RAVEL: *Tzigane.* SUK: *Four Pieces.* DINICU: *Hora staccato* (with Jean Neveu, piano).

(B) (***) Dutton (mono) CDEP 9710.

No sooner had Ginette Neveu established her claims as a great artist, mainly in her recordings in the immediate post-war period, than she was taken from us, together with her brother, Jean, in a tragic air accident. It makes these fine recordings the more precious, and they have been superbly transferred by Dutton, with the Brahms *Violin Concerto* sounding a degree more refined than in the earlier EMI transfer. Some of Neveu's recordings of the other items are new to CD, as for example the imaginative *Four Pieces* of Suk, with Neveu displaying her virtuoso flair in such showpieces as Dinicu's *Hora staccato*.

New London Orchestra, Ronald Corp

'British light music classics': Vol. 1: COATES: *Calling all workers.* TOYE: *The haunted ballroom.* COLLINS: *Vanity Fair.* FARNON: *Jumping bean.* BAYNES: *Destiny.* CURZON: *The Boulevardier.* LUTZ: *Pas de quatre.* BINGE: *The Watermill; Elizabethan serenade.* WILLIAMS: *The Devil's galop.* GIBBS: *Dusk.* WHITE: *Puffin' Billy.* KETELBEY: *Bells across the meadows.* Charles WILLIAMS: *The old clockmaker.* JOYCE: *Dreaming.* ELLIS: *Coronation Scot.* ANCLIFFE: *Nights of gladness.*

*** Hyp. CDA 66868.

Almost as soon as it was issued, Ronald Corp's stylish and beautifully played collection of inconsequential but engaging English miniatures rose up and held its place in the bestseller lists. This was the kind of music that used to be heard on seaside piers and which was played by spa orchestras in the years between the two World Wars – orchestras that have long since disappeared.

The robust *Nights of gladness* (1912) was composed by Charles Ancliffe on return from service as a bandmaster in India, while Sydney Baynes's *Destiny waltz*, from the same year, has a cello solo which, years later, was played by Sir John Barbirolli at Hallé balls; Archibald Joyce's *Dreaming* dates from the previous year, while two other hauntingly atmospheric pieces, *Dusk* by Armstrong Gibbs and Geoffrey Toye's *Haunted ballroom*, were both written in 1935. Vivian Ellis's *Coronation Scot*, a catchy sound-picture of a steam locomotive, dates from 1939 and became famous when it was used as the signature tune for BBC radio's 'Paul Temple' detective series. More recently, Ronald Binge has added his engaging *Elizabethan serenade* (1951) and a delicate portrait of *The Watermill* (1958). It was the famous Sibelius conductor, Anthony Collins, who wrote the delectable morsel, *Vanity Fair*, and he once said in a radio interview that he valued its composition above all his other achievements 'because it will keep my name alive long after my records have been forgotten'. The affectionate, polished performances here will certainly help to do that: they give much pleasure, and Tony Faulkner's recording balance is beautifully judged.

'British light music classics', Vol. 2: COATES: *London suite: Knightsbridge.* FLETCHER: *Bal masqué.* BUCALOSSI: *Grasshopper's dance.* Arthur WOOD: *'The Archers' theme': Barwick Green.* HARTLEY: *Rouge et Noir.* FARNON: *Peanut polka; Westminster waltz.* FRANKEL: *Carriage and pair.* Haydn WOOD: *The Horse Guards, Whitehall (Down your Way theme).* DUNCAN: *Little suite: March (Dr Finlay's Casebook theme).* BINGE: *Sailing by.* VINTER: *Portuguese party.* RICHARDSON: *Beachcomber.* FINCK: *In the shadows.* DOCKER: *Tabarinage.* KETELBEY: *Sanctuary of the heart.* ELGAR:

Carissima. **Charles** WILLIAMS: *Girls in grey.* WHITE: *The runaway rocking horse.* CURZON: *Robin Hood suite: March of the Bowmen.*

*** Hyp. CDA 66968.

Ronald Corp's second collection of popular evergreens is just as delightful as the first, for the supply of catchy and popular numbers shows no sign of drying up. Radio and television signature-tunes provide the cornerstones, with *Barwick Green (The Archers)* by Arthur Wood pointing the way, a piece inspired not by the West Country or the fictional world of Ambridge, but by a village near Leeds. From Eric Coates's *Knightsbridge march* onwards, chosen in the early 1930s to introduce the pioneering radio magazine programme *In Town Tonight*, here is a rich source of nostalgia, including Haydn Wood's *Horse Guards march (Down your Way)*, Ronald Binge's *Sailing by* (Radio 4 signing off) and Trevor Duncan's catchy *March (Dr Finlay's Casebook)*, which reminds one a little of the *Marcia* of Dag Wirén and is here played most delicately.

What comes out from every one of these twenty pieces is not just their catchy memorability and tunefulness, but the brilliance and subtlety of the instrumentations. They are full of the sort of effects that only a really practical musician, close to players, could think up; and they are here made the more enjoyable by the warmth and clarity of the sound. It is welcome that Elgar is this time included with one of his lesser-known pieces, *Carissima*, not to mention Ben Frankel with the jaunty *Carriage and pair*, with its clip-clopping rhythm vividly evoking the period Parisian atmosphere of the film *So Long at the Fair*. A must for anyone at all given to nostalgia.

'British light music classics', **Vol. 3:** HAYDN WOOD: *Montmartre.* CLIVE RICHARDSON: *Melody on the move.* TREVOR DUNCAN: *The girl from Corsica.* LIONEL MONCKTON: *Soldiers in the park.* FELIX GODIN: *Valse Septembre.* BINGE: *Miss Melanie.* IVAN CARYLL: *Pink Lady waltz.* FARNON: *Portrait of a flirt.* DEXTER: *Siciliano.* KETELBEY: *In a Persian market* (with chorus). JACK STRACHEY: *Theatreland.* ARCHIBALD JOYCE: *Songe d'automne.* VIVIAN ELLIS: *Alpine pastures.* TOMLINSON: *Little serenade.* MELACHRINO: *Woodland revel.* TOLCHARD EVANS: *Lady of Spain.* ANCLIFFE: *Smiles, then kisses.* TORCH: *On a spring note.* COATES: *Rediffusion march: Music everywhere.*

*** Hyp. CDA 67148.

Volume 3 is well up to the standard of its attractive predecessors, warmly and sparklingly played, with the orchestra clearly enjoying the melodic profusion. Haydn Wood's opening *Montmartre* would cheer anyone up, and the following *Melody on the move* and *In the party mood* maintain the spirited forward momentum. Many of the later items are justly famous. No collection of British light music would be complete without Ketèlbey, and the New London Light Opera Chorus makes a lusty contribution in the *Persian market.*

Farnon's *Portrait of a flirt*, Harry Dexter's delectably fragile *Siciliano* and Tomlinson's equally charming *Little serenade* are all winningly personable, while Melachrino's *Woodland revel* begins wittily with a simple interplay on a melodic fragment, which then flowers romantically, generating a rumbustious climax. The Ancliffe waltz is delightfully English in rhythmic inflection, and after Sidney Torch's catchy reminder of spring, Eric Coates provides a rousing conclusion. The recording is crisp and clear within a pleasingly warm ambience. Most refreshing.

'European light music classics': JESSEL: *Parade of the tin soldiers.* LEHAR: *Gold and silver* (waltz). PIERNE: *Album pour mes petits amis: Marche des petits soldats de plomb.* **Johann** STRAUSS Jr: *Tritsch-Tratsch polka.* LINCKE: *Glow worm idyll.* ALFVEN: *Swedish polka.* GOUNOD: *Funeral march of a marionette.* WALDTEUFEL: *The Skaters waltz.* HEYKENS: *Serenade.* PADILLA: *El relicaro.* BECUCCI: *Tesoro mio!* HELLMESBERGER: *Ball scene.* WEINBERGER: *Schwanda the Bagpiper: Polka.* FETRAS: *Moonlight on the Alster.* HALVORSEN: *Entry of the Boyars.*

**(*) Hyp. CDA 66998.

Although there is much to enjoy here, this is a less enterprising collection than usual in this series. The highlights are what one might call the Palm Court trifles, the two evocations of miniature soldiers (Pierné's unmistakably French), Lincke's exquisite *Glow worm idyll*, the Heykens *Serenade* and the *Entry of the Boyars*, which is most winningly played. *Moonlight on the Alster*, too, is a famous waltz by an unfamous composer and Waldteufel's *Skaters* are always welcome. But why choose the *Tritsch-Tratsch polka* and *Gold and silver* which are readily available elsewhere; the latter is one of Barbirolli's specials? Performances and recordings are pretty well up to standard.

'American light music classics'; SOUSA: *Washington Post.* **Kerry** MILLS: *Whistling Rufus.* GOULD: *American Symphonette No. 3: Pavane.* **Felix** ARNDT: *Nola (A silhouette).* PRYOR: *The whistler and his dog.* **Leroy** ANDERSON: *Belle of the ball; Plink, plank, plunk.* TRAD.: *The Arkansas traveller (The old fiddler's breakdown).* BRATTON: *Teddy bears' picnic.* MACDOWELL: *Woodland sketches: To a wild rose.* HOLZMANN: *Blaze away!* FRIML: *In love (Chanson).* **Raymond** SCOTT: *The toy trumpet.* GERSHWIN: *Promenade.* HERBERT: *Babes in Toyland: March of the toys.* ROSE: *Holiday for strings.* NEVIN: *Water scenes: Narcissus.* **Don** GILLIS: *Symphony No. 5 1/2 (A Symphony for fun).* RODGERS: *Carousel waltz.*

*** Hyp. CDA 67067.

The surprise here is instantly to recognize so many catchy tunes, and then find they come from the other side of the Atlantic. After the familiar Sousa march (played with spirit and a touch of panache, rather than Yankee bezaz), Kerry Mills's *Whistling Rufus*, with its cakewalk rhythm, is unmistakably American. Abe Holzmann's *Blaze away!*, complete with piccolo solo, is equally identifiable. So is the engaging Gould *Pavane* and the two witty Leroy Anderson encore pieces, while the New Yorker Edward MacDowell's tender little portrait of a wild rose, delightfully played here, remains his most famous piece. But *Nola, The whistler and his dog* (complete with 'barking' coda), Narcissus and David Rose's winning pizzicato *Holiday for strings* all seem so familiar that they feel more like local items.

The Teddy Bear's picnic, was an American instrumental piece, but became a British song, and a huge hit in England. Rudolf Friml's *Chanson (In Love)* also became famous when words were added to it – for its appearance in the Hollywood film *The Firefly*, and it was renamed the *Donkey serenade*. I. M. has a treasured childhood memory of seeing another 1930s film, *Babes in Toyland*, where Laurel and Hardy helped to defeat the evil Bogeymen to the strains of Victor Herbert's famous *March*. In that instance the toy soldiers were six feet tall, as Stanley, who had ordered them for Father Christmas, unfortunately got the measurements wrong! The music sounds as piquant as ever. Don Gillis's *Symphony for fun* doesn't seem as audacious as it once did, but still enjoyably bears out its descriptive title. As in the rest of this splendid Hyperion series, performances are as polished as they are spontaneous, and the recording is first class.

(i) New Philharmonia Orchestra, (ii) London Symphony Orchestra, Richard Bonynge

'Overtures and ballet music of the nineteenth century':

Disc 1: (i) Overtures: AUBER: *Marco Spada; Lestocq.* ADAM: *Giralda; La poupée de Nuremburg.* LECOCQ: *La fille de Madame Angot.* THOMAS: *Mignon.* PLANQUETTE: *Les cloches de Corneville.* BOIELDIEU: *Le calife de Bagdad; La dame blanche.* MEYERBEER: *Le Prophète: Coronation march.* MASSENET: *La Navarraise: Nocturne.* GOUNOD: *La Reine de Saba, Act II: Waltz.* BIZET: *Don Procopio, Act II: Entr'acte.*

Disc 2: (ii) Overtures: DONIZETTI: *Roberto Devereux.* ROSSINI: *Torvaldo e Dorliska.* MAILLART: *Les Dragons de Villars.* OFFENBACH: *La fille du tambour-major.* VERDI: *Giovanna d'Arco.* HEROLD: *Zampa.* WALLACE: *Maritana.* AUBER: *La Neige.* MASSENET: *Cherubin, Act III: Entr'acte. Don César de Bazan: Entr'acte Sevillana. Les Erinnyes: Invocation.* GOUNOD: *Le tribut de Zamora, Act III: Danse grecque.* SAINT-SAENS: *Henry VIII, Act II: Danse de la gypsy.* DELIBES: *Le roi l'a dit, Act II: Entr'acte.*

🅱 *** Double Decca (ADD) 466 431-2 (2).

By delving further into the back catalogue, Decca have come up with an even more delectable collection of overtures and orchestral sweetmeats than in the companion ECO eighteenth-century compilation above. The programme is again based on three Bonynge LPs, two from the LSO and one from the New Philharmonia Orchestra, again from the late 1960s and early 1970s. The format of the nineteenth-century overture is a pretty standard one, usually a potpourri, but sometimes more sophisticated in layout, as with Thomas's *Mignon*, and to a lesser extent, Hérold's *Zampa*. But it is the tunes that count.

Of the three Auber overtures *Marco Spada* has a wonderfully evocative opening, suggesting a sunrise, before bursting champagne-like into one of his typical galloping allegros; *Lestocq* contains a memorably wistful tune for the oboe, while *La Neige*, more subtle than usual, shows the composer's gift for writing catchy tunes quite early in his career. Adam's *Giralda* and *La poupée de Nuremburg* display all the delicacy and skill we know from his ballet scores, the former features glittering castanets, the latter an unexpected passage for string quartet. Boieldieu's charming *La dame blanche* is as light as thistledown and *The calife of Bagdad* has never sounded more resplendent. Lecocq's *La fille de Madame Angot* is quite delicious.

Among the LSO performances, *Maritana* stands out. Bonynge does this gorgeously, the melodramatic opening arresting, and the shaping of the hit tune *'Scenes that are brightest'* lusciously presented. Rossini's *Torvaldo e Dorliska* is interesting in including the second subject of the *Cenerentola* overture, while Donizetti's *Roberto Devereux* flagrantly draws on 'God save the King'. Offenbach's winning *La fille du tambour-major*, piquantly scored, ends with an exuberant can-can played with superb gusto.

We also turn to the LSO for the ballet music. Besides a brilliant account of Meyerbeer's *Coronation march*, there is a series of delightful *bon bouches* including a famous Massenet cello solo (the *Invocation* from *Les Erinnyes*) and the *Nocturne* from *La Navarraise*). Gounod's *Grande valse* from *La Reine de Saba* sounds as though it has been left over from the *Faust* ballet music, while Saint-Saëns's *Gypsy dance* from *Henry VIII*, with its ominous timpani strokes, turns into a tuneful valse-macabre. The programme ends with a charming pastiche *Minuet* from Delibes's *Le roi l'a dit*. Bonynge is a complete master of this repertoire, which he clearly loves, and all this music is so chic and poised in his hands and so brilliantly played and recorded, that enjoyment is assured.

New Symphony Orchestra, Sir Alexander Gibson

Concert: SAINT-SAENS: *Danse macabre.* HUMPERDINCK: *Hansel and Gretel: Witch's Ride.* LISZT: *Mephisto Waltz No. 1.* MUSSORGSKY: *Night*

on the Bare Mountain (arr. Rimsky-Korsakov).
SIBELIUS: *Symphony No. 5; Karelia Suite.*

(M) **(*) Decca (ADD) 468 488-2.

These recordings were part of a highly regarded early
LP Collection called 'Witches Brew', first issued by
RCA, although recorded by a top Decca team in the
Kingsway Hall in 1957. Alas the highlight of the programme, Malcolm Arnold's *Tam O'Shanter Overture*,
has been cut here to make room for Gibson's Sibelius
performances which are at a much lower level of tension. (They are discussed above under their composer
entry). The rest of the programme bubbles agreeably,
although the formidable *Witch's Ride* is too easy-
going, not a bit sinister in its progress. The recording
(engineered by Kenneth Wilkinson) is still in the
demonstration bracket for its period.

New World Symphony, Michael Tilson Thomas

CHAVEZ: *Symphony No. 2 (Sinfonia india).*
COPLAND: *Danzón cubano.* ROLDAN: *Suite de 'La
rebambaramba'.* REVUELTAS: *Sensemayá.*
CATURLA: *Tres danzas cubanas.* ROLDAN: *Ritmica V.*
PIAZZOLLA: *Tangazo.* GINASTERA. *Estancia, Op. 8a:
4 Dances.*

*** Australian Decca Eloquence (ADD) 467 603-2.

This disc seems to have had a short life in its full-price
incarnation, but returns in Australian Decca's Eloquence series. It demonstrates a titillating mixture of
South American influences, from the unashamedly
jazzy *Danzón cubano* of Copland, to more substantial
works, such as Chávez's *Second Symphony*. Its exotic
rarities include Revueltas's *Sensemayá*. This has a
delightful quirky opening with the bass drum, gong
and bassoon; then an ever-increasing collection of
instruments create an impressive cumulative effect.
The longest work here is *Tangazo*, first heard in 1988. A
celebration of the famous South American dance, it
begins slowly and broodingly, but gradually becomes
more vigourous and sensual. All the music here is colourful and vivid, and the performances and recordings
are excellent.

Noras, Arto (cello), Finnish Radio Symphony Orchestra, Oramo or Saraste; Norwegian Radio SO, Rasilainen

DVORAK: *Cello concerto* (with Finnish Radio
Symphony Orchestra, Oramo). DUTILLEUX: *Cello
concerto (Tout un monde lointain).* ELGAR: *Cello
concerto.* LALO: *Cello concerto in D min.* SAINT-
SAENS: *Cello concerto No. 1.* BARTOK: *Rhapsody No.
1* (originally for violin and orch.) (all with Finnish
RSO, Saraste). SHOSTAKOVICH: *Cello concertos Nos*

1 & 2. RICHARD STRAUSS: *Romanze in D* (1883)
(with Norwegian Radio Symphony Orchestra, Ari
Rasilainen).

(B) *** Finlandia 3984 26836-2 (3).

This fine collection of cello concertos comes in just
one of the many bargain-boxes issued to celebrate the
twentieth anniversary of the Finlandia label. The
Finnish cellist Arto Noras makes an outstanding soloist in this wide range of works, with his impressive
technique, flawless intonation and firm, full tone. In
generous couplings the Elgar concerto, dedicatedly
done, is just one of eight full concertos, all excellently
done in fresh, clear interpretations, as well as shorter
works by Bartók and Strauss. Brilliant, full sound.

Northern Ballet Theatre Orchestra, Pryce-Jones

Twentieth-century English ballets: FEENEY:
Cinderella. MULDOWNEY: *The Brontës.* Carl DAVIS:
A Christmas carol.

(BB) *** Naxos 8.553495.

This enterprising disc is of music taken from full-
length ballet scores commissioned by the Northern
Ballet Theatre. The most instantly appealing work is
Carl Davis's *A Christmas carol*, delightfully nostalgic
with its mixture of sentimental and vigorous numbers
– these include a lively, rustic-sounding dance as some
poor Londoners try to keep themselves warm. It is an
appealing score, with much piquant orchestration and
a neat use of the harpsichord. Davis introduces well-
known Christmas carols to present the story of Scrooge
in a fresh way.

Philip Feeney's *Cinderella* is more severe, reflecting
the story as told by the Brothers Grimm, rather than
the more romanticized version by Perrault. Feeney
uses a battery of percussion instruments to tell the
tale, and the result lacks really memorable tunes. But
it is not at all dull and has plenty of rhythm and colour. The *Courtly dances* begin with an array of bells,
percussion instruments and a gong, then the composer switches to the harpsichord halfway through to
striking effect. *The Red Ball*, where the prince introduces himself, is quirky in a haunting way, and the
finale an up-beat conclusion.

The Brontës, with music by Dominic Muldowney, is
a series of vignettes portraying the Brontë family, as
seen through the eyes of the father, Rev. Patrick
Brontë, who outlived all his six children. The opening
Toy soldiers' fantasy is charming, with its trumpet fanfares set against a robust marching tune; *The Moors*
and *Wuthering Heights* numbers are appropriately
broody, whilst *Charlotte in Brussels* is a jaunty little
waltz with witty writing throughout the orchestra. It
is thoroughly entertaining. The performances and
recording are outstanding.

Northern Philharmonia Orchestra of England, Leeds Festival Chorus, Paul Daniel

'*Rule, Britannia - The last night of the Proms*': WALTON: *Coronation marches: Crown imperial; Orb and sceptre.* PARRY: *Jerusalem.* ELGAR: *Enigma variations: Nimrod. Pomp and circumstance march No. 1.* WOOD: *Fantasia on British sea songs* (including *Rule, Britannia*). ARNOLD: *Overture Tam O'Shanter.* PARRY: *I was glad.*

(BB) **(*) Naxos 8.553981.

If it seems a little perverse to record such a programme without the contribution of the Prommers and the heady last-night atmosphere, it has to be said that this is a very good concert in its own right and the Leeds Chorus makes an impressive contribution in *Rule, Britannia* and especially in the reprise of the great *Pomp and circumstance* melody (which is the more effective at Paul Daniel's spacious tempo). The two Walton marches have panache and Arnold's *Tam O'Shanter* is splendidly done. Here the recording is of a spectacular demonstration quality. Excellent value.

Northern Sinfonia, David Lloyd-Jones

'*English String Miniatures*': HOPE: *Momentum Suite.* BRIDGE: *2 Pieces* (arr. Hindmarsh). CARSE: *2 Sketches.* TOMLINSON: *Graceful Dance.* HOLST: *A Moorside Suite.* DELIUS: *2 Aquarelles.* LEWIS: *English Suite.*

(BB) *** Naxos 8.555070.

Another enterprising programme of light but never trivial English music, all with a distinct pastoral feel. In Philip Hope's *Momentum Suite* the first movement, *Dance*, a lively rustic-sounding piece, has an especially attractive middle section, while the last movement, which gets faster and faster, gives the work its title. Paul Lewis's *English Suite* balances its lively *March, Jig* and *Jaunt* movements with a reflective *Meditation*. The two Frank Bridge *Pieces* are highly contrasted. The humour of the *Scherzo Phantastick* comes over well in Paul Hindmarsh's arrangement, including the 'sneeze' at the end of the mock *Trio* section; the *Valse-intermezzo* is delightful, too. *A Northern Dance* from Adam Carse's *Two Sketeches* has a quite haunting melancholy feel (with a tune rather similar to 'Danny Boy'). Tomlinson's *Graceful Dance* is slight, but pleasing. The better known Holst and Delius works are beautifully played, with the *Nocturne* from Holst's *A Moorside Suite* especially atmospheric. The recording is resonant but well detailed, and the performances are first class, as one might expect from Lloyd-Jones and his excellent northern players. Strongly recommended at super-bargain price.

Oistrakh, David (violin)

'*The Originals*' (with (i) VSO; (ii) Igor Oistrakh; (iii) RPO, Goossens; (iv) Dresden State O, Konwitschny): BACH: (i) *Violin concertos Nos. 1 in E; 2 in A min;* (ii-iii) *Double violin concerto in D min., BWV 1041-3.* (iii) BEETHOVEN: *Romances Nos. 1 in G, 2 in F, Opp. 40 & 50.* (iv) BRAHMS: *Violin concerto, Op. 77.* TCHAIKOVSKY: *Violin concerto, Op. 35.*

(M) (***) DG stereo/mono 447 427-2 (2).

In 'The Originals' series at mid-price, DG here offers reissues of classic Oistrakh recordings unavailable for years in any format. Rarest are the 1954 mono recordings of the Brahms and Tchaikovsky *Concertos*, more relaxed, more volatile readings than those Oistrakh recorded later in stereo. Oistrakh moves effortlessly from dashing bravura to the sweetest lyricism, the complete master. The Bach and Beethoven offerings are hardly less welcome.

Allowing for the practice of the time, these Bach performances are all strong and resilient, consistently bringing out the sweetness and purity of Oistrakh's playing, not least in the rapt accounts of the slow movements. Directing the Vienna Symphoniker from the violin, Oistrakh may make the tuttis in the two Bach solo concertos rather heavy, but he then transforms everything the moment he starts playing. The Bach *Double concerto* with Oistrakh father and son, accompanied by Goossens and the RPO, is more magnetic still, and they accompany him no less sympathetically in the warm, poised readings of the two Beethoven *Romances*.

Concertante works and Duos (with Igor Oistrakh): VIVALDI: *Concerto grosso in A min., Op. 3/8* (with RPO). SARASATE: *Navarra, Op. 33* (with Leipzig Gewandhaus Orchestra, Franz Konwitschny). BACH: *Sonata for 2 violins and harpsichord in C, BWV 1037* (with Hans Pischner, harpsichord). HANDEL: *Sonata for 2 violins and harpsichord in G min., Op. 2/7.* BENDA: *Trio sonata in E* (both with Wladimir Yampolsky, piano). WIENIAWSKI: *3 Etudes-caprices for 2 violins, Op. 18.*

(M) (***) DG mono/stereo 463 616-2.

The second Oistrakh reissue in DG's Original series, again joining father and son, gathers together an oddly assorted programme of recordings made in 1957/8 and 1960, with (surprisingly) only the Vivaldi item in stereo, although the sound throughout is very good indeed. The Bach hardly needs recommendation, the Handel sonata is a gem, and even the Benda – a slight but pleasing work – has its moments.

Orchestra of St John's, Smith Square, John Lubbock

'*On hearing the first cuckoo in spring*': VAUGHAN WILLIAMS: *Fantasia on Greensleeves; Rhosymedre.* GRIEG: *Peer Gynt: Morning.* RAVEL: *Pavane.*

DELIUS: *On hearing the first cuckoo in spring.*
FAURE: *Masques et bergamasques: Overture.*
Berceuse, Op. 56. SCHUBERT: *Rosamunde: Entr'acte*
No. 2; Ballet music No. 2. MOZART: *Divertimento in*
D, K.136: Presto.

(BB) **(*) ASV CDQS 6007.

An enjoyable bargain collection of essentially atmospheric music for late evening. Fine playing throughout: tempi are very relaxed, notably in the Grieg, Fauré and Schubert items, but the evocation is persuasive. The digital recording is first class, full and clear, yet not too clinical in its detail. Some might feel that the music-making here verges on the somnolent in its consistently easy-going manner – the Delius piece is indicative of the conductor's style – but the closing Mozart *Presto* ends the concert with a sparkle.

Orchestre National de France, Charles Munch

'*Hommage à Charles Munch*'.

BEETHOVEN: *Symphonies Nos. 4 in B flat; 7 in A*
Overture: Consecration of the house (*(*) V 4825).

BERLIOZ: *Symphonie fantastique, Op. 14; Overtures:*
Le Corsaire, Op. 21; Benvenuto Cellini, Op. 23 (* V
4826).

BRAHMS: *Symphony No. 2 in D, Op. 73.* SCHUMANN:
Symphony No. 4 in D min., Op. 120 (** V 4827).

DEBUSSY: *Images: Iberia; La Mer; Fantaisie for*
piano and orchestra (with Nicole Henriot) (** V
4828).

FRANCK: *Symphony in D min.* FAURE: *Pelléas et*
Mélisande: suite (** V 4829).

HONEGGER: *Symphony No. 1.* DUTILLEUX:
Symphony No. 2 (**(*) V 4830).

HONEGGER: *Symphonies Nos. 2 (for strings and*
trumpet obbligato); 5 (Di tre re); Le chant de
Nigamon; Pastorale d'été (** V 4831).

ROUSSEL: *Symphonies Nos. 3 in G min., Op. 42; 4 in*
A, Op. 53; Bacchus et Ariane: suite No. 2 (** V 4832).

'*Hommage à Charles Munch*' (complete).

(BB) ** Audivis Valois (ADD) V 4822 (8) (with the
complete set: SIBELIUS: *Legends: The swan of Tuonela;*
Lemminkäinen's return).

An eight-CD set called *Hommage à Charles Munch* commemorates his work with the Orchestre National after his return from Boston. If you buy the whole set – and it is very inexpensive – you get a 1964 recording of two of the *Four Legends* made while the orchestra was on tour in Finland. The discs are available separately and bring some outstanding performances, albeit in variable sound.

The Beethoven *Fourth* (V 4825) was recorded in Stockholm on the same Scandinavian tour and the *Seventh* and, appropriately enough, *The Consecration of the house* come from the inaugural concert in the *Maison de la Radio* in Paris in 1963. Not first-class but acceptable sound, as is the Berlioz (V 4826). The *Symphonie fantastique*, recorded in a rather dry acoustic in Lisbon in 1963, is a bit hard-driven, as was his Boston account. *Un bal* is horribly rushed.

Good though his Franck, Brahms and Schumann may be, it was for his Honegger and Roussel that Munch is best remembered. Always a champion of good contemporary music, he conducted the Honegger and Dutilleux (V 4830) in 1962. Both works are closely associated with Boston. Koussevitzky commissioned the Honegger *First Symphony* (along with the Roussel *Third*) for the 50th anniversary of the founding of the Boston *Symphony* and Munch conducted the première of the Dutilleux Symphony during his Boston years. The Honegger recording is not absolutely first class – a bit strident and narrower in frequency range than some of its companions – but the Dutilleux is very good, and what a performance!

Two other Honegger symphonies, Nos. 2 and 5 (V 4831), come from performances taken from the orchestra's 1964 European tour, the *Symphony for strings* in San Sebastien in Spain and the *Fifth* from Helsinki. The early *Le chant de Nigamon*, an amazingly original piece, was recorded at the Théâtre des Champs-Elysées two years earlier and though not first-class sound is perfectly acceptable (it briefly captures the conductor's vocalise!). Neither of the symphonies is superior to his Boston performances from the 1950s and the rather shrill-sounding *Symphony for strings* is nowhere near as impressive as his 1969 EMI recording with the Orchestre de Paris. The Helsinki recording of the *Fifth* sounds better.

The Roussel *Third* (V 4832) has plenty of drive, too, but the recording balance is poor. It comes from the 1964 Edinburgh Festival and the string melody at the opening has to struggle to make itself heard against the percussive accompaniment. The *Fourth Symphony*, recorded two years later at the Théâtre des Champs-Elysées, is better, though the *Bacchus et Ariane* suite, whose provenance is not given, is more transparent and present than either. Munch was closely identified with Roussel all his life and though this disc is better than nothing, if you can get hold of his commercial recording of the symphonies on Erato they are better served in terms of sound. All the same, despite its sonic limitations this is a set to have. Munch was a conductor of stature and his work with the Orchestre National is well worth commemorating.

Ormandy, Eugene (conductor and violinist)

'*The art of Eugene Ormandy*': Ormandy as violinist:
RIMSKY-KORSAKOV: *Le Coq d'Or: Hymn to the sun.*
Sadko: Song of India. Victor HERBERT: *Mlle.*
Modiste: Kiss me again. DRDLA: *Souvenir.* DVORAK:

Humoresque. **Ormandy and his Salon Orchestra:** BRAHMS: *Hungarian Dance No. 2 in D minor.* HOSMER: *Southern Rhapsody.* **With Dorsey Brothers' Concert Orchestra:** COSLOW-SPIER-BRITT: *Was it a dream?.* **With Minneapolis Symphony Orchestra:** ZEMACHSON: *Chorale and fugue in D min., Op. 4.* ZADOR: *Hungarian dance.* GRIFFES: *The Pleasure dome of Kubla Khan, Op. 8.* HARRIS: *When Johnny comes marching home.* **With Philadelphia Orchestra:** BARBER: *Essay No. 1, Op. 12.* MENOTTI: *Amelia goes to the ball overture.* MIASKOVSKY: *Symphony No. 21 in F sharp Min., Op. 51.* RICHARD STRAUSS: *Symphonia domestica, Op. 53.* **With Yeend, Beech, Coray, Kullman, Harrell, London, Los Angeles Chorus, Hollywood Bowl Symphony Orchestra: (vi)** MAHLER: *Symphony No. 8: 1st movement only.*

(***) Biddulph mono WHL 064/5.

This two-disc set gives a fascinating profile of Ormandy's early career. He arrived in America seeking a career as a violinist and in the first five tracks we hear him as a good deal more than capable in that role. These recordings, dating from the 1920s, have a warm nostalgic glow and the sound is generally good.

His next progression was conducting light classical and salon music for radio, of which there are three examples from the late 1920s, including a characteristic 1920s account (with vocals) of *Was it a dream?*

Ormandy's great turning point came when he stood in for Toscanini, who sudddenly pulled out of a Philadelphia Orchestral engagement, and Ormandy took over. His concerts were a triumph and, thanks to a talent scout, resulted in a series of recordings with the Minneapolis SO, of which four (from the mid 1930s) are included here. The repertoire is comparatively rare today, which makes their inclusion valuable, especially as they are so enjoyable.

But it is the Philadelphia recordings which are the glories of this set: Barber's *Essay No. 1* has rarely been equalled in performance, whilst the Menotti overture is brilliant as is could be. The Miaskovsky is magnetic in concentration and atmosphere, and one just has to hear the sumptuous string tone to appreciate why the Philadelphia sound is legendary. The *Symphonia domestica* is also perceptively characterized, and again, there is something quite magnetic about the performance.

The first movement of Mahler's *Eighth Symphony* is an interesting reminder of Ormandy's pioneering importance in this repertoire, but the recorded sound, from a live broadcast in 1948, leaves something to be desired. A fascinating collection just the same, with helpful sleeve notes and convenient slim-line packaging.

Osipov State Russian Folk Orchestra, Vitaly Gnutov

'Balalaika favourites': BUDASHIN: *Fantasy on two folk songs.* arr. GORODOVSKAYA: *At sunrise.* KULIKOV: *The Linden tree.* OSIPOV: *Kamarinskaya.*

MIKHAILOV/SHALAYEV: *Fantasy on Volga melodies.* ANDREYEV: *In the moonlight; Under the apple tree; Waltz of the faun.* SOLOVIEV/SEDOY: *Midnight in Moscow.* TCHAIKOVSKY: *Dance of the comedians.* SHISHAKOV: *The living room.* arr. MOSSOLOV: *Evening bells.* arr. POPONOV: *My dear friend, please visit me.* RIMSKY-KORSAKOV: *Flight of the bumblebee.*

✹ (M) *** Mercury 432 000-2.

The Mercury recording team visited Moscow in 1962 in order to make the first recordings produced in the Soviet Union by Western engineers since the Revolution. The spirit of that unique occasion is captured wonderfully here – analogue atmosphere at its best. The rippling waves of balalaika sound, the accordion solos, the exhilarating accelerandos and crescendos that mark the style of this music-making: all are recorded with wonderful immediacy. Whether in the shimmering web of sound of *The Linden tree* or *Evening bells*, the sparkle of the folksongs or the sheer bravura of items like *In the moonlight*, which gets steadily faster and louder, or in Rimsky's famous piece (sounding like a hive full of bumblebees), this is irresistible, and the recording is superbly real in its CD format.

Overtures

'Overtures' (with Chicago SO; LPO; LSO; Royal Opera House, Covent Garden Orchestra; VPO; Sir Georg Solti): SUPPE: *Light cavalry; Pique Dame; Morning, noon and night in Vienna; Poet and peasant.* GLINKA: *Ruslan and Ludmilla.* VERDI: *La Traviata: Prelude to Act I.* WAGNER: *Die Meistersinger von Nürnberg: Prelude to Act I; Der fliegende Holländer.* BERLIOZ: *Les Francs-juges.* MOZART: *Le nozze di Figaro.* BEETHOVEN: *Egmont; Leonora overture No. 3.* WEBER: *Oberon.* BRAHMS: *Academic festival overture.* ROSSINI: *Il barbiere di Siviglia.* GLAZUNOV: *Prince Igor.* BIZET: *Carmen: Prelude to Act I.* HUMPERDINCK: *Hänsel und Gretel.* MUSSORGSKY: *Khovanshchina: Prelude.*

(B) **(*) Double Decca (IMS) ADD/DDD 460 982-2 (2).

It was appropriate that this collection should include the four favourite Suppé overtures, as it was this repertoire in earlier mono versions with which Solti made his Decca orchestral début, and the virtuosity he generated with the LPO impressed Toscanini. These later (1960) VPO stereo versions are equally brilliant, but here Culshaw's recording balance was miscalculated, having an exceptionally wide dynamic range, too wide for the cello solos in *Morning, noon and night* and *Poet and peasant*, where the instrument is backward and sounds not unlike a viola. The rest of the collection ranges across Solti's recording career, through the 1960s and 1970s, including such highlights as his famous, fizzing LSO account of Glinka's *Ruslan and Ludmilla*, his electrifying *Les Francs-juges* and with several performances derived from his complete opera recordings, most recently the Act I *Prelude* from his outstanding 1995 version of Verdi's *La Traviata*. For the most part, vintage Decca recording of high quality.

Overtures: SUPPE: *Beautiful Galatea; Fatinitza; Jolly Robbers* (with Montreal SO, Dutoit); *Light Cavalry; Morning, Noon and Night; Pique Dame; Poet and Peasant* (with VPO, Solti). REZNICEK: *Donna Diana.* NICOLAI: *The Merry Wives of Windsor.* J. STRAUSS JR.: *Die Fledermaus* (with VPO, Boskovsky).

(BB) **(*) Decca (ADD/DDD) 467 438-2.

Solti's taut, high-powered approach to Suppé is not perhaps quite the right idiomatic style for this genially rumbustious music, but the results are very exciting indeed, and these four 1959 performances have long been famous for their orchestral bravura and exhilaration. Indeed, *Light Cavalry* musters up more energy than *The Charge of the Light Brigade*, while *Morning, Noon and Night* almost takes off altogether. The Boskovsky items have the authenticity of vintage champagne, and Dutoit's contributions are splendid – the *Fatinitza* overture ends with an irresistible *can-can*, which Offenbach would have been proud to own. Unless you resist Solti's Suppé (the dynamic range of their recordings is excessively wide), this is a fine bargain on the Eloquence label, all in excellent sound, although the packaging is minimal, to say the least.

'Famous Overtures': BIZET: *Carmen: Prélude.* BEETHOVEN: *Egmont; Fidelio.* BRAHMS: *Academic Festival Overture.* BERNSTEIN: *Candide* (with Met Op. O, VPO or LSO, Bernstein). ROSSINI: *Il barbiere di Siviglia.* MUSSORGSKY: *Khovanshchina: Prelude.* MOZART: *Le nozze di Figaro* (with COE, VPO or Vienna State Op. O, Abbado); *Die Zauberflöte* (with VPO, Karajan). VERDI: *La traviata: Act I Prelude.* WEBER: *Der Freischütz* (with Bav. State Op. O, Kleiber). OFFENBACH: *Orpheus in the Underworld.* J. STRAUSS JR: *Die Fledermaus.* SUPPE: *Light Cavalry* (with BPO, Karajan). REZNICEK: *Donna Diana* (with Gothenberg SO, Järvi). GLUCK: *Orfeo ed Euridice* (E. Bar. Sol., Gardiner). MENDELSSOHN: *A Midsummer Night's Dream.* GERSHWIN: *Cuban Overture* (with Chicago SO, Levine). VERDI: *La forza del destino:* WAGNER: *Die Meistersinger von Nürnberg* (with O de Paris, Barenboim). GLINKA: *Ruslan and Ludmilla* (Russian Nat. O, Pletnev).

(B) *** DG Panorama (ADD/DDD) 469 322-2 (2).

An outstandingly imaginative collection, with the advantage of a pair of discs that range more widely and more imaginatively than the Decca collection above and includes many outstanding performances. Karajan's sumptuously played Suppé and Offenbach overtures are more sophisticated than Solti's (if less visceral in their excitement); Bernstein's swaggering, though comparatively measured account of the *Carmen Prelude* and his warmly personal readings of the Beethoven and Brahms overtures are distinctive, not

to mention his own scintillating *Candide* overture. Pletnev's vibrant *Ruslan and Ludmilla* and Abbado's sparkling Rossini and Mozart items are most enjoyable, as is the latter's hauntingly atmospheric account of the *Khovanshchina Prelude*, one of the high points of the collection. Gardiner's period instrument account of Gluck's *Orfeo ed Euridice* is another highlight, as are Kleiber's *Der Freischütz* and Järvi's *Donna Diana*, a happy, light-hearted foil. The recordings, mainly digital, range from very good to excellent. This is the best compilation of its kind in the catalogue.

Perkins, Laurence (bassoon)

Bassoon Concertos (with Manchester Camerata, Douglas Boyd): M. HAYDN: *Concertino in B flat.* MOZART: *Concerto.* STAMITZ: *Concerto.* WEBER: *Concerto; Andante and Rondo ungarese.*

*** Hyp. CDA 72688.

If the bassoon has often been cast as the clown of the orchestra, the five concertante works on this disc demonstrate how much wider its role is, with Laurence Perkins as soloist bringing out the tender beauty of the muted slow movement of the Mozart *Bassoon Concerto*, an early work too often dismissed, but full of charm. The Stamitz *Concerto*, elegant in the slow movement, vigorous in the outer movements, is equally attractive, and the two Weber concertante works show him in relaxed mood, with the *Hungarian Rondo* and the finale of the *Concerto* winningly rumbustious. The *Concertino* by Michael Haydn is the slow movement of one of his orchestral *Serenades*. Perkins, with his crisp articulation, brings out the fun in much of the inspiration as well as the lyrical beauty, warmly accompanied by the Manchester Camerata (of which he is principal bassoon) under another leading wind-player, the oboist, Douglas Boyd.

Perlman, Itzhak (violin)

'A la carte' (with Abbey Road Ens., Lawrence Foster): MASSENET: *Thaïs: Méditation.* GLAZUNOV: *Mazurka-Obéreque; Méditation, Op. 32.* RACHMANINOV: *Vocalise, Op. 34/14.* SARASATE: *Zigeunerweisen, Op. 20; Introduction and Tarantelle, Op. 43.* RIMSKY-KORSAKOV: *Russian fantasy* (arr. KREISLER). TCHAIKOVSKY: *Scherzo, Op. 42/2* (orch. Glazunov). WIENIAWSKI: *Légende, Op. 17.* KREISLER: *The old refrain; Schön Rosmarin.*

**(*) EMI CDC5 55475-2.

Perlman is in his element in this luscious concert of mostly Russian lollipops – although, as it happens, the most delectable playing of all comes in the Sarasate *Zigeunerweisen*. But the pieces by Glazunov, Tchaikovsky's sparkling *Scherzo* and the Rimsky-Korsakov *Fantasy* also show the extraordinary range of colour and sheer charisma of this fiddling. Alas, as always, the violin is too closely balanced, and this is most disadvantageous in the Wieniawski *Légende*, which loses much of its romantic atmosphere. Perlman's closing solo encore, Kreisler's *Schön Rosmarin*, ends the programme with extraordinary panache. Otherwise Lawrence Foster accompanies discreetly.

'Concertos from my childhood' (with Juilliard Orchestra, Lawrence Foster): RIEDING: *Violin concerto in B min., Op. 25.* SEITZ: *Schuler-Konzert No. 2, Op. 13* (orch. ADOLPHE). ACCOLAY: *Violin concerto No. 1 in A min.* BERIOT: *Scenes de ballet, Op. 100.* VIOTTI: *Violin concerto No. 22 in A min.*

*** EMI CDC5 56750-2.

Itzhak Perlman here returns in nostalgia to the concertos which, from the age of six onwards, helped to shape his phenomenal technique. None of this is great music, not even the longest and best-known piece, the Viotti *Violin concerto No. 22*. But playing with obvious love, Perlman brings out freshness and sparkle in each of them. He turns even passing banalities into moments of joy. Oscar Rieding and Friedrich Seitz are so obscure that even their dates seem to be unknown, yet their miniature concertos here are totally charming, with Perlman springing rhythms infectiously. The student orchestra plays brilliantly too.

'Virtuoso Violin': SARASATE: *Carmen Fantasy, Op. 25* (with RPO, Lawrence Foster); *Zigeunerweisen, Op. 20* (with Pittsburg SO, André Previn). *Music for violin and piano* (with Samuel Sanders): *Malagueña & Habanera, Op. 21/1-2; Romanza Andaluza, Op. 22; Playera & Zapateado, Op. 23; Caprice basque, Op. 24; Spanish Dance, Op. 26/8.* FALLA: *Suite populaire espagnole* (arr. KOCHANSKI). GRANADOS: *Spanish Dance.* ALBENIZ: *Malagueña, Op. 165/3* (both arr. KREISLER). HALFFTER: *Danza de la Gitana* (arr. HEIFETZ).

(BB) *** EMI Encore (ADD) CDE5 74765-2.

Here is a recital for violin and piano, originally more appropriately entitled 'Spanish Album', framed by two of Perlman's most successful concertante recordings of Sarasate, the dazzling *Carmen Fantasy* and the equally beguiling *Zigeunerweisen*. Perlman is a violinist who on record demonstrate his delight in virtuosity in every phrase he plays. Yet he can also refine his timbre to be magically beguiling, as in the gentle Asturiano from Falla's *Suite populaire espagnole*. There are few more joyful records of violin fireworks than this, and the recording projects his playing vividly throughout, although the sound is a bit over-bright.

'The Art of Itzhak Perlman' (with Israel PO, Mehta; Pittsburgh SO, Previn; LPO, Ozawa; RPO, Foster; also Ashkenazy, Bruno Canino, Samuel Sanders, Previn (piano) and other artists): BACH: *Concerto, BWV 1056; Partita No. 3, BWV 1006.* VIVALDI: *Concerto, RV 199.* MOZART: *Oboe quartet, K.370.* BRAHMS: *Sonata No. 3; Hungarian dances 1-2, 7 & 9.* SINDING: *Suite, Op. 10.* WIENIAWSKI: *Concerto No. 1.* SIBELIUS: *Concerto.* KHACHATURIAN: *Concerto.* KORNGOLD: *Concerto.* STRAVINSKY: *Suite italienne.*

ANON.: *Doyna.* YELLEN/POLLACK: *My Yiddishe Momma.* FOSTER (arr. HEIFETZ): *The Old folks at home.* PONCE (arr. HEIFETZ): *Estrellita.* JOPLIN: *The Rag-time dance; Pineapple rag.* SMETANA: *Z domoviny.* KREISLER: *Liebesfreud; Liebesleid.* RACHMANINOV (arr. PRESS/GINGOLD): *Vocalise.* GRAINGER: *Molly on the shore.* PREVIN: *Look at him; Bowing and scraping.* TRAD. (arr. KREISLER): *Londonderry air.* SARASATE: *Carmen fantasy.*

(M) *** EMI ADD/DDD CMS7 64617-2 (4).

This box contains a feast of this great violinist's recordings. He made the choice himself and, while the concertos, particularly the Wieniawski, Sibelius, Khachaturian and Korngold (and not forgetting the dazzling concertante *Carmen fantasy* of Sarasate or the *Suite* of Sinding), are all indispensable, the shorter pieces on the last disc just as readily display the Perlman magic. They include the delectable jazz collaboration with Previn, the beautifully played Kreisler encores, and many popular items which are readily turned into lollipops. The stylish account of the Stravinsky *Suite italienne* which ends disc three is also one of the highlights of the set. For the most part the recordings have the violin very forwardly balanced, but that was Perlman's own choice; the sound is otherwise generally excellent.

'Great romantic violin concertos' (with (i) Chicago SO or (ii) Philh. O, Giulini; (iii) Concg. O, Haitink; (iv) RPO, Lawrence Foster; (v) Phd. O, Ormandy): (i) BRAHMS: *Concerto in D, Op. 77.* (iii) BRUCH: *Concerto No. 1 in G min., Op. 26.* (ii) BEETHOVEN: *Concerto in D, Op. 61.* (iv) PAGANINI: *Concerto No. 1 in D, Op. 6.* (iii) MENDELSSOHN: *Concerto in E min., Op. 64.* (v) TCHAIKOVSKY: *Concerto in D, Op. 35.*

(M) **(*) EMI ADD/DDD CMS7 64922-2 (3).

These major Perlman recordings include his earlier (1980) studio recording of the Beethoven *Concerto*; it is among the most commanding of his readings and the element of slight understatement, the refusal to adopt too romantically expressive a style, makes for a compelling strength, perfectly matched by Giulini's thoughtful, direct accompaniment. The (1976) Brahms is also a distinguished performance, again finely supported by Giulini, this time with the Chicago Orchestra, a reading of darker hue than is customary, with a thoughtful and searching slow movement rather than the autumnal rhapsody which it so often becomes. The (1983) Bruch *G minor Concerto* must be counted a disappointment, however, not helped by the harsh, early digital recording which gives an edge to the solo timbre. The performance is heavily expressive and, like the Mendelssohn (recorded at the same time), is not nearly as spontaneous as Perlman's earlier, analogue recording with Previn. The Paganini (1971) is one of Perlman's very finest records and, although the traditional cuts are observed, the performance has irresistible panache and has been transferred to CD very well. In the Tchaikovsky (1978) the soloist is placed less aggressively forward than is usual. Perlman's expressive warmth goes with a very bold orchestral texture from Ormandy and the Philadelphia Orchestra. However, admirers of these artists are unlikely to be disappointed.

'Cinema serenade': **Film themes (with Pittsburgh SO, John Williams):** TEMPERTON/ROSENBAUM: *The Color Purple.* GARDEL: *Scent of a Woman (Tango).* ELMER BERNSTEIN: *The Age of Innocence.* JOHN WILLIAMS: *Far and Away; Sabrina; Schindler's List.* LEGRAND: *The Umbrellas of Cherbourg.* PREVIN: *The Four Horsemen of the Apocalypse.* JOHN BARRY: *Out of Africa.* BONFA: *Black Orpheus.*

*** Sony SK 63005.

Over the centuries all the great violin virtuosi have indulged themselves with the popular tunes of the day, and in our time quite a few of the best of them come from film scores. Perlman relishes their melodiousness, playing them with an easy sophistication and an unashamed tonal succulence. He is immediately beguiling in the title theme from *The Color Purple* and then dances to the tango rhythms of *Pur una cabeza* from *Scent of a Woman.*

Most of these concertante arrangements have been skilfully managed by John Williams, and in his own score for *Far and Away*, he has created a sparkling scherzando to offset the lyrical melody. *Il Postero* and *Sabrina* bring a more delicate charm, but Elmer Bernstein's music for *The Age of Innocence* and John Barry's score for *Out of Africa* develop a Hollywoodian orchestral opulence. The engaging tune Michel Legrand was inspired to write for *The Umbrellas of Cherbourg* seems custom-made for Perlman's stylish languor, and for contrast *Black Orpheus* brings a more intimate duet for violin and guitar.

But our own favourite is the charmingly romantic music Andrea Morricone wrote for *Cinema Paradiso*, a nostalgic score for one of the more memorable films of the last decade. But there is too little of it, and there would have been room for more. Throughout, the easy bravura and panache of the solo playing recall Heifetz, and Williams and the excellent Pittsburgh Orchestra provide spectacular accompaniments. The recording is spacious with Perlman (as usual), upfront in a spotlight; the orchestra is full and warm, but could be better focused.

Petri, Michaela (recorder)

'English concertos' **(with Academy of St Martin-in-the-Fields, directed K. Sillito):** BABEL: *Concerto in C for descant recorder, Op. 3/1.* HANDEL: *Concerto in B flat for treble recorder and bassoon, Op. 4/6* **(with G. Sheene).** BASTON: *Concerto No. 2 for descant recorder in D.* JACOB: *Suite for treble recorder and strings.*

✪ *** Ph. (IMS) 411 056-2.

The *Concerto* by William Babel (c. 1690–1723) is a delight, with Petri's sparkling performance of the outer movements full of good humour and high

spirits, matched by Kenneth Sillito's alert accompaniments. The Handel is yet another arrangement of Op. 4/6, with the organ part felicitously re-scored for recorder and bassoon. The two instruments are nicely balanced and thus a familiar work is given an attractive new look. John Baston's Concerto has individuality and charm, and the finale is quirkily infectious. Gordon Jacob's *Suite* of seven movements balances a gentle bitter-sweet melancholy in the lyrical writing with a rumbustious, extrovert quality in the dances. Altogether a highly rewarding concert, beautifully played and recorded.

'The ultimate recorder collection': VIVALDI: *The Four Seasons: Spring* **(with Guildhall String Ens., George Malcolm).** *Concerto in D (Il gardellino), Op. 10/3: Finale. Concerto in G min. (La Notte), Op. 10/2, RV 439.* SAMMARTINI: *Recorder concerto in F* **(all with Moscow Virtuosi, Vladimir Spivakov).** SATIE: *Gymnopédie No. 1.* GLUCK: *Orfeo: Melody & Dance of the Blessed Spirits.* BACH: *Suite in D, BWV 1067: Air.* SCHEINDIENST: *Variations.* TARTINI: *Sonata in G min. (Devil's trill).* KOPPEL: *Nele's dances Nos. 15–18.* JACOB: *An encore for Michaela* **(all with Lars Hannibal, arr. for recorder and guitar).** GRIEG: *Peer Gynt: Solveig's song; Anitra's dance. Lyric pieces: Butterfly; Little bird, Op. 43/1 & 4; March of the Trolls, Op. 54/3; Once upon a time, Op. 71/1; 2 Norwegian dances, Op. 35/1-2* **(all arr. Langford).** KOPPEL: *Moonchild's dream: conclusion.* ARNOLD: *Recorder concerto, Op. 133: Lento.* CHRISTIANSEN: *Dance suite, Op. 29: Molto vivace* **(all with ECO, Okko Kamu).** HANDEL: *Sonata in G min., Op. 1/2.* BACH: *Sonata in E flat (transposed G), BWV 1031* **(with Keith Jarrett, harpsichord).** TELEMANN: *Trio sonata No. 3 in F min.* **(with Hanne Petri, harpsichord, David Petri, cello).** *Sonata No. 5 in D min. for 2 recorders* **(with Elisabeth Selin).** CORELLI: *Concerto grosso, Op. 6/8 (Christmas): Finale including Pastorale* **(with Nat. PO, Martin Neary).** BACH: *Cantata No. 140: Chorale: Wachet auf* **(with Westminster Abbey Ch., Alistair Ross, organ; cond. Neary).**

(B) ** RCA Twofer 74321 59112-2 (2).

This is a collection that will best appeal to amateur recorder players, and might make a good birthday present for a young beginner, who will surely be impressed by Michaela Petri's easy virtuosity and will respond to a string of such famous melodies. Not all of them transcribe too well, and many are far more effective on the instruments for which they were written. Vivaldi's *Spring* from *The Four Seasons* is indestructible, but Bach's famous *Air* sounds puny, while Grieg's *Second Norwegian dance* is much better suited to the oboe. However, there is quite a lot of genuine recorder repertoire here, stylishly presented, which hopefully should tempt any budding young soloist to explore further. The recording balance is generally well managed and the effect is truthful and not overblown.

Philadelphia Orchestra, Wolfgang Sawallisch

Stokowski orchestral transcriptions: BACH: Chorales from cantatas: *Sheep may safely graze; Wachet auf; Ein'feste Burg ist unser Gott. Toccata and fugue in D min., BWV 565.* BOCCHERINI: *Minuet, Op. 13/5.* BEETHOVEN: *Piano sonata No. 14 (Moonlight):* 1st movt. CHOPIN: *Prelude in E min., Op. 28/4.* FRANCK: *Panis angelicus.* TCHAIKOVSKY: *Andante cantabile, Op. 11; At the ball* (with Marjana Lipovšek). DEBUSSY: *Suite bergamasque: Clair de lune. Prélude: La cathédrale engloutie.* RACHMANINOV: *Prelude in C sharp min., Op. 3/2.*

(*) EMI CDC5 55592-2.

Though Stokowski's own recordings, even those he made in extreme old age, generally have a degree more flair and dramatic bite than any of these from the latterday Philadelphia Orchestra, this makes a fine tribute from the great orchestra he created. The selection of items is an attractive one, not least the Tchaikovsky song orchestration, with Marjana Lipovšek an aptly Slavonic-sounding soloist, though balanced too close.

Sawallisch brings out the evocative magic of Stokowski's impressionistic view of the *Moonlight sonata* movement, and *Clair de lune* is similarly free in its expressiveness. With warm, resonant sound, firmer in the bass than usual from this source, this makes a sumptuous collection, even if some will prefer the brighter, sharper focus of rival Stokowski collections such as Kunzel's on Telarc or Bamert's on Chandos. It is worth noting that Bamert's even more generous selection of fifteen encore pieces overlaps in only three items, and it includes more fun pieces.

Philadelphia Orchestra, Leopold Stokowski (see also under RCA Red Seal Century collection below)

'Fantasia': BACH, orch. Stokowski: *Toccata and Fugue in D min.* DUKAS: *L'Apprenti sorcier.* MUSSORGSKY, arr. Stokowski: *Night on the Bare Mountain.* STRAVINSKY: *The Rite of Spring.* TCHAIKOVSKY: *Nutcracker Suite.*

(M) (***) Pearl mono GEMMCD 4988.

A self-recommending disc. *The Rite of Spring* comes from 1929–30 and the *Nutcracker* from as early as 1926, though one would never believe it. Everything Stokowski did at this period was full of character, and the engineers obviously performed miracles. The latest recording is Stokowski's amazing arrangement of *Night on the Bare Mountain*, which dates from 1940. Such is the colour and richness of sonority Stokowski evokes from the fabulous Philadelphians that surface noise and other limitations are completely forgotten. The transfers are very good.

'Philadelphia rarities' (1928–1937): arr. STOKOWSKI: *2 Ancient liturgical melodies: Veni, Creator Spiritus; Veni, Emmanuel.* FALLA: *La vida breve: Spanish dance.* TURINA: *Gypsy dance, Op. 55/5.* DUBENSKY: *Edgar Allan Poe's 'The Raven'* (narr. Benjamin de Loache). arr. KONOYE: *Etenraku: Ceremonial Japanese prelude.* MCDONALD: *The legend of the Arkansas traveller; The Festival of the workers (suite): Dance of the workers. Double piano concerto* (with Jeanne Behrend & Alexander Kelberine). EICHHEIM: *Oriental impressions: Japanese nocturne. Symphonic variations: Bali.* SOUSA: *Manhattan Beach; El Capitan.*

(M) (***) Cala mono CACD 0501.

All these recordings show what splendid recorded sound Stokowski was achieving in Philadelphia as early as 1929. The opening Stokowski liturgical arrangements show how that master of orchestral sonority could make liturgical chants his very own, with a discreet tolling bell to indicate their source. Falla's *Spanish dance* shows him at his most sparklingly chimerical. Dubensky's music does not add a great deal to Edgar Allan Poe, but the narrator, Benjamin de Loache, certainly does, presenting the narrative with the essentially genial, melodramatic lubricity of Vincent Price.

Hidemaro Konoye and Stokowski and his players conspire between them to provide an extraordinarily authentic Japanese sound in *Etenraku*, and then in *The legend of the Arkansas traveller* we have a complete change of local colour for Alexander Hilsberg's folksy, sub-country-and-western violin solo. Henry Eichheim's Japanese and Balinese impressions are suitably exotic, but not music one would wish to return to. As for Harl McDonald's *Double piano concerto*, the piano writing is splashy and the finale is spectacularly based on the *Juarezca*, a jazzy Mexican dance.

The two soloists provide convincing, extrovert dash, and Stokowski obviously revels in what Noël Coward might have described as 'potent cheap music' if with nothing like the melodic appeal of Coward's own work. The two Sousa marches have both poise and élan, but here the sound is barely adequate – not the fault of the CD transfer. The programme lasts for 78 minutes and Stokowksi aficionados need not hesitate.

Philadelphia Orchestra, or (i) Minneapolis Orchestra, Eugene Ormandy

BEETHOVEN: *Piano Concertos Nos. 3 in C min., Op. 37* (with Arrau); *4 in G, Op. 58* (with Casadesus). BARBER: *Essay No. 1 for Orchestra, Op. 12.* BRAHMS: *Double Concerto in A min., Op. 102* (with Heifetz & Feuermann). BRUCKNER: *Symphony No. 7 in E.* DVORAK: *Cello Concerto in B min., Op. 104* (with Piatigorsky). (i) GRIEG: *Piano Concerto in A min., Op. 16* (with Rubinstein). GRIFFES: *The Pleasure Dome of Kubla Khan, Op. 8.* MAHLER: *Symphony*

No. 2 in C min. (Resurrection) (with Frank, O'Malley Gallogly; Twin City Symphony Ch.). MIASKOVSKY: *Symphony No. 21 in F sharp min. in One Movement, Op 51.* MUSSORGSKY: *Pictures at an Exhibition* (orch. Caillet). RACHMANINOV: *Piano Concertos Nos. 1 in F sharp min., Op. 1; 3 in D min., Op. 30* (with Composer). RAVEL: *Piano Concerto for the Left Hand* (with Casadesus). (i) SCHOENBERG: *Verklaerte Nacht, Op. 4.* SIBELIUS: *Symphony No. 1 in E min., Op. 39; Legend: Lemminkäinen's Homeward Journey, Op. 22/4.* RICHARD STRAUSS: *Don Quixote, Op. 35* (with Feuermann); *Symphonia domestica, Op. 53.* TCHAIKOVSKY: *Piano Concerto No. 1 in B flat min., Op. 23* (with Levant); *Symphony No. 6 in B min. (Pathéthique).*

(BB) (***) Brillante Maestro (mono) 205236/240-303 (10).

This is an amazing cornucopia of classic performances given by the Philadelphia Orchestra presided over by Eugene Ormandy. The Minneapolis Orchestra is represented by the electrifying 1935 Mahler *Second Symphony* and the 1934 Schoenberg *Verklaerte Nacht*, its première recording in the version for full strings. The earliest of the Philadelphia performances are *The Pleasure Dome of Kubla Khan* (1934) and the Bruckner *Seventh Symphony* (1935), the last being the Tchaikovsky *B flat minor Concerto* with Oscar Levant. Speaking of which, what a line-up of soloists is on offer: Jascha Heifetz and Emanuel Feuermann in the Brahms and the legendary 1940 *Don Quixote* also with Feuermann. Those who remember the Mahler will know how dramatic and intense was this performance. It is particularly good to have Robert Casadesus in Beethoven's *G major Concerto* and Louis Caillet's scoring of *Pictures at an Exhibition* recorded in 1937. Some of these performances (the Barber *Essay for Orchestra* and the Miaskovsky symphony) are already available in alternative transfers, but many are not. As far as we know, the *Verklaerte Nacht* makes its first appearance since the 1930s. It was a much sought-after import after the war and commanded what was then an astronomic price: £1 a disc! The whole treasure-house of ten CDs is marketed at under £20 (£2 a disc, each of which would encompass eight or nine 78s). Generally speaking the transfers are serviceable rather than distinguished: the Schoenberg does not noticeably improve on the original shellac discs, and the Rachmaninov concertos are not better than either the RCA or Naxos transfers. No matter; this is an incredible bargain, and some of the performances are alone worth the price of the whole box. Ormandy was taken for granted in the 1950s and 1960s, but he got a wonderful sound from his Philadelphia Orchestra; none of these performances falls below distinction.

Philharmonia Orchestra, Constant Lambert

'The Last Recordings': CHABRIER (orch. Lambert): *Ballabile.* SUPPE: *Overtures: Morning, Noon and Night in Vienna; Pique dame.* WALDTEUFEL: *Waltzes: Estudiantina, Les patineurs, Pomone, Sur la plage.* WALTON: *Façade Suites Nos. 1 and 2.*

(M) (***) Somm Celeste mono SOMMCD 023.

This charming disc offers a generous collection, very well-transferred, of the recordings Constant Lambert made just before his death. Lambert's flair as a ballet conductor is reflected in all the items here. Whether in Waldteufel waltzes, Suppé overtures or the orchestral *Façade* pieces (source of the highly successful ballet) Lambert is masterly at giving a spring to the dance-rhythms, while never indulging excessively in rubato. Lambert rivals even the composer himself in bringing out the fun of *Façade*. He was, after all, almost the work's surrogate creator – the friend of Walton who alongside him discovered the joys of jazz and syncopated rhythms in the early 1920s. It is remarkable too that even with the limitations of mono recording of 1950 Lambert keeps textures ideally clear and transparent, helped by the refined playing of the Philharmonia Orchestra, adding to the freshness of all these performances. As part of the documentation, Alan Sanders provides a most illuminating essay on Lambert's life and recording career.

Philharmonia Orchestra, Nicolai Malko

BORODIN: *Prince Igor: Overture; Polovtsian dances; Polovtsian march. Symphony No. 2 in A min.* RIMSKY-KORSAKOV: *Maid of Pskov (Ivan the Terrible): Overture.* LIADOV: *8 Russian folksongs.* GLAZUNOV (with Sokolov and Liadov): *Les vendredis: Polka.*

(**) Testament mono/stereo SBT 1062.

Nicolai Malko, from 1926 the chief conductor of the Leningrad Philharmonic and the first interpreter of Shostakovich's *First Symphony*, made all too few recordings; though some of these with the Philharmonia lack tautness, his feeling for the Slavonic idiom is unerring. This reading of the *Prince Igor overture* is light and transparent (in newly unearthed stereo) but lacks dramatic bite, and so do the *Polovtsian dances*, polished but not involving. The *Polovtsian march* is quite different: a tense, swaggering performance which reveals the true Malko. Then after an amiable, low-key account of the first movement of the Borodin symphony, the Scherzo second movement brings a virtuoso performance. Best of all is the Rimsky-Korsakov overture, in full-bodied stereo. After a relaxed, colourful account of the Liadov *Folksongs*, the corporately written *Polka* makes a charming encore, an Elgar-like salon piece.

Philharmonia Orchestra, Igor Markevitch

'Orchestral portrait': BARTOK: *Dance suite.* RAVEL: *La valse.* SATIE: *Parade.* BUSONI: *Tänzwalzer.* LIADOV: *Kikimora.* CHABRIER: *Le roi malgré lui: Fête polonaise.* LISZT: *Mephisto waltz.*

(***) Testament (mono) SBT 1060.

The seven varied items here make an illuminating portrait of a conductor who at the time seemed destined to be more central in the world of recording than he became. With immaculate transfers the 1950s mono recordings have astonishing vividness and presence. In the effervescent account of Satie's *Parade* (sadly cut in the last movement) the brass and percussion (including the celebrated typewriter) have wonderful bite, and so have the joyful brass fanfares at the start of the Chabrier *Polonaise*, done in Viennese style. Perhaps most vivid of all is the virtuoso performance of the *Mephisto waltz*.

Pierlot, Pierre (oboe)

'The magic of the oboe' (with Sol. Ven., Scimone; or Paillard CO, Jean-François Paillard): VIVALDI: *Concertos in C, RV 452; F, RV 455.* ALBINONI: *Concerto a cinque in D min., Op. 9/2.* CIMAROSA: *Concerto* (arr. BENJAMIN). ZIPOLI: *Adagio for oboe, cello, organ and strings* (arr. GIOVANNINI). MARCELLO: *Concerto in C min.* BELLINI: *Concerto.*

(M) *** Erato 4509 92130-2.

For once, a record company's sobriquet for a collection does not disappoint: this is indeed a magical and very generous (74 minutes) collection, well recorded. One might say the cream of baroque oboe concertos are included here, and Benjamin's arrangement of movements by Cimarosa with its delightful central *Siciliano* and spiccato finale is as engaging as any. The Albinoni and Marcello concertos have memorable slow movements, too, and the Bellini a catchy Polacca finale. The novelty is Zipoli's *Adagio*, sumptuously arranged by Francesco Giovannini after the manner of Giazotto's 'Albinoni *Adagio*'. It doesn't quite come off, but it is a very near miss. Throughout, Pierlot's sweet, finely focused timbre and graceful phrasing are a constant pleasure.

Radio Television Eireann Concert Orchestra, Dublin, Ernest Tomlinson

'British light music - Miniatures': ANTHONY COLLINS: *Vanity Fair.* MARK LUBBOCK: *Polka dots.* ARMSTRONG GIBBS: *Dusk.* BENJAMIN FRANKEL: *Carriage and pair.* VIVIAN ELLIS: *Coronation Scot.* ARTHUR BENJAMIN: *Jamaican song; Jamaican rumba.* ROBERT DOCKER: *Tabarinage.* ELGAR: *Beau Brummel.* HARRY DEXTER: *Siciliano.* KEN WARNER: *Scrub, brothers scrub!* GORDON JACOB: *Cradle song.* THOMAS ARNE, **arr.** TOMLINSON: *Georgian suite: Gavotte.* GILBERT VINTER: *Portuguese party.* GEOFFREY TOYE: *The Haunted ballroom* (concert waltz). EDWARD WHITE: *Puffin' Billy.* GEORGE MELACHRINO: *Starlight Roof waltz.* CLIVE RICHARDSON: *Beachcomber.*

**(*) Marco Polo 8.223522.

Anthony Collins was right to be proud of his delightful vignette 'Vanity Fair', for its theme is indelible, and it comes up very freshly here in a programme of unassuming orchestral lollipops, including many items with almost equally catchy musical ideas, even a *Gavotte* by Thomas Arne, arranged by the conductor to sound just a little like a caricature. The tunes are usually pithy and short, like Harry Dexter's daintily wispy *Siciliano*, but sometimes the writing is gently evocative, like the two romantic waltzes, *Dusk* by Armstrong Gibbs, and Geoffrey Toye's *Haunted ballroom*, and Gordon Jacob's delicate *Cradle song*.

Novelties like Benjamin Frankel's clip-clopping *Carriage and pair*, Edward White's *Puffin' Billy*, and Ken Warner's moto perpetuo, *Scrub, brothers scrub!* readily evoke the world of Leroy Anderson, while Clive Richardson's quirky *Beachcomber* makes one want to smile. The conductor, Ernest Tomlinson, understands that their very slightness is part of the charm of nearly all these pieces, and he presents them with a simplicity that is wholly endearing. The only relative disappointment is Vivian Ellis's wittily evoked *Coronation Scot*, which needs much more verve than it receives here. Good playing and good recording, although the acoustic effect noticeably becomes more brash for the second item, Mark Lubbock's breezy *Polka dots*.

Rahbari, Sohre (saxophone), Belgian Radio and TV Orchestra, Brussels, Alexander Rahbari

Music for saxophone and orchestra: MILHAUD: *Scaramouche (suite).* GLAZUNOV: *Concerto in E flat, Op. 109.* DEBUSSY: *Rapsodie.* IBERT: *Concertino da camera.* MUSSORGSKY: *Pictures at an exhibition: The old castle.* SOHRE RAHBARI: *Japanese improvisation for solo saxophones.*

(BB) ** Naxos 8.554784.

The Ibert is the most successful piece here and the concertante version of *Scaramouche* works well too, with its lively quotation of 'Ten green bottles', but the Glazunov rather outstays its welcome. Sohre Rahbari is a fine player and responds to Debussy's exoticism with an attractive freedom of line. Alexander Rahbari is at his best and the Belgian Orchestra gives quite persuasive support, although their playing could be more refined. The recording is good, but rather resonant. Value for money, but not distinctive.

Rampal, Jean-Pierre (flute)

'*Twentieth-century flute masterpieces*' (with (i) LOP, Froment; (ii) O de l'Ortf, Martinon; (iii) LOP, Jolivet; (iv) Robert Veyron-Lacroix): (i) IBERT: *Concerto.* (ii) KHACHATURIAN: *Concerto* (arr. from *Violin concerto*). (iii) JOLIVET: *Concerto.* (iv) MARTINU: *Sonata.* HINDEMITH: *Sonata.* PROKOFIEV: *Sonata in D.* POULENC: *Sonata.*

(M) **(*) Erato (ADD) 2292 45839-2 (2).

The concertos on the first CD have less than perfectly focused orchestral strings, and the Khachaturian arrangement is dispensable. But the Ibert Concerto is winning and the more plangent Jolivet not inconsiderable. The highlights of the collection are all on the second disc, three out of the four of them inspired works delightfully written for the instrument and marvellously played. Only the first movement of the Hindemith is a bit below par in its utilitarian austerity; the cool slow movement and more vigorous finale have something approaching charm. The Prokofiev *Sonata* (also heard in a version for violin – but the flute is the original) is a masterpiece, and Rampal makes the very most of it. Then comes the delightful Poulenc piece with its disarmingly easy-flowing opening, delicious central cantilena and scintillating finale with hints of *Les Biches*. The recording of the sonatas, made in 1978, is vividly firm and realistic. If this set is reissued later on a Bonsai Duo, it will be well worth seeking out.

RCA Red Seal Century

'RCA Red Seal Century': Soloists and Conductors.

Disc 1: (1911) KREISLER (after FRANCOEUR): *Sicilienne and Rigaudon* (Mischa Elman). (1912) CHOPIN: *Nocturne in G, Op. 37/2* (Vladimir de Pachmann). (1917) TCHAIKOVSKY: *Suite No. 1 in D, Op. 43: Marche miniature* (Boston SO, Karl Muck). (1924) TCHAIKOVSKY: *Violin concerto in D, Op. 35: Canzonetta:* abridged (Fritz Kreisler). (1925) SCHUBERT arr. CORTOT: *Litanei, D.343* (Alfred Cortot). (1927) WAGNER: *Götterdämmerung: closing scene* (Philadephia O, Leopold Stokowski). (1929) ARENSKY: *Suite for two pianos, Op.15: Valse* (Harold Bauer, Ossip Gabrilowitsch). (1930) CHOPIN: *Mazurka in D, Op. 33/2* (Ignace Jan Paderewski). (1935) BACH arr. RACHMANINOV: *Violin partita No.3 in E, BWV 1006* (Sergei Rachmaninov). (1935) CHOPIN: *Etude in E min., Op.25/11* (Josef Lhévinne). (1935) GADE: *Jalousie: Tango Tzigane* (Boston Pops O, Arthur Fiedler). (1942) HERBERT: *Cello concerto No. 2 in E min, Op. 30: Lento: Andante tranquillo:* abridged (Emanuel Feuermann). (1947) KREISLER: *Schön Rosmarin* (William Primrose). (1949) TCHAIKOVSKY: *Serenade for strings in C, Op. 48:*

Waltz (Boston SO, Serge Koussevitsky). (1949) BERLIOZ: *Béatrice et Bénédict: overture* (Boston SO, Charles Munch). (1950) HANDEL: *Messiah: Hallelujah Chorus* (Robert Shaw Chorale, Robert Shaw). (1950) SAINT-SAENS: *Carnival of the animals: The swan* (Gregor Piatgorsky). (1951) DONIZETTI: *Don pasquale: Overture* (NBC SO, Arturo Toscanini). (1951) CHOPIN: *Mazurka in A min., Op. 7/2* (William Kapell). (1952) ITURBI: *Cradle song: Canción de cuna* (José Iturbi).

Disc 2: (1953) DELIBES: *Coppélia: Prélude: Mazurka* (Boston SO, Pierre Monteux). (1957) CHOPIN: *Prelude in F sharp min., Op. 45* (Arthur Rubinstein). RUBINSTEIN: *Fantasy on Themes from Bizet's Carmen.* (1957) J. S. BACH: *Fantasia in C min., BWV 906* (Wanda Landowska). (1959) Kabalevsky: *Colas Breugnan: Overture* (Chicago SO, Fritz Reiner). (1975) GERSHWIN: *Porgy and Bess: Summertime; A Woman is a Sometime Thing* (Jascha Heifetz). (1973) WALTON: *Bagatelle No. 1* (Julian Bream). (1973) VERDI: *I Vespri Siciliani: The Four Seasons (Ballet): Winter* (New Philh. O, James Levine). (1975) DEBUSSY: *L'Isle Joyeuse* (Van Cliburn). (1983) MOUQUET: *La Flûte de Pan: Pan and the Birds* (James Galway). (1984) SCHUBERT: *Rosamunde, D.797: Ballet Music No. 2* (Cologne RSO, Günter Wand). (1987) SCHUMANN: *Fantasiestück, Op. 73/3: Rasch und mit Feuer* (Richard Stoltzman, clarinet). (1990) GLENNIE: *Light in the Darkness* (Evelyn Glennie). (1991) TOWER: *Fanfare for the Uncommon Woman No. 1* (Saint Louis SO, Leonard Slatkin). (1996) LISZT: *Transcendental Etude No. 5: Feux Follets* (Evgeny Kissin). (1996) WILLIAMS: *A Hymn to New England* (Boston Pops O, Keith Lockhart). (1999) COPLAND: *Fanfare for the Common Man* (San Francisco SO, Michael Tilson Thomas).

(**(*)) RCA 09026 63852-2 (2).

RCA's Centenary celebration comes in two boxes, each of a pair of CDs. The first pair covers instrumental soloists and conductors and the very first recording is a minor miracle, Mischa Elman playing a Kreisler piece in 1911, the image truthful, if fragile, but with an uncanny presence and the background noise minimized. After De Pachmann, quite well caught, there is 'the first commercial recording by a symphony orchestra', made in Boston in 1917. But of course Tchaikovsky's charming *Marche Miniature* is economically scored for the upper woodwind, a sound the recording horn could cope with. Even so the result is impressive. Kreisler playing the *Canzonetta* from the Tchaikovsky *Violin Concerto* in 1924 is another highlight, his rich tone well caught. Stokowski is predictably thrilling in the closing scene from *Götterdämmerung*, but the Philadelphia strings sound thin. After that the starry names come thick and fast, and it is good to have the Boston Pops in the first 'classical' million-seller: Gade's *Jealousy*. Among the other highlights are Toscanini's crisp *Don Pasquale Overture* and, unexpectedly, Reiner's fizzing *Colas Greugnon Overture*. James Galway captivates the ear in a little morsel by Mouquet and Kissin shows his mettle in Liszt; but there are some curious inclusions, and the later transfers are good rather than Dutton-standard. Quite good documentation, but sparse, and these discs come at full-price.

Reilly, Tommy (harmonica)

'*Harmonica concertos*' (with (i) Munich RSO, Gerhardt; (ii) Basel RSO, Dumont; (iii) SW German RO, Smola; (iv) Munich RSO, Farnon; (v) Farnon O, Farnon): (i) SPIVAKOVSKY: *Harmonica concerto.* (ii) ARNOLD: *Harmonica concerto, Op. 46.* (iii) VILLA-LOBOS: *Harmonica concerto.* (iv) MOODY: *Toledo (Spanish fantasy).* (v) FARNON: *Prelude and dance.*

*** Chan. 9248.

This is most attractive. The Spivakovsky is a particularly winning piece, with a catchy tune in the first movement, rather like a Leroy Anderson encore, a popular, romantic central interlude, marked *Dolce*, and a delicious moto perpetuo finale. Not surprisingly, the Malcolm Arnold is very appealing too, one of this composer's best miniature concertos, written in 1954 for the BBC Proms. The Villa-Lobos, written in 1955, should be much better known. Scored for a small orchestra of strings, single wind, harp, celesta and percussion, it has a neo-classical character. It produces a quite lovely melody for the *Andante*; only the finale, which moves along at a genial pace, has piquant hints of the composer's usual Brazilian preoccupation. James Moody's *Spanish fantasy* might be described as good cheap music, and it offers the soloist a glittering chance to demonstrate his bravura with infectious panache. Farnon's hauntingly nostalgic *Prelude and dance* (a charmingly inconsequential little waltz) brings a felicitous interleaving of both themes. The recording balance is surely as near perfect as one could wish.

Roscoe, Martin (piano), Guildhall Strings, Robert Salter

'*Peacock Pie*': JACOB: *Concertino.* ARMSTRONG GIBBS: *Concertino; Peacock Pie (suite).* ROOTHAM: *Miniature Suite.* MILFORD: *Concertino in E.* DRING: *Festival Scherzo.*

*** Hyp. CDA 67316.

A wholly delectable disc of piano concertinos with string orchestra, very English in character. The opening work by Gordon Jacob, characteristically well crafted, sets the scene with its spirited neoclassical outer movements, and a delicate morsel of a central Andante. Armstrong Gibbs opens and closes his *Concertino* (written at Windermere, in the Lake District in 1942) jauntily and is more romantic in the Andante, which yet has an English pastoral flavour. *Peacock Pie* is no less infectious, taking its title and inspiration from Walter de la Mare's book of rhymes; again the lyrical style is folksy, but the central picture of a *Sunken Garden* is mysteriously evocative and the the *Ride-by-Nights* finale gallops along with witches in mind, although there is nothing spooky in the music. Cyril Rootham's *Miniature Suite* is again very English in atmosphere, with a dainty opening *Allegretto*, a tripping third movement in a neatly contrived 5/4 rhythm and a distinct folksong idiom coming to the fore in the finale. Robin Milford's *Concertino* has a pleasing insouciance, and a charming siciliano as its central *Poco adagio*, which is recalled in the last movement. Madeleine Dring's *Festival Scherzo* makes a sparkling, debonair encore. Performances are light-hearted and polished, and beautifully recorded.

Rostropovich, Mstislav (cello and conductor)

'*The Russian years*'

BEETHOVEN: *Triple concerto in C, Op. 56* (with David Oistrakh, Sviatoslav Richter, Moscow PO, Kondrashin). SCHUMANN: *Cello concerto, Op. 129.* TCHAIKOVSKY: *Variations on a rococo theme, Op. 33* (both with USSR State O, Rozhdestvensky). STRAVINSKY: *Mavra: Russian song. Baiser de la fée: Pas de deux.* MILHAUD: *Saudades do Brasil: Tijuca.* FALLA: *El amor brujo: Ritual fire dance.* SINDING: *Suite im alten Stil, Op. 10: Presto.* FAURE: *Après un rêve.* DEBUSSY: *Clair de lune; Nocturne & Scherzo.* POPPER: *Dance of the elves.* SCHUBERT: *Impromptu in G flat, D.899/3* (trans. heifetz/rostropovich). HANDEL: *Sonata in D, HWV 371: Larghetto.* PROKOFIEV: *Cinderella: Adagio* (all with Alexander Dedyukhin, piano). *Waltz-Coda. Love for 3 Oranges: March* (with Alexei Zybtsev, piano). SCRIABIN: *Etude in B flat min., Op. 8/11.* DVORAK: *Silent woods.* RICHARD STRAUSS: *An einsamer Quelle.* SHAPORIN: *Romance: I see you; Elegy* (with Vladimir Yampolsky, piano); *Scherzo, Op. 25/5* (with Aza Amintayeva, piano).

(M) (**(*)) EMI mono CZS5 72294-2 (2).

SHOSTAKOVICH: *Cello concertos Nos. 1 in E flat, Op. 107* (with Moscow PO, Rozhdestvensky); *2 in G, Op. 126* (with USSR State SO, Svetlanov). *Cello sonata in D min., Op. 40* (with composer, piano). KABALEVSKY: *Cello sonata in B flat, Op. 71* (with composer, piano). KAREN KHACHATURIAN: *Cello sonata* (with composer, piano).

(M) (**(*)) EMI mono CZS5 72295-2 (2).

PROKOFIEV: *Cello sonata in C, Op. 119* (with Sviatoslav Richter, piano); *Symphony-concerto for cello and orchestra in E min., Op. 125* (with Israel Gusman & Rozhdestvensky); *Cello concertino, Op. 132* (orch. Kabalevsky) (with Moscow R & TV O, Rozhdestvensky). TANEIEV: *Canzona* (with Alexander Dedyukhin, piano). MIASKOVSKY: *Cello concerto in C min., Op. 66.* GLAZUNOV: *Concerto ballata, Op. 108* (both with USSR State SO, Svetlanov).

(M) (**(*)) EMI mono CZS5 72296-2 (2).

BRITTEN: *Suites Nos. 1-2 for solo cello, Op. 72 & Op. 80. Symphony for cello and orchestra* (with Moscow PO, composer). VILLA-LOBOS: *Bachianas brasileiras No. 1: Prelúdio for 8 cellos* (Rostropovich, cello/director). RESPIGHI: *Adagio con variazioni.* RICHARD STRAUSS: *Don Quixote, Op. 35* (both with Moscow PO, Kondrashin). HONEGGER: *Cello concerto* (with USSR State SO, Dubrovsky).

(M) (***) EMI mono CZS5 72297-2 (2).

LOPES-GRAÇA: *Concerto da càmera* (with Moscow PO, Kondrashin). KNIPPER: *Concerto-monologue for cello, 7 brass instruments and two kettledrums.* VAINBERG: *Cello concerto, Op. 43* (with USSR State SO, Rozhdestvensky). TISHCHENKO: *Concerto for cello, seventeen wind instruments, percussion & organ, Op. 23* (with Leningrad PO, Blazhkov). KHACHATURIAN: *Concert-rhapsody* (with Aza Amintayeva, piano). TOYAMA: *Cello concerto* (with Moscow R & TV O, composer).

(M) (**(*)) EMI mono CZS5 72298-2 (2).

In 1997 EMI marked the 70th birthday of Mstislav Rostropovich with an ambitious, celebratory survey called 'The Russian Recordings – 1950–74', which consisted of thirteen discs (EMI CZS5 72016-2) from which the present five two-CD sets are drawn. Rostropovich chose them himself from archival recordings in Russia. They range from such relatively familiar records as the 1964 Moscow première of Benjamin Britten's *Symphony for cello and orchestra*, which is available in other transfers, to more rare material like Moshei (now Mieczyslaw) Vainberg's *Cello concerto* and Tishchenko's *Concerto*, both dedicated to the great Russian cellist – as are many other pieces on these discs. All the performances are three star but the sound does not always do justice to his glorious tone.

CZS5 72294-2 brings commanding performances of the Beethoven *Triple concerto* with Oistrakh and Richter – made in 1970 just before the famous Karajan version – and the Schumann *A minor Concerto* and Tchaikovsky *Rococo variations*, both with Rozhdestvensky from 1960. These come with shorter pieces mainly recorded in the 1960s. Incomparable playing but variable recorded sound.

CZS5 72295-2 concentrates on Shostakovich and includes a 1961 concert performance of the *First Cello concerto* and the very first performance of the *Second*, in 1966, given under Svetlanov and in the presence of the composer, who was celebrating his 61st birthday. The accompanying sonatas were all recorded with their respective composers, though no date is given for the Shostakovich. Rostropovich recalls that some tempi are on the brisk side: 'it was a beautiful day and Shostakovich was anxious to visit friends in the country'. The performance sounds identical to the one

issued in the USA in 1958 on the Monitor label (MC 2021), though the sound has been rebalanced.

CZS5 72296-2 is mainly given over to Prokofiev. The *Symphony-concerto*, or as it is usually called, *Sinfonia concertante*, Op. 125, is a compilation, the first movement coming from a 1972 performance and the rest from 1964, both in the same hall. This set also includes the 1950 account of the Cello sonata with Richter made in Prokofiev's presence (which also appeared on MC 2021). The 1964 record of the Miaskovsky *Concerto* with Svetlanov conducting (the Glazunov comes from the same concert) is very fine, though not as well recorded as his early EMI recording with Sargent.

CZS5 72297-2 is self-recommending in bringing together the première of Benjamin Britten's *Cello Symphony* and two of the solo cello suites. Honegger's delightful 1929 concerto, and the Respighi *Adagio con variazione* are not to be missed either. The Honegger concerto comes off beautifully, and this is the set to go for if you want just one of these reissues, though it is a pity that space could not have been found for Sauguet's charming concerto (*Mélodie concertante*). EMI once coupled this with the Tishchenko *Concerto for cello, seventeen wind instruments, percussion and organ*, which is included on the last set.

CZS5 72298-2 offers a number of Russian works from the Soviet era. The finest piece on the last pair of discs is the Vainberg concerto rather than the somewhat unrewarding Tishchenko and Khachaturyan concertos.

'Masterpieces for cello' (with various orchestras and conductors): BERNSTEIN: *3 Meditations for cello and orchestra* (from *Mass*). BOCCHERINI: *Cello concerto No. 2.* GLAZUNOV: *Chant du Ménestrel.* SHOSTAKOVICH: *Cello concerto No. 2.* TARTINI: *Cello concerto.* TCHAIKOVSKY: *Andante cantabile; Variations on a rococo theme.* VIVALDI: *Cello concertos, RV 398 and RV 413.*

(B) *** DG Double (ADD) 437 952-2 (2).

A self-recommending set, with two CDs for the price of one. Each of the works included is discussed under its Composer entry in our main volume. The only drawback is the inadequate documentation.

'Slava 75' (75th Birthday Edition): Cello: BACH: *Suite No. 3 in C BWV 1003.* HAYDN: *Concertos Nos. 1-2* (with ASMF). DVORAK: *Concerto* (with LPO, Giulini). BEETHOVEN: *Triple Concerto, Op. 56* (with David Oistrakh, Sviatoslav Richter, Berlin Philharmonic Orchestra, Karajan). Conducting: DVORAK: *Symphony No. 9 (New World)* (LPO). GLINKA: *Overture Ruslan and Ludmilla; Valse-fantaisie.* BORODIN: *In the Steppes of Central Asia* (Orchestre de Paris). SHOSTAKOVICH: *Symphony No. 8* (National SO of Washington).

(M) **(*) EMI (ADD/DDD) CMS5 67807-2 (4).

This is a more ambitious coverage than that offered by DG below, and while its range is wider, not everything shows the great Russian musician at his finest and most illuminating. He is at his most brilliant and reponsive in the Bach's *Third Cello Suite*, and the recording is vividly present. The pair of Haydn concertos bring comparable virtuosity and even if his style is rather romantic, itis only too easy to be seduced by such genial and commanding music-making. The Beethoven *Triple Concerto* is a classic account which remains unsurpassed, and the 1969 recording, made in the Berlin Jesus-Christus Kirche, is generous in resonance and yet remains clear. It is rightly one of EMI's 'Great Recordings of the Century'. The Dvořák Concerto is another matter. Although it is beautifully recorded it is much too indulgently idiosyncratic to be really satisfying for repeated listening.

Turning now to Rostropovich as conductor, we find his interpretations consistently more wilful than his solo playing.

He directs the weightiest reading possible of the *New World Symphony*. The very opening chords of the slow introduction suggest an epic view, and from then on, with generally expansive tempi, the performance presents this as a genuine 'Ninth', a culmination to the cycle. In the first movement the exposition repeat brings a slight modification of treatment the second time round and some will resist such inconsistencies as that. The conscious weight of even the *Largo* is controversial too, though in all four movements Rostropovich contrasts the big tuttis – almost Straussian at times – with light pointing in woodwind solos. The recording is richly ample to match and certainly this account is an engulfing experience.

Of the Russian items, the most attractive is the Glinka *Valse-fantaisie* which is both elegant and lilting; the *Ruslan Overture* is very well played too, but lacks the kind of zest which makes it unforgettable. *In the Steppes of Central Asia* is poetically shaped but here the kind of heaviness experienced in the *New World Symphony* returns in the brass, the phrasing becomes too broad and the music's onward flow loses its simple forward impetus.

Fortunately the Shostakovich *Eighth* is in every way a success. This is Teldec recording, licensed to EMI for the occasion, and here Rostropovich's intensity and that of his American players does not spill over into excess. This is a gripping account that can rank alongside the best performances one has heard on or off record - Mravinsky, Rozhdestvensky, Kondrashin and the excellent Haitink - and it is very well recorded too.

'Rostropovich mastercellist (Legendary Recordings 1956–1978)': DVORAK: *Concerto.* TCHAIKOVSKY: *Andante cantabile for cello and string orchestra* **(with Berlin Philharmonic Orchestra, Karajan).** SCHUMANN: *Concerto* **(with Leningrad Philharmonic Orchestra, Rozhdestvensky).** GLAZUNOV: *Chant du ménéstral* **(with Boston Symphony Orchestra, Ozawa).** RACHMANINOV: *Cello Sonata, Op. 19; Vocalise, Op. 34/14.* CHOPIN: *Introduction and Polonaise brillante, Op. 3.* SCHUBERT: *Impromptu in D flat, D899/3.*

SCHUMANN: *Kinderszenen: Träumerei* **(all with Alexander Dedyukhin, piano).**

(M) *** DG stereo/mono DG 471 620-2 (2).

Of the two celebratory compilations issued to celebrate Rostropovich's 75th birthday, the DG two-disc package is undoubtedly the one to go for, unless you already have his incomparable 1969 recording of the Dvořák *Concerto* with Karajan or indeed the hardly less memorable account of the Schumann, imaginative and ever-communicative. The slighter, nostalgic Glazunov piece is also disarmingly attractive, and the great cellist can be readily forgiven for indulging himself a little in two of Tchaikovsky's loveliest lyrical melodies which together form the *Andante cantabile*. But what makes this programme even more enticing and valuable is the inclusion of the works with piano.

Recorded in Warsaw in 1956, with Alexander Dedyukhin, who was Rostropovich' regular partner in recitals over many years, these pieces have not been published in the U.K. before. They include a truly outstanding account of Rachmaninov's *Cello Sonata*, a romatically vibrant work in which a stream of irrepressible lyrical melodies contantly rise to the surface and blossom. Rostropovich plays with a rapt delicacy of feeling, his timbre in the upper range quite lovely, his at times phrasing slightly more restrained than in later years, echoed by the ever poetic Dedyukhin.

However, there is plenty of flair and gusto in the Chopin *Introduction and polonaise brillante*, and here the pianist, lets himself go brilliantly in the more extrovert bravura. The encores are played affectionately, with the Schubert *Impromptu* (transcribed first by Heifetz and then arranged by Rostropovich) quite unlike the piano original. The recordings are mono and truthful, closely but faithfully balanced.

Rotterdam Philharmonic Orchestra, Valéry Gergiev

STRAVINSKY: *Fireworks.* (i) *Piano Concerto* **(with Alexander Toradze).** PROKOFIEV: *Scythian Suite, Op. 20* **(with Rehearsal Feature).** DEBUSSY: *Le Martyre de Saint-Sébastien: Symphonic Fragments.* **(Director: Rob van der Berg. Video Director: Peter Rump.)**

⊕ *** Arthaus DVD 100 314.

The concert itself is just under an hour but also includes a rehearsal-feature in which Gergiev discusses Prokofiev and the *Scythian Suite*. What a relief to find a conductor championing this score with such eloquence! For too long it has been compared unfavourably with *The Rite of Spring* by English and American critics when no such comparison is called for. There are few pieces in twentieth-century music that are as imaginative as its third movement, *Night*, or as inventive as the first, *The Adoration of Vélèss and Ala*, with its extraordinarily lush contrasting group (fig. 8 onwards). There have been some fine CD versions by

Markevitch and Abbado, albeit none with the fervour of Koussevitzky and Désiré Defauw in the late 1940s. Gergiev comes nearest to them in his fervour and conviction, and it is good to hear him speak of the music with such warmth in the accompanying hour-long documentary. This includes some valuable archive material of Prokofiev himself and a contribution from his second son, the painter Oleg. (The programme was recorded in 1997, some time before Oleg's death.) The concert itself is imaginatively planned and Alexander Toradze is as impressive an exponent of the Stravinsky *Concerto* as he was of the Prokofiev Concertos he recorded with Gergiev and the Kirov Orchestra for Philips. The camera work is unobtrusive and intelligent though one could do without some of the aerial shots of the orchestra. The *Scythian Suite* is difficult to balance and some of the detail emerges in greater prominence than the main lines, but for the most part the sound balance is vivid and very present. This is an outstanding and valuable issue that is hugely enjoyable.

Rousseau, Eugene (saxophone), Paul Kuentz Chamber Orchestra, Kuentz

Saxophone concertos: IBERT: *Concertino da camera for alto saxophone and 11 instruments.* GLAZUNOV: *Alto saxophone concerto in E, Op. 109.* VILLA-LOBOS: *Fantasia for soprano saxophone, 3 horns and string orchestra.* DUBOIS: *Concerto for alto saxophone and string orchestra.*

(M) *** DG (ADD) 453 991-2.

An enterprising anthology. The Glazunov is a late work and the best known and most often recorded of the pieces here. However, both the Villa-Lobos *Fantasia* and the Ibert *Concertino da camera* are as appealing and exotic, and there is much to give pleasure. The longest work is the *Concerto for alto sax* by Max-Pierre Dubois, a pupil of Milhaud: fluent, well crafted and civilized. Eugene Rousseau is an expert and persuasive soloist and the recording, which dates from the early 1970s, is first class.

Royal Ballet Orchestra, David Lloyd-Jones

'English string miniatures': RUTTER: *Suite.* CHARLES ORR: *Cotswold hill tune.* MELACHRINO: *Les jeux.* PETER DODD: *Irish idyll.* ARMSTRONG GIBBS: *Miniature dance suite.* FRANK CORDELL: *King Charles's galliard.* DAVID LYON: *Short suite.* ROY DOUGLAS: *Cantilena.* PHILIP LANE: *Pantomime.*

(BB) *** Naxos 8.554186.

A delightful collection. John Rutter shows how artfully he can write for strings, using traditional tunes the invigorating '*A-Roving*', the gentle '*I have a bonnet trimmed with blue*', the touchingly simple *O, Waly,*

Waly and the fizzing energy of *Dashing away with the smoothing iron*. Much of the other music is permeated with influences from British folksong. Orr's *Cotswold hill tune* and Dodd's flimsy *Irish idyll* have much melodically in common, while George Melachrino's *Les jeux* makes an engaging contrast, a gossamer dance tapestry, alternating with a semi-luscious lyrical tune.

Frank Cordell's melancholy *Galliard*, of noble contour, and the *Miniature dance suite* of Armstrong Gibbs both have a hint of the pastiche flavour of Warlock's *Capriol suite*. The serene *Aria*, the penultimate movement of the equally attractive *Short suite* of David Lyon, shares an evocative link with the longer, gentle *Cantilena* of Roy Douglas. Philip Lane's *Pantomime* is another three-movement miniature suite of dainty charm and energy: its bouncing closing *Vivace* ends the concert winningly. Performances are persuasively polished and vivacious and the Naxos recording is excellent: this disc is rewarding value for money.

Royal Ballet Orchestra, Andrew Penny

'Welsh classical favourites': GRACE WILLIAMS: *Fantasia on Welsh nursery rhymes.* WALFORD DAVIES: *Solemn melody.* GARETH WALTERS: *Overture Primavera; A Gwent suite.* TREVOR ROBERTS: *Pastorale.* HODDINOTT: *Folksong suite.* MERVYN BURTCH: *Aladdin: overture.* MATHIAS: *Serenade.* IAN PARROTT: *Fanfare overture (for a Somerset festival).*

(BB) *** Naxos 8.225048.

The Welsh have a long and enduring vocal and choral heritage. But only in the twentieth century has there been an orchestral tradition, and so Welsh folk melodies had not received the concert-hall exposure of comparable English tunes. Then, in 1940, Grace Williams completed her *Fantasia*, using eight very attractive ideas, arranging them into a kind of pot-pourri, winningly scored. Walford Davies had preceded her in the 1930s and he left us the famous hymn-like *Solemn melody*. Trevor Roberts's delicate *Pastorale* readily evokes the Pembrokeshire countryside, with a lovely oboe solo and an expressive string climax, somewhat in the manner of George Butterworth.

Alun Hoddinott's *Folksong suite* is similarly felicitously scored. Mervyn Burtch's *Aladdin* concert overture has a syncopated main theme of considerable character, and Gareth Walters's vigorous spring-inspired overture is hardly less spontaneously inventive. The colourful orchestration of the latter's sets of dances is matched in the extrovert finale of Mathias's *Serenade*, where the main theme is presented in constantly changing colours, and in the exuberant opening and closing movements of the Walters *Gwent suite*. All this music is vividly played by Penny and his Royal Ballet Orchestra and given excellent recording, with a flattering ambience. The disc is generously full and good value. Worth exploring.

Royal Ballet Sinfonia, Gavin Sutherland

'British Light Overtures': BLEZARD: *Caramba.* BLACK: *Overture to a Costume Comedy.* LANGLEY: *Overture and Beginners.* DUNHILL: *Tantivy Towers.* CHAPPELL: *Boy Wizard.* CARROLL: *Festival Overture.* HURD: *Overture to an Unwritten Comedy.* MONCKTON: *The Arcadians* (arr. Wood). LANE: *A Spa Overture.* PITFIELD: *Concert Overture.* LEWIS: *Sussex Symphony Overture.*

(M) *** ASV CD WHL 2133.

A very promising start to an ASV series of British light overtures and including a modern recording of Stanley Black's delightful *Overture to a Costume Comedy*, a work of considerable charm, deftly scored. But there are many such delights in this programme: Michael Hurd's *Overture to an Unwritten Comedy* was written in 1970, yet sounds as though it could slot into an Ealing comedy of the 1950s. Lionel Monckton's *The Arcadians* is particularly tuneful and lively while William Blezard's *Caramba*, which opens the programme, has a distinct Latin-American flavour, and is well laced with rumba rhythms. Thomas Pitfield's *Concert Overture*, the longest work here, makes a charming use of French folk tunes (real or not), and is prettily orchestrated. Paul Lewis describes his *Sussex Symphony Overture* as 'seven minutes of joyful noise with a quiet bit in the middle'. This refers to some lovely nostalgic episodes, very imaginatively orchestrated, and proves that there are still composers who can write tunes (it was composed in 2000). Even more recent is Herbert Chappell's *Boy Wizard* overture from 2001, which is great fun. Philip Lane's *A Spa Overture* dates from 1982 and was written for the Cheltenham Ladies' College. It creates a romantic picture of that town, with a middle section evoking the spirit of Edward Wilson, Cheltenham's Antarctic explorer, whose statue looks down on the main Promenade. James Langley's *Overture and Beginners* has a theatrical atmosphere and a galumphing main theme. Thomas Dunhill's *Tantivy Towers* (reconstructed by Philip Lane from the piano score, plus a tape of a BBC broadcast from the 1970s) well captures the spirit of the early 1930s when it was written. Gavin Sutherland secures an excellent response from the orchestra, and the sound is just right for the music: bright, not too reverberant, warm, with plenty of detail emerging. Most entertaining!

'Brian Kay's British light music discoveries': ARNOLD: *The Roots of Heaven overture.* ALWYN: *Suite of Scottish dances.* SARGENT: *An impression on a windy day.* PARKER: *Overture: The Glass Slipper.* LANGLEY: *The coloured counties.* JACOB: *Overture: The Barber of Seville goes to town.* JOHNSTONE: *Tarn Hows (Cumbrian rhapsody).* LANGFORD: *Two worlds (overture).* R. R. BENNETT: *Little suite.* DYON: *Joie de vivre.*

(M) *** ASV CDWHL 2113.

Brian Kay (of BBC Radio 3) has certainly made some felicitous discoveries here: this is a most entertaining programme, summed up perfectly by Ernest Tomlinson's quoted definition of light music as 'where the melody matters more than what you do to it'. There are plenty of melodies here and the opening rumbustious Malcolm Arnold *Overture* (a concert work based on film music) has a characteristic share. William Alwyn's *Scottish dances* are charmingly scored, with *Colonel Thornton's* elegant *Strathspey* a highlight. Sir Malcolm Sargent's breezy scherzo *An impression on a windy day* follows, and after the frothy *Glass slipper overture*, James Langley's *Coloured counties* (which describes the spectacularly English view from Bredon Hill) brings an engaging oboe solo. Gordon Jacob's pastiche is agreeable enough and the whimsy of Langford's *Two worlds overture* leads neatly into Sir Richard Rodney Bennett's *Little suite* with its charming bird-imagery and delicate *Ladybird waltz*. The only disappointment is Maurice Johnstone's *Tarn Hows*, a pleasantly evocative pastoral idyll, but unworthy of that man-made gem, up in the hills above Hawkshead, perhaps the most beautiful tarn in the whole English Lake District.

British light music: MALCOLM ARNOLD: *Little suite No. 4, Op. 80a* (orch. Lane). BLEZARD: *The River.* CRUFT: *Hornpipe suite.* FENBY: *Overture: Rossini on Ilkla Moor.* WARREN: *Wexford Bells - suite on old Irish tunes.* ARTHUR BUTTERWORTH: *The Path across the moors.* HEDGES: *An Ayrshire serenade, Op. 42.* LEWIS: *An English overture.* LANE: *Suite of Cotswold folkdances.*

(M) *** ASV CDWHL 2126.

An excellent collection of British light music, all imbued with a strong rustic flavour, and valuable for rarities. Adrian Cruft's *Hornpipe suite* is nautically enjoyable, with each dance nicely contrasted; Raymond Warren's *Wexford Bells suite* draws on traditional melodies, yet with modest orchestral forces, each movement nicely atmospheric.

Arthur Butterworth's *The Path across the moors* is highly enjoyable – its title perfectly describing its content – and Fenby's witty *Rossini on Ilkla Moor* gives us an idea of what Rossini might have sounded like had he been a Yorkshireman! Robustly enjoyable is *An English overture* by Paul Lewis, written in 1971 for the opening of Westward TV in the west of England; it uses folk songs from that area.

William Blezard's *The River* is a beautiful, haunting, slightly melancholy piece, whilst Anthony Hedges's three-movement *Ayrshire Serenade*, with its breezy outer-movements and nostalgic centrepiece is a good find. Philip Lane's superb arrangements and reconstructions of film music are greatly valued, and it is good to hear some of his own music: his suite of *Cotswold folkdances* is piquantly orchestrated, as is his arrangement of Arnold's *Little suite*. Gavin Sutherland understands exactly how this music should go, and the recording is excellent.

Royal Ballet Sinfonia, John Wilson

'Scottish light music': DAVIE: *Royal Mile.* DODS: *Highland fancy.* HAMILTON: *Scottish dances.* MACCUNN: *The Land of the mountain and flood (overture); Highland memories.* MATHIESON: *From the Grampians (suite).* ORR: *Fanfare and Processional; Celtic suite.* ROBERTON: *All in the April evening.*

(M) *** ASV CDWHL 2123.

What a good idea to assemble a disc of comparatively rare light Scottish music, which with its characteristic folksy influences, proves most entertaining. The most famous piece here, MacCunn's *The land of mountain and flood overture*, begins the programme robustly, while the same composer's *Highland memories* (1897) for strings offers contrast: two rather nostalgic movements followed by a more lively *Harvest dance* (which is curiously reminiscent of the second movement of Schubert's *Ninth symphony*). Muir Mathieson is widely known for his work in countless films and the opening of the *Grampians suite* (1961) could well begin some Scottish swashbuckler; the rest of the *Suite* is thoroughly diverting too.

Buxton Orr's *Fanfare and Processional* (1968) is more angular than its companion pieces, while in his *Celtic suite* (1968), a four-movement work using dance rhythms as a basis, he pays tribute to his Celtic origins (the last movement, *Port-a-Beul*, means 'mouth music'). Cedric Thorpe Davie's robustly enjoyable *Royal Mile* (recorded complete for the first time) is subtitled 'a coronation march' and was written in 1952 for one of a series of concerts leading up to that celebrated event. Iain Hamilton's *Scottish dances* were, like Sir Malcolm Arnold's, composed for the BBC Light Music Festival and premièred on St Andrew's Day, 1956. They are comparably enjoyable. Marcus Dods's amusing *Highland fancy* and Sir Hugh Roberton's touching *All in the April evening* complete the programme. Full marks for an original collection, committed performances, a vibrant recording – and all at mid-price.

Royal Ballet Sinfonia, Barry Wordsworth

'Tribute to Madame': **Ballet Music**; BLISS: *Checkmate.* BOYCE-LAMBERT: *The Prospect Before us.* GORDON: *The Rake's Progress.* TOYE: *The Haunted Ballroom.*

(M) *** ASV CDWHLS 255.

'Madame' was of course Dame Ninette de Valois, the 'Mother' of British ballet, and she is rightly celebrated with these fine scores by Bliss and Gavin Gordon and Constant Lambert's elegant pastiche drawing on the music of Boyce. The surprise is Toye's *Haunted Ball-room*, much more than just a (very memorable) Waltz. First class performances and fresh, bright recording.

Royal Philharmonic Orchestra, Sir Thomas Beecham

'The RPO legacy,' Vol. 1: BERLIOZ: *Le Corsaire (overture).* SIBELIUS: *Tapiola, Op. 112.* MUSSORGSKY: *Khovanshchina: Dance of the Persian slaves.* DEBUSSY: *Printemps.* BACH: *Christmas oratorio: Sinfonia.* SMETANA: *The Bartered Bride: Overture; Polka; Dance of the Comedians.* CHABRIER: *Marche joyeuse.*

(M) (***) Dutton mono CDLX 7027.

With astonishingly full mono sound, this first disc in the 'RPO Legacy' series vividly captures the tense excitement of the months following Beecham's founding of the orchestra in 1946. It starts with the thrilling recording of the Berlioz *Corsaire overture*, which was the very first from the RPO to be published. *Tapiola*, recorded a few weeks later in November 1946, has a rugged intensity as well as polish, with the terracing of texture and dynamic beautifully brought out even in mono.

Finest of all in the collection is the Debussy *Printemps*, a work which Beecham conducted as early as 1913, but which he never recorded again. Bach, not a composer generally associated with Beecham, inspires him to a performance which suggests French rather than German music, sweet and elegant, and the Smetana and Chabrier are electrifying, not least the horn trills in the Chabrier. The Dutton transfers have a vivid sense of presence.

Royal Philharmonic Orchestra, Adrian Leaper

'Orchestral spectacular': CHABRIER: *España.* RIMSKY-KORSAKOV: *Capriccio espagnol.* MUSSORGSKY: *Night on the bare mountain* (arr. Rimsky-Korsakov). BORODIN: *Prince Igor: Polovtsian dances.* RAVEL: *Boléro.*

(BB) *** Naxos 8.550501.

Recorded in Watford Town Hall by Brian Culverhouse, this concert would be highly recommendable even if it cost far more. All these performances spring to life, and the brilliant, full-bodied sound certainly earns the record its title. The brass in the Mussorgsky/Rimsky-Korsakov *Night on the bare mountain* has splendid sonority and bite, and in the *Polovtsian dances* the orchestra 'sings' the lyrical melodies with such warmth of colour that the chorus is hardly missed. Leaper allows the *Capriccio espagnol* to relax in the colourful central variations, but the performance gathers pace towards the close. Chabrier's *España* has an attractive rhythmic lilt, and in Ravel's ubiquitous *Boléro* there is a strong impetus towards the climax, with much impressive playing on the way (the trombone solo, with a French-style vibrato, is particularly strong).

(i) Royal Philharmonic Orchestra or (ii) Philharmonia Orchestra, Vladimir Ashkenazy

'*Russian delights*': (i) TCHAIKOVSKY: *Capriccio italien, Op. 45; Francesca da Rimini, Op. 32.* (ii) RIMSKY-KORSAKOV: *The Tale of Tsar Saltan: suite, Op. 57; Flight of the bumblebee.* BORODIN: *Prince Igor: Polovtsian dances* (with Matthew Best, L. Opera Ch.).

(B) *** Decca 448 989-2.

This Ashkenazy compilation is first class in every respect, and the recordings (made between 1983 and 1988) are of Decca's finest vintage. *Capriccio italien* is superb, spectacular, elegant and possessed of exhilarating impetus. *Francesca da Rimini* is very exciting too, with much fine wind-playing from the RPO in the lyrical central section. Ashkenazy is also in his element in the dazzlingly scored *Tsar Saltan suite*, and the Philharmonia players obviously relish the good tunes, sonorous brass writing and glittering effects. In the *Polovtsian dances* the singing of the London Opera Chorus has striking fervour, with solo interjections from Matthew Best (normally not included) to bring an added edge of excitement, although it is a pity that the percussion-led opening dance is omitted.

St Paul Chamber Orchestra, Bobby McFerrin

'*Paper music*': MOZART: *Le nozze di Figaro overture; Serenade No. 13 in G (Eine kleine Nachtmusik).* BOCCHERINI: *String quintet in E: Minuet.* FAURE: *Pavane.* STRAVINSKY: *Pulcinella: Minuet and Finale.* VIVALDI: *Double cello concerto in G min., RV 531* (with Peter Howard). MENDELSSOHN: *A Midsummer Night's Dream: Scherzo.* BACH: *Violin concerto in A min., BWV 1041: 1st movt.* TCHAIKOVSKY: *Andante cantabile, Op. 11.*

**(*) Sony SK 63600.

Bobby McFerrin began his musical career in the world of pop music, and in 1988 had a hit single which reached No. 1. His background, however, included a father who was the first black singer at the Met. and a mother who was both a singer and a teacher. So it was not surprising that he found himself being drawn back to the classical sound-world. He made his début with the San Francisco Symphony in 1990 and went on to conduct most of America's top orchestras. Now he is director of the Saint Paul Chamber Orchestra and spends much of his time as a musical evangelist in schools. He is already a famous figure in the USA.

'Paper music' is an American jazz musician's term for music that is written down rather than impro-vised. If one hears McFerrin play this kind of popular repertoire at a concert, the effect of his personality is highly communicative; but here, although the music-making is alive, elegantly turned and aptly paced (especially *Eine kleine Nachtmusik*), there is nothing especially individual about it until he introduces his wordless vocal melismas in a voice a little like that of a counter-tenor. His feeling for dynamic nuance is remarkable, as is his range.

In the present concert he sweetly vocalizes the Boccherini *Minuet* and Fauré's *Pavane* in this way, then he replaces the solo violin line in the Bach concerto and follows up by taking over the second cello part in Vivaldi's *Double concerto*. He does this with such skill that one is almost convinced that it is a viable approach, especially if for the musical novice the result is often both magnetic and appealing. The highlight of his vocalizing here is Tchaikovsky's *Andante cantabile*, which he intones while conducting a refined accompaniment. This is obviously not a CD for general recommendation, but it speaks well for McFerrin's musicianship; if he can bring a new audience into the concert hall, then he has our full support.

Salvage, Graham (bassoon)

Bassoon Concertos (with Royal Ballet Sinfonia cond. (i) Sutherland (ii) Butterworth): (i) FOGG: *Concerto in D.* ADDISON: *Concertino.* HOPE: *Concertino.* (ii) A. BUTTERWORTH: *Summer Music, Op. 77.*

(M) *** ASV CD WHL 2132.

The three concerto/concertinos by John Addison, Eric Fogg and Peter Hope are all most enjoyable and are played with elegance, warmth and style by Graham Salvage, an outstandingly sensitive soloist, with lively and sympathic accompaniments from Gavin Sutherland and the Royal Ballet Sinfonia. The Addison *Concertino* opens in a mood of gentle melancholy, soon wittily dispelled, but returning later, and is quietly enjoyable. It is notable for the droll waltz that forms the second movement and the humorously quirky finale. Fogg's *Concerto* (1931) is essentially light-hearted and rhythmically sparkling, although there is a balancing dolour and solemnity in the central movement. The first movement cadenza is too long, but the rest of the movement, like the finale, is certainly entertaining.

Peter Hope's *Concertino*, written as recently as 2000, opens in a mood of romantic reverie. It is rather like a period film score (the composer worked with John Williams and James Horner), with gentle string ostinatos creating a haunting evocation, contrasted with a more lively middle section. But it has a blues centrepiece, replete with a 'walking bass' and vibraphone, while the finale delectably evokes a Latin American fiesta. But these very personable works are completely upstaged by Arthur Butterworth's masterly *Summer Music*, written in 1985, which is discussed under its separate composer entry. This work alone is well worth the cost of this disc. You will surely be drawn back to it, as we were. The other very entertaining pieces make an attractive programme overall. The performances and recordings are excellent, and this is a valuable addition to the catalogue.

Sargent, Sir Malcolm

'*Sir Malcolm Sargent conducts British music*' (with (i) LPO; (ii) LSO; (iii) Mary Lewis, Tudor Davies & O; (iv) Royal Choral Soc.; (v) New SO): (i) HOLST: *Perfect fool: suite.* (ii) BRITTEN: *Young person's guide to the orchestra.* (iii) VAUGHAN WILLIAMS: *Hugh the Drover: Love duet.* ELGAR: (iv) *I sing the birth*; (ii) *Pomp & circumstance marches Nos. 1 & 4.* (v) COLERIDGE TAYLOR: *Othello: suite.* (ii) BAX: *Coronation march.*

(***) Beulah mono 1PD13.

Sargent was at his finest in this repertory, and it is very welcome to have his personal electricity so vividly conveyed throughout the disc, and most of all in the recording, taken from the sound-track of the original COI film, of Britten's *Young person's guide*. The optical transfer by Martin Sawyer produces far more vivid and satisfyingly weighty results than one would ever expect. The *Love duet* from *Hugh the Drover* was recorded in 1924 in limited pre-electric sound, but the Elgar part-song, recorded live at the Royal Albert Hall in 1928, also soon after the first performance, is vividly atmospheric. The *Othello suite* of Coleridge Taylor, another première recording, is a sequence of brief genre pieces, with recording more than lively and colourful enough to make one forget the high surface-hiss. The three marches at the end were recorded for the Queen's coronation in 1953, with Sargent taking an uninhibitedly broad view of the great tunes in both the Elgar favourites, and with Bax doing a fair imitation of Walton.

La Scala Philharmonic Orchestra, Riccardo Muti

CATALANI: *Contemplazione; Scherzo.* PONCHIELLI: *Elegia.* PUCCINI: *Preludio sinfonico; Capriccio sinfonico; Le Villi: La tregenda.*

**(*) Sony SK 63025.

It makes an apt coupling having long-buried pieces by Ponchielli (Puccini's teacher) and Catalani (Puccini's contemporary from the same city, Lucca) alongside the three most impressive examples of Puccini's early orchestral writing. This easily lyrical music has been resurrected by the Italian musicologist Pietro Spada. The Ponchielli *Elegia* anticipates film music, and the Catalani pieces were both orchestrated from piano works, but the Puccini pieces are markedly more memorable. The *Capriccio sinfonico*, later to provide the opening theme of *La Bohème*, was written as a graduation exercise, very well orchestrated, with structure well controlled. Muti brings out the emo-

tional warmth in all these works, with Sony sound atmospheric rather than detailed.

'Serenade'

'*Serenade*': TCHAIKOVSKY: *Serenade for strings in C, Op. 48.* DVORAK: *Serenade for strings in E, Op. 22.* WIREN: *Serenade, Op. 11* (all with ASMF, Marriner). BRAHMS: *Serenade No. 2 in A, Op. 16.* DVORAK: *Wind serenade in D min., Op. 44* (both LSO, Kertész). SUK: *Serenade for strings in E flat, Op. 6* (Los Angeles Chamber Orchestra, Marriner).

(B) *** Double Decca (ADD) 466 459-2 (2).

A most enjoyable programme: it begins with Marriner's first-class 1969 performance of the Tchaikovsky *Serenade*, with its glowing sense of joy combined with the finest pointing and precision of ensemble. He is equally at home in the perennially fresh Wirén *Serenade*, recorded in 1977 and sounding rich and full. It is impossible to choose which of the two Bráhms *Serenades* is the more enjoyable. Here we have the *Second* in Kertész's fine LSO account from 1967 – wonderfully fresh playing and very good sound to match – and the Dvořák *Wind serenade* with the same forces is hardly less compelling. Suk's *Serenade* ought to be better known; it is a work of considerable charm, but has an underlying power and eloquence, as this fine account from Marriner demonstrates. The Los Angeles performance is more brightly lit than the ASMF recordings we are more used to, but the recording is of high quality and naturally balanced. Excellent value.

Serenades: 'Favourite serenades'

'*Favourite serenades*' (played by (i) Netherlands CO, Zinman; (ii) ECO, Leppard; (iii) I Musici; (iv) ASMF, Marriner; (v) Accardo, Leipzig GO, Masur; (vi) Netherlands Wind Ens., Edo de Waart; (vii) Catherine Michel, Monte Carlo Op. O, Almeida): (i) TCHAIKOVSKY: *String serenade, Op. 48.* (ii) DVORAK: *Serenade for strings, Op. 22.* (iii) MOZART: *Eine kleine Nachtmusik.* (iv) HOFFSTETTER/HAYDN: *Serenade from String quartet in F, Op. 3/5.* (v) BRUCH: *Serenade for violin and orchestra, Op. 75.* (iii) WOLF: *Italian serenade in G.* (vi) RICHARD STRAUSS: *Serenade for wind, Op. 7.* (vii) RODRIGO: *Concierto serenade for harp and orchestra.*

(B) **(*) Ph. (IMS) (ADD) 438 748-2 (2).

A generous 156-minute anthology about which there are few reservations. Zinman's account of the Tchaikovsky *Serenade* has not the very strongest profile, but it is polished and warmly recorded. I Musici play Wolf's infectiously gay little masterpiece extremely well, even if perhaps they do not do full justice to its effervescent spirit and sheer *joie de vivre*. Everything else here will certainly give pleasure, especially the rare Max Bruch concertante serenade, so enticingly tuneful with Accardo in ravishing form. Catherine Michel's account of Rodrigo's *Serenade concerto* for harp is not quite as enticing as Zabaleta's famous DG version, but the spicy harmonies are made to catch the ear with piquant abrasiveness. Excellent sound (mostly from the 1970s) and smooth remastering ensure aural pleasure throughout.

Slovak Philharmonic Orchestra

'Russian fireworks' (cond. (i) Richard Hayman; (ii) Kenneth Jean; (iii) Stephen Gunzenhauser; (iv) Michael Halász): (i) IPPOLITOV-IVANOV: *Caucasian sketches: Procession of the Sardar.* (ii) LIADOV: *8 Russian folksongs.* KABALEVSKY: *Comedians' galop.* MUSSORGSKY: *Sorochintsy Fair: Gopak. Khovanshchina: Dance of the Persian slaves.* (iii) LIADOV: *Baba Yaga; The enchanted lake; Kikimora.* (iv) RUBINSTEIN: *Feramor: Dance of the Bayaderes; Bridal procession. The Demon: Lesginka.* (ii) HALVORSEN: *Entry of the Boyars.*

(BB) *** Naxos 8.550328.

A vividly sparkling concert with spectacular digital sound, more than making up in vigour and spontaneity for any lack of finesse. The Liadov tone-poems are especially attractive and, besides the very familiar pieces by Ippolitov-Ivanov, Halvorsen and Mussorgsky, it is good to have the Rubinstein items, especially the *Lesginka*, which has a rather attractive tune.

Slovak State Philharmonic Orchestra (Košice), Mika Eichenholz

'Locomotive music (A musical train ride)', Vol. 1: LANNER: *Ankunfts waltz.* JOHANN STRAUSS SR: *Reise galop; Souvenir de Carneval 1847 (quadrille); Eisenbahn-Lust (waltz).* HOYER: *Jernban galop.* JOHANN STRAUSS JR: *Reiseabenteuer waltz.* MEYER: *Jernvägs-Galop.* EDUARD STRAUSS: *Glockensignale waltz; Mit Dampf polka; Lustfahrten waltz; Tour und Retour polka.* JOSEF STRAUSS: *Gruss an München polka.* GRAHL: *Sveas helsning till Nore waltz.* LUMBYE: *Copenhagen Steam Railway galop.*

** Marco Polo 8.223470.

'Locomotive music', Vol. 2: LANNER: *Dampf waltz.* FAHRBACH: *Locomotiv-Galop.* JOHANN STRAUSS JR: *Wilde Rosen waltz; Vergnügungszug polka; Spiralen waltz; Accelerationen waltz.* GUNGL: *Eisenbahn-Dampf galop.* EDUARD STRAUSS: *Polkas: Reiselust; Ohne Aufenthalt; Treuliebchen; Ohne Bremse; Von Land zu Land; Bahn frei; Feuerfunken waltz.* ZIEHRER: *Nachtschwalbe polka.*

** Marco Polo 8.223471.

This seems a happy idea on which to base a two-CD collection of Viennese-style dance music, but in the event the only piece which celebrates the effect of a train journey really successfully is the *Copenhagen Steam Railway galop.* The Slovak performance has rather a good whistle but seems more concerned with rhythm than with charm and cannot compare with the account included in the splendid Unicorn collection of Lumbye's dance music so beautifully played by the Odense Symphony Orchestra under Peter Guth (DKPCD 9089 - see our main volume). The first Marco Polo disc opens with Lanner's *Ankunfts* ('Arrival') *waltz*, which ironically dates from before the railway had even arrived in Vienna. It is enjoyable for itself; the other highlights are more descriptive. Frans Hoyer's *Jernban galop* makes a fair shot of a train starting up and has a rather engaging main theme, while Jean Meyer's *Jernvägs-Galop* follows Lumbye's pattern of an elegant opening and a whistle start, with the side-drum snares giving a modest railway simulation. This too is attractive melodically, but the coda is too abrupt. Eduard Strauss's *Mit Dampf polka* has a rather half-hearted whistle but plenty of energy, and his *Lustfahrten waltz* is lyrically appealing.

The second disc opens with Lanner again, but the *Dampf* refers to the steam of a coffee house! It is followed by Fahrbach's jolly *Locomotiv-Galop*, where the effects are minimal and primitive. However, Joseph Gungl does better, with an opening whistle which returns on a regular basis against supporting bass-drum beats. Johann Strauss's *Vergnügungszug polka* concentrates on the exhilaration of a day out on an excursion train, but Eduard Strauss's *Bahn frei*, comparably zestful, manages a cleverly brief introductory train imitation, and *Ohne Aufenthalt* has a gentle bell to set off. If most of this repertoire is unadventurous in terms of evocation, it is all tuneful and brightly presented; the playing is not without finesse and has plenty of zest, and the orchestra is very well recorded - and not in a train shed either. But these are full-priced CDs and one is plainly not travelling in a first-class carriage with the VPO.

Steele-Perkins, Crispian (trumpet)

'Six Trumpet Concertos' (with ECO, Anthony Halstead): J. HAYDN: *Concerto in E flat.* TORELLI: *Concerto in D..* M. HAYDN: *Concerto No. 2 in C.* TELEMANN: *Concerto for Trumpet, Two Oboes and Strings.* NERUDA: *Concerto in E flat.* HUMPHRIES: *Concerto in D, Op. 10/12.*

(BB) *** Regis (ADD) RRC 1053.

Collectors who have relished Håkan Hardenberger's famous collection of trumpet concertos might well go on to this equally admirable concert, which duplicates only the Joseph Haydn – and that in a performance hardly less distinguished. Crispian Steele-Perkins has a bright, gleaming, beautifully-focused timbre and crisp articulation, with easy command of the high tessitura of the Michael Haydn work and all the bravura necessary for the sprightly finales of all these concertos. His phrasing in the slow movement of Joseph Haydn's shapely *Andante* is matched by his playing of the *Largo* of the Neruda and the *Adagio-Presto-Adagio* of the

Torelli, another fine work. Anthony Halstead with the ECO gives him warmly sympathetic support. The recording balance gives the soloist plenty of presence, but the orchestra is recorded rather reverberantly, an effect similar to that on the Hardenberger record.

Stern, Isaac (violin), Franz Liszt CO, János Rolla

BEETHOVEN: *Romances Nos. 1 & 2, Op. 40 & 50.* HAYDN: *Violin concerto in G.* MOZART: *Serenata notturna; Adagio in E, K.261; Rondo in C, K.273.*

**(*) Sony SK 62693.

Balanced naturally, without the spotlighting that used to mark his concerto recordings, Isaac Stern gives fresh and stylish readings of this attractive collection of short concertante pieces, immaculately tuned, a tribute to his mastery even in his late seventies. True, these are not works which call for virtuoso flair, but in the little cadenza at the end of Mozart's *Rondo in C* you do have that sense of joyful freedom which has always marked Stern's playing. The speeds for both *Romances* are nicely flowing, not as slow as in most traditional performances. Sympathetic accompaniment from Rolla and the excellent Hungarian chamber orchestra, well recorded, though the timpani at the start of the *Serenata notturna* are disconcertingly boomy.

Stockholm Sinfonietta, Esa-Pekka Salonen

'*A Swedish serenade*': WIREN: *Serenade for strings, Op. 11.* LARSSON: *Little serenade for strings, Op. 12.* SODERLUNDH: *Oboe concertino* (with A. Nilsson). LIDHOLM: *Music for strings.*

**(*) BIS CD 285.

The most familiar piece here is the Dag Wirén *Serenade for strings*. Söderlundh's *Concertino for oboe and orchestra* has a lovely *Andante* whose melancholy is winning and with a distinctly Gallic feel to it. It is certainly played with splendid artistry by Alf Nilsson and the Stockholm Sinfonietta. The Lidholm *Music for strings* is somewhat grey and anonymous, though it is expertly wrought. Esa-Pekka Salonen gets good results from this ensemble and the recording lives up to the high standards of the BIS label. It is forwardly balanced but has splendid body and realism.

Stockholm Sinfonietta, Jan-Olav Wedin

'*Swedish pastorale*': ALFVEN: *The Mountain King, Op. 37: Dance of the cow-girl.* ATTERBERG: *Suite No. 3 for violin, viola and string orchestra.* BLOMDAHL: *Theatre music: Adagio.* LARSSON: *Pastoral suite, Op. 19; The Winter's Tale: Four vignettes.* ROMAN:

Concerto in D for oboe d'amore, string orchestra and harpsichord, BeRI 53. ROSENBERG: *Small piece for cello and string orchestra.*

*** BIS CD 165.

In addition to affectionate accounts of the Pastoral suite and the charming vignettes for *The Winter's Tale*, the Stockholm Sinfonietta include Atterberg's *Suite No. 3*, which has something of the modal dignity of the Vaughan Williams *Tallis fantasia*. It has real eloquence and an attractive melancholy, to which the two soloists, Nils-Erik Sparf and Jouko Mansnerus, do ample justice. The Blomdahl and Roman works are also given alert and sensitive performances; they make one think how charming they are. Hilding Rosenberg's piece is very short but is rather beautiful. A delightful anthology and excellent (if a trifle closely balanced) recording. Confidently recommended.

Stuttgart Chamber Orchestra, Münchinger

'*Baroque concert*': PACHELBEL: *Canon.* GLUCK: *Orfeo: Dance of the Blessed Spirits.* HANDEL: *Water music: Suite No. 3; Organ concerto in F (Cuckoo and the nightingale)* (with M. Haselböck); *Oboe concerto No. 3 in G min.* (with L. Koch). L. MOZART: *Toy Symphony.* ALBINONI: *Adagio in G min.* (arr. GIAZOTTO). BACH: *Suite No. 3, BMV 1068: Air.* BOCCHERINI: *Minuet (from String quintet in E, Op. 13/5).*

(B) **(*) Decca 448 239-2.

Beautifully recorded – this is an attractive concert with a very well-played suite from Handel's *Water music*, and the engaging *Cuckoo and the nightingale Organ concerto* (with Martin Haselböck an excellent soloist) to give a little ballast. The performance of Pachelbel's *Canon* is a little heavy-handed, but the strongly expressive account of Albinoni's *Adagio* is convincing. The *Toy Symphony* has some piquant special effects, and the shorter lollipops are played quite elegantly. The overall mood is a trifle serious, but that is Münchinger's way. For the Eclipse reissue, an elegant performance of a Handel *Oboe concerto* has been added.

Stuttgart Radio Symphony Orchestra, Celibidache

MUSSORGSKY: *Pictures at an exhibition.* STRAVINSKY: *Le Baiser de la fée; The Firebird: suite.* RIMSKY-KORSAKOV: *Scheherazade.* PROKOFIEV: *Romeo and Juliet: excerpts; Scythian suite; Symphony No. 5.*

(*) DG 445 139-2 (3).

One hardly knows were to begin with this set! The opening *Promenade* of *Pictures at an Exhibition* begins lethargically – but that is nothing compared to the ludicrous tempo distortions of the following *Gnomus* (marked *vivo*), which almost grinds to halt at one point.

Other eccentricities abound, and the result veers between the irritating and the boring: the finale is elongated beyond belief. Similar agogic distortions occur in the usually indestructible *Scheherazade*: the second movement, for example, begins rather beautifully, before rhythmic distortions utterly spoil the forward flow: the bassoon's lovely melody, 39 seconds in, is quite ruined. *The Firebird suite* opens with a certain amount of atmosphere, but very soon one has the urge to push the music forward; by 1 minute 50 seconds, the woodwind, in imitation, sound as though they are stuck in a groove. Reaction to the Prokofiev are more mixed. The *Scythian suite* is pretty feeble, the *Fifth symphony* is perhaps the best thing on this disc, but by no means overwhelming, and the *Romeo and Juliet* excerpts (three numbers on a free bonus CD) have a cool beauty, but again lack impetus. Every now and again, there are genuinely imaginative touches with Celibidache, but they are negated by his perverse eccentricity. The sound (these are all live recordings) is very average. This set is for total devotees of Celibidache only.

Swedish Chamber Orchestra, Petter Sundkvist

'*Swedish Orchestral Favourites*' Vol. 2: LARSSON: *Lyric Fantasy, Op. 54; Little Serenade, Op.12; Adagio for String Orchestra, Op. 48.* FRUMERIE: *Pastoral Suite, Op. 13b* (with Lindloff). BLOMDAHL: *The Wakeful Night: Adagio.* ATTERBERG: *Suite No. 3 for Violin, Viola and Orchestra, Op. 19/1* (with Tröback & Persson). RANGSTRÖM: *Divertimento elegiaco for Strings.*

(BB) *** Naxos 8.553715.

All the music on this inexpensive issue exerts a strong appeal. It is worth the modest outlay alone for Atterberg's poignant *Suite No. 3 for Violin, Viola and Orchestra, Op. 19*, which is one of his most poignant utterances, and for Gunnar de Frumerie's perennially fresh *Pastoral Suite* for flute and strings. Having been resistant over the years to Rangström's overblown symphonies but captivated by his songs, it is also a pleasure to welcome a new account of the *Divertimento elegiaco*, whose eloquence is well conveyed in this fine performance. Indeed, throughout this disc the Swedish Chamber Orchestra under Petter Sundkvist are first class.

Swedish Radio Symphony Orchestra, Sergiu Celibidache

DVORAK: *Cello Concerto in B min., Op. 104* (with du Pré). FRANCK: *Symphony in D min.* HINDEMITH: *Mathis der Maler Symphony.* SHOSTAKOVICH: *Symphony No. 9 in E flat, Op. 70.* SIBELIUS: *Symphonies Nos. 2 in D major, Op. 43; 5 in E flat, Op. 82.* R. STRAUSS: *Don Juan, Op. 20; Till Eulenspiegel, Op. 28.*

*(**) DG (ADD) Stereo/Mono 469 069-2 (4).

There are some good things here, and Jacqueline du Pré's many admirers will welcome the fiery eloquence this partnership brings to the Dvořák *Cello Concerto* (although this is available separately). After the war Celibidache was briefly with the Berlin Philharmonic, but he spent most of his time with radio orchestras, which could afford to indulge his inordinate and demanding rehearsal schedules. During the late 1960s he brought the Swedish Radio Orchestra to a high level of accomplishment, and these performances, made at various times between 1965 and 1971, show the refinement and sophistication of texture and sonority as well as the fine tonal blend he achieved. Celibidache may be idiosyncratic – some find his interpretations impossibly egocentric – but at its best his work could be tremendously vibrant. These performances are much more recommendable than some of his Stuttgart recordings, although they are by no means free from affectation. The Sibelius *Fifth Symphony* is curiously fascinating. His admirers will doubtless want this, but for others a certain caution may be advisable, particularly as the set is at premium price.

Symphonies: 'Great Symphonies'

BEETHOVEN: *Symphony No. 5 in C min., Op. 67* (Philharmonia Orchestra, Ashkenazy). BRAHMS: *Symphony No. 3 in F, Op. 90.* DVORAK: *Symphony No. 9 in E min. (From the New World), Op. 95.* (Vienna Philharmonic Orchestra, Kertesz). HAYDN: *Symphony No. 94 in G (Surprise)* (Philharmonia Hungarica, Dorati). MENDELSSOHN: *Symphony No. 3 in A min. (Scottish), Op. 56* (LSO, Abbado). MOZART: *Symphony No. 40 in G min., KV.550* (VPO, Karajan). SAINT-SAENS: *Symphony No. 3 in C min. (Organ), Op. 78* (Los Angeles PO, Mehta). SCHUBERT: *Symphony No. 9 in C (Great), D.944* (Israel PO, Mehta). SIBELIUS: *Symphony No. 7 in C, Op. 105* (VPO, Maazel). TCHAIKOVSKY: *Symphony No. 4 in F min., Op. 36* (LSO, Szell).

*** Australian Decca ADD/DDD 466 444-2 (5).

This set contains two really outstanding recordings: Szell's Tchaikovsky *Fourth*, and Maazel's Sibelius *Seventh*, with the Kertész *New World* not far behind. There is nothing substandard about anything else in this set either – most of the performances are well worth hearing, not least Ashkenazy's superbly recorded Beethoven *Fifth*, Dorati's Haydn *Surprise* and Mehta's vintage Decca version of the Saint-Saëns *Organ symphony*. He is less successful in Schubert's *Ninth*. The set includes excellent sleeve-notes.

Tancibudek, Jiri (oboe)

HAYDN: *Oboe Concerto in C, Hob. VIIg/C1* (with Adelaide CO, Duvall). MARTINU: *Oboe Concerto for Small Orchestra* (with Adeleide SO, Shapirra). BRITTEN: *6 Metamophoses after Ovid.* FELD: *Sonata*

for Oboe and Piano (with Blumenthal).
SUTHERLAND: *Sonatina for Oboe and Piano* (with Stokes).

**(*) Australian Universal Heritage ABC Classics (ADD) 461 703 2.

Part of the brief of the Australian Heritage series is to include recordings by important Australian residents even if they were not Australian born. One such is oboist Jiri Tancibudek, who was principal oboist for the Czech Opera and then the Czech Philharmonic under Kubelik. The Second World War caused him and his family to flee in a desperate night-time trek across the mountains, and they finally settled in Australia. This anthology is valuable for his agile playing of the Martinů *Oboe Concerto*, a work dedicated to him, as well as the Bartók-influenced *Sonatine* for oboe and piano by the Australian composer Margaret Sutherland, although the Haydn concerto and the Britten pieces also receive fine performances. The 1970s sound is good, but not outstanding.

Thames Chamber Orchestra, Michael Dobson

'*The baroque concerto in England*' (with Black, Bennett): ANON. (probably HANDEL): *Concerto grosso in F.* BOYCE: *Concerti grossi in E min. for strings; in B min. for 2 solo violins, cello and strings.* WOODCOCK: *Oboe concerto in E flat; Flute concerto in D.*

(M) *** CRD (ADD) CRD 3331.

A wholly desirable collection, beautifully played and recorded. Indeed, the recording has splendid life and presence and often offers demonstration quality – try the opening of the Woodcock *Flute concerto*, for instance. The music is all highly rewarding. The opening concerto was included in Walsh's first edition of Handel's Op. 3 (as No. 4) but was subsequently replaced by another work. Whether or not it is by Handel, it is an uncommonly good piece, and it is given a superbly alert and sympathetic performance here. Neil Black and William Bennett are soloists of the highest calibre, and it is sufficient to say that they are on top form throughout this most enjoyable concert.

Tokyo Metropolitan Orchestra, Ryusuke Numajiri

'Japanese Orchestral Favourites': TOYAMA: *Rhapsody for Orchestra.* KONOYE: *Etenraku.* IFUKUBE: *Japanese Rhapsody.* AKUTAGAWA: *Music for Symphony Orchestra.* KOYAMA: *Kobiki-Uta for Orchestra.* YOSHIMATSU: *Threnody to Toki for String Orchestra and Piano, Op.12.*

(BB) *** Naxos 8.555071.

There are now plenty of CDs devoted to British light classics, but this one of Japanese favourites is the first of its sort. It is everything one imagines Japanese light orchestral music to be: full of glittering percussion instruments, folk melodies and dance rhythms interspersed with more exotic elements. All these composers are professionals, writing for a modern symphony orchestra, so the music is well constructed and readily accessible. It is all entertainingly colourful, and well worth Naxos price for anyone wanting something fresh and off the beaten track. The performances and recordings are first class.

Toulouse Capitole Orchestra, Michel Plasson

French symphonic poems: DUKAS: *L'apprenti sorcier.* DUPARC: *Lénore; Aux étoiles.* FRANCK: *Le chasseur maudit.* LAZZARI: *Effet de nuit.* SAINT-SAENS: *Danse macabre.*

**(*) EMI CDC5 55385-2.

An interesting and (on the whole) successful programme, let down by the brilliant but unbeguiling account of *The Sorcerer's apprentice*. There is more fun in this piece than Plasson finds. Similarly, the humour of *Danse macabre* is not within Plasson's perceptions, although he gives an excitingly dramatic account of the piece and there is a seductive violin solo from Malcolm Stewart. There is plenty of gusto in *Le chasseur maudit*, where the opening horn-call is arresting, the chase is properly demonic and the malignant middle section masterful, when Christian stalwarts are sinisterly warned of the Satanic welcome waiting for those choosing the hunt rather than the church for their Sunday morning occupation.

Hardly less telling is Duparc's *Lénore*, an equally melodramatic scenario (also espoused by Liszt, with narrative included). This concerns a ghoulish midnight embrace with a skeleton after the eager heroine has been carried off on horseback by her dead lover. But the two most memorable pieces here are the radiantly serene *Aux étoiles* ('The astral light of dawn'), also by Duparc, and – most haunting of all – Sylvio Lazzari's impressionistic *Effet de nuit*, with its bleakly sinuous evocation on the bass clarinet of the scaffold silhouetted in the rain against the darkening evening sky. Its climax depicts 'three ghastly prisoners marching dejectedly' in the pitiless downpour, urged on by 225 halberdiers. The recording is excellent: spacious, yet vivid; it is a shame about *L'apprenti sorcier*.

Trumpet: 'The sound of the trumpet'

'*The sound of the trumpet*': CLARKE: *Trumpet voluntary.* M.-A. CHARPENTIER: *Te Deum: Prelude* (arr. Hazel). PURCELL: *Trumpet tune and air* (arr. Hurford) (all with Peter Hurford, organ, Michael Laird Brass Ens.). HAYDN: *Trumpet concerto in E flat* (Alan Stringer, trumpet, ASMF, Marriner).

BACH: *Christmas oratorio: Nun seid ihr wohl gerochen* (arr. Reeve). SCHEIDT: *Galliard battaglia.* HANDEL: *Occasional oratorio: March* (arr. Hazel); *Royal Fireworks music: Overture* (arr. & cond. Howarth) (all with Philip Jones Brass Ens.); *Messiah: The trumpet shall sound* (with Gwynne Howell, bass). VIVALDI: *Double trumpet concerto in C, RV 537* (with John Wilbraham, Philip Jones, trumpets). HUMMEL: *Trumpet concerto in E* (with John Wilbraham, trumpet) (all three with ASMF, Marriner). STANLEY: *Trumpet tune in D* (arr. Pearson; with Leslie Pearson, organ). ARBAN: *Carnival of Venice* (arr. & cond. Camarata; L. Festival O) (both with John Wilbraham, trumpet).

⊕ (M) *** Decca ADD/DDD 458 194-2.

The Decca production team are particularly adept at compiling an anthology like this, and there is simply no better single-disc recommendation for those who enjoy the sound of trumpets – regal and exciting – on the lips of true virtuosi. Such indeed are John Wilbraham and the individual players of the Michael Laird and Philip Jones Ensembles (especially in Elgar Howarth's highly effective brass arrangement of the *Overture* from Handel's *Royal Fireworks music*). The popular favourites by Jeremiah Clarke, once attributed to Purcell, and Purcell himself, his *Trumpet tune and air*, are equally appealing.

Wilbraham's account of the Hummel *Concerto* is among the finest ever recorded, elegant in the slow movement and with the finale sparkling irresistibly. Marriner and the ASMF, during their vintage period, accompany with comparable polish, as they do Alan Stringer, who plays the Haydn *Concerto* excellently, with a bolder and more forthright open timbre which is undoubtedly authentic. Peter Hurford, when he participates, is similarly stylish.

Almost every item here is a winner, and the stereo interplay in Scheidt's *Galliard battaglia* is indicative of the demonstration standard of many of the recordings included. The programme ends with a dazzling display from John Wilbraham in Camarata's lollipop arrangement of the most famous of all cornet solos, Arban's variations on the *Carnival of Venice*. The CD has good documentation and a particularly enticing frontispiece, with the title of the anthology embossed in gold lettering on the jewel-case – truly worthy of our Rosette.

Trumpet Concertos

'Virtuoso Trumpet Concertos': played by: Håkan Hardenberger: HAYDN: *Concerto in E flat* (with ASMF, Marriner). FRANZ XAVER RICHTER: *Concerto in D* (with LPO, Elgar Howarth). John Wilbraham: HUMMEL: *Concerto in E flat* (with ASMF, Marriner). Maurice André: MICHAEL HAYDN: *Concerto in D.* (with Munich Chamber Orchestr, Hans Stadmair). LEOPOLD MOZART: *Concerto in D* (with Rouen Chamber Orchestra, Albert Beaucamp).

(BB) *** Ph. Eloquence (ADD/DDD) 468 207-2.

While the first class individual collections by Hardenberger and Marsalis, on Philips and Sony respectively, are especially recommendable (see above), this inexpensive Eloquence CD is well worth its modest price, highlighting as it does three outstanding trumpeters of our time. Maurice André's performances have characteristic panache. The two-movement work by Michael Haydn is not as memorable as his brother's concerto, but it is a fine piece nevertheless, and Leopold Mozart's concerto has a similar layout and reminds the listener of Handel. Both works lie high up in the trumpet's register, yet offer André no problems.

If Hardenberger's supreme accounts of the most famous concerto of all – by Josef Haydn – and the unfamiliar but elegant work by Franz Xaver Richter (featuring more stratospheric trumpet writing) are among the highlights of the disc, John Wilbraham's brilliant account of the Hummel concerto, with its irresistible rondo finale, is also quite superbly played. (This version of the finale was once available separately on a 'World of the Academy of St Martin-in-the-Fields' compilation disc).

Tuckwell, Barry (horn), Academy of St Martin-in-the-Fields, Sir Neville Marriner or (i) with English Chamber Orchestra

Horn concertos: TELEMANN: *Concerto in D.* CHERUBINI: *Sonata No. 2 in F for horn and strings.* Christoph FORSTER: *Concerto in E flat.* WEBER: *Concertino in E min., Op. 45.* Leopold MOZART: *Concerto in D.* Giovanni PUNTO: *Concertos Nos. 5 in F; 6 in E flat; 10 in F; 11 in E.* (i) Michael HAYDN: *Concertino in D* (arr. SHERMAN). (i) Joseph HAYDN: *Concerto No. 1 in D.*

⊕ (B) *** EMI Double fforte (ADD) CZS5 69395-2 (2).

Barry Tuckwell readily inherited Dennis Brain's mantle and held his place as Britain's pre-eminent horn player for several decades before finally retiring in 1997. This EMI Double fforte set celebrates his supreme achievement in nearly a dozen of the finest concertos for his instrument; the Tuckwell recordings of the key works by Wolfgang Amadeus and Richard Strauss are of course available elsewhere. His supreme mastery and ease of execution, his natural musicality and warm lyricism of line – to say nothing of his consistent beauty of tone – make every performance here memorable, and he has the advantage of polished, graceful accompaniments from the ASMF under Marriner, except in the works by Michael and Joseph Haydn, in which he directs the ECO himself with comparable elegance.

The concerto of Telemann opens with a catchy moto perpetuo, despatched with aplomb; then comes a fine *Adagio* which often moves to the very top of the horn's upper range before the tension is released in the buoyant finale. The Cherubini *Sonata* opens with a melancholy *Largo*, then erupts into joyous high spirits, while the racing opening arpeggios of the concerto by Leopold Mozart and the tight trills in the finale (with harpsichord echoes) are managed with comparable exuberance. The Weber is an attractively diverse and extensive (17 minutes) set of variations and includes a good example of horn 'chords', where the soloist plays one note and hums another; it also has an exceptionally joyful finale.

One of the novelties is a delightful concerto by the virtually unknown Christoph Forster (1693–1745) with its amiably jogging first movement marked *Con discrezione* and its brief, disconsolate *Adagio* followed by a closing Rondo in which, though the clouds clear away, the lyrical feeling remains. In some ways most striking of all is the collection of four concertos by the Bohemian virtuoso Giovanni Punto, a successful and highly cultivated composer whose music is enjoyably distinctive, a mixture of Mozartean influences and Hummelian *galanterie*. The individual CD of these four works was issued to celebrate Barry Tuckwell's fiftieth birthday, and the performances show him at his finest. The recording throughout is of EMI's finest analogue quality, and the remastering retains the warmth and beauty of the originals.

Turner, John (recorder), Royal Ballet Sinfonia, Gavin Sutherland or Edward Gregson

English recorder music for recorder and strings: LANE: *Suite ancienne.* ARNOLD: *Concertino, Op. 41a.* PITFIELD: *Concerto for recorder, string orchestra and percussion; 3 Nautical sketches.* GREGSON: *3 Matisse impressions.* LYON: *Concertino.* PARROTT: *Prelude and Waltz.* BULLARD: *Recipes.*

*** Olympia OCD 657.

Who could have guessed that eight concertante works for recorder and strings would have been so entertainingly diverse? Philip Lane's *Suite* in the olden style is unrepentant pastiche with an irresistibly exuberant finale (*Beau Brummel's bath night*). Arnold's *Concertino* is even more quirky, with a haunting central *Chaconne*. Thomas Pitfield was a distinguished Professor of Composition at the Royal Manchester College and subsequently the Royal Northern College of Music, and his *Concerto*, which uses both treble and descant recorders, moves easily from English pastoralism to a *Tarantella* dance finale.

The *Nautical sketches* draw on sea-shanties with equally light touch. Edward Gregson cleverly catches the mood of three Matisse paintings: the evocative style is predictably French but also individual. David Lyon's *Concertino* is the most recent work (1999) and its wry opening movement nicely offsets the delicacy of the haunting central waltz. Parrott's *Prelude* opens more abrasively, bringing a welcome astringency,

then he relents into another delectably embroidered waltz. Bullard's very entertaining *Recipes* certainly titillates the palette, with a *Barbecue blues* wittily followed by a *Prawn* habanera, and, after a Chinese *Special chop suey*, ends with a circus galop enthusiastically celebrating *Fish and chips.*

The invention of all these works is consistently diverting and with a masterly soloist in John Turner, excellent accompaniments from the Royal Ballet Sinfonia under Gavin Sutherland (or Gregson, who conducts his own work) this is very enjoyable throughout and highly recommendable.

'Twilight Memories'

'Twilight Memories': WILLIAMSON: *Curtain Up.* WILLIAMS: *They Ride by Night; The Young Ballerina.* YORKE: *Fireflies.* ELLIS: *Muse in Mayfair.* TORCH: *Fandango; Wagon Lit* (with Queen's Hall Light O, Sydney Torch). VAUGHAN WILLIAMS: *Sea Songs: Quick March* (with New Concert O). FLETCHER: *Fiddle Dance; Folk Tune* (with Jay Wilbur O). COATES: *The 3 Bears: Waltz* (with Queen's Hall Light O, Composer). STRACHEY: *Ascot Parade.* BRIDGEWATER: *Prunella.* WHITE: *Caprice for Strings.* W. COLLINS: *Cumberland Green.* BANTOCK: *Twilight Memories* (London Promenade O, W. Collins). RICHARDSON: *Shadow Waltz.* CAMPBELL: *Cloudland.* MORLEY: *Mock Turtles.* SIDAY: *Petticoat Lane.* MACKINTOSH: *Strings on Wings* (with Queen's Hall Light O, King). CURZON: *Dance of an Ostracised Imp* (New Concert O, Wilbur). MILNER: *Downland* (with L'Orchestra de Concert, O'Henry). FARNON: *Goodwood Galop.* THOMAS: *Looking Around* (with Queen's Hall Light O, Farnon).

(M) (***) ASV mono CDAJA 5419.

Another collection of vintage nostalgia, dating from the late 1940s. The programme opens appropriately with Lambert Williamson's *Curtain Up*, a charming example of period writing, and a lively account of the *Quick March* from Vaughan Williams's *Sea Songs* follows. Percy Fletcher's *Folk Tune*, a piece of much charm, and Sidney Torch's catchy percussion rhythms in the jazzy *Fandango* are offset by Richardson's dainty *Caprice for Strings*. Farnon's *Goodward Galop* races along without a care in the world, and Angela Morely shows her gift for orchestral colour in the amusing *Mock Turtles*. Peter Yorke's *Fireflies* with its scurrying woodwind writing brings slinky strings into the middle section. Walter Collins's *Cumberland Green* is another joyful piece of tuneful writing, while Bantock's *Twilight Memories*, which gives this collection its title, is a rather haunting waltz. The recordings vary in quality, though none is below a decent standard for the period, and this disc is certainly recommended to those collectors with a nostalgic affection for the British light music tradition.

Ulsamer Collegium, Josef Ulsamer, with Konrad Ragossnig (lute), and Eduard Melkus Ensemble

'Dance music through the ages'

I: *Renaissance dance music:* ANON.: *Lamento di Tristano; Trotto; Istampita Ghaetta; Istampita Cominciamento di gioia; Saltarello; Bassa danza à 2; Bassa danza à 3.* GULIELMUS: *Bassa danza à 2.* DE LA TORRE: *Alta danza à 3.* ATTAIGNANT: *Basse danses: La brosse - Tripla - Tourdion; La gatta; La Magdelena.* DALZA: *Calata ala Spagnola.* NEUSIEDLER: *Der Judentanz; Welscher Tanz.* MILAN: *Pavana I/II.* MUDARRA: *Romanesca guarda me las vacas.* PHALESE: *Passamezzo - Saltarello; Passamezzo d'Italye - Reprise - Gallarde.* LE ROY: *Branle de Bourgogne.* B. SCHMIDT: *Englischer Tanz; Tanz: Du hast mich wollen nemmen.* PAIX: *Schiarazula Marazula; Ungaresca - Saltarello.* SUSATO: *Ronde.* GERVAISE: *Branle de Bourgogne; Branle de Champagne.*

II: *Early baroque dance music:* MAINERIO: *Schiarazula Marazula; Tedesca - Saltarella; Ungaresca - Saltarella.* BESARDO: *Branle - Branle gay.* MOLINARO: *Saltarello; Ballo detto Il Conte Orlando: Saltarello.* GESUALDO: *Gagliarda del Principe di Venosa.* CAROSO: *Barriera (Balletto in lode della Serenissima D. Verginia Medici d'Este, Duchessa di Modena); Celeste Giglio (Balletto in lode delli Serenissimi Signori Don Ranuccio Farnese, e Donna Margarita Aldobrandina Duca, e Duchessa di Parma e di Piacenza etc.).* CAROUBEL: *Pavana de Spaigne; 2 Courantes; 2 Voltes.* HOLBORNE: *Pavane: The Funerals; Noel's galliard; Coranto: Heigh ho holiday.* ANON.: *Kempe's jig.* DOWLAND: *Queen Elizabeth her galliard; Mrs Winter's jump.* SIMPSON: *Alman.* GIBBONS: *Galliard.* PRAETORIUS: *Galliarde de la guerre; Reprise.* HAUSSMANN: *Tanz; Paduan; Galliard; Catkanei.*

III: *High baroque dance music:* ANON.: *Country dances: Running footman; Greensleeves and Pudding eyes; Cobler's jigg; How can I keep my maiden head.* SANZ: *Canarios.* CORRETTE: *Menuet I/II.* HOTTETERRE: *Bourrée.* BOUIN: *La Montauban.* SANZ: *Pasacalle de la Cavalleria de Napoles; Españoletas; Gallarda y Villano.* CHEDEVILLE: *Musette.* REUSNER: *Suite Paduan (Allemande; Courantel Sarabande; Gavotte; Gigue).* POGLIETTI: *Balletto (Allemande; Amener; Gavotte; Sarabande; Gavotte).* DESMARETS: *Menuet; Passe-pied.* FISCHER: *Bourrée; Gigue.* ANON.: *Gavotte.* LOEILLET IL DE GANT: *Corente; Sarabande; Gigue.* LULLY: *L'Amour malade (opéra ballet): Conclusion; Une Noce de Village (dance suite).*

IV: *Rococo dance music* (Eduard Melkus Ensemble): C. P. E. BACH: *5 Polonaises, Wq.190; 2 Menuets with 3 Trios, Wq.189.* RAMEAU: *Zoroastre: Dances (Air tendre en Rondeau; Loure; Tambourin en Rondeau; Sarabande; Gavotte gaye avec Trio; Premier Rigaudon; Air en Chaconne).* STARZER: *Contredanse; Gavotte mit Trio; Pas de deux; Menuet; Gavotte mit Trio; Moderato; Gavotte; Menuet mit Trio; Gavotte mit Trio; Passe-pied mit Trio.*

V: *Viennese classical dance music:* EYBLER: *Polonaise.* HAYDN: *2 Menuets, Hob IX/11:4 & IX/16:12.* GLUCK: *Orfeo ed Euridice: Ballet; Don Juan (Allegretto).* MOZART: *6 Landerische, K.606; 5 Kontretänze, K.609.* ZEHN: *Deutsche.* BEETHOVEN: *4 Kontretänze, WoO 14/4, 5, 7 & 12.* SALIERI: *Menuetto.* WRANITZKY: *Quodlibet.*

VI: *Viennese dance music from the Biedermeier period (1815-48):* PALMER: *Waltz in E.* BEETHOVEN: *Mödlinger Tänze Nos. 1-8, WoO 17.* MOSCHELES: *German dances with trios and coda.* SCHUBERT: *5 Minuets with Trios, D.89; 4 komische Ländler, D.354.* ANON.: *Linzer Tanz; Vienna polka.* LANNER: *Hungarian galop in F.*

✿ (B) *** DG (ADD) 439 964-2 (4).

This collection, on four well-filled CDs (recorded between 1972 and 1974), explores the history of European dance music from the beginning of the fifteenth century right through to the first three decades of the nineteenth century, just about the time when Johann Strauss Senior was making his début. The members of the Ulsamer Collegium play an extraordinary range of authentic period instruments. Keyboards, strings, wind and plucked vihuela, as well as guitar, lute and hurdy-gurdy, are used with the greatest imagination, always to seduce the ear with variety of colour. There is not a whiff of pedantry or of abrasiveness of the kind that too often accompanies 'authentic' performances, yet the documentation is characteristically and fascinatingly thorough. The consistent tunefulness of the music is a continued source of pleasure and surprise.

Among the composers of early baroque dance music, Pierre Francisque Caroubel and Mario Fabrizio Caroso stand out: the suite of dances by the former, played variously on gambas and recorder consort, is most diverting. On the second CD, the keyboard, gamba and lute pieces from the English Elizabethan school hardly need advocacy, but they are beautifully played (the lute and guitar solos of Konrad Ragossnig are most distinguished throughout the set) as is the jolly suite of dances by Valentin Haussmann – another unfamiliar name to turn up trumps.

Among the high baroque composers Esaias Reusner (1636–79) provides another diverting dance suite which, like the ballet music of Alessandro Poglietti, proves as elegant and finished as the ballet suite of Lully. In the rococo era, Carl Philipp Emanuel Bach contributes five spirited *Polonaises*, and after a gracious interlude from Rameau there is a set of more robust and extrovert dances from Josef Starzer (1726–87). We enter the Viennese classical period with a clash of cymbals enlivening a *Polonaise* by Joseph Eybler (1764–1846), who sounds ahead of his time; but the two *Minuets* of Haydn stay well in period. At this stage of the proceedings the excellent Eduard Melkus Ensemble take over.

The first of the Mozart *Contredanses*, K.609, which opens the fifth CD makes reference to a famous tune from *Figaro*, and Paul Wranitzky quotes from the same opera in his *Quodlibet*. Beethoven produced irresistible music. Moscheles and Schubert follow his example, the latter providing some deliciously flimsy *Ländler*, while the delicate *E major Waltz* of Michael Palmer (1782–1827), the two anonymous dances from Linz and Vienna and the *Hungarian galop* of Joseph Lanner (which ends the programme) point onwards to the heyday of Viennese dance music, when Johann Strauss Junior was to reign supreme. Overall, this is a most stimulating and rewarding survey.

Vengerov, Maxim (violin)

'*Vengerov and Virtuosi*' (with Vag Papian, piano or Virtuosi): BAZZINI: *Le Ronde des lutins, Op. 25.* BRAHMS: *Hungarian Dances Nos. 1, 5 & 7.* DVORAK: *Humoresque No. 7 in G flat.* KHACHATURIAN: *Gayaneh: Sabre Dance.* MASSENET: *Thaïs: Méditation.* MONTI: *Csárdás.* NOVACEK: *Perpetuum mobile.* PONCE: *Estrellita.* RACHMANINOV: *Vocalise, Op. 34/14.* TCHAIKOVSKY: *Souvenir d'un lieu cher, Op. 42.* SCHUBERT (arr. Wilhelmi): *Ave Maria.*

*** EMI CDC5 57164-2.

With its odd accompaniment from Vengerov's chosen band of 11 Russian solo violins and piano, recorded live in the Musikvereinsaal in Vienna in April 2001, Vengerov's recital of violin lollipops is very much a fun record for those with a sweet tooth. The opening item, Rachmaninov's *Vocalise*, heavily inflected, leads to an account of Ponce's *Estrellita* that echoes Palm Court in its sweetness, Vengerov, full of spontaneous flair and encouraged by a live audience, allows himself extreme rhythmic freedom. Cheering greets the last item, Monti's famous *Csárdás*, with a big laugh from the audience as Vengerov plays around with bird imitations, but otherwise there is little evidence of the audience's presence. Tempo changes in almost every bar witness a young violinist at the peak of his form enjoying himself from first to last in music that is undemanding on the ear if not on the technique and outrageously showing off in a way that for many will be very endearing. Not that the playing is extrovert all the time. Vengerov's account of the *Méditation* from Massenet's *Thaïs* conveys a rare depth of feeling, making it more than just a lyrical interlude. Curiously, the coagulation of 11 solo violins often sounds rather like an accordion.

Vienna Philharmonic Orchestra, Sir John Eliot Gardiner

'*Vienna soirée*: SUPPE: *Overture Morning, noon and night in Vienna.* ZIEHRER: *Wiener Bürger waltz; Fächer-Polonaise; Schönfeld march.* LEHAR: *Waltzes: Ballsirenen; Gold and Silver.* LANNER: *Die Schönbrunner waltz; Tourbillon galopp.* HEUBERGER: *Der Opernball Overture.*

*** DG 463 185-2.

Sir John Eliot Gardiner here shows how the Viennese tradition might prosper even without a Strauss contribution. The Vienna Philharmonic is in scintillating form in this delightful collection of overtures, waltzes and shorter pieces, some of them rare, with one item not otherwise available, Lanner's dashing *Tourbillon-Galopp*. Gardiner's account of the Suppé overture is at once high-powered, highly polished and deliciously sprung, setting the pattern for the rest. This is playing of pin-point precision, gloriously resonant, and Gardiner, as in his Vienna recording of Lehár's *Merry Widow*, enters fully into the Viennese spirit. That same composer's *Ballsirenen waltz* is in fact a fantasy on themes from the operetta, refined and tender as well as ebullient. The other Lehár item too, the *Gold and silver waltz*, brings magical pianissimos. Most winning of all are the rarer, shorter items, with Ziehrer's *Fächer-Polonaise* and *Schönfeld march* played uninhibitedly with irresistible zest and bounce. The DG recording, made in the Vienna Musikverein, has ideal freshness and clarity.

Vienna Philharmonic Orchestra, Valéry Gergiev

'*Salzburg Festival Concert*': PROKOFIEV: *Symphony No. 1 in D (Classical) Op. 25.* SCHNITTKE: *Viola Concerto* (with Yuri Bashmet). STRAVINSKY: *The Firebird* (complete ballet).

plus feature: Stravinsky and Prokofiev (Gergiev) and Schnittke (Bashmet). (Director/Video Director: Brian Large.)

*** TDK **DVD** DV-VPOVG.

Gergiev and the Vienna Philharmonic are recorded at the Salzburg Festival in 2000 in an all-Russian programme. The excellence of the performances is enhanced by the visual direction, which, as so often with Brian Large, directs the listener's eyes where his ears want them to be. Gergiev has an excellent rapport with his Viennese players and *The Firebird*, for which most collectors will want this concert, is impressive both musically and, thanks to an excellent balance, aurally. There are times when one feels he could give his players just a little more time (the *Dance of the Princesses*) and conversely the first movement of the Prokofiev feels a little staid. However, for the most part, these are very fine readings with superb playing from the Viennese.

Schnittke's *Viola Concerto*, completed not long before his stroke, is generally thought to be among his most powerful compositions. Yuri Bashmet, who is the dedicatee, has recorded the concerto twice before, with Rozhdestvensky and Rostropovich. It is made up of two *Largos* surrounding a fast central movement, the mood swinging between a pensive brooding and a kind of frenetic activity. Whether one warms to Schnittke or not, it is a powerfully communicative performance. The TDK notes, incidentally, tell us that the '*Firebird Suite* exists in three versions … the second, *to be heard in the present recording* contains only seven numbers of the original 19 in the two-act (sic!) ballet version'. Not so, fortunately! The title-page lists the nineteen numbers of the full version and it is the complete score that is recorded here. TDK must look to their presentation.

Vienna Philharmonic Orchestra, Nikolaus Harnoncourt

'*Vienna New Year's Concert 2001*': J. STRAUSS SR: *Radetzky March* (original and revised versions). J. STRAUSS JR. *Overture: Eine Nacht in Vienna* (Berlin version). Polkas: *Electrofor; Electro-magnetic; Vergnügungzug (Excursion Train); Der Kobold; Luzifer.* Waltzes: *Morgenblätter; Seid umschlungen Millionen; An der schönen Blauen Donau (Blue Danube).* JOSEF STRAUSS: Polkas: *Harlekin; Ohne Sorgen.* Waltz: *Dorfschwalben aus Osterreich (Village Swallows).* LANNER: *Jägers Lust (galop); Die Schonbrunner Waltz; Steyrische Tanze.*

*** Teldec 8573 83563-2.

Harnoncourt may still be best known as a pioneer of period performance, but he is also dedicatedly Viennese, someone who as a young cellist once played in the orchestra. True to character, he introduces a fair sprinkling of novelties, starting with the original version of what by tradition has become the concert's final encore, the *Radetzky March*. Far more plainly orchestrated, it offers little rivalry for the established version. Other items new to the concerts include the *Electro-magnetic Polka* and *Electrofor Polka*, nicely contrasted, and the Polka-mazurka, *Der Kobold* ('The Goblin'), with charming pizzicato effects and a pianissimo coda. The three items by Joseph Lanner, stylistically well differentiated, celebrate that composer's bicentenary and include a jolly rarity, *Jägers Lust* ('Huntsman's Delight'), with hunting horns prominent and a shot simulated by the timpani. In a fascinating note on the history of the concerts the orchestra's chairman, Dr Clemens Hellberg, makes an illuminating comment on Harnoncourt from the players' point of view: that they were delighted to 're-examine the Philharmonic's Strauss tradition through the eyes of this analytical yet so impulsive conductor'. A vintage year, presented in sparklingly clear sound.

Vienna Philharmonic Orchestra, Herbert von Karajan

'*The great Decca recordings*': BRAHMS: *Symphonies Nos. 1 in C min., Op. 68; 3 in F, Op. 90; Tragic overture, Op. 81.* HAYDN: *Symphonies Nos. 103 in E flat (Drumroll); 104 in D (London).* MOZART: *Symphonies Nos. 40 in G min., K.550; 41 in C (Jupiter), K.551.* TCHAIKOVSKY: *Romeo and Juliet (fantasy overture); Nutcracker suite; Swan Lake (ballet): suite; Sleeping Beauty (ballet): suite.* ADAM: *Giselle (ballet; abridged).* BEETHOVEN: *Symphony No. 7 in A, Op. 92.* DVORAK: *Symphony No. 8 in G, Op. 88.* GRIEG: *Peer Gynt (incidental music): suite No. 1; suite No. 2: Ingrid's lament; Solveig's song.* HOLST: *The Planets (suite), Op. 31.* JOHANN STRAUSS JR: *Die Fledermaus: Overture and ballet music. Der Zigeunerbaron: Overture. Polkas: Annen; Auf der Jagd. Waltz: Geschichten aus dem Wiener Wald.* JOSEF STRAUSS: *Delirien waltz.* RICHARD STRAUSS: *Till Eulenspiegel; Salome: Dance of the 7 veils. Don Juan, Op. 20; Also sprach Zarathustra, Op. 30.*

(B) **(*) Decca (ADD) 448 042 (9).

Following directly on after his EMI Philharmonia recordings with Walter Legge, Karajan's five-year Decca period with the Vienna Philharmonic – master-minded by producers John Culshaw and Erik Smith – lasted from 1959 until 1964. Though the epithet 'great' can be applied to only a handful of the recordings in this box, almost all of them have far more character and musical appeal than many of the more anonymous records flooding the present-day CD market. Certainly Karajan's 1960 *Romeo and Juliet* stands the test of time, not only for its passion but also for its delicacy of feeling in the 'moonlight' music, and his virtually complete (1961) recording of Adam's *Giselle* (with sumptuous sound still approaching demonstration standard) shows what a fine ballet conductor he was, the playing combining affectionate warmth, elegance and drama.

The suites from the three Tchaikovsky ballets have comparable panache and generate considerable excitement; apart from the rather plangent timbre of the VPO's principal oboe, they have plenty of glowing colour, with the *Panorama* from *Sleeping Beauty* endearingly suave and the final climax from *Swan Lake* riveting in its histrionic power. The *Nutcracker suite* has more vivid characterization than the later, Berlin Philharmonic account, with the *Waltz of the flowers* lilting agreeably. The remastering scores over the analogue DG versions in its greater ambient depth.

The excerpts from *Peer Gynt* bring the freshest response from the VPO, with gusty Trolls galloping into the *Hall of the Mountain King*, and *Solveig's song* radiantly beautiful. Again, the 1961 Decca recording stands up well alongside the later DG analogue version (which we count as marginally the most alluring of his three stereo accounts) and in many ways is superior in body and naturalness. As for *The Planets*, dating from that same vintage year, this is certainly a great performance, with *Mars* among the most thrilling ever put on disc. With whining Wagnerian tubas it makes a terrifying impact; then *Venus* follows, transmuted into sensuous balm – the Venus of gentle ardour rather than mysticism. *Jupiter* is bucolic and breezy, the Vienna strings bringing their own characteristic tone-colour to the big central tune. *Saturn* with its slow, sad march and *Uranus* with superb VPO brass are no less outstanding, and the wordless chorus at the end of *Neptune* is more atmospheric than in almost any other version. The analogue recording is so stunningly vivid that it could have been made yesterday.

Karajan never surpassed his 1960 VPO collection of overtures, polkas and waltzes by Johann and Josef Strauss until he came to make his wonderful (DG) 1987 New Year concert with the same orchestra. His later, BPO records sound glossy by comparison, yet here his rhythmic touch is unerring in the two overtures, while the polkas have all the flair you could ask for. However, the highlight is the highly seductive account of *Tales from the Vienna woods*, played most beautifully, an account which may have been equalled, but has never been surpassed.

The superlative performances of the Richard Strauss tone-poems are hardly less remarkable, and they sound wonderfully fresh. In this repertoire no one can quite match Karajan in the panache and point of his conducting. This programme is available separately in Decca's Legends series and is discussed above under its Composer entry.

In the symphonic repertoire the results are less even. Of the two Haydn symphonies, No. 103 is more urbane than No. 104, though both offer enjoyably polished VPO playing: there is plenty of robust vigour in the latter and both slow movements are beautifully shaped. The same comments might apply to Mozart's *Fortieth* and *Jupiter Symphonies*. In the G minor every detail remains beautifully in place, each phrase nicely contoured and in perspective. Beautifully articulate, this performance has genuine dramatic power, even though one feels that it all moves within carefully regulated limits. The reading of the *Jupiter* is strong and direct and has breadth as well as warmth. Exposition repeats are observed in the first movements of each symphony, but not in the finale of the *Jupiter*.

Of the two Brahms symphonies, No. 1 gives the impression of being over-rehearsed. Its pacing does not always seem spontaneous, with an overall lack of tension; though towards the end of the finale Karajan cannot help creating genuine excitement, this is dissipated in a very slow chorale reference in the coda. The *Third* is much more successful. Here is another case in which the Vienna performance rivals the quality of the later, DG Berlin version. In both, Karajan takes the opening expansively; in both, he omits the exposition repeat. The third movement, too, is very slow, but the overall reading has plenty of grip and tension,

and the Decca recording has a fuller and more resonant bass than the DG, and this well suits Brahms.

The recording of Beethoven's *Seventh* is also full-bodied, though not as fine as that for the Dvořák *Eighth*. 1961 was certainly a vintage year for the Decca engineers. The Beethoven performance is massive rather than incandescent and refuses to catch fire or grip the listener emotionally. The Dvořák is another matter, a most winning performance with superb orchestral playing. There are moments of slight self-indulgence in the Trio of the Scherzo, but the result is delectable when the Vienna strings are at their creamiest; overall, this account blends polish and spontaneity in almost equal measure. The orchestra are clearly enjoying themselves and so do we.

Vienna Philharmonic Orchestra, Rudolf Kempe

'The Vienna Philharmonic on holiday': MASCAGNI: *Cavalleria rusticana: Intermezzo.* PONCHIELLI: *La Gioconda: Dance of the hours.* SCHMIDT: *Notre Dame: Intermezzo.* GOUNOD: *Faust: Waltz.* BAYER: *Die Puppenfee: suite.* OFFENBACH: *Orpheus in the Underworld: Overture.* GOTOVAC: *Ero the joker (dance).* SCHUBERT: *Rosamunde: Overture (Die Zauberharfe); Entr'acte in B flat; Ballet in G.* GLUCK: *Orfeo et Euridice: Dance of the Blessed Spirits.*

*** Testament (ADD) SBT 1127.

It is good to be reminded so vividly of an aspect of Rudolf Kempe's mastery too easily forgotten – his Beechamesque charm in light music. Waltz rhythms are given a delicious lilt not just in Viennese items like the delightful Josef Bayer suite, *Die Puppenfee*, but in Gounod too, with Kempe bringing out the delicacy as well as the vigour. Kempe's use of rubato is often extreme – arguably too much so in the Schubert *Rosamunde* music – but it never fails to be winning in a very Viennese way, as in the rare Franz Schmidt *Intermezzo*. The Ponchielli, once so popular, now neglected, sparkles with uninhibited joy, as does the Offenbach, and it is good to have such a rarity as the *Kolo* by the Zagreb conductor and composer Jakob Gotovac, rhythmic and colourful. The recordings were all made in the Musikvereinsaal in Vienna in December 1961, with the glowing EMI recording well caught in Testament transfers which bring out both warmth and depth of focus.

Vienna Philharmonic Orchestra, Carlos Kleiber

'1992 New Year Concert': J. STRAUSS JR: *Overture: Der Zigeunerbaron. Polkas: Neue pizzicato; Stadt und Land; Tritsch-Tratsch; Unter Donner und Blitz; Vergnügungszug.* WALTZES: *An der schönen, blauen Donau; Tausend und eine Nacht. Persischer march.*

J. STRAUSS SR: *Radetsky march.* JOSEF STRAUSS: Waltzes: *Dorfschwalben aus Osterreich; Sphärenklänge.* NICOLAI: *Overture: The Merry Wives of Windsor.*

*** Sony SK 48376.

When Carlos Kleiber conducted the 1989 event, he seemed at times a little stiff. But here he manages precision alongside lilt, discipline as well as verve. There is plenty of elegance and warmth too, in a programme entirely without novelties but where the waltzes nearly always go as spontaneously as the polkas, though the *Blue Danube* is no match for Karajan's version of two years earlier. The recording is well up to standard, vivid yet spacious and full.

Vienna Philharmonic Orchestra, Riccardo Muti

'1993 New Year Concert': J. STRAUSS SR: *Sperl-Galopp; Radetzsky march.* J. STRAUSS JR: *Klipp Klapp galop; Egyptische-Marsch; Overture Indigo und die Vierzig Räuber; Perpetuum mobile;* Polkas: *Auf der Jagd; Diplomaten; Pizzicato polka; Veilchen;* Waltzes: *Die Publicisten; An der schönen blauen Donau.* JOSEF STRAUSS: *Transaktionen.* LANNER: *Steyrische-Tänz; Hans-Jörgel.*

*** Ph. (IMS) 438 493-2.

Riccardo Muti seems an unlikely candidate for sweet-toothed Vienna *bon-bons*, but the atmosphere of this celebrated occasion has its usual effect and he clearly lets his hair down after a while. Once again there are novelties and they sparkle readily when Muti can produce such unselfconscious Straussian manners. Lanner's *Steyrische-Tänz* provides the surprise of the CD by unexpectedly turning out to be the source of the barrel-organ waltz in Stravinsky's *Petrushka*. The tension is not quite consistent throughout the concert, with the second half (beginning with the overture) setting an even more compelling atmosphere; but overall this is such a happy occasion that one cannot but enjoy the experience. Applause is nicely edited and is not too much of a problem. The documentation reveals the history of the event, fascinating in itself. Excellent recording.

Vienna Philharmonic Orchestra, Seiji Ozawa

'New Year Concert 2002': JOHANN STRAUSS SR: *Beliebte Annen Polka, Radetsky March.* JOHANN STRAUSS JR: *Carnevalbotschafter Waltz; Zivio! March; Kunstlerleben Waltz; Die Fledermaus Overture; Perpetuum mobile; Elisen-Polka;* Waltz: *Wiener Blut; Tik-tak Polka;* Waltz: *An die schönen Blauen Donau.* JOSEF STRAUSS: *Die Schwatzerin, Vorwarts!, Arm in Arm, Aquarellen Waltz, Die Libelle, Plappermaulchen, Im Pfluge.*

HELLMESBERGER: *Danse diabolique.* (Video Director Brian Large).

*** TDK **DVD** Mediactive DV-WPNK02.

With a large Euro sign in flowers on the organ pipes behind the orchestra in the Vienna Musikvereinsaal, this was a special New Year's concert, signalling the arrival that day of the new currency. One of the extra items in the 'Special Features' section of the disc is an alternative version of Johann Strauss's *Perpetuum mobile* showing what is described as the 'Dance of the Machines' with illustrations of Euro notes being printed and Euro coins being minted and stamped. Other additional items include alternative accounts of the *Blue Danube* with the ballet company of the Vienna State Opera and of two polkas, *Beliebte Annen* by Johann Strauss senior and the *Elisen Polka* by junior, with the Spanish Riding School performing wonders of equitation, a delightful extra.

Those extra items allow the main concert to be presented with no visual distraction from shots of the players, conductor, hall and audience, with almost every advantage for the DVD over the equivalent CD. Quite apart from the bonus of visual presentation the DVD offers five numbers omitted from the CD – two pieces by Josef Strauss, celebrating his 175th anniversary, the polkas *Arm in Arm* and *Im Pfluge*, and three Strauss numbers, the *Carnevalbotschafter Waltz,* the *Beliebte Annen Polka* and *Perpetuum mobile*.

Ozawa at his most relaxed is naturally idiomatic in his pauses and warm rubato, helped by not using a baton, relying on the innate expressiveness of the Viennese players to mould in perfect time. More than anyone since Karajan in his single New Year concert, Ozawa controls the clapping of the audience, limiting it to the proper passages in the final *Radetsky March.* The international credentials of the orchestra are demonstrated in the multilingual new year greetings from a dozen and more players just before the traditional *Blue Danube.*

(i) Vienna Philharmonic Orchestra, or (ii) Berlin Philharmonic Orchestra, Bruno Walter

(i) MAHLER: *Symphony No. 4 in G* (with Seefried).
(ii) R. STRAUSS: *Don Juan.*

(**) Urania mono URN 22156.

One of the glories of the post-war catalogue was Mahler's *Fourth Symphony* with Bruno Walter and the New York Philharmonic. Although the *Second* and *Ninth Symphonies* had been available, together with a Vienna *Das Lied von der Erde,* was a Society issue, available only by subscription. The appearance of the *Fourth* enthused music-lovers, but Walter's singer was Desi Halbein, whose colouring and timbre were somewhat uninviting. The Urania set comes from 1950 and has a rich-toned Irmgard Seefried and the Vienna Philharmonic. There is another

Walter recording with her in New York in 1953, while Music & Arts (see above) offers a 1952 live Concertgebouw recording with Elisabeth Schwarzkopf.

Virtuosi di Praga, Oldřich Vlček

Music for strings: GRIEG: *Holberg suite.* RESPIGHI: *Ancient airs and dances: Suite No. 3.* ELGAR: *Serenade in E min., Op. 20.* ROUSSEL: *Sinfonietta, Op. 52.*

(BB) **(*) Discover DICD 920236.

The Prague Virtuosi are an expert body of soloists who command an impressive sonority in spite of their modest size (here eleven players). Some ears might feel that the Elgar *Serenade* lacks ripeness of Elgarian feeling, yet the *Larghetto* is tenderly affecting. Equally, the Respighi suite of *Ancient airs* sounds fresher, less anachronistically voluptuous than usual. The chamber scale suits the *Holberg suite* admirably, with plenty of energy and bite. But undoubtedly the most effective performance here is the Roussel *Sinfonietta*, bracingly astringent and grippingly vital.

Wallfisch, Elizabeth (violin), Parley of Instruments, Peter Holman

'English classical violin concertos': JAMES BROOKS: *Concerto No. 1 in D.* THOMAS LINLEY JR: *Concerto in F.* THOMAS SHAW: *Concerto in G.* SAMUEL WESLEY: *Concerto No. 2 in D.*

**(*) Hyp. CDA 66865.

Peter Holman and his Parley of Instruments expend much energy and Elizabeth Wallfisch considerable musical sensibility to bring these concertos from the late eighteenth century fully to life. They succeed admirably in that, working hard over music which is usually felicitous and always well crafted but too often predictable. In first movements one keeps getting the impression of second-rate Haydn. However, the opening movement of the James Brooks *Concerto* is amiably pleasing in its melodic contours and offers the soloist plenty of lively bravura. Its brief *Largo affettuoso* is agreeable too, and the dancing finale sparkles on the Wallfisch bow, and she produces a neat cadenza.

Thomas Linley offers a *galant* Moderato first movement, another all-too-brief but graceful slow movement with a nice rhythmic snap; the finale is a charming gavotte. But Thomas Shaw goes one better in his *Adagio*, creating the best tune on the disc, for his slow movement, again with a Scottish snap, is most winning, very like a folksong. The finale bounces and the horns hunt boisterously. Wesley's first movement is vigorous and assured, if too long; and in the slow movement a pair of the orchestral violins join the soloist in a trio. The finale is very jolly and buoyant. The recording is excellent and, dipped into, this collection will give pleasure, providing you do not expect too much.

'Wedding Classics'

'Wedding Classics': MENDELSSOHN: *Midsummer Night's Dream: Wedding March* (OAE, Mackerras). ALBINONI: *Adagio* (L. Chamber O., Warren-Green). FAURE: *Pavane* (City of L Sinf., Hickox). MARCELLO: *Oboe Concerto: Adagio* (Ray Still, L. Academy, Stamp. MOZART: *Ave verum Corpus* (with Schütz Ch.). PURCELL: *The Fairy Queen, Part II: Overture* (both with L. Classical Players, Norrington). *The Indian Queen: Trumpet Overture.* PACHELBEL: *Canon.* HANDEL: *Messiah: Hallelujah Chorus; Dixit Dominus: excerpt.* BACH: *Jesu, joy of Man's desiring* (all by Taverner Players & Chorus, Parrott). *Suite No. 3: Overture; Air; Gavottes I & II* (ECO, Ledger); *Wedding Cantata (No. 202): Gavotte* (Nancy Argenta, Ens. Sonnerie, Huggett). BARBER: *Agnus Dei* (arr. of *Adagio for strings*) (Winchester Cathedral Ch., Hill). MOZART: *Alleluia* (Monika Frimmer); *Serenata notturna: Minuet* (Lausanne CO, Y. Menuhin). BACH/GOUNOD: *Ave Maria* (Sister Marie Keyrouz, Auvergne CO, Van Beck). ROSSINI: *Petite Messe solennelle: Prelude religioso* (Wayne Marshall, organ). RACHMANINOV: *Gloria in excelsis* (Swedish R Ch., Kaljuste). FRANCK: *Cantabile for organ* (Nicholas Danby). HAYDN: *The Seasons: excerpt* (Petite Band Kuijken). FALLA: *Three-Cornered hat (ballet): Miller's Dance* (Aquarius, Cleobury). HOLST: *The Planets; Venus* (RLPO, Mackerras). GRIEG: *Olav Trygvason: excerpts* (Trondheim Ch. & SO, Ruud). BORODIN: *Prince Igor: Polovtsian Dance* (RLPO Ch. & O, Mackerras). POULENC: *Organ Concerto: excerpts* (Weir; cond. Hickox). ORFF: *Carmina Burana: O Fortuna* (Bournemouth Ch. & SO, Hill).

(B) ** Virgin 2 X 1 VC5 61890-2 (2).

This curious Virgin collection of wedding music ('spiritual, contemplative or festive') was originally compiled in 1989, which perhaps accounts for the omission of the Widor *Organ Toccata*. But one wonders where music from Falla's *Three-Cornered Hat ballet* or Grieg's *Olav Trygvason* will fit into an English wedding celebration? However there are quite a number of more suitable items, and the performances and recordings are of a high standard. No doubt the inclusion of Orff's *O Fortuna* as the final item is intended to celebrate the 'luck' of the bride, and she will be glad to know that Holst's *Venus* represents 'the bringer of peace' rather than extra-marital temptation.

Williams, John (guitar)

Guitar concertos (with ECO, (i) Sir Charles Groves; (ii) Daniel Barenboim): (i) GIULIANI: *Concerto No. 1 in A, Op. 30.* VIVALDI: *Concertos in A and D.* RODRIGO: *Fantasia para un gentilhombre*; (ii) *Concierto de Aranjuez.* VILLA-LOBOS: *Concerto.* (i) CASTELNUOVO-TEDESCO: *Concerto No. 1 in D, Op. 99.*

(M) *** Sony M2YK 45610 (2).

This bouquet of seven concertante works for guitar from John Williams could hardly be better chosen, and the performances are most appealing. Moreover the transfers are very well managed and, if the guitar is very forward and larger than life, the playing is so expert and spontaneous that one hardly objects. All these performances are among the finest ever recorded, and Groves and Barenboim provide admirably polished accompaniments, matching the eager spontaneity of their soloist.

'The Seville concert' ((i) with Orquesta Sinfónica de Sevilla, José Buenagu): ALBENIZ: *Suite españolas: Sevilla; Asturias.* BACH: *Lute suite No. 4, BWV 1006a: Prelude.* D. SCARLATTI: *Keyboard sonata in D min., Kk 13* (arr. WILLIAMS). (i) VIVALDI: *Concerto in D, RV 93.* YOCUH: *Sakura variations.* KOSHKIN: *Usher waltz, Op. 29.* BARRIOS: *Sueño en la Floresta.* (i) RODRIGO: *Concierto de Aranjuez: Adagio.*

*** Sony SK 53359.

With so much reappearing from the Julian Bream archive, it is good to have a first-rate, modern recital from the estimable John Williams. It was recorded in Spain (in the Royal Alcázar Palace) as part of a TV programme, which accounts for its hour-long duration and the inclusion of the ubiquitous Rodrigo Adagio as the closing item. The recording is very realistic and present, yet the balance is natural and the effect not jumbo-sized. John Williams's intellectual concentration is as formidable as his extraordinary technique.

This playing comes as much from the head as from the heart. He is first rate in the Bach and brings a sense of keyboard articulation to the engaging *D minor Sonata* of Scarlatti (who was Bach's almost exact contemporary). His strength is felt in the flamenco accents of Albéniz's *Asturias*, a sense of the darkly dramatic is powerfully conveyed in Koshkin's *Usher waltz* (after Edgar Allan Poe). Yet his playing can be charmingly poetic, as in the delicate account of the *Largo* of the Vivaldi concerto; touchingly gentle, as in Yocuh's charming pentatonic evocation of cherry blossoms; or thoughtfully improvisational, as in the Barrios *Sueño en la Floresta*.

Zabaleta, Nicanor (harp)

'*Great concertante works for harp*': MOZART: *Flute and harp concerto, K.299* (with Karlheinz Zöller, BPO). BOIELDIEU: *Harp concerto.* RODRIGO: *Concierto serenata* (with Berlin RSO, Märzendorfer). HANDEL: *Harp concerto, Op. 4/6.* ALBRECHTSBERGER: *Harp concerto in C.* DITTERSDORF: *Harp concerto in A.* DEBUSSY: *Danse sacrée et danse profane.* RAVEL: *Introduction and allegro for harp, string quartet, flute and clarinet* (all with members of Paul Kuentz CO).

(B) *** DG Double (IMS) (ADD) 439 693-2 (2).

Zabaleta was an absolute master of his instrument and all these performances are touched with distinction. Johann Albrechtsberger taught Hummel and Beethoven, and his lightweight concerto is very pleasing when played with such flair and delicacy. The same might be said of the charming Boieldieu and Dittersdorf works, both of which display invention of some character, while the Handel and Mozart concertos are acknowledged masterpieces. In the latter, Karlheinz Zöller makes a distinguished partner.

When it was first issued on LP, we gave Zabaleta's version of Rodrigo's delectable *Concierto serenata* a Rosette. In the outer movements especially, the delicate yet colourful orchestration tickles the ear in contrast to the beautifully focused harp timbre. Zabaleta is marvellous too in Ravel's *Introduction and allegro*, with sensitive support from members of the Paul Kuentz Chamber Orchestra, and warmly atmospheric sound. The Mozart, Boieldieu and Rodrigo works come from the early 1960s; the others are later and, with excellent transfers, this 145 minutes of concertante harp music will surely offer much refreshment, though these are obviously not CDs to be played all at once.

Harp concertos: (i) BOIELDIEU: *Harp concerto in 3 tempi in C* (with Berlin RSO, Märzendorfer). SAINT-SAENS: *Morceau de concert in G, Op. 154.* TAILLEFERRE: *Concertino for harp and orchestra* (with ORTF, Martinon). RAVEL: *Introduction and allegro for harp, flute, clarinet and string quartet* (with members of the Kuentz CO).

(M) **(*) DG (IMS) (ADD) 463 084-2.

Two rarities – the Tailleferre and Saint-Saëns – make this collection interesting. Germaine Tailleferre's *Concertino* dates from 1927 and contains influences of Ravel, Poulenc and even Stravinsky peeping over the composer's shoulder. It is elegantly written and not without its own degree of urbanity, even if the lyrical element is comparatively diffuse. The three movements have an attractive impetus, with the jolly finale developing real exuberance. Saint-Saëns's *Morceau de concert* was written when he was 83 years old. Its four miniature movements – the dainty Scherzo only runs for 1' 54" – have a structure which has much in common with that of the *Second Piano concerto*. But the work's charm rests on its delicacy of texture and the skill with which the accompaniment is tailored, so that it supports but never overwhelms the soloist. Yet the invention has characteristic facility. Both performances are superb, with Martinon providing stylish accompaniments in good 1969 DG sound. The Ravel and Boieldieu performances are both stylish, but neither is quite the finest available, and the sound is not ideally full either. A pity that the Ginastera *Concerto*, originally on the Martinon disc, was dropped, for this disc plays for under 65 minutes.

INSTRUMENTAL RECITALS

The Art of the Piano

'*The Art of the Piano*': *Great pianists of the 20th Century*: (Paderewski; Hofmann; Rachmaninov; Moiseiwitsch; Horowitz; Cziffra; Myra Hess; Rubinstein; Planté; Cortot; Backhaus; Edwin Fischer; Gilels; Richter; Michelangeli; Gould; Arrau).

(*) Warner/NVC Arts **DVD 3984 29199-2; Video 3984 29199-3.

This fascinating video is in the line of '*The Art of Conducting*'. Unfortunately it is musically flawed because so many of the most interesting visual images are taken from old films and cinema sound-tracks which, with their inherent unsteadiness and fluctuations of timbre and pitch, have in the past been notoriously unkind to the piano. Most of the examples here offer marbled tone and harmonic distortion to varying degrees. However the video's introduction still brings a spectacular display of technical wizardry. We see and hear a kaleidoscope of stormy performances of Beethoven's *Appassionata Sonata* edited together in a rapid ongoing sequence, with Solomon first (in 1956), swiftly followed by Arrau (1983), then Dame Myra Hess (1945), Sviatoslav Richter (1992), and finally the aristocratic Artur Rubinstein (1975). Even with such short snippets, the different pianistic personalities of the five players emerge vividly.

We next focus on Paderewski, Prime Minister as well as a somewhat eccentric musician, but an artist whose personal magnetism projected strongly. Like Liszt, whose music he plays, he was irresistible to women. Hence his success in a 1936 Hollywood movie, *Moonlight Serenade*. Josef Hofmann, a legend among fellow pianists, is much more patrician: his approach to the ubiquitous Rachmaninov *C sharp minor Prelude* has no nonsense about it. Rachmaninov follows on playing his own music with natural authority, and then we meet one of his greatest contemporary interpreters, Moiseiwitsch. A pity there is not more of the *Second Piano concerto* (conducted by Constant Lambert) as the plum-label HMV records of this work were considered by some collectors even finer than the composer's own set with Stokowski.

The extraordinary dash of Horowitz (filmed in the Carnegie hall in 1968) in Scriabin and Bizet, his hands (to quote Támás Vásáry) 'like race horses!' virtually matched by those of the underrated Cziffra in Liszt.

Dame Myra Hess always felt intimidated by the recording studio, but here her performance of the first movement of Beethoven's *Appassionata Sonata* (of which we have previously heard a brief excerpt) demonstrates the full power and concentration of her live performances. Rubinstein follows magisterially with Chopin's *A flat Polonaise* (in 1953), then creates magic in the closing pages of the first movement of Beethoven's *Fourth concerto*, with Antal Dorati fifteen years later; and here the recording is faithful enough to make a real highlight.

But perhaps it is Cortot who provides the most intriguing cameo in the first part of the video. We see and hear him playing *The poet speaks* from *Kinderszenen* to a 1953 master class, commenting throughout Schumann's intimate reverie, and suggesting that the performer's aim should be 'to dream the piece rather than play it'.

Backhaus (filmed during his Decca recording sessions) now plays the slow movement of his favourite concerto, Beethoven's *Fourth*. He quotes Hans Richter who called it the 'Greek' concerto. In this central movement, Backhaus tells us 'Orpheus pleads to set Eurydice free; he meets with fierce resistance before his entreaties are answered'.

We move on to Edwin Fischer's pioneering Bach with its 'luminous' sound quality and intellectual spontaneity and then meet a very young Gilels in a Soviet wartime propaganda film playing Rachmaninov to a carefully staged group of Russian service personnel. Cut to his electrifying and extraordinarily imaginative 1959 performance of the cadenza from the first movement of Tchaikovsky's *B flat minor Piano concerto* (conducted by André Cluytens). This is followed immediately by Sviatoslav Richter, with his 'overwhelming presence' and extraordinary visceral bravura in the finale of the same work, and a comparable 'transcendental virtuosity' in a performance of Chopin's *Revolutionary* study.

After that Michelangeli's narcissistically self-aware keyboard personality makes a strange contrast, but his immaculate performance of a Scarlatti sonata is blurred by poor sound. Glenn Gould makes his entry playing Bach eccentrically, with intrusive vocalise, but is then heard at his most magnetically inspirational in partnership with Bernstein in the closing part of the first movement of the *D minor Clavier concerto*, where he is totally absorbed in creating an extraordinary diminuendo. But it is Claudio Arrau who has the last word, and is just as articulate talking about music-making as he is at the keyboard, where his closing except from Beethoven's last, *C minor Piano sonata* is played with a beauty and concentration to transcend the recorded sound.

'*The Art of the piano*' (CD supplement):

LISZT: *Hungarian rhapsody No. 2 in C sharp min.* (Paderewski). RACHMANINOV: *Prelude in C sharp min., Op. 3/2* (Josef Hofmann); *Moment musical No. 2 in E flat min., Op. 16* (Rachmaninov); *Prelude in B min., Op. 32/10* (Moiseiwitsch). CHOPIN: *Etude in F, Op. 10/8.* BIZET/HOROWITZ: *Variations on a theme from Carmen.* LISZT: *Grand galop chromatique* (Cziffra). BEETHOVEN: *Sonata No. 23 in F min., (Appassionata), Op. 57:* 1st movement only (Dame Myra Hess). CHOPIN: *Polonaises: in A flat, Op. 53; in A, Op. 40/1* (Rubinstein); *Etude in C, Op. 10/7* (Francis Planté). SCHUMANN: *Kinderszenen, Op. 15* (Cortot). BEETHOVEN: *Piano concerto No. 4 in G, Op. 58* (Backhaus, VPO, Schmidt-Isserstedt). BACH: *Well-tempered Clavier: Prelude and fugue in C, BWV 846; Prelude in E flat min.; Fugue in D sharp min., BWV 853* (Edwin Fischer). BEETHOVEN: *Sonata No. 23 in F min. (Appassionata), Op. 57* (Gilels).

(M) (***) Ph. mono/stereo 464 381-2 (3).

This three-disc set is surely an essential supplement to the video as most of the recordings, even the early ones, sound quite respectable and many of them, mono or stereo are very good. Highlights include Cortot's complete performances of *Kinderszenen* (EMI, 1935), Edwin Fischer's Bach (EMI, 1933), and Gilels's breathtaking *Appassionata Sonata* (DG, 1973). Sviatoslav Richter's 1959 recording of the entire Tchaikovsky *B flat minor concerto* is pretty riveting, and far preferable to his DG recording with Karajan, but Arrau's Philips reading of Beethoven's *Op. 111* fails to catch the spontaneous magic of the excerpt on the video.

The Art of Violin

The Art of Violin by Bruno Monsaingeon.

With Elman, Enescu, Ferras, Francescatti, Goldstein, Grumiaux, Heifetz, Kogan, Kreisler, Menuhin, Milstein, Neveu, Oistrakh, Rabin, Stern, Szeryng, Szigeti, Thibaud, Ysaÿe; and with commentaries by Itzhak Perlman, Ivry Gitlis, Ida Haendel, Hilary Hahn, Mstislav Rostropovich andYehudi Menuhin.

*** Warner/NVC Arts **DVD** 5 8573-85801-2.

Bruno Monsaingeon made a strong impression with his revealing studies of Sviatoslav Richter and David Oistrakh. As a glance at the list of artists here shows, he offers a glimpse of some of the great violinists of the last century and includes archival footage that will not only be new to many but, since some has only just come to light, new to all.

Virtuosity is common to all and transcendental in many, but it is the originality of their sound world that is at the centre of Monsaingeon's opening argument, which explores the expressive individuality and sonority of great violinists. No one listening to Szigeti or Kreisler, Oistrakh or Elman – and above all Heifetz – is ever in the slightest doubt as to who was playing. There are excellent commentaries by Itzhak Perlman, Ida Haendel and the splendid Ivry Gitlis; only Hilary Hahn is completely out of her depth in their company.

There is rare footage of Thibaud and Ginette Neveu playing the closing bars of the Chausson *Poème* in Prague and an interesting montage of part of the Mendelssohn concerto in which the soloists (Oistrakh, Stern, Christian Ferras, Milstein, Menuhin, Grumiaux, Heifetz and Elman) change, thus bringing home their differences in tonal production and their rich diversity of approach.

Other rarities include a glimpse of Ysaÿe from 1912, looking like an emperor! This thoughtful and intelligent production can be warmly recommended. Incidentally, on the credits nearly every European TV station is listed as supporting this venture, but neither the BBC nor Channel 4 is among them – further evidence, perhaps, of the declining cultural ambition of British television in the last decade.

Introduction

Tom Deacon's celebration on Philips of the hundred greatest pianists of the twentieth century was a laudable enterprise – to some extent inhibited by the availability of recordings. Of course, not everyone agreed with all his choices of artists for inclusion (or omission!), but certainly many of the CDs in this series were of great interest and many of the performances are of very high quality. Documentation is satisfactory, and the presentation in each volume of two discs for the price of one is generous enough. The only snag is that while for newcomers to CDs this surely proved a treasure trove, piano buffs who already had extensive collections found that the duplication of recordings which were already available presented a problem. Approximately three-quarters of the hundred original issues have now been withdrawn. Those that are still available – as we go to press – are listed below. However, the disappearance of such names as Argerich, Ashkenazy, Gilels, Kissin, Horowitz and Richter, to name but a few, indicates that most of the key issues have already disappeared. More will almost certainly have gone by the time we are in print.

Arrau, Claudio

Volume 4: BALAKIREV: *Islamey.* LISZT: *Rhapsodie Espagnole; Années de pèlerinages: Les Jeux d'eaux à la Villa d'Este. Bénédiction de Dieu; Danse de solitude.* BACH: *Chromatic Fantasia and Fugue, BWV 993.* ALBENIZ: *Iberia (Book I): Evocación; El puerto; Fête-Dieu à Seville.* BRAHMS: *Piano Concerto No. 1, Op. 15* (with Concertgebouw Orchestra, Haitink); *Variations on a Theme by Paganini, Op. 33.*

(B) **(*) Ph. mono/stereo 456 706-2 (2).

Starting with a breathtaking performance of Balakirev's *Islamey* – recorded in the 1920s – the first of these two discs is a revelation, presenting Arrau in his earlier years as a dazzling virtuoso, evidently uninhibited in the recording studio. That is so, whether in the Bach *Chromatic Fantasia* (aptly improvisatory in tone, with textures crystal clear), in Liszt (the *Spanish Rhapsody* given astonishing lightness and clarity in this 1936 performance), or Albéniz (with the mystery and keen originality of the piano-writing heightened). Rounding off the first disc, the three Liszt performances, recorded between 1969 and 1976, are among the finest Arrau did for Philips. The second disc of Brahms is more questionable. The 1969 account of the *First Piano Concerto* sounds sluggish in the first two

movements, though in the *Paganini Variations*, speeds on the slow side go with sprung rhythms and persuasive phrasing.

Barenboim, Daniel

Volume 9: MOZART: *Piano Concerto No. 25 in C, K.503.* BEETHOVEN: *Piano Concerto No. 1 in C* (with New Philh. O, Klemperer). LISZT: *Années de pèlerinage, 2nd Year (Italy): Sonette 47, 104 & 123 del Petrarca. Concert Paraphrase on Wagner's Tristan (Isoldens Liebestod).* BRAHMS: *Piano Concerto No. 1 in D min., Op. 15* (with Philh. O, Barbirolli).

(B) *** Ph. (ADD) 456 721-2 (2).

Two magisterial accounts of the Mozart K.503 and Beethoven's *C major concertos* by Barenboim, though the former is not so spontaneous as his ECO account, and his imposing Brahms *D minor concerto* with Barbirolli has great warmth and power plus an unforgettable slow movement. Those who do not have them in other incarnations can invest in these with confidence.

Bolet, Jorge

Volume 11: LISZT: *Années de pèlerinage: 2nd Year (Italy): Sonetto del Petrarca; Supplement: Venezia e Napoli: Gondoliera; Canzone; Tarantella. Années de pèlerinage: 1st Year (Switzerland). Consolation No. 3 in D flat; Deux études de concert: Gnomenreigen. Etudes d'exécution transcendante: Harmonies du soir; Ricordanza. Etudes d'exécution transcendante d'après Paganini: No. 3 (La campanella). Harmonies poétiques et religieuses: Funérailles. Hungarian rhapsody No. 12 in C sharp min.; Liebestraum No. 3 in A flat; Mephisto Waltz, No. 1. Trois études de concert: La leggierezza.* BELLINI/LISZT: *Réminiscences de 'Norma'.* VERDI/LISZT: *Rigoletto Paraphrase.* MOZART/LISZT: *Réminiscences de 'Don Juan'.*

(B) *** Ph. (ADD/DDD) 456 814-2 (2).

The bulk of these Liszt performances emanate from the recordings Bolet made in the Decca Studios in the late 1970s and 1980s. They exhibit qualities of clarity and lucidity; they are, for the most part, performances of refinement and culture that are missing the sheer abandon that marked the finest of his concert performances. Eminently satisfying, though readers who have collected the originals will not need to consider the present compilation. It is a pity that his 1974 Carnegie Hall recital (456 724-2) has been withdrawn. That was a dazzling affair and presents an altogether different picture of him from the more circumspect studio recordings.

Brendel, Alfred

Volume 14: MENDELSSOHN: *Variations Sérieuses, Op. 54.* WEBER: *Konzertstücke in F min., Op. 79* (with LSO, Abbado). BRAHMS: *Piano Concerto No. 1 in D min., Op. 15* (with Berlin Philharmonic Orchestra, Abbado). CHOPIN: *Polonaise in F sharp min., Op. 44.* LISZT: *Années de pèlerinage, 1st Year (Switzerland): Vallée d'Oberman; Orage; 2nd Year (Italy): Sposalizio. Totentanz* (with LPO, Haitink). *Bagatelle without Tonality. Hungarian Rhapsody No. 15 in A min. (Rákoczy march); La lugubre gondola.* BUSONI: *Toccata.*

(B) *** Ph. (ADD/DDD) 446 733-2 (2).

The *Totentanz* recorded with the LPO and Haitink in the late 1970s, along with the Liszt concertos, was one of Brendel's most electrifying performances, and his Weber *Konzertstücke* with Abbado as well as the Brahms *D minor Concerto* have much to recommend them. Brendel's Liszt has always been among the finest on record and those who haven't acquired this repertoire before, will find much to satisfy and nourish them.

Cherkassky, Shura

Volume 18: TCHAIKOVSKY: *Piano Concertos Nos. 1 in B flat min., Op. 23* (with Berlin Philharmonic Orchestra, Ludwig); *2 in G* (arr. Siloti), *Op. 44* (with Berlin Philharmonic Orchestra, Richard Kraus). LITOLFF: *Scherzo from Concerto Symphonique, Op. 102* (with LPO, Sir Adrian Boult). SCHUMANN: *Symphonic Studies, Op. 13; Kreisleriana, Op. 16.* JOHANN STRAUSS JR. (**arr.** SCHULT-EVLER): *Arabesques on An der schönen blauen Donau.* JOHANN STRAUSS JR (**arr.** GODOWSKY): *Wein Weib und Gesang.*

(B) *** Ph. mono/stereo 456 745-2 (2).

This compilation does sum up the personality of the artist and present him at his most mercurial and characteristic. His mono Tchaikovsky *B flat minor Concerto*, with a rather staid Leopold Ludwig, is full of those capricious flights of fantasy and spontaneity that made him such a delight in the concert hall. For a time during the 1950s his *Second* was the sole LP version to be had. The sound is more transparent than in the B flat minor. DG chose the Siloti version of the score with its truncated slow movement but Cherkassky's playing has warmth and in the finale dazzling high spirits. Cherkassky was more at ease in front of an audience than in the studio and that shows in the Schumann *Symphonic Studies* and *Kreisleriana*, which come from a 1975 recital at the Queen Elizabeth Hall, London, previously issued on the Oiseau Lyre label. An eminently satisfying set, if you do not mind the sluggish tempo for the first movement of Tchaikovsky's *Second Concerto*.

Cziffra, György

Volume 23: CHOPIN: *Etudes, Opp. 10 & 25. Polonaise No. 6 in A flat, Op. 53.* LISZT: *Etudes de concert No. 2 (La leggierezza) & 3 (Un sospiro). Etude d'exécution transcendante No. 12 (Chasse-neige); Fantasy and Fugue on the name of B-A-C-H; Légende No. 2 (St Francis de Paule marchant sur les flots). Mephisto Waltz No. 1. Polonaise No. 2 in E; Années de pèlerinages: Sonetto 123 del Petrarca. Supplement: Tarantella di bravura.*

(B) (***) Ph. (ADD) 456 760-2 (2).

A pupil of Dohnányi when he was nine, Cziffra's studies were broken off by military service during the Second World War and resumed in 1947–50, when he was arrested for political reasons. He won the Hungarian Liszt prize two years before the 1956 uprising, but his chequered career only took off after his escape from Hungary that year. These recordings, made in 1958–63, show Cziffra at his most dazzling and virtuosic. Not only are they exciting and brilliant in the true Hungarian style, but distinguished by great finesse and good taste. Marvellous, exhilarating playing, and very acceptable sound too.

Gieseking, Walter

Volume 33: MOZART: *Piano Sonata in C min., K.457.* BEETHOVEN: *Piano Sonatas in C (Waldstein), Op. 53; F min. (Appassionata), Op. 57.* RAVEL: *Gaspard de la nuit.* DEBUSSY: *Estampes; Préludes, Books 1–2.*

(B) (***) Ph. mono 456 790-2 (2).

Those who have acquired Gieseking's Debussy either in the four-CD box or the recent EMI set should not be deterred from investigating this. Those all emanate from the period 1951–5 and were produced by Walter Legge and Geraint Jones. The present set of the *Préludes* were legendary in their day, and were made in London in 1937–8, as was Ravel's *Gaspard de la nuit*. An invaluable insight into Gieseking's art before the war, and further proof, if that were needed, of the special authority he brought to French repertoire.

Gulda, Friedrich

Volume 41: BEETHOVEN: *Piano Concerto No. 1 in C, Op. 15* (with VPO, Karl Böehm). WEBER: *Konzertstück in F min., Op. 79* (with VPO, Volkmar Andrea). R. STRAUSS: *Burlesque* (with LSO, Collins). CHOPIN: *Piano Concerto No. 1 in E min.* (arr. Balakirev; with LPO, Boult). *4 Ballades.* SHEARING/FORSTER: *Lullaby of Birdland.*

(B) **(*) Ph. mono/stereo 456 820-2 (2).

The Gulda Volume presents this pianist to considerable effect. The present recordings all come from 1951–6 and show his youthful pianism at its best. One point of interest is that the Balakirev elaboration of Chopin's orchestration of the *E minor Piano Concerto* is used. *The Record Guide* much admired the delicacy of

Gulda's playing, though not in preference to Mewton Wood's poetic account; but compared with performances from later and greater pianists, there seems less cause for rapture. The Beethoven concerto is a very fluent and straightforward account, though the *Guide* was very critical of the somewhat shrill recording. The Strauss *Burlesque* is one of the more striking performances; obviously the partnership with Collins proved fruitful. But admirable though he is and of fine musical intelligence, one must question whether these performances can rank alongside the likes of Arrau, Gilels and Solomon.

Haebler, Ingrid

Volume 42: BACH: *French Suite No. 6 in E, BWV 817.* HAYDN: *Piano Concerto in D, Hob XVIII:11; Variations in F min., Hob. XVII: 6.* MOZART: *Piano Concerto No. 18 in B flat, K.456* (with LSO, Sir Colin Davis); *9 Variations on a Minuet by Duport, K.573.* SCHUBERT: *Sonata No. 14 in A min., D.784.* SCHUMANN: *Kinderszenen, Op. 15.* CHOPIN: *Waltz in E flat, Op. 18.*

(B) **(*) Ph. (ADD) 456 823-2 (2).

There is some musical playing here, but whether it can be described as great is a moot point! Ingrid Haebler has elegance and nimble fingers but many (including her admirers) would hesitate before placing her alongside such exalted company as Perahia, Richter and Horowitz. Having said that, this pair of CDs will undoubtedly give pleasure – particularly the *B flat Concerto*, K.456 – but that is another matter.

Haskil, Clara

Volume 43: MOZART: *Piano Concertos: Nos. 13 in C, K.415* (with Lucerne Festival Strings, Rudolph Baumgartner); *20 in D min., K.491; 24 in C min., K.491* (with Lamoureux Orchestra of Paris, Markevitch); *23 in A, K.488* (with Vienna SO, Paul Sacher); *27 in B flat, K.595* (with Bavarian State O, Fricsay). *Rondo in A, K.386* (with VSO, Bernhard Baumgartner).

(B) **(*) Ph. mono/stereo 456 826-2 (2).

Clara Haskil is a much venerated pianist and some of these recordings have already appeared in the Philips 'Clara Haskil Legacy'. Her refinement and grace are heard at their best in these Mozart concertos and the accompaniments are, on the whole, worthy of her. The performances are strong and classical, almost totally devoid of romanticism, but with the dramatic contrasts of light and shade made positive by the orchestra, especially under Markevitch and Fricsay. The recordings date from between 1954 and 1960; the coupling of K.466 and K.491 was made in the month before her death. Her somewhat cool approach rather suits the *Larghetto* of the *C minor*, and though some may find her a trifle unyielding in the slow movement of the *D minor*, K.488 suits her especially well. She is always stylish and musical, and there is usually ample spontaneity. Very good recording balances.

Hess, Myra

Volume 45: Domenico SCARLATTI: *Sonatas, K.11 & K.14.* SCHUMANN: *Carnaval, Op. 9; Symphonic Studies.* GRANADOS: *Goyescas: Quejas ó la maya y el ruiseñor.* MENDELSSOHN: *Song without Words, Op. 102/5.* BRAHMS: *Waltz in A flat, Op. 39/15; Intermezzo in C, Op. 119/3.* SCHUMANN: *Concerto in A min., Op. 54* (with Philharmonia Orchestra, Rudolf Schwarz). BEETHOVEN: *Sonatas Nos. 30 in E, Op. 109; 31 in A flat, Op. 110.* BACH, arr. HESS: *Jesu, Joy of Man's Desiring.*

(B) (***) Ph. mono 456 832-2.

As her account of the *Emperor Concerto* on BBC Legends shows, there was more to Myra Hess than the rather cosy *Jesu, Joy of Man's Desiring* halo that she came to acquire. Not only was she thoughtful and poetic but she commanded considerable intellectual strength. The two late Beethoven sonatas are unfailingly beautiful and have great tonal refinement and subtlety. The only disappointment, perhaps, is the Schumann *A minor Concerto* with Rudolf Schwarz conducting, which has less freshness and poetic spirit than her pre-war account with Walter Goehr. She was closely associated with this piece, making her Concertgebouw debut with it in 1912 under Mengelberg, and playing it in her first Queen's Hall appearance with Beecham four years later. As was customary in her day, she plays the *Symphonic Studies* without the five posthumous variations that Brahms published, and the 1938 account of *Carnaval*, of which she herself thought highly, was long (and rightly) regarded as a benchmark by which newcomers were judged.

Hofmann, Josef

Volume 46: SCHUBERT, arr. TAUSIG: *Marche Militaire No. 1.* LISZT: *Concert Paraphrases: of Schubert's Erlkönig; of Chopin's Chants Polonais: The Maiden's Wish; My Darling. Liebestraume No. 3; Années de pèlerinage (supplement: Venezia e Napoli): Tarantella. Hungarian Rhapsody No. 2 in C sharp min.; Concert Study No. 1: Waldesrauchen.* MENDELSSOHN: *Songs without Words: Hunting Song, from Op. 19; Spring Song, from Op. 62; Bee's Wedding (from Op. 67); Rondo capriccioso, Op. 14* (abridged). CHOPIN: *Polonaise No. 3 in A, Op. 40/1* (2 versions); *Waltzes: in A flat, Op. 34/1; in C sharp min., Op. 64/2; in E min., Op. posth.; Fantaisie-impromptu, Op. 66; Berceuse, Op. 57; Nocturne in F sharp min., Op. 15/2; Scherzo in B min., Op. 20* (abridged). RUBINSTEIN: *Valse caprice; Melody in F, Op. 3/1.* SCHUMANN: *Fantaisiestücke, Op. 12: Warum?;* STERNBERG: *Etude No. 3 in C min., Op. 120.* JOSEF HOFMANN: *The Sanctuary; Mignonettes: Nocturne.* GRIEG: *Lyric piece: Butterfly, from Op. 43.* MOSZKOWSKI: *Capriccio espagnol* (abridged). *La*

Jongleuse, Op. 52/4. PADEREWSKI: *Minuet in G, Op. 14/1.* PARKER: *Valse gracile.* DILLON: *Birds at Dawn, Op. 20/2.* GLUCK (arr. BRAHMS) *Pardie ed Elena: Gavotte in A.* D. SCARLATTI, arr. TAUSIG: *Pastorale e capriccio.* RACHMANINOV: *Preludes: in C sharp min., Op. 3/2; in G min., Op. 23/5.* WAGNER arr. BRASSIN: *Die Walküre: Magic Fire Music.* BEETHOVEN: *The Ruins of Athens: Turkish March* (arr. RUBINSTEIN).

(B) (***) Ph. mono 456 835-2 (2).

It was to Josef Hofmann that Rachmaninov dedicated the *Third Piano Concerto* and it was he who gave its New York première with Mahler conducting. His peers spoke of him as the greatest pianist of their time, and many pianists today regard him as the greatest of the twentieth century. His technique was incredible, his command of colour limitless and his memory prodigious (he once heard Godowsky playing his arrangement of melodies from *Fledermaus* and returned the following week and played the complete transcription from memory). His 1937 account of Rubinstein's *Fourth Concerto*, unfortunately not included here, leaves no doubt as to his stature and his magical delicacy of touch. Nor is his magical Chopin *G minor Ballade* here, but the collection is valuable in offering a wide range of his relatively few records from 1912–23, and his pioneering 1903 discs. Not exactly hi-fi but not to be missed.

Katchen, Julius

Volume 54: GERSHWIN: *Rhapsody in Blue* (with Mantovani). RAVEL: *Piano Concerto for the Left Hand; Piano Concerto in G.* PROKOFIEV: *Piano Concerto No. 3 in C, Op. 26* (all with LSO, Kertész). LISZT: *Piano Concerto No. 2 in A* (with LSO, Argenta). BEETHOVEN: *Rondo in B flat, WoO6* (with LSO, Gamba). RACHMANINOV: *Rhapsody on a Theme of Paganini.* DOHNANYI: *Variations on a Nursery Tune, Op. 25* (both with LPO, Boult).

(B) *** Ph. (ADD) 456 859-2 (2)

Katchen's career was sadly cut short by his premature death in 1969. Listening to his charismatic 1968 recordings of Gershwin and Prokofiev, both so vivid and exciting, no one would suspect that his health was anything but robust. The Ravel *Left-Hand Concerto* was his last recording: it is a brilliant account most expertly accompanied by Kertész and equally well served by the Decca engineers. The Liszt *A major Concerto* (with Argenta) is hardly less impressive, but perhaps his most successful coupling was of Rachmaninov and Dohnányi, with Boult and the LPO. The Rachmaninov is notable, not just for its virtuosity and romantic flair, but also for the diversity and wit displayed in the early variations. He made the Dohnányi *Nursery Rhyme Variations* his very own, recording the work twice with Boult, once in mono and once in stereo, and it is difficult to decide which is the more enjoyable.

Kempff, Wilhelm

Volume 55: BRAHMS: *4 Ballades, Op. 10; 7 Fantasias, Op. 116; 3 Intermezzi, Op. 117; 8 Pieces, Op. 76; 6 Pieces, Op. 118; 4 Pieces, Op. 119.* SCHUMANN: *Arabeske in C, Op. 18; Kreisleriana, Op. 16.*

(B) (***) Ph. mono (ADD) 456 862-2 (2).

We owe it to Alfred Brendel that this first of the Kempff selections is devoted to Brahms and Schumann. All the recordings here – except for the final item, Schumann's *Kreisleriana* – were recorded not for Kempff's regular recording company, DG, but for Decca, filling in on repertory he had not prevously tackled. Brendel counts that Decca period as 'in many ways the high point of Kempff's work in the recording studio,' at once authoritative, yet spontaneous-sounding, consistently bringing out his gift for producing a singing legato, while using the pedal lightly. The Philips transfers of mono recordings are superb, full and firm, bringing out the resonance and warmth of Kempff's piano sound, often giving the illusion of full stereo.

Volume 56: SCHUBERT: *Sonata No. 16 in A min., D.845.* BEETHOVEN: *Sonata No. 27 in E min., Op. 90.* MOZART: *Piano Concerto No. 23 in A, K.488* (with BPO, Ferdinand Leitner). LISZT: *Legends Nos. 1, St. Francis of Assisi Preaching to the Birds; 2, St. Francis of Paola Walking on the Waves. Années de Pèlerinage, 1st Year: Eglogue; Au lac de Wallenstadt; Au bord d'une source; 2nd Year: Il penseroso; Canzonetta del Salvator Rosa; Sonetti del Petrarca Nos. 47; 104; 123; Supplement: Gondoliera.* BACH, arr. KEMPFF: *Chorales: Jesu, Joy of Man's Desiring; Nun komm' der heiden Heiland; Watchet auf, ruft uns die stimme.*

(B) *** Ph. (ADD) 456 865-2 (2).

This selection includes Decca recordings Kempff made in the 1950s, less well known than those for DG. Guided by Alfred Brendel, the choice is weighted towards Kempff's poetry, notably in the Liszt and best of all in the two St *Legends* based on the two St Francises. Kempff's evocation of *St Francis of Assisi Preaching to the Birds* has never been matched on disc, a miraculous performance. Kempff's 1953 Decca recording of the Schubert *A minor Sonata*, D.845, provides a contrast with the one he recorded later for DG in his Schubert sonata cycle. Here in 1953, with speeds marginally broader, he is lighter and more transparent, bringing out the poetry more intensely. Among much else, the DG Mozart concerto recording is also uniquely individual. Excellent transfers.

Kocsis, Zoltán

Volume 59: GRIEG: *Lyric Pieces, Op. 43, Nos.: 1, Butterfly; 2, Solitary Traveller; 3, In my Native Country; 4, Little Bird; 5, Erotikon; 6, To the Spring.* BARTOK: *Romanian Folk Dances, Sz.56.* LISZT: *Années de pèlerinages: Les Jeux d'eaux à la Villa* *d'este.* DEBUSSY: *2 Arabesques; Estampes: Pagodes; Soirée dans Grenade; Jardins sous la pluie; Suite Bergamasque. Fantaisie for Piano and Orchestra.* DOHNANYI: *Variations on a Nursery Song* (both with Budapest Festival O, Iván Fischer). RACHMANINOV: *Piano Concerto No. 4 in G min., Op. 40* (with San Francisco SO, Edo de Waart); *Prelude in C sharp min., Op. 3/2; Vocalise, Op. 34/14* (arr. KOCSIS).

(B) *** Ph. 456 874 (2).

On the whole, a well-chosen anthology, though it is a pity that one of the leading Bartók interpreters of the day is not represented by something more substantial than the *Romanian Folk Dances.* A Bartók concerto would have made a better choice than his Debussy *Fantaisie.* All the same, the Debussy items are excellent and so is his Grieg and Dohnányi. The Rachmaninov *Fourth Concerto* is a particularly successful account which has been rather underrated. All the recordings are of a very high standard.

Larrocha, Alicia de

Volume 62: M. ALBENIZ: *Piano Sonata in D.* SOLER: *Piano Sonatas in C sharp min.; F; D.* GRANADOS: *Goyescas: El fandango de Candil; Quejas ó la maja y el ruiseñor; El pelele (Escena goyesca); Spanish Dance (Andaluza), Op. 37/5.* ALBENIZ: *Iberia: Book I: Evocación; El puerto; Fête-Dieu à Seville. Book II: Rondeña; Almeria; Triana. Book III: El Albaicin; El Polo; Lavapies. Book IV: Málaga; Jérez; Eritaña. Navarra.* HALFFTER: *Sonatina (ballet): Danza de la Pastora.* MOMPOU: *Cançons i dansas (excerpts) Nos. 1–6; 14.*

(BB) *** Ph. (ADD/DDD) 456 883-2 (2).

Most of this programme is already available reissued in Decca's 'Música española' series and is discussed above within the Composer Index. Born in Barcelona, Alicia de Larrocha is uniquely equipped to play everything here, and she does so with distinction, and the fullest Mediterranean atmosphere. She is given first-class recording too, but it seems a pity to duplicate so much repertoire rather than give a broader picture of her talents.

Pires, Maria João

Volume 76: BACH: *French Suite No. 2 in C min., BWV 813.* SCHUMANN: *Arabeske.* SCHUBERT: *Moment Musical in A flat, D.780/6.* CHOPIN: *Nocturnes: in C min.; in F sharp min., Op. 48/1–2; in E, Op. 62/2.* MOZART: *Piano Concerto No. 14 in E flat, K. 449* (with Vienna Philharmonic Orchestra, Abbado). *Piano Sonatas Nos. 4 in E flat, K.282; 11 in A, K.331; 13 in B flat, K.333; 16 in C, K.545.*

(B) *** Ph. (ADD) 456 928-2 (2).

An artist of strong personality and impeccable taste, Maria João Pires gives admirable accounts of all these pieces. Whether or not she belongs among the pantheon or not, she is a very distinguished pianist, and

this compilation will give great satisfaction to those who want an introduction to this artist.

Pletnev, Mikhail

Volume 77: TCHAIKOVSKY: *Capriccio in G flat, Op. 8; Piano Concerto No. 2 in G, Op. 44* (with Philharmonia Orchestra, Fedoseyev); *Nutcracker* (concert suite) (arr. PLETNEV); *Romance in F min., Op. 5; The seasons, Op. 37b; Sleeping Beauty* (excerpts) (arr. PLETNEV); *Valse-scherzo in A, Op. 7.*

(B) *** Ph. 456 931–2 (2).

Pletnev's playing here is not only masterly but demonstrates an exceptional affinity with Tchaikovsky. His performance of *The Seasons* is wonderfully poetic and illuminating, while the ballet transcriptions glitter and glow under his fingers. The one snag is that in the otherwise highly recommendable version of the *Second Piano Concerto* there is a small cut in the slow movement.

Pollini, Maurizio

Volume 78: SCHUMANN: *Arabeske in C, D.946; Piano Sonata No. 1 in F sharp min., Op. 11.* LISZT: *Piano Sonata in B min.* CHOPIN: *Scherzo No. 1 in B min., Op. 20.* SCHUBERT: *3 Klavierstücke, D.946 Nos. 1 in E flat min.; 2 in E flat, 3 in C.* WEBERN: *Piano Variations, Op. 27.* DEBUSSY: *Etudes pour piano pour les: egrés chromatiques; agréments; notes répétées; opposées sonorités; arpèges composés; accords.* STRAVINSKY: *Petrushka (3 movements): Russian Dance; Petrushka's Room; The Shrovetide Fair.*

(B) *** Ph. (ADD/DDD) 456 937-2 (2).

An outstanding collection, restoring to the catalogue some of Pollini's finest performances, and reminding us of others. If his Chopin *Scherzo* is brilliantly hard-edged, his account of the *F sharp minor Sonata* is among the most distinguished Schumann interpretations on disc. The playing throughout has both command and authority, and deep poetic feeling. The *Arabeske* is comparably fine, and the glorious *Drei Klavierstücke* of Schubert are hardly less masterly. Some might feel that in the *B minor Sonata* of Liszt the consistent rush of adrenalin sweeps the music forward too unrelentingly. But Pollini has a firm grasp on the structure and the final denouement is most compelling. *Petrushka* is simply dazzling, and the Webern *Variations* have never been presented with greater perception or given a stronger advocacy. Excellent sound throughout.

Rubinstein, Arthur

Volume 87: BEETHOVEN: *Sonata No. 18 in E flat, Op. 31/3.* FRANCK: *Prélude, Choral et Fugue.* SCHUBERT: *Sonata No. 21 in B flat, D.960.* BRAHMS: *Sonata No. 3 in F min., Op. 5; Ballade in B, Op. 10/4; Intermezzo in E, Op. 116/6; Romance in F, Op. 118/5.* SCHUMANN: *Fantasiestücke, Op. 12.*

(B) (***) Ph. mono/stereo 456 967-2 (2).

Rubinstein is best known as a Chopin pianist, but here he is heard in a wider range of repertoire, spontaneously authoritative in Beethoven, impulsive and mercurial in Brahms, aristocratic but ever poetic in Schumann, and at his most inspirational in Schubert's last and greatest Sonata. A treasurable programme with all the recordings faithfully remastered.

Uchida, Mitsuko

Volume 95: MOZART: *Adagio in B min., K.540; Rondo in A min., K.511; Sonata in D, K.311; 10 Variations in G 'Unser dummer Pabel meint', K.455;* (i) *Piano Concerto No. 9 in E flat (Jeunehomme), K.271* (with ECO, Jeffrey Tate). DEBUSSY: *12 Etudes.* SCHOENBERG: *3 Klavierstücke, Op. 12.*

(B) *** Ph. 456 982-2 (2).

Mitsuko Uchida, first prizewinner in the 1975 Leeds competition, came to public notice as a Mozartian when in 1985–6 she played all the Mozart concertos with the ECO. But on record it was a complete set of the sonatas which established her reputation as an impeccable Mozartian stylist, with slow movements bringing a sensibility of the highest order. She was equally impressive in the shorter pieces, and the present lightweight set of *Variations* is expertly managed, with absolutely no suggestion of triviality. The 'Jeunehomme' *Concerto* suits her especially well. Jeffrey Tate draws first-class playing from the orchestra and Uchida's response is spirited and elegant, while the *Andantino* brings lovely, refined playing, yet never sounds over-civilized. But it is her account of the Debussy *Etudes* which represents the very peak of her recording career so far, and is unsurpassed on CD. The Schoenberg *Klavierstücke*, recorded especially for this edition, are hardly less impressive, and throughout she is given the most natural piano recording, vividly coloured and beautifully focused.

Wild, Earl

Volume 98: 'The Art of the Transcription': GLUCK/SGAMBATI: *Melodie d'Orphée.* RAMEAU/GODOWSKY: *3 Pieces: Rigaudon, Elégie, Tambourin.* BACH/TAUSIG: *Toccata and Fugue in D min.* WAGNER/MOSZKOWSKI: *Liebestod from Tristan und Isolde.* RIMSKY-KORSAKOV/RACHMANINOV: *Scherzo from A Midsummer Night's Dream.* ROSSINI/THALBERG: *Grande Fantasie sur l'opera Semiramide.* CHOPIN/LISZT: *3 Polish Songs.* TCHAIKOVSKY/WILD: *Pas de quatre from Swan Lake.* STRAUSS/SCHUTZ-EVLER: *Concert Arabesques on Themes of the Beautiful Blue Danube.* GLINKA/BALAKIREV: *A Life for the Tsar.* HERZ: *Variations on 'Non piu mesta' from Rossini's La Cenerentola.* THALBERG: *Fantasy on Donizetti's Don Pasquale, Op. 67.* STRAUSS/GODOWSKI: *Symphonic Metamorphosis on an Artist's Life Waltz.* GERSHWIN/WILD: *7 Etudes on Popular Songs.*

(B) *** Ph. (ADD) 456 991-2 (2).

Earl Wild possesses a virtuosity that is second to none and a refined musicianship. This set concentrates on the transcriptions with which he dazzles his public. Unfortunately he has never enjoyed the advocacy of a major record company. The recordings on offer here emanate from the period 1964–76 and also include part of a live Carnegie Hall recital from 1981. His playing radiates a delight and pleasure in every bar.

Yudina, Maria

Volume 99: BACH: *Goldberg Variations, BWV 988.* BEETHOVEN: *Variations and Fugue on a Theme from Prometheus (Eroica Variations), Op. 35; Variations on a Waltz by Diabelli, Op. 120.*

(B) ** Ph. (ADD) 456 994-2 (2).

Maria Yudina studied with the legendary Essipova in St Petersburg and was particularly open to new music thanks to her contact with Klemperer and Hindemith. Her repertoire included Krenek, Bartók and Stravinsky; she had an extensive correspondence with the latter and played at his 80th birthday celebrations in 1962. (When Stalin heard a broadcast of her Mozart K.488, he asked Moscow Radio for a recording; not daring to confess that they did not have one, Yudina was summoned back to record it through the night!) The present recordings made in 1961 (Beethoven) and 1968 (Bach) show her in perhaps a less flattering light than the Hindemith, Krenek, Bartók and Stravinsky included in the BMG 'Great Russian Pianists'. The *Goldberg variations* are very plain and unadorned (there is none of Tureck's elegance and mastery of part-writing) and the piano in both sets of the Beethoven cries out for the ministrations of a technician.

Zimerman, Krystian

Volume 100: BRAHMS: *Piano Concerto No. 2 in B flat, Op. 83* (with Vienna PO, Bernstein); *Scherzo in E flat min., Op. 4.* CHOPIN: *Ballade No. 4 in F min., Op. 52; Fantaisie in F min., Op. 49.* LISZT: *Harmonies Poétiques et religieuses: Funérailles;* (ii) *Totentanz* (with Boston SO, Ozawa). DEBUSSY: *Préludes, Book 1: Danseuses de Delphes; Les Collines d'Anacapri; La Cathédrale engloutie; La Danse de Puck; Minstrels; Book 2: Hommage à Samuel Pickwick Esq., P.P.M.P.C.; Feux d'artifice.*

(B) **(*) Ph. 456 997-2 (2).

Krystian Zimerman's Chopin is undoubtedly touched with distinction, as is his Liszt: the *Totentanz* is very exciting yet fully controlled. The Debussy *Préludes*, though also very highly charged, are compellingly evocative and full of detailed insights. Only the Brahms concerto, in partnership with Bernstein, brings a measure of disappointment. Here the constant fluctuations of tempo in the first movement are disturbing, although there is charisma to spare from both artists, and no one could complain that this is dull, or indeed that there is a lack of poetic lyrical feeling. The recordings are all of high quality.

Other Instrumental Recitals

Alain, Marie-Claire (organ)

'*A Celebration*'.

(M) *** Erato/Warner ADD/DDD 0630 15343-2 (6).

CD 1: *J. S. Bach and his predecessors:* LEBEGUE: *Magnificat du premier ton; Noël: Où s'en vont ces gais bergers; Pour l'amour de Marie.* TUNDER: *Choral-fantasia: Jesu Christus, wahr' Gottes Sohn.* BRUHNS: *Prelude and fugue in E min.* BUXTEHUDE: *Chorales: In dulci jubilo, BuxWV 197; Der Tag, der ist so freudenreich, BuxWV 182; Magnificat primi toni, BuxWV 203.* BOHM: *Chorale: Gelobet seist du, Jesu Christ.* BACH: *Fuga sopra il Magnificat, BWV 733; Canonic variations on Vom Himmel hoch, BWV 769; Prelude and fugue in C, BWV 547.*

CD 2: *The late baroque:* BACH: *Toccata and fugue in D min., BWV 565; Trio sonata in C, BWV 529; Fugue in G min., BWV 578; Trio (Adagio) (after BWV 1027); (Allegro) BWV 1027a; Concerto in D min. (after Vivaldi), BWV 596.* HANDEL: *Concerto in B flat, Op. 4/6.* C. P. E. BACH: *Concerto in E flat, Wq. 35* (both with Paillard CO).

CD 3: *The 19th century:* BOELY: *Fantasia and fugue in B flat, Op. 18.* MENDELSSOHN: *Prelude and fugue in C min.* LISZT: *Prelude and fugue on B-A-C-H.* BOELLMAN: *Gothic suite, Op. 25.* WIDOR: *Symphony No. 5: Allegro cantabile; Toccata.* FRANCK: *Prélude, fugue et variation, Op. 18.* GUILMANT: *Sonata in D min. (Allegro assai).*

CD 4: *The 20th century:* VIERNE: *Suite No. 2, Op. 53: Toccata in B flat.* A. ALAIN: *Scherzo in E min.; Toccata on l'Antienne 'Cantemus Domino'.* J. ALAIN: *2 Danses à Agni Yavishta; Intermezzo; Litanies; Aria.* POULENC: *Concerto in G min. for organ, strings and timpani* (with ortf, Martinon). MESSIAEN: *La Nativité du Seigneur: Les bergers; Dieu parmi nous.*

CD 5: *Rare recordings: from Pachelbel to Mozart:* BACH: *Cantata No. 35: Sinfonia No. 2* (with Paillard CO); *14 Canons on the Goldberg bass* (with O. Alain). PACHELBEL: *Toccata in C; Prelude in D min.; Chorals: Vom Himmel hoch; Chaconne in F min.* bach: *10 Canons from The Musical offering, BWV 1079.* VIVALDI: *Concerto in D min. for violin, organ and strings, RV 541* (with Toso, Sol. Ven., Scimone). MOZART: *Fantasia for mechanical organ in F min., K.608; Sonata in C, K.336 (Allegro).*

Bonus disc: BACH: *Prelude and fugue in G, BWV 541; Chorale, BWV 721; Aria, BWV 587; Canzona, BWV 588.* C. P. E. BACH: *Sonata No. 6 in G min., Wq.70/6.*

Marie-Claire Alain's recording career is justly celebrated here by Erato, for she has been making recordings for this label since 1953. The sixth (bonus) CD offered here includes four works which were on that first Bach LP, plus a sampler of her latest recording of organ sonatas by Bach's son, Carl Philipp Emanuel, made in 1996. The other five discs survey her achievement over the intervening forty or so years. There is very little here that is not of high calibre and the range is remarkable, always using organs suitable for the repertoire.

The five recitals are arranged in historical order, beginning with Johann Sebastian and his predecessors, followed by a second disc of Bach but with concertos by Carl Philipp Emanuel and Handel. Then comes the nineteenth century, ranging from Boëly, Mendelssohn and Liszt to the French School – Boëllman, Widor, Franck and Guilmant. CD 4 moves on to the twentieth century but stays in France, and all of it is real music, by Vierne, Poulenc, Alain and – of course – Messiaen.

The fifth CD purports to be 'rare recordings', but they are not really so very rare, including Bach *Canons* and a Vivaldi *Concerto for violin, organ and strings* which is not one of the plums. But overall this set is well worth considering, especially by those who want some basic organ repertoire for a modest-sized collection. The reproduction is of a high standard.

Amato, Donna (piano)

'*A piano portrait*': LISZT: *Hungarian rhapsody No. 2* (cadenza by Rachmaninov); *Consolation No. 3; Liebestraum No. 3.* DEBUSSY: *Arabesque No. 1; Suite bergamasque: Clair de lune. Préludes: La fille aux cheveux de lin; La cathédrale engloutie.* RAVEL: *Pavane pour une infante défunte.* GERSHWIN: *3 Preludes; Rhapsody in blue (solo piano version). Song transcriptions: The man I love; Swanee; Oh, lady be good; I'll build a stairway to paradise; 'S wonderful; I got rhythm.*

*** Olympia OCD 352.

The young American pianist Donna Amato here proves her mettle in standard repertoire and, more importantly, confirms her ability to create 'live' performances in the recording studio. None of the readings is routine or conventional: the Liszt *Consolation* has an attractive simplicity and the famous *Liebestraum*, while not lacking romantic impulse, has an agreeable lack of gush. Her Debussy is particularly impressive: the *Arabesque* has a lightly chimerical variety of touch and colour and the two most famous pieces are made to seem refreshingly unhackneyed. The highlight, however, is *La cathédrale engloutie*, an unforgettably powerful evocation, played quite superbly. She is, not surprisingly, completely at home with Gershwin. The song transcriptions are splendidly stylish and sparkling and her solo account of the *Rhapsody in blue* is highly idiomatic. In its strong, natural impulse and rhythmic freedom it can be spoken of in the same breath as Bernstein's version, although it has completely its own character. Donna Amato's style is not that of a Horowitz, and so it was perhaps a pity she chose to open with the Liszt *Hungarian rhapsody*, which would have been better placed later on in the programme, while the Ravel *Pavane* is a little too sober; but as a whole this 76-minute recital, recorded very realistically indeed in Salen Church Hall, Ski, Norway, is most enjoyable.

Anderson, John (oboe), Gordon Back (piano)

'*Capriccio*': PONCHIELLI: *Capriccio.* HUE: *Petite pièce.* PALADILHE: *Solo.* KALLIWODA: *Morceau de salon, Op. 228.* PASCULLI: *Concerto sopra motivi dell'opera 'La Favorita' di Donizetti.* FAURE: *Pièce.* DONIZETTI: *Solo.* SCHUMANN: *3 Romances, Op. 94.* FRANCK: *Pièce No. 5.* SINIGAGLIA: *Variations on a theme of Schubert, Op. 19.*

(M) **(*) ASV CDWHL 2100.

The three *Romances* by Schumann are the highlight of the programme: they have more substance than the rest and are beautifully played, while Sinigaglia's ingenious variations on one of Schubert's most charming melodies make for an engaging finale. The decoratively florid *Capriccio* of Ponchielli which opens the recital receives the most stylish bravura from the soloist; but it is completely inconsequential. The *Petite pièce* of Georges Hue is more distinctive and Paladilhe's *Solo* (in fact a duo with piano) is amiable too, as is the Kalliwoda *Morceau*, although it is rather longer than a morceau.

When we come to Pasculli's cleverly contrived fantasia on Donizetti's *La Favorita*, the tunes are more indelible, and the resulting virtuosity is impressive. Donizetti's own *Solo* is another attractive miniature, as is the lilting Franck *Pièce*. John Anderson is a first-rate oboist and he is persuasively supported throughout by Gordon Back. The recording is very real and immediate. But this lightweight 75-minute concert needs to be dipped into rather than taken all at once.

Andreasen, Henri Wenzel (flute), Anna Oland (piano)

Flute music of the Danish Golden Age: HARTMANN: *Sonata in B flat, Op. 1; Prelude in G min.* FROLICH: *Sonata in A min.* WEYSE: *Rondeau in D min.* KUHLAU: *Duo brillant, Op. 110/1.*

(BB) *** Naxos 8.553333.

The Danish Golden Age is, roughly speaking, the period of the artists C. W. Eckersberg and Christen Købke (the first half of the nineteenth century) and it was then that the present repertoire was composed. It is best summarized as slight but pleasing music, and the performances are alert and fresh with good, bright – but not overbright – sound.

Andsnes, Leif Ove (piano)

'*The Long, long winter night*': GRIEG: *Norwegian folksongs, Op. 66; Peasant dances, Op. 72.* TVEITT: *Fifty folktunes from Hardanger, Op. 150.* JOHANSEN: *Pictures from Nordland: Suite No. 1, Op. 5.* VALEN: *Variations for piano, Op. 23.* SÆVERUD: *Tunes and dances from Siljustøl, Opp. 22, 24, 25; Peer Gynt: Hymn against the Boyg, Op. 28.*

✪ *** EMI Dig. CDC5 56541-2.

A recital of unusual excellence and distinction from Leif Ove Andsnes devoted to his fellow countrymen. The disc takes its title, 'The Long, long winter night', from one of the *Hardanger folktunes* by Geirr Tveitt. His programme ranges widely from some of the late and extraordinarily characterful *Slåtter* or *Peasant dances* of Grieg to the *Variations* by Fartein Valen, the pre-war Norwegian apostle of dodecaphony. Grieg's biographer David Monrad Johansen (best-known perhaps for his tone-poem, *Pan*) is represented by two early piano pieces that are of more than passing interest. He also includes seven of the Op. 150 set of *Hardanger folktunes*, which could be as popular here as they are in Norway if they were given the chance.

Although his symphonies are now gaining ground on CD, Harald Sæverud was arguably at his best as a miniaturist, and Andsnes gives us a handful of his distinctive, original *Slåtter og stev fra Siljustøl*, which have such winning titles as 'The cotton grass plays on a moonbeam fiddle' (variously translated as 'The windflowers twiddle the moonbeam fiddle'). He also includes *Kjæmpeviseslåtten* ('The Ballad of revolt') that came to symbolize Norwegian resistance to the Nazis during the occupation. A well-planned and imaginative recital, and an exhibition of masterly pianism. Very good recording indeed.

Antonelli, Claudia (harp)

Music for Harp and Violin: CLEMENTI: *Andante and Variations.* VIOTTI: *Harp Sonata.* POLLINI: *Capriccio and Aria with Variations; Theme and Variations.* ROSSINI: *Allegretto; Harp Sonata;* (i) *Violin and Harp Sonata.* DONIZETTI: (i) *Violin and Harp Sonata* (both with Alberto Ambrosini, violin). BOCHSA: *Fantasia on Bellini's I Capuleti e Montecchi.* ROCCHIS: *Fantasia on Bellini's Casta Diva.*

(BB) * Naxos 8.554252.

For the most part this is prettily attractive music, the most substantial work being the 16-minute Viotti

Sonata, which gives the programme a bit of weight. Claudia Antonelli plays well enough, though from time to time a hint of blandness creeps in, and, although the two short sonatas with violin add tonal variety, Alberto Ambrosini's timbre is hardly beautiful, with unstable intonation, and one or two really disagreeable passages. The harp is recorded adequately, but with the higher registers leaning towards harshness.

Argerich, Martha (piano)

CHOPIN: *Scherzo No. 3 in C sharp min., Op. 39; Barcarolle in F sharp min., Op. 60.* BRAHMS: *2 Rhapsodies, Op. 79.* PROKOFIEV: *Toccata, Op. 11.* RAVEL: *Jeux d'eau.* LISZT: *Hungarian rhapsody No. 6; Piano sonata in B min.*

(M) (**) DG 447 430-2.

This particular 'Legendary Recording' in DG's series of 'Originals' presents Argerich's remarkable début LP recital, recorded for DG in 1961. The phenomenal technique (she was twenty-one at the time) is as astonishing as the performances are musically exasperating. This artist's charismatic impulsiveness is well known, but in presenting Chopin and Brahms she is too impetuous by half, although *Jeux d'eau* brings a certain Ravelian magic. The Liszt *Sonata* has been added on; it dates from a decade later and yet again, although the bravura is breathtaking and there is no lack of spontaneity, the work's architecture and indeed its breadth are to some extent sacrificed to the insistent forward impulse of the playing. Good but not exceptional recording, a bit hard in the Liszt, though that may well reflect faithfully the percussive attack of Argerich's powerful hands.

'*Live from the Concertgebouw 1978 & 1979*':

CD 1: BACH: *Partita No. 2 in C min., BWV 826; English Suite No. 2 in A min., BWV 807.* CHOPIN: *Nocturne No. 13 in C min., Op. 48/1; Scherzo No. 3 in C sharp min., Op. 39.* BARTOK: *Sonata.* GINASTERA: *Danzas argentinas, Op. 2.* PROKOFIEV: *Sonata No. 7, in B flat, Op. 83.* D. SCARLATTI: *Sonata in D min., Kk.141.*

*** EMI CDC5 56975-2.

CD 2: RAVEL: *Sonatine; Gaspard de la nuit.* SCHUMANN: *Fantaisiestücke, Op. 12.*

*** EMI CDC5 57101-2.

Electrifying playing, even by Argerich's own standards. On the first disc the Prokofiev *Seventh Sonata* is given with demonic abandon, and the commanding performances by Horowitz, Pollini and Pletnev seem almost measured by comparison. The Bartók is hardly less astonishing and the same must be said of Ginastera's *Danzas argentinas*. The Scarlatti is wonderfully elegant, and the Bach and Chopin are gripping. On the second disc Ravel's *Gaspard de la nuit* is quite chilling in its intensity and the Schumann is incandescent. Fine though her studio recordings are, these have an inflam-

mable quality that is special. The recordings are a bit forward, but with playing like this, who cares!

Barere, Simon (piano)

'*The complete HMV recordings, 1934-6*': LISZT: *Etude de concert (La leggierezza), G.144/2. Années de pèlerinage, 2nd Year (Italy): Sonetto 104 del Petrarca, G.161/5. Gnomenreigen, G.145/2; Réminiscences de Don Juan, G.418 (2 versions); Rapsodie espagnole, G.254; Valse oubliée No. 1, G.215.* CHOPIN: *Scherzo No. 3 in C sharp min., Op. 39; Mazurka No. 38 in F sharp min., Op. 59/3; Waltz No. 5 in A flat, Op. 42.* BALAKIREV: *Islamey (2 versions).* BLUMENFELD: *Etude for the left hand.* GLAZUNOV: *Etude in C, Op. 31/1.* SCRIABIN: *Etudes in C sharp min., Op. 2/1; in D sharp min., Op. 8/12 (2 versions).* LULLY/GODOWSKI: *Gigue in E.* RAMEAU/GODOWSKI: *Tambourin in E min.* SCHUMANN: *Toccata in C, Op. 7 (2 versions).*

✪ (***) Appian mono CDAPR 7001 (2).

This two-CD set offers all of Barere's HMV recordings, made in the mid-1930s, including the alternative takes he made in the studio. What can one say of his playing without exhausting one's stock of superlatives? His fingerwork is quite astonishing and his virtuosity almost in a class of its own. The set contains an absolutely stunning account of the *Réminiscences de Don Juan*, and his *Islamey* knocks spots off any successor's in sheer virtuosity and excitement; it is altogether breathtaking, and much the same might be said of his *Rapsodie espagnole*. Nor is there any want of poetry – witness the delicacy of the Scriabin *C sharp minor Etude* or Liszt's *La leggierezza*. Readers wanting to investigate this legendary artist should start here. One of the most important functions of the gramophone is to chart performance traditions that would otherwise disappear from view, and this set is one to celebrate.

Barrueco, Manuel (guitar)

'*Cuba!*': LECUONA: *La Comparsa; Dana Lecami; A la Antiga.* BROUWER: *Preludio; Rito de los Orisbas.* FARINAS: *Cancón triste; Preludio.* UBIETA: *New York rush (Theme from El Super).* ANGULO: *Cantos Yoraba de Cuba.* ARDEVOL: *Sonata.*

**(*) EMI CDC5 56757-2.

Manuel Barrueco, Cuban by birth, is clearly at home in this late-evening programme of mostly gentle music. The three opening Lecuona pieces are totally seductive, as is Brouwer's lovely *Preludio* and the haunting *Theme from El Super*, which is built on a rhythmic bass ostinato of Caribbean extraction. Even the series of nine brief vignettes which make up Angulo's *Cantos Yoraba*, and which are based directly on folk melodies, are primarily evocative (No. 4, *Borotíti*, is like a berceuse). And it is only in Ardévol's *Sonata* with its central variations and vibrant closing *Danza* that the music becomes really animated.

This is maintained in the closing group of five Dances and Evocacións from Brouwer's *Rito de los Orisbas*, which bring plenty of chances for rhythmic bravura. (They should have been individually cued, however.) Barrueco plays with a spontaneous, ruminative style, and he is most naturally recorded (at Abbey Road).

VILLA-LOBOS: *Preludes Nos. 1-5; Chôros No. 1 in E min.* BROUWER: *Danza caracteristica; Canticum; Canción de cuna (Berceuse); Elogio de la danza; Ojos brujos; Guajira criolla. Julián orbon: Preludio y danza.*

(M) *** EMI CDM5 66576-2.

The Cuban guitarist Manuel Barrueco is the latest star in the line of great guitarists which began with Segovia and includes, of course, both John Williams and Julian Bream. His breadth of repertoire is remarkable and his playing is often electrifying, yet showing the most subtly imaginative touches in the control of rhythm, colour and dynamics. Barrueco is naturally at home in the music of his compatriots Leo Brouwer and the young Julián Orbon. The latter was a pupil of Aaron Copland, but his *Preludio y danza* comes nearer to the world of Villa-Lobos, with which Barrueco also has a ready affinity.

The Brouwer pieces, including the *Canticum* (dazzlingly vibrant and evocative by turns), the deliciously seductive *Canción de cuna*, the haunting *Elogio de la danza* and the *Guajira criolla* with its enticing opening pizzzicatos (violin style), are all marvellously done. Barrueco is perhaps not quite as winningly flexible as Bream in the famous *Third Prelude* of Villa-Lobos, but he makes No. 4 totally his own with a magical vibrato on the repeated tenutos. The *Chôros* is played with engaging intimacy, and the recording cannot be faulted.

FALLA: *The Three-cornered hat: Night; Miller's dance; Dance of the Corregidor; Dance of the Miller's wife. Omaggio per chitarra (Scritto per le tombeau de Debussy).* PONCE: *Sonatina meridional.* RODRIGO: *Invocación y danza (Homenaje a Manuel de Falla); 3 Piezas españolas.*

(M) *** EMI CDM5 66577-2.

What comes over here is not just the (often unostentatious) dazzling bravura and the evocative feeling, but the appealingly warm intimacy with which Barrueco communicates so directly to the listener. He finds all the colour and flamenco rhythms in Falla's *Three-cornered hat* ballet music without ever going over the top; but he is at his very finest in the delicate nocturnal evocation of Rodrigo's very personal tribute to Falla. Falla's own *Homenaje* for *Debussy* flashes vibrantly, as does the *Zapateado* finale of the Rodrigo *Spanish pieces*; but, for all the astonishing technical mastery of this playing, one always feels that Barrueco is looking beneath the music's surface and seeking to find added depth and atmosphere. If you enjoy Spanish guitar music, this recital is unmissable.

Bate, Jennifer (organ)

'From Stanley to Wesley' (Eighteenth-century organ music on period instruments from Adlington Hall, the Dolmetch Collection, St Michael's Mount, Kenwood House, Killerton House, Everingham Chapel).

(BB) **(*) Regis RRC 5002 (5).

Volume 1: READING: *Airs for French Horns & Flutes.* STANLEY: *Voluntaries, Op. 5/7 & 10; Op. 6/5 & 8; Op. 7/3.* HANDEL: *Fugues in G min.; in B flat.* ROSEINGRAVE: *Voluntary in G min.* TRAVERS: *Voluntary in D min. & major.* WALOND: *Voluntary in A min.* RUSSELL: *Voluntary in E min.;* WESLEY: *Short Pieces Nos. 7 & 12; Voluntary, Op. 6/1.*

(BB) *** Regis RRC 1113.

Volume 2: GREENE: *Voluntary in C min.* STANLEY: *Voluntaries, Op. 5/6 & 9; Op. 6/7 & 9; Op. 7/2.* HANDEL: *Voluntary in C; Fugue in A min.* LONG: *Voluntary in D min.* WALOND: *Voluntary in B min.* NARES: *Introduction & Fugue in F.* RUSSELL: *Voluntary in A min.* S. WESLEY: *Short Piece No. 9 in F; Voluntaries, Op. 6/3 & 9.*

Volume 3: GREENE: *Voluntary in B min.* STANLEY: *Voluntaries, Op. 6/1, 6 & 10; Op. 7/1 & 6.* WALOND: *Voluntary in G.* HANDEL: *Fugue in B min.; Voluntary in C.* BURNEY: *Voluntary No. 1: Cornet Piece in C.* RUSSELL: *Voluntary in A.* DUPUIS: *Voluntary in B flat.* S. WESLEY: *Short Pieces Nos. 6 & 8; Voluntary, Op. 6/6.*

(BB) **(*) Regis RRC 2058 (2).

Volume 4: CROFT: *Voluntary in D.* GREENE: *Voluntary in E flat.* STANLEY: *Voluntaries, Op. 5/1 & 8; Op. 6/4; Op. 7/8.* WALOND: *Voluntary in G.* HANDEL: *Fugue in C min.; Voluntary in G min.* BURNEY: *Fugue in F min.* KEEBLE: *Select Piece No. 1 in C.* S. WESLEY: *Voluntary, Op. 6/10.*

Volume 5: BOYCE: *Voluntary in D.* STANLEY: *Voluntaries, Op. 6/2; Op. 7/4, 7 & 9.* STUBLEY: *Voluntary in C.* HANDEL: *Fugue in G; Voluntary in C.* ROSEINGRAVE: *Fugue No. 8 in E min.* HERON: *Voluntary in G.* RUSSELL: *Voluntary in F.* HOOK: *Voluntary in C min.* S. WESLEY: *Voluntaries in B flat; in E flat, Op. 6/7.*

(BB) **(*) Regis RRC 2059 (2).

Jennifer Bate's survey of eighteenth-century English organ music uses six different organs from stately homes to secure maximum variety of presentation. But these instruments are without pedals, and each produces a sonority that is relatively light-textured, bright and sweet. The five programmes are each made up in the same way, usually opening with a voluntary by Maurice Greene (or alternatively Croft or Boyce), then offering a clutch of voluntaries by John Stanley, followed in most cases by music by Walond and Handel, among others, and usually ending with pieces by Samuel Wesley.

None of these are great composers, save Handel of course, and his chosen examples are extremely minor works. Jennifer Bate did much initial research into available instruments before undertaking the original project for Unicorn, and she plays all this music in impeccable style and is beautifully recorded. So the particular attractions of each volume depend on the items included. Easily the most engaging are the works which use cornet or trumpet stops, which are colourful and jolly, while the *Vox humana* stop, as in the finale of Stanley's Op. 6/5 of the first disc, is also ear-tickling.

Indeed the first volume is a good place to start, with Op. 5/7 by the same composer also quite engaging. The voluntaries are usually in two sections, but William Russell's E minor piece is in three, with an imposing opening, and the fugue used as a centrepiece. Samuel Wesley's *Short Piece No. 12* is a contrapuntal moto perpetuo.

The second volume offers more examples of Stanley's ready facility, notably Op. 7/2 and Op. 5/6, but on the whole this is a less interesting programme than the third which again shows Stanley at his more inventive in Op. 7/1, while Op. 6/1 begins with a pleasing *Siciliano*, and the trumpet theme of Op. 6/6 might have been written by Purcell. Handel's *Voluntary in C* brings an attractive interplay of parts in its second movement, while Burney's *Cornet Piece* has a whiff of the *Hallelujah Chorus*.

In Volume 4 Jennifer Bate registers Stanley's Op. 5/8 with piquant skill (this is a three-part work), and Volume 5 brings new composer names, adding music of Heron, Hook and Stubley, although the idiom remains much the same. Volume 1, however, is the CD to try first, and if you enjoy this go on to the 2-CD set including Volumes 3 and 4. But only the dedicated enthusiast attracted by the sounds of early English organs will want the complete set, for much of the music here is conventional.

'*Stanford and his contemporaries*' (British organ music played on the organs of Brangwyn Hall, Swansea; St James's Church, Muswell Hill, London and St Andrew's Parish Church, Plymouth): STANFORD: *Fantasia and toccata in D min., Op. 57; Preludes: in the form of a minuet; in the form of a chaconne; in the form of a toccata, Op. 88/1-3.* WHITLOCK: *Extemporisations Nos. 1 (Carol); 2 (Divertimento).* GRACE: *Psalm tune on 'Martyrs'.* PARRY: *Toccata and fugue in G (Wanderer).* C. WOOD: *Prelude on 'St Mary's'.* JACOB: *Festal flourish.* HARRIS: *A Fancy; Reverie.* BAIRSTOW: *Prelude in C; Evening song.* COCKER: *Tuba tune.*

(BB) *** ASV CDQS 6222.

Cocker's *Tuba tune* is one of the most brightly colourful of today's organ favourites, and alongside Gordon Jacob's *Festal flourish* it enlivens this collection of English organ music, framed by Stanford, and including three attractive genre pieces from his Op. 88 plus a number of other impressive and enjoyable items which suit the characteristically warm, full-bodied

sound of British organs. Parry's *Toccata and fugue* pictures an ocean voyage and Charles Wood's '*St Mary's*' *prelude* builds a solemn Elgarian march theme to a big climax. The *Psalm tune Postlude* of Harvey Grace is also quite memorable. Very well recorded, Jennifer Bate is thoroughly at home in the repertoire and she brings her comparatively lightweight programme fully to life.

Belgian Wind Quintet

'*Summer music*': BEETHOVEN: *Wind quintet in E flat.* HOLST: *Wind quintet in A flat, Op. 14.* BARBER: *Summer music, Op. 31.* ARRIEU: *Quintet in C.*

(BB) *** Koch Discover Dig. DICD 920322.

A delightful collection, well worth its modest price. The many felicities of the Barber *Summer music* are matched by those of the much less familiar work of Holst, contemporary with the *Military band suites*. Claude Arrieu (born 1903) also writes very engagingly: his *Quintet* is both elegant and witty. The playing of the Belgian group is polished and spontaneous, and they are very well recorded.

Bennett, Richard Rodney (piano)

'*British piano music of the '20s & '30s*': MAYERL: *Marigold; Punch; Ace of Hearts; Antiquary; Shallow Waters; Printer's Devil; Sleepy Piano; Railroad Rhythm.* BLISS: *The Rout Trot.* Gerrard WILLIAMS: *Déjeuner dansant: Valsette brute; Raguette extra-sec.* GOOSSENS: *Folk-tune.* WALTON **(arr. Rodney Bennett):** *Façade: Old Sir Faulk.* LAMBERT: *Elegiac blues; Elegy. Concerto for piano and nine players* **(with members of the English Sinfonia, Dilkes).**

(M) **(*) EMI (ADD) CDM 5 65596-2.

Constant Lambert's *Concerto for piano and nine players* presents a clever marriage between neo-classical and jazz manners. In a poor performance, the work can seem very dry indeed, but here (in 1974) Richard Rodney Bennett makes the music sparkle with wit, pointing the rhythms with subtle nuances that bring it to life. The sleight of hand pay-off endings to each movement are delectably done. The couplings could hardly be more apt: a collection of short pieces by Lambert and others with direct debts to jazz. The main addition to the original LP is eight characteristic pieces by Billy Mayerl – including his most famous, *Marigold*. Their carefree jazz style is neatly brought out by the pianist, even though here, the piano is too backwardly balanced. Lambert's *Elegiac blues* is rather leisurely, but very expressive, whilst the *Elegy*, which is more ambitious in scale, is less sharply inspired. The two miniatures by Gerrard Williams are slight but attractive. But every item here has a point: Bliss's piece is like a cross between Scott Joplin and Grainger's *Country gardens*, while Walton's *Old Sir Faulk* shines out as the finest example of all in this tiny but delightful genre. A most enjoyable collection which fully conjures up the spirit of the 1920s and

'30s, and the sound, with the caveat about the (1975) Mayerl pieces already mentioned, is remarkably good.

Bergen Wind Quintet

BARBER: *Summer music, Op. 31.* SÆVERUD: *Tunes and dances from Siljustøl, Op. 21a.* JOLIVET: *Serenade for wind quintet with principal oboe.* HINDEMITH: *Kleine Kammermusik, Op. 24/2.*

*** BIS CD 291.

Barber's *Summer music* is a glorious piece dating from the mid-1950s; it is in a single movement. Sæverud's *Tunes and dances from Siljustøl* derive from piano pieces of great charm and sound refreshing in their transcribed format. Jolivet's Serenade is hardly less engaging, while Hindemith's *Kleine Kammermusik*, when played with such character and finesse, is no less welcome. Throughout, the fine blend and vivacious ensemble give consistent pleasure.

Berman, Lazar (piano)

Live recital – 27 June 1992: SCHUBERT: *Piano sonata No. 21 in B flat, D.960.* LISZT: *Concert paraphrases of Schubert Lieder: Der Leiermann; Täuschung; Gretchen am Spinnrade; Die junge Nonne; Ave Maria; Erlkönig. Mephisto waltz; Années de pèlerinage, 1st Year: Chapelle de Guillaume Tell.* BEETHOVEN/RACHMANINOV: *Extract from The Ruins of Athens.*

(BB) ** Koch Discover DICD 920164/5 (2).

Berman's 1992 recital is uncommonly well recorded for a live occasion and the presence of the artist is in no doubt; indeed, we have to wait a full half-minute for him to start after the introductory applause. His account of Schubert's last and greatest sonata is obviously both felt and considered. It is certainly dramatic but also wayward, and not all will respond to Berman's agogic distortions of the flow, particularly in the first movement. The Liszt items provide repertoire for which he is famous and the *Mephisto waltz* shows him at his most commanding. Some of the Schubert song transcriptions may be felt to be over-dramatized, though no one could complain about the *Erl-King*. The Beethoven/Rachmaninov encore is properly piquant.

Bok, Henri (bass clarinet), Rainer Klaas (piano)

20th-century music for bass clarinet and piano: HINDEMITH: *Sonata.* SCHOECK: *Sonata, Op. 41.* SLUKA: *Sonata.* REHAK: *Sonnet III.* HEUCKE: *Sonata, Op. 23.* SOLL: *Lumen.*

*** Clarinet Classics CC 026.

A remarkably stimulating collection with a group of four diverse sonatas which between them explore every lyrical and virtuosic possibility of the bass clarinet's colour spectrum and virtuosic range. From Hindemith comes an unexpectedly enticing mixture of wit and wan pastoralism, while Rehak's *Sonnet III* is a darkly atmospheric interlude before the most ambitious piece here, by Stefan Heucke. It is in three sections, a *Ballade*, an extraordinary set of central *Variations* full of original and unexpected rhythms and sounds, followed by a plangent closing *Elegie*. Soll's *Lumen* then acts as a lighter, entertaining encore. The performances throughout are in every way superb and the recording excellent.

Bowyer, Kevin (organ)

'A feast of organ exuberance' (Blackburn Cathedral organ): LEIDEL: *Toccata Delectatione, Op. 5/35.* SWAYNE: *Riff-Raff.* BERVEILLER: *Suite; Cadence.*

(M) *** Priory Dig. 001.

The spectacular sound made by the magnificent 1969 Walker organ in Blackburn Cathedral is well demonstrated by this first-rate recital. Leidel is from the former East Germany, and his acknowledged influences from Messiaen and Scriabin are well absorbed into his own style. The *Toccata for pleasure* is titillating in its colouring and certainly exuberant in its extravagant treatment of its basic idea, which goes far beyond the minimalism achieved by many of his contemporaries. Giles Swayne is Liverpool-born and his quirky *Riff-Raff*, in the words of the performer, suggests 'isolated flashes of light of varying intensity'. Berveiller comes from the traditional French school of Dupré. His *Suite* is eminently approachable music, with a whimsical second-movement *Intermezzo* to remain in the memory, and a smoothly rich *Adagio*, before the Widorian finale. His *Cadence* provides a lightweight but by no means trivial encore. What one remembers most of all from this concert is the magnificent sonority of the organ, beautifully captured within its natural ambience, and that in itself shows how well composers and performer have combined their talents.

Brain, Dennis (horn)

Recital (with Dennis Brain Wind Quintet, Max Salpeter, violin, Wilfred Parry or Cyril Preedy, piano, English String Quartet): BEETHOVEN: *Piano and Wind Quintet, Op. 16.* MOZART: *Horn Quintet, K.407.* BRAHMS: *Horn Trio, Op. 40.* DUKAS: *Villanelle.* MARAIS: *Le Basque.*

(M) (***) BBC mono BBCL 4048-2.

Recital (with Marjorie Lempfert (viola), Alan Civil (horn), George Malcolm, Noel Mewton Wood (piano), Carter String Trio, English String Quartet, Dennis Brain Wind Quintet): BEETHOVEN: *Wind Sextet in E flat, Op. 81.* COOKE: *Arioso & Scherzo.* HAYDN: *Horn Concerto No. 1.* IBERT: *Trois pièces brèves.* MILHAUD: *La cheminée du Roi René, Op. 205.* MOZART: *Divertimento No. 14 in B flat, K.270.* SCHUBERT: *Auf der Strom, D 943* (with Peter Pears).

(M) (***) BBC mono BBCL 4066-2.

Who would have gussed that such bounty existed in the BBC archives: all the key works featuring the horn, played by the finest horn player of our time and with excellent support from other fine artists. The major chamber works by Beethoven, Brahms and Mozart are beautifully presented and the French repertoire is delightful too. The first disc also includes a wonderful lollipop by Marais, played with great wit and aplomb. On the second Brain is joined by Peter Pears for Schubert's *Auf der Strom*, with horn obbligato, and on the same disc he gives a brief demonstration of the different timbres of an 1812 French hand-horn, a modern Alexander wide-bore double horn, and finally a garden hosepipe!

Bream, Julian (guitar or lute)

❁ '*The Julian Bream Edition*' (BMG/RCA).

The Julian Bream Edition ran to some thirty CDs, representing three decades of a remarkably distinguished recording career. Bream has now moved over to EMI, so this edition is essentially retrospective. A few of the miscellaneous recitals are considered below, although most of the individual volumes have now been withdrawn. The concertante collections are listed as Composer entries in our main volume, and the Elizabethan lute songs are listed under Peter Pears among Vocal Recitals.

Bream, Julian (lute)

Volume 1. '*The golden age of English lute music*': Robert JOHNSON: *2 Almaines; Carman's whistle.* John JOHNSON: *Fantasia.* CUTTING: *Walsingham; Almaine; Greensleeves.* DOWLAND: *Mignarda; Galliard upon a galliard of Daniel Bachelar; Batell galliard; Captain Piper's galliard; Queen Elizabeth's galliard; Sir John Langton's pavan; Tarleton's resurrection; Lady Clifton's spirit.* ROSSETER: *Galliard.* MORLEY: *Pavan.* BULMAN: *Pavan.* BACHELAR: *Monsieur's almaine.* HOLBORNE: *Pavan; Galliard.* BYRD: *Pavana Bray; Galliard; Pavan; My Lord Willoughby's welcome home.*

(M) *** BMG/RCA (ADD) 09026 61584-2.

Bream is a natural lutenist and a marvellously sensitive artist in this repertoire, and here he conjures up a wide range of colour, matched by expressive feeling. Here Dowland is shown in more extrovert mood than in many of his lute songs, and overall the programme has plenty of variety. The CD combines two recitals, the first fifteen items recorded by Decca in London in September 1963, and the rest of the programme in New York City two years later. The recording is exemplary and hiss is minimal.

Bream, Julian (guitar)

'*Guitarra*' (Music of Spain): MUDARRA: *Fantasias X & XIV.* Luis DE MILAN: *Fantasia XXII.* Luis DE

NARVAEZ: *La canción del Emperador; Conde claros. Santiago de murcia*: *Prelude & Allegro.* BOCCHERINI: *Guitar quintet in D, G.448 (arr. for 2 guitars): Fandango.* SOR: *Gran solo, Op. 14; Variations on a theme of Mozart, Op. 9; Fantasie, Op. 7; Sonata, Op. 25: Minuet.* AGUADO: *Rondo in A min., Op. 2/3.* TARREGA: *Study in A; Prelude in A min.; Recuerdos de la Alhambra.*

(M) *** BMG/RCA DDD/ADD 09026 61610-2.

An admirable survey covering 400 years and featuring several different instruments, all especially built by José Ramanillos and including a Renaissance guitar and a modern classical guitar. Bream's natural dexterity is matched by a remarkable control of colour and unerring sense of style. Many of the earlier pieces are quite simple but have considerable magnetism. The basic recital was recorded digitally in 1983 at Bream's favourite venue, Wardour Chapel, Windsor, and is laid out chronologically. Two additional Sor items, the *Fantasie*, Op. 7 and the *Minuet* from Op. 25, were made eighteen years earlier in New York and, as they are analogue, have sensibly been added at the end.

'*Popular classics for Spanish guitar*': VILLA-LOBOS: *Chôros No. 1; Etude in E min.* TORROBA: *Madroños.* TURINA: *Homenaje a Tárrega, Op. 69: Garrotín; Solearas. Fandanguillo.* ALBENIZ: *Suite española, Op. 47: Granada; Leyenda (Asturias).* FALLA: *Homenaje pour le tombeau de Debussy.* TRAD., arr. LLOBET: *Canciones populares catalanas: El testament d'Amelia.*

(M) **(*) RCA (ADD) 09026 68814-2.

This outstanding early recital, recorded at Kenwood House in 1962, was one of Bream's very finest LP collections. The electricity of the music-making is consistently communicated, and all Bream's resources of colour and technical bravura are brought into play. The Villa-Lobos pieces are particularly fine, as is the Turina *Fandanguillo* (which comes at the end), and the Albéniz *Leyenda* is a *tour de force* and makes an almost orchestral effect. The recording (originally produced by James Burnett, with Bob Auger the engineer) has been splendidly remastered for RCA's 'Living Stereo' series (the equivalent of Decca's 'Classic Sound') and Bream is given a remarkable presence, with the analogue background noise all but vanquished. However, the playing time is only 42 minutes, and while Volume 8 of 'The Julian Bream Edition' (BMG/RCA 09026 61591-2) remains available (see above), this must take second place. That earlier reissue includes most of the present items, plus a great deal more music.

'*Baroque guitar*': SANZ: *Pavanos; Canarios.* J. S. BACH: *Prelude in D min., BWV 999; Fugue in A min., BWV 1000; Lute suite in E min., BWV 996.* SOR: *Fantasy and Minuet.* WEISS: *Passacaille; Fantaisie; Tombeau sur la mort de M. Comte de Logy.* VISEE: *Suite in D min.*

(BB) *** RCA Navigator (ADD) 74321 24195-2.

This is a shorter version of the baroque recital which forms Volume 9 of the 'Julian Bream Edition'. It still includes well over an hour of music as Bream's superb account of Bach's *E minor Lute suite* has been added. The recording is very natural, and this makes a fine recital in its own right, realistically recorded. A very real bargain in RCA's bargain-basement Navigator series.

Bream, Julian (guitar and lute)

'*The ultimate guitar collection*' ((i) with Monteverdi O, Gardiner): (i) VIVALDI: *Lute concerto in D, RV 93* (ed. Bream). Lute pieces: CUTTING: *Packington's round; Greensleeves*. DOWLAND: *A Fancy (Fantasia)*. Guitar pieces: SANZ: *Canarios*. M. ALBENIZ: *Sonata in D* (arr. PUJOL). I. ALBENIZ: *Suite española, Op. 47: Cataluña; Granada; Sevilla; Cádiz; Leyenda (Asturias). Mallorca, Op. 202. Cantos de España: Córdoba, Op. 232/4*. FALLA: *Three-cornered hat: Miller's dance*. TARREGA: *Recuerdos de la Alhambra*. VILLA-LOBOS: *Chôros No. 1; Preludes Nos. 1 in E min.; 2 in D*. RODRIGO: *En los trigales*; (i) *Concierto de Aranjuez. Tres piezas españolas*. GRANADOS: *Cuentos para la juventud: Dedicatoria. Tonadilla: La Maja de Goya. Danzas españolas Nos. 4 (Villanesca); 5 (Valses poéticos)*.

🔴 (B) *** RCA DDD/ADD 74321 33705-2 (2).

The extraordinary achievement of RCA's 'Julian Bream Edition' is admirably summed up by this inexpensive pair of CDs which include two and a half hours of the most popular repertoire for guitar, plus a small group of lute pieces for good measure. There is not a single item here that is not strong in musical personality, and every performance springs vividly and spontaneously to life. John Eliot Gardiner provides highly distinguished accompaniments for the two justly famous concertos by Vivaldi (for lute) and Rodrigo (for guitar).

The first of the two CDs provides a well-planned historical survey, opening with Elizabethan lute music and progressing through to include three magnetic pieces by Villa-Lobos. Highlights include an electrifying performance of Falla's *Miller's dance* from *The Three-cornered hat* and, of course, the most famous guitar piece of all, the *Recuerdos de la Alhambra* of Tárrega.

The second collection, which is entirely digital (from 1982–3), concentrates mainly on Isaac Albéniz and Granados (not forgetting the superb accounts of the *Córdoba* by the former and the *Danza española No. 5* by the latter, which are highly praised in our Composer section). It ends appropriately with Rodrigo's *Tres piezas españolas*, with its remarkable central *Passacaglia*. The recordings are of the highest quality and are excellently transferred to CD.

Bream, Julian and John Williams (guitar duo)

'*Together*': Disc 1: CARULLI: *Serenade in A, Op. 96*. GRANADOS: *Danzas españolas: Rodella aragonesa; Zambra, Op. 37/6 & 11*. ALBENIZ: *Cantos de España: Bajo la palmera, Op. 232/3. Ibéria: Evocación*. GIULIANI: *Variazioni concertanti, Op. 130*. JOHNSON: *Pavan & Galliard* (arr. BREAM). TELEMANN: *Partie polonaise*. DEBUSSY: *Rêverie; Children's corner: Golliwog's cakewalk. Suite bergamasque: Clair de lune*.

Disc 2: LAWES: *Suite for 2 guitars* (arr. BREAM). CARULLI: *Duo in G, Op. 34*. SOR: *L'encouragement, Op. 34*. ALBENIZ: *Cantos de España: Córdoba, Op. 232/4; Suite española: Castilla (Seguidillas)*. GRANADOS: *Goyescas: Intermezzo* (arr. PUJOL). *Danzas españolas: Oriental, Op. 37/2*. FALLA: *La vida breve: Spanish dance No. 1*. RAVEL: *Pavane pour une infante défunte*. FAURE: *Dolly (suite), Op. 56* (both arr. BREAM).

(B) *** RCA (ADD) 74321 20134-2 (2).

The rare combination of Julian Bream and John Williams was achieved by RCA in the studio on two separate occasions, in 1971 and 1973, providing the basic contents of these two recitals. Further recordings were made live in Boston and New York in 1978, during a North American concert tour.

Curiously, it is the studio programmes which seem the more spontaneous, and Fauré's *Dolly suite*, which sounds a little cosy, is the only disappointment (it also brings some audience noises). Highlights are the music of Albéniz and Granados (notably the former's haunting *Evocación* from Iberia, and *Córdoba*, which Bream also included on a very successful solo recital). The transcription of the *Goyescas intermezzo* is also very successful, as is Debussy's *Golliwog's cakewalk*, in a quite different way. Giuliani's *Variazioni concertanti*, actually written for guitar duo, brings some intimately gentle playing, as does the Theme and variations which forms the second movement of Sor's *L'encouragement*, while the *Cantabile* which begins this triptych is delightful in its simple lyricism.

The Carulli *Serenade* opens the first recital very strikingly, while on the second disc the performance of Ravel's *Pavane*, very slow and stately, is memorable. The Elizabethan lute music by Johnson and Lawes and the Telemann *Partie polonaise* (written for a pair of lutes) bring a refreshing change of style in what is predominantly a programme of Spanish music. The concert ends with Albéniz's *Seguidillas*, and an appropriately enthusiatic response from the audience. With the overall timing at a very generous 149 minutes, the pair of discs comes for the cost of a single premium-priced CD and can be recommended very strongly indeed. This is music-making of the very highest order, and the CD transfers bring fine presence and a natural balance.

Brendel, Alfred (piano)

Vanguard 'Alfred Brendel Collection'

Volume 1: MOZART: *Piano concertos Nos. 9 in E flat, K.271; 14 in E flat, K.449* (with I Solisti di Zagreb, Janigro); *Piano sonata No. 8 in A min., K.310; Fantasia in C min., K.396; Rondo in A min., K.511; 9 Variations on a Minuet by Duport, K.573.*

(M) *** Van. (ADD) 08 9161 71 (2).

Volume 2: CHOPIN: *Andante spianato et Grande polonaise brillante, Op. 22; Polonaises Nos. 4 in C min., Op. 40/2; 5 in F sharp min., Op. 44; 6 in A flat, Op. 53; 7 (Polonaise-fantaisie), Op. 61.* LISZT: *Hungarian rhapsodies Nos. 2-3, 8, 13, 15 (Rákóczy march); Csárdás obstinée.*

(M) **(*) Van. (ADD) 08 9163 72 (2) .

Volume 3: SCHUBERT: *Piano sonatas Nos. 15 in C (Unfinished), D.840; 19 in C min., D.958; 16 German dances, D.783.* SCHUMANN: *Etudes symphoniques; Fantasia in C.*

(M) *** Van. (ADD) 08 9165 72 (2).

Vanguard have now produced their own 'Alfred Brendel Collection' from recordings made in the 1960s. Each set of two CDs is offered in a slip-case but with no price saving. The separate discs are discussed in our main volume, under their Composer headings.

Britton, Harold (organ)

'Organ spectacular' (organ of Royal Albert Hall):

SUPPE: *Light Cavalry overture.* LEMARE: *Andantino in D flat.* VERDI: *Aida: Grand march.* ALBINONI: *Adagio* (arr. GIAZOTTO). WAGNER: *Ride of the Valkyries.* BACH: *Toccata and fugue in D min., BWV 565.* TCHAIKOVSKY: *None but the lonely heart.* ELGAR: *Pomp and circumstance march No. 1.* SOUSA: *Liberty Bell.* WIDOR: *Symphony No. 5: Toccata.*

(BB) *** ASV CDQS 6028.

If one is to have a collection mainly of arrangements of orchestral lollipops on an organ, the instrument at the Royal Albert Hall is surely an ideal choice: it offers the widest dynamic range, including an effective recession of quieter passages readily at the player's command – used to good purpose in *Light Cavalry* – but can also produce truly spectacular fortissimos, with a wide amplitude and a blaze of colour from its multitude of stops. Harold Britton is obviously fully at home on the instrument and plays in an aptly extrovert style for such a recital, obviously enjoying himself. The CD is in the demonstration class – there are few problems of muddying from reverberation.

Brodsky Quartet

'*Music from Vienna*', Volume I: SCHOENBERG: *String quartet in D.* WEBERN: *Langsamer Satz (Slow movement).* ZEMLINSKY: *String quartet No. 1 in A.*

(M) *** Vanguard 99208.

In the first of two discs titled 'Music from Vienna', the Brodsky Quartet have devised a fascinating grouping of early works by musical pioneers which give little idea of radical developments to come. The Schoenberg offers a surprising range of Dvořákian echoes from the opening onwards, and Dvořák is one of the influences too in the early Zemlinsky quartet, again with Brahms part of the mixture. The Webern (dated 1905, the same year as his earliest atonal works) is even more ripely romantic, with echoes of Schoenberg's *Verklärte Nacht* and little astringency. The Brodsky Quartet give flawless performances, at once stirring and subtle with superbly polished ensemble in deeply expressive music. For Volume 2, see in our main volume under composers Korngold and Kreisler.

Brüggen, Frans (recorder)

'The Frans Brüggen Edition' (complete)

(M) *** Teldec/Warner 4509 97475-2 (12).

Volume 1: TELEMANN (with Anner Bylsma, Gustav Leonhardt): *Essercizii musici: Sonatas in C, TWV 41:c5; in D min., TWV 41:D4. Fantasias in C, TWV 40:2; in D min., TWV 40:4; in F, TWV 40:8; in G min., TWV 40:9; in A min., TWV 40:11; in B flat, TWV 40:12. Der Getreu Musik-Meister: Canonic sonata in B flat, TWV 41:b3; Sonatas in C, TWV 41:c2; in F, TWV 41:f2; in F min., TWV 41:F1* (4509 93688-2).

Volume 2: *Italian recorder sonatas* (with Anner Bylsma, Gustav Leonhardt): CORELLI: *Sonatas: in F, Op. 5/4; La Follia (Variations in G min.), Op. 5/12.* BARSANTI: *Sonata in C.* VERACINI: *Sonatas in G; in A min.* (1716). BIGAGLIA: *Sonata in A min.* CHEDEVILLE: *Sonata in G min., Op. 13/6.* MARCELLO: *Sonata in D min., Op. 2/11* (4509 93669-2).

Volume 3: *English ensemble music* (with Kees Boeke, Walter van Hauwe, Anner Bylsma, Gustav Leonhardt, Brüggen Consort): HOLBORNE: *Dances and airs.* TAVERNER: *In nomine.* TYE: *In nomine (Crye).* BYRD: *In nomine; The leaves be green.* Thomas SIMPSON: *Bonny sweet Robin.* MORLEY: *La Girandola; Il Lamento; La Caccia.* JEFFREYS: *Fantasia.* PARCHAM: *Solo in G.* Robert CARR: *Divisions upon an Italian ground.* William BABELL: *Concerto in D.* PEPUSCH: *Sonata in F.* PURCELL: *Chaconne in F* (4509 97456-2).

Volume 4: *Early baroque recorder music* (with Kees Boeke, Walter van Hauwe, Anner Bylsma, Wouter Möller, Bob van Asperen, Gustav Leonhardt): Jacob VAN EYCK: *Batali; Doen Daphne d'over schoonne Maeght; Pavane Lachryme; Engels Nachtegaeltje.* FRESCOBALDI: *Canzon: La Bernadina.* Giovanni Paolo CIMA: *Sonatas in D & G.* Giovanni Battista RICCIO: *Canzon in A; Canzon in A (La Rosignola).* SCHEIDT: *Paduan a 4 in D.* ANON.: *Sonata in G* (4509 97466-2).

Volume 5: *Late baroque recorder music* (with Jeanette van Wingerden, Kees Boeke, Walter van Hauwe, Frans Vester, Joost Tromp, Brian Pollard, Anner Bylsma, Wouter Möller, Gustav Leonhardt, Bob van Asperen): TELEMANN: *Quartet in D min., TWV 43:D1.* FASCH: *Quartet in G.* LOEILLET: *Quintet in B min.* QUANTZ: *Trio sonata in C.* Alessandro SCARLATTI: *Sonata in F.* Johann MATTHESON: *Sonata No. 4 in G min.* (4509 97467-2).

Volume 6: *French recorder suites* (with Kees Boeke, Nikolaus Harnoncourt, Anner Bylsma, Gustav Leonhardt): Charles DIEUPART: *Suites in G min. & A.* HOTTETERRE: *Suite No. 1* (4509 97468-2).

Volume 7: *French recorder sonatas* (with Kees Boeke, Walter van Hauwe, Anner Bylsma, Gustav Leonhardt): Philibert DE LAVIGNE: *Sonata in C (La Barssan).* BOISMORTIER: *Sonata in F.* PHILIDOR: *Sonata in D min.* Louis-Antoine DORNEL: *Sonata (a 3 Dessus) in B flat.* François COUPERIN: *Le rossignol-en-amour* (4509 97469-2).

Volume 8: VIVALDI: *Chamber concertos* (with Jürg Schaefleit, Otto Fleischmann, Alice Harnoncourt, Walter Pfeiffer, Nikolaus Harnoncourt, Gustav Leonhardt): *in C, RV 87; in D, RV 92 & RV 94; in G min., RV 105; in A min., RV 108; in C min., RV 441; in F, RV 442* (4509 97470-2).

Volume 9: HANDEL: *Recorder sonatas* (with Alice Harnoncourt, Anner Bylsma, Nikolaus Harnoncourt, Gustav Leonhardt, Herbert Tachezi): *in G min., HWV 360; in A min., HWV 362; in C, HWV 365; in F, HWV 369, Op. 1/2, 4, 7 & 11; in F, HWV 389, Op. 2/4. Fitzwilliam sonatas Nos. 1 in B flat, HWV 377; 3 in D min., HWV 367a* (4509 97471-2).

Volume 10: TELEMANN: *Concertos and orchestral music* (with VCM, Harnoncourt): *Concertos in C; à 6 in F; Suite (Overture) in A min., TWV 55:A2* (4509 97472-2).

Volume 11: J. S. BACH: *Chamber and orchestral music* (with Jeanette van Wingerden, Leopold Stastny, Marie Leonhardt, Nikolaus Harnoncourt, Gustav Leonhardt, Herbert Tachezi): *Concertos in A min., BWV 1044; in F, BWV 1057; Sonata concerto from Cantata No. 182; Sonatina from Cantata No. 106; Trio sonata in G, BWV 1039* (4509 97473-2).

Volume 12: *Recorder sonatas and concertos* (with Frans Vester, Alice Harnoncourt, Nikolaus Harnoncourt, Anner Bylsma, Gustav Leonhardt, Herbert Tachezi, VCM; Amsterdam CO): LOEILLET: *Sonata in C min.; Sonata in G.* SAMMARTINI: *Concerto in F.* HANDEL: *Trio sonata in B min.* NAUDOT: *Concerto in G.* TELEMANN: *Double concerto in E min.* (4509 97474-2).

Frans Brüggen is perhaps the greatest master of the recorder of the post-war era. In his hands phrases are turned with the utmost sophistication, intonation is unbelievably accurate and matters of style exact. There is spontaneity too and, with such superb musicianship

and the high standard of recording we have come to expect from the Teldec Das Alte Werk series, these reissues in Brüggen's own special edition can almost all be recommended without reservation. He is equally at home in early or late baroque music. Throughout the collection, Frans Brüggen and his estimable colleagues demonstrate various period instruments; Anner Bylsma, Gustav Leonhardt and Bob van Asperen are present to provide a distinguished continuo, while Harnoncourt and the Vienna Concentus Musicus and Schröder's Amsterdam Chamber Orchestra are available for authentic concerto accompaniments.

Volume 1 is a single-disc anthology of Telemann's chamber music. Brüggen plays with his usual mastery and, as one would expect from Gustav Leonhardt's ensemble, the performances have polish and authority, and they are excellently recorded.

Volume 2 with its collection of Italian recorder sonatas is surely a perfect sampler for the whole edition, for it gives the opportunity for this king of recorder players to demonstrate his expertise and musicianship to maximum effect, admirably partnered by Anner Bylsma and Gustav Leonhardt. Corelli puts the famous 'Follia' melody through all possible hoops and Brüggen obliges with nimble virtuosity. The Veracini works are also primarily for violin, though the recorder is an optional alternative for the *G major Sonata*. All this music is played with exemplary skill, and no recorder enthusiast will want to be without this splendid example of Brüggen's art.

The collection of English ensemble music which constitutes Volume 3 is particularly diverting, opening with Holborne's *Suite of dances and airs* which alternates recorder and viols. The several *In nomines* are all differently scored and are very different in character too, while the folksong arrangements by Byrd and Simpson are touching. The *Solo* (Suite) by Andrew Parcham, the *Divisions* of Robert Carr and Pepusch's *Sonata* are all engaging and are played with characteristic skill and musicianship so that only occasionally does the ear detect the limitations of early instruments.

Volume 4 introduces works by Jacob Van Eyck, which are unaccompanied but are aurally titillating, particularly the primitive *Batali* with its 'bugle' calls, while the florid upper tessitura of Engels *Nachtegaeltje* really takes wing. The Frescobaldi *Canzon* and the works by Cima and Riccio use an organ and cello continuo, and the delightful *La Rosignola* is for recorder trio with cello and harpsichord.

Late baroque chamber music is represented on Volume 5, with works by Alessandro Scarlatti, Telemann and Johann Mattheson standing out, while Volume 6 brings entertainingly elegant and tuneful *Suites* by Dieupart (a French-born musician who taught in London around 1700 and whose harpsichord music influenced Bach) and Hotteterre (known as Le Romain). These suites are very much cast in the style favoured by Telemann, with an *Overture* and a collection of dances.

410 OTHER INSTRUMENTAL RECITALS

Volume 7 concentrates on French recorder sonatas and brings another vivid nightingale evocation – *Le rossignol-en-amour*, by François Couperin.

Volumes 8–10 are composer collections of music by Vivaldi, Handel and more Telemann, all discussed in detail under their Composer entries, in our main volume. Volume 11, offering a Bach collection, is the only relative disappointment. Two of the major works here are transcribed, and BWV 1044 comes off more effectively than BWV 1057. Best is the *Trio sonata in G*, BWV 1039, although the two cantata excerpts are pleasing.

A final excellent sampler is provided by the collection of *Recorder sonatas* and *concertos* which makes up Volume 12, featuring a chamber ensemble and both the Amsterdam Chamber Orchestra and the Vienna Concentus Musicus. The Telemann *Double concerto in E minor for recorder and flute* is a particularly fine one, and the dulcet duet in the slow movement begins rather like Handel's *Where'er you walk*. The Sammartini *Concerto* has an unexpectedly solemn *Siciliano* for its slow movement. The Handel *Trio sonata* is a splendid work, and the two Loeillet *Sonatas* are light and airy and full of charm, while even the less striking Naudot piece emerges as music of character. All these performances are outstandingly successful.

The recordings were nearly all made during the 1960s, with a few dating from the following decade, and they are of the highest quality, as are the vivid CD transfers. Documentation is very good. As we go to press, the individual issues are still available separately.

Byzantine, Julian (guitar)

ALBENIZ: *Rumores de la Caleta; Suite española No. 1; Torre bermeja.* TORROBA: *Madroños.* TARREGA: *La Alborada; Capricho árabe.* LAURO: *Vals venezolano No. 3.* VILLA-LOBOS: *Chôros No. 1 in G; 5 Preludes; Study No. 1 in E min.* RODRIGO: *En los trigales.* BORGES: *Vals venezolano.* GRANADOS: *Adaluza.* MALATS: *Serenata española.* FALLA: *The Three-Cornered Hat: Corregidor's Dance; Miller's Dance.*

(B) **(*) CfP (ADD/DDD) 575 140-2.

Julian Byzantine is a thoroughly musical player; his rubato and control of light and shade are always convincing. The playing may lack the last degree of individuality and electricity, and sometimes the listener may feel that the flow is too controlled, not absolutely spontaneous, but this remains an impressive recital, generous and varied in content and well recorded.

Campoli, Alfredo (violin)

'*Homage to Kreisler*': (with Eric Gritton; or Norihko Wada, piano): KREISLER: *Praeludium and allegro; Liebeslied; Liebesfreud; Polichinelle-serenade; Schön Rosmarin; Caprice viennois; Tamborin chinois; Rondo on a theme by Beethoven; La Chasse; La Gitana.* **Arrangements:** PADEREWSKI: *Minuet in G.* WIENIAWSKI: *Caprices in E flat; A min.* GRANADOS: *Dance Espagnole.* TARTINI: *Variations on a theme of Corelli.* ALBENIZ: *Tango.* BRAHMS: *Waltz in A flat.* YAMADA: *Akatonbo; Jogashima no ame.* BACH: *Arioso.* SCHUBERT: *Ave Maria.* MOZART: *Divertimento No. 17: Rondo.*

(***) Australian Decca Eloquence mono/stereo 466 666-2.

This disc not only pays 'Homage to Kreisler', but also to Alfredo Campoli. None of the music here is deeply profound, but it is all very entertaining – whether it be breathtakingly showy, or charmingly sentimental. Many of Kreisler's encore hits are included and Campoli's performances are full of flair, while the Decca recordings, both mono and stereo, are all characteristically vivid, though the stereo brings greater depth and richness.

Cann, Claire and Antoinette (piano duo)

'*Romantic favourites on 2 pianos*': SAINT-SAENS: *Danse macabre.* DEBUSSY: *Petite suite.* TCHAIKOVSKY (arr. CANN): *Nutcracker suite: excerpts.* BRAHMS: *Variations on a theme of Haydn (St Anthony chorale), Op. 56b; Waltzes, Op. 39/1-2, 5-6, 9-11 & 15.* MACDOWELL (arr. NIEMANN): *Hexentanz.* LISZT (arr. BRENDEL): *Hungarian rhapsody No. 2.*

✹ (M) *** Apollo Recordings ARCD 961.

We are glad to welcome the début recital of the Cann duo back to the catalogue. With the demise of the Pianissimo label it was unavailable for some time but it now returns on the Apollo label, distributed in the UK by Canterbury Classics. It is difficult to imagine a more scintillating piano duet record than this. Saint-Saëns's skeletons – summoned by an evocative midnight bell – dance as vigorously as do MacDowell's witches in the brilliant *Hexentanz*, while Debussy's delightful *Petite suite* – played here very effectively on two pianos, rather than with four hands on one – is full of charm. The Cann sisters then produce a rich-textured fullness of tone for the Brahms *Haydn variations*, which are every bit as enjoyable here as in their orchestral dress. Most remarkable of all are the excerpts from the *Nutcracker suite*, conceived entirely pianistically and glittering with colour. Indeed, the *Sugar plum fairy* has a much stronger profile than usual and the *Chinese dance* an irresistible oriental glitter. The *Hungarian dances* bring beguiling variety of mood and texture and display an easy bravura, ending with a lovely performance of the famous *Cradle song (No. 15 in A flat)*, while the dazzling Liszt *Hungarian rhapsody* ends the recital with great exuberance and much digital panache. The recording, made in Rosslyn Hill Chapel, is exceptionally real and vivid and is ideally balanced.

Casadesus, Robert and Gaby (piano)

'Two pianos and piano four hands': DEBUSSY: *Petite suite; En blanc et noir.* FAURE: *Dolly.* CASADESUS: *3 Danses Méditerranéennes.* SATIE: *3 Morceaux en forme de poire.*

(M) **(*) Sony stereo/mono MPK 52527.

These accounts come from 1959, save for Robert Casadesus's *Trois Danses Méditerranéennes,* which were recorded in 1950 and are in mono, and *En blanc et noir,* which is from 1963. Although the recording is not in the top bracket (the sound is a bit synthetic and hardens in fortissimo passages), the playing of Robert and Gaby Casadesus has such style and panache that technical limitations should not deter anyone with a taste for this repertoire. They have perfect unanimity and control, as well as wonderfully articulated rhythm. Casadesus's own *Danses Méditerranéennes* are inventive and attractive, distinctly Gallic though not highly personal, and the recording, though shallow, is perfectly acceptable. Fauré's *Dolly suite* is given with charm, and the Satie *Trois Morceaux en forme de poire* are also a delight. Some of the octave unisons in *En blanc et noir* are out of tune, but it is a fine performance for all that.

Casals, Pablo (cello)

Casals Edition (instrumental and chamber music)

BEETHOVEN: *Cello sonatas Nos. 1-5, Op. 5/1-2; Op. 69; Op. 102/1-2; 7 Variations on 'Bei Männern' (from Mozart's 'Die Zauberflöte'), WoO 46; 12 Variations on 'Ein Mädchen' (from Mozart's 'Die Zauberflöte'), WoO 66 (with Rudolf Serkin).*

(M) (**) Sony mono SM2K 58985 (2).

These Casals accounts of the Beethoven *Cello sonatas* come from 1953 and 1958 and exhibit strong personality but less finish, understandably so when one considers that by the latter date Casals was approaching eighty. In spite of the keyboard expertise of Serkin, these performances do not match his performances with Horszowski, made between 1931 and 1938 and now reissued on EMI, coupled with the Brahms *Second Cello sonata,* in which the pianist is Otto Schulhof, an altogether excellent set ((M) (***) CHS5 65185-2).

BEETHOVEN: *Piano trio No. 1 in E flat, Op. 1/1 (with Eugene Istomin, Joseph Fuchs).* SCHUBERT: *Piano trio No. 2 in E flat, D.929 (with Mieczyslaw Horszowski, Alexander Schneider).*

(M) (***) Sony mono SMK 58988.

The *E flat Piano trio,* Op. 1, No. 1 with the much and rightly admired Joseph Fuchs and Eugene Istomin is first class, and the Schubert *E flat Trio* with Horszowski and Schneider is a commanding account that is well worth considering.

BEETHOVEN: *Piano trio No. 2 in G, Op. 1/2.* SCHUBERT: *Piano trio No. 1 in B flat, D.898 (with Eugene Istomin, Alexander Schneider).*

(M) (**) Sony mono SMK 58989.

BEETHOVEN: *Piano trios Nos. 4 in B flat, Op. 11; 7 in B flat (Archduke), Op. 97 (with Eugene Istomin, Alexander Schneider).*

(M) (**) Sony mono SMK 58990.

The Schubert *B flat Trio* on SMK 58989 has its impressive insights, but the *Archduke* on the companion disc does not extinguish memories of the famous pre-war set with Thibaud and Cortot; but there is, as one might expect, perceptive and felicitous and touching phrasing. It comes with the *B flat Trio,* Op. 11, the transcription of the *Clarinet trio.*

BEETHOVEN: *Piano trios Nos. 5 in D (Ghost), Op. 70/1 (with Eugene Istomin, Joseph Fuchs); 6 in E flat, Op. 70/2 (with Eugene Istomin, Alexander Schneider); 12 Variations on a theme from Handel's 'Judas Maccabaeus', WoO 45 (with Rudolf Serkin).*

(M) (***) Sony mono SMK 58991.

The two Op. 70 *Trios,* the 'Ghost' with Fuchs and Istomin and the *E flat* with Istomin and Schneider, are given with great spirit and are arguably superior to Casals's later (1958) versions with Végh and Engel.

BRAHMS: *Piano trio No. 1 in B, Op. 8 (with Dame Myra Hess, Isaac Stern); String sextet No. 1 in B flat, Op. 18 (with Isaac Stern, Alexander Schneider, Milton Katims, Milton Thomas, Madeline Foley).*

(M) (***) Sony mono SMK 58994.

The Brahms performances, the *B major Trio,* Op. 8 and the *B flat Sextet,* Op. 18 are hardly less celebrated. The *Trio* with Isaac Stern and Myra Hess is a noble and beautifully phrased performance. The majestic and passionate account of the *Sextet* enjoyed cult status in France and elsewhere when it was used in Louis Malle's 1958 film *Les amants*; and it remains a classic of the gramophone – one of the artistic peaks of the Casals Edition.

Clarion Ensemble

'Trumpet collection': FANTINI: *Sonata; Brando; Balletteo; Corrente.* MONTEVERDI: *Et e pur dunque vero.* FRESCOBALDI: *Canzona a canto solo.* PURCELL: *To arms, heroic prince.* A. SCARLATTI: *Si suoni la tromba.* BISHOP: *Arietta and Waltz; Thine forever.* DONIZETTI: *Lo L'udia.* KOENIG: *Posthorn galop.* ARBAN: *Fantasia on Verdi's Rigoletto.* CLARKE: *Cousins.* ENESCU: *Legende.*

✪ *** Amon Ra (ADD) CD-SAR 30.

The simple title 'Trumpet collection' covers a fascinating recital of music for trumpet written over three centuries and played with great skill and musicianship by Jonathan Impett, using a variety of original instruments, from a keyed bugle and clapper shakekey cornopean to an English slide trumpet and a posthorn. Impett is a complete master of all these instruments, never producing a throttled tone; indeed, in the Purcell and Scarlatti arias he matches the soaring soprano line of Deborah Roberts with uncanny mirror-image precision. Accompaniments are provided by other members of the Clarion Ensemble. The Frescobaldi Canzona brings a duet for trumpet and trombone, with a background harpsichord filigree, which is most effective. With demonstration-worthy recording, this is as enjoyable as it is interesting, with the *Posthorn galop* and Arban's *Rigoletto variations* producing exhilarating bravura.

Cohler, Jonathan (clarinet)

'*Cohler on clarinet*' (with Judith Gordon, piano): BRAHMS: *Sonata No. 1 in F min., Op. 120/1.* WEBER: *Grand duo concertante, Op. 48.* BAERMANN: *Quintet No. 3, Op. 23: Adagio* (arr. for clarinet & piano). SARGON: *Deep Ellum nights (3 Sketches).*

*** Ongaku 024-101.

This fine collection marks the recording début of an outstanding, Boston-born, American clarinettist. He has a splendid technique and a lovely tone, and he is already master of an extraordinarily wide range of repertoire. The opening Brahms *F minor Sonata* is a supreme test, and he passes with distinction. The Weber *Grand duo concertante* is suitably good-natured, with a songful central cantilena and plenty of wit in the finale.

The Baermann *Adagio* shows how ravishingly Cohler can shape a melting legato line with a breath-catching pianissimo at its peak. He then throws his hat in the air in the three exuberant *Sketches* of Simon Sargon, where sultry melodic lines are interrupted by all kinds of jazzy glissandos and uninhibited syncopations, notably an explosive burst of energy intruding into the *Quiet and easy* central section. The finale is like a flashy cakewalk. The recording is truthful, but the piano is placed behind in a too resonant acoustic (the empty Paine Concert Hall at Harvard University), which is a tiresome misjudgement. Even so, Judith Gordon provides sympathetic support and the playing more than compensates.

'*More Cohler on clarinet*' (with Randall Hodgkinson, piano): BRAHMS: *Sonata No. 2 in E flat, Op. 120/2.* POULENC: *Sonata.* SCHUMANN: *Fantasiestücke, Op. 73.* MILHAUD: *Sonatina, Op. 100.* STRAVINSKY: *3 Pieces (for solo clarinet).*

*** Ongaku 024-102.

Cohler's second disc is much more satisfactorily balanced. His excellent partner, Randall Hodgkinson, is fully in the picture. The opening of the Brahms *E flat Sonata* is agreeably warm and relaxed, and the Theme and variations finale brings a pleasing interplay between the two artists. Poulenc's *Sonata* is beautifully done, the lovely *Romanza (Très calme)* is cool in the way only a player who knows about jazz can manage, while the fizzing finale also brings a hint of rapture in

its contrasting lyrical theme. The warmth of the Schumann pieces, for which Cohler imaginatively modifies his timbre, contrasts with the outrageous Milhaud sonatina, with both outer movements marked *Très rude* but the *Lent* centrepiece quite magical. The three dry Stravinsky fragments make a perfect close to a disc which is outstanding in every way.

Coletti, Paul (viola), Leslie Howard (piano)

'*English Music for Viola*': BRITTEN: *Elegy for Solo Viola.* VAUGHAN WILLIAMS: *Romance.* CLARKE: *Lullaby No. 1; Morpheus; Sonata.* GRAINGER: *Sussex Mummers' Carol; Arrival Platform Humlet for Solo Viola.* BAX: *Legend.* BRIDGE: *Pensiero; Allegro appassionato.*

(B) *** Hyp. Helios CDH 55085.

This attractive and important collection went unnoticed on its first issue and we are happy now to give it the strongest recommendation as an unmissable bargain. Paul Coletti is a first rate violist and a fine artist and he opens with an intensely compelling account of the *Elegy* which Britten wrote when he was only sixteen, but which was only recently discovered and premièred at the Aldeburgh Festival in 1984 by Nobuko Imai. The moving Vaughan Williams *Romance* was another posthumous discovery, found among the composer's effects after his death.

Like Vaughan Williams, Bax had a special feeling for the viola and his elegiac *Legend* is imbued with a mysterious Celtic atmosphere. The two folk inspirations of Grainger certainly suit the viola's rich cantilena, and Frank Bridge's *Pensiero* and *Allegro appasionato* make a perfect foil for each other. But the major work here and the most ambitious (21 minutes long) is Rebecca Clarke's three-movement *Sonata*. Not for nothing is the first movement marked *Impetuoso* and this mood interrups and engulfs the lyrical *Adagio* finale. Here (as elsewhere), Leslie Howard proves his mettle. Clarke's two shorter pieces, the lovely *First Lullaby* and the similarly reflective *Morpheus* are, like the *Sonata*, underpinned with English pastoral feeling. All in all a most stimulating and rewarding programme, played with great committment by both artists and vividly recorded.

Cortot, Alfred (piano), Jacques Thibaud (violin), Pablo Casals (cello)

BEETHOVEN: *Variations on Ich bin der Schneider Kakadu.* HAYDN: *Piano Trio No. 39 in G (Gypsy).* SCHUBERT: *Piano Trio No. 1 in B flat.*

(BB) (***) Naxos 8.110188

Although the piano trio Alfred Cortot formed with Pablo Casals and Jacques Thibaud was perhaps the most famous pre-war trio, it was extraordinarily short lived – in fact it lasted barely a decade, unlike the Beaux Arts which cover the best part of half a century, and (again unlike them) had a small repertoire and made few records. The claims of their solo careers meant that they had virtually stopped playing together by the mid-1930s. They are technically immaculate, supremely lyrical and with a spontaneity of feeling underpinned by firm yet flexible rhythm. Ward Marston's transfers give these exalted performances a new lease of life.

Crabb, James and Geir Draugsvoll (accordions)

Début recital: STRAVINSKY: *Petrushka* (ballet; complete). MUSSORGSKY: *Pictures at an exhibition* (both arr. CRABB/DRAUGSVOLL).

(B) **(*) EMI Début CDZ5 69705-2.

It seems impossible to believe that Stravinsky's brilliantly scored ballet, played on a pair of piano accordions, could sound remarkably like the orchestral version; but this phenomenal transcription brings all the colours of the Stravinskian palette vividly before the listener. Only the bold sound of unison horns and the bite of massed strings eludes these virtuosi, and they bring the ballet's drama and pathos fully to life. This is an extraordinary listening experience. Mussorgsky's *Pictures at an exhibition* is equally ingenious but is far less consistently effective, for one's ear is used to bold brass sonorities and spectacle. *Catacombs* and the big finale do not really come off, although the grotesque *Baba-Yaga* certainly does, played with proper rhythmic venom; otherwise the most effective pictures are those in which we normally expect woodwind chattering: *Tuileries, Limoges* and the cheeping chicks. Nevertheless it's a good try, and the playing itself has astonishing bravura. Well worth sampling on EMI's bargain Début label. The recording cannot be faulted.

Curley, Carlo (organ)

'Toccata: Organ favourites' (organ of Girard College Chapel, Philadelphia): BACH: *Toccata and fugue in D min., BWV 565; Cantata No. 22: Subdue us by thy kindness; Suite No. 3 in D: Air. Cantata No. 147: Jesu joy of man's desiring. Cantata No. 140: Wachet auf. Cantata No. 29: Sinfonia in D.* ALBINONI, arr. GIAZOTTO/CURLEY: *Adagio.* GUILMANT: *March on a theme by Handel, Op. 15.* SOLER/BIGGS: *Emperor's fanfare.* SCHUBERT, arr. CURLEY: *Ave Maria.* KARG-ELERT: *Chorale improvisation: Now thank we all our God (Trauung, Taufe, Emtefest).* LIDON: *Sonata on the first tone.* SAINT-SAENS: *Carnival of the animals: The Swan.* DUSSEK, arr. THALBEN-BALL: *Andante in F.* MOZART: *Fantasia in F min., K. 608.* WIDOR: *Organ Symphony No. 5: Toccata.* STANLEY: *Suite in D: Introduction & Trumpet tune, Op. 6/6.* MULET: *Tu es Petrus.* VIERNE: *Carillon de Westminster.* BEETHOVEN, arr. CURLEY: *Ruins of Athens: Turkish march.* SCHUBERT: *Moment musical in F min.* HANDEL: *Concerto in F, Op. 4/5:*

Allegro (both arr. CURLEY). RACHMANINOV, arr. BIRD: *Vocalise.* BOELLMANN: *Suite gothique, Op. 25.* HOLST: *The Planets: Jupiter* (theme, arr. CURLEY). SOUSA, arr. CURLEY: *Washington Post.*

(B) *** Double Decca 458 364-2 (2).

On the original issue which contained the *Emperor's fanfare* (an anachronistic but irresistible arrangement of Soler's music by E. Power Biggs, which provides an opportunity for great splashes of throaty timbre and uses the powerful *Tuba mirabilis* stop) the flamboyant Carlo Curley described with engaging enthusiasm the organ he plays here: 'Nearly one hundred feet from the [Girard] Chapel's marble floor and above the vast, coffered ceiling, entirely covered incidentally with real gold leaf, the organ, all thirty-five metric tonnes, and with 6,587 handmade pipes, is miraculously suspended. In a chapel so cavernous, and with such remarkable reverberation, it is well nigh impossible to identify the source of the sound.'

Yet the Decca (Argo) engineers manage to provide an excellent focus and capture the extremely wide range of Curley's playing with precision at both ends of the spectrum. The performances are full of drama and temperament, unashamedly romantic, yet very compelling. A great deal of this music is not ideally suited to the organ but Curley's panache almost convinces one that it is, and this collection cannot fail to entertain any organ fancier when the recording is so spectacularly vivid.

Curzon, Clifford (piano)

'Edinburgh Festival Recital': HAYDN: *Andante and Variations in F minor.* LISZT: *Années de pèlerinage; Sonetto del Patrarca No. 104; Berceuse* (2nd version); *Valse oubliée No. 1; Piano Sonata in B minor;* SCHUBERT: *Impromptus, D.899/2, 3 & 4.*

(M) (***) BBC Legends mono BBCL 4078-2.

When Clifford Curzon was always so reluctant to work in the recording studio, such a collection as this of live performances is most treasurable, despite any flaws. Curzon's account of the Liszt *Sonata*, given at the 1961 Edinburgh Festival, has obvious slips of finger, but is even more persuasively spontaneous than the Decca studio version of only a couple of years later. The impulsive energy lets us appreciate a side of Curzon's genius rarely revealed in his official recordings, the daring of the virtuoso. As for the other Liszt items they reveal Curzon's magic at its most intense, so that in the *Petrarch Sonnet* his velvet legato has one imagining a voice singing the words. In the Haydn *Variations*, a piece that can seem too formal and painstaking, Curzon similarly finds sparkle and fantasy, and the Schubert *Impromptus* – for him core repertory – show him at his happiest, though his breathtakingly fast tempo for No. 2 with its rippling scales in triplets may initially seem disconcerting. The singing legato of No. 3 is then all the more soothing, and the textural contrasts of No. 4 the more dramatic. The mono sound may be limited, but is very acceptable. An excellent note by

Jonathan Dobson movingly quotes a remark made by Curzon in 1981 that in his boyhood playing the piano became 'a lonely child's retreat from a happy family'. That sense of wonder was a quality he kept throughout his life.

Daniel, Nicholas (oboe), Julius Drake (piano)

– see below under Snowden, Jonathan (flute).

Danish Radio Wind Quintet

NIELSEN: *Wind Quintet, Op. 43.* MORTENSEN: *Wind Quintet.* JERSILD: *Serenade for Wind Quintet.* WELLERJUS: *Wind Quintet.*

*** dacapo 8.224151.

Recordings of the Nielsen *Quintet*, all variously coupled, are relatively plentiful. The fine wind players of the Danish Radio Orchestra give an expertly shaped and well-characterized account of the piece. In the finale the clarinet variation was not more vividly portrayed even by Aage Oxenvad himself, whose character it was supposed to enshrine. The expressive emphasis a few bars into the first movement and some rather too affectionate phrasing in the trio of the minuet must be mentioned, but one cannot imagine them causing serious concern. The Nielsen can be recommended alongside the Oslo Quintet on Naxos. Jørgen Jersild was born in 1913 and spent some years in France, studying briefly with Roussel. The *Serenade* (1947) confirms the positive impression so much of his music makes; it is impeccably crafted, intelligent and of some wit. The *Quintet* of 1944 by Otto Mortensen (1907–86) is pleasing, not wildly original perhaps, but civilized. The same goes for Henning Wellejus's slight and short *Quintet* from the mid-1960s. The performances are carefully prepared and strongly profiled, and the disc is worth having for the Nielsen and the Jersild. Good recording.

Claude Debussy Wind Quintet

'*The new interpreters*': LIGETI: *6 Bagatelles; 10 Pieces.* JANACEK: *Mládi; Concertino* (with Philippe Cassard, piano, Bruno Martinez & members of Parish Qt).

(B) *** HM (DDD) HMN 911624.

Anyone who thinks of Ligeti as a 'difficult' composer should sample this infectious performance of the *Six Bagatelles*, especially the riotous élan of the opening *Allegro con spirito* and the more wry wit of the finale. There is unexpected melodic charm too in the *Allegro grazioso* (No. 3), and the sombre tribute to Bartók is darkly memorable. The *Ten Pieces* are thornier, but still stimulating. The penultimate number is marked *Sostenuto stridente* and the finale *Presto bizzare*, but the music remains ear-catching. The two better-known Janáček works are also played with keen rhythmic feeling and, although this is in essence a

sampler, it makes a highly enjoyable concert; the recording gives these excellent players a very tangible presence within a nicely judged acoustic.

Demidenko, Nikolai (piano)

'*Live at Wigmore Hall*': VORISEK: *Fantasia in C, Op. 12.* HAYDN: *Variations in F min., Hob XVII/6.* D. SCARLATTI: *Sonatas Kk. 11, 377.* SCHUMANN: *Variations on a theme of Clara Wieck.* MENDELSSOHN: *Fantasy in F sharp min., Op. 28.* KALKEBRENNER: *Nocturne in A flat, Op. 129.* LISZT: *Concert paraphrase of Beethoven's An die ferne Geliebte.* BERG: *Sonata in B min., Op. 1.* BUXTEHUDE/PROKOFIEV: *Prelude & fugue in D min., BuxWV 140.* GUBAIDULINA: *Ciacona.* LISZT: *Funérailles.* SCHUBERT: *Impromptu, D.899/4.*

(B) **(*) Hyp. Dyad CDD 22024 (2).

With the advantage of the superb Wigmore Hall acoustics, Nikolai Demidenko, recorded live at a series of concerts between January and June 1993, comes over charismatically, and the programme is certainly diverse. Mendelssohn's *Fantasy* could hardly be played more brilliantly and this set, which has received an enthusiastic press, is a must for the pianist's admirers, even if perhaps the general collector would not be drawn to hearing some of this music very often. The Liszt/Beethoven song-cycle transcription, for instance, has not too much to offer compared with a vocal version. The Gubaidulina *Ciacona* is a stunning, indeed overwhelming, example of extrovert bravura and (like the spectacular Liszt *Funérailles*) receives a deserved ovation. But it leaves the listener somewhat battered! One welcomes the simpler appeal of the Schubert *Impromptu* with which the recital closes.

Duchable, François-René (piano)

Recital: CHOPIN: *Scherzi Nos. 1-4; Fantaisie in F min., Op. 49.* LISZT: *Etudes d'exécution transcendante Nos. 5, Feux follets; 10, Appassionata. Années de Pèlerinage, 2nd Year (Italy): Petrarch Sonnet No. 104. Grand Etude de Paganini: La Campanella. Nocturne No. 3 (Rêve d'amour). Polonaise No. 2 in E. Mephisto waltz. Consolation No. 3. Harmonies poétiques et religieuses: Funérailles. Concert paraphrase of Berlioz: Symphonie fantastique* (revised Duchable). DUKAS: *Sonata in B flat min.* SAINT-SAENS: *Etude en forme de valse, Op. 52/6; 6 Etudes, Op. 111; Allegro appassionato; Mazurka, Op. 66.*

(B) *** EMI (ADD) CZS5 72356-2 (3).

François-René Duchable's three-CD set is worth having, not so much for the Liszt – though that is brilliant enough – but for his commanding account of the Saint-Saëns rarities and, above all, for his magisterial Dukas *Sonata*. A pity that the French planners did not include *La plainte au loin du faune* and the *Prélude élégiaque sur le thème proposé Haydn*, which was on the original Dukas LP. Judged by modern standards, the 1978 sound is a bit synthetic. There is much more to admire here, including an impressive *Symphonie fantastique*.

Duo Reine Elisabeth (Wolfgang Manz and Rolf Plagge)

Russian music for two pianos: STRAVINSKY: *Petrushka.* SCRIABIN: *Romance in A min.* SHOSTAKOVICH: *Concertino, Op. 94.* RACHMANINOV: *6 Morceaux, Op. 11.*

(BB) *** Discover DICD 920150.

Petrushka has plenty of colour and a surprising degree of charm; the finale swings along infectiously. The melodically lavish, early Scriabin *Romance* then contrasts aptly with the wittily audacious Shostakovich *Concertino*, which has the temerity to open with an echo of the slow movement of Beethoven's *G major Piano concerto*. The six Rachmaninov *Morceaux* are strongly and colourfully characterized, and their diversity gives much pleasure. In short, Wolfgang Manz and Rolf Plagge create an impressive artistic symbiosis, playing with spontaneity as well as commanding impressive technical resource. Very good recording too – not too reverberant. A bargain.

Du Pré, Jacqueline (cello)

Recital (with (i) Gerald Moore (piano); (ii) Roy Jesson (organ); (iii) Osian Ellis (harp); (iv) John Williams (guitar)): (i) PARADIS: *Sicilienne.* SCHUMANN: *3 Fantasy pieces, Op. 73.* MENDELSSOHN: *Song without words in D, Op. 109.* FAURE: *Elégie in C min., Op. 24.* BRUCH: *Kol Nidrei, Op. 47.* (ii) BACH: *Adagio from BWV 564.* (iii) SAINT-SAENS: *The Swan.* (iv) FALLA: *Suite populaire espagnole: Jota.*

*** EMI (ADD) CDC5 55529-2 (with Delius: *Cello concerto* ***).

This heart-warming recital collects together more recordings Jacqueline du Pré made in her teens for EMI, plus the beautiful performance of Fauré's *Elégie* she recorded in 1969 with Gerald Moore for his seventieth-birthday record. There have been few performances of *The Swan* to match this in natural, unforced expressiveness (beautifully accompanied on the harp by Osian Ellis), and the other items all have one marvelling afresh at the maturity of so young a virtuoso. Excellent transfers.

BACH: *Cello suites Nos. 1 in G; 2 in D min., BWV 1007-8.* BRITTEN: *Cello sonata in C, Op. 65 (Scherzo and Marcia)* (with Stephen Kovacevich). FALLA: *Suite populaire espagnole.* BRAHMS: *Cello sonata No. 2 in F, Op. 99.* HANDEL: *Sonata in G min.* (all with Ernest Lush). F. COUPERIN: *Treizième concert (Les goûts-réunis)* (with William Pleeth).

(B) (***) EMI Double fforte mono CZS5 73377-2 (2).

Here are some of the radio performances which Jacqueline du Pré gave in her inspired teens. Her 1962

recordings of the first two Bach *Cello suites* may not be immaculate, but her impulsive vitality makes phrase after phrase at once totally individual and seemingly inevitable. In two movements from Britten's *Cello sonata in C*, with Stephen Kovacevich as her partner, the sheer wit is deliciously infectious, fruit of youthful exuberance in both players. The first of the two discs is completed by Falla's *Suite populaire espagnole*, with the cello matching any singer in expressive range and rhythmic flair. The second has fascinating Couperin duets played with her teacher, William Pleeth; the Handel *Sonata* is equally warm and giving. Best of all is the Brahms *Cello sonata No. 2*, recorded at the 1962 Edinburgh Festival.

Fanning, Diana (piano)

'Musical treasures': JANACEK: *On an overgrown path* (1911). DEBUSSY: *L'isle joyeuse.* CHOPIN: *Piano sonata No. 3 in B min., Op. 58.* ***

The American pianist Diana Fanning is a member of the music faculty at Middlebury College in Vermont and also a well-known soloist and chamber music performer in her native state. She has that special gift of being able to bring music spontaneously to life in the recording studio. The highlight of this recital is a splendidly alive and romantically compelling account of the Chopin *B minor Sonata*, which exerts more magnetism than many accounts by more famous artists. Her account of *L'isle joyeuse* is compellingly exciting too, and yet *On an overgrown path* has a pleasingly poetic intimacy. The recording is real and vivid, the ambience attractive, although a shade over-resonant for the fullest detail to emerge in the Debussy piece. The CD appears to have no catalogue number, but is available direct from Franck Publications, PO Box 96, Middlebury, Vermont 05753, USA.

Fergus-Thompson, Gordon (piano)

'Rêverie': DEBUSSY: *Rêverie; Arabesque No. 1; Suite bergamasque: Clair de lune.* SCRIABIN: *Etude, Op. 42/4.* BACH: *Chorales: Wachet auf* (trans. Busoni); *Jesu, joy of man's desiring* (trans. Hess). GLINKA: *The Lark* (trans. Balakirev). GODOWSKY: *Alt Wien.* SAINT-SAENS: *The Swan* (arr. GODOWSKY). SCHUMANN: *Arabeske in C, Op. 18; Kinderszenen: Träumerei.* BRAHMS: *Intermezzo in A, Op. 118.* GRIEG: *Lyric pieces: Butterfly, Op. 43/1; Nocturne, Op. 54/4.* RAVEL: *Le tombeau de Couperin: Forlane. Pavane pour une infante défunte.*

(M) *** ASV CDWHL 2066.

This 76-minute recital fills a real need for a high-quality recital of piano music for the late evening, where the mood of reverie is sustained without blandness. Gordon Fergus-Thompson's performances are of high sensibility throughout, from the atmospheric opening Debussy items to the closing Ravel *Pavane*. Perhaps his Bach is a little studied but the rest is admirably paced, and the two favourite Grieg *Lyric pieces* are particularly fresh. Excellent recording.

Fernández, Eduardo (guitar)

'*The World of the Spanish guitar*': ALBENIZ: *Sevilla; Tango; Asturias.* LLOBET: *6 Catalan folksongs.* GRANADOS: *Andaluza; Danza triste.* TARREGA: *Estudio brillante; 5 Preludes; Minuetto; 3 Mazurkas; Recuerdos de la Alhambra.* SEGOVIA: *Estudio sin luz; Neblina; Estudio.* TURINA: *Fandanguillo; Ráfaga.*

(M) *** Decca 433 820-2.

Fernández is most naturally recorded in the Henry Wood Hall. His programme is essentially an intimate one and centres on the highly rewarding music of Tárrega, although opening colourfully with items from Albéniz's *Suite española.* The Llobet group of *Folksongs,* and Segovia's hauntingly atmospheric *Neblina* ('Mist'), make further highlights. Later there is bravura from Turina, notably the spectacular *Ráfaga* ('Gust of wind') but even here, though the playing is vibrant, there is no flashiness. With an hour of music and digital sound, this well-chosen programme is excellent value.

Fierens, Guillermo (guitar)

'*Spanish guitar music*': VILLA-LOBOS: *Preludes Nos. 1-3.* PONCE: *Preludio, Balletto & Giga.* CASTELNUOVO-TEDESCO: *Capriccio diabolico; Sonata.* ALBENIZ: *Asturias.* TURINA: *Fandanguillo.* SOR: *Introduction and allegro (Gran solo), Op. 14.*

(B) *** ASV CDQS 6190.

Argentinian-born Guillermo Fierens studied under Segovia and has won several international prizes, including a First at Rio de Janeiro's Villa-Lobos competition. He is thoroughly sympathetic to that composer's music, and he presents this whole programme brightly and sympathetically, with plenty of personality and character. His technique is commandingly immaculate, his rubato nicely judged. He is very personable in the lively Ponce triptych (pastiche pieces of some charm) and the attractively spontaneous *Sonata* by Castelnuovo-Tedesco, particularly the two engaging central movements, and he finds plenty of bravura for the same composer's *Capriccio diabolico.* (Although it hardly matches Paganini in diabolism, it still makes a strong impression.) The *Gran solo* of Sor is equally appealing, but the highlight of a well-balanced programme is a magically evocative account of the famous *Asturias* of Albéniz. The recording has a vivid presence without being on top of the listener. Excellent value on all counts.

Fischer, Annie (piano)

BRAHMS: *Piano Sonata No. 3 in F min., Op. 5.* BARTOK: *15 Hungarian Peasant Songs.* LISZT: *3 Etudes de concert.* DOHNANYI: *Rhapsody in C, Op. 11/3.*

(M) (***) BBC mono BBCL 4054-2.

Annie Fischer is captured here in an Usher Hall recital at the 1961 Edinburgh Festival, albeit in mono sound. She was an artist of great musical insight, who steeped herself in each composer's sound world. Probably the best thing is the Bartók, which has never been played with greater imagination or sympathy (except, perhaps, by Kocsis). The Dohnányi encore is a delight. Such is the quality of Fischer's playing that the odd smudge or finger-slip to which she was prone in the concert hall do not more than marginally disturb.

'*Les Introuvables d'Annie Fischer*': BEETHOVEN: *Piano sonatas Nos. 8 in C min. (Pathétique), Op. 13; 14 in C sharp min. (Moonlight), Op. 27/2; 18 in E flat, Op. 31/3; 24 in F sharp, Op. 78; 21 in C (Waldstein), Op. 53; 30 in E, Op. 109; 32 in C min., Op. 111.* SCHUBERT: *Impromptus in A flat; F min., D. 935/2 & 4; Piano sonata in B flat, D.960.* SCHUMANN: *Fantaisie in C, Op. 17; Carnaval, Op. 9; Kinderszenen, Op. 15; Kreisleriana, Op. 16.*

(B) **(*) EMI stereo/mono CZS5 69217-2 (4).

Annie Fischer's Schumann is special, remarkably fine. *Kreisleriana,* recorded in Vienna in 1965 in a smallish studio, is magnificent, impassioned and full of fire, though one wishes that the sound had room in which to expand. Her Beethoven is perhaps less impressive and commanding – particularly the *Pathétique,* which, despite much sensitivity, suffers from a certain want of depth and sweep. Nevertheless whatever she does is distinguished by unfailing musicality.

Fretwork

'*In nomine*': 16th-century English music for viols: TALLIS: *In nomine a 4, Nos. 1 & 2; Solfaing song a 5; Fantasia a 5; Libera nos, salva nos a 5.* TYE: *In nomine a 5 (Crye); In nomine a 5 (Trust).* CORNYSH: *Fa la sol a 3.* BALDWIN: *In nomine a 4.* BULL: *In nomine a 5.* BYRD: *In nomine a 4, No. 2. Fantasia a 3, No. 3.* TAVERNER: *In nomine; In nomine a 4.* PRESTON: *O lux beata Trinitas a 3.* JOHNSON: *In nomine a 4.* PARSONS: *In nomine a 5; Ut re mi fa sol la a 4.* FERRABOSCO: *In nomine a 5; Lute fantasia No. 5; Fantasia a 4.*

*** Amon Ra (ADD) CD-SAR 29.

This was Fretwork's début CD. The collection is not so obviously of strong popular appeal as the later collections for Virgin but is nevertheless very rewarding and distinguished, and it includes the complete consort music of Thomas Tallis. The sound is naturally pleasing in a fairly rich acoustic and readers can be assured that there is no vinegar in the string-timbre here; indeed, the sound itself is quite lovely in its gentle, austere atmosphere.

'*Heart's ease*': HOLBORNE: *The Honiesuckle; Countess of Pembroke's paradise; The Fairie round.* BYRD: *Fantasia a 5 (Two in one); Fancy in C.* DOWLAND: *Mr Bucton, his galliard; Captaine Digorie Piper, his galliard; Lachrimae antiquae*

pavan; Mr Nicholas Gryffith, his galliard. BULL:
Fantasia a 4. FERRABOSCO: *In nomine a 5.* GIBBONS:
In nomine a 5; Fantasia a 4 for the great dooble base.
LAWES: *Airs for 2 division viols in C: Pavan of
Alfonso; Almain of Alfonso. Consort sett a 5 in C:
Fantasia; Pavan; Almain.*

*** Virgin VC7 59667-2.

An outstanding collection of viol consort music from
the late Tudor and early Stuart periods; the playing is
both stylish and vivacious, with a fine sense of the most
suitable tempo for each piece. The more lyrical music is
equally sensitive. This is a tuneful entertainment, not
just for the specialist collector, and Fretwork convey
their pleasure in all this music. The William Byrd *Fancy*
(from *My Ladye Nevells Booke*) is played exuberantly
on the organ by Paul Nicholson, to bring some contrast
before the closing Lawes *Consort sett*. The recording is
agreeably warm, yet transparent too.

'Portrait: Music for viols' ((i) with Michael Chance
(counter-tenor), Christopher Wilson (lute), Paul
Nicholson (organ)): BYRD: *Pavan a 6; Galliard a 6;*
(i) *Come to me, grief for ever; Ye sacred muses. bevin:
Browning a 3.* GIBBONS: *Go from my window a 6;
Fantasy a 6; In nomine a 5.* DOWLAND: *Lachrimae
antiquae; Lachrimae Coacte; Mr John Langtons
Pavan; The Earl of Essex galliard; Mr Henry Noell
his galliard.* (i) *Lasso vita mia.* LAWES: *Pavan a 5 in
C min.; Fantasy a 6 in F; Aire a 6 in F min.*
HOLBORNE: *The Honie-suckle; The Fairie-round.*

(M) *** Virgin/Veritas EMI VM5 61402-2.

A quite outstanding concert, with the consort music
nicely leavened by three vocal solos. Much of the
atmosphere is melancholic, but with the arrival of the
two dances by Holborne the mood (and timbre)
changes completely, while the following Dowland
Galliards, if less upbeat, bring yet another change of
character. The two vocal highlights are by Byrd, *Come
to me, grief for ever*, in which he outflanks Dowland in
dolour, and the beautiful *Ye sacred muses*, both sung
ravishingly by Michael Chance. Lawes's *Pavan a 5 in C
minor* which follows embroiders a particularly memorable theme and features the use of the chamber
organ subtly to fill out the sonority, as it does the
touching Gibbons *In nomine a 5*, while in the Lawes
Fantasy a 6 the organ has a delicate contrapuntal role.
Excellent – if close – recording.

Fromentin, Lawrence and Domenique Plancade (piano duo)

Début: 'French piano duets': POULENC: *Sonata.*
DEBUSSY: *Petite suite.* RAVEL: *Ma mère l'oye suite.*
FAURE: *Dolly (suite), Op. 56.* BIZET: *Jeux d'enfants
(complete).*

(B) *** EMI Début CDZ5 72526-2.

Lawrence Fromentin and Domenique Plancade, both
Gold Medal winners at the Paris Conservatoire and
pupils of Pascal Devoyon, decided to join together as a

duo in 1992, and this is their recording début. The
results are very impressive indeed. They encompass
the wide stylistic contrasts of their programme with
sympathy and panache, from the brittle wit of Poulenc
and its underlying innocence, to the exquisitely delicate Ravelian atmosphere of *Ma mère l'oye* and the
gentle charm of Fauré's *Dolly*. Debussy's *Petite suite* is
winningly spontaneous, while the perceptively characterized *Jeux d'enfants* of Bizet is the more valuable for
being complete, including all twelve movements, not
just those familiar in the orchestral suite. The recording is excellent. A genuine bargain in every sense.

Galimir Quartet

BERG: *Lyric suite.* MILHAUD: *String quartet No. 7 in
B flat.* RAVEL: *String quartet in F.*

(**) Rockport RR 5007.

Like the Hagens, the Galimir was a family quartet,
founded in 1929 by Felix Galimir with his three sisters.
They recorded the Milhaud and Ravel quartets in 1934
in the presence of their respective composers, and the
Lyric suite in 1935 just before Berg's death. Felix Galimir
emigrated to the United States just before the outbreak
of the Second World War and taught at the Juilliard
School until his death earlier this year. The performances naturally carry authority, though the somewhat
dry acoustic of the Berg calls for tolerance. The present
transfer of the latter is much better than the Contin-
uum version coupled with Louis Krasne's broadcast of
the violin concerto, with Webern conducting.

Goossens, Leon (oboe)

'The Goossens family' (with Lloyd, piano, Marie &
Sidonie Goossens, harps, Fitzwilliam Qt): BACH:
Easter Oratorio: Sinfonia. SOMER-COCKS: *Three
Sketches: No. 1.* STANTON: *Chanson pastorale.*
RICHARDSON: *Scherzino.* HENSCHEL: *Shepherd's
Lament.* PITFIELD: *Rondo Lirico.* HUGHES: *Bard of
Armagh.* DUNHILL: *Romance.* BOYCE: *Matelotte.*
FINZI: *Interlude.* KREIN: *Serenade for Oboe & Two
Harps.* NICHOLAS: *Melody.* SAUNDERS: *A Cotswold
Pastoral.* ELGAR (arr. Jacob): *Soliloquy* (with
Bournemouth Sinf., Del Mar).

(M) *** Chan. (ADD) 7132.

This touching tribute to Leon Goossens, a superstar
among oboists long before that term was invented, is
the more welcome when he made relatively few
recordings over his long career. The harpists, Marie
and Sidonie Goossens, accompany their brother in
two of the most charming items, the Krein *Serenade*
and Morgan Nicholas's *Melody*, but the rest of the
programme is devoted to Leon. These are mainly
recordings, first issued on RCA in the late 1970s,
which Goossens made after his amazing rehabilita-
tion following a serious car accident. Although the
technical facility may not be quite the same as earlier,
the warmth of tone and the ability to charm are undiminished. That he was in his late seventies at the time

only adds to the marvel. The two most extended items are the Elgar *Soliloquy*, which Elgar wrote for Goossens right at the end of his life, and the Finzi *Interlude*, superbly played by the Fitzwilliam Quartet, with contrasted sections covering a wide emotional range. Specially welcome is the carefree little *Rondo* by Thomas Pitfield with its witty pay-off.

Green, Gareth (organ)

English organ music (organ of Chesterfield Parish Church): LANG: *Tuba tune, Op. 15.* HOWELLS: *3 Psalm preludes, Op. 32.* ELGAR: *Sonata No. 1, Op. 28.* VAUGHAN WILLIAMS: *Rhosymedre (Hymn prelude).* WHITLOCK: *Hymn Preludes: on Darwell's 148th; on Song 13.* COCKER: *Tuba tune.*

(BB) *(*) Naxos 8.550582.

The organ as recorded here has no clarity of profile, and even the two characterful *Tuba tunes* fail to make their full effect. The sound in the *Hymn* and *Psalm Preludes* is washy and indistinct. Gareth Green plays the early Elgar *Sonata* very well but it makes an impact only in its more powerful moments, and it is difficult to find a volume level which reveals the unfocused, quieter detail while not having the climaxes too loud.

Grumiaux, Arthur (violin), István Hajdu (piano)

'Favourite violin encores': PARADIS: *Sicilienne.* MOZART: *Rondo, K.250; Divertimento in D, K.334: Minuet.* GLUCK: *Mélodie.* GRANADOS: *Danza española No. 5.* KREISLER: *Schön Rosmarin; Liebesleid; Liebesfreud; Rondino on a theme of Beethoven; Andantino in the style of Padre Martini.* VERACINI: *Allegro; Largo* (arr. CORTI). VIVALDI: *Siciliano* (arr. from Op. 3/11). LECLAIR: *Tambourin.* BEETHOVEN: *Minuet in G.* SCHUBERT: *Ave Maria; Ständchen.* DVORAK: *Humoresque in G flat, Op. 101/7; Songs my mother taught me, Op. 55/4; Sonatine in G, Op. 100: Larghetto.* MASSENET: *Thaïs: Méditation.* TCHAIKOVSKY: *Valse sentimentale, Op. 51/6.* ELGAR: *La Capricieuse.* FAURE: *Après un rêve, Op. 7/1; Les berceaux, Op. 23/1.* ALBENIZ: *Tango, Op. 165/2.* PONCE: *Estrellita.* SIBELIUS: *Nocturne, Op. 51/3.* PERGOLESI: *Andantino.* SCHUMANN: *Kinderszenen: Träumerei.* BACH/GOUNOD: *Ave Maria.* PAGANINI: *Sonata No. 12 in E min., Op. 3/6.* WIENIAWSKI: *Souvenir de Moscou, Op. 6.* RAVEL: *Pièce en forme de habanera; Tzigane.* SARASATE: *Zigeunerweisen, Op. 20/1.* FIOCCO: *Allegro.* BLOCH: *Baal Shem: Nigun.* KODALY: *Adagio.*

(B) *** Ph. Duo (ADD) 446 560-2 (2).

Marvellous fiddler as he is, Grumiaux is not an extrovert in the manner of a Perlman who likes to dazzle and be right on top of the microphones; instead, these are essentially intimate performances. Yet when fire is needed it is certainly forthcoming, as in the superb account of Ravel's *Tzigane*. But Grumiaux is completely at home in what are mostly elegant *morceaux de concert*, and especially the Kreisler encores. He brings a particularly nice touch of rubato to *Schön Rosmarin* and produces a ravishingly stylish *Liebesleid*, while the *Andantino in the style of Martini* is engagingly ingenuous. Schumann's *Träumerei* is made to sound as if originally conceived as a violin solo. The *Méditation* from *Thaïs* is delectably romantic without being oversweet, and the following *Valse sentimentale* of Tchaikovsky has just the right degree of restraint.

But Grumiaux's simplicity of style is heard at its most appealing in Wieniawski's *Souvenir de Moscou*, with its warm melody elegantly decorated and then let loose in a burst of Paganinian fireworks. István Hajdu accompanies with comparable taste, notably in Bach's unwitting contribution to Gounod's *Ave Maria*, while his simple introduction to Elgar's *La Capricieuse* is a model of how to set the scene for a salon piece of this kind. He is equally helpful in echoing Grumiaux in Schubert's lovely *Serenade* and in his discreet backing for Ponce's gently voluptuous *Estrellita*. The recording is most natural, without any edginess on the violin-tone, and the piano is pleasingly balanced within a warm acoustic.

Hamelin, Marc-André (piano)

'Live at Wigmore Hall': BEETHOVEN (arr. ALKAN): *Piano concerto No. 3: first movt.* CHOPIN (arr. BALAKIREV): *Piano concerto No. 1: Romanza.* ALKAN: *Trois grandes études.* BUSONI: *Sonatina No. 6 (Chamber fantasy on Carmen).* MEDTNER: *Danza festiva, Op. 38, No. 3.*

✪ *** Hyp. CDA 66765.

This is among the most spectacular piano issues of the last decade. It captures live one of the programmes given in June 1994 at Wigmore Hall by the French-Canadian pianist Marc-André Hamelin, in a series called 'Virtuoso Romantics'. Bizarre as the mixture is, it works magnificently, thanks not only to Hamelin's breathtaking virtuosity, finger-perfect, but to his magnetism. As well as the *Trois grandes études* of Alkan, he plays Alkan's arrangement of the first movement of Beethoven's *Third Piano concerto*. Thanks to his sharp clarity, one marvels afresh at the purposefulness of the writing, and he revels in Alkan's manic six-minute cadenza, which in dotty inspiration even quotes the finale of Beethoven's *Fifth Symphony*. Balakirev's arrangement of the Romanza from Chopin's *First Piano concerto* then offers yearning poetry, with two flamboyant display-pieces as encores: Busoni's *Carmen fantasy* and Medtner's *Danza festiva*.

'Kaleidoscope': WOODS: *Valse phantastique.* BEHR (trans. RACHMANINOV): *Polka de W.R.* HOFMANN: *Kaleidoskop; Nocturne.* HAMELIN: *Etudes Nos. 3 (d'après Paganini-Liszt) & 6 (Essercizio per pianoforte).* BLUMENFELD: *Etude pour la main gauche seule.* OFFENBACH: *Concert Paraphrase of 'The Song of the Soldiers of the Sea'.* MASSENET:

Valse folie. MOSZKOWSKI: *Etude in A flat min, Op. 72/13.* POULENC: *Intermezzo in A flat.* GODOWSKY: *Alt Wien.* MICHALOWSKI: *Etude d'après l'Impromptu en la bémol majeur de Fr. Chopin.* LOURIE: *Gigue.* BLANCHET: *Au jardin du vieux sérail, Op. 18/3.* CASELLA: *Deux contrastes.* VALLIER: *Toccatina.* GLAZUNOV (trans. HAMELIN): *Petit adagio.* KAPUSTIN: *Toccatina.*

*** Hyp. CDA 67275.

This collection of encores, most of them rarities, is a box of delights, with Marc-André Hamelin bringing out the fun as well as the brilliance. Consistently, one marvels that ten fingers can possibly play the notes involved, when the virtuosity demanded is almost beyond belief. Yet Hamelin is masterly at bringing out the wit of each piece, as in the opening item by a virtually unknown composer, Edna Bentz Woods, with waltz rhythms naughtily pointed. Hamelin's own tribute to Scarlatti in his *Etude No. 6* is in fact an amusing parody, very much tongue-in-cheek, and it is pure fun to have the American Marines' Hymn (drawn from Offenbach) elaborated as a virtuoso keyboard study. Hamelin also brings out the keyboard magic of such a piece as Blanchet's evocation of the garden of the seraglio or the transcription from Glazunov's ballet, *The Seasons*, with beauty as well as brilliance part of his message. Vivid recorded sound.

Hardenberger, Håkan (trumpet)

'*The virtuoso trumpet*' (with Roland Pöntinen): ARBAN: *Variations on themes from Bellini's 'Norma'.* FRANCAIX: *Sonatine.* TISNE: *Héraldiques.* HONEGGER: *Intrada.* MAXWELL DAVIES: *Sonata.* RABE: *Shazam!.* HARTMANN: *Fantasia brillante on the air Rule, Britannia.*

*** BIS CID 287.

This collection includes much rare and adventurous repertoire, not otherwise available and very unlikely to offer frequent access in live performance. Moreover, Hardenberger plays with electrifying bravura in the Maxwell Davies *Sonata* and the virtuoso miniatures. Antoine Tisné's five *Héraldiques* are eclectic but highly effective on the lips of such an assured player; *Scandé* and the following *Elégiaque* are notably characterful. But easily the most memorable item is the Françaix *Sonatine* (originally for violin and piano) in which two delicious brief outer movements frame a pleasing central *Sarabande.* Honegger's improvisatory *Intrada* is an effective encore piece. The recording is eminently realistic, with the CD giving superb presence.

Haskil, Clara (piano)

Clara Haskil: The Legacy:

Volume 1: Chamber music (with Arthur Grumiaux): BEETHOVEN: *Violin sonatas Nos. 1-10.* MOZART: *Violin sonatas Nos. 18; 21; 24; 26; 32; 34.*

(M) (***) Ph. (IMS) mono 442 625-2 (5).

Volume 3: Solo piano music: BEETHOVEN: *Sonatas Nos. 17 in D min. (Tempest), Op. 31/2; 18 in E flat, Op. 31/3 (two versions).* MOZART: *Sonata in C, K.330; 9 Variations on a Minuet by Jean-Pierre Duport, K.573.* RAVEL: *Sonatine.* Domenico SCARLATTI: *Sonatas in E flat, Kk. 193; B min., Kk. 87; F min., Kk. 386.* SCHUBERT: *Sonata No. 21 in B flat, D.960.* SCHUMANN: *Abegg variations, Op. 1; Bunte Blätter, Op. 99; Kinderszenen, Op. 15; Waldszenen, Op. 82.*

(M) **(*) Ph. (IMS) mono/stereo 442 635-2 (3).

Clara Haskil is a much-venerated pianist, as the very appearance of this 'Legacy' set shows. Each of the three volumes is available separately but single discs from the collection are not. The first volume (five CDs) is devoted to the Beethoven and Mozart sonatas with her long-standing partner, Arthur Grumiaux; the second (see above), of four CDs, is devoted to her various concerto recordings, including two of the Mozart *D minor*, K.466, one with the Wiener Symfoniker and Paul Sacher in mono (1954), the second with the Lamoureux Orchestra and Markevitch (1960); the third volume (three CDs) collects her solo repertoire, including two different accounts of the Beethoven sonatas (1955 and 1960).

The earliest recordings, the three Scarlatti sonatas, Ravel's *Sonatine* and the Schumann *Abegg variations* and *Piano concerto in A minor* (with Willem van Otterloo conducting the Hague Orchestra) come from 1951, and the last, the Mozart *Piano concertos in D minor*, K.466 and *C minor*, K.491, and the Beethoven *C minor Concerto*, from 1960, the year of her death. Although it is doubtless a truism, her playing is more private than public; hers is a reflective, inward-looking sensibility with nothing of the virtuoso or showman. Her musical dedication is total. Her Schumann is particularly searching and penetrating. And there is an innocence about her Mozart which makes it wonderfully fresh and immediate.

Perhaps part of the success of her partnership with Arthur Grumiaux in the cycle of Beethoven and Mozart sonatas may spring from the understanding she gained of the violin as well as the experience of her earlier partnerships with Enescu, Szigeti and Francescatti. Philips are reticent in disclosing whether they are mono or stereo: they are in fact mono. Notwithstanding, the sound is very pleasing indeed and the playing is beautifully natural yet innately aristocratic.

The solo recordings are equally self-recommending and her Schumann in particular is of exceptional insight. The set is accompanied by very perceptive notes by Max Harrison.

Headington, Christopher (piano)

British piano music of the twentieth century: BRITTEN: *Holiday diary.* DELIUS: *3 Preludes.* ELGAR: *Adieu; In Smyrna; Serenade.* HEADINGTON: *Ballade-image; Cinquanta.* IRELAND: *The island spell.* MOERAN: *Summer valley.* PATTERSON: *A Tunnel of time, Op. 66.*

*** Kingdom KCLD 2017.

The novelties here are fascinating. The Delius *Preludes* (1923) have much of the luminous atmosphere of the orchestral music, while Britten's *Holiday diary* (what a happy idea for a suite!), written when he was just twenty, is most winning. The Elgar pieces are well worth having, and Headington again reveals himself as an appealing composer. Both his pieces were written for fiftieth-birthday celebrations and the *Ballade-image* expressly seeks to conjure up an atmosphere combining the influences of Chopin and Debussy. It is most engaging. John Ireland's *Island spell* is beautifully played. A 69-minute recital which is skilfully planned to be listened to in sequence. Good, if not outstanding, recording.

Heifetz, Jascha (violin)

'*The Legendary Heifetz*' (with Emanuel Bay or Arpad Sandor piano): BAZZINI: *La ronde des lutins, Op. 25.* WIENIAWSKI: *Scherzo-tarantelle in G min., Op. 16.* DEBUSSY: *L'enfant prodigue; Prélude.* ALBENIZ: *Suite española: Sevillañas.* ELGAR: *La Capricieuse, Op. 17.* MOSZKOWSKI: *Guitarre, Op. 45/2.* FALLA: *Danza española No. 1.* Cyril SCOTT: *Tallahassee suite: Bygone memories.* DOHNANYI: *Ruralia hungarica, Op. 32a: Gypsy Andante.* CASTELNUOVO-TEDESCO: *Valse.* POULENC: *Mouvements perpétuelles No. 1.* VIVALDI: *Sonata in A, Op. 2/2.* PAGANINI: *Caprice, Op. 1/13.* BACH: *English suite No. 3 in G min., BWV 808: Gavottes Nos. 1 & 2 (Musette).* FRANCK: *Sonata in A: First movement Mosso* (with Artur Rubinstein).

(M) (**) EMI mono CDM5 67005-2.

Although the playing here offers the sophistication of bow-arm technique, and fabulous assurance for which Heifetz is famous, the recorded sound detracts very considerably from the listener's pleasure. All these recordings were made at Abbey Road (for the most part in 1934, and a few in 1937) but they are a credit neither to the original EMI engineers nor to the current EMI remastering process. The acoustic is dry, the violin uncomfortably close to the microphone, minimizing the breadth of tone, making it sound top-heavy and peaky. It is surely possible to do better than this! As it is, the extraordinary virtuosity of *La ronde des lutins*, Wieniawski's *Scherzo-tarantelle* and famous *Hora staccato*, the veiled beauty of tone in the Debussy *Prélude* to *L'enfant prodigue* and the evocation of Cyril Scott, are all but lost. The Vivaldi sonata, superbly stylish, and the excerpt from the Franck *Sonata* (with Rubinstein) seem almost to triumph over the sound, but, even so, one needs to replay this disc with the aural equivalent of top-quality dark-glasses to enjoy the music-making.

Hilton, Janet (clarinet), Keith Swallow (piano)

'*Rhapsodie*': POULENC: *Clarinet sonata.* RAVEL: *Pièce en forme d'habanera.* DEBUSSY: *Première rhapsodie.* SAINT-SAENS: *Clarinet sonata, Op. 167.* ROUSSEL: *Aria.* MILHAUD: *Duet concertante, Op. 351.*

(M) ** Chan. 6589.

There are some highly beguiling sounds here, and the languorous style adopted throughout is emphasized by the reverberant acoustic, which is less than ideal, creating the feeling of an empty hall. The Ravel and Debussy are given an evocative sentience and the Poulenc comes off very well too; overall, however, there is a feeling that a little more vitality and a more sharply focused sound-picture would have been advantageous.

Horowitz, Vladimir (piano)

'*The Horowitz Edition*': CHOPIN: *Sonata No. 2; Etudes, Opp. 10/12; 25/7; Scherzo No. 1.* RACHMANINOV: *Etudes-tableaux, Opp. 33/2; 39/5.* SCHUMANN: *Arabesque, Op. 18; Kinderszenen, Op. 15; Toccata, Op. 7.* LISZT: *Hungarian rhapsody No. 19* (trans. Horowitz). D. SCARLATTI: *Sonatas, Kk. 322, 455, 531.* BEETHOVEN: *Sonata No. 8.* SCHUBERT: *Impromptu No. 3.* DEBUSSY: *3 Préludes, Book II.* SCRIABIN: *Poème, Op. 32/1; Etudes, Opp. 2/1; 8/12* (S2K 53457 (2)). D. SCARLATTI: *Sonatas, Kk. 25, 33, 39, 52, 54, 96, 146, 162, 197, 198, 201, 303, 466, 474, 481, 491, 525, 547* (SK 53460). BACH/BUSONI: *Toccata, Adagio & Fugue, BWV 564.* SCHUMANN: *Fantaisie, Op. 17; Träumerei, Op. 15/7; Blumenstück, Op. 19.* SCRIABIN: *Sonatas Nos. 9-10; Poème, Op. 32/1; Etude in C sharp min., Op. 2/1.* CHOPIN: *Mazurkas, Opp. 30/4; 33/4; Etude, Op. 10/8; Ballade No. 1; Polonaise-fantaisie, Op. 61; Nocturne, Op. 72/1.* DEBUSSY: *Serenade for the doll; L'Isle joyeuse.* MOSZKOWSKI: *Etude in A flat, Op. 72/11.* MOZART: *Sonata No. 11, K.331.* HAYDN: *Sonata, Hob XVI/23.* LISZT: *Vallée d'Obermann.* (S3K 53461 (3)). CHOPIN: *Ballade No. 1; Nocturne, Op. 55/1; Polonaise, Op. 44.* D. SCARLATTI: *Sonatas, Kk. 55; 380.* SCHUMANN: *Arabeske, Op. 18; Traümerei.* SCRIABIN: *Etude, Op. 8/12.* HOROWITZ: *Variations on a theme from Carmen* (SK 53465). CLEMENTI: Excerpts from: *Sonatas, Opp. 12/2; 25/3; 50/1. Adagio sostenuto in F, from Gradus ad Parnassum, Book I/14.* J. S. BACH: *Chorale prelude: 'Ich ruf zu dir, Herr Jesu Christ'.* D. SCARLATTI: *Sonatas, Kk. 260; 319.* HAYDN: *Sonata, Hob XVI/48.* BEETHOVEN: *Sonata No. 28, Op. 101* (SK 53466). BEETHOVEN: *Sonatas Nos. 14, Op. 27/2 (Moonlight); 21, Op. 53 (Waldstein); 23, Op. 57 (Appassionata)* (SK 53467). CHOPIN: *Mazurkas, Opp. 7/3; 17/4; 30/3; 33/2; 41/2; 50/3; 59/3; Etudes, Op. 10/3-6, 12; 3 Nouvelles études: No. 2. Introduction & rondo, Op. 16; Waltzes, Op. 34/2; 64/2; Polonaises, Opp. 40/1; 53; Préludes, Op. 28/6, 15.* SCHUMANN: *Variations on a theme by Clara Wieck; Kreisleriana,*

Op. 16 (S2K 53468 (2)). SCHUBERT: *Impromptus, D.899/2, 4; D.935/1-2.* LISZT: *Consolation No. 2; Scherzo & Marsch.* DEBUSSY: *Pour les arpèges composées; La terrasse des audiences du clair de lune.* MENDELSSOHN: *Etude, Op. 104b/3* (SK 53471). SCRIABIN: *Feuillets d'album Opp. 45/1; 58; Etudes, Opp. 8/2, 8, 10-11; 42, 3-5; 65/3; 2 Poèmes, Op. 69; Vers la flamme.* MEDTNER: *Fairy tale, Op. 51/3.* RACHMANINOV: *Sonata No. 2; Prélude, Op. 32/12; Moment musical, Op. 16/3; Etudes-tableaux, Opp. 33/2, 5; 39/9.*

(M) (***) Sony mono SX13K 53456 (13).

The strength of this Sony box which runs to thirteen CDs and includes all Horowitz's recordings from 1962 to 1973 resides in the fact that nearly all these discs are essential repertory for Horowitz collectors but in any case are not now obtainable separately in the UK. Hardly any of these performances can be passed over, whether it be the Scarlatti sonatas or the stunning accounts of Scriabin's *Ninth* and *Tenth*. There is almost nothing that does not show him in top form – and the sound, though not ideal, is greatly improved.

'The Original Jacket Collection'

Disc 1: CHOPIN: *Sonata No. 2 in B flat min., Op. 35.* RACHMANINOV: *Etudes-tableaux, Op. 33/2 & Op. 39/5.* LISZT: *Hungarian Rhapsody No. 15.* (MS 6371).

Disc 2: SCHUMANN: *Kinderszenen, Op. 15; Toccata, Op. 7.* SCARLATTI: *Sonatas, L. 209, 430 & 483.* SCHUBERT: *Impromptu in G flat, D.899/3.* SCRIABIN: *Poème, Op. 32/1; Etudes, Op. 2/1 & Op. 8/12.* (MS 6411).

Disc 3: BEETHOVEN: *Sonata No. 8 (Pathétique), Op. 13.* DEBUSSY: *Préludes, Book II: Les Fées sont d'esquises danseuses; Bruyères; General Lavine – eccentric.* CHOPIN: *Etudes, Op. 10/12 & Op. 25/7; Scherzo No. 1, Op. 20.* (MS 6541).

Disc 4: SCARLATTI: *Sonatas, L. 21, 22, 118, 164, 187, 188, 203, 241, 349, 391, 424 & 465.* (MS 6658).

Disc 5: 'Historic Return to Carnegie Hall 1965': BACH/BUSONI: *Toccata in C.* SCHUMANN: *Fantasie in C, Op. 17.* SCRIABIN: *Sonata No. 9, Op. 68; Poème, Op. 32/1.* (MS 6765).

Disc 6: CHOPIN: *Mazurka, Op. 30/4; Etude, Op. 10/8; Ballade No. 1 in G min., Op. 23.* DEBUSSY: *Children's Corner: Serenade for the Doll.* SCRIABIN: *Etude, Op. 2/1.* MOSZKOWSKI: *Etude in A flat, Op. 72/11.* SCHUMANN: *Kinderszenen: Träumerei.* (MS 6766)

Disc 7: SCHUMANN: *Variations on a Theme by Clara Wieck; Kreisleriana, Op. 16.* (MS 7264).

Disc 8: RACHMANINOV: *Sonata No. 2 in B flat min., Op. 36; Prelude in C sharp min., Op. 32; Moment musical in B min., Op. 16. Etudes-tableaux: in B flat min. & C, Op. 33; in D, Op. 39.* (M 30464).

Disc 9: CHOPIN: *Polonaise-fantaisie, Op. 61; Mazurka in A min., Op. 17/4; Etude in G flat, Op.*

10/5; Introduction & Rondo, Op. 16; Waltz in A min., Op. 34/2; Polonaise in A flat, Op. 53. (M 30643)

Disc 10: SCRIABIN: *Feuillet d'album, Op. 45/1; Etudes: Op. 8/2, 8, 10 & 11; Op. 42/3, 4 & 5; Sonata No. 10, Op. 70; 2 Poèmes, Op. 69; Poème (Vers la flamme), Op. 72.* (M 31620).

(M) *** Sony (ADD) SX10K 89765 (10).

A welcome and attractive concept. The many treasures here are housed in their original LP covers (shrunk, of course, to CD size) and presented with their original 'liner notes'. (The print is very small indeed but legible with the aid of a magnifying glass.) There are essays by Goddard Lieberson and Thomas Frost and plenty of illustrations. The merits of the performances are too well known to need further exegesis, but the box reminds one of the sheer magic Horowitz commanded – the Rachmaninov is in a class of its own, the Scarlatti sonatas are of miraculous delicacy, and there has never been finer Scriabin (with the possible exception of Sofronitzky). But this will be familiar to most readers (except the most youthful), and the nostalgic presentation will lend it an additional lustre.

'Discovered treasures (1962-1972)': BACH/BUSONI: *Chorale prelude: Ich ruf zu dir, Herr Jesu Christ.* CHOPIN: *Nouvelle étude No. 1 in A flat; Etude in E flat min., Op. 10/6; Prelude in D flat (Raindrop), Op. 28/15.* CLEMENTI: *Piano sonata in E flat, Op. 12/2: Rondo. Gradus ad Parnassum, Book I, No. 14: Adagio sostenuto in F; Piano sonata in B flat, Op. 25/3: Rondo. Piano sonata in A, Op. 50/1: Adagio.* LISZT: *Consolation in E. medtner: Fairy tale in A, Op. 51/3.* D. SCARLATTI: *Sonatas in G, Kk. 547; B min., Kk. 197; F sharp min., Kk. 25; D min., Kk. 52; G, Kk. 201; C min., Kk. 303.* SCRIABIN: *Feuillet d'album, Op. 58; Etude, Op. 65/3.*

*** Sony (ADD) SK 48093-2.

The earliest of these recordings, the Liszt *Consolation*, comes from 1962, and the last, the Scriabin *Feuillet d'album* and *Etude*, Op. 65, No. 3, from 1972. All were made in the studio and were approved by Horowitz himself but were never included on records, purely for planning reasons. Horowitz was fastidious in seeing that each of the LPs he released made a logical programme, and hence there was in the Archives quite a lot of unused studio material.

'A Reminiscence': SCHUBERT: *Impromptu in G flat, D.899/3.* CHOPIN: *Waltz in C sharp min., Op. 64/2; Préludes in B min., Op. 28/6; D flat, Op. 13; Mazurka in E min., Op. 41/2.* SCARLATTI: *Sonata in D, Kk.491.* BACH (arr. BUSONI): *Chorale Prelude: Ich ruf' zu dir, Herr Jesus Christ (BWV 639).* RACHMANINOV: *Prelude in G sharp min., Op. 32; Moments musicaux, Op. 16/3.* BEETHOVEN: *Sonata No. 14 (Moonlight): 1st movement only.* LISZT: *Consolation No. 2 in E.* SCRIABIN: *Feuillets d'album, Op. 45/1 & Op. 58; Etude in A flat, Op. 8/8.* DEBUSSY: *Préludes, Book II: La terasse des audiences du clair de lune; Bruyères.*

SCHUMANN: *Kinderszenen*: **excerpts, including** *Träumerie.*

*** Sony (ADD) SK 89669.

The reminiscence (in the accompanying leaflet) is by Thomas Frost who was Horowitz's record producer from 1962 to 1974 and 1985 until the great pianist's death in 1989. It is he who has chosen the programme 'from some of Horowitz's favourite composers and pieces his audiences loved most'. It has been judiciously compiled opening with a miraculously lovely account of Schubert's *Impromptu in G flat*, as fine if not finer than any on record, and closing with the simple but no less haunting *Träumerie* of Schumann. The Scriabin pieces are exquisitely played too, indeed there is nothing here that is unmemorable. It is a pity that the whole of Beethoven's *Moonlight Sonata* was not included, for with only 62 minutes' playing time there was plenty of room for it. Nevertheless the recordings are of uniformly high quality and the only snag is the respiratory afflictions affecting the audience at the five live performances, recorded at Symphony Hall, Boston, or Carnegie Hall, New York. Included are the first of the two Debussy items and one wonders why audiences have such difficulty in containing their coughs during the music of this composer.

Recital: BACH/BUSONI: *Chorale prelude: Nun komm, der Heiden Heiland.* MOZART: *Piano sonata No. 10 in C, K.330.* CHOPIN: *Mazurka in A min., Op. 17/4; Scherzo No. 1 in B min., Op. 20; Polonaise No. 6 in A flat, Op. 53.* LISZT: *Consolation No. 3 in D flat.* SCHUBERT: *Impromptu in A flat, D.899/4.* SCHUMANN: *Novellette in F, Op. 21/1.* RACHMANINOV: *Prelude in G sharp min., Op. 32/12.* SCRIABIN: *Etude in C sharp min., Op. 2/1.* MOSZKOWSKI: *Etude in F, Op. 72/6* (**recording of performances featured in the film** *Vladimir Horowitz - The Last Romantic*).

*** DG (IMS) 419 045-2.

Recorded when he was over eighty, this playing betrays remarkably little sign of frailty. The Mozart is beautifully elegant and the Chopin *A minor Mazurka*, Op. 17, No. 4, could hardly be more delicate. The only sign of age comes in the *B minor Scherzo*, which does not have the leonine fire and tremendous body of his famous 1950 recording. However, it is pretty astonishing for all that.

'The studio recordings': SCHUMANN: *Kreisleriana, Op. 16.* D. SCARLATTI: *Sonatas in B min., Kk. 87; in E, Kk. 135.* LISZT: *Impromptu (Nocturne) in F sharp; Valse oubliée No. 1.* SCRIABIN: *Etude in D sharp min., Op. 8/12.* SCHUBERT: *Impromptu in B flat, D.935/3.* SCHUBERT/TAUSIG: *Marche militaire, D.733/1.*

✪ *** DG (IMS) 419 217-2.

The subtle range of colour and articulation in the Schumann is matched in his Schubert *Impromptu*, and the Liszt *Valse oubliée* offers the most delicious, twinkling rubato. Hearing Scarlatti's *E major Sonata*

played with such crispness, delicacy and grace must surely convert even the most dedicated authenticist to the view that this repertoire can be totally valid in terms of the modern instrument. The Schubert–Tausig *Marche militaire* makes a superb encore, played with the kind of panache that would be remarkable in a pianist half Horowitz's age. With the passionate Scriabin *Etude* as the central romantic pivot, this recital is uncommonly well balanced to show Horowitz's special range of sympathies.

'In Moscow': D. SCARLATTI: *Sonata in E, Kk. 380.* MOZART: *Sonata No. 10 in C, K.330.* RACHMANINOV: *Preludes in G, Op. 32/5; in G sharp min., Op. 32/12.* SCRIABIN: *Etudes in C sharp min., Op. 2/1; in D sharp min., Op. 8/12.* LISZT/SCHUBERT: *Soirées de Vienne; Petrarch Sonnet 104.* CHOPIN: *Mazurkas, Op. 30/4; Op. 7/3.* SCHUMANN: *Kinderszenen: Träumerei.*

*** DG 419 499-2.

This is familiar Horowitz repertoire, played with characteristic musical discernment and spontaneity. Technically the pianism may not quite match his finest records of the analogue era, but it is still both melting and dazzling. The sound too is really excellent, much better than he ever received from his American engineers in earlier days.

'The indispensable Horowitz': CHOPIN: *Polonaise-fantaisie in A flat, Op. 61; Scherzi Nos. 1 in B min., Op. 20; 2 in B flat, Op. 31; Etudes in C sharp min., Op. 10/4; in C sharp min., Op. 25/7; Nocturnes in B, Op. 9/3; in C sharp min., Op. 27/1; in E min., Op. 72/1; Barcarolle, Op. 60; Polonaise in A flat, Op. 53; Ballade No. 1 in G min., Op. 23.* D. SCARLATTI: *Keyboard sonatas, Kk. 87, 127, & 135.* RACHMANINOV: *Humoresque, Op. 10/5; Preludes in G min., Op. 23/5; in G, Op. 32/5; Barcarolle, Op. 10/3.* MOSZKOWSKI: *Etincelle, Op. 36/6; Etude in F, Op. 72/6.* LISZT: *Hungarian rhapsodies Nos. 2 & 15 (Rákóczy march)* (both arr. HOROWITZ); *Mephisto waltz No. 1.* BIZET/HOROWITZ: *Variations on a theme from Carmen.* SCRIABIN: *Etudes in C sharp min., Op. 2/1; in B flat min., Op. 8/7; in D sharp min., Op. 8/12; in C sharp min., Op. 42/5.* SOUSA/HOROWITZ: *The Stars and Stripes forever.*

✪ (B) *** RCA stereo/mono, 74321 63471-2 (2).

The notes with this remarkably generous collection include a quote from Neville Cardus, who once described Horowitz as 'the greatest pianist alive or dead'. Later he added that this comment 'perhaps was not positive enough about pianists still unborn'. His eulogy still holds true at the time of writing and the programme here demonstrates why. If you look for astonishing, barnstorming virtuosity you will find it in Horowitz's own *Carmen variations*, the Liszt *Hungarian rhapsody* 'arrangements' or the closing *Stars and Stripes*; but if you seek bravura delicacy, the Moszkowski *F major Etude* is a supreme example, while his Scarlatti is unforgettable. Romantic poetry constantly illuminates his Chopin (the *Barcarolle* and

G minor Ballade are especially memorable) and his Rachmaninov (the *G major Prelude* is exquisite), while throughout this is playing of unique distinction which offers infinite rewards.

Scriabin, another of Horowitz's special composers, is generously represented, not only by Horowitz's favourite, *D sharp minor Etude* (taken from a 1982 live recital), but also by the more prolix *C sharp minor*, recorded three decades earlier. What is surprising is the fairly consistent quality of the sound: one of the earliest mono recordings (from 1950), of Scriabin's Op. 2/1, is remarkably warmly coloured. Of course, the later stereo recordings are ever finer, as the commanding opening *Polonaise-fantaisie* of Chopin (1982) readily shows. But on sonic grounds there is little to criticize; artistically this pair of discs are in a class of their own.

Hough, Stephen (piano)

'Piano album':

Disc 1: MACDOWELL: *Hexentanz, Op. 12.* CHOPIN: *Chant polonaise No. 1.* QUILTER: *The crimson petal; The fuchsia tree.* DOHNANYI: *Capriccio in F min., Op. 28/8.* PADEREWSKI: *Minuet in G, Op. 14/1; Nocturne in B flat, Op. 16/4.* SCHLOZER: *Etude in A flat, Op. 1/2.* GABRILOVICH: *Mélodie in E; Caprice-burlesque.* RODGERS: *My favourite things.* WOODFORDE-FINDEN: *Kashmiri song.* FRIEDMAN: *Music box.* SAINT-SAENS: *Carnival of the animals: The Swan* (arr. GODOWSKY). ROSENTHAL: *Papillons.* GODOWSKY: *The Gardens of Buitenzorg.* LEVITZKI: *Waltz in A, Op. 2. palmgren: En route, Op. 9.* MOSZKOWSKI: *Siciliano, Op. 42/2; Caprice espagnol, Op. 37.*

Disc 2: CZERNY: *Variations brillantes, Op. 14.* LEVITZKI: *The Enchanted nymph.* SCHUMANN: *Der Kontrebandiste.* RUBINSTEIN: *Melody in F.* LIEBERMANN: *Gargoyles, Op. 29.* REBIKOV: *The Musical snuffbox.* RAVINA: *Etude de style (Agilité), Op. 40/1.* WOODFORDE-FINDEN: *Till I wake.* QUILTER: *Weep you no more.* RODGERS: *March of the Siamese children.* MOSZKOWSKI: *Valse mignonne; Serenata, Op. 15/1.* BACH: *Violin sonata No. 2: Bourrée.* GODOWSKY: *Erinnerungen.* BIZET: *L'Arlésienne: Adagietto.* TAUSIG: *Ungarische Zigeunerweisen.*

(BB) *** Virgin Classics VBD5 61498-2 (2).

There are few young pianists who can match Stephen Hough in communicating on record with the immediacy and vividness of live performance; this dazzling two-disc recital of frothy show-pieces presents the perfect illustration. Indeed, this Virgin Classics bargain Double captures more nearly than almost any other recent record – even those of Horowitz – the charm, sparkle and flair of legendary piano virtuosos from the golden age of Rosenthal, Godowsky and Lhévinne.

So many of the items are frivolous that it may be surprising that any serious pianist can stomach them;

yet on the first disc the very opening item, MacDowell's *Hexentanz (Witches' dance)*, launches the listener into pure pianistic magic, and the second, with Czerny's fizzing *Variations brillantes*, similarly offers totally uninhibited playing, with articulation and timing that are the musical equivalent of being tickled up and down the spine.

One would hardly expect Hough's own arrangements of sentimental little songs by Roger Quilter or Amy Woodforde-Finden to be memorable – yet, in their tender expressiveness, they are most affecting. In the grand tradition, Hough does a Valse-caprice arrangement he himself has made of *My favourite things* from *The Sound of Music*, as well as an equally attractive but simpler arrangement of Rodgers's *March of the Siamese children.* Firework pieces by Rosenthal and Moszkowski, among others, go along with old-fashioned favourites like Paderewski's *Minuet in G*, Rubinstein's *Melody in F* (here sounding fresh and unfaded) and Godowsky's arrangement of the Saint-Saëns *Swan*.

Not all of Lowell Liebermann's *Gargoyles* are menacing (there is a charming *Adagio semplice*) but the *Feroce* marking for the closing number is pungently realized. Then follow two different miniature portrayals of a *Musical snuffbox*, the first, by Vladimir Rebikov, not a whit less delightful than the more famous version by Liadov. The programme ends with an arresting account of Tausig's *Ungarische Zigeunerweisen*. Altogether it is a feast for piano lovers, very well recorded, the first disc in 1986 (in London and New York), the second in 1991 using the BBC's Manchester studio.

'New piano album':

LISZT: *Concert paraphrase of Schubert: Soirées de Vienne.* SCHUBERT (arr. GODOWSKY): *Moment musical in D min., D.780/3; Die schöne Müllerin: Morgengrüss.* GODOWSKI: *Alt Wien.* MOSZKOWSKI: *Etincelle Op. 36/6.* PADEREWSKI: *Mélodie in G flat, Op. 16/2.* CHAMINADE: *Pierrette (Air de ballet), Op. 41; Autrefois, Op. 87/4.* KALMAN (arr. HOUGH): *Hello young lovers; Carousel waltz.* TRAD. (arr. HOUGH): *Londonderry air.* RACHMANINOV: *Humoresque, Op. 10/5; Mélodie, Op. 3/3* (revised 1940 version). TCHAIKOVSKY: *Humoresque, Op. 10/2.* TCHAIKOVSKY, arr. WILD: *Swan Lake: Pas de quatre.* TCHAIKOVSKY/PABST (arr. HOUGH): *Sleeping Beauty paraphrase.*

*** Hyp. CDA 67043.

In his latest collection, Stephen Hough demonstrates yet again the flair with which he tackles trivial party pieces like the twenty varied items here. Such encore material has in his hands a sparkle and point that magick the ear whether in the virtuoso display of pieces by Godowsky, Moszkowski and Rachmaninov or in the loving lyricism of pieces by Chaminade, Kalman and others. As well as offering two witty showpieces of his own, Hough also plays his arrangements of two Richard Rodgers numbers and the *Londonderry air*. Among the four Tchaikovsky items, it is good to have the haunting little *Humoresque*, best known through Stravinsky's ballet *The Fairy's kiss*. Vivid sound.

'*English Piano Album*': RAWSTHORNE: *Bagatelles.* REYNOLDS: *2 Poems in Homage to Delius; 2 Poems in Homage to Fauré.* HOUGH: *Valses enigmatiques Nos. 1-2.* ELGAR: *In Smyrna.* BANTOCK: *Song to the Seals.* BOWEN: *Reverie d'amour, Op. 20/2; Serious Dance, Op. 51/2; The Way to Polden, Op. 76.* BRIDGE: *The Dew Fairy; Heart's Ease.* LEIGHTON: *6 Studies (Study-Variations), Op. 56.*

*** Hyp. CDA 67267.

This recital disc from Stephen Hough has a different aim from his previous collections of charmers, starting with four gritty and tough miniatures of Rawsthorne, thoughtful and intense, balanced at the end by Kenneth Leighton's *Study Variations*. Those do not make for easy listening either, inspiring Hough to superb pianism over six sharply characterized pieces, at times echoing Bartók in their angry energy, at others full of fantasy, with the second a slow and concentrated piece full of harmonic clusters, and with the final *Study* a breathtaking virtuoso exercise. What all these very varied items demonstrate is Hough's profound love of keyboard sound and textures, and his rare gift of bringing out the full beauty of that sound. His own pieces, the two *Valses enigmatiques*, each based on his own initials linked to those of friends, both bear that out, the one with light textures, the other with Debussian parallel chords. He also offers a warmly sympathetic arrangement of a song he recorded earlier with the tenor, Robert White, on a Hyperion disc of ballads, Bantock's *Song to the Seals*.

It is evidence too of Hough's wizardry that he makes the Elgar piece, *In Smyrna*, sound so bewitching, with echoes of the lovely solo viola serenade in the overture, *In the South*, written some two years before in 1903 and also with a Mediterranean inspiration. The four pieces by Stephen Reynolds, two with echoes of Delius, two of Fauré, are consciously relaxed exercises outside the composer's more astringent idiom. The two pieces by Frank Bridge bring out his love of delicate keyboard textures, while the three York Bowen pieces are simple and song-like using an almost cabaret-style of piano writing. In all this music Hough's magic is presented in full, clear Hyperion sound.

Hurford, Peter (organ)

'*Great Romantic organ works*' (played on organs at Ratzeburg Cathedral, the Royal Festival Hall, in the Basilica of Saint-Sermin, Toulouse): WIDOR: *Symphony No. 5: Toccata; Symphony No. 6, Op. 42: Allegro.* FRANCK: *Chorals Nos. 1-3; Pièce héroïque.* MENDELSSOHN: *Preludes and fugues: in C min., Op. 37/1 and D min., Op. 37/3; Sonata in A, Op. 65/3.* GIGOUT: *10 pièces: Scherzo.* KARG-ELERT: *March triomphale: on Nun danket alle Gott.* VIERNE: *24 pièces en style libre: Berceuse; Symphony No. 1, Op.*

14: Final. BRAHMS: *Choral preludes: Es ist ein Ros entsprungen; Herzlich tut mich verlangen; Schmücke dich.* LISZT: *Prelude and fugue on B-A-C-H.* SCHUMANN: *Four sketches, Op. 58/4: Allegretto.* REGER: *Introduction and passacaglia in D min.* BOELLMAN: *Suite gothique, Op. 25.*

(B) *** Double Decca 466 742-2 (2).

A self-recommending set of organ favourites at bargain price in splendid digital sound, for the most part played on the magnificent organ at Ratzeburg Cathedral. Not many collections of Romantic organ music match this in colour, breath of repertoire and brilliance of performance. Hurford's playing defies all considerations of Victorian heaviness, and the programme includes many key repertoire works. You cannot go wrong here.

'*Organ favourites*': Sydney Opera House organ: BACH: *Toccata and fugue in D min., BWV 565; Jesu, joy of man's desiring.* ALBINONI: *Adagio* (arr. GIAZOTTO). PURCELL: *Trumpet tune in D.* MENDELSSOHN: *A Midsummer Night's Dream: Wedding march.* FRANCK: *Chorale No. 2 in B min.* MURRILL: *Carillon.* WALFORD DAVIES: *Solemn melody.* WIDOR: *Organ Symphony No. 5: Toccata.* Royal Festival Hall organ: FRANCK: *Pièce héroïque.* Ratzeburg Cathedral organ: BOELLMANN: *Suite gothique.*

(B) **(*) Decca Eclipse 452 166-2.

Superb sound here, wonderfully free and never oppressive, even in the most spectacular moments. The Widor is spiritedly genial when played within the somewhat mellower registration of the magnificent Sydney instrument (as contrasted with the Ratzeburg Cathedral organ), and the pedals have great sonority and power. The Murrill *Carillon* is equally engaging alongside the Purcell *Trumpet tune*, while Mendelssohn's wedding music has never sounded more resplendent. The Bach is less memorable, and the Albinoni *Adagio*, without the strings, is not an asset to the collection either. The *Pièce héroïque* and the *Suite gothique* have been added for the Eclipse reissue.

Isbin, Sharon (guitar)

'*Latin romances*': de la MAZA: *Zapateado.* RODRIGO: *Invocación y Danza.* BARRIOS: *La Catedral.* ABREU: *Quejas (Lament).* JOBIM: *Estrada do Sol.* TARREGA: *Capricho árabe.* BROUWER: *El Decameron negro.* VILLA-LOBOS: *Sentimental melody; Etude No. 8.* ALBENIZ: *Mallorca; Asturias.*

(BB) *** Virgin Classics 2 x 1 VBD5 61627-2 (2) (with RODRIGO: *Concierto de Aranjuez; Fantasia para un gentilhombre* ***. SCHWANTNER: *From afar ...* (fantasy) **).

Sharon Isbin is a masterly guitarist and has inherited Segovia's gift of achieving natural spontaneity in the recording studio, so that this solo recital is consistently fresh and communicative, the playing brilliant and evocative by turns. Rodrigo's *Invocación y Danza* and Tárrega's *Capricho árabe* are only two of the familiar pieces which project magnetically, as does the Albéniz *Asturias* which ends the recital so vibrantly. The novelty is *The Black Decameron* of Leo Brouwer, a programmatic triptych which is sharply characterized and atmospherically realized. Isbin is given great presence by the recording, and he plays the key Rodrigo concertante works with no less distinction. The Schwantner piece is less recommendable, but this two-disc set remains a bargain.

Isoir, André (organ)

French Renaissance organ music (Koenig organ at Bon Pasteur, Angers): *Bransles, Galliards* and other dances by GERVAIS; FRANCISQUE; ATTAIGNANT. JANEQUIN: *Allez my fault.* SANDRIN: *Quand ien congneu.* **Eustache du** CAURROY: *Fantaisie sur une jeune fillette.* ATTAIGNANT: *3 Versets du Te Deum; Prélude aux treize motets; Kyrie cunctipotens. Fantaisies* **by** GUILLET; LE JEUNE; RACQUET. RICHARD: *Prélude in D min.* THOMELIN: *Duo.* LA BARRE: *Sarabande.* **Henri du** MONT: *Prélude No. 10 in D min.; Pavane in D min.* ANON.: *Fantaisie; Ave Maris Stella.* ROBERDAY: *Fugue et caprice No. 3 in C; Fugues Nos. 10 in G min.; 12 in D.*

(M) *** Cal. CAL 6901.

The Angers organ has a spicy régale stop which is used tellingly in several of the dance movements included in the programme, notably Gervaise's *Bransle de Bourgogne* and a *Basse dance, Bransle* and *Gaillarde* of Attaignant and also in Sandrin's *Quand ien congneu.* A warmer palette is found for Eustache du Caurroy's agreeable *Fantaisie sur une jeune fillette.* This is a French equivalent to the divisions found in Elizabethan music, whereas the piquant *Fantaisie sur orgue ou espinette* of Guillaume Costeley is very succinct. Attaignant's *Kyrie cunctipotens* and the *Third Fantaisie* of Charles Guillet are essentially chorale preludes, as is the more elaborate *Fantaisie* of Charles Racquet, but the *Second Fantaisie* of Claude Le Jeune, a remarkable piece, anticipates the chorale variations of Bach, but using two different fugal subjects. Joseph Thomelin's (two-part) *Duo* is a winning miniature and Joseph de la Barre's *Sarabande* also has a gentle charm, while the three *Fugues* of François Roberday show impressive craftsmanship. No. 12, which ends the recital resplendently, is a good example of Isoir's imaginative registrations, which find ear-tickling contrasts between the plangent and mellow timbres that this organ offers, while the music is kept very much alive. A generous (76 minutes) and stimulating recital, although not to be played all at one sitting.

Isserlis, Steven (cello)

'Cello world' (with Thomas Adès, Maggie Cole, Michael Tilson Thomas, Dudley Moore): BEETHOVEN: *Andante and Variations.* SCHUMANN: *Violin sonata: Intermezzo.* FAURE: *Morceau de concours.* LEONARD: *L'âne et l'ânier.* DVORAK: *Romantic piece.* SEIBER: *Dance suite* (all arr. ISSERLIS). DEBUSSY: *Nocturne et Scherzo.* BERLIOZ: *La captive.* TAVENER: *The child lives* (both with Felicity Lott). SAINT-SAENS: *Le Cygne.* VILLA-LOBOS: *O canto do cisne negro.* MARTINU: *Duo.* RACHMANINOV: *Lied.* SCRIABIN: *Romance.* POPPER: *Dance of the elves.* ISSERLIS: *Souvenir russe.* TSINTSADZE: *Chonguri.* VINE: *Inner world.*

*** RCA 09026 68928-2.

This is a cello recital with a difference, attractive in an off-beat way. The last and longest item, *Inner world*, by the Australian Carl Vine, is for amplified cello with electronic support, a cult piece, modern but not difficult. Otherwise, there are only two regular cello show-pieces, Saint-Saëns's *Swan*, exquisitely portrayed, and Popper's *Dance of the elves*, with Isserlis flamboyant. The Beethoven *Variations*, with harpsichord accompaniment, were transcribed from a *Sonatina for mandolin and piano* (1796), but most of the transcriptions are from violin originals, including the comic Leonard piece, full of ever more exaggerated hee-haws, set against the carter's song in the middle. In most items, Thomas Adès is the inspired accompanist and inspired too is the accompaniment by Maggie Cole, relishing the witty 1920s parodies in Matyas Seiber's *Dance suite.* The two items with Felicity Lott bring extra freshness and beauty, not just in the Berlioz song but also in the Tavener piece with accompaniment for cello alone. First-rate sound.

(i) Jackson, Francis (organ of York Minster), (ii) Michael Austin (organ of Birmingham Town Hall)

'Pipes of splendour': (i) COCKER: *Tuba tune.* PURCELL: *Trumpet tune and almand.* JACKSON: *Division on 'Nun Danket'.* LEIGHTON: *Paean.* DUBOIS: *Toccata in G.* GUILMANT: *Allegretto in B min., Op. 19.* GIGOUT: *Scherzo in E.* MULET: *Carillon-Sortie.* **(ii)** REGER: *Toccata and fugue in D min./major, Op. 59/5-6.* DUPRE: *Prelude and fugue in B, Op. 7.* FRANCK: *Final in B flat.*

(M) *** Chan. (ADD) 6602.

It was Francis Jackson who made Cocker's *Tuba tune* (with its boisterous, brassy, principal theme) justly famous, and it makes a splendid opener. But the entire programme shows that it is possible to play and record an English organ without the result sounding flabby. The *Toccata* of Dubois is very winning and, in its quieter central section, the detail is beautifully clear, as it is in the charming Guilmant *Allegretto* and the lightly articulated Gigout *Scherzo.* Mulet's *Carillon-Sortie* rings out gloriously and Leighton's *Paean* brings a blaze of tone. The items played in Birmingham by Michael Austin are no less stimulating, especially the two French pieces, which have a fine piquant bite, while the Reger isn't in the least dull. Superb transfers of demonstration-standard analogue recording from the early 1970s.

Jacoby, Ingrid (piano)

MUSSORGSKY: *Pictures at an Exhibition.* PROKOFIEV: *Piano Sonata No. 7.* TCHAIKOVSKY: *The Seasons: excerpts.*

*** Dutton CDSA 6802.

There are few keyboard warhorses to compare with Mussorgsky's *Pictures at an Exhibition.* Quite apart from the virtuoso demands of piano writing with its chunky chords that rarely fit under the fingers, there is always the colourful rivalry of the ever-popular orchestral arrangement by Ravel. It says much not just for the brilliant technique but also the artistry of the American pianist, Ingrid Jacoby, that she so clarifies textures, with pedal lightly used, making the writing seem far more pianistic than usual, yet retaining the vivid pictorial detail and the tension and excitement of the final sequence leading to the culminating evocation of *The Great Gate at Kiev.* The Prokofiev *Sonata*, another warhorse, arguably his most striking piano work, demands great virtuosity, yet brings similar clarity and incisiveness, with four of the most memorable movements from Tchaikovsky's suite, *The Seasons*, as an agreeable interlude. Exceptionally vivid piano sound.

John, Keith (organ)

'*Great European organs No. 10*': Tonhalle, Zurich: MUSSORGSKY (trans. John): *Pictures at an exhibition.* ALAIN: *3 Danses (Joies; Deuils; Luttes).*

*** Priory PRCD 262.

Keith John has made his own transcription of Mussorgsky's *Pictures* – and pretty remarkable it sounds. Only the pieces like *Tuileries* that require pointed articulation come off less well than on orchestra or piano, but *Gnomus* and *Bydlo* and, especially, the picture of the two Polish Jews are all remarkably powerful, while the closing sequence of *Catacombs*, *The Hut on fowl's legs* and *The Great Gate of Kiev* are superb. The three Alain pieces make a substantial encore. This is as much a demonstration CD as an orchestral version of the Mussorgsky.

'*Great European organs No. 26*': Gloucester Cathedral: STANFORD: *Fantasia and toccata in D min., Op. 57.* REGER: *Prelude and fugue in E, Op. 56/1.* SHOSTAKOVICH: *Lady Macbeth of Mtsensk: Passacaglia.* SCHMIDT: *Chaconne in C min.* RAVANELLO: *Theme and variations in B min.*

*** Priory PRCD 370.

Keith John, having shown what he can do with Mussorgsky, turns his attention here to little-known nineteenth- and twentieth-century organ pieces. The programme is imaginatively chosen and splendidly played – indeed, the bravura is often thrilling – and most realistically recorded on the superb Gloucester organ. Both the Schmidt *Chaconne* and Ravanello *Theme and variations* are fine works,

and the Shostakovich *Passacaglia*, an opera entr'acte, was originally conceived as a work for organ.

'*Toccata!*' (organ of St Mary's, Woodford): BACH/BUSONI: *Partita No. 2 in D min., BWV 1004: Chaconne* (trans. K. John). BACH/RACHMANINOV: *Partita No. 3 in E, BWV 1006: suite* (trans. K. John). GUILLOU: *Sinfonietta.* HEILLER: *Tanz-Toccata.*

(M) *** Priory PRCD 002.

It was a most imaginative idea to use Busoni's arrangement of Bach's famous *D minor Partita for unaccompanied violin* as a basis for an organ transcription, and the result is like nothing you have ever heard before – especially when Keith John gets cracking on the pedals. The three excerpts from the *E major Partita* (as originally transcribed by Rachmaninov) are hardly less successful: how well the opening *Prelude* sounds on the organ, and one can forgive Keith John's affectionately mannered touch on the famous *Gavotte*. We then have a dramatic, almost bizarre change of mood and colour with Jean Guillou's 'neoclassical' (more 'neo' than 'classical') *Sinfonietta*. Even though it opens with a Bachian flourish, its colouring and atmosphere are highly exotic, the austere central *Allegretto* leading to a somewhat jazzy but naggingly insistent, partly contrapuntal and plangent, *Gigue*. Heiller's *Tanz-Toccata*, with its complex rhythms and chimerical changes of time-signature, finally brings a positive link with Stravinsky's *Rite of spring* during the insistent motoric final pages. After his remarkable Bach performances, Keith John's kaleidoscopic registration here shows how adaptable and versatile is the modern (1972) organ at St Mary's, Woodford.

Johnson, Emma (clarinet)

'*A clarinet celebration*' (with Gordon Back, piano): WEBER: *Grand duo concertante; Variations concertantes.* BURGMULLER: *Duo.* GIAMPIERI: *Carnival of Venice.* SCHUMANN: *Fantasy pieces, Op. 73.* LOVREGLIO: *Fantasia de concerto, La Traviata.*

*** ASV CDDCA 732.

ASV have reissued and repackaged Emma Johnson's outstanding 72-minute collection, dating from 1990. It is still at full price but is worth it. These are party pieces rather than encores, all of them drawing electric sparks of inspiration from this winning young soloist. Even in such virtuoso nonsense as the Giampieri *Carnival of Venice* and the Lovreglio *Fantasia* Johnson draws out musical magic, while the expressiveness of Weber and Schumann brings heartfelt playing, with phrasing creatively individual. Gordon Back accompanies brilliantly, and the sound is first rate.

'*British clarinet music*' (with Malcolm Martineau (piano); (i) Judith Howard (soprano)): IRELAND: *Fantasy sonata in E flat.* VAUGHAN WILLIAMS: *6 Studies in English folksong;* (i) *3 Vocalises for soprano voice and clarinet.* BAX: *Clarinet sonata.* BLISS: *Pastoral;* (i) *2 Nursery rhymes.* STANFORD: *Clarinet sonata.*

*** ASV CDDCA 891.

Stanford's *Sonata* has the usual Brahmsian flavour but uses an Irish lament for the expressive central *Adagio*; then the finale has the best of both worlds by combining both influences. Vaughan Williams's *Six Studies in English folksong* (1927) are beguilingly evocative, while the *Vocalises* for soprano voice and clarinet are brief but rather touching; they were written in the last year of the composer's life. Both the Bax two-movement *Sonata* and the Ireland *Fantasy sonata* are fine works, and Bliss's *Pastoral* is wartime nostalgia, written while the composer was in France during the First World War. Needless to say, Emma Johnson plays everything with her usual spontaneity and musicianship, and she has a fine partner in Malcolm Martineau, while Judith Howard's contribution is pleasingly melismatic. Excellent, atmospheric recording, made in the London Henry Wood Hall.

Juilliard String Quartet

'*50 Years*', Volume 1: BARTOK: *String quartets Nos. 3-4; 6.*

(M) *** Sony mono/stereo SMK 62705.

This CD collects three Bartók performances, one from each of the Juilliards' cycles, in 1949, 1963 and 1981. It is discussed in our main volume under the composer.

'*50 Years*', Volume 2: BACH: *The Art of fugue: Contrapuncti 1-4.* BEETHOVEN: *String quartets Nos. 9 in C (Rasumovsky), Op. 59/3; 16 in F, Op. 135.* HAYDN: *String quartet in D, Op. 76/5: Largo (only).*

(M) ** Sony mono/stereo SMK 62706.

The first four *Contrapuncti* of *The Art of fugue* come from the impressive set the Juilliards made in 1987, to which we awarded three stars. The two Beethoven *Quartets* are drawn from different cycles: the *C major Rasumovsky*, Op. 59, No. 3 comes from 1964 and its companion, the *F major*, Op. 135, from 1982. Both are played with the formidable technical address the Juilliards command, but the acoustic in neither the CBS Studios nor the Coolidge Auditorium of the Library of Congress is ideal. One thinks longingly of the transparency and warmth of the old Quartetto Italiano set on Philips.

'*50 Years*', Volume 3: MOZART: *String quartet No. 19 in C (Dissonance), K.465.* SCHUBERT: *String quartet No. 15 in G, D.887.*

(M) ** Sony (ADD) SMK 62707.

The Mozart was recorded in the CBS Studios in New York in 1977 and the Schubert two years later. Perhaps owing to the group's generous vibrato, the opening of the Mozart is not as mysterious as it could be, though the playing is of the highest order of accomplishment. Tempi are well judged and the first-movement exposition repeat is observed. The Schubert is high-powered and at times sounds too well-upholstered in tone, perhaps the fault of the closer balance; but there are many sympathetic and imaginative moments and much to

admire. However, there are deeper and more penetrating accounts on disc.

'*50 Years*', Volume 4: DEBUSSY: *String quartet in G min.* HAYDN: *String quartet in D (Frog), Op. 50/6.* VERDI: *String quartet in E min.*

(M) ** Sony (ADD) SMK 62708.

Sony have chosen the 1970 performance of the Debussy rather than the 1989. It is immaculate technically but a trifle overblown; the upfront recording renders the aural image oversized rather than intimate. However, the slow movement is wonderful and manages to shake off the impression of 'public' music-making rather than music played in the home. The Haydn quartet performance is new to the catalogue and was recorded in 1985, again in a rather resonant acoustic; a very enjoyable performance, though again it is almost symphonic and some will want a greater lightness of touch. The Verdi, recorded in 1989 (and previously coupled with the Sibelius *Voces intimae*), is impeccable in technical address – perhaps less winning in terms of charm. All the same, those wanting this particular coupling will find much to reward them.

'*50 Years*', Volume 5: DVORAK: *Piano quintet in A, Op. 81* (with Rudolf Firkušný, piano). BARBER: *Dover Beach, Op. 3* (with Dietrich Fischer-Dieskau). SCHOENBERG: *Verklärte Nacht* (with Walter Trampler, viola). SCHUMANN: *Piano quintet in E flat, Op. 44* (with Leonard Bernstein, piano). COPLAND: *Sextet for clarinet, piano and string quartet* (with Harold Wright, clarinet, and the composer, piano). FRANCK: *Piano quintet in F min.* (with Jorge Bolet, piano).

(M) ** Sony (ADD) SM2K 62709 (2).

Apart from the Bartók, this is probably the most desirable of the Juilliard's fiftieth anniversary set. The Dvořák *Piano quintet* is marvellously played by Rudolf Firkušný (recorded in 1975), and so, too, is the magnificent Franck *Piano quintet* with Jorge Bolet (recorded in 1978), which this fine pianist plays with a restrained ardour that is impressive, though at times the Juilliard emote rather too much for comfort. The Copland *Sextet* with the composer himself (1966) and Samuel Barber's absurdly neglected and noble setting of *Dover Beach* with Fischer-Dieskau (1967) are valuable additions to the current catalogue and sound considerably better than on LP. The 1991 *Verklärte Nacht* is a little too over-heated to be ideal, with rather too much vibrato, but it still gives pleasure, while the 1964 version of the Schumann *Quintet* with Bernstein as pianist is coarsely recorded.

'*50 Years*', '*The Scherzo through time*': Minuets and Scherzi by HAYDN; BEETHOVEN; SCHUBERT; MENDELSSOHN; BRAHMS; FRANCK; RAVEL; SIBELIUS; BARTOK; SCHOENBERG; BERG; CARTER.

(M) * Sony (ADD) SMK 62712.

There is some splendid playing here, but it is difficult to imagine any but a few collectors wanting isolated Scherzos from great string quartets, however superbly they are played.

Kang, Dong-Suk (violin), Pascal Devoyon (piano)

French violin sonatas: DEBUSSY: *Sonata in G min.* RAVEL: *Sonata in G.* POULENC: *Violin sonata.* SAINT-SAENS: *Sonata No. 1 in D min.*

(BB) *** Naxos 8.550276.

One of the jewels of the Naxos catalogue, this collection of four of the finest violin sonatas in the French repertoire is self-recommending. The stylistic range of this partnership is evident throughout: they seem equally attuned to all four composers. This is warm, freshly spontaneous playing, given vivid and realistic digital recording in a spacious acoustic. A very real bargain.

Katchen, Julius (piano)

The art of Julius Katchen

Volume 1: BEETHOVEN: *Piano concertos Nos. 1-3; 5 (Emperor), Rondo in B flat for piano and orchestra* (with LSO, Piero Gamba).

*** Australian Decca Double 460 822-2 (2).

Volume 2: BEETHOVEN: *Piano concerto No. 4, Op. 58* (with LSO, Gamba); *Choral fantasia, Op. 80* (also with LSO Ch.). MOZART: *Piano concertos No. 13 in C, K. 415* (with New SO of London, Peter Maag); *20 in D min., K. 466; 25 in C, K. 503* (with Stuttgart Chamber Orchestra, Karl Münchinger).

*** Australian Decca Double 460 825-2 (2).

Volume 3: BRAHMS: *Piano concertos Nos. 1* (with LSO, Monteux); *2* (with LSO, János Ferencsik). SCHUMANN: *Piano concerto in A min.* (with Israel PO, Kertész); *Fantasia in C, Op.17.*

*** Australian Decca Double 460 828-2 (2).

Volume 4: LISZT: *Piano concertos Nos. 1-2* (with LPO, Argenta). *Mephisto waltz No. 1; Harmonies poétiques et religieuses: Funérailles; Hungarian rhapsody No. 12.* GRIEG: *Piano concerto in A min., Op. 16* (with Israel PO, István Kertész). BALAKIREV: *Islamey.* MUSSORGSKY: *Pictures at an exhibition.*

*** Australian Decca Double stereo/mono 460 831-2 (2).

Volume 5: TCHAIKOVSKY: *Piano concerto No. 1 in B flat min., Op. 23.* LISZT: *Hungarian fantasia* (both with LSO, Gamba). PROKOFIEV: *Piano concerto No. 3 in C, Op. 26* (with LSO, Kertéz). RACHMANINOV: *Piano concerto No. 2 in C min., Op. 18* (with LSO, Solti). *Rhapsody on a theme of Paganini, Op 43.* DOHNANYI: *Variations on a nursery theme* (both with LPO, Sir Adrian Boult).

*** Australian Decca Double mono/stereo 460 834-2 (2).

Volume 6: GERSHWIN: *Piano concerto in F* (with Mantovani and his Orchestra). BARTOK: *Piano concerto No. 3.* RAVEL: *Piano concerto in G; Piano concerto for the left hand* (all with LSO, Kertész).

BRITTEN: *Diversions for piano (left hand) and orchestra, Op. 21* (with SO, composer).

*** Australian Decca Double 460 837-2 (2).

Katchen's very distinguished 15-year recording career spanned the end of the mono LP era and the first decade of stereo. He was for most of that time Decca's star pianist, and we must be grateful to the Australian Repertoire Manager of Universal Music, Cyrus Meher-Homji, for providing what is to become a complete survey of his Decca recordings on a series of well-filled Doubles with the brightly lit transfers adding to the vividness, and the piano timbre of consistent high quality. As can be seen above, and from the four CDs (2 Volumes) included in Philips's 'Great Pianists' series above, Katchen's range of repertoire was as wide as his technique was brilliant, and he never delivered an unstimulating or unspontaneous performance. For his concerto recordings Decca provided him with a fine roster of conductors. The unexpected choice of Mantovani for the early LP of Gershwin's *Concerto in F* worked quite well, for he had fine soloists in his orchestra, and many may prefer the compilations offered here on Volumes 5 and 6 to the content of Volume 54 of the Philips series, particularly as the wonderfully imaginative performance of Britten's *Diversions* (with the composer conducting) is an indispensable highlight.

In the Beethoven concertos Katchen's partnership with Gamba worked particularly well, and the performances are fresh and commanding. Tempi are often on the fast side, but Katchen keeps a classical firmness and provides the necessary contrast in relaxed, poetic accounts of slow movements and sparkling readings of finales. In No. 1 he uses the longest and most impressive of Beethoven's own cadenzas for the first movement. The opening atmosphere of No. 4 is beautifully caught, while the *Emperor* is characteristically full of animal energy. The first and last movements are taken at a spanking pace, but not so that Katchen sounds at all rushed. Plainly he enjoyed himself all through, and in the very relaxed slow movement he seems to be coaxing the orchestra into matching his own delicacy, with the tension admirably sustained. The *Rondo* and the *Choral fantasia* too, are both very successful.

In the Brahms *First Concerto* the solo playing is superb, especially in the first movement, and Katchen is well partnered by Monteux (with the LSO), as he is by Ferencsik in No. 2, where he again gives an impassioned and exciting account of the solo piano part, here combining tremendous drive with the kind of ruminating delicacy Brahms so often calls for. These recordings are less successfully balanced than the Beethoven. However, in the Grieg and Schumann concertos the sound is clear and brilliant, with both performances strong, any willfulness tempered by a natural flexibility and the feeling for the music's poetry. Kertész provides plenty of life in the accompaniments. In Schumann, Katchen's virtuosity does not eschew romantic charm, the first movement more rhapsodical than usual, and throughout there is a pervading freshness. The Mozart performances, with Münchinger not always an ideally resilient conductor, yet have character (as does the solo sonata), and in the *D minor* there is strength as well as plenty of life and spirit.

In Liszt, Katchen is in his element. He is superb in the *E flat concerto* and by any standards these are commanding performances. The Bartók, Prokofiev and Ravel concertos are among his finest records, with Kertész especially compelling in his native Hungarian music, the playing combining intensity with brilliance and sparkle, and the Rachmaninov and Dohnányi performances are hardly less celebrated. The Tchaikovsky *Piano concerto* offers equally prodigious pianism, but is alas mono, and although the recording is basically rich and full, and the piano timbre is real and well balanced, the high violin timbre is thin and glassy, though not disastrously so, except perhaps at the very opening. Some might feel that in the finale Gamba broadens the reprise of the grand tune rather more than necessary. An exciting account just the same. Of the other solo performances Katchen's almost unbelievable technique is well demonstrated in Balakirev's *Islamey*. Even in an age of technicians few pianists could play the piece like this. The *Mephisto waltz* and Mussorgsky *Pictures* are also pretty remarkable, but in the latter the rather dry mono sound does not help Katchen to colour the music as he might. *Goldenberg and Schmuyle* and the *Chicks*, are highlights, but the finale could ideally be more expansive.

Volume 7: BEETHOVEN: *Piano sonatas Nos. 23 in F min. (Appassionata), Op. 57; 32 in C min., Op. 111.* MOZART: *Piano sonatas Nos. 13 in B flat, K.388; 16 in C, K.545. 33 Variations on a waltz by Diabelli, Op. 129; 6 Bagatelles, Op. 126; Polonaise in C, Op. 89.*

*** Australian Decca Double mono/stereo 466 714-2 (2).

Katchen recorded his impressive (mono) *Appassionata* in 1956 and his sparkling account of the *Diabelli variations* (a work that proved ideal for his pianistic talents) in 1961, but Opus 111 dates from the year before his death. Already the cancer which would kill him was taking its toll, for the playing, although still prodigious, is no longer immaculate. But the performance has great power, total spontaneity and a profound searching inner quality in the *Adagio*. The Mozart sonatas, also from 1956 and mono, are sheer delight, wonderfully crisp and stylish, yet with just the right degree of underlying expressive feeling. All the recordings have come up well and Katchen is given a very real presence.

Volume 8: SCHUBERT: *Fantasy in C (Wanderer), D.760.* SCHUMANN: *Carnaval, Op. 9; Toccata in C, Op. 7; Arabeske in C, Op. 18.* DEBUSSY: *Suite bergamasque: Clair de lune.* FALLA: *El amor brujo: Ritual fire dance.* CHOPIN: *Piano sonatas Nos. 2 in B flat min. (Funeral march), Op. 36; 3 in B min., Op. 58; Fantaisie-impromptu, Op. 66; Polonaise No. 6 in A flat (Heroic), Op. 53.* MENDELSSOHN: *Rondo*

capriccioso, Op. 14. LISZT: *Concert paraphrase of Mendelssohn's On wings of song.* BACH, arr. HESS: *Jesu, joy of man's desiring.*

*** Australian Decca Double mono/stereo 466 717-2 (2).

Volume 8 is another Double showing the remarkable range of a great pianist who died sadly young at the age of 42. The performance of *Carnaval* is striking for its skittishness as well as its infinite variety of mood and colour, while the *Arabeske* has a delighful sense of fantasy. The *Wanderer fantasia* also shows both Katchen's imaginative range, and his feeling for Schubert. But what stands out here is the Chopin, powerful yet with a natural lyrical feeling. His virtuosity comes into play too, in the dazzling account of the *Fantaisie-impromptu*, while the finale of the *B flat minor Sonata* is quite breathtaking in its evenness and clarity, and the *Scherzo* of the *B minor* just as remarkable in its clean articulation. Yet both slow movements are deeply felt. The famous *A flat Polonaise* is arresting and the two Mendelssohn pieces which follow show in turns sparkling dexterity and an unsentimentally bold romantic impulse, while Debussy's *Clair de lune* has an exquisite simplicity. The sound throughout is excellent.

Kempff, Wilhelm (piano)

Recital in Queen Elizabeth Hall, London, 5 June 1969: BACH: *Chromatic Fantasia and Fugue, BWV 903.* BEETHOVEN: *Sonata No. 22 in F, Op. 54.* SCHUBERT *Sonata No. 11 in F min., D.625; 3 Klavierstücke, D.946; Impromptus Nos. 3 & 4, D.899/3–4.*

(M) *** BBC (ADD) BBCL 4045.

This recital was one of the finest examples of Kempff's inspired pianism that London ever heard. He was still at the height of his powers, and inspiration did not desert him on this occasion. Brendel spoke of his *cantabile* with reverence and as being the essence of his art, which made him such a great Schubert interpreter and makes his *Klavierstücke* so special. (Oddly enough, the cover does not refer to the *F minor Sonata*.) But the Bach and Beethoven are hardly less magnificent, and they enhance the value of this invaluable BBC archive series. This playing really is the stuff of legends.

Kennedy, Nigel (violin), Lynn Harrell (cello)

Duos for violin and cello: RAVEL: *Sonata.* HANDEL: *Harpsichord suite No. 7 in G min.: Passacaglia (arr.* HALVORSEN/PRESS). KODALY: *Duo.* BACH: *2-Part Invention No. 6 in E.*

❂ *** EMI CDC5 56963-2.

An extraordinarily successful collaboration between the extrovert Kennedy and the more reticent Harrell, in which the listener has the constant impression of inspirational live intercommunication, and no suggestion whatsoever of the recording studio. The Ravel

Sonata opens with disarming simplicity and immediately takes off, producing an enormous intensity of feeling – whether in the sheer gutsy energy and fireworks of the *Très vif Scherzo*, or the veiled delicacy of the slow movement, begun very gently by Harrell.

The playing in the first movement of the masterly Kodály *Duo* is so closely and powerfully intertwined, so completely integrated in its ebb and flow of phrasing, dynamic and tension, that it is as if violin and cello were the flip-sides of the same coin. The superb Handel *Passacaglia* is played with confident and captivating bravura and the programme ends coolly and satisfyingly with simple Bach polyphony, the interchange quite perfectly balanced. The recording is forward and gives the illusion of an extremely vivid presence, within an open acoustic.

King, Thea (clarinet), Clifford Benson (piano)

English clarinet music: STANFORD: *Sonata, Op. 29.* FERGUSON: *4 Short pieces, Op. 6.* FINZI: *5 Bagatelles, Op. 23.* HURLSTONE: *4 Characteristic pieces.* HOWELLS: *Sonata.* BLISS: *Pastoral.* REIZENSTEIN: *Arabesques.* COOKE: *Sonata in B flat.*

(B) *** Hyp. Dyad CDD 22027 (2).

This Hyperion Dyad aptly combines two separate recitals, now offered for the price of one. They were recorded at the beginning of the 1980s and are in many ways complementary. Stanford's *Clarinet sonata* is clearly influenced by Brahms but has plenty of character of its own. The other works on the first disc are all appealingly communicative, lighter in texture and content, but well crafted.

The second CD opens with the Howells *Sonata*, among the finest written since Brahms, a warmly lyrical piece in two extended movements that bring out the instrument's varied colourings. Bliss's early *Pastoral* follows, thoughtful and unassuming, improvisatory in feeling. Reizenstein's short piece then acts as an interlude before the Cooke *Sonata*, strong but undemanding, with a darkly nostalgic *Adagio* and a chirpy finale. Thea King's warm, naturally expressive playing makes her an ideal advocate, not only for the music, but for her instrument; and her partner, Clifford Benson, is no less eloquent. Smooth, natural, analogue recording.

Kipnis, Igor (harpsichord)

'First solo recordings (1962)': BACH: *French suite No. 6 in E, BWV 817; Fantasia in G min., BWV 917; Prelude, fugue and allegro in E flat, BWV 998. Toccata in E min., BWV 914.* HANDEL: *Suite No. 5 in E (HWV 430).* SOLER (attrib.): *Fandango in D min.* DUSSEK: *The sufferings of the Queen of France.*

*** VAI Audio VAIA 1185.

With a photo of the young Kipnis as the frontispiece, this superb recital demonstrates a prodigious keyboard talent, and playing that is thoughful, scholarly yet alive.

His Bach is of a high calibre, and equally impressive is the Handel suite (which includes a breathtaking account of the *Harmonious blacksmith*). Soler's extended *Fandango* is equally brilliant and diverting, and he ends with his own edition of Dussek's vividly pictorial programmatic fantasia, describing the suffering, imprisonment and execution of Marie Antoinette – played with great imaginative flair, and bravura. The harpsichord is not named, but it is a most attractive instrument, with a wide range of colour and is most naturally recorded.

Kissin, Evgeni (piano)

'Carnegie Hall début' (30 September 1990), *Highlights:* LISZT: *Etude d'exécution transcendante No. 10; Liebestraum No. 3; Rhapsodie espagnole.* SCHUMANN: *Abegg variations, Op. 1; Etudes symphoniques, Op. 13; Widmung* (arr. LISZT).

*** BMG/RCA 09026 61202-2.

Evgeni Kissin has phenomenal pianistic powers; this is a *tour de force* not only in terms of technical prowess but also in sheer artistry. Both sets of Schumann *Variations* are remarkable. The Liszt *Rhapsodie espagnole* is played with superb bravura. Kissin's range of colour and keyboard command throughout are dazzling. The Carnegie Hall was packed and the recording balance, while a bit close, is perfectly acceptable. The excitement of the occasion is conveyed vividly.

BEETHOVEN: *Piano sonata No. 14 in C sharp min. (Moonlight), Op. 27/2.* BRAHMS: *Variations on a theme of Paganini, Op. 35.* FRANCK: *Prélude, chorale et fugue.*

*** RCA 09026 68910-2.

Strongly projected playing from this outstanding (and still young) artist. There is impressive concentration in the Beethoven, an effortless virtuosity in the Brahms, and great poetic feeling in the Franck. Everything here bears witness to a powerful musical mind allied to consummate pianistic mastery. Excellent recorded sound.

'In Tokyo' (12 May 1987): CHOPIN: *Nocturne in A flat, Op. 32/2; Polonaise in F sharp min., Op. 44.* LISZT: *Concert studies Nos. 1 in D flat (Waldesrauschen); 2 in F min. (La Leggierezza).* PROKOFIEV: *Sonata No. 6 in A, Op. 82.* RACHMANINOV: *Etudes tableaux, Op. 39/1 & 5; Lilacs.* SCRIABIN: *Etude in C sharp min., Op. 42/5; Mazurka in E min., Op. 25/3.*

*** Sony SK 45931.

Kissin was only fifteen at the time of his Tokyo début, but he sounds fully mature throughout this recital. He plays Prokofiev's *Sixth Sonata* for all it is worth with no holds barred, and the effect is altogether electrifying – one finds oneself on the edge of one's chair. He is no less at home in the Rachmaninov *Etudes tableaux* and the Liszt *La Leggierezza*, which he delivers with marvellous assurance and poetic feeling. His Scriabin, too, is pretty impressive. The microphone placing is too close – but no matter, this is breathtaking piano playing.

Labèque, Katia and Marielle (piano duo)

'*Encore!*': A. BERIO: *Polka; Maria Isabella (Waltz); La Primavera (Mazurka).* BACH: *Jesu, joy of man's desiring* (arr. HESS). GERSHWIN: *Preludes Nos. 1-3; Promenade (Walking the dog).* STRAVINSKY: *Tango; Waltz.* L. BERIO: *Wasserklavier.* BRAHMS: *Waltz in A flat.* TCHAIKOVSKY: *The Seasons: June.* BERNSTEIN: *West Side story: Jet song; America.* JOPLIN: *Bethena (Ragtime waltz); The Entertainer.* JAELL: *Valse.* BARTOK: *New Hungarian folksong.* SCHUMANN: *Abendlied.*

*** Sony SK 48381.

The Labèque sisters have never made a better record than this; the playing scintillates, especially the Bernstein and Stravinsky items, while the Labèques' Scott Joplin is admirably cool and the account of Myra Hess's arrangement of the famous Bach chorale is gentle and quite beautiful. Luciano Berio's evocative *Wasserklavier* is a real lollipop, but the surprise is the selection of four catchy and often boisterous pieces by his grandfather, Adolfo, a church organist 'of doubtful faith' (according to his grandson). Luciano gives his imprimatur to the lively Labèque performances, even while he feels that their 'modern and uninhibited pianism' might not have suited his more conventional grandfather.

Landowska, Wanda (harpsichord)

'*Portrait*': F. COUPERIN: *La favorite; Les moissonneurs; Les Langueurs-Tendres; Le gazouillement; La commère; Le moucheron; Les bergeries; Les tambourins; Les fastes de la grande ménestrandise; Le dodo, ou l'amour au berceau; Musette de Taverny; Les folies françaises ou les Dominos; Les calotins et les calotines; Les vergers fleuris; Soeur Monique.* RAMEAU: *Suite in G min.* BACH: *Goldberg variations, BWV 988.* HANDEL: *Suites Nos. 2 in F, HWV 427; 5 in E, HWV 430; 7 in G min., HWV 432.*

(M) (***) Grammofono 2000 mono AB 78715/6.

It is good to have a representative collection of the art of Wanda Landowska, who put the harpsichord back on the musical map in the twentieth century. She was not the first to try to do so; Violet Gordon Woodhouse actually made earlier acoustic recordings of some distinction, but it was Landowska's larger-than-life personality that soon made her a star. She gave her first performances on this instrument in 1903, and she toured Europe over the next two decades, visiting the United States from 1923 onwards. She persuaded Falla and Poulenc to write concertos (in 1926 and 1927 respectively) and had Pleyel build a large, modern instrument especially for her concerts.

Yet, as is readily apparent here, in the music of Couperin and Rameau she could articulate with the greatest delicacy (*La Poule* is delightful), and she kept her big guns in reserve for appropriate moments. Her *Goldberg variations* was rightly celebrated, the playing robust when required but suitably restrained at other times. Her overall timing is surprisingly close to Leonhardt's but her approach, without any loss of seriousness of purpose, is freer and more imaginative, and her reprise of the *Aria* reminds one of Rosalyn Tureck in its delicacy of feeling.

The recordings of French music were made in 1934, the *Goldberg* in 1933, and the quality is excellent, although in the French *pièces de clavecin* there are pitch differences between some items. The Handel *Suites* are a little more variable in sound, but still impressive, and in No. 5 *The harmonious blacksmith* (1935) strikes his anvil at first robustly but later with varying degrees of delicacy: there is no more spontaneous account in the catalogue. In the *Overture* which opens Handel's *Seventh Suite*, Landowska flamboyantly sounds like a full orchestra, and she plays the closing *Passacaglia* with similar satisfying weight, but in between there is a wider range of dynamic. Above all, this great artist communicated her joy in everything she played, and these excellent transfers ensure that we fully share it.

Larrocha, Alicia de (piano)

'*Música española*': Piano music, Volume IV: FALLA: *The Three-cornered hat: 3 Danzas. El amor brujo: suite.* TURINA: *Sacro Monte; Zapateado.* HALFFTER: *Danza de la pastora; Danza de la gitana.* MONTSALVATGE: *Sonatina para Yvette; Divertimento No. 2 'Habanera'.* NIN-CULMELL: *6 Tonadas.* SURINACH: *3 Canciones y danzas españolas.* MOMPOU: *Impresiones intimas; Preludio a Alicia de Larrocha; Música callada, IV; Canciones y danzas.*

✿ (B) *** Double Decca (IMS) (ADD) 433 929-2 (2).

Alicia de Larrocha is ideally cast here. Much of the music is delightful and all of it interesting. Joaquín Nin-Culmell's *6 Tonadas* are flashingly characterful in their folk feeling: the closing *Muñeira (Galicia)* brings spectacular flamenco fireworks. Xavier Montsalvatge's *Sonatina* in its finale quotes 'Twinkle twinkle little star', yet its audaciously quirky satire has more in common with Poulenc and Satie than Debussy's *Children's corner*. Alicia de Larrocha plays the whole sonata with breathtaking virtuosity. The coupled Mompou pieces, which are superbly played, have much charm and an atmosphere all their own – they are discussed in more detail under their Composer entry. They are digitally recorded; the rest of the recital is analogue, but hardly less real.

LaSalle Quartet

Chamber music of the Second Viennese School:
BERG: *Lyric suite; String quartet, Op. 3.*
SCHOENBERG: *String quartets: in D; No. 1 in D min.,
Op. 7; No. 2 in F sharp min., Op. 10/3 (with Margaret
Price); No. 3, Op. 30; No. 4, Op. 37.* WEBERN: *5
Movements, Op. 5; String quartet (1905); 6
Bagatelles, Op. 9; String quartet, Op. 28.*

(M) *** DG (IMS) 419 994-2 (4).

DG have compressed their 1971 five-LP set onto four
CDs, offering them at a reduced and competitive
price. They have also retained the invaluable and
excellent documentary study edited by Ursula Rauch-
haupt – which runs to 340 pages! It is almost worth
having this set for the documentation alone. The
LaSalle Quartet give splendidly expert performances,
even if at times their playing seems a little cool; and
they are very well recorded. An invaluable issue for all
who care about twentieth-century music.

Lawson, Peter, and Alan MacLean
(piano duet)

English music for piano duet: BERNERS: *Valses
bourgeoises; Fantasie espagnole; 3 Morceaux.*
LAMBERT: *Overture (ed. Lane); 3 Pièces nègres pour
les touches blanches.* RAWSTHORNE: *The Creel.*
WALTON: *Duets for children.* LANE: *Badinages.*

*** Troy TROY 142.

This collection centres on Lord Berners, who had a
recurring twinkle in the eye and loved to parody;
moreover his inspiration regularly casts a glance in the
direction of Satie and Poulenc, as the *Trois Morceaux*
readily demonstrate. Both Walton and Constant Lambert were his friends, admired his individuality and
came under his influence. Lambert's *Trois Pièces nègres*
have a Satiesque title, yet they are all the composer's
own work: the *Siesta* is quite haunting and the catchy
Nocturne brings sparkling Latin-American rhythmic
connotations, far removed from Chopin.

The four engaging Rawsthorne miniatures,
inspired by Izaak Walton's *Compleat Angler*, fit
equally well into the programme. The Walton *Duets
for children* have a disarming simplicity and often a
nursery rhyme bounce: *Hop scotch* is particularly
delightful, and vignettes like *The silent lake* and *Ghosts*
will surely communicate very directly to young performers. Walton's final *Galop* was arranged by Philip
Lane, who also provides four of his own pieces to
close the concert with a strongly Gallic atmosphere.
The performances by Peter Lawson and Alan
MacLean are strong on style yet also convey affection.
Excellent recording in a nicely resonant but not
muddy acoustic.

Leach, Joanna (piano)

'Four square': SOLER: *Sonata No. 90 in F sharp.*
HAYDN: *Sonata in C, Hob XVI/1.* J. S. BACH: *Partita
No. 1 in B flat: Prelude; Minuets I & II; Gigue.*
MOZART: *Fantasia in D min., K.397; Sonata No. 11 in
A, K.331.* SCHUBERT: *Impromptu in A flat, D.899/4.*
MENDELSSOHN: *Songs without words, Op. 19/1.*

*** Athene CD 3.

There is no more convincing fortepiano recital than
this. Joanna Leach uses an 1823 Stodart with its effectively dark lower register for the Soler *Sonata*, then
plays the same instrument later to show its attractive
upper range in an almost romantic performance of
Mozart's *Fantasia in D minor*; she ends the recital with
the *A major Sonata*, K.331, with the introductory variations particularly inviting. For the Haydn, she chooses
a 1789 Broadwood, a more brittle sound, and for the
Bach a very effective 1787 instrument made by Long-
man & Broderip. In the Schubert and Mendelssohn
pieces an 1835 D'Almaine brings us that bit nearer a
modern piano. Fine performances throughout, and
excellent recording. A fascinating way of discovering
what the modern piano's ancestors could do best.

Léner Quartet

HAYDN: *String Quartets: Nos. 76 in D min., Op. 76/2:
Andante; 77 in C (Emperor), Op. 76/3; 79 in D, Op.
76/5 (2 versions).*

(**) Rockport mono RR 5004.

HAYDN: *String Quartets in 17 in F, Op. 3/5 (2
versions); 67 in D (Lark), Op. 64/5: Minuet.* MOZART:
*Divertimento No. 17 in D, K.334 (with Aubrey &
Dennis Brain).*

(N) (**) Rockport mono RR 5006.

SCHUBERT: *Octet in F, D.803 (with Draper, Aubrey
Brain, Hinchcliff, Hobday).* SCHUMANN: *String
Quartet No. 3 in A, Op. 41/3.*

(N) (**) Rockport mono RR 5008.

MOZART: *Oboe Quartet in F, K.370 (with Goossens);
String Quartet No. 17 in B flat (Hunt), K.458; String
Quintet No. 3 in G min., K.516 (with d'Oliviera).*

(N) (**) Rockport mono RR 5010.

These are the first four CDs in what is to be a complete
reissue of all the Léner Quartet recordings on CD. The
scale of the enterprise is daunting, as the Léners
recorded no fewer than 210 shellac discs. The planners
of the series estimate that the final set will run to 30
CDs. Only a few of their recordings are currently available: the Brahms quartets, the Mozart and Brahms
Clarinet Quintets and the Mozart *Oboe Quartet* with
Leon Goossens (also included here). The Léners began
recording in 1924 and were the first to record a
complete Beethoven cycle. One unusual feature of this
venture is to juxtapose their acoustic recordings with
later electrical versions on the same CD. The first disc
brings Haydn's *Emperor Quartet, Op. 76, No. 3*, made in

1935, and contrasts their 1924 and 1928 versions of the *D major Quartet, Op. 76, No. 5*. Similarly, the third disc brings two versions of the *Op. 3, No. 5* (now attributed to Roman Hofstetter).

Those who think of the Léner as oversweet in tone with too much vibrato and cloying portamento should hear the *Hunt Quartet*, recorded in 1924. The sound is frail and wanting in body, but the quartet's purity of style is quite striking. Later on, in the 1930s, Jenö Léner developed a much wider vibrato, witness the *D major Divertimento, K.334*, from 1939 (with Aubrey and Dennis Brain) and again in the *G minor Quintet, K.516*, of 1930, with Louis d'Oliviera as second viola. Contrasts between their approach in the same works are often quite marked. In the first movement of *Op. 3, No. 5* they are faster in their 1924 acoustic recording, although the famous *Serenade* movement is slower in 1928 and much pulled around. The Schumann *Quartet in A, Op. 41, No. 3* is wonderfully rhapsodic in feeling, with little sense of the bar-line. Indeed, this is the sort of approach that seems totally idiomatic. Léner shows great imagination and poetic feeling in the *Adagio*, and there is an aristocratic poise that distinguishes his playing throughout. His style is very personal, whether or not you like it, and, on its own terms, is completely natural in approach, with, above all, no playing to the gallery. The Schubert *Octet*, with such distinguished figures as Charles Draper and Aubrey Brain, has some lovely playing, though the sound is pretty frail. Allowances have to be made for the actual quality, but then that is the case throughout the set. Robert Philip in his *Grove* article rightly speaks of the 'unusually homogeneous blend' of the Léners and the 'extraordinary smoothness and finish of their performances'. What is equally striking are their matchless sense of legato, a sophisticated lyricism (some might say over-sophisticated) and a generally unhurried and civilized approach. An important project.

Leonhardt Consort, Gustav Leonhardt (director, and playing: harpsichord, organ, virginal, viol)

Leonhardt Edition

(B) **(*) Teldec (ADD) 3984 21349-2 (21).

Gustav Leonhardt has made an exceptionally distinguished contribution to period-instrument performances of baroque music. During the 1960s he directed and performed in many first recordings for Das Alte Werk label, and it is appropriate that Teldec should have celebrated the fortieth anniversary of that label with a 21-disc Leonhardt Edition. The excellent Ensemble which bears his name always sought to make a sound which, although transparent, also had body, as well as being in believable period style. Similarly for his own many keyboard recordings, he chose instruments which would colour the music pleasingly as well as authentically.

Leonhardt's scholarship, his understanding of the finer points of baroque performance detail, not least ornamentation, showed a remarkable combination of musicality and scholarship. If his readings sometimes erred on the side of literal directness and sobriety, he could never be accused of self-regarding eccentricity, and it is apt that these reissued records should carry with their documentation printed tributes from such current experts in the period-instrument field as Bob van Asperen and Ton Koopman. Although we have reservations about recommending the set as a whole, certain of these CDs are very desirable indeed, for the technical standard of the recordings is remarkably high. All these discs are available separately.

BACH: **Harpsichord concertos (with (i) Frans Brüggen (flute), Marie Leonhardt (violin); (ii) Eduard Müller; (iii) Anneke Uittenbosch; (iv) Alan Curtis; (v) Janny van Wering). *Concertos: (i) in A min., for flute, violin and harpsichord, BWV 1044; Nos. 2 in E; 3 in D; 4 in A; 5 in F min., for solo harpsichord, BWV 1053-6; 6 for harpsichord and 2 recorders in F, BWV 1057; 7 in G min.; 8 in D min., for solo harpsichord, BWV 1058-9; Double harpsichord concertos Nos. (ii) 1 in C min., BWV 1060; (iii) 2 in C, BWV 1061; (ii) 3 in C min., BWV 1062; (iii-iv) Triple harpsichord concertos Nos. 1 in D min.; 2 in C, BWV 1063-4; (ii-iii; v) Quadruple harpsichord concerto in A min., BWV 1065***

((M) *(*) Teldec (ADD) 3984 21350-2 (3)).

The one clear drawback to this Edition as a complete set (apart from the curious omission of the *First Concerto*, BWV 1052) is Leonhardt's set of harpsichord concertos; this has many fine qualities, including Brüggen's contribution (immediately apparent in the *A minor Concerto*, BWV 1044), but it is surprisingly lacking in imagination and spontaneity. The recording is warm and resonant (comparable with the sound we usually expect from the Collegium Aureum) and reproduces smoothly, but inner clarity leaves much to be desired and the keyboard reproduction in the multiple concertos is much too opaque. In the solo works Leonhardt's steady – at times seemingly unrelenting – progress in allegros wearies the ear and, although he can be sensitive enough in slow movements (witness the famous *Largo* of the *F minor Concerto*), this is very disappointing, all things considered.

BACH: *Goldberg variations, BWV 988*

((M) ** Teldec (ADD) 3984 21351-2).

There are no complaints about the recording of the *Goldberg variations* (from 1965, using Leonhardt's favourite copy of a Dulcken harpsichord), which sounds fresh and vivid in its present incarnation. The reading is clear and direct, if not producing any especially individual resonances. Leonhardt was to re-record the work later for Deutsche Harmonia Mundi, and that version has a more spontaneous feeling; but it is not currently available.

BACH: **Works for harpsichord: *Chromatic fantasia and fugue in D min., BWV 903; Sonata in D min., BWV 964; Sonata in G, BWV 1005; Suite in E min., BWV 996; Toccata in G, BWV 916***

((M) ** Teldec (ADD) 3984 21352-2).

It has to be said that Bach's music does not always show Leonhardt at his very best. This miscellaneous recital is played on a modern harpsichord, but one which is a reproduction of a mid-eighteenth-century Dulcken. The sounds are authentic and attractive; unquestionably Leonhardt's playing reflects what would have been possible in Bach's time and, with judicious ornamentation of repeated sections, the scholarship behind the playing is impeccable. The opening *Chromatic fantasia and fugue* brings exciting dexterity, and so does the *Allegro assai* finale of the *Sonata in G*, which is an arrangement of the work for unaccompanied violin in C, BWV 1005. In between, however, a good deal of the playing is rather metronomic, and the *Suite in E minor* (which Bach probably intended for the now obsolete lute-harpsichord) could do with a lighter touch. The recording is rather close, but the CD transfer cannot be faulted.

BACH: *Violin sonatas* (for violin and harpsichord) *Nos. 1-6, BWV 1014-19* (with Lars Frydén)

((M) **(*) Teldec (ADD) 21353-2 (2)).

The six *Sonatas for violin and harpsichord* are far less well known than the works for unaccompanied violin or cello, and their relative obscurity is quite undeserved. They contain music of great character and beauty: who could forget the beautiful *Siciliana* which opens the *C minor* (No. 4) (played most persuasively here by Lars Frydén) or the more solemn dignity of the first movement of the *B minor Sonata* (No. 1), which Leonhardt opens very simply and which glows with life at the violin entry.

Frydén proves to be a most stylish and sympathetic exponent. He uses a baroque violin, made in London in 1767, and lets it sing and dance, just as Bach intended. Although he is balanced fairly closely, if not at the expense of his partner, his timbre is full and cleanly formed and never sounds scratchy – witness his *Dolce* opening of the *A major Sonata* (No. 2). Throughout these works the polyphony of the allegros is always engagingly fresh, and the continuo offers plenty of opportunities to the imaginative harpsichordist.

Alas, Leonhardt does not always take them, for the most part being content to provide ongoing background support. When he is on his own (as again at the opening of the *F minor*, No. 5) he proceeds uneventfully onwards until the warm entry of the solo violin transforms the music. In a flowing *Andante*, as in the A major work, he is content to provide a straightforward accompaniment and let his partner soar above him. However, better this than eccentric rubato, and in the jolly second movement of the *E major* (No. 3), the players work well together, while

the finale sparkles with energy. An excellent transfer to CD, but don't play the disc at too high a volume.

BACH: *Quodlibet, canons, chorales, songs and keyboard works* (with Anner Bylsma (cello), Agnes Giebel, Marie Luise Gilles, Bert van t'Hoff, Peter Christoph Runge): *Canons in 2 parts, BWV 1075; in 7 (8) parts, BWV 1078; in 4 parts, BWV 1073; in 4 (5) parts, BWV 1077;* (Keyboard) *Capriccio in B flat (sopra la lontananza del suo fratello dilettissimo), BWV 992; Preludes in F, BWV 927; in E, BWV 937; in G min., BWV 929; in D, BWV 925; in C, BWV 939; Fugue in C, BWV 952; Prelude and Fugue in A min., BWV 895; Prelude and Fughetta in D min., BWV 899; Suite in F min., BWV 823. Quodlibet, BWV 524.* Arias: *Erbauliche Gedanken eines Tobackrauchers, BWV 515a; Gieb dich zufrieden und sie stille, BWV 511; Vergiss mein nicht, mein allerliebster Gott! BWV 505.* Chorales: *O Herzensangst, o Bangigkeit und Zagen! BWV 400; Nicht so traurig, nicht so sehr, BWV 384; Dir, dir Jehova, will ich singen, BWV 452; Was betrübst du dich, mein Herze, BWV 423; Wer nur den lieben Gott lässt walten (3 versions), BWV 691 BWV 434*

(M) *** Teldec (ADD) 3984 21354-2.

Much of this material comes from Anna Magdalena's *Klavierbüchlein*, intended for use by Bach's sons: keyboard pieces, together with simple chorales and songs for domestic entertainment rather than public performance. They show another side of Bach, as a genial but painstaking family man, and the music brings out the best in Leonhardt, who plays the brief keyboard pieces in an appropriately light-hearted manner.

He gives a colourful account of the designedly programmatic *Capriccio in B flat* ('On the departure of a beloved brother'), personally announcing the title of each section in German. The brief *Canon in 2 parts* wittily introduces a recorder, while the *Canon in 7 (8) parts* fills out quickly and ends in mid-air.

The arias and chorales are agreeably outgoing. In *So oft ich meine Tobacks-Pfeife* (subtitled 'The edifying thoughts of a tobacco-smoker') Bert van t'Hoff (or Peter Runge – it is not quite clear which) genially reflects on Bach's 'contented puffing on my small pipe', while the serene *Gieb dich zufrieden und sie stille* ('Be of good cheer and hold your peace') is sung delightfully by Agnes Giebel. The chorale *Was betrübst du dich, mein Herz* ('Why are you sad, my heart?') touchingly appears to reflect on a family crisis.

But the highlight of the concert is the *Quodlibet* ('As you wish') for vocal quartet, which by definition is an informal, light-hearted piece, but here is a true musical joke, originally intended for performance at a wedding. The manuscript is incomplete (both the beginning and the end are missing) but what there is (about 10 minutes) is set to outrageous words which flit from image to image, not unlike Gilbert's famous Nightmare song, and ending with the observation, 'Oh what a delightful fugue this is!' The whole piece is captivating, especially when sung so freshly. To end the collection, Leonhardt returns to his more didactic Bach keyboard style for

BWV 823, BWV 895 and BWV 899, but the closing *Fughetta* of the latter work is pleasingly jaunty. The recording throughout is excellent, and altogether this is a most entertaining concert.

English consort and keyboard music: DOWLAND: *Pavan in C.* LAWES: *Suites Nos. 1 in C min.; 2 in F; Sonata No. 7 in D min.; Suite No. 3 in B flat: In nomine.* COPRARIO: *Fantasia; Suite.* BYRD: *Pavan; Galliard; Fantasia No. 3.* Thomas SIMPSON: *Ricercar: Bonny sweet robin.* Thomas LUPO: *Fantasia.* BYRD: *Pavan; Galliard; Miserere.* MORLEY: *Nancie; Fantasia.* John BULL: *Hexachord fantasia; The Duchesse of Brunswick's toye.* William RANDALL: *Dowland's Lachrymae; Galliard: Can't she excuse my wrongs.* TOMKINS: *Pavan; Galliard; A sad pavan for these distracted times.* GIBBONS: *Pavan.* FARNABY: *Fantasia; Spagnioletta.* William TISDALE: *Mrs Katherin Tregians pavan.* ANON.: *A toye*

((M) *** Teldec (ADD) 3984 21760-2 (2)).

This two-CD compilation draws on three Das Alte Werk LPs from 1965–6 and 1970, and the result is an unusually comprehensive survey which gives an excellent overall picture of the various composers writing music in Elizabethan and Jacobean England. The programme opens appropriately with Byrd, a consort *Pavane*, and later we are to have a harpsichord *Pavane and Galliard* and two consort *Fantasias*. In between come the highly individual *Suites* of William Lawes, who was a member of the Chapel Royal and a very considerable contributor to early seventeenth-century consort music. His *In nomine* (taken from the *Third Suite*) is particularly eloquent. But the surprise is perhaps the music of William Coprario (Cooper), whose *Fantasia* (for two violins, viola, viol and cello) is very striking indeed, to be followed by a tuneful and light-hearted *Suite in three parts* and the equally engaging *Ricercar on Bonny sweet Robin* by Thomas Simpson.

The first CD ends with Lupo's *Fantasia*, another piece of real quality. There could perhaps be more ornamentation in these performances, but on the whole they are in excellent taste and style. There is nothing anaemic about the string textures, nor are they edgy, while the playing itself has plenty of life and spirit. The recording is impeccable.

The music of Byrd again opens the second disc with a consort pavane and galliard to introduce his beautiful *Miserere*, which is most touchingly played by Leonhardt on a chamber organ. He continues with a series of keyboard pieces, alternating harpsichord (choosing between two different instruments) and virginal. All come from the Fitzwilliam Virginal Book, except for the Gibbons *Pavane* and the two pieces by Randall. Predictably fine are the Bull *Fantasia* and the three pieces by Thomas Tomkins: here Leonhardt changes instruments for the third, *A sad pavane for these distracted times*. Farnaby's jolly *Spagnioletta* makes a spirited contrast and the programme ends with an encore - a brief, anonymous *Toye*.

Consort music: BIBER: *Harmonia artificiosa-ariosa: diversi mode accordata: Partita No. 3 in A; Mensa sonora: Part 3; Fidicinium sacro-profanum: Sonatas 3-6.* MUFFAT: *Armonico tributo: Sonata No. 2 in G min.* ROSENMULLER: *Sonata No. 7 a 4.* SCHEIDT: *Paduan a 4.* SCHMELZER: *Sacro-profanus concentus musicus: Sonatas Nos. 7, 9*

(M) *** Teldec (ADD) 3984 21761-2.

It was Leonhardt who introduced us (in the late 1960s) to much of Biber's instrumental music, the excellence of which is only now being fully explored. The best-known set is the *Harmonia artificiosa-ariosa*, a collection of seven *Partitas* or suites for strings (published posthumously), and here we are offered the *Third* with its remarkable finale, an elaborately decorated *Chaconne/Canon*.

The *Mensa sonora* sonatas (from 1680) are – as the title suggests – essentially homophonic, more concerned with richness of texture and harmony than with contrapuntal ingenuity. Again we are offered Partita III, in five movements, written for a modest chamber ensemble and continuo. The music is warmly expressive: even the fourth-movement *Chaconne* is mellow.

Four of the twelve *Fidicinium sacro-profanum* sonatas follow. They were published three years later and are scored for 2 violins, 2 violas, 2 cellos and continuo. As their title suggests, contrast is the order of the day, with the expressive movements quite dolorous, while allegros are lively and light-hearted. The *Sixth Sonata* (the last here) opens quite solemnly, and Leonhardt fills out the texture with an organ continuo.

The following Muffat *Sonata* opens even more sombrely, but it becomes an inventive series of linked movements alternating Grave slow sections with buoyant allegros. The two Schmelzer *Sonatas* (1662) for two violins, viola and continuo seek contrast in the same way as Biber's music and are similarly entitled *Sacro-profanus concentus musicus*. They are of high quality, as is the briefer work by Johann Rosenmüller and the stately *Paduan* (Pavane) of Samuel Scheidt. As can be seen, all this music, much of which is well off the beaten track, comes from the same fertile period, and Leonhardt and his players (six in all) are persuasive advocates. They use period instruments which are tuned to seventeenth-century pitch, but the sounds they make are full-timbred, and expressive phrasing is not eccentric but warmly musical.

FROBERGER: **Organ and harpsichord works: Organ:** *Capriccio II; Fantasia III; Toccata XI alla levazione; Ricercar II; Canzona II.* **Harpsichord:** *Toccata IX; Suite XVIII; Toccata XVIII; Suite XII*

((M) *** Teldec (ADD) 3984 21762-2).

Froberger was a pupil of Frescobaldi and one of the most exploratory and inward-looking composers of the seventeenth century. Leonhardt, who is an authoritative guide, offers here two groups of pieces, the first five played on the now familiar eighteenth-century organ (at the Waalse Kerk, Amsterdam), and the second group on a modern harpsichord, copied from an Italian instrument from the same period. The opening organ *Capriccio* is joyously buoyant, but the *Chorale fantasia* is more thoughtful and in its steady progress anticipates Bach. The *Toccata alla levazione* has much of Frescobaldi's improvisatory feeling, while the *Ricercar II* brings a remarkably solemn profundity. The *Harpsichord suites*, skilfully decorated, are more lively and outgoing and readily show the composer's resourceful melodic and harmonic flare. Most striking is the opening movement of the *Twelfth Suite*, which laments the death of King Ferdinand IV in 1654. The closing *Sarabande* has comparable regal dignity. Excellent recording of both instruments.

KUHNAU: *Musikalische Vorstellung einiger biblischer Historien: Sonatas 1-6 (1: The combat between David and Goliath; 2: Saul healed by David with the help of music; 3: Jacob's marriage; 4, Hezekiah is mortally ill and restored to health; 5: Gideon, the saviour of Israel; 6: The death and burial of Jacob)*

(M) *(*) Teldec (ADD) 3984 21763-2 (2).

Johann Kuhnau was Bach's predecessor at St Thomas's, Leipzig, and this is his fourth and last keyboard work. The *Musical depiction of some biblical stories* (in six *Sonatas*) dates from 1700. Each programmatically illustrates a story from the Old Testament, which is filled out by a narrative – an introduction at the beginning of each work, plus titles for each section, the latter usually spoken over the music. Here these introductions, recounting each biblical story in full, given in German – and, fortunately, separately banded on the CDs – are written and spoken by Leonhardt himself, and they are very subjective.

Alas, Kuhnau's musical resources are not equal to the pictorial task he has set himself: they are most striking for their naïvety and seldom show much descriptive skill: *The combat between David and Goliath* is depicted with singular lack of imagination. However, when Gideon leads the Israelites into battle, the 'blast of trombones and trumpets' is more tellingly depicted, and the scalic flight of pursued enemy forces, both here and earlier in the David/Goliath narrative, is effective enough.

Kuhnau is also rather better at portraying melancholy, as in Saul's rather extended bout of it, before David's not very believable musical cure, and again during Hezekiah's mournful sickness before God relents and restores him to health. In the most intriguing story of all, *Jacob's marriage*, the devious Laban, using the cover of darkness, places his elder, ugly daughter, Leah, in the bridal bed instead of the younger, the beautiful Rachel (whom Jacob is expecting). Such duplicity is represented with melodramatically florid flourishes. Then, in a section lasting two minutes, Jacob's relishing of the wedding night consummation is depicted with an amiable little theme, until 'his heart tells him something is amiss'. But in the dim light his misgivings cannot be confirmed and he 'finally falls asleep' – to a single chord. The next morning he discovers his mistake and is none

too pleased about it. However, he agrees to keep Leah after the promise that in seven years he can have Rachel too; so the piece ends with a second wedding and repeated celebrations!

The organ is used for *Sonatas Nos. 1, 2* and *4*, the harpsichord for the remainder. Generally it is the latter instrument which works best in the primitive narrative detail, as Leonhardt brings a certain improvisational feeling to the disconsolate music. But to claim this as a 'great work', as Lothar Hoffmann-Erbrecht does in his accompanying note, is singularly misguided. It has historical interest, to be sure, but little else, although one wonders whether a more extrovert account would bring it more fully to life. The documentation is good, if a little unwieldy, with full narrative translations, and the titles given for each section.

MONDONVILLE: (with Lars Frydén) *Violin sonatas Op. 3, Nos. 1 in G min.; 2 in F; 3 in B; 4 in C; 5 in G; 6 in A*

(M) **(*) Teldec (ADD) 3984 21765-2.

Mondonville's *Violin sonatas* are important in that they helped the development away from the violin-plus-continuo style to the form as we know it today. Thus both instruments are given proper 'solo' parts to play, and they are often very florid parts. One might be forgiven for occasionally thinking that the composer had forgotten himself and allotted two accompaniment parts instead! But generally the music is inventive enough, and the disc has real historical interest in demonstrating the duet sonata when ideas concerning the marriage of two instruments were very much in the melting pot. Opus 3 dates from about 1734 and predates by fourteen years the fascinating Opus 5 set, which also includes the human voice and which is listed and discussed in our main volume. The recording here, made in 1966, is good but is rather more forward than the earlier (1963) recording by these same artists of the Bach *Violin and harpsichord sonatas*. This means that the full timbre of Lars Frydén's baroque violin is less flattered, although he can still be serenely expressive in the *Arias* which form the slow movements – witness the fine flowing melody of No. 4 in C major – and Leonhardt's harpsichord (a Kirckman, made in London in 1766) is a little sharp-toned. But the two instruments are generally well balanced – and the players seem pretty sure of themselves. Tempi are often brisk and very lively (try the infectious *Giga* finale of that same *C major Sonata*).

Organ and harpsichord music: F. COUPERIN: *Messe à l'usage ordinaire des Paroisses: Offertoire sur les grands jeux. L'Art de toucher le clavecin: 8 Préludes.* Alessandro POGLIETTI: *Ricercar primi toni.* Nicolas DE GRIGNY: *Cromorne en taille à deux parties.* RAMEAU: *Pièces de clavecin.* ANON.: *Daphne; Resonet in laudibus*

(M) **(*) Teldec (ADD) 3984 21766-2.

This collection creates a stimulating variety of timbres and textures from the various keyboard instruments which Leonhardt chooses. He first seeks a French association rather than a specific French accent in presenting the Couperin *Offertoire* rather grandly on the Müller organ at the Waalse Kerk (or French church) in Amsterdam, which dates originally from 1680. The instrument has clarity and all the necessary bite in the reeds. He then plays eight *Préludes* from *L'Art de toucher le clavecin* very stylishly and pleasingly on a copy of a Rück harpsichord by an eighteenth-century Dresden maker, C. A. Gräbner, which works equally well.

The solemn *Ricercar* by Alessandro Poglietti, an influential Italian who became organist at the Viennese Imperial Chapel, follows on yet another organ, which it suits admirably. Leonhardt then returns to Amsterdam to find an engaging registration for Nicolas de Grigny's gentle *Cromorne en taille*.

According to the documentation, the same Rück/Gräbner harpsichord is used for the six *Pièces de clavecin* of Rameau as for the Couperin *Préludes*, but the recordings were made two years apart and the Rameau (from 1962) is mono, and is less easy on the ear: brighter, harsher and at times even clattery. But one soon adjusts, and the effect is certainly lively and characterful. The anonymous portrait of *Daphne* has a gentle melancholy, and for this Leonhardt uses a noticeably mellower 1648 Ruckers, a stereo recording of five years later, closing with the divisions on *Resonet in laudibus* played on the deliciously reedy Arp Schnitger organ at Noordbroek, Gronnigen. Most entertaining.

RAMEAU: *Pièces de clavecin en concerts: Premier concert; Deuxième concert; Troisième concert; Quatrième concert; Cinquième concert* (with Frans Brüggen, Wieland and Sigiswald Kuijken)

(M) *** Teldec (ADD) 3984 21767-2.

These ensemble versions of the *Pièces de clavecin en concerts*, published in 1741, were not pioneered by Leonhardt on LP: there were two previous recordings by Rampal, one on Nonesuch with Robert Veyron-Lacroix and the other on Fontana with Ruggiero Gerlin. But the present (1971) performance trumped its predecessors: it has a surer sense of style and a deeper understanding of the niceties of the period. It is a period-instrument performance, but a thoroughly stimulating and enjoyable one, beautifully recorded.

PURCELL: **Anthems, instrumental music and songs** (with Leonhardt Consort): Anthems (with James Bowman, Nigel Rogers, Max van Egmond, King's College, Cambridge, Choir, Willcocks): *Rejoice in the Lord alway; Blow up the trumpet in Sion; O God, thou art my God; O God, thou hast cast us out; My heart is inditing; Remember not, Lord, our offences.* Consort music: *Chacony in G min.; Overture in D min.; Pavan in B flat; Overture (with Suite) in G; Pavan in A min.; Fantasia (Chaconne): 3 Parts on a ground in D; Overture in G min.; Pavan of 4 parts in G min.; Sonata in A min.; Ground in D min.* Harpsichord music: *Suite in D; Sefauchi's farewell in D min.; A new ground in E min.* Songs: *Fly swift, ye hours; The Father brave; Return, revolting rebels*

(with Max van Egmond, Leonhardt Consort). Consort music: *Fantasia a 4 No. 7* (Brüggen Consort)

● (M) *** Teldec (ADD) 3984 21768-2 (2).

This Purcell collection is the pick of the bunch and should not be missed. The anthems are all very well sung indeed, with the King's College Choir's penchant for tonal breadth and beauty. Not all of them have instrumental accompaniments, but those that do enjoy a distinctive sound, with period instruments used in such a way that the performances overall happily blend scholarship and vigour, warmth and spontaneity. The recordings were not made at King's College, but in Holland, in 1969, and the acoustic is ideal, not too resonant, so that the effect is uncommonly fresh and clear. The delightful *Blow up the trumpet in Sion* has splendid antiphonal effects which remind one of Purcell's famous directional chorus in *King Arthur*. But the highlight must be *My heart is inditing*, an extended work, also for double chorus, in which the polyphony is a thing of wonder. It is superbly integrated and the choir conclude with a very beautiful performance of the unaccompanied *Remember not, Lord, our offences*.

Leonhardt's excellent Dutch ensemble experiences no difficulty in getting right inside the spirit of Purcell's instrumental music, which they perform with admirable taste and finesse of style. The *Fantasia on a ground*, a brilliant work exploiting the special sound of three violins above a repeated bass motive, is one of the best recorded versions of this piece, as is that of the famous *Chacony in G minor*. The two *Overtures* are less familiar; while they may not rank, like the *Pavans* and *Sonatas* here, among Purcell's best music, it is good to have them in such neat and sparkling performances, and Leonhardt's intepretations of the harpsichord solos leaves little to be desired. The stereo sound from the late 1960s is warm and lively, and very successfully transferred.

Organ and harpsichord music: Organ: REINCKEN: *An den Wasserflüssen Babylon*. SCHEIDEMANN: *Praeambulum in D*. BACH: *Prelude and fugue in D min., BWV 539*. Harpsichord: BOEHM: *Suites Nos. 6 in E flat; 8-9 in F min*. HANDEL: *Suite No. 8 in F min*. J. C. BACH: *Sonata in D, Op. 5/2*

(M) *** Teldec (ADD) 3984 21769-2.

Johann Adam Reincken was a famed improviser, and Bach travelled to Hamburg to hear him play. Not surprisingly, his *Chorale fantasia* on *An den Wasserflüssen* is an ingeniously crafted work that projects readily in Leonhardt's fine performance. The following *D minor Prelude and fugue* of Bach might have been moved on a little more swiftly, yet Leonhardt certainly holds the listener's attention at his chosen pace.

He then turns to the harpsichord for the three attractive suites of Georg Böhm (French in form and layout, but German in sensibility) and the splendid work of Handel, and he closes with a remarkably modern-sounding *D major Sonata* of J. C. Bach, with its pair of *Allegro di molto* movements (played with great flair), followed by a closing minuet. Leonhardt uses two different organs and (more importantly) three different harpsichords: two copies and, for the J. C. Bach work, an original instrument made in London in 1775. The basic sound of each is quite different (the Boehm and Handel suites appear to be very good mono recordings), and Leonhardt makes the most of his colouristic opportunities. The balance is close but otherwise the CD transfer produces first-class results. Very stimulating.

Harpsichord and consort music: FRESCOBALDI: *Toccata settima; Toccata undecima in C; Canzona terza; Toccata in G; Fantasia sesta sopra doi soggetti; 5 Galliards.* TURINI: *Sonata in A.* CACCINI: *Amarilli mia bella.* Biagio marini: *Balletto secondo a tre & a quattro.* D. SCARLATTI: *Sonatas in A min., Kk. 3: Presto; in D min., Kk. 52: Andante moderato; in E, Kk. 215: Andante; in E, Kk. 216: Allegro*

(M) *** Teldec (ADD) 3984 21770-2.

Another very enjoyable recital, in which Leonhardt uses four different early harpsichords. Frescobaldi's music suits him admirably, for he obviously relishes its improvisational freedom of style and its ability to take the listener by surprise. Alternating an Italian instrument and a sonorous London Kirkman, he plays the *Toccatas* with an entirely appropriate freedom and is equally appealing in the *Canzona*; it is only in the *Fantasia* that he progresses somewhat deliberately. But he finds an appropriately buoyant rhythmic touch for the five brief *Galliards*. Turini's Trio sonata, alternately expressive and vigorous, makes a strong contrast, played with elegance and spirit, while the following *Amarilli mia bella* of Caccini has a certain lovelorn air when played so responsively on a fine Ruckers.

The Ensemble returns for Marini's ballet suite, which has a surprisingly grave concluding *Pretirata*. The programme ends with nicely turned performances of four choice keyboard sonatas of Scarlatti, using a characterful instrument made by R. Schütz of Heidelberg. These appear to be more mono recordings (from 1962) but of high quality. The closing work in *E major*, Kk. 216, with its swirling bravura scales, is particularly engaging.

Lidström, Mats (cello), Bengt Forsberg (piano)

'*Smorgåsbord*': KORNGOLD: *Mummenschant; Romance Impromptu in E flat.* GRAINGER: *Sussex Mummers' Christmas Carol.* SIBELIUS: *Rondino; Berceuse.* GODOWSKY: *Larghetto lamentoso.* JONGEN: *Valse; Habanera.* MONTSALVATGE: *Canto negro.* HALFFTER: *Habanera.* MOERAN: *Prelude.* KREISLER: *Liebesleid.* SCRIABIN: *Poème in F sharp, Op. 32/1; Romance in A min.* MARTINU: *Arabesque No. 1.* TORTELIER: *Pishnetto.* HAGG: *Andante; Albumblatt.* LENNOX BERKELEY: *Andantino, Op. 21/2a.* LIDSTROM: *The Sea of Flowers is Rising Higher (Elegy).* RAMEAU: *Air vif; 'Torture d'Alphise'.*

TILLE: *Courante.* OFFENBACH: *Souvenir du val, Op. 29/1.* FAURE: *Pièce (Papillon), Op. 77.* STENHAMMAR: *Adagio.*

*** Hyp. CDA 67184.

This fine Swedish partnership has given us some enterprising issues ranging from Saint-Saëns to Boëllman and Benjamin Godard, but on this disc they assemble some 25 *bonnes bouches* lasting in all not much longer than an hour. They call it '*Smörgåsbord*' (the table of Scandinavian hors d'oeuvres that used to precede but sometimes also comprises the main course) although many of the pieces here, such as Ernesto Halffter's *Habañera* and Kreisler's *Liebesleid* could just as well be petits fours. In any event, whether they be sweet or savoury, they are all delicious as served here. As a glance at the listing above shows, their choice of repertoire is highly enterprising and ingenious. The thought of hearing so many miniatures puts one in mind of Bernard Shaw's celebrated remark about Grieg: 'His sweet but very cosmopolitan modulations, and his inability to get beyond a very pretty snatch of melody do not go very far with me … Give me a good, solid, long-winded classical lump of composition with time to go to sleep and wake up two or three times in each movement.' Well, there is no time to doze off here and no inducement to do so either. Everything is compellingly and exquisitely played, and beautifully recorded too. Almost all these pieces are worthwhile, though one is not altogether sure about Lidström's own work, written soon after the death of Diana, Princess of Wales. But that is the single exception and this is a highly enjoyable issue.

Lim, Dong-Hyek (piano)

CHOPIN: *Ballade No. 1 in G min., Op. 23; Etude in C, Op. 10./1; Scherzo No. 2 in B flat min., Op. 31.* RAVEL: *La Valse* (trans. composer); SCHUBERT: *Four Impromptus, D.899/1–4.*

❂ (M) *** EMI CDM5 67933-2.

Magnificent! This recital by the South Korean pianist Dong-Hyek Lim is as virtuosic as were some of his footballing countrymen at the recent World Cup. He was seventeen last year when this recital was recorded, and is presently studying in Moscow with Lev Naumov. From the very first bar to the last, he has the listener in his grip, such is the strength of his musical personality. A real artist and not just a brilliant pianist, he brings a commanding narrative power to this repertoire. The Chopin is electrifying, sensitive, poetic and has an authority that is unexpected in one so young, and the Schubert has depth and poignancy. He is one of the artists who appear under Martha Argerich's banner and has the same youthful flair she had in the beginning of her career as well as ardour, effortless technique and sensitivity.

Lipatti, Dinu (piano)

CHOPIN: *Sonata No. 3 in B min., Op. 58.* LISZT: *Années de pèlerinage: Sonetto del Petrarca, No. 104.* RAVEL: *Miroirs: Alborada del gracioso.* BRAHMS: *Waltzes, Op. 39/1, 2, 5, 6, 10, 14 & 15* (with Nadia Boulanger). ENESCU: *Sonata No. 3 in D, Op. 25.*

(M) (***) EMI mono CDH7 63038-2.

The Chopin is one of the classics of the gramophone, and it is good to have it on CD in this excellent-sounding transfer. The Brahms *Waltzes* are played deliciously with tremendous sparkle and tenderness; they sound every bit as realistic as the post-war records. The Enescu *Sonata* is an accessible piece, with an exuberant first movement and a rather atmospheric *Andantino*, but the sound is not as fresh as the rest of the music on this valuable CD. A must for all with an interest in the piano.

Recital: BACH: *Partita No. 1 in B flat, BWV 825. Chorale preludes: Nun komm, der Heiden Heiland; Ich ruf zu dir, Herr Jesu Christ; Jesu, joy of man's desiring. Flute sonata No. 2 in E flat, BWV 1031: Siciliana* (arr. KEMPFF). D. SCARLATTI: *Sonatas, Kk. 9 & 380.* MOZART: *Sonata No. 8 in A min., K. 310.* SCHUBERT: *Impromptus in E flat; G flat, D.899/2-3.*

(M) (***) EMI mono CDM5 66988-2 [CDM 67003].

No collector should overlook this Lipatti CD. Most of the performances derive from the pianist's last recital in Besançon and have scarcely been out of circulation since their first appearance in the 1950s: the haunting account of the Mozart *A minor Sonata* and the Bach *B flat Partita* have both had more than one incarnation on LP and CD. The Schubert *Impromptus* are equally treasurable, and the Scarlatti sonatas have been added for the present reissue in EMI's 'Great Recordings of the Century' series. The remastering is well done; and one notices that, among his other subtleties, Lipatti creates a different timbre for the music of each composer.

Little, Tasmin (violin), Piers Lane (piano)

'Virtuoso violin': KREISLER: *Prelude and allegro in the style of Pugnani; Caprice viennois.* BRAHMS: *Hungarian dances Nos. 1 & 5.* SHOSTAKOVICH: *The Gadfly: Romance.* DRIGO: *Valse bluette.* FIBICH: *Poème.* FALLA: *La vida breve: Spanish dance.* WIENIAWSKI: *Légende, Op. 17.* SARASATE: *Introduction and Tarantelle, Op. 43.* BLOCH: *Baal Shem: Nigun.* DEBUSSY: *Beau soir.* RIMSKY-KORSAKOV: *Flight of the bumblebee* (both arr. HEIFETZ). DELIUS: *Hassan: Serenade* (arr. TERTIS). KROLL: *Banjo and fiddle.* RAVEL: *Tzigane.*

(B) *** CfP 574 9492.

A pretty dazzling display of violin fireworks from a brilliant young fiddler who conveys her delight in her own easy virtuosity. The opening Kreisler pastiche, *Prelude and allegro*, is presented with real style, and later the *Caprice viennois* has comparable panache

and relaxed charm. The schmaltzy daintiness of Drigo's *Valse bluette* is followed by an unexaggerated but full-timbred warmth in Fibich's *Poème*. The gypsy temperament of the Falla and the ready sparkle of Sarasate's *Tarantelle* and Kroll's *Banjo and fiddle* are offset by the lyrical appeal of the more atmospheric pieces. The violin is very present – perhaps the microphones are a fraction too close, but the balance with the piano is satisfactory and there is not an exaggerated spotlight here.

Lloyd Webber, Julian (cello)

'British cello music' ((i) with John McCabe, piano): (i) RAWSTHORNE: *Sonata for cello and piano.* ARNOLD: *Fantasy for cello.* (i) IRELAND: *The holy boy.* WALTON: *Passacaglia.* BRITTEN: *Tema (Sacher); Cello suite No. 3.*

*** ASV CDDCA 592.

A splendid recital and a most valuable one. Julian Lloyd Webber has championed such rarities as the Bridge *Oration* at a time when it was unrecorded and now devotes this present issue to British music that needs strong advocacy; there is no alternative version of the Rawsthorne *Sonata*, in which he is most ably partnered by John McCabe. He gives this piece – and, for that matter, the remainder of the programme – with full-blooded commitment. Good recording.

'British cello music', Vol. 2 (with John McCabe, piano): STANFORD: *Sonata No. 2, Op. 39.* BRIDGE: *Elegy; Scherzetto.* IRELAND: *Sonata in G min.*

✪ *** ASV CDDCA 807.

The Stanford *Second Cello sonata* (1893 – written between the *Fourth* and *Fifth Symphonies*) is revealed here as an inspired work whose opening theme flowers into great lyrical warmth on Lloyd Webber's ardent bow. The focus of the recording is a little diffuse, but that serves to add to the atmosphere. Ireland's *Sonata*, too, is among his most richly inspired works, a broad-spanning piece in which ambitious, darkly intense outer movements frame a most beautiful *Poco largamente*. Again Lloyd Webber, who has long been a passionate advocate of the work, conveys its full expressive power. The Bridge *Elegy* (written as early as 1911) is another darkly poignant evocation which points forward to the sparer, more austere style of the later Bridge, and the *Scherzetto* (even earlier, 1902) makes a winning encore: it should ideally have been placed at the end of the recital. John McCabe is a sympathetic partner – in spite of the balance – but this collection offers what are among Lloyd Webber's finest performances on disc.

London Wind Trio

'20th-century miniatures': IBERT: *5 Pièces en trio.* MILHAUD: *Pastorale; Suite d'après Corrette, Op. 161b.* TOMASI: *Concert champêtre.* POULENC: *Sonata for clarinet and bassoon.* VILLA-LOBOS: *Trio.*

*** Somm SOMMCD 013.

The personnel of the London Wind Trio consists of Neil Black, Keith Puddy and Roger Birnstingl, who are as adroit individually as they are perfectly matched as a team. They give attractively deft and fresh performances of these finely crafted French works, conveying their enjoyment of the music's melodic felicity. The wit, charm and nostalgia of Ibert's *Cinq Pièces* contrast with Milhaud's *Pastorale* which is more brazenly prolix, yet his *Suite d'après Corrette* has an ingenuous simplicity, while offering a neat condiment of dissonance in its Menuet, before the chirping of 'Le coucou'.

No less diverting is the cheeky Poulenc duo *Sonata* with its rueful central 'Nocturne' (*très doux*). Tomasi's rustic *Concert champêtre* is hardly less engaging, with its droll *Nocturne* temporarily interrupting the good humour before the folksy closing 'Vif'. The Villa-Lobos *Trio* is the most ambitious piece, fascinatingly intricate in its rhythmic and harmonic texture, evoking the exotic, vividly colourful sounds of the Brazilian jungle, with the central *Languissamente* a darker, but still restless, tropical nocturnal. It is played with great character and unforced virtuosity. The well-balanced, natural recording gives these artists a fine presence and altogether this is a most diverting and rewarding recital.

Ma, Yo-Yo (cello), Lynn Chang, Ronan Lefkowitz (violins), Jeffrey Kahane, Gilbert Kalish (pianos)

IVES: *Trio for violin, clarinet and piano.* BERNSTEIN: *Clarinet sonata (arr.* MA). KIRCHNER: *Triptych.* GERSHWIN: *3 Preludes* (arr. HEIFETZ/MA).

*** Sony SK 53126.

An unexpectedly rewarding and beguiling mix which is more than the sum of its parts. The whole 65-minute recital is just the thing for late-evening stimulation. The early Bernstein sonata transcription is full of that ready melodic and rhythmic appeal which makes the composer's concert music so individual, and the Gershwin encore, equally felicitously transcribed, is hardly less appealing. The meat of the programme is in the Kirchner *Triptych*, while the jokesy Ives provides a *Trio* (quoting corny 'folk' tunes with relish), bringing the usual audacious 'remembering', this time picturing 'Sunday evening on the campus', thus concluding the entertainment with much spirit and aplomb.

McLachlan, Murray (piano)

Piano music from Scotland: SCOTT: *8 Songs* (trans. Stevenson): *Since all thy vows, false maid; Wha is that at my bower-door?; O were my love yon lilac fare; Wee Willie Gray; Milkwort and bog-cotton; Crowdieknowe; Ay waukin, O; There's news, lasses, news.* CENTER: *Piano sonata; 6 Bagatelles, Op. 3.; Children at play.* STEVENSON: *Beltane bonfire. 2 Scottish ballads: The Dowie Dens O Yarrow; Newhaven fishwife's cry.*

⚙ *** Olympia OCD 264.

Francis George Scott (1880–1958) was a prolific and striking composer of songs and Ronald Stevenson's very free transcriptions, somewhat after the fashion of Liszt's concert paraphrases, are imaginatively creative in their own right. Ronald Center's *Piano sonata* is restless and mercurial, lacking much in the way of repose, but the joyous syncopations of the first movement are infectious and the work is a major contribution to the repertory and not in the least difficult to approach. The *Six Bagatelles* are even more strikingly diverse in mood. *Children at play* is an enchanting piece, with a musical-box miniaturism of texture at times, yet the writing is by no means inconsequential. All this music is played with commitment and considerable bravura by Murray McLachlan, who is clearly a sympathetic exponent, and the recording is extremely vivid and real. Our Rosette is awarded not just for enterprise, but equally from admiration and pleasure.

Malcolm, George (harpsichord)

'*The world of the harpsichord*': BACH: *Italian concerto, BWV 971; Chromatic fantasia and fugue in D min., BWV 903; French suite No. 5 in G, BWV 816; Toccata in D, BWV 912.* PARADIES: *Toccata.* DAQUIN: *The cuckoo.* RIMSKY-KORSAKOV: *Flight of the bumblebee* (arr. MALCOLM). RAMEAU: *Pièces de clavecin: La Poule; Le rappel des oiseaux; Tambourin.* François COUPERIN: *Pièces de clavecin: Le rossignol-en-amour; Le carillon de Cithère.* TEMPLETON: *Bach goes to town.* MALCOLM: *Bach before the mast.*

⚙ (M) *** Decca (ADD) 444 390-2.

This is a delectable collection, a CD of harpsichord music that should be in even the smallest collection, spanning as it does the full range of the late George Malcolm's wide repertory. His Bach performances are very considerable indeed: the *Chromatic fantasia* has an appropriate improvisatory element, the *Italian concerto* is full of vitality, and the best known of the *French suites* has a genial, lyrical intimacy to offset the buoyant *Toccata in D*. The comparative gravitas of Bach goes well with the charm of Rameau and Couperin, with their descriptive pieces realized with flair, notably *Le rappel des oiseaux* and *Le carillon de Cithère*.

The two witty Bach imitations make a tempting hors d'oeuvre and the Rimsky-Korsakov is similarly a fun piece, played with great bravura; but no one should dismiss the mixture, for there is plenty of real substance here and playing of great distinction. The 1960s recording of the harpsichord (unnamed, but almost certainly a modern copy of a fine baroque instrument) is in the demonstration class, beautifully balanced – not too close – and natural within an airy but not over-resonant acoustic.

Marsalis, Wynton (trumpet), Judith Lynn Stillman (piano)

'On the 20th century': RAVEL: *Pièce en forme de Habanera.* HONEGGER: *Intrada.* TOMASI: *Triptyque.* STEVENS: *Sonata.* POULENC: *Eiffel Tower polka* (trans. Stewart). ENESCU: *Légende.* BERNSTEIN: *Rondo for Lifey.* BOZZA: *Rustiques.* HINDEMITH: *Sonata.*

*** Sony SK 47193.

What a wonderful player Wynton Marsalis is! His instrumental profile is so strong and stylish, his basic timbre unforgettably full of character, as at the very opening with the quiet, stately presentation of Ravel's *Pièce en forme de Habanera.* The Enescu *Légende* is hardly less distinctive, while the melodic line of Bozza's *Rustiques*, though not in the Ravel class, yet sounds remarkably special, and the jolly roulades of the finale bring the easy manner of true virtuosity. Yet for fizzing bravura turn to the witty Poulenc polka – like a silent movie speeded up (*Discours du général* from *Les mariés de la Tour Eiffel* – transcribed by Don Stewart for two trumpets in which Wynton takes both parts, with a little electronic help). The Halsey Stevens *Sonata* is a first-class piece, and Marsalis makes the Hindemith, which has an effectively dry slow movement and a *Trauermusik* finale, sound almost like a masterpiece, helped by the fine piano contribution of Judith Stillman. The recording has an uncanny presence and realism: it is as if this superb artist were just out beyond the speakers.

Mayer, Albrecht (oboe), Markus Becker (piano)

COSSART: *Liebesgedicht, Op. 23/4.* DAELLI: *Fantasy on themes from Verdi's Rigoletto.* KOECHLIN: *Le repos de tityre - Monodie, Op. 216/10.* NIELSEN: *2 Fantasy pieces, Op. 2.* SCHUMANN: *Abendlied, Op. 107/6; Ihre Stimme, Op. 96/3; Romanzen, Op. 94; Stille tränen, Op. 35/10.* YVON: *Sonata in F.*

🌠 (B) *** EMI Début CDZ5 73167-2.

Albrecht Mayer is an artist of exceptional quality and his partnership with Markus Becker the meeting of true minds. Their playing on this EMI Début recital gives enormous pleasure for its subtlety, refinement and musicianship. Their choice of repertoire is unfailingly enterprising and the Schumann and Nielsen are as well played as we have ever heard. Mayer is principal oboe of the Berlin Philharmonic and will obviously be one of the great players of the next decade or so. Excellent recording.

Melos Ensemble

18th- and 19th-century chamber music: MOZART: *Piano and wind quintet in E flat, K.452.*

BEETHOVEN: *Piano and wind quintet in E flat, Op. 16; Sextet in E flat for 2 horns, 2 violins, viola & cello, Op. 81b; March for wind sextet in B flat, WoO 29; Rondino in E flat, WoO 25; Duo No. 1 for clarinet and bassoon, WoO 27.* SCHUMANN: *Fantasiestücke for clarinet and piano, Op. 73. Märchenerzählungen, Op. 132.* BRAHMS: *Clarinet quintet in B min., Op. 115.* REGER: *Clarinet quintet in A: 2nd movement: Vivace.*

(B) *** EMI Double fforte (ADD) CZS5 72643-2 (2).

This collection, like its companion below, dates from the late 1960s when the Melos Ensemble gathered together some of London's finest orchestral musicians to make a series of recordings for EMI. There is plenty of individual personality in the music-making here, but how beautifully these fine musicians blend together as a group! The polished elegance and charm of their playing cannot be heard to better effect than in the Mozart *Piano and wind quintet*, dominated by the splendid musicianship of the pianist, Lamar Crowson, and with some particularly felicitous oboe playing from Peter Graeme. Its Beethoven successor follows on naturally, played with a lighter touch than usual to emphasize the Mozartean influences.

The *Sextet* brings some splendid bravura from the two horn players, Neil Sanders and James Buck, while the *March* (for wind alone) is very jolly. The *Duo* for clarinet and bassoon is now thought not to be by Beethoven but is very agreeable nevertheless. Schumann's rarely heard *Märchenerzählungen* ('Fairy-tales') is late (1853) and is almost unique in being scored for the same combination as Mozart's *Trio* for clarinet, viola (here Gervase de Peyer and Cecil Aronowitz) and piano. The *Fantasiestücke*, for clarinet and piano, was written four years earlier. Both performances are persuasively warm and mellow, although Lamar Crowson again achieves a strong backing profile.

For all their lyricism, these artists don't miss Schumann's marking, '*mit Feuer*', in the finale of Op. 73, and the second movement of Op. 132 is strongly accented to make a bold contrast with the flowingly romantic third, before the similarly bold finale. Gervase de Peyer then relaxes completely to present an essentially lyrical view of the Brahms *Clarinet quintet*. It is a lovely performance, achieving a wistful nostalgia in the slow movement, but it is perhaps in the rippling execution of the arpeggios of the finale that his playing is particularly individual. The Reger lollipop *Scherzo*, which acts as an encore, may be as light as thistledown, but its central trio has a beguiling richness of style in the post-Brahms tradition. All the recordings were made at Abbey Road, and the sound is excellent throughout; only in the Beethoven Sextet is there a hint of thinness in the violins. Overall this will give much refreshment and pleasure.

20th-century chamber music: RAVEL: *Introduction and allegro for flute, clarinet, harp and string quartet.* POULENC: *Trio for oboe, bassoon and piano; Sonata for clarinet and bassoon.* FRANCAIX: *Divertissement for oboe, clarinet and bassoon;*

Divertissement for bassoon and string quintet.
MILHAUD: *Suite for violin, clarinet and piano.*
BARTOK: *Contrasts for violin, clarinet and piano.*
SKALKOTTAS: *Octet; 8 Variations on a Greek tune.*
KHACHATURIAN: *Trio for clarinet, violin and piano.*
PROKOFIEV: *Overture on Hebrew themes.*

(B) *** EMI Double fforte (ADD) CZS5 72646-2 (2).

If anything, the Melos survey of twentieth-century music is even more enjoyable than their classical programme. It opens with Ravel's sublime *Septet* (with Richard Adeney, Gervase de Peyer and Osian Ellis in the lead). The performance is very fine indeed, and the 1967 Abbey Road recording is that bit warmer and smoother than their earlier version for Oiseau-Lyre/Decca, even if that might have a degree more subtlety (Decca 452 891-2). Both the Poulenc pieces are delightful, particularly the delicious *Trio for oboe, bassoon and piano*, which has an admirably dry wit and unfailing inventiveness; the playing is above reproach. The two *Divertissements* of the always elegant Jean Françaix have much inconsequential charm, and the *Ouverture* and *Finale* of the irrepressible Milhaud *Suite* sparkle lustrously, while the inner movements produce an engaging, gentle melancholy. The other masterpiece here is the Bartók *Contrasts*, for the same combination as the Milhaud but of altogether stronger fibre. Both are played superbly. The works by the neglected Greek composer Nikolaos Skalkottas (a Schoenberg pupil who died not long after the Second World War) show a fairly strong personality, the *Octet* abrasively neo-classical, and both pieces revelling in a mordant harmonic dissonance. The surprise is Khachaturian's remarkably cultivated *Trio*, laced with attractively sinuous Armenian ideas. Finally comes Prokofiev's *Overture on Hebrew themes*, another highly spontaneous piece, presented with real style. The recording is excellent throughout.

Menuhin, Yehudi and Stéphane Grappelli (violins)

'*Menuhin and Grappelli play*' (with rhythm group; Alan Clare Trio; Orchestral Ensemble; cond. Nelson Riddle and Max Harris): GERSHWIN: *Fascinatin' rhythm; Soon; Summertime; Nice work if you can get it; Embraceable you; Liza; A foggy day; 'S wonderful; The man I love; I got rhythm; He loves and she loves; They can't take that away from me; They all laughed; Funny face; Our love is here to stay; Lady be good.* STRACHEY: *These foolish things.* RASKIN: *Laura.* HARBURG & DUKE: *April in Paris.* KOSMA, PREVERT & MERCER: *Autumn leaves.* DUKE: *Autumn in New York.* BERLIN: *Cheek to cheek; Isn't this a lovely day; Change partners; Top hat, white tie and tails; I've got my love to keep me warm; Heat wave.* KERN: *The way you look tonight; Pick yourself up; A fine romance; All the things you are; Why do I love you?* PORTER: *I get a kick out of you; Night and day; Looking at you; Just one of those things.* RODGERS &

HART: *My funny Valentine; Thou swell; The lady is a tramp; Blue room.* GADE: *Jealousy.* CARMICHAEL: *Skylark.*

(B) *** EMI Double fforte Analogue/Dig. CZS5 73380-2 (2).

The partnership of Menuhin and Grappelli started in the television studio, many years before Menuhin was ennobled. Their brief duets (tagged on to interviews) were so successful that the idea developed of recording a whole recital (and then several), with each maestro striking sparks off the other in style, but matching the other remarkably closely in matters of tone and balance. One of the secrets of success of this partnership lies in the choice of material. All these items started as first-rate songs, with striking melodies which live in whatever guise, and here with ingenious arrangements (mostly made by Max Harris, but some by Nelson Riddle) which spark off the individual genius of each violinist, acting as a challenge, and inviting the players' obvious enjoyment. The result is delightful, particularly in numbers such as *Pick yourself up* where the arrangement directly tips a wink towards Bachian figuration. The CD transfers are immaculate and the high spirits of the collaboration are caught beautifully.

Michelangeli, Arturo Benedetti (piano)

BEETHOVEN: *Piano Sonatas Nos. 4 in E flat, Op. 7; 12 in A flat, Op. 26.* DEBUSSY: *Hommage à Rameau.* RAVEL: *Gaspard de la nuit.*

*** BBC Legends (ADD) BBCL 4064-2.

The Ravel *Gaspard de la nuit* has been in circulation on various labels, most recently in the Philips '*Great Pianists of the Twentieth Century*' series. Recorded in the Concert Hall of Broadcasting House in 1959, it was a legendary account of *Gaspard*, which left all who heard it spellbound. But, of course, there have been many *Gaspards*: the balance renders Michelangeli's enormous dynamic range less wide than usual (the opening of *Ondine* is not as *pianissimo* as one remembers it being in the Concert Hall). Those who recall Michelangeli's marmoreal account of the *E flat Sonata*, Op. 7, which bestrode two sides of a DG LP way back in the early 1970s, will find the 1982 Festival account more involving – but then, it had to be! Generally speaking, Michelangeli is commanding in both sonatas and produces some lovely sounds in the Debussy *Hommage à Rameau*. Admirers of the great pianist will want this, and the sound is very acceptable indeed.

Miolin, Anders (ten-stringed guitar)

'*The Lion and the Lute*': WALTON: *5 Bagatelles.* RAWSTHORNE: *Elegy.* LENNOX BERKELEY: *Sonatina, Op. 51; Theme and variations, Op. 77.* TIPPETT: *The Blue guitar.* BRITTEN: *Nocturnal, Op. 70.*

*** BIS Dig. CD 926.

Anders Miolin, born in Stockholm, designs his own guitars, allowing a greater compass and creating a richer palette. That is well borne out here by this unsurpassed collection of British twentieth-century guitar music; indeed, the colour inherent in the five Walton *Bagatelles* has never glowed so brightly, and this comment might also be applied to the whole programme, so attractively recorded in an open acoustic. The Rawsthorne *Elegy* is darkly expressive and both the Tippett and Britten works are highly charged and atmospheric. The Tippett was inspired indirectly by a Picasso painting, which stimulated Wallace Stevens to write a poem called 'The man with the blue guitar'. The Britten night music is a set of seven variations and a passacaglia on Dowland's song *Come heavy sleep*. Both make considerable imaginative as well as technical demands on the player, and they could hardly be more persuasively presented or recorded. If you enjoy guitar music, this is not to be missed.

Mogilevsky, Alexander (piano)

BACH **arr.** SILOTI: *Prelude in B min.* BRAHMS: *Fantasias, Op. 116/2, 4 & 5.* PROKOFIEV: *Sonata No. 7.* SCHUMANN: *Kinderszenen.*

(M) *(*) EMI CDM5 67934-2

Alexander Mogilevsky is one of the young artists to enjoy the advocacy of Martha Argerich in EMI's midprice series. Born in Odessa twenty-five years ago he is Moscow-trained and has already appeared at the Théâtre du Châtelet in Paris and at the Wigmore Hall. He possesses excellent fingers and an impressive range of keyboard colour but he is far from self-effacing in his approach to these pieces. In the three Brahms *Intermezzi* from the *Fantasien, Op. 116* he produces beautifully inward, withdrawn sound and the intrusive rubati which are so ruinous in Schumann's *Kinderszenen* are less disturbing. Nothing is left to speak for itself in the Schumann, which is at times unbearably affected and even in the slow movement of the Prokofiev *Seventh Sonata* he manages to insert all sorts of little expressive hesitations into the melodic line. The recording made in the studios of Radio della Svizzera Italian in Lugano is excellent.

Moiseiwitsch, Benno (piano)

1938-1950 recordings: MUSSORGSKY: *Pictures at an exhibition.* BEETHOVEN: *Andanti favori, WoO 57; Rondo in C, Op. 51/1.* WEBER: *Sonata No. 1: Presto; Invitation to the dance* (**arr.** TAUSIG). MENDELSSOHN: *Scherzo in E min., Op. 16.* SCHUMANN: *Romanzen: No. 2, Op. 28/2.* CHOPIN: *Nocturne in E flat, Op. 9/2; Polonaise in B flat, Op. 71/2; Barcarolle, Op. 60.* LISZT: *Liebestraum No. 3; Etude de concert: La leggierezza. Hungarian rhapsody No. 2 in C sharp min. Concert paraphrase of Wagner's Tannhäuser overture.* DEBUSSY: *Pour le piano: Toccata. Suite bergamasque: Clair de lune.*

Estampes: Jardins sous la pluie. RAVEL: *Le tombeau de Couperin: Toccata.*

(**(*)) APR mono CDAPR 7005 (2).

Moiseiwitsch never enjoyed quite the exposure on records to which his gifts entitled him, though in the earlier part of his career he made a great many. Later, in the electrical era, he was a 'plum-label' artist and was not issued on the more prestigious and expensive 'red label'. In this he was in pretty good company, for Solomon and Myra Hess were similarly relegated. This anthology gives a good picture of the great pianist in a wide variety of repertory: his *Pictures at an exhibition*, made in 1945, was for some time the only piano version; and those who identify him solely with the Russians will find his Chopin *Barcarolle* and Debussy *Jardins sous la pluie* totally idiomatic. The transfers are variable – all are made from commercial copies, some in better condition than others.

Mordkovitch, Lydia (violin), Gerhard Oppitz (piano)

BRAHMS: *Violin Sonatas Nos. 1–3.* PROKOFIEV: *Violin Sonatas Nos. 1–2.* SCHUBERT: *Fantasie in C, Op. post. 159 D.934; Violin Sonata in A, Op. post. 162 D.574.* R. STRAUSS: *Violin Sonata in E, Op. 18.* SCHUMANN: *Violin Sonatas Nos. 1–2.* FAURE: *Violin Sonata in A, Op. 13.*

(B) **(*) Chan. 6659 (4).

Chandos has collected Lydia Mordkovitch's sonata recordings made with Gerhard Oppitz in the 1980s into this one bargain box. It is an inexpensive way of acquiring this artist's often exciting violin playing, very Russian, full of temperament, and never dull. The Brahms *Sonatas* are without question amongst the finest performances of this repertoire, with Mordkovitch's imaginative and subtle phrasing a constant source of pleasure. Both she and Oppitz give authoritative and perceptive accounts of all three sonatas, which could almost be a top choice were it not for the over-reverberant sound. If her accounts of the Prokofiev *Sonatas* do not displace versions by Oistrakh and Perlman, they can be placed alongside them. These are thoughtful readings with vital contributions from both partners. They have the measure of the darker, more searching side of the F minor, and are hardly less excellent in the companion work. The recording is excellent and the insights both artists bring to this music make these performances well worth exploring. The popular Fauré *Sonata* is given a sensitive account by Mordkovitch, but her otherworldly, disembodied pianissimo tone does not always draw comparable playing from the pianist, though the acoustic may have posed problems. All the same, the performance gives pleasure. The Strauss *Sonata* is certainly compelling, though here too the recording, which tends to make the piano a little overpowering, is not ideal. The Schubert pieces receive lovely performances, though yet again the over-reverberant recording, which draws attention to the fact that it was recorded in an empty church, does not help – for this is above all intimate music, and the sound – which even blurs details in places – precludes that. The quality for the Schumann is much better, and one enjoys the rich colours Mordkovitch finds in these richly rewarding Sonatas.

Moyse, Marcel (flute)

'The Recorded Legacy' (with Louise Moyse, piano and others): DRIGO: *Les millions d'Arlequin: Serenade.* HUE: *Fantaisie.* COUPERIN: *Le rossignol en amour.* SEGHERS: *Souvenir de Gand.* DOPPLER: *Fantaisie pastorale hongroise, Op. 26.* FERROUD: *3 Pièces for solo flute.* WETZGER: *By the Brook.* BIZET: *L'Arlésienne: Minuet.* IBERT: *Piece for Solo Flute.* GÉNIN: *Carnaval de Venise, Op. 11; Fantasy with Variations on a Neapolitan Air, Op. 8.* DVORAK: *Humoresque, Op. 101/7.* REICHERT: *Fantaisie mélancolique, Op. 1.* LALO: *Namouna suite No. 1: Parade de Foire* (with Paris Conservatoire Orchestra, Pierre Coppola). TCHAIKOVSKY: *Andante cantabile.* TELEMANN: *Esercizi musici No. 9: Trio in E min.* (with Blanche Honegger).

(B) (***) Dutton mono CDLX 7041.

Marcel Moyse was a legendary figure in the 1920s and '30s when these recordings were made, and (because the timbre of the flute is harmonically so pure) his characteristically French clear, sweet tone could be captured very realistically in the early days of electric recording. Moyse was soloist in the pioneering records of the Bach *Brandenburgs* by the Busch Chamber Players, his 1930 recording of the Mozart *D major Concerto* received a 'Grand Prix du Disque', and he later recorded Debussy's *Syrinx* and the *Sonata for Flute, Viola and Harp.* But alas, most of the music included here (including much music written or arranged especially for him) is trivial, including the most substantial work, Döppler's (11-minute) *Fantaisie pastorale hongroise,* which neverthless displays astonishing virtuosity.

Moyse's remarkable technical facility is certainly displayed here, but is best heard in the lollipops. However, Pierre Ferroud's *Trois pièces pour flûte seul* make a haunting interlude of some musical distinction, as does the performance of Couperin's *Le rossignol en amour.* The solo *Pièce* by Ibert, recorded in 1935, has cuts when compared with the published score. Conjecturally this may have been because Moyse used the composer's early pre-publication draft, or it could have been brought about by the time limitations of the 78 rpm disc – most likely both factors contributed.

It is good to hear Moyse as an orchestral soloist in the delicious excerpt from Lalo's *Namouna.* Otherwise the accompaniments of Louise Moyse are simple and supportive, but the unidentified pianist backing the dazzling *Carnaval de Venise* is almost comically square. After so much triviality, the final item in the programme offers a tantalizing excerpt from Tele-

mann's *Esercizi musici* which engagingly shows Moyse as a fine chamber-music player. In many ways it is the most rewarding piece on the disc. As expected from this source the transfers are impeccable.

'Música española' for guitar

'Música española' for guitar, Volume I (played by: William Gómez, Timothy Walker, John Williams, Eduardo Fernández, Carlos Bonell): ANON.: *Romance.* MUDARRA: *Fantasía X.* SOR: *Minuets Nos. 9, 25; Introduction and variations on a theme by Mozart; Gran solo; Sonatas in C min., Op. 15/2; in C, Op. 25; Estudios, Op. 35/16, 17; Op. 6/4, 6, 8; Op. 29/23; Les Adieux, Op. 21; Fantasía elegíaca.* TARREGA: *Recuerdos de la Alhambra; Estudio brillante; 5 Preludes; Minuet; 3 Mazurkas; Lágrima (Andante); La alborada; Introduction and fantasia on themes from La Traviata.* CHAPI: *Serenata morisca.* GRANADOS: *Goyescas: La Maja de Goya; Danzas españolas Nos. 5 (Andaluza); 10 (Melancólica).*

(B) *** Double Decca (IMS) DDD/ADD 433 932-2 (2).

This generous collection centres on a pair of outstanding digital recitals from the highly musical Eduardo Fernández of the music of Sor and Tárrega. Sor gets the lion's share including the two *Sonatas,* Op. 15/2 and Op. 25, 6 *Estudios* and the *Fantasía elegíaca* (with its remarkable 14-minute *Marcha fúnebre*), which Fernández plays with a characteristic, restrained eloquence. Much of Sor's writing has a melancholy trait. The one-movement *Sonata in C* is thoroughly classical, but the *C minor Sonata* opens darkly and has an appealingly lyrical Theme and variations for its finale. The Tárrega pieces include, of course, the famous fluttering *Recuerdos de la Alhambra,* and the diverting *Introducción y fantasia sobre temas de La Traviata,* while John Williams plays Sor's famous *Variations on a theme of Mozart.* The other players who contribute include William Gómez, who opens the programme with the anonymous but indelible *Jeux interdits,* Carlos Bonell in Granados, and Timothy Walker (who seems to be recorded at a fractionally lower pitch than his colleagues).

'Música española' for guitar, Volume II (played by Eduardo Fernández, John Williams, Carlos Bonell, William Gómez, Sergio and Eduardo Abreu, Timothy Walker): ALBENIZ: *Sevilla; Tango; Asturias; Cádiz. Torre bermeja.* VALVERDE: *Clavelitos.* LLOBET: *Scherzo-vals; 6 Canciones catalanas.* FALLA: *Homenaje a Debussy.* TURINA: *Homenaje a Tárrega; Fandanguillo; Ráfaga.* DE LA MAZA: *Habanera.* SEGOVIA: *Oración; Estudio; Neblina; Estudio sinz luz; Divertimento.* TORROBA: *Madroños; Fandanguillo; La danza; Canción y danza No. 1.* RODRIGO: *3 Piezas españolas. Concierto de Aranjuez; Fantasia para un gentilhombre* (both with Montreal SO, Charles Dutoit).

(B) **(*) Double Decca ADD/DDD 433 935-2 (2).

Fernández shares the limelight here with Carlos Bonell, and the other players listed make more modest contributions to what is certainly a well-varied programme (149 minutes). Fernández opens with Albéniz and continues with Llobet's *6 Canciones catalanas*. Bonell makes a vivid entry with Valverde's *Clavelitos* and then after Fernández has returned to play Tórroba's *Sonatina* and Rodrigo's *3 Piezas españolas*, Bonell is joined by Charles Dutoit and the Montreal Orchestra for Rodrigo's two most popular concertante works, splendidly played and recorded; but these are works which many collectors will have already.

Nakariakov, Sergei (trumpet), Alexander Markovich (piano)

'*Trumpet works*': GERSHWIN: *Rhapsody in blue* (arr. DOKSHITSER). ARENSKY: *Concert waltz.* ARBAN: *Carnival of Venice.* RAVEL: *Pavane pour une infante défunte.* BERNSTEIN: *Rondo for Lifey.* GLAZUNOV: *Albumblatt.* STOLTE: *Burleske.* HARTMANN: *Arbucklenian polka.* FIBICH: *Poème.* RIMSKYKORSAKOV: *Flight of the bumblebee.* DINICU: *Hora staccato.* GLIÈRE: *Valse.* RUEFF: *Sonatina.*

*** Teldec 9031 77705-2.

An astonishing CD début by a brilliant Russian schoolboy virtuoso, barely fifteen at the time. Nakariakov's supreme command of the instrument is matched by instinctive musicality and taste. He manages to sound suitably transatlantic in an incredible full-length arrangement of Gershwin's *Rhapsody in blue*, and is even better in Bernstein's entertainingly ebullient *Rondo for Lifey*. Lovely tone and simplicity of line make Fibich's *Poème* sound appealingly restrained, and in the bandstand variations by Arban and Hartmann the playing is stylishly infectious. Highlights are Stolte's witty *Burleske* and the very considerable *Sonatina* by Jeanine Rueff in which trumpeter and pianist, as elsewhere, make a genuine partnership. But for ear-tickling bravura try Dinicu's *Hora staccato*, which surely would have impressed Heifetz. Excellently balanced and realistic recording.

ARBAN: *Variations on a theme from Bellini's 'Norma'; Variations on a Tyrolean song.* BIZET, arr. WAXMAN: *Carmen fantasy.* BRANDT: *Concert piece No. 2.* FALLA: *Spanish dance.* FAURE: *Le réveil.* PAGANINI: *Caprice, Op. 1/17; Moto perpetuo, Op. 11.* SARASATE: *Zigeunerweisen, Op. 20/1.* SAINT-SAENS: *Le cygne.*

**(*) Teldec 4509 94554-2.

Sergei Nakariakov exhibits some stunning technique in his second Teldec recital, coupling various trifles including Franz Waxman's *Carmen fantasy* and Paganini's *Moto perpetuo*, as well as the remainder of his programme. He was only seventeen when this recording was made and, although not many will want to hear more than a few of these pieces at a time, there is much to enjoy. He is a veritable Russian

Håkan Hardenberger, save for the fact that, on the evidence of this disc, he does not always command the latter's extraordinary variety of tonal colour or his impeccable taste.

Navarra, André (cello), Erika Kilcher (piano)

Recital: Sonatas by: LOCATELLI; VALENTINI; BOCCHERINI: *in A & G.* GRANADOS: *Goyescas: Intermezzo.* FALLA: *Suite populaire espagnole* (arr. Maurice MARECHAL). NIN: *Chants d'Espagne: Saeta; Andalousie.*

(M) *** Cal. (ADD) CAL 6673.

Navarra's recital dates from 1981 and shows this fine cellist in top form. He is splendidly partnered by Erika Kilcher, who, although she is backwardly balanced in relation to the up-front cello (recorded somewhat dryly), makes a highly artistic contribution with her sympathetic accompaniments. This is immediately noticeable in the splendid opening sonata of Locatelli.

But it is the four-movement work by Giuseppe Valentini which is the highlight of the Italian repertoire, a most engaging piece with an elegant *Gavotte* and an aria-like *Largo*, framed by two energetic outer movements in which Navarra's spiccato-like articulation of moto perpetuo allegros is most infectious. He is equally at home in the Spanish half of the programme, and Kilcher joins him in providing colourful characterization of the five miniatures which make up the Falla suite. In the second of the two Nin pieces, *Andalousie*, Navarra's cello sounds like a larger-than-life Spanish guitar. However, it is a pity that the documentation does not identify the Italian sonatas more positively.

New Century Saxophone Quartet

'*Main Street USA*': GOULD: *Pavane. Main Street waltz; Main Street march.* GERSHWIN: *Promenade; Three quartet blues; Merry Andrew. Porgy and Bess: Clara, Clara; Oh, I got plenty o' nuttin'; Bess, you is my woman now; Oh, I can't sit down; It ain't necessarily so; Summertime; There's a boat dat's leavin' for New York; Oh Lawd, I'm on my way.* BERNSTEIN: *West Side story: I feel pretty; Balcony scene; Tonight; Cha-cha/Meeting scene; Jump; One hand, one heart; Gee, officer Krupke; Scherzo; Somewhere.*

*** Channel Classics CCS 9896.

Uncommonly fine playing, with superbly blended timbres and a subtly appealing melodic lead from Michael Stephenson on the soprano saxophone, means that this collection of famous show melodies is very appealing. Gould's delightful *Pavane* is presented with a neat degree of whimsy and the three Gershwin instrumental numbers have a pleasing sophistication. Stephenson's line in the songs is quite remarkably vocal in feeling. 'It ain't necessarily so' recalls Fats Waller, and the Balcony scene from *West Side story* is really touching. Steven Kirkman gives admirably restrained support on percussion, when needed, and the balance and recording could hardly be bettered.

Nishizaki, Takako (violin)

'*Romantic violin favourites*': trans. Fritz Kreisler (with Wolf Harden, piano): SCHUBERT: *Rosamunde: Ballet music.* BIZET: *L'Arlésienne: Adagietto.* RIMSKY-KORSAKOV: *Le coq d'or: Hymn to the sun. Sadko: Hindu song. Scheherazade: Oriental dance.* DVORAK: *Songs my mother taught me.* GLUCK: *Orfeo ed Eurydice: Dance of the Blessed Spirits.* HAYDN: *Piano trio in G: Hungarian rondo. Austrian imperial hymn.* MOZART: *Haffner serenade: Rondo.* SCHUMANN: *Romance, Op. 94.* GRIEG: *Lyric piece: To the spring.* RAMEAU: *Tambourin.* GRAINGER: *Molly on the shore.* TRAD.: *Song of the Volga boatmen; Londonderry air.*

(BB) **(*) Naxos Dig. 8.550125.

'*Violin miniatures*' (with Jenö Jandó, piano): KREISLER: *Schön Rosmarin; Rondino; Liebesleid; Liebesfreud; Caprice viennois.* RACHMANINOV: *Rhapsody on a theme by Paganini: Variation No. 18.* FIBICH: *Poème.* ELGAR: *Salut d'amour.* GRANADOS: *Spanish dance: Andaluza, Op. 37/5.* BRAHMS: *Hungarian dance No. 1.* SCHUBERT: *Moment musical in F min.* DVORAK: *Humoresque, Op. 101/7; Slavonic dance No. 1 in G min.* (all trans. Kreisler). BOCCHERINI: *Minuet.* DEBUSSY: *Clair de lune.* MASSENET: *Thaïs: Méditation.* TCHAIKOVSKY: *Chant sans paroles, Op. 2/3; Chanson triste, Op. 40/2.*

(BB) **(*) Naxos 8.550306.

Takako Nishizaki is a highly accomplished player who has recorded prolifically on the Marco Polo and Naxos labels. She has recorded Mozart sonatas with Jenö Jandó and a host of rare works, from Respighi's *Concerto gregoriano* to César Cui's *Suite concertante.* She delivers these miniatures with considerable charm and aplomb. Good recording – no one investing in these CDs is likely to be disappointed and, were there not even more virtuosic and authoritative versions in the catalogue, they would warrant an unqualified three stars.

O'Dette, Paul (lute)

'*Alla Venetiana*': DALZA: *Pavana alla veneziana; Saltarello; Piva I; Piva II; Piva III Ricercar; Calata ala spagnola ditto terzetti; Tastar de corde - Recercar dietro; Pavana alla ferrarese; Saltarello.* ANON. arr. DALZA: *Laudate Dio.* CAPIROLA: *Recercar primo; Recercar secondo; Recercar quinto; Non ti spiaqua l'ascoltar; La vilanela; Padoana belissima; Spagna seconda; Tientalora (Balletto da ballare).* VAN GHIZEGHEM: *De tous bien playne; De tous bien playne nel ton del primo recercar.* CARA: *O mia ciecha, e dura sorte.* PESENTI: *Che farala.* SPINACINO: *Recercare I; Recercare II.* MARTINI:

Malor me bat. JOSQUIN DESPREZ: *Adieu mes amours; Qui tolis pechata mondi.*

*** HM HMU 907215.

The expert lutenist Paul O'Dette seldom disappoints. He draws here mainly on the very first Venetian books of solo lute music to be published, by Francesco Spinacino (1507) and Joan (Zuan) Ambrosio Dalza (1508). Lively dance pieces by the latter, who has a comparatively strong musical personality, are used to frame this varied 73-minute programme. The early repertory comes in three main categories, the improvisatory ricercare, and arrangements of vocal music and dances. O'Dette shows himself a master of the ruminative improvisatory style, but adding some splendid bravura flourishes, as in the first of Spinacino's *Recercare*; and his virtuosity is just as striking in the *Spagna seconda* of Capirola and Dalza's sparkling *Calata ala spagnola* (which must have been a hit in its day).

One of the most touching pieces is Martini's melancholy *Malor me bat*, which is followed by a most extrovert *Piva* by Dalza, and the darker mood then returns with the reflective Anonymous *Laudate Dio*. Capirola's haunting *La vilanela* is matched by the two reflective vocal transcriptions from Josquin Desprez.

This discerningly selected recital is beautifully played and recorded, and admirably documented. A sample page (in colour) from Capirola's richly illuminated Lute Book is upstaged by the frontispiece (taken from a miniature by Philippe de Mazerolles) elegantly picturing a Venetian brothel. A colourfully garbed lutenist is accompanying the less venial pleasures: the naked men are clearly enjoying themselves, the young ladies are hardly more modest in their apparel, but look more circumspect.

Ogden, Craig (guitar), Alison Stephens (mandolin)

'*Music from the novels of Louis de Bernières*': VIVALDI: *Concerto in C, RV 425* (arr. BEHREND). HUMMEL: *Mandolin concerto in G: Andante with variations.* GIULIANI: *Grand duo concertante.* PERSICHINI: *Polcha variata.* CALACE: *Amor si culla, Op. 133.* PALUMBO: *Petite bolero.* SAGRERAS: *El Colibri (The humming bird).* LAURO: *4 Venezuelan waltzes.* BARRIOS: *Choro de Saudade; Las Abejas.* LLOBET: *El noi de la mare; El testament d'Amelia; El mestre.* ANON.: *Mis dolencias.* Celedonio ROMERO: *Suite andaluza: Soleares.* TURINA: *Homenaje a Tárrega: Soleares.*

*** Chan. 9780.

Not many gimmicky discs work as well as this. It makes a delightful mixture having the metallic 'plink plonk' of the mandolin set against the rich twanging of the guitar. The author of *Captain Corelli's Mandolin* has helped the two talented young performers here, Craig Ogden and Alison Stephens, in making a wide selection of music from Vivaldi to Villa-Lobos, mainly of works specifically mentioned in de Bernières' novels – not just *Captain Corelli's Mando-*

lin but also the Latin trilogy – as well as of related pieces. Starting with Vivaldi's *Mandolin concerto* with the string accompaniment arranged for solo guitar, each of the twenty-three items is a charmer, not least those from unknown composers like Persichini, Calace and Sagreras.

Ogdon, John and Brenda Lucas
(pianos)

RACHMANINOV: *Suites for 2 pianos Nos. 1 (Fantasy), Op. 5; 2 in C, Op. 17; Six pieces for piano duet, Op. 11; Polka italienne.* ARENSKY: *Suite for 2 pianos, Op. 15.* KHACHATURIAN: *Sabre dance.* SHOSTAKOVICH: *Concertino, Op. 94.* DEBUSSY: *Petite suite; Fêtes.* BIZET: *Jeux d'enfants.*

(B) **(*) EMI (ADD) Double fforte CZS5 69386-2 (2).

John Ogdon and Brenda Lucas's readings of the two Rachmaninov *Suites*, not ideally imaginative but enjoyable nevertheless, are aptly coupled with other duet recordings made by them, including the delightful Arensky *Suite* which includes the famous waltz. It is good too to have the long-neglected *Concertino* of Shostakovich and the anything-but-neglected *Sabre dance*, which is rather heavy-going here. However, the Debussy *Petite suite* is very engaging, and most valuable of all is the complete recording of Bizet's *Jeux d'enfants* – all twelve movements. Only the five included by the composer in his orchestral suite are at all well known, and many of the others are equally charming, not least the opening *Rêverie (L'Escarpolette)*, the *Scherzo (Les chevaux de bois)* and the *Nocturne (Colin-Mainard - 'Blind man's buff')*. Fine ensemble and sparkling fingerwork, but just occasionally a touch of rhythmic inflexibility. Good, mid-1970s recording.

Oslo Wind Ensemble

Scandinavian wind quintets: FERNSTROM: *Wind quintet, Op. 59.* KVANDAL: *Wind quintet, Op. 34; 3 Sacred folktunes.* NIELSEN: *Wind quintet, Op. 43.*

(BB) ** Naxos 8.553050.

A super-bargain account of the Nielsen Quintet, more relaxed in its tempi and measured in approach than the account by the Scandinavian Quintet on Marco Polo. Very decently recorded, too. The Swedish musician John Fernström was a prolific composer whose output runs to twelve symphonies and much else besides. He was for years solely represented in the catalogue by a *Concertino for flute, women's choir and small orchestra*. This *Wind quintet* is not quite so charming, but is well worth hearing – as, for that matter, is the *Wind quintet* by the Norwegian Johan Kvandal, a thoughtful figure who is a composer of imagination and substance.

Paik, Kun Woo (piano)

Recital: LISZT: *Années de pèlerinage: Au bord d'une source; Au lac de Wallenstadt; Les jeux d'eau à la Villa d'Este. Harmonies poétiques et religieuses: Bénédiction de Dieu dans la solitude. Liebestraum No. 3; Mephisto waltz No. 1; Hungarian rhapsody No. 12; Variations on B-A-C-H. French music:* POULENC: *Nocturnes Nos. 1, 5 & 6; Presto; Improvisations Nos. 10, 12 & 15; Intermezzo No. 2; Mouvements perpétuels Nos. 1-3.* DEBUSSY: *Pour le piano; Suite bergamasque: Clair de lune.* SATIE: *Gnossiennes Nos. 4 & 5; Ogives Nos. 1-2; Descriptions automatique: Sur un vaisseaux; Sur un casque. Chapitre tourné en tous sens: Celui qui parle trop. Croquis et agaceries d'un gros bonhomme en bois: Españaña. Embryons desséchés: D'Edriophtalma; De Podophtalma. Gymnopédies Nos. 1-3.*

(BB) *** Virgin Classics 2 x 1 Dig. VBD5 61757-2 (2).

This Virgin 2 x 1 reissue pairs two outstanding individual recitals, a distinguished Liszt collection discussed under the composer, and the present grouping of French repertoire, which is slightly more idiosyncratic, even including individual movements from suites of miniatures meant to be played as a group. However, the mixture works well when the playing is consistently magnetic. There is much to relish, notably Poulenc's *Mouvements perpétuels* and indeed other pieces by this composer. Kun Woo Paik's withdrawn performance of *Clair de lune* is a little indulgent and the *Gnossiennes* also find him a shade mannered, while the *Gymnopédies* are very languorous. But the outer movements of Debussy's *Pour le piano* bring some electrifying bravura and his imagination is given full rein in the quirkier Satie miniatures. There are 154 minutes of music here and, even if the back-up documentation is fairly sparse, the value is obvious, for the recording is excellent.

Parker-Smith, Jane (organ)

'Popular French romantics' (organ of Coventry Cathedral): WIDOR: *Symphony No. 1: Marche pontificale. Symphony No. 9 (Gothique), Op. 70: Andante sostenuto.* GUILMANT: *Sonata No. 5 in C min., Op. 80: Scherzo.* GIGOUT: *Toccata in B min.* BONNET: *Elfes, Op. 7.* LEFEBURE-WELY: *Sortie in B flat.* VIERNE: *Pièces de fantaisie: Clair de lune, Op. 53/5; Carillon de Westminster, Op. 54/6.*

*** ASV CDDCA 539.

The modern organ in Coventry Cathedral adds a nice bite to Jane Parker-Smith's very pontifical performance of the opening Widor *March* and creates a blaze of splendour at the close of the famous Vierne *Carillon de Westminster*, the finest performance on record. The detail of the fast, nimble articulation in the engagingly Mendelssohnian *Elfes* of Joseph Bonnet is not clouded; yet here, as in the splendid Guilman *Scherzo* with its wider dynamic range, there is also a nice atmospheric effect. Overall, a most entertaining recital.

'Popular French Romantics', Vol. 2 (organ of Beauvais Cathedral): FRANCK: *Prélude, fugue et variation, Op. 18.* GUILMANT: *Grand choeur in D* (after Handel). MULET: *Carillon-Sortie.* RENAUD: *Toccata in D min.* SAINT-SAENS: *Prelude and fugue.* VIERNE: *Symphony No. 1: Finale. Stèle pour un enfant défunt.* WIDOR: *Symphony No. 4: Andante and Scherzo.*

*** ASV CDDCA 610.

With his *Prelude and fugue*, Saint-Saëns is in more serious mood than usual but showing characteristic facility in fugal construction; Widor is first mellow and then quixotic – his *Scherzo* demands the lightest articulation and receives it. High drama and great bravura are provided by the Vierne *Finale* and later by Albert Renaud's *Toccata* and Henri Mulet's *Carillon-Sortie*, while Franck's *Prélude, fugue et variation* and the poignant Vierne *Stèle pour un enfant défunt* bring attractive lyrical contrast: here Jane Parker-Smith's registration shows particular subtlety. The organ is splendidly recorded.

Perahia, Murray (piano)

25th Anniversary Edition: D. SCARLATTI: *Sonatas in B min., Kk. 27; A, Kk. 212.* MOZART: *6 German dances, K.509; Adagio, K.540. Piano concerto No. 27 in B flat, K.595* (with COE). SCHUBERT: *Impromptu in A flat, D.899/4.* SCHUMANN: *Papillons, Op. 2.* CHOPIN: *Ballade No. 1 in G min., Op. 23. Piano concerto No. 2 in F min., Op. 21* (with Israel PO, Zubin Mehta). LISZT: *Gnomenreigen.* RACHMANINOV: *Etudes-tableaux: Nos. 5 in E flat; 6 in A min., Op. 39/5-6.* BARTOK: *Suite, Op. 14; Improvisations on Hungarian peasant songs, Op. 20; Out of doors suite.* BERG: *Sonata, Op. 1.* TIPPETT: *Sonata No. 1.* BEETHOVEN: *Piano and wind quintet in E flat, Op. 16* (with members of ECO). SCHUMANN: *5 Lieder, Op. 40.* BRAHMS: *Piano quartet No. 1 in G min., Op. 25* (with members of Amadeus Qt).

(M) *** Sony DDD/ADD SX4K 63380 (4).

This 1997 anthology effectively celebrates Murray Perahia's fiftieth birthday and his 25-year recording association with CBS/Sony. Opening delightfully with two Scarlatti sonatas, the variety of music here readily confirms Perahia's pianistic and artistic mastery over the widest musical range, with the Berg *Sonata* (attractively lyrical) and the Tippett (with its haunting *Andante tranquillo*) new to the catalogue. The recordings are technically a little variable but always good, often excellent, notably those made at the Maltings: the Mozart solo works, Liszt and Rachmaninov and the Beethoven *Piano and wind quintet*. The inclusion of the latter makes one wish that its Mozartian predecessor had also been featured, for that omission highlights the problem for many collectors: that, attractive as this mid-priced compilation is, it cuts across other issues which admirers of this great pianist may already possess.

Peyer, Gervase de (clarinet), Gwenneth Pryor (piano)

French music for clarinet and piano: SAINT-SAENS: *Sonata, Op. 167.* DEBUSSY: *Première rhapsodie; Arabesque No. 2; Prélude: La fille aux cheveux de lin.* POULENC: *Sonata.* SCHMIDT: *Andantino, Op. 30/1.* RAVEL: *Pièce en forme de habanera.* PIERNE: *Canzonetta, Op. 19.*

✪ *** Chan. 8526.

A gorgeous record. The Saint-Saëns *Sonata* is an attractively crafted piece, full of engaging invention. Poulenc's *Sonata* is characteristically witty, with contrast in its lovely central *Romanza* (*très calme*); and the other short pieces wind down the closing mood of the recital, with De Peyer's luscious timbre drawing a charming portrait of *The girl with the flaxen hair* before the nimbly tripping closing encore of Pierné. This is a quite perfect record of its kind, the programme like that of a live recital and played with comparable spontaneity. The recording is absolutely realistic; the balance could hardly be improved on.

Pinnock, Trevor (harpsichord or virginals)

'At the Victoria and Albert Museum': ANON.: *My Lady Wynkfylds rownde.* BYRD: *The Queens alman; The Bells.* HANDEL: *Harpsichord suite No. 5 in E.* CROFT: *Suite No. 3 in C min.* ARNE: *Sonata No. 3 in G.* J. C. BACH: *Sonata in C min., Op. 5/6.*

(M) *** CRD (ADD) CRD 3307.

Trevor Pinnock recorded for CRD before he moved over to the DG Archiv label and this was his first solo recital, made at the Victoria and Albert Museum using virginals and other period harpsichords. He opens with three very colourful pieces played on an instrument originally belonging to Queen Elizabeth I, who was an accomplished virginal player. It is in splendid condition and has a most attractive sound. Pinnock plays it with enthusiasm and his performance of Byrd's extraordinarily descriptive *The Bells* is a *tour de force*. For the rest of the recital he uses two different harpsichords. His style in the works of Handel, Croft, Arne and J. C. Bach is less flamboyant, more circumspect, but the music is strongly characterized and boldly recorded. The Handel suite is the one which has the *Harmonious blacksmith* as its finale, which is played with considerable flair.

Pletnev, Mikhail (piano)

'Hommage à Rachmaninov': RACHMANINOV: *Variations on a theme of Corelli, Op. 42; 4 Etudes-tableaux, Op. 39/5; Opp. 44/6, 8-9.* BEETHOVEN: *Piano sonata No. 26 (Les Adieux), Op. 81a.* MENDELSSOHN: *Andante cantabile & Presto agitato; Andante & Rondo capriccioso, Op. 14.*

CHOPIN: *Andante spianato et Grande polonaise brillant, Op. 22.*

✿ *** DG 459 634-2.

Way back in 1982, when Pletnev was in his early twenties, Dr Mark Zilberquist (in *Russia's Great Modern Pianists*, New York) noted the young pianist's affinities with his aristocratic and patrician compatriot, Rachmaninov: 'discreet, reserved, outwardly restrained in showing emotion'. Pletnev certainly has something of the same commanding keyboard authority, the extraordinary range of colour and clarity of articulation of Rachmaninov. This recital is recorded at Rachmaninov's own summer home, the Villa Senar on the Vierwaldstätter See, near Lake Lucerne, using the composer's newly restored American Steinway. The playing is breathtaking, worthy of the composer at his best, and dazzling but never ostentatious. The delicacy of the Mendelssohn and the introductory *Andante cantabile* to the Chopin is magical. A quite exceptional recital even by the standards of this exceptional pianist.

'Carnegie Hall Recital' (1 November 2000): **BACH/BUSONI:** *Chaconne in D min., BWV 1004.* **BEETHOVEN:** *Sonata No. 32 in C min., Op. 111.* **CHOPIN:** *4 Scherzi: Op. 20; Op. 31; Op. 39; Op. 54.* **Plus encores: BALAKIREV:** *Islamey.* **MOSZKOWSKI:** *Etude de virtuosité, Op. 72/6.* **RACHMANINOV:** *Etude-tableau, Op. 39/5.* **SCARLATTI:** *Sonata in D min., Kk 9.* **SCRIABIN:** *Poème, Op. 32/1.*

✿ *** DG 471 157-2 (with encores bonus CD).

Mikhail Pletnev made his Carnegie Hall debut when he was in his early forties, relatively late in his career, but the wait should not have disappointed his many American admirers. 'He links arms with such stalwarts of the Russian school as Horowitz, Richter and Gilels,' wrote the *New York Times*, and his programme has all the dazzling command and authority not to mention virtuosity we would expect. The Beethoven *Op. 111 Sonata* has tremendous power and concentration and comes up sounding altogether fresh, while the four Chopin *Scherzi*, which comprised the second half, are quite thrilling and brought the house down. The five encores that followed come on an extra CD, and the *Islamey* belongs among the great performances of this work. Some recital this, and very decently recorded too!

Pollini, Maurizio (piano)

STRAVINSKY: *3 movements from Petrushka.* **PROKOFIEV:** *Piano sonata No. 7 in B flat, Op. 83.* **WEBERN:** *Variations for piano, Op. 27.* **BOULEZ:** *Piano sonata No. 2.*

(M) *** DG 447 431-2.

The Prokofiev is a great performance, one of the finest ever committed to disc; and the Stravinsky *Petrushka* is electrifying. Not all those responding to this music will do so quite so readily to the Boulez, fine though the playing is; but the Webern also makes a very strong

impression. This is the equivalent of two LPs and is outstanding value. It is a natural candidate for reissue in DG's set of 'Originals' of legendary performances.

Preston, Simon (organ)

'The world of the organ' (organ of Westminster Abbey): **WIDOR:** *Symphony No. 5: Toccata.* **BACH:** *Chorale prelude, Wachet auf, BWV 645.* **MOZART:** *Fantasia in F min., K.608.* **WALTON:** *Crown imperial* (arr. **MURRILL**). **CLARKE:** *Prince of Denmark's march* (arr. **PRESTON**). **HANDEL:** *Saul: Dead march.* **PURCELL:** *Trumpet tune* (arr. **TREVOR**). **ELGAR:** *Imperial march* (arr. **MARTIN**). **VIERNE:** *Symphony No. 1: Finale.* **WAGNER:** *Tannhäuser: Pilgrims' chorus.* **GUILMANT:** *March on a theme of Handel.* **SCHUMANN:** *Study No. 5* (arr. **WEST**). **KARG-ELERT:** *Marche triomphale (Now thank we all our God).*

(M) *** Decca (ADD) 430 091-2.

A splendid compilation from the Argo catalogue of the early to mid-1960s, spectacularly recorded, which offers 69 minutes of music and is in every sense a resounding success. Simon Preston's account of the Widor *Toccata* is second to none, and both the Vierne *Finale* and the Karg-Elert *Marche triomphale* lend themselves admirably to Preston's unashamed flamboyance and the tonal splendour afforded by the Westminster acoustics. Walton's *Crown imperial*, too, brings a panoply of sound which compares very favourably with an orchestral recording. The organ has a splendid trumpet stop which makes both the Purcell piece and Clarke's *Prince of Denmark's march*, better known as the 'Trumpet voluntary', sound crisply regal.

Prometheus Ensemble

'French impressions': **RAVEL:** *Introduction & allegro for harp, flute, clarinet and string quartet.* **DEBUSSY:** *Danses sacrée et profane; Sonata for flute, viola and harp.* **ROUSSEL:** *Serenade.*

*** ASV CDDCA 664.

This young group gives eminently well-prepared and thoughtful accounts of all these pieces. The *Danses sacrée et profane* sound particularly atmospheric and the Debussy *Sonata* is played with great feeling and sounds appropriately ethereal. The Roussel, too, is done with great style and, even if the *Introduction and allegro* does not supersede the celebrated Melos account, the Prometheus do it well.

Purcell Quartet, Purcell Band, with Robert Wooley (harpsichord)

'La Folia (variations on a theme)': **CORELLI:** *Violin sonata in D min., Op. 5/12.* **MARAIS:** *Les folies d'Espagne.* **VIVALDI:** *Trio sonata in D min. (Variations on La Folia), Op. 1/12 (RV 63)* (Purcell Quartet). **GEMINIANI:** *Concerto grosso (La Folia)* *(after Corelli)* (Purcell Quartet & Purcell Band). Alessandro SCARLATTI: *Toccata No. 7 (Primo tono): Folia.* C. P. E. BACH: *12 Variations on Folies d'Espagne, Wq.118/9 (H.263)* (Robert Wooley).

*** Hyp. CDA 67035.

Just as the chanson *L'homme armé* was popular among composers as a basis for mass settings in the fifteenth and early sixteenth centuries, so at the very end of the seventeenth and throughout the eighteenth, *La Folia* was in constant use for instrumental variations. The word '*folia*' is Portuguese in origin and means 'empty-headed', but also refers to a dance in triple time, which originated around the same time as that famous chanson. It changed its rhythmic accents over the years and the special character of the format we now recognize seems to have first come into use by Lully for an oboe tune around 1672.

Corelli probably appropriated it from Lully in 1700, resourcefully turning the piece into a chaconne, but Marais probably beat him to it: even though his *Folies d'Espagne* was not published until 1701, it was probably written some years earlier. Thereafter composers seemed to almost fall over each other to put it to good use in their instrumental music. The above six listings are excellent examples, among which Vivaldi's highly entertaining *Trio sonata* stands out alongside Carl Philipp Emanuel Bach's superb set of variations for the keyboard, which ought to be much better known. But all the versions here are stimulating, and played with fine, expressive vitality. The recording too is excellent. This is not a recital to play continuously, but dipped into a version at a time it will give much pleasure.

Puyana, Rafael (harpsichord)

'*The Golden Age of harpsichord music*': ANON.: *My Lady Carey's Dompe.* BULL: *Les Buffons; The King's hunt.* PEERSON: *The Primerose; The fall of the leafe.* BYRD: *La Volta.* PHILIPS: *Pavana dolorosa; Galliard dolorosa.* BESARD: *Branle gay.* L. COUPERIN: *Tombeau de M. de Blancrocher; Pavane.* FRANCISQUE: *Branle de Montiradé.* BACH: *Keyboard concerto in D min., after Marcello.* FREIXANET: *Sonata in A.* M. ALBENIZ: *Sonata in D.* CHAMBONNIERES: *Le Moutier (after Louis Couperin).* RAMEAU: *Gavotte et Doubles.* DIEUPART: *Passepied.* F. COUPERIN: *La Pantomime.*

◉ (M) *** [Mercury 434 364-2].

If you think you don't enjoy listening to the harpsichord, Rafael Puyana, who was a pupil of Landowska, will surely persuade you otherwise in this remarkably diverse, 75-minute recital, for he is a supreme master of his instrument. He plays a large, modern, double-keyboard Pleyel harpsichord (replicating one of Landowska's own instruments). In his bravura hands it produces an astonishingly wide range of dynamic, colour and sonority, no better demonstrated than in the *Gavotte et Doubles* of Rameau, which is a continuously inventive set of variations, running on for about ten minutes. Puyana effectively uses every possible device to divert his listeners, to say nothing of demonstrating his own dexterity, which he does again more simply in the engagingly brief *Passepied* of Charles Dieupart (who died in 1740). Martin Peerson's modest variations on a popular song of the period, *The Primerose*, and his more dolorous evocation of *The fall of the leafe* both feature the highly effective dynamic contrasts which this instrument can provide.

The programme opens with the piquant *My Lady Carey's Dompe*, a lollipop if ever there was one, presented with great panache. John Bull's divisions on *Les Buffons* and *The King's hunt* have never sounded more vital, while Puyana's account of the charming *La Volta* of William Byrd makes one appreciate why it was reputedly a favourite dance of Queen Elizabeth I. Perhaps Puyana goes over the top a bit in his robust presentation of the pieces by Peter Philips, and he plays Bach's *Concerto in D minor* (supposedly after Alessandro Marcello, but sounding more like Vivaldi) in such a robust manner that it is almost if he were sitting at the keyboard of an organ. But the crisply articulated *Sonata* of Freixanet is very effective indeed, and the *Sonata* of Mateo Albéniz is a *tour de force*.

The instrument's resonant lower octave is really made to tell in Louis Couperin's *Tombeau*; while the elegant *Le Moutier* of Jacques Champion de Chambonnières brings a nice sonic contrast on three different levels, within a time period of just over two minutes. The Mercury recording is real and vivid, but please don't set the volume level too high. This is one of two harpsichord compilations that deserve a place in every collection: the other is George Malcolm's Decca anthology 'The world of the harpsichord', utterly different but equally rewarding – see above. Alas, the Puyana disc has now been withdrawn in the UK.

Rév, Lívia (piano)

'*For children*': BACH: *Preludes in E, BWV 939; in G min., BWV 930.* DAQUIN: *Le coucou.* MOZART: *Variations on Ah vous dirai-je maman, K.265.* BEETHOVEN: *Für Elise.* SCHUMANN: *Album for the young, Op. 63: excerpts.* CHOPIN: *Nocturne in C min., Op. posth.* LISZT: *Etudes, G. 136/1 & 2.* BIZET: *Jeux d'enfants: La Toupie.* FAURE: *Dolly: Berceuse.* TCHAIKOVSKY: *Album for the young, Op. 39: Maman; Waltz.* VILLA-LOBOS: *Prole do bebê: excerpts.* JOLIVET: *Chansons naïve 1 & 2.* PROKOFIEV: *Waltz, Op. 65.* BARTOK: *Evening in the country; For Children: excerpts.* DEBUSSY: *Children's corner: excerpts.* MAGIN: *3 Pieces.* MATACIC: *Miniature variations.*

*** Hyp. CDA 66185.

A wholly delectable recital, and not just for children either. The whole is more than the sum of its many parts, and the layout provides excellent variety, with the programme stimulating in mixing familiar with unfamiliar. The recording is first class. Highly recommended for late-evening listening.

Reykjavik Wind Quintet

Jean-Michel DAMASE: *17 Variations*. DEBUSSY (arr. BOZZA): *Le petit nègre*. FAURE (arr. WILLIAMS): *Dolly suite: Berceuse, Op. 56/1*. FRANCAIX: *Quintet No. 1*. IBERT: *3 Pièces brèves*. MILHAUD: *La Cheminée du Roi René, Op. 205*. PIERNE: *Pastorale, Op. 14/1*. POULENC (arr. EMERSON): *Novelette No. 1*.

*** Chan. 9362.

A delightful recital for late-night listening. Elegant, crisp playing from this accomplished Icelandic ensemble. The Damase *Variations* are delightful, as indeed are the Françaix and Milhaud pieces, and the Chandos recording is in the best traditions of the house.

'*Nordic music for Wind Quintet*': RASMUSSEN: *Quintet in F*. LARSSON: *Quattro tempi (Divertimento), Op. 55*. NIELSEN: *Quintet, Op. 43*. HALLGRIMSSON: *Intarsia*.

(N) *** Chan. 9849.

The quintets by Peter Rasmussen and Haflidi Hall-grímsson are new to CD. Rasmussen comes between Gade and Nielsen, though if you heard this music without knowing what it was, you could be forgiven for thinking it was by Reicha and Danzi or one of their contemporaries. It is well written for the instruments but pleasingly inconsequential. Haflidi Hallgrímsson, who was born in 1941, is Icelandic. His *Intarsia* is a witty and inventive score, expertly laid out for wind. Its title derives from knitting, and the ideas bubble away in a diverting and inventive way. Well worth trying out. Lars-Erik Larsson's evocation of the four seasons, *Quattro tempi*, is an imaginative and individual score. This version more than holds its own against the earlier 1983 version by the Stockholm Wind Quintet (Caprice). With the Nielsen *Quintet* competition is very stiff, and though the Reykjavik players do it well, the Oslo Quintet (Naxos) and the Wind Quintet of the Danish Radio Orchestra (dacapo – see above) have the greater personality and finesse. Enjoyable and recommendable, though the sound is a bit upfront.

Ricci, Ruggiero (violin), Louis Persinger or Ernest Lush (piano)

PAGANINI: *Witches dance, Op. 8; Fantasia on the G string after Rossini's Mosè in Egitto; Moto perpetuo in C; Variations on 'Nel cor più mi sento' from Paisiello's La Molinara; Variations on God Save the Queen; La Campanella (from Violin concerto No. 2); Sonata No. 12 in E min, Op. 3/6; I Palpiti: Variations after Rossini's Tancredi* (arr. KREISLER). WIENIAWSKI: *Scherzo-Tarentelle in G min*. ELGAR: *La capricieuse*. VECSEY: *Caprice No. 1 (Le vent)*. KROLL: *Banjo and fiddle*. CHOPIN: *Nocturne No. 20 in C sharp min*. (arr. MILSTEIN). SMETANA: *Má Vlast: Andantino*. SARASATE: *8 Spanish dances; Caprice basque; Introduction et Tarantelle; Zigeunerweisen; Jóta Aragonesa*. SUK: *Burleska*.

ACHRON: *Hebrew Melody*. HUBAY: *The Zephyr*. MOSZKOWSKI: *Guitarre*. BAZZINI: *La Ronde des lutins: scherzo fantastique*.

*** Australian Double Decca mono/stereo 458 191-2 (2).

Ricci gives us a dazzling displays of violin pyrotechnics in all these pieces much prized by violinists, from Heifetz downwards – music to show off the virtuoso possibilities (and improbabilities) of the instrument, and this they it surely do. Ricci uses every trick in the book to make one gasp at the sheer technical brilliance – try the final Bazzini number first, and then the music of Sarasate in which he was a specialist. The mono sound is naturally a little thin, but has transferred very well to CD, and half the programme is in excellent stereo. As much of this repertoire is rare in the concert hall these days, this collection is especially valuable, and this is the first time, thanks to Australian Decca, that it has appeared on CD. Thoroughly recommended.

Richter, Sviatoslav (piano)

Sviatoslav Richter (1913–97) – The Enigma. Documentary by Bruno Monsaingeon.

*** Warner NVC Arts **DVD** 3984 23029-2.

In this altogether remarkable and revealing film Bruno Monsaingeon draws on rare archive material as well as the testimony of the great pianist himself. The result will be a revelation, even to those well informed about the great pianist: Richter speaks of his early years and his parents, of the privations of the years leading up to the war and of the war years themselves. His father, a pupil of Franz Schreker, disappeared during that period, and his relationship with his mother was obviously not untroubled after her remarriage.

Richter's own development was quite unique. He was self-taught and worked as a coach at the opera in Odessa, turning up in Moscow in 1937 (partly to avoid induction into the military), where he became a student of Heinrich Neuheus, who took him under his wing. In 1941 Prokofiev about whom, incidentally, Richter is distinctly unflattering, asked him to play his *Fifth Piano Concerto*, which was an immediate success and launched him on his career. There is an astonishing clip of a 1958 Warsaw performance of it.

During the course of two-and-a-half hours there are innumerable excerpts from his vast repertoire, ranging over Rachmaninov, Liszt and Debussy to Shostakovich, all of which are carefully indexed by chapter and time code and most of which are pretty breathtaking. There is archive material garnered from broadcast and private sources, which will be new to music-lovers.

There are some haunting images of wartime Russia and glimpses of Richter playing with others, including Rostropovich and Benjamin Britten. We also see his appearance at Stalin's funeral and his first tours abroad. Although he loved three things about America – its museums, its great orchestras and its cocktails – he disliked most other things and declined to revisit it after his fourth tour.

The portrait that emerges is indeed enigmatic, and the frail expression as he says, 'I don't like myself,' is painful and haunting. Moving, concentrated and frankly indispensable, this is a documentary that can, without fear of contradiction, be called great. This scores over its video not only in the sharper focus of the images but in the greater ease of access.

'*Sviatoslav Richter in the 1950s*', Volume 1:
PROKOFIEV: *Cinderella: 5 Pieces; Visions fugitives, Op. 22: excerpts; Piano sonata No. 7 in B flat, Op. 83.* SCHUMANN: *Toccata in C, Op. 7.* DEBUSSY: *Images, Book II: Cloches à travers les feuilles (2 performances).* CHOPIN: *Etudes in C & E (2 performances), Op. 10/1 & 3.* RACHMANINOV: *Preludes in F sharp min., Op. 23/1; in B flat, Op. 23/2; in D, Op. 23/4; in G min., Op. 23/5; in C min., Op. 23/7; in A flat, Op. 23/8; in A, Op. 31/9; in C, Op. 32/1; in B flat min., Op. 32/2; in F, Op. 32/7; in B min., Op 32/10; in G sharp min., Op. 32/12; in G sharp min., Op. 32/15.* TCHAIKOVSKY: *Piano sonata in G, Op. 37.* LISZT: *Valse oubliée No. 1.*

(M) (***) Parnassus mono PACD 96-001/2 (2).

We owe this double-pack of Richter to the dedication of some enthusiasts who have tracked down a considerable number of live performances from the 1950s, before his star had risen in the West, recordings which have never been issued before. The unsigned liner-note claims that Richter was at this time 'perhaps even more of a virtuoso than the more mature artist' and that 'he was more willing to dazzle audiences with his facility'. Another claim the producer makes, and one that must be upheld, is that 'the recorded sound while not the ultimate in fidelity is superior to what we might have expected from early Russian tapes'.

The first CD brings some dazzling Prokofiev, recorded in Moscow in April 1958. The transcriptions from *Cinderella*, the excerpts from *Visions fugitives* and the *Seventh Sonata* are little short of amazing. (The sonata was recorded two months before the BMG/Melodiya version made at a recital in the Great Hall of the Moscow Conservatoire, and is every bit as electrifying, though the BMG is better recorded.) The producer's claim that Richter took more risks in this concert performance of the Schumann Toccata than in the safer but still stunning DG studio recording later the same year is also on target.

The Tchaikovsky *G major Sonata*, Op. 37 comes from another Moscow recital, in December 1954, two years before the BMG account, as do two other pieces also played at that later recital, the *Cloches à travers les feuilles* and the Chopin *E major Study*, Op. 10, No. 3. Richter also recorded the Tchaikovsky sonata in the studio in the mid-1950s (it was issued in the UK on Parlophone). We would not wish to choose between the two presently before the public; what is undeniable is that both are pretty sensational. (There are some barely discernible bumps in the slow movement but the transfers are otherwise excellent.) So, for that matter, are the thirteen Rachmaninov *Preludes* in this recital. What pianisim!

'*Sviatoslav Richter in the 1950s*', Volume 2:
MUSSORGSKY: *Pictures at an exhibition.* SCHUMANN: *Abegg variations, Op. 1; 3 Fantasiestücke, Op. 12; Humoreske in B flat, Op. 20.* SCRIABIN: *12 Preludes, Op. 11; Sonatas Nos. 2 in G sharp min., Op. 19; 6, Op. 62.* TCHAIKOVSKY: *Piano concerto No. 1 in B flat min., Op. 23* (with USSR State SO, Nathan Rachlin).

(M) (**(*)) Parnassus mono PACD 96-003/4 (2).

The earliest performances here are the Mussorgsky *Pictures* and the Scriabin *Sixth Sonata*, which come from a 1952 Moscow recital. The BMG/Melodiya account comes from 1958, the same year as the famous Sofia recital, while their recording of the Scriabin comes three years later, in 1955. The other Scriabin repertoire, along with the Schumann pieces, come from June 1955 and the Tchaikovsky concerto with Nathan Rachlin from 1957. Though the playing is again dazzling, the orchestral recording is coarse and climaxes discolour, and in the climaxes the engineers can be heard reducing the level to avoid overloading. Apart from this, Richter is in a class of his own, and *aficionados* will surely want this.

'*In Memoriam - Legendary recordings (1959–1962)*':
BACH: *Well-tempered Clavier, Book I: Preludes and fugues Nos. 1, 4-6 & 8, BWV 846, 849-51 & 853.* HAYDN: *Sonata in G min., Hob XVI/44.* CHOPIN: *Ballades Nos. 3 in A flat, Op. 47; 4 in F min., Op. 52; Polonaise-fantaisie in A flat, Op. 61; Etudes in C; C min. (Revolutionary), Op. 10/1 & 12.* SCHUBERT: *Allegretto in C min., D.915. Ländler, D.366/1, 3 & 4-5.* SCHUMANN: *Abegg variations, Op. 1.* DEBUSSY: *Estampes; Préludes, Book I: Voiles; Le vent dans la plaine; Les collines d'Anacapri.* RACHMANINOV: *Preludes Nos. 3 in B flat; 5 in D; 6 in G min.; 8 in C min., Op. 23/2, 4-5 & 7; 12 in C; 13 in B flat; 23 in G sharp min., Op. 32/1-2 & 12.* PROKOFIEV: *Visions fugitives, Op. 22/3, 6 & 9.*

(B) *** DG Double 457 667-2 (2).

Over the years DG have made a number of different collections from the recordings Richter made at live recitals while on tour in Europe between 1959 and 1962. The present programme extends the Chopin coverage to include two *Ballades*, volatile, highly individual performances; the number of Rachmaninov *Preludes* is also increased to cover virtually all the favourites. The remastered recordings – the quality varies somewhat between items – are for the most part very good, though audience noises inevitably intrude at times.

The compelling accounts of the Scriabin and Prokofiev *Sonatas* previously included are here omitted. Each disc is generously full and the set is highly recommendable. The discography details are as follows: Rachmaninov *Preludes* (except Op. 32/12): Warsaw, 1959; Haydn *Sonata*, Chopin Op. 47, Debussy *Préludes*: Wembley Town Hall, 1961; Bach, Prokofiev, Chopin (except Op. 47), Debussy *Estampes*, Rachmaninov Op. 32/12, Schubert, Schumann: Italian tour, 1962.

CHOPIN: *Ballade No. 3 in A flat, Op. 47; Barcarolle in F sharp, Op. 60; Etudes, Op. 10/12 (2 versions) 1; 4; 6; & 10; Mazurkas, Op. 24/1–4; Scherzo No. 4 in E min., Op. 54.* DEBUSSY: *Images, Book ll: Cloches à travers les feuilles. L'Isle joyeuse; Préludes, Book l: l Danseuses de Delphes; ll Voiles; lll Le Vent dans la plaine; lV Les Sons et les parfums tournent dans l'air du soir; Vl Des pas sur la neige; lX La Sérénade interrompue (2 versions); V Les Collines d'Anacapri; Xl La Danse de Puck; Vll Ce qu'a vu le vent d'ouest; X La Cathédrale engloutie. Préludes, Book ll: l Brouillards; ll Feuilles mortes; lll La Puerta del Vino; lV Les Fées sont d'exquises danseuses; Bruyèrea; Vl General Lavine – eccentric; Vll La Terrasse des audiences du clair de lune; Vlll Ondine; lX Hommage à Pickwick Esq. P.P.M.P.C.; X Canope; Xl Les tierces alternées; Xll Feux d'artifice.* PROKOFIEV: *Dance, Op. 32/1.*

(M) (***) BBC mono BBCL 4021-2 (2).

These archive recordings offer a unique glimpse of Richter's art in the early 1960s. The Chopin and the ten *Préludes* from Book I plus *L'Isle joyeuse* and *Cloches à travers les feuilles* come from a 1961 relay of his Festival Hall recital; Book 2 comes from a 1967 recital at the Maltings, Snape. He was very much at his peak at this time, and no Richter admirer or lover of the piano will want to be without this invaluable memento. As a Debussy interpreter, Richter gave a powerfully concentrated distillation that brought the atmosphere of these miniature tone-poems before our eyes with greater refinement of colour and touch than almost all his colleagues. Sonic limitations are surprisingly few and matter little given the distinction and stature of this playing.

BEETHOVEN: *Piano Sonata No. 11 in B flat, Op. 22; Eroica Variations, Op. 35.* CHOPIN: *Nocturnes, Op. 15/1; Op. 72/2.* HAYDN: *Piano Sonata No. 37 in E, Hob.XVI/22.* RACHMANINOV: *12 Preludes, Op. 23/1, 2, 4, 5 & 8; Op. 32/1, 2, 6, 7, 9, 10 & 12.* SCHUMANN: *Etudes Symphoniques.*

(M) *** BBC (ADD) BBCL 4090-2.

These performances are assembled from various broadcasts: the Rachmaninov from the Free Trade Hall, Manchester in 1969; the Beethoven and Schumann from a Festival Hall recital in the previous year, and the Haydn Sonata and one of the Chopin Nocturnes from the Snape Maltings in 1967. This was a period when Richter was at the height of his powers: the Rachmaninov *Preludes* particularly draw from him playing of exceptional eloquence and concentration. However the Beethoven and Schumann are hardly less impressive, and the Haydn *E major Sonata (No. 37 in E, Hob.XVI/22)* has tremendous character too. The recordings are excellent for their period and enhance the attractions of a most distinguished compilation.

BEETHOVEN: *Piano sonatas Nos. 3 in C, Op. 2/3; 4 in E flat, Op. 7; 27 in E min., Op. 90.*

**(*) Olympia (ADD) OCD 336.

SCHUBERT: *Piano sonatas Nos. 19 in C min., D.958; 21 in B flat, D.960.*

**(*) Olympia OCD 335.

RACHMANINOV: *Etudes-tableaux, Opp. 33 & 39; 6 Preludes, Op. 23/1-2, 4-5, 7-8; 7 Preludes, Op. 32/1-2, 6-7, 9-10, 12.*

**(*) Olympia DDD/ADD OCD 337.

Sonically these recordings leave a good deal to be desired: in most instances the balance is fairly close and the acoustic on the dry side, without being unacceptably so. They call for tolerance, but this is well worth extending for the sake of this music-making. The early Beethoven sonatas are from 1975 and the *E minor*, Op. 90 comes from 1971. The *C major Sonata*, Op. 2, No. 3 is far more powerful than one is used to encountering, particularly in the intensity of the slow movement; Richter's view of the *E flat*, Op. 7, familiar from an earlier recording Philips issued in the 1960s, is further deepened. There is a marvellously inward feeling and a sense of profound euphony in the *E minor*, Op. 90.

The Schubert sonatas were recorded in the early 1970s; the *C minor Sonata*, D.958 in 1973, the *B flat*, D.960 in the previous year; neither has been in currency in the UK. Richter's way with Schubert is well known. Some listeners have difficulty in coming to terms with the sheer scale of his first movement: it seems almost timeless, just as the almost static inwardness of the slow movement is not for those in a hurry.

Some of the Rachmaninov *Etudes-tableaux* have been available before, but again most are new to this country. The majority of the pieces were recorded in 1971 but others are later. The playing is of a rare order of mastery and leaves strong and powerful resonances. Richter's conception goes far beyond the abundant virtuosity this music calls for, and the characterization of the music is strong and searching. If you invest in no other of these Olympia CDs, this is the one that is unique – which makes the poor sound quality particularly regrettable.

'The Philips Richter Authorized Edition'

BACH: *Concerto in the Italian style, BWV 971; 4 Duets, BWV 802-5; English suites Nos. 3 in G min., BWV 808; 4 in F, BWV 809; 6 in D min., BWV 811; Fantasy in C min., BWV 906; French suites Nos. 2 in C min., BWV 813; 4 in E flat, BWV 815a; 6 in E, BWV 817; Overture (Partita) in the French style, BWV 831; Toccatas in D min., BWV 913; in G, BWV 916.*

**(*) Ph. (IMS) (ADD) 438 613-2 (3).

BEETHOVEN: *Piano sonatas Nos. 19 in G min.; 20 in G, Op. 49/1-2; 22 in F, Op. 54; 23 in F min. (Appassionata), Op. 57; 30 in E, Op. 109; 31 in A flat, Op. 110; 32 in C min., Op. 111.*

**(*) Ph. (IMS) 438 486-2 (2).

BEETHOVEN (with (i) Moraguès Qt; (ii) members of the Borodin Qt): (i) *Piano quintet in E flat, Op. 16;*

(ii) *Piano trio in B flat, Op. 97. Rondos in C; in G, Op. 51/1-2; Piano sonatas Nos. 18 in E flat, Op. 31/3; 28 in A, Op. 101.*

**(*) Ph. (IMS) 438 624-2 (2).

BRAHMS: *Ballade in G min., Op. 118/3; Capriccio in C, Op. 76/8; Intermezzo in E min., Op. 116/5; Rhapsody in E flat, Op. 119/4; Piano sonatas Nos. 1 in C, Op. 1; 2 in F sharp min., Op. 2; Variations on a theme by Paganini, Op. 35.* SCHUMANN: *Blumenstück, Op. 19; 3 Concert Etudes on Caprices by Paganini, Op. 10/4-6; Fantasy in C, Op. 17; March in G min., Op. 76/2; 4 Nachtstücke, Op. 23; Novelette in F, Op. 21/1.*

**(*) Ph. (IMS) 438 477-2 (3).

CHOPIN: *Barcarolle in F sharp, Op. 60; Etudes, Op. 10/1-5, 10-12; Etudes, Op. 25/5-8, 11-12; Nocturne in F, Op. 15/1; Polonaises in C sharp min., Op. 26/1; in C min., Op. 40/2; Polonaise-fantaisie in A flat, Op. 61; Preludes, Op. 28/6-11, 17, 19, 23-24.* LISZT: *Consolation No. 6; Etudes d'exécution transcendante, Nos. 1-3, 5, 7-8, 10-11; Etudes de concert: 'Un sospiro'; 'Gnomenreigen'; Hungarian rhapsody No. 17; Klavierstück in F sharp; Mephisto-Polka; Polonaise No. 2 in E; Piano sonata in B min.; Scherzo in G min.; Trübe Wolken.*

**(*) Ph. (IMS) 438 620-2 (3).

SCRIABIN: *2 Dances: 'Guirlandes'; 'Flammes sombres', Op. 73; Fantaisie in B min., Op. 28; Poème-Nocturne; Vers la flamme, Op. 72.* PROKOFIEV: *Cinderella: excerpts, Op. 87; Danza and waltz, Op. 32/1 & 4; Légende, Op. 26/6; Piano sonatas Nos. 4 in C min., Op. 29; 6 in A, Op. 82; Visions fugitives, Op. 22/3-6, 8-9, 11, 14-15; 18.* SHOSTAKOVICH: *Preludes and fugues, Op. 87/4, 12, 14-15, 17, 23.*

*** Ph. (IMS) (ADD) 438 627-2 (2).

Unusually for Philips, the documentation concerning the date and provenance of these records is meagre or non-existent. So, although many of the recordings appear to be digital, the quality of the sound is extremely variable. But, generally speaking, these are self-recommending performances which admirers of this pianist will want to have anyway. In Beethoven, Richter's voice is uniquely authoritative.

The indispensable compilation of Prokofiev, Scriabin and Shostakovich is a combination of studio recordings and live recitals. The Liszt playing is little short of inspired, especially the *Sonata*, but the recordings are again confined. The Schumann performances, too, inhabit an area of repertoire in which Richter has something very special to say, and the playing triumphs over any sonic limitations; the Brahms sonatas, on the other hand, are made to sound hard at higher dynamic levels. All the Bach performances, aristocratic and masterly, were recorded live, and these superbly controlled interpretations, unashamedly pianistic, are often surprisingly generous with repeats.

Robles, Marisa (harp)

'*The world of the harp*': FALLA: *Three-cornered hat: Danza del corregidor.* ALBENIZ: *Rumores de la Caleta; Torre Bermeja.* BIDAOLA: *Viejo zortzico.* EBERL (attrib. Mozart): *Theme, variations and rondo pastorale.* BEETHOVEN: *Variations on a Swiss song.* BRITTEN: *Ceremony of carols: Interlude.* FAURE: *Impromptu, Op. 86.* PIERNE: *Impromptu-caprice, Op. 9.* SALZEDO: *Chanson de la nuit.* BRAHMS: *Lullaby.* BACH: *Well-tempered Clavier: Prelude No. 1.* CHOPIN: *Mazurka, Op. 7/1; Prelude, Op. 28/15 (Raindrop).* HASSELMANS: *La source.*

(M) *** Decca (ADD) 433 869-2.

The artistry of Marisa Robles ensures that this is a highly attractive anthology and the programme is as well chosen as it is beautifully played. As ex-Professor of the harp at the Madrid Conservatory, Miss Robles has a natural affinity for the Spanish music that opens her programme, and other highlights include a magnetic account of the Britten *Interlude* and the Salzedo *Chanson de la nuit* with its bell-like evocations. The Eberl *Variations* are highly engaging. The excellent recordings derive from the Argo catalogue of the 1960s and '70s, except for the Chopin, Brahms, Bach and Hasselmans pieces, which have been added to fill out the present reissue (75 minutes). The delicious Hasselmans roulades are the epitome of nineteenth-century harp writing. The CD has a most realistic presence.

'*Música española*': NARVAEZ: *Variaciones populares sobre 'Guárdame las vacas'.* CABEZON: *Pavana y variaciones.* SANZ: *La serenissima.* M. ALBENIZ: *Sonata in G.* I. ALBENIZ: *Torre Bermeja.* FALLA: *The Three-cornered hat: Danza del corregidor.* GURIDI: *Viejo zortzico; Nere Maitea; Aritz Adarean; Ator, Ator Mutil; Agura Zarkilun; Garizuma Luzerik; Zorabitatua Naiz.* GOMBAU: *Apunte bético.* ALFONSO: *Cadenza.* FRANCO: *Canción y danza.*

(B) *** Double Decca (IMS) ADD/DDD 433 938-2 (2). – RODRIGO: *Concierto de Aranjuez* (trans. for harp) (with Philh. O, Dutoit). SARASATE: *Music for violin and piano.* ***

The harp is without the vibrant quality of the guitar in Spanish music, but in the hands of a master (or perhaps one should say a mistress) its swirling liquidity can have a magic of its own. Certainly Marisa Robles shows herself an artist of uncommon stamp in her subtlety in matters of colour. Her Spanish world is a personal one, its atmosphere contrasting vivid splashes of colour with the most delicate nuances of half-lighting, and her intimate musical feeling ensures the listener's continued fascination and pleasure. The music-making is entirely spontaneous and whether in the familiar writing of Falla or the piquant world of Basque folk music, this makes entirely delightful listening. She is beautifully recorded and the inclusion of Rodrigo's own arrangement for harp of his *Concierto de Aranjuez* is another plus point for this set, which also offers Campoli and Ricci at their finest in the violin and piano music of Sarasate.

Romero, Pepe (guitar)

Spanish music ((i) with Celín Romero): ANON.: *Jeux interdits*. ALBENIZ: *Suite española, Op. 47: Sevilla; Granada. Recuerdos de viaje, Op. 71: Rumores de la caleta. Mallorca (barcarolle), Op. 202. España (6 hojas de álbum), Op. 165: Asturias*; (i) *Tango*. GRANADOS: (i) *Danzas españolas, Op. 37: Andaluza.* (i) *Goyescas: Intermezzo.* CELEDONIO ROMERO: *Malagueña; Romantico.* TARREGA: *Capricho árabe; Pavana.* SOR: *Introduction & variations on a theme by Mozart, Op. 9.*

(M) **(*) Ph. (IMS) 434 727-2.

A thoroughly professional and immaculately played collection of favourites. The effect is intimate, pleasing rather than electrifying – the virtuoso showing his paces in familiar pieces. The flamenco-based pieces by the performer's father, Celedonio, bring a sudden hint of fire. For the reissue Celín Romero joins his brother for three duets, and this brings added spontaneity, although the intimate mood remains – witness the Granados *Spanish dance* which does not have the electricity of Julian Bream's solo version. The recording is very natural, but no information is provided about the music (except titles).

Los Romeros

Spanish guitar favourites (with Pepe Romero, Celín Romero, Celedonio Romero, Celino Romero): GIMONEZ: *La boda de Luis Alonso: Malagueña-Zapateado. El baile de Luis Alonso: Intermedio.* BOCCHERINI: *Guitar quintet No. 4 in D, G.448: Grave-Fandango.* CELEDONIO ROMERO: *Fantasia Cubana; Malagueñas.* FALLA: *El amor brujo: Ritual fire dance.* SOR: *L'encouragement, Op. 34.* PRAETORIUS: *Bransle de la torche; Ballet; Volta.* TARREGA: *Capricho árabe.* TURINA: *La oración del torero.* TORROBA: *Estampas.*

✪ *** Ph. (IMS) 442 781-2.

Opening with a compelling *Malagueña-Zapateado* of Jerénimo Gimónez and closing with an engaging and lighter *Intermedio* encore by the same composer, both from zarzuelas, this 74-minute collection of mainly Spanish music grips and entertains the listener as at a live concert. Celedonio contributes two pieces of his own, a charming solo lightweight *Fantasia Cubana*, and the others join him for his glittering flamenco *Malagueñas*, which has an improvisatory central section before the dashing coda with castanets.

Among the more famous pieces arranged for the four players are the very effective Falla *Ritual fire dance* and Turina's *La oración del torero* (full of evocation), while Sor's *L'encouragement*, with its ingenuous lilting *Cantabile*, a simple but artful *Theme and variations* and elegant closing *Valse*, is played as a duet by Pepe and Celino. Tárrega's haunting *Capricho árabe* is exquisitely phrased by Celino. The arrangement of the three Praetorius dances, with an added condiment of percussion, is colourfully in period. Tórroba's *Estampas* brings a highly imaginative response from the group, making this a highlight of the concert. The recording gives the guitars splendid presence against the attractively warm ambience, which in no way blurs the sharpness or focus of the players' attack.

Rosenthal, Moritz (piano)

CHOPIN: *Piano concerto No. 1 in E min., Op. 11* (with Berlin State Opera Orchestra, Frieder Weissmann); *Romanze only* (with NBC SO, Frank Black). *Berceuse, Op. 57; Chants polonais* (arr. LISZT); *Etudes, Op. 10/1; 10/5* (twice); *Mazurkas, Opp. 63/3* (three versions); *67/1; Waltz in C sharp min., E min. Op. posth.*

(***) Biddulph mono LHW 040.

Rosenthal was a pupil of Karl Mikuli, who was himself a Chopin pupil, and his Chopin is quite out of the ordinary. The *E minor Concerto* was made in 1930 and the ritornello is cut, but what pianism! (The alternative slow movement was recorded in New York on Rosenthal's 75th birthday.) Rosenthal's effortless virtuosity, lightness of touch, legatissimo and tonal subtlety are altogether remarkable. Playing of great culture from a distant age and beautifully transferred by Ward Marston.

Rossetti-Bonell, Dario (guitar)

'Début': BARRIOS: *2 Valses, Op. 8/3-4; Mazurka appassionata; Aconquija.* VIVALDI: *Mandolin concerto in C, RV 425* (transcribed for solo guitar by Rossetti-Bonell). VILLA-LOBOS: *Preludes Nos. 1-5.* GRANADOS: *Valses poéticos.*

(B) **(*) EMI CDZ5 73499-2.

Dario, son of Carlos Bonell, proves to be a masterly guitarist, and by no means in the shadow of his father. His technique is consummate and he knows just how to seduce the ear with subtle rubato, as in the Barrios *Mazurka appassionata*, or with a magnetically gentle melodic ebb and flow, as in the A minor or E major Villa-Lobos *Preludes*, and how to hold the listener with dramatic use of light and shade as in No. 4 in E minor. The engaging closing Granados *Valses poéticos* are presented with charm and much expertise in the matter of colour. However, the inclusion of the Vivaldi *Mandolin concerto*, arranged for guitar without orchestra, was a curious indulgence. It is very well played of course, but fails to make a case for a guitar taking over the orchestral as well as solo mandolin roles. The recording, made in Forde Abbey, Somerset, is wholly natural with a most pleasing acoustic.

Rothwell, Evelyn (oboe)

Recital: C. P. E. BACH: *Sonata in G min.* TELEMANN: *Sonata in E flat.* M. HEAD: *Siciliana* (all with Valda Aveling, harpsichord, Dennis Nesbitt, viola da

gamba). LOEILLET: *Sonata in C* (arr. ROTHWELL).
HANDEL: *Air & Rondo* (arr. & ed. ROTHWELL).
MORGAN: *Melody* (all with Wilfred Parry, piano).

(M) ** Dutton Lab./Barbirolli Soc. (ADD) CDSJB 1016.
(with CORELLI; HAYDN; MARCELLO: *Oboe concertos* ***).

Evelyn Rothwell, as always, plays expressively with
charm and poise. But the recording of Valda Aveling's
harpsichord seems unnecessarily recessed and insubstantial. Even so the Telemann *Sonata* is enjoyable
enough, and the Michael Head *Siciliana* brings a more
positive effect. The items accompanied on the piano by
Wilfred Parry are more successful. He is still rather
backwardly placed but emerges with a stronger personality and the delightful Handel titbits and the Nicholas
Morgan *Melody* are the highlights of the recital.

Russian Baroque Ensemble

'*Chamber music from the court of St Petersburg*':
STARTZER: *Divertimento in A min.* TITZ: *String
quartet in G; Violin sonata in F sharp min.* BAILLOT:
Russian air. MADONIS: *12 Diverse symphonies.*
BEREZOVSKY: *Violin sonata in C.* STEIBELT:
Variations on 2 Russian folksongs.

(BB) **(*) Arte Nova 74321 51626-2 (2).

All but one of these still obscure composers came
from outside the Russian empire but gravitated to the
court in St Petersburg, writing attractive and civilized,
if hardly original, music like this. The exception,
Maxim Berezovsky, represented here by a fresh, lively
Violin sonata, came from the Ukraine. In this two-
disc collection, much the longest and most impressive
work is the *Quartet in G* by the German, Anton Titz
(1742–1810), with an extraordinarily ambitious first
movement which alone lasts 20 minutes. He is also
represented by a fine *Violin sonata in F sharp minor*.
The only signs of ethnic Russian influence come in
three sets of variations on Russian themes, and they
are just as completely translated to the Viennese tradition as those in Beethoven's *Rasumovsky Quartets*.
The performances on period instruments are lusty
and heartfelt rather than subtle, given close recording
to match. A fascinating, unusual offering.

Salomon Quartet

'*The string quartet in 18th-century England*': ABEL:
Quartet in A, Op. 8/5. SHIELD: *Quartet in C min.,
Op. 3/6.* MARSH: *Quartet in B flat.* WEBBE:
Variations in A on 'Adeste fidelis'. S. WESLEY:
Quartet in E flat.

** Hyp. CDA 66780.

A good idea, let down by the indifferent invention of
much of the music itself. The amateur, John Marsh,
stands up very well alongside his professional companions, and his five-movement *Quartet in B flat*
(modelled on Haydn's Op. 1/1 and almost as pleasing)
is the first piece to catch the listener's attention, for
Abel is a very dull dog indeed. Samuel Webbe's *Varia-*

tions on '*O come all ye faithful*' does little but repeat
the melody with decorations. Samuel Wesley begins
conventionally and agreeably, then produces a real
lollipop as the Trio of the Minuet and a similarly winning finale. No complaints about the performances:
the Salomon Quartet play everything freshly and with
total commitment, using original instruments stylishly and in the sweetest possible manner. They are
very realistically recorded, too. Three stars for the performers but not the programme.

Satoh, Toyohiko (lute)

'*Gaultier and the French lute school*': E. GAULTIER:
*Tombeau de Mezangeau; Courante; Carillon;
Rossignol; Testament de Mezangeau; Canarie.* D.
GAULTIER: *Tombeau de Mademoiselle Gaultier;
Cleopâtre amante (Double).* J. GALLOT: *Prélude; Le
bout de l'an de M. Gaultier; Courante la cigogne;
Sarabande la pièce de huit heures; Volte la
Brugeoise.* DUFAUT: *Prélude; Tombeau de M.
Blanrocher; Dourante; Sarabande (Double); Gigue.*
MOUTON: *Prélude. Tombeau de Gogo (Allemande);
La belle homicide/Courante de M. Gaultier (Double
de la belle homicide); Gavotte; La Princesse
sarabande; Canarie.* DE VISEE: *Tombeau de M.
Mouton (Allemande).*

*** Channel Classics Dig. CCS 8795.

Toyohiko Satoh has already given us a collection of the
music of Robert de Visée (CCS 7795), whose *Tombeau
de M. Mouton* provides one of the most affecting
pieces here, to close a recital which is in essence a survey of French lute music of the seventeenth century.
Satoh is clearly an expert in this field, and he plays an
original lute made by Laurentius Grieff of Ingolstadt
in 1613, which was modified into an eleven-course
French baroque instrument around 1670.

It took four years for the Dutch lute-maker Van der
Waals to restore it to playing condition, and its gut
strings create a pleasingly warm sonority. Satoh's
playing is robust yet thoughtful and it has an improvisatory freedom which extends even to the dance
movements. (Dufaut's *Gigue*, for instance, is jolly
enough but would be difficult to dance to.) This is
apparently possible because, around 1630, a new
French tuning was developed within the lute school
centring round Le vieux Gaultier (Ennemond Gaultier of Lyon, 1575–1651). This allowed more freedom for
the fingers of the left hand, enabling lutenists to write
their music in a *style brisé* (broken style), which was
later to spread across Europe.

Gaultier and his cousin Denis (Gaultier le Jeune)
were important innovators in their time and they also
introduced the idea of the dignified 'tombeau'
mementos, as well as vignettes with sobriquets like *Le
rossignol* and *Carillon*, yet which are in no way imitative. The two versions of the *Canarie* (by Ennemond
Gaultier and Mouton respectively) are based on the
same melody and dance form, with a dotted rhythm,
and both are among the more striking items here,

alongside the expressive *Sarabande* of Dufaut and Mouton's *La Princesse*, which features the famous *La Folia*. Rather unexpectedly, the same composer's *La belle homicide* is a cheerful piece.

Scandinavian Wind Quintet

Danish concert: NIELSEN: *Wind quintet, Op. 43.* HOLMBOE: *Notturno, Op. 19.* NORGARD: *Whirl's world.* ABRAHAMSEN: *Walden.*

*** dacapo 8.224001.

The Scandinavian Wind Quintet give an eminently acceptable account of the Nielsen which can stand up to most of the competition. The Holmboe *Notturno* is a beautiful piece from 1940 whose language blends the freshness of Nielsen with the neo-classicism of Hindemith yet remains totally distinctive. The Nørgård is less substantial but is not otherwise available; Hans Abrahamsen's *Walden* is thin but atmospheric. Very present and lifelike recording.

Schiff, András and Peter Serkin
(piano duo)

Music for 2 pianos: MOZART: *Fugue in C min., K. 426; Sonata in D, K.448.* REGER: *Variations and fugue on a theme of Beethoven, Op. 86.* BUSONI: *Fantasia contrappuntistica.*

*** ECM 465 062-2 (2).

András Schiff and Peter Serkin join here in a symbiotic partnership to give a quite superb and certainly gripping account of Busoni's formidable *Fantasia contrappuntistica* in which they find as wide a range of mood and colour as in Max Reger's *Variations* (on a Beethoven *Bagatelle* from Op. 119). The theme is presented with a disarming simplicity, but Reger soon introduces characteristically florid textures, yet returning to simplicity in the *Andante* and *Sostenuto* variations. These alternate with *Agitato* and *Vivace* sections leading to the spirited closing *Fugue*. The pair of early twentieth-century works are framed by two-piano music of Mozart. Here the opening *Fugue in C minor* is strong and positive, and the first movement of the *D major Sonata*, too, is taken very seriously, not emphasizing what Alfred Einstein called its 'gallant character' until the arrival of the second subject, and then only momentarily. However, the mood lightens in the central *Andante*, in which the two players exchange phrases very beguilingly, and the finale is rhythmically most winning. Excellent, well-focused and not too resonant recording.

Schiller, Allan (piano)

'Für Elise': Popular piano pieces: BEETHOVEN: *Für Elise.* FIELD: *Nocturne in E (Noontide).* CHOPIN: *Mazurka in B flat, Op. 7/1; Waltz in A, Op. 34/2. 3 Ecossaisen, Op. 72/3; Fantaisie-impromptu, Op. 66.* MENDELSSOHN: *Songs without words: Venetian gondola song, Op. 19; Bees' wedding, Op. 67.* LISZT: *Consolation No. 3 in D flat.* DE SEVERAC: *The music box.* DEBUSSY: *Suite bergamasque: Clair de lune. Arabesques Nos. 1 and 2. Prélude: The girl with the flaxen hair.* GRIEG: *Wedding day at Troldhaugen; March of the dwarfs.* ALBENIZ: *Granada; Tango; Asturias.*

(BB) *** ASV CDQS 6032.

A particularly attractive recital, diverse in mood, spontaneous in feeling and very well recorded. The acoustic is resonant, but the effect is highly realistic. There are many favourites here, with Allan Schiller at his most personable in the engaging Field *Nocturne*, De Severac's piquant *Music box* and the closing *Asturias* of Albéniz, played with fine bravura. The Chopin group, too, is most successful, with the Scottish rhythmic snap of the *Ecossaisen* neatly articulated and the famous *B flat Mazurka* presented most persuasively.

Segovia, Andrés (guitar)

'The Legendary Segovia': BACH: *Cello suite in G, BWV 1007: Prelude* (arr. PONCE); *(Unaccompanied) Violin Partita No. 3 in E, BWV 1006: Gavotte & Rondo; Prelude in C min. for lute, BWV 999* (both arr. SEGOVIA). SOR: *Thème varié, Op. 9.* Robert DE VISEE: *Minuet.* FROBERGER: *Gigue.* CASTELNUOVO-TEDESCO: *Hommage à Boccherini: Vivo e energico.* MENDELSSOHN: *String quartet No. 1 in E flat, Op. 12: Canzonetta* (arr. SEGOVIA). MALATS: *Serenata.* ALBENIZ: *Suite española: Granada; Sevilla.* GRANADOS: *Danza española No. 10 in G, Op. 37.* TURINA: *Fandanguillo.* TORROBA: *Suite castellana: Fandanguillo. Sonatina in A: Allegretto. Preludio; Notturno.* PONCE: *Petite valse; Suite in A.* TARREGA: *Recuerdos de la Alhambra.*

(M) (***) EMI mono CDM5 67009-2.

It was Segovia's pioneering recitals in the 1930s that re-established the guitar in the public mind as a serious solo instrument. This collection consists of his early recordings, made over a span of twelve years from 1927 to 1939 either at Abbey Road or the Small Queen's Hall in London. There are quite a few transcriptions, including several Bach items, where the style of the playing is romantic (though never showing lapses of taste). However, the second part of the programme includes a high proportion of Spanish repertoire either written for or naturally suited to the guitar. What is so striking throughout this collection is the way all the music, slight or serious, springs vividly to life. Segovia had the gift of natural spontaneity in all he played, and he was in his prime at this period, so that technically this is wonderfully assured. His performance of Tárrega's famous *Recuerdos* is quite individual, with the underlying melodic line shaped like a song, rather than treated seamlessly. Guitar fans will find this generous 74-minute recital an essential purchase; others will be surprised to discover that no apologies need be made for the sound, which is natural in timbre and gives the instrument a ready projection.

Shifrin, David (clarinet), Lincoln Center Chamber Music Society

Five American clarinet quintets: CORIGLIANO: *Soliloquy for clarinet and string quartet.* ZWILICH: *Clarinet quintet.* TOWER: *Turning points.* SHENG: *Concertino for clarinet and string quartet.* ADOLPHE: *At the still point there the dance is.*

*** Delos DE 3183 (2).

A remarkable group of five surprisingly lyrical works, often searching and all readily approachable. John Corigliano's *Soliloquy*, adapted from the second movement of his *Concerto*, is essentially a haunting interplay between solo clarinet and violin. It was written in memory of his father, who was concertmaster of the New York Philharmonic, and is passionately elegiac. While sustaining its mood of desolation throughout, it leaves the listener uplifted rather than depressed.

Ellen Zwilich's *Quintet* opens with stabbing aggression from the strings and a continuing restlessness from the soloist, with moments of wildness carried through into the pungent second movement. Finally, relative calm is reached in the third, but its language becomes increasingly plangent, until relative serenity returns towards the close. The brief *Scherzo* is ironically jocular, followed by an atmospheric epilogue.

Joan Tower's *Turning points* immediately features the device of a long slow crescendo for the soloist: its style is at first rhapsodic, with a central cadenza-like virtuoso display for the soloist and increasing agitation towards the end. The remaining two works are primarily atmospheric. Bright Sheng's attractively lyrical *Concertino* brings an exotic influence from Chinese folk music. It opens and closes reflectively, but its serenity does not run an even course, with energetic bursts from the clarinet. The Chinese influence is most strongly felt in the repeated scherzando ostinatos of the second movement.

Bruce Adolphe's *At the still point* is also ruminative, the first two movements, *Aria* and *Meditation*, move hauntingly towards the 'still point', though not without interruption, and then are released into the dance, which swirls, but in a relatively gentle minimalist manner. It is a work of immediate appeal. David Shifrin's performances are masterly and the recording is excellent. A most stimulating collection.

(i) Snowden, Jonathan (flute), Andrew Litton (piano), (ii) Nicholas Daniel (oboe), Julius Drake (piano)

'*French music for flute and oboe*': (i) WIDOR: *Suite for flute and piano, Op. 34.* FAURE: *Fantaisie, Op. 79; Morceau de concours.* DEBUSSY: *Syrinx.* HONEGGER: *Danse de la chèvre.* ROUSSEL: *Jouers de flûte, Op. 27.* MESSIAEN: *Le Merle noir.* POULENC: *Flute sonata.* (ii) SAINT-SAENS: *Oboe sonata.* DUTILLEUX: *Oboe sonata.* KOECHLIN: *Oboe sonata, Op. 28.* POULENC: *Oboe sonata.*

(BB) *** Virgin VBD5 61495-2 (2).

This Virgin Double aptly and inexpensively pairs two outstanding recitals of French instrumental music, originally issued separately, but which in this format complement each other admirably. Jonathan Snowden, deftly accompanied by Andrew Litton, a formidable pianist, first gathers a vintage collection of French works for flute. The Poulenc *Sonata* is dazzlingly done, and so are the other virtuoso pieces, all strongly characterized. The surprise is the opening item, by Widor, delicate and pointed, charmingly lyrical, a suite by a composer now remembered for his heavyweight organ works.

On the second disc Nicholas Daniel and Julius Drake concentrate equally persuasively on four major French oboe sonatas. Once again the Poulenc proves highly diverting, its outer movements, *Elégie paisiblement* and *Déploration: très calme*, proving as unpredictable as ever. The opening piece, by Saint-Saëns, is captivating but by no means trivial, with its central *Allegretto* framed by two sections giving the soloist a great deal of freedom.

Dutilleux's *Sonata* typically combines subtlety of colour and expressive depth with ingenuity. However, the most ambitious work is by Koechlin, its four movements running for 28 minutes. It opens in pastoral evocation, but afterwards the writing often becomes very prolix, the range of mood remarkably wide. The Daniel/Drake duo play it expertly and sympathetically, but they do not entirely erase one's suspicion that it would have been a stronger piece if more concise. Yet overall these paired recitals, well balanced and truthfully recorded, give much pleasure.

Staier, Andreas (harpsichord)

'*Variaciones del fandango español*': SOLER: *Fandango.* ALBERO: *Recercata, fuga y sonata in G; Recercata, fuga y sonata in D.* GALLES: *Sonatas Nos. 9 in C min.; 16 in F min.; 17 in C min.* LOPEZ: *Variaciones del fandango español.* FERRER: *Adagio in G min.; Sonata, Andantino in G min.* BOCCHERINI: *Fandango, Grave assai* (with Christine Schornheim, harpsichord & Adela Gonzáles Cámpa, castanets).

*** Teldec 3984 21468-2.

Framed by two great *Fandangos* by Soler and Boccherini, and with a sparkling further set of *Fandango* variations by Félix López as centrepiece, this is a fascinatingly conceived recital, superbly played on an ideal harpsichord – a modern French copy of an early eighteenth-century German instrument (associated with Silbermann). The rest of the programme includes a pair of inventive triptychs by Sebastián de Albero (1722-56) – 'polyphony used in a very Mediterranean way' (to quote Staier) – and three delightful miniature sonatas by Joseph Gallés: No. 16 in F minor (a single movement) is particularly winning, as are the two short pieces by José Ferrer.

Staier plays with fine sensibility and great virtuosity, always retaining the listener's interest. For the spectacular finale (which he has freely arranged from the finale of Boccherini's *D major Guitar quintet*, G.448) Staier is joined by an excellent second player, with a third artist to decorate the thrilling climax with castanets. The result is a semi-improvisational *tour de force*. The only small snag is that the recording is somewhat over-resonant – thus, setting a modest volume level is important, though not, of course, in the *Fandangos*.

Steele-Perkins, Crispian (trumpet), Stephen Cleobury (organ)

'*The King's trumpeter*': MATHIAS: *Processional*. L. MOZART: *Concerto in E flat*. BOYCE: *Voluntaries in D*. ANON.: *3 16th-century dances*. TELEMANN: *Concerto da caccia in D*. GOUNOD: *Méditation: Ave Maria*. STEELE: *6 Pieces, Op. 33*.

**(*) Priory PRCD 189.

Crispian Steele-Perkins is here given a chance to show his paces on a modern trumpet. The programme opens with Mathias's distinctly catchy *Processional* and covers a fairly wide range of repertoire, ending with the six characterful pieces by Christopher Steele. The disc is relatively short measure (53 minutes), but the playing is first class and the balance most convincing.

Stringer, Alan (trumpet), Noel Rawsthorne (organ)

'*Trumpet and organ*' (organ of Liverpool Cathedral): M.-A. CHARPENTIER: *Te Deum: Prelude*. STANLEY: *Voluntary No. 5 in D*. PURCELL: *Sonata in C; Two Trumpet tunes and Air*. BOYCE: *Voluntary in D*. CLARKE: *Trumpet voluntary*. BALDASSARE: *Sonata No. 1 in F*. ROMAN: *Keyboard suite in D: Non troppo allegro; Presto (Gigue)*. FIOCCO: *Harpsichord suite No. 1: Andante*. BACH: *Cantata No. 147: Jesu, joy of man's desiring*. attrib. GREENE: *Introduction and trumpet tune*. VIVIANI: *Sonata No. 1 in C*.

(M) **(*) CRD CRD 3308.

This collection is extremely well recorded. The reverberation of Liverpool Cathedral is under full control and both trumpet and organ are cleanly focused, while the trumpet has natural timbre and bloom. Alan Stringer is at his best in the classical pieces, the *Voluntary* of Boyce, the *Trumpet tunes* and *Sonata* of Purcell and the stylishly played *Sonata* of Viviani, a most attractive little work. He also gives a suitably robust performance of the famous *Trumpet voluntary*. Elsewhere he is sometimes a little square: the Bach chorale is rather too stiff and direct. But admirers of this repertoire will find much to enjoy, and the *Andante* of Fiocco has something in common with the more famous *Adagio* attributed to Albinoni in Giazotto's famous arrangement.

Swiss Wind Quintet

20th-century wind quintets: JANACEK: *Mládi*. NIELSEN: *Wind quintet, Op. 43*. HINDEMITH: *Kleine Kammermusik, Op. 24/2*. LIGETI: *6 Bagatelles*.

(BB) *** Koch Discover Dig. DICD 920395.

Mládi isn't, strictly speaking, a quintet, as it has an additional bass clarinet part. But it is uncommonly well played by this excellent Swiss group, and they give an equally sympathetic account of the Nielsen *Quintet*, most winning in the *Minuet* as well as in the third-movement Theme and variations. The Hindemith *Kleine Kammermusik* is hardly less successful, notably the dolorous *Waltz* which hints at Walton's *Façade*, and the pensive nostalgia of the third movement, although there is plenty of sparkling vitality elsewhere. The riotously witty opening movement of Ligeti's *Six Bagatelles* is splendidly done. There is little to choose between this performance of an unexpectedly entertaining work and that by the competing Claude Debussy Quintet on Harmonia Mundi (see above). In some ways the programme on this excellently recorded Discover disc is the more tempting, but both CDs are equally recommendable.

Tal, Yaara and Andreas Groethuysen (piano duo)

DVORAK: *From the Bohemian forest, Op. 68*. RUBINSTEIN: *6 Characteristic pictures, Op. 50*. RACHMANINOV: *6 Pieces, Op. 11*.

*** Sony SK47199.

Anything that this remarkably musical and sensitive partnership has recorded is special, and this programme – and in particular the Rachmaninov Op. 11 pieces – proves no exception. They make every phrase breathe naturally and freshly.

Tetzlaff, Christian (violin), Lars Anders Tomter (viola), Leif Over Andsnes (piano)

JANACEK: *Violin Sonata*. DEBUSSY: *Violin Sonata*. RAVEL: *Violin Sonata*. NIELSEN: *Violin Sonata No. 2, Op. 38*. BRAHMS: *Viola Sonatas Nos. 1 & 2*. SCHUMANN: *Märchenbilder*.

◉ (BB) *** Virgin VBD5 62016-2 (2).

Virgin has here brought together two outstanding recital discs from the 1990s, of which the Brahms and Schumann coupling originally received a ◉. There is no need to modify that judgement, and in view of the overall excellence of this combined release, it is extended to this double-CD as a whole. In the Janáček *Sonata*, Christian Tetzlaff and Leif Ove Andsnes show a complete understanding of the score. They play with commitment and dedication while there are no more imaginative accounts of either the Debussy or Ravel couplings.

Nielsen's *G minor Sonata* is a transitional work in which the composer emerges from the geniality of the *Sinfonia espansiva* into the darker, more anguished world of the *Fourth Symphony*. It has much of the questing character of the latter and much of its muscularity, and Tetzlaff and Andsnes give a very distinguished – at times inspired – performance. They also provide one of the best accounts in the catalogue of the Brahms sonatas in their viola form. Theirs is playing of great sensitivity and imagination. These Norwegian artists bring a wide range of colour to this music and phrase with an unforced naturalness that is very persuasive, and their fresh account of the Schumann gives much pleasure too. The sound is natural and well balanced throughout this programme (in the Brahms and Schumann, there is a slight bias towards the piano), and this is altogether a rather special CD Double and remarkably inexpensive.

Thurston Clarinet Quartet

'*Clarinet masquerade*': FARKAS: *Ancient Hungarian dances from the 17th century.* MOZART (arr. WHEWELL): *Divertimento No. 2.* TOMASI: *3 Divertissements.* GARNER (arr. BLAND): *Misty.* JOBIM (arr. BLAND): *The Girl from Ipanema.* DESPORTES: *French suite.* ALBINONI (arr. THILDE): *Sonata in G min.* STARK: *Serenade.* GERSHWIN (arr. BLAND): *Rhapsody: Summertime.* PHILLIPS (arr. HARVEY): *Cadenza;* (arr. FERNANDEZ): *Muskrat Sousa.*

(M) *** ASV CDWHL 2076.

A light-hearted concert, but an entertaining one which will especially appeal to those who like the clarinet's sonority, reedier than the flute's and with more character. The opening suite of Hungarian folk dances (with the chirps and cheeps in the finale very engaging) leads on to a Mozart *Divertimento* for basset horns. The other pieces, the insouciant Tomasi and the Desportes suite (full of Ravelian elegance) are all amiable, and the arrangement of Gershwin's *Summertime* has the famous opening swerve of *Rhapsody in blue* as its introduction. Finally there is the exuberant *Muskrat Sousa* which features a combination of *12th Street Rag* and *South Rampart Street Parade*. The recording is immaculately vivid.

Troussov, Kirill (violin), Alexandra Troussova (piano)

BEETHOVEN: *Violin sonata No. 5 in C min., Op. 30/2.* BRAHMS: *Violin sonata No. 3 in D min., Op. 108.* WIENIAWSKI: *Fantaisie brillante on themes from Gounod's 'Faust'.* ZIMBALIST: *Fantasy on Rimsky-Korsakov's 'The Golden Cockerel'.*

(B) *** EMI Début CDZ5 73212-2.

One of the best of the valuable EMI Début series. Kirill Troussov and Alexandra Troussova are a brother-and-sister team of remarkable skill. They are Russian and were both in their teens when this outstanding recital was recorded. Vibrant and committed playing from both artists and excellent recordings.

Trpčeski, Simon (piano)

PROKOFIEV: *Piano Sonata No. 6 in A.* SCRIABIN: *Piano Sonata No. 5.* STRAVINSKY: *Three Movements from Petrushka.* TCHAIKOVSKY (trans. PLETNEV): *Nutcracker Concert Suite.*

(B) *** EMI Début CDZ5 75202-2.

Simon Trpčeski is Macedonian-born and twenty-three, making his record debut in virtuoso Russian repertoire. He is obviously a pianist of awesome technical prowess and it is a tribute to his pianism and artistry that only the most exalted comparisons come to mind. The Scriabin *Sonata No. 5* is very impressive indeed, sounds freshly experienced and has great inner vitality. The Prokofiev *Sixth* does not have quite the abandon of Kissin's Tokyo version (at least in the finale) but is among the very finest all the same. Trpceski plays the Stravinsky with great abandon and does very well in Mikhail Pletnev's arrangement of movements from the *Nutcracker*, though without perhaps having quite the range of colour and dynamics that the latter demands.

Tureck, Rosalyn (piano)

'*Live at the Teatro Colón*': BACH: *Adagio in G, BWV 968; Chromatic fantasia and fugue, BWV 903; Partita No. 1, BWV 825: Gigue. Goldberg variation No. 29, BWV 988; Klavierbüchlein for Anna Magdalena Bach: Musette in D.* MENDELSSOHN: *Songs without words, Op. 19/1.* SCHUBERT: *Moments musicaux Nos. 2 in A flat; 3 in F min.* BACH/BUSONI: *Chaconne* (from BWV 1004). BRAHMS: *Variations and fugue on a theme by Handel, Op. 24.*

**(*) VAI Audio VIAI 1024-2 (2).

Rosalyn Tureck has lost none of her magic, as this Buenos Aires (1992) live recital demonstrates, and it is good to find her so sympathetic in Schubert and Mendelssohn, as well as in Bach. Her articulation in the Brahms *Handel variations* suggests she is thinking as much of Handel as of Brahms, but that is a comment, not a criticism. The Bach/Busoni *Chaconne* is splendid. Excellent recording, but there are two snags: the almost hysterical applause which bursts in as soon as a piece has ended and the fact that this recital would almost have fitted on one CD. These two play for just 83 minutes 31 seconds.

Vieaux, Jason (guitar)

Recital: MERLIN: *Suite del recuerdo*. PUJOL: *Preludios Nos. 2, 3 , & 5*. ORBON (de SOTO): *Preludio y Danza*. KROUSE: *Variations on a Moldavian hora*. BARRIOS: *Valses, Op. 8/3 & 4; Julia Florida: Barcarola*. MOREL: *Chôro; Danza Brasileira; Danza in E min*. BUSTAMENTE: *Misionera*.

✿ (BB) *** Naxos 8.553449.

This is the finest début guitar recital we have heard for some years. Jason Vieaux is a young American musician, already a prize-winner – and no wonder. This Latin-American repertoire is unfailingly diverting in his hands: there are no familiar names here except that of Barrios, yet almost every item is either memorably evocative or it makes the pulse quicken. Vieaux's completely natural rubato at the opening *Evocación* of José Luis Merlin's *Suite del recuerdo* is quite masterly and the slow crescendos in the final *Carnavalito* are thrilling; then there is a complete change of mood and the *Evocación* makes a haunting return before the final *Joropo*. The *Preludios* of Pujol are quite magical; Vieaux then lets his hair down for the *Candombe*. The two *Valses* of Barrios are deliciously fragile, with the central *Barcarola* hardly less subtle, while the more robust Brazilian dances of Jorge Morel have real panache. The Naxos recording has good ambience and is present yet not too closely balanced. Unforgettable.

Wagler, Dietrich (organ)

'*Great European organs No. 24*': Freiberg Dom, Silbermann organ: SCHEIDT: *Magnificat Noni toni*. CLERAMBAULT: *Suite de premier ton*. BUXTEHUDE: *Prelude and fugue in D min*. KREBS: *Choral preludes: Mein Gott, das Herze bring ich dir; Herr Jesus Christ, dich zu uns wend; Herzlich tut mich verlangen; O Ewigkeit, du Donnerwort*. J. S. BACH: *Fantaisie in G; Prelude and fugue in C*.

**(*) Priory PRCD 332.

The organ, rather than the player, is the star of this record; the latter's performances are sound but very much in the traditional German style. But he knows his instrument and the opening *Magnificat Noni toni* of Scheidt sounds resplendent, with the following Clérambault *Suite* also very effectively registered. A well-balanced programme, lacking only the last degree of flair in presentation.

Weir, Gillian (organ)

'*King of instruments: The art of Dame Gillian Weir (A Feast of organ music from the 16th to 20th centuries)*'

Volume I: BACH: *Toccata, adagio and fugue in C, BWB 564; Fantasia in G, BWV 572; Trio sonata No. 1 in E flat, BWV 525; Passacaglia in C min., BWV 582* (Organ of St Lawrence, Rotterdam). MARCHAND: *Pièces d'Orgue, Premier Livre: Dialogue sur les grands jeux; Récit de tierce en taille; Basse et dessus de trompette et de cornet; Récit de voix humaine; Cinquième Livre: Bass de coumorne ou de trompette; Duo; Récit; Plein-jeu; Fugue; Basse de trompette ou de cromorne; Récit de tierce en taille* (Organ of St Maximin, Thionville, France). BULL: *Dr Bull's my selfe; Dr Bull's jewell* (Organ of Hexam Abbey).

Volume II: CLERAMBAULT: *Suite de premier ton; Suite de deuxième ton* (Organ of St Leonard Kirche, Basel, Switzerland). BRUHNS: *Praeludium Nos. 1-3; Chorale: Nun komm, der Heiden Heiland* (Organ of Clare College, Cambridge).

Volume III: ROBERDAY: *Fuges et caprices pour orgue Nos. 1-12* (Organ of St Leonhardkirche, Basel, Switzerland). LANGLAIS: *Dialogue sur les mixtures* (Organ of Hexam Abbey). SCHEIDT: *Passamezzo* (Variations 1-12) (Organ of Clare College, Cambridge).

Volume IV: DANDRIEU: *Premier Livre de Pièces d'Orgue: Pièces en A, Mi, La. Magnificat* (Organ of St Leonard, Basel, Switzerland); *Pièces en G, Ré, Sol minuer; Magnificat II*. MARCHAND: *Pièces d'Orgue, Troisième Livre: Dialogue sur les grands jeux; Quatrième Livre: Duo; Fugue; Trio; Récit; Duo; Basse et trompette; Récit de tierce en taille* (Organ of St Maximin, Thionville, France). DE GRIGNY: *Tierce en taille*. MULET: *Toccata Tu es Petrus* (Organ of Hexam Abbey).

Volume V: CAMILLERI: *Missa Mundi* (Organ of Royal Festival Hall). WIDOR: *Symphony No. 6: Allegro*. VIERNE: *Impromptu*. DAQUIN: *Noël suisse*. DUPRE: *La Fileuse*. TOMKINS: *Worcester braules*. SWEELINCK: *Chorale: Mein junges Leben hat ein End*. DUBOIS: *Toccata* (Organ of Hexam Abbey).

*** Australian Argo/Decca (ADD) 460 185-2 (5).

Gillian Weir made her début at the 1965 season of Proms, and soon established a formidable reputation over the widest range of organ repertoire, but especially in music of the French school. Over a period of five years in the latter half of the 1970s, she made a series of major recordings for Decca's Argo label and it is good that this logo has been retained for the present superbly remastered five-disc survey.

Her Bach, recorded on an ideal Dutch organ in Rotterdam, is cool and poised. The bravura in the deliciously registered *Fantasia in G* cannot escape the listener, yet there is no sense of the virtuosity being flaunted. The *Trio sonata* is equally colourful, but the remorseless tread of the *Passacaglia in C minor*, taken very steadily, is undoubtedly compelling, and the *Toccata, adagio and fugue* is hardly less telling in its sense of controlled power.

Louis Marchand (1669–1732) was Bach's French contemporary: his suites are not learned but meant to divert, which they certainly do here and especially the delectably registered *Basse et dessus de trompette et de cornet* from the first book and the comparable pieces in the second, again played on a highly suitable organ in France. The brief encores by John Bull are equally tangy and spirited.

Clérambault's *Livre d'orgue* dates from 1710 and follow the same layout as those of Marchand: the music has slightly more formality, yet the influences of French dance music remain, and once again Weir's sparkling registration tickles the ear. The Swiss organ also features an authentic 'tremblant fort' stop, used in the piece called *Flûtes*, with a suprisingly modern effect, followed by the charming dialogue of the *Récit de Nazard* and a powerful closing *Caprice*.

Nikolaus Bruhns (1665–97) died young and left only five organ works, of which four are recorded here. His individuality is striking, and so is the quirky originality of his musical style, which freely interchanges fugal passages and sections of the most florid bravura. The *First Praeludium in G major* has the kind of immediate appeal which could make it famous if regularly heard; its memorable fugal subject is even more jaunty than Bach's *Fugue à la gigue*. Gillian Weir has the full measure of this music, finding a perfect balance between the fantasy and the structural needs of each piece. She dazzles the ear not only with her vigour and virtuosity but also with some quite scrumptious registration on an organ at Clare College, Cambridge that seems exactly right for the music. The recording is marvellous, a demonstration of clarity and sonority admirably combined.

François Roberday (1624–80) will be little more than a name – if that – to most readers. He is a *petite maître* who occasionally figures in recitals, but has until now not made a very striking presence in the CD catalogue. This recording of his twelve *Fugues et caprices* (over an hour of music) is made on a modern instrument in Basel which produces very authentic-sounding timbres. As usual Gillian Weir plays with enormous style and aplomb, but it would be idle to maintain that this is music of more than passing interest, except to the specialist collector. Once again the Argo recording has splendid range and presence.

On the other hand, Samuel Scheidt's *Passamezzo Variations*, taken from the first Volume of his *Tablatura nova* has a more general appeal, readily demonstrating the composer's mastery of variation technique, with imaginative invention throughout. Gillian Weir helps a great deal, not only by playing the music splendidly but by again choosing registrations with great flair and a marvellous sense of colour. The piquancy of several of her combinations is unforgettably apt and she is superbly recorded. This music was originally coupled with the Bruhns *Preludes* above but now it is joined with Roberday, with Langlais's rhythmically quirky *Dialogue for the mixtures* used as a colourful intermezzo.

Dandrieu was a younger contemporary of Couperin le Grand and, like him, came from a musical family. He spent most of his life as organist at Saint-Barthélemy in Paris and at the Royal Chapel. The First Book of organ pieces, published in 1739 a year after his, death, contains a number of suites; two are recorded here, consisting of an offertory, several other short movements, and a series of couplets which comprise the organ's contribution to a pair of settings of the *Magnificat*.

The music is more than just historically interesting; the invention is full of individual character and resource. Gillian plays each *Suite* and *Magnificat* on a different instrument, both of them recorded in a lively acoustic and her interpretations are marked by a vivid palette, authority and taste. There follows a further selection of *Pièces* by Louis Marchand and a move forward in time for Nicolas de Grigny's serene *Tierce en Taille* (effectively decorated). The programme of this most stimulating disc ends with a famously brilliant twentieth-century Toccata, *Tu es petrus*, by Henri Mulet.

The composer who dominates the final disc, Charles Camilleri, is Maltese, but his background influence comes as much from the East as the West. The (45-minute) *Missa Mundi* is a highly mystical work, inspired by a meditative prose-poem by Teilhard de Chardin, *La Messe sur le Monde*, written in the middle of the Ordos Desert area of China in 1923. The music follows the five sections of the meditation: *The offering; Fire over earth; Fire in the earth; Communion; Prayer*. The poem introduces an astonishing range of organ technique and sonority from the frenzied *Fire in the earth* to the simplistic closing *Prayer*. Weir gives a thrillingly dedicated performance which immediately grabs the listener.

Certainly this playing offers both a personal identification with the music and great bravura in equal measure; at times it is as overwhelming as the composer envisaged, at others its simple statements show an eloquence that is notable for its gentleness. The recording is superb. It is as clear and clean as a whistle, immensely wide in dynamic range, and there is not a ripple of distortion of any kind. The rest of the programme is made up of a skilfully chosen selection of genre pieces, among which Vierne's rippling *Impromptu*, Daquin's charming fanfare-like *Noël suisse* and Dupré's delicate evocation of *La Fileuse* stand out. The jolly closing *Toccata* of Theodor Dubois (which has a whiff of Widor) makes an exhilarating finale.

Almost all this repertoire is most rewarding and can be cordially recommended even to those who normally fight shy of early organ composers. It could hardly be played more masterfully and the engineers provide first-class sound throughout. Readers interested in this repertory (and even those who are not) should investigate this thoroughly satisfying survey.

Whiteley, John Scott (organ)

'*Great romantic organ music*' (organ of York Minster): TOURNEMIRE: *Improvisation on the Te Deum.* JONGEN: *Minuet-Scherzo, Op. 53.* MULET: *Tu es Petra.* DUPRE: *Prelude and fugue in G min., Op. 3/7.* R. STRAUSS: *Wedding prelude.* KARG-ELERT: *Pastel in B, Op. 92/1.* BRAHMS: *Chorale prelude: O Gott, du frommer Gott, Op. 122/7.* LISZT: *Prelude and fugue on bach, G.260.*

*** York CD 101.

A superb organ recital, with the huge dynamic range of the York Minster organ spectacularly captured on CD and pianissimo detail registering naturally. John Scott Whiteley's playing is full of flair: the attractively complex and sparklingly florid *Prelude and fugue* of Marcel Dupré is exhilarating and reaches a high climax, while the grand Liszt piece is hardly less overwhelming. The opening Tournemire *Improvisation* is very arresting indeed, while Jongen's *Minuet-Scherzo* displays Whiteley's splendidly clear articulation.

Williams, John (guitar)

'*Spanish guitar music*': I. ALBENIZ: *Asturias; Tango; Córdoba; Sevilla.* SANZ: *Canarios.* TORROBA: *Nocturno; Madroños.* SAGRERAS: *El Colibri.* M. ALBENIZ: *Sonata in D.* FALLA: *Homenaje; Three-cornered hat: Corregidor's dance; Miller's dance. El amor brujo: Fisherman's song.* CATALAN FOLKSONGS: *La Nit de Nadal; El noy de la mare; El testaman de Amelia.* GRANADOS: *La Maja de Goya. Spanish dance No. 5.* TARREGA: *Recuerdos de la Alhambra.* VILLA-LOBOS: *Prelude No. 4 in E min.* MUDARRA: *Fantasia.* TURINA: *Fandanguillo, Op. 36.*

(B) *** Sony (ADD) SBK 46347.

John Williams can show strong Latin feeling, as in the vibrant *Farruca* of the *Miller's dance* from Falla's *Three-cornered hat,* or create a magically atmospheric mood, as in the hauntingly registered transcription of the *Fisherman's song* from *El amor brujo.* He can play with thoughtful improvisatory freedom, as in the Villa-Lobos *Prelude,* with its pianissimo evocation, or be dramatically spontaneous, as in the memorable performance of Turina's *Fandanguillo,* which ends the recital magnetically. The instinctive control of atmosphere and dynamic is constantly rewarding throughout a varied programme, and the technique is phenomenal, yet never flashy, always at the service of the music. The remastering brings a clean and truthful, if very immediate, image. Background is minimal and never intrusive.

Recital: THEODORAKIS: *3 Epitatios.* DOMENICONI: *Koyyunbaba, Parts 1-4.* ANON.: *Lamento di Tristan; Ductia; Saltarello.* HOUGHTON: *Stélé.* SATIE: *Gnossiennes Nos. 1-2. Gymnopédie No. 3* (arr. for guitar and small orchestra). WILLIAMS: *Aeolian suite* (for guitar and small orchestra) (both with orchestra cond. William Goodchild).

**(*) Sony SK 60585.

An insubstantial recital perhaps, but quite an attractive one, with every piece showing John Williams's supreme and easy mastery, and his ability to make music in front of studio microphones with concert-hall-like spontaneity. The three vivid miniatures by Theodorakis are followed by what is essentially an atmospheric set of variations by an Italian composer, Carlo Domeniconi, who lived in Istanbul. The result sounds curiously Andalusian. The three medieval dances then make a good foil (the *Ductia* is like a nursery rhyme) and lead naturally to John Williams's own *Aeolian suite,* a colourful pastiche, mixing original and borrowed ideas to good effect. With its simple orchestration it sounds rather like film music. Phillip Houghton's four evocations called *Stélé* (which translates as 'headstone') have Grecian influences and are slightly more plangent. It cannot be said that the orchestra adds much to the famous Satie *Gymnopédie,* pleasing as it is, and the two *Gnossiennes* which close the programme are played ruminatively in solo arrangements. The recording is remarkably real and present.

Wilson, Christopher (lute)

'*La Magdalena*' (*Lute music in Renaissance France*): BLONDEAU (publ. ATTAIGNANT): *La brosse (Recoupe et Tourdion); La Magdalena (Recoupe et Tourdion).* ANON. (publ. ATTAIGNANT): *Bransle de Poictou; Tant que vivray; Pavane; Gaillarde; Prelude; Une bergerotte.* DE PARIGI: *2 Recercars.* BERLIN: *Fantaisie No. 3; Trio No. 2.* PALADIN: *Anchor che col partir; Fantaisie.* MORLAYE: *Bransle d'Ecosse No. 1; Bransle gay; Fantaisie; Sans liberté; Pavane; Gaillarde piemontoise.* DE RIPPE: *Pleurés mes yeux; 2 Fantaisies; Galliarde.* LE ROY: *Passemeze; La souris.* BAKFARK: *Si grand è la pietà.*

*** Virgin VC5 45140-2.

An agreeable, unassertive, hour-long programme for the late evening, although perhaps a few more lively dances would have made the recital even more attractive. Certain items stand out, like the anonymous portrayal of *Une bergerotte,* the title-piece and the two works of Jean Paul Paladin (although *Anchor che col partir* is a transcription of a famous madrigal of the period – by Cipriano da Rore). Valentin Bakfark's *Si grand è la pietà* brings yet another madrigal arrangement (by Jacques Arcadelt). Most of this music has a character of gentle melancholy, so the exceptions, like the *Bransle gay* and the *Gaillarde piemontoise* (both by Morlaye), make a welcome diversion. The two pieces by Adrian Le Roy are also rather more extrovert, but the pervading atmosphere is doleful. Christopher Wilson plays with much sensitivity and he is beautifully recorded, provided one accepts the rather misty, ecclesiastical acoustic.

Yates, Sophie (virginals)

English virginals music: BYRD: *Praeludium - Fantasia; The barley breake; The Tennthe pavan (Sir William Petre); Galliard to the Tennthe pavan; The woods so wild; Hugh Aston's ground; The Bells.* DOWLAND: *Lachrymae pavan* (arr. BYRD). HARDING: *Galliard* (arr. BYRD). GIBBONS: *Fantasia.* ANON.: *My Lady Careys dompe.* TOMKINS: *Barafostus's dreame.* ASTON: *Hornepype.* BULL: *In nomine.*

** Chan. 0574.

Sophie Yates is a thoughtful and accomplished player and she uses a modern copy by Peter Bavington of an Italian instrument made at the very beginning of the seventeenth century. Her programme is well thought out and, even though it is dominated by the music of Byrd, it is musically well balanced. The snag is the resonant recording, which gives a larger-than-life impression of the instrument which even the lowering of the volume control does not entirely diminish.

Yepes, Narciso (guitar)

'The art of the guitar': SANZ: Suite española: Españoletas; Canarios. PISADOR: Pavana muy llana para tañer. MUDARRA: Fantasia que contrahaza la harpa en la manera de Ludovico. NARVAEZ: La canción del emperador: Mille regretz (Josquin Desprez). Diferencias sobre Guádame las vacas. ANON.: Irish march (11th century); Saltarello (both arr. YEPES). DOWLAND: The King of Denmark his galliard. SOR: Studies in A; in C, Op. 6/6 & 8; in B flat; in G, Op. 29/1 & 11. TARREGA: Lágrima; Recuerdos de la Alhambra; Adelita. GRANADOS: Danza española No. 5. TURINA: Fandanguillo, Op. 36. ALBENIZ: Suite española: Asturias.

*** DG CD PlusScore ADD/DDD 459 613-2.

Many of these recordings have appeared before and some already exist on bargain labels. But this recital has been carefully planned, expertly remastered, and affords great naturalness and presence. Moreover the special logo indicates that the CD can also be played via a CD-ROM drive on a PC, enabling the listener to follow the musical scores simultaneously on the screen while listening to the performances. The programme has been selected in an approximately historical sequence to show the great guitarist at his finest, whether in the delightful Sanz Canarios, the noble Pavana of Pisador, the two melancholy miniatures of Tárrega, which are perhaps less familiar than the famous Recuerdos. The Diferencias of Narváez (written for the vihuela) is one of the earliest Spanish examples of variation form; Mudarra's Fantasia is more complex; but later the Dowland Galliard (where Yepes simulates a bolder keyboard image) admirably demonstrates Elizabethan divisions. The kernel of the recital is provided by the four diverse Sor Studies, which are marvellously played, but then so is Turina's Fandanguillo, which follows the Granados Spanish dance, the latter more robust than Julian Bream's famous recording, offering a refreshingly different interpretation.

'Malagueña' (Spanish Guitar Music): ALBENIZ: Malagueña, Op. 165/3; Suite española: Asturias (Leyenda). TARREGA: Recuerdos de la Alhambra; Marieta (Mazurka); Capricho árabe. RODRIGO: En los trigales. RUIZ-PIPO: Cancion y danza No. 1. SOR: Introduction & Variations on a Theme of Mozart, Op. 9. SANZ: Suite española: Españoletas; Gallarda y villano; Danza y villano; Danza de las hachas; Rujero y paradetas; Zarabanda al ayre español;

Passacalle; Folias; La miñona de Cataluña; Canarios. MUDARRA: Fantasia que contrahaza la harpa en la manera de Ludovico. SOLER: Sonata in E. GRANADOS: Danza española No. 4 (Villanesca). FALLA: El sombrero de tres picos: Danza del mólinero (Farruca). ANON.: Romance (from the film: Forbidden Games).

⊕ (BB) *** DG Eloquence (ADD) 469 649-2.

With repertoire recorded between 1968 and 1977, this Eloquence reissue is based on a long-standing DG recital showing this great Spanish guitarist at his very peak, which now has been expanded to a playing time of 76 minutes. Yepes was not only an outstanding exponent of this repertoire but also had that rare gift of constantly creating electricity in the recording studio, no more thrillingly than in Falla's Miller's Dance from the Three-Cornered Hat, in which he creates an orchestral range of colour. But all this music springs vividly to life and popular favourites like Tárrega's Recuerdos de la Alhambra (presented with unostentatious bravura) and the engagingly ingenuous Mozart Variations of Sor are wonderfully fresh. The earlier music is also very appealing, the Sanz Suite – ten through-composed miniatures of which Canarios is probably the best-known – is delightful. The final item, an anonymous Romance used in the film, Forbidden Games, makes a real lollipop encore. Throughout, Yepes's assured, vibrant and always stylish advocacy brings consistent pleasure and stimulation: there are few solo guitar records to match this, particularly as the Eloquence transfers are so present and realistic and the cost so reasonable.

Zabaleta, Nicanor (harp)

'Arpa española': ALBENIZ: Malagueña, Op. 165/3; Suite española: Granada (Serenata); Zaragoza (Capricho); Asturias (Leyenda). Mallorca, Op. 202; Tango español. FALLA: Serenata andaluza. TURINA: Ciclo pianistico No. 1: Tocata y fuga. GOMBAU: Apunte bético. GRANADOS: Danza española No. 5. HALFFTER: Sonatina (ballet): Danza de la pastora. LOPEZ-CHAVARRI: El viejo castillo moro.

⊕ (M) *** DG (IMS) (ADD) 435 847-2.

A good deal of the music here belongs to the guitar (or piano) rather than the harp, but Nicanor Zabaleta, with his superb artistry and sense of atmosphere, makes it all his own. Throughout this delightful programme, Zabaleta gives each piece strong individuality of character. In the Granados Spanish dance No. 5 he matches the magnetism of Julian Bream's famous recording, and Manuel de Falla's Serenata andaluza is hardly less captivating. DG's sound balance is near perfection, as is the choice of acoustic, and the magic distilled by Zabaleta's concentration, often at the gentlest levels of dynamic, is unforgettable.

VOCAL RECITALS AND CHORAL COLLECTIONS

The Art of Singing

'*The Art of Singing*': Video: '*Golden voices of the century*' (Björling, Callas, Caruso, Chaliapin, Christoff, Corelli, De los Angeles, De Luca, Di Stefano, Flagstad, Gigli, Martinelli, Melchior, Olivero, Pinza, Ponselle, Leontyne Price, Schipa, Stevens, Supervia, Sutherland, Tauber, Tebaldi, Tetrazzini, Tibbett, Vickers, Wunderlich): Excerpts: PUCCINI: *La Bohème*. SAINT-SAENS: *Samson et Dalila*. VERDI: *Rigoletto*. LEONCAVALLO: *I Pagliacci* (all silent film excerpts with Caruso). DONIZETTI: *Lucia di Lammermoor*: sextet with Caruso, mimed. DE CURTIS: song *Torna a Surriento* (Giovanni Martinelli). HANDEL: *Xerxes: Ombra mai fù* (Beniamino Gigli). FLOTOW: *Martha: M'appari* (Tito Schipa). ROSSINI: *Il barbiere di Siviglia: Largo al factotum* (Giuseppe de Luca). FLOTOW: *Martha: M'appari* (Luisa Tetrazzini). PUCCINI: *La Bohème: Quando me'n vo* (Conchita Supervia). BIZET: *Carmen: Chanson Bohème; Habanera* (Rosa Ponselle). SCHUBERT: *Ständchen* (Richard Tauber). RIMSKY-KORSAKOV: *The Maid of Pskov*. IBERT: *Chanson du duc* (both with Fyodor Chaliapin). WAGNER: *Die Walküre: Hojotoho!* (Kirsten Flagstad). BIZET: *Carmen: Chanson du toréador* (Lawrence Tibbett). SAINT-SAENS: *Samson et Dalila: Mon coeur s'ouvre* (Risë Stevens). WAGNER: *Die Walküre: Winterstürme* (Lauritz Melchior). MUSSORGSKY: *Boris Godunov: Coronation scene* (Ezio Pinza). PUCCINI: *La Bohème: Che gelida manina; Mi chiamano Mimì; O soave fanciulla* (Jussi Björling, Renata Tebaldi). FALLA: *La vida breve: Vivan los que rien* (Victoria de los Angeles). MEYERBEER: *Les Huguenots: O beau pays* (Joan Sutherland). VERDI: *Aida: O patria mia* (Leontyne Price). MUSSORGSKY: *Boris Godunov: Death scene* (Boris Christoff). PUCCINI: *Tosca: Vissi d'arte*; (i) Act III duet (Magda Olivero, (i) with Alvinio Misciano). MOZART: *Die Zauberflöte: Dies Bildnis ist bezaubernd schön* (Fritz Wunderlich). BEETHOVEN: *Fidelio: In des Lebens* (Jon Vickers). PUCCINI: *Turandot: Non Piangere, Liù* (Franco Corelli). LEONCAVALLO: *I Pagliacci: Vesti la giubba* (Giuseppe di Stefano). (i) VERDI: *La Traviata: Parigi, o cara*. (ii) PUCCINI: *Tosca: Duet and Vissi d'arte* (both Maria Callas, with (i) Alfredo Kraus, (ii) Tito Gobbi). (Commentary by Magda Olivero, Thomas Hampson, Schuyler Chapin, Kirk Browning, Nicola Rescigno.)

*** Teldec VHS 0630 15893-3.

This is Teldec's vocal equivalent of 'The Art of Conducting'. While almost all the film excerpts included here are fascinating, this comparable vocal survey proves less uniformly compulsive than its orchestral equivalent. Moreover, while almost all the comments on the earlier video concerning the conductors themselves and their various idiosyncrasies proved very perceptive, the commentaries here, especially the contributions by the singers themselves, seem much less illuminating. Thomas Hampson's definition of the meaning of *legato*, a term which almost explains itself, is perversely over-complicated. But now to the singing.

Two performances stand out above the rest in magnetism. A live telecast, with good sound, from the Met. in 1956 brought Renata Tebaldi and Jussi Björling together in virtually the whole of the great Act I love scene in *La Bohème*, from *Che gelida manina* to their final exit, with their glorious voices ending the Act from offstage. They are dressed in a curiously formal way – one might even say overdressed – and Tebaldi is not shown to be the greatest actress in the world, but their voices match superbly. The other scene is even more electrifying – a live telecast made in December of the same year for which obviously no expense was spared, and the set and production were fully worthy. Boris Christoff's Death scene from *Boris Godunov* is deeply moving; Nicola Moscona is a hardly less resonant Pimen, and an unnamed boy is very touching as Boris's young son. Hardly less impressive is the great Kirsten Flagstad (at her vocal peak), introduced by Bob Hope, who manages to keep a straight face, in a Paramount movie, *The Big Broadcast of 1938*. She sings *Hojotoho!* thrillingly from *Die Walküre*, waving her spear with remarkable conviction.

Risë Stevens, Lauritz Melchior, Victoria de los Angeles in Falla and Joan Sutherland in Meyerbeer coloratura add to the vocal pleasures, and Leontyne Price's gloriously full-voiced *O patria mia* from *Aida* is engulfing. What a stage presence she has! Another highlight is Magda Olivero's charismatically seductive *Vissi d'arte* from *Tosca*. The great Callas ends the programme by singing the same aria (in 1964) but, although her presence is commanding, the actual singing, with its wobbling vibrato, is no match for Olivero.

The early recordings are interesting, but the sound is such that they are usually less than overwhelming vocally, with Gigli and Tito Schipa possible exceptions. A hilarious interlude is provided by a 1908 silent film with professional actors hopelessly overacting and miming the words of the Sextet (*Chi mi frena*) from *Lucia di Lammermoor*, designed to accompany the famous 1911 RCA recording by Caruso, Daddi, Journet, Scotti, Sembrich and Severina. Another smile comes when Rosa Ponselle is shown singing *Carmen* for an MGM screen test in 1936 and her fan gets in the way of the camera! All in all, this is a considerable entertainment, but one hoped, unrealistically perhaps, for more items like *Boris* and *Bohème*.

Historical Vocal Recitals

'The EMI Record of Singing'

Volume 3 (1926–39): Part 1: The German school: Arias and excerpts from WAGNER: *Tannhäuser* (Lauritz Melchior; Göta Ljungberg with Walter Widdop); *Die Walküre* (Max Lorenz; Kirsten Flagstad); *Lohengrin* (Franz Völker); *Die Meistersinger* (Rudolf Bockelmann; Delia Reinhardt); *Das Rheingold* (Hans Hermann Nissen); *Der fliegende Holländer* (Elizabeth Ohms); *Siegfried* (Nanny Larsen-Todsen). WILLIE: *Königsballade* (Helge Rosvaenge). D'ALBERT: *Tiefland* (Torsten Ralf). JOHANN STRAUSS JR: *Die Fledermaus* (Richard Tauber with Vera Schwarz). KIENZL: *Der Evangeligmann* (Marcel Wittrisch with Children's chorus). RICHARD STRAUSS: *Der Rosenkavalier* (Herbert Ernst Groh; Lotte Lehmann); *Arabella* (Alfred Jerger with Viorica Ursuleac; Tiana Lemnitz); *Daphne* (Margarete Teschemacher); *Die ägyptische Helena* (Rose Pauly). KORNGOLD: *Die tote Stadt* (Joseph Schmidt; Karl Hammes). MOZART: *Die Entführung aus dem Serail* (Julius Patzak). HUMPERDINCK: *Hänsel und Gretel* (Gerard Hüsch). KREUTZER: *Das Nachtlager in Granada* (Willi Domgraf-Fassbaender). MENDELSSOHN: *Elijah* (Friedrich Schorr); *Saint Paul* (Jo Vincent). LORTZING: *Zar und Zimmermann* (Heinrich Schlusnus; Leo Schützendorf); *Der Wildschütz* (Alexander Kipnis). NICOLAI: *Die lustigen Weiber von Windsor* (Wilhelm Strienz). VERDI: *Macbeth* (Ivar Andresen); *Un ballo in maschera* (Adele Kern). MEYERBEER: *Le Prophète* (Sigrid Onegin); *L'Africaine* (Elisabeth Rethberg). PONCHIELLI: *La Gioconda* (Karin Branzell). SAINT-SAENS: *Samson et Dalila* (Kerstin Thorborg). MOZART: *La clemenza di Tito* (Rosette Anday). FLOTOW: *Alesandro Stradella* (Fritz Jold). RIMSKY-KORSAKOV: *The Tsar's bride* (Miliza Korjus; Meta Seinemeyer). ADAM: *Le Postillon de Longumeau* (Felicie Hüni Mihacsek). PUCCINI: *Turandot* (Luise Helletsgruber); *La Bohème* (Maria Cebotari). GOLDMARK: *Die Königen von Saba* (Maria Nemeth). Lieder: BEETHOVEN: *Der Wachtelschlag* (Karl Erb). SCHUMANN: *Liederkreis: Mondnacht* (Leo Slezak); *Die Lotusblume* (Ursula van Diemen). WOLF: *Vers hwiegene Liebe* (Heinrich Schlusnus). SCHUBERT: *Die Stadt* (Herbert Jannsen); *Aufenthal* (Maria Olczewska); *Die Allnacht* (Marta Fuchs). BRAHMS: *Nicht mehr zu dir zu gehen* (Margarete Klose); *Feldeinsamkeit* (Elena Gerhardt); *Volkslieder: Schwesterlein* (Lulu Mysz-Gmeiner).

SCHOECK: *Mit einem gemalten Bande* (Ria Ginster); *Nachtlied* (Margherita Perras). MARX: *Marienlied* (Elisabeth Schumann). ROSSINI: *Soirrées musicales; L'invito.* (Lotte Schöne). OBOUSSIER: *Weine du nicht* (Erna Berger). LISZT: *Es muss ein Wunderbares sein* (Emmy Bettendorf). REGER: *Waldeinsamkeit; Zum Schlafen* (Maria Müller). WAGNER: *Wesendonck Lieder: Schmerzen* (Frida Leider).

Part 2: The Italian school: Arias and excerpts from: PAISIELLO: *I zingari infiera* (Conchita Supervia). BIZET: *Carmen* (Giannina Pederzini). VERDI: *Requiem* (Irene Minghini-Catteneo; Ezio Pinza); *I Lombardi* (Giannina Aranji-Lombardi); *La forza del destino* (Dusolina Giannini); *Ernani* (Iva Pacetti). *Otello* (Hina Spani; Renato Zanelli); *Rigoletto* (Lina Pagliughi); *Falstaff* (Mariano Stabile). SAINT-SAENS: *Samson et Dalila* (Ebe Stignani). DONIZETTI: *La Favorita* (Florica Cristoforeanu); *Don Pasquale* (Afro Poli with Ernesto Badini). BOITO: *Mefistofele* (Pia Tassinari; Nazzareno de Angelis). CATALANI: *Loreley* (Bianca Scacciati). GIORDANO: *Siberia* (Maria Caniglia); *Andrea Chénier* (Lina Bruna Rasa; Cesare Formichi; Benvenuto Franci; Antonio Cortis); *Il Re* (Mercedes Capsir). PUCCINI: *La fanciulla del West* (Gina Cigna); *Madama Butterfly* (Margaret Sheridan); *Turandot* (Maria Zamboni; Magda Oliviero; Alessandro Ziliani); *Manon Lescaut* (Licia Albanese; Francesco Merli; Giacomo Lauri-Volpi); *La Bohème* (Tancredi Pasero); *Tosca* (Giovanni Inghilleri). PIETRI: *Maristella* (Rosetta Pampanini). MASCAGNI: *Iris* (Maria Farneti); *Lodeletta* (Malfada Favero; Galliano Masini); *Guglielmo Ratcliffe* (Carlo Galeffi). GOMES: *Il Guarany* (Bidù Sayão). CILEA: *Adriana Lecouvreur* (Adelaide Saraceni; Aurelio Pertile). RICCI: *Crispino e la comare* (Salvatore Baccaloni). PONCHIELLI: *Il figliuol prodigo* (Mario Basiola). LEONCAVALLO: *Zazà* (Apollo Granforte). BELLINI: *La sonnnambula* (Dino Borgioli with Maria Gentile, Ida Mannarini, Gina Pedroni; also Enzo de Muro Lomanto). MASSENET: *Werther* (Tito Schipa). GUERRERO: *Los Gavilanes* (Tino Folgar). VITTADINI: *Anima allegra* (Luigi Fort). OFFENBACH: *La Belle Hélène* (Jussi Bjoerling). Songs: TRAD: *Have you seen but a whyte lilie grow?* (Conchita Supervia); BUZZI-PECCIA: *Colombetta* (Claudia Muzio). GRANADOS: *Tonadillas: El majo discreto; El majo timido* (Conchita Badia). JAMES: *Maori lullaby* (Toti da Monte). TIRINDELLI: *Mistica* (Carlo Tagliabue). TOSTI: *Ideale* (Riccardo Stracciari); *Aprile* (Beniamino Gigli). : *Do not go, my love* (Dino Borgioli). HAGEMAN LONGAS: *En effeuillant la marguerite* (Tito Schipa).

Part 3: The French school: Arias from: RAMEAU: *Hippolyte et Aricie* (Leila Ben Sedira). OFFENBACH: *Les Brigands* (Emma Luart); *Contes d'Hoffmann* (André Pernet); *La Grande Duchesse de Gérolstein* (Yvonne Printemps); *Le Boulangère a des écus* (Reynaldo Hahn). DELIBES: *Lakmé* (Germaine Feraldy). ROSSINI: *Guillaume Tell* (Eidé Norena). MASSENET: *Marie-Magdeleine* (Germaine Martinelli); *Hérodiade* (René Maison). GOUNOD: *Sapho* (Suzanne Cesbron-Viseur; Germain Cernay); *Polyucte* (José Luccioni); *Mireille* (Gaston Micheletti). DUKAS: *Ariane et Barbe-Bleu* (Suzanne Balguerie). WAGNER: *Lohengrin* (Germaine Lubin). GLUCK: *Orphée* (Alice Raveau). REYER: *Sigurd* (Georges Thill; César Vezzani). HALEVY: *La Juive* (René Verdière). LAPARRA: *L'illustre Fregona* (Miguel Villabella). BAZIN: *Maître Pathelin* (André d'Arkor). VERDI: *Luisa Miller* (Giusppe Lugo). LALO: *Le Roi d'Ys* (Joseph Rogatchewsky). BERLIOZ: *L'enfance du Christ* (Jean Planel); *La Damnation de Faust* (Charles Panzéra). MAGNARD: *Guercoeur* (Arthur Endrèze). PALADILHE: *Patrie!* (Robert Couzinou). BERTHOMIEU: *Robert Macaire* (André Balbon). FLOTOW: *L'Ombre* (Lucien Fugère). Songs: SAINT-SAENS: *Le rossignol et la rose* (Lily Pons). FAURE: *Les berceux* (Ninon Vallin); *Aurore* (Pierre Bernac); *Lydia* (Roger Bourdin). TORELLI: *Tu lo sai* (Povla Frijsh). DEBUSSY: *Chansons de Bilitis: Le chevelure* (Jane Bathori). RAVEL: *Chants hébraïques: Kaddisch* (Madeleine Grey); *Don Quichotte à Dulcinée: Chanson épique* (Martial Singher). DE BREVILLE: *Une jeune fille parle* (Claire Croiza). HAHN: *D'un prison* (Charles Panzéra). MARTINI: *Plaisir d'amore* (Jean-Emil Vanni-Marcoux).

Part 4: The Anglo-American school: Arias and excerpts from: VERDI: *Falstaff* (Lawrence Tibett). THOMAS: *Hamlet* (John Charles Thomas; John Brownlee). ROSSINI: *Il barbiere di Siviglia* (Dennis Noble); *Stabat Mater* (Florence Austral). Songs: COWAN: *Onaway, awake, beloved* (Harold Williams). HANDEL: *Messiah* (Peter Dawson). OFFENBACH: *Contes d'Hoffmann* (Charles Kullman). BIZET: *La jolie fille de Perth* (Heddle Nash); *Carmen* (Marguerite D'Alvarez). Goring THOMAS: *Esmeralda* (Thomas Burke). PUCCINI: *Tosca* (Richard Crooks); *La Bohème* (Grace Moore; Ina Souez); *Madama Butterfly* (Joan Cross); *Turandot* (Eva Turner). HANDEL: *Acis and Galatea* (Walter Widdop). PURCELL: *The Tempest* (Norman Allin). MENDELSSOHN: *St Paul* (Muriel Brunskill). HANDEL: *Theodora* (Isobel Baillie). DELIUS: *Irmelin* (Dora Labbette). SPONTINI: *La Vestale* (Rosa Ponselle). REYER: *Sigurd* (Marjorie Lawrence). Songs: DUNN: *The bitterness of love* (John McCormack). MONTEVERDI: *Maladetto sia l'aspetto* (Roland Hayes). MARTINI: *Minuet* (Mme Charles Cahier). SULLIVAN: *The lost chord* (Dame Clara Butt). SCHUBERT: *Der Tod und das Mädchen* (Marian Anderson). FAURE: *Le secret* (Susan Metcalfe-Casals). CANTELOUBE: *Baïlero* (Gladys Swarthout). PALADILHE: *Psyché* (Maggie Teyte). HAYDN: *My mother bids me bind my hair* (Florence Easton).

Part 5: The East European/Slavic school: Arias and excerpts from: DVORAK: *Rusalka* (Jarmila Novotná; Ada Nordenova). RIMSKY-KORSAKOV: *The Tsar's bride* (Nathalie Vechor). GOMES: *Salvator Rosa* (Mark Reisen). KODALY: *Háry János* (Imry Palló). Songs: GRETCHANINOV: *The wounded birch; Snowflakes* (Maria Kurenko with Composer, piano); *Lullaby* (Oda Slobodskaya). RIMSKY-KORSAKOV: *The rose and the nightingale* (Xenia Belmas). KARLOWICZ: *I remember golden days* (Ada Sari). DVORAK: *Leave me alone* (Maria Krasová). arr. BARTOK: *2 Hungarian folk songs* (Maria Basildes). DARGOMIJSKY: *Bolero* (Feodor Chaliapin). CUI: *Hunger* (Vladimir Rosing). KASHEVAROV: *Tranquility* (Sergei Lemeshev).

✿ (M) (***) Testament mono SBT 0132 (10).

The importance of EMI's monumental series, 'The Record of Singing', cannot be exaggerated, and it is sad that although the fourth volume was issued on CD, covering the period from the start of electrical recording up to the end of the 78 era, the others have been allowed to languish. That fact makes it all the more creditable that Stewart Brown of Testament has boldly issued this beautifully produced CD reissue of the third volume, the work of Keith Hardwick, both in the selection of items, often unexpected but always keenly perceptive, and in the actual transfers, which set standards in clarity and accuracy too rarely matched by others. Inevitably in a very compact format, the background material is not quite so lavish as in the original LP issue, with separate booklets included covering details of recording and biographies of the 200 or so singers covered. Even so, essential details are all here, and the methodical covering of so many singers from so many different schools, divided mainly by nationality, could not be more illuminating. In a note written especially for this CD reissue Hardwick confesses that though initially he had misgivings over following up the earlier two volumes of golden age material with recordings from a period generally regarded as one of decline, he has more and more come to revise that opinion. Certainly, thanks to his brilliant choice of items, one has much to admire in every school represented, with reservations not so much over quality of singing as of performance style, where inevitably modern taste differs greatly, notably on such composers as Mozart. A magnificent achievement. One hopes that Testament may have the courage to bring out CD versions of the first two volumes of this indispensable series.

Other Historical Reissues

Ancona, Mario (baritone)

'*The Complete Victor recordings (1907–08)*': Arias and duets from: LEONCAVALLO: *I Pagliacci.* GOUNOD: *Faust.* VERDI: *La traviata; Ernani; Un ballo in maschera; Era la notte; Rigoletto* (with Bessie Abbot); *Il trovatore.* BELLINI: *I Puritani* (with Journet). BIZET: *I pescatore di perle* (with Caruso). DONIZETTI: *La Favorita.* MEYERBEER: *Dinorah.* GIORDANO: *Andrea Chenier.* Songs by: TOSTI: *Mattinata; Invano. Rotoli: Mia sposa sarà la mia bandiera.* TCHAIKOVSKY: *Sérénade de Don Juan.*

(***) Romophone mono 82013-2.

The Romophone series is favoured by many vocal collectors, for the transfers are straightforwardly done, seeking as clear as possible a focus for the voice, aiming to match closely the original recording quality, and in so doing accepting a fairly high degree of background noise. But as always with transfer technology, it is the ear of the transfer engineer that is paramount and in many cases make the vocal impression here is impressively vivid.

Born in 1860 Mario Ancona came to prominence as the first Silvio in the premiere of *I Pagliacci* in 1892, and had a distinguished career for another twenty-five years. His was a firm clear baritone, marked by flawless control and clean attack. He was more concerned with fine singing than strong characterization, so that Iago's *Era la notte* is hardly sinister. A fascinating supplement offers three Pathé recordings of 1906 including stirring accounts of Rigoletto's solos, but which fail to convey any anger. Good transfers by Ward Marston with the voice clearly caught, and with surface noise that one quickly forgets.

Battistini, Mattia (baritone)

'*The Complete recordings (1902–11)*': Arias, duets and scenes from: MOZART: *Don Giovanni* (with Emilia Corsi). WAGNER: *Tannhäuser.* TCHAIKOVSKY: *Eugene Onegin.* RUBINSTEIN: *The Demon.* ROSSINI: *Il barbiere di Siviglia.* GOUNOD: *Faust.* DONIZETTI: *La favorita; Don Sebastiani; Maria di Rohan.* COCCHI: *Per la patria.* VERDI: *Ernani* (with Emilia Corsi, Aristodemo Sillich, Luigi Colazza); *Un ballo in maschera.* FLOTOW: *Martha.* BERLIOZ: *La damnation de Faust.* HEROLD: *Zampa.* LEONCAVALLO: *I Pagliacci.* MASSENET: *Werther; Thaïs* (with Ebe Boccolini, Attilia Janni). BELLINI: *I puritani.* THOMAS: *Hamlet.* PUCCINI: *Tosca.* Songs

by: ALVAREZ: *Lamantilla.* DENZA: *Occhi di fata.* TOSTI: *Ancora; Amour, amour.* GOUNOD: *Le soir.*

(***) Romophone mono 82008-2 (2).

As Michael Scott's note points out in this magnificent collection of Battistini's early recordings, he is the oldest great singer (he was born in 1856) to have made records whilst still at the peak of his powers. Not that the first disc represents him at all fairly, characterful as it is, for it consists of a double rendering of Don Giovanni's 'champagne' aria astonishingly fast, so that even he with his dark, agile voice has to slide sketchily over many of the notes. The magnetism and projection make one share his obvious joy in the new medium, a fun occasion, and almost all the rest are a delight, for this was one of the finest baritone voices ever put on disc. Those sessions took place in Warsaw in 1902, then under the control of Imperial Russia, and that may account for the Tchaikovsky and Rubinstein items. Here was a singer who did not limit himself to the central nineteenth-century Italian repertory, for it was not until his next set of sessions in 1906 that he began to record Verdi, and even then not obvious arias, for six of them are from *Ernani* and two from *Ballo*, with *Eri tu* gloriously resonant and finely shaded, if again hardly conveying anger. The rare aria from Herold's *Zampa* is included, and it is good too to have among these 1902 recordings so poised an account of Wolfram's *O star of eve* from *Tannhäuser*, sung in Italian. Ward Marston's transfers give a vivid idea of the commanding voice, though he has not been able to eliminate the heavy surface noise on some of the rarer items.

Bori, Lucrezia (soprano)

'*The Victor Recordings (1914–25)*': Arias, duets and scenes from: LEONCAVALLO: *I Pagliacci.* VERDI: *La traviata* (with John McCormack); *Rigoletto* (with John McCormack, Josephine Jacoby and Richard Werrenrath). PUCCINI: *La bohème* (with John McCormack and with Tito Schipa). VALVERDE: *Nina Pancha.* MASCAGNI: *Iris; L'amico Fritz* (with Miguel Fleta). OFFENBACH: *Les contes d'Hoffmann.* CHAPI: *La revoltosa; El puñao de rosas* (both with Andrea Perello de Segurolla). MOZART: *Le nozze di Figaro; Don Giovanni; Così fan tutte.* WOLF-FERRARI: *Il segreto di Susanna.* DONIZETTI: *Don Pasquale.* RIMSKY-KORSAKOV: *The Snow Maiden.* GOUNOD: *Roméo et Juliette* (with Beniamino Gigli). MASSENET: *Manon.* DELIBES: *Lakmé.* BIZET: *Carmen* (with Miguel Fleta). VARNEY: *L'amour*

Mouillée. Songs by: ROSSINI: *La danza.* PAGANS: *Malagueña.* YRADIER: *La paloma.* MARSHALL: *I hear you calling me.* VALVERDE: *Clavelitos.* SIBELLA: *Villanella.* MOORE: *When love is kind.* ARDITI: *Il bacio.* GRANADOS: *El majo discreto.* PESTALOZZI: *Ciribiribin.* DELFINO: *Milonguita.* NOVELLO: *The Little Damozel.*

(***) Romophone mono 81016.

'*The Victor Recordings (1925–37)*': Arias and duets from: CHARPENTIER: *Louise.* PUCCINI: *La bohème; Madama Butterfly; La rondine.* OFFENBACH: *Les contes d'Hoffmann.* VARNEY: *Amour mouilée.* VERDI: *La traviata.* THOMAS: *Mignon.* MOZART: *Don Giovanni; Le nozze di Figaro.* MASSENET: *Manon.* DE FALLA: *La vida breve.* WOLF-FERRARI: *Il segreto di Susanna.* LITERES (arr. NIN): *Acis y Galatea.* LASERNA: *Amantes chasqueaos.* OBRADORS: *Don Quixote de la Mancha.* Songs by: GLAZUNOV: *La primavera d'or.* STRAUSS: *Tales from the Vienna Woods* (three versions). VALVERDE: *Cruz de majo; Clavelitos.* JOVES: *Patoteres sentimental.* RUMBOLD: *Simonetta.* SCHUMANN: *Into the woods* (with John McCormack). GORING-THOMAS: *Night hymn at sea* (two versions with McCormack). ARDITI: *Il bacio* (two versions). PESTALOZZA: *Ciribiribin.* PAGANS: *Malagueña.* GOETZ-PADILLA: *La violetera.* RIEMANN (arr.): *Seguidilla.* DE FALLA: *Jota; Seguidilla murciana.* NIN: *Malagueña; Jota tortosina; Copias de curro dulce; Canto andaluz.*

(***) Romophone mono 81017-2 (2).

Lucrezia Bori, a favourite at the Met in New York from her début in 1912 through to the 1930s, was a sparkling characterful singer, whose agility in coloratura went with clear, fresh projection, belying the size of voice. That quality is beautifully caught here in excellent Ward Marston transfers which characteristically prefer to keep the voice vivid rather than eliminating surface hiss. The first of the two double-disc boxes covers all Bori's pre-electric recordings – including some fine duets with McCormack, as well as her first four electric recordings of 1925. The second double-disc box containing the rest, demonstrates her later development, when with the voice as pure and sweet as ever she brought an extra emotional intensity into such numbers as 'Mimi's farewell', taken slower in 1926 than in 1914, singing with extra poise in Louise's *Depuis le jour*. Her gift of characterization comes out vividly in the contrast of the two solos from Thomas's Mignon, the one tender, the other sparkling. As usual with Romophone issues, it is fascinating to compare different versions of various numbers, many unpublished.

Caruso, Enrico (tenor)

'*The Legendary Caruso*': Opera arias and songs: Arias from: MASCAGNI: *Cavalleria Rusticana; Iris.* PONCHIELLI: *La Gioconda.* LEONCAVALLO: *I Pagliacci*; and song: *Mattinata.* BOITO: *Mefistofele.* PUCCINI: *Tosca.* GIORDANO: *Fedora.* CILEA:

Adriana Lecouvreur. VERDI: *Rigoletto; Aida.* BIZET: *Les pêcheurs de perles.* MASSENET: *Manon.* DONIZETTI: *L'Elisir d'amore.* MEYERBEER: *Les Huguenots.* Songs: TOSTI: *La mia canzone.* DENZA: *Non t'amo più*; and by ZARDO & TRIMARCHI.

(M) (***) EMI mono CDM5 67006-2.

The EMI collection was originally on the Références label and has now been again remastered. It brings together Caruso's earliest recordings, made in 1902, 1903 and 1904 in Milan with at times misty piano accompaniment. The very first pieces were done impromptu in Caruso's hotel, and the roughness of presentation reflects that; but the voice is glorious in its youth, amazingly well caught for that period and now remarkably fresh and free from horn resonances, even if the background noise, not always regular, is still obvious. But it was the vocal quality of these very recordings which, more than anything else, first convinced a wide public that the gramophone was more than a toy.

Christoff, Boris (bass)

'*The early recordings (1949–52)*': excerpts from: MUSSORGSKY: *Boris Godunov; Khovanshchina.* BORODIN: *Prince Igor.* RIMSKY-KORSAKOV: *Sadko; The Legend of the invisible city of Kitezh.* TCHAIKOVSKY: *Eugene Onegin.* MUSSORGSKY: *Songs. Russian folksongs.*

(M) (***) EMI mono CDH7 64252-2.

The magnetic quality of Christoff's singing is never in doubt here, and the compulsion of the singer's artistry as well as the vivid individuality of his bass timbres make this a real portrait, not just a collection of items. These were his first recordings of the *Boris Godunov* excerpts (in which he assumes three different characters), and in musical terms he probably never surpassed them. But his characterization here is just as impressive as the singing itself, full of variety. The EMI transfers are bold and brightly focused, with the most vivid projection.

'*Russian songs*' (with LOP, Tzipine; Paris Conservatoire O, Cluytens; Alexandre Labinsky, Alexandre Tcherepnine, Janine Reiss, Serge Zapolsky, or Nadia Gedda-Nova (piano); Gaston Marchesini, Maud-Martin Tortelier (cello)): GLINKA: *The Midnight review; Cradle song; What, young beauty; Where is our rose?; The Lark; Ah, you darling, lovely girl; Doubt; Grandpa, the girls once told me; How sweet to be with thee; Do not say the heart is sick; Hebrew song; Elegy; I remember the wonderful moment.* BORODIN: *Those folk; Song of the dark forest; From my tears; The Sea princess; The Pretty girl no longer loves me; The Magic garden; Arabian melody; The false note; The fishermaiden; Listen to my song, little friend; The Sleeping princess; Pride; For the shores of thy far native land; The sea; Why art thou so early, dawn?; My songs are poisoned.* CUI: *Songs, Op. 44: Le Hun; Berceuse; Le*

*ciel est transi; Les songeants. Ici-bas; The tomb and
the rose; The Love of a departed one; A Recent
dream; Pardon!; Desire; Conspiracy; Song of Mary;
The Imprisoned knight; Album leaf; The Prophet;
The Statue of Tsarskoïe; In Memory of V. S. Stassov.*
BALAKIREV: *Prologue; Song of Selim; Song: The
Yellow leaf trembles; The Pine tree; Nocturne;
Starless midnight, coldly breathed; The Putting-
right; November the 7th; Dawn; Hebrew melody; The
Wilderness; The Knight; The Dream; Look, my
friend.* RIMSKY-KORSAKOV: *The Pine and the palm;
On the hills of Georgia; The Messenger; Quietly
evening falls; Hebrew song; Zuleika's song; Across the
midnight sky; I waited for thee in the grotto at the
appointed hour; The sea is tossing; The Upas tree;
The Prophet; Quiet is the blue sea; Slowly drag my
days; Withered flower; The rainy day has waned.*
TCHAIKOVSKY: *Don Juan's serenade; The Mild stars
shone for us; Child's song; Cradle song; Night; Do not
ask; As they kept on saying, 'Fool'; To sleep;
Disappointment; the canary; None but the weary
heart; Again, as before, alone; A Legend.*
RACHMANINOV: *Fate; How fair is this spot; When
yesterday we met; All once I gladly owned; Morning;
All things depart; Thy pity I implore; Christ is risen;
Loneliness; O never sing to me again; The dream;
The soldier's wife; The Harvest of sorrow; Oh stay,
my love; The world would see thee smile; Night is
mournful. Folksongs: arr.* SEROV: *The Evil power.*
TRAD.: *Doubinouchka: Song of the Volga; The
Bandore; Down Peterskaya Street; Going down the
Volga; Notchenka* (Folksongs with Russian Ch.,
Potorjinsky).

(B) *** EMI mono/stereo CZS7 67496-2 (5) [CDZE
67496].

This survey covers recordings by the great Bulgarian
bass made between 1954 and 1969. The great majority
come from the 1960s, the earliest are the Russian folksongs recorded in 1954 and the Rachmaninov and
Rimsky-Korsakov (1959). But throughout this remarkably extensive programme, the magnificent voice is in
perfect shape and the recordings are faithfully transferred. Some might think a big voice like Christoff's
would be unsuitable for art songs, but his sensitivity is
never in question and, whenever necessary, he scales it
down, especially (for instance) in several of the Glinka
songs where he has a cello obbligato. This repertoire is
enormously rich in melody and, just as in the opera
house, Christoff's art demonstrates the widest emotional range. Characterization is always strong and his
feeling for words is just as striking here as in his performances of the stage repertory. Most of the songs are
piano accompanied (with a whole range of excellent
accompanists) but occasionally orchestral versions are
used, as in Rimsky-Korsakov's *The Prophet* or Balakirev's *Prologue*, when the orchestra is vividly balanced.
The collection ends with an exhilarating half-dozen
traditional Russian folksongs in which Christoff is
joined by an enthusiastic (if backwardly balanced)
Russian chorus and balalaika ensemble. The result is

irresistible, with melancholy and joy side by side in a
wonderfully Slavonic way. These five well-filled discs
not only demonstrate some of the riches hitherto hidden in EMI's international vaults; they also give us
unique performances of repertoire most of which is
otherwise totally inaccessible. The snag lies in the documentation. As this derives from EMI's French stable,
even the song-titles are given in French. (It was a
major task identifying and translating them!) No texts
are provided, simply a two-page biographical note.

Destinn, Emmy (soprano)

'*The Complete Victor Recordings (1914–21)*': **Arias
and duets from:** THOMAS: *Mignon.* PUCCINI:
Madama Butterfly; Tosca. VERDI: *Aida; Il trovatore.*
PONCHIELLI: *La gioconda.* WAGNER: *Allmächt'ge
Jungfrau.* GOMES: *Il guarany* (with Caruso).
MOZART: *Die Zauberflute.* DVORAK: *Rusalka.*
KOVAROVICH: *Nazarene.* TCHAIKOVSKY: *The Queen
of Spades.* SCHUBERT: *Wiegenlied.* BACH-GOUNOD:
Ave Maria. MOZART: *Wiegenlied.* Czech folk songs
(all with Dinh Gilly). **Songs by:** TOSTI; GOUNOD;
STANGE; LISZT; JINDRICH; DESTINN; HESS;
STEPAN; SMETANA; VERDI; DVORAK.

(M) (***) Romophone mono 81002-2 (2).

Emmy Destinn was the leading dramatic soprano of
her day, the choice of Strauss for the role of Salome
and of Puccini for Minnie, the Girl of the Golden
West. Yet as this wide-ranging collection makes clear,
the poise of her singing, with its perfect control, was
at least as remarkable as the power.

The finest examples here, all of them flawlessly
controlled, include Aida's *O patria mia* and Tosca's
Vissi d'arte. Pamina's *Ach ich fühl's* is similarly poised,
with a superb trill at the end. The thirty-seven items
offer Destinn's complete Victor recordings made
between 1914 and 1921, but the choice of the opening
item is unfortunate, when the aria from Thomas's
Mignon (in German, not French) has Destinn singing
with an ugly yodelling tone, using excessive portamento. As a Czech, she includes a number of Czech
folksongs, but then sings the *Rusalka* aria in German,
not Czech. The transfers capture the voice vividly, but
surface hiss tends to be high.

Eames, Emma (soprano)

'*The Complete Victor Recordings (1905–11)*': **Arias
and duets from:** GOUNOD: *Faust; Roméo et Juliette.*
PUCCINI: *Tosca.* MOZART: *Don Giovanni; Il flauto
magico* (both with Emilio de Gogorza). VERDI:
Otello; Il trovatore (with Gogorza). BIZET: *Carmen.*
MASCAGNI: *Cavalleria rusticana; Le nozze di Figaro*
(with Marcella Sembrich and with Gogorza).
MASSENET: *Chérubin.* DELIBES: *Lakmé.* WAGNER:
Lohengrin. MESSAGER: *Véronique.* BOHM: *Still wie
die nacht* (two versions). BACH-GOUNOD: *Ave
Maria.* FAURE: *Crucifix* (three versions with

Gogorza). **Songs by:** HAHN; TOSTI; MASSENET; SCHUBERT; ARNOLD; EMMETT; HOLLMAN; PARKER; NEVIN; KOECHLIN; HENSCHEL; BEACH; BEMBERG. **(Includes extracts of Calvé commenting on her records.)**

(**(*)) Romophone mono 81001-2 (2).

Most of these recordings of the American soprano Emma Eames date from 1905 and 1906, the earlier ones involving piano accompaniment, even in operatic items. The voice in these transfers is variably caught, sometimes rather faint, behind heavy surface-hiss. Yet the flexibility of the voice, as well as its purity and projection, come out splendidly in such items as the two versions of the *Jewel song* from *Faust* and duplicate versions of the *Ave Maria* from Verdi's *Otello*, as well as a rapt account of Tosca's *Vissi d'arte*. Some of the most attractive excerpts are the duets with the superb baritone, Emilio de Gogorza.

Galli-Curci, Amelita (soprano)

'*The Complete acoustic recordings (1916–20)*': **Arias, duets and scenes from:** VERDI: *Rigoletto* (with Caruso, Flora Perini, Giuseppi De Luca, Marcel Journet and Angelo Bada); *La traviata* (with De Luca). DONIZETTI: *Lucia di Lammermoor* (with Caruso, Minnie Egener, etc.); *Don Pasquale*. GOUNOD: *Roméo et Juliette*. AUBER: *Manon Lescaut*. GRIEG: *Peer Gynt*. DELIBES: *Lakmé*. ROSSINI: *Il barbiere di Siviglia*. MEYERBEER: *Dinorah*. BELLINI: *La sonnambula*. FLOTOW: *Martha*. MOZART: *Le nozze di Figaro*. DAVID: *La perle du Brésil*. BELLINI: *I puritani*. THOMAS: *Mignon*. **Songs by:** ALVAREZ; BISHOP; BUZZI-PECCIA; GIORDANI; SEPPILLI; PROCH; MASSENET; BENEDICT; CHOPIN; SAMUELS; DELIBES; DELL'ACQUA; VALVERDE.

(***) Romophone mono 81003-2 (2).

'*The Complete acoustic recordings (1920–24)*': **Arias and duets from:** BELLINI: *I puritani; La sonnambula* (with Tito Schipa). RIMSKY-KORSAKOV: *Le coq d'or; Sadko*. ADAM: *Le toréador*. BIZET: *Les pêcheurs de perles*. FLOTOW: *Martha*. PUCCINI: *Madama Butterfly*. MEYERBEER: *L'étoile du nord; Le pardon de Ploérmel (Dinorah)*. DONIZETTI: *Lucia di Lammermoor; Don pasquale* (both with Schipa); *Linda di Chamounix*. VERDI: *Rigoletto; La traviata* (both with Schipa); *Il trovatore*. HERBERT: *Orange blossoms; Mlle Modiste*. MASSENET: *Don César de Bazan; Manon*. ROSSINI: *Semiramide*. **Songs by:** COOKE; BISHOP; FOSTER; MOLLOY; DYKES; DANKS; PIERNE; STRICKLAND; RUSSELL; BISHOP; TRADITIONAL: ARR. GUERVOS; DELIBES; CONRAD; PONCE.

(***) Romophone mono 81004-2 (2).

'*The Complete Victor Recordings (1925–28)*': **Arias and duets and scenes from:** MEYERBEER: *Dinorah*. THOMAS: *Amleto (Hamlet)*. VERDI: *Il trovatore; Rigoletto* (with Giuseppi de Luca, Louise Horner

and Beniamino Gigli, and with Tito Schipa); *La traviata* (with de Luca and with Schipa). CHAPI: *Las hijas del Zebedeo*. GRETRY: *Zémire et Azor*. ROSSINI: *Il barbiere di Siviglia*. DONIZETTI: *Lucia di Lammermoor* (with Gigli, Horner, de Luca, Ezio Pinza and Angelo Bada); *Don Pasquale* (With Schipa). THOMAS: *Mignon*. **Songs by:** MONK: arr. SAMUELS; DYKES; STRICKLAND; TOSTI; BENEDICT; ARDITI; PROCH; ALABIEV; YRADIER; GREIG; BISHOP; MOLLOY; BAILY; MOORE; SCARLATTI: arr. Ary VAN LEEUWEN; VALVERDE; PONCE; FOSTER.

(***) Romophone mono 81020-2 (2).

'*The Victor recordings (1930)*': **Arias and duets from:** RIMSKY-KORSAKOV: *Sadko*. GOUNOD: *Philémon et Baucis; Roméo et Juliette*. VERDI: *Rigoletto; Il trovatore*. MEYERBEER: *L'étoile du nord*. DONIZETTI: *Lucia di Lammermoor* (with Tito Schipa). **Songs by:** ROSSINI; DELIBES; FOSTER; BISHOP; MOORE; GREVER and TRADITIONAL. **(Includes excerpt of Galli-Curci radio interview.)**

(***) Romophone mono 81021-2.

Amelita Galli-Curci was among the most vivacious singers of her time. It was not just the beauty and brilliance of her coloratura that captivated audiences, but also the caressing way she had with phrasing conveying a poignancy in cantilena, which made her flights of coloratura brilliance sound all the more carefree and charming by contrast. She was naturally characterful, and projected well, even if it was a relatively small voice. All those qualities come over impressively in this comprehensive collection of her recordings for Victor, seven discs in all. The pre-electric recordings, less well-known than the popular electrical issues from the late 1920s contained on the third of the four issues here, are just as impressive; both in the showpiece arias and in the many trivial items which were at the core of Galli-Curci's popular success, not least those in which she exploited the purity and sweetness of her topmost register in imitation birdsong. The last, single disc of her 1930 recordings contains, as a delightful supplement, a radio interview recorded in 1963, the year she died, confirming in her spoken words everything about her character that her singing suggests.

Garden, Mary (soprano)

'*The Complete Victor recordings (1926–29)*': **Arias and duets from:** CHARPENTIER: *Louise*. ALFANO: *Résurrection*. BIZET: *Carmen*. **Songs by:** CADMAN; HAHN; ROGERS; TATE; HUME; HARRISON; DEBUSSY; SZULE; GRETCHANINOV and TRADITIONAL.

(***) Romophone mono 81008.

The Scottish soprano Mary Garden, Debussy's first and favourite Mélisande, made sadly few recordings, but those here reveal a fresh, bright voice in performances marked by clean, fearless attack. If those are not quite the mysterious qualities one expects of the ideal Mélisande, these items effectively dispatch the idea, sometimes suggested, that the voice was undistinguished, and that she relied for her impact on her acting. Though she was a lyric soprano, it is striking how strong and characterful her reading is of Carmen's 'Card scene' solo. It is fascinating too to compare the three contrasted versions of Louise's *Depuis le jour*, only one of them previously published. Fine Ward Marston transfers.

Gigli, Beniamino (tenor)

'*The Complete Victor recordings (1921–25)*': Arias and duets from: BOITO: *Mefistofele*. PUCCINI: *Tosca*. PONCHIELLI: *La gioconda*. DONIZETTI: *La favorita; L'elisir d'amore; Lucia di Lammermoor*. GOUNOD: *Faust; Roméo et Juliette* (with Lucrezia Bori). MASCAGNI: *Iris*. DRIGO: *I millioni d'Arlecchino*. LALO: *Le roi d'Ys*. LEONCAVALLO: *I Pagliacci*. GIORDANO: *Andrea Chénier*. PUCCINI: *Tosca*. MEYERBEER: *L'africana*. CATALANI: *Loreley*. FLOTOW: *Martha*. Songs by: DE CURTIS; MARIO; TOSELLI; SAINT-SAENS; BUZZI-PECCIA; CARNEVALI; TAGLIAFERRI; DE CRESCENZO; DI CAPUA.

(***) Romophone mono 82003-2 (2).

'*The Complete Victor recordings (1926–28)*': Arias, duets and scenes from: VERDI: *La forza del destino*. PUCCINI: *La bohème*. PONCHIELLI: *La gioconda* (all three with Titta Ruffa and with Giuseppe de Luca). PUCCINI: *Tosca; Manon Lescaut*. BOITO: *Mefistofele*. DRIGO: *I millioni d'Arlecchino*. BIZET: *I pescatori di perle*. DONIZETTI: *Lucia di Lammermoor* (with Ezio Pinza and with Amelita Galli-Curci, Louise Homer, Angela Bada, Pinza and de Luca). VERDI: *Rigoletto* (with Galli-Curci, Homer, and de Luca); *La traviata*. MASCAGNI: *Cavalleria rusticana*. THOMAS: *Mignon*. MEYERBEER: *L'africana*. Songs by: TOSELLI; BUZZI-PECCIA; MASCAGNI; MARIO; DE CRESCENZO; COTTRAU; DONNAUDY; DE CURTIS.

(***) Romophone mono 82004-2 (2).

'*The Complete Victor recordings (1929–32)*': Arias and scenes from: FLOTOW: *Martha*; PONCHIELLI: *La gioconda*; BIZET: *Pearlfishers*; DONIZETTI: *L'elisir d'amore*; VERDI: *I Lombardi & Attila* (both with Rethberg & Pinza); RIMSKY-KORSAKOV: *Sadko*. Songs by DEDA; DENZA; GASTALDON; DE CURTIS; KREISLER; NUTILE; SIMONS; ALBENIZ; SANDOVAL' DE CRESCENZO.

(***) Romophone mono 82005-2 (2).

'*The Complete HMV recordings (1918–32)*': Arias and duets from: BOITO: *Mefistofele* (with Carlo Scattola and with Gemma Bosini). PUCCINI: *Tosca; La bohème* (with Maria Zamboni). PONCHIELLI: *La Gioconda* (with Dario Zani and with Elvira Casazza). DONIZETTI: *La Favorita* (with Casazza). MASCAGNI: *Lodoletta; Iris; L'amico Fritz* (with

Naldira Baldisseri); *Cavalleria rusticana* (with Dusolina Giannini and with Zamboni). GOUNOD: *Faust* (with Zamboni). BIZET: *Les pêcheurs des perles* (with Adolfo Pacini). GIORDANO: *Fedora*. MASSENET: *Manon*. ROSSINI: *Stabat Mater*. Songs by: CANNIO; TOSTI; SULLIVAN; SCHUBERT; NIEDERMEYER; DE CURTIS.

(***) Romophone mono 82011-2 (2).

'*The complete HMV recordings (1933–35)*': LEONCAVALLO: *I Pagliacci* (complete) (with Iva Pacetti, Mario Basiola and Giuseppe Nessi). Arias and duets from: GIORDANO: *Andrea Chénier*. MASCAGNI: *Cavalleria rusticana*. HANDEL: *Serse*. LEONCAVALLO: *I Pagliacci*. DONIZETTI: *L'elisir d'amore*. PUCCINI: *Tosca*. VERDI: *Rigoletto*. BIZET: *Carmen*. GLUCK: *Paride ed Elena*. Songs by: COTTRAU; DI CAPUA; DE CURTIS; BIXIO; LEONCAVALLO; MARTINI; MASSENET; SCHUBERT; MELICHAR.

(***) Romophone mono 82017-2 (2).

These five sets, nine discs in all, magnificently cover the recording activity up to the mid 1930s of Beniamino Gigli, both in Europe and America; more than any tenor, he was the successor to Caruso. It is striking throughout that Gigli with his honeyed, golden-toned voice was one who unlike so many other Italian tenors positively thrived on not singing at a consistent *fortissimo*. He is hardly a stylist, or the connoisseur's favourite, but no Italian tenor of his generation quite compared with Gigli in the magic quality he could give to a song or aria, both in his colouring of tone and in the warm-hearted magnetism which marked all his singing. It follows that his forte lies in Puccini and Neapolitan song, with 'Arie antiche' or Mozart revealing his stylistic weaknesses, thanks to heavily aspirated divisions and the occasional sob. His headily beautiful soft singing can also turn into a near-croon. Whatever those shortcomings, the results are consistently magical, so that *M'appari tutt'amor* from *Martha* may be aspirated, but its golden beauty has you charmed. As usual in Romophone issues alternative takes, usually unpublished, are included, often with fascinating results, as with the two versions of the *Pearl fishers'* aria on the 1929–32 Victor set. In that same issue it is good too to have side-by-side versions of the *Lombardi* and *Attila* trios with Rethberg and Pinza. Italian is the preferred language but the *Chanson hindoue* from Sadko comes in French. Excellent transfers by Mark Obert-Thorn.

Opera arias from: GOUNOD: *Faust*. BIZET: *Carmen; Les Pêcheurs de perles*. MASSENET: *Manon*. HANDEL: *Serse*. DONIZETTI: *Lucia di Lammermoor; L'Elisir d'amore*. VERDI: *Rigoletto; Aida*. LEONCAVALLO: *I Pagliacci*. MASCAGNI: *Cavalleria Rusticana*. PUCCINI: *La Bohème; Tosca*. GIORDANO: *Andrea Chénier*. PIETRI: *Maristella*.

(M) (***) EMI mono CDH7 61051-2.

No Italian tenor has sung with more honeyed beauty than Beniamino Gigli. His status in the inter-war period as a singing superstar at a time when the media were less keenly organized is vividly reflected in this Références collection of eighteen items, the cream of his recordings made between 1927 and 1937. It is especially welcome to have two historic ensemble recordings, made in New York in 1927 and originally coupled on a short-playing 78-r.p.m. disc – the *Quartet* from *Rigoletto* and the *Sextet* from *Lucia di Lammermoor*. In an astonishing line-up Gigli is joined by Galli-Curci, Pinza, De Luca and Louise Homer. Excellent transfers.

Arias from: VERDI: *Aida; La forza del destino; Un ballo in maschera; Rigoletto; Requiem.* DONIZETTI: *L'elisir d'amore.* PUCCINI: *La Bohème; Tosca.* CILEA: *L'Arlesiana.* GIORDANO: *Andrea Chénier.* BIZET: *Carmen.* LEONCAVALLO: *Pagliacci.* MASCAGNI: *Cavalleria rusticana; Isabeau.* ROSSINI: *Stabat Mater.* HANDEL: *Serse; Atalanta.* Songs: SCHUBERT: *Ave Maria.* BIZET: *Agnus Dei.* GIORDANO: *Caro mio ben.* DE CURTIS: *Torna a Surriento.* TOSTI: *L'untima canzone; La serenata; Aprile.* CARDILLO: *Core'ngrato.* DENZA: *Funiculi, funicula.* FRANCK: *Panis angelicus.* BACH/GOUNOD: *Ave Maria.* CACCINI: *Amarilli.* MARTINI: *Plaisir d'amore.* DI CAPUA: *O sole mio.* ROSSINI: *La danza.* LEONCAVALLO: *Mattinata.*

(BB) (***) Disky Royal Classics Vocal Double mono DCL 706652.

This very inexpensive Royal Classics Double involves some duplication with the Références disc above but not enough to matter, and the present collection extends to include recordings pulished in the late 1930s and early 1940s, when the voice was still sounding warm and fresh: the 1941 *E la solita storia del pastor* from Cilea's *L'Arlesiana* is particularly affecting. It is good too, to have the songs, richly lyrical performances like Schubert's *Ave Maria*, and the glorious *Caro mio ben* (published in 1947), while Gigli shows he can let himself go splendidly in the Neapolitan favourites, especially *O sole mio*. The transfers are first class, but there is no documentation beyond a list of titles, accompaniment details, and publishing dates.

Jurinac, Sena (soprano)

Opera arias from: MOZART: *Così fan tutte; Idomeneo.* SMETANA: *The Bartered Bride; The Kiss.* TCHAIKOVSKY: *Joan of Arc; Queen of Spades.* R. STRAUSS: *Four Last Songs (Vier letzte Lieder).*

(M) (***) EMI mono CDH7 63199-2.

This EMI Références issue, very well transferred, celebrates a magical, under-recorded singer. It brings together all of Jurinac's recordings for EMI outside the complete operas, and adds a live radio recording from Sweden – with Fritz Busch conducting the Stockholm Philharmonic Orchestra – of Strauss's *Four Last songs*, most beautifully done, if with rather generalized expression. Busch was also the conductor for the Glyndebourne recordings of excerpts from *Così fan tutte* and *Idomeneo*.

Lehmann, Lotte (soprano)

'*The Complete RCA Victor recordings (1947–49)*': SCHUBERT: *Ständchen: Leise flehen meine Lieder; An den Mond; An die Musik; Der Jüngling an der Quelle; An die Nachtigall; Der Männer sind méchant; Nacht und Träume; Der Erlkönig.* BRAHMS: *Ziegeunerlieder* (excerpts); *Feldeinsamkeit; Der Kranz; Wiegenlied.* TRADITIONAL: *Adeste fideles.* GRUBER: *Stille Nacht, heilige Nacht.* BERLIN: *God bless America.* MOLLOY: *The Kerry dance.* SCHUMANN: *Träumerei.* DUPARC: *La vie antёrieure.* PALADILHE: *Psyché.* RICHARD STRAUSS: *Die Zeitlose; Wozu noch, Mädchen; Du meines Herzens Krönelein.*

(***) Romophone mono 81033-2

Most of these post-war Victor recordings by Lotte Lehmann date from 1947, mostly of lieder with Paul Ulanowski accompanying her. Though the acoustic is uncomfortably dry, allowing little bloom on the voice, the singing is still magnetic, while the items with orchestra include such an oddity as Irving Berlin's *God bless America*, with Lehmann appropriately fervent. The Lieder and French mélodies from 1949 are better balanced, with the voice more persuasively caught. Transfers by Mark Obert-Thorn, which accurately convey the original recording quality.

'*The Victor recordings (1935–40)*': Lieder and songs: MOZART: *An Chloë; Die Verschweigung.* SCHUBERT: *Ungeduld; Im Abendrot; Gretchen am Spinnerade; Schlafe, schlafe; Die Nebensonnen; Die Post; Der Stürmische Morgen; Der Lindenbaum; Der Wegweiser; Die Krähe; Das Wirtshaus; Täuschung; Mut!; Im Dorfe; Rückblick.* SCHUMANN: *Die Kartenlegerin; Waldgespräch; Du bist wie eine Blume; Frühlingsnacht; Alte Laute; Er und sie; So wahr die Sonne scheinet; Unterm Fenster; Familien-Gemälde; Ich denke dein.* BRAHMS: *Der Tod das ist die kühle Nacht; Therese; Meine Liebe ist grün; Botschaft; Das Mädchen spricht; Mein Mädchen hat einen Rosenmund.* WOLF: *Anakreons Grab; In der Schatten meiner Locken; Storchenbotschaft; Der Gärtner; Du denkst mich zu fangen; Gebert; Früling übers Jahr; Auf ein altes Bild; In der Frühe; Auch kleine Dinge; Willst du Deinen Liebsten sehen; Peregrini I; Der Knabe und das Immlein; Heimweh.* BALOGH: *Do not chide.* GRETCHANINOFF: *My native land.* WORTH: *Summer.* SODERO: *Fa la Nanna, Bambin.* CIMARA: *Canto di primavera.* BEETHOVEN: *Ich liebe dich.* HAHN: *D'une prison.* GOUNOD: *Vierge d'Athènes.* PFITZNER: *Gretel.* MARX: *Selige Nacht.* FRANZ: *Für Musik; Gute Nacht.* JENSEN: *Lehn' deine Wang' an meine Wang'.* SJOBERG: *Visions.* CALCOTT: *Drink to me only.* TRADITIONAL: *Schlafe, mein süsses Kind.*

(***) Romophone mono 81013-2 (2).

These Victor recordings of Lehmann in Lieder present the voice at its freshest, superbly controlled, and the recordings, less dry than the 1947 sessions and far more sympathetic. The singer's enjoyment as well as her understanding consistently come out both there and in the recordings she went on to make in 1937, 1939 and finally 1940, when she essayed what only Elena Gerhardt had attempted before her, a woman's interpretation of Schubert's *Winterreise*, and it is sad that she covered only eleven of the songs. Though the voices are recorded close with thin orchestral accompaniments, the five Schumann duets with Melchior make a vividly characterful supplement to the Lieder, with operatic manners charmingly emerging.

Lieder, Frida (soprano)

'*The Singers*' (Decca series): Arias from: MOZART: *Le nozze di Figaro*. BEETHOVEN: *Fidelio*. WEBER: *Oberon*. WAGNER: *Götterdämmerung; Parsifal; Siegfried; Tristan und Isolde; Die Walküre*.

(M) (**) Decca mono 467 911-2.

Frida Lieder was born in Berlin in 1888 and made that city the centre of her career, dying there in 1975. In her day, she received tremendous accolades. 'The greatest Isolde of them all,' wrote Lauritz Melchior, one of the outstanding Tristans of his day (heard here in the *Die Walküre* excerpt). What one notices in these historic recordings from the 1920s are the tremendous firmness as well as the freshness in her voice – combined with an intelligence in her approach – which gives an idea of what she must have been like 'live'. One can only say 'gives an idea', as these pre-electric recordings are simply not able to capture the true power of her voice, and the small and thin-sounding, scrappy orchestra will horrify anyone who hasn't experienced pre-electric recording before. But for all its technical inadequacies, this remains one of the more interesting releases in Decca's 'The Singers' series, although the texts and translations are available, along with a photo-gallery, only via a CD ROM drive. The transfers are acceptable, and the voice is certainly immediate.

Martinelli, Giovanni (tenor)

'*The Complete acoustic recordings (1912–1924)*': Arias, duets and scenes from: PUCCINI: *La bohème; Madama Butterfly* (both with Frances Alda); *Manon Lescaut; Tosca*. PONCHIELLI: *La Gioconda*. VERDI: *Rigoletto; Aida* (with Rosa Poncelle); *Un ballo in maschera; Il trovatore* (with Emmy Destinn); *Ernani; La traviata*. LEONCAVALLO: *I Pagliacci; Zazà*. MASCAGNI: *Cavalleria rusticana; Iris*. MEYERBEER: *L'africana*. DONIZETTI: *Lucia di Lammermoor; Don Pasquale*. FLOTOW: *Marta*. ROSSINI: *Guglielmo Tell* (with Marcel Journet and with Giuseppe de Luca and José Mardones). GOUNOD: *Faust*. MASSENET: *Werther*. HALEVY: *La Juive*. Songs by: TOSTI; MASCAGNI; BIZET; LEONCAVALLO; ROXAS; GASTELDO. (Includes extended excerpts from BIZET: *Carmen* with Geraldine Farrar.)

(***) Romophone mono 82012-2 (3).

Giovanni Martinelli, often described as Toscanini's favourite tenor, is more renowned for his electric recordings, but this comprehensive collection of his pre-electrics is most revealing in the way it shows how he developed into such a commanding singer. The voice was heroic and distinctive from the start, but the opening item, *Recondita armonia*, from Puccini's *Tosca*, recorded in 1912, finds him disconcertingly effortful, while Cavaradossi's Act III aria, *E lucevan le stelle*, is slow and heavy. His remakes of those arias only two years later show how quickly he learnt from his recordings, making them both more flowing and more characterful. As usual on Romophone these alternative takes are included, and it is good to have the five items from Bizet's *Carmen*, recorded in 1915 with Farrar singing the title role.

McCormack, John (tenor)

'*The Acoustic Victor and HMV recordings (1910–11)*': Arias, duets and scenes from: DONIZETTI: *Lucia di Lammermoor; L'elisir d'amore; La fille du régiment*. BIZET: *Carmen*. DELIBES: *Lakmé*. VERDI: *La traviata; Rigoletto* (with Nellie Melba, Edna Thornton and Mario Sammarco). PUCCINI: *La bohème*. BIZET: *Les Pêcheurs de perles*. ROSSINI: *Il barbiere di Siviglia*. PONCHIELLI: *La gioconda*. GOUNOD: *Faust* (with Melba and all five with Sammarco). Songs by: BALFE; BARNARD; ANNE; LADY JOHN SCOTT; MARSHALL; CHERRY; BARKER; CROUCH; OLCOTT AND BALL; HERBERT; MACMURROUGH; BLUMENTHAL; PARELLI; ROSSINI **and** TRADITIONAL.

(***) Romophone mono 82006-2 (2).

'*The Acoustic Victor and HMV recordings (1912–14)*': Arias from: HERBERT: *Natoma*. WOLF-FERRARI: *I gioielli della Madonna*. BOITO: *Mefistofele*. BIZET: *Les pêcheurs de perles; Carmen*. WALLACE: *Maritana*. MASSENET: *Manon*. VERDI: *Rigoletto*. GODARD: *Jocelyn*. Irish traditional songs including: *Eileen Aroon; The wearing of the Green; The harp that once through Tara's halls; Mollie Brannigan*. Songs and Ballads by: STERNDALE BENNETT; MARSHALL; TROTERE; LIDDLE;. CLUTSAM; DANKS; TOSTI; TUCKER; SCOTT; MARSHALL; FOX; BIMBONI; KENNEDY; SILESU; THOMAS; HATTON; PARKYNS; LEROUX; NEVIN: *The Rosary*. DANKS: *Silver threads among the gold*. CADMAN: *At dawning*. ADAMS: *Nirvana; Nearer my God to thee*. CLAY: *I'll sing thee songs of Araby*. TOURS: *Mother o'mine*. RONALD: *Down in the forest*. BRAGA: *Angel's serenade* (with Kreisler, violin). SCHUBERT: *Ave Maria*. BACH-GOUNOD: *Ave Maria*.

(***) Romophone mono 82007-2 (2).

Born in 1884, John McCormack developed early, belonging more to the age of Caruso than of Gigli. He used his heady, ringing Irish tenor, always distinctive, to produce singing of wonderful purity and evenness, whether in a Mozart aria or in the many popular ballads which were the staple of his repertory. His main achievement lay more in recital than on the opera stage, so that his accounts of popular arias, though always stylish tend to be emotionally restrained, even in Rodolfo's *Che gelida manina*. Unlike Gigli he would produce the smoothest legato line for *Una furtiva lagrima* with no hint of an aspirate. The first of the two Romophone sets of his acoustic recordings is the one which has the more substantial items, where the second two-disc box includes only nine operatic arias among the forty-nine items, among them rare arias by such composers as Victor Herbert and Wolf-Ferrari. First-rate transfers by Ward Marston.

'Songs of my heart': TRAD.: *The garden where the praties grow; Terence's farewell to Kathleen; Believe me if all those endearing young charms; The star of the County Down; Oft in the stilly night; The meeting of the waters; The Bard of Armagh; Down by the Salley Gardens; She moved thro' the fair; The green bushes.* BALFE: *The harp that once through Tara's halls.* ROECKEL: *The green isle of Erin.* SCHNEIDER: *O Mary dear.* LAMBERT: *She is far from the land.* HAYNES: *Off to Philadelphia.* MOLLOY: *The Kerry dance; Bantry Bay.* MARSHALL: *I hear you calling me.* E. PURCELL: *Passing by.* WOODFORD-FINDEN: *Kashmiri song.* CLUTSAM: *I know of two bright eyes.* FOSTER: *Jeannie with the light brown hair; Sweetly she sleeps, my Alice fair.*

⚘ (M) (***) EMI mono CDM7 64654-2.

In Irish repertoire like *The star of the County Down* McCormack is irresistible, but in lighter concert songs he could also spin the utmost magic. *Down by the Salley Gardens* and Stephen Foster's *Jeannie with the light brown hair* are superb examples, while in a ballad like *I hear you calling me* (an early pre-electric recording from 1908) the golden bloom of the vocal timbre combining with an artless line brings a ravishing frisson on the closing pianissimo. Many of the accompaniments are by Gerald Moore, who proves a splendid partner. Occasionally there is a hint of unsteadiness in the sustained *piano* tone, but otherwise no apology need be made for the recorded sound which is first class, while the lack of 78-r.p.m. background noise is remarkable.

Melba, Nellie (soprano)

Arias from: VERDI: *Rigoletto; La traviata.* DONIZETTI: *Lucia di Lammermoor.* HANDEL: *Il Penseroso.* THOMAS: *Hamlet.* MOZART: *Le Nozze di Figaro.* PUCCINI: *La Bohème.* Songs: TOSTI: *Goodbye; Mattinata.* BEMBERG: *Les anges pleurent; Chant Vénitien; Nymphes et sylvains.* TRAD.: *Comin' thro' the Rye.* ARDITI: *Se saran rose.*

D'HARDELOT: *Three Green Bonnets.* HAHN: *Si mes vers avaient des ailes.* BACH/GOUNOD: *Ave Maria.*

(BB) (***) Naxos mono 8.110737.

From the moment she made her debut in Brussels as Gilda in *Rigoletto* in 1887 Helen Porter Mitchell, better known as Nellie Melba, became an operatic star of stars, particularly at Covent Garden, but also at the Met and in Europe. She retired in 1926. Her first records, of which 19 items are included here, were made privately at her home in 1904, when she was 43. They were not originally intended for public release, but later she approved fourteen for publication, though in the case of the Act I *La traviata* aria she only permitted the release of *Ah! fors è lui* (simply and beautifully sung) and not the cabaletta, though both are included here. Another fascinating item from those first sessions is Handel's *'Sweet Bird'* from *Il Penseroso*, where during the first take the flautist played incorrectly, causing Melba to stop and say *'Now we'll have to do it over again'*. Fortunately the second take is flawless, for she was good at trilling with a flute, as is shown in the brief excerpt from Donizetti's Mad scene (*Lucia de Lammermoor*). Although the voice is obviously showing signs of wear, the agility is unimpaired, as the arias from Thomas's *Hamlet* demonstrate. *Et maintenant, écoutez ma chanson!* is a real bravura example. Some of the items suffer from distortion or excess, uneven surface noise, but not this, and *Caro nome* (with more background and some slight distortion), is also pretty impressive. Mozart's *Porgi amor* is not really stylish by today's standards but shows Melba's quality of tone and line. Ward Marston's fine transfers certainly bring this legendary figure fully to life, and the Naxos documentation is well up to standard for this enterprising series.

Piccaver, Alfred (tenor)

'The Son of Vienna' Arias and duets from: VERDI: *Rigoletto; Trovatore; In ballo in maschera; Aida.* MEYERBEER: *L'africaine.* MASCAGNI: *Cavalleria rusticana.* LEONCAVALLO: *I Pagliacci.* WAGNER: *Die Meistersinger; Lohengrin.* GOUNOD: *Faust.* PONCHIELLI: *La Gioconda.* PUCCINI: *Tosca; Turandot.* Song: GEEHL: *For You Alone.*

(BB) (***) Dutton mono CDPB 9725.

Though born in England, Alfred Piccaver was brought up in the United States, and then in his mid-twenties settled permanently in Vienna, where he was a stalwart of the Vienna State Opera for almost thirty years. This disc of his relatively rare recordings in every item explains his success. His was a ringingly clear tenor, with no hint of strain even in the high registers. His style was Germanic, at times suggesting similarities with his Viennese contemporary, Richard Tauber, yet Piccaver's repertory was far wider, extending to most of the principal lyrico-dramatic tenor parts, as the items here suggest. The recordings are divided sharply into two sections, the first eight numbers recorded in 1923 by the acoustic process – with the voice yet ringingly clear – and eight recorded electrically in 1928. The Dutton transfers are excellent, though it is a pity that background details of each recording are very limited.

RCA Red Seal Century: The Vocalists

'RCA Red Seal Century': The Vocalists.

Disc 1: (1903) THOMAS: *Le Caïd: Je comprends que la belle aime le militaire* (Pol Plançon). (1906) VERDI: *Otello: Ave Maria* (Emma Eames). (1908) WAGNER: *Die fliegende Holländer: Senta's Ballad: Traft ihr das Schiff* (Johanna Gadski). (1908) BIZET: *Carmen: Gypsy Song: Les Tringles des Sistres* (Emma Calvé). (1908) VERDI: *Aida: Celeste Aida* (Enrico Caruso). (1909) DONIZETTI: *Lucretia Borgia: Il segreto per essere felice.* (Ernestine Schumann-Henk). (1911) ROSSINI: *Il barbiere di Siviglia: Una voce poco fa* (Luisa Tetrazzini). (1911) RAMEAU: *Hippolyte et Aricie: Rossignols Amoureux* (Alma Gluck). (1912) J. STRAUSS arr. La Forge: *Tales from the Vienna Woods: Storielle del Bosco Viennese, Op. 325* (Marcella Sembrich). (1912) PONCHIELLI: *La Gioconda: Voce di donna* (Louise Homer). (1913) PUCCINI: *Tosca: Vissi d'arte* (Geraldine Farrar). (1914) VERDI: *Un ballo in maschera: Eri tu* (Pasquale Amato). (1915) TCHAIKOVSKY: *Pique Dame: It is almost Midnight* (Emmy Destinn). (1916) MOZART: *Don Giovanni: Il mio tesoro* (John McCormack). (1917) MOZART: *Le nozze di Figaro: Bravo, signor padrone!* (Giuseppe de Luca). (1919) VERDI: *La traviata: Follie! Follie! … Sempre libera* (Amelita Galli-Curci). (1920) ROSSINI: *Il barbiere di Siviglia: Largo al factotum* (Titta Ruffo). (1925) GIORDANO: *La cene delle beffe: Ed io non ne godevo* (Frances Alda). (1926) VERDI: *Falstaff: E sogno, o realtà* (Lawrence Tibbett). (1927) MUSSORGSKY: *Boris Godunov: (Vaarlam's Song) In the Town of Kazan* (Feodor Chaliapin). (1927) LEONCAVALLO: *Pagliacci: Vesti la giubba* (Giovanni Martinelli).

Disc 2: (1925) PUCCINI: *La Bohème: Sono andati* (Lucrezia Bori, Tito Schipa). (1928) VERDI: *La forza del destino: Pace, pace mio dio* (Rosa Ponselle). (1930) VERDI: *I Lombardi: Qual voluttà trascorrere* (Elisabeth Rethberg, Beniamino Gigli, Ezio Pinza). (1934) MASSENET: *Hérodiade: Ce breuvage … Vision fugitive* (John Charles Thomas. (1936) SIBELIUS: *Säv, säv, susa, Op. 36/4* (Marian Anderson). (1937) WAGNER: *Die Walküre: Du bist der lenz* (Kirsten Flagstad). (1938) WAGNER: *Die Walküre: Winterstürme* (Lauritz Melchior). (1940). WAGNER: *Lohengrin: (Elsa's Dream) Einsam in trüben Tagen* (Helen Traubel). (1946) VERDI: *Il trovatore: Vanne, lasciami … D'amor sull'ali rosee* (Zinka Milanov). (1950) VERDI: *Rigoletto: Cortigiani, vil razza dannata* (Leonard Warren). (1951) BIZET: *Les Pêcheurs des perles: Au fond du temple saint* (Jussi

Bjoerling, Robert Merrill). (1952) CILEA: *L'Arlesiana: (Lamento di Federico) E la solita storia* (Mario Lanza). (1958) BARBER: *Vanessa: Do not utter a word, Anatole* (Eleanor Steber). (1960) PUCCINI: *La rondine: Che il bel sogno di Doretta* (Leontyne Price). (1963) MASSENET: *Manon: (Obéissons quand leur voix appelle): Gavotte* (Anna Moffo). (1967) VERDI: *Il corsaro: No so le tetre immagini* (Montserrat Caballé). (1978) VERDI: *Otello: Ah! Mille vite … Sì pel ciel marmoreo giuro!* (Placido Domingo, Sherrill Milnes). (1996) MOZART: *Le nozze di Figaro: Non so più cosa son, cosa faccio* (Vesselina Kasarova). (1998) MASSENET: *Werther: Traduire! … Pourquoime réveiller* (Ramón Vargas). (1999) BIZET: *Carmen: (Habanera): Quand je vous aimerais? … L'amour est un oiseau rebelle* (Denyce Graves).

(***) RCA 09026 63860-2 (2).

There is little to quibble at in this vocal celebration of the RCA Century. The galaxy of singers offered here is almost overwhelming, the transfers are generally good with no great background noise problems. To the modern non-specalist ear some of the sounds made by the female singers in the early years of the century sound curiously dated, rather in the way that portamenti on a stringed instrument are no longer expected. But Tetrazzini, Alma Gluck and Sembrich are very impressive and Galli-Curci and Geraldine Farrar always delight the ear. Among the men Chaliapin in *Boris Godunov* stands out for sheer drama. As we come nearer our own time there is much to enchant. Rosa Ponselle sings gloriously and Marian Andersen's Sibelius song is captivating. A relatively unfamiliar name among the men is John Charles Thomas, whose voice is pleasingly full-bodied and warm in Massenet. Lauritz Melchior's *Die Wälkure* excerpt is one of the few items where there is real distortion, but Flagstad sounds wonderful, as does Milanov in *Il trovatore*. An obviously indispensable item is the famous duet from the *Pearl Fishers* with Bjoerling and Merrill, but Domingo and Milnes are just as impressive in their Act II duet from *Otello*. All-in-all a fine selection, endng with a most seductive *Carmen* in Denyce Graves. But the documentation is sparse for a full-priced set.

Schmidt, Joseph (tenor)

Complete EMI recordings: Arias (sung in German) from: MEYERBEER: *L'africaine.* FLOTOW: *Martha; Alessandro Stradella.* KIENZL: *Der Evangelimann.* KORNGOLD: *Die tote Stadt.* ADAM: *Der Postillon von Longjumeau.* MASSENET: *Manon; Der Cid.* TCHAIKOVSKY: *Eugene Onegin.* MORY: *La Vallière.* GOTZE: *Der Page des Königs.* JOHANN STRAUSS JR: *1001 Nacht; Der Zigeunerbaron; Simplicus.* LEHAR: *Zigeunerliebe.* TAUBER: *Der Singende Traume.* DONIZETTI: *Der Liebestrank (L'elisir d'amore).* VERDI: *Rigoletto; Der Troubadour (Il trovatore).* LEONCAVALLO: *Der Bajazzo (Pagliacci).* PUCCINI:

La Bohème; Tosca; Das Mädchen aus dem Goldenen Westen (Fanciulla del West); Turandot. SERRANO: *El Trust de Los Tenorios.* SPOLIANSKY: *Das Lied einer Nacht* (**film**). **Lieder & Songs:** SCHUBERT: *Ständchen; Ungeduld.* BENATZKY: *Wenn du treulos bist.* NIEDERBERGER: *Buona notte, schöne Signorina.* LEONCAVALLO: *Morgenständchen.* LABRIOLA: *Serenata.* BISCARDI: *L'ariatella.* DENZA: *Funiculi, funicula.* BUZZI-PECCIA: *Lolita.* DI CAPUA: *O sole mio.*

(M) (***) EMI mono CHS7 64676-2 (2).

Joseph Schmidt, born in 1904 in what is now Romania, studied in Berlin, and developed what by any standards is one of the most beautiful German tenor voices ever recorded, less distinctive than that of Richard Tauber, but even more consistently honeyed and velvety in the upper registers, exceptionally free on top, so that the stratospheric top notes in *Le Postillon de Longjumeau* have never sounded so beautiful and unstrained. This is the ideal lyric tenor voice, not just for the German repertory, including operetta, but for the Italian; it was tragic that, standing less than five foot high, he was precluded from having an operatic career. Nevertheless, he was most successful in his concert work as well as in his recording career, as this glowing collection demonstrates. He even had a brilliantly successful American tour in 1937; but sadly, as a Jew, he got caught up in Europe during the Second World War, and died from a chest complaint in a Swiss refugee camp in 1942. The records – with informative notes – make a superb memorial, here at last given full prominence in excellent transfers.

Schumann, Elisabeth (soprano)

Lieder: MENDELSSOHN: *Auf Flügeln des Gesanges.* SCHUMANN: *Schneeglöckchen; Der Nussbaum; Er ist's; Aufträge; Mondnacht; Ständchen; O ihr Herren; Röselein, Röselein.* BRAHMS: *Wiegenlied; Vergebliches Ständchen; Nachtigall; Der Jäger; Sandmännchen; Der Tod das ist die kühle Nacht; Immer leiser wird mein Schlummer; Das mädchen spricht; Der Mond steht über dem Berge; Die schone Magelone: Ruhe, Süssliebchen; An eine Aolsharfe; Bitteres zu sagen denkst du; Blinde Kuh; Erlaube mir, fein's Mädchen; Wie komm' ich denn zur Tür herein?; In stiller Nacht; Mein Mädel hat einen Rosenmund; Schwesterlein; Och Moder, ich well en Ding han!*

(***) Romophone mono 81018-2.

Over two-thirds of the songs here are by Brahms – delectable performances, intimate and engaging – with Schumann charming the listener with her individual pointing of words and phrase. Two of the most popular songs, *Wiegenlied* and *Immer leiser*, are with orchestra but the rest have the original piano accompaniment. The one Mendelssohn item, *On wings of song* (in the original German), also has orchestral accompaniment but the remaining nine songs, all by Schumann, have piano. Recorded between 1930 and 1938, this has the singer at her peak, with the voice angelically pure but with nuances of tone and phrase that are totally individual.

Arias from: MOZART: *Il re pastore; Le nozze di Figaro; Don Giovanni.* JOHANN STRAUSS JR: *Die Fledermaus.* ZELLER: *Der Vogelhändler; Der Obersteiger.* ZIEHRER: *Der Landstreicher; Der Fremdenführer.* SCHUBERT: *Das Dreimäderlhaus.* HEUBERGER: *Der Opernball.* KREISLER: *Sissy.* BENATZKY: *Ich muss wieder einmal in Grinzing sein.* SIECZNSI: *Wein du Stadt meiner Träume.* Joseph STRAUSS: *Sphärenklänge waltz.*

(**(*)) Romophone mono 81019-2.

No German singer exuded quite such charm as Elisabeth Schumann, with her sweet, silvery soprano and sparkling manner. Nowhere does this come over more vividly than in this magical collection of Viennese operetta arias, deliciously idiomatic in their pointing. In such a favourite as *Sei nicht bös* from *Der Obersteiger* by Zeller, the element of naughtiness is beautifully caught, with a sparkle in the eye as well as the voice, and Adèle's arias from *Die Fledermaus* have never been so delectably characterized as here. Those thirteen numbers are preceded by eight of Mozart, recorded not in Vienna like most of the operetta items but in London. In contrast with her pre-electric versions, the original Italian is used, and though the portamento is still obtrusive, the point and control are keener. The only reservation is that the transfer brings out an extra brightness in the voice not quite true to life.

'*The Complete Edison and Polydor recordings (1915–23)*': **Arias from:** BEETHOVEN: *Fidelio.* WEBER: *Der Freischütz.* THOMAS: *Mignon.* MOZART: *Le nozze di Figaro; Don Giovanni; Die Entführung auf dem Serail; Die Zauberflöte; Exsultate jubilate.* LORTZING: *Der Wildschütz.* GOUNOD: *Faust.* AUBER: *Fra Diavolo.* HUMPERDINCK: *Hansel und Gretel.* R. STRAUSS: *Die heiligen drei Könige aus Morgenland.*

(***) Romophone mono 81028-2.

This collection of rarities brings together Elisabeth Schumann's pre-electric recordings for the Edison and Polydor labels before she turned to HMV. Maybe because copies are so rare, surfaces are very intrusive, particularly on the four Pathés, recorded in 1915. Yet behind the heavy hiss you can hear the unmistakable magic voice in different repertory from her usual - Marzelline's aria from *Fidelio* and Aennchen's from *Der Freischütz*, more than just a soubrette. Also Mignon's *Connais-tu le pays*, translated back (awkwardly for the music) as '*Kennst du das Land*'. Most of the Polydor recordings are of Mozart, all in German, as is the *Jewel song* from *Faust* and *Quel bonheur* from Auber's *Fra Diavolo*. The Mozart is charming, as one would expect, but like many singers of that period she had not yet learnt to limit the swoop of portamentos.

Schumann-Heink, Ernestine
(contralto)

'The Complete recordings (1900–09)': Arias from: MEYERBEER: *Le prophète.* DONIZETTI: *Lucrezia Borgia.* SAINT-SAENS: *Samson und Dalila.* J. EDWARDS: *Love's lottery.* MENDELSSOHN: *Saint Paul.* HANDEL: *Rinaldo.* THOMAS: *Mignon.* GLUCK: *Orpheus und Euridike.* WAGNER: *Das Rheingold* (with Herbert Witherspoon); *Rienzi.* GOUNOD: *Sapho.* MOZART: *La clemenza di Tito.* Songs by: ARDITI; SCHUBERT; BRAHMS; TCHAIKOVSKY;. R. BECKER; NEVIN; BOND; MENDELSSOHN; LANG: Folk songs: GRUBER; CHADWICK; MILLOCKER; SCHUMANN; REGER; WEINGARTNER; HERMANN.

(***) Romophone mono 81029-2 (2).

Ernestine Schumann-Heink was the outstanding operatic contralto of her time, and the recordings here vividly explain why. Hers was a voice of extraordinary range, firm and clear in every register; on the one hand weighty and powerful, on the other extraordinarily agile, as is demonstrated in the four versions of the 'Drinking song' from Donizetti's *Lucrezia Borgia*, the first two from 1903 with piano, the last of 1909 brighter, clearer and freer and even more characterful. It is fascinating too to compare the five versions of Delilah's *Softly awakes my heart* (all in German), with the singer learning to reduce the swooping portamentos of the first of 1903. Not only was Schumann-Heink's voice a unique instrument, she was vividly characterful in everything she sang, projecting magnetically her involvement. The first Zonophone item from 1900 brings dim sound, and the Columbia recordings of 1906 (with piano) are restricted too, but the voice comes over splendidly, and the rest are treated to excellent Ward Marston transfers.

Sembrich, Marcella (soprano)

'The Victor recordings (1904–08)': Arias from: VERDI: *La traviata; Rigoletto; Ernani.* BELLINI: *La sonnambula; Norma; I puritani.* GOUNOD: *Faust.* MOZART: *Don Giovanni; Le nozze di Figaro* (with Emma Eames). DONIZETTI: *Lucia di Lammermoor; Don Pasquale.* HANDEL: *Alessandro.* FLOTOW: *Martha.* ROSSINI: *Il barbiere di Siviglia.* MONIUSZKO: *Halka.* THOMAS: *Hamlet* (with Emilio de Gogorza); *Mignon.* LEHAR: *Die lustige Witwe.* Songs by: JOHANN STRAUSS JR; RICHARD STRAUSS; SCHUMANN; CHOPIN; ARDITI; BISHOP; ARNE; ALABIEV; HAHN; SCHUBERT.

(**(*)) Romophone mono 81026-2 (2)

'The Victor recordings (1908–19)': With appendix of cylinder and grand opera recordings (c. 1900-03). Arias, duets and scenes from: VERDI: *Rigoletto* (with Mario Sammarco); *I vespri siciliani; Ernani; La traviata.* DONIZETTI: *Lucia di Lammermoor* (with Enrico Caruso, Gina Severina Francesco Daddi, Antonio Scotti and Marcel Journet); *Linda di*

Chamounix; La fille du régiment. ROSSINI: Semeramide. LEHAR: *Die lustige Witwe.* BARBIERI: *Barbarillo de lavapies.* FALL: *Dollar princess.* OSCAR STRAUS: *Waltz dream.* MOZART: *Il flauto magico.* Songs by: JOHANN STRAUSS JR; LILLEJEBJORN; HEINE-RUBENSTEIN; MANNEY; SARA TEASDALE-WILLIAM; ARMS FISHER; STEBBINS; RUBINSTEIN; MASSENET; LA FORGE; PADEREWSKI; ARDITI and TRADITIONAL.

(***) Romophone mono 81027-2 (2).

Marcella Sembrich is a singer whose reputation – as the supreme coloratura soprano of her day – is hardly borne out by her recordings. There are many fine qualities here, but her undoubted daring in tackling coloratura results in some astonishingly sketchy passages with the notes skated over, whether in the early recordings of 1904–8 or the later recordings made up to her retirement after the First World War. She was not as ready as some other singers to learn from her earliest recordings that swooping protamentos needed to be avoided, but there are many impressive points to note, such as the tight, clean trills. The second of the pair of two-disc boxes has a higher proportion of trivial items, but offers a charming appendix in a series of Mapleson cylinder recordings of live performances, dim in sound but very revealing, as well as six rare recordings of 1903 from the Columbia Grand Opera series. The later recordings offer fine transfers with the voice bright and clear, with the voice in sharp focus, but with high hiss.

Tauber, Richard (tenor)

Arias from: AUBER: *Fra Diavolo.* FLOTOW: *Martha.* KORNGOLD: *Die tote Stadt.* KIENZL: *Der Evangelimann.* PUCCINI: *La Bohème; Tosca.* ROSSINI: *Il Barbiere di Siviglia.* SMETANA: *The Bartered Bride.* RICHARD STRAUSS: *Der Rosenkavalier.* TCHAIKOVSKY: *Eugene Onegin.* THOMAS: *Mignon.* VERDI: *La forza del destino; La Traviata; Il Trovatore.* WOLF-FERRARI: *Jewels of the Madonna.*

(B) (***) Naxos mono 8.110729.

These acoustic recordings, made between 1919 and 1926, offer a totally different view of Richard Tauber and his art from the usual one, revealing the range of his sympathies in the world of opera. A complete musician, an excellent pianist and conductor as well as singer, he here tackles a formidable list of arias, including even Siegmund's *Wintersturme* solo from Wagner's *Die Walküre*, not a role he ever sang on stage. While in the 1920s he was establishing his unique reputation in operetta, he was also much admired for his performances in opera, a career that had begun in 1913, first in Chemnitz with *Zauberflöte* and then on contract in Dresden with Thomas's *Mignon.* The distinctive warmth of Tauber's tenor was ideally suited to recording, and though these acoustic examples do not generally capture the timbre we associate with his singing of Lehár, the sweetness is beautifully caught in Ward Marston's fine transfers. It is good too to be without the kind of distortion characteristic of some of his later electric recordings. The disc comes with a highly informative note by Peter Dempsey.

MOZART: *Don Giovanni: Il mio tesoro. Die Zauberflöte: Dies Bildnis.* Arias from: PUCCINI: *La Bohème; Madama Butterfly; Tosca; Turandot.* LEONCAVALLO: *Pagliacci.* VERDI: *Il Trovatore.* MEHUL: *Joseph in Aegypten.* OFFENBACH: *Contes d'Hoffmann.* THOMAS: *Mignon.* TCHAIKOVSKY: *Eugene Onegin.* SMETANA: *Bartered bride* (all sung in German). WEBER: *Der Freischütz.* LORTZING: *Undine.* KIENZL: *Der Evangelimann.* WAGNER: *Die Meistersinger.* RICHARD STRAUSS: *Der Rosenkavlier.* KORNGOLD: *Die tote Stadt.* LEHAR: *Die lustige Witwe (Lippen schweigen; Vilja-Lied); Paganini; Friederike (O Mädchen, mein Mädchen); Das Land des Lächelns* (4 excerpts, including *Dein ist mein ganzes Herz); Giuditta; Die Zarewitsch.* KALMAN: *Die Zirkusprinzessin; Gräfin Mariza.* HEUBERGER: *Der Opernball (Im chambre séparée).* STOLZ: *Adieu, mein kleiner Gardeoffizier; Im Prater blühn wieder die Bäume.* SIECZYNSKI: *Wien, du Stadt meiner Träume.* JOHANN STRAUSS JR: *Geschichten aus dem Wienerwald; Rosen aus dem Süden.* ZELLER: *Der Vogelhändler.* DOELLE: *Wenn der weisse Flieder wider blüht.* ERWIN: *Ich küsse Ihre Hand, Madame.* Lieder: SCHUBERT: *Ständchen; Der Lindenbaum.*

(M) (*(**)) EMI mono CMS5 66692-2 (2).

If one begins with the second of these two CDs, it becomes immediately obvious why Tauber established his reputation with the wider public largely in the field of operetta. The uniquely honeyed voice makes simple melodies like *Lippen schweigen* from *The Merry Widow*, with its magical final cadence, or the *Vilja-Lied* utterly seductive, and that despite often inadequate transfers, with thin, whistly orchestral sound and plenty of distortion, even on the voice itself. One wonders why Tauber, more than most singers of his generation, so regularly suffers from this problem. It isn't that the basic recordings are bad, except for the thin orchestra (though there are frequent moments of blasting); usually the magic and power of the voice are well conveyed; yet the original sources too often seem prone to distortion. The first disc concentrates on opera and opens with a glowingly lyrical 1939 *Il mio tesoro*, but again there is distortion. *Dies Bildnis* (from *Die Zauberflöte*) is acoustic (1922) and rather better, and Tauber then makes *Your tiny hand is frozen* sound beguiling even in German! – the chosen language for most of his records. There are many remarkable performances here, from the lilting *Legend of Kleinsach* (1928) to a stirring *Di quella pira* (1926) with a comic wind band accompaniment; there are also equally moving versions of Lenski's aria from *Eugene Onegin* (1923), when the band is less clumsy, and the ardent *On with the motley* (recorded in London in 1936 and sung in English). It is a pity the

recordings are technically so inadequate, but the voice still enthrals the listener.

Tetrazzini, Luisa (soprano)

'*The Complete Zonophone (1904) and Victor recordings (1911–20)*': Arias from: VERDI: *Un ballo in maschera; La traviata; Rigoletto* (with Enrico Caruso, Josephine Jacoby and Pasquale Amato); *Il trovatore; La forza del destino; I vespri siciliani.* BELLINI: *La sonnambula.* BENEDICT: *Il carnavale di Venezia.* DONIZETTI: *Lucia di Lammermoor* (with Caruso, Jacoby, Amato, Marcel Journet and Angelo Bada); *Linda di Chamounix.* ROSSINI: *Il barbiere di Siviglia.* DAVID: *La perle du Brésil.* THOMAS: *Mignon.* CHAPI: *Las hijas del Zebedeo.* DELIBES: *Lakmé.* MEYERBEER: *Dinorah.* VERACINI: *Rosalinda.* BIZET: *Carmen.* MOZART: *Il flauto magico.* GOUNOD: *Romeo e Guilietta.* Songs by: MOORE; ECKERT; PROCH; COWAN; DE KOVEN; BRAHMS; VENZANO; GILBERT; CIAMPI; GRIEG.

(***) Romophone mono 81025-2 (2).

If Marcella Sembrich brings a fair measure of disappointment in her recordings, Luisa Tetrazzini is the coloratura, bright, clear and characterful, who consistently bewitches one not only with her dazzling technique but with her sparkle, charm, vivacity and vivid projection. Her singing is individual in every phrase, so that one readily forgives the stylistic flaws. The range was wide, so that the chest notes of Rosina's *Una voce poco fa* were rich and firm, and the recordings confirm as far as anything can that the size of the voice was greater than one would expect: it was sometimes described as a dramatic soprano with agility. Tetrazzini in *Ah non giunge* from Bellini's *Sonnambula* remains unsurpassed, and her portrayal of Violetta in her 1910 version of *Ah forse'è lui* brings out the degree of pathos she could convey, no mere canary-bird. First-rate Ward Marston transfers with the surface hiss kept under fair control.

Teyte, Maggie (soprano)

'*The Singers*' (Decca series): Arias from: OFFENBACH: *La Périchole.* MESSAGER: *Véronique.* Songs: FAURE: *Après un rêve.* HAHN: *Si mes vers avaient des ailes.* DVORAK: *Christina's Lament; Songs My Mother Taught Me.* GIBSON: *Carefree; Sweet Mistress Prue.* ROMBERG: *Deep In My Heart Dear.* CUVILLIER: *What Is Done You Never Can Undo.* COWARD: *I'll Follow My Secret Heart; Nevermore.* SCHUMANN: *Aufträge; Der Nussbaum.* BRAHMS: *An die Nachtigall; Die Mainacht; Meine Liebe ist grün.* QUILTER: *Now Sleeps the Crimson Petal.* DELIUS: *Indian Love Song.* GIBBS: *The Fields are Full of Summer Still.* BRIDGE: *E'en as a Lovely Flower.* WEBBER: *The Nightingale Sings to His Mate in the Tree.* PEEL: *Wander-Thirst.*

⊛ (M) (*(**)) Decca mono 467 916-2.

This is one of the highlights in Decca's very uneven 'The Singers' series. These rare recordings date from the 1930s, yet the freshness of Maggie Teyte's singing, her beautiful characterizations and impeccable diction shine through all the technical limitations of the sound. In operetta she displays the lightest of touches, though there is little wanting in sensuousness or depth of feeling too – the simple *Songs My Mother Taught Me* has one close to tears. Texts and translations can be seen only via a CD ROM drive, but this CD is an essential purchase for all those who love singing of great character, of which little today rivals this. The transfers are good rather than outstanding.

'The Pocket Prima Donna' (with various accompanists): RAVEL: *Shéhérazade.* BERLIOZ: *Nuites d'été: Le spectre de la rose; Absence.* DUPARC: *L'invitation au voyage; Phidylé.* DEBUSSY: *Proses lyriques.* Arias from: PERGOLESI: *La serva padrona* (in French); MONSIGNY: *Rose et Colas; Le déserteur;* GRETRY: *Zémire et Azore; Le tableau parlant;* DOURLEN: *Les oies de Frère Philippe.* OFFENBACH: *La Périchole.*

(BB) (***) Dutton mono CDBP 9274.

Maggie Teyte, born in Wolverhampton, yet made a speciality of the French repertory. In 1908 at the age of twenty she sang Mélisande in Debussy's opera with great success, the second singer after Mary Garden to tackle the role. Though there was a gap in her career after she got married, she returned, and made most of her recordings – including the majority of those here – in the 1940s. Hers is an exceptionally sweet soprano, ideally suited to the microphone in its purity, while her sense of style is unerring, whether in the songs of Ravel, Berlioz and Debussy or the lighter operatic and operetta

repertory represented here, always sung with character and vivacity. The Dutton transfers are first-rate.

Thill, Georges (tenor)

French opera arias (with orchestras conducted by Bigot; Heurteur; Gaubert; Szyfer; Frigara): BERLIOZ: *La Damnation de Faust: Nature immense, impénétrable et fière. Les Troyens à Carthage: Inutiles regrets.* BIZET: *Carmen: La fleur que tu m'avais jetée.* GLUCK: *Alceste: Bannis la crainte et les alarmes.* GOUNOD: *Faust: Quel trouble inconnu me pénètre. Roméo et Juliette: L'amour, l'amour* (with Germaine Feraldy). MASSENET: *Le Cid: O noble lame étincelante; O souverain! O Juge! O père. Werther: Invocation à la nature; Un autre est son époux!.* ROSSINI: *Guillaume Tell: Asile héréditaire.* SAINT-SAENS: *Samson et Dalila: Air de la meule.*

(M) (***) EMI mono CDM7 69548-2.

Georges Thill left an enormous discography, and this selection of 78-r.p.m. discs made between 1927 and 1936 will come as a revelation to younger collectors unacquainted with his work. He made his début at the Paris Opéra in 1924 and soon established himself as the greatest French tenor of his day. The tone is splendidly full and round and the phrasing masterly. In an age when one is lucky to make out what language is being sung, let alone the actual words, his diction is an object lesson. Every word resonates, and yet it is the musical line which remains paramount. At 74 minutes, this is a generous sampling of his recorded legacy, very well transferred and absolutely indispensable to anyone who cares about singing.

Other Vocal and Choral Recitals

Alagna, Roberto (tenor)

'*Sanctus*': *Sacred songs* (with Toulouse Ch. and O, Plasson): BACH/GOUNOD: *Ave Maria.* GOUNOD: *Repentance (O divine Redeemer); St Cecilia Mass: Sanctus; Angelic greeting (Ave Maria).* FRANCK: *Panis angelicus; The Procession.* ADAM: *Midnight, Christians.* FAURE: *O salutaris hostia; Crucifix.* BERLIOZ: *Requiem: Sanctus.* SAINT-SAENS: *Panis angelicus.* BIZET: *Agnus dei.* CAPLET: *Panis angelicus.* L. BOULANGER: *Piè Jesu.*

* EMI CDC5 56206-2

This sumptuously over-produced record has already been a big hit in France. After the opening *Ave Maria*, however, Alagna's singing gets buried in an over-resonantly unclear chorus until the Caplet *Panis angelicus* near the end. The Gounod items are unbelievably mushy.

French opera arias (with ROHCG, O, de Billy) from: BAZIN: *Maître Pathelin.* BERLIOZ: *La Damnation de Faust.* BIZET: *The Pearl Fishers.* BRUNEAU: *L'Attaque du Moulin.* CHERUBINI: *Les Abencerrages.* GLUCK: *Iphigenie en Tauride.* GOUNOD: *Mireille.* GRETRY: *L'Amant jaloux.* HALEVY: *La Juive.* LALO: *Le Roi d'Ys.* MASSENET: *Le Cid.* MEHUL: *Joseph.* MEYERBEER: *L'Africaine.* SAINT-SAENS: *Samson et Dalila* (with London Voices). THOMAS: *Mignon.*

*** EMI CDC5 57012-2.

It was a bold venture for such a leading tenor as Roberto Alagna to present such a formidable collection of fifteen arias, many of which are rarities. From the start his forte has been the French repertory, and here he displays his versatility in operatic excerpts that cover the widest range of styles and periods. They also make dauntingly contrasted demands on any single tenor, from the lyric purity of Bizet's *Pearl Fishers* aria to the heroic scale of Samson's aria in the Saint-Saëns opera, the longest item here, with Alagna's singing not just powerful but finely shaded. The title role in an earlier biblical opera, Méhul's *Joseph*, also demands a heroic style, yet Alagna, a devoted admirer of the legendary French tenor Georges Thill, copes superbly both stylistically and vocally. The high tessitura of some of these arias, demanding in quite a different way, has Alagna producing beautiful head-tones when required. It is especially good to the work of such little-known composers as François Bazin (1816–78) and Massenet's pupil, Alfred Bruneau (1857–1934), while other charming rarities include the Lalo aria and Grétry's *Sérénade*, with its accompanying mandolin. The warmly understanding accompaniment is

from the Covent Garden Orchestra under the brilliant young French conductor, Bertrand de Billy.

Allen, Thomas (baritone)

'*French and English Songs*': (with (i) Roger Vignoles or (ii) Geoffrey Parsons, piano). (i) FAURE: *Automne; Chanson d'amour; Clair de lune; Fleur jetée; L'aurore; 5 Mélodies 'de Venise'; Prison; Le secret; Spleen; Le voyageur.* RAVEL: *Don Quichotte à Dulcinée; 5 Mélodies populaires grecques.* POULENC: *Le travail du peintre.* (ii) VAUGHAN WILLIAMS: *The House of Life; Linden Lea.* PEEL: *In Summertime on Bredon.* BUTTERWORTH: *On the Idle Hill of Summer; 6 Songs from 'A Shropshire Lad'.* QUILTER: *7 Elizabethan Lyrics, Op. 12; Now Sleeps the Crimson Petal.*

(M) *** Virgin VBD5 62059-2 (2).

This two-disc box neatly brings together recitals recorded by Thomas Allen at his full maturity, the French songs in 1993, the English in 1989. Allen's feeling for idiom is unerring, and though no texts are included in this mid-price issue, with just a sketchy note about the repertory, there is compensation when Allen's diction allows every word to be heard, whether in French or English. The selection of items too cannot be faulted, with the fourteen Fauré songs including eight settings of Verlaine, most of them favourites. The stillness of *Prison* for example, so simple and so moving, brings an instant chill of self-identification more intense than the original poem. The Ravel and Poulenc songs, more robust, bring out Allen's vigour and that of Roger Vignoles. Equally sympathetic, Geoffrey Parsons accompanies Allen in the English songs, with Vaughan Williams's *House of Life*, six settings of Rossetti, played with commitment. The Housman settings, the one popular Peel song alongside six by Butterworth, have winning freshness, and it is good to have the inspired Quilter songs so persuasively performed, each of them striking and individual. Well-balanced sound.

'*Songs My Father Taught Me*' (with Malcolm Martineau, piano): PURCELL: *Passing By.* TATE: *The Lark in the Clear Clean Air.* SULLIVAN: *The Lost Chord; My Dearest Heart.* SANDERSON: *Until.* HAYDN WOOD: *Bird of Love Divine; A Brown Bird Singing; It is Only a Tiny Garden; Love's Garden of Roses.* QUILTER: *Drink to Me Only.* CAPEL: *Love, Could I Only Tell Thee.* TRAVERS: *A Mood.* PENN: *Smilin' Through.* S. ADAMS: *The Holy City.* ROBSON: *The Cheviot Hills.* DRESSER: *On the Banks of the*

Wabash, Far Away. LAMBERT: *God's Garden; She is Far from the Land.* PEEL: *In Summertime on Bredon.* DIX: *The Trumpeter.* NOVELLO: *Till the Boys Come Home.* RASBACH: *Trees.* O'CONNER: *The Old House.* COATES: *Bird Songs at Eventide.* MURRAY: *I'll Walk Beside You.*

*** Hyp. CDA 67290.

Sir Thomas Allen explains that in this collection of drawing-room ballads he has tried to 'recapture memories of amateur singers coming to our house in Seaham Harbour', when his father would supervise at the piano. The disc, he says, marks something of a watershed for him, with 'nostalgia and sentiment almost entirely responsible'. Thanks to the singer's mastery and his winningly intimate, intense manner, speaking from the heart, there is not a suspicion of sentimentality even in such numbers as *Love's Garden of Roses, Smilin' Through* or *The Lost Chord*, which could so easily have seemed mawkish. Instead through his magnetism, as Allen intends, one wonders at the simple beauty of the melodies in these once-popular songs. Malcolm Martineau is the most understanding accompanist, equally sensitive in taking a fresh, unexaggerated approach.

American Boychoir, Atlantic Brass Quintet, James Litton

'Trumpets sound, voices ring: A joyous Christmas': arr. WILLCOCKS: *O come all ye faithful; Once in Royal David's city.* RUTTER: *Angel tidings; Star carol; The Lord bless you and keep you.* BRAHMS: *Regina coeli.* ELGAR: *The snow.* GAWTHROP: *Mary speaks.* MENDELSSOHN, arr. WILLCOCKS: *Hark! the herald angels sing.* VAUGHAN WILLIAMS: *Hodie; Lullaby.* FRASER: *This Christmastide (Jessye's carol).* CORELLI: *Concerto grosso in G min. (Christmas), Op. 6/8.* MANZ: *E'en so, Lord Jesus, quickly come.* TELEMANN: *Lobet den Herrn, alle Heiden; Meine Seele, erhebt den Herrn.* CASALS: *Nigra sum. Spiritual: Go tell it on the mountain.*

*** MusicMasters 01612 67076-2.

Gleaming brass fanfares introduce this lively and attractively diverse American collection featuring a gleaming treble line against full brass sonorities. The Americans follow the English King's College tradition at the opening of *Once in Royal David's city* but cap its climax resplendently. The three Rutter carols are ideal for boy trebles and the infectious *Star carol* brings an engagingly light rhythmic touch. Elgar's much less well-known portrayal of *The snow* is very touching, while *Jessye's carol* has one of those gentle but haunting melodies that persist in the memory: its descant is particularly apt, and it builds to an expansive climax. Both *Mary speaks* and Paul Manz's *E'en so, Lord Jesus* are modern carols with an appealing simplicity, matched by Pablo Casals's better-known *Nigra sum.* The two Telemann items featuring famous chorales

are both floridly testing of the boys' resources, and here the faster passages are not always completely secure. But they provide a nice baroque contrast, and it was a happy idea to include a brass transcription of Corelli's famous *Christmas concerto grosso* which, if sounding comparatively robust, is still highly effective when played so well. The choral singing is generally of a high calibre and the recording has a natural, warm ambience and is admirably clear.

Ampleforth Schola Cantorum, Ian Little

'Carols from Ampleforth': arr. WILLCOCKS: *O come all ye faithful; Once in Royal David's city; Unto us a son is born; Sussex carol; God rest you merry, gentlemen.* arr. HOLST: *Personent Hodie.* arr. JACQUES: *Good King Wenceslas.* arr. STAINER/WILLCOCKS: *The first Nowell.* PRAETORIUS: *A great and mighty wonder.* arr. RUTTER: *Angel tidings.* STEWART: *On this day earth shall ring.* WARLOCK: *Adam lay ybounden.* MATHIAS: *Sir Christèmas.* arr. WOOD: *Past three o'clock; Ding, dong! merrily on high.* arr. SULLIVAN: *It came upon the midnight clear.* arr. LEDGER: *Still, still, still.* arr. LITTLE: *Come with torches.* arr. PETTMAN: *The infant king.* GRUBER, arr. LITTLE: *Silent night.* MENDELSSOHN, arr. WILLCOCKS: *Hark! the herald angels sing.*

*** Ampleforth Abbey Records Dig. AARCD 1.

A splendidly robust selection of favourites, with the expansive Abbey acoustic and the superb organ adding much to the listener's pleasure. The sound itself is often thrilling with men and boys both singing ardently; there are a few minor blemishes of ensemble, but nothing to worry about when the projection is so vigorously communicative. Perhaps the rhythm of Mathias's *Sir Christèmas* is a bit heavy, but *On this day earth shall ring* makes a magnificent effect, with the organ adding a final blaze of sound at the close. There are gentler carols too, of course, though not all will like Ian Little's added harmonies at the end of *Silent night*.

Angeles, Victoria de los (soprano)

Opera arias from: VERDI: *Ernani; Otello.* PUCCINI: *La Bohème.* BOITO: *Mefistofele.* ROSSINI: *La Cenerentola.* MASCAGNI: *Cavalleria Rusticana.* CATALANI: *La Wally.* MOZART: *Le nozze di Figaro.* WAGNER: *Tannhäuser; Lohengrin.* MASSENET: *Manon.* GOUNOD: *Faust.*

(M) (***) EMI mono CDH7 63495-2.

Most of the items here are taken from an early LP recital by de los Angeles that has rarely been matched in its glowing beauty and range of expression. The *Willow song* and *Ave Maria* from *Otello* have never been sung with more aching intensity than here, and the same goes for the Mascagni and Catalani arias. The final cabaletta from *Cenerentola* sparkles deliciously with de los Angeles, as so often, conveying the purest of smiles in the voice. The CD reissue is augmented by the valuable Mozart, Massenet, Gounod and Wagner items, all recorded in the days of 78s.

'*Diva*': Arias from ROSSINI: *Il barbiere di Siviglia.* GOUNOD: *Faust.* VERDI: *La Traviata; Otello.* PUCCINI: *La Bohème; Madama Butterfly; Suor Angelica; Gianni Schicchi.* MASCAGNI: *Cavalleria rusticana.* LEONCAVALLO: *Pagliacci.* CATALANI: *La Wally.* MASSENET: *Manon.* BIZET: *Carmen.* GIMENEZ: *La Tempranica.* CABALLERO: *Gigantes y Cabezudos.* BARBIERI: *Il barberillo de Lavaplés.*

(M) *** EMI mono/stereo CDM5 65579-2.

This splendid compilation brings it home how many of the classic sets of the 1950s and 1960s have Victoria de los Angeles as a golden-toned heroine, responding with heartfelt expressiveness. These include the two incomparable Beecham sets of Puccini's *La Bohème* and Bizet's *Carmen*, Gui's Glyndebourne-based set of Rossini's *Barbiere*, Monteux's magical set of Massenet's *Manon*, Cluytens's recording of *Faust*, Serafin's of Puccini's *Il Trittico*, not to mention the RCA New York recording in 1953 of *I Pagliacci*, in which de los Angeles sings charmingly as Nedda communing with the birds – not the role one expects from her. These are well supplemented by two items from her superb (1954) opera recital, including a tenderly beautiful *Ave Maria* from *Otello* and three final numbers from Spanish zarzuelas, making a winning collection overall.

Songs of Spain: **Disc 1: *Traditional songs* (arr. Graciano Tarragó; with Renata Tarragó & Graciano Tarragó, guitars); *Medieval songs* (early 14th century); *Renaissance and Baroque songs* (15th–18th centuries; with Ens., José María Lamaña).**

Disc 2: *Medieval and Renaissance songs of Andalusia; Renaissance songs* (with Ars Musicae de Barcelona, Enrique Gisbert & José María Lamaña).

Disc 3: *19th- and 20th-century arrangements and art songs: Canciones Sefardies* (arr. Manuel Valls; with Jean-Claude Gérard, flute & Oscar Ghighia, guitar); *Canciones populares españoles* (arr. Lorca; with Miguel Zanetti, piano). Songs by MOMPOU; TOLDRA; MONTSALVATGE; RODRIGO **(all with Gonzalo Soriano, piano);** GRANADOS; GURIDU; HALFFTER; TURINA; NIN; VALVERDE **(all with Gerald Moore, piano);** BARRERA & CALLEJA **(arr. Los Angeles, guitar);** MONTSALVATGE: *Madrigal* **(with Barcelona City Orchestra, Garcia Navarro).**

Disc 4: *Songs and opera arias:* GRANADOS: *Colección de tonadillas; Tres majas dolorosa* **(with Gonzalo Soriano, piano);** *Goyescas: La Maja y el ruiseñor.* FALLA: *La vida breve:* excerpts **(with New Philharmonia Orchestra or Paris Conservatoire Orchestra, Rafael Frühbeck de Burgos. 1971 New York Recital (with Alicia de Larrocha, piano): Songs by** LITERES; DE LASERNA; GIMENEZ. GRANADOS:

Canciones amatorias. FALLA: *7 Canciones populares españolas.*

(M) *** EMI mono/stereo CMS5 66937-2 (4).

Issued to celebrate the singer's seventy-fifth birthday in November 1998, this four-disc compilation of de los Angeles in her native Spanish repertory is a delight. Two of the four discs are devoted to traditional, medieval and renaissance songs, accompanied by the guitarist Renata Tarragó, as well as by her mentor in early music, José María Lamaña, with his own Ars Musicae of Barcelona and a British group. Recorded over two decades between 1950 and 1971, the set also includes de los Angeles's contribution to the closing ceremony of the 1992 Barcelona Olympic Games (the folk/madrigal *El cant dels ocells* of Montsalvatge), the voice carefully husbanded but still golden.

Overall, this lavish survey represents a cross-section of the varied types of art song which were current in the rich period of Spanish music between the thirteenth and sixteenth centuries, and then moves on to include key nineteenth- and twentieth-century repertoire. Earliest are monodic cantigas associated with the Virgin Mary, but most of the rest are secular, including a group of songs of the Sephardic Jewish tradition, also romances and villancicos (brief ballads), songs with vihuela accompaniments and madrigals – one might quibble about their presentation by a solo voice – of a later period. The first disc opens with eighteen traditional songs arranged by Graciano Tarregó, with guitar accompaniments, and the result has a captivating simplicity; moreover the mono recordings (from 1950–52) give a most natural presence for the voice.

Since the early days of her career, de los Angeles has been associated with the Ars Musicae ensemble of Barcelona. They play here on authentic instruments – fidulas, recorders, lute, vihuela de mano, viols and lira da braccio – and if the more complex later songs from the Courts of Charles V and Philip II hardly match the finest of our own Elizabethan songs, they are exquisitely done by de los Angeles and her friends. The Spanish folksongs arranged by the poet Lorca are mainly dance-songs, while the main Sephardic collection, arranged by Valls, gives an admirable sample of the music which was developing among Spanish Jews in the late Middle Ages, exotic and individual. The later Granados and Falla items are better known and no less winning.

De los Angeles made her recording début with the two Falla arias years ago; these later versions come from 1962. The collection ends with her live New York recital of 1971, where she forms a symbiotic partnership with her Catalan contemporary, Alicia de Larrocha, as accompanist, including the best loved of her encore numbers, Valverde's *Clavelitos* and *Adios Granada*, and ending with a riotous *Zapateado*. The voice is as fresh as ever. What matters most is that this is all music which inspires the singer to her fullest, most captivating artistry. The documentation could be more extensive, but full texts and translations are included.

Arias from: FAURE: *Requiem.* HANDEL: *Acis and Galatea.* ROSSINI: *Il barbiere di Siviglia.* PUCCINI: *La Bohème; Madama Butterfly; Suor Angelica; Gianni Schicchi.* LEONCAVALLO: *Pagliacci.* MASSENET: *Manon; Werther.* PURCELL: *Dido and Aeneas.* OFFENBACH: *Les contes d'Hoffmann.* VERDI: *La Traviata; Simon Boccanegra.* BIZET: *Carmen.* GOUNOD: *Faust.* **Lieder and songs:** MENDELSSOHN: *Auf Flügeln des Gesanges.* GRIEG: *Ich liebe dich.* BRAHMS: *Wiegenlied.* DVORAK: *Als die alte Mutter.* MARTINI: *Plaisir d'amour.* DELIBES: *Les filles de Cadiz.* YRADIER: *La Paloma.* CHUECA/VALVERDE: *Tango de la menegilda.* LORENTE: *Canción de la gitana.* FALLA: *El amor brujo:* excerpts; *Siete canciones populares españolas.* CANTELOUBE: *3 Chants d'Auvergne.* MOZART: *Exsultate jubilate, K.165.*

(BB) *** Disky Royal Classics Vocal Double (ADD) DCL 703972 (2).

The Royal Classics series of Vocal Doubles is just as enticing with its portraits of star singers as it is in the comparable coverage of conductors listed above, and there is surely no better place to start than with the golden-voiced Victoria de los Angeles. The well-chosen and remarkably comprehensive selection above takes a broad swath through her wide-ranging repertoire, from opera to Lieder, not forgetting Spanish song, happily framed by famous ecclesiastical items by Fauré and Mozart. As expected in this fine series, the EMI transfers are of the highest quality, there is charm in plenty, and this makes for a generous, treasurable and inexpensive collection, even if the documentation is limited to titles and publication dates.

Anonymous 4

'The Lily and the lamb' (Chant and polyphony from medieval England): *Conducti, Hymns, Motets, Sequences; Antiphon: Ave regina coelorum.*

*** HM HMU 907125.

The Anonymous Four (Ruth Cunningham, Marsha Genensky, Susan Hellauer and Johanna Rose) are an American vocal quartet whose voices merge into a particularly pleasing blend. They came together in 1986, bringing with them a variety of musical skills, including instrumental proficiency and a musicological background. The group focuses on medieval music, mainly sacred, spanning 500 years, from the eleventh to the fourteenth century. It is perhaps appropriate that this first collection should be devoted to hymns, sequences and motets dedicated to the Virgin Mary.

Women in medieval times identified with Mary and in particular her suffering as she saw her son dying on the cross. The second item in this programme, a monodic hymn, begins with the words 'The gentle lamb spread on the cross, hung all bathed with blood'. For women of those times, death was an everyday event, especially since only a small propor-

tion of their many children survived into adulthood and they saw their young loved ones succumb to disease and other causes. The singers here blend their voices into one, whether singing monody or in simple polyphony, as in the sequence *Stillat in stelam radium*, or the beautiful motet *Veni mater gracie*. The voices are heard floating in an ecclesiastic acoustic and the effect is mesmeric.

'An English Ladymass' (13th- and 14th-century chant and polyphony in honour of the Virgin Mary): *Alleluias, Gradual, Hymn, Introit, Kyrie, Motets, Offertory, Rondellus, Sequences, Songs.*

**(*) HM HMU 907080

In medieval times most large churches and cathedrals had a lady chapel, where a Ladymass could be sung regularly to the Virgin Mary. And these still exist today in larger Catholic cathedrals, like Chartres in France. They usually have an extraordinary atmosphere and one watches with respect as young mothers not only attend alone but also bring their children to present to the statue of the Virgin. Here the Anonymous Four have arranged their own Mass sequence with the Propers interspersed with appropriate motets, hymns, a Gradual and Alleluia, finally concluding with the hymn *Ave Maris stella*. In doing so they make their own homage to the Virgin Mother which is well planned. The music is beautifully sung, although this is perhaps not one of their most potent collections.

'Miracles of Sant'Iago' (Medieval chant and polyphony for St James from the Codex Calixtinus): *Agnus dei trope, Benedicamus tropes, Kyrie trope, Antiphon, Conducti, Hymns, Invitatory, Offertory, Prosae, Responsories.*

*** HM HMU 907156.

The Cathedral of Santiago in Compostela is the home of a manuscript of five books called collectively *Jacobus*, and its music was designed to be sung by groups of young French boy-trebles. It proves ideal material for the Anonymous Four and its musical interest is immediately demonstrated by the brilliantly decorated Benedicamus trope *Vox nostra resonet*. Much of the music is plainchant, but the early examples of two-part polyphony are very striking. Again the singing here is magnetic and the warm resonance of the recording very flattering.

'Love's illusion' (French motets on courtly love texts from the 13th-century Montpellier Codex): *Plus bele que flor / Quant revient / L'autrier joer; Puisque bele dame m'eime; Amours mi font souffrir / En mai; Ne sai, que je die; Si je chante / Bien doi amer; Or ne sai je que devenir / puisque d'amer; Hé Dieus, de si haut si bas / Maubatus; Celui en qui / La bele estoile / La bele, en qui; Qui d'amours se plaint; Amours, dont je sui / L'autrier, au douz mois / Chose Tassin; Au cuer ai un mal / Ja ne m'en repentirai / Jolietement; Quant voi la fleur; Quant se depart / Onques ne sai amer; Joliement / Quant voi la florete / Je sui joliete; Amor potest conqueri / Adamorem sequitur; Ce que je tieng*

/ Certes mout / Bone compaignie; J'ai si bien mon cuer assiz / Aucun m'ont; Ne m'oubliez mie; J'ai mis toute ma pensee / Je n'en puis; Blanchete / Quant je pens; Dame, que je n'os noumer / Amis donc est / Lonc tans a; Li savours de mon desir / Li grant desir / Non veul mari; Entre Copin / Je me cuidoie / Bele Ysabelos; S'on me regarde / Prennés i garde / Hé, mi enfant; Quant yver la bise ameine; Ne m'a pas oublié; On doit fin[e] Amor / La biauté; Ja n'amerai autre que cele; Quant je parti de m'amie.

*** HM HMU 907109.

For this programme the Anonymous Four have moved away from liturgical music and chosen twenty-nine thirteenth-century motets from the Montpellier Codex, setting courtly love texts with simple and affecting polyphony. It is remarkable how the atmosphere of this music brings a more secular, plaintive quality. The means are the same but the expressive result is different, for the words are about the joys and regrets and the feelings of love. Many of these songs are dolorous but *Ne sai, que je die* (about pride, hypocrisy and avarice) and *Qui l'amours se plaint* are both dance songs. This is one of the most attractive of this fine group's collections. They are obviously moved, as women, by the words they sing, and they find remarkable variety of expressive feeling here. Occasionally a drone is added under the melodic line to telling effect, and one never misses an instrumental backing. The recording is well up to standard. A splendid disc.

'On Yoolis night' (Medieval carols and motets): Antiphons, Carols, Hymns, Motets, Responsory, Rondella, Songs.

*** HM HMU 907099.

This is a delightful collection. The carol *Alleluia, A new work* and the anonymous setting of *Ave Maria* are both enchanting discoveries, and many of these items have that curious, Christmassy colouring. The dance song *Gabriel from heaven-king* and the lovely *Lullay: I saw a sweet seemly sight* are matched by *As I lay on Yoolis night*, while the closing *Nowel* is wonderfully joyful. The simple medieval implied harmonies in no way inhibit the character but increase the special colour of these carols, which are sung tenderly or with great spirit by this excellent group. Here is a record to lay in store for next Christmas, but to play at other times too.

'A Star in the East' (Medieval Hungarian Christmas music): Alleluias, Antiphons, Communion, Evangelium, Gradual, Hymns, Introit, Lectio, Motet, Offertory, Sanctus, Songs, Te Deum.

*** HM HMU 907139.

The repertoire here is comparatively unsophisticated but full of charm, and the singing has the right kind of innocence. The programme came about by accident. While one of the group was researching the music of Hildegard of Bingen at Columbia University Library, a book of Hungarian Christmas music fell off the shelf at the researcher's feet, inviting its performance. There is not a great deal of polyphony here, but that is not a feature of many of our own favourite Christmas carols either. There is no lack of melody. Excellent recording and splendid documentation.

'A Portrait': excerpts from 'Miracles of Sant'Iago'; 'The Lily and the lamb'; 'A Star in the East'; 'Love's illusion'; 'An English Ladymass'; 'On Yoolis night'.

(B) *** HM HMX 2907210.

Here is a carefully chosen selection of highlights from the six CDs listed above. It's well worth sampling to find out whether the pure yet richly expressive vocal style of this remarkable female group will tempt you to explore further in one direction or another.

Anthony, Susan (soprano)

'Portrait': Scenes and arias (with Slovak Radio Symphony Orchestra, Angelov) from: R. STRAUSS: *Salome; Ariadne auf Naxos; Elektra; Die Frau ohne Schatten.* WAGNER: *Tannhäuser; Lohengrin.* CHAUSSON: *Le roi Arthaus.* MENOTTI: *The Consul.*

(BB) *** Arte Nova 74321 86894-2.

Not many sopranos sing with such firm purity as the American, Susan Anthony, in this demanding repertory, with the four Strauss heroines including Salome, Ariadne, Chrysothemis in *Elektra* and the Empress in *Die Frau ohne Schatten*. It is particularly good to have a portrait of Salome in the final ghoulish scene which retains something girlish in the characterization, even if the result is less sinister than it can be. The two Wagner items, *Elsa's Dream* from *Tannhäuser* and *Elisabeth's Prayer* from *Lohengrin*, are more predictably suited to such a creamy voice, with phrasing immaculately moulded. It is good too to have such a rarity as the heroine's big aria from Chausson's *Le roi Arthus* and two poignant numbers from Menotti, including Magda's heartfelt plea in *The Consul*, 'To This We've Come'. This is outstanding among soprano recital discs on bargain label, with full, clear sound.

Ars Nova, Bo Holten

Portuguese polyphony: CARDOSO: *Lamentatio; Magnificat secundi toni.* LOBO: *Audivi vocem de caelo; Pater peccavi.* MAGALHAES: *Vidi aquam; Missa O Soberana luz; Commissa mea pavesco.* MANUEL DA FONSECA: *Beata viscera.* BARTOLOMEO TROSYLHO: *Circumdederunt.* PEDRO DE ESCOBAR: *Clamabat autem mulier.*

(BB) *** Naxos Dig. 8.553310.

In every respect this is an outstanding anthology. Apart from the major items from the Portuguese 'famous three' contemporaries, Cardoso, Lôbo and (the least-known) Filippe de Magalhães, which are discussed above under their respective Composer entries in our main volume, the motets by the earlier figures, Pedro de Escobar (c. 1465–1535), Bartolomeo

Trosylho (c. 1500–c. 1567) and Manuel da Fonseca (*maestre da capela* at Braga Cathedral in the mid-sixteenth century), are all touchingly, serenely beautiful, if perhaps less individual. The singing of this Danish Choir is superb and so is the Naxos recording. Texts and translations are provided, although for some reason they are printed separately. A unique bargain of the highest quality.

Augér, Arleen (soprano)

'*Love songs*' (with Dalton Baldwin, piano): COPLAND: *Pastorale; Heart, we will forget him.* OBRADORS: *Del Cabello más sutil.* OVALLE: *Azulao.* R. STRAUSS: *Ständchen; Das Rosenband.* MARX: *Selige Nacht.* POULENC: *Fleurs.* CIMARA: *Stornello.* QUILTER: *Music, when soft voices die; Love's philosophy.* O. STRAUS: *Je t'aime.* SCHUMANN: *Widmung; Du bist wie eine Blume.* MAHLER: *Liebst du um Schönheit.* TURINA: *Cantares.* LIPPE: *How do I love thee?* COWARD: *Conversation piece: I'll follow my secret heart.* GOUNOD: *Serenade.* SCHUBERT: *Liebe schwärmt auf allen Wegen.* BRIDGE: *Love went a-riding.* FOSTER: *Why, no one to love.* DONAUDY: *O del mio amato ben.* BRITTEN (arr.): *The Salley Gardens.* LOEWE: *Camelot: Before I gaze at you again.*

✿ *** Delos Dig. D/CD 3029.

This extraordinarily wide-ranging recital is a delight from the first song to the last. Arleen Augér opens with Copland and closes with *Camelot*, and she is equally at home in the music by Roger Quilter (*Love's philosophy* is superbly done), Noël Coward and the *Rückert* song of Mahler. Britten's arrangement of *The Salley Gardens*, ravishingly slow, is another highlight. The layout of the recital could hardly have been managed better: each song creates its new atmosphere readily, but seems to be enhanced by coming after the previous choice. Dalton Baldwin's accompaniments are very much a partnership with the singing, while the playing itself is spontaneously perceptive throughout. With a good balance and a very realistic recording, this projects vividly like a live recital.

(i) Bach Choir, Sir David Willcocks; (ii) Philip Jones Brass Ensemble, Philip Jones

'*In dulci jubilo – A Festival of Christmas*': (i; ii) arr. WILLCOCKS: *Fanfare – O come all ye faithful; Gabriel's message; Angelus ad Virginem; Ding dong! merrily on high; God rest you merry, gentlemen; Unto us a son is born; Once in Royal David's city; Hush my dear, lie still and remember; Away in a manger; Sussex carol.* TRAD.: *A virgin most pure; In dulci jubilo.* RUTTER: *Shepherd's pipe carol; Star carol.* GRUBER: *Stille Nacht.* MENDELSSOHN: *Hark the herald angels sing.* (ii) BACH: *Christmas oratorio: chorales: Nun seid Ihr wohl gerochen; Ach, mein herzliebes Jesulein.* TRAD.: *Lord Jesus hath a garden; Come all ye shepherds; Il est né.* arr. IVESON: *We three kings; Jingle bells – Deck the hall; The holly and the ivy.* arr. RUTTER: *Wassail song; We wish you a merry Christmas.*

(B) **(*) Decca Eclipse (IMS) 448 980-2.

The titling and documentation of this otherwise admirable Eclipse collection is misleading. It is basically an early (1980) digital concert by the Bach Choir, colourfully accompanied by the Philip Jones Brass Ensemble, conducted by Sir David Willcocks. Fresh simplicity is the keynote: the brass fanfares bring a touch of splendour, but the accompaniments are not over-scored. *Silent night* has never sounded more serene, and the other carols bring a wide variety of mood, while the two engaging Rutter pieces make a further refreshing contrast. However, as a central interlude there is a selection of ten items taken from a separate collection of Christmas music by Philip Jones and his Brass Ensemble without the choir, recorded two years later, also in the Kingsway Hall. Once again sound and playing are of very high quality. Appropriately framed by two chorales from Bach's *Christmas oratorio*, these arrangements are again effectively varied, with *Jingle bells* and *We wish you a merry Christmas* making a sparkling contrast with the gentler and more solemn music. But it must be said that carols are meant to include the words!

Baker, Dame Janet (mezzo-soprano)

Radio Recordings: HAYDN: *Arianna a Naxos* (cantata). SCHUMANN: *Frauenliebe und Leben, Op. 42.* SCHUBERT: *Der blinde Knabe; Totengräber-Weise.* WOLF: *Die ihr schwebet; Geh', Geliebter, geh'jetzt!* SCHUMANN: *Meine Rose; Der Page.* R. STRAUSS: *Befreit; Heimliche Aufforderung; Morgen!.*

(M) *** BBC (ADD) BBCL 4049-2.

These vintage radio recordings from 1968–70 find Dame Janet Baker in glorious voice. Both the Haydn scena and Schumann song-cycle were recorded live at Snape Maltings, while the mixed Lieder recital was done in the studio, with all three conveying the urgency and spontaneity of live performance. Compared with Dame Janet's studio recordings of this same repertory they bring out even more strikingly the vehement intensity of her singing as well as its heart-stopping beauty and glorious contrasts of tone-colour. Never have the changing emotions of *Frauenliebe und Leben* been so vividly conveyed on disc, from ecstasy to exhilaration to agony. It is a pity no texts are given.

HAYDN: *19 Scottish Folk Songs* (with Yehudi Menuhin & George Malcolm, harpsichord). BEETHOVEN: *5 Scottish Folk Songs* (with Ross Pople). CAMPIAN: *Never Love Unless you can; Oft have I Sighed; If Thou Longest so Much to Learn; Fain Would I Wed;* DOWLAND: *Come Again* (with

Robert Spencer, lute); ARNE: *Where the Bee Sucks* (with Spencer & Douglas Whittaker, flute). BOYCE: *Tell me Lovely Shepherd.* MONRO: *My Lovely Celia.* PURCELL: *Sleep, Adam, Sleep, Lord, What is Man?* (with Isepp & Gauntlett)

*** Testament SBT 1241.

This Testament issue, superbly transferred, generously brings together two of Dame Janet Baker's most charming discs, long neglected. The Haydn and Beethoven folk-song settings accompanied by Yehudi Menuhin and George Malcolm (on the harpsichord in Haydn, on the piano in Beethoven) stem from a project at the Windsor Festival in the 1970s, when Menuhin was music director. These studio recordings reflect the joy of discovery and corporate music-making on the highest level. The English songs come from a recording which Dame Janet made earlier in 1967 with the Elizabethan songs by Dowland and Campian accompanied on the lute by Robert Spencer and with the flautist, Douglas Whittaker joining the team in the popular Arne setting of *Where the Bee Sucks*. Dame Janet is in glorious voice, with well-balanced EMI sound still very vivid.

'*Janet Baker sings*' (with Gerald Moore, piano): FAURE: *Automne; Prison; Soir; Fleur jetée; En sourdine; Notre amour; Mai; Chanson du pêcheur; Clair de lune.* STANFORD: *La belle dame sans merci.* PARRY: *Proud Masie; O mistress mine.* William BUSCH: *Rest.* WARLOCK: *Pretty ringtime.* VAUGHAN WILLIAMS: *Linden Lea.* GURNEY: *Fields are full.* BRITTEN: *Corpus Christi carol.* IRELAND: *Sally Gardens.* QUILTER: *Love's Philosophy.* SCHUBERT: *Am Grabe; Anselmos; Abendstern; Die Vögel; Strophe aus Die Götte; Griechenlands; Gondelfahrer; Auflösung.* Richard STRAUSS: *Morgen!; Befreit.*

✪ (M) *** EMI (ADD) CDM5 65009-2.

Just after he had officially retired, in the late 1960s, Gerald Moore returned to the recording studio to accompany Janet Baker, an artist whom he counted high among the many great singers he had accompanied in his career. This recital brings together a sequence of magical perfomances of songs especially dear to Dame Janet, with the voice consistently golden in tone. The Fauré group brings out her intense love of singing in French, and her devotion to the German Lied shines out equally in Schubert and Strauss. The group of ten English songs demonstrates that this neglected genre has comparable claims in beauty and intensity, with such favourite items as Vaughan Williams's *Linden Lea* and Quilter's *Love's Philosophy* given heartfelt performances. Even this singer rarely sang with more beauty than here.

RAVEL: *Shéhérazade* (with New Philh. O, Barbirolli). CHAUSSON: *Poème de l'amour et de la mer.* DUPARC: *Phidylé; La vie antérieure; Le manoir de Rosamonde; Au pays où se fait la guerre; L'invitation au voyage* (all with LSO, Previn). SCHUMANN: *Frauenliebe und Leben* (with

Barenboim). BRAHMS: *Vier ernste Gesänge, Op. 121* (with Previn); *2 Lieder, with viola, Op. 91* (with Aronowitz, Previn); *4 Duets, Op. 28* (with Fischer-Dieskau, Barenboim).

(B) *** EMI Double Fforte (ADD) CZS5 68667-2 (2).

Dame Janet Baker was always at her finest in French music, and with her 1967 performance of *Shéhérazade* she inspired Barbirolli to one of his most glowing performances in this atmospherically scored music; her range of tone and her natural sympathy for the French language make for heartwarming singing which has a natural intensity. The account of Chausson's *Poème de l'amour et de la mer* is comparably glorious and heartfelt, both radiant and searching, so that this picture of love in two aspects, first emergent, then past, has a sharpness of focus often denied it; in this she is superbly supported by Previn and the LSO. Their partnership is hardly less persuasive in the five Duparc *mélodies* which the composer orchestrated himself – each a jewelled miniature of breathtaking beauty, with the extra richness and colour of the orchestral accompaniment adding to the depth and intensity of the exceptionally sensitive word-settings, especially in the greatest of them all, *Phidylé*.

It was Schumann's *Frauenliebe und Leben* that helped to establish Baker's early reputation, and she returned to this favourite cycle in early maturity with renewed freshness in the light of deeper experience. Where on her Saga record (now deleted) she transposed most of the earlier songs down a full tone, the later version keeps them in the original keys. Then by contrast it is the later songs which she transposes, reserving her warmer tones for those expressions of motherhood. The wonder, the inwardness, are even more intense, while the final song in some ways brings the most remarkable performance of all ('Now you have hurt me'), not at all a conventional expression of mourning. With Barenboim an endlessly imaginative – if sometimes reticent – accompanist, this is another classic example of Baker's art.

The Brahms Lieder were the last to be recorded, in 1977, and the gravity and nobility of her singing in the *Four Serious Songs* underline the weight of the biblical words while presenting them with a far wider and more beautiful range of tone-colour than is common. André Previn's piano is placed rather backwardly, but his rhythmic control provides fine support, and in the two viola songs, which are ravishingly sung and played, these artists are partnered by the late Cecil Aronowitz, making his last appearance on record.

To cap the recital come the four varied duets of Op. 28, in which Baker is joined by Dietrich Fischer-Dieskau, recorded at a live recital at London's Queen Elizabeth Hall in 1969. The vivacious closing *Der Jäger und sein Liebchen* makes a spiritedly vivacious coda to a collection which could hardly be bettered. Even if the presentation here omits texts and translations, this set still makes an amazing bargain.

'*Italian love songs*' (with ASMF, Marriner, James Tyler, lute, Nicholas Kraemer, harpsichord):

GIORDANI: *Caro mio ben.* CACCINI: *Amarilli mia bella.* STRADELLA: *Ragion sempre addita.* SARRI: *Sen corre l'agnelletta.* CESTI: *Intorno all'idol mio.* LOTTI: *Pur dicesti, o bocca bella.* A. SCARLATTI: *Già il sole dal Gange; Sento ne core.* BONONCINI: *Deh più a me non v'ascondete.* DURANTE: *Danza fanciulla gentile.* CALDARA: *Sebben crudele me fai languir; Selve amiche.* PERGOLESI: *Ogni pena più spietata.* MARTINI: *Plaisir d'amore.* PICCINI: *O notte o dea del mistero.* PAISIELLO: *Nel cor più non mi sento.*

(B) **(*) Ph. Virtuoso (ADD) 434 173-2.

A delightful collection of Italian classical arias (the original title of the CD was '*Arie amorose*'), marred only by the absence of libretti and translations. The documentation is a marginal improvement on the original LP, but still inadequate when, apart from *Caro mio ben* and *Plaisir d'amore*, most of these pieces are better known to singers than the wider musical public. However, the programme is cleverly arranged to contrast expressive with sprightly music, and Baker's wide range of tonal gradation and beautiful phrasing are matched by an artless lightness of touch in the slighter numbers. The accompaniments are intimate and tasteful: there is no more fetching example than Pergolesi's *Ogni pena più spietata* with its deft bassoon obbligato (Graham Sheen) or the short closing song with harpsichord – Paisiello's *Nel cor più non mi sento*. The recording has a warm acoustic and the resonance is kind to the voice without loss of orchestral detail.

'*The Legendary Dame Janet Baker*' (with various orchestras and conductors): HANDEL: *Joshua: O had I Jubal's lyre. Atalanta: Care selve. Serse: Ombra mai fù. Judas Maccabaeus: Father of Heav'n. Ariodante: Dopo notte. Rodelinda: Dove sei, amato bene?* ELGAR: *Sea pictures: Where corals lie.* GLUCK: *Orfeo ed Euridice: Che faro senza Euridice; Che puro ciel.* MARTINI: *Plaisir d'amore.* MOZART: *Così fan tutte: E amore un ladroncello; Ah, scostati! Smanie implacabili. mozart: La clemenza di Tito: Non più di fiori.* CACCINI: *Amarilli mia bella.* PURCELL: *Dido and Aeneas: When I am laid in earth.* GIORDANO: *Caro mio ben.*

*** Ph. (ADD) 465 253-2.

There are a number of outstanding Baker recitals available, at least two of which have earned Rosettes. Most of them are better documented than this, which although offered at premium price offers nothing but titles and performance details. But it cannot be said that the present 74-minute collection is not well compiled, with all the items except two dating from between 1972 and 1978 when the voice was warm and fresh and Dame Janet's interpretations had the maturity of experience. The two earlier exceptions are even more desirable, her very moving account of Purcell's *Dido's lament* from 1962, and the memorable *Where corals lie* from *Sea pictures*, recorded with Barbirolli in 1965, kindly contributed by EMI. As for the rest, the Handel arias are all gloriously sung, and the two

excerpts from *Orfeo ed Euridice* are superb. It hardly needs saying that Dame Janet is a fine Mozartean, and the Italian songs are delightful, especially Giordano's *Caro mio ben.*

DUPARC: *L'invitation au voyage; Philydé.* SCHUBERT: *Die Forelle; Ave Maria; An die Musik; An Sylvia.* R. STRAUSS: *Befreit; Morgen!* HAYDN: *O can ye sew cushions.* BEETHOVEN: *The sweetest lad was Jamie.* DEBUSSY: *Chansons de Bilitis.* FAURE: *Notre amour; Clair de lune.* Excerpts and arias from: ELGAR: *Sea Pictures; The Dream of Gerontius.* MAHLER: *Rückert Lieder.* HANDEL: *Messiah.* BERLIOZ: *La damnation de Faust; Nuits d'été.* RAVEL: *Shéhérazade.* MENDELSSOHN: *Elijah.* BACH: *Christmas oratorio; Cantata No. 161.* WAGNER: *Wesendonck Lieder.* MONTEVERDI: *L'incoronazione di Poppea.*

(BB) *** Disky Royal Classics Vocal Double DCL 703942 (2).

Although many collectors will already have some of these items in the complete recordings from which they are taken (Elgar's *Sea Pictures* with Barbirolli, for instance), this is hard to surpass as a summary of Dame Janet's achievement over a wide range of repertoire. For whether it is in French *mélodie*, Schubert and Mahler Lieder, or the glorious *He was despised* from Handel's *Messiah*, the touching *Wo unto them who forsake Him* from Mendelssohn's *Elijah*, or the sensuous delicacy and passion of Ravel's *La flûte enchantée*, the vocal richness and artistry emerge as individually as ever. The programme ends rapturously with the Angel's farewell and the closing pages of Elgar's *Gerontius*. The selection is generous and inexpensive, the transfers excellent, but no back-up documentation or texts and translations are included.

'*The Very Best of Janet Baker*': BACH: *Christmas Oratorio: Bereite dich, Zion* (with ASMF, Marriner). HANDEL: *Messiah: He Was Despised* (with ECO, Mackerras). MENDELSSOHN: *Elijah: O Rest in the Lord* (with New Philh. O, Burgos). *On Wings of Song* (with Parsons, piano). BRAHMS: *Alto Rhapsody* (with John Aldis Choir, LPO, Boult). *Geistliches Wiegenlied* (with Previn, piano and Aronowitz, viola). MAHLER: *Rückert Lieder: Ich bim der Welt abhanden gekommen* (with Hallé O, Barbirolli). DUPARC: *L'Invitation au voyage* (with LSO, Previn). DURUFLÉ: *Requiem: Pie Jesu* (with Butt, organ, cond. Ledger). ELGAR: *The Dream of Gerontius: Angel's Farewell* (with Ambrosian Singers, Sheffield Philh. Ch., Hallé O, Barbirolli); *Sea Pictures* (with LSO, Barbirolli). VAUGHAN WILLIAMS: *Linden Lea.* BRITTEN: *A Boy Was Born: Corpus Christi Carol.* WARLOCK: *Pretty Ring Time.* FAURE: *Clair de Lune; Prison; Soir.* SCHUBERT: *Ave Maria; Gretchen am Spinnrade; Wiegenlied* (with Moore, piano); *An die Musik; An Sylvia; Auf dem Wasser zu singen; Du bist die Ruh'; Die Forelle; Heidenröslein; Nacht und Träume* (with Parsons, piano). SCHUMANN: *Du Ring an meinem Finger; Mondnacht* (with

Barenboim, piano). R. STRAUSS: *Befreit; Morgen* (with Moore, piano).

(B) *** EMI (ADD) CZS5 75069-2 (2).

A self-recommending recital, imaginatively chosen and well assembled, logically progressing from Dame Janet's deeply moving performances of Bach and Handel, to her incomparable accounts of Elgar's *Sea Pictures* and the *Angel's Farewell* from *Gerontius* – both offering the finest accounts yet committed to disc – as well as some of her finest Lieder performances. Her extraordinary ability to communicate is apparent throughout this programme and as gives the music a fresh perspective; her strongly characterized reading of *Die Forelle* makes it much more of a fun song than usual, and similarly, Geoffrey Parson's naughty springing of the accompaniment of *An Sylvia* (echoed by the singer) gives a twinkle to a song that can easily be treated too seriously. Her heartfelt expressiveness in such numbers as *Gretchen am Spinnrade* and her equal mastery of the French repertoire complete the picture. There are no texts or translations, but a well-written biography relevant to the music is included, and the CD is inexpensive while the transfers are excellent.

Baroque opera: 'Treasures of baroque opera'

'*Treasures of baroque opera*': MONTEVERDI: *L'Orfeo: Toccata* (New London Consort, Pickett); *Prologo: Ritornello . . . Dal mio Permesso amato* (Catherine Bott). ARNE: *Rosamond: Rise, glory, rise* (Emma Kirkby). *Artaxerxes: The soldier tir'd.* PICCINI: *La buona figliuola: Furia di donna.* HANDEL: *Alcina: Tornami a vagheggiar* (Dame Joan Sutherland). *Rinaldo: March and Battle* (ECO, Bonynge); *Armida dispietatat! … Lascia ch'io pianga* (Bernadette Greevy). *Rodelinda: Vivi, tiranno* (Marilyn Horne). *Atalanta: Care selve* (Luciano Pavarotti). PURCELL: *Dido and Aeneas: Dido's lament.* CAVALLI: *La Calisto: Ardo, sospiro e piango* (Dame Janet Baker). RAMEAU: *Hippolyte et Aricie: Puisque Pluton est inflexible* (John Shirley-Quirk). *Le Temple de la gloire: Overture* (ECO, Raymond Leppard). *Les indes galantes: Soleil on a détruit tes superbes asiles* (Gérard Souzay). *PERGOLESI: a serva padrona: Stizzoso, mio stizzoso* (Teresa Berganza).

❀ (M) *** Decca ADD/DDD 458 217-2.

This is truly a treasure-chest – one of the finest collections of baroque arias ever assembled on disc, and certainly the most generous, with sixteen excerpts, all performed superbly. The overall standard is astonishingly high, with almost every item a plum. After Philip Pickett's dramatic opening *Toccata*, Catherine Bott is in glorious voice as La Musica in *Orfeo* and Emma Kirkby's Arne is equally fresh. The inclusion of Dame Janet Baker's achingly vulnerable portrayal of the betrayed Dido is predictable, but her account of

Diana's *Ardo, sospiro e piango* from Cavalli's *La Calisto* is hardly less moving. On a lighter note comes Teresa Berganza's deliciously coquettish *Stizzoso, mio stizzoso* from Pergolesi's *La serva padrona*. Richard Bonynge introduces the Handelian sequence with the *March and Battle* from *Rinaldo* which is more familiar as 'Let us take the road' in *The Beggar's Opera*, and then Bernadette Greevy richly reminds us that Almirena's *Lascia ch'io pianga* is as noble a melody as Handel ever wrote (undecorated, but none the worse for that).

She is followed by Marilyn Horne's astounding demonstration of vocal bravura as she leaps from one register to another and back again in *Vivi, tiranno* from *Rodelinda*. The art of Joan Sutherland is well represented (with all the recordings coming from the early 1960s, when the voice was at its sweetest) and it is she who ends the programme with sparkling virtuosity in *Tornami a vagheggiar*. The recording throughout is brilliant and atmospheric in Decca's best manner; the disc is handsomely packaged and full translations are included. Not to be missed!

Bartoli, Cecilia (mezzo-soprano)

Italian songs (with András Schiff): BEETHOVEN: *Ecco quel fiero istante!; Che fa il mio bene?* (2 versions); *T'intendo, si, mio cor; Dimmi, ben mio; In questa tomba oscura.* MOZART: *Ridente la calma.* HAYDN: *Arianna a Naxos.* SCHUBERT: *Vedi quanto adoro ancora ingrato!; Io vuo'cantar di Cadmo; La pastorella; Non t'accostar all'urna; Guarda, che bianca luna; Se dall'Etra; Da quel sembiante appresi; Mio ben ricordati; Pensa, che questo istante; Mi batte'l cor!*

*** Decca 440 297-2.

Bartoli and Schiff make a magical partnership, each challenging the other in imagination. These seventeen Italian songs and one cantata by the great Viennese masters make a fascinating collection, not just Haydn and Mozart but Beethoven and Schubert as well. Beethoven's darkly intense *In questa tomba oscura* is well enough known but, as sung by Bartoli, with András Schiff adding sparkle, the lighter songs are just as magnetic, with Beethoven showing his versatility in two astonishingly contrasted settings of the same love-poem.

'*A Portrait*': Arias from: MOZART: *La clemenza di Tito; Così fan tutte; Le nozze di Figaro; Don Giovanni. Concert aria: Ch'io mi scordi di te?* ROSSINI: *Semiramide; Maometto II; La Cenerentola. Songs: Bella crudèle.* PARISOTTI: *Se tu m'ami.* GIORDANO: *Caro mio ben.* CACCINI: *Amarilli.* SCHUBERT: *La pastorella; Metastasio: Vedi quanto adoro ancora ingrato!*

*** Decca 448 300-2.

Cecilia Bartoli's portrait, covering a recording period from 1991 to 1995, could hardly be more enticing. Every lyrical aria displays her truly lovely voice with astonishing consistency. The very opening *Parto,*

parto, ma tu ben mio from *La clemenza di Tito* could hardly be more inviting, with its engaging basset clarinet obbligato from Lesley Schatzberger, and *Come scoglio* shows her dramatic and vocal range to powerful and moving effect.

There is a delicious combination of charm and sparkle in Despina's *In uomini, in soldate* (wonderfully crisp trills echoing the orchestral violins), while Cherubino's *Voi che sapete* brings delightful innocence, and Susanna's *Deh vieni* the sunny joy of loving anticipation which ravishes the ear, especially at the leisurely close. The simpler classical songs bring contrast, with the silken line of *Caro mio ben* followed by the very touching and gloriously sung *Amarilli* of Caccini.

Finally Rossini, where Bartoli is unsurpassed among the present generation of mezzos (and measures up impressively to famous names from the past). After the beautifully spun line of the aria from *Maometto II* (with choral support) she captivates with a fizzing, crisply articulated and joyfully humorous *Non più mesta.* Top-class Decca recording throughout ensures the listener's pleasure and this hugely enjoyable collection would have earned a Rosette but for the totally inadequate documentation, with no translations – unacceptable in a premium-priced record.

'Chant d'amour'(with Myung-Whun Chung, piano): BIZET: *Mélodies: Adieux de l'hôtesse arabe; Chant d'amour; La coccinelle; Ouvre ton coeur; Tarantelle.* BERLIOZ: *La Mort d'Ophélie; Zaïde.* DELIBES: *Les filles de Cadiz.* VIARDOT: *Les filles de Cadiz; Hai luli!; Havanaise.* RAVEL: *4 Chansons populaires; 2 Mélodies Hébraïques; Tripatos; Vocalise-etude en forme de Habanera.*

*** Decca 452 667-2.

This is a delectable disc, a winning collection of French songs, many of them unexpected, which inspire Bartoli to the most seductive singing. One would have predicted that Delibes's sparkling setting of Musset's poem *Les filles de Cadiz* would draw out Carmen-like fire from her, but here that charming song is set alongside the setting of the same poem made by the great prima donna Pauline Viardot, giving a refreshingly different view. The other Viardot items too come as a delightful surprise, as do the Bizet songs, including *La coccinelle,* 'The Ladybird', a sparkling waltz, superbly characterized here. The better-known Berlioz and Ravel songs are beautifully done too, with Myung-Whun Chung revealing himself just as inspired in the role of pianist as of conductor. Excellent sound.

'Live from Italy' (with Jean-Yves Thibaudet (piano), Sonatori de la gioiosa marca): BELLINI: *Malinconia ninfa gentile; Ma rendi pur contento.* BERLIOZ: *Zaïde.* BIZET: *Carmen: Près des ramparts de Séville.* CACCINI: *Al fonte al prato; Tu ch'hai le penne; Amarilli mia bella.* DONIZETTI: *La conocchia; Me voglio fa'na casa.* GIORDANI: *Caro mio ben.* HANDEL: *Il Trionfo del Tempo e del Disinganno: Lascia la spina.* MONTSALVATGE: *Canto negro.* MOZART: *Le nozze di Figaro: Voi che sapete. Concert aria: Oiseaux, si tous les ans.* ROSSINI: *Mi Lagnerò tacendo, Book I/2, 3 & 4. L'orpheline du Tyrol. Zelmira: Riedi al soglio. Canzonetta spagnuola.* SCHUBERT: *La pastorella al Prato.* VIARDOT: *Havanaise; Hai luli!* VIVALDI: *Griselda: Agitata da due venti.*

*** Decca 455 981-2.

Recorded live at the Teatro Olimpico in Vicenza, this recital vividly conveys the high-powered magnetism of Cecilia Bartoli. Encouraged by the rapturous audience, Bartoli may in some items go over the top in her individual characterization, but magic is there from first to last. The opening group of baroque items comes with string accompaniment, but then Thibaudet at the piano takes over as the most sympathetic partner, whether in the characterful little Schubert song, *La pastorella,* the tango-like *Havanaise* of Pauline Viardot or Berlioz's *Zaïde,* with Bartoli herself playing castanets. It is fascinating to have three widely contrasted settings by Rossini of the same Metastasio text, and crowning the whole recital – before a sparkling sequence of encores – is the longest item, a spectacular aria from Rossini's *Zelmira* with a breathtaking display of coloratura at the end. A fun disc, atmospherically recorded.

Bartoli, Cecilia (mezzo-soprano), Bryn Terfel (baritone)

'Cecilia and Bryn': Duets (with Santa Cecilia National Academy Orchestra, Myung-Whun Chung) from: MOZART: *Le nozze di Figaro; Così fan tutte; Don Giovanni; Die Zauberflöte.* ROSSINI: *Il barbiere di Siviglia; L'Italiana in Algeri.* DONIZETTI: *L'elisir d'amore.*

*** Decca 458 928-2.

The friendly title, 'Cecilia and Bryn', though suggesting a crossover disc, is well justified when in each of these operatic duets these two charismatic singers are so characterful in their performances, both musically and dramatically. At times they come near to overacting but, with brilliant support from Chung and the orchestra, that goes with the virtuoso flair. Warm, full sound, though Bartoli is made to sound breathy.

Berganza, Teresa (mezzo-soprano)

'The Singers' (Decca series): Arias from: MOZART: *La clemenza di Tito; Così fan tutte; Le nozze di Figaro* (with LSO, Pritchard). ROSSINI: *Il barbiere di Siviglia; La Cenerentola; L'Italiana in Algeri; Semiramide* (with LSO, Gibson). Songs: GRANADOS: *La maja dolorosa* (with Lavilla, piano).

(M) **(*) Decca (ADD) 467 905-2.

Berganza's Rossini and Mozart items were recorded in 1959 and 1963 respectively, when her voice was at its most beautiful. The musical intensity combines formidably with an amazing technique (listen to *Bel raggio* from *Semiramide*), and only occasionally does once sense a lack of warmth. There is plenty of sparkle in the fast Rossini numbers as there is consistent voice control in the long legato lines of the slower arias. The Granados items, recorded by DG in 1975, provide a colourful contrast. All of these recordings won great praise in their day, and there is no reason to modify that view now. Texts and translations, as usual in 'The Singers' series, can be obtained only via a CD ROM drive, which will be counted a great drawback by many collectors. Even if a photo-gallery is included, this is no substitute for printed texts and translations. Decca has, over the years, given us more varied Berganza recital LPs and CDs, but this one is acceptable enough, and the sound is excellent.

'*Canciones españolas*' (with Narciso Yepes, guitar, Félix Lavilla, piano): SABIO: *Rosa das rosas; Santa Maria.* FUENLLANA: *Pérdida de Antequera.* ANON.: *Dindirindin; Nuaves te traygo, carillo; Los hombres con gran plazer.* MUDARRA: *Triste estava el rey David; Si me llaman a mi; Claros y frescos rios; Ysabel, perdiste la tu faxa.* TORRE: *Dime, triste corazón; Pámpano verde.* VALDERRABANO: *De dónde venis, amore?* MILAN: *Toda mi vida os amé; Aquel caballero, madre.* TRIANA: *Dinos, madre del donsel.* ENCINA: *Romerico.* VAZQUEZ: *Vos me matastes; En la fuente del rosel.* NARVAEZ: *Con qué la lavaré?* ANCHIETA: *Con amores, la mi madre.* ESTEVE: *Alma sintamos.* GRANADOS: *La maja dolorosa: Oh, muerte cruel!; Ay, majo de mi vida!; De aquel majo amante. El majo discreto; El tra la lá y el punteado; El majo timido.* GURIDI: *Canciones castellanas: Llámale con el pañuelo; No quiero tus avellanas; Cómo quieres que adivine!* FALLA: *7 Canciones populares españolas.* LORCA: *13 Canciones españolas antiquas.* TURINA: *Saeta en forma de Salve a la Virgen de la Esperanza; Canto a Sevilla: El fantasma. Poema en forma de canciones: Cantares.* MONTSALVATGE: *5 Canciones negras.*

(M) *** DG (IMS) (ADD) 435 848-2 (2).

This collection dates from the mid-1970s when Berganza was at her peak, the voice fresh, her artistry mature. In essence she provides here a history of Spanish song, opening with two pieces taken from the *Cantigas de Santa Maria*, dating from the thirteenth century, and moving on through Renaissance repertory and, with only one song from the eighteenth century, to the nineteenth and twentieth, traditional settings by Lorca, Falla's *7 Spanish popular songs* and the engaging *Canciones negras* of Montsalvatge. The collaboration with Narciso Yepes seems ideal, for he is an inspirational artist, while her husband, Félix Lavilla, provides the later piano accompaniments. This is not a specialist recital: the music communicates readily in the most direct way, and excellent notes and translations are provided. The balance is very natural and the CD transfers are immaculately managed. This is repertoire one first associates with Victoria de los Angeles, but Berganza makes it her own and there are not many more attractive Spanish song-recitals than this.

Berger, Erna (soprano)

'*The Singers*' (Decca series): Arias from: FLOTOW: *Martha.* GRIEG: *Peer Gynt.* MOZART: *Don Giovanni; Le nozze di Figaro.* DONIZETTI: *Don Pasquale; La Fille du régiment.* AUBER: *Fra Diavolo.* BIZET: *Les Pêcheurs de perles.* J. STRAUSS JR: *Die Fledermaus.* VERDI: *Rigoletto; La traviata.* Songs: FLIES: *Wiegenlied: Schlafe mein Prinzchen.* BRAHMS: *Wiegenlied.* REGER: *Mariä Wiegenlied.* PUCCINI: *Madama Butterfly.* R. STRAUSS: *Der Rosenkavalier.*

(M) (***) Decca mono 467 917-2.

One of the best in Decca's uneven 'The Singers' series finds Erna Berger in her prime in these (mainly) 1930s recordings, largely with the Berlin State Opera orchestra. Berger's pure tone and beautiful legato are apparent throughout, and, as John Steene writes in the notes, if her range of expression was not especially wide, she excelled within her limits and 'there was from the start a smile in her voice', which is captivating. These recordings also capture several of her most distinguished contemporary singers, such as Viorica Ursuleac, Tiana Lemnitz, Julius Patzak and Gino Sinimberghi, among others, making this CD even more desirable to collectors of historical voice. The transfers are fine, although texts and translations can be seen, annoyingly, only via a CD ROM drive, where a photo-gallery is also included.

Berger, Erna (soprano), Sebastian Peschko (piano)

Arias from: PERGOLESI: *Il Flaminio.* VERACINI: *Rosalinda.* HANDEL: *Semele.* GLUCK: *Die Pilger von Mekka.* Arias: CACCINI: *Amarilli mia bella.* A. SCARLATTI: *La Violetta.* TELEMANN: *Trauer-Music eines kunsterfahrenen Canarienvogels.* J. C. BACH: *Midst Silent Shades.* MOZART: *Abendempfindung; Oiseaux, si tous les ans; Ridente la calma; Der Zauberer.* SCHUBERT: *Im Abendrot; An die untergehende Sonne; Am Grabe; Schäfers Klagelied; Suleika I & II.*

(M) (**) Orfeo mono C 556021B.

This recital was recorded in Hanover in 1962. Erna Berger too, was 62, and while the voice still sounds remarkably fresh, a close vibrato is used to maintain the tonal bloom. There is more than a hint of strain in Johann Christian Bach's *Midst silent shades.* However she is at her charming best in the Italian arias (especially the Veracini and Scarlatti) and still impresses in Mozart and Schubert. But the highlight is the winning Telemann cantata about the canary's funeral. It is a great pity that no texts and translations are provided, either here or elsewhere, and the notes are entirely biographical. Handel's famous aria from *Semele* is engagingly listed (although not sung) as '*Wher'are you walking*'. However this is a recital for Berger admirers, rather than the general collector.

Bergonzi, Carlo (tenor)

Italian songs (with John Wustman, piano): BELLINI: *Vaga luna che inargenti.* VERDI: *Stornello.* DENZA: *Se …; Occhi fi fata.* DONIZETTI: *Me voglio fa'na casa.* DONAUDY: *O del mio amato ben; Vaghissima sembianza.* TITIRINDELLI: *O primavera!* ROSSINI: *La Promessa; La danza.* MASCAGNI: *Serenata.* TOSTI: *Tormento!; L'Iba sepera dalla luce l'ombra; Ideale.* BUZZI-PECCIA: *Lolita.* DE CURTIS: *Non ti scordar di me.* PUCCINI: *Edgar: Orgia, chimera dall'occhio vitreo* (with NY Opera Orchestra, Eve Queler).

(M) *(*) Sony (ADD) SMK 60785.

This is repertoire with which the golden-voiced Gigli could continually ravish the ear and make one think every number a gem. Bergonzi was still in good voice when he made these recordings in 1977 (and he has a splendid accompanist in John Wustman), but as the opening Bellini song demonstrates, his phrasing is unmagical. He is better in the lighter, livelier songs like Verdi's *Stornello*, or the more ardent popular songs by De Curtis and Denza, and he does very well by Tosti, with whom he readily identifies. But when he begins the closing aria from Puccini's *Edgar*, he is on home ground and the singing really takes hold of the listener.

'*Grandi voci*': Arias from: VERDI: *Aida; Luisa Miller; La forza del destino; Il Trovatore; Un ballo in maschera; Don Carlos; La Traviata.* MEYERBEER: *L'Africana.* GIORDANO: *Andrea Chénier.* CILEA: *Adriana Lecouvreur.* PUCCINI: *Tosca; Manon Lescaut; La Bohème.* PONCHIELLI: *La Gioconda.*

(M) **(*) Decca (ADD) 440 417-2.

This recital, consisting mainly of Bergonzi's early stereo recordings, a dozen arias recorded with the Orchestra of the Santa Cecilia Academy, Rome, under Gavaazeni in 1957, shows him on consistently peak form. He does not attempt the rare pianissimo at the end of *Celeste Aida*; but here among Italian tenors is a thinking musical artist who never resorts to vulgarity. The lovely account of *Che gelida manina* (with Serafin) comes from two years later. The early stereo has transferred well and retains a bloom on the voice. The other recordings also derive from sets: *La Traviata* (1962), *Un ballo* (1960–61), *Don Carlos* (1965), all with Solti, while the stirring *Cielo e mar* from *La Gioconda* (1967) shows that Bergonzi's tone retained its quality. These added items help to make up a generous playing time of 71 minutes, besides adding variety to what was originally essentially a collection of favourites. Everything sounds fresh.

Bernac, Pierre (baritone)

'*The essential Pierre Bernac*' (with Francis Poulenc, Gerald Moore, Graham Johnson, piano): GOUNOD: *Sérénade; Ce que je suis sans toi; Au rossignol. 6 Mélodies* (cycle). DUPARC: *Soupir; L'invitation au voyage.* CHABRIER: *L'île heureuse.* CHAUSSON: *Le Colibri.* ROUSSEL: *Le Jardin Mouillé; Coeur en Péril.* SCHUMANN: *Dein Angesicht. Dichterliebe* (cycle), *Op. 48.* LISZT: *Freudvoll und Leidvoll; Es muss ein Wunderbares; Nimm einen Strahl der Sonne.* MILHAUD: *La Tourterelle.* VELLONES: *A mon fils.* BEYDTS: *La lyre et les amours* (cycle). FAURE: *Après un rêve; Le secret; Aurore; Prison; Soir; Jardin nocturne.* DEBUSSY: *3 Chansons de France. Fêtes galantes: Colloque sentimental. 3 Ballades de François Villon.* SATIE: *Mélodies Nos. 1 & 3.* RAVEL: *Don Quichotte à Dulcinée* (cycle). POULENC: *2 Chansons gailliards; Métamorphoses; Le bestiaire* (cycles). *2 Mélodies de Guillaume Apollinaire: Montparnasse. 2 Poèmes de Guillaume Apollinaire: Dans le jardin d'Anna. 2 Poèmes de Louis Aragon* (with O, Louis Beydts); *Telle jour telle nuit* (cycle). *Le Travail du peintre* (cycle). *L'Histoire de Babar, le petite éléphant.*

(***) Testament mono SBT 3161 (3).

When the duo of Pierre Bernac and Francis Poulenc provided a French equivalent of Pears and Britten, it is especially valuable to have this distinctive and often magical collection of recordings, made between 1936 and 1958. Most were recorded for EMI, notably those made in London just after the end of the Second World War. But the core of the collection, the late recordings made in 1957–8, come from BBC sources, recorded from broadcast concerts.

The distinctive voice, with its flicker of vibrato, was not quite so evenly produced as earlier, but the artistry remains magical. As a supplement comes a broadcast interview, with Bernac questioned by Graham Johnson, and finally comes a performance of Poulenc's *Babar the elephant* with Johnson at the piano and Bernac a magnetic narrator. On the first disc as a sample of Bernac's Lieder-singing comes an EMI recording with Gerald Moore of Schumann's *Dichterliebe*, while as the perfect introduction there is Bernac's uniquely charming account with Poulenc of Gounod's *Sérénade*. Most moving of all are the readings of such deeper Poulenc songs as the first of the two *Poèmes de Louis Aragon*, '*C*', inspired by the Nazi occupation of France.

Björling, Jussi (tenor)

Bjoerling Edition: (Studio recordings 1930–59; with O, Nils Grevillius): Disc 1 (1936–41): Arias from VERDI: *Aida; Rigoletto; Requiem; La Traviata; Il Trovatore.* PUCCINI: *La Bohème; Tosca; La fanciulla del West.* PONCHIELLI: *La Gioconda.* MEYERBEER: *L'Africaine.* MASSENET: *Manon.* BIZET: *Carmen.* GOUNOD: *Faust.* FLOTOW: *Martha.* ROSSINI: *Stabat Mater.* FRIML: *The Vagabond King.* Songs by TOSTI; DI CAPUA; GEEHL. Disc 2 (1941–50): Arias from: PUCCINI: *La Bohème; Turandot; Manon Lescaut; Tosca.* VERDI: *Rigoletto; Un ballo in maschera.*

GIORDANO: *Andrea Chénier, Fedora* MASCAGNI: *Cavalleria rusticana.* LEONCAVALLO: *Pagliacci* (also song: *Mattinata*). DONIZETTI: *L'elisir d'amore.* BIZET: *Les Pêcheurs de perles.* GOUNOD: *Roméo et Juliette.* MASSENET: *Manon.* CILEA: *L'arlesiana.* GODARD: *Jocelyn (Berceuse).* Song: TOSTI: *L'alba separa.* Disc 3: Arias (sung in Swedish) from: GOUNOD: *Roméo et Juliette.* VERDI: *Rigoletto; Il Trovatore.* LAPARRA: *L'illustre Fregona.* BORODIN: *Prince Igor.* PUCCINI: *Tosca; La fanciulla del West.* LEONCAVALLO: *Pagliacci.* MASCAGNI: *Cavalleria rusticana.* ATTERBERG: *Fanal.* RIMSKY-KORSAKOV: *Sadko.* OFFENBACH: *La belle Hélène.* JOHANN STRAUSS JR: *Der Zigeunerbaron.* MILLOCKER: *Der Bettelstudent.* Traditional songs (in Swedish) and by PETERSON-BERGER; SJOBERG; SCHRADER; STENHAMMAR; ALTHEN; WIDE. Disc 4: Lieder and songs (1939–59): BEETHOVEN: *Adelaide.* R. STRAUSS: *Morgen; Cäcile.* RACHMANINOV: *In the silence of the night; Lilacs.* FOSTER: *Jeannie with the light brown hair.* D'HARDELOT: *Because.* SPEAKS: *Sylvia.* CAMPBELL-TIPTON: *A spirit flower.* BEACH: *Ah, love but a day.* SJOBERG: *I bless ev'ry hour.* SIBELIUS: *The diamond in the March snow.* ADAM: *O holy night.* Songs by NORDQVIST; SALEN; PETERSON-BERGER; SODERMAN; ALFVEN.

(M) (***) EMI mono/stereo CMS5 66306-2 (4).

All admirers of the great Swedish tenor should consider this comprehensive compilation, eighty-nine items chosen by Harald Henrysson from EMI's Swedish archives and admirably remastered at Abbey Road. The voice is caught freshly and truthfully. Björling's wife, Anna-Lisa, also participates in duets from *La Bohème* and *Roméo et Juliette*, towards the end of the second disc. The selection of arias is almost entirely predictable (and none the worse for that); a number of the key items are offered twice, and sometimes again in Swedish (where they sound surprisingly effective, even an excerpt from Offenbach's *La belle Hélène*). All the songs have a direct popular appeal. Björling opens Disc 4 with a winning account of Beethoven's *Adelaide*, and many will welcome the lighter songs, and particularly the English ballads. However, the closing group of eight Scandinavian songs is memorable: romantic and dramatic by turns, and closing with a bold final contrast, *The diamond in the March snow* of Sibelius, which is capped by Björling's ardent version of Adam's *Cantique de Noël* in Swedish. Excellent documentation, with photographs and full translations.

Opera arias from: DONIZETTI: *L'Elisir d'amore.* VERDI: *Il Trovatore; Un Ballo in maschera; Aida.* LEONCAVALLO: *I Pagliacci.* PUCCINI: *La Bohème; Tosca; La Fanciulla del West; Turandot.* GIORDANO: *Fedora.* CILEA: *L'Arlesiana.* MEYERBEER: *L'Africana.* GOUNOD: *Faust.* MASSENET: *Manon.* FLOTOW: *Martha.* ROSSINI: *Stabat Mater.*

(M) (***) EMI mono CDH7 61053-2.

The EMI collection on the Références label brings excellent transfers of material recorded between 1936

and 1947 on the tenor's home-ground in Stockholm. The voice was then at its very peak, well caught in those final years of 78-r.p.m. discs, with artistry totally assured over this wide range of repertory.

Arias and excerpts from: VERDI: *Rigoletto* (with Hjördis Schymberg); *Requiem.* BIZET: *Les pêcheurs de perles; Carmen.* OFFENBACH: *La belle Hélène.* GOUNOD: *Roméo et Juliette.* MASSENET: *Manon.* PONCHIELLI: *La Gioconda.* MASCAGNI: *Cavalleria rusticana.* BORODIN: *Prince Igor.* PUCCINI: *Manon Lescaut; La Bohème* (with Anna-Lisa Bjoerling). GIORDANO: *Andrea Chénier.* Songs: RACHMANINOV: *In the silence of the night; Lilacs.* LEONCAVALLO: *Mattinata.* TOSTI: *Ideale.* BEETHOVEN: *Adelaide.* R. STRAUSS: *Morgen.*

(M) (**(*)) EMI mono CDH7 64707-2.

The second Références collection – particularly generous, with a 77-minute programme – is if anything even more attractive than the first, offering recordings over the full range of the great tenor's 78-r.p.m. recording career with EMI, from 1933 (*Vladimir's Cavatina* from *Prince Igor*) to 1949 (*O soave fanciulla* from *La Bohème*, with Anna-Lisa Björling). Again the voice is in peak form, ringing out with that penetrating yet glowing vocal production that was the hallmark of Björling's timbre, while the singing itself has that innate sense of style which made him such a satisfying artist.

It is a pity that the CD transfers are so very bright and edgy, affecting the orchestra as well as the voice. This is particularly annoying in the delicate *Manon* excerpt (*Instant charmant . . . En fermant les yeux*) from 1938, where the violins are particularly tiresome; but the overall tendency to shrillness tends to tire the ear before the recital is halfway through. One wonders why this effect cannot be mitigated – the voice does not lack either vividness or presence without artificial enhancement.

'Great opera arias' (with RCA Victor Orchestra, Robert Shaw Chorale, Cellini or Rome Opera Orchestra, Perlea or Leinsdorf or (i) Frederick Schauwecker (piano)): MEYERBEER: *L'Africana: O paradiso.* VERDI: *Aida:* excerpts. *Il Trovatore:* excerpts (with Zinka Milanov, Fedora Barbieri, Leonard Warren). *Rigoletto:* excerpts (with Roberta Peters, Robert Merrill, Anna Maria Rota). PUCCINI: *La Bohème: Che gelida manina. Tosca: E lucevan le stelle; Amaro sol per te* (with Milanov). *Manon Lescaut: Ah! Manon mi tradisce* (with Licia Albanese); *No! no! pazzo son!* (with Enrico Campo). MASCAGNI: *Cavalleria rusticana:* excerpts (with Milanov). (i) BIZET: *Carmen: Flower song.* (i) MOZART: *Don Giovanni: Il mio tesoro.* (i) MASSENET: *Manon: Instant charmant; En fermant les yeux.* (i) GIORDANO: *Fedora: Amor ti vieta.* (i) PUCCINI: *Turandot: Nessun dorma.*

(M) *** RCA mono/stereo 09026 68429-2.

If you want a single disc to represent Jussi Björling, this is the one to have. The recordings date from between 1951 and 1959, the last decade of his life, when the voice was still astonishingly fresh. Most of the excerpts come from distinguished complete recordings, when the great tenor was partnered by artists of the calibre of Zinka Milanov and Licia Albanese (the duets from *Tosca* and *Manon Lescaut* are electrifying and the excerpts from *Aida*, *Il Trovatore* and *Cavalleria rusticana* are hardly less thrilling). The recordings, splendidly transferred, are all of high quality and show the great tenor in the very best light: even the 1958 live recital, with just a piano accompaniment, is treasurable for its famous arias from *Carmen* and *Manon*, and the closing, passionate *Nessun dorma*.

Operatic recital: Arias from: PONCHIELLI: *La Gioconda*. puccini: *La Fanciulla del West; Manon Lescaut*. GIORDANO: *Fedora*. CILEA: *L'Arlesiana*. VERDI: *Un ballo in maschera; Requiem*. MASCAGNI: *Cavalleria rusticana* (with Tebaldi). LEHAR: *Das Land des Lächelns*.

(M) *** Decca (IMS) (ADD) 443 930-2.

Jussi Björling provides here a flow of headily beautiful, finely focused tenor tone. These may not be the most characterful renderings of each aria, but they are all among the most compellingly musical. The recordings are excellent for their period (1959–60). The Lehár was the last solo recording he made before he died in 1960. The transfers to CD are admirably lively and present.

Bocelli, Andrea (tenor)

Operatic arias (with Maggio Musicale Fiorentino O, Gianandrea Noseda): PUCCINI: *La Bohème, Tosca, Madama Butterfly*. LEONCAVALLO: *La Bohème*. CILEA: *Andriana Lecouvreur*. BELLINI: *I puritani*. R. STRAUSS: *Der Rosenkavalier*, Etc.

(*) Ph. 462 033-2.

'Viaggio Italiano' (with Academy of Choir Art, Moscow RSO, Vladimir Fedoseyev): Arias from: PUCCINI: *Turandot*. CILEA: *L'Arlesiana*. VERDI: *Macbeth; Rigoletto*. DONIZETTI: *L'Elisir d'amore*. Songs: FRANCK: *Panis angelicus*. SCHUBERT: *Ave Maria*. DI CAPUA: *O sole mio; L' te vurria vasà*. CARDILLO: *Core n'grato*. MARIO: *Santa Lucia luntana*. DE CURTIS: *Tu'ca nun chiagne!* GAMBARDELLA: *Marinariello* TAGLIAFERRI: *Piscatore'e pusilleco*. TRAD.: *Adeste fidelis*. Spoken message.

(*) Ph. 462 196-2.

Trumpeted as one of today's greatest tenors, having emerged from a pop background, Andrea Bocelli on the first disc here shows his paces in a formidable collection of arias including even the tenor's aria from *Der Rosenkavalier*. Bocelli's great natural gift is a tenor of very distinctive timbre, not conventionally rounded in a Pavarotti-like way but above all virile with a baritonal tinge, used over a wide tonal range

with not a suspicion of strain. He soars readily to a top C or even a C sharp, as in *A te o cara* from Bellini's *I Puritani*.

There is fair evidence too of lessons well learnt. Werther's *Pourquoi me reveiller* – among the most testing of French arias – inspires Bocelli to produce very refined mezza voce, beautifully sustained, and the *Flower song* from *Carmen* too is subtler than most. Yet there is a sequence of Puccini arias – the two from *Tosca*, one from *Butterfly* – which are disappointingly slow and heavy, though *Che gelida manina* is nicely detailed. And though in the nine top Cs of Tonio's *Pour ton âme* from *La fille du régiment* – the final rip-roaring item here – he cannot quite match the flamboyance of Pavarotti, there are all too few recording tenors who could do it so confidently, or even at all.

The second disc was recorded in Moscow in 1994, and offers no vocal disappointments, with the darker timbre particularly striking in the arias from *Macbeth* and notably *Una furtiva lagrima* from *L'Elisir d'amore*, which is strikingly different from a honeyed Gigli-like account. Franck's *Panis angelicus* and Schubert's *Ave Maria* are not sentimentalized. But not everyone will welcome the fact that half the recital is taken up with Neapolitan popular songs which are all rather similar in their ardent declarations. Bocelli sings them persuasively and the recital ends with a passionate 'live' recording of *Adeste fidelis*, where the choral contribution is made very spectacular by the resonance.

Bonney, Barbara (soprano)

'Diamonds in the snow' (with Antonio Pappano, piano): GRIEG: *Spring; I love you; With a water-lily; The princess; A swan; From Monte Pincio; 6 Lieder, Op. 48; Peer Gynt: Solveig's song*. SIBELIUS: *The diamond in the snow; Lost in the forest; Sigh, rushes, sigh; Was it a dream?; The girl came home from meeting her lover*. STENHAMMAR: *The girl came home from meeting her lover; Adagio; Sweden; Guiding spirit; In the forest*. ALFVEN: *Take my heart; The forest sleeps*. SJOBERG: *Music*.

*** Decca 466 762-2.

Barbara Bonney, with her warm understanding of Scandinavia and its music, offers the most seductive choice of songs in this inspired collection. The Grieg group includes most of the well-known favourites, but with Antonio Pappano proving just as understanding a piano accompanist as he is a conductor, they all emerge fresh and new, animated and strongly characterized. There is a sensuousness and passion behind the love songs in particular, with free rubato sounding spontaneous, never studied. The Sibelius set brings ravishing tonal contrasts too, and it is fascinating to hear the settings of the same Swedish poem, first by Sibelius, then more simply but with warm feeling by Stenhammar. More than anything the disc disproves the idea of coldness in the Nordic make-up. Warm, full sound with Bonney's lovely voice glowingly caught.

Bostridge, Ian (tenor), Julian Drake (piano)

'The English Songbook': STANFORD: *La belle dame sans merci.* GURNEY: *Sleep; I will go with my father a-ploughing.* DUNHILL: *The cloths of heaven.* WILLIAM DENIS BROWN: *To Gratiana dancing and singing.* SOMERVELL: *To Lucasta, on going to the wars.* DELIUS: *Twilight fancies.* GERMAN: *Orpheus with his lute.* WARLOCK: *Jillian of Berry; Cradle song.* FINZI: *The dance continued (Regret not me); Since we loved.* VAUGHAN WILLIAMS: *Linden Lea; Silent noon.* Irish air, arr. STANFORD: *My love's an arbutus.* Irish tune, arr. BRITTEN: *The Salley Gardens.* TRAD./ANON.: *The death of Queen Jane; The little turtle dove.* PARRY: *No longer mourne for me.* WARLOCK: *Rest, sweet nymphs.* QUILTER: *Come away death; Now sleeps the crimson petal.* GRAINGER: *Bold William Taylor; Brigg Fair.*

*** EMI CDC5 56830-2.

Ian Bostridge with his clear, honeyed tone is in his element in this collection of twenty-four English songs, almost all of them neglected. He and his keenly responsive accompanist, Julius Drake, have made an imaginative, far from predictable choice of items, with only the two Vaughan Williams songs, *Linden Lea* and *Silent noon*, qualifying as popular favourites. It is good to find the collection delving as far back as Parry and Stanford (the first and most ambitious of the songs, memorably setting Keats's *La belle dame sans merci*), and including composers like Edward German, generally celebrated for his light music. It is a reflection on the singer's personality too that there is a high proportion of thoughtful, introspective songs, most sensitively matched by Drake in his accompaniments. One hopes that EMI's inclusion of French and German translations alongside the English texts will encourage new discovery outside Britain of a genre seriously underappreciated, one which directly reflects the magic of English lyric poetry.

Bott, Catherine (soprano)

ANON: *Carmina Burana: Axe Phebus aureo. The Pilgrimage to Santiago (Navarre and Castile): Non e gran causa.* WOLKENSTEIN: *Der mai mit lieber zal.* DE FOURNIVAL: *Onques n'amai tant que jou fui amee.* MARINI: *Con le stelle in ciel che mai.* FRESCOBALDI: *Se L'aura spira.* MONTEVERDI: *L'Orfeo: Ritornello ... Dal mio Permesso amato.* BLOW: *Venus and Adonis: Adonis! Adonis! Adonis!* BACH: *Christmas Oratorio: Herr, dein Mitleid, dein Erbarmen.* VIVALDI: *Introduzione al Dixit: Ascende laeta.* ECCLES: *Cease of Cupid to Complain; Let's all be Gay; I Burn, my Brain Consumes to Ashes.* PURCELL: *The Indian Queen: They Tell Us that You Mighty Powers Above; Dido and Aeneas: Thy Hand, Belinda ... ; With Drooping Wings.*

(B) *** Decca 470 121-2.

This splendid collection begins with the rustically vibrant account *Non e gran causa*, which tells of a pilgrim who, having sinned carnally, meets the devil, kills himself, is jailed by Saint Mary and is then (improbably) restored to life! Catherine Bott beautifully shades and characterizes this ten-minute work against a background array of colourful instruments, vibrantly played by Pickett's New London Consort. This soloist has made a speciality of Renaissance and early Baroque music, and there are many typical examples of her imaginative art found here. The Eccles items – all of them 'mad songs' – are most appealing, with Bott decorating the vocal line with taste and style, as she also does in the perky Vivaldi item. She is no less successful in sustaining long vocal lines, never more so than in *Dido and Aeneas*, which shows her at her moving best. With excellent orchestral accompaniments and recordings, this is a superb bargain CD, and although there are no texts, her diction is generally clear.

Bott, Catherine (soprano), New London Consort, Philip Pickett

'Music from the time of Columbus': VERARDI: *Viva El Gran Re Don Fernando.* ANON.: *A los Maytines era; Propinan de Melyor; Como no le andare yo; Nina y viña; Calabaza, no sé, buen amor; Perdi la mi rueca; Al alva venid buen amigo; Dale si la das.* URREDA: *Muy triste.* J. PONCE: *Como esta sola mi vida.* ANCHIETA: *Con amores mi madre.* ENCINA: *Triste españa; Mortal tristura; Mas vale trocar; Ay triste que vengo; Quedate carillo.* MEDINA: *No ay plazer en esta vida.* DE LA TORRE: *Danza alta.* DE MONDEJAR: *Un sola fin des mis males.*

*** Linn CKD 007.

The songs offered here are broadly divided into two groups, the romantic ballads, usually of a melancholy disposition (the word 'triste' occurs frequently), and the usually jollier *villancio* form, which brings a repeated refrain. Catherine Bott is the most delightful soloist, singing freshly and simply, often with a ravishing tone, and there is much to give pleasure. In the anonymous songs it is fascinating to discover just how international medieval folk music was, for more than once the listener is reminded of the Auvergne songs collected later in France by Canteloube. The two most delightful items are saved until the end, first a truly beautiful love song, *Al alva venid buen amigo* ('Come at dawn my friend'), in which a young woman reflects on her lover's visits, and then lets her thoughts change to consider the birth from the Virgin Mary of 'him who made the world'. In complete contrast is the robust and charmingly naughty villancio, *Dale si das* ('Come on, wench of Carasa'). The recording is first class, naturally balanced in a pleasing acoustic, and full documentation is provided.

Bowman, James (counter-tenor)

'*The James Bowman collection*' (with The King's Consort, Robert King): BACH: *Erbarme dich; Stirb in mir.* HANDEL: *Almighty power; Crueltà nè lontananza; Impious mortal; Tune your harps; Welcome as the dawn of day; Thou shalt bring them in; Or la tromba; Eternal source of light.* PURCELL: *Britain, thou now art great; O solitude; By beauteous softness mixed; An Evening hymn; On the brow of Richmond Hill; Vouchsafe, O Lord.* ANON.: *Come tread the paths.* GABRIELI: *O magnum mysterium.* FORD: *Since I saw your face.* F. COUPERIN: *Jerusalem, convertere.*

(BB) *** Hyp. KING 3.

Apart from the opening Bach item, which has not previously been published and which is not entirely flattering, this admirable 78-minute sampler will delight fans of James Bowman as it shows his art and fine vocal control over a wide range of repertoire at which he excelled. Robert King and his Consort provide admirable support.

Caballé, Montserrat (soprano)

'*Diva*': Arias from: PUCCINI: *Madama Butterfly; Tosca; Manon Lescaut; La Bohème; Turandot; La Rondine.* ROSSINI: *William Tell.* BELLINI: *Il Pirata; I Puritani.* VERDI: *Giovanna d'Arco; Macbeth; Don Carlos; Aida.* BOITO: *Mefistofele.* MASCAGNI: *Cavalleria rusticana.*

(M) *** EMI (ADD) CDM5 65575-2.

This fine compilation is framed by items from Caballé's 1970 Puccini recital in which she impersonates Mimì, Tosca and Butterfly, singing more impressively than she characterizes. Otherwise these are items from complete sets made between 1970 (Giulini's *Don Carlos*) and 1980 (Muti's *I Puritani*). The items are not always the obvious choices from each opera but from first to last they demonstrate the consistent beauty of her singing at that period, responding to a wide range of conductors.

Arias from: PUCCINI: *La Bohème; Madama Butterfly; Tosca; Gianni Schicchi; Le Villi.* BELLINI: *Il Pirata; I Puritani.* VERDI: *Aida; La forza del destino; Giovanna d'Arco; Macbeth.* BOITO: *Mefistofele.* ROSSINI: *Guillaume Tell.* MEYERBEER: *Les Huguenots* (with MONTSALVATGE: *Canción.* R. STRAUSS: *Zueignung; Ruhe, meine Seele*).

(BB) *** Disky Royal Classics Vocal Double (ADD) DCL 703962 (2).

This two-disc collection expands the programme offered in Caballé's single-disc EMI recital above, including as it does her glorious Puccini recordings, made when the voice was at its freshest. The cost is rather less and a pair of highly desirable Strauss songs are thrown in for good measure. There are no texts, but the transfers are excellent and at its very low cost

this remains a prime choice among the various Caballé recitals on offer.

'*Opera arias and duets*' (with Luciano Pavarotti) from: VERDI: *Luisa Miller.* BELLINI: *Norma.* BOITO: *Mefistofele.* PUCCINI: *Turandot.* GIORDANO: *Andrea Chénier.* PONCHIELLI: *La Gioconda.*

(M) *** Decca DDD/ADD 458 231-2.

Although this disc centres on Caballé there are plenty of duets here and ensembles too. All the excerpts come from highly recommendable complete sets, and Pavarotti figures often and strongly. In Bellini, Giordano or Boito, and especially as Liù in *Turandot*, Caballé is often vocally ravishing, and she finds plenty of drama and power for Verdi and Ponchielli. There are at least two and sometimes three and four items from each opera, admirably chosen to make consistently involving entertainment. The presentation on this Opera Gala reissue is admirable, with full translations included.

Callas, Maria (soprano)

'*La Divina I*': Arias from: PUCCINI: *Madama Butterfly; La Bohème; Gianni Schicchi; Turandot; Tosca.* BIZET: *Carmen.* CATALANI: *La Wally.* ROSSINI: *Il barbiere di Siviglia.* BELLINI: *Norma.* SAINT-SAENS: *Samson et Dalila.* VERDI: *Rigoletto; La Traviata.* GOUNOD: *Roméo et Juliette.* MOZART: *Don Giovanni.* MASCAGNI: *Cavalleria rusticana.* PONCHIELLI: *La Gioconda.*

**(*) EMI stereo/mono CDC7 54702-2.

'*La Divina II*': Arias from: GLUCK: *Alceste; Orphée et Eurydice.* BIZET: *Carmen.* VERDI: *Ernani; Aida; I vespri siciliani; La Traviata; Don Carlos.* PUCCINI: *Manon Lescaut; La Bohème.* CHARPENTIER: *Louise.* THOMAS: *Mignon.* SAINT-SAENS: *Samson et Dalila.* BELLINI: *La Sonnambula.* CILEA: *Adriana Lecouvreur.* DONIZETTI: *Lucia di Lammermoor.*

*(*) EMI stereo/mono CDC5 55016-2.

'*La Divina III*': Arias and duets from: GIORDANO: *Andrea Chénier.* SPONTINI: *La vestale.* MASSENET: *Manon.* PUCCINI: *Manon Lescaut; La Bohème* (with Giuseppe di Stefano); *Madama Butterfly* (with Nicolai Gedda); *Turandot.* BIZET: *Carmen* (with Nicolai Gedda). ROSSINI: *Il barbiere di Siviglia* (with Tito Gobbi). DELIBES: *Lakmé.* VERDI: *Aida; Il Trovatore.* LEONCAVALLO: *Pagliacci.* MEYERBEER: *Dinorah.*

*** EMI stereo/mono CDC5 55216-2.

These three recital discs (with nearly four hours of music) cover Callas's recording career pretty thoroughly, although the first two are inadequately documented, giving only the date each recording was *published*. 'Divina III', however, provides both the actual dates and venues of the recordings and details of the other artists involved. Throughout the three programmes, results are inevitably uneven and if at times the rawness of exposed top-notes mars the lyrical beauty of her singing, equally often her dramatic magnetism is such that many phrases stay indelibly in the memory.

Each disc has its share of highlights, with the earlier recordings usually the more memorable. What is perhaps surprising are the omissions: nothing, for instance, from the collection of 'Mad scenes' she recorded with Rescigno. However, many of the choices are apt. 'La Divina I', for instance, includes her sharply characterful, early 1954 recording of *Una voce poco fa* from Rossini's *Barbiere*, and 'La Divina III' draws on the later, complete set for the duet *Dunque io son*, with Tito Gobbi. 'La Divina II' consistently shows her at her finest or near it. The recordings cover a decade from 1954 to 1964 and include much that is arrestingly dramatic (Gluck and Verdi) and ravishing (Puccini and Cilea), while everything shows that special degree of imagination which Callas brought to almost everything she did. The *Mignon Polonaise* is not ideally elegant but it has a distinctive character and charm, and it is almost irrelevant to criticize Callas on detail when her sense of presence is so powerful. The excerpt from *La Traviata* was recorded live in Lisbon in 1958 and even the audience noises cannot detract from its magnetism. All three recital discs are available separately at full price, with the third certainly the place to start, as it centres on early recordings, including the excerpt from *La vestale*, and opens with the movingly intense *La mamma morta* from *Andrea Chénier*. However, it is astonishing that, having provided so much information about the singer, EMI chose not to include any translations, resting content with a brief synopsis of each aria.

Callas Edition

'*Callas at La Scala*' (with La Scala, Milan O, Tullio Serafin): CHERUBINI: *Medea: Dei tuoi figli.* SPONTINI: *La Vestale: Tu che invoco; O nume tutelar; Caro oggetto.* BELLINI: *La Sonnambula: Compagne, teneri amici . . . Come per me sereno; Oh! se una volta solo . . . Ah! non credea mirati.*

(M) (***) EMI mono CDM5 66457-2.

These recordings were made at La Scala in June 1955 and feature extracts from three operas which at the time Callas had made all her own. However, for some unexplained reason, the diva refused to sanction publication of the *Sonnambula* items, so the original LP was released in 1958 with substituted performances, taken from her complete set, made the previous year. Yet, with Callas in her prime, if anything more relaxed than in those later versions, the remarkable quality is the total consistency: most details are identical in both performances. *Aficionados* will surely be delighted that the original performances have been restored alongside the Cherubini and Spontini arias. Throughout, Callas is heard at her most magnetic. As usual in this series, the CD transfers are very impressive.

'*Lyric and coloratura arias*' (with Philh. O, Tullio Serafin): CILEA: *Adriana Lecouvreur: Ecco, respiro*

appena . . . *Io son l'umile; Poveri fiori.* GIORDANO: *Andrea Chénier: La mamma morta.* CATALANI: *La Wally: Ebben? Ne andrò lontana.* BOITO: *Mefistofele: L'altra notte.* ROSSINI: *Il barbiere di Siviglia: Una voce poco fa.* MEYERBEER: *Dinorah: Shadow song.* DELIBES: *Lakmé: Bell song.* VERDI: *I vespri siciliani: Bolero: Mercè, dilette amiche.*

(M) (***) EMI mono CDM5 66458-2.

Recorded at the same group of sessions in September 1954 as her very first (Puccini) recital for EMI, this is another of the classic early Callas records, ranging extraordinarily widely in its repertory and revealing in every item the uniquely intense musical imagination that set musicians of every kind listening and learning. Coloratura flexibility here goes with dramatic weight. Not all the items are equally successful: the *Shadow song* from *Dinorah*, for example, reveals some strain and lacks charm, but these are all unforgettable performances. Callas's portrait of Rosina in *Una voce poco fa* was never more viperish than here, and she never surpassed the heartfelt intensity of such numbers as *La mamma morta* and *Poveri fiori*. This mono reissue is well balanced and cleanly transferred with the voice vividly projected against a convincing orchestral backdrop.

'*Mad scenes*' (with Philh. Ch. & O, Nicola Rescigno): DONIZETTI: *Anna Bolena: Piangete voi?. . . Al dolce guidami castel natio.* THOMAS: *Hamlet: A vos jeux . . . Partagez-vous mes fleurs . . . Et maintenant écoutez ma chanson.* BELLINI: *Il Pirata: Oh! s'io potessi . . . Cor sorriso d'innocenza.*

(M) *** EMI (ADD) CDM5 66459-2.

Recorded in the Kingsway Hall in September 1958, this is the record which, Desmond Shawe-Taylor suggested, more than any other summed up the essence of Callas's genius. If the rawness of exposed top notes mars the sheer beauty of the singing, few recital records ever made can match – let alone outshine – this collection of 'Mad scenes' in vocal and dramatic imagination.

Recital (with Paris Conservatoire O, Nicola Rescigno): BEETHOVEN: *Ah! perfido* (scena and aria), Op. 65. WEBER: *Oberon: Ocean! thou mighty monster.* MOZART: *Le nozze di Figaro: Porgi amor. Don Giovanni: Or sai chi l'onore; Crudele?. . . Non mi dir; In quali eccessi, O numi! . . . Mi tradi quell'alma ingrate.*

(M) ** EMI (ADD) CDM5 66465-2.

The 1963–4 recording sessions in Paris which produced these Beethoven, Mozart and Weber arias also included arias by Verdi which were not to appear until a decade later. They were to be among Callas's very last recordings, and the Beethoven scena immediately exposes the flaws that sadly emerged in the great voice towards the end of her career. Yet her fire-eating manner remains irresistible.

'*Callas à Paris*', Volume I (with Fr. Nat. R. O, Georges Prêtre): GLUCK: *Orphée et Euridice: J'ai perdu mon Euridice. Alceste: Divinités du Styx.*

BIZET: *Carmen: Habanera; Seguidilla.* SAINT-SAENS: *Samson et Dalila: Printemps qui commence; Amour! viens aider ma faiblesse! Mon coeur s'ouvre à ta voix.* GOUNOD: *Roméo et Juliette: Ah! je veux vivre dans ce rêve.* THOMAS: *Mignon: Ah, pour ce soir . . . Je suis Titania.* MASSENET: *Le Cid: De cet affreux combat . . . pleurez.* CHARPENTIER: *Louise: Depuis le jour.*

(M) *** EMI (ADD) CDM5 66466-2.

'*Callas à Paris*', Volume II (with Paris Conservatoire O, Georges Prêtre): GLUCK: *Iphigénie en Tauride: O malheureuse Iphigénie.* BERLIOZ: *Damnation de Faust: D'amour l'ardente flamme.* BIZET: *Les Pêcheurs de perles: Me voilà seule . . . Comme autrefois.* MASSENET: *Manon: Je ne suis que faiblesse . . . Adieu notre petite table. Suis-je gentille ainsi?. . . Je marche sur tous les chemins. Werther: Werther! Qui m'aurait dit . . . Des cris joyeuse (Air des lettres).* GOUNOD: *Faust: Il était un Roi de Thulé . . . O Dieu! que de bijoux . . . Ah! je ris.*

(M) ** EMI (ADD) CDM5 66467-2.

The first LP collection, *Callas à Paris*, dating from 1961, has the singer at her most commanding and characterful. The sequel disc was recorded two years later when the voice was in decline. The vocal contrast is clear enough, and the need at the time to patch and re-patch the takes in the later sessions makes the results sound less spontaneous and natural. But the earlier portraits of Carmen, Alceste, Dalila and Juliette find Callas still supreme, and her mastery of the French repertoire provides a fascinating slant on her artistry.

'*Romantic arias*': PUCCINI: *Gianni Schicchi: O mio babbino caro. Manon Lescaut: In quelle trine morbide. La Bohème: Donde lieta uscì. Madama Butterfly: Un bel dì vedremo.* VERDI: *Rigoletto: Caro nome. Il Trovatore: D'amor sull'ali rosee. Otello: Ave Maria.* BELLINI: *La Sonnambula: Come per me sereno.* MEYERBEER: *Dinorah: Ombra leggiera (Shadow song).* DELIBES: *Lakmé: Bell song.* MOZART: *Le nozze di Figaro: Porgi amor.* DONIZETTI: *L'elisir d'amore: Prendi, per me sei libro. Lucia di Lammermoor: Spargi d'amaro piano (excerpt from Mad scene).*

(B) *** EMI (ADD) Eminence CD-EMX 2243.

A comparatively recent bargain assembly of Callas arias, attractively designed to show her lyrical gifts. The Puccini, Verdi and Meyerbeer recordings date from the 1950s, except for the *Ave Maria* from *Otello* which, like the *Nozze di Figaro* and *L'elisir d'amore* arias, comes from a decade later. The brief excerpt from the *Lucia* Mad scene is drawn from the 1960 complete set, and the Bellini *La Sonnambula* excerpt, although originally recorded in 1955, was not passed for publication by Callas until near her death.

'*Music from Films*': Arias from: BELLINI: *Norma.* CATALANI: *La Wally.* PUCCINI: *Gianni Schicchi.* GIORDANO: *Andrea Chénier.* PUCCINI: *La Bohème; Madama Butterfly; Manon Lescaut; Tosca;*

Turandot. VERDI: *Otello; Rigoletto; La traviata; Il trovatore.* CILEA: *Adriana Lecouvreur.* DONIZETTI: *Anna Bolena; Lucia di Lammermoor.* GLUCK: *Orphée et Eurydice.* BIZET: *Carmen.* ROSSINI: *Il barbiere di Siviglia.* MEYERBEER: *Dinorah.* GOUNOD: *Roméo et Juliette.* SAINT-SAENS: *Samson et Dalila.* MASSENET: *Le Cid; Manon.* CHARPENTIER: *Louise.* SPONTINI: *La Vestale.* BELLINI: *La sonnambula.* MOZART: *Le Nozze di Figaro.*

(M) *(**) EMI mono/stereo CMS5 57062-2 (2).

'*Romantic Callas*': Arias from: PUCCINI: *La Bohème; Madama Butterfly; Manon Lescaut; Tosca.* BELLINI: *La Sonnambula.* VERDI: *Aida; Un ballo in maschera; La traviata; Il trovatore.* LEONCAVALLO: *Pagliacci.* DONIZETTI: *Lucia di Lammermoor.* SAINT-SAENS: *Samson et Dalila.* BIZET: *Carmen; Les Pêcheurs de perles.* BERLIOZ: *La Damnation de Faust.* MASSENET: *Werther.* MOZART: *Don Giovanni.* SPONTINI: *La Vestale.* MASCAGNI: *Cavalleria rusticana.* CILEA: *Adriana Lecouvreur.*

(M) *(**) EMI mono/stereo CMS5 57205-2 (2).

There have probably been more Maria Callas compilations than of any other female opera singer, and of the two latest two-CD sets listed above, there is nothing that has not been compiled several times before. However, never have they been presented more extravagantly. Both releases feature lavish booklets ('*Romantic Callas*' is in hardback) containing over 45 high-quality photographs (in black and white and colour), biographical information, full texts and translations, a discography and something of the opera's plots, which places each aria in context. Each CD contains plenty of examples of Callas at her commanding best: she never surpassed the dramatic intensity she showed in such numbers as *La mamma morta* (from *Andrea Chénier*), or *Poveri fiori* (from *Adriana Lecouvreur*), even if some of the French arias and the Mozart recordings show the voice in decline. However, the majority of items are from her classic complete opera recordings and recital discs from the 1950s.

'*Music from Films*' draws from music featured in various film and TV programmes, filled out with various other arias, to form an attractive compilation, and it contains some of her best-known numbers, including the *Habanera* from *Carmen* and *Casta Diva* (from *Norma*). The booklet also includes photographs of some of her classic record sleeves. Both sets include a wide repertoire, and although some items, such as *Vissi d'arte*, are common to both sets (but taken from different recordings), little directly overlaps. Neither set is particularly recommendable over the other, and the Callas devotee will surely want both. The transfers are excellent.

Cambridge Singers, John Rutter

'*There is sweet music*' (English choral songs): STANFORD: *The blue bird.* DELIUS: *To be sung of a summer night on the water I & II.* ELGAR: *There is sweet music; My love dwelt in a Northern land.* VAUGHAN WILLIAMS: *3 Shakespearean songs: Full fathom five; The cloud-capp'd towers; Over hill, over dale.* BRITTEN: *5 Flower songs, Op. 47. Folksongs:* arr. MOERAN: *The sailor and young Nancy.* arr. GRAINGER: *Brigg Fair; Londonderry air.* arr. CHAPMAN: *Three ravens.* arr. HOLST: *My sweetheart's like Venus.* arr. BAIRSTOW: *The oak and the ash.* arr. STANFORD: *Quick! We have but a second.*

❀ *** Coll. COLCD 104.

Opening with an enchanting performance of Stanford's *The blue bird* followed by equally expressive accounts of Delius's two wordless summer evocations, this most attractive recital ranges from Elgar and Vaughan Williams, both offering splendid performances, to various arrangements of folksongs, less fashionable today than they once were, but giving much pleasure here. The recording, made in the Great Hall of University College, London, has an almost ideal ambience: words are clear, yet the vocal timbre is full and natural. A highly recommendable anthology.

'Flora gave me fairest flowers' (English madrigals): MORLEY: *My bonny lass she smileth; Fyer, fyer!; Now is the month of Maying.* EAST: *Quick, quick, away dispatch!* GIBBONS: *Dainty fine bird; Silver swan.* BYRD: *Though Amaryllis dance in green; This sweet and merry month of May; Lullaby.* WEELKES: *Hark, all ye lovely saints.* WILBYE: *Weep, weep, mine eyes; Flora gave me; Draw on sweet night; Adieu sweet Amaryllis.* TOMKINS: *Too much I once lamented; Adieu ye city-prisoning towers.* FARMER: *Little pretty bonny lass.* BENNETT: *Round about.* WEELKES: *Ha ha! this world doth pass; Death hath deprived me.* RAMSEY: *Sleep, fleshly birth.*

*** Coll. COLCD 105.

John Rutter's Cambridge Singers bring consistent unanimity of ensemble and a natural expressive feeling to this very attractive programme of madrigals. Perhaps the first group, devoted to love and marriage, may be thought rather too consistently mellifluous; but the second, 'Madrigals of times and season', is nicely contrasted, with the clean articulation of Morley's *Now is the month of Maying* made the more telling by the lightness of the vocal production. John Wilbye's lovely *Draw on sweet night*, which follows, makes a perfect contrast. After two items about 'Fairies, spirits and conceits', the concert closes in a mood of moving Elizabethan melancholy with a group devoted to mourning and farewell. Superb recording in a most flattering acoustic makes this collection the more enjoyable, though one to be dipped into rather than heard all at once.

'Faire is the Heaven' (Music of the English Church): PARSONS: *Ave Maria.* TALLIS: *Loquebantur variis linguis; If ye love me.* BYRD: *Misere mei; Haec dies; Ave verum corpus; Bow thine ear.* FARRANT: *Hide not thou thy face; Lord, not thou thy face; Lord for thy tender mercy's sake.* GIBBONS: *O clap your hands; Hosanna to the Son of David.* PURCELL: *Lord, how long wilt thou be angry; Thou knowest, Lord; Hear my prayer, O Lord.* STANFORD: *Beati quorum via.* arr. WOOD: *This joyful Eastertide.* HOWELLS: *Sing lullaby; A spotless rose.* WALTON: *What cheer?* VAUGHAN WILLIAMS: *O taste and see.* BRITTEN: *Hymn to the Virgin.* POSTON: *Jesus Christ the apple tree.* HARRIS: *Faire is the Heaven.*

*** Coll. COLCD 107.

These recordings were made in the Lady Chapel of Ely Cathedral, and the ambience adds beauty to the sound without in any way impairing clarity of focus. The music ranges from examples of the Roman Catholic Rite as set by Tallis, Byrd and Robert Parsons (with a touch of almost Latin eloquence in the presentation), through widely varied Reformation music, to the Restoration, represented by three Purcell anthems, and on to the Anglican revival and the twentieth century. The Reformation group is particularly successful, with the opening Tallis and closing Gibbons works rich in polyphony and Byrd's *Bow thine ear* wonderfully serene. Of the modern items, the Howells pieces are quite lovely and Walton's *What cheer?*, with its engaging imitation, is attractively genial. The Britten and Poston items, both well known, are hardly less engaging; and the concert ends with the ambitious title-number, William Harris's *Faire is the Heaven*, sung with great feeling and considerable power. There is no more successful survey of English church music in the current catalogue and certainly not one presented with more conviction.

'The lark in the clear air' (Traditional songs; with members of the London Sinfonia): *I know where I'm going; She moved through the fair; The lark in the clear air; Down by the Salley Gardens; Dashing away with the smoothing iron; The sprig of thyme; The bold grenadier; The British Grenadiers; The keel row; The girl I left behind me; The cuckoo; O waly waly; Willow song; The willow tree; The Miller of Dee; O can ye sew cushions.* arr. VAUGHAN WILLIAMS: *The spring time of the year; The dark-eyed sailor; Just as the tide was flowing; The lover's ghost; Wassail song.*

**(*) Coll. COLCD 120.

Most of these songs are arranged by Rutter himself, often with simple and characteristic instrumental backings – the opening *I know where I'm going* has an oboe introduction, *Down by the Saley Gardens* a clarinet, and *The Miller of Dee* a genial bassoon. *The cuckoo* brings a harp, and in *The keel row* the woodwind interjections are delightful, while the evocative introduction to *Afton water* is particularly beautiful. Even so, several more memorable items, *O waly waly* for instance, are unaccompanied. The five arrangements by Vaughan Williams bring welcome contrast. The choir sings beautifully, but most of the programme is flowing and mellifluous and one would have welcomed more robust items like *Dashing away* with the smoothing iron and *The British Grenadiers*. The recording is richly atmospheric.

'Christmas day in the morning' (with City of London Sinfonia; (i) Stephen Varcoe): TRAD., arr. RUTTER: *I saw three ships; Sans day carol; Un flambeau, Jeannette, Isabelle; Wexford carol; Quittes pasteurs; Go tell it on the mountain; Deck the hall; We wish you a merry Christmas; (i) Riu, riu, chiu.* RUTTER: *Mary's lullaby; Star carol; Jesus child; Donkey carol; Wild wood carol; The very best time of year; Shepherd's pipe carol; Christmas lullaby.* WILLAN: *What is this lovely fragrance?* WARLOCK: *Balulalow; I saw a fair maiden.* TAVENER: *The Lamb.* VAUGHAN WILLIAMS: (i) *Fantasia on Christmas carols.* TRAD., arr. WILLCOCKS: *Blessed be that maid Mary.*

**(*) Coll. COLCD 121.

Admirers of Rutter's own carols will certainly be drawn to his latest Christmas collection, for alongside the favourites there are several new ventures in his inimitably lively rhythmic style. The *Donkey carol*, too, becomes more passionate than in previous accounts. But in general, although the whole programme is enjoyable, beautifully sung and smoothly recorded, the feeling of spontaneous freshness, so enticing on his earliest Decca collection (currently withdrawn), made with the choir from Clare College, is less apparent here, and at times there is a hint of blandness (noticeable with the ritardando at the close of Tavener's *The Lamb*). *Go tell it on the mountain* does not sound entirely idiomatic, and while *We wish you a merry Christmas* ends the concert spiritedly, the Vaughan Williams *Fantasia*, even though it has a fine climax, does not quite match the King's College version (see below) in robust, earthy vigour.

'A Banquet of voices' (Music for multiple choirs): GUERRERO: *Duo seraphim.* ALLEGRI: *Miserere.* CALDARA: *Crucifixus.* SCHEIDT: *Surrexit pastor bonus.* TALLIS: *Spem in alium* (40-part motet). PHILIPS: *Ave Regina caelorum.* BRAHMS: *3 Fest-und Gedenksprücke.* MENDELSSOHN: *Mitten wir im Leben sind; Heilig.* BACH: *Motet: Singet dem Herrn, BWV 225.*

** Coll. COLCD 123.

The resonant acoustic of the Great Hall of University College, London, does not really suit the complex early polyphonic music here, often clouding the detail of writing for double or triple choir and producing a poorly focused climax in the spectacular Tallis *Spem in alium*. The singing too could be more robust in the Scheidt motet. The choir, seem much more at home in Brahms and Mendelssohn and the closing section of the Bach motet, *Singet den Herrn*, is vigorously joyful.

'Portrait': BYRD: *Sing joyfully; Non vos relinquam.* FAURE: *Cantique de Jean Racine; Requiem: Sanctus.* RUTTER: *O be joyful in the Lord; All things bright and beautiful; Shepherd's pipe carol; Open thou mine eyes; Requiem: Out of the deep.* PURCELL: *Hear my prayer, O Lord.* STANFORD: *Beati quorum via; The blue bird.* TRAD.: *This joyful Eastertide; In dulci jubilo.* HANDEL: *Messiah: For unto us a child is born.* FARMER: *A pretty bonny lass.* MORLEY: *Now is the month of maying.* DELIUS: *To be sung of a summer night on the water I & II.* VICTORIA: *O magnum mysterium.* TERRY: *Myn lyking.*

(M) *** Coll. DDD/ADD CSCD 500.

John Rutter has arranged the items here with great skill so that serene music always makes a contrast with the many exuberant expressions of joy, his own engaging hymn-settings among them. Thus the bright-eyed hey-nonny songs of John Farmer and Thomas Morley are aptly followed by the lovely wordless *To be sung of a summer night on the water* of Delius, and Stanford's beautiful evocation of *The blue bird* (one of Rutter's own special favourites). The sound, vivid and atmospheric, suits the colour and mood of the music quite admirably. Not to be missed!

'The Cambridge Singers Collection' (with Wayne Marshall, City of L. Sinf.): DEBUSSY: *3 Chansons d'Orléans.* Folksongs (arr. RUTTER): *The keel row; The willow tree.* Gregorian chant: *Regina caeli laetare.* BRUCKNER: *Ave Maria.* VERDI: *Laudi alla Vergine Maria.* STANFORD: *Magnificat in D; Te Deum in C.* PURCELL: *Remember not, Lord, our offences.* TAVERNER: *Christe Jesu, pastor bone.* PHILIPS: *O Beatum et sacrosanctum diem.* PEARSALL: *Lay a garland.* RUTTER: *Riddle song; Waltz; Magnificat* (1st movement); *The Wind in the Willows* (excerpt, with The King's Singers, Richard Baker, Richard Hickox). TRAD. (arr. RUTTER): *Sing a song of sixpence.*

(M) Coll. CSCD 501.

Here is an attractively chosen, 64-minute sampler, including a wide range of tempting repertoire from arrangements of folksongs to Stanford and Verdi. The Taverner and Philips items are particularly welcome. Rutter includes a fair proportion of his own music, but the opening (only) from his setting of *The Wind in the Willows* will not be something one would want to return to very often.

Carewe, Mary (soprano)

'Tell me the truth about love' (with Blue Noise, Philip Mayers, piano): GERSHWIN: *Blah, blah, blah; Embraceable you; They all laughed; Summertime; Love is here to stay; By Strauss.* WAXMAN: *Alone in a big city.* HOLLAENDER: *Chuck out the men.* SPOLIANSKY: *The smart set.* WEILL: *Speak low; The saga of Jenny; It never was you.* MULDOWNEY: *In Paris with you.* BRITTEN: *Tell me the truth about love; Funeral blues; Johnny; Calypso; When you're feeling like expressing your affection.*

(M) *** ASV CDWHL 2124.

In her brilliantly chosen collection of cabaret songs, Mary Carewe hits an ideal balance between cabaret style - with a touch of the old-fashioned 'belter' – and art-song style – with clean, firm vocal attack. Too often, Britten's five settings of Auden poems emerge as too refined. Carewe's full-blooded approach brings them to life in a new way, not just as anaemic pastiche. The first and longest of them is what gives the collection its title, but the six Gershwin numbers which frame the programme at beginning and end are just as stylish, though Philip Mayers' sophisticatedly smoochy arrangement of *Summertime* from *Porgy and Bess* makes it almost unrecognizable. In some ways the most moving item is one of the three Kurt Weill songs, *It never was you*, and it is good to have Dominic Muldowney represented in nicely turned pastiche, the more impressive when set against numbers by such exiles in Hollywood as Waxman, Hollaender and Spoliansky. The only snag is the overblown recording, which emphasizes the pop style in aggressive closeness for voice and instruments.

Cathedral Choirs of Winchester, St Paul's and Christ Church, Oxford

English Cathedral Music: PURCELL: *Rejoice in the Lord Always* (with Brandenburg Consort). SCHUBERT: *German Mass: Sanctus.* LOTTI: *Crucifixus.* ALLEGRI: *Miserere mei.* HAYDN: *Missa Rorate coeli desuper: Kyrie; Gloria; Credo* (with Academy of Ancient Music, Preston). BYRD: *Bow thine ear, O Lord; Turn Our Captivity, O Lord.* WEELKES: *Alleluia, I Heard a Voice; Lord Arise Into Thy Resting-Place* (with London Cornet & Sackbut Ens.). VAUGHAN WILLIAMS: *O Clap Your Hands.* SAINT-SAENS: *Messe à quatre voix, Op. 4: Sanctus; Benedictus; O salutaris.* WALTON: *Coronation Te Deum* (with Bournemouth SO, Hill).

(B) **(*) Decca (ADD/DDD) 470 124-2.

This collection, though diverse, works well as a 70-minute anthology of choral favourites, plus a few less familiar pieces. Mixing organ-accompanied items with the full orchestral numbers, as well as others with baroque orchestral accompaniments, means that the results are well contrasted. The performances range from good to outstanding, and the recordings are all excellent. At bargain price this is attractive enough.

Cerquetti, Anita (soprano)

'Grandi voci': Arias from: VERDI: *Aida; I vespri siciliani; Nabucco; Ernani; La forza del destino.* BELLINI: *Norma.* SPONTINI: *Agnes von Hohenstaufen.* PUCCINI: *Tosca.* PONCHIELLI: *La Gioconda* (with Giulietta Simionato, Mario del Monaco, Ettore Bastianini, Florence Festival Ch. & O, Gianandrea Gavazzeni).

(M) ** Decca (IMS) (ADD) 440 411-2.

This recital sports a really fearsome portrait of Madame Cerquetti with raspberry lips pouting furiously – a Casta diva indeed! In the aria of that name, Cerquetti's entrance is rather marred by an unforgivably flat flute obbligato. Cerquetti's half-tone at the beginning of the aria is most ingratiating (if not entirely free of squelching in toothpaste bursts), but the voice hardens when pressed. With such a big voice the degree of flexibility is credible, but ideally Bellini requires even greater sense of style.

The rare aria, *O re dei cieli*, from Spontini's *Agnes von Hohenstaufen* also brings shrill fortissimo attack, but the *Nabucco* excerpt shows up Cerquetti's voice more impressively, with a fine sense of attack in the dramatic recitative, and her richly spun *Vissi d'arte* suggests she was a formidable Tosca. The most impressive items here come from her 1957 complete set of *La Gioconda*; they are rather fine and certainly powerful. The recording is spacious and free without being markedly brilliant. In 1961 Cerquetti withdrew from the operatic stage (temporarily, as she thought) but her attempts to return were thwarted by the pre-eminence of Callas and Tebaldi.

Chadwell, Tracy (soprano), Pamela Lidiard (piano), John Turner (recorders)

'Songbook': MACONCHY: *Sun, moon and stars; Three songs.* LEFANU: *I am bread; A penny for a song.* WHITEHEAD: *Awa Herea.* CRESSWELL: *Words for music.* LUMSDAINE: *Norfolk songbook* (with John Turner, recorders). LILBURN: *3 Songs.* FARQUHAR: *6 Songs of women.* JOUBERT: *The turning wheel.* Rodney BENNETT: *A Garland for Marjory Fleming.*

British Music Society BMS 420/1 (2).

Tracey Chadwell, whose career was tragically cut short by leukaemia when she was still in her mid-thirties, was an exceptional singer, as this generous two-disc collection of songs makes plain. Hers was a light, bright soprano of extraordinary flexibility and sweetness. She might have become an operatic coloratura, but her special love was for new music. She had an extraordinary gift for making the most impossibly craggy vocal lines sound grateful and expressive, as she does in many of the challengingly difficult songs here. Three of the song-cycles in the collection, by Elizabeth Maconchy, David Lumsdaine and the New Zealand composer Gillian Whitehead, were specially written for her, as well as one of the separate songs, and one can understand the enthusiasm of composers to write for a singer so responsive. Not only did she sing with keen musical imagination, she projected her sparkling personality with a zest that matched the sparkle in her voice.

The recordings, drawn from BBC sources, are all first-rate, with Pamela Lidiard as her understanding piano accompanist, and with the recorder-player, John Turner, as her partner in the Lumsdaine cycle. The collection comes to a charming conclusion with Richard Rodney Bennett's settings of poems by an early-nineteenth-century child-poet, *A Garland for*

Marjory Fleming. An illuminating collection of modern songs as well as a fitting memorial.

Chanticleer

'Sing we Christmas': PRAETORIUS: *Es ist ein Ros' entsprungen.* VICTORIA: *O magnum mysterium.* TRAD.: *In dulci jubilo* (with verse 2 arr. M. PRAETORIUS; verse 3 arr. H. PRAETORIUS; verse 4 arr. BACH). *O Jesuslein süss, O Jesuslein mild* (verse 1 arr. SCHEIDT; verse 2 arr. BACH). JOSQUIN DES PRES: *O virgo virginum.* HANDEL: *Hodie Christus natus est; Mirabile mysterium.* ANON.: *Verbo caro factum est: Y la Virgen le dezia.* GUERRERO: *A un niño llorando.* HOWELLS: *Here is the little door.* SAMETZ: *Noel canon.* arr. WILLCOCKS: *Quelle est cette odeur agréable.* arr. RIBO: *El Noi de la mare.* IVES: *A Christmas carol.* BILLINGS: *A virgin unspotted.* HOLST: *In the bleak midwinter.* arr. JENNINGS: *Glory to the newborn king* (fantasia on four spirituals). GRUBER: *Stille Nacht.*

** (*) Teldec 4509 94563-2.

The rich sonority of the very familiar opening Praetorius carol immediately demonstrates the body and homogeneity of the singing of this fine choral group of a dozen perfectly matched male voices; but while the choir's dynamic contrasts are not in question, the close balance prevents an absolute pianissimo, and the resonance brings a degree of clouding when lines interweave swiftly, as in Jacob Händl's *Hodie Christus natus est.* The lush blend of the slowly flowing *Mirabile mysterium,* with its haunting momentary stabs of dissonance, shows the choir at its finest, as does Victoria's contemplatively gentle setting (*O magnum mysterium*) and the rapt, interweaving polyphony of Josquin's *O virgo virginum,* where the depth of sonority is extraordinary.

If Herbert Howells's *Here is the little door* and Holst's *In the bleak midwinter* are made to seem too static, the *Ives Christmas carol* suits the sustained style, while Sametz's ingenious *Noel canon* is admirably vigorous, as is William Billings's *A virgin unspotted.* The extended sequence of four traditional gospel songs, arranged by Joseph Jennings, is perhaps the highlight of the concert, sung colloquially with some fine solo contributions, especially from the bass; and the closing *Stille Nacht* brings an unforgettably expansive resonance, with the voices blending like a brass chorale.

'Christmas' (also with Dawn Upshaw, soprano): Arr. VAUGHAN WILLIAMS: *This the Truth Sent from Above.* TAVENER: *A Christmas Round; Today the Virgin.* DISTLER: *Es ist ein Ros entsprungen (Fantasy).* Arr. HUMPHRIES: *Noël nouvelet.* BOLD/KIRKPATRICK: *Lullaby/Away in a manger.* Arr. WILLCOCKS: *The First Nowell.* WILLAN: *Three Kings.* MANTYJARVI: *Die Stimme des Kindes.* TRAD. Welsh: *Sio Gân.* GRUBER: *Silent Night.* TRAD.: *Mary and the Baby Medley.*

*** Teldec 8573 85555-2.

An essentially intimate collection, beautifully sung and recorded. But the mixture, with its fair sprinkling of favourites, does not always gell readily. John Tavener, as always, manages stimulatingly to look backwards in time, with his bare medieval harmonies; but some of the other modern settings are quite luscious, notably Hugo Distler's vocal divisions on *Es ist ein Ròs entsprungen* and Jaakko Mäntyjärvi's *Die Stimme des Kindes.* Healy Willan's *The Three Kings* is refreshingly original, and Dawn Upshaw contributes serenely to Vaughan Williams's lovely arrangement of *This is the Truth Sent from Above* and vivaciously to the Spanish carol. However not all will want the elaborate treatment of Grüber's *Silent Night,* and the American gospel sequence, *Mary and the Baby Medley,* spirited as it is, does not fit readily into the programme's overall mood.

Christ Church Cathedral Choir, Oxford, Francis Grier

'Carols from Christchurch' (with Harry Bicket, organ): GARDNER: *Tomorrow shall be my dancing day.* trad.: *O thou man; In dulci jubilo.* HADLEY: *I sing of a maiden.* HOWELLS: *Sing lullaby; Here is the little door; A spotless rose.* WARLOCK: *Bethlehem Down.* MATHIAS: *Sir Christèmas.* arr. BACH: *O little one sweet.* TCHAIKOVSKY: *The crown of roses.* WISHART: *Alleluya, a new work is come on hand.* BRITTEN: *A ceremony of carols* (with Frances Kelly, harp); *Shepherd's carol; A Boy was born: Jesu, as Thou art our Saviour.*

(M) *** ASV (ADD) CDWHL 2097.

This is among the most attractive of mid-priced reissues of carol collections, the more particularly as it includes not only a first-class account of Britten's *Ceremony of carols,* plus *Jesu, as Thou art our Saviour,* with its piercing momentary dissonances, but also the dialogue *Shepherd's carol,* so effectively featuring four soloists. The dozen other carols also bring some radiantly expressive singing, particularly in the three inspired Howells works; the Hadley carol, too, is delightful. They are framed by the admirably lively items by Gardner and Wishart, with Mathias's buoyant *Sir Christèmas* as a centrepiece. Generally good, analogue sound from the early 1980s.

Christofellis, Aris (sopraniste)

'Farinelli et son temps' (with Ensemble Seicentonovecento, Flavio Colusso): Arias from: DUNI: *Demofoonte.* GIACOMELLI: *Merope.* METASTASIO: *La Partenza.* HANDEL: *Ariodante; Serse.* BROSCHI: *Artaserse.* HASSE: *Artaserse; Orfeo.* ARIOSTI: *Artaserse.* PERGOLESI: *Adriano in Siria.*

*** EMI CDC5 55250-2.

What did operatic castratos sound like in the eighteenth century? The only recording of a genuine castrato, made at the turn of the last century, is a travesty, merely the squawking of an old man. By any reckoning, here is a much closer answer, a finely trained high falsettist who, in the beauty and evenness of the sound, with a minimum of ugly hooting, suggests that this may well approximate to the sound of a castrato.

A recording may exaggerate the size of Christofellis's voice – by report the singing of the great castratos was exceptionally powerful – but he is artist enough, with a formidable technique, to make a splendid show in this dazzling series of arias originally written for the great castrato Farinelli. Some of his cadenzas are breathtaking. One brief song is by Farinelli's greatest friend, the librettist Metastasio, and Farinelli's own setting of the same words is also included. The items from Handel's *Ariodante* and *Serse*, better known than the rest, come in performances which stand up well against those we have had from female singers, and Christofellis in his note pays tribute to the pioneering work of Marilyn Horne. The performances are all lively and alert, and the recording of the voice is full and vivid, though the instrumental accompaniment is backwardly placed.

'Coloratura spectacular'

'Coloratura spectacular' (with (i) Joan Sutherland; (ii) Sumi Jo (sopranos); (iii) Marilyn Horne (mezzo)): (i) OFFENBACH: *Contes d'Hoffmann: Doll song.* (ii) *Un mari à la porte: Valse tyrolienne.* (iii) PERGOLESI/LAMPUGNANI: *Meraspe o l'Olimpiade: Superbo di me stesso.* (i) VERDI: *Attila: Santo di patria … Allor che i forti corrono.* (ii) AUBER: *Le Domino noir: La belle Inès fait florès; Flamme vengeresse.* (i; iii) ROSSINI: *Semiramide: Serbami ognor si fido il cor.* (ii) MASSE: *La Reine Topaze: Ninette est jeune et belle.* (iii) ARDITI: *Bolero: Leggero, invisibile qual aura sui fiori.* (i) GLIERE: *Concerto for coloratura soprano, Op. 82;* (iii) DONIZETTI: *Lucrezia Borgia: Il segreto per esse felici.* (ii) MOZART: *Die Zauberflöte: Der Hölle Rache.*

(M) *** Decca ADD/DDD 458 240-2.

'Coloratura spectacular' is a dazzling display of vocal feux d'artifice from Decca's three top female vocal virtuosi, opening appropriately with Sutherland's sparklingly precise *Doll song*, followed by Sumi Jo's glittering and no less charming displays in Offenbach and Auber, plus an amazing *Carnaval de Venise*, where the flexibility of her upper tessitura has to be heard to be believed. Vibrant drama comes from Sutherland in Verdi's *Attila*, and Marilyn Horne shows her vocal range and fire-eating strength in a thrilling pastiche Pergolesi aria, Arditi's *Bolero* and *Il segreto per esse felici* from Donizetti's *Lucrezia Borgia*. The two divas then join together for a famous duet from Rossini's *Semiramide*, while Glière's two-movement *Concerto for coloratura soprano* again shows Sutherland at her most nimble and personable. Overall this is a remarkable demonstration to confirm that the present-day coloraturas can hold their own with the best from the so-called Golden Age. Full translations are included.

Columbus Consort

'Christmas in early America' (18th-century carols and anthems): BELCHER: *How beauteous are their feet.* HOLYOKE: *How beauteous are their feet; Th'Almighty spake and Gabriel sped; Comfort ye my people.* CARR: *Anthem for Christmas.* STEPHENSON: *If angels sung a Saviour's birth.* HUSBAND: *Hark! The glad sound.* HEIGHINGTON: *While shepherds watched their flocks by night.* FRENCH: *While shepherds watched their flocks by night.* BILLINGS: *While shepherds watched their flocks by night.* PETER: *Unto us a child is born.* ANTES: *Prince of Peace, Immanuel.* MICHAEL: *Hail Infant newborn.* HERBST: *To us a Child is born.* SCHULZ: *Thou Child divine.* DENCKE: *Meine Seele erhebet den Herrn.* GREGOR: *Hosanna! Blessed he that comes in the name of the Lord.* Charles PACHELBEL: *Magnificat anima mea Dominum.*

*** Channel Classics Dig. CC 5693.

A fascinating look back to the celebration of Christmas in the New World in the late eighteenth century, both by the British colonial settlers in New England and by their Moravian counterparts in Pennsylvania and North Carolina, where the inheritance was essentially in the European tradition. The English style is usually fairly simple and hymn-like, but with overlapping part-writing and occasional solo dialogues (as in the rhythmically interesting *Th'Almighty spake*).

Samuel Holyoke shows himself to be a strikingly fresh melodist; while, of the three settings of *While shepherds watched* to different tunes, William Billings's emerges as the most striking and imaginative. Benjamin Carr's *Anthem for Christmas* is a musical pastiche (indeed, a kind of 'musical switch' with brief quotations from Corelli's *Christmas concerto* and Handel's *Messiah* among other works). The Moravian/German music is usually more elaborate. Johann Peter's delightful motet-like carol, *Unto us a Child is born*, has characteristically resourceful accompanimental string-writing and those who follow him – David Moritz Michael, Johannes Herbst, J. A. P. Schulz and Jeremiah Dencke – all write in a tradition descended from the great German composers, capped by Charles Pachelbel (son of the Johann Pachelbel of *Canon* fame). He played the organ in Boston, New York and Charleston in the 1730s and 1740s, and his *Magnificat* for double chorus celebrates a much more florid style, utterly different from the music which opens this programme.

The surprise is that this concert is performed not by American singers but by a Dutch group of expert vocal soloists, with a choral and string ensemble who sing and play with convincing authenticity and an agreeably stylish spontaneity. The recording is realistic and clear and made within a perfectly judged acoustic.

Consort of Musicke, Anthony Rooley

'The World of the Consort of Musicke': DOWLAND: Come away, come sweet love; Fine knacks for ladies; Me, me, and none but me; Praise blindness eyes; Rest awhile, you cruel cares; Say, Love, if ever thou didst find; When Phoebus first did Daphne love; White as lilies was her face. GIBBONS: Dainty fine bird; Fair is the Rose; Fair ladies that to Love; 'Mongst thousand good; The Silver Swan; Trust not too much, fair youth. WILBYE: Ah, cannot sighs, nor tears; Die, Hapless man; Lady, I behold; Lady, your words do spite me; Lady, when I behold the Roses; Softly, o softly drop, mine eyes; Thus saith my Cloris bright; Why dost thou shoot; Ye that do live in pleasures. MORLEY: Arise, awake; Deep lamenting Hard by a crystal fountain; Hark! Alleluia; No, no, no, no, Nigella; Stay heart, run not so fast.

(B) *** Decca (ADD/DDD) 467 786-2.

These fine performances emanate from various LPs of the 1970s and early 1980s. The collection is well planned, and these are sensitive and stylish performances, excellently recorded, with moments of great beauty. One may complain about odd points: the diction is not always what it might be, for example, although the director is at pains to avoid obtrusive consonants, but there is much to delight the ear, and at its modest price, this is well worth exploring.

Corelli, Franco (tenor)

'The Singers' (Decca series): Arias from: VERDI: Otello. PONCHIELLI: La Gioconda. PUCCINI: Manon Lescaut; Tosca. ZANDONAI: Francesca da Rimini. GOUNOD: Faust.

(M) **(*) Decca (ADD) 467 918-2.

The dashingly handsome tenor Franco Corelli certainly cut a striking figure on stage, and he was described by Karajan as having 'heroic power, yet with great beauty of tone; darkly sensuous, mysteriously melancholic ... but above all a voice of thunder and lightning, fire and blood!' There are few tenors today who can match him, and his records are nearly always exciting. Even when one has quibbles stylistically – such as his French in the vivid Faust excerpt from 1966 – the sheer exhilaration of his approach wins out. Curiously, three of the items in this Corelli tribute – La Gioconda, Manon Lescaut and Francesca da Rimini – are duets with Renata Tabaldi, recorded in 1972, when the great soprano was unfortunately somewhat past her best, although she is certainly passionate. While there is much to enjoy here, the programme does not make a very satisfying whole. The texts and translations, as always in 'The Singers' series, are available only via a CD ROM drive, but the recordings, bar the odd minor bit of distortion, are vivid.

Arias from: VERDI: Il Trovatore; Aida. MASCAGNI: Cavalleria rusticana. PUCCINI: Turandot; Manon Lescaut; Tosca. GOUNOD: Roméo et Juliette. LEONCAVALLO: Pagliacci. GIORDANO: Andrea Chénier. BELLINI: Norma. DONIZETTI: La Favorita. PONCHIELLI: La Gioconda. CILEA: Adriana Lecouvreur. MEYERBEER: Les Huguenots. HANDEL: Serse (with SCHUBERT; BACH/GOUNOD: Ave Maria. ROSSINI: Petite messe SOLENNELLE: Domine Deus. FRANCK: Panis angelicus. DE LARA: Granada. CARDILLO: Core 'ngrato. DE CURTIS: Torna a Surriento).

(BB) **(*) Disky Royal Classics Vocal Double (ADD) DCL 704812 (2).

At his powerful best, Corelli was a really heroic if not a subtle tenor, as the opening Di quella pira and the following Celeste Aida lustily demonstrate. He is in equally good form as Turiddù in Cavalleria rusticana, and even finer as Canio in Pagliacci. Throughout this recital the glorious flow of tone and a natural feeling for the Italianate phrase (as in Come un bel dì di maggio from Andrea Chénier or the equally stirring Cielo e mar from La Gioconda) compensate for any lack of imagination. This together with the Donizetti, Puccini, and Meyerbeer items come from a 1962 recital, when Corelli was in excellent voice. The religious numbers (from the same period) are sung in a similar declamatory style, but Corelli's sense of line prevents vulgarization and he is in his element in the Neapolitan songs which close the programme. Accompaniments are sympathetic throughout, and the transfers project the voice vividly. There are no texts or translations.

Cotrubas, Ileana (soprano)

'Famous opera arias and duets' (with (i) Philharmonia Orchestra or (ii) Royal Opera House, Covent Garden, Orchestra, Sir John Pritchard): (i) Arias from DONIZETTI: Don Pasquale. MOZART: Le nozze di Figaro; Die Zauberflöte; Die Entführung aus dem Serail. PUCCINI: Turandot; La Rondine; La Bohème. Gianni Schicchi (with LSO, Maazel). VERDI: Rigoletto; La forza del destino. CHARPENTIER: Louise (cond. George Prêtre). Arias & duets from DONIZETTI: L'elisir d'amore (with Plácido Domingo or Sir Geraint Evans).

(M) *** Sony (ADD) SMK 60783.

Ileana Cotrubas recorded this basic recital in 1976, when she was at her prime. She was performing all the roles in the opera house at the time (except Leonora in Forza del destino) and the performances are beautifully sung (often ravishingly so, as in Deh vieni, Caro nome and the excerpt from La Rondine) and almost always dramatically convincing. The original LP collection is there supplemented with excerpts from her complete recordings, and Cotrubas makes a seductive Louise, and a delightfully vivacious Adina in L'elisir d'amore, well partnered by Domingo and Sir Geraint Evans. It was sensible that such an extended selection was included from this latter set, in which she was at her very best. It is perhaps a pity that the final bonus item, *O mio babbino caro* from Maazel's *Gianni Schicchi*, shows a flutter in the voice, but this is a tiny blemish, and there are few singers whose talents have been more comprehensively covered on a single CD. The accompaniments are very supportive, and the voice beautifully caught by the recording team, led by the late Bob Auger.

Crespin, Régine (mezzo-soprano)

'*French songs*': BERLIOZ: *Les nuits d'été.* RAVEL: *Shéhérazade* (with Suisse Romande Orchestra, Ansermet). DEBUSSY: *3 Chansons de Bilitis.* POULENC: *Banalités: Chanson d'Orkenise; Hôtel. La Courte Paille: Le Carafon; La Reine de coeur. Chansons villageoises: Les gars qui vont à la fête. 2 Poèmes de Louis Aragon: C; Fêtes galantes* (with John Wustman, piano).

⊕ (M) *** Decca Legends (ADD) 460 973-2.

Régine Crespin's recordings with Ansermet of the Berlioz and (especially) Ravel song cycles are classics of the gramophone and sound marvellous in these new Decca transfers. The other songs were originally part of a 1967 song cycle recorded in the Kingsway Hall with John Wustman. Crespin cleverly chose repertoire to suit her voice and all come over vividly, particularly the Debussy *Chansons de Bilitis* and the charming Poulenc song about *Le Carafon* – 'The little water jug' – who wants (like the giraffe at the zoo) to have a baby water jug and, with the magical assistance of Merlin, succeeds, much to the astonishment of the lady of the house.

Cura, José (tenor)

'*Anhelo*': Argentinian songs (with Ernesto Bitetti, guitar; Eduardo Delgado, piano; and orchestra).

** (*) Erato/Warner 3984-23138-2.

In his disc of Argentinian songs José Cura not only sings but directs the performances – seven of them involving a small orchestra – and arranges some of the pieces, two of them his own compositions. It makes a crossover disc that is not just 'middle-of-the-road' but 'easy listening', evidently designed to provide a sweet and unobtrusive background. The bright little Ginastera song is one of the few which, with its tango rhythm, has a Hispanic flavour. Most of the rest are yearningly melancholy, with *La campanilla*, the fifth of eight songs by Carlos Guastavino, a charming exception. In face of the general mood, the title, *Anhelo*, 'Vehement desire', taken from the last of the Guastavino songs, seems hardly appropriate. Though the recording acoustic and close balance do not allow the full bloom of Cura's fine tenor to come out, these are warmly expressive performances, not just from him but from his associates too.

Danco, Suzanne (soprano)

'*The Singers*' (Decca series): Arias from: PURCELL: *Dido and Aeneas.* GLUCK: *Alceste.* VERDI: *La traviata.* MASSENET: *Manon.* BIZET: *Carmen.* CHARPENTIER: *Louise* (with Suisse Romande O, Erede). MOZART: *Così fan tutte; Le nozze di Figaro* (with La Scala O, Perlea). Lieder and mélodies: R. STRAUSS: *Freundliche Vision; Morgen; Ständchen; Traum durch die Dämmerung; Zueignung.* DEBUSSY: *Ariettes oubliées* (with Agosti, piano).

(M) (**) Decca mono 467 909-2.

'Elegant, cool – paradoxically – at the same time passionate; technically accomplished and a mistress of pointed diction and immaculate phrasing,' writes Alan Blyth in the sleeve note, qualities all apparent on this disc from the very opening with Purcell's poignant *Thy hand, Belinda*. Famous in particular for both her Mozart and Debussy, as well as her supremacy in the French repertoire – all found here – one finds Danco also convincing in Lieder, using her fresh, pure voice with tremendous style, yet sounding very different from the sort of voices we often hear in this repertoire today, making this disc all the more cherishable. The 1950s sound is variable: the earliest items, the 1949 Mozart, are taken from 78s and have a scrawny orchestra, and the quality in the Suisse recordings is rather thin in tone. However, that is nothing compared to that frightful orchestral playing under Erede – Danco's beautifully poised *Depuis le jour* is almost totally destroyed by the strings at 1′49″ in one of the most scrappily played passages ever to be committed to disc! Goodness knows how it was passed by the producer, never mind the conductor. Texts and translations are available only through a CD ROM drive, along with a photo-gallery, as usual in 'The Singers' series. The three stars are for Danco only!

Daniels, David (counter-tenor), Orchestra of the Age of Enlightenment, Harry Bicket

'*Sento amor*': Operatic arias from: MOZART: *Mitridate; Ascanio in Alba* (also Concert aria: *Ombra felice … Io ti lascio, K.255*). GLUCK: *Telemaco; Orfeo ed Euridice.* HANDEL: *Tolomeo; Partenope.*

*** Virgin VC5 45365-2.

There are few discs of counter-tenor arias to match this. The American David Daniels uses his exceptionally beautiful and even voice with flawless artistry and imagination, whether in Handel, Gluck or Mozart. Even such a well-known aria as *Che faro* from Gluck's *Orfeo* emerges with fresh individuality, and the coloratura is breath-taking in its precision and fluency throughout, not just a brilliant technical exercise but a musical delight. One can imagine singing like this from castratos of the time delighting eighteenth-century audiences. Even those who usually resist the falsetto voice will find Daniels on this disc an exception in his naturalness and freshness. Excellent sound.

Danish National Radio Choir, Stefan Parkman

'*Scandinavian contemporary a cappella*': TORMIS: *Raua needmine.* NORGARD: *And time shall be no more.* RAUTAVAARA: *Suite de Lorca, Op. 72.* SANDSTROM: *A cradle song.* JERSILD: *3 Romantike korsange.*

*** Chan 9264.

Tormis is an honorary Scandinavian: he hails from Estonia. Jørgen Jersild and Per Nørgård are both Danish, Sven-David Sandström Swedish (and mightily overrated in his homeland), and Einojuhani Rautavaara comes from Finland. Stefan Parkman has brought the Danish National Radio Choir to considerable heights and now it almost (but not quite) rivals the Swedish Radio Choir in its heyday under Eric Ericsson. None of the music is quite good enough to enter the permanent repertory in the way that the sublime motets of Holmboe's *Liber canticorum* should and doubtless will. By their side, this is all pretty small beer, but the Jersild and Rautavaara are worth investigating.

Dawson, Lynne (soprano), Malcolm Martineau (piano)

'*On this Island*': BRITTEN: *On this Island.* WARLOCK: *Lilligay My Own country; The Night.* QUILTER: *Fair House of Joy; My Life's Delight.* PARRY: *Armida's Garden; My Heart is like a Singing Bird.* STANFORD: *La belle dame sans merci; 3 Edward Lear Limericks; Limmerich ohne Worte* (piano solo). GURNEY: *Sleep.* HOWELLS: *King David.* VAUGHAN WILLIAMS: *Silent Noon; The Lark in the Clear Air; Through Bushes and through Briars.* FINZI: *Oh Fair to See; Since we Loved; As I Lay in the Early Sun.*

*** Hyp. CDA 67227.

Lynne Dawson, singing with golden tone and sparklingly clear diction offers one of the most delectable recitals of English song. In addition to well-known favourites like Vaughan Williams's *Silent Noon* and Howells's *King David*, Dawson and Martineau include a whole sequence of brief, intensely tuneful songs that are totally charming and deserve to be far better known, from Parry's *Armida's Garden* to Gurney's rapt setting of John Fletcher's, *Sleep.* Stanford is represented not only by the substantial *La belle dame sans merci*, but by three witty settings of Edward Lear limericks, which he used as comic party-pieces, full of parodies, together

with a brief piano solo designed as an accompaniment to any other limerick required. The recital ends with the Britten cycle of Auden settings that gives the disc its title; this is tougher, more incisive music than most of the rest. Dawson and Martineau are inspired throughout and beautifully recorded.

Robert DeCormier Singers and Ensemble, Robert DeCormier

'*Children go where I send thee*' (*A Christmas celebration around the world*) (with soloists from the Choir): Traditional songs and carols from: Sweden (arr. DECORMIER): *Ritsch, ratsch, filibon.* Italy: *Dormi, dormi, O bel bambin.* Austria: *Da Droben vom Berge.* Nigeria: *Betelehemu.* Spain: *A la nanita, nanita*; (Catalonia): *El noi de la mare.* USA: *Children go where I send thee; Poor little Jesus*; (Appalachian): *In the valley.* Puerto Rico: *La Trulla.* Germany: *Es ist ein' Ros' entsprungen.* France: *Ecoutons donc les aubades.* India: *Lína avatárá.* Canada: *Huron carol.* Syria: *Miladuka.* Argentina: *La peregrinacion.* West Indies: *The Virgin Mary had a baby boy.*

*** Arabesque Z 6684.

The excellent Robert DeCormier Singers have already recorded a number of fine collections, including a John Dowland anthology ('Awake sweet love': Z 6622) and two previous Christmas collections ('A Victorian Christmas': Z 6525 and 'The first nowell': Z 6526), but none has been more attractive than this geographically wide-ranging programme of Christmas songs with children in mind. The arrangements are simple, for every number has great character and needs no embellishment.

The programme opens enticingly with a tick-tock (*Ritsch, ratsch*) Swedish carol which is immediately captivating; it is followed with an exquisite Italian lullaby. The oldest item is a Syrian Christmas hymn, *Miladuka* ('The Nativity'), which, based on plainchant, is thought to be more than 1,000 years old. It is presented here in harmonized form and is quite haunting, as is the example from Northern India, *Lína avatárá* ('He chose to be among us'), which is introduced softly on flute and chiming percussion. When the voices enter, the harmonies are bare, whereas the Nigerian song about Bethlehem has rich upper intervals above the sonorous repeated bass and soon becomes exultant. The Argentinian carol, *The Pilgrimage*, is lusciously Latin, while the Spanish examples are simpler but lilting. The only really familiar carol is from Germany and it is beautifully and serenely presented. The concert ends swingingly with the more familiar West Indian *The Virgin Mary had a baby boy*, which is given the lightest, most infectious rhythmic touch. Altogether this splendidly recorded anthology, with its nicely judged instrumental accompaniments, will give great pleasure - to grown-ups as well as to children.

Deller, Alfred (counter-tenor)

Alfred Deller Edition

'*Western wind and other English folksongs and ballads*' (with Desmond Dupré, lute & guitar, John Southcott, recorder): *Western wind; Early one morning; Black is the colour; All the pretty little horses; Lowlands; The Sally gardens; Bendemeer's Stream; Annie Laurie; The Miller of the Dee; Cockles and mussels; Drink to me only; The foggy, foggy dew; The frog went a-courtin'; The turtle dove; Pretty Polly Oliver; The carrion crow; The wife of Usher's Well; Henry Martin; I am a poor wayfaring stranger; Cold blows the wind; Skye boat song; Every night the sun goes down; Song of a wedding.*

(M) *** Vanguard (ADD) 08.5032.71.

A ravishing collection of folksongs, recorded in 1958 when the great counter-tenor was at the very peak of his form. The early stereo gives a lovely bloom to his voice, and here, as throughout this fine series, the CD transfers are of a high calibre. The opening *Western wind* is justly another of Deller's 'hits', but *Lowlands* is hardly less beautiful, and many other items here show the magic of his tonal nuancing and his natural, spontaneous musicianship. *Annie Laurie* is wonderfully fresh and brings a frisson as he soars up to the top of his range, while the irrepressible *Miller of Dee*, the petite *Pretty Polly Oliver*, and jaunty *Foggy, foggy dew* show him well able to lighten his presentation in the most sparkling manner. *Every night when the sun goes down* brings an almost Gershwinesque, bluesy feeling. In the charming *All the pretty little horses*, *The Frog went a-courtin'* and the *Skye boat song*, John Southcott touches in discreet obbligati on the recorder, and throughout Desmond Dupré provides persuasive lute accompaniments. The last four songs listed appear on record for the very first time in any format.

'*The Silver swan and other Elizabethan and Jacobean madrigals*' (with the Deller Consort): GIBBONS: *The Silver swan; What is our life?; Ah! Dear heart; Dainty fine bird.* FRANCIS PILKINGTON: *Rest, sweet nymphs; Diaphenia like the daffdowndilly; Have I found her; O softly singing lute; Amyntas with his Phyllis fair.* BYRD: *Though Amaryllis dance; This sweet and merry month.* WARD: *Retrie, my troubled soul; Upon a bank with roses; Out from the vale.*

(M) **(*) Vanguard (ADD) 08.5038.71.

This collection comes from 1962 when the Deller Consort included April Cantelo, Eileen McLoughlin, Wilfred Brown and Maurice Bevan. The opening Gibbons title-number (in five parts) with its gentle passing dissonances is particularly beautiful, with the lullaby of Francis Pilkington, *Rest, sweet nymphs*, following on naturally; the same composer's lively portrait of the fair *Diaphenia* brings a lively contrast. Yet later *O softly singing lute* is ravishingly expressive, and an even deeper note is struck with Orlando Gibbons's ques-tioning *What is our life?* (with the poem, surprisingly, by Sir Walter Raleigh), sung with considerable intensity, as is *Ah! dear heart*. This composer's madrigals bring out the best in the Deller Consort. Byrd's *Sweet and merry month of May* might have had more sparkle, and the programme overall could have included more jolly numbers with advantage. The group's intonation is true and the vocal blending cannot be faulted, but the close recording means a comparatively restricted dynamic range, and the playing time is only 43 minutes. Full texts are included.

'*Catches, glees and other divers entertainments*': Tavern songs (with the Deller Consort): PURCELL: *Man is for woman made; Sir Walter; To thee and to the maid; Chiding catch; Once, twice, thrice; When the cock begins to crow; Epitaph, Under this stone; An ape, a lion, a fox, and an ass; True Englishmen; Young Collin; If all be true.* EARL OF MORNINGTON: *'Twas you, sir.* SAVILE: *Had she not care enough.* TURNER: *Young Anthony.* TRAD.: *Amo amas, I love a lass.* CORNYSHE: *Ah, Robin; Hoyda, jolly Rutherkin.* LAWES: *Bess Black; Sing fair Clorinda; The captive lover.* ANON.: *I am athirst; Troll the bowl; We be soldiers three; He that will an alehouse keep; Inigo Jones; Summer is icumen in.* ECCLES: *Wine does wonders.* TRAVERS: *Fair and ugly, false and true.* BENNET: *Lure, falconers, lure.* ROGERS: *In the merry month of May.* SPOFFORTH: *L'ape e la serpe.* HILTON: *Call George again.* ATTERBURY: *As t'other day.* ARNE: *The street intrigue; Which is the properest way to drink.* BLOW: *Bartholomew Fair; The self banished; Galloping Joan.* BOYCE: *John Cooper.* BARNABY: *Sweet and low.*

(M) **(*) Vanguard (ADD) 08.5039.71 [id.].

In this extraordinarily generous 78-minute collection from 1956, forty items in all, the Deller Consort consisted of Gerald English, Wilfred Brown, Maurice Bevan, Edgar Fleet and Owen Grundy, and they sing, unaccompanied, various catches and glees, part-songs, rounds (of which *Summer is icumen in* is a prime example) and semi-madrigals from both Elizabethan and Restoration England, right up to the pre-Victorian period. The opening 'Choice collection of the most diverting catches', attributed to Purcell, are mainly bawdy, explicitly about the joys of love-making in an age of frankness. The Elizabethan romantic lute-songs had an essential finesse and delicacy of feeling, so the more robust dialogue pieces acted as a healthy counterbalance. The popular ballads could also be restrained, and this opening group ends with a touching glee, *Under this stone*, about the late-lamented Gabriel John. There are many other part-songs intended to charm with their vivacity, and *Young Anthony peeping through the keyhole*, by William Turner (1651–1740), becomes more complex as its hero eagerly joins the two ladies he has overheard discussing their probity. *Ah, Robin*, a lovely glee by William Cornyshe, is better known today, slightly altered in rhythm, as *Sing we Nowell*, while the music for the glee/madrigal *Amo, amas, I love a lass*, with its naughty Latin parody text, could have come straight out of *HMS Pinafore*. Purcell's 'patter' trio, *True Englishmen*, also shows how much Sullivan borrowed from this fertile source. *We be soldiers three* even quotes doggerel French in the way of British soldiers who, in this instance, have returned from the Flemish wars, while *L'ape e la serpe*, a late-eighteenth-century glee by Reginald Spofforth, is sung in Italian. The performances are suitably direct, never prissy, and this especially applies to the robust drinking songs, although occasionally one would have welcomed a more spontaneously earthy bite. The recording is clear and immediate, the ambience dry but pleasing.

'The Connoisseur's Handel': excerpts from opera and oratorio (with Eileen Poulter, Wilfred Brown, Maurice Bevan, Handel Festival O, Anthony Lewis):
HANDEL: *Jephtha: 'Tis Heav'n's all ruling power; O spare your daughter; Laud her all ye virgins. Serse: Ombra mai fù. Orlando: Ah! stigie larve; Cielo! se tu il consenti. L'Allegro: Let me wander. Rinaldo: Lascia ch'io pianga. Theodora: Kind Heaven; Wide spread his name; Sweet rose and lily; To thee thou glorious son of worth.*

(M) **(*) Vanguard (ADD) 08.5043.71.

The highlight here is Deller's remarkable account of one of opera's first great mad scenes, Orlando's *Ah! stigie larve*, which is sung both dramatically and with passages of touching lyrical beauty. He also gives us the later florid *Cielo! se tu il consenti* from the same opera, the opening *'Tis heav'n's all ruling power* from *Jephtha* and, even more memorably, *Kind Heaven* and *Sweet rose and lily from Theodora*. The concert ends with a duet from the same oratorio, *To thee thou glorious son of worth*, shared with the radiant-voiced Eileen Poulter, who has previously given an equally beautiful account of the touching *Lascia ch'io pianga* from *Rinaldo*. But unexpectedly it is Wilfred Brown who sings *Ombra mai fù*, and the other solos are well shared with Maurice Bevan. There is less ornamentation than we would expect today, although Deller never puts a note wrong in this respect. Not surprisingly, Anthony Lewis provides stylish and pleasing accompaniments with the excellent strings of the 1960 Handel Festival Orchestra. Full texts and translations (where needed).

HANDEL **(with Oriana Concert Ch. & O, Honor Sheppard, Mary Thomas, Mark Deller, Maurice Bevan):** *Ode for the birthday of Queen Anne. Coronation anthems: The King shall rejoice; Let thy hand be strengthened; Zadok the Priest.*

(M) ** Vanguard (ADD) 08.5045.71.

In the Ode the highlight is Alfred Deller's opening solo, *Eternal source of light divine*, with his dueting melisma with the solo trumpet (the splendid Harold Lester). Otherwise the performance is only made distinctive by Deller's contributions: apart from the excellent Honor Sheppard, he is partnered by good, rather than outstanding, soloists, so the performance is enjoyable but not memorable. The *Coronation anthems* could do with more vitality in the accompa-

niments, especially the opening of *Zadok the Priest*, which has little anticipatory tension.

Italian songs (with Desmond Dupré, lute and viola da gamba; George Malcolm, harpsichord):
CACCINI: *Pien d'amoroso affetto; Amarilli.* SARACINI: *Pallidetto qual viola; Da te parto.* DA GAGLIANO: *Valli profonde.* A. SCARLATTI: *Difesa non ha; O, cessate di piagarmi; Bellezza che s'ama; O dolcissima speranza; La speranza mi tradisce.* BERTI: *Da grave incendio.* DONATO: *Dolce mio ben.* WERT: *Dunque basciar* (with harpsichord pieces by PARADISI **and** Michelangelo ROSSI).

(M) *** Vanguard (ADD) 08.5056.71.

This is another early collection from 1957. Deller is in freshest voice and top lyrical form here, and this repertoire suits him admirably. His phrasing is a model of melancholy elegance, as two Caccini songs immediately demonstrate, especially the lovely *Amarilli*, and as the poignant closing *Dunque basciar* (by Giaches Wert) readily shows. It is by no means a predictable programme, and there are two attractive harpsichord interludes from George Malcolm. Both he and Desmond Dupré provide admirable accompaniments. Full texts and translations are included, and the only criticism (apart from a curious drop in pitch at the opening of Berti's ambitiously sorrowful *Da grave incendio*) is Deller's repeated use of a very familiar (and authentic) cadential decoration. Recommended.

'Deller's choice' (with Gustav Leonhardt, organ or harpsichord; Marie Leonhardt, violin; Robert Scheiwein, cello): VIADANA: *Exaudi me Domine.* schutz: *In te Domine speravi.* PURCELL: *The Queen's Epicedium.* HUMFREY: *A Hymn to God the Father.* DE RORE: *Ancor che c'ol partire.* BLOW: *The Self-banished.* WELDON: *The Wakeful nightingale.* HANDEL: *Rodelinda: Dove sei.* bach (attrib.): *Bist du bei mir.* LOCKE: *Voluntaries in G and F.* FRESCOBALDI: *Toccata terza.* FROBERGER: *Toccata in D min.*

(M) *** Vanguard (ADD) 08.5059.71.

Another quite outstanding solo recital from 1960, with a most imaginative programme interspersed with organ and harpsichord pieces, all very well played indeed. The effect is highly spontaneous and there are some remarkable examples of Deller's art here, including a superb account of Purcell's beautiful *Elegy on the death of Queen Mary* and – no less memorable – Cipriano de Rore's *Ancor che c'ol partire*, with ornaments by Bovicelli. Blow's *The Self-banished* is also very touching, then Weldon's *Wakeful nightingale* provides a charming interlude before Handel's famous aria *Dove sei*, simply and gloriously sung, while the closing *Bist du bei mir* is hardly less eloquent. The accompaniments are very distinguished indeed, and the recording balance could hardly be bettered. Excellent notes and full translations.

'Madrigal masterpieces', Vol. 1: The Renaissance in France, Italy and England (with Eileen Poulter,

Mary Thomas, Wilfred Brown, Gerald English, Maurice Bevan, Geoffrey Coleby, Deller Consort): JANEQUIN: *Ce moys de may; La bataille de Marignan; Au joly boys.* LASSUS: *Mon coeur se recommande à vous; Matona mia cara.* MARENZIO: *Scaldava il sol.* MONTEVERDI: *Baci, soavi, e cari; Ecco mormorar l'onde; A'un giro sol bell'occhi; Non piu guerra!; Sfogava con le stelle.* BYRD: *My sweet little baby* (lullaby). MORLEY: *Now is the month of maying.* GESUALDO: *Ecco moriro dunque/Hai gia mi disco loro.* tomkins: *When David heard that Absolom was slain.*

(M) ** Vanguard (ADD) 08.5061.71.

We have moved on in the style of performance of Italian madrigals since this collection was (excellently, if closely) recorded in 1959. The Deller Consort are entirely happy in the English repertoire. Morley's *Now is the month of maying* almost explodes with spring-like vitality, and the Byrd and Tomkins items are beautiful. The Lassus *Mon coeur se recommande à vous* is touchingly serene in the same way, and *Matona mia cara* is freshly presented, but the Janequin and Monteverdi items are less successful, although *Baci, soavi, e cari* has an appealing simplicity.

'Madrigal masterpieces', Vol. 2 (with the Deller Consort): COSTELEY: *Allons, gay bergères; Mignonne, allons voir si la rose.* PASSEREAU: *Il est bel et bon.* MONTEVERDI: *Lagrime d'amante al sepolcro dell'amata; Incenerite spoglie; Ditelo voi; Dara la notte il sol; Ma te raccoglie; Ochioma d'or; Dunque amate reliquie; Zefiro torna e'l bel tempo rimena.* MARENZIO: *Solo e pensoso; Leggiadre Ninfe.* DE RORE: *Ancor che c'ol partire.* GESUALDO: *Morro lasso al mio duolo.* ARCADELT: *Il bianco e dolce cigno.* Robert JONES: *Fair Oriana seeming to wink at folly.*

(M) **(*) Vanguard (ADD) 08.5057.71.

For this 1963 collection the Deller Consort consisted of Mary Thomas, Honor Sheppard, Deller himself, Robert Tear, Max Wortley and Maurice Bevan, and once again the ear is struck by how well these highly individual artists can blend their voices together. The opening three chansons are charmingly sung as is the penultimate madrigal, Arcadelt's *Il bianco e dolce cigno*, yet one would have welcomed a more robust approach at times, especially to Passereau's delicious *Il est bel et bon* (with its hens cackling while the wife takes her pleasure with her cousin, and the play on the word 'coquette') after the more extrovert manner of David Munrow. However, the Monteverdi items are most expressively done and Gesualdo's *Morro lasso* is quite profound in its despair. Not unusually with this group they respond best to the melancholy numbers, not least the glorious rise and fall of the closing madrigal by Robert Jones, *Fair Oriana, seeming to wink at folly.* Excellent documentation as usual.

'Madrigal masterpieces', Vol. 3 (with the Deller Consort): MONTEVERDI: *Lamento d'Arianna; Ohimè il bel viso.* MARENZIO: *Cedan l'antiche tue chiare vittorie.* GESUALDO: *Belta poi che t'assenti.* JANEQUIN: *Le chant des oiseaux; Le chant de l'Alouette.* JOSQUIN DES PRES: *La déploration de Jehan Ockeghem; Parfons regretz.* LASSUS: *La nuit froide et sombre.*

(M) *** Vanguard 08.5092.71.

Volume 3, from 1965, is the finest of these three discs of 'Madrigal masterpieces' and brings a further regrouping of the singers in the Consort, with Honor Sheppard joined by Sally le Sage, and Max Worthley and Maurice Bevan by Philip Todd, all in their finest form. This repertoire clearly suits them admirably, for they sing with vitality – comparatively robustly where needed, and always with deep feeling. While including earlier music by Josquin, the programme concentrates on Flemish and Italian madrigals from the 'golden age' of the late sixteenth century. But the famous opening work dates from 1614: Monteverdi's four-part cycle *Lamento d'Arianna* originated as the heroine's key arioso in the opera of the same name written six years earlier. The complex writing, alternating drama and espressivo brings out the very best from the group and Deller directs the work with a natural spontaneity.

Marenzio's glorious *Cedan l'antiche* is hardly less successful and Gesualdo's remarkable *Belta poi che t'assenti*, with its plangent harmonic dissonances is also very finely sung. The delightful Janequin *Chant des oiseaux* ('Wake up sleepy hearts') with its ingenious polyphonic bird calls, makes a perfect interlude before Josquin's profound lament for his older contemporary, Ockeghem. The dolorous mood is then sustained with most beautiful singing and perfect tonal matching in *Parfons regretz* and the sombre *Le nuit froide* of Lassus, which evokes the darkness just before sunrise. Again Janequin lifts our spirits with more charming bird imitations and the programme ends with another of Monteverdi's finest madrigals, *Ohimè ilo bel viso*, like the *Lamento* coming from Book VI.

Beautifully recorded, this is one of the very finest of all the collections from Deller's Consort, and his direction shows supreme understanding and musicianship. As usual with this series, full texts are included.

TALLIS (with Wilfred Brown, Gerald English, Eileen McLoughlin, Maurice Bevan, Deller Consort): *Lamentations of Jeremiah the Prophet.* 5 hymns alternating plainchant and polyphony: *Deus tuorum militum; Jam Christus astra ascenderat; Jesu Salvator Saeculi; O nata lux de lumine; Salvator mundi Domine.*

(M) ** Vanguard (ADD) 08.5062.71.

Alfred Deller pioneered so much repertoire on LP, and even today Tallis's settings of the *Lamentations of Jeremiah* are not generously represented on disc. They are given poised, expressive performances and the motets are presented with their alternating plainsong, but the close recording robs the music-making of atmosphere and the dynamic range is very limited.

MONTEVERDI: *Il ballo delle Ingrate* (with Eileen McLoughlin, David Ward, April Cantelo, Amb. S., L. Chamber Players, Denis Stevens); *Lamento d'Arianna* (with Honor Sheppard, Sally le Sage, Max Worthley, Philip Todd, Maurice Bevan, Deller Consort).

(M) ** (*) Vanguard (ADD) 08.5063.71.

Deller's pioneering 1956 stereo recording of Monteverdi's *Il ballo delle Ingrate* would not, perhaps, be a first choice today, but at the time he had the advantage of Denis Stevens's scholarly assistance, and the performance has remarkable authenticity as well as considerable dramatic life. The famous *Lamento d'Arianna* is slightly less successful.

'*The three ravens': Elizabethan folk and minstrel songs* (with Desmond Dupré, guitar & lute): *The three ravens; Cuckoo; How should I your true love know; Sweet nightingale; I will give my love an apple; The oak and the ash;* (Lute) *Go from my window; King Henry; Coventry carol; Barbara Allen; Heigh ho, the wind and the rain; Waly, waly; Down in yon forest; Matthew, Mark, Luke and John;* (Lute) *A Toye; The Tailor and the mouse; Greensleeves; The Wraggle Taggle Gipsies; Lord Rendall; Sweet Jane; The frog and the mouse; The seeds of love; Near London town; Who's going to shoe your pretty little foot?; Blow away the morning dew; Searching for lambs; Sweet England; Dabbling in the dew; Just as the tide was flowing.*

(M) ** (*) Vanguard (ADD) 08.5064.71.

Opening charismatically with *The three ravens*, this very early (1956) recital contains some outstanding performances, notably of *Barbara Allen*, the delightful *Tailor and the mouse*, *The frog and the mouse*, and the captivating *Who's going to shoe your pretty little foot?*. *Searching for lambs* brings another favourite melody, and Deller's inimitable *Greensleeves* is certainly memorable. As before, Desmond Dupré provides highly sympathetic accompaniments, and here he also has a couple of solo opportunities in which to shine. But although the recording is admirably truthful, this collection is not quite so spontaneously appealing as the '*Western Wind*' recital listed above, even if it is comparably generous (73 minutes).

FRANCOIS COUPERIN: *Leçons de ténèbres I-III* (excerpts) (with Wilfred Brown, Desmond Dupré, viola da gamba, Harry Gabb, organ).

(M) *(*) Vanguard (ADD) 08.5066.71.

Although there is some remarkable singing here, Deller cannot compare with Gérard Lesne in this repertoire – his manner is curiously histrionic and self-aware, unusually so for this artist. Harry Gabb's discreet organ accompaniment is to be commended, but Dupré's viola da gamba is too backwardly balanced.

'*Duets for counter-tenors*' (with Mark Deller & Bar. Ens.): MORLEY: *Sweet nymph, come to thy lover; Miraculous love's wounding; I go before my darling.* PURCELL: *Sweetness of nature.* SCHUTZ: *Erhöre mich wenn ich; Der Herr ist gross.* JONES: *Sweet Kate.* ANON.: *Ah, my dear son.* MONTEVERDI: *Currite populi; Angelus ad pastores ait; Fugge, fugge, anima mea; Salve Regina.* BLOW: *If my Celia could persuade; Ah, heaven, what is't I hear.* DEERING: *O bone Jesu; In coelis.*

(M) *(*) Vanguard (ADD) 08.5067.71.

Deller's style needs no advocacy, and he has trained his son well to follow faithfully in his footsteps. But although Mark has a fine (treble rather than alto) voice, he does not have his father's subtle instinct for light and shade. So in this case a succession of duets for counter-tenors proves far from ideal planning for a whole recital. Moreover the voices are placed very forwardly, somewhat edgily recorded, and robbed of a convincing dynamic range; there are no possibilities for pianissimo singing here.

'*Byrd and his age*' (with Wenzinger Consort of Viols of Schola Cantorum Basiliensis, August Wenzinger). WILLIAM BYRD: *My sweet little darling; Lullaby, my sweet little baby* (both arr. FELLOWES); *Fantasia for viols in G min.; Ye sacred muses (Elegy on the death of Thomas Tallis); Come pretty babe* (arr. PETER LE HURAY & THURSTON DART). ANON.: *Guishardo; Ah, silly poor Joas; O Death, rock me asleep.* WHYTHORNE: *Buy new brooms.* RICHARD NICHOLSON: *In a merry May morn.* ROBERT PARSONS: *Pandolpho* (all six arr. PETER WARLOCK). WILLIAM CORKINE: *What booteth love?* (arr. THURSTON DART). FERRABOSCO: *Fantasias for viols in F & G.*

(M) ** Vanguard (ADD) 08.5068.71.

The advantage of accompaniments from the excellent Schola Cantorum Basiliensis under Wenzinger is reduced by the rather forward balance of the voice in relation to the string group, and when the viols play alone the effect is rather dry. It is on the whole a melancholy programme, although *Buy new brooms* comes centrally as a bright diversion. But it is *Ah, silly poor Joas*, the Byrd *Lullaby*, and especially the very touching *Pandolpho* that are memorable, while the closing *O Death, rock me asleep* shows Deller at his most moving.

BACH: *Cantata No. 170: Vergnügte Ruh', beliebte Seelenlust* (with Leonhardt Bar. Ens.); *Cantata No. 54: Widerstehe doch: Aria: Widerstehe doch; Recitative: Die Art verruchter Sünden; Aria: Wer Sünde tut, der ust vom Teufel. Mass in B min.: Agnus Dei.* HANDEL: *Arias: Orlando: Ah! stigie larve* (Mad scene). *Jephtha: Tis heav'n's all ruling power. Theodora: Kind Heaven; Sweet rose and lily.*

(M) ** Vanguard (ADD) 08.5069.71.

These are among Deller's earliest recordings for Vanguard, dating from 1954. In the Bach cantatas Leonhardt provides dull, plodding accompaniments, and his ensemble of original instruments is uninspiringly meagre. The interest of this collection then centres on Deller himself, and he rises to the occasion, especially in the *Agnus Dei* from the *Mass in B minor*, which is most beautifully sung. The Handel accompaniments are more robust and it is good to hear Deller in these operatic excerpts, especially in Orlando's mad scene, but he is also at his finest in both the excerpts from *Theodora*.

DOWLAND **(with the Deller Consort and Desmond Dupré, lute): Airs and partsongs: *Wilt thou, unkind, thus reave me?; Awake, sweet love; In darkness let me dwell; Me, me, and none but me!; Go, nightly cares; If my complaints could passions move; Sleep, wayward thoughts; Flow not so fast, ye fountains; Come again! Sweet love doth now invite; Sorrow, stay; If that a sinner's sighs; Fine knacks for ladies; Flow, my tears; Can she excuse my wrongs; (Lute) Queen Elizabeth's galliard.***

(M) **(*) Vanguard (ADD) 08.5071.71.

For this 1965 collection, Honor Sheppard, Deller and Maurice Bevan are joined by Philip Todd. The performances are stylish enough but perhaps just a little cosy. *Go, nightly cares*, which is sung by Honor Sheppard as a solo with continuo, is most touching. Deller's solo contributions, *If my complaints could passions move, Flow not so fast, ye fountains, Sorrow, stay, If that a sinner's sighs*, and *Flow, my tears*, are the memorable items here, although *Fine knacks for ladies* and *Can she excuse my wrongs* are engagingly presented by the full group.

'The Cries of London and English ballads and folksongs': The Cries of London (with April Cantelo, Wilfred Brown, Amb. S., Deller Consort, L. Chamber Players): JOHN COBB: *These are the cries of London.* RAVENSCROFT: *New oysters; Bellman's song; The painter's song; Brooms for old shoes.* DERING: *The cries of London* (all ed. Stevens); *Country cries* (ed. Revell). ANON.: *A quart a penny; I can mend your tubs and pails.* NELHAM: *Have you any work for the tinker?* (all ed. Stevens). WEELKES: *The cries of London* (ed. Noble). **English ballads and folksongs (with Deller Consort; Desmond Dupré, lute):** *When cockleshells turn silver bells; An Eriskay love lilt; Peggy Ramsay* (arr. GERARD WILLIAMS); *Bushes and briars; Brigg Fair; The cruel mother; A sweet country life* (arr. IMOGEN HOLST); *The bitter withy; Lang a-growing; The lover's ghost; Lovely Joan; She moved through the fair; A brisk young lad he courted me* (arr. NORMAN STONE); *Geordie.*

(M) **(*) Vanguard (ADD) 08.5072.71.

Richard Dering's *Fantasia* is sophisticated and creates a continuous ten-minute musical kaleidoscope, ingeniously linking the airs in a seemingly natural sequence, ending with a melodious apotheosis on the words 'and so good night'. Weelkes's selection is little more than half as long, using one soloist, here the fresh-voiced April Cantelo. Even so, she gets through a great many lyrical exhortations to buy, ending with a gentle *Alleluia*.

The second half of the recital brings Deller back (in 1959) to the world of ballads and folksongs, opening

with a bewitchingly gentle account of *When cockleshells turn silver bells*. Both *The lover's ghost* and the *Eriskay love lilt* take him soaringly upwards, rapturously comparable with *Annie Laurie* on an earlier recital. He is effectively joined by the Consort in *Peggy Ramsay* and they bring variety to the collection with characteristic accounts of *A sweet country life* and *A brisk young lad*. Dupré and his lute set the scene for the lovely *Bushes and briars*. *The cruel mother*, which tells a dreadful story of infanticide, also shows him imaginatively stretched, while *Lang a-growing* with its neat Scottish snap is most effectively done.

VAUGHAN WILLIAMS: **Arrangements of folksongs (with Deller Consort, Desmond Dupré, lute): *An acre of land; Bushes and briars; Ca' the yowes; The cuckoo and the nightingale; The dark-eyed sailor; Down by the riverside; A farmer's son so sweet; Greensleeves; John Dory; Just as the tide was flowing; The jolly ploughboy; Loch Lomond; The lover's ghost; My boy Billy; The painful plough; The spring time of the year; The turtle dove; Ward the Pirate; Wassail song.***

(M) ** Vanguard (ADD) 08.5073.71.

These highly artistic folksong settings can be effectively performed either by choir or by soloists, and here Deller often alternates his own estimable solo contributions with choral versions. The recording is a little dry, but the stereo adds to the sense of atmosphere. An enjoyable collection, but not one of the finest of the series.

'A Musical portrait of Shakespeare's England': (with the Deller Consort, Desmond Dupré, lute, Taylor Recorder Consort, Ambrosian Singers, Wenzinger Consort of Viols): ANON.: *We be soldiers three; The Wind and the rain; Munday's Joy and Watkins ale; Have you seen but a whyte lillie grow; Frog galliard, Coranto and borey, 'Mr Tollett'* (arr. DOLMETSCH); *Greensleeves; The Boar's head carol; The Agincourt song; O Death, rock me asleep* (arr. WARLOCK); *He who will an alehouse keep; Lord Rendall.* DOWLAND: *My Lady Hunsdon's Puffe.* WILBYE: *Ye that do live in pleasures.* RAVENSCROFT: *New oysters.* TALLIS: *O nata lux de lumine.* JOHNSON: *Alman. bennet: Lure, falconers, lure.* MORLEY: *Sweet nymph.* FERRABOSCO: *Fantasia* in G. BYRD: *Non nobis Domine.*

(M) **(*) Vanguard (ADD) 08.5075.71.

Another fairly early (1959) collection – which is particularly well planned – immediately invites the criticism that the opening *We soldiers three*, though admittedly sung in West-Country accents, needs to be more earthily robust; a comment which applies equally to *He who will an alehouse keep*. However, Deller's own contributions with Dupré, *The wind and the rain*, the lovely *Have you seen but a whyte lillie grow* and *Lord Rendall*, are all of the utmost distinction. In *O Death, rock me asleep* he is joined by Wenzinger's Viol Consort, who also play a solo *Fantasia* of Ferrabosco. April Cantelo and Eileen McLoughlin join to sing Morley's *Sweet nymph*, and there are diverting instrumental interludes from an accomplished recorder consort and also from Gustav Leonhardt. The full Deller Consort contribute impressively in darker music of Tallis and Byrd.

WILBYE: *Madrigals* (with the Deller Consort): *Thus saith my Cloris bright; Happy, O happy he, who not affecting; Ye that do live in pleasures plenty; Ah, cannot sighs, nor tears, nor aught else move thee; Stay, Corydon, thou swain; Draw on, sweet Night, best friend unto those cares; Lady, your words do spite me; As fair as morn, as fresh as May; Weep, weep, mine eyes, my heart can take no rest; I always beg, yet never am relieved; Thus Love commands that I in vain complain me; Oft have I vowed how dearly I did love thee; Come, shepherd swains, that wont to hear me sing; The Lady Oriana.*

(M) **(*) Vanguard (ADD) 08.5080.71.

This pioneering collection from 1957 is especially welcome, as even now Wilbye is not generously represented in the catalogue and the quality of his madrigals is consistently high. Gerald English here joins the other regulars and the vocal matching remains smoothly integrated. As ever it is the deeply expressive settings that are the most memorable, with *Ah, cannot sighs, nor tears, Draw on, sweet Night* and *Weep, weep mine eyes* all particularly beautiful. But the singing is always fresh and well captures the changing character of each item, revealing a composer who, if not as prolific as some of his contemporaries, was their equal in all other respects.

Elizabethan and Jacobean music (with Desmond Dupré, lute; Consort of Viols; Gustav Leonhardt, harpsichord; Nikolaus Harnoncourt, bass viol): DOWLAND: *Can she forgive my wrongs?; If my complaints could passions move. My Lady Hunsdon's puffe* (lute). *From silent night.* MORLEY: *Air for 3 viols.* BARTLETT: *Of all the birds that I do know.* JOHNSON: *Alman for harpsichord.* JENKINS: *Pavan and Fantasia in C, for 4 viols.* CAMPION: *I care not for these ladies.* PARSONS: *Pandolpho.* FARNABY: *Variations for harpsichord on Up tails all.*

(M) *** Vanguard (ADD) 08.5094.71.

One of the earliest recorded of the series (1954), though the recording is remarkably natural, this collection is in every way outstanding. Deller is in superb voice and the whole programme is glowingly fresh. There are novelties too. Parsons's air, *Pandolpho* (taken from a stage play), brings just as touching a melancholy as Dowland's *If my complaints could passions move*, and Bartlett's air, *Of all the birds that I do know*, and Campion's *I care not for these ladies* are delightfully light-hearted. The programme is attractively interspersed with music for viols (both bright and sombre) and a couple of lively harpsichord pieces. One small point: the vocal programme ends with a most moving account of Dowland's *From silent night* from *The Pilgrim's Solace*, but then the closing

harpsichord *Variations* brings a disconcerting slight change of pitch.

English lute songs and In nomines (with Desmond Dupré, lute, and the In Nomine Players): Francis PILKINGTON: *Rest, sweet nymphs.* DOWLAND: *What if I never speed?; Shall I sue?; Come again! Sweet love doth now invite; Me, me and none but me; Wilt thou unkind.* CAMPION: *Care-charming sleep; Shall I come sweet love to thee?* ANON.: *Have you seen but a whyte lillie grow.* ROSSETER: *When Laura smiles.* John DANYEL: *Chromatic tunes.* MORLEY: *Will ye buy a fine dog?* (*In nomines* by John BULL; TOMKINS; WHITE; TYE; TAVERNER).

(M) *** Vanguard (ADD) 08.5095.71.

This outstandingly well-balanced programme dates from 1958 and again finds Deller in exquisite voice in (among other items) his performances of Dowland's *Shall I sue?* and the traditional *Have you seen but a whyte lillie grow* (most subtly decorated), which is immediately followed by Rosseter's happy *When Laura smiles*. Morley's *Will ye buy a fine dog?* has an even lighter touch, but perhaps the most remarkable (and rarest) work here is John Danyel's *Chromatic tunes*, a highly expressive fantasia-like melisma in three sections for solo voice and lute, showing Deller and Dupré in total symbiosis.

The six *In nomines* are used as interludes and are varied in mood and colour. The two by Christopher Tye (*Trust* and *Crye*), both in five parts, are particularly engaging, but the most profound, which ends the concert, is by John Taverner. The instrumental playing is worthy of Deller's supreme vocal art and with excellent documentation this is another of the great counter-tenor's very finest discs.

Music of Purcell, John Jenkins and Matthew Locke (with Leonhardt Baroque Ensemble; Consort of Viols; Gustav Leonhardt, harpsichord; Nikolaus Harnoncourt, bass viol): PURCELL: *The Fairy Queen: Secrecie's song; Mystery song; The plaint. Fantasia for 4 viols. If ever I more riches did desire* (cantata): *Here let my life. Welcome to all pleasures: Here the Deities approve. History of Dioclesian: Since from my dear Astrea's sight. Keyboard: Prelude, air and hornpipe; Suite in D min.* LOCKE: *Consort of 4 parts for viols.* JENKINS: *Pavane for 4 viols.*

(M) *** Vanguard (ADD) 08.5104.71.

Deller did so much to revive interest in Purcell's stage works (as well as his songs and instrumental music) that it is meet and right that the last disc of the Vanguard series – although one of the first to be recorded, in 1954 – should be devoted to the music of England's greatest composer. Of the three items from *The Fairy Queen*, the opening *Secrecie's song* (with its accompanying pair of recorders) is delightful, but it is *The plaint* that stands out, one of the most masterly of all Purcell's songs. It is here superbly sung over a firm chromatic ground bass (Nikolaus Harnoncourt) and with a delicate violin obbligato. *Since from my dear Astrea's sight* is also memorable and *Here let my life* has a melancholy worthy of Dowland. The inclusion of music by Locke and Jenkins means that the songs can be interleaved with impressively performed instrumental pieces.

Other recordings

'*O ravishing delight*' (with David Munrow, Richard Lee, Desmond Dupré, Robert Elliott): ANON.: *Miserere my Maker.* DOWLAND: *Shall I sue?; Come heavy sleep; I saw my lady weep; Wilt thou unkind; Fine knacks for ladies; Flow my tears.* CAMPION: *I care not for these ladies; The Cypress curtain.* BARTLETT: *Of all the birds.* ROSSETER: *What then is love; What then is love but mourning.* FRANCIS PILKINGTON: *Rest, sweet nymphs.* BLOW: *The fair lover and his black mistress; The Self-banished.* CLARKE: *The glory of the Arcadian groves; In her brave offspring.* ECCLES: *Oh! the mighty pow'r of love.* CROFT: *My time, o ye Muses.* DANIEL PURCELL: *O ravishing delight.* HUMFREY: *A Hymne to God the Father.*

(B) **(*) HM Musique d'abord (ADD) HMA 190215.

Deller's recording contract with Vanguard lasted from 1954 to 1965 and he made more than sixty LPs for this label. Then he had a second, shorter recording period with Harmonia Mundi. The present collection dates from 1969 and one can hear him husbanding his voice, using it lightly where possible.

Many of the songs here are available in earlier performences above, but they still sound pleasingly fresh, and as can be heard in the very lovely opening *Miserere my Maker*, he has not lost his magic touch. Dowland's *Come heavy sleep* and *I saw my lady weep* and Campion's *Cypress curtain of the night* certainly bring the 'ravishing delight' of the title. It is good to have also a pair of songs from Jeremiah Clarke (of *Trumpet voluntary* fame), and *The glory of the Arcadian groves* features a charming recorder obbligato. The programme closes with a beautifully refined performance of Dowland's famous *Flow my tears*. Throughout, the accompaniments are of the highest quality, as is the recording, and as texts are included, this makes a fine bargain sampler of Deller's later achievement.

Del Monaco, Mario (tenor)

'*The Singers*' (Decca series) (with various conductors): Arias from: GIORDANO: *Andrea Chénier.* PUCCINI: *La Bohème; Madama Butterfly.* HALEVY: *La Juive.* BELLINI: *Norma.* VERDI: *Un ballo in maschera; Macbeth; Otello.* WAGNER: *Lohengrin; Die Walküre.* Songs: BIZET: *Agnus Dei.* FRANCK: *Panis angelicus.* GASTALDON: *Musica proibita.* BERNSTEIN: *West Side Story: Tonight.* BRODSZKY: *Be My Love.*

(M) (*) Decca stereo/mono 467 919-2.

Mario Del Monaco, a star at the Met, mainly because he could fill the house with his voice without difficulty, earned himself a reputation in the studio for all but shouting his way through many a recorded opera recording, particularly the later ones on Decca. He is at his best on this CD in the blood-and-thunder verismo excerpts represented by the *Andrea Chénier* aria and the Puccini items, which are not exactly vocally subtle. Under Karajan, he does, at last, show that he was capable of tender singing with a degree of characterization, which is not much in evidence in the other Verdi items under Rescigno. Perhaps the earliest excerpt here, from *La Juive* (mono), is the most enjoyable aria. The Wagner excerpts sound unidiomatic, but the lighter items, such as the *Agnus Dei* and *Panis angelicus*, show him at his very worst: loud and sloppy singing, even slightly embarrassing. As usual in Decca's 'The Singers' series, texts and translations, along with the usual photo-gallery, are available only via a CD ROM drive.

Domingo, Plácido (tenor)

'Vienna, City of My Dreams' (with Ambrosian Singers, ECO, Rudel): Arias from: LEHAR: *Das Land des Lächelns; Die lustige Witwe; Paganini.* ZELLER: *Der Vogelhändler.* KALMAN: *Gräfin Mariza.* FALL: *Der fidele Bauer; Die Rose von Stambul.* SIECZYNSKI: *Wien, du Stadt meiner Träume.* O. STRAUS: *Ein Walzerstaum.* J. STRAUSS JR: *Eine Nacht in Venedig.*

(BB) *** EMI Encore CDE5 75242-2.

Having such a golden tenor sound in Viennese operetta makes a winning combination, and Domingo, always the stylist, rebuts the idea that only a German tenor can be really idiomatic. A delightful selection, including one or two rarities, which is very well recorded and now offered at budget price.

'*Domingo favourites*' Arias from: DONIZETTI: *L'elisir d'amore.* VERDI: *Ernani; Il Trovatore; Aida; Nabucco; Don Carlos.* HALEVY: *La Juive.* MEYERBEER: *L'Africaine.* BIZET: *Les Pêcheurs de perles; Carmen.* PUCCINI: *Tosca; Manon Lescaut.*

(M) *** DG 445 525-2.

The greater part of this collection is taken from a 1980 digital recital, recorded in connection with yet another gala in San Francisco. The result is as noble and resplendent a tenor recital as you will find. Domingo improves in detail even on the fine versions of some of these arias he had recorded earlier, and the finesse of the whole gains greatly from the sensitive direction of Giulini. Though the orchestra is a little backward, the honeyed beauty of the voice is given the greatest immediacy. The other items are taken from Domingo's complete sets of *Don Carlos* (with Abbado), *Nabucco*, *Manon Lescaut* and *Tosca* (with Sinopoli), and are well up to the high standards this great tenor consistently sets for himself.

'Duets of love and passion'

Duets from: PUCCINI: *La bohème; Madama Butterfly; Manon Lescaut; Turandot.* VERDI: *Otello.* GOUNOD: *Faust.* SAINT-SAENS: *Samson and Dalila.*

(M) **(*) Decca (ADD) 458 241-2.

This collection starts well with Butterfly's duet with Pinkerton, from Serafin's classic 1958 account with Tebaldi and Bergonzi, but the *Otello* duet, with Margaret Price and Cossutta (Solti, 1977) is not quite so successful: Price is in lovely voice, but Cossutta does not quite match her in character. The 1972 Tebaldi/Corelli duet from *Manon Lescaut* is certainly passionate, but Tebaldi is a little past her prime here. The *Faust* excerpt is taken from Bonynge's lively 1966 set, and if one forgets the questionable French, it is most enjoyable – how could it fail with Sutherland, Corelli and Ghiaurov? It was imaginative of Decca to use the Josephine Barstow recording (1989) for the *Turandot* number: this was the first recording of Alfano's completion of the opera in its original full form, and is much longer than the version we are used to. The *Samson and Delila excerpt* is strongly performed with Sandra Warfield and McCracken (1966), and the programme ends with another classic Tebaldi/Bergonzi duet from *Bohème* (1959). Full texts and translations are included in this mid-price Opera Gala collection.

Early Music Consort of London, David Munrow

'*Music of the Gothic era*' (excerpts): **Notre Dame period:** LEONIN: *Organum Viderunt omnes.* PEROTIN: *Organum Viderunt omnes.* **Ars Antiqua:** *Motets from the Bamberg and Montpellier Codices* by PETRUS DE CRUCE, Adam DE LA HALLE and ANON. **Ars Nova:** *Motets from the Roman de Fauvel. Chantilly/Ivrea Codices* by MACHAUT: DE VITRY.

(B) *** DG (ADD) 469 027-2.

'Music of the Gothic era' is particularly valuable in providing a remarkably lively survey of medieval music during the two centuries when it was developing at a comparatively swift rate from early organa to the thirteenth-century motet, 'from the monumental to the miniature'. David Munrow had exceptional powers, both as scholar-performer and as a communicator. These performances are wonderfully alive and vital and the digital remastering is expert as one would expect.

'*The Art of the Netherlands*': **Secular songs (vocal and instrumental versions):** JOSQUIN DESPREZ: *Scaramella va alla guerra; Allegez moy, doulce plaisant brunette; El grillo è buon cantore; Adieu mes amours.* ISAAC: *Donna di dentro della tua casa.* VAN GHIZEGHEM: *De tous biens plaine.* BRUMEL: *Du tout plongiet – Fors seulement l'attente.*

OCKEGHEM: *Prenez sur moi vostre exemple amoureux; Ma bouche rit.* BUSNOIS: *Fortuna desperata* (with others by GHISELIN; ANON.). **Sacred music:** TINCTORIS: *Missa sine nomine:* Kyrie. BRUMEL: *Missa Et ecce terrae motus:* Gloria. JOSQUIN desprez: *Credo super De tous biens; De profundis; Benedicta es caelorum regina.* DE LA RUE: *Missa Ave sanctissima Maria: Sanctus.* ISAAC: *Missa La bassadanza: Agnus Dei.* OBRECHT: *Haec Deum caeli; Laudemus nunc Dominum.* MOUTON: *Nesciens mater virgo virum.* OCKEGHEM: *Intemerata Dei mater* (with anon.).

(M) *** Virgin (ADD) VED5 61334-2 (2).

The coverage here concentrates on the latter half of the fifteenth century, and the first disc is devoted to secular songs and instrumental arrangements. Josquin immediately makes his presence felt with an ear-catching opening item, *Scaramella is off to war*, for vocal quartet with recorders, bass viol, guitar, harp and tambourine, and later he is to return with the unaccompanied *El grillo*, where the vocal interchanges are equally lively. As most of these vocal numbers are short, what follows is a kaleidoscope of concerted and solo items, alongside instrumental arrangements (for lute duet, recorder consort, broken consorts or keyboard), providing plenty of contrast. Heinrich Isaac's jubilant quodlibet feaures nine singers, while Hayne van Ghizeghem's touching chanson, *De tous biens plaine*, is first sung as an accompanied counter-tenor solo, and then heard in three different instrumental arrangements. Many of the songs are richly expressive, Ockeghem's canon *Prenez sur moi vostre exemple amoureux* and Brumel's *Du tout plongiet* are memorably poignant examples. Busnois's *Fortuna desperata* is first presented in a three-part vocal presentation, then in six parts (three singers with a trio of viols), and finally on a combination of tenor dulcian, recorder, rebec and two lutes.

The second section, a group of Mass movements, immediately brings a greater degree of gravitas with Johannes Tinctoris's *Kyrie*, solemnly presented by four low male voices, yet Brumel's robust *Gloria* is memorably gutsy. Pacing never drags; indeed, Isaac's six-part *Agnus Dei* flows forward strongly. The motets in the third section, many of them Marian, are more consistently expressively solemn, but all are strikingly beautiful, with Josquin's *De profundis*, with its firm bass line, particularly eloquent. Full texts and translations are included and this seems an excellent way to explore this repertoire as a prelude to acquiring CDs concentrating on a single composer. The standard of singing and playing is high, and the recording is as vivid as you could wish.

'*The Art of courtly love*' (with James Bowman, Charles Brett, Martyn Hill, Geoffrey Shaw): I: '*Guillaume de Machaut and his age*': JEHAN DE LESCUREL: *A vous douce debonaire* (chanson). MACHAUT: *Amours me fait desirer; Dame se vous m'estés lointeinne; De Bon Espoir – Puis que la douce rousee; De toutes flours; Douce dame jolie; Hareu! hareu! le feu; Ma fin est mon commencement; Mes esperis se combat; Phyton le mervilleus serpent; Quant j'ay l'espart; Quant je suis mis au retour; Quant Theseus – Ne quier veoir; Se ma dame m'a guerpy; Se je souspir; Trop plus est belle – Biauté paree – Je ne sui mie certeins.* P. DES MOLINS: *Amis tout dous vis.* ANON.: *La Septime estampie real.* F. ANDRIEU: *Armes amours – O flour des flours.* II: 'Late 14th century avant-garde': GRIMACE: *A l'arme a l'arme.* FRANCISCUS: *Phiton Phiton.* BORLET: *2 Variants on the tenor 'Roussignoulet du bois'; Ma tedol rosignol.* SOLAGE: *Fumeux fume; Helas! je voy mon cuer.* Johannes de MERUCO: *De home vray.* ANON.: *Istampitta Tre fontane; Tribum quem; Contre le temps; Restoés restoés.* HASPROIS: *Ma douce amour.* VAILLANT: *Trés doulz amis – Ma dame – Cent mille fois.* PYKINI: *Plasanche or tost.* Anthonello DE CASERTA: *Amour m'a le cuer mis.* Matteo da PERUGIA: *Andray soulet; Le greygnour bien.* III: 'The Court of Burgundy': DU FAY: *Ce moys de may; La belle se siet; Navré ju sui d'un dart penetratif; Lamention Sanctae Matris Ecclesiae Constantinopolitaine (O tres piteulx - Omnes amici); Par droit je puis bien complaindre; Donnés l'assault; Helas mon dueil; Vergine bella.* BINCHOIS: *Je ne fai tousjours que penser; Files a marier; Amoreux suy et me vient toute joye; Je loe Amours et ma dame mercye; Vostre trés doulx regart; Bien puist.* ANON.: *La Spagna* (basse danse) *Variants I & II.*

(M) *** Virgin (ADD) VED5 61284-2 (2).

David Munrow's two-disc set 'The Art of courtly love' spans the period 1300-1475 in some depth. The survey is divided into three sections: 'Guillaume de Machaut and his age', 'Late fourteenth-century avant-garde' and 'The Court of Burgundy'. The first section is introduced arrestingly by two cornetts and an alto shawm, who accompany a striking chanson of Jehan de Lescurel (died 1304) which must have had 'hit' status in its time (*A vous douce debonaire*). The bare harmonies give a real tang to the tune. Then comes the first of many numbers by the justly famous Guillaume de Machaut, *Hareu! hareu! le feu . . . le feu d'ardant desir* which one hardly needs to translate, and it is certainly ardent!

But it is the expressive romantic chansons of Machaut that make one appreciate how readily the composer came to dominate the combination of lyric poetry and music in fourteenth-century France and to epitomize the title, 'The Art of courtly love'. The virelais *Se ma dame m'a guerpy* ('If my lady has left me') and *Quant je suis mis au retour*, for solo tenor and chorus, with its sad introductory bass rebec solo, surely anticipate the melancholy eloquence of Dowland, while Machaut could also be attractively lighthearted as in *Se je souspir* ('If I sigh'), or robustly jolly and spiritedly extrovert (*Douce dame jolie*).

The second CD opens with a particularly lovely vocal trio by Jehan Vaillant (?1360–90) which anticipates *The first nowell* in its vocal line, and a following ballade, *Amour m'a la cuer mis*, by Anthonello de

Caserta (whose career spanned the turn of the century) demonstrates how forward-looking were other composers of 'the late fourteenth-century avant-garde', while Solage is no less enterprising (flourished 1370-90) in providing lugubrious humour with his baritone solo *Fumeux fume* ('He who fumes and lets off steam provokes hot air') with its unlikely melodic line. (Not surprisingly, Munrow gives this rondeau an appropriately bizarre instrumental backing.) 'A man's true worth' (*De home vray*), a ballade by the late-fourteenth-century Johannes de Meruco, also brings lively melodic twists and turns.

Gilles Binchois (c. 1400–60) was another leading figure of the time, well represented here, and, like Machaut, he had a wide range. But it is the lovely rondeau duet *Amoreux suy et me vient toute joye* ('Filled with love, I am overjoyed, hoping that your kindness might bring sweet comfort') that one especially remembers. With its expressive pleading so direct in its appeal, it is one of the set's highlights and is ravishingly sung here. With the music from 'The Court of Burgundy' we also meet the remarkable Guillaume Du Fay, with his exhilarating rondeau *Ce moys de may*, so different in mood from his Masses, followed by an engagingly melancholy echoing duet for two counter-tenors, *La belle se siet au piet de la tour* ('The maiden sits . . . weeping, sighing and venting her grief'), while the virelai *Helas mon dueil*, a rejected lover's lament, is infinitely touching.

However, the collection ends in lively fashion with the anonymous basse danse *La Spagna*, and here (as in the other instrumental items) Munrow's choice of colour brings an extra dimension to what is basically a very simple dance. All the soloists are distinguished and at their finest. Incidentally, although the translations are not affected, the documentation for this set has the list of titles for the second disc mixed up, starting with bands 12–15, then following with 1–11, but they are all there.

'Monteverdi's contemporaries' (with James Bowman, Martyn Hill and Paul Elliott):

MAINERIO: *Il primo libro di balli: 10 Dances.* GUAMI: *Canzoni per sonar: Canzona a 8.* LAPPI: *Canzoni per sonar: La negrona.* PRIULI: *Sacrorum Concentuum: Canzona prima a 12.* PORTA: *Sacro convito musicale: Corda Deo dabimus.* BUSATTI: *Compago ecclesiastico: Surrexit Pastor bonus.* DONATI: *Concerti ecclesiastici, Op. 4: In te Domine speravi.* D'INDIA: *Novi concentus ecclesiastici; Isti sunt duae olivae.* GRANDI: *Motetti con sinfonie, Libro I: O vos omnes; Libro III: O beate Benedicte.*

✪ (M) *** Virgin VER5 61288-2.

Munrow's art is shown to even greater advantage in his collection of music by Monteverdi's contemporaries, which has a comparatively short time-span (1535–1644). Opening with five dances from Giorgio Mainerio's *Il primo libro di balli*, vividly scored, mainly for wind and brass, but unexpectedly bringing a xylophone solo in the *Ballo francese*, the programme continues with other impressive instrumental pieces by Gioseffo

Guami, Pietro Lappi and Giovanni Priuli. Then come five more of the Mainerio dances, two of which are solos for the cittern, notably the brilliant and catchy *Schiarazula marazula*, which is as intricately titillating as its title suggests.

But this all serves to act as a prelude to a superb collection of vocal music, nearly all of which is entirely unknown. Ercole Porta's sonorous setting of *Corda Deo dabimus* has the counter-tenor (James Bowman) and tenor (Martyn Hill) sonorously underpinned by sackbuts; Cherubino Busatti's *Surrexit Pastor bonus* which follows (James Bowman at his most inspired) is unforgettable. The setting of this short but deeply poignant motet dramatically alternates moods: bright and lighthearted for 'The good shepherd is risen – Alleluia' and then (with a sudden change) movingly eloquent in telling of the crucifixion, with a despairing downward scale for the word '*mori*' (die) which is infinitely touching. Ignazio Donati's tenor duet *In te Domine speravi* (Martyn Hill and Paul Elliott) is almost equally eloquent.

There is a fine motet from Sigismondo d'India, then comes the other highlight, Alessando Grandi's tragically beautiful *O vos omnes*, gloriously sung by Bowman. This too is unforgettable. The concert ends happily in celebration with Grandi's *O beate Benedicte*, with counter-tenor and tenor duetting happily, sometimes in harmony, at others in felicitous imitation, with the accompaniment for cornett, tenor sackbut, organ and bass violin adding to the simple polyphony. Here as elsewhere Munrow's instrumentation has an imaginative flair matched by no other exponent of this repertoire. The recording is superb and this collection, including several out-and-out masterpieces among much else that is rewarding, is on no account to be missed.

(i) Early Music Consort of London, David Munrow; (ii) Musica Reservata, John Beckett

'*Early music festival*': (i) *Florentine music of the fourteenth century* (with James Bowman, counter-tenor, Nigel Rogers and Martyn Hill, tenors): LANDINI: *Ecco la primavera; Giunta vaga biltà; Questa fanciull' amor; De! dinmi tu; Cara mie donna; La bionda treçça; Donna 'l tuo partimento.* ANON.: *Lamento di Tristano; Trotto; Due saltarelli; Quan ye voy le duç; La Manfredini; Istampita Ghaetta; Biance flour.* PIERO: *Con dolce brama.* TERAMO: *Rosetta.* LORENZO DI FIRENZE: *Chon brachi assai; Dà, dà, a chi avaregia.* JACOBO DE BOLOGNA: *Fenice fu' e vissi.* (ii) *Florentine music of the sixteenth century* (with Jantina Noorman, mezzo-soprano, Grayston Burgess, counter-tenor, Nigel Rogers, tenor, John Frost, bass baritone): MONTEVERDI: *Orfeo: Toccata.* Music for Ferdinando de' Medici (incidental music for the play *La Pellegrina*): MARENZIO: *Second Intermedio.*

MALVEZZI & CAVALIERI: *Sesto Intermedio.* FESTA: *Quando ritova.* ANON.: *Allemana-ripresa; Pavana: La cornetta; Gagliarda Giorgio; Ahimè sospiri; Pavana: Forze d'Ercole; Orsù, orsù, car'Signori; Pavana: El colognese. Dance songs* (vocal and keyboard settings): *Era di Maggio; El marchesse di Salluzzo; In questo ballo; Non ci vogliam' partire; Bussa la porta; La pastorella; E su quel monte; Maggio valente; Sorella mi piacente.* TROMBONCINO: *Frottola: Io son l'occello.* NOLA: *Tri ciechi siamo.* CARA: *Frottola: Io non compro.*

(B) *** Double Decca (ADD) 452 967-2 (2).

This Decca Double happily combines two collections of Florentine music from two different authentic groups recording for the Argo label in the late 1960s and early 1970s. The repertoire may be a century apart, but this means that the contrast is the more striking. The fourteenth-century collection has a wide general appeal. Its key figure, Francesco Landini, has an immediate approachability, and this extends to much else here, especially when the variety of presentation, both vocal and instrumental, is so stimulating.

No one knows exactly how or on what instruments accompaniments would have been performed, but David Munrow and his Early Music Consort solve the problems with their usual combination of scholarship and imagination. The singers include artists of the distinction of James Bowman, and the players are first rate. David Munrow's recorder playing is virtuosic, and Andrea Zachara da Teramo's *Rosetta*, played on a chamber organ, is most piquant. Attractive music, expertly transcribed and beautifully recorded.

The sixteenth-century collection from Musica Reservata opens with a *Toccata* from Monteverdi's *Orfeo*, vigorously played on a colourful combination of baroque trumpet, sackbuts and percussion, which shows how much more elaborate musical presentation had become in the intervening century. The earthy style of Musica Reservata may be typified by the throaty roaring of the unforgettable Jantina Noorman, but the opening vocal number from Luca Marenzio's *Second Intermedio* (incidental music for the play *La Pellegrina*) is charmingly presented by three boy trebles, accompanied by lyra, viol and harp, and later the choruses (sometimes for double or triple choirs) are both expansive and beautiful.

The collection ranges wide in mood among vigorous dances, popular songs and ceremonial music, all of it refreshing to the modern ear. Full translations are included and both programmes can be highly recommended to anyone who wants to explore painlessly and with delight a rich period of musical history. Again the recording is excellent, and the only possible criticism about this straight reissue of a pair of highly recommended LPs is to mention that other explorations were made by Argo at that time; with 51 minutes' playing time on the first disc and 53 on the second, there would have been room to include more music, from the intervening period. But each concert here is self-sufficient in itself, and this Double is still worth its cost.

Emmanuel College, Cambridge, Chapel Choir, Timothy Prosser

'*Carols from Cambridge*': TRAD.: *Veni, veni Emmanuel; The Angel Gabriel; In dulci jubilo.* RUTTER: *What sweeter music.* GAUNTLETT: *Once in Royal David's city.* arr. WILLCOCKS: *Ding dong! merrily on high; O come all ye faithful.* BRITTEN: *A Hymn to the virgin; Friday afternoons, Op. 7: New Year carol.* arr. JACKSON: *Noël nouvelet.* arr. VAUGHAN WILLIAMS: *This is the truth sent from above; Wither's rocking hymn.* MATHIAS: *Sir Christèmas.* WARLOCK: *Bethlehem Down; Benedicamus Domino.* arr. HAMMOND: *Swete was the song the Virgin Soong.* GARDNER: *Tomorrow shall be my dancing day.* BERLIOZ: *L'enfance du Christ: Shepherds' farewell.* LEIGHTON: *Lully, lulla, thou tiny Child.* RAVENSCROFT: *Remember, O thou man.* HOPKINS: *We three kings.* ORD: *Adam lay y-bounden.* GRUBER: *Stille Nacht.* arr. RUTTER: *Wexford carol.*

(M) *** ASV CDWHL 2104.

Opening with the famous melodic chant *Veni, veni Emmanuel*, which turns out to be medieval in origin and not a Victorian hymn, this is a particularly appealing mid-priced collection, beautifully recorded. Although it includes (as the third item) *Once in Royal David's city*, sung in crescendo in the Willcocks arrangement, a strongly expressed *O come all ye faithful*, and Mathias's jovial *Sir Christèmas*, as outgoing and vigorous as one could wish, the style of performance, as befits a smaller chapel choir, is for the most part a pleasingly intimate one.

Unlike King's College, Emmanuel uses women's voices, but they are as sweet and pure as any boy trebles', the overall blending and ensemble are nigh perfect and the effect is disarmingly simple, notably so in the lovely *Shepherds' farewell* from Berlioz's *L'enfance du Christ*. Anna Dennis is a pleasingly fragile soloist in Vaughan Williams's setting of *Wither's rocking hymn*; Rutter's *What sweeter music* and Warlock's *Bethlehem Down* are especially touching.

Enterprisingly, the famous *Stille Nacht* is presented in its charming original version for two solo voices (Julia Caddick and Sarah Fisher) and guitar. Grüber hastily scored it in this fashion when the organ broke down just before its first performance on Christmas Eve 1818 – in the appropriately named Church of St Nicholas (Oberndorf, Austria). Not all the choices are obvious, and Britten's *New Year carol*, taken from *Friday afternoons*, is an engaging novelty. Prosser and his splendid singers are equally impressive in the livelier carols: the rhythmic syncopations of Gardner's *Tomorrow shall be my dancing day* are as sparkling as the bounce of *We three kings*, and the choir's lightness

of touch is equally appealing in Warlock's *Benedicamus Domino*, which ends the concert joyfully.

English opera: 'Stars of English opera'

'*Stars of English opera*' Arias and excerpts from: HANDEL: *Alessandro* (Isobel Baillie). VERDI: *Simon Boccanegra* (Joyce Gartside; James Johnston; Arnold Matters; Frederick Sharp; Howell Glynne); *Un ballo in maschera* (Jean Watson). GOUNOD: *Faust* (Joan Hammond; Owen Brannigan; Heddle Nash); *La reine de Saba* (Norman Allin). PUCCINI: *La Bohème* (Lisa Perli (Dora Labbette); Gerald Davies). MOZART: *Le nozze di Figaro* (Miriam Licette). TCHAIKOVSKY: *The Maid of Orleans* (Maggie Teyte). GLUCK: *Orfeo ed Euridice* (Kathleen Ferrier). CILEA: *L'Arlesiana.* MASSENET: *Werther* (Tano Ferendinos). DONIZETTI: *L'elisir d'amore* (Heddle Nash).

(B) (***) Dutton mono CDLX 7024.

The sixteen tracks here – including three devoted to a rare 1948 recording, celebrating the first British production of Verdi's *Simon Boccanegra*, at Sadler's Wells – demonstrate what outstanding singers, almost all of them technically immaculate, were active in the years immediately after the Second World War. It is striking what clarity of focus marks almost all the singing, with hardly a wobble throughout and with words exceptionally clear, usually but not always involving an English text.

Isobel Baillie was never strictly an opera-singer, but it is good to hear her in an aria from Handel's *Alessandro*. The Ferrier recording of Orfeo's great aria, *What is life?*, from Gluck's opera was from a test disc she made with Gerald Moore at the piano, anticipating her Decca recordings, and the *Boccanegra* excerpts feature an excellent team of singers whose careers centred on Sadler's Wells: Joyce Gartside, James Johnston, Arnold Matters and Frederick Sharp, with Michael Mudie conducting, as in the theatre. Another fine ensemble recording of 1948 has Joan Hammond, Heddle Nash and Owen Brannigan in the garden scene from Gounod's *Faust*, and two tracks celebrate the superb voice of the long-neglected Greek–Welsh tenor Tano Ferendinos. Perhaps most striking of all is the pure, bright singing of Lisa Perli (pseudonym of Dora Labbette), with Beecham conducting, in *Mimi's Farewell* from Puccini's *La Bohème*. Transfers are vivid, full and immediate.

Estampie, John Bryan

'*Under the greenwood tree*' (with Deborah Catterall, Graham Derrick): WALTHER VON VOGELWEIDE: *Palästinalied.* Richard COEUR DE LION: *Ja nuis homs pris.* BLONDEL DE NESLE: *A l'entrant d'este.* Raimbault DE VAQUERIAS: *Kalenda Maya.*

CORNYSHE: *Ah! Robin.* STONINGES: *Browning my dear* (on the theme *The leaves be green*). GERVAISE: *4th Livre de Danceries: La Venissienne. 6th Livre de Danceries: Gailliarde.* PLAYFORD: *The Dancing Master: Greenwood; Nottingham Castle; Green Goose Fair; The green man.* SIMPSON: *Ricercar on Bonny sweet Robin.* WEELKES: *When Kempe did dance alone, or Robin Hood, Maid Marian and Little John are gone.* ANON.: *Novus miles sequitur; Estampie; Clap, clap un matin s'en aloit Robin; Robin Hood; The Wedding of Robin Hood; Under the greenwood tree; Sellenger's round; Greensleeves* (lute and vocal versions); *Robin Hood and the Curtal Friar; Robin Hood and the Tanner; Robin Hood and Maid Marian; Sweet angel of England* (to the tune *Bonny sweet Robin*); *O lusty May.*

(BB) ** Naxos 8.553442.

With John Bryan as music director and Graham Derrick as arranger and main performer, the early-music group Estampie here offer a well-devised group of dances and instrumental pieces, interspersed with songs, broadly inspired by the legend of Robin Hood and the ballad *Robin is to the greenwood gone* in its various forms. That in turn leads to celebrations in song and dance of Maytime and the annual revival of the Green Man. Items range from a song attributed to King Richard the Lionheart in the twelfth century to four items drawn (in arrangements by Graham Derrick) from John Playford's collection *The Dancing Master*, in the seventeenth.

The sequence is most illuminating, but the performances, always tasteful, rather lack the bite and earthiness which can make medieval music so invigorating. The final item, a Scottish song, *O lusty May*, is anything but that, though there and in the other songs the mezzo, Deborah Catterall, sings with a fresh, clear tone. Aptly intimate recorded sound.

Evans, Sir Geraint (baritone)

'*Arias and sacred songs*' (with (i) SRO, Balkwill; (ii) Shelley Singers, Lyrian Singers, Glendower Singers, BBC Welsh SO, Mansel Thomas). (i) HANDEL: *Berenice: Si trai ceppi. Semele: Leave me radiant light.* MOZART: *Le nozze di Figaro: Non più andrai. Don Giovanni: Madamina, il catalogo. L'oca del Cairo: Ogni momento. Die Zauberflöte: Der Vogelfänger.* BEETHOVEN: *Fidelio: Ha! welch'ein Augenblick!* LEONCAVALLO: *Pagliacci: Prologue.* DONIZETTI: *Don Pasquale: Un fuoco insolito.* VERDI: *Otello: Credo. Falstaff: Ehi! Paggio . . . l'onore! Ladri.* BRITTEN: *A Midsummer Night's Dream: Bottom's dream.* MUSSORGSKY: *Boris Godunov: Tchelkalov's aria.* (ii) MENDELSSOHN: *Elijah: Lord God of Abraham; Is not His word like a fire?* HANDEL: *Judas Maccabaeus: Arm, arm ye brave. Messiah: The Trumpet shall sound.* ROSSINI: *Requiem: Pro peccatis.*

(BB) *** Belart (ADD) 461 492-2.

This is a marvellous display of wide-ranging virtuosity, of artistic bravura such as we know from almost any performance that this ebullient and lovable singer gave. Part of Evans's mastery lay in the way he could convey the purest comedy, even drawing laughs without ever endangering the musical line through excessive buffoonery. His Mozart characters are almost unmatchable – Figaro, Leporello, Papageno – while it is good to be reminded that here is a singer who could be a formidable Iago as well as the most complete Falstaff of his day. Good accompaniment and recording, with a richly atmospheric orchestral backing, of one of Britain's greatest singers at the peak of his form.

Evans, Nancy (mezzo-soprano)

'*The Comely Mezzo*' (with various accompanists including Ivor Newton, Gerald Moore, Hubert Foss, piano): BEECHAM: *Outward Bound; Otello: Willow Song; O Mistress Mine.* DELIUS: *Indian Love Song; Irmelin Rose.* PARRY: *Armida's Garden.* BURY: *There is a Lady.* VAUGHAN WILLIAMS: *The Water Mill; How Can the Tree but Wither?* WARLOCK: *Rest, Sweet Nymphs; St Anthony of Padua.* HAGEMAN: *Do not Go my Love.* GURNEY: *The Scribe; Nine of the Clock O; All Night Under the Moon; Blaweary; You are my Sky; Latmian Shepherd.* FALLA: *7 Spanish Popular Songs.* BLISS: *Pastoral: Pigeon Song.* D'HARDELOT: *Wait.* FISHER: *An Old Violin.* ELGAR: *Land of Hope and Glory* (with Dennis Noble & Chorus).

(BB) (**(*)) Dutton mono CDBP 9723.

As Alan Blyth's note rightly says, Nancy Evans was for sixty years 'one of the best-loved personalities on the British musical scene', one who followed up her singing career with untiring work as a teacher, administrator and adjudicator, helping generations of young singers. She was married in turn to the recording producer, Walter Legge, and to Eric Crozier, collaborator with Britten on such operas as *Albert Herring* and *Billy Budd*. It was for Nancy Evans that Britten wrote the role of Nancy in *Albert Herring*, and in his preceding chamber opera, *The Rape of Lucretia*, Evans alternated with Kathleen Ferrier in the title role. When far too few of her recordings have appeared on CD, it is good to welcome this collection of rarities, even though the close balance of most of the pre-war recordings takes the bloom from the voice, giving it a raw quality in places and undermining the beauty. Nonetheless, the artistry and technical security come out from first to last, whether in the songs by Adrian Beecham (with the composer's father, Sir Thomas, at the piano), a sequence of songs by Ivor Gurney or the well-known Falla songs, which she delivers with Spanish fire. Most beautiful is *The Pigeon Song* from Bliss's *Pastoral*, with accompaniment for flute and strings, set in a more open acoustic, and the programme ends with two ballads and a stirring account of Elgar's *Land of Hope and Glory* with chorus and military band accompaniment.

Evans, Rebecca (soprano), Michael Pollock (piano)

'*Début*': BELLINI: *6 Ariette da camera.* VERDI: *Stornella.* RESPIGHI: *Notturno; Storia breve; Tanto bella; Lagrime; L'ultima ebbrezza; Luce.* ROSSINI: *Serate musicale, Vol. 1: L'invito; La pastorella delle Alpi; La promessa.* DONIZETTI: *Ah! rammenta, o bella Irene; A mezzanotte; La ninn-nanna.* WOLF-FERRARI: *4 Rispetti, Op. 11.*

(B) **(*) EMI CDZ5 69706-2.

The young Welsh soprano Rebecca Evans makes an excellent choice of artist for the EMI Début series. This programme, devised by the excellent accompanist Michael Pollock, a specialist in this area, consists almost entirely of miniatures, chips off the workbenches of great opera-composers, which consistently flaunt the Italian love of lyricism. It is striking how, after the opening Bellini group, Verdi immediately has one listening with new attention, when his two lively songs make the singer sparkle. The three Rossini items too – from the *Serate musicale* – bring extra vigour and striking tunes. Two of the Donizetti songs are longer and much closer to operatic models, but the Wolf-Ferrari group brings a charming conclusion, ending with a tiny squib of a tarantella. The recording is bright and forward, even if it does not quite catch the full beauty of Rebecca Evans's voice.

I Fagiolini, Robert Hollingsworth with David Miller (lute)

The Triumphs of Oriana (compiled by Thomas Morley): WILBYE: *The Lady Oriana.* NICHOLSON: *Sing, Shepherds All.* MUNDY: *Lightly she Whipped o'er the Dales.* CARLTON: *Calm was the Air and Clear the Sky.* HOLBORNE: *Lute Fantasias Nos. 2 & 3; Galliard No. 8 (Clark's Galliard).* EAST: *Hence Stars too Dim of Light.* CAVENDISH: *Come, Gentle Swains and Shepherds' Dainty Daughters.* KIRBYE: *With Angel's Face and Brightness.* MARSON: *The Nymphs and Shepherds Danced.* HOLBORNE: *Galliard.* BENNET: *All Creatures Now are Merry Minded.* FARMER: *Fair Nymphs, I Heard Calling.* R. JONES: *Fair Oriana, Seeming to Wink at Folly.* TOMKINS: *The Fauns and Satyrs Tripping.* E. GIBBONS: *Round About her Cherret; Long live Fair Oriana.* COBBOLD: *With Wreaths of Rose and Laurel.* HOLMES: *Thus Bonny-boots the Birthday Celebrated.* MORLEY: *Arise, Awake, Awake; Hard by a Crystal Fountain.* HUNT: *Hark! Did ye Ever Hear so Sweet a Singing?* MILTON: *Fair Oriana in the Morn.* NORCOME: *With Angel's Face and Brightness.* JOHNSON: *Come Blessed Bud.* BYRD: *Galliard.* HILTON: *Fair Oriana, Beauty's Queen.* LISLEY: *Fair Cytherea Presents her Doves.* WEELKES: *As Vesta was from Latmos Hill Descending.*

*** Chan. 0682.

This outstanding collection of madrigals in praise of Oriana (a poetic image for Queen Elizabeth I), compiled by Thomas Morley in 1601, has been seriously neglected on disc for many years, making this fine new version from I Fagiolini very welcome. Drawing on the talents of a wide range of his friends and contemporaries, including Wilbye, Tomkins and Weelkes, as well as his own work, Morley presents a superb overview of the art of the Elizabethan madrigal at its peak. Though the talented singers of I Fagiolini have a tendency to squeeze notes in pursuit of authenticity, this is refined singing, polished and expressive. The sequence of twenty-five madrigals is nicely punctuated by lute solos played by David Miller, four by Holborne, one by Byrd. The recording is both warm and immediate in an intimate acoustic.

Ferrier, Kathleen (contralto)

Lieder, arias, songs and duets: MAHLER: *Kindertotenlieder* (with Vienna Philharmonic Orchestra, Bruno Walter). HANDEL: *Ottone: Spring is coming; Come to me.* MAURICE GREENE: *O praise the Lord; I will lay me down in peace.* PURCELL: *Ode for Queen Mary: Sound the trumpet. The Indian Queen: Let us not wander. King Arthur: Shepherd, shepherd cease decoying.* MENDELSSOHN: *I would that my love; Greeting* (all with Gerald Moore, piano; Purcell & Mendelssohn duets with Isobel Baillie). GLUCK: *Orfeo ed Euridice: excerpts including Che farò and Che puro ciel.* (with Netherlands Opera Ch. & O, Charles Bruck).

(M) (***) EMI mono CDM5 66911-2.

It was especially tragic that Kathleen Ferrier made so few recordings in which the technical quality matched her magical artistry. This collection, rightly reissued as one of EMI's 'Great Recordings of the Century', includes many of her mono records from this source, which generally sound better than the Decca repertoire listed below. The Gluck *Orfeo* excerpts (deriving from an indifferent recording of a broadcast) have undoubtedly been enhanced for this reissue, although the choral entry in *Deh! placetevi con me* is still very fierce, and the Maurice Greene items are ill-focused. However, fortunately the 1949 *Kindertotenlieder* comes over very well. Particularly worth having are the duets with Isobel Baillie, as these artists obviously worked especially well together. The new transfers are vivid and show an enhancement of their early LP incarnations.

'*The world of Kathleen Ferrier*', Volume 1: TRAD.: *Blow the wind southerly; The Keel row; Ma bonny lad; Kitty my love.* arr. BRITTEN: *Come you not from Newcastle.* HANDEL: *Rodelinda: Art thou troubled? Serse: Ombra mai fù.* GLUCK: *Orfeo ed Euridice: What is life?* MENDELSSOHN: *Elijah: Woe unto them; O rest in the Lord.* BACH: *St Matthew Passion: Have mercy, Lord, on me.* SCHUBERT: *An die Musik; Gretchen am Spinnrade; Die junge Nonne; Der Musensohn.* BRAHMS: *Sapphische Ode; Botschaft.* MAHLER: *Rückert Lieder: Um Mitternacht.*

✹ (M) (✲✲✲) Decca mono 430 096-2.

This selection, revised and expanded from the original LP issue, admirably displays Kathleen Ferrier's range, from the delightfully fresh folksongs to Mahler's *Um Mitternacht* in her celebrated recording with Bruno Walter and the VPO. The noble account of *O rest in the Lord* is one of the essential items now added, together with an expansion of the Schubert items (*Die junge Nonne* and *An die Musik* are especially moving). The CD transfers are remarkably trouble-free and the opening unaccompanied *Blow the wind southerly* has uncanny presence. The recital plays for 65 minutes and fortunately there are few if any technical reservations to be made here about the sound quality.

'*The world of Kathleen Ferrier*' , Volume 2: TRAD.: *Ye banks and braes; Drink to me only* (both arr. QUILTER); *I have a bonnet trimmed with blue; Down by the Sally Gardens; The stuttering lovers* (all arr. HUGHES). PURCELL: *The Fairy Queen: Hark! the echoing air.* HANDEL: *Atalanta: Like the love-lorn turtle.* GLUCK: *Orfeo ed Euridice: Che puro ciel.* MAHLER: *Rückert Lieder: Ich bin der Welt abhanden gekommen.* SCHUMANN: *Frauenliebe und Leben: Er, der Herrlichste von allen.* BRAHMS: *Geistliches Wiegenlied; Von ewiger Liebe.* SCHUBERT: *Du bist die Ruh'; Rosamunde: Romance.* BACH: *Mass in B min.: Agnus Dei.* HANDEL: *Messiah: He was despised.*

(M) (✲✲✲) Decca mono 448 055-2.

Volume 2 offers a comparable mixture, opening with more delightful folksongs, notably the charming *Stuttering lovers*, although it is *Ye banks and braes* and *Drink to me only* that show the full richness of this glorious voice. *Che puro ciel* stands out among the opera arias for its simple eloquence, and the Brahms *Geistliches Wiegenlied*, with its somewhat wan viola obbligato, is gently ravishing. The passionate *Du bist die Ruh'*, the *Rosamunde Romance* and *Von ewiger Liebe* come from a BBC acetate disc of her 1949 Edinburgh Festival recital with Bruno Walter at the piano, and here there is some uneven background noise and the quality deteriorates in the Brahms song. But the CD closes with one of her very last recordings, her unforgettably poignant *He was despised*, with those words given an uncanny presence.

'*What is Life?* (with Phyllis Spurr or John Newmark, piano; Jacques Orchestra, Jacques; Nat. SO or LSO, Sargent; Boyd Neel Orchestra, Neel or Roy Henderson): TRAD.: *Blow the Wind Southerly; The Keel Row; Down by the Sally Gardens; Ma Bonny Lad; Ca' the Yowes.* SCHUBERT: *Die junge Nonne; Gretchen am Spinnrade.* SCHUMANN: *Volksliedchen; Widmung.* BACH: *St Matthew Passion; Grief for Sin; Have Mercy Lord; Cantata No. 11: Ah, Tarry Yet, my Dearest Saviour.* GLUCK: *Orfeo: What is Life?* HANDEL: *Xerxes: Ombra mai fu; Rodalinda: Art thou troubled.* PERGOLESI: *Stabat Mater; Fac et*

portem. MENDELSSOHN: *Elijah: Woe unto Them; O Rest in the Lord.* GRUBER: *Silent Night.*

(BB) (✲✲✲) Regis mono RRC 1057.

This disc does not replace the two Decca Volumes of '*The World of Kathleen Ferrier*', where the recordings have been transferred with greater range and, as in the first item, a remarkable presence. But for the Regis anthology, offering many of the same recordings, Tony Watts has taken great care to smooth out the sound from the original masters: it is always warm and pleasing, the vocal quality rich, and the extraneous noises have been virtually eliminated. So if you want an inexpensive single disc assembling some of the very finest records made by this great artist, comfortably presented (and in some items, *Ombra mai fu* for instance, the quality is particularly warm and beautiful), this disc can be cordially recommended. And it is good to have Ferrier's lovely performance of the most magical carol of all, Grüber's *Silent Night*.

Fischer-Dieskau, Dietrich (baritone)

'*Fischer-Dieskau Lieder Edition*'

SCHUBERT: Lieder (with Gerald Moore, piano): Volume I (1811-17); Volume II (1817-28); Volume III: Song cycles: *Die schöne Müllerin; Schwanengesang; Winterreise.*

(B) ✲✲✲ DG (ADD) 437 214-2 (21).

Lieder, Volume I (1811-17): *Ein Leichenfantasie; Der Vatermörder* (1811); *Der Jüngling am Bache* (1812); *Totengräberlied; Die Schatten; Sehnsucht; Verklärung; Pensa, che questo istante* (1813); *Der Taucher* (1813-15); *Andenken; Geisternähe; Erinnerung; Trost, An Elisa; Die Betende; Lied aus der Ferne; Der Abend; Lied der Liebe; Erinnerungen; Adelaide; An Emma; Romanze: Ein Fräulein klagt' im finstern Turm; An Laura, als sie Klopstocks Auferstehungslied sang; Der Geistertanz; Das Mädchen aus der Fremde; Nachtgesang; Trost in Tränen; Schäfers Klagelied; Sehnsucht; Am See* (1814); *Auf einen Kirchhof; Als ich sie erröten sah; Das Bild; Der Mondabend* (1815); *Lodas Gespenst* (1816); *Der Sänger* (1815); *Die Erwartung* (1816); *Am Flusse; An Mignon; Nähe des Geliebten; Sängers Morgenlied; Amphiaraos; Das war ich; Die Sterne; Vergebliche Liebe; Liebesrausch; Sehnsucht der Liebe; Die erste Liebe; Trinklied; Stimme der Liebe; Naturgenuss; An die Freude; Der Jüngling am Bache; An den Mond; Die Mainacht; An die Nachtigall; An die Apfelbäume; Seufzer; Liebeständelei; Der Liebende; Der Traum; Die Laube; Meeres Stille; Grablied; Das Finden; Wandrers Nachtlied; Der Fischer; Erster Verlust; Die Erscheinung; Die Täuschung; Der Abend; Geist der Liebe; Tischlied; Der Liedler; Ballade; Abends unter der Linde; Die Mondnacht; Huldigung; Alles um Liebe; Das Geheimnis; An den Frühling; Die Bürgschaft; Der Rattenfänger; Der Schatzgräber; Heidenröslein; Bundeslied; An den Mond; Wonne der Wehmut; Wer kauft Liebesgötter?* (1815); *Der Goldschmiedsgesell* (1817); *Der Morgenkuss; Abendständchen: An Lina; Morgenlied: Willkommen, rotes Morgenlicht; Der Weiberfreund; An die Sonne; Tischlerlied; Totenkranz für ein Kind; Abendlied; Die Fröhlichkeit; Lob des Tokayers; Furcht der Geliebten; Das Rosenband; An Sie; Die Sommernacht; Die frühen Gräber; Dem Unendlichen; Ossians Lied nach dem Falle Nathos; Das Mädchen von Inistore; Labetrank der Liebe; An die Geliebte; Mein Gruss an den Mai; Skolie - Lasst im Morgenstrahl des Mai'n; Die Sternenwelten; Die Macht der Liebe; Das gestörte Glück; Die Sterne; Nachtgesang; An Rosa I: Warum bist du nicht hier?; An Rosa II: Rosa, denkst du an mich?; Schwanengesang; Der Zufriedene; Liane; Augenlied; Geistes-Gruss; Hoffnung; An den Mond; Rastlose Liebe; Erlkönig* (1815); *Der Schmetterling; Die Berge* (1819); *Genügsamkeit; An die Natur* (1815); *Klage; Morgenlied; Abendlied; Der Flüchtling; Laura am Klavier; Entzückung an Laura; Die vier Weltalter; Pflügerlied; Die Einsiedelei; An die Harmonie; Die Herbstnacht; Lied: Ins stille Land; Der Herbstabend; Der Entfernten; Fischerlied; Sprache der Liebe; Abschied von der Harfe; Stimme der Liebe; Entzückung; Geist der Liebe; Klage: Der Sonne steigt; Julius an Theone; Klage: Dein Silber schien durch Eichengrün; Frühlingslied; Auf den Tod einer Nachtigall; Die Knabenzeit; Winterlied; Minnelied; Die frühe Liebe; Blumenlied; Der Leidende; Seligkeit; Erntelied; Das grosse Halleluja; Die Gestirne; Die Liebesgötter; An den Schlaf; Gott im Frühling; Der gute Hirt; Die Nacht; Fragment aus dem Aeschylus* (1816); *An die untergehende Sonne* (1816/17); *An mein Klavier; Freude der Kinderjahre; Das Heimweh; An den Mond; An Chloen; Hochzeitlied; In der Mitternacht; Trauer der Liebe; Die Perle; Liedesend; Orpheus; Abschied; Rückweg; Alte Liebe rostet nie; Gesänge des Harfners aus Goethes Wilhelm Meister: Harfenspieler I: Wer sich der Einsamkeit ergibt; Harfenspieler II: An die Türen will ich schleichen; Harfenspieler III: Wer nie sein Brot mit Tränen ass. Der König in Thule; Jägers Abendlied; An Schwager Kronos; Der Sänger am Felsen; Lied: Ferne von der grossen Stadt; Der Wanderer; Der Hirt; Lied eines Schiffers an die Dioskuren; Geheimnis; Zum Punsche; Am Bach im Frühling* (1816); *An eine Quelle* (1817); *Bei dem Grabe, meines Vaters; Am Grabe Anselmos; Abendlied; Zufriedenheit; Herbstlied; Skolie: Mädchen entsiegelten; Lebenslied; Lieden der Trennung* (1816); *Alinde; An die Laute* (1827); *Frohsinn; Die Liebe; Trost; Der Schäfer und der Reiter* (1817); *Lob der Tränen* (1821); *Der Alpenjäger; Wie Ulfru fischt; Fahrt zum Hades; Schlaflied; Die Blumensprache; Die abgeblühte Linde; Der Flug der Zeit; Der Tod und das Mädchen; Das Lied vom Reifen; Täglich zu singen; Am Strome; Philoktet; Memnon; Auf dem See; Ganymed; Der Jüngling und der Tod; Trost im Liede* (1817).

(B) *** DG (ADD) 437 215-2 (9).

Lieder, Volume II (1817-28): *An die Musik; Pax vobiscum; Hänflings Liebeswerbung; Auf der Donau; Der Schiffer; Nach einem Gewitter; Fischerlied; Das Grab; Der Strom; An den Tod; Abschied; Die Forelle; Gruppe aus dem Tartarus; Elysium; Atys; Erlafsee; Der Alpenjäger; Der Kampf; Der Knabe in der Wiege* (1817); *Auf der Riesenkoppe; An den Mond in einer Herbstnacht; Grablied für die Mutter; Einsamkeit; Der Blumenbrief; Das Marienbild* (1818); *Litanei auf das Fest Allerseelen* (1816); *Blondel zu Marien; Das Abendrot; Sonett I: Apollo, lebet noch dein Hold verlangen; Sonett II: Allein, nachdenken wie gelähmt vom Krampfe; Sonett III: Nunmehr, da Himmel, Erde schweigt; Vom Mitleiden Mariä* (1818); *Die Gebüsche; Der Wanderer; Abendbilder; Himmelsfunken; An die Freunde; Sehnsucht; Hoffnung; Der Jüngling am Bache; Hymne I: Wenige wissen das Geheimnis der Liebe; Hymne II: Wenn ich ihn nur hab; Hymne III: Wenn alle untreu werden; Hymne IV: Ich sag es jedem; Marie; Beim Winde; Die Sternennächte; Trost; Nachtstück; Prometheus; Strophe aus Die Götter Griechenlands* (1819); *Nachthymne; Die Vögel; Der Knabe; Der Fluss; Abendröte; Der Schiffer; Die Sterne; Morgenlied* (1820); *Frühlingsglaube* (1822); *Des Fräuleins Liebeslauschen* (1820); *Orest auf Tauris* (1817); *Der entsühnte Orest; Freiwilliges Versinken; Der Jüngling auf dem Hügel* (1820); *Sehnsucht* (1817); *Der zürnenden Diana; Im Walde* (1820); *Die gefangenen Sänger; Der Unglückliche; Versunken; Geheimes; Grenzen der Menschheit* (1821); *Der Jüngling an der Quelle* (1815); *Der Blumen Schmerz* (1821); *Sei mir gegrüsst; Herr Josef Spaun, Assessor in Linz; Der Wachtelschlag Ihr Grab; Nachtviolen; Heliopolis I: Im kalten, rauhen Norden; Heliopolis II: Fels auf Felsen hingewälzet; Selige Welt; Schwanengesang: Wie klage'ich's aus; Du liebst mich nicht; Die Liebe hat gelogen; Todesmusik; Schatzgräbers Begehr; An die Leier; Im Haine; Der Musensohn; An die Entfernte; Am Flusse; Willkommen und Abschied* (1822); *Wandrers Nachtlied: Ein Gleiches; Der zürnende Barde* (1823); *Am See* (1822/3); *Viola; Drang in die Ferne; Der Zwerg; Wehmut; Lied: Die Mutter Erde; Auf dem Wasser zu singen; Pilgerweise; Das Geheimnis; Der Pilgrim; Dass sie hier gewesen; Du bist die Ruh'; Lachen und Weinen; Greisengesang* (1823); *Dithyrambe; Der Sieg; Abendstern; Auflösung; Gondelfahrer* (1824); *Glaube, Hoffnung und Liebe* (1828); *Im Abendrot; Der Einsame* (1824); *Des Sängers Habe; Totengräbers Heimwehe; Der blinde Knabe; Nacht und Träume; Normans Gesang; Lied des gefangenen Jägers; Im Walde; Auf der Bruck; Das Heimweh; Die Allmacht; Fülle der Liebe; Wiedersehn; Abendlied für die Entfernte; Szene I aus dem Schauspiel Lacrimas; Am mein Herz; Der liebliche Stern* (1825); *Im Jänner 1817 (Tiefes Leid); Am Fenster; Sehnsucht; Im Freien; Fischerweise; Totengräberweise; Im Frühling; Lebensmut; Um Mitternacht; Uber Wildemann* (1826); *Romanze des*

Richard Löwenherz (1827); Trinklied; Ständchen; Hippolits Lied; Gesang (An Silvia); Der Wanderer an den Mond; Das Zügenglöcklein; Bei dir allein; Irdisches Glück; Wiegenlied (1826); Der Vater mit dem Kind; Jägers Liebeslied; Schiffers Scheidelied; L'incanto degli occhi; Il traditor deluso; Il modo di prender moglie; Das Lied im Grünen; Das Weinen; Vor meiner Wiege; Der Wallensteiner Lanzknecht beim Trunk; Der Kreuzzug; Das Fischers Liebesglück (1827); Der Winterabend; Die Sterne; Herbst; Widerschein (1828); Abschied von der Erde (1825/6).

(B) *** DG (ADD) 437 225-2 (9)

Lieder, Volume III: Song cycles: *Die schöne Müllerin; Schwanengesang; Winterreise.*

(M) *** DG (ADD) 437 235-2 (3).

SCHUMANN: **Lieder (with Christoph Eschenbach, piano):** *Myrthen, Op. 25/1-3; 5-8; 13; 15-19; 21-2; 25-6. Lieder und Gesänge, Op. 27/1-5; Op. 51/4; Op. 77/1 & 5; Op. 96/1-3; Op. 98/2, 4, 6 & 8; Op. 127/2-3. Gedichte, Op. 30/1-3; Op. 119/2. Gesänge, Op. 31/1 & 3; Op. 83/1 & 3; Op. 89/1-5; Op. 95/2; Op. 107/3 & 6; Op. 142/1, 2 & 4; Schön Hedwig, Op. 106. 6 Gedichte aus dem Liederbuch eines Malers, Op. 36. 12 Gedichte aus Rückerts Liebesfrühling, Op. 37. Liederkreis, Op. 39. 5 Lieder, Op. 40. Romanzen und Balladen, Op. 45/1-3; Op. 49/1-2; Op. 53/1-3; Op. 64/3; Belsatzar, Op. 57. Liederkreis, Op. 24. 12 Gedichte, Op. 35. Dichterliebe, Op. 48. Spanisches Liederspiel, Op. 74/6, 7 & 10. Liederalbum für die Jugend, Op. 79; Der Handschuh, Op. 87. 6 Gedichte von Nikolaus Lenau und Requiem (Anhang, No. 7), Op. 90. Minnespiel, Op. 101. 4 Husarenlieder, Op. 117. Heitere Gesänge, Op. 125/1-3. Spanische Liebeslieder, Op. 138/2, 3, 5 & 7. Balladen, Op. 122/1-2. Sechs frühe Lieder, Op. posth. (WoO 21).*

(B) *** DG (ADD) 445 660-2 (6).

BRAHMS: **Lieder (with Daniel Barenboim, piano):** *Gesänge, Op. 3/2-6; Op. 6/2-6; Mondnacht, Op. 7/1-4 & 6; Op. 43/1-4; Op. 46/1-4; Op. 70/1-4; Op. 71/1-5; Op. 72/2-5. Lieder und Romanzen, Op. 14/1-8; Gedichte, Op. 19/1-2, 3 & 5; Lieder und Gesänge, Op. 32/1-9; Op. 57/2-8; Op. 58/1-8; Op. 59/1-4, 6-7; Op. 63/1-9; Romanzen, Op. 33/1-15; Lieder, Op. 47/1-4; Op. 48/1, 2, 5-7; Op. 49/1-5; Op. 85/1-2, 4-6; Op. 86/2-5; Op. 94/1-3 & 5; Op. 95/2, 3 & 7; Op. 96/1-4; Op. 97/1-3, 5-6; Op. 105/4-5; Op. 106/1-5; Op. 107/1-2 & 4. Neuen Gesänge, Op. 69/3, 5 & 7. Vier ernste Gesänge, Op. 121.*

(B) *** DG (ADD) 447 501-2 (6).

Richard STRAUSS: **Lieder (with Wolfgang Sawallisch, piano):** *5 kleine Lieder, Op. 69; Lieder, Op. 10/2-7; Op. 15/2 & 5; Op. 17/2; Op. 19/1-6; Op. 26/1-2; Op. 27/1, 3 & 4; Op. 29/1 & 3; Op. 31/4; Op. 32/1-5; Op. 36/1 & 4; Op. 37/1-2, 5-6; Op. 49/6; Op. 56/1 & 3; Op. 67/6. Schlichte Weisen, Op. 21; Vier Gesänge, Op. 87.*

(M) *** DG (IMS) (ADD) 447 512-2 (2).

WOLF: **Lieder (with Daniel Barenboim, piano):** *23 Eichendorff Lieder; 42 Goethe Lieder; 7 Heine*

Lieder; 4 Lenau Lieder; 3 Gedichte von Michelangelo; Mörike Lieder (complete); *6 Reinick Lieder; 4 Gedichte von Robert Reinick. 3 Gedichte nach Shakespeare und Lord Byron.* Miscellaneous Lieder by Peitl; Von Matthisson; Körner; Herlossohn; Hebbel; Von Fallersleben; Sturm; Von Scheffel.

(B) *** DG (ADD) 447 515-2 (6).

To celebrate the seventieth birthday of the great German baritone, DG published a justifiably extravagant Lieder Edition, summing up the astonishing achievement of the greatest male Lieder singer of our time.

Each individual composer grouping is available separately, very competitively priced. With consistent artistry from all concerned and with first-class transfers, these CDs are self-recommending. We have discussed the Schubert in previous volumes, and much else, too, in individual issues. Fischer-Dieskau's mastery never ceases to amaze. Sample this set at almost any point and the same virtues emerge: characteristic beauty of vocal tone and an extraordinarily vivid power of characterization and vocal colouring. No less remarkable are his accompanists, including the incomparable Gerald Moore and Daniel Barenboim, whose sensitivity and command of keyboard colour make for consistently memorable results. The Liszt collection has alas, been withdrawn. The sheer originality of thought and the ease of the lyricism are a regular delight. Fischer-Dieskau's concentration and inspiration never seem to falter, especially in the most famous of the songs, the *Petrarch Sonnets*, and Barenboim's accompaniments could hardly be more understanding.

Fischer-Dieskau Edition

🏵 (B) *** DG mono/stereo 463 500-2 (21).

This self-recommending set was a follow-up to the Lieder Edition above and was also released to celebrate Fischer-Dieskau's 75th birthday. The Rosette is surely obligatory for the sheer scope of this achievement, not only for the great baritone's consistent supreme artistry and astonishingly varied repertoire, but also in appreciation to DG for releasing over 300 works on CD for the first time – with a recording of *Die schöne Müllerin* which had never before been released. One of the other joys of this Fischer-Dieskau Edition is that it has included a great deal of music, much of it little known, either side of his core nineteenth-century repertoire.

Of course, it will be a personal choice which of the various recordings of individual works one prefers, but there is nothing remotely sub-standard here. DG are also to be congratulated for their superb transfers, many of which seem to defy time, and also in providing full texts and translations. The twenty CDs are available as a boxed set at bargain price (with a Volume 21 offered as a bonus CD), or individually at mid-price.

Volume 1: SCHUBERT: *Winterreise, D.911.*

(M) *** DG (ADD) 463 501-2. with Daniel Barenboim.

This is Fischer-Dieskau's fifth recording of Schubert's greatest cycle (1979), with the voice still in superb condition. It is perhaps the most inspirational, prompted by Barenboim's spontaneous-sounding, almost improvisatory accompaniment. In expression, this is freer than the earlier versions, and though some idiosyncratic details will not please everyone, the sense of concentrated development is irresistible. The recording is excellent.

Volume 2: SCHUBERT: *Die schöne Müllerin, D.795.* **Lieder:** *Du bist die Ruh; Erlkönig; Nacht und Träume; Ständchen.*

(M) *** DG (ADD) 463 502-2. with Jörg Demus.

This fascinating disc makes available Fischer-Dieskau's 1968 recording of *Die schöne Müllerin* with one of his favourite pianists, Jörg Demus, for the first time. The reason for its previous non-apperance were not artistic: Dieskau regards it as one of his most successful interpretations of this cycle, and edited and approved the disc for release. It seems that DG, understandably, wanted to concentrate on the Gerald Moore recordings which were then being undertaken, and with whom he recorded the same cycle just three years later. The result was that this version was never issued. Comparisons with the 1971 Moore version are fascinating: the earlier version has a greater feeling of risk, with the dynamics noticeably more pointed, and as Alan Newcombe says in the sleeve note 'the result is starker, more elemental, less comfortable, and conceived on a larger scale'. Whereas the later version offers the more rounded polish – from both artists – and for many will be the safer recommendation, this 'new' version is just as compelling. The recording is excellent, and the four extra songs included on this disc are supremely done.

Volume 3: SCHUBERT: *Schwanengesang, D.957.* **Lieder:** *Im Abendrot; An die Musik; An Sylvia; Die Erde; Die Forelle; Heidenröslein; Der Musensohn; Der Tod und das Mädchen; Vollendung.*

(M) *** DG (ADD) 463 503-2 with Gerald Moore.

Fischer-Dieskau's and Gerald Moore's 1972 performance of *Schwanengesang* – a work not conceived as a cycle by Schubert but grouped together by his publisher – is masterly. The singer may occasionally over-emphasize individual words, but the magnetism, poetry and insight – matched by Moore's playing – has one consistently marvelling. The remaining songs are superbly done, and both *Vollendung* and *Die Erde*, also recorded in 1972, receive their first release here. Excellent recording.

Volume 4: SCHUBERT: **Lieder:** *An die Leier; Aus Heliopolis I; Der entsühnte Orest; Fahrt zum Hades; Fragment aus dem Aeschylus; Freiwilliges Versinken; Frühlingslied; Jägers Liebeslied; Der Kreuzzug; Lied des Orpheus, als er in die Hölle ging; Lied eines Schiffers an die Dioskuren; Memnon; Orest auf Tauris; Philoktet; Schiffers Scheidelied; Vor meiner Wiege; Das Weinen; Der zürnenden Diana.*

(M) *** DG (ADD) 463 504-2 with Jörg Demus.

Fischer-Dieskau was most adept at compiling recital discs, and this one comprises songs which conjures up evocations of antiquity. These recordings, dating from 1961 and 1965, receive their CD debut here, and have transferred very well. Both artists are on top form and there is nothing to quibble about artistically. This is a highly stimulating CD, and although the thread of antiquity gives the programme a slightly dark quality, this disc cannot fail to reward the listener.

Volume 5: SCHUMANN: (i) *Dichterliebe, Op. 48;* (ii) *12 Gedichte, Op. 35.* **Lieder:** *Freisinn; Schneeglöckchen; Des Sennen Abschied; Ständchen; Talismane; Venezianisches Lied I & II.*

(M) *** DG Stereo/mono 463 505-2 with (i) Jörg Demus; (ii) Günter Weissenborn.

The beautifully intense and expressive performance of *Dichterliebe* – perhaps the most concentrated of all song cycles – was taped in 1965. Here, Fischer-Dieskau surpassed his famous mono version, with the voice sounding if anything in better condition here, and with an even more tragic account of *Iche grolle nicht*. The other Lieder (mono) are no less attractive, and they all make their debut on CD here.

Volume 6: SCHUMANN: *Liederkreis, Op. 24; Myrten, Op. 25* (selection). **Lieder:** *Abends am Strand; Die beiden Grenadiere; Die feindlichen Brüder; Geständnis; Der Hidalgo; Der Kontrabandiste; Mein schöner Stern; Mein Wagen; Melancholie; O wie lieblich ist das Mädchen; Romanze; Sehnsucht; Tief im Herzen trag ich Pein; Weh, wie zornig ist das Mädchen; Zigeunerliedchen I & II.*

(M) *** DG (ADD) 463 506-2 with Jörg Demus.

In *Liederkreis*, Fischer-Dieskau vividly conveys the range of emotion from the anguish of the spurned lover to the delight of the traveller. The rest of the programme is a typically judicious collection, dating from the early to the mid-sixties, and sounding rich and full on this, its first release on CD.

Volume 7: BEETHOVEN: *An die ferne Geliebte, Op. 98; Drei Gesänge, Op. 83.* **Lieder:** *Adelaide; Abendlied unterm gestirnten Himmel; Adelaide; L'amante impaziente (Nos 3 & 4); Andenken; An die Hoffnung; Ariette (Der Kuss); Aus Goethes Faust; Die Ehre Gottes aus der Natur; Ich liebe dich, so wie du mich; In questa tomba oscura; Der Jüngling in der Fremde; Der Liebende; Lied aus der Ferne; Maigesang; Marmotte; Seufzer eines Ungeliebten - Gegenliebe; Der Wachtelschlag.*

(M) **(*) DG (ADD) 463 507-2 with Jörg Demus.

This Beethoven collection was recorded in 1966, finding Fischer-Dieskau at his vocal peak, especially in the song cycle which he made his very own. Though Demus's accompaniments are not quite so imaginative as the singer has received on other versions of these songs, Fischer-Dieskau's individuality is as positive as ever, with detail touched in as with few other singers. Excellent recording.

Volume 8: LISZT: **(i)** *Der Alpenjäger; Blume und Duft; Die drei Zigeuner; Es muss ein Wunderbares sein, S.314; Ihr Glocken von Marling; Oh, quand je dors; 3 sonetti di Petrarca, S270 Tristesse; Die Vätergruft; Vergiftet sind meine Lieder.* **(ii)** *Ein Fichtenbaum steht einsam; Hohe Liebe; Im Rhein, in schönen Strome; Morgens steh ich auf und frage; O lieb, so lang du lieben kannst; Der traurige Mönch.*

(M) *** DG (ADD) 463 508-2 with (i) Jörg Demus; (ii) Daniel Barenboim.

This collection comprises Fischer-Dieskau's 1961 Liszt recital (with Demus), making its first appearance on CD here, with others he made with Barenboim in 1979 and 1981. One is struck at the consistent freshness of the singer, in performance and in sound, throughout this disc. The later performances if anything have even more richness and expressiveness, even if the voice is obviously has not quite the youthful ardour of the earlier ones. The DG recording is impressive throughout, with the 1961 recordings defying its age. A superb collection.

Volume 9: BRAHMS: *Vier ernste Gesänge, Op. 121. Lieder: Abenddämmerung; Alte Liebe; Auf dem Kirchhofe; Auf dem See; Es liebt sich so lieblich im Lenze; Es schauen die Blumen; Feldeinsamkeit; Frühlingslied; Heimweh II; Herbstgefühl; Kein Haus, keine Heimat; Meerfahrt; Mein Herz ist schwer; Mit vierzig Jahren; Mondenschein; Nachklang; Regenlied; Steig auf, geliebter Schatten; Sommerabend; Der Tod, das ist die kühle Nacht; Verzagen.*

(M) *** Mono/Stereo 463 509-2 with Jörg Demus.

At the opening of this recital, with the *Four serious songs*, the commanding eloquence of Fischer-Dieskau's singing is gripping, and this level of concentration is maintained throughout, with Dieskau exploiting his range of tone colour in interpreting the fullest meaning of the words. The recordings were made from 1957 to 1960, and are strikingly full and vivid – both in stereo and mono.

Volume 10: WOLF: *Mörike Lieder: Abschied; An die Geliebte; Auf einer Wanderung; Begegnung; Bei einer Trauung; Der Feuerreiter; Fußreise; Der Genesene an die Hoffnung; Im Frühling; In der Frühe; Der Jäger; Jägerlied; Lebewohl; Neue Liebe; Peregrina I and II; Storchenbotschaft; Verborgenheit.*

(M) **(*) DG (ADD) 463 510-2 with Sviatoslav Richter.

The combination of Fischer-Dieskau and Richter is fascinating – this 55-minute recital was recorded live in 1973, but the sound is good, there are few distractions from the audience, and no clapping. Although the performances have that spontaneity which one expects in live recordings, the surprising thing is that the actual expression is so consistent. Richter proves a lyrical magician, bringing out hidden inner lines of melody – a remarkable CD indeed – though it does

not eclipse the singer's other versions of these songs, not least those with Barenboim.

Volume 11: RICHARD STRAUSS: **(i)** *Krämerspiegel, Op. 66. Lieder: Der Arbeitsmann; Blindenklage; Einerlei; Gefunden; Heimkehr; Das Rosenband; Stiller Gang; Winterweihe;* **(ii)** *Drei Lieder aus den Büchern des Unmuts des Rendsch Nameh, Op. 67.*

(M) *** DG (ADD) 463 511-2 with (i) Jörg Demus; (ii) Karl Engel.

Fischer-Dieskau's Straussian credentials are well known: he has recorded much of the composer's repertoire over the years, but this collection is quite rare, and is released on CD for the first time. The bulk of it was recorded in 1964, with the *Op. 67* taped in 1959. They are superb performances of these marvellously varied songs, and the transfers are excellent.

Volume 12: REGER: **(i)** *Aeolsharfe; Im April; Das Blatt im Buche; Ein Drängen; Einsamkeit; Flieder; Glückes genug; Gottes Segen; Grablied; Heimat; Der Himmel hat eine Träne geweint; Ihr, ihr Herrlichen!; Minnelied; Nelken; Schlecht Wetter; Das sterbende Kind; Traum durch die Dämmerung; Trost; Waldeinsamkeit; Winterahnung; Der zerrissne Grabkranz.* PFITZNER: **(ii)** *An die Mark; Eingelegte Ruder; Hussens Kerker; In Danzig; Säerspruch; Sie haben heut Abend Gesellschaft; Tragische Geschichte; Zorn; Zum Abschied meiner Tochter;* **(iii)** *Sonett nach Petrarca.*

(M) *** DG (ADD) 463 512-2 with (i) Günther Weissenborn; (ii) Karl Engel; (iii) Jörg Demus.

Another collection which makes its debut on CD. Reger was one of the most prolific of all masters and his songs are in particular need of advocacy. Some of them are little masterpieces and there is an original and memorable quality which runs through all those here. The 1966 recording has emerged stronger on CD than it was on LP, though the piano still sounds just a bit too much in the background. The Pfitzner songs were recorded, with the exception of the *Sonett nach Petrarca*, in 1959, though one would never guess the early date from the recorded sound. They are memorable works – more approachable for the non-German listener than you might think – and if they are not in the masterpiece class, they are well worth exploring. It would be hard to imagine a more persuasive advocate than Fischer-Dieskau, and this is altogether a valuable addition to the CD catalogue.

Volume 13: SCHOECK: **(i)** *Ach, wie schön ist Nacht und Dämmerschein; Auf ein Kind; Dämmrung senkte sich von oben; Das Ende des Festes; Ein Tagewerk I and II; Frühgesicht; Höre den Rat; Jetzt rede du! Jugendgedenken; Nachklang; Nachruf; Peregrina II; Reisephantasie; Venezianisches Epigramm;* **(ii)** *Liederzyklus, Op. 44. Lieder: Auskunft; Aus zwei Tälern; Im Kreuzgang von Santo Stefano; Keine Rast; Kennst du das auch?; Kindheit; Ravenna I; Das Ziel.*

(M) *** DG (ADD) 463 513-2 with (i) Margrit Weber; (ii) Karl Engel.

Though Schoeck's songs haven't yet attained the universal popularity of, say, Schubert or Wolf, they certainly follow that lieder tradition in its fullest sense, with nicety of expression and aptness of music to word. It is arguable that Schoeck is the finest German song composer after Wolf, and those who know these examples will testify to their rare qualities. They provide a wonderful vehicle for Fischer-Dieskau's art. *Liederzyks* was recorded in 1977, and the rest of the programme in 1958, though the sound in both is excellent, and this is the first time they have been made available on CD.

Volume 14: DEBUSSY: **(i)** *Trois Ballades de François Villon.* IVES: **(ii)** *Abide with me; Ann Street; At the river; Autumn; The children's hour; A Christmas carol; Disclosure; Elégie; A farewell to land; Feldeinsamkeit; From 'The Swimmers'; Ich grolle nicht; In Flanders fields; Tom sails away; Two little flowers (and dedicated to them); Weil' auf mir; West London; Where the eagle; The white gulls.* RAVEL: **(i; iii)** *Chansons madécasses;* **(i)** *Cinq Mélodies populaires grecques; Don Quichotte à Dulcinée.*

(M) *** DG (ADD) 463 514-2 with (i) Karl Engel (ii) Michael Ponti; (iii) Aurèle Nicolet; Irmgard Poppen.

A fascinating disc, offering some unexpected repertoire. Anyone who has fought shy of sampling the work of Ives should hear this delightful and often moving collection of his songs. Some of them are typically rumbustious, but equally memorable and ultimately more telling still are the reflective, poetic ones like *Feldeinsamkeit* or *Elégie*, or the very simple ones like *A Christmas carol*. They were recorded in 1975 and sound as fresh as paint. The French *Mélodies* have plenty of atmosphere and great colour; they were recorded in 1959 and the sound is astonishingly modern. The performances throughout his disc once again show Fischer-Diskau's supreme artistry in both the dramatic and reflective writing, and if his French doesn't always sound totally idiomatic, that becomes a secondary consideration in music making of this standard. The disc plays for just under 81 minutes.

Volume 15: BUSCH: **(i)** *Aus den Himmelsaugen droben; Nun die schatten dunkeln; Wonne der Wehmut.* BUSONI: **(i)** *Lied des Mephistopheles; Lied des Unmuts; Schlechter Trost; Zigeunerlied.* KEMPFF: **(ii)** *Alle; Der Gesang des Meeres; In einer Sturmnacht (Nikodemus); Liederseelen.* MAHLER: **(iii)** *Des Knaben Wunderhorn* (selection)*; Phantasie aus Don Juan.* MINARDI: **(i)** *Con una fronda di mirto; Uomo del mio tempo.* REZNICEK: **(iv)** *Vier Bet- und Bussgesänge.* BRUNO WALTER: **(i)** *Der junge Ehemann; Musikantengruss; Der Soldat.*

(M) *** DG (ADD) 463 515-2 with (i) Jörg Demus; (ii) Wilhelm Kempff; (iii) Karl Engel; (iv) Günter Weissenborn.

This collection comprises the music of artist-composers and was recorded between 1960 and 1964. With the exception of the Kempff items, this is all new to CD, and is a doubly important release for including so many interesting rarities – there is nothing here which is not worth having. How fascinating to hear some of Bruno Walter's songs – *Musikantengruss ('Musicians' greeting')* is quite magical, whilst the Kempff items are most animated and full of imagination. This is definitely a CD to sample, and the performances and recordings are first-rate.

Volume 16: MAHLER: **(i)** *Kindertotenlieder;* **(ii)** *Lieder eines fahrenden Gesellen;* **(i)** *Rückert Lieder: Blicke mir nicht in die Lieder; Ich atmet' einen linden Duft; Ich bin der Welt abhanden gekommen; Um Mitternacht.*

(M) *** DG (ADD) 463 516-2 with (i) BPO, Boehm; (ii) Bavarian Radio SO, Kubelik.

Mahler was another composer in which Fischer-Dieskau excelled. Few can rival him in his range and beauty of tone in conveying the heartache of the young traveller the *Lieder eines fahrenden Gesellen*. Kubelik is a most persuasive Mahlerian too, and the 1968 sounds quite excellent. The *Kindertotenlieder* receives a superb performance too, and was recorded in 1963, with Boehm providing imaginative accompaniment. The *4 Rückert Lieder* complete a totally successful collection.

Volume 17: BACH: **(i)** *Ich habe genug, BWV 82; Ich will den Kreuzstab gerne Tragen, BWV 56.* BUXTEHUDE: **(ii)** *Ich bin eine Blume zu Saron, BuxWV 45; Ich suchte des nachts, BuxWV 50.*

(M) (***) Mono/Stereo DG 463 517-2 with (i) Munich Bach Orchestra, Karl Richter; (ii) Helmut Krens, Berlin Bach Orchestra, Carl Gorvin.

The Buxtehude items were recorded in 1957 (mono) and make their CD debut here, with the singer emerging most vividly, and only a slight thinness in the orchestra betraying their age. This is ravishing singing, with the music imbued with a radiantly relaxed quality which is totally unaffected. The Bach performance were recorded in the late sixties and are rich and full in sound. If the orchestra here sounds a little earthbound at times, it is all most beautiful, with Fischer-Dieskau's usual colour and imagination ensuring the constant pleasure of the listener. Well worth considering.

Volume 18: Arias from: BACH: **Cantatas:** *Christ lag in Todesbanden, BWV 4; Meine Seufzer, meine Tränen, BWV 13; Wachet auf, ruft uns die Stimme, BWV 140. Mass in B minor; St Matthew Passion.* **(ii)** BRAHMS: *A German Requiem.* **(iii)** HANDEL: *Belshazzar.* **(iv)** HAYDN: *(The Creation) Die Schöpfung.* **(v)** STOLZEL: *Cantata: Aus der Tiefe rufe ich.*

(M) *** DG (ADD) 463 518-2 with (i) Munich Bach Orchestra, Karl Richter; (ii) Edinburgh Festival Ch., LPO, Barenboim; (iii) Munich Chamber O, Stadlmair; (iv)

Janowitz, BPO, Karajan; (v) Lucerne Festival Strings, Baumgartner.

This disc, titled 'Sacred arias', offers further examples of Fischer-Dieskau's sublimely beautiful and characterful way with baroque repertoire. The Bach excerpts are all most persuasively done, as is the rare Stölzel item, which is new to CD. The recordings are up to DG's high analogue standard, and the CD plays for just under 80 minutes.

Volume 19: Arias from: BEETHOVEN: *Fidelio.* CIMAROSA: *Il matrimonio segreto.* GLUCK: *Orfeo ed Euridice.* HANDEL: *Apollo e Dafne; Giulio Cesare; Serse.* MOZART: *Don Giovanni; Le nozze di Figaro; Die Zauberflöte.* WAGNER: *Die Meistersinger; Das Rheingold; Tannhäuser.*

*** DG mono/stereo 463 519-2 (with various orchestras and conductors).

Heard live on the operatic stage, Fischer-Dieskau's vocal image was sometimes too intimate for the bigger dramatic roles, but with the help of the recording microphone, these problems disappear, and one can do nothing but take pleasure in the singer's feeling for the words and dramatic situations. In Mozart, of course, Fischer-Dieskau has few peers, and the selection here includes his delightful Papageno arias from the *Magic flute*, as well as a beautifully turned performance of Don Giovanni's *Serenade*. The Wagner selection shows his warmly illuminating approach to this repertoire, with Wolfram's lovely solo from *Tannhäuser* quite magical, and the sharply individual Hans Sachs arias from *Die Meistersinger* equally unforgettable (if in some ways controversial). The bubbly Cimarosa aria is a joy and all the baroque arias are quite superb. The recordings, though, are excellent.

Volume 20: Arias from: BIZET: *Carmen; Les Pêcheurs de perles.* GIORDANO: *Andrea Chénier.* GOUNOD: *Faust.* LEONCAVALLO: *Pagliacci.* PUCCINI: *La Bohème.* ROSSINI: *Guglielmo Tell.* VERDI: *Falstaff; La forza del destino; Rigoletto; La Traviata.*

(M) *** DG mono/stereo 463 520-2 (mainly with Berlin RIAS Chamber Ch.& RSO, Fricsay).

This second volume of arias concentrates on the French and Italian opera, and although he may not be totally idiomatic in all this repertoire, Fischer-Dieskau's unique artistry tends to disarm criticism, and one wonders if in fact there has ever been a more versatile artist. Just how good a Verdian he is can be heard in *Di Provenza il mar* from *La Traviata*, in which the lyrical phrasing is most beautiful. The vigorous characterisation in the lively numbers is equally illuminating, and even though one might expect a darker voice in Gérard's monologue from *Andrea Chénier*, Dieskau's unique feeling for characterisation enables him to carry it off with total success. Most of the items are from a 1961 recital disc conducted by Fricsay, whilst others are drawn from complete opera recordings. The Quartet from *La Bohème* (with

Tröschel, Fehenberger, Streich, conducted by Schmitz fascinatingly) dates from 1949, and sounds very good for its period. It marked Fischer-Dieskau's debut as an opera singer on record. All the items here are presented on CD for the first time.

Bonus CD

Volume 21: BEETHOVEN: **Folksongs: (i)** *Da brava, Catina; Horch auf, mein Liebchen; Kommt, schließt mir einen frohen; Kreis; O köstliche Zeit; Der treue Johnie; Trinklied;* **(ii)** *Could this ill world; Oh, had my fate; Once more I hail thee; The pulse of an Irishman; The return to Ulster; Sunset; Put round the bright wine.* HAYDN: **Scottish songs:** *Dort, wo durchs Ried; Fliess leise, mein Bächlein; Heimkehr; Maggy Lauder; Schläfst oder wachst du?* WEBER: **(iii; iv) Scottish songs:** *Bewunderung; Ein beglückter Liebender; Ein entmutigter Liebender; Glühende Liebe; Trinklied;* **(iii)** *Weine, weine, weine nur nicht.*

(M) *** DG (ADD) 463 521-2. (i) Helmet Heller (violin), Irmgard Poppen (cello); (ii) Andreas Röhn (violin), Georg Donderer (cello); (iii) Karl Engel; (iv) Aurèle Nicolet (flute).

The bonus CD, offered free to those who buy the complete Fischer-Dieskau Edition, is a sheer delight. These folk-like songs are completely unpretentious, utterly enchanting pieces, full of lovely ideas and fresh melody. Their relative neglect is unaccountable, and this recital makes a hugely enjoyable hour of engaging music. The recordings date from 1961 and 1970 and all sound first class in this, their first CD incarnation.

Arias from: VERDI: *Otello; Il Trovatore; Rigoletto; Don Carlos; Un ballo in maschera; Falstaff.* WAGNER: *Der Fliegende Hollander; Die Walküre.* HANDEL: *Rinaldo.* BACH: *Christmas oratorio.* MAHLER: *Das Lied von der Erde: Von der Schönheit.* **Lieder:** SCHUBERT: *Das Lied im Grünen; Der Tod und das Mädchen; Du bist die Ruh'; Heidenröslein; Ständchen; Die Forelle.* BRAHMS: *Von ewige Liebe; Die Mainacht; Wiegenlied.* RICHARD STRAUSS: *Morgen!; Freundlich Vision; Mit deinen blauen Augen.*

(BB) *** Disky Royal Classics Vocal Double (ADD) DCL 706672 (2).

Even among the plethora of Fischer-Dieskau reissues currently reappearing, this inexpensive Double is not to be missed. Opening with Iago's two key scenes from Barbirolli's superb complete *Otello*, the selection continues with a number of arias taken from an early (1960) Verdi recital. Here Fischer-Dieskau is giving the most stylish and convincing performances and only the attention to detail betrays him as non-Italian. It is not, of course, the conventional baritone voice, but in *Il balen*, for example, there is a natural feel for the waltz rhythm as it picks up; throughout, the range of characterization is astonishing on any count. Then follow thrilling performances of the Dutchman's *Die frist ist um* and Wotan's tender farewell from *Die*

Walküre, both excitingly supported by Kubelik and the Bavarian Radio Orchestra.

The second disc ranges wide, from stylish Bach and Handel to the excerpt from Kletzki's engagingly imaginative *Das Lied von der Erde*, six favourite Schubert Lieder (from 1965) and three of Strauss (1970), with Gerald Moore playing the introduction to *Morgen!* with the utmost magic, and three of Brahms (1974), including the *Wiegenlied* (with Sawallisch). The programme then ends with a brilliant account of *Ehi Paggio!* from *Falstaff*. Excellent, vivid transfers, but no texts.

Lieder (with Reimann or Reutter, piano): FRANZ: *Auf dem Meeere* (3 versions); *Wie des Mondes Abbild; Gewitternacht; Bitte; Für Musik; Abends; Wonne der Wehmut; Mailied.* GRIEG: *Dereinst, Gedanke mein; Lauf der Welt; Wo sind sie hin?; Hör'ich das Liedchen klingen; Morgentau; Abschied; Jägerlied.* KIRCHNER: *Sie weiss es nicht; Frühhlingslied* (3 versions). HILLER: *Gebet.* JENSEN: *Lehn deine Wang' an meine Wang'.* A. RUBINSTEIN: *Es blinker der Tau.* LISZT: *Es rauschen die Winde; Wieder möcht'ich dir begegnen; Ständchen; Uber allen Gipfeln ist Ruh'.* WAGNER: *Der Tannenbaum.* BERLIOZ: *Auf den Lagunen.* CORNELIUS: *Liebe ohne Heimat; Sonnenuntergang.* NIETZSCHE: *Nachtspiel; Wie sich Rebenranken schwingen; Verwelkt.* WEINGARTNER: *Liebesfeier.* RITTER: *Primula veria.* STREICHER: *Ist die ein getreues, liebevolles Kind beschert.* RAFF: *Unter den Palmen.* EULENBURG: *Liebessehnsucht.* VON SCHILLINGS: *Freude soll in deinen Werken sein.* SCHOECK: *Abendwolken; Reiselied; Peregrina II.* WETZEL: *An miene Mutter; Der Kehraus.* MATTIESEN: *Heimgang in der Frühe; Herbstgefühl.* PFITZNER: *An den Mond; Mailied; Hussens Kerker.* TIESSEN: *Vöglein Schwermut.* R. STRAUSS: *Wer hat's getan?* REGER: *Warnung; Sommernacht.* SCHREKER: *Die Dunkelheit sinkt schwer wie Blei.* DEBUSSY: *Pour ce que plaisance est morte; Le temps a laissie son manteau.* MILHAUD: *Lamentation.* MAHLER: *Des Knaben Wunderhorn: Wo die schönen Trompeten blasen.* HINDEMITH: *Fragment.* REUTTER: *Johann Kepler; Lied für ein dunkles Mädchen; Trommel.* FORTNER: *Abbitte; Hyperions Schicksalslied; Lied vom Weidenbaum.* BARTOK: *Im Tale.* BLACHER: *Gedicht; Worte.* HAUER: *Der gefesselte Strom; An die Pasrzen.* SCHOENBERG: *Warnung; Traumleben.* WEBERN: *4 Lieder* (with George). APOSTEL: *Nacht.* KRENEK: *Die frühen Gräber; Erinnerung.* VOM EINEM: *Ein junger Dichter denkt an die Geliebte; In der Fremde.* EISLER: *An die Hoffnung; In der Frühe; Spruch 1939.* DESSAU: *Noch bin ich eine Stadt; Sur nicht mehr, Frau.* BECK: *Herbst.*

(M) **(*) EMI (ADD) CMS5 67349-2 (3).

With Fischer-Dieskau at his most inspired in this rare repertory, it would be hard to devise a more imaginative survey of the German Lied after Schumann. Ranging astonishingly widly in its coverage of the genre between 1850 and 1950, it generally bypasses obvious names, celebrating instead such composers as Franz, Kirchner, Cornelius and even Nietzsche (Wagner's pupil) in the nineteenth century and Weingartner, Schreker and Apostel in the twentieth. It is fascinating to have Wagner himself represented, Grieg and Berlioz (in German) as well as Debussy, Milhaud and even Bartok in songs with Lieder-like aim. Never issued on CD before, this makes a memorable celebratory issue, timed for Fischer-Dieskau's 75th birthday in May 2000. Sadly, this mid-price issue earns a big black mark for giving no texts or translations, leaving one in the dark over much rare material, even though the singer's diction is excellent.

Flagstad, Kirsten (soprano)

'The Flagstad Legacy', Volume 1: Opera arias from: BEETHOVEN: *Fidelio.* WAGNER: *Götterdämmerung; Lohengrin; Parsifal; Tannhäuser; Tristan und Isolde; Die Walküre.* WEBER: *Oberon.* **Songs and arias by** ALNS; BEETHOVEN; BISHOP; BRAHMS; BULL; FRANZ; GRIEG; GRONDAHL; HURUM; LIE; NORDRAAK; PALENZ; ROSENFELDT; SCHUBERT; SINDING; R. STRAUSS; THOMMESEN; THRANE.

(***) Simax mono PSC 1821 (3).

These three Simax CDs make up the first of five sets, running to thirteen CDs in all, which promise the most comprehensive overview of this great singer's legacy on records. It comes with a substantial article by Arne Dørumsgaard, himself a composer and translator. The contents range from the period of the First World War through to 1941, though the 1940 *Haugtussa* is not included. There is a thrilling *Dich, teure Halle* from *Tannhäuser*, recorded in New York in 1935 (hardly surprising that Flagstad took America by storm) and a *Liebestod* from the same year, as well as the 1936 Copenhagen recordings of Grieg and other Norwegian songs.

There are some Philadelphia and San Francisco Opera recordings under Ormandy with Melchior, and many feature her lifelong accompanist, Edwin McArthur. In Norwegian song, Grieg is not the whole story even if he is most of it. Flagstad included a number of her other and less familiar countrymen in her discography. These include Ole Bull, the violinist-composer who encouraged Grieg's family to send the boy to Leipzig, and whose *Sæterjentens Søndag* ('The Herd Girl's Sunday') would have been mandatory at the time. Eyvind Alnæs's song *Lykkan mellem To Mennseskor* ('Happiness between two people') was also a favourite of hers.

Dørumsgaard tells of the 'disarming simplicity' of her 1929 version, the finest of her early electrics, released 'before fame struck'. It is indeed quite amazing and fresher than the 1936 record, which also suffers from the rather dry acoustic of the Copenhagen studio. The Simax will be indispensable to the serious collector, both for its comprehensiveness and for the generally high standard of its transfers.

'Grieg's Haugtussa and the complete 1937 Victor Recordings': Arias from: BEETHOVEN: *Fidelio.*

WEBER: *Oberon*. WAGNER: *Lohengrin; Die Walküre; Gotterdämmerung*. **Songs by:** GRIEG: *Haugtussa*. BEETHOVEN: *Ah, Perfido!*.

(***) Romophone mono 81023-2.

Kirsten Flagstad with her dramatic soprano on a heroic scale may not have been a natural Lieder singer, but Grieg's warmly characterful cycle, *Haugtussa*, plainly brings out her natural warmth, and with Edwin McArthur as her sympathetic accompanist she gives a magnetic performance. The recording favours the voice, which is placed rather close, but the Romophone transfer brings out bloom and warmth. Flagstad's 1937 recording of Brünnhilde's Immolation scene has been preferred, never issued at the time. It is very commanding, with the voice fresh and full throughout.

Fleming, Renée (soprano)

Great opera scenes (with LSO, Solti) from: MOZART: *Le nozze di Figaro*. TCHAIKOVSKY: *Eugene Onegin*. DVORAK: *Rusalka*. VERDI: *Otello*. BRITTEN: *Peter Grimes*. RICHARD STRAUSS: *Daphne*.

✿ *** Decca 455 760-2.

Solti, in one of his very last recordings, here pays tribute to a soprano he especially admired and the wide choice of repertory movingly reflects an inspired collaboration. Far more than most operatic recitals, this presents fully rounded characterizations in extended scenes, from the Countess in *Figaro* through two Slavonic roles Tatiana and Rusalka (Fleming's favourite) to a tenderly girlish portrait of Verdi's Desdemona, wonderfully poised. Most moving of all is the final item – in effect a valediction – a ravishing, sensuous account of the heroine's final transformation into a tree in Strauss's late opera, *Daphne*.

'I want magic!': American opera arias (with Met. Op. O, James Levine) from: HERRMANN: *Wuthering Heights*. MOORE: *The Ballad of Baby Doe*. MENOTTI: *The Medium*. GERSHWIN: *Porgy and Bess*. BERNSTEIN: *Candide*. FLOYD: *Susannah*. STRAVINSKY: *The Rake's progress*. BARBER: *Vanessa*. PREVIN: *A Streetcar named Desire*.

*** Decca 460 567-2.

The title, 'I want magic!', is from André Previn's opera based on Tennessee Williams's *Streetcar named Desire*. Blanche Dubois's climactic aria – recorded even before the world première of the opera in 1998 – makes a moving conclusion to a varied and characterful collection. The beauty and power of Fleming's singing transforms arias from such operas as Bernard Herrmann's *Wuthering Heights*, Douglas Moore's *Ballad of Baby Doe* and Carlisle Floyd's *Susannah*, bringing out their lyricism. In arias from *Porgy and Bess* she is totally in style, and has both weight and brilliance in the big show-piece arias from Stravinsky's *Rake's progress*, Barber's *Vanessa* and Bernstein's *Candide*.

Fleming, Renée (soprano), Jean-Yves Thibaudet (piano)

'Night Songs': FAURE: *Après un rêve; Clair de lune; Mandoline; Nell; Soir*. DEBUSSY: *Apparition; Beau soir; Mandoline; Chansons de Bilitis*. MARX: *Nachtgebet; Nocturne; Pierrot Dandy; Selige Nacht*. R. STRAUSS: *Cäcilie; Leise Lieder; Leises Lied; Ruhe, meine Seele!; Schlechtes Wetter*. RACHMANINOV: *In the Silence of Mysterious Night; It is Beautiful Here; Sleep; Oh Do Not Sing To Me; These Summer Nights; The Waterlily*.

*** Decca 467 697-2.

Whilst it is possible to imagine a classic French singer bringing more authenticity to the French songs, there is no doubting Renée Fleming's understanding of the idiom. Her performances bring a genuine warmth which is most attractive, and her subtle colourings are a delight. In such numbers as Debussy's *Beau soir* she sings with a dreamy delicacy, whilst the following *Mandoline* is animated and lively, and her voice remains rich and well focused throughout her range in both. The Strauss songs have much atmosphere and character, from the hushed still of *Ruhe, meine Seele!* (*Rest, my Soul*) to the more dramatic *Cäcilie*, in which the strong emotions in the text are well conveyed. The yearning Russian qualities of Rachmaninov are well captured too, and the selection included finds the composer at his most persuasive. The Marx songs are an unexpected but welcome inclusion, especially the wild and quirky *Pierrot Dandy*. Much of the overall success of this disc is due to the superlative accompaniments from Jean-Yves Thibaudet who plays with great understanding and style. Full texts and translations are included, and the recording is warm and perfectly balanced.

Freni, Mirella (soprano), Luciano Pavarotti (tenor)

Arias and duets from: PUCCINI: *Tosca; La Bohème*. ROSSINI: *Guglielmo Tell*. BOITO: *Mefistofele*.

(M) *** Decca 458 221-2.

Both artists come from the same small town in Italy, Modena, where they were born in 1935; less surprisingly, they studied under the same singing teacher. Their artistic partnership on record has always been a happy one, and perhaps reached its zenith in their 1972 *Bohème* with Karajan (unexpectedly, recorded in the Jesus-Christus Kirche, Berlin).

Their great introductory love-duet as Mimì and Rodolfo, perhaps the most ravishing in all opera (from *Che gelida manina*, through *Sì, mi chiamano Mimì* to the soaring *O soave fanciulla*) is an obvious highlight here, but the much less familiar *Lontano, lontano* from *Mefistofele* shows no less memorably that the voices were made for each other. It was a very good idea to include a substantial selection from their 1978–9 *Tosca* (recorded in the Kingsway Hall), not a first choice as a complete set, but with some marvellous singing in Act III, of which some 17 minutes is offered (including *E lucevan le stelle* and the dramatic finale of the opera).

The recital opens very spontaneously with 13 minutes from Act I (*Mario! Mario!*), the engagingly temperamental interplay between the lovers, in the Church of Sant'Andrea della Valle. The only slight disappointment is Freni's *Vissi d'arte*; otherwise this is 70 minutes of vintage material, given Decca's top-drawer sound. Full translations are included.

Fretwork

'*The English viol*' (with Catherine Bott, soprano, Jeremy Budd, treble, Michael Chance, countertenor and (i) Red Byrd): ANON.: *The dark is my delight; Allemande and Galliard* (from *Lumley Books*); *In paradise.* FERRABOSCO I: *In Nomine a 5.* HOLBORNE: *Pavan and Galliard.* BYRD: *Christe redemptor a 4; In nomine a 5 No. 4; Ah silly soul.* DOWLAND: *Lachrimae gementes; Semper Dowland, semper dolens; M. Bucton his Galiard. ferrabosco II: Pavan and Alman.* GIBBONS: *Fantasia a 6 No. 2; Fantasia a 3 for the 'Great dooble bass'; The silver swan; Fantasia a 2.* (i) *The cry of London, Part II.* LAWES: *Fantasy a 5' on the playnesong' in G min.; Gather ye rosebuds; Aire a 6 in G min.* LOCKE: *Consort of 4 parts in F.* PURCELL: *Fantasia a 4 in B flat No. 5; In nomine a 6.*

✪ (M) *** Virgin VER5 61173-2.

Fretwork was one of the really outstanding groups of artists which Virgin Records promoted from their inception and they offer viol playing which is in a class of its own. This superb 77-minute anthology draws on recordings made between 1988 and 1994: the excellence is unvarying: these players catch perfectly the spirit of the late-Tudor and early-Stuart periods. The playing itself has immaculate ensemble and intonation, restrained feeling and great freshness. Much of the music is relatively austere but the effect on the listener is hypnotic.

The special character of Elizabethan romantic melancholy is well caught by Dowland (especially in his autobiographical *Semper Dowland, semper dolens*), but there is lively part-writing too, notably from Lawes and Locke. Lawes's *Fantasy a 5 'on the playnesong'* is touchingly expressive, the music's sonority coloured subtly by an (uncredited) chamber organ continuo, while the two pieces by Purcell are also quietly moving. The instrumental music is sprinkled with brief, cheerful, vocal items, delightfully sung, and the selection includes an excerpt from *The cry of London*, where the vocal group, Red Byrd, offer every conceivable commodity for sale, from a pair of oars and a good sausage to bread and meat 'for the prisoners of the Marshalsea'. Altogether an ideal introduction to a

period in English history which was musically very productive. The recording could hardly be bettered.

Gabrieli Consort & Players, Paul McCreesh

'*A Venetian coronation (1595)*': GIOVANNI GABRIELI: *Canzonas Nos. XIII a 12; IX a 10; XVI a 15; Deus qui beatum Marcum a 10 Intonazione ottavo toni; Intonazione terzo e quarto toni; Intonazioni quinto tono alla quarta bassa; Omnes gentes a 16; Sonata No. VI a 8 pian e forte.* ANDREA GABRIELI: *Intonazione primo tono; Intonazione settino tono; Mass excerpts: Kyrie a 5-12; Gloria a 16; Sanctus a 12; Benedictus a 12; O sacrum convivium a 5; Benedictus dominus Deus sabbaoth.* BENDINELLI: *Sonata CCCXXXIII; Sarasinetta.* THOMSEN: *Toccata No. 1.*

*** Virgin VC7 59006-2.

This recording and its DG successor below won *Gramophone* Early Music Awards in two consecutive years. '*A Venetian coronation*' is a highly imaginative if conjectural reconstruction of the Mass and its accompanying music as performed at St Mark's for the ceremonial installation of Doge Marino Grimaldi in 1595. The evocation begins with sounding bells (Betjeman would have approved) and the choice of music is extraordinarily rich, using processional effects to simulate the actual scene, like a great Renaissance painting. The climax comes with the Mass itself; and the sounds here, choral and instrumental, are quite glorious. The spontaneity of the whole affair is remarkable and the recording superb.

'*Venetian Vespers*', including: MONTEVERDI: *Laudate pueri; Laudate dominum; Deus qui mundum; Laetatus sum.* GIOVANNI GABRIELI: *Intonazione* (for organ). RIGATTI: *Dixit dominus; Nisi dominus; Magnificat; Salve regina.* GRANDI: *O intemerata; O quam tu pulchra es.* FASALO: *Intonazione* (for organ). BANCHIERI: *Suonata prima; Dialogo secondo* (for organ). FINETTI: *O Maria, quae rapis corda hominum.* CAVALLI: *Lauda Jerusalem.* MARINI: *Sonata con tre violini in eco.* ANON.: *Praeambulum.*

(M) *** DG 459 457-2 (2).

Sequels can sometimes fall flat (as Hollywood so often demonstrates), but this one certainly doesn't, for the musical intensity of the performance is no less vivid here, and the spatial effects and polychoral interplay are equally impressive in this hypothetical re-creation of a Vespers at St Mark's. Grandiose effects alternate with more intimate sonorities, but the feeling of drama which was part and parcel of the Venetian Renaissance tradition is fully conveyed. Once again all the participants are on their toes, and playing and singing (soloists as well as chorus) are transcendent with detail in the accompaniment always effective and stylish. The recording is splendidly opulent, yet never loses its definition. This fine set is the more welcome, reissued at mid-price.

Gallardo-Domas, Cristina (soprano)

'Bel sogno' (with Munich Radio Orchestra, Maurizio Barbacini): Arias from: BELLINI: *I Capuletti ed I Montecchi.* CATALANI: *La Wally.* CILEA: *Adriana Lecouvreur.* DONIZETTI: *Anna Bolena.* PUCCINI: *Madama Butterfly; La Bohème; Manon Lescaut; Suor Angelica; Gianni Schicchi.* VERDI: *La Traviata; Simon Boccanegra; Otello.*

**(*) Teldec 8573 86440-2.

Cristina Gallardo-Domas made her first big impact on disc with her deeply moving assumption of the title-role in Antonio Pappano's prize-winning version of Puccini's *Suor Angelica.* Here it is in the Puccini items above all that she shines out, giving portraits of each heroine that are not just beautiful and sensitive but bring out the words too. Yet this collection demonstrates the breadth of her sympathies in a formidable range of arias, and though she is not quite so much at home in Bellini or Donizetti, there too one recognises the warmth and responsiveness of her singing. The only slight disappointment is that the Munich recording brings out an occasional unevenness in her vocal production, though that will matter little to anyone finding her distinctive timbre attractive.

Gedda, Nicolai (tenor)

Songs and Lieder: VERACINI: *Meco verrai.* RESPIGHI: *Notte; Stornellatrice.* PRATELLA: *La strada bianca.* CASELLA: *La storia della fanciulla rapita.* CARNEVALI: *Stornelli capriccioso.* TURINA: *Poema en forma de canciones, Op. 19.* RACHMANINOV: *Frühlingsfluten; Hier ist es schön; Lied des jungen Zigeuners; O singe nicht, du schönes Mädchen.* BEETHOVEN: *Andanken; An die Geliebte; Der Floh; Der Kuss; Der Liebende; 3 Gesänge von Goethe; Lied aus der Ferne; Mailied; Neue Liebe, neues Leben; Zärtliche Liebe; Der Zufriedene.* SCHUBERT: *Nachthelle; Trinklied.* Arias from: ADAM: *Le Postillon de Lonjumeau.* MEYERBEER: *L'Africaine.* MASSENET: *Werther.* BORODIN: *Prince Igor.* RIMSKY-KORSAKOV: *Sadko.* TCHAIKOVSKY: *Eugene Onegin.* RACHMANINOV: *Aleko.* VERDI: *Aida.* PONCHIELLI: *La Gioconda.* PUCCINI: *La Bohème; Turandot.* HAYDN: *L'Infedeltà delusa.* BEETHOVEN: *Fidelio.* SCHUBERT: *Die Verschworenen.* FLOTOW: *Martha.* MOZART: Concert arias: *Clarice cara mia sposa; Con ossequito, con rispetto; Müsst ich auch durch tausend Drachen.*

(BB) **(*) EMI (ADD) CZS5 67684-2 (2).

Gedda – every producer's ideal of a recording tenor – has encompassed an astonishingly wide range of repertoire in his long recording career, and these two discs cover it splendidly. Among the French items one especially marvels at the heady freedom on top in the jolly Adam aria, recorded early in his career. Other items give a hint of the strain, which marred some of his later recordings, but by no means is there any serious flaw. Whether in operetta, song or in full-blooded opera arias, he has an innate sense of idiomatic style, a claim few tenors can boast today. The recordings, which cover a wide range and period, are generally fine, with just one or two items showing their age. The blot on this CD, and others in this series, is the pitiful packaging, which has the scantiest of biographies possible, and, needless to say, no texts or translations. The two CDs are inexpensive, but we are sure most of Gedda's admirers would be prepared to pay extra for some decent notes, translations and packaging.

FAURE: *Nell; Aprés un rêve; Fleur jetée.* POULENC: *A sa guitare; Hôtel.* DEBUSSY: *Mandoline.* HAHN: *L'heure exquise.* RACHMANINOV: *Spring waters; How fair this spot.* BEETHOVEN: *Adelaïde.* R. STRAUSS: *Ständchen; Befreit.* TCHAIKOVSKY: *Sérénade de Don Juan.* GRIEG: *Ich liebe dich.* Arias from: MUSSORGSKY: *Boris Godunov.* R. STRAUSS: *Capriccio.* GOUNOD: *Mireille.* BERLIOZ: *La damnation de Faust.* BIZET: *Carmen; Les Pêcheurs de perles.* CORNELIUS: *Der Barbier von Bagdad.* PUCCINI: *La Bohème.* WEBER: *Der Freischütz.* ROSSINI: *Il barbiere di Siviglia.* DONIZETTI: *L'elisir d'amore.* MOZART: *Idomeneo.* OFFENBACH: *La Belle Hélène.* ADAM: *Le postillon de Longjumeau.* LEHAR: *Giuditta; Der Graf von Luxemburg; Das Land des Lächelns.* LORTZING: *Undine.* AUBER: *Fra Diavolo.* FLOTOW: *Martha.*

(BB) *(**) Disky Royal Classics Vocal Double (ADD) DCL 704802 (2).

The present survey covers a period of three decades from 1955 (the *Mireille* excerpt, transferred very fiercely here) to 1985 (Lehár's *Giuditta*).

However, the opening group of French songs are not very flatteringly transferred and Ciccolini, though characterful, proves a less than subtle accompanist. Rachmaninov fares better, as does Berlioz, and once we reach the *Flower song* from *Carmen* with Beecham (1969) the quality improves, and Donizetti's *Una furtiva lagrima* is agreeably caught. But the fierceness returns in the *Der Freischütz* excerpt. The second disc opens with honeyed performances of songs by Beethoven and Strauss, but the peakiness then returns in Tchaikovsky, and ruins Grieg's *Ich liebe dich.* Among the operetta items which follow one admires Gedda's freedom on top in the Adam aria from *Le postillon de Longjumeau* and after the attractive Lehár selection the arias from Auber's *Fra Diavolo* and Flotow's *Martha* are particularly fresh. It is a great pity that the transfers are of such uneven quality.

Gens, Véronique (soprano)

'Nuit d'étoiles' (with Roger Vignoles): Songs: DEBUSSY: *3 Chansons de Bilitis etc.* FAURE: *Aprés un rêve, etc.* POULENC: *Banalités etc.*

***Virgin (ADD) VC5 45360-2.

This is one of the very finest of all discs of French mél-odies, an inspired choice of well-known and rare songs sung with exceptional imagination and feeling for the idiom. Best known for her brilliant perform-ances of baroque music, Gens here sings with a tone at once firmly focused and sensuously beautiful. In her distinctive and idiomatic characterization of each composer she is greatly helped by Roger Vignoles, by the brilliant accompaniment adding to the element of fantasy that runs through the whole sequence. The point and wit found in such a popular song as Fauré's *Mandoline* are exceptional, making one appreciate it afresh, and the waltz numbers from the Poulenc group, *Voyage à Paris* and *Les chemins de l'amour*, are equally seductive in their idiomatic lilt. The poise of Gens in the more serious songs is also exemplary, with the voice flawlessly placed. A magical disc.

Gheorghiu, Angela (soprano)

Arias (with Ch. & O of Teatro Regio, Turin, John Mauceri) from: VERDI: *Falstaff.* MASSENET: *Hérodiade; Chérubin.* CATALANI: *La Wally.* BELLINI: *I Capuleti e i Montecchi.* PUCCINI: *La Bohème.* BOITO: *Mefistofele.* GOUNOD: *Faust.* DONIZETTI: *Don Pasquale.* GRIGORIU: *Valurile Dunarii.*

**(*) Decca 452 417-2.

The star of Decca's *La Traviata* here makes her solo début in a recital which offers much lovely singing - the very opening excerpt from Verdi's *Falstaff* brings a ravishing line (and some fine orchestral playing, too) and the Massenet aria is quite melting and full of charm. But there is too little difference of characteri-zation between the different heroines, not enough fiery passion or, indeed, displays of temperament, which means that the *Jewel song* from *Faust* fails to sparkle as it should. Nevertheless the sample of Mimì in *La Bohème* promises well. The back-up here, from John Mauceri and the Turin chorus and orchestra, is impressive, and so is the glowing Decca recording.

'Casta Diva' (with ROHCG Ch. & O, Pidó): Arias from: BELLINI: *Norma; I puritani; La sonnambula.* ROSSINI: *L'assedio di Corinto; Il barbiere di Siviglia; Guglielmo Tell.* DONIZETTI: *Anna Bolena; Lucia di Lammermoor.*

*** EMI CDC 5 57163-2.

Not since Joan Sutherland has a disc of *bel canto* arias inspired such glorious singing as from Angela Gheo-rghiu in repertory with which she has not till now been associated. The flexibility of her voice has been amply demonstrated in her regular lyric repertory, whether as Gounod's Marguerite in *Faust* or Verdi's Violetta in *La traviata*, and this translates perfectly to Rossini, Bellini and Donizetti at their most demand-ing. Ravishing tone, finely shaded, marks the opening item, *Casta diva*, with poised legato that yet allows moving characterization. In the other great Bellini

arias tenderness goes with depth of feeling, with a hint of flutter heightening the emotion in Amina's *Ah, non credea mirarti* from *La sonnambula*, and with spar-kling coloratura in all the cabalettas. In Rossini she is just as commanding, whether in the *Guglielmo Tell* aria, the fine aria from *L'assedio di Corinto* or Rosina's *Una voce poco fa* from *Il barbiere di Siviglia*, sparkily characterful. In Donizetti the scena from *Anna Bolena* leads naturally to the great Act I aria from *Lucia di Lammermoor*. The top of the voice may not be quite as free as Sutherland's was, but this is comparably assured. Perhaps wisely, Gheorghiu has opted not to include the Mad Scene from *Lucia* as well. Warm, sym-pathetic accompaniment and vivid recording.

'Angela Gheorghiu Live at Covent Garden' (with Royal Opera House, Covent Garden Orchestra, Ion Marin) : Arias from: BELLINI: *Norma.* BREDICEANU: *La seceris.* CHARPENTIER: *Louise.* CILEA: *Adriana Lecouvreur.* HANDEL: *Rinaldo.* LOEWE: *My Fair Lady.* MASSENET: *Manon.* MOZART: *Le nozze di Figaro.* PUCCINI: *Gianni Schicchi; Madama Butterfly; Turandot.*

**(*) EMI CDC5 57264-2.

It was a striking enough development when Angela Gheorghiu, a soprano geared to Verdi, Puccini and Massenet, displayed such formidable mastery in the bel canto repertory, as captured on her recital disc of Rossini, Bellini and Donizetti. Even more remarkable is the classical poise and purity of her singing here in *Lascia ch'io pianga* from Handel's *Rinaldo* and the Countess's aria, *Porgi amor*, from Mozart's *Figaro*. This recording was made at her Covent Garden recital in June 2001, demonstrating throughout that unlike so many operatic prima donnas she has not forgotten her early lessons. Her assurance and tech-nical mastery go with a magnetic ability to project character with musical imagination, not just in favourite romantic arias, including Norma's *Casta diva* and Louise's *Depuis le jour*, but in the encores which include a charming Romanian song and *I Could have Danced all Night* from *My Fair Lady*. Marred slightly by intrusive applause.

'Angela Gheorghiu Live' (with Royal Opera House Covent Garden Orchestra, Ian Marin): Arias from: HANDEL: *Rinaldo.* MOZART: *Le nozze di Figaro.* CHARPENTIER: *Louise.* PUCCINI: *Madama Butterfly; Gianni Schicchi.* CILEA: *Adriana Lecouvreur.* BELLINI: *Norma.* Encores: BREDICEANU: *La Seçeris.* LOEWE: *My Fair Lady: I Could have Danced all Night.*

*** EMI DVD 4 92695-9.

This DVD offers a visual recording of the live recital given at Covent Garden by Gheorghiu in June 2001, which has also been issued on audio CD (see above). The bonus on DVD, as well as having the vision of an exceptionally beautiful woman, is that among the special features is an interview with Gheorghiu, in which she confirms some of the points implied by the CD version, notably that when she was a student she knew and loved the two opening arias, not generally part of her latter-day repertory, *Lascia ch'io pianga* from Handel's *Rinaldo* and the Countess's *Porgi amor* from Mozart's *Marriage of Figaro* (as she explains, the very first Mozart aria she ever sang). The poise of those performances, the stylish concern for vocal purity, leads on to moving accounts of arias more usually associated with her, as well as an extrovert group of encores executed with commanding artistry, even if during *I Could have Danced all Night* she has to prompt herself with the music. As to the video production, having multi-coloured back lighting for each aria – pink, blue or a mixture of both – takes us near the pop world, but it gives variety!

Gheorghiu, Angela (soprano), Roberto Alagna (tenor)

Opera arias and duets from: MASCAGNI: *L'amico Fritz.* MASSENET: *Manon.* DONIZETTI: *Anna Bolena; Don Pasquale.* OFFENBACH: *La belle Hélène.* BERNSTEIN: *West Side story.* GOUNOD: *Faust.* G. CHARPENTIER: *Louise.* BERLIOZ: *Les Troyens.* PUCCINI: *La Bohème.*

*** EMI CDC5 56117-2.

If Angela Gheorghiu's Decca solo début is a little disappointing, this record of duets with her husband, Roberto Alagna, is not. Clearly they are a natural couple as artists as well as human beings. There is much here to delight, not least the opening *Cherry duet* from *L'amico Fritz*, in which the voices blend delightfully. *Manon* brings a comparable symbiosis, and the Donizetti items are as winning as the unexpected excerpt from *Les Troyens*. Solo arias also come off well here, notably Gheorghiu's aria from *Anna Bolena*, which suits her exactly; Alagna turns in a stylishly heady account of the delicious Waltz song from *La belle Hélène*. The excerpt from *West Side story* is tenderly touching but, as nearly always, the voices sound too mature for these star-crossed young lovers. Again the promise of that future complete *Bohème* comes in the closing all-too-short *O soave fanciulla*. First-rate accompaniments under Richard Armstrong and superb sound contribute to the great success of this immensely pleasurable operatic hour.

Ghiaurov, Nicolai (bass)

'The Singers' (Decca series): Arias (with LSO, Downes) from: MOZART: *Don Giovanni.* GOUNOD: *Faust.* MASSENET: *Manon.* MEYERBEER: *Les Huguénots.* BIZET: *Carmen; La Jolie Fille de Perth.* GLINKA: *A Life for the Tsar.* RUBINSTEIN: *The Demon.* TCHAIKOVSKY: *Yolanta; Eugene Onegin.* BORODIN: *Prince Igor.* RIMSKY-KORSAKOV: *Sadko.* MUSSORGSKY: *Boris Godunov.* RACHMANINOV: *Aleko.*

(M) *** Decca (ADD) 467 902-2.

This superb Ghiaurov CD, with plenty of colourfully contrasting arias, is drawn from two LPs dating from 1962 and 1964. At the time, he was rather unfairly compared to Boris Christoff, who had just made some classic recitals of Russian arias, but the distance of time allows us to appreciate just how good Ghiaurov is in his own right, even if he does yield to his fellow Bulgarian in sheer artistry, particularly in detail. Ghiaurov's rich bass is always commanding, and his musicianship is never in doubt. The Decca recording is rich and vivid, but texts and translations are (irritatingly) available only via a CD ROM drive.

Gloriae Dei Cantores, Elizabeth Patterson

'By the rivers of Babylon (American Psalmody II)' (with James E. Jordan, organ): LOEFFLER: *By the rivers of Babylon, Op. 3* (with P. Clark, E. Ingwersen (flutes), M. Buddington (harp), H. Vacarro (cello)). Virgil THOMSON: *3 Antiphonal Psalms (Nos. 123, 133 & 136); De profundis.* SCHOENBERG: *De profundis.* TAYLOR: *Sing to the Lord a new song.* BERGER: *The eyes of all wait upon Thee.* NEWBURY: *Psalm 150.* NEAR: *My song shall be alway of the loving-kindness of the Lord.* ADLER: *Psalm triology (Nos. 42, 84 & 113).* NESWICK: *Hallelujah! Sing to the Lord a new song.* WHITE: *Cantate Domino* (with brass Ens.).

**(*) Paraclete Press Gloriae Dei Cantores Dig. GDCD 027.

This collection of twentieth-century psalm settings includes music by 'those who are native Americans by birth or citizenship', which covers both Charles Loeffler, a late nineteenth-century émigré, and Schoenberg, who became an American citizen in 1941. The latter's atonal setting of the original Hebrew text of Psalm 120 (commissioned by Koussevitzky), with its dramatic spoken acclamations adding to the music's emotional impact, is the one really avant-garde piece here. It comes immediately after Virgil Thomson's admirably fresh but much simpler setting in English.

Loeffler's sensuously lush *By the rivers of Babylon*, which introduces the programme and gives the disc its title, is the most ambitious piece, very Gallic in feeling. It is richly sung and has a beautiful postlude for two flutes and cello, let down by imperfect intonation from the solo cellist. This closing section should have been re-recorded, for it all but spoils a superb performance. The rest of the music is traditional, but individually so, especially the very striking *Psalm triology* by Samuel Adler and the pieces by Clifford Taylor, Jean Berger (gently touching) and Bruce Neswick, his joyous *Hallelujah!*.

The choral singing is very fine and deeply committed throughout, and the choir has the advantage of the ideal acoustics of the Methuen Music Hall in Massachusetts, while James Jordan's organ accompaniments (when required) give admirable support, using the superb organ now located there. Even with the reservation about the Loeffler postlude, this splendid collection is well worth having. (Volume I, which we have not received for review, is available on GDCD 025.)

Gobbi, Tito (baritone)

'*Heroes*': Arias and excerpts from: ROSSINI: *Il barbiere di Siviglia.* DONIZETTI: *Lucia di Lammermoor.* VERDI: *Rigoletto; La Traviata; Simon Boccanegra; Un ballo in maschera; Don Carlos; Otello; Falstaff.* LEONCAVALLO: *Pagliacci.* PUCCINI: *Tosca* (with Callas).

(M) (***) EMI (ADD) CDM5 66810-2.

Tito Gobbi is not usually a hero figure in opera, although his portrayal of Rodrigo in Verdi's *Don Carlos* (sombre and powerful) undoubtedly has a heroic ring to it, and his uniquely charismatic portrayal of Verdi's Falstaff (the closing item) is heroic in its way, good-humouredly so. No other version of Rossini's *Largo al factotum* on record effervesces with such wit, yet has such subtle vocal inflection. Gobbi's portrayal of Rigoletto has a moving resonance, his Germont père in *La Traviata* and Tonio in *Pagliacci* are hardly less eloquent and his *Eri tu* in *Simon Boccanegra* is most soberly powerful of all. But the roles for which he is most celebrated on disc are darker (Scarpia in de Sabata's 1953 *Tosca*) and cruel (Iago in Verdi's *Otello*) and these are superb examples of his supreme mastery.

Arias from: LEONCAVALLO: *Pagliacci.* ROSSINI: *Il barbiere di Siviglia; Guglielmo Tell.* DONIZETTI: *L'elisir d'amore.* CILEA: *Adriana Lecouvreur.* GIORDANO: *Fedora; Andrea Chénier.* VERDI: *Macbeth; Otello; Nabucco; Simon Boccanegra.* PUCCINI: *Tosca; La fanciulla del West.* WOLF-FERRARI: *I gioielli della Madonna.* CAVALLI: *Serse.* VIVALDI: *Cantata: Piango, gemo.* PAISIELLO: *L'amor contrastato (La molinara).* A. SCARLATTI: *Il Pompeo.* MONTEVERDI: *Orfeo.* BERLIOZ: *La damnation de Faust.* Songs by COTTRAU; LAMA; PIGARELLI; TAGLIAFERRI; D'ANZI; SADERO; TOSTI; CARISSIMI; DURANTE; GIORDANI; GASTALDON; RESPIGHI; TRAD.; ANON.

(BB) *** Disky Royal Classics Vocal Double (ADD) DCL 706662 (2).

This remarkably varied compilation has many treasures, mostly on the operatic side (recorded between 1958 and 1965), showing the range of Gobbi's expression based on a unique range of such diverse characters as Boccanegra, Iago, Scarpia, Jack Ranch in *Fanciulla del West* and the swaggering Belcore in *L'elisir d'amore.* The excerpt from *The Jewels of the Madonna* is a welcome bonus. The songs are of lesser interest, although all are compellingly sung, especially those of Tosti. However, the *arie antiche* bring some exquisite performances, and any unstylishness can be forgiven when the singing itself is so fine, and the accompaniments often very well managed. The programme closes with an engaging version of Berlioz's *Song of the Flea* and *Tre sbirri* from Gobbi's later stereo *Tosca.* Transfers are

good, but documentation sadly lacking. Even so this is an indispensable reissue.

Gothic Voices, Christopher Page

'*The Guardian of Zephirus*' (Courtly songs of the 15th century, with Imogen Barford, medieval harp): DU FAY: *J'atendray tant qu'il vous playra; Adieu ces bons vins de Lannoys; Mon cuer me fait tous dis penser.* BRIQUET: *Ma seul amour et ma belle maistresse.* DE CASERTA: *Amour ma' le cuer mis.* LANDINI: *Nessun ponga speranza; Giunta vaga bilta.* REYNEAU: *Va t'en mon cuer, avent mes yeux.* MATHEUS DE SANCTO JOHANNE: *Fortune, faulce, parverse.* DE INSULA: *Amours n'ont cure le tristesse.* BROLLO: *Qui le sien vuelt bien maintenir.* ANON.: *N'a pas long temps que trouvay Zephirus; Je la remire, la belle.*

*** Hyp. CDA 66144.

In 1986 the Gothic Voices began what was to become a large-scale survey of medieval music, secular and sacred – for the two are inevitably intermingled. From the beginning, the project was an adventure in exploration, as much for the artists as for the listener, for comparatively little is known about how this music sounded on voices of the time.

The songs of the troubadours or trouvères – outside the church – sometimes drew on ecclesiastical chant, but other such chansons had a modal character of their own. They were essentially monophonic, i.e. a single line of music, perhaps with an instrumental accompaniment, but the rhythmic patterns were unrecorded and, like much else in this repertoire, are inevitably conjectural in modern re-creative performance.

Much of the repertoire on this first disc (and indeed elsewhere) is unfamiliar, with Du Fay the only famous name; but everything here is of interest, and the listener inexperienced in medieval music will be surprised at the strength of its character. The performances are naturally eloquent and, although the range of colour is limited compared with later writing, it still has immediacy of appeal, especially if taken in short bursts. The recording balance is faultless and the sound first rate. With complete security of intonation and a chamber-music vocal blend, the presentation is wholly admirable. There is full back-up documentation.

'*The Castle of Fair Welcome*' (Courtly songs of the late 15th century, with Christopher Wilson, lute): ANON.: *Las je ne puis; En amours n'a si non bien; Mi ut re ut.* MORTON: *Le souvenir de vous me tue; Que pourroit plus; Plus j'ay le monde regardé.* REGIS: *Puisque ma dame.* BEDYNGHAM: *Myn hertis lust.* BINCHOIS: *Deuil angoisseux.* VINCENET: *La pena sin ser sabida.* FRYE: *So ys emprinted.* ENRIQUE: *Pues servicio vos desplaze.* CHARLES THE BOLD: *Ma dame, trop vous mesprenés.* DU FAY: *Ne je ne dors.*

*** Hyp. CDA 66194.

Christopher Page has by now established a basic procedure for his presentation of this early vocal repertoire: he has decided that it will be unaccompanied and usually performed by a modest-sized vocal group. So, in the present collection, further variety is provided with four instrumental pieces (played on harp and lute). Not surprisingly, the two most striking works here are by Du Fay (remarkably compelling) and Binchois; but the programme overall has been carefully chosen and it is given a boldly spontaneous presentation which cannot but intrigue the ear. As always, the recording is first class.

'*The Service of Venus and Mars*': DE VITRY: *Gratissima virginis; Vos quie admiramini; Gaude gloriosa; Contratenor.* DES MOLINS: *De ce que fol pense.* PYCARD: *Gloria.* POWER: *Sanctus.* LEBERTOUL: *Las, que me demanderoye.* PYRAMOUR: *Quam pulchra es.* DUNSTABLE: *Speciosa facta es.* SOURSBY: *Sanctus.* LOQUEVILLE: *Je vous pri que j'aye un baysier.* ANON.: *Singularis laudis digna; De ce fol, pense; Lullay, lullay; There is no rose; Le gay playsir; Le grant pleyser; Agincourt carol.*

*** Hyp. CDA 66283.

The subtitle of this collection is 'Music for the Knights of the Garter, 1340-1440'; few readers will recognize many of the names in the list of composers above. But the music itself is fascinating and the performances bring it to life with extraordinary projection and vitality. The recording too is first class, and this imaginatively chosen programme deservedly won the 1988 *Gramophone* award for Early Music. Readers interested in trying medieval repertoire could hardly do better than to start here.

'*A song for Francesca*': ANDREAS DE FLORENTINA: *Astio non mori mai. Per la ver'onesta.* JOHANNES DE FLORENTINA: *Quando la stella.* LANDINI: *Ochi dolenti mie. Per seguir la speranca.* ANON.: *Quando i oselli canta; Constantia; Amor mi fa cantar a la Francesca; Non na el so amante.* DU FAY: *Quel fronte signorille in paradiso.* RICHARD DE LOQUEVILLE: *Puisquie je suy amoureux; Pour mesdisans ne pour leur faulx parler; Qui ne veroit que vos deulx yeulx.* HUGO DE LATINS: *Plaindre m'estuet.* HAUCOURT: *Je demande ma bienvenue.* GROSSIN: *Va t'ent souspir.* ANON.: *O regina seculi; Reparatrix Maria; Confort d'amours.*

*** Hyp. CDA 66286.

The title, 'A Song for Francesca', refers not only to the fourteenth-century French items here, but to the fact that the Italians too tended to be influenced by French style. More specifically, the collection is a well-deserved tribute to Francesca MacManus, selfless worker on behalf of many musicians, not least as manager of Gothic Voices. The variety of expression and mood in these songs, ballatas and madrigals is astonishing, some of them amazingly complex. The Hyperion recording is a model of its kind, presenting this long-neglected music most seductively in a warm but clear setting.

'*Music for the Lion-hearted King*' (Music to mark the 800th anniversary of the coronation of Richard I): ANON.: *Mundus vergens; Noves miles sequitur; Anglia planctus itera; In occasu sideris.* BRULE: *A la douçour de la bele saison; Etas auri reditu; Pange melos lacrimosum; Vetus abit littera; Hac in anni ianua.* LI CHASTELAIN DE COUCI: *Li nouviauz tanz; Soi sub nube latuit.* BLONDEL DE NESLE: *L'amours dont sui espris; Ma joie me semont; Purgator criminum; Ver pacis apperit; Latex silice.*

*** Hyp. CDA 66336.

Partly because of the intensity, partly because of the imaginative variety of the choral response, all this twelfth-century music communicates readily, even though its comparatively primitive style could easily lead to boredom. The performances are polished but vital, and there is excellent documentation to lead the listener on. This may be a specialist record, but it could hardly be better presented.

'*The marriage of Heaven & Hell*' (Anonymous motets, songs and polyphony from 13th-century France). Also: BLONDEL DE NESLE: *En tous tans que vente bise.* MUSET: *Trop volontiers chanteroie.* BERNART DE VENTADORN: *Can vei la lauzeta mover.* GAUTIER DE DARGIES: *Autre que je laureta mover.*

*** Hyp. CDA 66423.

The title of this collection dramatically overstates the problem of the medieval Church with its conflicting secular influences. Music was universal and the repertoire of the trouvère had a considerable melodic influence on the polyphonic motets used by the Church, though actual quotation was very rare. Nevertheless, on occasion, vulgar associations in a vocal line could ensue and the clergy tore their hair. It all eventually led to the Council of Trent when, the story goes, the purity of Palestrina's contrapuntal serenity saved the day. Certainly medieval church music was robust and full of character, but here one is also struck by its complexity and intensity. The performances have a remarkable feeling of authenticity, and the background is admirably documented.

'*The Medieval romantics*' (French songs and motets, 1340-1440): ANON.: *Quiconques veut; Je languis d'amere mort; Quant voi le douz tanz; Plus bele que flors; Degentis vita; Mais qu'il vous viegne.* SOLAGE: *Joieux de cuer.* DE PORTA: *Alma polis religio.* MACHAUT: *C'est force; Tant doucement; Comment qu'a moy lonteinne.* TENORISTA: *Sofrir m'estuet.* SENLECHES: *En ce gracieux temps.* DU FAY: *Je requier a tous; Las, que feray.* VELUT: *Je voel servir.* LYMBURGIA: *Tota pulchra es.*

*** Hyp. CDA 66463.

Machaut (fourteenth century) and Du Fay (fifteenth) are names which have now become individually established. Du Fay was master of the secular song-form called the 'virelai' (opening with a refrain, which then followed each verse) and Machaut was one of the first (if not *the* first) composers to set the Ordinary of the Mass; he too wrote chansons and virelais. But of course there is also much music here by other (unknown) composers and our old friend, Anon. The virelais are sung unaccompanied. Sometimes there are vocal melismas (extra parts without words) set against the textual line. So this collection represents the medieval blossoming of songs and part-songs alongside the motets, for secular and sacred never really grew apart. As usual, the Gothic Voices perform this repertoire with skill and confidence and lots of character, and the splendid documentation puts the listener fully in the historical picture.

'Lancaster and Valois' (French and English music, 1350-1420): MACHAUT: *Donnez, signeurs; Quand je ne voy; Riches d'amour; Pas de tor en thies pais.* SOLAGE: *Tres gentil cuer.* PYCARD: *Credo.* STURGEON: *Salve mater domini.* FONTEYNS: *Regail ex progenie.* CESARIS: *Mon seul voloir; Se vous scaviez, ma tres douce maistresse.* BAUDE CORDIER: *Ce jour de l'an.* ANON.: *Sanctus; Soit tart, tempre, main ou soir; Je vueil vivre au plaisir d'amours; Puis qu'autrement ne puis avoir; Le ior; Avrai je ja de ma dame confort?*

*** Hyp. CDA 66588.

This stimulating series has always been essentially experimental, for we do not know just how unaccompanied medieval voices were balanced or how many were used. In the documentation with this record, Christopher Page suggests that on this disc he feels he has the internal balance just about right, and the vocal mix varies, sometimes led by a female voice, sometimes by a male. More Machaut here, some slightly later French settings, and the usual balance between sacred and secular. Everything sounds vital and alive.

'The study of love' (French songs and motets of the 14th century): ANON.: *Pour vous servir; Puis que l'aloe ne fine; Jour a jour la vie; Combien que j'aye; Marticius qui fu; Renouveler me feist; Fist on dame; Il me convient guerpir; Le ior; En la maison Dedalus; Combien que j'aye; Le grant biauté; En esperant; Ay las! quant je pans.* MACHAUT: *Dame, je suis cilz – Fin cuers; Trop plus – Biauté paree – Je ne suis; Tres bonne et belle; Se mesdisans; Dame, je vueil endurer.* SOLAGE: *Le basile.* PYCARD: *Gloria.*

*** Hyp. CDA 66619.

The Gothic Voices' exploration is moving sideways rather than forward, for Machaut is still with us. The present collection of settings demonstrates the medieval literary and poetic understanding of 'love' - romantic and spiritual. The Anonymous examples are often as stimulating as any of the songs and motets here by named composers, and the Pycard *Gloria* is obviously included to remind us again that church music is about the love of God. This and the previous three CDs should be approached with some caution, starting perhaps with 'The Medieval romantics'.

'The voice in the garden' (Spanish songs and motets, 1480-1530): JUAN DEL ENCINA: *Mi libertad; Los sospiros no sosiegan; Triste España sin ventura.* LUIS DE NARVAEZ: *Fantasias;* (after) *Paseávase el rey Moro.* FRANCISCO DE PENALOSA: *Precor te, Domine; Ne reminiscaris, Domine; Por las sierras de Madrid; Sancta Maria.* JULIUS DE MODENA: *Tiento.* PALERO: (after) *Paseávase el rey Moro.* ENRIQUE: *Mi querer tanto vos quiere.* LUIS MILAN: *Fantasias Nos. 10; 12; 18.* GABRIEL: La Bella Malmaridada; *Yo creo que n'os dió Dios.* ANON.: *Dentro en el vergel; Harto de tanta porfia; Entra Mayo y sale Abril; Dindirin; Ave, Virgo, gratia plena; A la villa voy; Pasa el agoa.*

*** Hyp. CDA 66653.

Here the Gothic Voices travel to Spain and take with them Christopher Wilson (vihuela) and Andrew-Lawrence King (harp). Their earlier concerts have included instrumental items, kept separate from the vocal music, and here the same policy is followed, but the mix of sacred, secular and instrumental is more exotic than usual. As throughout this series, the recording is of the highest quality.

'The Spirits of England and France' (Music of the Middle Ages for court and church, with Pavlo Beznosiuk, medieval fiddle): ANON.: *La uitime estampie real; La quarte estampie real; La septime estampie real; Credo; Virelais; Songs; Conducti; Conductus motets.* Matteo Da PERUGIA: *Belle sans per.* MACHAUT: *Ay mi! dame de valour.* PYKINI: *Plaissance, or tost.* PEROTINUS: *Presul nostri temporis.* ANON.: *Ave Maria.*

*** Hyp. CDA 66739.

This is the first of a series of CDs covering French and English music between the twelfth and fifteenth centuries. The first half of the present collection explores the sonorities of three- and four-part writing during the last decades of the fourteenth century and the first decades of the fifteenth. The second group goes back in time to anonymous settings from the twelfth and thirteenth centuries, although including one memorable piece possibly written by Perotinus. Although the items by Machaut (monodic) and Pykini (in four parts) are particularly striking, 'Anonymous' does not mean that the music is not full of character and individuality and the closing *Ave Maria*, with its series of triads, is as beautiful as many later settings. Pavlo Beznosiuk provides three instrumental interludes, a series of *Estampie*, winningly played on a medieval fiddle. The recording is excellent.

'The Spirits of England and France' (Songs of the trouvères, with Emma Kirkby, Margaret Philpot, Roger Covey-Crump, Leigh Nixon, Henry Wickham, Instrumental Ensemble): RICHART DE SEMILLI: *Je chevauchai.* BRULE: *Desconfortez plais de dolor; Quant define feuille et flor; De bien amer grant joie atent; Cil qui d'amours;* ANON.: *Estampie 1-3; Donna pos vos ay chausida; Quant voi la fleur nouvelle; Amors m'art con fuoc am flama.* GONTIER

DE SOIGNES: *Dolerousement commence.*
KAUKESEL: *Un chant novel; Fins cuers enamourés.*
GAUTIER DE DARGIES: *La doce pensee.* ADAM DE LA
HALLE: *Assénes chi, Grievilier.* ERNOUS LI VIELLE:
Por conforter mon corage. AUDEFROI: *Au novel tens pascor.*

*** Hyp. CDA 66773.

The songs of the troubadours were inevitably mono-phonic, usually offering an expressive and touching melisma, lightly ornamented. To quote Christopher Page's excellent notes: 'their supreme genre was the *grand chant*, a protracted meditation upon the fortunes of loving'. One of the key composers in this style was Gace Brulé, and examples such as *Desconfortez plais de dolor, Quant define feuille et flor and De bien amer grant joie atent* convey an almost desperate melancholy. However, not all is despair: the opening *Je chevauchai* ('I rode out the other morning'), with its repeated refrain, is as spirited as it is optimistic – and rightly so, for the amorous singer has his way with with the shep-herdess he encounters by chance in the wood.

Ernous Li Vielle's *Por conforter mon corage* has a similar theme, only this time the seduction is more forceful. In contrast Wibers Kaukesel's *Fins cuers enam-ourés* ennobles the theme of love and being loved, while finally Audefroi tells of a husband who, after his wife Argentine, has borne him six sons, tires of her and takes a concubine, banishing her when she objects. The ingenuous moral of the tale is repeated after each verse: 'Whoever is wed to a bad husband often has a sad heart'. The singing and presentation here are admira-ble, and there are instrumental *Estampie* to provide interludes. A fascinating collection.

'*The Spirits of England and France*' (Binchois and his contemporaries, with Shirley Rumsey, Christopher Wilson, Christopher Page, lute):
BINCHOIS: *Qui veut mesdire; Amoreux suy; Adieu mon amoreuse joye; Ay! doloureux; Magnificat secundi toni; Se la belle.* CARDOT: *Pour une fois.*
VELUT: *Un petit oyselet; Laissiés ester.* ANON.:
Abide, I hope; Exultavit cor in Domino. LE GRANT:
Se liesse. DE LYMBURGIA: *Descendi in ortum meum.*
POWER: *Gloria.* DUNSTABLE: *Beata Dei genitrix.*
FONTAINE: *J'ayme bien celui.* MACHAUT: *Il m'est avis.* BITTERING: *En Katerina solennia.*

*** Hyp. CDA 66783.

Christopher Page and his group have been exploring early English and French repertoire in a number of earlier Hyperion anthologies. Here they turn to the early decades of the fifteenth century and to the music of Binchois (who died in 1460) and his contemporar-ies. Binchois is represented by a series of medieval love songs, all in three parts, very word-sensitive, even poignant in feeling, climaxed by the remarkably expressive *Ay! doloureux*, the most expansive and the most memorable. Then we turn to religious music and, besides a fine Binchois *Magnificat*, there is also Power's eloquent *Gloria* in five voices and fine exam-ples of the music of Dunstable and even of Machaut. It

is a heady mix, and it is the contrast here that makes this finely sung and recorded collection so stimulating.

'*The Spirits of England and France*' (with Shirley Rumsey, Christopher Wilson, Christopher Page, lute): ANON.: *The Missa Caput*: an English Mass setting from c. 1440 interspersed with the story of the Salve Regina. Carols: *Jesu for thy mercy; Jesu fili Dei; Make us merry; Nowell, nowell, nowell; Clangat tuba; Alma redemptoris mater; Agnus Dei* (Old Hall Manuscript).

*** Hyp. CDA 66857.

The inclusion here of the anonymous English *Missa Caput* gives a special interest to this collection. Com-posed around 1440, it survived in seven different manuscripts, and it is credited with having had a strong influence on the Masses of Ockeghem. The quality of the music is sure – it has long been attributed to Du Fay. Indeed, it is a remarkable and powerful setting, well worth discovering, and it is given added impact by the urgency of Christopher Page's direction.

The performance intersperses the Mass Propers with verses from a recently discovered Latin song nar-rating the origins of the Marian antiphon *Salve Regina*, with a view to alternating monody and polyphony, and this works remarkably well. The rest of the concert, a collection of early carols, makes an attractively lightweight pendant to the major work. The Gothic Voices sing with great eloquence through-out this 66-minute programme and this is one of their most attractively conceived collections. The record-ing, as ever with this series, is first class.

'*The Spirits of England and France*': ANON.: *Missa Veterum hominem; Jesu, fili Virginis; Doleo super te; Gaude Maria virgo; Deus creator omnium; Jesu salvator; A solis ortuas; Salvator mundi; Christe, Qui lux es; To many a well; Sancta Maria virgo; Mater ora filium; Ave maris stella; Pange lingua.*
DUNSTABLE: *Beata mater.*

*** Hyp. CDA 66919.

The *Missa Veterum hominem* might be considered as complementary to the *Missa Caput*, offered on the previous CD from the Gothic Voices, and the present compilation is equally successful. Both Masses were composed at about the same time, in the late 1440s; both were written for four voices. Once again, in performing this work (with comparable urgency) Christopher Page seeks to vary the vocal texture by opening with an early, three-part carol, *Jesu, fili Vir-ginis*, and alternating the Mass polyphony with monodic plainchant hymns. There are three of these, the last of which, *Deus creator omnium*, uses the same liturgical text as is employed in the Kyrie of the Mass.

'*Jerusalem: the vision of peace*' ANON.: *Luto carens et latere; Jerusalem! grant damage me fais; Te Deum; O levis aurula!; Hac in die Gedeonis; In Salvatoris; Veri vitis germine.* GUIOT DE DIJON: *Chanterau pour mon corage.* Easter Day Mass in Church of Holy Sepulchre, Jerusalem (c. 1130): *Gradual;*

Alleluia; Gospel. HUON DE ST QUENTIN: *Jerusalem se plaint et li pais; Luget Rachel iterum; Incocantes Dominum/Psalm: Deus, qui venerunt; Congaudet hodie celestis curia.* HILDEGARD OF BINGEN: *O Jerusalem.*

*** Hyp. CDA 67039.

'Jerusalem: the vision of peace' was the underlying ideal which motivated the Crusades, as medieval pilgrims believed that such an armed expedition, with papal blessing – killing Saracens on the way – would lead to universal peace and harmony! Anti-Semitism was another factor in the crusading spirit, expressing Christian anger and contempt for the Jews' denial of Christ. *Veri vitis germine* calls strongly on Judaea to return to the Cross.

On a personal level was the tragedy of separation for women whose lovers and husbands had departed for the Holy Land, perhaps never to return. All these elements are reflected in the present diverse anthology, from the opening three-part song of confidence in the power of God, to Hildegard's rhapsodic closing monody, an ecstatic eulogy of longing for Jerusalem and all it represented. The melancholy of a deserted woman's loss is lamented in *Jerusalem! grant damage me fais*, while the *Te Deum*, heard against tolling bells, and the excerpts from the Easter Day Mass represent the liturgy of the period. Harmony, where it occurs, is organum and has great character, and certainly all the music here has great vitality, and is splendidly sung.

'Master of the Rolls' (Music by English composers of the 14th century, with Catherine King, Steven Harrold, Julian Podger, Leigh Nixon, Charles Daniels, Steven Charlesworth): ANON.: *Ab ora summa nuncius; Inter usitata/Inter tot et tales; Vexilla regni prodeunt; Singularis laudis digna; Dulcia [dona redemptoris]; Summum regen honoremus; Omnis terra/Habenti dabitur; Copiose caritatis; Missa Gabriel de celis; Pura, placens/ Parfundement plure; Letetur celi cura; Salve Regina; Jesu fili Virginis* (Plainsong); *Jesu fili/Jesu lumen; Jesu fili Virginis; Sospitati dat egrotos; Exultemus et letemur; Stella maris illustrans omnia; Veni dilectus meus; Pange lingua; O sponsa dei electa; Generosa Jesse plantula; Musicorum collegio/ In templo dei.*

*** Hyp. CDA 67098.

Very few English composers of the fourteenth century are remembered by name. The word used to describe accomplished musicians of the period was magister (master): hence the title of this collection. Only six items here are monodic and what is remarkable is how individual are some of these compositions. *Singularis laudis digna*, for instance, with its whirls of parallel writing, or the simple but touching harmonization of the Marian *Dulcia [dona redemptoris]* and the lovely, lilting *Missa Gabriel de celis*, while *Jesus fili* (a trio) has some engaging rhythmic triplets. Perhaps the most remarkable, original and forward-looking of all is *Stella maris illustrans omnia*, where a highly unu-

sual text is matched by a comparably unpredictable use of chromatics.

Graham, Susan (mezzo-soprano)

'French Operetta' (with CBSO, Abel). Arias from: SIMON: *Toi c'est moi.* MESSAGER: *L'Amour masqué; Coups de roulis; Les Dragons de l'Impératrice; Fortunio; Passionnément; Le Petit Fonctionnaire; Les P'tites Michu.* YVAIN: *Yes* HONNEGER: *Les Aventures du roi Pausole..* HAHN: *Brummell; o mon bel inconnu; Ciboulette.* MOZART *O mon bel inconnu.*

*** Erato 0927 42106-2.

In every way this is an enchanting disc, bringing together in sparkling performances a sequence of rare items which richly deserve revival. Messager's *Fortunio* has been rediscovered in recent years, largely thanks to the complete recording from Sir John Eliot Gardiner. Yet as the items here demonstrate, this amazing figure who, as well as conducting the first performance of Debussy's *Pelléas et Mélisande*, was in turn musical director of the Paris Opéra and Covent Garden, and also composed a sequence of other operettas. Reynaldo Hahn is also well-represented with charming items from four operettas, and it is good to be reminded that even Honneger made an unexpected foray into the genre. The Cuban composer, Moises Simon, has been even more neglected, yet his colourful Spanish-American items equally add to the joy of this frothy collection, idiomatically accompanied and well-recorded. The documentation of the actual arias on this CD leaves much to be desired, but the notes contain an excellent essay by Patrick O'Connor.

'Gramophone Greats'

'Twenty Gramophone All-time Greats' (original mono recordings from 1907–1935): LEONCAVALLO: *Pagliacci: Vesti la giubba* (Caruso); *Mattinata* (Gigli). BISHOP: *Lo here the gentle lark* (Galli-Curci with flute obbligato by Manuel Beringuer). PURCELL: *Nymphs and shepherds* (Manchester Schools Children's Choir (Choir Mistress: Gertrude Riall), Hallé O, Harty). MENDELSSOHN: *Hear my prayer – O for the wings of a dove* (Ernest Lough, Temple Church Ch., Thalben Ball). MARSHALL: *I hear you calling me* (John McCormack). ELGAR: *Salut d'amour* (New SO, composer). J. STRAUSS JR: *Casanova: Nuns' Chorus* (Ch. & O of Grossen Schauspielhauses, Berlin, Ernst Hauke). RACHMANINOV: *Prelude in C sharp min., Op. 3/2* (composer). TRAD.: *Song of the Volga boatmen* (Chaliapin). KREISLER: *Liebesfreud* (composer, Carl Lamson). MOSS: *The floral dance* (Peter Dawson, Gerald Moore). BACH: *Chorale: Jesu, joy of man's desiring* (arr. & played Dame Myra Hess). HANDEL: *Messiah: Come unto Him* (Dora Labette, O, Beecham). SAINT-SAENS: *Samson and Delilah: Softly awakes my heart* (Marian Anderson). BIZET:

Fair Maid of Perth: Serenade (Heddle Nash).
CHOPIN: *Waltz in C sharp min., Op. 64/2* (Cortot).
LEHAR: *Land of Smiles: You are my heart's delight*
(Richard Tauber). KERN: *Showboat: Ol' man river*
(Paul Robeson). SULLIVAN: *The lost chord* (Dame
Clara Butt).

(M) (***) ASV mono CDAJA 5112.

It seems strange and somewhat sad that this marvellous
collection of classical 78-r.p.m. hit records, covering a
period of three decades, should be coming from ASV
rather than HMV (EMI), who are responsible for so
many of the actual recordings. Their amazing technical
excellence means that they can be enjoyed today as they
were then, with only occasional clicks and generally not
too intrusive a background 'surface' noise to create the
right ambience.

Caruso still projects vividly from a 1907 acoustic
master and Amelita Galli-Curci's soprano is as clear
and sweet as the day the recording was made (1919).
Other highlights (for us) include the Manchester
Schools Children's Choir of 250 voices, electrically
recorded in Manchester's Free Trade Hall in 1929. The
story goes that, just before the record was made, Sir
Hamilton Harty bought cream buns and pop for every
child, and that accounts for the warm smile in the
singing. Master Ernest Lough's *O for the wings of a
dove* is another miracle of perfection from a young boy
treble, and Peter Dawson's exuberant *Floral dance* has
astonishing diction – you can hear every word – and
here Gerald Moore's bravura accompaniment is a key
part of the sheer pleasure this performance still gives.

Finally, Dame Clara Butt with her deep masculine
contralto, clanging like a bell in its lowest register,
delivers the sacred piece so beloved of Victorians, Sullivan's *Lost chord*. The transfers are all good (except
perhaps for Dame Myra Hess's *Jesu, joy of man's desiring*, where the background noise surely could have
been cut back a bit more).

Gray, Emily (soprano), Manchester Cathedral Choir, Christopher Stokes

'*Passiontide*' (with Claire Buckley, Jeffrey
Makinson): MENDELSSOHN: *Hear my Prayer.*
VAUGHAN WILLIAMS: *O Taste and See.* HURFORD:
Litany to the Holy Spirit. WESLEY: *Wash me
Throughly.* PERGOLESI: *Stabat Mater.* BYRD: *Civitas
sancti tui.* BACH: *O Sacred Head Sore Wounded; Bist
du bei mir.* CASALS: *O vos omnes.* LOTTI: *Crucifixus.*
DERING: *O bone Jesu.* GIBBONS: *Drop, Drop, Slow
Tears.* IRELAND: *Ex ore innocentiam.* GREENE: *Lord
Let me Know mine End.* MILLER: *When I Survey the
Wonderous Cross.*

(BB) *** Naxos 8.557025.

In this wide-ranging collection the 15-year-old Emily
Gray (who won BBC Radio 2's 'Choirgirl of the Year'
in 2000) produces the firm traditional sound of the
Anglican choirboy, slightly hooty, seemingly all the
more powerful from a female throat, using her voice
with care and taste. The sequence starts with the longest item, the one associated with Master Ernest Lough
and his 1927 recording with the Temple Church Choir,
Mendelssohn's *Hear my Prayer*, here more sharply dramatic under Christopher Stokes' direction, sweet and
pure in the concluding section, *O for the Wings of a
Dove*. The other major item brings together four sections of Pergolesi's *Stabat Mater* in which Gray is
joined by another young soprano, Claire Buckley, similar in style but nicely contrasted. The choir is first-rate
too in that item, and generally they sing with fresh,
clear tone and crisp ensemble, very well-recorded in
Manchester Cathedral. Only in the Byrd Latin setting,
Civitas sancti tui, does it rather lack variety. Rounding
off the sequence comes Maurice Greene's weighty
psalm-setting, *Lord, Let me Know mine End*. The traditional congregational hymn, *When I Survey the
Wondrous Cross*, to the tune *Rockingham*, then provides a rousing conclusion at a rich fortissimo.

Gueden, Hilde (soprano)

'*Operetta favourites*' (with Vienna State Opera
Chorus and Orchestra, Max Schönherr or New
Promenade Orchestra, Hans May): Excerpts from
JOHANN STRAUSS JR: *Wiener Blut* (arr.
SCHONHERR); *Die Fledermaus (Entr'acte); Die
Tänzerin Fanny Elssler* (arr. STALLA). KREISLER:
Sissy. LEHAR: *Die lustige Witwe; Zigeunerliebe. Der
Zarewitsch; Schöne ist die Welt; Paganini.* KALMAN:
Gräfin Mariza. Oscar STRAUS: *Der Tapfere Soldat
(Chocolate soldier); Ein Walzertraum.* FALL:
Madame Pompadour; Die Dollarprinzessin.
ASCHER: *Hoheit Tanzi Walzer.* ZIEHRER: *Der
Schätzmeister.* STOLZ: *Der Favorite.* DOSTAL: *Clivia;
Die Flucht ins Glück.* GROTHE: *Die Schmedische
Nachtigall.*

(BB) (***) Belart mono 461 623-2.

Hilde Gueden's many delightful gramophone contributions to operetta tended latterly to rest in the
shadow of Elisabeth Schwarzkopf, who brought a
Lieder-like skill with words even to relatively banal
lyrics. Gueden's approach was more direct, but she
had this repertoire in her very being, a lilting feel for a
Viennese melodic line and a natural stage presence,
which comes over on recordings too. Her lovely voice
is heard here at its freshest in an early Decca mono
recital from the beginning of the 1950s, when the full
vocal bloom was winningly apparent. The chorus
sounds well too, but the orchestra brings whistly violins, characteristic of Decca records of this period.
Nevertheless this is an enchanting recital, with many
delights in the key numbers from *Wiener Blut, Gräfin
Mariza* and *The Chocolate Soldier*, and of course the
greatest melody of all, *Lippen Schweigen*, the Merry
Widow's Waltz song. Lehár, Fall and Kálmán are well
represented, but there are also rarer items which are
little known outside Vienna, by composers like

Ascher, Dostal and Grothe. Alas the documentation is hopeless, listing twenty-six titles when there are only ten tracks; so you will have to find your way about in spite of this. But with such enchanting singing it's well worth it!

Gunn, Nathan (baritone), Kevin Murphy (piano)

'*American anthem: From ragtime to art song*':
TRAD.: *Shenandoah.* GORNEY: *Brother can you spare a dime.* ROREM: *Early in the morning; The Lordly Hudson.* SCHEER: *At Howard Hawks' house; Holding each other; Lean away; American anthem.* NILES: *The lass from the low countree; I wonder as I wander.* MUSTO: *Recuerdo.* BARBER: *Nocturne; Sure on this shining night.* BOLCOM: *Fur (Murray the Furrier); Over the piano; Black Max (As told by the De Kooning Boys).* IVES: *Slugging a vampire; Two little flowers* (and dedicated to them); *General William Booth enters into heaven.* HOIBY: *The Lamb.* arr. COPLAND: *At the river; Long time ago.*

(B) *** EMI Début Dig. CDZ5 73160-2.

The subtitle, 'From ragtime to art song', sums up the breadth of this delightful collection, the imaginative choice of Nathan Gunn – as he describes it himself, 'a beautiful forest of songs'. Gunn is one of the most promising of young American singers, possessor of a glorious baritone of a velvety beauty, consistent throughout its range. If anyone is disconcerted to have *Brother can you spare a dime* early on the list, it leads brilliantly to the most eclectic sequence, a reflection of Gunn's keen perception as well as of his musicianship. How welcome to have the work of such composers as Gene Scheer and William Bolcom well represented, alongside such predictable names as Charles Ives, Aaron Copland and Samuel Barber. The title, 'American anthem', comes from the last song on the CD, a surging expression of patriotism worthy of an American 'Last Night of the Proms'. Sensitive accompaniment and well-balanced recording.

Hagegård, Håkan (baritone)

'*Dedication*' (with Thomas Schuback, piano):
BRAHMS: *An die Nachtigall; An ein Veilchen; An die Mond.* FOERSTER: *An die Laute.* GOUNOD: *A toi mon coeur.* HAHN: *A Chloris.* MOZART: *An Chloë, K.524; Ich würd' auf meinem Pfad (An die Hoffnung), K.390.* R. SCHUBERT: *An Mignon; An den Tod; An den Mond; An den Leier; An die Musik; Am mein Herz.* RICHARD STRAUSS: *Zueignung.* WOLF: *An eine Aeolsharfe.*

**(*) BIS (ADD) CD 54.

This recital is called 'Dedication' and it begins with the Strauss song of that name. The collection first appeared in LP form in 1976 but was in circulation only intermittently in this country. The record was made at the outset of the distinguished Swedish bari-

tone's career when he was in his mid-twenties and in wonderfully fresh voice. He sounds very much like a youthful Fischer-Dieskau but is at times a trace too studied, colouring the voice rather too expressively and adopting rather self-consciously deliberate tempi. There are times when one longs for him to be a little more unbuttoned. However, there is far more to admire and relish than to criticize, in particular the gloriously fresh vocal tone, and the sensitive playing of Thomas Schuback. Admirers of Hagegård will probably have this on LP; others need not hesitate.

German and Scandinavian Songs (with Warren Jones, piano) BRAHMS: *5 Songs, Op. 105; Vier ernste Gesänge, Op. 121.* SIBELIUS: *Black roses (Svarta rosor), Op. 36/1; The dream (Drömmen), Op. 13/5; The first kiss (Den första kyssen), Op. 37/1; Sigh, sedges, sigh (Säv, säv, susa), Op. 36/4; The diamond in the March snow (Diamanten på marssnön), Op. 36/6; Was it a dream? Op. 37/4.* STENHAMMAR: *Adagio, Op. 20/5; Florez and Whiteflower (Florez och Blanzeflor), Op. 3; Prince Aladdin of the Lamp (Prins Aladin av lampen), Op. 26/10; Starry eye (Stjärnöga), Op. 20/1.*

**(*) RCA 09026 68097-2.

The distinguished Swedish baritone is on home territory in Stenhammar's and Sibelius's Swedish settings, and his sense of style and phrasing are unerring, both here and in the wonderful Brahms *Vier ernste Gesänge*. The voice has inevitably lost something of the youthful bloom that made his singing so radiant but the musical intelligence and artistry are unimpaired. He is well partnered by Warren Jones and excellently recorded.

Hampson, Thomas (baritone)

'*German opera arias*' from: KORNGOLD: *Die tote Stadt.* LORTZING: *Zar und Zimmermann; Der Wildschütz.* MARSCHNER: *Hans Heiling; Der Vampyr.* WEBER: *Euryanthe.* SPOHR: *Faust.* KREUTZER: *Das Nachtlager in Granada.* SCHREKER: *Der ferne Klang.* HUMPERDINCK: *Königskinder.* WAGNER: *Tannhäuser; Die Walküre.*

*** EMI Dig. CDC5 55233-2.

Hampson here presents a fascinating collection of rarities, many of them otherwise unavailable on disc, making one wonder, while listening to his red-blooded performances, why most of these items are so neglected. Anyone wanting to investigate the byways of German opera in the nineteenth and early twentieth centuries will find much treasure here, starting with a charming Korngold waltz song from *Die tote Stadt*. Returning to familiar repertory, giving perspective, he rounds the recital off with two Wagner items, *O star of Eve* from *Tannhäuser* and then – invading what is officially the Heldentenor repertory – Siegmund's 'Spring greeting' from *Walküre*. A recital to treasure, beautifully recorded.

'*Leading man (Best of Broadway)*': KERN: *All the things you are.* KRETZMER: *Les Misérables: Bring him home.* LLOYD WEBBER: *Phantom of the Opera: Music of the night.* RODGERS: *Carousel: Soliloquy.* LOEWE: *Gigi; Camelot: If ever I would leave you.* ADLER: *The Pajama Game: Hey there.* SONDHEIM: *Unusual way; Not a day goes by.* NORMAN: *The Secret Garden: How could I ever know?* MENKEN: *Beauty and the Beast: If I can't love he.*

*** EMI CDC5 55249-2.

Starting with a classic number by Jerome Kern, *All the things you are*, Hampson's Broadway selection ranges on up to *The Phantom of the Opera* and *Les Misérables*, where atmosphere and evocation seem to weigh more heavily than good tunes. The *Soliloquy* from *Carousel* – one of the few numbers from that great musical without a big tune – here can be seen to point forward, but one number (among the most recent here, dating from 1991) unashamedly returns to older standards of tunefulness, *How could I ever know?* from *The Secret Garden* by Marsha Norman and Lucy Simon. Hampson with his rich, dark voice seems totally at home in each number, finding no problems in adapting to this idiom, switching easily and aptly to half-speech in such a patter-number as the title-song from *Gigi*. Paul Gemignani conducts what is called the American Theater Orchestra, though you have to look through the small print to learn that information. Full, immediate recording.

Disc 1: Mélodies and Lieder (with Geoffrey Parsons, piano): BERLIOZ: *Irlande, Op. 2: La belle voyageuse; Adieu, Bessy!; Le coucher du soleil; L'origine de la harpe; Elégie.* WAGNER: *Lieder: Mignonne; Tout n'est qu'imagines fugitives; Les deux Grenadiers; 2 Lied des Mephistopheles: Es war einmal ein König; Was machst du mir; Der Tannenbaum.* LISZT: *Die Vätergruft; Go Not, Happy Day; Es rauschen die Winde; Ihr Auge; Uber alln Gipfein ist Ruh (Wanderers Nachtlied); Im Rhein, im schönen Strome; Es muss ein Wunderbares sein; Vergiftet sind meine Lieder; La tombe et la rose; 'Comment', disaient-ils; Oh, quand je dors.*

Disc 2: Edinburgh Festival Recital, 20–21 August 1993: FRANZ: *Nun holt mir eine Kanne Wein; Ihr Auge; Die süisse Dirn' von Inverness; Findlay.* SCHUMANN: *Niemand; Dem roten Röslein gleicht mein Lieb; Hochländers Abscheid; Dichterliebe* (song cycle), *Op. 48.* GRIEG: *Gruss; Dereinst; Lauf der Welt; Die verschwiegene Nachtigall; Zur Rosenzeit; Ein Traum.* BEETHOVEN: *An die ferne Geliebte* (song cycle), *Op. 98.*

(B) *** EMI double fforte CZS5 75187-2 (2).

This EMI double fforte reissue joins together two quite different recitals, the second recorded live in the Usher Hall at the 1993 Edinburgh Festival. This includes as an engaging novelty – so appropriate for the occasion – settings of Robert Burns in German translation, including attractive items by the little-known Robert Franz. The six rare German-language

songs by Grieg are a comparable success, as is the freshly spontaneous account of Beethoven's cycle, *An die ferne Geliebte*. However, what should be the highlight but proves a considerable disappointment is Schumann's *Dichterliebe* which, with curiously measured tempi, refuses to spring to life and lacks both ironic subtlety and real depth of feeling.

Never mind, the companion collection is a different matter and received a ✪ on its first premium-priced appearance (with full texts). Hampson begins with glowing performances of five of the nine songs from Berlioz's *Irlande*, using translations from English texts by the poet, Thomas Moore. The Liszt collection is equally magnetic, ending with a memorable performance of his setting of Victor Hugo, *Oh, quand je dors*, and the Wagner songs are equally winning showing him unexpectedly and light-heartedly setting French love-songs. Hampson is in superb voice and at his most imaginative, while throughout both CDs Geoffrey Parson is the ideal accompanist, and the recording cannot be faulted. The only snag, and it is a serious one, is the absence of texts and translations.

Hemsley, Thomas (baritone)

Mélodies (with Hamburger or (i) Gürtler, piano): DUPARC: *Chanson triste; Elégie; Extase; L'Invitation au voyage, Lamento; Le Manoir de Rosemonde; Phidylé; La Vie antérieure.* FAURE: *5 Verlaine Songs, Op. 58; L'Horizon chimérique, Op. 118.* (i) ROUSSEL: *Odes anacréontique, Op. 31 & Op. 32.*

*** Amphion PHI CD 166.

Although he was represented in the days of LP in operatic repertoire, Thomas Hemsley enjoyed scant exposure in Lieder or mélodie. BBC listeners will, of course, recall his broadcasts, some of which are found here. He proves as masterly an interpreter of French song as he is of Schubert and Wolf. The Roussel *Odes anacréontiques* are not otherwise available on disc and, apart from their artistic merits, sound excellent in these 1978 BBC recordings. The Fauré and Duparc come from 1973 with Paul Hamburger as pianist and are no less fine. Why has the BBC label not issued them?

Hendricks, Barbara (soprano)

Spirituals (with Dimitri Alexeev, piano): *Deep river; Ev'ry time I feel the spirit; Fix me, Jesus; Git on boa'd little child'n; His name is so sweet; Hold on!; Joshua fit de battle of Jericho; Nobody knows de trouble I've seen; Oh what a beautiful city!; Plenty good room; Roun' about de mountain; Sometimes I feel like a motherless child; Swing low, sweet chariot; Talk about a child that do love Jesus; Were you there?; When I lay my burden down.*

*** EMI CDC7 47026-2.

So often spirituals can be made to seem too ingenuous, their deep reserve of feeling degraded into sentimentality. Not so here: Barbara Hendricks' vibrant identification with the words is thrilling, the jazz inflexions adding natural sophistication, yet not robbing the music of its directness of communication. Her lyrical singing is radiant, operatic in its eloquence of line, yet retaining the ecstasy of spirit, while the extrovert numbers – *Joshua fit de battle of Jericho* a superb example – are full of joy in their gutsy exuberance. Dmitri Alexeev accompanies superbly and the very well-balanced recording has remarkable presence.

Hespèrion XX

'**Llibre Vermell de Montserrat**' (A fourteenth-century pilgrimage): *O Virgo splendens; Stella splendens in monte; Laudemus Virginem Mater est; Los set goyts recomptarem; Splendens ceptigera; Polorum regina omnium nostra; Cincti simus concanentes: Ave Maria; Mariam Matrem Virginem; Imperayritz de la ciutat joyosa; Ad mortem festinamus; O Virgo splendens hic in monte celso.*

(M) *** Virgin VER5 61174-2.

In the Middle Ages the Spanish monastery of Montserrat was an important place of pilgrimage and, although a great deal of the music held in the library there was lost in a fire at the beginning of the nineteenth century, one early manuscript, the Llibre Vermell (Red Book), has survived to remind us of the music of that period. It dates from 1400 and is especially fascinating in including ten anonymous choral songs for the use of the pilgrims 'while holding night vigil' who may 'sometimes desire to sing and dance in the Church Square (where only respectable and pious songs may be sung)'.

The music is extraordinarily jolly and robust, often written in the style of the French virelais (featuring alternating musical lines, with the first framing a central repeated tune). Canonic devices are also used and the effect is often quite sophisticated. There is no better example of this spirited music than *Los set goyts*, an infectious round dance complete with refrain. Various instrumental groupings add lively colour and support to the vocal line; the performances are full of joy, though at times emotionally respectful too. The analogue recording was made in France, but the resonant acoustic seems perfectly judged. This is a life-enhancing collection to cheer one up, and it shows that life in the Middle Ages was not always grim.

Hilliard Ensemble

English and Italian Madrigals:

English madrigals: MORLEY: *O griefe even on the bud; When loe, by breake of morning; Aprill is in my mistris face; Sweet nimphe, come to thy lover; Miraculous love's wounding; Fyer and lightning in nets of goulden wyers.* WEELKES: *Thule, the period of cosmographie; O care thou wilt dispatch mee; Since Robin Hood; Strike it up tabor.* WILBYE: *Sweet hony sucking bees; Adew sweet Amarillis; Draw in sweet night.* J. BENNET: *Weepe O mine eyes.* GIBBONS: *The silver swanne.* TOMKINS: *See, see the shepherd's*

queene. WARD: *Come sable night.* VAUTOR: *Sweet Suffolk owle.*

Italian madrigals: GASTOLDI: *Cantiam lieti cantiamo.* CAPRIOLI: *E d'un bel matin d'amore; Quella bella e biancha mano; Una leggiadra nimpha.* COMPERE: *Venite amanti insieme.* VERDALOT: *Divini occhi sereni; Con l'angelico riso; Madonna, il tuo bel viso; Fuggi, fuggi, cor mio; Si liet'e grata morte.* ARCALDET: *Se la dura durezza; Ahimé, dové, bel viso; Madonna, s'io v'offendo; Il bianco e dolce cigno.* PATAVINO: *Donne, venete al ballo.* CASUALANA: *Morir non pué il mio cuore.* MARENZIO: *Se la mia vita.* RORE: *Mia benigna fortuna; Ancor che col partire; O sonno.* NOLA: *Chi la gagliarda; Medici noi siamo; Tre ciechi siamo.* WILLAERT: *Madonna mia fa.* BELL'HAVER: *Quando saré mai quel zorno.* LASSUS: *Matona, mia cara.*

(BB) *** Virgin Veritas 2 x 1 VBD5 616710-2 (2).

The first of these two discs is of English madrigals and was recorded in 1987. It is an enchanting disc; and, as might be guessed from the above spelling, Tudor pronunciation is used which adds extra bite to the vocal timbre. Intonation and ensemble are flawless, and some of the songs are in five or six parts. If one feels that they could be a shade more unbuttoned at times, and they do not always reflect the lighter moments with quite enough sparkle, there is so much here to beguile the ear that few will grumble. The Italian madrigals were recorded in 1991, and are hardly less enjoyable. Indeed, this second collection is is perhaps even more beautiful, and the programme is as rich and varied as in the English collection. A pity that there are no texts or translations and little about the music, but at super-bargain price one only expects such extras from Naxos.

'**A Hilliard Songbook**': New music for voices: GUY: *Un coup de dès.* FELDMAN: *Only.* MOODY: *Endechas y Canciones; Canticum Canticorum I.* HELLAWELL: *True Beautie* (cycle of 8 songs). ROBINSON: *Incantation.* TORMIS: *Kullervo's message.* ANON.: *Adoro te devote.* MACMILLAN: *... here in hiding ...* PART: *And one of the Pharisees ...; Summa.* LIDDLE: *Whale rant.* METCALF: *Music for The Star of the Sea.* FINNISSY: *Stabant autem iuxta cruceme.* CASKEN: *Sharp Thorne.*

*** ECM 453 259-2 (2).

The Hilliard Ensemble are best known for exploring the world of early music. In this CD, however, they survey modern trends and at times they find a surprising affinity with the repertoire with which they are more familiar. The opening number here is avant-garde with a vengeance. Extraordinary instrumental noises (contrived from an amplified double-bass) act as a prelude to *Un coup de dès*, and the performance appears to turn into a fight among the participants, with animal noises thrown in.

Then we turn to real music, Morty Feldman's touching, unaccompanied solo soliloquy *Only*, about flight (Rogers Covey-Crump). Ivan Moody's set of four *Endechas y Canciones* chime with the current trend towards medievalism, very bare in their part-writing but spiced with dissonances. Piers Hellawell's melodic lines are unpredictable, but his eight vignettes are all very brief and concentrated: the music fits the Elizabethan texts, which are about colours. The set is held together effectively by four different settings of *True Beautie*, which are quite haunting, and it is made the more effective by alternating baritone, tenor and counter-tenor soloists. The closing concerted number, *By falsehood*, is genuinely poignant.

Paul Robinson's *Incantation* (the text is Byron's) is an ambitious (15-minute) dialogue between lead singer (a bit like a cantor) and the main group, usually moving chordally using a spiced modal harmony. *Kullervo's message* is a lively ballad, setting an English translation from *The Kalevala*.

The second disc opens with Gregorian chant, then shocks the listener with the pungent fortissimo dissonance at the opening of James MacMillan's ingeniously woven motet. After the more familiar style of Arvo Pärt we move on to Elizabeth Liddle's mournful *Whale rant*, in which two texts are presented in bravura juxtaposition, one set to a famous hymn with the harmony touched up, the other a plangent soliloquy. The result is something of a *tour de force*. John Casken's *Sharp Thorne* brings exuberant bursts of sound, and we finally return to Ivan Moody setting texts from *The Song of Songs* which emphasize the link modern composers have found with the past. The whole programme is sung with great eloquence and is beautifully recorded, and no one could accuse any of the composers here of writing in a routine manner.

Holst Singers, Stephen Layton

'*Ikon*' (with (i) James Bowman, counter-tenor): SVIRIDOV: *Three choruses from Tsar Feodor Ioannovich; Four choruses from Songs of Troubled Times.* GRETCHANINOV: *The cherubic hymn;* (i) *The Creed. Our Father.* KALINNIKOV: *Radiant light.* TCHAIKOVSKY: *We hymn Thee; The cherubic hymn; Blessed are they.* PART: *Magnificat.* GORECKI: *Totus Tuus.* NYSTEDT: *Immortal Bach.*

*** Hyp. CDA 66928.

The Orthodox tradition has regularly inspired Russian composers to write with a rare fervour for unaccompanied chorus. This hauntingly beautiful disc was inspired by live performances given by the Holst Singers, beginning with pieces of extraordinary, dark intensity by Gyorgy Sviridov. Born in 1915, he defied all Soviet bans on religious music, echoing Tchaikovsky in his exotic harmonies and dramatic contrasts but with a twentieth-century flavour. A sequence of inter-linked items by Tchaikovsky and Gretchaninov brings fascinating contrasts, leading to a fine *Magnificat* by Arvo Pärt and a long piece by Gorecki in the Polish Catholic tradition, touchingly simple in harmony. Radiant performances and recording, with James Bowman soaring away as counter-tenor soloist.

Huddersfield Choral Society, Brian Kay; Phillip McCann; Simon Lindley

'*A Christmas celebration*' (with Sellers Engineering Band): TRAD.: *Ding dong merrily on high; Kumbaya; Joys seven; Away in a manger; Deck the hall; O Christmas tree (Tannenbaum); Coventry carol.* JAMES: *An Australian Christmas.* GRUBER: *Silent night.* BACH: *Cantata No. 140: Zion hears the watchmen's voices.* GARDNER: *The holly and the ivy.* arr. RICHARDS: *A merry little Christmas.* HOLST: *In the bleak mid-winter.* arr. WILLCOCKS: *Tomorrow shall be my dancing day.* BRAHMS: *Lullaby.* arr. SMITH: *Santa Claus-Trophobia.* MATHIAS: *Sir Christèmas.* LANGFORD: *A Christmas fantasy.*

(M) *** Chan. 4530.

Sumptuously recorded in the generous acoustic of Huddersfield Town Hall, opening with a spectacular arrangement of *Ding dong merrily* and closing with Gordon Langford's colourful pot-pourri *Fantasy*, this CD offers rich choral tone, well laced with opulent brass. There are simple choral arrangements too, beautifully sung by the Huddersfield choir, like Stephen Cleobury's *Joys seven*, Langford's *Deck the hall* and David Willcocks's slightly more elaborate *Tomorrow shall be my dancing day*, while Grüber's *Silent night* remains the loveliest of all serene carols.

In other favourites the brass is nicely intertwined, as in *Away in a manger* and the *Coventry carol*, or it provides a sonorous introduction, as in Holst's *In the bleak mid-winter*. Mathias's rhythmically energetic *Sir Christèmas* provides a little spice. The brass are given their head in a solo spot, an effective novelty number, *Santa Claus-Trophobia*, arranged by Sandy Smith, which brings an impressive contribution from the solo tuba. Undoubtedly the brass contribution adds much to the entertainment value of this superbly recorded and well-presented 70-minute concert.

Hvorostovsky, Dmitri (baritone)

'*Passione di Napoli*' (with Russian Philh. O, Orbelian) BIXIO: *Parlami d'amor; Mariù.* CANNIO: '*O surdato 'nnamurato.* CARDILLO: *Core 'ngrato; Cottrau Santa Lucia.* DE CURTIS: *Canta pe'me!; Non ti scordar di me; Torna a Surriento; Voce 'e notte!* DI CAPUA: *Maria, Marì; O sole mio.* FALVO: *Dicetencello vuie.* GAMBARDELLA: *Comme facette mammeta?* GASTALDON: *Musica proibita.* TAGLIAFERRI: *Passione.* TOSTI: *A Vucchella; Marechiare.* TRAD.: *Fenesta che lucive; Logi; Medvedev; Mnatsakanov.*

**(*) Delos DE 3290.

The Siberian baritone Dmitri Hvorostovsky has here clearly wondered why tenors should have all the fun in the Neapolitan song repertory. Maybe Italian baritones are too firmly conditioned towards villainy by

Italian opera to think of themselves as passionate lovers. Hvorostovsky points out that this repertory has been in his blood from his early days as a student, and the performances bear that out. As well being physically a glamorous figure, he sports a voice with all the regulation heart-throb required for this repertory, rich and firm. In this collection, recorded in Moscow, he pulls out all the stops without ever resorting to coarseness, even if understandably he comes close in his outburst over 'O sole mio'. He characterizes well, bringing out distinctions of mood and timbre, and the voice is more Italianate than Slavonic. Though this will delight both devotees of Neapolitan song and fans of the singer, the snag lies in the soupy orchestrations with sound 'enhanced' through an echo chamber to create a swimming-bath acoustic.

Janowitz, Gundula (soprano)

'The Singers' (Decca series): Arias from: WEBER: Der Freischütz; Oberon. WAGNER: Lohengrin; Tannhäuser (with Berlin Opera O, Leitner). Lieder: SCHUBERT: Die bist die Ruh'; Die Forelle (with Gage, piano). R. STRAUSS: Four Last Songs (with BPO, Karajan).

(M) **(*) Decca (ADD) 467 910-2.

Janowitz's beautiful flow of creamy tone is well maintained in her contribution to Decca's 'The Singers' series (although the recordings are borrowed from DG). Her beautiful version of the Four Last Songs dates from 1974 and is understandably admired. Perhaps the music's deeper and subtler emotions are under-exposed in this account, but it still ranks near the top of the list. The bulk of the CD is from a 1967 recital LP with Ferdinand Leitner, recorded when the voice was at its freshest. These are lovely, unforced performances, even if they miss that last ounce of colour and depth. It is perhaps surprising that none of her superb Mozart recordings was chosen, but there is much fine singing to enjoy here, and the sound is excellent. As usual with this series, texts and translations, along with the usual photo-gallery, are available only through a CD ROM drive.

Jo, Sumi (soprano)

'Les bijoux': Arias from: GOUNOD: Roméo et Juliette; Faust. THOMAS: Mignon; Hamlet; Mirielle. MEYERBEER: L'Etoile du nord; Les Huguenots. G. CHARPENTIER: Louise. MASSENET: Manon. BIZET: Les Pêcheurs de perles. OFFENBACH: Robinson Crusoé.

*** Erato 3984 23140-2.

For all the delights of French operetta and opéra-comique, it is good to hear the breadth of Sumi Jo's artistry when taking mature operatic roles. The famous Polonaise from Mignon sparkles iridescently, Gounod's waltz songs have both grace and charm, and in Meyerbeer's L'Etoile du nord the vocal/flute duet is as captivating as ever. But Louise's Depuis le jour brings an additional dimension in its warmly sympathetic phrasing, and Jo's portrait of Manon is equally touching, as is Leila's Cavatina from Les Pêcheurs de perles, with its characteristic Bizet horn writing. But perhaps the highlight is the Mad scene from Thomas's Hamlet, far more than a coloratura display. Here Jo is given fine support by the conductor, Giuliano Carella, with the opening beautifully prepared. The recital finishes on an upbeat with a charming Offenbach waltz song made famous by Joan Sutherland. As with the Decca disc below, this is a voice that takes naturally to recording, especially when the acoustic is pleasingly warm.

Virtuoso arias (with Monte Carlo PO, Olmi) from: ROSSINI: Il barbiere di Siviglia. BELLINI: La Sonnambula. DONIZETTI: Lucia di Lammermoor. DELIBES: Lakmé. RICHARD STRAUSS: Ariadne auf Naxos. VERDI: Rigoletto. MEYERBEER: Dinorah. BERNSTEIN: Candide. MOZART: Die Zauberflöte (with O de Paris Ens., Jordan). YOUNG-HA HOON: Song: Boribat.

*** Erato 4509 97239-2.

This is among the most brilliant and commanding recitals of coloratura arias made in the 1990s. Though the recording brings out a slight flutter in Sumi Jo's lovely voice, the sweetness and tenderness of her singing, so different from the hardness of many coloratura sopranos, are formidably established over the widest range of arias. Sumi Jo's clarity, with no hint of stridency, coupled with a dreamy quality in the delivery, reminds one of the remark of an opera critic many years ago, that Galli-Curci sounded like 'a nightingale half-asleep'.

Not that there is anything sleepy in Sumi Jo's singing, which is beautifully controlled. That is so both in firework arias like Rosina's Una voce poco fa from Rossini's Barber and over the sustained spans of the big aria in Bellini's La Sonnambula (full recitative leading to Ah non credea mirarti and Ah! non giunge) and the Mad scene from Donizetti's Lucia di Lammermoor. Though Glitter and be gay from Bernstein's Candide lacks a little in fun, Delibes' Bell song from Lakmé is aptly sensuous and Zerbinetta's aria from Ariadne auf Naxos aptly extrovert, while the reading of the Queen of the Night's second aria from Mozart's Zauberflöte is lighter and even faster than with Solti in his Decca set. With tenderness and poise regular ingredient, alongside brilliance, not least in the honeyed sounds of the final, Korean song, all ten arias are to be cherished. The voice is well caught, though the orchestral accompaniment has less presence.

'Carnaval!' (with ECO, Richard Bonynge): French coloratura arias from: OFFENBACH: Un mari à la porte. MASSENET: Don César de Bazan. Félicien DAVID: La Perle du Brésil. GRETRY: L'Amant jaloux. BALFE: Le puits d'amour. MESSAGER: Madame Chrysanthème. THOMAS: Le songe d'une nuit d'été. ADAM: Les pantins de Violette; Si j'étais roi. HEROLD: Le pré aux clercs. DELIBES: Le roi l'a dit.

BOIELDIEU: *La fête du village voisin.* MASSE: *La Reine Topaze: Carnaval de Venise.*

✪ *** Decca (IMS) 440 679-2.

If anything, this singing is even more astonishing than Sumi Jo's Erato recital, above. The music may be more frivolous, but what delectable freshness and vocal sparkle there is in every number! And this repertoire is far rarer. After the frothy Offenbach introduction, the nightingale lightness and precision in Massenet's *Sevillana* from *Don César de Bazan* are matched by the vocal poise in the *Couplets du Mysoli* from David's *La Perle du Brésil,* with William Bennett playing the flute solo. Equally, Jo trills along seductively in Adams *Chanson du canari,* in which the song's pensive quality is also nicely caught.

This is Galli-Curci territory, and Sumi Jo doesn't come off second best; moreover her voice is fuller and warmer. The softness and delicious ease of her pianissimo top notes also recall Rita Streich at her finest, in both Adam and Thomas, and in the Grétry *Je romps la chaîne qui m'engage.* Her ravishingly easy legato in Balfe's *Rêves d'amour* is a joy, while Hérold's *Jours de mon enfance* brings a duet with a solo violin (the excellent Anthony Marwood), and here one is reminded of the young Sutherland. Delibes' *Waltz song* from *Le roi l'a dit* is bewitching, and the recital ends with a sparkling *Boléro* of Boieldieu and an unforgettable interpolation of the *Carnival of Venice* into an aria by Victor Massé, with astonishingly free divisions. Throughout, Bonynge provides stylish and beautifully pointed accompaniments, as he has done for Sutherland in the past, and the Decca recording could hardly be bettered.

'The Art of Sumi Jo' (with English Chamber Orchestra, Welsh National Opera Orchestra, Richard Bonynge): Arias from AUBER: *Le Domino noir.* GRETRY: *L'Amant jaloux.* MOZART: *Die Zauberflöte.* OFFENBACH: *Le mari à la porte.* ADAM: *Le Toréador.* MASSENET: *Don César de Bazan.* DAVID: *La Perle du Brésil.* BOIELDIEU: *La fête du village voisin.* MASSE: *La Reine Topaz: Carnaval de Venise.*

*** Decca 458 927-2.

This is another of the most astonishing displays of light-voiced soprano coloratura ever put on record: even Galli-Curci is outshone. Sumi Jo's voice is not only wonderfully agile and pretty, it can deepen and become tender. Even in the middle of the unbelievable fireworks of David's *Couplets du Mysoli* (where the solo flute is quite upstaged in the many vocal interchanges), Jo can suddenly touch the listener with her gentleness. Five of the key items here are understandably also included in Decca's 'Coloratura spectacular' (above), including a thrilling *Der Hölle Rache* from *Die Zauberflöte,* the delicious Offenbach *Valse tyrolienne* and the closing *Carnaval de Venise,* which has to be heard to be believed. But there are many other delights, including exquisite singing in *Je romps la chaîne qui m'engage* from Grétry's *L'Amant jaloux,*

and the excerpts from the recent complete recording of Adam's *Le Toréador,* where *Flamme vengeresse* is utterly winning, and the ensemble *Ah! vous dirai-je maman* is unforgettable for its light-hearted sparkle. Richard Bonynge, ever affectionate, displays the lightest touch in the accompaniments and the Decca recording projects the voice warmly without the slightest suspicion of edge or hardness.

Jones, Della (mezzo-soprano)

Arias, Duets and Ensembles (sung in English, with Plazas, Miles, Mason, Magee, Shore, Bailey, LPO, Parry) from: ROSSINI: *The Barber of Seville; The Italian Girl in Algiers; Tancredi; William Tell.* HANDEL: *Rodelinda; Xerxes.* MOZART: *The Clemency of Titus.* DONIZETTI: *La favorita; Lucrezia Borgia.* BELLINI: *Norma.* GERMAN: *Merrie England.* PONCHIELLI: *La Gioconda.* Song: BISHOP: *Home Sweet Home.*

(M) *** Chan. 3049.

Recorded in 2000, this formidable collection of 14 arias and ensembles testifies to the continuing vocal health of this ever-characterful singer, whether in the legato of Handel's *Largo* or the coloratura of the Rossini, Donizetti and Bellini cabalettas. It was daring of this mezzo to include among the ensemble numbers the celebrated Norma/Adalgisa duet (rounded with a joyous account of the cabaletta), in which she takes the title role with Anne Mason as her partner. The *Brindisi* from *Lucrezia Borgia* brings more exuberance, and it is a charming touch to have the collection lightly rounded off with Queen Elizabeth's song from *Merrie England* (*With Sword and Buckler by her Side*) and *Home Sweet Home,* with the singer accompanying herself at the piano. Clear, well-balanced sound.

Joyful Company of Singers, Peter Broadbent

'A Garland for Linda' (with: Phillippa Davies, flute; Robert Cohen, cello: TAVENER: *Prayer for the healing of the sick.* JUDITH BINGHAM: *Water lilies.* JOHN RUTTER: *Musica Dei donum.* DAVID MATTHEWS: *The doorway of the dawn.* MCCARTNEY: *Nova.* ROXANA PANUFNIK: *I dream'd.* MICHAEL BERKELEY: *Farewell.* GILES SWAYNE: *The flight of the swan.* RODNEY BENNETT: *A Good-night.*

*** EMI CDC5 56961-2.

The tragic death of Linda McCartney led to this remarkable commemorative collection of music, notable for its serenity and lyrical beauty, with Paul McCartney's own piece, *Nova,* standing out alongside Michael Berkeley's moving *Farewell* and Richard Rodney Bennett's touchingly simple *Good-night.* The programme opens with Vaughan Williams's lovely *Silence and music,* for which his wife, Ursula, appropriately wrote the words. John Rutter's offering characteristically has a flute introduction, as does Giles Swayne's quite different, haunting evocation of *The flight of the Swan*, but every piece here is moving and beautifully sung and recorded; they will not only serve as a remembrance, but also give much pleasure to a great many listeners.

Kanawa, Dame Kiri Te (soprano)

'*Classics*': Arias from: MOZART: *Die Entführung aus dem Serail; Idomeneo; Don Giovanni; Vesperae solennes de Confessore; Die Zauberflöte; Exsultate, jubilate.* HANDEL: *Samson.* GOUNOD: *Messe solennelle de Saint Cécile; Faust.* SCHUBERT: *Ave Maria.* J. STRAUSS JR: *Die Fledermaus.*

(M) *** Ph. (ADD/DDD) 434 725-2.

Admirers of Dame Kiri will find this a pretty good sampler of her diverse talents, including as it does Mozart's *Exsultate, jubilate* with its famous *Alleluia* and the similarly beautiful *Laudate dominum* from the *Solemn Vespers*, plus Handel's brilliant *Let the bright seraphim.* An excellent 74-minute selection from recordings made over two decades from the early 1970s onwards. The notes, however, concentrate on the singer rather than the music.

'*Greatest hits*': Arias from: PUCCINI: *Suor Angelica; Turandot.* CILEA: *Adriana Lecouvreur.* BOITO: *Mefistofele.* GIORDANO: *Andrea Chénier* (with LSO, Myung-Whun Chung). G. CHARPENTIER: *Louise.* BIZET: *Les Pêcheurs de perles* (with Royal Opera House, Covent Garden, Orchestra, Jeffrey Tate). KORNGOLD: *Die tote Stadt* (with Philharmonia Orchestra, Julius Rudel). Songs: MOORE: *The last rose of summer.* TRAD.: *Greensleeves; Annie Laurie* (with Nat. PO, Gamley). KERN: *All the things you are; Smoke gets in your eyes.* BERLIN: *Always* (with Orchestra, Jonathan Tunick).

**(*) EMI CDC5 56722-2.

This collection certainly gives a rounded picture of the glorious voice and vocal art of Dame Kiri. But while the lovely aria from Korngold's *Die tote Stadt* is especially welcome, some ears will find the silky phrasing and voluptuous tone not quite idiomatic in the popular ballads of Jerome Kern and Irving Berlin, and certainly the traditional items like *Greensleeves* and *Annie Laurie* call for a more artless approach, even though all these songs bring a ravishing beauty of line. Four of the Italian and French arias are included on the mid-priced 'Diva' collection below, and this would seem an even more recommendable disc.

'*Diva*': Arias from: CHARPENTIER: *Louise.* MASSENET: *Manon; Hérodiade.* BERLIOZ: *La Damnation de Faust.* GLUCK: *Iphigénie en Tauride.* PUCCINI: *Suor Angelica.* LEONCAVALLO: *Pagliacci.* GIORDANO: *Andrea Chénier.* CILEA: *Adriana Lecouvreur.* RICHARD STRAUSS: *Der Rosenkavalier.* TCHAIKOVSKY: *Eugene Onegin.*

(M) *** EMI CDM 65578-2.

Like others in EMI's 'Diva' series of compilations, this selection has been shrewdly drawn from the limited

number of recordings Dame Kiri has made for that company, principally a recital of French opera arias recorded in 1988 and an Italian opera recital made in 1989. These provide a fruitful source for the first nine items, but they are crowned by excerpts from two complete opera sets, the Marschallin's monologue and final solo from Act I of *Der Rosenkavalier* and (in English) *Tatiana's Letter scene* from *Eugene Onegin*, a recording made with Welsh National Opera forces. The beauty of the voice is beautifully caught.

Karnéus, Katarina (mezzo-soprano), Roger Vignoles (piano)

Lieder: RICHARD STRAUSS: *Die Nacht; Meinem Kinde; Begegnung; Nachtgang; Ruhe, meine Seele! Allerseelen; Mein Herz ist stumm; Morgen!; Wie sollten wir geheim sie halten.* MAHLER: *Frühlingsmorgen; Erinnerung; Hans und Grethe; Des Knaben Wunderhorn: Ich ging mit Lust durch einen grünen Wals; Ablösung in Sommer; Scheiden und Meiden. 4 Rückert Lieder.* MARX: *Und gestern hat er mir Rosen gebracht; Malenblüten; Hat dich die Liebe berührt; Wofür; Venetianisches Wiegenlied.*

(B) *** EMI Début CDZ5 73168-2.

Winner of the Cardiff Singer of the World competition in 1995, Katerina Karnéus was born in Stockholm, but completed her singing studies in London. Hers is a beautifully warm and even mezzo which she uses with great imagination and fine attention to detail, in both words and music. This is a formidable Lieder collection in EMI's Début series, with the golden beauty of Strauss songs leading to a wide-ranging selection of Mahler songs, with charming early songs leading to four of the five *Rückertlieder* (*Um Mitternacht* the one left out). The Joseph Marx songs, simpler in style, provide an apt and attractive tailpiece. Roger Vignoles is the most sensitive partner. Well-balanced sound.

Kiehr, Maria Cristina (soprano)

'*Cantala la Maddalena*' (with Concerto Soave, Jean-Marc Aymes): Arias and scenas by: AGNELETTI; LUIGI ROSSI; FRESCOBALDI; GRATIANI; MAZZOCCI; BEMABEL; FERRARI. Lute pieces by: FRESCOBALDI; Michelangelo ROSSI; KAPSBERGER.

**(*) HM HMC 901698.

After her two superb recitals of the music of Strozzi and Monteverdi (in our main volume) this is a disappointment. The performances are altogether plainer, Kiehr's voice less honeyed. The repertoire is concerned with the subject of the many *Stabat Mater* settings – Mary in despair, grieving at the foot of the cross, and is of considerable interest, but the music itself is expressively sung rather than greatly moving the listener.

King's College, Cambridge, Choir, Stephen Cleobury and Boris Ord

'Carols from Kings': Festivals of Lessons and Carols (Recorded live in the Chapel, 1954 & 2000).

Includes from 1954 & 2000 services: GAUNTLETT: *Once in Royal David's City; Bidding Prayer.* 1954: BACH: *Christmas Oratorio: And there were Sheperds; Up! Good Christian Folk!* 1954 & 2000: TRAD.: *In dulci jubilo.* 1954: *Hail! Blessed Mary!; A Virgin most Pure.* 1954 & 2000: *While Shepherds Watched.* 1954: CORNELIUS: *The Three Kings.* TRAD.: *Sing Lullaby; O Come all ye Faithful.* 2000: *Quem pastores laudavere; Angels from the Realms of Glory.* DARKE: *In the Bleak Midwinter.* TRAD.: *Quitter pasteurs.* GRUBER: *Silent Night.* CHILCOTT: *Shepherd's Carol.* TRAD.: *The Angels and the Shepherds; Riu, riu, riu; O little town of Bethlehem.* BERLIOZ: *Childhood of Christ: Shepherd's Farewell.* RUTTI: *I Wonder as I Wander.* EDWARDS: *Small Wonder the Star.* TRAD.: *Sussex Carol; Gloria in excelsis Deo; God Rest ye Merry Gentlemen.* 1954 & 2000: *Blessing; Benediction.* 2000: MENDELSSOHN: *Hark the Herald Angels sing;* (Organ) *Chorale: Vom Himmel hoch.* (Includes discussion by Sir David Willcocks, Sir Philip Ledger and Stephen Cleobury).

(*) BBC Opus Arte **DVD OA 0815 D. Producer: James Whitbourn. V/D: David Kremer.

Splendid singing throughout by the Choir, of course, and the visual images of the Chapel are eye-catchingly beautiful. The recording also is very fine, and is available either in stereo (which is excellent) or surround sound. However at the opening of the 2000 service, rather than creating a distant processional image, the camera focuses closely on the choirboy who introduces *Once in Royal David's City;* and elsewhere, because the cameras are placed and moved to maximize the visual imagery, the actual singing within the expansive King's ambience (although synchronized) often does not seem sharply to relate to what one sees. One has the paradoxical impression of simultaneous audio and visual images, often closely observed, that are somehow not intrinsically connected, although of course they are.

But when one turns to the black-and-white film of the 1954 service, with its very simple camera technique, the magic of the occasion is tellingly projected, even though the sound itself is not absolutely secure. As the choir begins its processional through the arch towards the viewer and the Provost, standing beside the treble soloist, gently conducts his solo, the effect is most moving, and the singing of Boris Ord's choir is luminous throughout. Indeed the whole of this much shorter earlier service is engrossing, not least because of the recognizable linguistic mode of the BBC announcer's introduction, and the equally characterful reading of the lessons by unnamed lay readers in the style of English as it was spoken in Cambridge fifty

years ago. The shots of the congregation when they join in *O Come all ye Faithful* are similarly nostalgic.

The music is followed by an extended dialogue between the three directors of the Choir, which makes a further valuable record of the occasion. The various facilities offered by the DVD include the opportunity to listen only to the carols or choose the full service, including the lessons.

King's College, Cambridge, Choir, Stephen Cleobury

'Best Loved Hymns' (with The Wallace Collection, Sioned Williams, harp, Benjamin Bayl & Thomas Williamson, organ): *A mighty fortress is our God; All my hope on God is founded; All people that on earth do dwell; Be thou my vision; Come down, O love divine; Dear Lord and Father of mankind; Glorious things of thee are spoken; Let all mortal flesh keep silent; My song is love unknown; Morning has broken; O what their joy and their glory must be; Praise to the Lord, the Almighty, the King of creation; Praise, my soul, the King of heaven; The day thou gavest, Lord, is ended; The lord is my shepherd; Thine be the glory; Drop, drop, slow tears; When I survey the wondrous Cross.*

*** EMI CDC 5 57026-2.

Best-loved hymns and some lesser-known ones, introduced by brass (which returns in one or two of the more ambitious hymns and to close the concert with the Old Hundredth). But for the most part they are presented simply, with full choir sometimes alternating with the men or boys, and refined harp accompaniments to contrast with the organ. Magnificent singing, splendid recording, a perfect acoustic and what tunes they are! If you like hymns they could not be better presented.

'Anthems from Kings: English Choral Favourites': WOOD: *Hail, Gladdening Light.* IRELAND: *Greater Love hath no Man.* PARRY: *I was Glad.* HARRIS: *Bring us, O Lord God; Faire is the Heaven.* BAINTON: *And I Saw a New Heaven.* HOWELLS: *Like as the Hart.* STANFORD: *Gloria in Excelsis; Beati quorum vita.* BALFOUR GARDINER: *Evening Hymn.* WALFORD DAVIES: *God be in my Head.* NAYLOR: *Vox dicentis clama.* VAUGHAN WILLIAMS: *Let all the World.*

*** BBC Opus Arte **DVD** OS 0934 D.

With a delightful supplementary half-hour feature on the King's Choir and its sixteen talented boy trebles, this is a charming recital disc of English church music. Parry's coronation anthem, *I was glad,* and Walford Davies's *God be in my Head* are favourites with more than specialist listeners, but all the items here are most attractive and superbly done, leading up to the culminating item, Vaughan Williams's striking setting of George Herbert's Antiphon, *Let all the world.* With evocative camera-work, most items are sung by the choir in their regular choir-stalls, but several of the more intimate numbers have them grouped at the far end of the sanctuary in King's Chapel in front of the altar, with the Rubens painting of the Nativity behind them. As the extra feature brings out, the boy choristers are boarders in the Choir School, which also has many day-students from the Cambridge area. The life of the school and the training of these young musicians is fascinating, demonstrating that though their routine is rigorous, they find it all fun.

'Ikos': Alma Redemptoris mater (Marian antiphon). GORECKI: Totus tuus; Amen. Ave Maria (Offertory antiphon); Regina coeli laetare (Marian antiphon); Alleluia – Venite ad me. PART: Magnificat; The Beatitudes. Beati mondo corde (Communion antiphon). TAVENER: Magnificat and Nunc dimittis (Collegium Regale); Funeral Ikos. Requiem aeternam (Introit antiphon with verse); Ego sum resurrectio et vita; In paradisum – Chorus angelorum (Funeral antiphons).

(M) *** EMI CDC5 55096-2.

In the notes for this admirable collection of modern liturgical settings, John Milsom suggests that their connecting link is 'ritual detachment'. He continues: 'Everything inclines to modesty, to mystery, to meditation, to musical refinement – and to the model of the past.' And that final comment is surely the key to this remarkably communicative a cappella music of our time which, for all its modernity, constantly seeks to identify with a medieval atmosphere of unquestioning faith.

Each of the composers here occupies ecclesiastical space with floating threnodies. Pärt's comparatively static Magnificat relies on intensity of sonority rather than movement; his better-known Beatitudes, gentle and rippling, is regularly pierced by dissonance, with the organ entering briefly and unexpectedly at the close to add a florid postlude and then disappear into infinity. Górecki's Amen is vocally much more dramatic and, although only having one word of text, continually explores its emotional potential, moving from serenity to sudden bursts of passion.

Tavener's undulating Magnificat is given its special character by flitting references to Byzantine chant. His simple and beautiful Funeral Ikos brings a haunting mixture of monody and chordal progressions on the word 'Alleluia', just occasionally touched with dissonance, and recalling his famous carol The Lamb. Górecki's masterly Totus tuus opens stirringly and is a superbly concentrated example of his minimalist choral progression. The music constantly redefines the intensity of the repetitions of the text, ending with a haunting diminuendo on Mater mundi ... Totus sum Maria!, then with the constantly recurring name 'Maria' fading gently into silence.

The conductor, Stephen Cleobury, directs glorious, deeply felt performances of all this music and emphasizes the medieval associations by placing Latin chants before and after each piece, ending with two touching Funeral antiphons, the first sung by the men alone, the second, In paradisum, soaring radiantly

with the trebles. The recording is superb: the famous King's acoustic adds much to the music.

'The King's Collection' (with James Vivian or Robert Quinney, organ): PARRY: I was glad. MOZART: Ave verum corpus. ALLEGRI: Miserere (ed. Guest). MENDELSSOHN: Hear my prayer: O for the wings of a dove (both with Alastair Hussain, treble). HANDEL: Coronation anthem: Zadok the Priest. BACH: Cantata 147: Jesu, joy of man's desiring. FAURE: Cantique de Jean Racine. FRANCK: Panis angelicus. WALTON: Jubilate Deo (with Edward Saklatvala, treble). BRITTEN: Hymn to the virgin. WALFORD DAVIES: God be in my head. BURGON: Nunc dimittis (woth Thomas Hopkinson, treble). TAVENER: Song for Athene. WIDOR: Organ Symphony No. 5: Toccata (Stephen Cleobury, organ).

**(*) Decca (ADD/DDD) 460 021-2.

Magnificently recorded, with the choral tone sumptuous and clear, and resplendent sound from the organ, this unashamedly popular collection of choral favourites is bound to be a success. Certainly Handel's Zadok the Priest comes off exultantly, even if one misses the orchestral strings. Parry's I was glad is robustly presented, and so is the Mozart Ave verum corpus, which is just a shade stolid. However, Alastair Hussain is a true and pure treble soloist in the famous Allegri and Mendelssohn works, even if he is not quite so magical as Roy Goodman in the former, and Master Lough in the latter; and Thomas Hopkinson is genuinely touching in Burgon's equally famous Nunc dimittis.

The Walton and Britten pieces suit the King's style and acoustic particularly well, as does the lovely Tavener Song for Athene. This is well sustained, and its climax is powerful, but the last degree of spontaneity is missing. However, Walford Davies's simple setting of God be in my head is another highlight, and Franck's Panis angelicus is a surprising success. As a central interlude Cleobury gives a rousing, bravura account of Widor's famous Toccata.

TALLIS: Spem in alium (40-part motet). BACH: Cantata 147: Jesu, Joy of Man's Desiring. VERDI: Pater Noster. HANDEL: Israel in Egypt: The Sons of Israel do Mourn. Messiah: And the Glory of the Lord; Lift Up Your Heads, Oh ye Gates. BRAHMS: Geistliches Lied, Op. 30. GOMBERT: Chanson – Triste départ. BRITTEN: A Ceremony of Carols: There is no Rose. LASSUS: Vinum Bonum (motet). DAVIS: Hymn to the Word of God. HOWELLS: Take Him, Earth, for Cherishing. TAVENER: Song for Athene.

(B) *** Decca 470 122-2.

A self-recommending anthology, made all the more interesting for scanning music written from the Renaissance to the present day. The modern Britten and Tavener pieces suite the King's style and the warm acoustic particularly well, as, needless to say, do the popular numbers. Tallis's 40-part motet is much faster than this same choir's magical account from the 1960s with Willcocks, although it is just as memorable in a different way. It is especially welcome that the nineteenth century is not forgotten, and the lovely Brahms and Verdi pieces are among the highlights. The performances are superb, and the 1990s sound is magnificent.

King's College, Cambridge, Choir, (i) Stephen Cleobury with David Briggs (organ), (ii) Sir David Willcocks, (iii) Anthony Way (treble), St Paul's Cathedral Ch. and CO, John Scott

'The ultimate carol collection': (i) GAUNTLETT, arr. LEDGER: Once in Royal David's city. arr. WILLCOCKS: O come all ye faithful; The first nowell; (ii) Unto us is born a son; (i) God rest ye merry, gentlemen; I saw three ships; (ii) See amid the winter's snow; Rocking; (i) The infant King. (i) MENDELSSOHN, arr. LEDGER: Hark! the herald angels sing. DARKE: In the bleak midwinter. arr. VAUGHAN WILLIAMS: O little town of Bethlehem. (ii) arr. PEARSAL: In dulci jubilo. PRAETORIUS: A great and mighty wonder. (i) arr. LEDGER: Sussex carol. (ii) TATE: While shepherds watched. (i) arr. CLEOBURY: Away in a manger. arr. WOOD: Ding dong! Merrily on high; (ii) King Jesus hath a garden; Shepherds in the field abiding. arr. WALFORD DAVIES: The holly and the ivy. arr. WOODWARD: Up, good Christian folk. (ii) arr. SHAW: Coventry carol. (i) GRUBER, arr. CLEOBURY: Silent night. (iii) SHANE, arr. ALEXANDER: Do you hear what I hear?

(M) **(*) Decca ADD/DDD 458 863-2.

Decca's 'Ultimate' carol collection (issued in 1997) is hardly that, but it will suit those looking for an essentially atmospheric concert of tested favourites for Christmas Day. It centres on a 1984 compilation directed by Stephen Cleobury with Once in Royal David's city presented not as a processional but as an interplay between treble soloist (Robin Barter) and full choir. The choir is backwardly placed and the atmosphere overall is slightly subdued. However, the organ contribution from David Briggs (uncredited in the documentation) always makes its presence felt and is strongly featured in Willcocks's dramatic arrangement of Unto us is born a son and the powerful close of God rest ye merry, gentlemen. Philip Ledger's version of Hark! The herald angels sing also has a spectacular climax.

However, in general the recording does not seek to clarify textures but concentrates on capturing the ambient atmosphere. Thus the older recordings conducted by Willcocks, which are interspersed, match up well to the later collection. The modern carol Do you hear what I hear?, featuring the eloquent Anthony Way and opulently presented with orchestral accompaniment, while it may be a highlight for some listeners, fits rather uneasily in the middle of the programme (following

after the Sussex carol), and not everyone will respond to Cleobury's elaboration of the closing Silent night, which takes an original turn after the opening verse.

King's College, Cambridge, Choir, Sir David Willcocks

'Noël': Disc 1: MENDELSSOHN: Hark the herald angels sing. TRAD.: The first nowell; While shepherds watched; I saw three ships; Ding dong! merrily on high; King Jesus hath a garden; Unto us a son is born; O come all ye faithful; Away in a manger; The holly and the ivy; God rest ye merry, gentlemen; See amid the winter's snow; Past three o'clock. arr. BACH: In dulci jubilo. arr. VAUGHAN WILLIAMS: O little town of Bethlehem.

Disc 2: TRAD.: Once in Royal David's city; Sussex carol; Rocking; Rejoice and be merry; Joseph was an old man; As with gladness men of old; The infant King; Christ was born on Christmas day; Blessed be that maid Mary; Lute-book lullaby; Personent hodie; In the bleak midwinter; Coventry carol; Shepherds, in the field abiding. CORNELIUS: The three kings; A great and mighty wonder. WARLOCK: Balulalow. TCHAIKOVSKY: The crown of roses. TERRY: Myn lyking. JOUBERT: Torches. VAUGHAN WILLIAMS: Fantasia on Christmas carols (with Hervey Alan & LSO).

(B) **(*) Double Decca (ADD) 444 848-2 (2).

This Decca Double is essentially a combined reissue of a pair of bargain-priced LP collections, made over a span of eight years at the end of the 1950s and the beginning of the 1960s. They were counted excellent value when they first appeared in Decca's 'World of' series. The 50-minute programme on the first disc concentrates on established King's favourites; the second is not only more generous (66 minutes), but also includes novelties which are designed to get the listener inquiring further, such as Warlock's Balulalow, the engaging Lute-book lullaby and Joubert's Torches.

This collection opens with the famous processional version of Once in Royal David's city and closes with a superbly joyful performance of Vaughan Williams's Fantasia on Christmas carols, very well recorded, with Hervey Alan the excellent soloist. The sound is always pleasingly full and atmospheric, but with some of the earlier recordings from the late 1950s not quite as clean in focus as those made in the mid-1960s.

'Great choral classics': ALLEGRI: Miserere (with Roy Goodman, treble). PALESTRINA: Stabat Mater. TALLIS: Spem in alium (40-part motet; with Cambridge University Musical Society); Sancte Deus. BYRD: Ave verum corpus. VIVALDI: Gloria in D, RV 589 (with Elizabeth Vaughan, Dame Janet Baker, Roger Lord, ASMF). GIBBONS: This is the record of John (with unnamed soloist and Jacobean Consort of Viols). BACH: Jesu, priceless treasure (Jesu meine Freude), BWV 227. HANDEL: 4

Coronation anthems: Zadok the Priest; My heart is inditing; Let thy hand be strengthened; The King shall rejoice (with ECO).

(B) *** Double Decca (ADD) 452 949-2 (2).

An admirably chosen group of choral masterpieces spanning the riches of the sixteenth and seventeenth centuries and the first half of the eighteenth, opening with Allegri's *Miserere* with its soaring treble solo, so confidently sung here by the same Roy Goodman who was later to make his mark as a conductor. Palestrina's *Stabat Mater* which follows is no less arresting in its bold contrasts, and the richness of texture of Tallis's *Spem in alium* is little short of astonishing. The resonant King's acoustic prevents sharp linear clarity, but it underlines the work's spiritual power and extraordinarily expansive sonority.

Byrd's beautiful *Ave verum corpus* then brings a serene simplicity, with Vivaldi's exuberant *Gloria* rounding off the first CD. The second programme opens with music by Orlando Gibbons, himself a chorister at King's, a delightfully intimate viol-accompanied solo motet with brief choral echoes. Bach's most famous motet follows, sung in English (none too clearly, because of the reverberation), and the concert closes resplendently with Handel's four *Coronation anthems*, including the most famous, *Zadok the Priest*. Here the sound is quite excellent.

King's College, Cambridge, Choir, Willcocks or Philip Ledger

'Favourite carols from Kings': GAUNTLETT: *Once in Royal David's city.* TRAD., arr. VAUGHAN WILLIAMS: *O little town of Bethlehem.* TRAD., arr. STAINER: *The first nowell.* TRAD., arr. LEDGER: *I saw three ships.* TRAD. German, arr. HOLST: *Personent hodie.* TERRY: *Myn Lyking.* HOWELLS: *A spotless rose.* KIRKPATRICK: *Away in a manger.* HADLEY: *I sing of a maiden.* TRAD. French, arr. WILLCOCKS: *O come, o come Emmanuel.* TRAD., arr. WILLCOCKS: *While shepherds watched; On Christmas night.* arr. WOODWARD: *Up! Good Christian folk and listen.* DARKE: *In the bleak midwinter.* GRUBER: *Silent night.* TRAD., arr. WALFORD DAVIES: *The holly and the ivy.* TRAD., arr. SULLIVAN: *It came upon the midnight clear.* CORNELIUS: *Three kings.* SCHEIDT: *A Child is born in Bethlehem.* TRAD. German, arr. PEARSALL: *In dulci jubilo.* WADE: *O come, all ye faithful.* MENDELSSOHN: *Hark! the herald angels sing.*

(M) *** EMI (ADD) CDM5 66241-2.

With 71 minutes of music and twenty-two carols included, this collection, covering the regimes of both Sir David Willcocks and Philip Ledger, could hardly be bettered as a representative sampler of the King's tradition. Opening with the famous processional of *Once in Royal David's city*, to which Willcocks contributes a descant (as he also does in *While shepherds watched*), the programme is wide-ranging in its historical

sources, from the fourteenth century to the present day, while the arrangements feature many famous musicians. The recordings were made between 1969 and 1976, and the CD transfers are first class. The two closing carols, featuring the Philip Jones Brass Ensemble, are made particularly resplendent.

'A Festival of Lessons and Carols from King's' (1979) includes: TRAD.: *Once in Royal David's city; Sussex carol; Joseph and Mary; A maiden most gentle; Chester carol; Angels, from the realms of glory.* HANDEL: *Resonet in laudibus.* ORD: *Adam lay ybounden.* GRUBER: *Stille Nacht.* MATHIAS: *A babe is born.* WADE: *O come all ye faithful.* MENDELSSOHN: *Hark! the herald angels sing.*

(M) *** EMI (ADD) CDM5 66242-2.

This 1979 version of the annual King's College ceremony has the benefit of fine analogue stereo, even more atmospheric than before. Under Philip Ledger the famous choir keeps its beauty of tone and incisive attack. The opening processional, *Once in Royal David's city*, is even more effective heard against the background quiet of CD, and this remains a unique blend of liturgy and music.

'Procession with carols on Advent Sunday' includes: PALESTRINA (arr. from): *I look from afar; Judah and Jerusalem, fear not.* PRAETORIUS: *Come, thou Redeemer of the earth.* TRAD.: *O come, o come, Emmanuel!; Up, awake and away!; 'Twas in the year; Cherry tree carol; King Jesus hath a garden; On Jordan's bank the Baptist's cry; Gabriel's message; I wonder as I wander; My dancing day; Lo! he comes with clouds descending.* BYRT: *All and some.* P. NICOLAI, arr. BACH: *Wake, o wake! with tidings thrilling.* BACH: *Nun komm' der Heiden Heiland.*

(M) *** EMI (ADD) CDM5 66243-2.

This makes an attractive variant to the specifically Christmas-based service, though the carols themselves are not quite so memorable. Beautiful singing and richly atmospheric recording; the wide dynamic range is demonstrated equally effectively by the atmospheric opening and processional and the sumptuous closing hymn.

'Christmas music from King's' (with Andrew Davis, organ, D. Whittaker, flute, Christopher van Kampen, cello and Robert Spencer, lute): SWEELINCK: *Hodie Christus natus est.* PALESTRINA: *Hodie Christus natus est.* VICTORIA: *O magnum mysterium; Senex puerum portabat.* BYRD: *Senex puerum portabat; Hodie beata virgo.* GIBBONS: *Hosanna to the Son of David.* WEELKES: *Hosanna to the Son of David; Gloria in excelsis Deo.* ECCARD: *When to the temple Mary went.* MACONCHY: *Nowell! Nowell!.* arr. BRITTEN: *The holly and the ivy.* PHILIP (The Chancellor): *Angelus ad virginem.* arr. POSTON: *Angelus ad virginem; My dancing day.* POSTON: *Jesus Christ the apple tree.* BERKELEY: *I sing of a maiden.* TAYLOR: *Watts's cradle song.* CAMPION: *Sing a song of joy.* PEERSON: *Most* *glorious Lord of life.* Imogen HOLST: *That Lord that lay in Assë stall.* WARLOCK: *Where riches is everlastingly.*

(M) *** EMI CDM5 (ADD) 66244-2.

A happily chosen survey of music (63 minutes), inspired by the Nativity, from the fifteenth century to the present day. As might be expected, the King's choir confidently encompasses the wide variety of styles from the spiritual serenity of the music of Victoria to the attractive arrangements of traditional carols by modern composers, in which an instrumental accompaniment is added. These items are quite delightful and they are beautifully recorded (in 1965). The motets, from a year earlier, were among the first recording sessions made by the EMI engineers in King's College Chapel, and at the time they had not solved all the problems associated with the long reverberation period, so the focus is less than sharp. Even so, this group demonstrates the unique virtuosity of the Cambridge choir, exploiting its subtlety of tone and flexibility of phrase.

'Choral favourites from King's': HANDEL: *Messiah: Hallelujah chorus.* BACH: *Cantata 147: Jesu, joy of man's desiring.* HAYDN: *The Creation: The heavens are telling.* PURCELL: *Rejoice in the Lord alway.* BRITTEN: *Saint Nicholas: The birth of Nicholas* (all three excerpts with soloists). FAURE: *Requiem: Sanctus* (all seven excerpts with ASMF). SCHUBERT: *Psalm 23: Gott ist mein Hirt* (with Philip Ledger, piano). ELGAR: *Coronation Ode: Land of hope and glory* (with soloists, Band of Royal Military School of Music, Cambridge University Musical Society). DELIUS: *To be sung of a summer night on the water* (with Robert Tear). BRITTEN: *Ceremony of carols: There is no rose* (with Osian Ellis, harp). William HARRIS: *Faire is the heaven.* Charles WOOD: *Hail, gladdening light.* John DYKES: *Holy, holy, holy* (with Philip Jones Brass Ens.; Ian Hare, organ).

(M) *** EMI (ADD) CDM5 72812-2.

Even though it is a mid-priced sampler, this King's collection makes a satisfying concert in its own right, besides tempting the listener to explore further. Opening with a joyful version of the *Hallelujah chorus*, with the radiant treble contribution very striking, the coverage is wide-ranging. Schubert's delightful setting of the Psalm 23 (with Philip Ledger's piano accompaniment) makes an ideal foil for the preceding Purcell anthem and the following excerpt from the Fauré *Requiem*. Similarly the introduction of *Land of hope and glory* into Elgar's *Coronation ode* begins a delightful sequence of music by Delius and Britten. The concert then closes with three fine examples of the continuing Anglican choral tradition from William Harris, Charles Wood and, ending more conventionally, John Dykes, with his familiar hymn *Holy, holy, holy*, but in Willcocks's imaginative arrangement with a descant. The warmly atmospheric King's ambience adds much to the music throughout; only in *The heavens are telling*

from *The Creation* might one have liked a bit more choral bite.

King's Consort, Robert King

'Great Baroque Arias' (with Gillian Fisher, soprano, John Mark Ainsley, tenor, James Bowman, alto, Michael George, bass) from: HANDEL: *Ode for St Cecilia's Day; Serse; Semele; Acis and Galatea; Joshua; Jephtha; Alexander's Feast; Samson.* BACH: *Cantata No. 208.* PURCELL: *Dido and Aeneas.* VIVALDI: *Orlando Furioso.*

(BB) *** Regis RRC 1062.

A more successful budget collection of popular Baroque arias (thirteen altogether) would be hard to find. The great majority are by Handel (including *Ombra mai fu* and *Wher'er you Walk*), but then he wrote many of the best tunes. Apart from the consistently fine singing, Robert King's accompaniments are both stylish amd full of life and he has splendid obbligato soloists, not least Crispian Steele-Perkins, whose vibrant playing is just right to set the scene for the opening *Let the Trumpet's Loud Clangour* (John Mark Ainsley). He returns equally vigorously for *Revenge Timotheus Cries* (the exultant Michael George), and the closing *Let the Bright Seraphim*, gleamingly bright as sung by Gillian Fisher. She is equally impressive in her eloquent account of *Dido's Lament* and the delightful *Sheep May Safely Graze* of Bach, with Lisa Beznosiuk providing the flute/recorder obbligato, as she does in the lovely alto aria from Vivaldi's *Orlando Furioso* where she is completely at one with James Bowman. Another highlight in which Beznosiuk participates is Michael George's genially exuberant *O Ruddier than the Cherry*. The recording is in the demonstration bracket, vivid but most believably balanced.

King's Consort and Choir, Robert King

The Coronation of George II 1727 (includes: HANDEL: *4 Coronation Anthems.* BLOW: *Behold, o God our Defender; God Spake Sometime in Visions.* CHILD: *O Lord, Grant the King a Long Life.* FARMER: *Come Holy Ghost.* GIBBONS: *2nd Service: Te Deum.* PURCELL: *I was glad.* TALLIS: *O God, the Father of Heaven*).

*** Hyp. SACD 67286 or CDA 67286 (2).

The idea of recreating on disc great ceremonial occasions of the past from Rome, Venice or Salzburg has already been established, and here Robert King and the King's Consort bring the process nearer home by recreating the grandest of all Coronation services, the one for George II in 1727. Ambitious as it was, the occasion was chaotic, but King and his fellow researchers have put together a vividly atmospheric sequence, punctuated by fanfares, pealing bells and processional pieces. So Handel's four great *Coronation Anthems*, including *Zadok the Priest*, are the more characterful set in context, matched by equally inspired items by Purcell, Gibbons and, above all, John Blow.

Kirkby, Emma (soprano)

'*Madrigals and wedding songs for Diana*' (with David Thomas, bass, Consort of Musicke, Rooley): BENNET: *All creatures now are merry-minded.* CAMPION: *Now hath Flora robbed her bowers; Move now measured sound; Woo her and win her.* LUPO: *Shows and nightly revels; Time that leads the fatal round.* GILES: *Triumph now with joy and mirth.* CAVENDISH: *Come, gentle swains.* DOWLAND: *Welcome, black night ... Cease these false sports.* WEELKES: *Hark! all ye lovely saints; As Vesta was.* WILBYE: *Lady Oriana.* EAST: *Hence stars! too dim of light; You meaner beauties.* LANIER: *Bring away this sacred tree; The Marigold; Mark how the blushful morn.* COPERARIO: *Go, happy man; While dancing rests; Come ashore, merry mates.* E. GIBBONS: *Long live fair Oriana.*

*** Hyp. CDA 66019.

This wholly delightful anthology celebrates early royal occasions and aristocratic weddings, and in its choice of Elizabethan madrigals skilfully balances praise of the Virgin Queen with a less ambivalent attitude to nuptial delights. Emma Kirkby is at her freshest and most captivating, and David Thomas, if not quite her match, makes an admirable contribution. Accompaniments are stylish and well balanced, and the recording is altogether first rate.

'*O tuneful voice*' (with Rufus Müller, Timothy Roberts (fortepiano or harpsichord), Frances Kelley (harp)): HAYDN: *O tuneful voice; She never told her love; Sailor's song.* SAMUEL ARNOLD: *Elegy.* PINTO: *Invocation to Nature; A Shepherd lov'd a nymph so fair; From thee, Eliza, I must go; Eloisa to Abelard; Minuet in A.* STORACE: *The curfew.* LINLEY THE ELDER: *The lark sings high in the cornfield; Think not, my love.* JACKSON: *The day that saw thy beauty rise; Time has not thinn'd my flowing hair.* SHIELD: *Ye balmy breezes, gently blow; Hope and love; 'Tis only no harm to know it, you know.* CARDON: *Variations on 'Ah vous dirai-je, maman'.* HOOK: *The emigrant.* SALOMON: *Go, lovely rose; Why still before these streaming eyes; O tuneful voice.*

*** Hyp. CDA 66497.

This programme is centred in eighteenth-century England, although Haydn could be included because of his London visits. Indeed, Salomon, his impresario, is featured here as a composer, and a very able one, too; but it is Haydn's comparatively rare song which gives the CD its title and shows Emma Kirkby on top form, just as charming but with greater depth of expression than in her companion Hyperion and Oiseau-Lyre collections, the latter having the same geographical basis but offering repertoire from an earlier period. Kirkby sings like a lark in the cornfield, and Rufus Müller joins her

in some duets by William Jackson and also shares the solo numbers. There are innocently rustic songs from William Shield in which each artist participates, and much else besides: this 74-minute programme has a wide range of mood and style.

'*A Portrait*' (with AAM, Hogwood): HANDEL: *Disseratevi, o porte d'Averno; Gentle Morpheus, son of night.* PURCELL: *Bess of Bedlam; From rosie bow'rs.* ARNE: *Where the bee sucks there lurk I; Rise, glory, rise.* DOWLAND: *I saw the lady weepe.* D'INDIA: *Odi quel rosignuolo.* TROMBONCINO: *Se ben hor non scopro il foco.* VIVALDI: *Passo di pena in pena.* J. S. BACH: *Ei! wie schmeckt der Coffee süsse.* HAYDN: *With verdure clad.* MOZART: *Laudate Dominum; Exsultate, jubilate, K.165.*

✪ (M) *** O-L 443 200-2.

Admirers of Emma Kirkby's style in early and baroque music will delight in this well-chosen 76-minute sampler of her work. L'Oiseau-Lyre have altered and expanded the original issue and the excerpt from Handel's *Messiah* has been replaced by the remarkable Angel's aria, *Disseratevi, o porte d'Averno*, from Part I of *La Resurrezione* (calling on the gates of the Underworld to be unbarred, to yield to God's glory). It opens with joyous baroque trumpets and oboes, and Emma Kirkby shows with her florid vocal line that anything they can do, she can do better.

This is rather effectively followed by Purcell's melancholy Mad song, *Bess of Bedlam*, and the equally touching *From rosie bow'rs*. Music by Arne lightens the mood and later there are excerpts from Bach's *Coffee cantata* and popular solos by Haydn and Mozart. This recital is as well planned as it is enjoyable, and Hogwood ensures that accompaniments are consistently fresh and stylish. First-class sound.

Arias (with AAM, Hogwood): HANDEL: *Alessandro Severo: Overture.* Arias from: *Alcina; Alexander's Feast; L'Allegro, il penseroso ed il moderato; Saul; March in D; Hornpipe.* LAMPE: *Britannia: Welcome Mars. Dione: Pretty warblers.* ARNE: *Comus. Rosamond: Rise, glory, rise. By the rusty-fringed bank; Brightest lady. The Tempest: Where the bee sucks.* HAYDN: *The Creation: With verdure clad; On mighty pens.* MOZART: *Concert arias: Voi, avete un cor fedele; Nehmt meinen Dank, ihr holden Gönner! Ch'io mi scordi di te?* Arias from: *Il rè pastore; Zaïde.*

(B) *** Double Decca 458 084-2 (2).

Two of the Arne arias and one of Haydn's are included in the 'Portrait' (see previous entry), and Arne's *Rise, glory, rise* (showing the singer at her very finest) also rightly appears in Decca's 'Treasures of baroque opera' (see above). The rest is new. Of the novelties Lampe's charming *Pretty warblers*, like Handel's *Sweet bird* from *L'Allegro, il penseroso ed il moderato*, brings an illustrative aviary from the solo flute, with Kirkby then adding her own exquisite roulades. *Credete al mio dolore* from *Alcina* has an important cello obbligato. Kirkby's smooth sweet line and easy coloratura give consistent pleasure, and the two famous arias from Haydn's *Creation* are gloriously sung.

Throughout, Hogwood's accompaniments are light and stylish and give the singer every support, and one's only criticism is that the Handel and Mozart selections would have benefited from more instrumental music in between the arias to add variety. But individually every item here is treasurable and the recording is first class, giving plenty of space and a fine bloom to the voice.

'*The sweet voice of Emma Kirkby*' (with AAM, Hogwood/Preston; or Consort of Musicke, Rooley): Arias from: HANDEL: *Alcina; Alceste; Esther.* ARNE: *Rosamond.* PERGOLESI: *Stabat Mater:* excerpt (with James Bowman). MOZART: *Le nozze di Dorina.* Also Concert aria: *Nehmt meinen Dank, K.383.* BACH: Excerpts from: *Cantata, BWV 202; Wedding cantata, BWV 509.* VIVALDI: *Gloria: Laudamus te* (with Judith Nelson). TROMBONCINO: *Vergine bella.* MONTEVERDI: *O come sei gentile.* PURCELL: *If music be the food of love; Pausanias: Sweeter than roses.* WILBYE: *Draw on sweet night.*

**(*) Decca 466 322-2.

The voice is certainly as sweet as ever, the singing full of vitality and character. The accompaniments are just as sparkling as the singing, the recording is first class, and there is again not too much duplication here. Whether in the spectacular and charming little-known Mozart aria from *Le nozze di Dorina*, the flamboyant Handel and Arne arias with trumpets and, in the case of *Praise the Lord* from *Esther* (where Kirkby herself opens like a trumpet), a harp too, the lovely Bach cantata excerpts, including the famous *Bist du bei mir* (now attributed to G. H. Stölzel), or the duets by Pergolesi, Vivaldi and Tromboncino, the ear is constantly ravished, as it is again in the closing group of songs by Purcell and Wilbye. However, there seems no reason for paying full price for a sampler which is inadequately documented and contains no texts or translations. Indeed, the brief note is biographhical only, and tells the collector nothing whatsoever about the music beyond a list of titles.

'*The World of Emma Kirkby*': Arias from: HANDEL: *Alcina; Messiah.* PURCELL: *Dido and Aeneas.* LAMPE: *Dione.* VIVALDI: *Nulla in mundo pax sincera.* PERGOLESI: *Salve Regina.* ARNE: *Comus.* HAYDN: *The Creation.* Songs: DOWLAND: *I saw my Ladye Weepe.* GIBBONS: *The Silver Swan.* MORLEY: *With my Love.* MOZART: *Ch'io mi scordi di te?*

(M) *** Decca (ADD/DDD) 467 781-2.

During the last 25 years Emma Kirkby has won the affections of not only aficionados of the early music world but the music-loving public in general. This recital clearly shows why. Her voice is not large, but it projects vividly, is unself-consciously beautiful, fresh sounding and imbued with an obvious sense of joy. This CD charts her career from 1975 to the present, in a varied programme, from full *da capo* arias to art

songs. She manages both the challenging coloratura of *Torami a vagheggiar* (from *Alcina*) with the same conviction as she presents the simple rustic charm of Arne's *By the rushy-fringed bank* (from *Comus*). The recordings are excellent, the programme varied and the CD inexpensive.

Kraus, Alfredo (tenor)

Arias and excerpts from: VERDI: *Rigoletto; La Traviata.* DONIZETTI: *Don Pasquale; Lucia di Lammermoor.* PUCCINI: *La Bohème.* BELLINI: *I Puritani.* MOZART: *Così fan tutte: Un'aura amorosa.*

(BB) ** Royal Classics Vocal Double (ADD) DCL 706642 (2).

Alfredo Kraus, a light tenor and a stylish one, always gives pleasure, if at times one misses the thrill of a really big voice. These five sets of excerpts come from complete recordings in which he participated in the late 1970s and early 1980s, in partnership with Beverly Sills, Renata Scotto and others. He is heard at his stylish best in *Rigoletto*, is a tender Rodolfo in *Bohème* and is equally touching in *Traviata*, although here the voice sounds thinner. He is also impressive alongside Edita Gruberová in *Lucia di Lammermoor*. Most of these recordings are far from first choices, so his admirers will be glad to have his contributions available separately.

Larin, Sergej (tenor), Eleonora Bekova (piano)

'*Songs by the Mighty Handful*': RIMSKY-KORSAKOV: *It was not the wind blowing from above; The octave; The nymph; Clearer than the singing of the lark; The scurrying bank of clouds disperses; On the hills of Georgia; Of what in the silence of the night; Captivated by the rose, the nightingale; Silence descends on the yellow cornfields; A pressed flower.* CUI: *A statue at Tsarskoye Selo; The burnt letter.* BORODIN: *The fair maid has stopped loving me; For the shores of the distant homeland.* BALAKIREV: *You are full of captivating bliss; Barcarolle; Look, my friend.* MUSSORGSKY: *Songs and dances of Death.*

*** Chan. 9547.

Sergej Larin with his outstandingly beautiful and expressive tenor presents vivid portraits of the five Russian composers grouped as 'The Mighty Handful', all but Mussorgsky here represented in miniatures. The ten Rimsky-Korsakov songs are totally unpretentious, simple ballads that he wrote in joyful relaxation, a mood which is reflected in the music. The two Cui songs are far more intense, as are the two by Borodin, one of them, *The fair maid has stopped loving me*, with cello obbligato played by Alfia Bekova. The three Balakirev songs are tiny chips from the workbench, beautifully crafted. Only Mussorgsky is presented at full stretch with the greatest and best known of the items here, the *Songs and dances of Death*. Larin, having for the earlier songs used his most honeyed tones and velvety, seamless production, including a wonderful head-voice on top, here darkens his tone thrillingly, ending with a searing account of *The Field Marshal Death*. A superb disc, revealing a great artist.

Laudibus, Michael Brewer

'*All in the April evening*': ROBERTON: *All in the April evening.* arr. ROBERTON: *The banks o'Doon; An Eriskay love lilt; Dream Angus; All through the night. The wee Copper o'Fife; Drink to me only with thine eyes.* arr. VAUGHAN WILLIAMS: *Ca' the yowes; The turtle dove.* VAUGHAN WILLIAMS: *3 Shakespeare songs: Full fathom five; The cloud-capp'd towers; Over hill, over dale.* arr. BANTOCK: *O can ye sew cushions?* arr. MANSFIELD: *Wi' a hundred pipers.* MORLEY: *Fyer! fyer!* BENNET: *All creatures now are merry-minded.* BYRD: *Ave verum corpus.* GRANT: *Crimond.* PARRY: *Never weather-beaten sail.* ELGAR: *My love dwelt in a northern land; As torrents in summer.* arr. WARLOCK: *Corpus Christi.* STANFORD: *The blue bird.* SULLIVAN: *The long day closes.*

*** Hyp. CDA 67076.

The twenty-two members of Laudibus are all recruited from the National Youth Choir. Their tuning is impeccable and they blend together with the natural flexibility which established the international reputation of Sir Hugh Roberton's Glasgow Orpheus Choir. The programme here is based on repertoire made famous by that now disbanded group, opening appropriately with the title piece, one of the simplest and loveliest examples of four-part writing in the English language. The programme is for the most part composed of similarly serene and evocative music, but every so often there is a lively item like *Wi' a hundred pipers*, Morley's *Fyer! fyer!*, or Bennet's *All creatures now are merry-minded*, to interrupt the reverie momentarily. The various soloists are drawn from the choir and very good they are too (sample the treble solo in Stanford's *Blue bird*). Beautifully recorded, this is a choral record for the late evening, and its consistency of mood is one of its virtues. The playing time is a generous 72 minutes.

Legge, Walter (producer)

'*Les introuvables de Walter Legge*': Disc 1: Lieder: WOLF: *Eichendorff Lieder: Der Freund; Der Musikant* (Herbert Janssen with Gerald Moore; 1937). *Mörike Lieder: In der Frühe; Mausfallen-Sprüchlein. Spanisches Liederbuch: In dem Schatten meiner Locken.* Italienisches Liederbuch: *Auch kleine Dinge; Und willst du deinen Liebsten. Wie glänzt der helle Mond.* HAYDN: *Canzonetta: She never told her love; Sailor's song.* MOZART: *Das Veichen* (Elisabeth Schumann with Gerald Moore; 1945/6). SCHUBERT: *Der Musensohn.* YRYO KILPINEN: *6 Lieder um den Tod, Op. 62* (Gerhard Hüsch with Hanns Udo Müller or Margaret Kilpinen; 1934/5). BRAHMS: *2 Lieder with viola, Op.*

91 (Kirsten Flagstad with Herbert Downes and Gerald Moore; 1949). WOLF: Goethe Lieder: *Mignon II: Nur wer die Sehnsucht kennt.* SCHUMANN: *Die Kartenlegerin* (Elisabeth Höngen with Hans Zipper; 1946). SCHUBERT: *Der Wanderer* (Hans Hotter with Hermann von Nordberg; 1947). BRAHMS: *Feldeinsamkeit* (Tiana Lemnitz with Herta Klust; 1948). RICHARD STRAUSS: *Cäcile* (Hilde Konetzni with Hermann von Nordberg; 1948).

Disc 2: *Voices*: O'CONNOR: *The old house.* THAYER: *A child's prayer* (John McCormack with Gerald Moore; 1939). ADRIAN BEECHAM: *The willow song; O mistress mine* (Nancy Evans, Sir Thomas Beecham; 1940). PURCELL: *The Blessed Virgin's expostulation* (Isobel Baillie with Arnold Goldsbrough, organ; 1941). GLUCK: *Orpheus and Eurydice: What is life to me without thee?* BRAHMS: *Liebestreu; Deutsche Volkslieder: Feinsliebchen* (sung in English). ELGAR: *The Dream of Gerontius: My work is done … It is because then thou didst fear.* MAURICE GREENE: *I will lay me down in peace; O praise the Lord* (Kathleen Ferrier with Gerald Moore; 1944). GOUNOD: *Au rossignol* (Pierre Bernac with Francis Poulenc; 1945). RICHARD STRAUSS: *Ariadne aux Naxos: Es gibt ein Reich … In den Schönen Feierkleidern* (Maria Cebotari, VPO, Karajan; 1948). *Salome*: Final scene, excerpt: *Sie ist ein Ungeheuer* (Ljuba Welitsch, Gertrud Schuster, Josef Witt, VPO, Karajan; 1948). WAGNER: *Tristan und Isolde: Tod denn Alles!* (Ludwig Weber, Elisabeth Schwarzkopf, Philh. O, Schüchter; 1951); *Die Meistersinger: Fliedermonologue* (Hans Hotter, VPO, Karajan; 1948). BOITO: *Mefistofele: L'altra notte* (Renata Scotto, Philh. O, Manno Wolf-Ferrari; 1958). MOZART: *Il rè pastore: L'amerò, sarò costante* (Anna Moffo, Philh. O, Galliera; 1958).

Disc 3: *Instruments*: BACH: *Toccata and fugue in D min., BWV 565* (Albert Schweitzer, organ of All Hallows by the Tower, Barking, Essex; 1935). MENDELSSOHN, arr. RACHMANINOV: *A Midsummer Night's Dream: Scherzo* (Moiseiwitch; 1939). SARASATE: *Danzas españolas: Playera; Zapateado* (Josef Hassid with Gerald Moore; 1940). SHOSTAKOVICH: *Prelude No. 24, Op. 34/24* (Harriet Cohen; 1942). SCHUBERT: *String quartet No. 14 (Death and the Maiden): Andante* (Philharmonia Qt; 1942). SZYMANOWSKI: *Notturno e Tarantella, Op. 28: Tarantella* (Arthur Grumiaux, Gerald Moore; 1945). WEBER: *Invitation to the dance.* BACH: *Chromatic fantasia and fugue, BWV 903* (Artur Schnabel; 1947/8). D. SCARLATTI: *Sonata in F, Kk. 7.* BACH/BUSONI: *Cantata No. 140: Chorale: Wachet auf* (Solomon; 1948). D. SCARLATTI: *Sonatas in D min., Kk. 9; in D, KK. 33.* HANDEL: *Suite No. 5: The Harmonious blacksmith* (Walter Gieseking; 1951).

Disc 4: *Orchestral*: BEETHOVEN: *Overture: The Ruins of Athens* (LSO, Weingartner; 1940). LISZT: *Fantasia on a theme from Beethoven's 'Ruins of Athens'* (Egon Petri, LPO, Leslie Heward; 1938).

WALTON: *Henry V* (film score): *Passacaglia: The death of Falstaff; Touch her soft lips and part* (Philh. O strings, composer; 1945). BLISS: *March: The Phoenix* (Philh. O, Constant Lambert; 1946). DVORAK: *Carnaval overture, Op. 9* (Czech PO, Kubelik; 1946). MOZART: *Serenade No. 7 (Haffner): Rondo* (Willi Boskovsky, VPO, Karl Boehm; 1947). BORODIN: *Overture: Prince Igor* (Philh. O, Issay Dobrowen; 1949). PROKOFIEV: *Symphony No. 1 in D (Classical), Op. 25* (BPO, Sergiu Celibidache; 1948).

(B) (***) EMI mono CZS5 69743-2 (4).

Many of the items here may be so offbeat as to seem perverse in celebration of the work of the greatest of recording producers. The key word is '*introuvables*', recordings so rare that hardly anyone knows of them. It is surprising for example to have Legge's second wife, Elisabeth Schwarzkopf – she as much an inspiration to him as he always was to her – celebrated with an odd fragment from Wagner's *Tristan*. In the passage leading up to the final *Liebestod*, she acts as foil for the bass, Ludwig Weber, in the brief, poignant duet, *Tod denn Alles!*, between King Mark and Brangäne, a touching performance. It is good to have Legge's first wife also remembered, a lovely singer far less celebrated but much loved, Nancy Evans, who, accompanied at the piano by Sir Thomas Beecham, sings two Shakespeare settings by Beecham's son, Adrian.

Each of the four CDs is devoted to a different category: Lieder, Voices, Instruments and Orchestral. Rightly, the first disc begins with some of the Hugo Wolf recordings, part of the Hugo Wolf Society Edition – the project which first made Legge's reputation – with Herbert Janssen and Elisabeth Schumann the singers chosen here. One might have expected some songs from Elena Gerhardt, but maybe her recordings were counted too '*trouvable*'. A fascinating rarity follows, reminding us that, along with the most prominent Society editions promoted by Legge, covering Beethoven, Bach, Mozart, Sibelius, Delius and others, there was a celebration of a most sensitive Finnish composer, still largely unappreciated by the Yrjö Kilpinen Society edition, with his songs recorded by the great Lieder-singer Gerhard Hüsch, the central figure in Legge's Lieder projects in the 1930s.

The Voices disc ranges from John McCormack to Anna Moffo (enchanting in Mozart's *Il rè pastore*) by way of Ferrier, Cebotari and many others; and the Instruments disc goes from Albert Schweitzer in Bach to Walter Gieseking in Handel, by way of such neglected artists as the violinist Josef Hassid. The Orchestral disc then ranges from Weingartner in Beethoven's *Ruins of Athens* and Egon Petri's recording of Liszt's *Variations* on a theme from that work to Celibidache doing Prokofiev's *Classical Symphony* in a typically idiosyncratic way. Karajan, one supposes, was also too 'trouvable' to be included - though, as he always resisted being anthologized next to others on disc, maybe that rule still applies. In the booklet Alan Sanders writes a searching and informative (if brief) essay on Legge, and there are some delightful photos, though no texts of vocal items. An offbeat, very enjoyable tribute, though no such compilation could adequately convey a full portrait of such a figure.

Lemalu, Jonathan (bass-baritone)

'*Lieder, Mélodies and English Songs*' (with Roger Vignoles, piano): BRAHMS: *4 Serious Songs.* SCHUBERT: *Der Wanderer; Auf der Donau; Der Schiffer; Der Wanderer an den Mond.* FAURE: *L'horizon chimérique* (song-cycle). FINZI: *Rollicumrorum; To Lizbie Brown.* IRELAND: *Sea Fever.* KEEL: *Trade Winds.* HEAD: *The Estuary.* TRAD. (arr. VIGNOLES): *Lowlands.*

(B) *** EMI Début CDZ5 75203-2.

This is an outstanding disc in EMI's Début series, a wide-ranging recital from one of the most talented singers of the younger generation, Jonathan Lemalu, a New Zealand-born Samoan with a magnificent natural voice and artistry to match. In 2002 he won the Royal Philharmonic Society's 'Young Artist Award', and here demonstrates his versatility over some very demanding repertory. He seems just as much at home in the dark cadences of Brahms's *Four Serious Songs* as in late Fauré – *L'horizon chimérique*, a cycle of four songs, three of which are connected with the sea, was written by the aged composer in 1921 for Charles Panzéra. The sea and water connection is carried through many of the other songs, even the Schubert group with the vigorous *Der Schiffer* given a rousing performance. The final group of four songs, which come almost as encores, is also nautical, with John Ireland's masterpiece, *Sea Fever*, matched by the hauntingly evocative *Trade Winds* by Frederick Keel, which deserves to be far better known. In all these songs Roger Vignoles is an unfailingly imaginative and sympathetic accompanist. Being a budget issue, this has no texts in the booklet, but Lemalu's diction is excellent.

Lemper, Ute, Matrix Ensemble, Robert Ziegler

'*Berlin cabaret songs*' (sung in German) by SPOLIANSKY; HOLLAENDER; GOLDSCHMIDT; BILLING; NELSON.

*** Decca 452 601-2.

The tangy, sexy voice of Ute Lemper is here caught at its most provocative in a colourful sequence of cabaret songs reflecting the sleazy, decadent atmosphere of Berlin under the Weimar Republic, as observed in the popular cabarets of the city. With Lemper characterizing delectably, with German consonants adding extra bite, often 'over the top' as in the delightful *Ich bin ein Vamp*, the authentic flavour is here presented in music with new vividness.

The conductor, Robert Ziegler, has restored the original orchestrations as closely as he can (no scores survive, only piano reductions), and the result is a valuable addition to the 'Entartete Musik' series. Not only is the music fascinating and characterful, so are the words, including even a gay anthem, with oom-pah bass, *Das lila Lied*, written by Mischa Spoliansky under a pseudonym. It is good too to have included a song by Berthold Goldschmidt which he wrote for his wife in 1930.

'Berlin cabaret songs' (sung in English):
SPOLIANSKY: *It's all a swindle; The smart set; When the special girlfriend; I am a vamp; L'heure bleue; Maskulinum.* HOLLAENDER: *Sex appeal; Take it off Petronella!; Chuck out the men!; Oh just suppose; I don't know who I belong to; A little yearning; Oh, how we wish that we were kids again; Munchausen.* NELSON: *Peter, Peter; A little Attila.* GOLDSCHMIDT: *The washed-up lover.* BILLING: *The Lavender song.*

*** Decca 452 849-2.

This offers the same programme as the disc above, but in English translation. Inevitably some of the bite is lost with softer English consonants, but it is amazing how much of the original tang and snarl Lemper manages to inject, and there is much to be said for having the words instantly identifiable to the English speaker, with diction crystal clear.

(i) Leonard, Sarah (soprano), (ii) Paul Leonard (baritone), Malcolm Martineau (piano)

'A Century of English song', Volume II: (i) PARRY: *My heart is like a singing bird; From a city window; The maiden; Armida's garden; My true love hath my heart; Goodnight; Crabbed age and youth.* Sir Arthur SOMERVELL: **(ii)** *A Shopshire lad* (cycle); **(i)** *Young love lies sleeping; Shepherd's cradle song; Come to me in my dreams.* STANFORD: **(ii)** *The fair; To the soul; The calico dress:* **(i)** *An Irish idyll* (cycle).
**(*) Somm SOMMCD 214.

Sarah Leonard with her fresh, bright soprano and her brother Paul with his cleanly focused baritone are persuasive advocates in these largely neglected songs, helped by the imaginative accompaniments of Malcolm Martineau. All three composers rise above the limitations of the drawing-room ballad thanks to musical finesse and sensitive response to words, though Somervell's *Shropshire lad* cycle, open in its lyricism, completely misses the darkness implied behind seemingly innocent verses. Parry owes most to the example of Brahms, while Stanford, with Irish as well as English overtones, finds a personal magic in such songs as *The fairy lough*, the second song in the *Irish idyll*. Well-balanced recording, but with edge on the top of the soprano's voice.

London, George (bass)

'The Singers' (Decca series): Arias from: WAGNER: *Der fliegende Holländer; Die Meistersinger von Nürnberg; Die Walküre* (with VPO,

Knappertsbusch). **Songs from musicals:** RODGERS AND HAMMERSTEIN: *Carousel; Oklahoma; South Pacific.* LERNER AND LOEWE: *Brigadoon; My Fair Lady.* WEILL: *Knickerbocker Holiday.* KERN AND HAMMERSTEIN: *Show Boat; Very Warm for May* (with the Ronald Shaw O).

(M) **(*) Decca (ADD) 467 904-2.

George London's distinctive, rich-hued voice could be capable of sounding very dramatic, even sinister, and with his dark good looks and magnetic presence he was indeed a commanding figure. The Wagner items demonstrate a vigorous personality, and if characterization is not his strong point, he is dramatic in the broadest sense. The gritty sound of his vibrato is not to our tastes, but we are the first to admit that others hear it differently. The singing certainly communicates excitement, but it is rather tiring when the singing is so consistently loud. The 1958 recording is warm and vivid, and only a little dated.

It is something of a shock that the remaining half of the programme is devoted to musicals. Nothing wrong with that in principle, but if you play *O What a Beautiful Morning* straight after *Die Walküre*, it can cause a severe aural 'double-take'. As for the performances, they are strongly sung. Even if one doesn't always like full operatic voices in this repertoire London's Canadian accent is certainly an asset here, and the 1957 sound captures the voice well. Once again in this series, texts and translations, along with a photo-gallery, are available only via a CD ROM drive.

Lott, Felicity (soprano), Graham Johnson (piano)

Mélodies on Victor Hugo poems: GOUNOD: *Sérénade.* BIZET: *Feuilles d'album: Guitare. Adieux de l'hôtesse arabe.* LALO: *Guitare.* DELIBES: *Eclogue.* FRANCK: *S'il est un charmant gazon.* FAURE: *L'absent; Le papillon et la fleur; Puisqu'ici-bas.* WAGNER: *L'attente.* LISZT: *O quand je dors; Comment, disaient-ils.* SAINT-SAENS: *Soirée en mer; La fiancée du timbalier.* M. V. WHITE: *Chantez, chantez jeune inspirée.* HAHN: *Si mes vers avaient des ailes; Rêverie.*

(B) *** HM Musique d'Abord HMA 901138.

Felicity Lott's collection of Hugo settings relies mainly on sweet and charming songs, freshly and unsentimentally done, with Graham Johnson an ideally sympathetic accompanist. The recital is then given welcome stiffening with fine songs by Wagner and Liszt, as well as two by Saint-Saëns that have a bite worthy of Berlioz. It makes a headily enjoyable cocktail. Now reissued in the Musique d'Abord series, this is a bargain not to be missed.

'Summertime': ARNE: *Where the Bee Sucks.* BARBER: *Sure on this Shining Light; The Monk and his Cat.* BERLIOZ: *Nuites d'été: L'Île inconnue; Villanelle.* BERNSTEIN: *My House.* BRAHMS: *Meine Liebe ist* grun. BRIDGE: *Go not Happy Day.* DELIUS: *To Daffodils.* ELGAR: *The Shepherd's Song.* FAURE: *Clair de lune; Soir; Notre amour.* FRASER-SIMPSON: *Vespers.* GERSHWIN: *Summertime.* HEAD: *The Little Road to Bethlehem.* IRELAND: *The Trellis.* LEHMANN: *Ah, Moon of my Delight.* PORTER: *The Tale of the Oyster.* QUILTER: *Now Sleeps the Crimson Petal. Love's Philosophy.* RUTTER: *The Lord Bless you.* SCHUBERT: *Who is Sylvia? Auf dem Wasser zu singen.* SCHUMANN: *Der Nussbaum.* TRAD: *The Lark in the Clear Air.* VAUGHAN WILLIAMS: *Orpheus with his Lute.* WARLOCK: *Sleep.* HAYDN WOOD: *A Brown Bird Singing.*

*** Black Box BBM 3007.

It would be hard to devise a song-miscellany more attractive than this programme, which brings together so many popular favourites as well as some welcome rarities. It is Graham Johnson's genius pointfully to juxtapose so many different areas of song, with such an item as Cole Porter's cabaret-song, *The Tale of the Oyster,* adding an extra, unexpected dimension, as do Haydn Wood's *Brown Bird Singing* and Fraser-Simpson's setting of one of A. A. Milne's Christopher Robin poems, *Vespers.* Dame Felicity rightly presents it straight as a child might, punctuating it with little staccato cries of '*oh!*' (of which there are perhaps one or two too many).

In every way she is a charmer, which makes this disc self-recommending, and her voice is at its freshest, even girlish. Yet the recording tends to highlight a brightness in both the voice and the piano that limits her range of tone and makes it seem less varied than usual. The information on the two-page leaflet is very limited indeed, and Schumann's most popular song, *Der Nussbaum,* is attributed to Schubert. As a CD-ROM the disc offers more information, including translations, yet even for those with access to a computer that is no substitute for a printed note, which provides you with texts and translations while you are actually listening. Even so, it is a delight to go from one jewel of a song to another, and it is good to have a spicing of American items, not just Gershwin, Barber (with two songs) and Cole Porter, but Bernstein too, with one of his early songs for Barrie's *Peter Pan.*

Ludwig, Christa (mezzo-soprano)

'*The Art of Christa Ludwig*' (with Gerald Moore or Geoffrey Parsons (piano) & (i) Herbert Downes (viola); (ii) with Philh. O, Klemperer; (iii) with Berlin SO, Stein or Forster): BRAHMS: *Sapphische Ode; Liebestreu; Der Schmied; Die Mainacht. 8 Zigeunerlieder. 4 Deutsche Volkslieder: Och mod'r ich well en Ding han!; We kumm ich dann de Pooz erenn?; In stiller Nacht; Schwesterlein. Lieder: Dein blaues Auge; Von ewiger Liebe; Das Mädchen spricht; O wüsst ich doch; Wie Melodien zieht es mir; Mädchenlied; Vergebliches Ständchen; Der Tod, das ist die kühle Nacht; Auf dem See; Waldeinsamkeit; Immer leiser wird mein Schlummer; Ständchen;*

Gestillte Sehnsucht; (i) *Geistliches Wiegenlied.* MAHLER: *Hans und Grete; Frühlingsmorgen; Des Knaben Wunderhorn: Ich ging mit Lust durch einen grünen Wald; Wo die schönen Trompeten blasen; Der Schildwache Nachtlied; Um schlimme Kinder; Das irdische Leben; Wer hat dies Liedlein erdacht; Lob des hohen Verstandes;Des Antonius von Padua Fischpredigt; Rheinlegendchen.* Rückert Lieder: *Ich atmet' einen linden Duft; Liebst du um Schönheit; Um Mitternacht; Ich bin der Welt abhanden gekommen.* SCHUMANN: *Frauenliebe und -Leben, Op. 42.* REGER: *Der Brief; Waldeinsamkeit.* SCHUBERT: *Die Allmacht; Fischerweise; An die Musik; Der Musensohn; Ganymed; Auf dem Wasser zu singen; Ave Maria; Die Forelle; Gretchen am Spinnrade; Frühlingsglaube; Der Tod und das Mädchen; Lachen und Weinen; Litanei auf das Fest Aller Seelen; Erlkönig; Der Hirt auf dem Felsen.* WOLF: *Gesang Weylas; Auf einer Wanderung.* RICHARD STRAUSS: *Die Nacht; Allerseelen; Schlechtes Wetter.* RAVEL: *3 Chansons madécasses.* SAINT-SAENS: *Une flûte invisible.* RACHMANINOV: *Chanson géorgienne; Moisson de tristesse.* ROSSINI: *La regata veneziana* (3 canzonettas). (ii) WAGNER: *Wesendonk Lieder.* (iii) HANDEL: *Giulio Cesare: Cleopatra's aria.* BACH: *St John Passion: Aria: Es ist vollbracht!.* (ii) WAGNER: *Tristan und Isolde: Mild und leise.*

(M) *** EMI (ADD) CMS7 64074-2 (4).

Christa Ludwig is an extraordinarily versatile artist with a ravishing voice, readily matched by fine intelligence and natural musical sensitivity which place her among the special singers of our time, including De los Angeles and Schwarzkopf (to name two from the same EMI stable). She was as impressive in Schubert as she was in Strauss and Brahms, and her Mahler is very special indeed. This compensates for the below-par Schumann song cycle. Her voice took naturally to the microphone, so this four-disc set is another source of infinite musical pleasure to be snapped up quickly before it disappears. The recordings come from the 1950s and 1960s and are very well transferred indeed.

Magdalen College Choir, Oxford, Dr John Harper

'*The English Anthem Collection*' complete; (with Goffrey Webber or Paul Brough, organ).

(BB) *** Regis (ADD/DDD) RRC 4001 (4) (2 x 2).

Volume 1 (1540–1870): Disc 1: BYRD: *O Lord Turn Thy Wrath; Teach Me O Lord; Exalt Thyself O God; Sing Joyfully unto God.* MORLEY: *Out of the Deep; Nolo mortem peccatoris.* VAN WILDER: *Blessed Art Thou.* TYE: *I Will Exalt Thee.* TALLIS: *I Call and Cry to Thee; O Lord, Give Thy Holy Spirit. Purge Me, O Lord.* SHEPHERD: *The Lord's Prayer.* GIBBONS: *O Lord in Thy Wrath Rebuke me not; O Lord, I Lift my Heart to Thee.* WEELKES: *Hosanna to the Son of David; O Lord Arise into Thy Resting Place.*

TOMKINS: *Then David Mourned; O Praise the Lord.* BLOW: *My God, my God, Look Upon Me.* PURCELL: *I was Glad.*

Disc 2: PURCELL (cont.): *Hear my Prayer, O Lord; O God Thou has Cast us Out; Remember Not, O Lord our Offences.* CROFT: *God is Gone Up.* GREENE: *Lord, Let Me Know Mine End.* BOYCE: *O Where shall Wisdom be Found?* BATTISHILL: *Look, Look Down from Heaven.* ATTWOOD: *Come Holy Ghost.* S. S. WESLEY: *Blessed be the Lord and Father; The Wilderness.* OUSELEY: *Is it Nothing to You?; O Saviour of the World.* STAINER: *I Saw the Lord.*

(BB) *** Regis ADD/DDD RRC 2030 (2).

Since these recordings were made for the Alpha label between 1963 and 1969, Dr Harper has been appointed Director of the Royal School of Church Music. Here he and his splendid choir offer a survey spanning four-and-a-half centuries, covering 67 anthems (or motets) written by 42 composers. With a very high overall standard of performance and recording, it is an astonishing achievement, which Regis have conveniently made available in two seperate budget Duos, with the complete anthology also available together in a slipcase, at a comparable low cost.

Opening with three magnificent examples by William Byrd, the first and third unaccompanied, the choir moves on to Morley and Farmer, including an attractively intimate setting of *The Lord's Prayer*. One of the early surprises is the fresh, uncomplicated imitation of *Blessed art Thou* (Psalm 128) by Philip van Wilder, a Netherlander who served at the Court of Henry VIII. Of the Tallis items *Purge Me O Lord* is particularly touching, while *O Lord Give Thy Holy Spirit*, radiantly serene, is spiced with a twinge of dissonace.

If Byrd was the father of English Renaissance polyphony, Weelkes brought real drama into his settings, and his *Hosanna to the Son of David* is a thrillingly vibrant example. Tomkins's simple, melancholy lament by David for Jonathan then contrasts with his contrapuntal *O Praise the Lord*, for twelve independent voices, which recalls Tallis's *Spem in alium*. The first disc then ends with John Blow, direct and eloquent in *My God, my God, Look Upon Me* and Purcell's jubilant *I was Glad*.

With the three Purcell works which open the second disc we are on more familiar territory, but then come two of the highlights, Croft's joyful three-verse *God is Gone Up*, followed by Greene's richly expressive *Lord, Let Me Know Mine End*, with its imitative duet for a pair of trebles. Boyce's use of solo voices in dialogue contrasted with the full choir later brings a flavour of Handel. Thomas Battishill was a pupil of Mozart and he builds a fine intense climax in *Lord Look Down from Heaven*.

The move forward to the nineteenth century brings an obvious change of style. Wesley's *Blessed be the God and Father* is an eloquent example, while *The Wilderness*, at fourteen minutes, is more like a miniature cantata, and with its finely-sung treble solos might almost be by Mendelssohn. Ouseley's style is much simpler: his richly homophonic textures look back as

well as forward, while the dramatic closing work of Stainer for double choir and organ shows the Victorian tradition at its most flamboyant.

Volume 2 (1870–1988): Disc 1: STANFORD: *The Lord's my Shepherd; Glorious and powerful God.* PARRY: *My Soul, there is a Country.* WOOD: *O Thou, the Central Orbe; Hail, Gladdening Light; Expectans expectavi.* BAIRSTOW: *Blessed City, Heavenly Salem; Let all Mortal Flesh keep Silent.* IRELAND: *Greater Love hath No Man.* VAUGHAN WILLIAMS: *Whitsunday Hymn.* FINZI: *Welcome Sweet and Sacred Feast.* HOLST: *The Evening Watch.* HOWELLS: *Like as the Hart.*

Disc 2: HOWELLS (cont.): *Thee will I Love; Come my Soul.* WALTON: *Set Me as a Seal upon Thine Heart.* STEWART: *King of Glory, King of Peace.* ROSE: *O Praise ye the Lord.* JOUBERT: *O Lord the Maker of All Things.* BRITTEN: *Hymn to St Peter.* HARRIS: *Bring us, O Lord God.* HARVEY: *Come Holy Ghost; The Tree.* BERKELEY: *Thou has Made Me.* TAVENER: *Hymn to the Mother of God.* BENNETT: *Verses 1–3.* HARPER: *Salve Regina; Ubi caritas.* LEIGHTON: *Drop, Drop, Slow Tears; Give Me the Wings of Faith.*

☉ (BB) *** RRC 2031 (2).

If in Volume 1, fine though it is, the Magdalen Choir face competition from other specialist groups in the early music (which they meet admirably), in Volume 2, which spans the late nineteenth and twentieth centuries, they are unsurpassed. The remarkable range of music included is matched by the quality of performances, and one is again struck by the secure solo contributions by the unnamed treble soloists, for example at the opening of the beautiful and rejoicing closing anthem by Kenneth Leighton, *Give Me the Wings of Faith*.

The opening unaccompanied works by Stanford and Parry readily demonstrate the vocal riches of the Victorian era, while Charles Wood uses the organ to underpin his exultant *Hail Gladdening Light*, with its lively antiphonal interplay for two four-part choirs. Dr Harper's notes make a special case for what he calls the (relative) 'modernism' of Howells, here eloquently represented, suggesting he is still underestimated (but not by us). Bairstow's *Blessed City, Heavenly Salem*, is less familiar than *Let all Mortal Flesh keep Silence*, but no less impressive. Vaughan Williams's *Whitsunday Hymn* is comparably memorable, as are the contributions of Finzi and the harmonically lavish *Evening Watch* of Holst, which seems to anticipate the later music of John Tavener.

The second disc opens tellingly with Walton's wedding anthem (which draws on the *Song of Songs*), but the following settings by Stewart, Joubert (harmonically tangy) and Rose, the latter joyfully spirited, and the more restrained Harris, are no less individual. Bennett's *Three Verses* (of John Donne) open radiantly but establish their cool beauty with relatively austere harmony. Lennox Berkeley's *Thou has Made Me* is also a setting of Donne. It opens and closes wistfully, but has a forceful central section in which the organ participates strongly. But it is in Jonathan Harvey's *The Tree* that the organ is used (in its upper range) with striking imagination, creating an atmosphere for this poignant setting (for trebles alone) within the framework of a 12-note chromatic pitch series. *Come Holy Ghost*, a set of variations on the Pentecost Hymn, is hardly less arresting, with its complex writing for up to sixteen independent vocal lines.

Edward Harper's Latin settings were written for the Magdalen Choir and their overlapping part-writing hauntingly makes use of the cathedral resonance. He uses plainsong melodies as a source of inspiration and although the harmonic style is comparatively avant garde, these works look back to the very roots of English church music. They bring a powerfully committed response from the Magdalen Choristers and the whole programme is superbly sung and recorded in what is surely an ideal acoustic.

Matteuzzi, William (tenor)

'*Fermé tes yeux*': Arias, duets and ensembles (with Scano, Cullagh, Shkosa, Ford, Wood, Geoffrey Mitchell Choir, ASMF, Parry) from ADAM: *Le Postillon de Longjumeau.* AUBER: *La Muette de Portici.* CARAFA: *Gabriella di Vergi.* DONIZETTI: *Il castello di Kenilworth; La Fille du regiment.* OFFENBACH: *Le Pont des soupirs.* PACINI: *Alessandro nell' Indie.* ROSSINI: *Le Comte Ory; Il viaggio a Reims.*

*** Opera Rara ORR 216.

The title for this intensely imaginative recital, '*Fermé tes yeux*', comes from Masaniello's aria in Auber's opera, best known through its overture. What is striking about this selection of items (with the choice master minded by the sponsor, Peter Moores) is that only three items out of the nine are solo arias. The ensembles just as much as the arias brilliantly exploit Matteuzzi's glorious tenor, honey-toned even up to the highest register. That register is spectacularly in evidence in the best-known item here, the Postilion's song from Adam's opera (done with more character than in the classic versions of Roswaenge and Gedda), but just as winning is the opening item, the hilarious Act II trio from *Le Comte Ory*, with Matteuzzi the most seductive Count. The beauty of Matteuzzi's timbre is well contrasted with the more sinewy tenor of Bruce Ford in the Carafa duet, every one of these items brings illumination, both for the music and for the singing. Strong, well-paced conducting from David Parry and full, brilliant recording.

McKellar, Kenneth (tenor)

'*The Decca Years 1955–1975*': TRAD., arr. KENNEDY-FRASER: *Kishmul's galley; An island sheiling song; The Christ-child's lullaby; The peat fire flame; To people who have gardens; Skye fisher's song; Sleeps the noon in the clear blue sky; An Eriskay love lilt.* TRAD., arr. SHARPLES; *An island sheiling song; Wi' a hundred pipers; The De'ils awa' wi' the exciseman; There was a lad was born in Kyle; Mary Morison; Ye banks and braes; Ca the Ewes.* TRAD.. arr. KNIGHT: *Think on me; Ae fond kiss* (with Patricia Cahill); *Kalinka.* TRAD., arr. ROBERTON: *Dream Angus; Lewis bridal song.* TRAD., arr. STANFORD: *Trottin' to the fair.* TRAD., arr. BRITTEN; *Down by the Sally Gardens.* TRAD., arr. HUGHES: *She moved thro' the fair.* TRAD., arr. LAWSON: *Skye boat song.* FARNON: *Country girl.* DI CAPUA: *O sole mio.* HANDEL: *Xerxes: Ombra mai fù. Acis and Galatea: Love in her eyes sits playing.* MASSENET: *Manon: En fermant les yeux (Dream song).* BIZET: *The Fair maid of Perth: Serenade.* ELLIS: *This is my lovely day* (with Patricia Cahill). ANKA: *The longest day.* HOPPER: *By the short cut to the Rosses.* DONIZETTI: *L'elisir d'amore: Una furtiva lagrima.* MENDELSSOHN: *On wings of song.* BOUGHTON: *The Immortal hour: Faery song.* MURRAY: *I'll walk beside you.* SPEAKS: *On the road to Mandalay.* HARTY: *My lagen love.* BOCK: *Sunrise, sunset.* BERNSTEIN: *West Side story: Maria.* LAUDER: *Roamin' in the gloamin'.* GOULAY: *Song of the Clyde.* BANNERMAN, arr. ROBERTON: *Uist tramping song.* MURDOCH: *Hame o'mine.* OGILVIE: *Hail Caledonia.* SCHUBERT: *Great is Jehova.* TRAD., arr. MCPHEE: *I to the hills.* arr. WALFORD DAVIES: *God be in my head* (all three with Paisley Abbey Choir, George McPhee). LEMON: *My ain folk.* TRAD., arr. KNIGHT: *Will ye no come back again.*

(M) *** Decca (ADD) 466 415-2 (2).

Both artistically and vocally, Kenneth McKellar's lovely singing of Scottish folksongs can be ranked alongside Count John McCormack's instinctive response to similar Irish melodies. Like McCormack, he had a natural feeling for their simplicity of line, and his artless phrasing and ravishingly beautiful upper range, together with splendid diction, and a spirited sense of fun, made him a uniquely gifted exponent, whether the song be lyrical or rhythmically catchy in its ready tunefulness. The sparkling *Lewis bridal song* was a BBC radio hit at one time, although the voice reproduces curiously here in this particular number. But McKellar's range was far wider than that.

Early in his career he played the Count in Rossini's *Barber of Seville* with the touring Carl Rosa Opera Company and, as Donizetti's *Una furtiva lagrima* shows, he could certainly spin an Italian lyric melody. But even finer is the delightful *Faery song* from *The Immortal hour*, and the *Dream song* from *Manon* brings a comparable delicacy of feeling and lovely tone. He could sing a sentimental ballad like *I'll walk beside you* with real style, and every word is clear in *The Road to Mandalay*. The duets with the charming soubrette Patricia Cahill show him in even lighter vein, while *God be in my head* (recorded in Paisley Abbey) has a touching combination of warmth and sincerity.

He was pretty good too at an Irish inflection. *Trottin' to the fair*, *By the short cut to the Rosse*, the memorable *My lagen love*, and (especially) the touching, unaccompanied *She moved thro' the fair* are splendid examples of his art. But it is the Scottish repertoire for which he will be uniquely remembered, and in which he had no peer, and this extremely generous concert ends very appropriately with *Will ye no come back again*. Accompaniments (often by Bob Sharples) are mostly well managed, the CD transfers are good and the set has an interesting extended reminiscence by McKellar's producer, Raymond Herricks.

'**Kenneth McKellar's Scotland - Sleeps the noon in the clear blue sky**' (with accompaniments directed by Robert Sharples): Disc 1: '*Songs of the Hebrides*' (arr. KENNEDY-FRASER): *Sleeps the noon in the clear blue sky; The peat fire flame; Land of heart's desire; The reiving ship; Aignish of the Machair; A fairy's love song; Skye fisher's song; A Clyde-side love lilt; Heart of fire love; Sea longing; To the people who have gardens; The Bens of Jura; The Birlinn of the White shoulders; Isle of my heart; Kirsteen; Ye Highlands and ye Lowlands.* '*Roamin' in the gloamin*': arr. KENNEDY-FRASER: *The road to the isles: An Eriskay love lilt; The cockle gatherer.* TRAD.: *Bonnie Mary of Argyle.* THOMSON: *The star o' Robbie Burns.* HANLEY: *Scotland the brave.* FOX: *Bonnie wee thing.* ROBERTON: *Westering home.* HUME: *Afton Water.* GOULAY: *Song of the Clyde.* LAUDER: *Roamin' in the gloami'; Keep right on to the end of the road.*

Disc 2: '*The Tartan*': TRAD.: *The March of the Cameron Men; Kishmul's Galley; The flowers of the forest; Lochnagar; Wi' a hundred pipers; Air Falalolo; An island sheiling song; Scots wha ha'e wi' Wallace bled.* SMITH: *Jessie, the flower of Dunblane.* SCOTT: *Annie Laurie.* MCKELLAR: *The Tartan; The Royal mile.* Folksongs (arr. SHARPLES): *McGregor's gathering; The Laird o'Cockpen; The bonnie Earl of Moray; O Gin I were a baron's heir; Turn ye to me; Hey, Johnny Cope; Ho-ro, my nut-brown maiden; Bonnie Strathyle; The wee Cooper o'Fife; Isle of Mull; A pair of nicky tams; The proud peaks of Scotland; Auld Lang Syne.*

🌑 *** Australian Decca 844 840-2 (2).

Concurrently with the wider coverage above, Australian Decca have issued a second two-CD collection, entirely devoted to the finest of Kenneth McKellar's Scottish repertory. It is compiled from his most beautiful LP, '*Songs of the Hebrides*', plus three others, '*Folk songs from Scotland's heritage*' with much of the programme dealing with Scotland's colourful history, '*The Tartan*', which is essentially a collection of Scottish popular genre songs, with elaborately arranged accompaniments, and '*Roamin' in the gloamin*', McKellar's first stereo recital. This was recorded early in his career, when the voice was at its peak, with a marvellous freshness and bloom.

His simple presentation has a natural, spontaneous warmth and ardour, and the jaunty songs are most engagingly infectious, especially the wittily descriptive *Song of the Clyde*, with every word as clear as a bell. *Scotland the brave* and *Westering home* swing

along splendidly, and the slightly sentimental Burns setting *Bonnie wee thing* could not be more charming. McKellar also includes the two most famous songs of his illustrious predecessor, Sir Harry Lauder, ending with a bold account of *Keep right on to the end of the road* of which that famous Scotsman would have surely approved. The orchestral arrangements here are nicely judged and show none of the inflation that marks the 'Tartan' collection, which is still very enjoyable for a' that.

But it is the ravishingly lovely collection of Hebridean songs which earns the set its Rosette. It opens with the sound of surf on sand, and this evocation returns between the items, many of which McKellar introduces himself, warmly and intimately. The lovely opening title song is followed by *The Peat fire flame*, sung with the lightest rhythmic touch, and then comes the most beautiful song of all, *Land of heart's desire*.

Here the voice is slightly backwardly balanced, and McKellar's gently curving upward line is utterly melting. The melancholy *Aignish of the Machair* is another highlight and *The Fairy lover* (charmingly introduced) brings a delightful, lilting melody. Throughout, the accompaniments are delicately scored, often using pipes, and the voice itself is most naturally caught. But all these CD transfers are superb, the quality enhanced over the original LPs. Like the other Australian Decca issues, this set can be obtained to special order from the address given in the Introduction.

Mera, Yoshikazu (counter-tenor), Bach Collegium Japan, Masaaki Suzuki

Baroque arias: J. S. BACH: *Cantatas Nos. 12: Wir müssen durch viel Trübsal; Krenz und krone; 54: Widerstehe doch der Sünde; Die art verruchter Sünde; Wer Sünde tut; 132: Ich will, mein Gott; Christi Glieder, ach bedenket; 161: Komm, du süsse Todesstunde; Mein Jesus, lass mich nicht; In meinem Gott.* HANDEL: *Messiah: But who may abide; He was despised; Thou art gone up on high; Behold, a virgin; O Thou that tellest.* ahle: *Prima pars; Secunda pars.* SCHUTZ: *Geistliche chormusik, Op. 11: Auf dem Gebirge hat man ein geschrei gehört.*

*** BIS CD 919.

The Japanese counter-tenor Yoshikazu Mera is one of the most impressive soloists on Suzuki's excellent recordings of choral works for BIS. This compilation drawn from various sources consistently displays his exceptionally sweet and even tone, even though his performances are not very sharply characterized. The voice is set against a helpfully reverberant acoustic.

Metropolitan Opera (artists from)

'**Metropolitan Opera Gala**': Arias from BIZET: *Les Pêcheurs de perles* (Roberto Alagna; Bryn Terfel). G. CHARPENTIER: *Louise* (Renée Fleming). GOUNOD: *Faust* (Samuel Ramey; Plácido Domingo); *Roméo et*

Juliette (Ruth Ann Swenson). LEHAR: *Giuditta* (Ileana Cotrubas). VERDI: *Don Carlos* (Dolora Zajick). MOZART: *Don Giovanni* (Fleming, Terfel, Jerry Hadley, Kiri Te Kanawa, Hei-Kyung Hong, Julien Robbins). JOHANN STRAUSS JR: *Die Fledermaus* (Håkan Hagegård; Karita Mattila). MASSENET: *Werther* (Alfredo Kraus). SAINT-SAENS: *Samson et Dalila* (Grace Bumbry). WAGNER: *Tannhäuser* (Deborah Voight). OFFENBACH: *La Périchole* (Frederica von Stade). RICHARD STRAUSS: *Der Rosenkavalier* (Fleming, Anne Sofie Von Otter, Heidi Grant Murphy). *Tribute to James Levine* (Birgit Nilsson).

**(*) DG 449 177-2; Video VHS 072 451-3.

Recorded live at James Levine's twenty-fifth anniversary gala in April 1996, this offers an extraordinary galaxy of stars, often teamed up in unexpected ways - as, for example, Alagna and Terfel in the first item, the *Pearl fishers* duet. The singers represented a range from such relative newcomers as those rising stars to veterans like Alfredo Kraus and Grace Bumbry. Few of the voices are heard at their very finest, not helped by a rather hard acoustic, but the variety of party pieces here is enough of a delight. The video re-creates the occasion the more satisfactorily, but it is worth hearing the disc for the end of Birgit Nilsson's speech, involving a shattering cry of 'Hojotoho!'.

Miles, Alastair (bass)

Arias and ensembles, sung in English, with Ch. and Philh. O, Parry), from: VERDI: *The Lombards at the First Crusade; Luisa Miller; Nabucco; The Sicilian Vespers.* ROSSINI: *Mohamet II; Moses in Egypt; Zelmira.* BELLINI: *Norma; The Puritans.* GOMES: *Salvator Rosa.*

(M) *** Chan. 3032.

Alastair Miles here formidably enhances his reputation as a powerful recording artist, exploiting his firm, well-focused bass in a wide range of 11 arias and ensembles, starting with the *Chorus of Hebrew Slaves* from *Nabucco*, which then leads into Miles's noble and sonorous account of Zaccaria's Prophecy. The biting incisivensss of that and much else, as for example the protagonist's aria from *Mahomet II*, is thrilling, and he is well matched in the duets from *Luisa Miller* and *I Lombardi* by his fellow bass, Clive Bayley, crisply dramatic in their exchanges. Garry Magee is also a fine foil in the final long excerpt from *I puritani*. All but the *Nabucco* item have never been recorded in English before, and the clarity of diction adds to the intensity. There are excellent sound and understanding direction from David Parry.

Minstrelsy

'Songs and dances of the Renaissance and Baroque' (Carole Hofsted-Lee (soprano), Nancy Froseth, David Hays, David Livingstone (viola da gamba, baroque violin, recorders), Philip Rukavina (lute, archlute): SIMPSON: *Ballet.* ANON.: *2 Ballets; Mascarada; Volta.* arr. MCLACHLAN: *When she cam ben, she bobbat.* PRAETORIUS: *Dances from Terpsichore* (suite). PACHELBEL: *Partita in C.* SALAVERDE: *Canzon a 2.* LAWES: *Suite in G min.* Songs: ROSSETER: *When Laura smiles.* DOWLAND: *I saw my lady weep; Shall I sue.* ARNE: *Under the greenwood tree.* CAMPION: *It fell upon a summer's day.*

*** Lyrichord LEMS 8018.

A most entertaining, lightweight consort, full of life and charm, although one wonders if Renaissance and Baroque musicians could have achieved such sophistry of intonation, blending and playing! The period instruments here are made to integrate smoothly and without any rough edges. The singing of Carole Hofsted-Lee too is pure in tone and line. She is naturally at home in the simplicity of Arne, and her lovely voice caresses the songs of Dowland and Campion with considerable feeling, even if her range of vocal colour is less intense than that of, say, Alfred Deller. There is much to delight in the instrumental music.

Some half-a-dozen of the ensemble pieces come from the *Taffel-Consort*, published by Thomas Simpson in 1621, a collection which has much in common with Praetorius's *Terpsichore*. John McLachlan's *When she cam ben, she bobbat* is very Scottish, a treble to a ground, with sparkling divisions. But perhaps the highlight is Pachelbel's *Partita*, which is not unlike his more famous Canon in making use of an ostinato bass, but is a more elaborate chaconne, with a dozen variations. The recording is beautifully balanced to match this sprightly and elegant music-making.

Miricioiu, Nelly (soprano)

'Bel canto portrait': Scenes (with Plazas, Holland, Coote, Wood, Janes, Geoffrey Mitchell Ch., LPO. or Philh O, Parry) from: MERCADANTE: *Emma d'Antiochia.* COSTA: *L'assedio di Corinto.* DONIZETTI: *Belisario; Parisina.*

*** Opera Rara ORR 217.

The Romanian soprano Nelly Miricioiu, now resident in London, gives a formidable display of both technique and dramatic flair in this fascinating collection of rare arias and scenes from *bel canto* operas of the 1830s. Hers is not just a flexible voice but also one with plenty of character, full and vibrant with a good cutting edge and occasional echoes of Callas. Thanks to the researches of Jeremy Commons, who provides excellent notes as supplement to the full texts, these long-buried pieces are revealed as far more than merely conventional examples of the genre. The aria from *L'assedio di Corinto*, one of Rossini's operas, was written by Sir Michael Costa as an alternative aria for the heroine, Pamira, when it was sung by the prima donna, Giulia Grisi, at the King's Theatre in London, where Costa was music director when he was a young man. The Mercadante and the extract from Donizetti's *Belisario* lead from the soprano's arias to impressive final ensembles, while most inspired of all is the aria from Donizetti's *Parisina*, which is fairly described by Commons as 'one of the most sustained and consistently beautiful flights of *bel canto* that Donizetti ever achieved'.

Mitchell, Leona (soprano)

Arias (with New Philh. O, Adler) from: MOZART: *Le nozze di Figaro.* PUCCINI: *La Bohème; Gianni Schicchi; Madama Butterfly; La Rondine; Turandot.* MASCAGNI: *L'amico Fritz.* ROSSINI: *William Tell.* VERDI: *Ernani.*

** (*) Australian Decca Eloquence (ADD) 466 903-2.

It's good to have this 1980 recital, Leona Mitchell's debut LP, back in the catalogue – the first time on CD. Its appeal is in its freshness, with her naturally dark vocal colouring most appealing. The charming *La Rondine* aria (*Il bel sogno di Doretta*) is a highlight, as is the gentle lilt she finds in the final *Ernani* aria (*Ernani! Ernani, involami*). *Dove sono* is movingly done, and the reverie-like aria from *L'amico Fritz* is lovely too. There is nothing here to mar one's enjoyment, and it is the lyrical moments on this recital that are particularly memorable. The recorded sound is rich and full, though the disc has a short playing time.

Montague, Diana (mezzo-soprano)

'Bella imagen': Arias, duets and ensembles (with Kenny, Ford, Lewis, Geoffrey Mitchell Ch., ASMF, Philh or RPO, Parry) from BENEDICT: *l'inganno felice.* DONIZETTI: *Zoraida di Granata.* MAYR: *Alfredo Grande.* MERCADENTE: *Amleto.* MEYERBEER: *Il crociato di Egitto.* MOSCA: *Le bestie in uomini.* PAER: *Sofonisba.* ROSSINI: *Il trionfo di Quinto Fabio.* VON WINTER: *Zaira.*

*** Opera Rara ORR 210.

Who ever would have thought that Mayr had written an opera about Alfred the Great or that Mercadante had written one about Hamlet? The answer is: those who have been collecting the brilliant series from Opera Rara, '100 Years of Italian Opera', with each decade covered separately. Diana Montague has been a regular contributor, and this compilation of her outstanding recordings is very welcome indeed. Although the recordings were made over a wide period, from 1983 to 1998, the clear, firm voice remains gloriously consistent throughout – as Hugh Canning says in his note, with not only 'the voluptuous warmth of a mezzo, but the shining top of a true soprano'. The title, 'Bella imagen', comes from the Benedict opera, in a 1994 recording that illustrates those qualities perfectly, and one of the 1983 recordings, of the heroine's aria from Von Winter's *Zaira*, had previously demonstrated what dramatic dedication she naturally conveys. Diana Montague has made far too few recordings, but this splendidly fills an important gap, with David Parry providing strong support, mainly with the Philharmonia.

Monteverdi Choir, John Eliot Gardiner

'Once as I Remember ... (The Story of Christmas)' (with cornetts and sackbuts, recorder, drum): COWPER: *Gloria in excelsis Deo.* PLAINSONG: *Ave Maria, gratia plena.* TRAD.: *Angeles ad Virginem; Jolly Shepherd; Past Three o'clock; There is No Rose of Such Virtu; Once as I Remember; The King of all Kings* (English carols); *Entre le boeuf; Psalite* (French carols); *Gabriel's Message* (Basque carol); *Est ist ein Ros' entsprungen* (German); *Guillô, pran ton tamborin* (Provençal) *The Cradle* (Austrian). PALESTRINA: *Alma Redemptoris Mater.* BASSANO: *Hodie Christus natus est.* PIETERSON: *Hodie Christus est.* BARDOS: *Ave maris stella.* HOWELLS: *A Spotless Rose.* BYRD: *O magnum mysterium; Lullaby.* SCHUTZ: *Ach Herr, Du Schöpfer.* Arr. VAUGHAN WILLIAMS: *This Endris Night.* DERING: *Quem vivistis pastores?* TAVENER: *The Lamb.* WALTHER: *Joseph lieber, Joseph mein.* GARDINER: *Entry of the Three Kings* (with John Anderson, cor anglais). ARMSTRONG: *Ring Out ye Crystal Spheres.* WEELKES: *Gloria in excelsis Deo.*

*** Ph. 462 050-2.

Gardiner's 'Story of Christmas', among the finest and most imaginatively varied of all carol collections, remembers a nativity play performed by the Gardiner family each year at Fontmell Magna, Dorset. The programme is arranged to follow the Christmas story, from the Annunciation and Birth to the Adoration of the Magi, with a closing Epilogue of recessional hymns by Robert Armstrong and Thomas Weelkes. The radiant opening *Gloria in Excelcis Deo* of Robert Cowper leads to a series of enchanting regional carols, often very simple, contrasting with more spectacular renaissance settings with brass from Bassano and Sweelinck. Byrd's radiant *O magnum mysterium* is all but upstaged by his own beautiful echoing *Lullaby* and it is fascinating to realise that memorable tunes like *Joseph lieber Joseph mein, Es ist ein Ros' entsprungen* and *There is No Rose of Such Virtu* go back at least as far as the sixteenth century. Among modern settings, Tavener's serene *The Lamb* is an obvious choice, but Gardiner's own *Entry of the Three Kings*, with its haunting cor anglais obbligato, is almost as memorable. The singing is glorious throughout – full of joy, and the recording in the demonstration bracket.

'Música española'

'Música española': Canciones: GRANADOS: *Goyescas: La maja y el ruiseñor.* FALLA: *La vida breve: Vivan los que rien; Allí está, riyendo.* TURINA: *Canto a Sevilla* (Pilar Lorengar, SRO, López Cobos). GRANADOS: *9 Tonadillas; 3 Majas dolorosas; 6 Canciones amatorias* (with Alicia de Larrocha). OBRADORS: *5 Canciones clásicas españolas* (Kiri Te Kanawa, Roger Vignoles). FALLA: *7 Spanish popular* *songs.* NIN: *4 Villancicos españoles* (Marilyn Horne, Martin Katz). GURIDI: *Cómo quieres que adivine; Mañanita de San Juan.* LAVILLA: *4 Canciones vascas.* TURINA: *Saeta en forma de salve; Farruca* (Teresa Berganza, Félix Lavilla).

(B) ** Double Decca ADD/DDD 433 917-2 (2).

With a celebrated Spanish soprano, accompanied in Granados by the most vividly characterful of Spanish pianists or, alternatively, by the highly sympathetic López-Cobos, and the Suisse Romande Orchestra providing a vivid orchestral backcloth in Falla and Turina, the casting might seem ideal. But Pilar Lorengar's tone, seldom perfectly steady, has grown slacker with the years and her vibrato more intrusive. Thanks to de Larrocha, Spanish fire is rarely lacking, but the partnership is unequal.

Granados's *La maja y el ruiseñor* is comparatively voluptuous, but too often the singing is squally and uncomfortable. Turina's *Canto a Sevilla* is a song cycle framed by an orchestral introduction and epilogue, with a central interlude: these are omitted here. Lorengar sings vibrantly, but again her voice hardens to shrillness under pressure, and the bold vibrato means that the pitch is not always perfectly focused. However, lyrical charm is certainly present when Kiri Te Kanawa (partnered by Roger Vignoles) contributes Fernando Obradors's *5 Canciones clásicas españolas*.

But the highlight of the set comes on the second disc, with the vibrant mezzo of Marilyn Horne. She sings Falla's *7 Canciones populares españolas*, and *4 Villancicos españoles* of Joaquín Nin, with real flamenco fire, and yet can be just as lyrically appealing as Te Kanawa. Her accompanist, Martin Katz, gives strong support. Teresa Berganza (with Félix Lavilla at the piano) then charms the listener with two of Guridi's *Canciones castellanas*, including the tenderly sung *Mañanita de San Juan*, four of Lavilla's own charming *Canciones vascas*, and two memorably contrasted songs by Turina.

Nash, Heddle (tenor)

'*Serenade*': Arias from: BIZET: *The Fair Maid of Perth; The Pearl fishers.* ROSSINI: *The Barber of Seville.* MOZART: *Don Giovanni; Le nozze di Figaro* (both sung in Italian). BALFE: *The Bohemian Girl.* LEHAR: *Frederica.* OFFENBACH, arr. KORNGOLD: *La belle Hélène.* GOUNOD: *Faust.* DONIZETTI: *Elixir of love.* HANDEL: *Judas Maccabaeus.* MASSENET: *Manon.* Songs: TRAD. *Annie Laurie* (all with orch.). BENEDICT: *Eily Mavoureen.* BISHOP: *The bloom is on the rye.* MORGAN: *My sweetheart when a boy.* MCGEOCH: *Two eyes of grey.* MACDOWELL: *To a wild rose.* WHITAKER: *Diaphenia.* DELIUS: *To the queen of my heart; Love's philosophy.* WHITE: *To Mary.* MOERAN: *Diaphenia; The sweet o' the year* (all with Gerald Moore).

(M) (**(*)) ASV mono CDAJA 5227.

Although there are a few (obvious) duplications, this ASV compilation nicely supplements the finer Dutton Lab. collection below. The transfers of the orchestral accompaniments, which often sound boxy and confined, are much less sophisticated, but the voice emerges naturally, even if it is projected with less uniform vividness. But there are genuine treasures here, not least the songs, with Gerald Moore, who is more faithfully caught. The delightful *To a wild rose*, the Delius and Moeran songs and the splendid excerpt from *Judas Maccabaeus* are among the highlights.

'*The incomparable Heddle Nash*': PUCCINI: *La Bohème, Act IV* (complete; with Lisa Perli, Brownlee, Alva, Andreva, LPO, Beecham). Arias from: MOZART: *Così fan tutte* (with Ina Souez); *Don Giovanni* (all in Italian). ROSSINI: *The Barber of Seville.* VERDI: *Rigoletto.* BIZET: *The Fair Maid of Perth.* JOHANN STRAUSS JR: *Die Fledermaus* (with Dennis Noble) (all in English).

(M) (***) Dutton Lab. mono CDLX 7012.

Once again Dutton Laboratories provide incomparable transfers from 78s – of such quality that Beecham's extraordinarily theatrical (1935) Act IV of *La Bohème*, sung in Italian, communicates like a modern recording. Heddle Nash sings ardently, but Lisa Perli (Dora Labette) as Mimì is equally touching and, if the rest of the cast are less distinctive, Beecham's direction carries the day. Nash's four Mozart recordings (also sung in Italian) are included, notably the 1929 *Il mio tesoro*. Most cherishable of all is the *Serenade* from *The Fair Maid of Perth* from 1932, but there is some very striking Verdi in English, full of flair (in spite of awkward words), and a sparkling Johann Strauss duet with Dennis Noble. It seems carping to point out that, with only 69 minutes, there would have been room for more. But what there is is technically state of the art.

New College, Oxford, Choir, Higginbottom

'*Carols from New College*': *O come, all ye faithful; The angel Gabriel; Ding dong! merrily on high; The holly and the ivy; I wonder as I wander; Sussex carol; This is the truth; A Virgin most pure; Rocking carol; Once in Royal David's city.* ORD: *Adam lay y-bounden.* Richard Rodney BENNETT: *Out of your sleep.* HOWELLS: *A spotless rose; Here is the little door.* DARKE: *In the bleak midwinter.* MATHIAS: *A babe is born; Wassail carol.* WISHART: *Alleluya, A new work is come on hand.* LEIGHTON: *Lully, lulla, thou little tiny child.* JOUBERT: *There is no rose of such virtue.*

(M) *** CRD (ADD) CRD 3443.

A beautiful Christmas record, the mood essentially serene and reflective. Both the Mathias settings are memorable and spark a lively response from the choir; Howells' *Here is the little door* is matched by Wishart's Alleluya and Kenneth Leighton's *Lully, lulla, thou little tiny child* in memorability. Fifteen of the twenty-one items here are sung unaccompanied, to maximum effect. The recording acoustic seems ideal and the balance is first class. The documentation, however, consists of just a list of titles and sources – and the CD (using the unedited artwork from the LP) lists them as being divided onto side one and side two!

New Company, Harry Bicket

'*Sacred voices*': ALLEGRI: *Miserere.* LOBO: *Versa est in luctum.* PALESTRINA: *The Song of Solomon: Quae est ista; Descendit in hortum nocum; Quam pulchri sunt gressus tui; Duo ubera tue.* BYRD: *Haec dies.* PHILIPS: *Ascendit Deus.* MUNDY: *Vox Patris caelestis.* TALLIS: *Spem in alium* (40-part motet). DERING: *Factum est silentium.*

(M) *** Classic fm 75605 57029-2.

A splendid recording début for The New Company, a professional chamber choir of twelve, directed by Harry Bicket, which is expanded here to forty voices for a thrilling performance of Tallis's *Spem in alium*, one of the great masterpieces of Elizabethan music. The programme opens with a double choir version of Allegri's justly famous *Miserere*, with the second group atmospherically recessed alongside the confident soprano soloist, who soars up again and again to what the conductor calls that 'exquisitely floaty top C': and she hits the spot beautifully every time.

Then follows Lobo's hardly less ethereal *Versa est in luctum* and a characteristic sequence of four serenely flowing five-part motets from Palestrina's *Song of Solomon*, sensuously rich in harmonic implication, all written around 1583-4. Suddenly the mood changes and the pace quickens for William Byrd's *Haec dies*, with its joyful cross-rhythms and an exultant concluding *Alleluia*. Peter Philips's *Ascendit Deus* is similarly full of life and energy and it prepares the way for the contrasting three-part anthem by the lesser-known William Mundy. Its serene simplicity has great beauty, and it again offers a chance for a celestial soaring solo soprano.

After the climactic Tallis work, the programme ends with a short, but thrillingly jubilant, six-part Matins responsory by Richard Dering. The choir were recorded at Temple Church, London, the venue some ten decades earlier for one of the most famous choral recordings of all time: Mendelssohn's *Hear my Prayer*, with its famous solo from Master Ernest Lough, 'Oh for the wings of a dove'. The treble soloist here is a worthy successor.

New London Consort, Philip Pickett

'*The Pilgrimage to Santiago*' (21 cantigas from the collection of King Alfonso el Sabio).

*** O-L 433 148-2 (2).

Philip Pickett and his brilliant team of singers and players present what is described as 'a musical journey along the medieval pilgrim road to the shrine of St James at Santiago de Compostela'. The twenty-one pieces, lasting over two hours, together provide a mosaic of astonishing richness and vigour, directly related to the four main pilgrim routes to the shrine, via Navarre, Castile, Leon and Galicia.

Pickett argues the importance of the Islamic influence in Spain, with bells and percussion often added to the fiddles, lutes, tabors and other early instruments. So the long opening cantiga, *Quen a virgen ben servira*, begins with an instrumental introduction, where (echoing Islamic examples) the players attract attention with tuning-up and flourishes, before the singing begins. The main cantiga then punctuates the twelve narrative stanzas sung by the solo soprano with a catchy refrain, *Those who serve the virgin well will go to paradise*. Standing out among the singers is the soprano Catherine Bott, the soloist in most of the big cantigas, warm as well as pure-toned, negotiating the weird sliding portamentos that, following Islamic examples, decorate some of the vocal lines. Vivid sound, though the stereo spread of the chorus is limited.

Nilsson, Birgit (soprano)

'*The Singers*' (Decca series): Arias from: BEETHOVEN: *Fidelio.* WEBER: *Der Freischütz.* VERDI: *La forza del destino; Nabucco.* WAGNER: *Tristan und Isolde; Tannhäuser; Die Walküre* (with ROHCG, Downes or Quadri); *Götterdämmerung* (with Bayreuth Festival O, Boehm). Songs: ADAM: *O Holy Night.* FRANCK: *Panis angelicus.* GRUBER: *Silent Night* (with Levén, organ)

(M) **(*) Decca (ADD) 467 912-2.

The sheer power of Nilsson's voice is always impressive. These recordings date from the 1960s, and, with the exception of the Boehm *Götterdämmerung* items (both superb), which were recorded by Philips and DG respectively, the rest are Decca, and the sound is top drawer (the Decca ones are especially brilliant). Nilsson cuts through the textures with a knife-edge, not always sweet on the ear by any means, but usually thrilling and commanding. Occasionally she indulges herself in the deliberate flattening of notes (intended to soften tone colour), which can be distressing, but only in *Leise, leise* from *Der Freischütz* and the Verdi excerpts does her approach seem too wilful. *Pace pace*, too, is hard and unyielding, and these are the least agreeably sung items here, but the rest are very impressive indeed. As usual with this series, the texts and translation are available only via a CD ROM drive, along with a photo-gallery.

Nilsson, Birgit, & Kirsted Flagstad

(sopranos)

'**Land of the Midnight Sun**': Birgit Nilsson: SIBELIUS: *Demanten på marssnön; Flickan kom ifran sin alsklings mote; Höstkväll; Säv, Säv, Susa; Svarta rosor; Var deten drom; Våren flyktar hastigt.* GRIEG: *En svane; Fra monte pincio; Våren.*

RANGSTROM: *Bön till natten; En gammal dansrytm; Melodi; Sköldmön* (all with Vienna Opera Orchestra, Bokstedt). Kirsten Flagstad: EGGEN: *Aere det evige forår i livet.* ALNAES: *Februarmorgen ved Golfen; De hundrede fioliner; Nu brister alle de klofter; Vårlaengsler.* LIE: *Nykelen; Skinnvengbrev* (all with LSO, Oivin Fjelstad).

*** Australian Decca (ADD) 466 657-2.

The Birgit Nilsson items, recorded in the late 1950s, show her art at its most eloquent. One does not primarily think of Sibelius as a song composer, yet every one of the songs is memorable, often in a highly characteristic way. *Flickan kom ifran,* contemporary with the *Second Symphony,* has a power and dramatic passion with which any lover of Sibelius's orchestral music will find an immediate affinity. *Säv, Säv* too is especially imaginative in its creation of atmospheric tension, but all the songs offer something to the listener, and all are superbly sung. In the lighter Greig items, Nilsson shows loving affection, and though the Rangstrom songs are slighter in their quality, they are still rewarding.

Flagstad's contribution was recorded a few years later and is just as compelling: one can hear why she so spellbound listeners by her performances of songs in her first London recital in 1936. Any doubts about the size of the voice being too unwieldy for this comparatively intimate programme are swept away by the eloquence and commitment of the singing. Oivin Fjeldstad's contribution too is an outstanding one. Few of the songs are well-known but with such deeply-felt advocacy they are all worth getting to know. The recordings emerge warm and vivid in this transfer, and whilst texts are not provided (nor were they on their original LP releases), this Australian Eloquence CD comes complete with sleeve notes (written, unlike this entry, by our own R.L.). Alas, as an import it will cost more in the UK, but it is well worth it.

Norman, Jessye (soprano)

'*Diva*': Arias from WAGNER: *Tannhäuser; Der fliegende Holländer; Tristan und Isolde.* OFFENBACH: *Contes d'Hoffmann; La belle Hélène.* BERLIOZ: *Roméo et Juliette.*

(M) *** EMI (ADD) CDM5 65576-2.

This is a magnificent compilation, framed by four items from Jessye Norman's Wagner recital of 1987 with Klaus Tennstedt: Elisabeth's two arias from *Tannhäuser,* Senta's Ballad from *Der fliegende Holländer* and Isolde's Liebestod, all superb. Her formidable powers of characterization in tragedy and comedy alike are illustrated in the sequence of excerpts from Offenbach's *Contes d'Hoffmann* (four, including long-buried material from the Oeser Edition) and *La belle Hélène* (three), vocally flawless too. It is also good to have her Juliet represented, taken from Muti's otherwise flawed version of Berlioz's *Roméo et Juliette.*

More than with most issues in this well-planned 'Diva' series, it is a snag to have no texts provided.

Lieder and songs: SCHUBERT: *Dem Unendlichen; Der Winterabend; Auflösung.* WAGNER: *Wesendonck Lieder.* POULENC: *Tu vois le feu du soir; La fraîcheur et le feu, Nos. 1-7* (all with Irwin Gage). RAVEL: *Chanson de rouet; Si morne* (with Dalton Baldwin). Arias from: WAGNER: *Tristan und Isolde; Tannhäuser; Die fliegende Holländer.* BRAHMS: *Ein deutsches Requiem* (with LPO, Tennstedt). BERLIOZ: *Roméo et Juliette* (with Philadelphia Orchestra, Muti). OFFENBACH: *Les contes d'Hoffmann* (with Brussels Opera Orchestra, Cambreling).

(BB) *** Disky Royal Classics Vocal Double DDD/ADD DCL 703952 (2).

One snag for the compilers of this EMI anthology is having only a limited range of recordings to draw from. But this selection is comprehensive enough, with the Wagner Tennstedt items plus the *Wesendonck Lieder* (with piano), songs by Schubert, Poulenc and Ravel, plus a curious mixture of Brahms (from the Tennstedt *German Requiem*), Berlioz (the usual Juliet aria) and an ongoing selection from Offenbach's *Contes d'Hoffmann.* There are genuine treasures here and this is more comprehensive than the 'Diva' compilation above and costs less, but again no texts are provided.

Oberlin, Russell (counter-tenor)

'*Troubadour and trouvère songs*' Volume 1 (with Seymour Barab, viol): BRULE: *Cil qui d'amor me conseille.* DE BORNEIL: *Reis glorios, verais lums e clartatz.* DANIEL: *Chanson do - Ih mot son plan e prim.* D'EPINAL: *Commensmens de dolce saison bele.* RIQUIER: *Ples de tristor, marritz e doloires; de ventadour: Can vei la lauzeta mover.*

*** Lyrichord LEMS 8001.

It is good to see the legendary Russell Oberlin return to the catalogue. Older readers will recall his Covent Garden appearance as Oberon in Britten's *Midsummer Night's Dream.* Unfortunately his concert career was cut short and he has since pursued a distinguished career as a scholar. This 1958 recital of 'Troubadour and trouvère songs' first appeared on the Experiences Anonymes label and, like so many of his all-too-few recordings (including an incredible Handel aria disc), has long been sought after. This voice was quite unique, a real counter-tenor of exquisite quality and, above all, artistry. The disc is expertly annotated and is of quite exceptional interest. LEMS stands for Lyrichord Early Music Series, and the discs we have heard so far are artistically impressive.

'*Las Cantigas de Santa Maria*' (with Joseph Iadone, lute): *Prologo; Cantigas Nos. 7, 36, 97, 111, 118, 160, 205, 261, 330, 340 & 364.*

✪ *** Lyrichord LEMS 8003.

The 400 *Cantigas de Santa Maria,* all of which have music, come from the time of Alfonso El Sabio, king of

Spain (1221–84). He is credited with being their composer, but that seems unlikely since they are very diverse. The texts are in Galician, a language in general use in medieval Spain for literary and artistic purposes.

They are all concerned with miracles associated with the Virgin Mary, but the music itself has considerable variety and, while the basic style may come from European monodic chant, the melisma has a distinctly Spanish colouring, which in itself has Arab influences. The selection of a dozen items is very well made, for these simple strophic songs have an instant appeal when sung with such lyrical ease by the incomparable Russell Oberlin. The character of the *Cantigas* seems to suit his special timbre especially well, and he has made no finer record than this.

The recital opens with a Prologue in which the singer relates the qualities necessary to be a good troubadour and invokes the Virgin's acceptance of his skills with some confidence. Two of the settings are lively dance songs, Cantiga 36 telling how Mary appeared in the night on the mast of a ship journeying to Brittany and saved it from danger, and Cantiga 205 about the rescue of a Moorish woman with her child who were sitting on top of a tower which collapsed – yet neither she nor the child came to any harm. But it is the beauty of the lyrical music which is so striking, notably so in Cantigas 118 and 330, which are concerned with the restoration of a dead child to life and a simple song of praise for the Virgin herself. The recording is natural and vivid and, as with the other discs in this Series, the CD remastering by Nick Fritsch is first class. The content of this reissue is not generous in playing time, but it is of the very highest musical quality and interest.

'*Troubadour and trouvère songs*', Volume 5: *English medieval songs* (with Seymour Barab, viol): *The St Godric songs. Worldes blis ne last no throwe. Bryd one breve; Man mei longe him liues wene; Stond wel moder under rode.*

*** Lyrichord LEMS 8005.

The *St Godric Songs* are the earliest known songs in the English language. St Godric died in 1170, so they date from halfway through the twelfth century. The other items here belong to the latter part of the century. As with his first disc, above, Russell Oberlin is completely convincing in this repertoire, the purity of line and beauty of timbre consistently appealing. The accompanying viol is discreet and the sound is remarkably clear and vivid.

Opera choruses

'*Grand opera choruses*': VERDI: *Nabucco: Va pensiero (Chorus of the Hebrew slaves). Il Trovatore: Vedi! le fosche (Anvil chorus).* BEETHOVEN: *Fidelio: O welche Lust (Prisoners' chorus)* (Chicago Ch. & SO, Solti). BELLINI: *Norma: Squilla il bronzo del dio! … Guerra, guerra!* (Welsh Nat. Op. Ch. & O, Bonynge). WAGNER: *Lohengrin: Prelude to Act III and Bridal chorus. Tannhäuser: Pilgrims' chorus* (V.

State Op. Konzertvereinigung or V. State Op. Ch., VPO, Solti). GOUNOD: *Faust: Soldiers' chorus* (Ambrosian Op. Ch., LSO, Bonynge). PUCCINI: *Madama Butterfly: Humming chorus* (V. State Op. Ch., VPO, Karajan). LEONCAVALLO: *Pagliacci: I zampognari! … Don, din, don (Bell chorus)* (Santa Cecilia, Rome, Ac. Ch. & O, Gardelli). BIZET: *Carmen: Toreador chorus* (John Alldis Ch., LPO, Solti). WEBER: *Der Freischütz: Huntsmen's chorus.* NICOLAI: *Die lustigen Weiber von Windsor: O süsser Mond* (Bav. R. Ch. & O, Kubelik). BERLIOZ: *Les Troyens: Dieux protecteurs de la ville éternelle* (Montreal Schubert Ch. & SO, Dutoit). MUSSORGSKY: *Boris Godunov: Coronation scene* (Ghiaurov, V. Boys' Ch., Sofia R. Ch., V. State Op. Ch., VPO, Karajan).

(M) *** Decca DDD/ADD 458 205-2.

This 75-minute collection re-assembled for reissue in Decca's Opera Gala series is exceptional value and offers vivid, and often demonstration worthy sound throughout. Most of the excerpts come from distinguished complete sets, notably the *Pilgrims' chorus* from Solti's *Tannhäuser*, which has a memorable sense of perspective, while the *Lohengrin* excerpt is hardly less impressive. However, that also means that they are not always cleanly tailored and sometimes there are soloists too.

A high proportion of the items are from Solti, but other highlights include Karajan's *Humming chorus* from *Madama Butterfly*, which is so warmly atmospheric, and the expansive *Coronation scene* from *Boris Godunov*. Bonynge conducts the *War chorus* from *Norma* and the *Soldiers' chorus* from *Faust*. Since the disc's previous issue additional items have been added, notably the excerpts from *Der Freischütz* and Nicolai's *Merry Wives of Windsor* (from Kubelik) and the *Hymn of deliverance* from *Les Troyens* (Dutoit). Good documentation and translations are provided, an exception rather than the rule for this kind of operatic collection.

Opera love songs

'*Amor – Opera's great love songs*': VERDI: *Aida: Celeste Aida. Luisa Miller: Quando le sere al placido* (Pavarotti). *Rigoletto: Caro nome* (Sutherland). PUCCINI: *Gianni Schicchi: O mio babbino caro* (Tebaldi). *Manon Lescaut: Donna non vidi mai* (Carreras). *Tosca: Recondita armonia* (Corelli); *Vissi d'arte* (Kiri Te Kanawa); *E lucevan le stelle* (Domingo). *La Bohème: Musetta's waltz song* (Elizabeth Harwood). *Madama Butterfly: Un bel dì* (Mirella Freni). *Turandot: Signore ascolta!* (Caballé); *Nessun dorma* (Pavarotti). DONIZETTI: *La Favorita: O mio Fernando* (Cossotto). *L'elisir d'amore: Una furtiva lagrima. Fedora: Amor ti vieta.* PONCHIELLI: *La Giaconda: Cielo e mar.* MASSENET: *Werther: Pourquoi me réveiller* (all Pavarotti). BIZET: *Carmen: Habanera* (Troyanos);

Flower song (Domingo). MOZART: *Nozze di Figaro: Voi che sapete* (Frederica von Stade).

(M) *** Decca (ADD) 458 201-2.

Brimming over with stellar performances, this generous (76-minute) collection is a true 'Opera gala'. Pavarotti dominates and seldom lets us down, and he ends the disc with a thrilling performance of his great showpiece, *Nessun dorma*, from his complete set conducted by Mehta. Many of the other excerpts too are drawn from outstanding sets, including Caballé's beautiful *Signore ascolta!* (taken from the same source), Freni's passionately expansive *Un bel dì* from Karajan's *Madama Butterfly*, Domingo's outstanding *Flower song* and Troyanos's *Habanera*, both from Solti's *Carmen*, and Frederica von Stade's delightful *Voi che sapete*, taken from the same conductor's highly successful *Nozze di Figaro*. Tebaldi's ravishing *O mio babbino caro* dates from 1962 when the voice still had all its bloom, while Marilyn Horne's dark-voiced *Softly awakes my heart* comes from a 1967 recital. Nicely packaged in a slip case, the documentation includes full translations.

Otter, Anne Sofie von (mezzo-soprano)

'*Wings in the night*' (Swedish songs; with Bengt Forsberg, piano): PETERSON-BERGER: *Aspåkerspolska* (*Aspåker's polka*); *Aterkomst* (*Return*); *Böljeby-vals* (*Böljeby waltz*); *Like the stars in the sky* (*Som stjärnorna på himmeln*); *Marits visor* (3 songs, Op. 12*); *Nothing is like the time of waiting* (*Intet är som väntanstider*); *When I walk by myself* (*När jag går för mig själv*). SJOGREN: *6 Songs from Julius Wollf's Tannhäuser.* SIGURD VON KOCH: *In the month of Tjaitra* (*I månaden Tjaitra*); *Of lotus scent and moonshine* (*Af Lotusdoft och månens sken*); *The wild swans* (*De vilda svanarna*) (3 songs). STENHAMMAR: *Miss Blond and Miss Brunette* (*Jungfru blond och jungfru brunett*); *In the maple's shade* (*I lönnens skymning*); *Jutta comes to the Volkungs* (*Jutta kommer till Folkungarna*); *A seaside song* (*En strandvisa*); *A ship is sailing* (*Det far ett skepp*); *The wanderer* (*Vandraren*). RANGSTROM: *The farewell* (*Afskedet*); *Old Swedish* (*Gammalsvenskt*); *Melodi; Pan; Supplication to night* (*Bön till natten*); *Wings in the night* (*Vingar i natten*). ALFVEN: *The forest is asleep* (*Skogen sover*); *I kiss your white hand* (*Jag kysser din vita hand*).

✪ *** DG 449 189-2.

So often Swedish singers, once they have made a name for themselves in the world, neglect their native repertoire in favour of Schumann, Brahms, Strauss and Wolf. Anne Sofie von Otter is an exception and, fresh from her recent successes in Scandinavian repertoire, above all her Grieg *Haugtussa* and her Sibelius recitals on BIS, she gives us a splendid anthology of Swedish songs. The disc takes its name from one of Ture Rangström's most haunting songs, *Vingar i natten* (*Wings in the night*), and, indeed, his are some of the loveliest songs in the Swedish *romans* repertoire. (*Romans* is

the Nordic equivalent of *Lied.*) *Bön till natten* (*Supplication to the night*) is arguably the most beautiful of all Swedish songs and has the innocence and freshness of Grieg combined with a melancholy and purity that are totally individual.

Von Otter also includes songs by the composer-critic Wilhelm Peterson-Berger, whose criticism was much admired in his native Sweden and who was compared with Bernard Shaw (he is in fact an opinionated windbag) and whose songs have a certain wistful charm. The Stenhammar songs are among his finest, and von Otter adds some familiar Alfvén and less familiar repertoire by Emil Sjögren and Sigurd (not to be confused with Erland) von Koch. A disc to be treasured.

'*Folksongs*' (with Forsberg piano): DVORAK: *Gypsy Songs, Op. 55.* GRAINGER: *The Sprig of Thyme; Died for Love; British Waterside; The Pretty Maid Milkin' her Cow.* LARSSON: *Watercolour; The Box Painter; The Girl with the Divining Herb.* G. HAHN: *The Heart's Prey: A Song from Lapland.* R. HAHN: Songs in Venetian dialect: *On the Drowsy Waters; The Little Boat; The Warning; The Fair Maid in the Gondola; What a Shame!* KODALY: Hungarian folk music: *Little Apple Fell in the Mud; Drinking Wine on Sunday; Youth is Like a Falcon; Let No-one's Bride Bewail; All Through the Vineyard; Hey, the Price of Wine from Mohovce Hill; Beneath the Csitár Hills.* BRITTEN: arr. of French folksongs: *La Noël passée; Voice le printemps; La Fileuse; Le Roi s'en va-t'en chasse; La Belle est au jardin d'amour; Il est quelqu'un sur terre; Eho! Eho!; Quand j'etais chez mon père.*

*** DG 463 479-2.

An enterprising and rewarding recital from the great Swedish mezzo, this covers a wide range of songs from the Slavonic to Kodály and Britten rarities. Her impeccable artistry is given excellent support from Bengt Forsberg and the DG engineers.

Oxford Camerata, Jeremy Summerly

'*Lamentations*': WHITE: *Lamentations.* TALLIS: *Lamentations, Sets I & II.* PALESTRINA: *Lesson I for Maundy Thursday.* LASSUS: *Lessons I & III for Maundy Thursday.* ESTAVAO DE BRITO: *Lesson I for Good Friday.*

✪ (BB) *** Naxos 8.550572.

On the bargain Naxos label come nearly 70 minutes of sublime polyphony, beautifully sung by the fresh-toned Oxford Camerata under Jeremy Summerly. All these *Lamentations* (*Lessons* simply means collection of verses) are settings from the Old Testament book, *The Lamentations of Jeremiah.* They were intended for nocturnal use and are usually darkly intense in feeling. The English and Italian *Lamentations* have their own individuality, but the most striking of all is the

Good Friday Lesson by the Portuguese composer Estâvão de Brito. This is very direct and strong in feeling for, as the anonymous insert-note writer points out, Portugal was under Spanish subjugation at the time and de Brito effectively uses dissonance at the words *non est lex* ('there is no law') to assert his nationalistic defiance. The recorded sound is vividly beautiful within an ideal ambience.

Palmer, Felicity (soprano), John Constable (piano)

'*Love's old sweet song*': Victorian and Edwardian ballads: SULLIVAN: *My dearest heart.* HAYDN WOOD: *A Brown bird singing; Bird of love divine.* EDEN: *What's in the air today.* TRAVERS: *A Mood.* MOIR: *Down the vale.* SQUIRE: *If I might come to you.* BRAHE: *Two little words.* D'HARDELOT: *Three green bonnets.* EVERARD: *It's all right in the summertime.* MOLLOY: *Love's old sweet song.* SPEAKS: *Morning.* MURRAY: *I'll walk beside you.* SANDERSON: *The valley of laughter.* LAO SILESU: *Love, here is my heart.* LEHR: *Whatever is – is best.* BEHREND: *Daddy.*

(BB) *** Belart (ADD) 461 490-2.

The ear-catching item here is Everard's *It's all right in the summertime*, which Felicity Palmer delivers in true music-hall style with a cor-blimey Cockney accent. Even if the off-key piano postlude is also off-key (not matching the humour of the rest at all), the result is a glorious *tour de force* and sets the tone for one of the most warmly characterful recitals of its kind. These were all drawing-room songs which for decades were despised; now, in performances like these, their overtly sentimental charm can be enjoyed afresh as a delightful period offering, superbly accompanied by John Constable. The acoustic is reverberant, not like a drawing-room at all, but the sound is full and vivid.

Panzéra, Charles (baritone)

French and German Songs: FAURE: (i) *La bonne chanson, Op. 61; L'horizon chimérique; Au cimetière; En Sourdine.* DUPARC: *Extase; Lamento; L'invitation au voyage; Sérénade Florentine; La vie antérieure* (with Magda Panzéra-Baillot, piano). SCHUMANN: *Dichterliebe, Op. 48* (with Alfred Cortot, piano).

☻ (B) (***) Dutton mono CDBP 9726.

What a glorious voice – and apart from the tonal beauty, it is a joy to hear every syllable with such clarity. The Swiss-born French baritone, Charles Panzéra (1896–1976) was closely associated with Fauré's songs (and gave the first performance of *L'horizon chimérique*). During the 1930s when most of these records were made, he was the foremost interpreter of the French repertoire, and in particular Duparc, whose songs have a special eloquence. His selfless artistry is everywhere in evidence and not even Pierre Bernac or

Gérard Souzay surpass him. The Dutton transfers bring his voice to life as no others before them!

Paul Hofhaimer Consort, Salzburg, Michael Seywald

'*Fedelta d'amore*' (Music at the court of Salzburg): Motets, madrigals & dances by ANON.; GASTOLDI; SENFL; KOTTER; UNTERHOLZER; VECCHI; HOFHAIMER; PERKIN; BUCHNER; NEGRI.

(BB) *** Arte Nova 74321 61338-2.

Around 1600, the Archbishop's court in Salzburg was one of the great centres of European music, for which a range of composers, now half-forgotten, wrote not just religious but secular music like the twenty-one items here. Many are anonymous, with Paul Hofhaimer (1459–1537) providing five items and most of the others one each. Under Michael Seywald the talented group named after Hofhaimer give aptly vigorous, well-disciplined performances, with their impact heightened by the upfront sound, warm and intimate. An excellent bargain, offering one or two jewels like Ludwig Senfl's poignant lament, *Unsäglich Schmerz*.

Pavarotti, Luciano (tenor)

'*The Pavarotti Edition*'

Volume 1: DONIZETTI. Arias from: *Don Pasquale; La Fille du régiment; L'elisir d'amore; La Favorita; Linda di Chamounix; Lucia di Lammermoor; Maria Stuarda.* (ADD 470 001-2).

Volume 2: Arias from: BELLINI: *I Capuleti e i Montecchi; Beatrice di Tenda.* DONIZETTI: *Don Sebastiano; Il Duca d'Alba.* VERDI: *Norma; I puritani; La sonnambula; Attila; I due Foscari; Ernani; I Lombardi.* (ADD/DDD 470 002-2).

Volume 3: VERDI. Arias from: *Luisa Miller; Macbeth; Rigoletto; Il trovatore; La traviata; I vespri siciliani.* (ADD/DDD 470 003-2).

Volume 4: VERDI. Arias from: *Aida; Un ballo in maschera; Don Carlos; La forza del destino; Otello; Requiem.* (ADD/DDD) 470 004-2).

Volume 5: PUCCINI. Arias from: *La Bohème; Madama Butterfly; Turandot.* (ADD/DDD 470 005-2).

Volume 6: Arias from: PUCCINI: *Manon Lescaut; Tosca.* MASCAGNI: *Cavalleria rusticana.* LEONCAVALLO: *Pagliacci.* GIORDANO: *Andrea Chénier.* (ADD/DDD 470 006-2).

Volume 7: Arias from: A. SCARLATTI: *L'Onestà negli amori.* BONONCINI: *Griselda.* HANDEL: *Atalanta.* GLUCK: *Orfeo ed Euridice.* MOZART: *Così fan tutte; Don Giovanni; Idomeneo.* ROSSINI: *Guglielmo Tell; Stabat Mater.* Songs: CALDARA: *Alma del core.* CIAMPI: *Tre giorni son che Nina.* GIORDANI: *Caro mio ben.* MERCADANTE: *Qual giglio candido.* STRADELLA: *Pietà, Signora.* (ADD/DDD 470 007-2).

Volume 8: Arias from: FLOTOW: *Martha.* GOUNOD: *Faust.* MEYERBEER: *L'Africaine.* BOITO: *Mefistofele.* PONCHIELLI: *La Gioconda.* BIZET: *Carmen.* MASSENET: *Manon; Werther.* GIORDANO: *Fedora.* MASCAGNI: *Iris; L'amico Fritz.* CILEA: *Adriana Lecouvreur; L'Arlesiana.* PUCCINI: *La fanciulla del West.* R. STRAUSS: *Der Rosenkavalier.* PIETRI: *Maristella.* (ADD/DDD 470 008-2).

Volume 9: *Italian Songs:* DONIZETTI: *Il barcaiolo; Me voglio fà 'na casa.* ROSSINI: *La danza; La promessa.* BELLINI: *Malinconia, ninfa gentile; Vanne, o rosa fortunata.* LISZT: *Tre sonetti di Petrarca.* RESPIGHI: *Nebbie; Nevicata; Pioggia.* MASCAGNI: *Serenata.* LEONCAVALLO: *Mattinata.* TOSTI: *'A vucchella; Aprile; L'alba sepàra della luce l'ombra; Malia; Marechiare; Non t'amo più!; La serenata; L'ultima canzone* (also with BEETHOVEN: *In questa tomba oscura).* (ADD/DDD 470 009-2).

Volume 10: *Popular Italian and Neapolitan Songs:* DI CAPUA: *O Sole Mio.* CURTIS: *Non ti scordar di me; Torna a Surriento; Ti voglio tanto bene; Tu, ca nun chiagne; Voce'e notte!.* CARDILLO: *Core 'ngrato.* D'ANNIBALE: *'O paese d'o sole.* VALENTE: *Passione.* MARIO: *Santa Lucia luntana.* DENZA: *Funiculì funiculà.* CRESCENZO: *Rondine al nido.* BIXIO: *Mamma; La mia canzone al vento; Vivere.* MODUGNO: *Volare.* SIBELLA: *La Girometta.* MARTUZZI: *La Graunadora.* CASARINI: *Fra tanta gente.* MARIA FERILLI: *Un amore così grande.* LAZZARO: *Chitarra romana.* (ADD/DDD 470 010-2).

❂ (M) *** Decca (ADD/DD) 470 011-2 (10). (with Bonus CD: Arias from: PUCCINI: *La Bohème; Tosca.* VERDI: *Rigoletto).*

'The Pavarotti Edition' is a well-produced and comprehensive set (including several items new to CD), which offers good documentation, full texts and translations and excellent transfers. As the Donizetti items in the first volume show, Pavarotti quickly became a singer of impressive style as well as one with a honeyed tenor voice, and he soon carved a distinctive niche in the operatic world. The breadth of his achievement is well demonstrated here and surely earns him a ❂ for its range as well as its consistency.

Volumes 1 and 2 concentrate mainly on the bel canto recordings from the late 1960s and 1970s, celebrating his partnership with Joan Sutherland and Richard Bonynge. They include some of the finest things he has ever done in the studio, his stylish vocal production often demonstrating sparkling vivaciousness, as in the series of spectacular high Cs in his key aria from *La Fille du régiment,* or genuine feeling, as in his touching Nemorino in *L'elisir d'amore* where, for once, *Una furtive lagrima* is sensitive, not cloyingly sentimental. The 1976 *La sonnambula* excerpt makes its CD debut here.

The second volume includes excerpts from recital discs (with Downes and Abbado) from 1968, and an *I Lombardi* extract from 1996 with Levine – the voice not

so golden but remarkably intact after all those years. Verdi presides over volumes 3 and 4, again selected largely from Pavarotti's complete opera recordings. The *Rigoletto, Il trovatore* and *La traviata* selections come from the Bonynge sets, and he is particularly memorable as a characterful Duke in *Rigoletto.* The 'live' 1992 *Don Carlos* excerpt, which is borrowed from EMI, is an exciting performance by any standards. The *Un ballo in maschera* and *Otello* arias come from Solti's 1983 and 1991 sets, respectively, and usually show Pavarotti at his extrovert best.

The *La Bohème* and *Madama Butterfly* excerpts in volume 5 derive from Karajan's famous early 1970s Decca sets and find Pavarotti as an intensely imaginative Pinkerton and as a Rodolfo of comic flair and expressive passion. He is hardly less impressive in *Turandot,* as Calif in Mehta's classic 1972 set: rich-timbred and strong on detail.

The 1978 *Tosca* conducted by Rescigno on volume 6 proved to be less inspired, although he is back on form in his powerful 1992 portrayal of Des Grieux in *Manon Lescaut* (with Levine). The rest of the verismo performances again show Pavarotti at his most extrovert, if not always his most subtle, reluctant to sing anything other than loud. He is less at home in Mozart in volume 7: he even sounds a little strained at times and obviously is not really in tune with Mozartian sensibilities. But the rest of the excerpts are generally enjoyable, the baroque repertoire surprisingly so, with the simpler items, such as the minor-key *Tre giorni son che Nina,* coming across very effectively. The CD ends with a rousing *Guglielmo Tell* highlight.

A myriad sources is used for volume 8, although many are taken from Pavarotti's first digital recital LP in 1980. Here he is splendid in the breast-beating numbers, such as Des Grieux's plea in Act III of *Manon,* which has great emotional force. If some of the lighter numbers would benefit from a easier touch, a more blithe approach, in such arias as *M'appari* from *Martha* one is caught up in the vibrant ardour, and there are still plenty of things to enjoy.

The final two volumes are of inconsequential, yet highly tuneful repertoire. Volume 9 brings songs by Rossini, Donizetti and Bellini, which have a pleasing, easy charm, while the famous Tosti numbers are sung with all the Italian passion you could wish for – with rich orchestral accompaniments, too.

Volume 10 is mainly devoted to popular Neapolitan songs, given the grand treatment in ardent, forthright, very Italian performances, missing some of the charm, but none of the red-blooded fervour. The first 11 numbers are conducted by Guadagno, while the remaining ten are, more surprisingly, conducted by Henry Mancini in his own unashamedly popular and highly effective arrangements. Although memories of Di Stefano are not effaced, it is all very enjoyable.

The edition is perhaps not aimed at the general collector, but Pavarotti's admirers are well served. The complete set comes with an album of 76 colour photographs of Pavarotti's recording and operatic career, as well as a reproduction of his first Decca recording in its original 45rpm packaging – a nice idea, neatly done, which will make vintage aficionados feel very nostalgic. The original Penguin Review (of Decca 45 SEC 5532) said: 'As Italian tenors go Pavarotti is comparatively tasteful in the use of his voice, and although there are no special touches of imagination here, they are all clean and enjoyable performances, beautifully recorded'.

'The Singers' (Decca series): Arias from: GLUCK: *Orfeo ed Euridice.* DONIZETTI: *La Fille de régiment; Linda di Chamounix.* VERDI: *Aida; Otello.* PUCCINI: *Turandot.* Songs: BEETHOVEN: *In questa tomba oscura.* BELLINI: *Vaga luna.* DONIZETTI: *Me voglio fà'na casa.* TOSTI: *Aprile.* LEONCAVALLO: *Mattinata.* YON: *Gesù bambino.* BACH/GOUNOD: *Ave Maria.* ADAM: *O Holy Night.*

(M) *** Decca (ADD) 467 920-2.

Pavarotti was bound to feature in Decca's 'The Singers' series, and this CD concentrates on lighter repertoire, with popular Italian songs and charming Bellini and Donizetti items, including Tonio's fizzing aria *Ah! mes amis* from the classic *La Fille du régiment*, with its now almost legendary top Cs. The Verdi and Puccini arias balance the collection with more serious items. If the programme appeals, then this CD is recommendable, though much of the same repertoire appears in the 'Pavarotti Edition' which includes texts and translations, unlike this series, which requires the use of a CD ROM drive. Full, vivid sound in the Decca manner.

'Pavarotti's greatest hits': PUCCINI: *Turandot: Nessun dorma. Tosca: Recondita armonia; E lucevan le stelle. La Bohème: Che gelida manina.* DONIZETTI: *La fille du régiment: O mes amis … Pour mon âme. La Favorita: Spirito gentil. L'elisir d'amore: Una furtiva lagrima.* RICHARD STRAUSS: *Der Rosenkavalier: Di rigori armato.* LEONCAVALLO: *Mattinata.* ROSSINI: *La Danza.* DE CURTIS: *Torna a Surriento.* BIZET: *Carmen: Flower song.* BELLINI: *I Puritani: A te o cara; Vanne, O rose fortunata.* VERDI: *Il Trovatore: Di qual tetra … Ah, si ben mio; Di quella pira. Rigoletto: La donna è mobile; Questa o quella. Requiem: Ingemisco. Aida: Celeste Aida.* FRANCK: *Panis angelicus.* GOUNOD: *Faust: Salut! Demeure.* SCHUBERT: *Ave Maria.* LEONCAVALLO: *I Pagliacci: Vesti la giubba.* PONCHIELLI: *La Gioconda: Cielo e mar.* DENZA: *Funiculì, funiculà.*

*** Decca (IMS) (ADD) 417 011-2 (2).

This collection of 'greatest hits' can safely be recommended to all who have admired the golden beauty of Pavarotti's voice. Including as it does a fair proportion of earlier recordings, the two discs demonstrate the splendid consistency of his singing. Songs are included as well as excerpts from operas, including *Torna a Surriento, Funiculì, funiculà*, Leoncavallo's *Mattinata* and Rossini's *La Danza.* However, this is at premium price and there are plenty of less expensive collections.

'Tutto Pavarotti': VERDI: *Aida: Celeste Aida. Luisa Miller: Quando le sere al placido. La Traviata: De'*

miei bollenti spiriti. Il Trovatore: Ah si ben mio; Di quella pira. Rigoletto: La donna è mobile. Un ballo in maschera: La rivedrà nell'estasi. DONIZETTI: *L'elisir d'amore: Una furtiva lagrima. Don Pasquale: Com'è gentil.* PONCHIELLI: *La Gioconda: Cielo e mar.* FLOTOW: *Martha: M'appari.* BIZET: *Carmen: Flower song.* MASSENET: *Werther: Pourquoi me réveiller.* MEYERBEER: *L'Africana: O paradiso.* BOITO: *Mefistofele: Dai campi, dai prati.* LEONCAVALLO: *Pagliacci: Vesti la giubba.* MASCAGNI: *Cavalleria rusticana: Addio alla madre.* GIORDANO: *Fedora: Amor ti vieta.* PUCCINI: *La Fanciulla del West: Ch'ella mi creda. Tosca: E lucevan le stelle. Manon Lescaut: Donna non vidi mai. La Bohème: Che gelida manina. Turandot: Nessun dorma.* ROSSINI: *Stabat Mater: Cuius animam.* BIZET: *Agnus Dei.* ADAM: *O holy night.* DI CAPUA: *O sole mio.* TOSTI: *A vucchella.* CARDILLO: *Core 'ngrato.* TAGLIAFERRI: *Passione.* CHERUBINI: *Mamma.* DALLA: *Caruso.*

(M) *** Decca (ADD) 425 681-2 (2).

Opening with Dalla's *Caruso*, a popular song in the Neapolitan tradition, certainly effective, and no more vulgar than many earlier examples of the genre, this selection goes on through favourites like *O sole mio* and *Core 'ngrato* and one or two religious items, notably Adam's *Cantique de Noël*, to the hard core of operatic repertoire. Beginning with *Celeste Aida*, recorded in 1972, the selection of some twenty-two arias from complete sets covers Pavarotti's distinguished recording career with Decca from 1969 (*Cielo e mar* and the *Il Trovatore* excerpts) to 1985, although the opening song was, of course, recorded digitally in 1988. The rest is a mixture of brilliantly transferred analogue originals and a smaller number of digital masters, all or nearly all showing the great tenor in sparkling form. The records are at mid-price, but there are no translations or musical notes.

'The greatest ever Pavarotti' (with various orchestras and conductors): Arias from: VERDI: *Rigoletto; Il Trovatore; La Traviata; Aida.* PUCCINI: *La Bohème; Turandot; Tosca; Fanciulla del West; Manon Lescaut.* DONIZETTI: *L'elisir d'amore.* FLOTOW: *Martha.* BIZET: *Carmen.* LEONCAVALLO: *I Pagliacci.* GIORDANO: *Fedora.* MEYERBEER: *L'Africana.* MASSENET: *Werther.* Songs: DALLA: *Caruso.* LEONCAVALLO: *Mattinata.* TOSTI: *Aprile; Marechiare; La Serenata.* CARDILLO: *Core 'ngrato.* ROSSINI: *La Danza.* MODUGNO: *Volare.* DENZA: *Funiculì, funiculà.* DE CURTIS: *Torna a Surriento.* DI CAPUA: *O sole mio!* SCHUBERT: *Ave Maria.* FRANCK: *Panis angelicus.* MANCINI: *In un palco della Scala* (with apologies to Pink Panther). GIORDANO: *Caro mio ben.* BIXIO: *Mamma.*

(M) *** Decca ADD/DDD 436 173-2 (2).

Such a collection as this is self-recommending and scarcely needs a review from us, merely a listing. The first disc opens with *La donna è mobile* (Rigoletto), *Che gelida manina* (La Bohème), *Nessun dorma*

(Turandot), all taken from outstandingly successful complete recordings, and the rest of the programme, with many favourite lighter songs also given the golden touch, is hardly less appealing. The second CD includes Pavarotti's tribute to the Pink Panther and ends with a tingling live version of *Nessun dorma*, to compare with the studio version on disc one. Vivid, vintage Decca recording throughout.

Pears, Peter (tenor), Julian Bream (lute)

Julian Bream Edition, Volume 19. Elizabethan lute songs: MORLEY: *Absence; It was a lover and his lass; Who is it?.* ROSSETER: *What then is love?; If she forsake me; When Laura smiles.* DOWLAND: *I saw my lady weep; Dear, if you change; Stay, Time; Weep you no more; Shall I sue?; Sweet, stay awhile; Can she excuse?; Come, heavy sleep; Wilt thou unkind, thus leave me?; Sorrow stay; The lowest trees have tops; Time's eldest son, Old Age; In darkness let me dwell; Say, love, if ever thou didst find.* ford: *Come Phyllis; Fair, sweet, cruel.*

(M) *** BMG/RCA (ADD) 09026 61609-2.

This vintage collection was recorded between 1963 and 1969 when Pears was at the peak of his form. The Dowland songs are particularly fine, sung with Pears's usual blend of intelligence and lyrical feeling, their nostalgic melancholy tenderly caught. Excellent, vivid, well-balanced recording, with Bream's expert accompaniments well in the picture. Most refreshing.

Pears, Peter (tenor), Benjamin Britten (piano)

Lieder: SCHUMANN: *Liederkreis, Op. 39;* FAURE: *La bonne chanson;* PURCELL: *5 songs;* SCHUBERT: *3 Songs;* BRITTEN: *4 Folksongs.*

(M) (***) BBC mono BBCB 8006-2.

Britten as pianist is, if anything, even more individual than Britten as conductor. With Pears in glowing voice (1958/9) he sparkles in his own realizations of Purcell songs and folksongs, while in Schumann's Eichendorff song cycle he makes the poetic piano-writing glow, as in *Frühlingsnacht* ('Spring night'), where the notes shimmer distinctively. The Fauré cycle too reminds one that as a fourteen-year-old Britten also set Verlaine's poetry. Clean focus in mono radio recording.

Petibon, Patricia (soprano)

'Airs Baroques Français' (with Paris Chamber Ch, Les Folies Françaises, Patrick Cohen-Akenine) from: M-A. CHARPENTIER: *David et Jonathas.* LULLY: *Armide.* RAMEAU: *Les indes galantes; Platée; Les fêtes de l'Hymen et de l'Amour.* GRANDVAL: *Rien du tout.*

*** Virgin VC5 45481-2.

Not helped by excessively arch portraits of the singer on front and back covers of the disc, Patricia Petibon's disc yet offers fresh and brilliant performances of an attractive collection of arias by the leading French composers of the late 17th and early 18th centuries. Petibon, a member of the outstanding team of Les arts florissants assembled by William Christie, with her bright and clear if slightly hooty soprano gives characterful and stylish readings of each item, and it is good to find her responding so positively to the less serious items which add a sparkle to the collection. A delightful disc, very well recorded.

Polyphony, Stephen Layton

'O magnum mysterium' (A sequence of twentieth-century carols and Sarum chant): Plainchant: *O radix lesse; O magnum mysterium; Puer natus est nobis; Reges Tharsis; Verbum caro factum est.* WISHART: *3 Carols, Op. 17, No. 3: Alleluya, A new work is come on hand.* HOWELLS: *3 Carol-anthems: Here is the little door; A spotless rose; Sing lullaby.* RICHARD RODNEY BENNETT: *5 Carols: There is no rose; Out of your sleep; That younge child; Sweet was the song; Susanni.* KENNETH LEIGHTON: *Of a rose is my song; A Hymn of the Nativity; 3 Carols, Op. 25: The Star song; Lully lulla, thou little tiny child; An Ode on the birth of our Saviour.* WARLOCK: *As dew in Aprylle; Bethlehem Down; I saw a fair maiden; Benedicamus Domino; A Cornish Christmas carol.* BYRT: *All and some.* WALTON: *What cheer?*

*** Hyp. CDA 66925.

A gloriously sung collection in which (what Meurig Bowen's extensive notes describe as) 'the magnificent corpus of British carols' is alive and still impressively expanding in the twentieth century. The atmosphere is readily set by the opening plainchant, which frames and punctuates the concert with appropriate liturgical texts. Peter Wishart's exuberant *Alleluya* and the poignant *A spotless rose* immediately catch up the listener. This is the first of Howells's *Three Carol-anthems*, of which the others are equally lovely (especially the rocking *Sing lullaby*). The five Richard Rodney Bennett carols have their own particular brand of cool dissonance, with *There is no rose* and *Sweet was the song* particularly haunting.

But perhaps it is the series of beautiful Peter Warlock settings one remembers most for their ready melodic and harmonic memorability (notably *As dew in Aprylle*, the lovely *Bethlehem Down* and the serene *Lullaby my Jesus*) alongside the soaring music of Kenneth Leighton, helped in the ambitious *Nativity hymn* and the *Ode on the birth of our Saviour* by the rich, pure line of the soloist, Libby Crabtree, and in *Lully, lulla* by the equally ravishing contribution of Emma Preston-Dunlop. Walton's *What cheer?* brings an exuberant rhythmic spicing, but for the most part this programme captures the tranquil pastoral mood of Christmas Eve. The recording could hardly be bettered, clear yet with the most evocative ambience.

Popp, Lucia (soprano)

MOZART: *Exsultate jubilate.* SCHUBERT: *Die Forelle; Gretchen am Spinnrade; An Sylvia.* RICHARD STRAUSS: *Zueignung; Wiegenlied.* **Songs and arias from:** LEHAR: *Die lustige Witwe.* JOHANN STRAUSS JR: *Casanova; Die Fledermaus.* ZELLER: *Der Obersteiger.* ORFF: *Carmina burana.* MOZART: *Le nozze di Figaro; Così fan tutte; Die Entführung aus dem Serail; Die Zauberflöte.* GRIEG: *Peer Gynt.* PUCCINI: *La Bohème.* RICHARD STRAUSS: *Vier letzte Lieder; Intermezzo.* DVORAK: *Rusalka.* TCHAIKOVSKY: *Eugene Onegin.* WAGNER: *Tannhäuser.* HANDEL: *Joshua.* ROSSINI: *Petite messe solennelle.* MAHLER: *Des Knaben Wunderhorn; Symphony No. 4.*

(BB) *** Disky Royal Classics Vocal Double (ADD) DCL 703932 (2).

Lucia Popp, Czechoslovakian born, finds an eastern-European lilt for the music of Lehár and sparkles in the other operetta items, takes just as readily to Mahler, and Richard Strauss, yet is a natural in Mozart, whether in the passion of *Come scoglio* or the mellow beauty of line of *Voi che sapete*. The two excerpts from Grieg's *Peer Gynt* are ravishingly sung. Throughout, Popp's musical imagination and concern for word meaning effectively counteract any feeling of sameness.

In Slavic repertoire, her portrayal of the water-sprite in *Rusalka* is a highlight, but the one disappointment of the collection is the famous scena from *Eugene Onegin*; it opens well but later on, Tatiana's outbursts sound rather constricted, and both singer and conductor do not let the music expand enough.

The second disc opens with *Dich teure Halle* from *Tannhäuser*, splendidly sung, with vibrant support from Haitink, and the five Lieder of Schubert and Strauss (accompanied by Sawallisch) are simply and appealingly sung, though not as memorable as the lovely excerpt from Strauss's *Intermezzo* and the Mahler items. The programme ends with the finale of Mahler's *Fourth Symphony*, for which Popp is ideally cast. The voice is often recorded rather close, which only occasionally exaggerates her tendency to squeeze salient notes. Good transfers, but no texts.

Prey, Hermann (bass-baritone)

'*The Singers*' (Decca series): **Arias from:** ROSSINI: *Il barbiere di Siviglia* (with LSO, Abbado). MOZART: *Le nozze di Figaro* (with VPO, Solti); *Die Zauberflöte* (with German Opera O, Boehm). **Lieder:** SCHUBERT: *Im Abendrot; Erlkönig; An Silvia; Der Wanderer an den Mond.* SCHUMANN: *Der Hidalgo; Meine Rose; Der Spielmann.* BRAHMS: *Dein blaues Auge; Die Mainacht; Sonntag; Ständchen; Wiegenlied.* R. STRAUSS: *Allerseelen; Heimkehr; Heimliche Aufforderung; Ständchen* (with Engel, piano).

(M)**(*) Decca (ADD) 467 901-2.

The bulk of this recital CD is drawn from a 1962 Decca record made with Karl Engel. The nicely contrived programme demonstrates the wide range of sympathies Herman Prey encompassed at this early stage of his career. Quick to match his vocal timbre with the mood of the poem, he also possessed a dynamic range of amazing breadth, so that prolonged *mezza voce* sections may lull the listener into thinking the volume has been cut down. Don't turn it up, because Prey will surprise you and launch into a spine-tingling crescendo that builds up into a powerful yet always quite stylish *forte*, as in the second of the Brahms songs. The accompaniments are excellent, although the piano tone seems a mite thin in this transfer, even if the voice is captured well. The opera arias, recorded in the late 1960s and early 1970s, are taken from his complete opera recordings (the Abbado and Boehm are DG recordings and the sound is a little dry in these transfers) and are most enjoyable; the Mozart is especially distinguished, but the Rossini is fun and stylish, too. One of the better 'The Singers' compilations then, although one can gain access to the texts and translations and a photo-gallery, only via a CD ROM drive.

'*Bravo Figaro*': **Arias and excerpts from:** ROSSINI: *Il barbiere di Siviglia* (with Luigi Alva). MOZART: *Le nozze di Figaro* (with Edith Mathis); *Così fan tutte* (with Brigitte Fassbaender). WEBER: *Oberon* (with Judith Hamari). JOHANN STRAUSS JR: *Die Fledermaus* (with Julia Varady, Bernd Weikl). **Lieder:** MOZART: *Die Zufriedenheit; An die Freude* (with Bernhard Klee, piano). BRAHMS: *All'mein Gedanken; In stiller Nacht* (with Karl Engel, piano); *Volkslied* (with Leonard Hokanson, piano).

(BB) *** Belart (ADD) 461 060-2.

This engaging collection is happily titled, for Hermann Prey was surely born to play Figaro, whether in Rossini's original (with Luiga Alva) or Mozart's sequel (with Edith Mathis). The excerpts from Kleiber's *Die Fledermaus* also scintillate, and the other Mozart and Weber excerpts, if not quite as distinctive, are all characterful. The Lieder are sung with a pleasing directness. A most winning recital.

Price, Leontyne (soprano)

'*Ultimate Collection*': **Arias from:** BERLIOZ: *Les nuits d'été.* BIZET: *Carmen.* BARBER: *Antony and Cleopatra.* GERSHWIN: *Porgy and Bess.* MASSENET: *Manon.* MOZART: *Le nozze de Figaro; Il rè pastore.* PUCCINI: *Madama Butterfly; Manon Lescaut; La Rondine; Suor Angelica; Tosca; Turandot.* PURCELL: *Dido and Aeneas.* R. STRAUSS: *Im Abendrot (Vier letzte Lieder No. 1); Ariadne auf Naxos.* VERDI: *Aida; Un ballo in maschera; Don Carlos; La forza del destino; Il Trovatore.*

(M) **(*) RCA 74321 63463-2.

This CD may appeal to those who want some of Leontyne Price's most famous roles, or those who simply want a marvellously sung soprano operatic compilation. It is well programmed and includes some unlikely repertoire for Price (including Purcell), as well as many of the things you would expect. The recordings and performances are generally excellent, often brilliant. What is shabby about this release is that there is nothing in the documentation about the recordings, dates, conductors, orchestras, or the music. As for texts and translations, you must be joking!

'*The Singers*' (Decca series): Arias from: VERDI: *Aida; Un ballo in maschera. Ernani; Otello* (with Israel PO, Mehta). HANDEL: *Messiah* (with Montreal SO, Dutoit). Songs: FRANCK: *Panis angelicus.* TRAD.: *I Wonder as I Wonder; What Child is This?* MURRAY: *Away in a Manger.* WADE: *O Come, All Ye Faithful.*

(M) *(*) Decca (ADD/DDD) 467 913-2.

Considering the great recordings available to Decca of Leontyne Price at the height of her considerable powers, it is curious that the compiler of this CD should have choosen two LP excerpts made in the early 1980s, near the end of her career. Here the voice is really not what it was in its glorious prime, although her commanding personality and warmth are some compensation. Unfortunately, the characteristically dry Tel Aviv acoustic does not help the diminished vocal bloom in the big operatic numbers, nor does her forward placement in the Christmas items. As with other CDs in this series, no texts and translations are provided.

Psalmody, Parley of Instruments, Peter Holman

'*While shepherds watched*' (Christmas music from English parish churches and chapels 1740-1830): BEESLY: *While shepherds watched.* ANON.: *Let an anthem of praise; Hark! how all the welkin rings.* J. C. SMITH: *While shepherds watched.* HELLENDAAL: *Concerto in E flat for strings, Op. 3/4: Pastorale.* KEY: *As shepherds watched their fleecy care.* ARNOLD: *Hark! the herald angels sing.* CLARK: *While shepherds watched.* HANDEL: *Hark! the herald angels sing; Hymning seraphs wake the morning.* JARMAN: *There were shepherds abiding in the field.* S. WESLEY: *(Piano) Rondo on 'God rest you merry, gentlemen'* (Timothy Roberts). MATTHEWS: *Angels from the realms of glory.* FOSTER: *While shepherds watched.*

*** Hyp. CDA 66924.

This is a Christmas collection of genuine novelty. None of the settings of *While shepherds watched* uses the familiar tune: the regal closing version from John Foster of Yorkshire is remarkably lively, as is the lighter variation from Joseph Key of Northampton, *As shepherds watched their fleecy care* with woodwind accompaniment. There are other things too. Handel's *Hark! the herald angels* is neatly fitted to *See the conqu'ring hero comes*, and *Hymning seraphs* (presented as a tenor solo with fortepiano) turns out to be

our old keyboard friend, 'The harmonious blacksmith'. Peiter Hellendaal's *Pastorale for strings* is in the best concerto grosso tradition, although Samuel Wesley's variations on *God rest you merry* are merely ingenious. Nevertheless the whole programme is presented with pleasing freshness and is very well sung, played and recorded.

Ramey, Samuel (bass)

'*A Date with the Devil*' (with Munich Radio Symphony Orchestra, Julius Rudel): Arias from BERLIOZ: *La damnation de Faust.* MEYERBEER: *Robert le diable.* BOITO: *Mefistofele.* OFFENBACH: *Les contes d'Hoffmann.* GOUNOD: *Faust.* STRAVINSKY: *The Rake's Progress.* LISZT: *Mephisto Waltz* (orchestra only).

(BB) *** Naxos 8.555355.

Samuel Ramey has had great success in the concert hall with this collection of devilish portraits, most of them from French sources. Here in a composite recording, partly live, partly under studio conditions, he sings and acts with fine flair, bringing out the wry humour in many of the items. Mephistopheles' *Serenade* and the *Calf of Gold* aria from Gounod's *Faust* provide a fine climax before the tailpiece solos from *The Rake's Progress*. He is well supported by Julius Rudel and the Munich Radio Orchestra, springing rhythms crisply, with well-balanced sound. The orchestral showpieces by Berlioz and Liszt provide a nice contrast. An outstanding Naxos bargain.

Resnik, Regina (mezzo-soprano), Richard Woitach (piano)

Song recital: RAMEAU: *Le Grillon.* SPONTINI: *Les riens d'amour.* MARTINI: *Plaintes de Marie Stuart.* GAVEUX: *Dieu d'Israel.* TURINA: *Homenaje a Lope de Vega, Op. 90; Poema: Tu pupila es azul, Op. 81/2; Soneta: Vade retro!, Op. 54/2.* TCHAIKOVSKY: *At the ball; Can it be day?; The bride's lament.* PROKOFIEV: *The grey-eyed king; Thoughts of the sunlight; Stolby.* MAHLER: *Des Knaben Wunderhorn: Das irdisch Leben; Nicht wiedershen!; Lob des hohen Verstandes. Hans und Grete; Erinnerung.* MENOTTI: *The Medium: Afraid, am I afraid* (with Columbia Chamber Ensemble, Jorge Mester).

(M) *(*) Sony SMK 60784.

This recital was made just after Regina Resnik's début New York recital in 1967 and the first four French and Italian songs show her lack of experience in their lack of charm; they are further flawed by the quick vibrato, which the close microphones do not flatter. She is much more colloquially at home in the Spanish repertoire, and at her very best in the Russian songs. Here the vibrato is an asset, and the drama and dark melancholy are powerfully caught. The Mahler Lieder are more problematic. *Erinnerung* is all but ruined by the intrusive vibrato, and *Hans und Grete* is over-characterized, but the others are more successful. The excerpt from *The Medium* is splendidly histrionic. But this disc is only really recommendable to the singer's admirers.

Riedel, Deborah (soprano), Australian Opera and Ballet Orchestra, Richard Bonynge

'British Opera Arias': Arias from: WALLACE: *The Amber Witch; Love's Triumph; Lurline; Maritana.* BALFE: *The Maid of Artois; The Puritan's Daughter; The Rose of Castille; Satanella; The Siege of Rochelle; Il Talismano.* SULLIVAN: *Ivanhoe; The Rose of Persia.* FARADAY: *Amasis.*

*** Australian Melba 301082.

It is astonishing, considering how much nineteenth-century opera has been resurrected on CD, that there has been no such revival in English opera of that period. Although the composers featured here embraced current (Italian) operatic trends, their art retained an attractive home-spun quality, but was eventually eclipsed by more inflated operatic traditions later in the century. Balfe achieved considerable success both in England and internationally in his day with his ability to write attractive melody of great charm. The first of the *Il Talismano* (1874) arias included here starts most beguilingly with a horn solo followed by a flute, before the voice enters, whilst the other aria, *Nella dolce trepidanza*, is most memorable for its swinging cabaletta. Many of his arias, such as the numbers from *The Rose of Castille* and *Satanella*, have a simple, almost folk-like quality that is most fetching, whilst *The rapture dwelling in my heart* from *The Maid of Artois* is a delicious coloratura waltz song.

Wallace is remembered today mainly for *Maritana*, from which the charming *Tis the harp in the Air* and *Scenes that are brightest* are included, but the more substantial items from *Lurline*, the waltz song *The Naiad's Spell*, *These withered flowers* from *Love's Triumph* and *My long hair Is braided* from *The Amber Witch* – a brilliant coloratura aria – are all greatly enjoyable. The Sullivan items come from his 'serious' attempts at grand opera and are not quite so rare these days, but their inclusion is welcome – *Neath My Lattice* from *The Rose of Persia* is very winning, as is the rare Faraday number from his musical comedy of 1906, *Amasis*, which has a nice period charm. This is an important as well as an enjoyable collection which gives us a fuller picture of English operatic history, and a CD which makes one want to hear some of the complete operas. The performances are excellent: Deborah Riedel sings with warmth and real understanding of the idiom and meets the challenges of the virtuoso passages, whilst Bonynge provides his usual sterling support with his Australian Orchestra, who make a fine contribution. The recording is atmospheric, perhaps a touch backwardly balanced, but not seriously so. Full texts are included.

Roswaenge, Helge (tenor)

'The Dane with the High D': Arias from: VERDI: *Aida; La traviata; Il trovatore.* CORNELIUS: *Der Barbier von Bagdad.* ADAM: *Le Postillon de Longjumeau.* AUBER: *Fra Diavolo.* MOZART: *Cosi fan Tutte.* BEETHOVEN: *Fidelio.* WEBER: *Der Freischütz; Oberon.* TCHAIKOVSKY: *Eugene Onegin.* R. STRAUSS: *Der Rosenkavalier.* WILLE: *Königsballade.*

❂ (BB) (***) Dutton mono CDBP 9728.

Helge Roswaenge had one of the most thrilling voices of the twentieth century. He began singing professionally in 1921 and was still on excellent form nearly half a century later. But most of these recordings were made in the 1930s, when was at his peak, and although Mozart was perhaps not his strongest suit, he was chosen by Beecham as Tamino for his famous 1937 *Zauberflöte*. As Alan Blyth comments in the excellent insert note, his amazing voice has a 'gleaming trumpet-like quality at the top' – reminiscent of Tamagno – 'yet was mellifluous in quieter moments'. He was also a superb stylist, whether in Verdi or in operetta for which his fresh, ringing upper register was especially suitable. The most famous item here, which gives the disc its title, is the sparkling excerpt from Adam's *Le Postillon de Longjumeau*, which is electrifying, but he shows his lyrical grace in the *Fra Diavolo* aria with which this was paired on the original 78 shellac disc. This warm, lyrical quality appears again and again in this generous selection, notably in Lensky's ardent aria from *Eugene Onegin*.

In the rare excerpts from Cornelius's *Barbier von Bagdad* he is joined by his first wife, Ilonka, not a great singer but a charming partner. Almost all his recordings were made in German, yet he somehow does not sound Germanic in the French and Italian repertoire, and his ardent account of *Di rigor armato* from *Der Rosenkavalier is* sung in Italian, and how marvellously passionate it is! He was ideal for Weber (the *Oberon* excerpt is another highlight), and his dramatic entry on the word '*Gott*' in the Fidelio excerpt (the only opera he sang at Covent Garden) is characteristic of him at his very finest, and is alone worth the price of the disc. Most of the recordings were made in the 1930s and were of high quality. But the miraculous Dutton transfers enhance them further, and the voice projects with the utmost realism throughout, and with its full bloom remaining. An unforgettable and treasurable collection.

Rouen Chambre Accentus Choir, Eric Ericson

ALFVEN: *Aftonen; Uti vår hage;* JERSILD: *Min yndlingsdal (My dear valley);* NYSTEDT: *O Crux;* SANDSTROM: *Two Poems;* STENHAMMAR: *Tre körvisor (Three choral pieces);* WERLE: *Canzone 126 del Petrarcha;* WIKANDER: *Kung Liljekonvalje (King of the Lily-of-the-valley)*; *Förårskväll* **(Spring evening)**.

**(*) Assai 207 182.

The Rouen-based Chœur de Chambre Accentus was founded in 1991 by Laurence Equilbey, herself an Ericson pupil, and they tackle this predominantly Swedish repertoire with complete sympathy. In the 1960s and 1970s, Eric Ericson brought the Swedish Radio Choir to an unrivalled excellence (it was the Berlin Philharmonic of choirs). These French singers produce the beautifully blended and finely nuanced sound one associates with him. He has recorded Stenhammar's glorious choral songs to texts by the Danish poet J. P. Jaocbsen many times. Wikander's *Kung Liljekonvalje* (*King of the Lily-of-the-Valley*) and Alfvén's *Aftonen* (*The Evening*) are affecting pieces and are beautifully done.

For most collectors the surprise will be *Min yndlingsdal* (*My dear valley*) by the Dane Jørgen Jersild, a contemporary of Vagn Holmboe, though less prolific. During the 1930s he studied with Roussel, and his writing has almost luminous quality. Jan Sandström is not to be confused with Sven David and is still in his mid-forties, and these two pieces, *Anrop* (*Call*) and *Två japanska landskap* (*Two Japanese landscapes*), date from his student years and are quite haunting. By its side Werle's Petrach setting seems more self-conscious. At less than 50 minutes this is short measure, but his repertoire is not widely known and is immensely rewarding.

Royal Liverpool Philharmonic Choir and Orchestra, St Ambrose R. C. Junior School Choir, Speake, Edmund Walters

'*A Festival of Christmas*' (with Jocelyn Bell, girl soprano): arr. WALTERS: *Ding dong! merrily on high; The boar's head; Buenos Reyes; Deck the hall.* arr. PETTMAN: *The Infant King.* WALTERS: *Where was Jesus born?; The carol singers; Dance little goatling; As Joseph was a-walking; Three little birdies; Little Robin redbreast; Hop-hop-hop; Little one sleep.* BYRD: *Cradle song.* BACH: *O little one sweet.* DARKE: *In the bleak midwinter.* GRUBER: *Silent night.* arr. WALLACE: *O come, all ye faithful.*

(M) *** Chan. 7111.

The introductory woodwind in the scoring of Edmund Walters's opening arrangement of *Ding dong! merrily on high*, and the light-hearted touches of syncopation, suggest that his approach to Christmas music has much in common with that of John Rutter. His own carols are jauntily engaging, helped by the freshness of the excellently trained St Ambrose Junior School Choir, who sing them with vigour and enthusiasm. *Little one sleep* (a treble solo) verges on sentimentality. But the Spanish carol *Buenos Reyes*, with its castanets, is most piquant and the two Basque

carols *The Infant King* and *I saw a maiden* are most eloquently sung, as are the settings by Bach and Byrd. Fine recording too.

Russian opera: 'The splendours of Russian opera'

'*The splendours of Russian opera*': GLINKA: *Overture: Ruslan and Ludmilla.* BORODIN: *Prince Igor: Polovtsian dances* (with London Symphony Chorus; both LSO, Solti); *Galitzky's aria.* RIMSKY-KORSAKOV: *Sadko: Song of the Viking Guest.* RACHMANINOV: *Aleko: Aleko's cavatina* (all three, Nicolai Ghiaurov). TCHAIKOVSKY: *Eugene Onegin: Tatiana's letter scene* (Teresa Kubiak); *Entr'acte and Waltz scene* (Soloists, ROHCG Ch. & O, Solti). *The Maid of Orleans: Farewell to the forests* (Regina Resnik). MUSSORGSKY: *Boris Godunov: Coronation scene* (Ghiaurov, V. State Op. Ch., VPO, Karajan).

(M) **(*) Decca (IMS) (ADD) 458 216-2.

Issued at the same time as Decca's outstanding Baroque opera collection, this Russian compilation cannot match it, either in imaginative choice of items (here rather predictable) or in the consistent excellence of the performances. Solti opens the proceedings with his famous dashing account of the *Ruslan and Ludmilla overture* (although the transfer isn't very glamorous), and Ghiaurov's three arias certainly show the richness of his magnificent voice.

But it is Teresa Kubiak's memorable account of *Tatiana's letter scene* from *Eugene Onegin* that is the highlight of the concert, and this is neatly linked to the opera's *Waltz scene* by the *Entr'acte* based on Tatiana's music. It is good also to have Regina Resnik's fine *Farewell* aria from *The Maid of Orleans* (which musically has much in common with *Eugene Onegin*). But the present transfer of the choral *Coronation scene* from *Boris Godunov* seems to have lost some of the rich amplitude of Karajan's 1970 complete recording from which it is taken. As with the rest of Decca's current Opera Gala releases, the presentation is attractive, and full translations are included.

St George's Canzona, John Sothcott

Medieval songs and dances: Lamento di Tristano; L'autrier m'iere levaz; 4 Estampies real; Edi beo thu hevene quene; Eyns ne soy ke plente fu; Tre fontane. PERRIN D'AGINCOURT: *Quant voi en la fin d'este. Cantigas de Santa Maria: Se ome fezer; Nas mentes semper teer; Como poden per sas culpas; Maravillosos et piadosos.*

(M) *** CRD (ADD) CRD 3421.

As so often when early music is imaginatively re-created, one is astonished at the individuality of many of the ideas. This applies particularly to the second item in this collection, *Quant voi en la fin d'este*, attributed to the mid-thirteenth-century trouvère, Perrin d'Agincourt, but no less to the four *Cantigas de*

Santa Maria. The instrumentation is at times suitably robust but does not eschew good intonation and subtle effects. The group is recorded vividly and the acoustics of St James, Clerkenwell, are never allowed to cloud detail. The sound is admirably firm and real in its CD format.

St John's College Choir, Cambridge, George Guest

'Christmas carols from St John's' (with Philip Kenyon, organ): TRAD.: *Unto us a boy is born; Ding dong! merrily on high; Good King Wenceslas; There is no rose.* arr. WALFORD DAVIES: *The holly and the ivy.* arr. WILLCOCKS: *Sussex carol; God rest you merry, gentlemen; O come, all ye faithful.* WARLOCK: *Balulalow.* HOLST: *In the bleak mid-winter.* HADLEY: *I sing of a maiden.* RUTTER: *Shepherd's pipe carol.* GRUBER: *Silent night.* MENDELSSOHN, arr. WILLCOCKS: *Hark! the herald angels sing.* arr. VAUGHAN WILLIAMS: *O little town of Bethlehem.* POSTON: *Jesus Christ the apple tree.* Raymond WILLIAMS: *2 Welsh carols.* KIRKPATRICK: *Away in a manger.*

(M) *** Chan. 7109.

An essentially traditional concert and none the worse for that when so beautifully sung and recorded. Among the more modern carols, Elizabeth Poston's beautiful *Jesus Christ the apple tree* stands out. Many of the arrangements are famous, notably the spectacular Willcocks versions of *Hark! the herald angels sing* and *O come, all ye faithful*, but some of the gentler, atmospheric items (*There is no rose*) are just as memorable. A most enjoyable hour of music.

La Scala, Milan, Chorus and Orchestra, Arturo Toscanini

'The reopening of La Scala, 12 May 1946' (with soloists including Renata Tebaldi, Mafalda Favero and Tancredi Pasero): ROSSINI: *La gazza ladra: Overture. William Tell: Wedding chorus; Act I: Dance; Act III: Soldiers' dance. Mosè in Egitto: Prayer.* VERDI: *Nabucco: Overture & Chorus of Hebrew slaves. Overture: I vespri siciliani. Te Deum.* PUCCINI: *Manon Lescaut, Act III (complete).* BOITO: *Mefistofele: Prologue.*

(BB) (**(*)) Naxos mono 8.110821/22 (2).

The radio recording may be close, harsh and boxy, but it is firm and clear, so giving a vivid idea of one of the great musical events of post-war Europe. This marked Toscanini's return to the opera house where he had had his greatest triumphs. Each performance here is incandescent. The manner may often be uncomfortably taut, as it regularly was in his New York performances, but there is an extra warmth here too. Such items as the *Dance* from Rossini's *William Tell* are most delicately pointed, and the articulation

throughout has a pin-point precision of a kind rarely heard from an Italian orchestra.

It is good too to hear the chosen soloists, with the emergent Renata Tebaldi shining alongside established colleagues like Mafalda Favero and Tancredi Pasero. The short items by Rossini and Verdi on the first disc are then nicely contrasted against the three major items on the second. Toscanini's electrifying readings of Verdi's *Te Deum* and the *Prologue* from Boito's *Mefistofele* are both well known from RCA recordings, but it is especially good to have Act III of Puccini's *Manon Lescaut*, plainly a Toscanini favourite: uniquely powerful, this was the work which brought reconciliation between the conductor and composer after an estrangement.

The Scholars of London

French chansons: JOSQUIN: *Faute d'argent; Mille regretz.* JANEQUIN: *Le chant des oiseaux; Or vien ça.* SANDRIN: *Je ne le croy.* GOMBERT: *Aime qui vouldra; Quand je suis aupres.* SERMISY: *Tant que vivrai; Venez regrets; La, la, maistre Pierre.* ARCADELT: *En ce mois délicieux; Margot, labourez les vignes; Du temps que j'estois amoureux; Sa grand beauté.* TABOUROT: *Belle qui tiens ma vie.* VASSAL: *Vray Dieu.* CLEMENS: *Prière devant le repas; Action des Graces.* PASSEREAU: *Il est bel et bon.* LE JEUNE: *Ce n'est que fiel.* LASSUS: *Bonjour mon coeur; Si je suis brun; Beau le cristal; La nuit froide; Un jeune moine.* BERTRAND: *De nuit, le bien.* COSTELY: *Arrête un peu mon coeur.*

(BB) *** Naxos 8.550880.

This disc offers a representative selection from the thousands of sixteenth-century French polyphonic chansons, and ranges from the devotional to the amorous, the bawdy and the bucolic. It includes some of the best known, such as the ubiquitous Janequin *Le chant des oiseaux*, and features such familiar masters as Josquin, Sermisy and Claude Le Jeune. It encompasses Flemish masters writing in the language such as Gombert and Lassus. The Scholars of London are expressive and persuasive guides in this repertoire and are decently recorded at St Silas the Martyr in Kentish Town. There is an all-too-short but thoughtful introduction, and the booklet then reproduces texts and translations. What more can you ask from a disc that would undoubtedly cost less than admission to a concert plus the programme?

Scholl, Andreas (counter-tenor)

'Heroes' (with Orchestra of the Age of Enlightenment, Sir Roger Norrington): Arias from HANDEL: *Giulio Cesare; Rodelinda; Saul; Semele; Serse.* HASSE: *Artaserse.* GLUCK: *Orfeo; Telemaco.* MOZART: *Ascanio in Alba; Mitridate.*

*** Decca 466 196-2.

'There is more to heroism than winning fearlessly … My heroes have moments of weakness and must overcome their difficulties,' comments Andreas Scholl about the operatic characters represented in his Decca recital. Indeed it is the lovely tender singing in the lyrical arias that one remembers most, as in the familiar *Where'er you walk*, and *Oh Lord whose mercies numberless* (from *Saul*, with its delicate closing harp solo from Frances Kelly), or *Con rauco mormorio* from *Rodelinda*.

In spite of the prevalence of Handel in the programme, Scholl overlaps with his Harmonia Mundi disc on only one aria, *Ombra mai fù*, just as characterful though less forwardly recorded. The other items range from Hasse (wonderfully light and nimble) to dramatic early Mozart. Altogether this is a formidable collection of arias designed originally for castrato, all performed characterfully with a firm, clear tone and virtuoso agility. *Che farò* from Gluck's *Orfeo* is on the slow side, but no less impressive for that. Clear, open sound, the voice caught brightly and naturally. Norrington's accompaniments are light-textured and fresh. But Scholl's earlier Harmonia Mundi Handel collection, including instrumental music also, is in many ways even more seductive – see under Handel in the Composer index of our main volume.

Schwarzkopf, Dame Elisabeth
(soprano)

'Diva': Arias from: MOZART: *Le Nozze di Figaro; Don Giovanni; Così fan tutte.* BEETHOVEN: *Fidelio.* WEBER: *Der Freischütz.* WAGNER: *Lohengrin.* SMETANA: *The Bartered Bride.* RICHARD STRAUSS: *Der Rosenkavalier; Ariadne auf Naxos; Arabella.* HEUBERGER: *Der Opernball.* JOHANN STRAUSS JR: *Die Fledermaus.*

(M) *** EMI stereo/mono CDM5 65577-2.

Elisabeth Schwarzkopf, married to the recording producer and impresario Walter Legge, had a uniquely intensive recording career from the 1940s onwards. This single CD in EMI's 'Diva' series offers an excellent and shrewdly selected survey of her opera and operetta recordings. Mozart is very well represented, with Schwarzkopf as both Susanna and the Countess in *Figaro*, as Donna Elvira in *Don Giovanni* (from the masterly Giulini recording) and as Fiordiligi in *Così fan tutte* (commanding in *Come scoglio* under Boehm). From Richard Strauss there is not only the Marschallin's monologue (from the Karajan recording of *Rosenkavalier*) but also Ariadne's lament and Arabella's final solo, another of her most compelling Strauss performances. Immaculate accounts of Weber (Agathe's *Leise, leise* from *Freischütz*) and of Wagner (*Elsa's Dream* from *Lohengrin*) have been drawn from one of the finest of all her discs, with Heuberger's *Im chambre séparée* as an enchanting operetta tailpiece. Excellent transfers.

'Elisabeth Schwarzkopf sings operetta' (with Philharmonia Ch. and O, Ackermann): Excerpts from: HEUBERGER: *Der Opernball.* ZELLER: *Der Vogelhändler.* LEHAR: *Der Zarewitsch; Der Graf von Luxembourg; Giuditta.* JOHANN STRAUSS JR:

Casanova. MILLOCKER: *Die Dubarry.* SUPPE: *Boccaccio.* SIECZYNSKY: *Wien, du Stadt meiner Träume.*

✿ (M) *** EMI CDM5 66989-2 [567004].

This is one of the most delectable recordings of operetta arias ever made, and it is here presented with excellent sound. Schwarzkopf's 'whooping' manner (as Philip Hope-Wallace called it) is irresistible, authentically catching the Viennese style, languor and sparkle combined. Try for example the exquisite *Im chambre séparée* or *Sei nicht bös*; but the whole programme is performed with supreme artistic command and ravishing tonal beauty. This outstanding example of the art of Elisabeth Schwarzkopf at its most enchanting is a disc which ought to be in every collection. The CD transfer enhances the superbly balanced recording even further; it manages to cut out nearly all the background, gives the voice a natural presence and retains the orchestral bloom.

'Lieder recital' (with Gerald Moore, piano): BACH: *Bist du bei mir.* PERGOLESI: *Se tu m'ami, se tu sospiri.* HANDEL: *Atalanta: Care selve.* GLUCK: *Die Pilger von Mekka: Einam Bach der fliesst.* BEETHOVEN: *Wonne de Wehmut.* SCHUBERT: *An Sylvia; Romanze aus Rosamunde; Die Vögel; Der Einsame; Vedi quanto adoro.* WOLF: *Kennst du das Land; Philine; Nachtzauber; Die Zigeunerin.* RICHARD STRAUSS: *Ruhe meine Seele; Wiegenlied; Schlechters Wetter; Hat gesagt, bleibt's nicht dabei.* Encores: MOZART: *Warnung.* SCHUMANN: *Der Nüssbaum.* SCHUBERT: *Ungeduld.*

(M) (**(*)) EMI mono CDH5 66084-2.

Schwarzkopf's 1956 Salzburg recital with Gerald Moore is the third to have appeared on CD, more varied than the earlier two, another great occasion caught on the wing. It ranges from Bach and Handel arias, expansive and poised, through a Schubert-like Gluck song and rare Beethoven to Schwarzkopf's regular repertory of Schubert, Wolf and Strauss, delectably done. Wolf's *Kennst du das Land*, greatest of all Lieder for a woman, here comes not as a climax but at the start of a group, building up with biting intensity. No texts are provided.

'Unpublished recordings' (with (i) Philh. O, Thurston Dart; (ii) Kathleen Ferrier, VPO, Karajan; (iii) Philh. O, Galliera; (iv) Walter Gieseking, Philh. O, Karajan): J. S. BACH: (i) *Cantata No. 199: Mein Herze schwimmt im Blut: Auf diese Schmerzens Reu; Doch Gott muss mir genädig sein; Mein Herze schwimmt im Blut.* (ii) *Mass in B min.: Christe eleison; Et in unum Dominum; Laudamus te.* (iii) MOZART: *Nehmt meinen Dank, K.383.* (iv) GIESEKING: *Kinderlieder.* RICHARD STRAUSS: *4 Last songs.*

(M) (**(*)) EMI mono (ADD) CDM7 63655-2.

Long-buried treasure here includes Bach duets with Kathleen Ferrier conducted by Karajan, a collection of charming children's songs by Gieseking, recorded almost impromptu, and, best of all, a live performance of Strauss's *Four Last songs* given under Karajan at the Festival Hall in 1956, a vintage year for Schwarzkopf. Sound quality varies, but the voice is gloriously caught.

Unpublished recordings 1946–52: BACH: *Cantata No. 51: Jauchzet Gott* (with Philh. O, Susskind). MOZART: *Exsultate jubilate, K.165; Das Veilchen. Die Zauberflöte:* excerpts (with piano); Schwarzkopf talks about the *Die Zauberflöte* recordings. Arias from VERDI: *La Traviata.* PUCCINI: *La Bohème.* BACH/GOUNOD: *Ave Maria.* ARNE: *When dasies pied.* MORLEY: *It was a lover and his lass.* SCHUBERT: *Gretchen am Spinnrade; Der Musensohn; Wiegenlied.* RICHARD STRAUSS: *Hat gesagt, bleibt's nicht dabei; Schlechtes Wetter.* WOLF: *Storchenbotschaft* (2 versions); *Epiphanias; Mein Liebster hat zu Tische; Du denkst mit einem Fädchen; Schweig'einmal still; Wer tat deinem Füsslein weh?; Bedeckt mich mit Blumen; Mögen alle bösen Zungen; Elfenlied; Nixe Binserfuss; Im Frühling; Die Spröde; Die Bekehrte; Mausfallensprüchlein; Wiegenlied in Sommer.*

☉ *** Testament mono/stereo SBT 2172 (2).

Here we have a magnificent store of the recordings made when her glorious voice was at its most radiant. For any lover of singing this is buried treasure when many of these items have an immediacy and freshness even more winning than later, published versions. Parallel versions of the jolly little Wolf song *Storchenbotschaft* demonstrate how rapid her development was between 1948 and 1951, leading to a whole collection of Wolf recorded in 1951, every one a jewel.

The three Schubert songs include *Der Musensohn*, joyfully buoyant, and *Gretchen am Spinnrade*, brighter and more passionate than in later recordings, with a little spontaneous gasp of emotion after the climax on '*sein Kuss!*'. Bach and Mozart too have an extra urgency compared with later, and Violetta's aria from Verdi's *La Traviata* is all the more intense, done in English. Most revealing of all is the private recording, some half-hour of music, made with piano accompaniment when Schwarzkopf was preparing to sing Pamina in English in a Covent Garden revival of Mozart's *Magic Flute*, a 'glimpse into the singer's workshop' centring on a ravishing account of *Ach ich fühls*.

The Unpublished EMI Recordings 1955–64 (with Moore, piano): BIZET: *Pastorale.* BRAHMS: *In stiller Nacht; Sandmannchen; Von ewige Liebe; Wiegenlied.* FLIES: *Wiegenlied.* MOZART: *Un moto di gioia; Warnung.* PARISOTTI: *Se tu m'ami.* SCHUBERT: *Claudine von villa bella; Du bist der Ruh; Die Forelle; Der Jungling an der Quelle; Lachen und Weinen; Die Vogel; Wiegenlied.* SCHUMANN: *Widmung.* STRAUSS: *Ruhe, meine Seele; Wiegenlied; Zueignung.* WAGNER: *Traume.* WOLF: *Der Kohlerweib; Nachtzauber; Treten ein; Die Zigeunerin.*

(***) Testament SBT 1206.

This makes a superb follow-up to Testament's previous delving into the archive of Schwarzkopf's unpublished recordings, which covered Bach, Handel and opera. She and her husband, the recording producer, Walter Legge, were the most exacting critics, and the reasons for rejection (if that is what it was) are not at all evident from these inspired performances of Lieder. That is the area where Schwarzkopf was supreme, above all in Schubert and Wolf, who are well represented here in intense, characterful performances, with the voice at its freshest. One attractive touch is the inclusion of no fewer than four, nicely contrasted cradle-songs. Excellent transfers.

Scotto, Renata (soprano)

Italian Opera Arias (with Philharmonia Orchestra, Manno Wolf-Ferrari or (i) Rome Opera Orchestra, Barbirolli): from ROSSINI: *Il barbiere di Siviglia.* BELLINI: *I puritani.* PUCCINI: *Gianni Schicchi; Turandot;* (i) *Madama Butterfly.* DONIZETTI: *Lucia di Lammermoor.* VERDI: *La traviata.* BOITO: *Mefistofele.*

(BB) **(*) EMI Encore (ADD) CDE5 74766-2.

Apart from two outstanding excerpts from Scotto's complete 1967 *Madama Butterfly* with Carlo Bergonzi, conducted by Barbirolli, this recital dates from 1959, early in her career. The widely-ranging programme has the voice at its freshest and most agile, giving an idea of the later dramatic developments which changed the character of the voice and filled it out (as is shown by the *Butterfly excerpts*).

Seefried, Irmgard (soprano), Erik Werba (piano)

Lieder: BRAHMS: *Es träumte mir; Nicht mehr zu dir zu gehen; Ständchen; Trost in Tränen; Unbewegte laue Luft; 6 Volkslieder: In stiller Nacht; Schwesterlein; Die Sonne scheint mehr; Die Trauernde; Der Versuchung; Volkslied.* SCHUBERT: *Mignon Lieder: Heiss mich nicht reden; Kennst du das Land; Nur wer die Sehnsucht kennt; So lasst mich scheinen.* WOLF: *Mignon Lieder I–IV: Heiss mich nicht reden; Kennst du das Land; Nur wer die Sehnsucht kennt; So lasst mich scheinen.* (Irmgard Seefried in conversation with John Amis).

(***) BBC mono BBCL 4040-2.

Recorded by the BBC in the studio in January 1962, this recital brings out the open charm of Irmgard Seefried as a winning Lieder singer. Her Brahms group sets the pattern, bringing out the links with German folksong, fresh and tuneful. There is no lack of detail in her pointing of words, but she takes a direct view of even such a deeply meditative song as *In stiller Nacht*, singing with concentration but little mystery.

Such songs as *Schwesterlein* and *Ständchen* are given with such urgency that one holds one's breath, half expecting disaster. Seefried's forte is her full, strong creamy voice, here recorded rather close, so that Schubert's *Gretchen am Spinnrade* brings little build-up, and Wolf's supreme Lied, *Kennst du das Land*, remains fresh and forthright in its lyricism rather than offering darker emotions. The interview with John Amis, which comes as a delightful supplement, bears out the joyful enthusiasm of the singer, whose strength, beauty and openness defy any detailed reservations.

(Robert) Shaw Festival Singers, Robert Shaw

'*O Magnum mysterium*': GORECKI: *Totus tuus.* LAURIDSEN: *O magnum mysterium.* POULENC: *O magnum mysterium.* RACHMANINOV: *Praise the name of the Lord.* SCHUBERT: *Der Ernfernten.* TALLIS: *If ye Love Me; A New Commandment.* TRAD: *Amazing Grace. Sometimes I Feel like a Moanin' Dove. Wondrous Love.* VICTORIA: *O vos omnes. O magnum mysterium.*

*** Telarc CD 80531.

This compilation of unaccompanied choral music pays tribute to Robert Shaw as one of the world's great choir-trainers, who first made his name in the 1940s, when Toscanini chose the Robert Shaw Chorale for major choral recordings. Then, towards the end of his career, after two decades as music director of the Atlanta Symphony Orchestra, Shaw once again had time for unaccompanied choral music, establishing in 1989 a summer festival of choral workshops as well as performance at Quercy in the south of France and using a choir of students from American universities. His Telarc recordings made with that festival choir provide most of the items here, which were atmospherically recorded in the church of St Pierre at Gramat. The Tallis and Victoria motets, recorded in 1989, are an exception; they appear on disc for the first time in immaculate performances from a relatively large choir, which demonstrate the consistent refinement of the matching and balance that are characteristic of Shaw's choral work. The Schubert part-song and the Lauridsen motet, recorded in the United States with Shaw's chamber singers, readily match the rest in beauty of sound, particularly the Lauridsen, a fine piece by a composer, born in 1943, who spices a traditional idiom with clashing intervals in a way that Purcell would have enjoyed.

Shuard, Amy (soprano)

Recital (with Royal Opera House, Covent Garden Orchestra, Edward Downes or RPO, George Weldon): Arias from: VERDI: *Aida; Un ballo in maschera.* MASCAGNI: *Cavalleria rusticana.* PUCCINI: *Turandot; Gianni Schicchi; Tosca; La Bohème.* GIORDANO: *Andrea Chénier.* TCHAIKOVSKY: *Eugene Onegin (Letter scene).*

(M) **(*) Dutton Lab. CDCLP 4006.

What this formidable aria collection triumphantly demonstrates is that Amy Shuard, for many years the leading soprano in the Covent Garden company, has been seriously underestimated. Her premature death at the age of 50 compounded what was already sadly evident, that this home-grown singer was not going to be fully appreciated. Even when originally issued on two LPs in the early 1960s, the recordings did not appear on a premium label, yet the singer, at once gloriously firm and strong, yet sensitively shaded and deeply expressive, whether as Aida, Turandot or Tatiana, can bear international comparision with other recording artists. The timbre may not have been of the most distinctive, but she amply compensated in the central strength and precision of everything she sang. There are few Turandots quite so incisive as this one. The Dutton transfer here is immaculate, with the voice vivid and clear.

Sills, Beverly (soprano)

'*The Singers*' (Decca series): **Arias from:** MOZART: *Die Entführung aus dem Serail.* MEYERBEER: *Les Huguenots; Robert le diable.* THOMAS: *Hamlet; Mignon.* CHARPENTIER: *Louise.* ADAM: *Le Toréador.* **Arias:** MOZART: *Vorrei spiegarvi, Oh Dio!, K.418.* BISHOP: *Lo! Hear the Gentle Lark.* R. STRAUSS: *Amor; Breit' über mein Haupt dein schwarzes Haar, Op. 19/2.*

(M) **(*) Decca (ADD) 467 906-2.

Decca curiously gives no published dates for this CD. The bulk of it comes from a 1969 recital LP of French arias (with the RPO under Mackerras), which, even more curiously, first appeared on HMV (ASD 2513). It was made at the time Beverly Sills emerged as an international star after she had already established her place as a favourite singer on the New York musical scene. The vocal facility is phenomenal, and a natural expressiveness is always part of Sills's performances. Her complete involvement is never in doubt, although when it comes to the voice itself, one cannot help but notice patches of comparatively sour tone and intrusive vibrato, notably at the top of the stave. But these are still enjoyable performances of tuneful music. This new compilation adds the engaging Adam aria (a set of variations on 'Twinkle, twinkle, little star') and Bishop's *Lo! Hear the Gentle Lark* (both with flute and piano accompaniment), as well as some lightly sung German repertoire. As usual, texts and translations and photographs are available only via a CD ROM drive.

Sinfonye, Stewart Wishart

'*Gabriel's greeting*' (Medieval carols) including: *Gabriel framevene king; Salva Virgo virginium; Ave Maria virgo virginium; Ther is no rose of swych vertu; Lolay, lolay; Nowell, nowell.*

**(*) Hyp. CDA 66685.

Unlike the Taverner Consort, who range over many centuries of music, Sinfonye concentrate on vocal and instrumental music from the thirteenth, fourteenth and fifteenth centuries, which usually consists of simple ostinato-like rhythmic ideas with a very distinctive melodic and harmonic character. These five singers and instrumentalists present their programme with spirit and vitality, but the range of the music is necessarily limited. Those who take to the repetitive medieval style will undoubtedly find this refreshing, and the recording is pleasingly live and atmospheric.

Söderström, Elisabeth (soprano)

'A Swedish song collection' (with Westerberg, Eyron, piano): ALMQVIST: *The Listening Maria; The Startled Maria; You are not Walking Alone; Why did you not Come to the Meadow?* BERGER: *Aspåkerspolka; Longing is my Inheritance.* LINDBLAD: *By Aarensee; I Wonder.* JOSEPHSON: *Serenade.* RANGSTROM: *Pan; Villema; The Girl under the New Moon; The Only Moment.* STENHAMMAR: *The Girl on Midsummer Eve; The Girl Returned from Meeting her Loved One; Adagio.* SJOGREN: *Sound, Sound my Pandero!; In the Shade of my Curls; I would Hold you Forever.* FRUMERIE: *A Letter Arrived; The Song of Love.*

*** Swedish Soc. SCD 1117.

These songs find Söderström at her finest in repertoire that she made very much her own in the late 1950s and 1960s, when she was in her prime. Songs like *Månntro (I Wonder)* by Adolf Fredrik Lindblad have an affecting simplicity that is quite haunting, and the Rangström songs, in particular *Den enda stunden (The Only Movement)*, have not been surpassed. Much of this wonderful repertoire will be new to collectors, as the original LPs enjoyed limited currency in the UK. They still sound wonderfully fresh.

Soprano arias

'20 Great soprano arias' from: MOZART: *Le nozze di Figaro* (Kiri Te Kanawa; Ileana Cotrubas). *Die Entführung aus dem Serail* (Kathleen Battle). *Die Zauberflöte* (Sumi Jo). PUCCINI: *Madama Butterfly* (Régine Crespin). *Turandot* (Caballé; Virginia Zeani). *La Rondine* (Renata Tebaldi). *Tosca* (Leontyne Price). *Gianni Schicchi* (Felicia Weathers). *La Bohème* (Mirella Freni; Elizabeth Harwood). VERDI: *I vespri siciliani* (Anita Cerquetti). *Un ballo in maschera* (Margaret Price). CATALANI: *La Wally* (Maria Chiara). PONCHIELLI: *La Gioconda* (Elena Souliotis). DONIZETTI: *La figlia del reggimento* (Graziella Sciutti). GOUNOD: *Faust* (Joan Sutherland). DVORAK: *Rusalka* (Pilar Lorengar). WAGNER: *Die Walküre* (Kirsten Flagstad).

(M) *** Decca (ADD) 458 230-2.

Decca's collection of '20 Great soprano arias' is made the more interesting by its use of twenty different singers, and the choices are not always obvious ones; for instance Régine Crespin's very individual and very touching *Un bel dì* from *Madama Butterfly*, Elena Souliotis's searingly powerful *Suicido* from *La Gioconda* and the beautifully spun line of Maria Chiara's *Ne andrò lonata* from *La Wally*.

Opening with Kiri Te Kanawa's moving *Dove sono*, other highlights include Kathleen Battle's vivacious portrayal of Blonde in *Die Entführung*, Kirsten Flagstad as Sieglinde in *Die Walküre*, the charming Graziella Sciutti, in *La figlia del reggimento*, and Joan Sutherland's scintillating (1960) *Jewel song*. Both Margaret and Leontyne Price are included, and of course Freni.

Alongside these familiar names come rather less well-known singers, all in excellent voice (Anita Cerquetti in *I vespri siciliani*; Felicia Weathers as Lauretta in *Gianni Schicchi*; Pilar Lorengar no less striking in Rusalka's famous Moon invocation, and Virginia Zeani alongside Caballé – two very contrasted voices – as Liù in *Turandot*). The programme ends with Sumi Jo's sparklingly precise coloratura in the most familiar of the Queen of the Night's arias from *Die Zauberflöte*. This famous show-piece has never been better sung on record – it has drama as well as extraordinary bravura.

Souzay, Gérard (baritone)

Early records including *Boîte à Musique* recordings: BASSANI: *Posate dormite.* A. SCARLATTI: *O cessate.* LULLY: *Air de ballet.* DURANTE: *Vergin tutt'amor.* POULENC: *Le Bestaire; La Grenouillère; Reine des mouettes.* SCHUMANN: *Der arme Peter; Der Sandman; Dein Angesicht.* BACH: *So oft ich meine Tabakspfeife; Willst du dein Herz mir schenken; Gedenke doch, mein Geist; Wie wohl ist mir, o Freund der Seelen.* LEGUERNEY: *7 Poèmes de François Maynard* (all with Bonnard, piano). PURCELL: *Sound the Trumpet; My Dearest, my Fairest* (with Touraine, piano). TCHAIKOVSKY: *Ah! Qui brula d'amour; Pendant le bal* (with Aitoff, piano). FAURE: *Mandoline; Le Plus doux chemin.* FRANCK: *Nocturne* (with Damase, piano). RAVEL: *Don Quichotte à Dulcinée* (with Paris Conservatoire O, Lindenberg).

✪ (M) (***) Dutton mono CDLX 7036.

These recordings come from the period when the great French baritone was at his freshest and most youthful. While his early Decca recordings have been available here, those for the Boîte à Musique label are rarities and should be snapped up. This is wonderful singing, well recorded and impeccably transferred to CD. A very special set.

Souzay, Gérard (baritone), Dalton Baldwin (piano)

Mélodies françaises: FAURE: *Chanson du pêcheur; Poème d'un jour, Op. 21; Les berceaux; Le secret;*

Aurore; Fleur jetée; La rose; Madrigal; 5 Mélodies de Venise, Op. 58; La bonne chanson, Op. 61; Le parfum impérissable; Arpège; Prison; Soir; Dans la forêt de septembre; La fleur qui va sur l'eau; Le don silencieux; La chanson d'Eve, Op. 95, excerpts (Eau vivante; O mort, poussière d'étoiles). Le jardin clos, Op. 106, excerpts (Exaucement; Je me poserai sur ton cœur). Mirages, Op. 113; L'horizon chimérique, Op. 118. POULENC: Chansons villageoises; Calligrammes; Le travail du peintre; La fraîcheur et le feu; Airs chantés: Air vif. La grenouillère; Métamorphoses: Reine des mouettes. Priez pour paix. RAVEL: 5 Mélodies populaires grecques; Epigrammes de Clément Marot; Histoires naturelles; Chansons madécasses; 2 Mélodies hébraïques; Don Quichotte à Dulcinée; Les grands vents venus d'outre-mer; Sainte; Sur l'herbe. LEGUERNEY: 20 Poèmes de la Pléiade, excerpts (Ma douce jouvence est passée; A son page). HAHN: L'heure exquise. DUPARC: L'invitation au voyage; Sérénade florentine; La vague et la cloche; Extase; Le manoir de Rosemonde; Lamento; La vie antérieure; Testament; Phidylé; Chanson triste; Elégie; Soupir. GOUNOD: L'absent; Sérénade. CHABRIER: Les cigales; Chanson pour Jeanne. BIZET: Chanson d'avril. FRANCK: Nocturne. ROUSSEL: Le jardin mouillé; Le bachelier de Salamanque.

⚫ (M) *** Ph. (ADD) 438 964-2 (4).

Now here is something to make the pulse quicken: Gérard Souzay recorded while still in his prime and in repertoire in which he was unmatched in his day. Only Bernac had as refined an interpretative intelligence and, of an older generation, only Panzera commanded an equal authority and tonal beauty. Souzay's 1963 recording of Fauré's La bonne chanson is one of the classics of the gramophone and has been extensively discussed in the Stereo Record Guide over the years. It was chosen by RL as one of his 'desert-island' discs in 'The Great Records' ('rich in artistry, imagination and insight').

The recording of the Deux Mélodies hébraïques is captivating, though Souzay made an even more haunting version for French EMI in the late 1950s; and one is hard pressed to choose between his Don Quichotte à Dulcinée and those of Panzera and Bernac. After Souzay's Philips disc with La bonne chanson came further recordings of Fauré, an anthology of other French mélodies and an LP of the Duparc songs, in every way superior to his later, EMI re-make in the early 1970s. This is treasure-trove which no lover of the French repertoire should be without. It is essential acquisition for Souzay admirers. Not everyone can afford four CDs all at one go, even at mid-price, and Philips would be wise to re-package the Fauré songs as part of their bargain Duo series, and issue the Duparc separately as well.

Stader, Maria (soprano)

'In memoriam': Arias from BACH: St. John Passion; St. Matthew Passion. HANDEL: Joshua; Messiah.

HAYDN: The Creation; The Seasons; MENDELSSOHN: Elijah. MOZART: Die Entführung aus dem Serail; Don Giovanni; Le nozze di Figaro; Die Zauberflöte; Vesperae solennes de confessore. Concert arias: Un moto di gioia, K.579; A questo seno deh vieni, K.375; Esxultate, jubilate. MENDELSSOHN: songs: Es weiss und röt es doch keiner; Nachtlied; Neue Liebe; Schilflied; Wanderlied.

(B) ** DG Double (IMS) Mono/Stereo 447 334-2 (2).

Although Maria Stader's reputation is in no doubt, this double-disc set is a mixed success. Perhaps best known as a Mozartian, some of her singing in this repertoire is a little variable: the Entführung aria, for example, sounds rather strained – the voice a bit shrill under pressure – though other examples show why her Mozart was so admired. In the oratorio extracts she is more secure, and there is also much to enjoy in the intimate Mendelssohn songs too. Whilst this set is not particularly recommendable to the general collector, admireres of this artist will be glad to have it, especially as some of the repertoire is available on CD for the first time. The recordings range from average to good, but the sleeve notes are restricted to biographical details only.

Stefano, Giuseppe di (tenor)

'The Singers' (Decca series): Arias (with Orchestra del Maggio Musicale Fiorentino, Bartoletti): VERDI: Aida; Luisa Miller; Otello. BOITO: Mefistofele. MEYERBEER: L'Africaine. PONCHIELLI: La Gioconda. PUCCINI: La fanciulla del West. CILEA: Adriana Lecouvreur. LEONCAVALLO: La Bohème. PIETRI: Maristella; GIORDANO: Fedora. PIZZETTI: Il calzare d'argento. Traditional Sicilian songs (arr. Favara, with Orchestra conducted by Olivieri): A la barcillunisa; A la vallelunghisa; Cantu a timuni; Chiovu Abballati; Muttetti di lu paliu; Nota di li lavannari.

(M) *** Decca 467 908-2.

The Bartoletti items come from a 1963 DG recital, and, if the sound is rather dry and unyielding, it is certainly bright and lively. Di Stefano is hardly subtle, but one is easily caught up in his vibrant and lusty music-making. His flamboyancy is certainly enjoyable, if a little wearing. The popular Neapolitan songs were recorded by Decca in 1959 and project vividly: these simple and endearing tunes, in colourful orchestrations, remain a joy; just sample the infectiously jolly Chiovu Abballati. As always in Decca's 'The Singers' series, texts and translations are available only via a CD ROM drive.

'Heroes': Arias and excerpts from: VERDI: Rigoletto; Il Trovatore; La Traviata; Un ballo in maschera. DONIZETTI: Lucia di Lammermoor. PUCCINI: Manon Lescaut; La Bohème; Tosca; Madama Butterfly. LEONCAVALLO: Pagliacci. MASCAGNI: Cavalleria rusticana.

(M) (***) EMI mono CDM5 66808-2.

Except for those demanding stereo, this is an out-standing demonstration of di Stefano's open-throated vocal ardour. The recordings date from between 1953 and 1956 when the voice was at its finest. Certainly the heroic side of his vocal personality comes over splendidly in Verdi (especially in *Di quella pira*) but he is at his finest and most responsive in the Puccini excerpts, the superb *Tosca* with de Sabata (1953), *Madama Butterfly* (1953), and *La Bohème* (1958). He is ideally cast as Turiddù, and his two arias from *Cavalleria rusticana*, which end the recital, are passionately moving, while the *Pagliacci Prologue* brings compellingly vibrant vocal histrionics. Excellent, vivid transfers which make one forget the age of the recordings.

Arias from: VERDI: *La Traviata; Un ballo in maschera; Rigoletto; Il Trovatore; La forza del destino.* PUCCINI: *La Bohème; Tosca; Manon Lescaut; Turandot; Madama Butterfly; La Fanciulla del West; Gianni Schicchi.* DONIZETTI: *Lucia di Lammermoor.* LEONCAVALLO: *Pagliacci.* MASCAGNI: *Cavalleria rusticana.* BIZET: *Les Pêcheurs de perles.* Songs: DI CAPUA: *O sole mio!* CARDILLO: *Core 'ngrato.* LEONCAVALLO: *Mattinata.* TOSTI: *La serenata.* DENZA: *Funiculì, funiculà.*

(BB) (***) Disky Royal Classics Vocal Double mono/stereo DCL 704822 (2).

Giuseppe di Stefano made his finest complete opera recordings for EMI at the end of the mono era, when he was usually partnered by Callas. Though he was not the subtlest of tenors, he was often in splendid voice and there is no doubting the visceral thrill of the key arias in the favourite Puccini roles, especially in *Manon Lescaut,* and the famous De Sabata *Tosca,* while he made a heroic figure of Pinkerton in *Butterfly* and he could be a tender Rodolfo in *La Bohème.* In Verdi he was both a crisply stylish Duke in *Rigoletto* and arresting as Manrico in *Il Trovatore.* Not everything here is equally distinctive, but he is obviously at home in the Neapolitan songs. The recording quality is variable but often the transfers are surprisingly successful.

'Torna a Surriento' (songs of Italy and Sicily): CD 1 (with New SO of London, Iller Pattacini): DE CURTIS: *Torna a Surriento; Tu ca' nun chiagne; Sonta chitarra!* BUONGIOVANNI: *Lacreme napulitane.* TAGLIAFERRI: *Napule canta; Pusilleco … califano: O 'surdato 'nnamurato.* CARDILLO: *Catari, Catari.* COSTA: *Era di maggio matenata; Scetate.* VALENTE: *Addio mia bella Napoli.* CD 2 (with Orchestra, Dino Olivieri): BIXIO: *Parlami d'amore Mariù.* BARBERIS: *Munasterio'e Santa-Chiara.* CESARINI: *Firenze sogna.* DE CURTIS: *Canta pe'me; 'A canzone'e Napule; Ti voglio tanto bene.* NARDELLA: *Che t'aggia di!* SIMI: *Come è bello far l'amore quanno è sera.* VANCHERI: *Sicilia bedda.* BUONGIOVANNI: *Fili d'oro.* DI LAZZARO: *Chitarra romana.* RIVI: *Addio, sogni di gloria.* TRAD., arr. FAVARA: *A la barcillunisi; Nota di li lavannari; A la vallelunghisa; Muttètti di lu pàliu; Chiovu 'abballati'; Cantu a timùni.*

(B) *** Double Decca (ADD) 455 482-2 (2).

Giuseppe di Stefano was still in magnificent voice when, in the summer of 1964, he recorded the collection of popular Italian songs assembled on the first disc of this Decca Double. He projects the ardent numbers such as the title-song with characteristic lustiness but less subtlety; despite the inevitable touches of vulgarity, the singing is rich-toned and often charming, and a famous Neapolitan hit like *Catari, Catari* is winningly done. Pattacini's accompaniments are vividly idiomatic.

The second collection is even more generous, offering eighteen songs (against eleven on the first disc). This dates from 1958, when the voice was even more honeyed, so that Bixio's opening *Parlami d'amore Mariù* sounds almost like operetta and brings an engaging pianissimo ending. The luscious Mantovani-styled accompaniments are certainly seductive, and very well recorded, while in *Come è bello far l'amore quanno è sera* the use of the mandolin is particularly atmospheric.

Besides the popular Neapolitan numbers, there are many comparative rarities here, often coming from Venice, Florence or Sicily, with their respective dialects. There are no translations, but none are really needed. As Frank Granville Barker observes in his note: 'Strong emotions are the concern of all these songs, expressed in no less straightforward melodies. The mood is intense, the singer declaring his devotion to his loved one, or despairing when it is not returned. Parting from home inspires as much anguish as parting from the loved one, as we hear in *Addio mia bella Napoli.*'

The group of six traditional songs arranged by Favara, which close the recital, are particularly fine; *Muttètti di lu pàliu* (introduced by a fine horn solo) is really memorable, with di Stefano responding to its plaintive melancholy with a very gentle closing cadence. He then follows with a sparkling tarantella, Chiovu 'abballati'. This is not a collection to play all at once (and memories of Gigli in this repertory are not vanquished), but in its field it is currently unsurpassed.

Streich, Rita (soprano)

'Waltzes and arias' (with Berlin RSO, RIAS Berlin, Kurt Gaebel): JOHANN STRAUSS JR: *Frühlingsstimmen; Draussen in Sievering.* SAINT-SAENS: *Le rossignol et la rose.* VERDI: *Lo spazzacamino.* ARDITI: *Parla waltz.* JOSEF STRAUSS: *Dorfschwalben aus Osterreich.* ALABIEV: *The Nightingale.* DELIBES: *Les filles de Cadiz.* CZERNIK: *Chi sa?* MARCHESI: *La folletta.* FLOTOW: *Last rose of summer.* DELL'ACQUA: *Villanelle.* ARDITI: *Il bacio.* Arias from: GODARD: *Jocelyn.* SUPPE: *Boccaccio.* DVORAK: *Rusalka.* MEYERBEER: *Dinorah.*

✪ (M) *** DG mono/stereo 457 729-2 (2).

Possessing the prettiest coloratura soprano voice of the second half of the twentieth century (and she was hardly less attractive to look at!), Rita Streich measured up well to all the competition from the 'Golden Age'. It was a small voice but perfectly formed, and it recorded marvellously well. Many of the most memorable pieces included here come from a recital she recorded in 1958 in the Jesus Christus Kirche, Berlin.

Included were the Strauss waltzes, Dvořák's *Invocation to the moon*, the charming *Hab' ich nur deine Liebe* from *Boccaccio* and the equally delightful *Shadow song* from *Dinorah*. Godard's highly romantic *Berceuse* is the most famous item, but it is in the deliciously fragile Saint-Saëns vocalise, *Le rossignol et la rose*, and in Verdi's captivating song of the chimney sweep (*Lo spazzacamino*) that her magic sends a shiver of special pleasure to the nape of the neck. A worthy vocal addition for DG's series of 'Originals'.

'*Folk songs and lullabies*': *Du, du liegst mir im Herzen; O du liabs Angeli; Frère Jacques; L'Amore de moi; Canto delle risaiole; Z'Lauterbach; Schlof sche, mein Vögele; Drink to me only with thine eyes; Nobody knows the trouble I've seen; Sakura, Sakura; Tschubtschik; Spi mladenez; In mezo al mar; Wenn ich ein Vöglein wär'; Der mond ist aufgegangen; Muss I denn zum Städtele 'maus* (with Rudolf Lamy Choir and instrumental accompaniment, Michalski). *Weisst Du, wieviel Sterne stehen; O wie wohl ist mir Abend; Wo e kleins Hüttle steht; All mein Gedanken; Glockenruf; Der Bürgermeister von Wesel; Der Wechsel der Jahreszeiten; Schlaf, Herzenssöhnchen; Schlafe, mein Prinzchen, schlaf ein; Sandmännchen; Der Kuckuck; Schwesterlein!; Ach Modr, ick will en Ding han; In der Fruah; Abendlied; Ave Maria* (with Regenszburger Domspatzen, Bavarian Radio SO, Kurt Gaebel).

(M) *** DG (ADD) 457 763-2.

This disc is a delight. Every song is most winning and it is difficult to say which is the more captivating, the Russian, French, English or Swiss folk songs, all dressed up in freshly colourful orchestrations, and the delectable *Frère Jacques* presented in canon with the choir. Rita Streich sings with obvious affection, with her legendary creaminess of vocal timbre tickling the ear throughout the two collections, which were recorded in 1963 and 1964. Their remarkable variety, to say nothing of the vocal charm, prevents any sense that 79 minutes of folk-song is too much. It is regretted that DG, in these beautifully transferred recordings on their Originals label, has failed to provide any texts or translations. But this is still a reissue not to be missed.

Sutherland, Dame Joan (soprano)

'*The Art of Joan Sutherland*':

Volume 1: Arias from: HANDEL: *Alcina; Giulio Cesare; Samson.* MOZART: *Die Entführung; Il Re Pastore; Die Zauberflöte.*

Volume 2: Arias from French operas: OFFENBACH: *Le Grande-Duchesse de Gérolstein; Robinson Crusoé.* MEYERBEER: *Dinorah; Robert le Diable.*

CHARPENTIER: *Louise.* AUBER: *Manon Lescaut.* BIZET: *Les Pêcheurs de Perles; Vasco de Gama.* MASSENET: *Cenrillon.* GOUNOD: *Faust; Mireille; Le Tribut de Zamora.* LECOCQ: *Le Coeur et la main.* MASSE: *Les Noces de Jeanette.*

Volume 3: 'Command Performance': WEBER: *Oberon.* MASSENET: *Le Cid.* MEYERBEER: *Dinorah; L'Étoile de Nord.* LEONCAVALLO: *Pagliacci.* VERDI: *I Masnadieri.* BELLINI: *Beatrice di Tenda.* DONIZETTI: *La Fille du Regiment.* OFFENBACH: *Contes d'Hoffman.* GOUNOD: *Faust.*

Volume 4: 'Rarities and surprises': Arias from WAGNER: *Der fliegende Holländer; Lohengrin; Die Meistersinger; Rienzi; Tannhäuser; Tristan und Isolde; Die Walküre.* MOZART: *Le Nozze di Figaro*: **arias.** GLIERE: *Concerto for coloratura soprano.* STRAVINSKY: *Pastorale.* CUI: *Ici bas.* GRETCHANINOV: *Lullaby.*

Volume 5: 'Great Operatic Scenes' from: MEYERBEER: *Les Huguenots.* BELLINI: *Norma.* DONIZETTI: *Lucia di Lammermoor.* VERDI: *Atilla; Ernani; I vespri siciliani; Traviata.*

*** Australian Decca (ADD) 466 474-2 (5)

For Decca, Joan Sutherland was one of their most important recording artists, particularly during the analogue LP era. In return, often with the prompting, and careful and imaginative planning of her husband and musical partner Richard Bonynge, they provided an extraordinary wide-ranging discography over her remarkably long recording career. This bargain box from Decca's Australian branch is important for including many recordings not otherwise available on CD.

Volume 1 is a reminder of her excellent Handel performances, with the arias mainly taken from her complete opera recordings, although the ringing account of *Let the bright seraphim* is from 'The Art of the Prima Donna', as is the Mozart *Die Entführung* aria. The other Mozart items are from her 1979 Mozart LP: not one of her best discs, but one which Sutherland admirers will surely want.

The French arias on Volume 2 were recorded in 1968 and sound sparklingly vivid and fresh in this new transfer. This was one of her most successful and infectiously tuneful recital discs: highlights include swirling coloratura waltzes from *Robinson Crusoé* and *Mireille*, a sparkling bolero by Lecocq, and spectacular set-piece arias by Meyerbeer, Auber and Charpentier.

Volume 3, '*Command Performance*' is hardly less succesful: the showy numbers of Meyerbeer, Donizetti and Offenbach display her virtuoso singing to the full, whilst her hauntingly exquisite bel canto in the Bellini item is another highlight.

Volume 4 includes her 1979 Wagner recital, and more items from the Mozart recital from the same year: this is not top-drawer Sutherland, but it is fascinating to hear (this is their CD debut); the Glière *Concerto for coloratura soprano* is quite superb.

The final volume, a collection of operatic scenes, includes the great 1959 Paris recording of the *Mad scene* from *Lucia*, as well as the arias from *Ernani* and the splendidly crisp bolera from *I vespri siciliani* from the same disc. All in all, a splendid collection of some great singing and interesting repertoire, with stylish orchestal contributions, mainly from Richard Bonynge, and although no texts are provided, there are good sleeve notes.

'*Grandi voci*': BELLINI: *Norma: Sediziose voci ... Casta diva ... Ah! bello a me ritorna. I Puritani: Qui la voce sua soave ... Vien, diletto* (with ROHCG O, Molinari-Pradelli). VERDI: *Attila: Santo di patria ... Allor che i forti corrono ... Da te questo or m'è concesso* (with LSO, Bonynge); *Ernani: Surta è la notte ... Ernani! Ernani, involami. I vespri siciliani: Mercè, dilette amiche (Boléro).* DONIZETTI: *Lucia di Lammermoor: Ancor non giunse! ... Regnava nel silenzio; Il dolce suono mi colpi di sua voce! ... Ardon gl'incensi (Mad scene). Linda di Chamounix: Ah! tardai troppo ... O luce di quest'anima.*

✿ (M) *** Decca (ADD) 440 404-2.

Sutherland's '*Grandi voci*' disc is one of the most cherishable of all operatic recital records, bringing together the glorious, exuberant items from her very first recital disc, made within weeks of her first Covent Garden success in 1959, and – as a valuable supplement – the poised accounts of *Casta diva* and *Vien, diletto* she recorded the following year as part of 'The Art of the prima donna'.

It was this 1959 recital which at once put Sutherland firmly on the map among the great recording artists of all time. Even she has never surpassed the freshness of these versions of the two big arias from *Lucia di Lammermoor*, sparkling in immaculate coloratura, while the lightness and point of the jaunty *Linda di Chamounix* aria and the *Boléro* from *I vespri siciliani* are just as winning. The aria from *Attila* comes from 'The age of bel canto' (1963). The sound is exceptionally vivid and immediate, though the accompaniments under Nello Santi are sometimes rough in ensemble.

'*Love live forever (The Romance of musical comedy)*' (with Ambrosian Light Opera Chorus, New Philharmonia Orchestra, Bonynge): Excerpts from: ROMBERG: *The Student prince; The Desert song.* RODGERS: *The Boys from Syracuse.* KERN: *Music in the air; Show Boat.* FRIML: *Rose Marie.* HERBERT: *The Only girl.* FRASER-SIMPSON: *The Maid of the Mountains.* GERMAN: *Tom Jones.* OFFENBACH: *La Périchole.* MASSENET: *Chérubin.* ZELLER: *Der Vogelhändler.* MILLOCKER: *The Dubarry.* FALL: *Die geschiedene Frau; Die spanische Nachtigall; Die Dollarprinzessin; Madame Pompadour; Die liebe Augustin.* LEHAR: *Eva; Die lustige Witwe; Paganini.* STRAUS: *Ein Walzertraum; The Chocolate soldier.* HEUBERGER: *Der Opernball.* JOHANN STRAUSS JR: *Casanova.* KREISLER: *The King steps out.* POSFORD: *Balalaika.*

(B) *** Double Decca (ADD) 452 955-2 (2).

Beginning with an exuberant account of the opening chorus from *The Student prince* and including a glorious performance of the title number from *The Desert song (Blue heaven)*, this is a lilting, whooping recital to set against the superb Schwarzkopf record of operetta favourites which covers some of the same ground. Sutherland may not always match Schwarzkopf in the haunting Viennese quality which inhabits such an enchanting number as *Im chambre séparée*, but her range of repertoire here is far wider, including as it does a pair of Offenbach items, not to mention the songs from American and British musicals down to *The Boys from Syracuse*.

Above all it is the tune that counts and there are plenty of good ones, not least *Make believe* from *Show Boat* and the unforgettable *Love will find a way* from *The Maid of the Mountains*. Bonynge's sparkling selection ranges into the easily melodious world of Romberg and Friml, Fraser-Simpson and Oscar Straus, and most enterprisingly includes a potpourri from the German operettas of Leo Fall. What is immediately obvious is Sutherland's own delight in singing this music, with no apology whatever. Produced by Christopher Raeburn, the sumptuous Kingsway Hall recording catches the glory of Sutherland's voice (in the mid 1960s) to perfection against appropriately rich accompaniments all specially arranged by Douglas Gamley.

'*Greatest hits*': Excerpts from: HANDEL: *Samson.* PICCINNI: *La buona figliuola.* BELLINI: *Norma; I Puritani.* DONIZETTI: *La fille du régiment; Lucia di Lammermoor: Mad scene.* DELIBES: *Lakmé.* VERDI: *Rigoletto; La Traviata.* GOUNOD: *Faust.* OFFENBACH: *Contes d'Hoffmann.*

(M) *** Decca (ADD) 458 209-2.

A 76-minute collection like this, well chosen to entertain, is self-recommending at mid-price. It has been nicely repackaged in a slip-case for this reissue in Decca's Opera Gala series, and translations are now included. The chosen recordings have been slightly amended since the previous issue but all come from the period when the voice was at its freshest: *Let the bright seraphim*, the delectable *Caro nome* and the vivacious *Jewel song* from Faust date from 1960, but here the justly famous 1959 Mad scene from *Lucia di Lammermoor* has been substituted for the performance in the complete set under Pritchard. The lively excerpt from *La fille du régiment* (1967) and the *Doll song* from *Contes d'Hoffmann* (1972) come from the complete sets, as does the famous Act I *La Traviata* scena (1962), which is now added. The sound is consistently vivid.

'*Mad scenes*' from: BELLINI: *I Puritani.* MEYERBEER: *Dinorah; L'Etoile du Nord.* DONIZETTI: *Lucia di Lammermoor.* THOMAS: *Hamlet.*

(M) *** Decca (ADD) 458 243-2.

No Sutherland 'mad scene' recital would be complete without her *Lucia* portrayal and here we have the 1971 version from the complete set. It is generally considered that her early 1959 Paris recording is her finest, but this one is equally compelling: her voice is richer, more characterful – and is better recorded and conducted. If it doesn't quite have the girlish quality which made the early one so remarkable, it makes up for it in maturity of interpretation.

The *Hamlet* scene is now a relative rarity: it is remarkably effective, with some particularly imaginative writing from Thomas: the humming chorus creates a haunting effect and the orchestration throughout is piquantly telling. As for Sutherland, it is remarkable how youthful she sounds. Considering that this digital recording was made when she was in her fifties, her coloratura is still effortlessly beautiful.

The *Puritani* excerpt is taken from the 1973 complete recording – one of the most successful of all the Bonynge-Sutherland sets. The two Meyerbeer showpieces are as charming as they are brilliant, and complete this well-planned 'Opera Gala' compilation. Full texts and translations are included, which makes this especially recommendable among the current Sutherland single-disc anthologies.

'The Singers' (Decca series): Arias from: DONIZETTI: *Lucia di Lammermoor.* WAGNER: *Lohengrin; Tannhäuser.* Concert aria: MOZART: *Vorrei spiegarvi, K.418.* Songs: ROSSINI: *La danza (Tarantella napoletana); L'Orgia.* DAVID: *Les Hirondelles.* GOUNOD: *Au Printemps; O Divine Redeemer.* MASSENET: *Oh! si les fleurs avaient des yeux.* HAHN: *Si mes vers avaient des ailes.* LA FORGE: *I Came with a Song.* DEL RIEGO: *Homing.* COWARD: *Conversation Piece: I'll Follow My Secret Heart. Bitter Sweet: I'll See You Again; Zigeuner.* ADAM: *Holy Night.*

(M) ** Decca (ADD) 467 914-2.

This compilation includes Sutherland's famous early version of the Mad Scene from *Lucia* from the Paris 1959 recital conducted by Santi and also some lush arrangements by Douglas Gamley of songs by Coward (rather diverting), Hahn, Adam and Gounod. It seldom shows Sutherland at her brilliant best. Some of the songs (Rossini, David, Gounod and Massenet), charming though they be, were recorded (with Bonynge as accompanist) at her home in 1978, and the sound here is very dry and with virtually no ambience, making somewhat tiring listening. The Wagner items are fascinating, although this is hardly repertory that suits her. Without printed texts and translations, this is a disc for the Sutherland specialist rather than the general collector, although most of the items are available more usefully coupled on other CDs.

Sutherland, Joan (soprano), Marilyn Horne (mezzo-soprano), Luciano Pavarotti (tenor)

'Live from the Lincoln Center, New York' (Duets and trios): VERDI: *Ernani: Solingo, errante e misero.*

Otello: Già nella notte densa. Il Trovatore: Madre non dormi? BELLINI: *Norma: Adalgisa! ... Oh! rimembranza! Ma di' ... Oh non tremare.* PONCHIELLI: *La Gioconda: Ecco la barca ... addio; Deh! non turbare.*

(M) *** Decca (IMS) (ADD) 458 207-2.

Not all gala concerts make good records, but this 1981 occasion is an exception; almost every item here puts an important gloss on the achievements of the three stars, not least in the concerted numbers which have been separated off for this single-disc reissue in Decca's Opera Gala series. It is good to have a sample not only of Sutherland's Desdemona, but also of Pavarotti's Otello (not at that time heard, either on stage or in the studio) in their account of the Act I duet. The final scene from *Il Trovatore* is more compelling than on the complete set made by the same soloists five years earlier. At times the microphones catch a beat in the voices of both Sutherland and Horne, but not as obtrusively as on some studio discs. Lively accompaniments under Bonynge, bright, vivid, digital recording, but over-loud applause. The documentation includes full translations and a picture of the celebrated occasion.

Sutherland, Joan (soprano), Luciano Pavarotti (tenor)

'Love duets' (with National PO, Richard Bonynge from VERDI: *La Traviata; Otello; Aida* (with chorus). BELLINI: *La Sonnambula.* DONIZETTI: *Linda di Chamounix.*

(M) *** Decca (ADD) 458 235-2.

This collection, recorded in the Kingsway Hall in 1976, offers a rare sample of Sutherland as Aida (*La fatale pietra ... O terra, addio* from Act IV), a role she sang only once on stage, well before her international career began; and with this and her sensitive impersonations of Desdemona, Violetta (generously represented) and the Bellini and Donizetti heroines, Sutherland might have been expected to steal first honours here. In fact these are mainly duets to show off the tenor, and it is Pavarotti who runs away with the main glory, though both artists were plainly challenged to give their finest. The result, with excellent accompaniment, is among the most attractive and characterful duet recitals in the catalogue. The recording is admirably clear and well focused, and the sophistication of orchestral detail is striking in the *Otello* and *Aida* scenes which close the recital, with the singers given remarkable presence.

Tallis Scholars, Peter Phillips

'Western Wind Masses': SHEPPARD: *Mass, The Western wynde.* TAVERNER: *Mass, Western Wynde.* TYE: *Mass, Western wind.*

*** Gimell CDGIM 027.

It was a splendid idea for Gimell to gather together the three key Mass settings which use the well-known source theme, the *Western Wynde*. The performances are as eloquent as we would expect from this source and they are beautifully recorded. Taverner's setting emerges as the most imaginative, but Tye comes pretty close. A most enterprising issue which deserves support.

'*Live in Oxford*': OBRECHT: *Salve Regina*. JOSQUIN DESPREZ: *Gaude Virgo; Absalon fili mei*. TAVERNER: *Gaude plurium*. BYRD: *Tribus, Domine*. TALLIS: *O sacrum convivium*. MUNDY: *Adolescentulus sum ego; Vox Patris caelestis*.

*** Gimell CDGIM 998-2.

The fledgling Tallis Scholars gave their first concert, in 1973, in the Church of St Mary Magdalen, but have chosen the Chapel of Merton College for this, their twenty-fifth-anniversary programme. The beauty of its acoustic, resonant but unclouding, is ideal for their flowing style in this survey of fifteenth- and sixteenth-century masterpieces, ending with Mundy's spectacularly ambitious *Vox Patris caelestis*, with its vocal complexities confidently encompassed, especially by the soaring trebles.

Talvela, Martti (bass)

'*The Singers*' (Decca series): *Song Recital* (with Gage or Gothoni, piano): SCHUMANN: *12 Gedichte, Op. 35*. MUSSORGSKY: *Songs and Dances of Death; The Flea*. RACHMANINOV: *Christ is Risen; Night is Mournful; Oh Never Sing to Me Again; Oh Stay My Love Forsake Me Not!*

(M) **(*) Decca (ADD) 467 903-2.

The Russian items were recorded in 1980 and find Martti Talvela's magnificent bass voice superbly caught. His Mussorgsky is dark and intense, immediate and involving – a singer with an operatic background gains enormously here – and at the time this was the finest version to appear since Boris Christoff's: no praise could be higher. The Rachmaninov is not quite so successful, as Talvela modifies his dark tones to suit the gentler lines of this music, and, as recorded, the voice acquires a plaintive quality, which is not as pleasing. However, it remains a commanding account. The Finnish bass is similarly rich and vibrant in the Schumann Lieder, recorded in 1969 and excellently accompanied by Irwin Gage. This is a very individual performance, striking in its depth. If heavier than classic accounts by Fischer-Dieskau, it is equally valid and certainly gives these wonderful songs another dimension. There is vivid sound throughout in this transfer, and this is one of the best in Decca's 'The Singers' series. Even if texts and translations (and photos) are available only by using a CD ROM drive, this must still be given a pretty strong recommendation.

Taverner Consort and Choir, Andrew Parrott

'*The promise of ages*': A Christmas collection (with members of New London Chamber Choir & Henrietta Barnett School Choir & (i) Frances Kelly, Welsh harp; (ii) Paul O'Shaughnessy, Irish fiddle): CHARLES BURNEY: *Hark! The herald angels sing*. Arr. EDWARD JONES: (i) *Deck the hall*. NILES: (ii) *Lullay, thou tiny child; I wonder as I wander; Sing we the Virgin Mary*. TRAD.: *There is no rose of swych vertu; Lullay, lullow, I saw a swete semly syght; Song of the Nuns of Chester; Hayl, Mary, ful of grace; Hodie Christus natus est*; (ii) *The seven joys of Mary; Good people all, this Christmastide; Christmas eve*. HOLST: *I sing of a maiden; Jesu, thou the Virginborn*. BRITTEN: (i) *Ceremony of carols: There is no rose; As dew in Aprille*. MAXWELL DAVIES: *O magnum mysterium; The Fader of heven*. WEIR: *Illuminare, Jerusalem*. VAUGHAN WILLIAMS: *In Bethlehem City*. MADAN: *Lo! he comes with clouds descending*.

*** Sony SK 60713.

Opening with an engagingly unfamiliar setting of *Hark! the herald angels sing* (perhaps by Charles Burney) this is an extraordinarily varied selection, ranging from very early carols and chants to striking modern settings from Holst, Britten, Maxwell Davies and Judith Weir. Further diversity is provided by delicate solo peformances on the Welsh harp (*Deck the hall*) and traditional Irish fiddle solos (*Good people all, this Chrismastide*). Indeed, this beautifully played, sung and recorded programme offers much pleasure from its very range and unexpected juxtapositions.

Many of the items are given as solos, while *There is no rose* is presented very touchingly as a vocal trio. Among the modern settings, *The Fader of heven* and *Illuminare, Jerusalem* stand out as hauntingly individual, but then so do the simpler medieval carols. The presentation in the resonant acoustic of St Jude-on-the-Hill, Hampstead Garden Suburb, could not be more evocative. Altogether this is a Christmas Eve entertainment of distinction, and it will give great pleasure.

Taverner Consort, Choir and Players, Andrew Parrott

'*The Christmas Album*' (Festive music from Europe and America): BILLINGS: *Methinks I see an heav'nly host; A virgin unspotted*. FOSTER: *While shepherds watched their flocks*. CEREROLS: *Serafin, quin con dulce harmonia*. Francisco DE VIDALES: *Los que fueren de buen gusto*. PRAETORIUS: *Magnificat super Angelus ad pastores*. MARC-ANTOINE CHARPENTIER: *In nativitatem Domini nostri Jesu Christi canticum*. PASCHA: *Gloria*. arr. GREATOREX: *Adeste fidelis*.

(M) *** Virgin VC5 45155-2.

Another refreshing Christmas collection which treads much unfamiliar territory. Opening and closing with jolly carols that sound almost like rustic drinking songs, from the New England composer William Billings – with the chorus giving their pronunciation an appropriate transatlantic twang – the concert moves from a bright baroque setting of *While shepherds watched their flocks*, a new tune, with Bachian trumpets, by John Foster (1762–1822) to a haunting *Gloria* by Edmund Pascha. This represents Slovakia; from France there is a charming Christmas sequence by Marc-Antoine Charpentier.

In between comes a gloriously sonorous *Magnificat* by Michael Praetorius and, at last something familiar, *Adeste fidelis*, arranged by Thomas Greatorex in a choral concerto grosso style. Best of all are the *Villancicos*, one by Joan Cererols from Catalonia, one even jollier by the seventeenth-century Mexican Francisco de Vidales, which in their colour and vitality reflect the popular dance music of the time. Performances are as lively as they are stylish and the soloists are excellent. The 1991 recording, made at St John's at Hackney, London, has plenty of atmosphere and presence.

Tear, Robert (tenor)

'**English baroque recital**' (with Iona Brown, violin, Kenneth Heath, cello, Simon Preston and Colin Tilney, harpsichord continuo, ASMF, Marriner): HANDEL: *Look down, harmonious Saint; Meine Seele hört im Sehen; Süsse Stille*. ARNE: *Bacchus and Ariadne*: excerpts; *Fair Caelia love pretended*: excerpts. BOYCE: *Song of Momus to Mars*. JAMES HOOK: *The Lass of Richmond Hill.*

(B) *** Double Decca (ADD) 452 973-2 (2) (with HANDEL: *Acis and Galatea* ***).

Robert Tear's 1969 recital offers a rare Handel cantata and two of his German songs, followed by an even rarer and certainly delightful collection of music by his English successors. This may in essence be a scholarly compilation, but it is one which imparts its learning in the most painless way, including as it does the vigorous Boyce song and the original, bouncing setting of *The Lass of Richmond Hill*, beautifully pointed. The *harmonious Saint* of the Handel cantata is of course St Cecilia, while Arne too is in Italianate mood in *Bacchus and Ariadne* – until he ends with a galumphing final number with ripe horn parts – very English. Robert Tear is in excellent voice and the recording has all the atmospheric warmth one associates with Argo's recordings of the ASMF in St John's, Smith Square.

Tebaldi, Renata (soprano)

'**The Singers**' (Decca series): Arias from: GOUNOD: *Faust*. PUCCINI: *La Bohème; Gianni Schicchi; Madama Butterfly; Manon Lescaut*. CATALANI: *La Wally*. VERDI: *Aida*. CILEA: *Adriana Lecouvreur*.

HANDEL: *Serse*. PAISIELLO: *La molinara*. PERGOLESI: *La serva padrona*. Songs: GLUCK: *Paride ed Elena*. MARTINI: *Piacer d'amor*. ADAM: *O Holy Night*. GOUNOD: *O Divine Redeemer*. RODGERS: *If I Loved You.*

(M) *(*) Decca mono/stereo 467 915-2.

Once again, as with Sutherland and Leontyne Price, Decca has chosen examples from a great singer late in her career. The songs, as well as the Paisiello and Handel numbers, derive from a 1973 LP with the New Philharmonia Orchestra, conducted by Richard Bonynge, in arrangements by Douglas Gamley. Although they have undoubted charm, with the artist making the most of the souped-up arrangements, Tebaldi is past her prime, although her obvious love of the music makes one forget some of the technical deficiencies. Only the Puccini items, recorded between 1950 and 1962, find Tebaldi at her best, but the rest of the programme was recorded from 1969 to 1972, again at the end of her career. With texts and translations available only via a CD ROM drive, readers would do far better to turn to the more comprehensive collection below: 'The Great Renata Tebaldi'. Generally vivid sound.

'**The Great Renata Tebaldi**' (recordings made between 1949 and 1969): Arias and excerpts (with various artists, orchestras and conductors) from: PUCCINI: *Gianni Schicchi; Tosca; Suor Angelica; Il tabarro; La fanciulla del West; Turandot; La Bohème; Manon Lescaut; Madama Butterfly*. CATALANI: *La Wally*. PONCHIELLI: *La Gioconda*. CILEA: *Adriana Lecouvreur*. GIORDANO: *Andrea Chénier*. BOITO: *Mefistofele*. VERDI: *Aida; Il trovatore; La traviata; La forza del destino; Otello; Don Carlos; Un ballo in maschera*. LEHAR: *The Merry Widow: Vilja* (sung in Italian). ROSSINI: *La regata veneziana: Anzoleta avant la regata.*

(M) *** Decca mono/stereo 470 280-2 (2).

For I.M. during the years following the end of the Second World War, the discovery of Tebaldi was something of a revelation. He purchased her first Decca mono LP, which was recorded by Decca, in 1949 and was immediately entranced by the sheer lyrical beauty of her voice. Two of the items on that LP (Verdi's *Ritorna vincitor* from *Aida* and *Tacea la notte placida* from *Il trovatore*) are used to open the second of the two discs of this set, and the vocal magic is immediately apparent. The ffrr mono recording, made in the Victoria Hall, Geneva, still sounds pretty remarkable, and one feels that it was a pity that Decca chose not to assemble this collection in historical order, for the third item on disc two is an infinitely touching account of *Parigi o cara, noi lasceremo* from *La traviata*, with Gianni Poggi a remarkably sympathetic Alfredo. Then comes a famous aria from *La forza del destino* (*Ma pellegrina ed orfana … Pace, pace, mio Dio!*) in which Tebaldi produces one of those exquisite sudden pianissimos in her upper range that was one of the frisson-making hallmarks of her vocal line. The scene from *Don Carlos*, with Nicolai Ghiaurov, conducted by Solti a decade later, follows soon afterwards, demonstrating that, under the right conductor, she could also rise to thrilling drama in Verdi.

But it was not for Verdi that she was most renowned. Her great contemporary, Maria Callas, could upstage her there, for she was a much greater stage actress. But in Puccini (especially) and comparable Italian bel canto roles Tebaldi was unsurpassed in the 1950s and 1960s, recording the principal roles more than once.

If her Mimì was unforgettable (touchingly remembered here in the Love Scene from Act I of *La bohème*, with Carlo Bergonzi, dating from 1959), she was also a delightful Lauretta, and *O mio babbino caro* (1962) opens the first disc ravishingly. The following *Vissi d'arte* (*Tosca*, 1959) is equally lovely. Other highlights include the key arias from *Suor Angelica, Manon Lescaut* and a splendid excerpt from *La fanciulla del West* (with Cornell MacNeil as Jack Rance). In *Turandot* she chose the lesser part of Liù, and *Signore, ascolta, Tu che di gel sel cinta* is characteristically melting.

Her rather stiff acting meant that she was perhaps a less than ideal *Madama Butterfly*, but even so the Love Scene from Act I (again with Bergonzi) is vocally spellbinding, and many other key arias from comparable non-Puccini repertoire are no less bewitching and certainly dramatic, notably the excerpts from *La Wally* and *La Gioconda* (which demonstrate her rich lower range), *Adriana Lecouvreur* and *Andrea Chénier*. She was fortunate that the Decca engineers recorded her voice with complete naturalness, as the current CD transfers (which are excellent) so uniformly show. This is not a set to play through all at once, for subtlety of characterization was not Tebaldi's strong suit; if it is dipped into judiciously, however, one is consistently seduced by Tebaldi's beauty of tone and simplicity of line.

'Grandi voci': Arias and excerpts from: PUCCINI: *Madama Butterfly; La Bohème* (with Carlo Bergonzi); *Turandot* (with Mario del Monaco); *Tosca; Gianni Schicchi; Suor Angelica; La Fanciulla del West* (with Cornell MacNeil); *Manon Lescaut.* VERDI: *Aida; Otello* (with Luisa Ribacci); *La forza del destino.* CILEA: *Adriana Lecouvreur.* GIORDANO: *Andrea Chénier.* BOITO: *Mefistofele.* CATALANI: *La Wally.*

(M) *** Decca (ADD) (IMS) 440 408-2.

Those wanting a single-disc, stereo representation of Tebaldi's vocal art could hardly do better than this. It is good that her early mono complete sets of *La Bohème* and *Madama Butterfly* are now again available, and the selection here rightly concentrates on her stereo remakes of the key Puccini operas in the late 1950s, when the voice was still creamily fresh. *Vissi d'arte* (1959) is particularly beautiful. She could be thrilling in Verdi too, as the splendid *Ritorna vincitor!* vibrantly demonstrates, taken from Karajan's complete *Aida*, made in the same year. With a playing time of 75 minutes, this recital should disappoint no one, for the Decca recordings come up as vividly as ever.

Songs and arias (with Giorgio Favaretto, piano): Recital I: Songs: ANON.: *Leggiadri occhi bello.* A. SCARLATTI: *Le violette.* ROSSINI: *Soirées musicales: La promessa.* BELLINI: *Dolente immagine di fille mia; Vanne, o rosa Fortunata.* MARTUCCI: *La canzone dei recordi (Al folto bosco; Cavanta il ruscello; Sul mar la navicella).* TRAD., arr. FAVARA: *A la barcillunisa.* MASETTI: *Passo e non ti vedo.* TURINA: *Poema en forma de canciones: Cantares.* Arias: HANDEL: *Giulio Cesare: Piangerò la sorte mia.* SARTI: *Giulio Sabino: Lungi dal caro bene.*

Recital II: Songs: A. SCARLATTI: *Chi vuole innamorarsi.* ROSSINI: *Péchés de vieillesse: 3 Songs in Venetian dialect (Anzoleta avanti La Regata; Anzoleta co passa la Regata; Anzoleta dopo la Regata).* Arias: A. SCARLATTI: *Il Seddecia, Re di Gerusalemme: Caldo sangue.* HANDEL: *Armadigi de Gaula: Ah! spietato.* MOZART: *Ridente la calma, K.152; Un moto di gioia, K.579.* BELLINI: *Vaga luna che inargenti; Per pietà, bell'idol mio.* MASCAGNI: *M'ama ... non m'ama.* RESPIGHI: *Notte.* TOSTI: *'A vucchella.* DAVICO: *O luna che fa lum.*

(B) ** Double Decca (ADD) 452 472-2 (2).

Here combined on a Decca Double are a pair of song recitals which Tebaldi recorded fairly early in her career, in 1956 and 1957 respectively, and which have been out of the catalogue for forty years, although four items – by Scarlatti, Rossini, Mozart and the charming Favara folksong arrangement – were put out on a stereo '45' disc at the beginning of the 1960s. The voice sounds young and fresh but, like many another Italian opera singer, Tebaldi proved hardly a stylist in eighteenth-century music, and the lighter songs do not always suit her big voice.

But when she comes to the arias it is a different matter. Cleopatra's lament from the third Act of Handel's *Giulio Cesare* brings a natural, flowing legato, and Sarti's *Lungi dal caro bene* is gently ravishing. The two Bellini ariettas are also appealingly sung, and Verdi's *Stornella* makes a light-hearted contrast, while the three excerpts from Martucci's seven-part mini-cycle about another forsaken maiden, sadly and affectionately remembering past times with her lover, produces a charming and touching response. The following Sicilian folksong, *A la barcillunisa*, soars like a Puccini aria, and the first disc ends seductively with Turina's *Cantares*.

The second recital opens with a vivacious canzonetta, nicely articulated, warning of the dangers of falling in love, and the following Scarlatti and Handel arias do not disappoint. Tebaldi obviously had a soft spot for Rossini's songs in Venetian dialect (which come from his 'Sins of my old age') and she sings them with a lighter touch here than in her later recording (see above).

Tebaldi's Mozart singing is freely peppered with intrusive aitches and occasional swerves, but she is back on form in the two Bellini songs and, after a rich-voiced if a very operatic version of Respighi's *Notte*, she finishes in lighter vein with a lilting Tosti favourite – another song she included in her later recital – and a meltingly affectionate account of a colloquial Tuscan song, arranged by Vincenzo Davico. Throughout, Giorgio Favaretto accompanies quite supportively, if without producing a distinctive personality, but the recording balance does not flatter him and the piano sounds rather withdrawn at times.

Terfel, Bryn (bass-baritone), Malcolm Martineau (piano)

'*The vagabond and other English songs*': VAUGHAN WILLIAMS: *Songs of travel (The vagabond; Let beauty awake; The roadside fire; Youth and love; In dreams; The infinite shining heavens; Whither must I wander; Bright in the ring of words; I have trod the upward and the downward slope).* G. BUTTERWORTH: *Bredon hill (Bredon hill; Oh fair enough; When the lad for longing sighs; On the idle hill of summer; With rue my heart is laden); The Shropshire lad (6 songs): Loveliest of trees; When I was one-and-twenty; Look not in my eyes; Think no more, lad; The lads in their hundreds; Is my team ploughing?* FINZI: *Let us garlands bring (Come away, death; Who is Silvia?; Fear no more the heat of the sun; O mistress mine; It was a lover and his lass).* IRELAND: *Sea fever; The vagabond; The bells of San Marie.*

🌑 *** DG 445 946-2.

No other collection of English songs has ever quite matched this one in its depth, intensity and sheer beauty. Terfel, the great Welsh singer of his generation, here shows his deep affinity with the English repertory, demonstrating triumphantly in each of the twenty-eight songs that this neglected genre deserves to be treated in terms similar to those of the German Lied and the French mélodie. The Vaughan Williams songs are perhaps the best known, nine sharply characterized settings of Robert Louis Stevenson which, thanks to Terfel's searching expressiveness matched by Martineau's inspired accompaniments, reveal depths of emotion hardly suspected.

The five Shakespeare settings by Finzi are just as memorable in their contrasted ways, five of the best-known lyrics from the plays that have been set countless times but which here are given new perspectives, thanks both to the composer and to the singer. The eleven Butterworth settings of Housman are among the finest inspirations of this short-lived composer, and it is good to have three sterling Ireland settings of Masefield, including the ever-popular *Sea fever*, which with Terfel emerges fresh and new. The singer's extreme range of tone and dynamic, down to the most delicate, firmly supported half-tones, is astonishing, adding intensity to one of the most felicitous song-recital records in years. The warm acoustic of the Henry Wood Hall gives a glow both to the voice and to the piano.

'*Impressions*' (with (i) E. Bar. Soloists, Gardiner; (ii) Malcolm Martineau, piano; (iii) Philh. O, Sinopoli; (iv) BPO, Abbado): (i) MOZART: *Le nozze di Figaro: Se vuol ballare; Non più andrai; Aprite un po' quegli occhi.* (ii) SCHUBERT: *Litanei auf das Fest Allerseelen; Die Forelle; An die Musik; Erlkönig.* (iii) MAHLER: *Kindertotenlieder.* (ii) VAUGHAN WILLIAMS: *The vagabond; The roadside fire.* (iv) WAGNER: *Die Meistersinger: Wie duftet doch der Flieder. Tannhäuser: O! du mein holder Abendstern.*

*** DG 449 190-2.

Ranging over the recordings made for DG up to his English song disc, this sampler gives a formidable idea of this brilliant young singer's powers, very well chosen not just from his solo discs but from complete opera sets and discs with orchestra.

'*A night at the opera*': Disc 1: Operatic arias (with Metropolitan Opera Orchestra, James Levine) from: MOZART: *Le nozze di Figaro; Così fan tutte; Don Giovanni; Die Zauberflöte.* WAGNER: *Tannhäuser; Der fleigende Holländer.* OFFENBACH: *Contes d'Hoffmann.* GOUNOD: *Faust.* BORODIN: *Prince Igor.* DONIZETTI: *Don Pasquale.* ROSSINI: *La Cenerentola.* VERDI: *Macbeth; Falstaff.*

Disc 2: Arias from: HANDEL (with Scottish Chamber Orchestra, Mackerras): *Acis and Galatea; Alcina; Alexander's feast; Berenice; Dettingen Te Deum; Giulio Cesare; Judas Maccabaeus; Messiah; Orlando; Samson; Semele; Serse.*

(M) *** DG 467 092-2 (2).

This two-disc compilation brings together without amendment Bryn Terfel's two impressive recital discs: the first of opera, from Mozart and Donizetti to Wagner, Verdi and Borodin, recorded in New York with James Levine conducting, and the second devoted to Handel, thirty-four arias in all. The miscellaneous recital, keenly enjoyable, offers, in Terfel's own words, 'a future diary of my opera plans' and demonstrates not just the warmth and musical imagination of this brilliant singer, but his range and power too.

The account of *Non più andrai* is weightier, marginally broader and even more characterful than the one he recorded as part of John Eliot Gardiner's complete set and that is typical of his development. Though Mozart is central to his repertory, it is striking that the most thrilling items of all are those which test him most severely, such as Igor's aria from Borodin's *Prince Igor* and the Dutchman's monologue. The *Falstaff* excerpt from Act I of Verdi's comic masterpiece similarly find him presenting a larger-than-life portrait with no holds barred over the widest dynamic range.

The Handel collection makes no distinction between those arias for oratorio or opera, both equally dramatic, particularly as Terfel interprets them. The range of expression is wide, with Terfel using a beautiful head-voice for such favourite lyrical arias as *Ombra mai fù* and *Where'er you walk*, both hushed and poised. More typical is his fire-snorting manner in such powerful arias as *Revenge, Timotheus cries* from *Judas Maccabaeus*, and the three arias from *Messiah*, which with Terfel sound fresh and new. This is singing that is not just strong, varied and imaginative, but consistently beautiful too.

Tomlinson, John (bass)

Opera arias and scenes (with Geoffrey Mitchell Ch., Philh O, Parry) from HANDEL: *Acis and Galatea; Samson.* MOZART: *Abduction from the Seraglio* **(with Williams, Banks).** VERDI: *Simon Boccanegra; Ernani.* BORODIN: *Prince Igor.* DARGOMIZHSKY: *Rusalka.* SULLIVAN: *The Mikado; The Pirates of Penzance.* OFFENBACH: *Geneviève de Brabant* **(with Shore).** MUSSORGSKY: *Mephistopheles: Song of the Flea.* LEHMANN: *In a Persian Garden: Myself when Young.*

(M) *** Chan. 3044.

The versatility of John Tomlinson is breathtaking, and here he tackles the widest range of bass arias. It adds to the characterful tang and sparkle of the performances that all 17 items are in English on one of the 'Opera in English' discs sponsored by the Peter Moores Foundation. One might have expected this singing actor, today's greatest Wotan, to be attuned to Verdi and the Russians, with an attractive aria from Dargomizhky's *Rusalka* in addition to the well-known Mussorgsky and Borodin items, but he is just as stylish in Handel (both comic and heroic), as well as in Mozart (a characterful Osmin in three items from *Seraglio*). He is full of fun in Offenbach (the Gendarmes' duet from *Geneviève de Brabant* with Andrew Shore) and G. & S. (the Policeman's song from *The Pirates of Penzance*) winningly sung in a bluff northern accent. There is brilliant accompaniment under David Parry.

'German Operatic Arias' (sung in English, with LPO or Philharmonia Orchestra, David Parry) from: MOZART: *The Abduction from the Seragio; The Magic Flute.* BEETHOVEN: *Fidelio.* WEBER: *Der Freischütz.* WAGNER: *The Rheingold; The Flying Dutchman; The Mastersingers of Nuremberg.* R. STRAUSS: *Der Rosenkavalier.* LORTZING: *The Armourer.*

(M) *** Chan. 3073.

Opening with great gusto in an exhilarating account of Osmin's 'vengeance' aria, John Tomlinson, in splendid voice, shows how effective opera in English can be, sung by a master of characterization with a rich voice. Whether in the deep sonorities of 'Sarastro's Prayer' from *The Magic Flute*, as Caspar in *Der Freischütz*, as an unforgettable Wotan in the 'Rainbow Bridge' sequence from *Rheingold* (to gorgeous sound from the LPO); as Hans Sachs in *Mastersingers* or a highly individual Baron Ochs in *Rosenkavalier*, Tomlinson's projection is matched by the resonant quality of the singing, and only occasionally does a minor excess of vibrato have any adverse effect on a firmly

supported vocal line. There is always fine orchestral support from David Parry. The recordings (of typical Chandos excellence) were made at Blackheath Halls between 1998 and 2001. A most enjoyable collection, with Hans Stadlinger's '*I used to be young with a fine head of hair*' from Lortzing's *Der Waffenschmied (The Armourer)* included as a final jest; for, as can be seen by the photographs, there is nothing sparse about Tomlinson's current mop!

Tourel, Jennie (mezzo-soprano)

'The Singers' (Decca series) (with (i) Ulanovsky or (ii) Smith, piano): (i) ROSSINI: *La regatta veneziana.* GLUCK: *Paride ed Elena.* VIVALDI: *L'Atenaide.* BIZET: *Adieux de l'hotesse arabe.* LISZT: *Oh! quand je dors.* RAVEL: *Deux Mélodies hébraïques: Kaddisch; Trois Chansons: Nicolette.* POULENC: *Violon.* BERLIOZ: *Les Nuits d'été.* (ii) TCHAIKOVSKY: *Amid the Noise of the Ball; None But the Lonely Heart; To Forget So Soon; It Was in Early Spring.* GRECHANINOV: *Over the Steppe.* RACHMANINOV: *In the Silence of Mysterious Night; Oh, Do Not Sing to Me, Fair Maiden; The Soldier's Wife.* BALAKIREV: *Beneath the Mask.* DARGOMIZHSKY: *Look, Darling Girls.* RIMSKY-KORSAKOV: *More Sonorous Than the Lark's Singing.*

(M) (**) Decca mono 467 907-2.

Russian-born mezzo-soprano Jennie Tourel was a successful and characterful singer who had the longest possible stage career – she was appearing in *La Fille du régiment* in the year of her death in 1973 (she was born in 1900). At the height of her powers, her repertoire ranged from Rossini and Bellini to the twentieth century (she created Baba the Turk in *The Rake's Progress*), but later, when these American Decca recordings from the 1950s were made, she concentrated on recitals. While this 'The Singers' CD is enjoyable, it must also be reported that her voice does sound rather old, with a thinness of timbre that is at times very noticeable, though with many of her virtues remaining.

Her personality is always apparent, be it in the lively and animated mélodies, such as Ravel's *Nicolette*, or in the more romantic songs, where she responds with warm understanding, especially in the Russian repertoire. Not a disc to take on all at one time, but the richly varied repertoire and excellent transfers makes this CD a fair tribute, even if it invariably misses the brilliance of her earlier performances. Texts, translations and photos are available only via a CD ROM drive.

Vyvyan, Jennifer (soprano), Norma Procter (contralto)

'Songs of England': Jennifer Vyvyan (with Ernest Lush, piano): ANON., arr. DOLMETSCH: *Lye still my*

deare. PURCELL: *Nymphs and shepherds; Fairest isle.*
MORLEY: *Now is the month of Maying.* arr.
VAUGHAN WILLIAMS: *I will give my love an apple.*
ARNE: *Where the bee sucks; O ravishing delight.* arr.
WHITTAKER: *Bobby Shaftoe.* arr. LEHMANN: *Cherry ripe.* arr. GRAINGER: *The sprig o'thyme.* arr.
BRITTEN: *Sweet Polly Oliver.* HEAD: *Foxgloves.*
HOWELLS: *Gavotte.* VAUGHAN WILLIAMS: *The new ghost.* HOPKINS: *Melancholy song.* QUILTER: *Love's philosophy.* Norma Procter (with Alec Redshaw, piano): TRAD.: *Lord Rendell; Soldier, soldier.* arr.
SHARP: *I'm seventeen come Sunday; O no John!* arr.
HUGHES: *How deep in love am I.* arr. BENJAMIN: *Jan.* arr. TAYLOR: *O can ye sew cushions?*

(BB) *** Belart 461 625-2.

Jennifer Vyvyan and Norma Procter were among the distinguished soloists in Boult's much admired mid 1950s Decca *Messiah*, and here they delight us with a most attractive and wide-ranging collection of English songs. Both singers have a natural feeling for the folk material, and the recital opens with Vyvyan's glorious performance of the melancholy *Lye still my deare*. *Now is the month of Maying, I will give my love an apple* and *The sprig o'thyme* are equally lovely, while the livelier numbers, sung with superb diction, *Bobby Shaftoe* and Britten's arrangement of *Sweet Polly Oliver* are just as winning. Purcell's *Fairest isle* and Arne's *O ravishing delight* are well described by the latter title. Other highlights include Vaughan Williams's haunting *New ghost* and Quilter's lightly lilting *Love's philosophy*. When the rich-voiced Norma Procter takes over with *Lord Rendell*, the engaging *I'm seventeen come Sunday*, the emphatic *O no John!* and the superb *Soldier, soldier*, one thinks readily of Kathleen Ferrier's comparable affinity with this repertoire and there can be no higher praise. Benjamin's arrangement of *Jan* is very touching as is the closing *O can ye sew cushions?* The recording gives both singers splendid presence, but curiously the CD transfer of the earlier (1958) Procter sessions brings a slight loss of focus at times, and a hint of distortion. Never mind, this is still a delightful collection, and for once no texts are needed, for every word is clear. The piano accompaniments by Ernest Lush and Alec Redshaw are admirable.

Walker, Sarah (mezzo-soprano)

'*Blah, blah, blah*' (with Roger Vignoles, piano, in cabaret at the Wigmore Hall): GERSHWIN: *Blah, blah, blah; They all laughed; Three times a day; Boy, what love has done to me.* PORTER: *Tale of the oyster; Where O where?.* BERNSTEIN: *Who am I?*
NICHOLAS: *Place settings; Usherette's blues.* DRING: *Song of a nightclub proprietress.* BOLCOM: *Lime jello, marshmallow, cottage-cheese surprise.*
FLANDERS and SWANN: *A word on my ear.*
LEHMANN: *There are fairies at the bottom of my garden.* WRIGHT: *Transatlantic lullaby.* BAKER:

Someone is sending me flowers. SCHOENBERG: *3 Brettl Lieder.*

*** Hyp. CDA 66289.

Recorded live at the Wigmore Hall in London, Sarah Walker's recital of trifles is one of the happiest records you could wish to find, as well as one of the funniest. Her comic timing is masterly in such delectable revue numbers as Cole Porter's *Tale of the oyster* or William Bolcom's culinary patter-song, *Lime jello, marshmallow, cottage-cheese surprise*. Perhaps surprisingly, she does such a song as *There are fairies at the bottom of my garden* straight, restoring its touching quality in defiance of Beatrice Lillie's classic send-up.

Also, by treating a popular number such as *Transatlantic lullaby* as a serious song, she not only underlines purely musical qualities but touches a deeper vein than one might expect in a cabaret sequence. Three of Schoenberg's *Brettl Lieder*, in deft English translations by Michael Irwin, are sung just as delightfully – and more provocatively than the German versions which were recorded by Jill Gomez in her delectable 'Cabaret classics' recital.

The title, *Blah, blah, blah*, comes from the opening number, a witty concoction by George Gershwin with words by his brother, Ira, which reduces the popular love-song lyrics to the necessary - and predictable - rhymes. Roger Vignoles, always an understanding accompanist, here excels himself with playing of flair and brilliance, exuberantly encompassing every popular idiom in turn. The recording, unlike most made at the Wigmore Hall, captures some of the bloom of its acoustic; but that means that the voice is set slightly at a distance. Texts are provided but, with such clear diction from the singer, they are needed only occasionally.

Walker, Sarah (mezzo-soprano), Thomas Allen (baritone)

'*Dreams and fancies*' (Favourite English songs) with Roger Vignoles, piano: IRELAND: *If there were dreams to sell.* DELIUS: *Twilight fancies.*
ARMSTRONG GIBBS: *Silver; Five eyes.* VAUGHAN WILLIAMS: *Silent noon; The water mill.* WARLOCK: *The fox; Jillian of Berry; The first mercy; The night.*
SULLIVAN: *Orpheus with his lute.* HOWELLS: *King David; Gavotte; Come sing and dance; The little road to Bethlehem.* STANFORD: *The monkey's carol.* BRIDGE: *Isobel.* CLARKE: *The seal man; The aspidistra.* HAVELOCK NELSON: *Dirty work.* HOIBY: *Jabberwocky.* QUILTER: *Now sleeps the crimson petal.* GURNEY: *Sleep.* DUNHILL: *The cloths of heaven.*

(M) *** CRD CRD 3473.

A well-designed and delightful programme, and it is good to see the Roger Quilter favourite, *Now sleeps the crimson petal*, back in favour alongside both the familiar and unfamilar items included here. Dunhill's

The cloths of heaven, too, leaves the listener wanting more. The secret of a miscellaneous (72 minutes) recital like this is for each song to lead naturally into the next, and that is what happens here, while the listener relaxes and enjoys each contrasted setting as it flows by. Sarah Walker is in inspired form and is very well accompanied.

'*The Sea*' (with Roger Vignoles, piano): IRELAND: *Sea fever.* HAYDN: *Mermaid's song; Sailor's song.* DIBDIN: *Tom Bowling.* WALTON: *Song for the Lord Mayor's table; Wapping Old Stairs.* WOLF: *Seemanns Abschied.* FAURE: *Les Berceaux; Au cimetière; L'horizon chimerique.* SCHUBERT: *Lied eines Schiffers an die Dioskuren.* BORODIN: *The Sea; The Sea Princess.* DEBUSSY: *Proses lyriques: De grève.* IVES: *Swimmers.* SCHUMANN: *Die Meersee.* BERLIOZ: *Les Nuits d'été: L'ile inconnue.* MENDELSSOHN: *Wasserfahrt.* BRAHMS: *Die Meere.* TRAD.: *The Mermaid.* Arr. BRITTEN: *Sail on, sail on.*

✪ *** Hyp. CDA 66165.

With Roger Vignoles as master of ceremonies in a brilliantly devised programme, ranging wide, this twin-headed recital celebrating 'The Sea' is a delight from beginning to end. Two outstandingly characterful singers are mutually challenged to their very finest form, whether in solo songs or duets. As sample, try the setting of the sea-song *The Mermaid*, brilliantly arranged by Vignoles, with hilarious key-switches on the comic quotations from *Rule, Britannia*. Excellent recording.

Wedding music

'*The world of wedding music*': WAGNER: *Lohengrin: Wedding march.* BACH: *Suite No. 3: Air* (Stephen Cleobury). CLARKE: *Prince of Denmark's march (Trumpet voluntary).* PURCELL: *Trumpet tune* (Simon Preston). BACH/GOUNOD: *Ave Maria* (Kiri Te Kanawa). SCHUBERT: *Ave Maria.* MOZART: *Alleluja* (Leontyne Price). *Vespers: Laudate dominum* (Felicity Palmer). KARG-ELERT: *Marche triomphale: Nun danket alle Gott.* BRAHMS: *Chorale prelude: Es ist ein Ros entsprungen.* WIDOR: *Symphony No. 5: Toccata.* MENDELSSOHN: *Midsummer Night's Dream: Wedding march* (Peter Hurford). WALFORD DAVIES: *God be in my head.* Hymn: *The Lord's my shepherd* (Huddersfield Choral Soc., Morris). STAINER: *Love divine.* Hymn: *Praise my soul, the King of heaven* (King's College Ch., Cleobury). BACH: *Cantata No. 147: Jesu, joy of man's desiring.* Hymn: *Lead us, Heavenly Father, lead us* (St John's College Ch., Guest). HANDEL: *Samson: Let the bright seraphim* (Joan Sutherland).

(B) ** Decca (ADD) 436 402-2.

An inexpensive present for any bride-to-be, with many traditional suggestions, well played and sung, though it would have been better to have omitted the Karg-Elert *Marche-triomphale* in favour of Handel's *Arrival of the Queen of Sheba*, to which many a contemporary bride trips down the aisle. Good sound.

Westminster Cathedral Choir, David Hill

'*Treasures of the Spanish Renaissance*': GUERRERO: *Surge propera amica mea; O altitudo divitiarum; O Domine Jesu Christe; O sacrum convivium; Ave, Virgo sanctissima; Regina coeli laetare.* LOBO: *Versa est in luctum; Ave Maria; O quam suavis es, Domine.* VIVANCO: *Magnificat octavi toni.*

*** Hyp. CDA 66168.

This immensely valuable collection reminds us vividly that Tomás Luis de Victoria was not the only master of church music in Renaissance Spain. Francisco Guerrero is generously represented here, and the spacious serenity of his polyphonic writing (for four, six and, in *Regina coeli laetare*, eight parts) creates the most beautiful sounds. A criticism might be made that tempi throughout this collection, which also includes fine music by Alonso Lobo and a superb eight-part *Magnificat* by Sebastian de Vivanco, are too measured, but the tension is held well, and David Hill is obviously concerned to convey the breadth of the writing. The singing is gloriously firm, with the long melismatic lines admirably controlled. Discreet accompaniments (using Renaissance double harp, bass dulcian and organ) do not affect the essentially a cappella nature of the performances. The Westminster Cathedral acoustic means the choral tone is richly upholstered, but the focus is always firm and clear.

Westminster Cathedral Choir, James O'Donnell

'*Masterpieces of Mexican polyphony*': FRANCO: *Salve regina.* PADILLA: *Deus in adiutorium; Mirabilia testimonium; Lamentation for Maundy Thursday; Salve Regina.* CAPILLAS: *Dis nobis, Maria; Magnificat.* SALAZAR: *O sacrum convivium.*

*** Hyp. CDA 66330.

The Westminster Choir under James O'Donnell are finding their way into hitherto unexplored Latin vocal repertoire – and what vocal impact it has! These musicians were employed in the new cathedrals when Spain colonized Mexico; only Capillas was native-born (though of Spanish descent). Padilla shows he had brought over a powerful Renaissance inheritance with him and uses double choir interplay to spectacularly resonant effect. Not all the other music is as ambitious as this, but there is a devotional concentration of feeling which illuminates even the simpler settings. The singing has the body and fervour this music needs, and the choir is splendidly recorded.

'*Masterpieces of Portuguese polyphony*': CARDOSO: *Lamentations for Maundy Thursday; Non mortui; Sitvit anima mea; Mulier quae erat; Tulerunt lapides; Nos autem gloriosi.* REBELO: *Panis angelicus.* DE CRISTO: *3 Christmas responsories;*

Magnificat a 8; Ave Maria a 8; Alma redemptoris mater; Ave maris stella; O crux venerabilis; Sanctissima quinque martires; Lachrimans sitivit; De profundis.

*** Hyp. CDA 66512.

With the help of the Tallis Scholars we have already discovered Manuel Cardoso and the unique character of Portuguese Renaissance music. The present collection duplicates four of the motets on the Tallis Scholars' CD (see our main volume), but the Westminster performances are slightly more robust and add to their character. The *Lamentations for Maundy Thursday* show the composer at his most imaginatively expressive, 'a resplendent example of his chromatic serenity', as Ivan Moody, the writer of the excellent notes on this CD, aptly puts it.

The music of Cardoso's contemporary, Pedro de Cristo (c. 1550–1618) is hardly less individual. His *Magnificat a 8* for two choirs is particularly arresting, as is the much simpler *O magnum mysterium*, while the *Sanctissimi quinque martires* (celebrating five Franciscans who were killed in 1220 while attempting to convert Moroccan Moslems) has a radiant, flowing intensity. Rebelo's *Panis angelicus* is rich in its harmonic feeling, and Fernandez's *Alma redemptoris mater* ends the programme in a mood of quiet contemplation.

'*Adeste fidelis*' (with Ian Simcock): WADE: *O come, all ye faithful.* TRAD.: *Gabriel's message; O come, O come Emanuel; Ding dong! merrily on high; A maiden most gentle; I wonder as I wander; O little town of Bethlehem; In dulci jubilo; The holly and the ivy.* GAUNTLETT: *Once in Royal David's city.* DARKE: *In the bleak mid-winter.* CORNELIUS: *The three kings.* PETRUS: *Of the Father's love begotten.* KIRKPATRICK: *Away in a manger.* WARLOCK: *Bethlehem Down.* HADLEY: *I sing of a maiden.* GRUBER: *Silent night.* HOWELLS: *Sing lullaby.* TAVENER: *The Lamb.* PARRY: *Welcome yule.* MENDELSSOHN: *Hark! the herald Angels sing.*

*** Hyp. CDA 66668.

An extremely well-sung traditional carol collection. Although many of the arrangers are distinguished names, the arrangements of traditional carols are essentially simple, and the concert makes a great appeal by the quality of the singing and the beautiful digital recording, with the choir perfectly focused and realistically set back just at the right distance within the cathedral acoustic. The programme is spiced with one or two attractive modern settings, notably Patrick Hadley's ravishing *I sing of a maiden* and John Tavener's familiar and highly individual carol, *The Lamb.*

'*Favourite motets from Westminster Cathedral*': MENDELSSOHN: *Ave Maria; Hymn of Praise: I waited for the Lord.* BACH: *Cantata No. 147: Jesu, joy of man's desiring.* FRANCK: *Panis angelicus.* MAWBY: *Ave verum corpus.* ROSSINI: *O salutaris hostia.* HARRIS: *Faire is the heaven.* HOLST: *Ave Maria; Nunc dimittis.* GOUNOD: *Ave Maria.* FAURE: *Maria Mater gratiae.* ELGAR: *Ave verum corpus.* MOZART:

Ave verum corpus. GRIEG: *Ave maris stella.* DE SEVERAC: *Tantum ergo.* VILLETTE: *Hymne à la Vierge.* SCHUBERT: *The Lord is my Shepherd.*

*** Hyp. CDA 66669.

The Westminster Cathedral Choir is a traditional men's and boys' choir of the highest calibre. The treble line is particularly rich, and this is essentially a satisfyingly full-throated concert, although there is no lack of dynamic nuance, and phrasing always flows naturally and musically. Franck's *Panis angelicus*, which gives the collection its sobriquet, is splendidly ripe, and other favourites like Bach's *Jesu, joy of man's desiring* and Mozart's *Ave verum* are most satisfyingly done.

Elgar's *Ave verum* too is a highlight, and Schubert's lovely setting of *The Lord is my Shepherd* is very successful in its English version. Among the novelties, De Séverac's *Tantum ergo* and the touching *Hymne à la Vierge* of Pierre Villette stand out, and the concert ends with a memorable account of Holst's setting of the *Nunc dimittis*, which opens ethereally and then soars into the heavens: the trebles are superbly ardent at the climax. The recording is outstandingly full and the cathedral ambience is caught without too much blurring.

Wunderlich, Fritz (tenor)

'*Great voice*': Arias and excerpts from: MOZART: *Die Zauberflöte; Die Entführung aus dem Serail.* VERDI: *La Traviata* (with Hilde Gueden); *Rigoletto* (with Erika Köth); *Don Carlos* (with Hermann Prey). TCHAIKOVSKY: *Eugene Onegin.* LORTZING: *Zar und Zimmermann; Der Waffenschmied.* ROSSINI: *Il barbiere di Siviglia.* PUCCINI: *La Bohème* (with Hermann Prey). *Tosca.* Lieder: SCHUBERT: *Heidenröslein.* BEETHOVEN: *Ich liebe dich.* TRAD.: *Funiculì-funiculà; Ein Lied geht um die Welt* (with R. Lamy Ch.).

(B) *** DG Classikon (ADD) 431 110-2.

Here is 70 minutes of gloriously heady tenor singing from one of the golden voices of the 1960s. Mozart's *Dies Bildnis* makes a ravishing opener, and *Hier soll ich dich denn sehen* from *Die Entführung* is equally beautiful. Then come two sparkling excerpts from *La Traviata* with Hilde Gueden and some memorable Tchaikovsky, like all the Italian repertoire, sung in German. The Rossini excerpt is wonderfully crisp and stylish.

Wunderlich is joined by the charming Erika Köth in *Rigoletto* and by Hermann Prey for the rousing *Don Carlos* duet (*Sie ist verloren ... Er ist's! Carlos!*) and the excerpt from *Bohème*. Last in the operatic group comes the most famous *Tosca* aria, *Und es blitzen die Sterne* (not too difficult to identify in Italian) sung without excessive histrionics. The Schubert and Beethoven Lieder are lovely and, if the two final popular songs (with chorus) bring more fervour than they deserve, one can revel in everything else. Excellent recording throughout. It is a pity there are no translations or notes, but with singing like this one can manage without them. A splendid bargain.

DOCUMENTARIES

Beethoven; Wagner

BBC Documentaries in the Great Composer series. Narrated by Kenneth Branagh, with artists and orchestras including: Vladimir Ashkenazy; Lindsay Quartet; Chicago Symphony Orchestra, Solti; Chamber Orchestra England, Harnoncourt; Berlin State Opera Orchestra, Barenboim; Munich State Opera Orchestra, Mehta; Prague Symphony Orchestra, Norrington. Video Directors Jill Marshall, Kriss Rusmanis.

*** Warner Music Vision/NVC Arts **DVD** 0927-42871-2.

These two hour-long features, packaged on a single DVD, crisply and efficiently tell the life-stories of Beethoven and Wagner with the help not only of the artists mentioned above, each performing relevant passages from the composers' works, but of a whole range of experts and authorities who irritatingly are not identified. The visual illustrations for each sequence are well-chosen and atmospheric, often very illuminating, as when one is taken to the Beethoven-haus in Bonn where the composer was born (now a place of pilgrimage) or the staircase of Wagner's house at Triebchen in Switzerland, where musicians gathered to give the first informal performance of the *Siegfried Idyll* composed for his wife, Cosima, after the birth of their son, Siegfried. One might occasionally quarrel with the proportion of each film given over to particular works – as for example the rather paltry treatment of *Meistersinger* in the Wagner film – but the commendable thing is how much has been included, not how much has been left out, even if the Wagner film concentrates rather obsessively on the composer's anti-semitism.

Concours d'une Reine

Le Concours d'une Reine (A Queen's Competition) 1951–2001. (Documentary by Michel Stockhem, Benoît Vietinck.)

*** Cypres **DVD** CYP1101.

This absorbing and fascinating documentary brings some invaluable footage of Le Concours Reine Eliza-beth, one of the major international competitions. There are glimpses of the 1937 performance, in which David Oistrakh triumphed, and the commentary throughout is of unfailing interest. Marcel Poot, Arthur Grumiaux and other distinguished musicians have much to say about music competitions that is both perceptive and humane, and we see something of the queen herself, who studied with Ysaÿe, taking a

keen interest in the young artists. In addition to the violin, there is, of course, a piano competition and, recently added, a vocal one. Some tantalizing glimpses of the final concerts engage the viewer almost as much as if they were going on now.

There is, incidentally, an accompanying 12-CD set (Cypres CYP 9612): its material is too diverse and wide-ranging even to list! It includes Leonid Kogan playing the cadenza of the Paganini *Concerto No. 1 in D major* in 1951 (otherwise all the repertoire is complete) and some rarer material from the same decade: Jaime Laredo plays the Milhaud *Concert Royal*, Op. 373, not otherwise available on CD, and Julian Sitko-vetsky (father of Dmitry) the Ysaÿe *Sixth Sonata*.

When the competition was broadened in 1952 to include the piano, Leon Fleischer was the winner with an impressive Brahms *D minor Concerto* (with Franz André conducting the Belgian Orchestre National). The Belgian composer Marcel Poot, for long the chairman of the competition, is represented by a *Piano Concerto*, heard in the late Malcolm Frager's 1960 performance, again with Franz André.

There are many mouth-watering opportunities to hear and see artists now famous at the early stages of their careers: Ashkenazy, the 19-year-old first-prize winner in 1956 in the Liszt *E flat Concerto*, the 20-year-old Gidon Kremer (ranked third in 1967) playing Schumann, and Mitsuko Uchida, also 20 years of age, playing the Beethoven *C minor Concerto* – she was ranked tenth in 1968!

Some will feel that the 12-CD set is too much of a good thing and too substantial an outlay, even at its competitive price. But the DVD is extraordinarily fas-cinating and involving – and often quite moving. Strongly recommended. The languages used are Dutch and French, with subtitles in English, German and Spanish.

Fonteyn, Margot

Margot Fonteyn – A Portrait. **Documentary produced and directed by Particia Foy (with Frederick Ashton, Ida Bromley, Robert Gottlieb, Nicola Kathak, Andrey King, Robert Helpmann, Rudolf Nureyev, Ninette de Valois).**

*** Arthaus **DVD** 100 092.

Margot Fonteyn dominated the ballet scene in Britain for more than 40 years, and she capped her career in 1961 by creating her legendary partnership with Rudolph Nureyev. Here in 1989, only two years before her death, she tells her life story. Not only was she will-ing to talk about the tragic death of her huband, but she also tells us about the background to her long career, and there are contributions from most of those who played an important part in it. With plenty of clips, including legendary archive material, this will be an essential purchase for anyone interested in ballet.

Great Composers: Mahler, Puccini, Tchaikovsky

BBC Documentaries narrated by Kenneth Branagh, featuring various artists and orchestras (with biographical amd critical commentaries). Executive Director: Kriss Rusmanis.

MAHLER: **Filmed in Prague, Budapest and Vienna. Director: Kriss Rusmanis. Includes excerpts from** *Symphonies Nos. 1–3, 5 & 9; Das Lied von der Erde; Des Knaben Wunderhorn; Lieder eines fahrenden Gesellen & Kindertotenlieder* **(with Charlotte Hellekant, Thomas Hampson, BBC SO, Sir Georg Solti).**

PUCCINI: **Filmed in Italy. Director Chris Hunt/Iambic. Includes excerpts from:** *Manon Lescaut; La Bohème; Tosca; Madama Butterfly; La Fanciulla del West; Il Tabarro; Turandot* **(with José Cura, Leontina Vaduva, Julia Migenes, BBC PO, Richard Buckley).**

TCHAIKOVSKY: **Filmed in Russia and America. Director: Simon Broughton. Includes excerpts from:** *Symphonies Nos. 2, 4, 5 & 6; The Voyevoda; Piano Concerto No. 1* **(with Mikhail Rudy);** *Violin Concerto* **(with Maxim Vengerov);** *Ballet Music; Eugene Onegin, Queen of Spades* **(with St Petersburg PO, Yuri Temirkanov).**

*** Warner NVC Arts **DVD** 0927-43538-2.

This group of three television portraits, taken from the BBC's 'Great Composers' series, brings out the parallels between these three musical geniuses, all three of them high neurotics who translated their inner problems into music of overwhelming emotional thrust. The approach with three different television directors is helpfully direct, linking the careers in outline to the principal works, including interviews with artists involved as well as various scholarly authorities.

The works chosen for coverage in the Tchaikovsky portrait are fairly predictable, with the exception of the symphonic ballad *Voyevoda*, written after Mme von Meck had put an end to their long relationship by correspondence: as David Brown puts it, containing 'some of his most ferocious and dissonant music'. The choice of works in the Puccini and Mahler portraits is less complicated, when the majority of Puccini's operas and of Mahler's symphonies and song-cycles can readily be included. In Chris Hunt's evocative Puccini film it is particularly effective to have interviews with some of the Torre del Lago villagers who actually remembered Puccini, and who could characterize him with his foibles. Puccini's granddaughter is also a valuable contributor, now custodian of the Puccini museum in

Torre del Lago. The evocative shots of the composer's haunts and homes are nicely linked to passages in the operas, the offstage bell effects in Act 3 of *Tosca*, or the boatmen's cries at the equivalent point of *Butterfly*, and the lapping water of *Il Tabarro*. The principal singers involved are José Cura and Julia Migenes.

Though Mahler died only 13 years before Puccini, that has evidently undermined any idea in Kriss Rusmanis's portrait of providing interviews with people who actually knew him like those in the Puccini film. The shots of Mahler's early homes and haunts as well as those later in his life, many of them turned into museums, are equally vivid. In the musical analyses Michael Tilson Thomas is particularly perceptive, and the character analyses bring out the way that Mahler, devastated by his daughter's death, selfishly left it to his young wife, Alma, to cope with the resulting problems. A whole sequence of contributors, arguably too many, put forward contrasting analyses of what motivated Mahler at various points. With Sir Georg Solti responsible for most of the musical excerpts, the principal singers, both excellent, are Thomas Hampson and the mezzo Charlotte Hellekant.

Grieg, Edvard

Edvard Grieg – What price immortality? **(Film by Thomas Olofsson & Ture Rangström).**

With Staffan Scheja & Philip Branmer. Directed by Thomas Olofsson.

Arthaus **DVD** 100 236.

This film sets some biographical impressions of Grieg against the background of two works, the *Ballade, Op. 24*, arguably his greatest keyboard piece, and the *String Quartet in G minor*, both of which are heard complete. The *Ballade* is an outpouring of grief at the death of his parents, and such was the emotion it aroused and the pain that accompanied its composition that in later life Grieg himself could hardly bear to play it. Incidentally, it is played here with much sensitivity by Staffan Scheja, who also plays the composer in the mimed dramatic episodes that make up the film. The Auryn Quartet play the *G minor Quartet*, a work with distinctly autobiographical overtones. But those looking for illumination will turn to this in vain. Neither Ibsen nor Bjørnson features; nor do his struggles with the orchestras in Christiania and Bergen. Despite the pretty costumes, there is curiously little period atmosphere. Much is made of the tension between Grieg and his wife, Nina, and his infatuation with Elise (or Leis) Schjelderup, under whose spell he came in the early 1880s. She was an artist in her mid-twenties living in Paris, and her brother, Gerhard, was later to become Grieg's first biographer, in Norwegian at least.

Otherwise you are left with little idea of what Grieg was like and how his life unfolded. One wonders what a viewer completely innocent of any biographical background will make of it all. Take one small example among many: we see Grieg as a boy standing under a drainpipe, the significance of which will escape viewers. When Edvard came to school soaking wet from the Bergen rain, he was often sent back home, and he once stood under a drainpipe in the hope of this happening. Viewers who don't know this will be as puzzled by this image as they will be by much else. We catch a brief glimpse of the famous 1888 lunch party with Brahms and Tchaikovsky, though little sense of the great feeling Grieg had for the Russian master is conveyed. Episodes in Grieg's life are sensitively mimed for the most part, but the Grieg we see does not correspond to the personality we know from the letters and diaries and from Finn Benestad and Schjelderup-Ebbe's authoritative biography or any other study for that matter! The film does not bring one closer to a composer whose naturalness of utterance was so disarming. Not recommended. No stars.